THE
FamilyCircle
ENCYCLOPEDIA
OF COOKING

THE FamilyCircle ENCYCLOPEDIA OF COOKING

From the Editors of Family Circle

Editorial Director Donald D. Wolf
Design and Layout Margot L. Wolf

Lexicon Publications, Inc.
95 Madison Avenue New York, N.Y. 10016

Opposite title page:
Mama's Chicken Soup with Fluffy Matzo Balls, page 727;
Orange-Glazed Baked Chicken, page 664; Carrot-Yam
Tzimmes, page 764; Dilled Green Beans, page 760; Matzo
Honey Cake, page 167.

ISBN: 0-7172-4578-0

CONTENTS

Accompaniments 7

Appetizers 25

Beverages 57

Breads 83
- YEAST and QUICK BREADS 83
- COFFEE CAKES 132
- BREAD LEFTOVERS 138

Cakes and Tortes 143

Cookies and Candies 205

Desserts 259

Eggs and Cheese 347

Fish and Shellfish 383

Meat 413
- BEEF and VEAL 413
- GROUND and VARIETY MEATS 454
- LAMB 484
- PORK, HAM and SAUSAGES 496

Microwave 545

Pasta, Grains and Dumplings 599

Pies 621
- MAIN-DISH PIES 621
- DESSERT PIES 629
- PIZZAS 642

Poultry 647

Salads and Salad Dressings 687

Sauces, Glazes, Frostings and Stuffings 713

Soups and Snacks 723

Vegetables 753

Metric Charts 788

Index 789

ACCOMPANIMENTS

Mustard   Prepared mustard, dry mustard, mustard seeds and mustard greens are the products derived from several varieties of the mustard plant. It is a pungent herb belonging to the vast *Brassica* or cabbage family.

Prepared mustard, which can be hot or mild, spicy or sweet, is made by grinding mustard seeds and adding vinegar, water and seasonings. It is widely used as a table condiment and in cooking. Dry mustard is blended from a number of varieties of mustard seeds and can be hot or mild too. Blending achieves full flavor and desirable characteristics. Dry mustard is used in salad dressings, cream sauces, egg or cheese dishes.

In making prepared mustard or dry mustard, the degree of hotness comes from the varieties of mustard seeds used as well as the portion of the seed. The layer under the skin or hull of a mustard seed is hotter than the center of the seed. The two varieties of mustard seeds commonly used are the black and white or yellow mustard seeds.

Black mustard seed is yellowish-brown in color and has a very pungent flavor. White or yellow mustard seed is pale yellow with a less pungent taste than the black variety. Mustard seeds are used primarily when making pickles at home.

The word mustard comes from the French word *moustarde*. Mustard has been used as a condiment and a medicine since 75 A.D.

Mustard Trio

Makes 3 six-ounce jars.

2 cups dry white wine	**2 teaspoons salt**
1 large onion,	**Liquid hot pepper**
chopped (1 cup)	**seasoning**
2 cloves garlic,	**1 tablespoon tomato**
minced	**paste**
1 can (4 ounces) dry	**1 teaspoon leaf**
mustard	**tarragon, crumbled**
2 tablespoons honey	**1 tablespoon grated**
1 tablespoon	**orange rind**
vegetable oil	

1. Combine wine, onion and garlic in a medium-size saucepan; bring to boiling; lower heat; simmer 5 minutes. Strain; cool.

Pictured opposite: Basic French Mustard, page 7; Sweet 'n' Hot Mustard, page 7; Carrot-Pineapple Marmalade, page 8; Lemon Curd, page 8; Lemon-Lime Marmalade, page 8; Papaya Chutney, page 12; Strawberry-Orange Marmalade, page 8; Cranberry-Apple Glaze, page 717; Apricot-Orange Winter Barbecue Sauce, page 716.

2. Mix dry mustard and strained wine in medium-size saucepan until very smooth; blend in honey, oil, salt and few drops pepper seasoning.
3. Cook over medium heat, stirring constantly, until mixture thickens; remove from heat and pour into 3 hot sterilized 6-ounce jars. Stir tomato paste into one jar, tarragon into a second and orange rind into the third; seal and refrigerate at least 1 week.

Basic French Mustard

Makes 1 cup.

¹/₄ cup dry mustard	**wine**
1 tablespoon sugar	**¹/₄ cup white wine**
¹/₂ teaspoon salt	**vinegar**
¹/₃ cup dry white	**3 egg yolks**

1. Combine mustard, sugar and salt in a small saucepan. Stir in wine and wine vinegar until smooth. Let stand, uncovered, for 2 hours.
2. Beat egg yolks in a small bowl until light. Stir into mustard mixture. Cook over low heat, stirring constantly, until slightly thickened, about 5 minutes. Do not allow to boil. Cool; pour into small jars; cover. May be stored in refrigerator for up to 1 month. Use as is or as a base for Tomato Mustard.

Tomato Mustard: Add 1 teaspoon paprika and 4 tablespoons tomato paste with the egg yolks. Nice with shrimp, hamburgers, frankfurters, and baked ham.

Sweet 'n' Hot Mustard

Makes 1 cup.

1 medium-size onion,	**1¹/₂ teaspoons**
finely chopped	**vegetable oil**
(¹/₂ cup)	**1 tablespoon honey**
1 clove garlic, minced	**1 teaspoon salt**
1 cup dry white wine	**2 to 3 drops liquid hot**
²/₃ cup dry mustard	**pepper seasoning**

1. Combine onion, garlic and wine in a small saucepan. Bring to boiling; lower heat; simmer 5 minutes.
2. Pour mixture into a small bowl; cool. Strain wine mixture into dry mustard in a small saucepan, beating constantly until smooth. Beat in oil, honey, salt and pepper seasoning.
3. Cook over low heat, stirring constantly, until mixture thickens. Cool; pour into small jars; cover.
4. May be stored in refrigerator for up to 1 month.

Lemon Curd

Makes about 4½ cups.

2 whole eggs	⅔ cup lemon juice
2 egg yolks	1 cup (2 sticks) butter
1½ cups sugar	or margarine,
2 tablespoons grated	melted
lemon rind	

Beat eggs, yolks and sugar in the top of a double boiler with electric mixer until light and fluffy, 3 to 5 minutes. Beat in rind, juice and butter. Cook, stirring constantly, over hot, not boiling, water until mixture thickens, about 15 minutes. Remove from heat; cool. Spoon into jars; seal; refrigerate for up to 2 weeks.

Lemon-Lime Marmalade

Makes 5 half pints.

3 large lemons	5 cups sugar
6 limes	¼ cup shredded
6 cups water	preserved ginger

1. Wash, seed and slice thinly 2 of the lemons and 3 of the limes. Pack tightly to make 1½ cups.
2. Use vegetable parer to remove rind (colored part only, no white) from remaining lemon and 3 limes. Cut into thin strips 1/16-inch wide and 2-inches long to make ½ cup.
3. Place slices and rind in large kettle with water. Bring to boiling; boil 20 minutes. Stir in sugar and ginger. Boil 20 more minutes until jelly sheets from cold metal spoon.
4. Skim off foam; ladle into 5 hot 8-ounce jars. Seal.
5. Process 10 minutes in *simmering* water bath (185°). Cool; label and store in a cool, dry place.

Carrot-Pineapple Marmalade

Makes 4 half pints.

2 lemons	1 can (15¼ ounces)
½ pound carrots,	crushed pineapple
shredded (2 cups)	in pineapple juice
2 cups water	½ 6-ounce package
1¾ cups sugar	liquid pectin

1. Shred rind from lemons, about ¼ cup, and combine with carrots in large saucepan.
2. Squeeze juice from lemons, about ⅓ cup; add to saucepan with water. Simmer 20 minutes until tender.
3. Stir in sugar and pineapple; bring to a full boil; boil 1 minute, stirring constantly. Remove from heat; stir in liquid pectin (1 pouch).
4. Skim off foam and stir about 8 minutes to cool. Ladle into 4 hot 8-ounce jars; seal. Process 10 minutes in *simmering* water bath (185°). Cool; label and store in cool, dry place.

Strawberry-Orange Marmalade

Makes 5 half pints.

3 oranges	frozen whole
2 lemons	unsweetened
6 cups water	strawberries,
4 cups sugar	partially thawed
1 bag (1 pound)	

1. Cut 2 oranges into quarters; remove seeds. Slice thinly (about 2 cups).
2. Cut 1 lemon in half lengthwise; slice thinly, removing seeds.
3. Remove rind from remaining orange and lemon with vegetable parer. Cut into thin strips 1/16-inch wide and 2-inches long.
4. Combine slices and rind in large kettle with water. Bring to boiling; boil 30 minutes until soft.
5. Combine sugar and strawberries in large bowl; mash slightly; stir into kettle. Boil 30 more minutes until liquid sheets from spoon.
6. Skim off foam; ladle into 5 hot 8-ounce jars. Seal. Process 10 minutes in *simmering* water bath (185°). Cool; label and store in cool, dry place.

Jam   Making jam is one of the oldest ways of preserving fresh fruit, made by crushing fruit and cooking it with sugar. Jam can be made with or without the addition of commercial pectin, which is a substance found in plant tissue that causes the mixture to gel when mixed with acid and sugar. Underripe fruit contains more pectin than ripe fruit and should be included with ripe fruit when making jams without added pectin. With commercial pectin, you can use fully ripened fruit but more sugar is needed to assure gelling.

How to Make Jam

1. Use 8-ounce jars with 2-piece lids and process jam in boiling water after filling for better keeping qualities (preventing mold). Processing the jam in a water-bath canner can be omitted, but jars and lids must be sterilized. Do not seal jam in jelly glasses covered with paraffin. Wash and rinse jars and lids.
2. To sterilize jars, place jars on a rack in a water-bath canner or deep kettle. Fill canner with water to a depth 2 inches above level of the jars. Bring water to boiling; boil 10 minutes. Turn off heat but keep jars in water until ready to fill. Put lids in a small pan; cover with

boiling water shorlty before using. Aways use new lids.

3. Prepare fruit as directed in recipe. Do not double recipe.

4. Ladle jam into drained hot jars leaving 1/4 -inch space at top. Wipe jar rims with damp toweling. Cover jars with hot lids; screw bands on firmly.

5. If processing, place jars in boiling water bath and add more water, if needed, to cover jars by 1 inch. Cover canner and bring to boiling; boil 5 minutes. Remove to wire rack.

6. Let jam stand until cool. Label and store jam in a cool, dry place.

How to Make Freezer Jam

A freezer jam requires little or no cooking of the crushed fruit and therefore has the flavor of fresh fruit and a brighter color and softer consistency than nonfrozen jam. Store in the freezer or keep in the refrigerator for up to 3 weeks.

1. Use glass or plastic containers with tight lids. Wash; scald in boiling water and drain.

2. Prepare fruit as directed in recipe. Ladle into containers leaving 1/2-inch space at top. Cover with lids. Let stand at room temperature 24 hours. Store jam in the freezer.

Scotch Rhubarb and Ginger Jam

Makes 8 half pints.

3 1/2 pounds rhubarb, cut into 1-inch pieces
OR: 3 packages (about 1 pound each) frozen rhubarb
7 cups sugar
1/2 cup chopped preserved ginger
6 tablespoons lemon juice

1. Combine rhubarb and sugar in a large saucepan; let stand 3 hours. Stir in ginger and lemon juice. Heat to boiling; lower heat; simmer about 1 hour or until thermometer registers 220° or jam sheets from spoon. Skim off foam.

2. Ladle hot jam into 8 hot, scalded 8-ounce jars, filling to within 1/4 inch of tops. Wipe rims and seal.

3. Process for 10 minutes in a boiling water bath (212°). Remove jars from water bath; cool to room temperature; check seals, then label and store in a cool, dry place.

Blueberry Jam

Makes 8 half pints.

12 cups blueberries (3 quarts)
1/4 cup lemon juice
6 cups sugar
1/2 teaspoon ground mace

1. Wash berries and place in a large kettle with lemon juice; cook slowly, stirring constantly, until juice flows from berries; stir in sugar and mace.

2. Bring to boiling; lower heat; simmer 20 minutes, stirring often, until mixture thickens.

3. Ladle into 8 hot, sterilized 8-ounce jars. Wipe rims and seal. Cool; label.

Sweet Pepper and Orange Jam

Makes 7 half pints.

25 red peppers (about 6 pounds)
1 large seedless orange, peeled and cut into pieces
4 1/2 cups sugar
2 cups cider vinegar
1 teaspoon salt

1. Wash peppers; cut in half; remove seeds and white membranes; cut into large pieces; put through food chopper using coarsest blade.

2. Drain peppers well and discard liquid. Grind orange.

3. Combine peppers, orange, sugar, vinegar and salt in a large kettle. Bring quickly to boiling, stirring. Cook over high heat, stirring often, 30 minutes or just until thick and as clear as jam; don't overcook.

4. Ladle into 7 hot, sterilized 8-ounce jars. Wipe rims and seal. Cool; label.

Apricot-Pineapple Jam

Makes 8 half pints.

2 packages (11 ounces each) dried apricots
5 cups water
3 cups sugar
1 can (20 ounces) crushed pineapple in pineapple juice
1/2 cup thawed, frozen orange juice concentrate
1 teaspoon grated lemon rind

1. Soak apricots in water overnight. Next day, simmer apricots with the water in a large saucepan or Dutch oven until tender, about 10 minutes.

2. Mash apricots with their liquid; add sugar, pineapple and juice, orange concentrate and lemon rind.

3. Heat, stirring constantly, until sugar dissolves. Continue cooking over medium heat, stirring occasionally, until thickened, about 20 minutes. Skim off foam. Ladle into 8 hot, sterilized 8-ounce jars. Seal; cool and label.

Overleaf (from top left): Winter Salad of Julienne Vegetables, page 696; Stuffed Turkey Breast; page 680, Zucchini Boats with Red Pepper Bulgur Pilaf, page 614; Boiled New Potatoes and Onions, page 539; Holiday Punch, page 69; Gorgonzola Toast, page 30; Champagne Choucroute with Smoked Meats, page 537; Pear-Ginger Pudding with Lemon and Nesselrode Sauces, page 311; Cranberry Linzer Torte, page 189.

Strawberry-Pineapple Freezer Jam

Makes 7 half pints.

1 pint (2 cups) strawberries OR: 1 package (pound) frozen unsugared strawberries, thawed 1 can (8 ounces)	crushed pineapple in pineapple juice Water 4 cups sugar 1 package (1¾ ounces) powdered pectin

1. Wash, hull, slice and crush strawberries in a large bowl.
2. Drain pineapple juice (about ⅓ cup) into a measuring cup. Add enough water to make ¾ cup liquid.
3. Add pineapple and sugar to strawberries. Stir; let stand 10 minutes.
4. Stir pineapple juice and water mixture into powdered pectin in a small saucepan. Heat to boiling, stirring constantly. Boil 1 minute. Stir mixture into fruit. Stir 3 minutes.
5. Ladle at once into 7 scalded 8-ounce jars; cover. Let stand at room temperature until set, up to 24 hours. Store in freezer.

Jelly   A clear fruit spread made by cooking fruit juices with sugar and sometimes commercial pectin, then allowing it to set or gel. Vegetables such as green peppers and herbs such as mint are sometimes made into jelly and served as an accompaniment to meat. Wine can be substituted for fruit juice in making jelly.

How to Make Jelly

1. Use jelly glasses or jars with 2-piece lids. Wash and rinse glasses or jars and lids.
2. To sterilize glasses or jars, place on a rack in a water-bath canner or deep kettle. Fill canner with water to a depth 2 inches above level of the jars. Bring water to boiling; boil 10 minutes. Turn off heat but keep glasses or jars in water until ready to fill. If using jars, put lids in a small pan; cover with boiling water shortly before using. If using glasses, melt paraffin in a double boiler or coffee can placed in hot water; keep hot.
3. Prepare jelly mixture as directed in recipe. Do not double recipe.
4. Ladle jelly into drained hot glasses or jars leaving ½-inch space at top of glasses or ⅛-inch hot paraffin

onto hot jelly surface. Make sure paraffin touches rim of glass and there are no air bubbles. Seal jars with hot lids; screw bands on firmly.
5. Let jelly cool. Label. Cover paraffin-sealed glasses with caps. Store jelly in a cool, dry place.

Basil Jelly

Makes 4 half-pint jars.

1½ cups firmly packed fresh basil leaves, finely chopped 1¾ cups water	3½ cups sugar 2 tablespoons lemon juice 1 packet (3 ounces) fruit pectin

1. Place chopped basil in a saucepan. Add water. Bring to boiling. Remove from the heat. Set aside, covered, for 15 minutes.
2. Wash 4 half-pint canning jars. Sterilize in boiling water for 10 minutes. Keep hot.
3. Strain the basil mixture into a 2-cup glass measure. Add water to measure 1¾ cups, if necessary. Return the mixture to the saucepan. Stir in sugar and lemon juice.
4. Bring basil mixture to full boil over high heat, stirring constantly. When the mixture reaches boiling, immediately stir in pectin. Return to full boil; boil for 1 minute, stirring constantly. Remove from the heat.
5. Skim foam from the top of the jelly. Pour jelly into prepared jars, leaving at least 1/4-inch headspace. Wipe rims and threads clean. Cover jars with hot lids; screw on bands firmly. Let jelly stand until completely cool. Tighten bands, if necessary.
6. Store in cool dry place for several months. After opening, store in refrigerator for up to several weeks.

Cranberry-Apple Jelly

Two flavors in one glass for very little extra effort.

Makes 8 half pints.

2 cups bottled apple juice 7 cups sugar 1 package (6 ounces) liquid pectin	(2 pouches) 2 cups cranberry-juice cocktail Red food coloring

1. Prepare apple jelly layer: Measure apple juice and 3½ cups of the sugar into a large saucepan. Bring to boiling over high heat, stirring constantly.

2. Stir in 1 pouch of the liquid pectin. Bring to a full, rolling boil; boil hard 1 minute.

3. Remove from heat; skim off foam with a metal spoon. Ladle hot jelly into 8 hot, sterilized 8-ounce glasses, filling each half full. Allow to cool slightly while continuing recipe.

4. Prepare cranberry jelly layer: Follow recipe for apple jelly, substituting cranberry juice for apple juice and using remaining sugar and pectin. After skimming foam from jelly, stir in a little red food coloring to tint a deep pink.

5. Carefully ladle hot cranberry jelly over slightly cooled apple jelly in glasses, dividing evenly. Seal with paraffin. Allow to cool completely before moving the glasses. Label; store in a cool, dry place. The jelly takes a week or longer to become firmly set.

Parsleyed Vermouth Jelly

A sprightly, flavorful jelly, just right for an important dinner party.

Makes 5 half pints.

2 cups dry vermouth
3 cups sugar
1 package (6 ounces) liquid pectin
(2 pouches)
1/2 cup chopped fresh parsley

1. Combine vermouth and sugar in top of a double boiler. Place over boiling water; cook, stirring constantly, until sugar is dissolved. Continue cooking until very hot, about 5 minutes; skim off foam on top.

2. Remove from heat; stir in liquid pectin and parsley; mix well. Allow to stand 5 minutes.

3. Ladle jelly into 5 hot, sterilized 8-ounce jars. Wipe rims and seal. Cool; label.

Vin Rosé Jelly

Since the days of Victorian England, wine jellies have been considered a special treat for family and friends.

Makes 4 half pints

3 1/2 cups sugar
1 1/2 cups bottled red grape juice
1/2 cup water
1 3-inch piece stick
cinnamon
3/4 cup rosé wine
1/2 a 6-ounce package liquid pectin (1 pouch)

1. Combine sugar, grape juice, water and cinnamon stick in a large heavy saucepan.

2. Place saucepan over high heat; bring to a full rolling boil; add wine; return to a full rolling boil and boil hard, stirring constantly, for 1 minute. Remove from heat; stir in 1 pouch liquid pectin; remove cinnamon stick with a slotted spoon.

3. Ladle into 4 hot, sterilized 8-ounce jars; wipe rims and seal. Cool on wire rack until room temperature, then refrigerate. Jelly takes about a week to set firmly.

Vin Chablis Jelly: Substitute white grape juice for the red, 4 whole allspice for the cinnamon and white wine for the rosé. Proceed as for Vin Rosé Jelly.

Note: For a two-tone effect, make up a batch of Vin Rosé Jelly and ladle into 8 hot, sterilized jars, filling each half full. Allow to stand until room temperature, then make up a batch of Vin Chablis Jelly and ladle over Vin Rosé Jelly.

Hot Pepper Jelly

Makes about 8 half pints.

2 green peppers, halved, seeded and finely chopped
6 1/2 cups sugar
1 1/3 cups white vinegar
1 1/2 tablespoons
crushed red pepper
Green food coloring
2 packages (6 ounces each) liquid pectin (4 pouches)

1. Combine peppers, sugar, vinegar and pepper in a large heavy saucepan. Bring to boiling; lower heat; simmer 10 minutes.

2. Line a colander with several layers of cheesecloth; pour pepper mixture through cloth into a large saucepan.

3. Add a few drops green food coloring to mixture. Add pectin; bring to boiling over high heat for 1 minute.

4. Ladle jelly into 8 hot, sterilized 8-ounce jars. Wipe rims and seal. Turn upside down on a folded clean dish towel. Turn upright after a few minutes. Cool; label. Keep refrigerated.

Low-Calorie Grape Jelly

There are only 19 calories per tablespoon.

Makes 2 half pints.

1 envelope unflavored gelatin
2 cups unsweetened grape juice
1/2 a 6-ounce package liquid pectin (1 pouch)
5 tablespoons sugar

1. Stir gelatin into grape juice in a large saucepan. Bring to boiling, stirring constantly. Stir until gelatin is dissolved.

2. Add pectin and sugar to juice mixture. Reheat to a rolling boil; boil for 1 minute, stirring constantly. Remove from heat; skim off any foam. Pour into two hot, sterilized 8-ounce jars. Wipe rims and seal. Cool; label. Store in refrigerator.

Champagne Jelly

Makes 6 half pints.

1²/₃ cups champagne OR: 1²/₃ cups dry white wine 1¹/₃ cups orange juice	4 cups sugar 1 package (6 ounces) liquid pectin (2 pouches)

1. Combine champagne or wine, orange juice and sugar in top of a double boiler. Place over boiling water; cook, stirring constantly, until sugar is dissolved. Continue cooking until very hot, about 5 minutes; skim off foam on top.
2. Remove from heat; stir in liquid pectin. Mix well.
3. Ladle into 6 hot, sterilized 8-ounce glasses. Seal with paraffin; cool. Label and date; store in the refrigerator. Jelly takes a week or longer to set firmly.

Papaya Chutney

Makes 9 half pints.

2 large papayas (3 pounds total), pared, seeded and chopped (about 5 cups) 2 large onions, chopped (2 cups) 3 apples, pared and chopped (3 cups) 1 cup golden raisins	1 sweet red pepper, chopped (1 cup) 1¹/₂ teaspoons mustard seeds 1 cup cider vinegar 2 cups sugar 2 teaspoons salt ¹/₄ cup shredded preserved ginger

1. Combine all ingredients in kettle or Dutch oven. Bring to boiling, stirring often; lower heat and simmer 30 minutes until mixture is thickened. Stir often to prevent scorching.
2. Ladle into 9 hot 8-ounce jars leaving ¹/₄-inch head space. Seal jars. Process for 10 minutes in boiling water bath (212°). Cool; check seals; label and store in cool, dry place.

Plum Chutney

Makes 5 pints.

4 pounds purple plums, halved, pitted and diced (8 cups) 2 large onions, chopped (2 cups) 1 cup raisins	1 clove garlic, minced 2 cups firmly packed brown sugar 1 tablespoon chili powder 1¹/₂ teaspoons salt 4 cups cider vinegar

1. Combine plums, onions, raisins, garlic, brown sugar, chili powder and salt in a large kettle; stir in cider vinegar.
2. Bring to boiling, stirring often; lower heat; simmer 1 hour, stirring often or until mixture thickens.

3. Ladle into 5 hot 16-ounce jars, leaving ¹/₄-inch head space. Seal and process 5 minutes in boiling water bath (212°). Remove; cool; label.

Special Low-Cal Pancake Syrup

Makes 1 cup at 14 calories a tablespoonful.

1 tablespoon cornstarch 5 tablespoons sugar Pinch salt	1 cup cold water 2 teaspoons maple flavoring

1. Combine cornstarch, sugar, salt and water in a small saucepan; mix to dissolve cornstarch.
2. Cook mixture over medium heat, stirring constantly, until syrup thickens and bubbles. Lower heat; simmer 1 minute. Remove from heat; stir in maple flavoring.
Low-Calorie Honey Syrup: Substitute ¹/₄ cup honey for the sugar and omit the maple flavoring. Makes 1 cup at 18 calories a tablespoonful.
Ten-Calorie Maple Syrup: Reduce sugar to 2¹/₂ tablespoons. After removing syrup from heat, stir in sugar substitute to equal 4 tablespoons sugar. Makes 1 cup at 10 calories a tablespoonful.
Pineapple or Orange Pancake Sauce: Substitute unsweetened pineapple or orange juice for the water and reduce the sugar to 2 tablespoons. Makes 1 cup at 13 calories a tablespoonful.

Preserves A fruit spread made of whole berries or large pieces of fruit cooked with sugar until the mixture is of a syrupy consistency. The word "preserves" is often used interchangeably with jam.

Tomato Preserves

Makes 6 half pints.

1 tablespoon mixed pickling spices 1 1-inch piece fresh ginger root OR: ¹/₂ teaspoon ground ginger 4 cups sugar	2 lemons, thinly sliced and seeded ³/₄ cup water 6 medium-size tomatoes (2 pounds), peeled, cored and quartered

1. Tie pickling spices and ginger root in a small piece of cheesecloth. Combine with sugar, lemons and water in a large, heavy enamel or stainless steel kettle. Bring slowly to boiling, stirring. Lower heat; simmer 15 minutes.
2. Add tomatoes; simmer about 1¹/₂ hours, stirring

occasionally to prevent sticking, until tomatoes become clear. Remove from heat; cover. Let stand 12 to 18 hours in a cool place.

3. Wash and rinse six 8-ounce jars and their 2-piece lids. Keep jars and their lids in separate pans of hot water until you are ready to use them.

4. Drain jars; with a slotted spoon, pack tomatoes and lemons into hot jars, filling half full.

5. Remove spice bag from syrup; boil syrup 3 to 5 minutes or longer, if too thin. Pour, boiling hot, over tomatoes, leaving 1/4-inch head space.

6. Run a thin wooden or plastic spoon handle or other non-metallic utensil between tomatoes and jar to release air bubbles. Add more syrup, if needed. Wipe jar rims and seal.

7. Process 20 minutes in boiling water bath (212°). Remove jars from water bath; cool; check seals; label and store on a cool, dark, dry shelf.

Cranberry Relish

Makes 4 cups.

4 cups (1 pound) fresh or frozen cranberries
1 large orange, quartered and seeded
1 lemon, quartered
and seeded
1 1/2 cups sugar
1 teaspoon ground cinnamon
1/2 teaspoon ground cloves

1. Wash cranberries; drain and remove any stems. Put 1 cup of the cranberries in the container of an electric food processor fitted with metal chopping blade. Cover; process until cranberries are coarsely chopped. Empty cranberries into a bowl. Repeat with remaining berries.

2. Chop orange and lemon in food processor fitted with metal chopping blade. Add chopped fruit to berries.

3. Add sugar, cinnamon and cloves to cranberry mixture; mix thoroughly. Cover. Refrigerate several hours or overnight.

Carrot-Raisin Relish

Serve this old favorite as is, or spoon into lettuce cups, salad style.

Makes 6 servings.

3 cups shredded carrots
1 cup seedless raisins
1 tablespoon sugar
6 tablespoons mayonnaise or salad dressing
6 tablespoons light cream or half-and-half
1 tablespoon lemon juice
Dash salt
Dash pepper

1. Mix carrots and raisins in a bowl; sprinkle with sugar; toss lightly to mix. Chill at least 30 minutes.

2. Combine mayonnaise, cream, lemon juice, salt and pepper in a small bowl; stir into carrot mixture just before serving.

Onion-Lemon Relish

Serve with meat or poultry.

Makes about 1 1/2 cups.

2 large lemons
6 green onions with green tops, cut up
1/2 green pepper, seeded
1/4 cup parsley sprigs
1 cup chopped celery
1/2 teaspoon dry mustard
1/4 teaspoon ground
cardamom
1 teaspoon salt
1 small hot red pepper, seeded and chopped
OR: 1/2 teaspoon liquid hot pepper seasoning
1 tablespoon sugar

1. Grate lemons and reserve the grated rind. Cut off all the remaining white membrane of lemons.

2. Put lemons, green onions, pepper, parsley and celery through the coarse blade of a meat grinder, or whirl in a food processor until coarsely chopped. Stir in grated lemon rind.

3. Add mustard, cardamom, salt, chopped pepper and sugar. Refrigerate, covered, overnight to blend flavors.

Yankee Corn Relish

Makes 8 half pints.

12 ears corn
2 large red or green peppers, halved, seeded and chopped
1 large Bermuda onion, chopped
1 cup sliced celery
2 cups cider vinegar
2 cups water
2 tablespoons mustard seeds
4 teaspoons salt
1 1/2 teaspoons turmeric
1 1/2 cups sugar
1/2 cup all-purpose flour

1. Peel husks and silk from corn. Place corn in a kettle of boiling water; return to boiling; simmer 5 minutes; drain and cool. Cut corn kernels from cobs.

2. Combine kernels, peppers, onion, celery, vinegar, water, mustard seeds, salt and turmeric in a large kettle. Bring to boiling; lower heat; simmer 20 minutes. Combine sugar and flour in a small bowl; stir into kettle slowly. Cook, stirring constantly, until mixture thickens and bubbles 3 minutes.

3. Ladle into 8 hot 8-ounce jars, leaving 1/2-inch head space. Seal and process 15 minutes in boiling water bath (212°). Cool; label.

Quick Corn Relish

Makes 5 cups.

2 cans (12 ounces each) whole-kernel corn
²/₃ cup diced onion
²/₃ cup diced green pepper
²/₃ cup diced canned pimiento
¹/₂ cup distilled white vinegar
2 tablespoons vegetable oil
¹/₄ cup sugar
2 teaspoons dry mustard
¹/₂ teaspoon salt
¹/₂ teaspoon pepper

1. Drain liquid from corn, reserving ¹/₂ cup. Combine corn with onion, green pepper and pimiento in a large bowl.
2. Combine the reserved corn liquid, vinegar, vegetable oil, sugar, dry mustard, salt and pepper in a small saucepan. Bring to boiling; pour over vegetables. Cover with plastic wrap. Refrigerate overnight, stirring occasionally.

Ripe Tomato-Pear Relish

Makes 9 half pints.

3 pounds firm ripe tomatoes
3 pounds firm ripe pears
2 large yellow onions
2 large sweet green peppers
2 large sweet red peppers
1 cup raisins
1¹/₂ cups sugar
1¹/₂ cups light corn syrup
1¹/₂ cups cider vinegar
2 teaspoons salt
1 teaspoon dry mustard
1 teaspoon curry powder
1 teaspoon ground ginger
¹/₄ teaspoon ground cloves
¹/₄ teaspoon crushed red pepper

1. Rinse tomatoes; cut away stem portions; peel and cut into wedges (about 5 cups).
2. Rinse, pare and core pears; cut into ¹/₂-inch cubes (about 5 cups).
3. Peel onions; cut into ¹/₂-inch cubes (about 2 cups).
4. Rinse peppers; remove stems, seeds and white membranes; cut into ¹/₂-inch pieces (about 1¹/₂ cups each).
5. Place tomatoes, pears, onions, peppers and raisins in an 8-quart stainless steel or enamel pan. Stir in sugar, corn syrup, vinegar, salt, mustard, curry, ginger, cloves and red pepper. Bring to boiling; boil uncovered about 1 hour until thickened. Stir often as syrup thickens.
6. While relish cooks, prepare jars: Wash nine 8-ounce jars and their lids in hot, soapy water; rinse; keep jars and lids in hot water until ready. Start heating water in canner for processing in water bath.
7. Ladle relish into drained hot jars leaving ¹/₄-inch head space. Wipe rims with damp cloth; seal. Place jars in boiling water to cover by 2 inches in canner or other large, heavy kettle. When water returns to boiling, cover pan; process for 5 minutes. Remove to wire rack; cool completely. Check seals, label and store on cool, dry shelf.

Note: Process in 2 batches if canner will not hold all the jars. If you have a bit more relish after filling nine jars, place extra in refrigerator and use first.

Celery Relish

Makes 4¹/₂ cups.

4 cups sliced celery
1 large onion, cut into sixths
1 jar (4 ounces) pimiento, drained
1 envelope unflavored gelatin
1 bottle (8 ounces) Italian salad dressing

1. Put celery, onion and pimiento into the container of an electric blender; reserve.
2. Mix gelatin and salad dressing in small saucepan. Stir over low heat just until gelatin is dissolved.
3. Pour gelatin mixture over vegetables in blender. Cover; whirl at low speed until ingredients are coarsely chopped.
4. Pour mixture into a bowl, cover and chill until thick. Serve as an accompaniment to hamburgers, frankfurters or fried fish. This relish keeps well for about a week.

Baked Apple Relish

A pungent accompaniment to roast chicken.
Bake at 350° for 25 minutes.

Makes 6 servings.

6 small baking apples
2 tablespoons butter or margarine
1 large onion, finely chopped
1 tomato, peeled and chopped (1 cup)
¹/₄ cup raisins
1 tablespoon finely chopped preserved ginger
¹/₄ teaspoon crushed red pepper
¹/₄ teaspoon dry mustard
4 tablespoons red currant jelly
4 tablespoons cider vinegar

1. Cut a slice from top of each apple; remove core with apple corer or small knife. Scoop out apples with the tip of a small spoon, leaving a shell about ¹/₂ to ³/₄-inch thick. Chop the scooped-out apple (about 1 cup).
2. Heat butter in large skillet; add onion and sauté 5 minutes. Stir in chopped apple, tomato, raisins, ginger, crushed red pepper, mustard, 1 tablespoon of the currant jelly and 1 tablespoon of the vinegar. Cook, stirring often, 5 minutes longer or until slightly thickened.

Baked Apple Relish with Roast Chicken.

3. Spoon cooked mixture into hollowed-out apples; arrange apples in shallow baking pan. Add remaining jelly and vinegar to skillet; heat just until melted; spoon over and around apples.

4. Bake uncovered and baste once or twice in a moderate oven (350°) for 25 minutes or until apples are glazed and tender. Let cool 15 minutes before serving while basting with juices in pan.

Crisp Cranberry Relish

Be sure to add the apple and celery no more than an hour or two before serving to ensure that the relish is crispy.

Makes 12 servings (3 cups).

1 package (12 ounces) fresh or frozen cranberries	1 tablespoon lemon juice
1 cup sugar	1 cup diced green eating apple
2 teaspoons grated lemon rind	1 cup sliced celery

1. Place half the cranberries in the container of a blender or food processor. Turn on and off until the cranberries are evenly chopped. Transfer to a bowl. Repeat with the remaining berries.

2. Stir in sugar, lemon rind and juice. Refrigerate overnight or for up to 1 week.

3. Add apple and celery 1 to 2 hours before serving.

Sauerkraut Relish

Makes about 1 quart.

1 can (27 ounces) sauerkraut, drained (about 3 1/2 cups)	seeds
	1/4 teaspoon salt
	Dash pepper
1/4 cup sugar	1/3 cup finely chopped onion
1/4 cup honey	
2 tablespoons vegetable oil	3 tablespoons chopped canned pimiento
1 teaspoon caraway	

Combine sauerkraut, sugar, honey, oil, caraway seeds, salt, pepper and onion in a large saucepan. Simmer, covered, 20 minutes; stir in pimiento. Turn into a jar. Cover. Cool; chill at least 4 hours. Keep refrigerated. Will keep for about a week.

Hot Dog Relish

Makes 9 half pints.

2 pounds medium-size green tomatoes (about 6)
3 medium-size yellow onions
1 pound cabbage (1/2 head)
1 1/2 pounds sweet green peppers (about 6)
3/4 pound sweet red peppers (about 3)
1/4 cup salt
1 cup sugar
2 cups cider vinegar
1 cup light corn syrup
1 tablespoon mustard seeds
1 tablespoon celery seeds
1 teaspoon turmeric

1. Rinse and remove stem portions from green tomatoes; cut into pieces that will fit food grinder.
2. Peel and quarter onions. Remove core from cabbage; cut into pieces that will fit food grinder.
3. Rinse peppers; remove stems, seeds and white membranes; cut into pieces.
4. Put all vegetables through food grinder, using coarse blade. Place in large bowl. Sprinkle with salt; mixing well. Cover and refrigerate overnight.
5. The next day, wash nine 8-ounce jars and lids in hot, soapy water; rinse; keep jars in hot water until ready. Start heating water in canner for processing in water bath.
6. Put vegetables into a large colander; rinse with running cold water; drain well, pushing vegetables against sides of colander.
7. Combine sugar, vinegar, corn syrup, mustard seeds, celery seeds and turmeric in a 5-quart stainless steel or enamel pan. Bring to boiling; lower heat; boil gently 5 minutes. Stir in vegetables. Return to boiling; lower heat; simmer 10 minutes.
8. Ladle into drained, hot jars, leaving 1/4-inch head space; wipe rims; seal. Place jars in boiling water to cover by 2 inches in canner or other large, heavy kettle. Cover; when water returns to boiling, process for 5 minutes. Remove to wire rack; cool completely; check seals, label jars and store on cool, dry shelf.

California Pepper Relish

A new treat to serve with hamburgers. Have no red peppers? Green peppers will do just as well -- or, mix them.

Makes 8 half pints.

12 large red peppers
3 tablespoons salt
6 large tomatoes, peeled and chopped
2 large onions, chopped (2 cups)
3 cups sugar
1 cup cider vinegar
2 tablespoons mixed pickling spices

1. Halve, seed and chop peppers. (You should have 9 cups.) Layer with salt in a large glass bowl. Allow to stand at room temperature, stirring several times, for 3 hours. Drain peppers well to remove all liquid.

2. Combine drained peppers, tomatoes and onions in a large kettle; stir in sugar and vinegar. Tie mixed pickling spices in cheesecloth and crack with hammer. Add to kettle.
3. Bring to boiling, stirring often. Lower heat; simmer, stirring frequently near the end of the cooking time to prevent scorching, 30 minutes or until mixture thickens. Remove spice bag.
4. Ladle into 8 hot, sterilized 8-ounce jars; seal; cool. Label and date.

Tangerine and Cranberry Mold

Spoon the mixture into a relish dish instead of a mold, if you wish.

Makes 4 cups.

2 cups sugar
1 1/2 cups water
4 cups fresh or frozen cranberries (about 1 pound)
1 tangerine, peeled, seeded and finely chopped (2/3 cup)
Leaf lettuce

1. Combine sugar and water in medium-size saucepan; bring to boiling, stirring constantly. Boil, uncovered, for 5 minutes.
2. Add cranberries and tangerine. Cook 15 minutes until berries pop and mixture thickens slightly. Pour into a 4-cup mold or bowl; chill overnight.
3. To serve: Unmold onto serving plate. Garnish with lettuce and tangerine sections, if you wish.

Chow Chow

Makes about 3 quarts.

2 cups coarsely chopped celery
2 cups sliced carrots
2 cups coarsely chopped red and green peppers
2 cups cauliflowerettes (1/2 head)
2 cups small white onions, peeled
1 package (9 ounces) frozen cut green beans
1 package (10 ounces) frozen lima beans
1 can (16 ounces) yellow wax beans, drained
2 jars (8 ounces each) sweet gherkins
3 cups sugar
2 cups cider vinegar
1 cup water
1 1/2 tablespoons mustard seeds
1 tablespoon celery seeds
1/2 teaspoon turmeric

1. Cook each vegetable except yellow wax beans separately in boiling salted water until just tender but still firm. Drain. Combine in a large bowl. Add canned beans. Drain juice from gherkins into bowl; chop gherkins finely and add to bowl.
2. Combine sugar, vinegar, water, mustard seeds, celery seeds and turmeric in large kettle. Bring to boiling, stirring constantly until sugar dissolves. Add

vegetable mixture. After mixture comes to boiling again, boil 5 minutes, stirring often.

3. Ladle into hot, sterilized jars to within 1/4 inch from top. Seal, following manufacturer's directions; process in hot water bath 15 minutes. Let jars cool. Label, date and store in a cool place.

Red Beet Eggs

Makes 10 servings.

10 hard-cooked eggs, peeled	1/2 cup cider or distilled white vinegar
2 cans (16 ounces each) sliced beets with juice	1/2 teaspoon salt
1 cup water	1/4 teaspoon pepper
	Curly endive

1. Combine eggs, beets, water, vinegar, salt and pepper in a large bowl. Cover; Refrigerate at least 8 hours or overnight.
2. To serve: Drain eggs and beets. Line a serving plate with endive. Cut eggs in half; arrange on plate with sliced beets. Serve immediately.

Garlic Butter

Makes 1/2 cup (enough for 2 pounds grilled chicken, beef, veal or lamb). Combine 1/2 cup (1 stick) softened butter with 1 clove crushed garlic in a small bowl. Place butter mixture on wax paper and shape into a log. Refrigerate until firm. Cut log into "pats." Place a pat of butter on each serving as it comes off the grill.

Chili Butter

Makes 1/2 cup (enough for 2 pounds grilled chicken, beef, or veal). Combine 1/2 cup (1 stick) softened butter and 1 tablespoon chili powder in a small bowl; blend well. Place butter mixture on wax paper and shape into a log. Refrigerate until firm. Cut log into "pats." Place a pat of butter on each serving as it comes off the grill.

Pimiento and Pepper Butter

Makes 1/2 cup (enough for 2 pounds grilled chicken, beef, veal or lamb). Blot 1 tablespoon chopped pimiento and 1 tablespoon chopped canned jalapeño peppers dry on paper toweling. Combine pimiento, peppers and 1/2 cup (1 stick) butter, softened, in a small bowl; blend well. Place butter mixture on wax

paper and shape into a log. Refrigerate until firm. Cut log into "pats." Place a pat of butter on each serving as it comes off the grill.

Tarragon Butter

Makes 1/2 cup (enough for 2 pounds grilled chicken, beef, veal or lamb). Combine 1/2 cup (1 stick) softened butter and 1 tablespoon chopped fresh tarragon or 1 teaspoon crumbled leaf tarragon in a small bowl; blend well. Place butter mixture on wax paper and shape into a log. Refrigerate until firm. Cut log into "pats." Place a pat of butter on each serving as it comes off the grill.

Plum Butter

Makes about 1 3/4 cups.

2 pounds ripe red or purple plums, halved, pitted and	sliced
	1/4 cup apple juice
	1 cup sugar

1. Combine plums and juice in large saucepan; cook, covered, over moderate heat until fruit is soft, about 10 minutes. Puree in an electric blender or food processor until smooth; return to saucepan.
2. Stir in the sugar and cook puree over low heat until it becomes quite thick, about 1 hour, stirring frequently to prevent scorching.
3. Pour into small plastic containers and refrigerate up to 2 weeks or freeze.

Blue Cheese Butter

Makes 3/4 cup.

1/4 cup (1/2 stick) butter, softened	2 ounces blue cheese, crumbled

1. Combine butter and blue cheese in a small bowl until well mixed. Place butter mixture on wax paper and shape into a log.
2. Refrigerate until firm. Slice log. Serve cheese slices on grilled or broiled beef, chicken or veal.

Maitre d'Hotel Butter

Makes about 2/3 cup.

1/2 cup (1 stick) butter	2 tablespoons finely minced chives
2 tablespoons finely minced fresh parsley	2 tablespoons lemon juice

Blend butter, parsley and chives in a small bowl. Add lemon juice, a little at a time. Turn out onto wax paper; shape into a 1 1/2-inch roll. Wrap tightly and refrigerate until firm. Cut into slices and serve 1 slice on each serving of grilled or broiled meat or poultry.

Basil Butter

Spread on bread or place a pat on grilled steak, grilled chicken or hot vegetables.

Makes 1/2 cup.

1 tablespoon fresh basil, finely chopped	juice
	1/2 cup unsalted butter, softened
2 teaspoons lemon	

Stir the basil and lemon juice into the softened butter in a small bowl. Spoon into a serving container. Store, tightly covered, in the refrigerator.

Basil Butter, page 20; Basil Jelly, page 10.

Brandied Apple Slices

Serve as an accompaniment to pork, ham or poultry or as a dessert.

Makes 5 cups (10 to 12 servings).

6 Golden Delicious apples	stick cinnamon
1 cup orange juice	3/4 cup sugar
2 3-inch pieces	1/2 cup brandy

1. Pare, halve, core and cut apples into eighths.

Place in a large saucepan; add orange juice and cinnamon sticks. Bring to boiling; lower heat and simmer, covered, for 10 minutes or until apples are tender but still firm.
2. Remove from heat; stir in sugar and brandy. Cool; spoon into a container. Can be stored in refrigerator up to 1 month.

Dill Pickles, Kosher Style

Makes 6 quarts.

30 to 36 Kirby cucumbers or other small cucumbers (3 to 4 inches long)	6 cups water
	3/4 cup canning salt
	Fresh or dried dillweed
6 cups cider or distilled white vinegar	Garlic cloves, halved
	Mustard seeds

1. Wash and rinse six 32-ounce jars and their closures. Keep jars and closures immersed in separate kettles of hot water until you are ready to use them.
2. Wash cucumbers thoroughly. Combine vinegar, water and salt in a kettle and bring to boiling.
3. Remove jars, one at a time, from water. Place a generous layer of dill, 1/2 to 1 clove garlic and 1 1/2 teaspoons whole mustard seeds on bottom of each jar.
4. Pack cucumbers into jars. When the jars are half-filled, add more dill and complete the packing of the jars.
5. Pour hot brine over pickles, filling to 1/2 inch of top. Run a thin wooden or plastic spoon handle or other nonmetallic utensil around edge of jars between food and jar to release any trapped air bubbles. Wipe jar rims and seal.
6. Process 20 minutes in boiling water bath (212°). Remove jars from water bath; cool. Pickles will shrivel after processing, but will plump in sealed jar. Check seals, label; store on a cool, dark, dry shelf.

Overnight Pickled Vegetables

Serve with grilled hamburgers, roast meats or an afternoon sandwich.

Makes about 1 quart, 8 servings.

1 cup water	zucchini
1 cup sugar	3 medium-size carrots
2 teaspoons pickling spice	2 medium-size sweet red peppers
2/3 cup white vinegar	1 small yellow squash
2 medium-size	

1. Stir together water, sugar and pickling spice in a medium-size saucepan. Bring to boiling. Lower heat;

Overnight Pickled Vegetables.

Sweet Pickle Chips

Remember to keep these on hand for holiday gifts. They'll remind you of the pickles Grandma used to make.

Makes 5 pints.

1 quart distilled white vinegar	firm cucumbers, sliced 1/4-inch thick (12 cups)
3/4 cup sugar	5 cups sugar
3 tablespoons canning salt	2 cups distilled white vinegar
2 teaspoons mustard seeds	1 tablespoon whole allspice
5 3-inch pieces stick cinnamon	2 teaspoons celery seeds
4 pounds small,	

1. Wash and rinse five 16-ounce jars and their closures. Keep jars and closures immersed in separate kettles of hot water until you are ready to use them.
2. Combine 1 quart vinegar, the 3/4 cup sugar, canning salt, mustard seeds and stick cinnamon in a large, heavy, enamel or stainless steel kettle. Add cucumbers. Bring to boiling, stirring occasionally. Adjust heat; simmer 5 minutes; drain cucumbers; discard liquid but reserve cinnamon.
3. Combine remaining sugar and vinegar, allspice and celery seeds in kettle; bring to rolling boil over high heat.
4. Pack cucumbers into hot preserving jars, using a wide-mouth funnel, to within 1/4 inch of tops; add 1 cinnamon stick to each jar. Pour hot liquid over pickles filling to 1/4 inch of top, making sure there is enough syrup to cover pickles. Run a thin wooden or plastic spoon handle or other nonmetallic utensil around edge of jars between food and jar to release any trapped air bubbles. Wipe jar rims and seal.
5. Process 10 minutes in a boiling water bath (212°). Remove jars from water bath; cool; check seals, then label and store on a cool, dark, dry shelf.

Pickled Beets

You can eat these beets ten days after you make them, or you can "put them up" and eat them all winter.

Makes 1 quart or 4 half-pints.

8 small beets (2 pounds)	5 peppercorns
1 cup cider vinegar	1 teaspoon pickling spice
1 teaspoon salt	1 bay leaf
1/4 cup sugar	Fresh dill (*optional*)

1. Wash and rinse a 1-quart canning jar and lid, or, if "putting up," 4 half-pint jars and lids. Keep jars in simmering water.

simmer, uncovered, without stirring, for 5 minutes. Cool to room temperature. Pour in vinegar.
2. Slice zucchini into 1/2-inch-thick rounds. Pare carrots. Halve and seed red peppers. Cut carrots and peppers into 1 1/2 × 1/2-inch sticks. Slice yellow squash into 1/2-inch-thick rounds. You should have a total of about 4 cups of vegetables.
3. Pack the zucchini tightly, with round cut-sides facing outward, in bottom of a 1-quart glass or clear plastic container with a tight-fitting lid.
4. Mix together carrot and red pepper sticks. Arrange, standing upright, on top of zucchini; pack tightly.
5. Pack yellow squash, round cut-sides facing outward on top of carrot and red pepper sticks. Make sure all the vegetables are tightly packed in the container, or they will float to the top when the pickling liquid is added.
6. Slowly pour enough of the pickling liquid into the container to cover the vegetables. Gently move vegetables so some of the spices fall between the vegetables. Cover tightly; refrigerate overnight. Vegetables can be stored in the refrigerator for up to 3 days.

(continued)

2. Scrub beets; trim, leaving 1 inch of the tops and the root ends attached. Cook, covered, in boiling salted water to cover, 40 minutes or until barely tender. Beets should be somewhat firm. Drain, reserving 1 cup of the cooking liquid. Rinse beets in cold running water; slip off skins, roots and tops; slice.
3. Fill the jar or jars with beet slices. Combine the reserved cup of cooking liquid with vinegar, salt, sugar, peppercorns, pickling spice and bay leaf. Bring to boiling; pour into filled jars to 1/4-inch from tops.
4. Seal jar and refrigerate for 10 days before serving.
5. For canning, seal the half-pint jars. Process for 10 minutes in boiling water bath. Cool; check seals. Label and store in a cool, dry place.

Pickled Mushrooms

A tempting appetizer to serve.

Makes 5 cups.

2 cups water	**1/8 teaspoon fennel**
3/4 cup vegetable oil	**seeds**
1/2 cup lemon juice	**1/2 teaspoon salt**
3 celery stalks, cut	**8 peppercorns**
into 3-inch pieces	**1 1/2 pounds small**
1 clove garlic, halved	**mushrooms**
1/2 teaspoon ground	**1 jar (4 ounces)**
coriander	**pimientos, drained**
1/4 teaspoon leaf	**and sliced**
thyme, crumbled	

Combine water, oil, lemon juice, celery, garlic, coriander, thyme, fennel, salt and peppercorns in a medium-size saucepan; bring to boiling. Lower heat; add mushrooms; simmer 5 minutes. Pour into a large bowl. Cool. Add pimientos. Cover; refrigerate. Will keep for up to 1 week.

Pickled Peaches and Pears

Makes 5 pints peaches and 6 pints pears.

12 cups sugar	**peeled, halved and**
4 cups cider vinegar	**pitted (about 6**
4 3-inch pieces stick	**pounds)**
cinnamon	**24 medium-size pears**
2 tablespoons whole	**1 1-inch piece ginger**
cloves	**root** *(optional)*
14 large peaches,	

1. Combine sugar, vinegar, cinnamon and cloves in a large kettle. Bring to boiling; simmer 5 minutes.
2. Lower peach halves into kettle with a slotted spoon; bring to boiling; lower heat; simmer 15 minutes or just until peaches are tender.
3. Remove kettle from heat; cover; let stand 12 to 18 hours at room temperature. Next day, bring mixture to boiling. Ladle into 5 hot, 16-ounce jars, leaving

1/2-inch head space. Seal and process in boiling water bath for 20 minutes. Remove; cool; label.
4. Pare, halve and core pears. Add dry ginger root to remaining syrup in kettle, if you wish. (You should have about 8 cups of syrup left.) Bring to boiling; lower pear halves into kettle with a slotted spoon; bring to boiling; lower heat; simmer 10 minutes or just until pears are tender.
5. Remove kettle from heat; cover; let stand 12 to 18 hours at room temperature. Next day, bring mixture to boiling. Ladle into 6 hot, 16-ounce jars, leaving 1/2-inch head space. Seal and process in boiling water bath for 20 minutes. Remove; cool; label.

Garden Mustard Pickles

Makes 7 pints.

1 small cauliflower,	**cut into 1-inch**
separated into	**pieces**
flowerets	**1/3 cup kosher or**
1 pound small white	**canning salt**
onions, peeled	**1/2 cup firmly packed**
6 green tomatoes,	**brown sugar**
cored and cut into	**3 tablespoons dry**
wedges	**mustard**
6 pickling cucumbers,	**2 teaspoons turmeric**
cut into 1-inch	**2 teaspoons mustard**
pieces	**seeds**
2 large green peppers,	**2 teaspoons celery**
halved, seeded and	**seeds**
cut into 1-inch	**6 cups cider vinegar**
pieces	**1/2 cup all-purpose**
2 large red peppers,	**flour**
halved, seeded and	**1 cup cold water**

1. Combine vegetables with salt in a large glass or ceramic bowl.
2. Cover bowl with plastic wrap; let stand 12 to 18 hours at room temperature. Next day, drain vegetables; spoon into a large kettle. Add brown sugar, mustard, turmeric, mustard and celery seeds; stir in cider vinegar.
3. Bring to boiling, stirring often; lower heat; simmer 15 minutes or until vegetables are tender. Combine flour and cold water in a small bowl to make a smooth

paste. Stir slowly into bubbling liquid; cook, stirring, until mixture thickens and bubbles 3 minutes.
4. Ladle into 7 hot, 16-ounce jars, leaving 1/2-inch head space. Wipe rims and seal. Process in boiling water bath for 5 minutes. Remove; cool; label.

Piccalilli

Makes 6 half pints.

1 pound green tomatoes (3 medium-size)
1 large red pepper, seeded and chopped (3/4 cup)
1 large green pepper, seeded and chopped (3/4 cup)
1 to 2 tablespoons finely chopped hot pepper
2 large onions,
chopped (2 cups)
1 small head cabbage, cored and chopped (6 cups)
1 tablespoon salt
1 cup sugar
1 tablespoon mustard seeds
1 tablespoon celery seeds
1 cup light corn syrup
2 cups cider vinegar

1. Core tomatoes; chop coarsely (you should have 3 cups). Combine tomatoes with remaining ingredients in a large stainless steel or enamel kettle.
2. Bring mixture to boiling, stirring occasionally. Lower heat and cook about 30 minutes or until syrup is slightly thickened and vegetables are crisp-tender.
3. Ladle vegetables into 6 hot, 8-ounce jars with a slotted spoon, leaving 1/2-inch head space. Pour the syrup into jars, covering vegetables and leaving 1/4-inch head space. Wipe rims and seal.
4. Process in boiling water bath for 10 minutes. Remove; cool; label.

Marinated Cucumber Slices

Makes 6 servings.

2 small or 1 large cucumber, unpeeled, halved lengthwise, seeded and very thinly sliced
1 1/2 teaspoons salt
1/2 cup white vinegar
1/4 cup chopped fresh parsley
1/2 teaspoon sugar
1/4 teaspoon white pepper

1. Layer cucumber slices with 1 teaspoon of the salt in a 9-inch pie plate. Let stand 10 minutes.
2. Press cucumbers into plate; pour off liquid that accumulates.
3. Sprinkle vinegar, parsley, sugar, pepper and remaining salt over cucumbers, tossing gently to mix well.
4. Marinate, covered, for at least 30 minutes to let flavors blend before serving.

Horseradish

The thick taproot of a mustard plant which is ground and served as is or mixed with vinegar. It is used as a condiment or made into sauces for serving with roast beef and other meat entrees.

Horseradish probably originated in eastern Europe, although it was brought to America from Great Britain. The plant grows wild in the moist areas of some of the northeastern United States.

Fresh horseradish root is available in the fall. The root is grated and mixed with vinegar or beet juice, bottled and sold for year-round use. Commercially made horseradish is called prepared horseradish.

Capers

The flower buds of a wild Mediterranean shrub, which are salted and preserved in vinegar. They are used as a condiment or for seasoning sauce. Capers are sold in small bottles, usually imported from Spain, France or Italy. Refrigerate them once the bottle is opened; use to add a unique flavor to mayonnaise sauces and seafood or veal dishes.

Spicy Tomato Ketchup

Makes 4 half pints.

16 large ripe tomatoes
1 cup cider vinegar
1/2 cup firmly packed brown sugar
2 tablespoons salt
1 tablespoon mixed pickling spices tied in cheesecloth

1. Wash and core tomatoes; cut into chunks; place in a large kettle. Bring slowly to boiling, stirring often; lower heat; simmer 30 minutes.
2. Press tomatoes through strainer or food mill, a few cups at a time, into a large *heavy* kettle; bring slowly to boiling; lower heat; simmer, uncovered, 1 hour or until reduced by half.
3. Stir in vinegar, brown sugar, salt and mixed pickling spices. Cook, stirring frequently to prevent sticking, about 1 hour or until mixture has thickened as you like it. (An asbestos pad placed under the kettle will help prevent scorching.)
4. Remove spice bag. Ladle into 4 hot, sterilized 8-ounce jars, leaving 1/8-inch headspace. Seal; process 10 minutes in boiling water bath.

APPETIZERS

Appetizer
Everyone likes a party, especially when there are plenty of appetizers and conviviality. But appetizers are not just for parties. They can be served as the first course of a meal as well. Appetizers are any foods that stimulate the appetite.

APPETIZERS FOR A PARTY
• *Dips* are for dipping, not dripping. Make them thick enough to cling to vegetables, crackers, chips or fruit. Instead of the usual bowl, hollow out vegetables such as eggplant, squash, cabbage, peppers or even a sweet Spanish onion. A fresh hollowed out pineapple makes a nice bowl for a fruit dip.
• *Spreads* should glide over bread or crackers, not shatter them. You can choose from meat or poultry spreads, cheese, seafood or even vegetable spreads.
• *Canapés* are miniature, open-face, hot or cold sandwiches on a base of either bread, pastry, cracker or sliced vegetable. They should be small enough to eat in two bites.
• *Hors d'oeuvres* are any other bite-size finger foods not served on a base.
• *Relishes* such as pickled mushrooms, onions, peppers, olives. Fresh carrot sticks, radishes, green onions and celery are simple relishes.
• *Cheese* with bread, crackers or fruit and nuts can make an easy-on-the-host appetizer. Choose several different-looking cheeses with sharp or very distinct flavors. Let them warm to cool room temperature before serving.
• *Nibblers* are chips, pretzels, nuts or homemade tidbits.

When choosing an appetizer for a first course, consider it as part of the meal. A light appetizer such as a clear soup goes with a heavy meal. An elegant holiday meal requires a special first course, not a jiffy dip and chips. Consider the weather too. Cold finger foods and icy soups are more enjoyable when it's warm outside.

APPETIZERS FOR A FIRST COURSE
• *Fruit or Seafood Cocktail*
• *Pâtés* can be made of meat, poultry, game, seafood or vegetables
• *Soup* can be hot or cold
• *Marinated vegetables or seafood*
• *Smoked fish* such as salmon, trout
• *Pasta* in a light sauce
• *Shellfish* on the half shell

Antipasto
An Italian word, meaning "before the meal." Antipasto foods are usually tart or biting and are served as appetizers before the main course. The most typical antipasto consists of salami, olives, marinated mushrooms, peppers, tuna or anchovies and artichokes. The Italian cured ham, prosciutto, combined with fresh melon or figs is also very popular as an antipasto.

Country Pâté

This smooth, mellow pâté can be baked a day or two in advance and served cold or warmed in a slow oven.

Bake at 350° for 1 1/2 hours.

Makes 16 servings.

1 pound beef liver	**1 teaspoon ground**
3/4 pound boneless	**allspice**
pork shoulder	**1/4 teaspoon ground**
1/4 pound pork fat back	**cloves**
1 large onion,	**1/2 teaspoon pepper**
quartered	**2 cups milk**
3 tablespoons butter	**2 eggs**
or margarine	**Crisp bacon strips**
1/4 cup all-purpose	**Sautéed mushrooms**
flour	**Watercress or parsley**
3 teaspoons salt	

1. Soak liver in cold water for 30 minutes; pat dry on paper toweling. Trim fat and membranes from liver. Grind liver, pork, pork fat and onion twice through the fine blade of meat grinder. Place in large bowl.
2. Melt butter or margarine in medium-size saucepan; stir in flour, salt, allspice, cloves and pepper. Gradually add milk. Cook, stirring constantly, until sauce thickens and bubbles 1 minute; cool slightly. Stir hot sauce into ground liver-meat mixture; add eggs and beat with a wooden spoon until thoroughly mixed. Turn mixture into a greased 6-cup shallow baking dish.
3. Place dish in larger pan; pour boiling water into outer pan to come halfway up the side of pâté dish.
4. Bake in a moderate oven (350°) for 1 1/2 hours or until juices run clear when pâté is pierced with a fork or a thin-bladed knife.
5. Remove from water bath and allow to cool; when pâté is cool, drain off juices; cover and refrigerate overnight or longer. Garnish with bacon, mushrooms and watercress or parsley.

Pictured opposite: Country Pâté.

Elegant Pâté

Makes about 2 cups.

1 1/2 pounds chicken livers	Dash cayenne
1/2 small onion	1 tablespoon dry mustard
1 cup (2 sticks) butter or margarine, softened	1/4 teaspoon ground nutmeg
1/2 cup minced onion	1/8 teaspoon ground cloves
1 teaspoon salt	

1. Cook livers with the onion half in boiling salted water to cover until tender, about 15 minutes; drain.
2. Place chicken livers, butter, minced onion, salt, cayenne, mustard, nutmeg and cloves in container of an electric blender or food processor. Cover and whirl until smooth. Turn into a serving bowl. Cover; chill for several hours. Serve with assorted crackers.

Shrimp Pâté Canapes

Makes 6 to 7 dozen.

1 1/2 pounds cooked, shelled and deveined shrimp	1 jar (6 ounces) tartar sauce
2 tablespoons lemon juice	1 teaspoon salt
2 tablespoons prepared horseradish	4 large cucumbers OR: Crackers or slices of toast
1/4 cup chili sauce	1 jar (4 ounces) red caviar

1. Place shrimp, lemon juice, horseradish, chili sauce, tartar sauce and salt in container of electric blender; whirl until smooth; cover and chill.
2. Cut unpeeled cucumbers into 1/4-inch diagonal slices; chill.
3. When ready to serve, spread cucumber with pâté. Top each with a tiny spoonful of red caviar.

Sausage Pâtè en Croûte

Makes about 12 servings.

1 large loaf rye, white or Italian bread OR: 2 loaves (7 ounces each) French bread	2 tablespoons brandy
	1/4 cup pistachio nuts (optional)
1 package (8 ounces) cream cheese	1/4 pound unsliced ham, tongue or bologna, cut into 1/2-inch cubes
1 pound liver sausage	

1. Slice about 1/2 inch off each end of loaf of bread. Hollow out inside with serrated knife and long-handled fork, leaving 1/2-inch crust all around. (Use crumbs for another recipe.)
2. Soften cream cheese in a large bowl. Cut sausage in chunks and add to cheese; add brandy. Beat with electric mixer until smooth; stir in pistachios. Fold diced meat into sausage mixture.
3. Pack pâtè mixture into hollowed bread. Press both end slices back onto loaf. Wrap loaf in foil and chill several hours. Cut loaf in slices about 1/2-inch thick and garnish with parsley and tomatoes or, for a festive touch, fresh grapes.

Chicken Pâté With Port Wine Aspic

Bake at 350° for 1 1/2 hours.

Makes 12 servings.

1 chicken breast half (about 8 ounces), skinned and boned	1/2 teaspoon leaf thyme, crumbled
1/2 cup white or tawny port wine	1/2 teaspoon pepper
2 tablespoons butter or margarine	2 eggs
3/4 pound chicken livers	3/4 cup heavy cream
1 pound ground turkey, pork or veal	3 tablespoons pistachio nuts or almonds
1 medium-size onion, minced (1/2 cup)	2 bay leaves
2 teaspoons salt	Port Wine Aspic (recipe follows)
1 teaspoon ground coriander	1 whole canned pimiento
	Parsley stems and sprigs

1. Cut chicken breast into long thin strips. Place in a small bowl; add port wine; let marinate several hours. Drain, reserving wine. Sauté chicken in butter in small skillet just until no pink remains. Remove to plate. Deglaze pan with reserved wine; cook until reduced to 1/4 cup.
2. Chop chicken livers finely. Combine with ground turkey, onion, salt, coriander, thyme and pepper in a large bowl. Beat with wooden spoon until well blended. Gradually beat in eggs and cream. Stir in nuts and wine mixture from skillet.
3. Layer pâté mixture with chicken breast pieces in 1 1/2-quart baking dish or loaf pan. Arrange bay leaves on top; cover with foil. Set dish in larger pan on oven shelf; fill pan half full with boiling water.
4. Bake in a moderate oven (350°) for 1 1/2 hours until juices are no longer pink. Remove to wire rack. Cool, then chill overnight in refrigerator. Remove from pan.
5. Prepare Port Wine Aspic. Place pâté on rack over a platter to catch gelatin that drips down. Spoon a thin coating of aspic over paté. Cut pimiento into flower-petal shapes. Arrange on top of pâté. Use parsley for stems and leaves. Brush or spoon several layers of aspic over decorations. Chill several hours. Chill remaining aspic in shallow bowl or pie plate; chop and spoon around pâté.

Port Wine Aspic: Pour 1 cup chicken broth through paper filter or double layer of cheesecloth in small saucepan; sprinkle 1 envelope unflavored gelatin over. Let stand 5 minutes to soften. Heat, stirring constantly, until gelatin is completely dissolved; remove from heat; stir in 1/2 cup white or tawny port wine. Place pan in larger pan of ice and water to speed thickening. Chill, stirring until syrupy.

Greek Cucumber Dip

In Greece, this dip is made with thick, rich yogurt. Here, a blend of yogurt plus sour cream is the best way to achieve the authentic flavor and texture of this delicious dipping sauce.

Makes about 2 1/2 cups.

2 large cucumbers, pared and coarsely grated	garlic, finely chopped
1 cup low-fat yogurt	1 teaspoon salt
1 cup dairy sour cream	1/4 teaspoon pepper
1 small clove	Paprika *(optional)*
	Pita Crisps *(recipe follows)*

1. Enclose 1/4 of the grated cucumbers in the corner of a clean disk towel and wring out to remove as much moisture as possible. Put the drained cucumbers in a bowl and repeat with the remainder.
2. Stir the yogurt, sour cream, garlic, salt and pepper into the cucumbers. Sprinkle lightly with paprika, if you wish. Serve with Pita Crisps.
Pita Crisps: Split small pita breads in half with scissors, forming two thin rounds. Cut rounds in quarters, place on cookie sheet and bake 7 to 10 minutes at 325° until crisp and very lightly browned.

Creamy Herb Dip

Serve this with an assortment of fresh vegetables for dipping.
Makes about 1 1/2 cups.

2 to 3 cloves garlic	1 teaspoon leaf basil, crumbled
2 tablespoons lemon juice	1/2 teaspoon salt
1 egg	Dash cayenne pepper
1/2 cup grated Parmesan cheese	1/2 cup olive or vegetable oil
1/2 cup small parsley sprigs	1/2 cup plain yogurt

1. Place garlic, lemon juice, egg, cheese, parsley, basil, salt and cayenne in the container of an electric blender; cover. Whirl until smooth, scraping down sides of blender.
2. Remove the center of the blender cover. With the blender running, pour oil in a thin stream into mixture, stopping once or twice to scrape down sides of blender; mixture should be thick. Stir in yogurt. Scrape into serving bowl. Cover; refrigerate 2 hours.

Fresh Dill Dip

A charming way to serve this dip is in a small new and well scrubbed flowerpot, surrounded by vegetables.

Makes about 2 cups.

1 1/2 cups dairy sour cream	dillweed
1/2 cup mayonnaise	1/4 cup thinly sliced green onions
2 tablespoons Dijon mustard	2 teaspoons lemon juice
1/3 cup chopped fresh dill	1/2 teaspoon salt
OR: 1 tablespoon	1/4 teaspoon pepper

1. Combine all ingredients in a medium-size bowl and blend thoroughly.
2. Spoon into serving bowl, cover and refrigerate 1 hour or longer.
Dipper Tips: Good with raw green beans, carrot sticks, red pepper strips, any chips.

Chick-Pea Dip

Makes 2 cups.

1/4 cup sesame seeds	cumin
2 tablespoons water	1 can (16 ounces) chick-peas, undrained
1/2 teaspoon vegetable oil	
3 tablespoons lemon juice	Chopped fresh parsley
1 clove garlic, crushed	Assorted raw vegetables
1/4 teaspoon ground	

1. Place sesame seeds in container of electric blender or food processor; whirl until ground. Add water and oil; whirl until smooth paste forms.
2. Add lemon juice, garlic and cumin. Drain chick-peas, reserving liquid. Add chick-peas to sesame mixture; whirl until smooth. Add as much liquid as is necessary to make a dip consistency.
3. Pour dip into a small serving bowl; cover and chill several hours.
4. To serve: Place bowl of dip on a large plate. Garnish dip with chopped parsley. Surround bowl with raw vegetables—celery or carrot sticks, cherry tomatoes, edible-podded peas, green or red pepper strips, broccoli or cauliflowerets.

Jalapeño Refried Bean Dip

The best dipper to use is freshly fried corn tortilla chips, but you can also use ready-to-eat corn or tostado chips.

Makes about 2 cups.

1/4 cup lard or bacon drippings	green (jalapeño) chilies, seeded and diced
1 small onion, minced (1/4 cup)	1/2 teaspoon salt
1 small clove garlic, minced	1/2 cup shredded longhorn or mild Cheddar cheese
1 can (16 ounces) refried beans or cooked pinto beans, mashed with liquid	Tortilla Chips (*recipe follows*) or packaged corn chips
1 to 2 canned hot	

Heat lard in a small skillet. Add onion and garlic; sauté 1 minute. Add refried or mashed pinto beans. Cook, stirring frequently, until well mixed and lard is absorbed. Stir in chile to taste, salt and 1/4 cup of the cheese. (If dip is too firm for dipping, add a little water.) Garnish with remaining cheese and serve with corn chips.

Tortilla Chips: From 1 dozen fresh or thawed, frozen corn tortillas, cut each tortilla into 8 triangles. Heat 1/4 inch vegetable oil in a large skillet until hot. Fry tortillas, a few at a time, in hot oil, turning once or twice, until crisp and golden brown. Drain on paper toweling.

Note: These are perfect keepers so you can make them ahead. Store in an airtight container so they'll stay crisp.

Guacamole

Makes 2 cups.

2 medium-size ripe avocados	1/4 cup dairy sour cream
2 tablespoons chopped canned mild green chilies	2 tablespoons lime juice
1 tablespoon grated onion	1 teaspoon salt
1 clove garlic, minced	1/4 teaspoon liquid hot pepper seasoning
	Tortilla or corn chips

Mash avocados in a medium-size bowl until smooth. Stir in chilies, onion, garlic, sour cream, lime juice, salt and hot pepper seasoning. Cover tightly with plastic wrap. Refrigerate about 1 hour or until well chilled. Garnish with chopped onion, if you wish. Serve with tortilla or corn chips. Or, serve as a sauce with tacos or tostadas.

Olive-Tuna Dip

Makes about 2 cups.

1/2 cup (1 stick) butter or margarine	juice
1 can (6 1/2 ounces) water-pack tuna, drained and flaked	1/4 cup mayonnaise or salad dressing
4 teaspoons lemon	2 tablespoons chopped, stuffed green olives

1. Cream butter until soft in a small bowl; beat in tuna, lemon juice and mayonnaise; fold in olives. Cover. Chill. Serve with vegetables, if you wish.

Garlic Cheese Dip

Makes 2 cups.

1 container (16 ounces) dairy sour cream	garlic salad dressing mix
1 envelope cheese-	1/2 teaspoon dried parsley flakes

Combine sour cream, salad dressing mix and parsley flakes in a small bowl; chill for several hours to blend flavors.

Bagna Cauda

Translated "hot bath," bagna cauda is an Italian sauce flavored with anchovies and garlic. It is served over cooked vegetables, fish or meats, or as a dip for bread sticks and raw vegetables.

Bagna Cauda

Here's a party dip with pizzazz.

Makes 8 servings.

3 cups heavy cream	slender wedges
6 tablespoons (3/4 stick) unsalted butter	1 bunch young green onions, cut into 3-inch lengths
1 can (2 ounces) anchovy fillets, drained and mashed	1/2 pint cherry tomatoes
1 clove garlic, minced	1/2 pound very fresh mushrooms, quartered—if large, or halved, leave stems on
2 cucumbers, pared, cut into bite-size sticks	Italian bread sticks or 1 loaf crusty Italian bread, cubed
2 heads fennel, washed, trimmed and cut into	

1. Simmer heavy cream in a small saucepan, stirring occasionally, until reduced to half its volume (1 1/2 cups). This will take about 20 minutes.

use as the container for the spread. Cut removed circle of bread into thin slices; wrap and chill. Wrap ring of bread.

2. Combine salmon, cheese, milk, onions and lemon juice in the container of an electric blender or food processor; whirl until smooth. Scrape into a bowl; cover and chill. When ready to serve, place ring of bread on a large platter. Fill center with salmon spread. Surround loaf with slices of bread. Sprinkle top of spread with capers.

Liptauer Cheese Spread

A Middle European recipe, temptingly good on crisp crackers. It was originally made with a goat's milk cheese, called Liptauer.

Makes 1 1/2 cups.

1/2 cup small curd cottage cheese	paste
1/2 cup (4 ounces) cream cheese, softened	1 teaspoon Dijon mustard
1/2 cup (1 stick) butter or margarine, softened	1 tablespoon grated onion
1 teaspoon paprika	1/2 teaspoon caraway seeds
1 teaspoon anchovy	Chopped radishes
	Chopped chives

1. Beat cottage and cream cheeses, butter, paprika, anchovy paste and mustard in small bowl with electric mixer until smooth; stir in onion and caraway. Cover; refrigerate.

2. Remove from refrigerator 1 hour before serving. Garnish with chopped radishes and chives; serve with crackers or pumpernickel bread, if you wish.

Note: This spread may be made up to a week in advance.

Sausage Stuffed Onions, page 587.

2. Melt butter in a skillet; add anchovies and garlic; cook 2 minutes, stirring often. Stir in hot cream. Pour into chafing dish. Keep warm over low heat while dipping vegetables or bread.

3. Arrange vegetables and bread on tray around chafing dish.

Spread A food soft enough to apply to bread, crackers or other foods. Cheese, butter, jams or jellies are popular bread or cracker spreads.

Smoked Salmon Spread in Pumpernickel

A great way to stretch smoked salmon.

Makes 2 1/2 cups spread.

1 unsliced loaf round pumpernickel, about 1 pound	1/2 cup milk
1/2 pound smoked salmon	1/3 cup chopped green onions
1 package (8 ounces) cream cheese	1 tablespoon lemon juice
	Drained capers

1. With a sharp knife, cut a circle out of center of bread, leaving a narrow, but sturdy, ring of bread to

Herring Apple Spread

Makes 2 cups.

1 jar (8 ounces) herring party snacks in wine sauce, drained and cut into 1/4-inch cubes	chopped (1/2 cup)
	1 tablespoon minced fresh dill
1 eating apple, quartered, cored and finely chopped	OR: 1 teaspoon dillweed
	1 tablespoon Dijon mustard
1 medium-size red onion, finely	1/2 cup dairy sour cream
	Lettuce leaves

1. Combine herring, apple, onion and dill in a medium-size bowl. Stir mustard into sour cream; stir into

(continued)

herring mixture; cover. Refrigerate several hours before serving.

2. To serve: Stir herring mixture. Line serving bowl with lettuce leaves; mound mixture in center. Garnish with red apple slices (dipped in lemon juice) and dill sprigs. Serve with thin pumpernickel bread slices.

Parsleyed Blue Cheese Spread

This spread features a duet of two cheeses plus herbs and tangy olives.

Makes 2 cups.

4 ounces blue cheese, softened	**green olives**
2 packages (3 ounces each) cream cheese, softened	**1¹/₂ teaspoons chopped chives**
¹/₂ cup (1 stick) butter or margarine, softened	**³/₄ cup chopped fresh parsley**
¹/₃ cup chopped pimiento-stuffed	**1 small clove garlic, minced**
	1 tablespoon brandy (optional)

1. Combine blue cheese, cream cheese, butter, olives, chives, 1¹/₂ teaspoons of the parsley, garlic and brandy in a medium-size bowl; blend well.
2. Line a 2-cup bowl with plastic wrap. Turn cheese mixture into bowl, packing it down firmly; refrigerate.
3. To serve: Turn cheese ball out onto serving platter. Peel off plastic wrap. Sprinkle with remaining parsley and garnish with pimiento, if you wish.

Gorgonzola Toast

These tangy, Christmas tree-shaped cheese toasts are guaranteed to whet the appetite.

Bake at 400° for 5 to 8 minutes.

Makes 18 to 24 servings.

18 to 24 slices very thin-sliced bread	**Gorgonzola cheese OR: blue cheese**
¹/₄ cup crumbled	**¹/₄ cup (¹/₂ stick) butter**

1. Preheat the oven to hot (400°).
2. Cut each bread slice into a tree shape, using 3- or 4-inch cookie cutter.
3. Melt together the cheese and butter in a small skillet over low heat. Dip each tree shape quickly into the cheese mixture, coating one side only. Place, cheese-side up, on cookie sheet.
4. Bake in preheated hot oven (400°) for 5 to 8 minutes until toasty and golden. Remove the breads to wire racks to cool.

Note: Use trimmings from bread to make bread crumbs for another use.

Salmon Appetizer, page 547.

Cheese Crisp

This is a quick and irresistible appetizer or snack. Traditionally, it is served whole at the table and everyone breaks off a piece but it may be precut into wedges like pizza.

Makes about 8 servings.

1 large flour tortilla (about 14-inches in diameter)	**softened**
1 tablespoon butter or margarine,	**¹/₂ cup shredded longhorn or mild Cheddar cheese**

Spread tortilla with butter or margarine. Heat on hot griddle or very large skillet until crisp and firm. Sprinkle with cheese; bake just until cheese melts. Garnish with strips of green chile, if you wish.

Gorgonzola Logs

Nippy Gorgonzola teams with butter and Cheddar for a zesty spread.

Makes 2 logs.

1 package (6 ounces) Gorgonzola cheese, softened	**2 tablespoons brandy**
¹/₂ cup (1 stick) butter, softened	**1 teaspoon Worcestershire sauce**
1 stick (10 ounces) extra sharp Cheddar cheese, shredded	**²/₃ cup chopped walnuts**
	¹/₃ cup chopped fresh parsley

1. Beat Gorgonzola and butter until light and fluffy in large bowl with electric mixer. Stir in Cheddar, brandy and Worcestershire.
2. Divide mixture in half. Turn each half onto wax

paper and roll, shaping into a log 1 inch in diameter. Twist ends of wax paper closed. Refrigerate several hours until firm.

3. Combine nuts and parsley. Roll cheese logs in mixture, pressing firmly. Roll up in wax paper; refrigerate. Soften slightly before serving with crackers.

Cheddar Poppy Strips

Bake at 425° for 10 minutes.

Makes 16 strips.

2 cups buttermilk baking mix	**melted**
1/2 teaspoon leaf basil, crumbled	**1 package (4 ounces) shredded Cheddar cheese (1 cup)**
1/2 cup milk	**1 teaspoon poppy seeds**
2 tablespoons butter or margarine,	

1. Preheat oven to 425°. Place baking mix and basil in a large bowl. Stir in milk with fork until a soft dough forms.
2. Knead dough 3 to 4 times on a floured board. Roll out into a 16 × 10-inch rectangle; brush with 1 tablespoon of the melted butter; sprinkle cheese evenly over dough.
3. Fold in thirds lengthwise. You will have a 16 × 3-inch strip.
4. Brush with remaining butter; sprinkle with poppy seeds; cut crosswise into 16 1-inch strips. Place on ungreased cookie sheet.
5. Bake in a preheated hot oven (425°) for 10 minutes or until strips are golden brown. Serve warm.

Three-Cheese Tart

Serve slivers of this rich appetizer with grapes.
Bake pastry at 425° for 10 minutes, then bake tart at 400° for 15 minutes.

Makes 12 servings.

1 1/2 cups *sifted* all-purpose flour	**mustard**
1/4 teaspoon salt	**1/4 teaspoon salt**
9 tablespoons butter or margarine	**Dash cayenne**
1 egg yolk	**3 ounces Danish Fontina or Swiss cheese, shredded (3/4 cup)**
1 package (3 ounces) cream cheese	
1 egg	**1 ounce blue cheese, crumbled (1/4 cup)**
1 egg yolk	**3/4 cup heavy cream, whipped**
2 tablespoons aquavit or vodka	**Seedless grapes**
1/4 teaspoon dry	

1. Mix flour and salt in a medium-size bowl. Cut in butter with a pastry blender until mixture is crumbly.

Add one egg yolk; mix lightly with a fork, then knead until pastry holds together and leaves side of bowl clean. Chill 30 minutes or until ready to use.

2. Preheat oven to 425°. Roll pastry out to an 11-inch round on a lightly floured surface. Carefully slip the bottom from a 9-inch fluted quiche pan under pastry; lift bottom with pastry into pan; turn edge of pastry under; press against side of pan. Or, if quiche pan or dish does not have a removable bottom, lift pastry into pan and press onto bottom or side, leveling off at edge of dish. Prick bottom and side with a fork. Chill 30 minutes.
3. Bake pastry shell in preheated hot oven (425°) for 10 minutes or until golden. Cool on wire rack. Lower oven temperature to hot (400°).
4. Beat cream cheese until smooth in large bowl; gradually blend in egg, egg yolk, aquavit, mustard, salt and cayenne. Fold in Fontina, blue cheese and cream. Pour into partially baked pastry shell.
5. Bake in a preheated hot oven (400°) for 15 minutes or until top is golden and quiche is almost set. (A knife blade inserted 1 inch from edges will come out clean.) Cool completely on wire rack. Chill until ready to serve. Garnish with grapes.

Sweet and Sour Meatballs, page 570.

Cheese Rolls

For a large crowd make the recipe two or three times. These easy-to-make rolls can be prepared a day or two ahead. Save any leftovers for a delicious sandwich filling.

Makes 2 cheese rolls, 12 servings each.

- 2 packages (8 ounces each) cream cheese, softened
- 2 tablespoons prepared horseradish
- 2 tablespoons Dijon-style mustard
- 2 tablespoons finely chopped onion
- 2 jars (2.5 ounces each) sliced dried beef, finely chopped
- 3/4 cup finely chopped pecans
- 3/4 cup finely chopped chives or parsley

1. Beat together the cream cheese, horseradish, mustard and onion in a small bowl with wooden spoon until well blended. Stir in beef.
2. Chill for about 1 hour or until the mixture is firm enough to be shaped into 2 equal size rolls, each about 1 1/2 inches in diameter.
3. Roll one log in the chopped pecans and the other in the chopped chives. Serve with crackers or party rounds.

Chili-Cheese Rolls with Avocado Dip

Try the Avocado Dip with fresh vegetables or tortilla chips as dippers.

Makes 50 rolls.

- 50 wonton skins (1-pound package)*
- 2 egg whites beaten with 1 tablespoon water
- 8 ounces Monterey Jack cheese cut into 1/2×1/2×1/4-inch cubes
- 3/4 cup finely chopped drained green chilies
- Vegetable oil for frying
- Avocado Dip (recipe follows)

1. Place wonton skin on work surface with a point facing you. (Keep the remaining skins covered with plastic wrap while you work.) Brush lightly with the beaten egg white.
2. Place a cheese cube in the center of the wrapper; top with 1/4-teaspoon of the chilies. Bring one corner up and over the filling; repeat with the adjacent corners, one at a time, pressing down the points firmly together over the filling. Roll into a neat package. Place on a cookie sheet, cover with plastic wrap to prevent drying. Repeat with the remaining wonton wrappers, cheese cubes and chopped chillies.
3. Pour the oil into an electric skillet or deep saucepan to a depth of 3 inches. Heat to 375°. Deep-fry 8 rolls at a time for 30 seconds or until golden brown; keep the rolls submerged with a slotted spoon. Drain on paper toweling. Serve immediately with Avocado Dip.

Avocado Dip: Combine 1 cup mashed avocado, 1 finely chopped clove of garlic, 2 tablespoons dairy sour cream, 2 tablespoons yogurt, 1 teaspoon lemon juice and 1/4-teaspoon pepper.

*You can find wonton skins in the freezer or produce section of your supermarket.

To Make Ahead: Prepare the recipe through step 2. When ready to serve proceed as the recipe directs. The Avocado Dip may also be prepared in advance. If preparing in advance cover the surface with plastic wrap and refrigerate until ready to serve.

Cheese Puffs

Bake at 350° for 15 minutes.

Makes about 4 dozen.

- 1/2 cup (1 stick) butter or margarine, softened
- 8 ounces process American cheese, shredded
- 1 cup *unsifted* all-purpose flour
- 1/4 teaspoon salt

1. Preheat oven to 350°. Beat butter and cheese in a medium-size bowl with electric mixer until smooth. Stir in flour and salt until well mixed; knead lightly with hands to form a soft dough.
2. Roll into balls, 1 teaspoon at a time; place on greased cookie sheets.
3. Bake in a preheated moderate oven (350°) for 15 minutes or until golden. Serve hot.

Deviled Eggs

Makes 6 servings.

- **Basic Recipe:**
- 6 large hard-cooked eggs, halved horizontally
- 2 tablespoons mayonnaise (or enough to give
- yolks a nice creamy consistency)
- 1 teaspoon prepared mustard
- 1 teaspoon grated onion

1. Remove yolks from whites; press yolks through sieve and blend with mayonnaise, mustard and onion.
2. Stuff yolk mixture into whites, mounding it up softly. Refrigerate until ready to serve.

Stuffed Pickled Eggs: Prepare as directed, but to the yolk mixture add 1 tablespoon sweet pickle relish.

Nippy Deviled Eggs: Prepare as directed, but add 1 teaspoon prepared horseradish and 1/2 teaspoon dry mustard to yolk mixture.

Herbed Deviled Eggs: Prepare as directed, but add 2 tablespoons *each* chopped parsley and minced chives to yolk mixture.

Chili-Cheese Rolls with Avocado Dip, page 32.

Deviled Ham Eggs: Prepare as directed, but to the yolk mixture add 1 tablespoon deviled ham.

Stuffed Curried Eggs: Prepare as directed, but to the yolk mixture add 1 teaspoon curry powder.

Capered Eggs: Prepare as directed, but to the yolk mixture add 1/4 teaspoon crumbled leaf marjoram and 2 teaspoons minced capers.

Anchovy Eggs: Prepare as directed, but omit mustard and use 1 tablespoon *each* mayonnaise and dairy sour cream or milk instead of 2 tablespoons mayonnaise; blend in 1/4 to 1/2 teaspoon anchovy paste (according to taste).

Blini   Russian or Polish yeast pancake, usually made with buckwheat flour. Blini, sometimes spelled blinys, are served in a stack, wrapped in a cloth napkin to keep them warm, and offered with a variety of toppings. They can be spread with butter or sour cream, and topped with sliced smoked fish, pickled herring, hardcooked eggs or caviar. They are served as an appetizer when made as small silver-dollar-size pancakes.

Blini

The perfect way to serve caviar, and well worth the time it takes.

Makes about 6 servings or 4 1/2 dozen pancakes.

1 envelope active dry yeast	**3 tablespoons butter, melted**
2 cups very warm milk	**1/2 teaspoon salt**
2 cups *sifted* all-purpose flour	**Butter**
1 tablespoon sugar	**Dairy sour cream**
3 eggs, separated	**Caviar or smoked fish for topping**

1. Sprinkle yeast over very warm milk in large bowl. ("Very warm milk" should feel comfortably warm when dropped on wrist.) Beat 1 1/2 cups of the flour and the sugar. Cover the bowl and allow the sponge to rise in a warm place about 1 hour or until double in volume.

2. Beat egg yolks, melted butter and the salt in a small bowl. Beat in the remaining flour until smooth. Beat this mixture into the sponge. Let rise again, about 30 minutes or until batter is doubled and bubbly.

(continued)

3. Beat the egg whites until soft peaks form; fold into batter. Allow the batter to stand 15 minutes, then cook the blini.

4. Butter a hot large skillet and drop batter by 1$^1/_2$ tablespoonfuls; cook until golden brown on bottom. Turn and cook until golden on second side. Add butter to pan each time before cooking pancakes.

5. Keep blini warm, covered, in oven or chafing dish while the remaining are being cooked. Serve blini hot from chafing dish with caviar or smoked fish and sour cream or just with sour cream.

Pickled Bologna

Makes 4 cups.

2$^1/_2$ cups water	1 ring bologna
1$^3/_4$ cups distilled	(1 pound)
white vinegar	1 large onion, sliced
2 tablespoons sugar	and separated into
1$^1/_2$ teaspoons salt	rings
20 peppercorns	1 jar (7$^1/_2$ ounces)
16 whole allspice	roasted peppers

1. Combine water, vinegar, sugar, salt, peppercorns and allspice in a medium-size saucepan. Bring to boiling; lower heat; cover; simmer 10 minutes. Remove from heat; cool.

2. Slice bologna diagonally into $^1/_2$-inch pieces. Layer bologna, onion rings and roasted peppers in a large glass or ceramic casserole; pour cooled pickling liquid over. Cover; chill at least 3 days before serving.

Danish Meatballs with Dill Sauce

Bake at 375° for 35 minutes.

Makes about 75 meatballs and 4 cups sauce.

1 pound ground	butter or
beef	margarine
$^1/_2$ pound ground	$^1/_4$ cup all-purpose
veal	flour
$^1/_2$ pound ground	2 cups chicken
pork	broth
2 teaspoons salt	1 carton (16
$^1/_4$ teaspoon pepper	ounces) dairy
2 eggs	sour cream
$^1/_3$ cup finely	$^1/_4$ cup chopped
chopped onion	fresh dill
$^1/_2$ cup heavy cream	OR: 1$^1/_2$
Packaged bread	tablespoons
crumbs	dried dillweed
1 cup (2 sticks)	

1. Mix beef, veal, pork, salt, pepper, eggs, onion and cream in a large bowl; beat until very smooth and well blended. Shape mixture with wet hands into 1-inch balls. Roll balls in bread crumbs; place side by side in a shallow baking pan; cover and chill.

2. Melt 1 stick of the butter in a large saucepan; stir in flour; gradually stir in broth. Cook over low heat, stirring constantly, until sauce bubbles and thickens. Stir in sour cream and dill. Taste; add additional salt and pepper, if you wish. Cool and chill.

3. When ready to serve, melt remaining stick of butter. Drizzle butter over the meatballs.

4. Bake in a moderate oven (375°) for 35 minutes or until meatballs are brown. Turn meatballs occasionally during cooking for even browning. Reheat sauce until bubbly. Place meatballs in chafing dish; pour sauce over and serve hot with skewers for spearing. Sprinkle meatballs with additional chopped fresh dill, if you wish.

Oysters Rockefeller

This appetizer was invented at Antoine's, the famous New Orleans restaurant, by Jules Alciatore in the 1850's.

Makes 6 servings.

6 tablespoons	2 tablespooons diced
($^3/_4$ stick) butter or	onion
margarine	1 tablespoon Pernod
$^1/_2$ cup packaged	liqueur
bread crumbs	$^1/_4$ teaspoon salt
2 cups fresh spinach	3 drops liquid hot
leaves, washed and	pepper seasoning
stemmed	18 large oysters on the
$^1/_2$ cup parsley sprigs	half shell (*See Note*)
$^1/_2$ cup diced celery	Rock salt

1. Melt butter in a small saucepan; add bread crumbs; sauté for 1 minute. Remove from heat.

2. Combine buttered crumbs, spinach, parsley, celery, onion, Pernod, salt and pepper seasoning in container of an electric blender. Cover and whirl, stopping to stir contents several times, until the mixture is smooth. Pour into a small bowl; refrigerate until ready to use.

3. Arrange oysters in shells on a bed of rock salt in six individual, heatproof dishes, placing 3 in each dish. (Rock salt steadies oyster shells and retains heat.) Top each oyster with a tablespoonful of the spinach mixture.

4. Broil 4 inches from heat for 3 minutes or just until topping is lightly browned and heated through. Serve at once.

Note: If oysters in the shell are not available, place well-drained shucked oysters in scallop shells or in small, heatproof serving dishes. Add topping and broil as above.

Pictured opposite: Oysters Rockefeller.

Canapé

Canapé   A small, decorative, open-face "sandwich" served with cocktails. Canapés may be cut or shaped in a variety of attractive ways. You can use many foods for the base of canapés—as the base of the sandwich—bread, crackers, split tiny cream puffs, even sliced cucumbers. The base is spread with butter or mayonnaise before being topped with different tidbits. Almost any garnish can be used.

Party Canapés

These appetizers can be made ahead and frozen to have on hand.

Makes 2 dozen.

1/4 cup (1/2 stick) butter or margarine, softened	Worcestershire sauce
1 package (3 ounces) cream cheese, softened	2 hard-cooked eggs
	3 slices white bread
1/2 teaspoon	3 slices whole-wheat bread
	Various garnishes

1. Blend butter or margarine, cream cheese and Worcestershire sauce until smooth in a medium-size bowl; spoon half into a second bowl.
2. Halve eggs; remove yolks; press through a sieve and blend into mixture in one bowl. Cover bowl and set aside with whites for decorating canapés.
3. Trim crusts from bread; cut 12 rounds out with 1 1/2-inch cutter from 3 slices; cut 12 diamond shapes from remaining slices. Spread each with plain cheese mixture. Decorate with various garnishes as directed.

How to Decorate and Freeze Canapés
● *To Decorate:* Fill a cake-decorating bag with cream-cheese-egg mixture; fit with star tip; pipe an edging around each canapé.
● *To Garnish:* Arrange on each canapé any of the following: small whole shrimp, slivers of rolled smoked salmon, bits of king crab meat or lobster, sliced stuffed green olives or ripe olives, capers, cut-up gherkins, diced pimiento, small pickled onions or diced cooked egg whites.
● *To Freeze:* Place in a single layer in a large, shallow pan; cover tightly with plastic wrap; freeze. Pack in boxes no more than 2 layers deep with plastic wrap between layers. Use canapés within 2 weeks.
● *To Thaw:* Remove canapés from freezer 1 hour before serving; place in a single layer; let stand at room temperature.

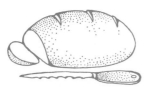

Smoked Salmon and Cheese Canapés

Makes about 30 canapés.

1 package (8 ounces) cream cheese	1/4 cup chopped fresh dill
1/4 pound sliced smoked salmon	Pumpernickel bread
1 tablespoon lemon juice	Red or black lumpfish caviar
	Fresh dill sprigs

1. Soften cream cheese and spread on wax paper to an 8- or 9-inch square. Chop salmon finely; spread evenly over cream cheese, pressing down slightly. Sprinkle with lemon juice. Roll up, jelly-roll fashion, scraping cheese from paper with small spatula as you roll. Roll in chopped dill. Wrap in foil. Chill several hours or until firm enough to slice.
2. To serve: Slice with a thin-bladed sharp knife into about 1/4-inch-thick rounds. Arrange on thin slices of party pumpernickel bread. Garnish each with caviar and a small sprig of dill.

Piquant Pickled Olives

Perk up ripe olives with this spicy marinade.

Makes about 3 cups.

2 cans (5 3/4 ounces each) pitted ripe olives, drained	crushed
	1 teaspoon crushed red pepper
2 teaspoons mixed pickling spice	1/4 cup vegetable oil
1 large clove garlic,	1/4 cup red wine vinegar

Combine all ingredients in a large jar with a screw top; shake gently. Refrigerate several days, shaking jar occasionally. Drain olives just before serving.

Tartare Steak Canapés

Makes 8 servings.

1/2 pound top round, ground twice	square pumpernickel bread
1 egg yolk	1 tablespoon butter or margarine, softened
1/2 teaspoon salt	
1/8 teaspoon freshly ground pepper	1/2 cup finely chopped fresh parsley
1 tablespoon chopped chives	1 jar (2 ounces) black caviar
6 slices thinly sliced	

1. Combine ground round, egg yolk, salt, pepper and chives in a small bowl.
2. Cut each bread slice into 4 rounds with a 2-inch cutter. Spread edge of each round with softened butter or margarine; roll in parsley to coat.
3. Spread each bread round with a heaping

tablespoonful of the beef mixture. Place a dab of caviar in center of each round.
4. Arrange on serving platter and cover with transparent wrap. Chill until serving time.

Poppy Seed-Onion Crackers

Bake at 350° for 15 minutes.

Makes about 5½ dozen.

2 cups *sifted* unbleached all-purpose flour	pepper
1 teaspoon baking powder	⅓ cup poppy seeds
	1 tablespoon instant minced onion
1 teaspoon sugar	¼ cup warm water
1 teaspoon salt	2 eggs, slightly beaten
⅛ teaspoon white	6 tablespoons vegetable oil

1. Sift flour, baking powder, sugar, salt and pepper into a large bowl; stir in poppy seeds.
2. Combine onion with water; let stand 5 minutes; drain thoroughly. Preheat oven to 350°.
3. Add onion, eggs and oil to flour mixture; mix thoroughly with fork until moistened. Gather into a ball.
4. Roll out to ⅛-inch thickness on a floured surface. Cut with a 1½-inch round cutter. Place on ungreased cookie sheets 2 inches apart. Reroll and cut trimmings.
5. Bake in a preheated moderate oven (350°) for 15 minutes or until edges of crackers are a light brown. Remove from cookie sheets to wire racks to cool completely. Store in tightly covered containers.

Pork Balls en Brochette

Bake at 400° for 15 minutes.

Makes 24 servings.

24 pitted prunes	pepper
½ cup port wine	1 egg
¾ pound ground pork	½ cup chili sauce
¼ cup bread crumbs	½ cup red currant jelly
¼ cup finely chopped walnuts	1 tablespoon Worcestershire sauce
¼ cup chopped green onions	1 orange, peeled, cut into 24 equal pieces, seeded
¾ teaspoon salt	
¼ teaspoon ground	

1. Soak the prunes in the port wine in a small bowl for several hours or overnight. Drain, reserving the liquid and prunes separately.
2. Preheat the oven to hot (400°).
3. Combine the pork, bread crumbs, walnuts, green onions, salt, pepper and egg in a medium-size bowl; mix well. Shape into about 24 equal balls. Arrange on an oiled rack in broiler pan.

4. Bake in the preheated hot oven (400°) for 15 minutes or until browned and no longer pink in the center. Place on a pie plate.
5. Combine the chili sauce, currant jelly, Worcestershire and 2 tablespoons of the port wine from the prunes in a small saucepan. Bring to boiling, stirring, until the jelly is melted. Add just enough sauce to the pork balls to coat.
6. Thread the orange, prunes and pork balls onto 24 short bamboo skewers. Serve hot or warm. Pass the sauce for dipping.

To Make Ahead: Prepare the pork balls, prunes, sauce and orange a day ahead; refrigerate. Bake the pork balls, reheat the sauce and assemble the brochettes 30 minutes before serving.

Peeling an Orange: For more colorful orange pieces, peel an orange with a small sharp paring knife, removing the thin, white pith layer as you peel.

Party Pork Balls

Bake at 350° for 20 minutes.

Makes 12 servings.

1 pound ground pork	1 tablespoon soy sauce
1 can (8 ounces) water chestnuts, drained and minced	1 egg, lightly beaten
½ cup minced green onions	½ cup packaged bread crumbs
	Cornstarch
1 teaspoon minced fresh or preserved ginger	3 tablespoons vegetable oil
¾ teaspoon salt	Sweet and Sour Sauce *(recipe follows)*

1. Combine pork, water chestnuts, onions, ginger, salt, soy sauce, egg and bread crumbs in a large bowl; mix well. Shape into 36 balls. Roll in cornstarch to coat lightly, shaking off excess.
2. Brown in oil in a large skillet. Remove balls to a roasting pan as they brown; cover loosely with foil.
3. Bake in a moderate oven (350°) for 20 minutes or until thoroughly cooked. Combine pork balls with Sweet and Sour Sauce in a serving bowl. Serve with cocktail picks.

Sweet and Sour Sauce: Sauté ½ cup *each* cubed sweet green and sweet red pepper, and 2 large carrots, thinly sliced, in 2 tablespoons vegetable oil in a large saucepan until tender, 3 minutes. Stir in 1 can (20 ounces) sliced pineapple in pineapple juice (each slice quartered), ¼ cup cider vinegar, 1 tablespoon soy sauce, 2 tablespoons sugar, ½ cup beef broth and 2 teaspoons minced fresh ginger. Combine 2 tablespoons cornstarch with ⅓ cup water in a cup; stir into saucepan. Cook, stirring constantly, until mixture thickens.

Overleaf: Party Pork Balls.

Butterflied Coconut Shrimp

Makes about 24 appetizers.

1 pound large raw shrimp	2 tablespoons cream or milk
Vegetable oil for frying	3/4 cup flaked coconut
1/4 cup all-purpose flour	1/3 cup packaged bread crumbs
1/2 teaspoon salt	Chinese Mustard Sauce *(recipe follows)*
1/2 teaspoon dry mustard	
1 egg	

1. Shell and devein shrimp, leaving tails on. Slit shrimp with sharp knife along curved side, cutting almost through. Place on paper toweling.
2. Pour oil into a medium-size saucepan to a depth of 2 inches. Heat to 350° on deep-fat frying thermometer.
3. While oil is heating, combine flour, salt and dry mustard in one small bowl; beat egg and cream in second small bowl. In third bowl, combine coconut and bread crumbs.
4. Dip shrimp in flour mixture, then in egg-cream mixture, then in coconut-crumb mixture, coating well. Refrigerate until ready to cook.
5. When oil is hot, fry shrimp, a few at a time, turning once, for 2 minutes or until golden. Remove with slotted spoon and drain on paper toweling. Keep warm in oven. Serve with Chinese Mustard Sauce and bottled duck sauce, if you wish.

Chinese Mustard Sauce: Mix 1/3 cup dry mustard with 1 tablespoon honey, 2 teaspoons vinegar and 1/4 cup cold water until well blended. Keep refrigerated. Makes about 1/3 cup.

Shrimp Toast

In America, Shrimp Toast is very popular as an appetizer. In China, it is used as one of the many dishes in a banquet, usually served after four to eight cold dishes. It is prepared in all provinces.

Makes 24 pieces.

1 package (8 ounces) frozen, shelled and deveined shrimp, thawed	1 teaspoon salt
	1/2 teaspoon sugar
	1 teaspoon dry sherry
4 canned water chestnuts, finely minced	1 tablespoon cornstarch
	6 slices of bread, at least two days old
1 egg, slightly beaten	2 cups vegetable oil

1. Chop shrimp until paste-like. Mix with water chestnuts, egg, salt, sugar, sherry and cornstarch.
2. Trim crusts from bread and cut each slice into 4 triangles. Spread a teaspoon of the shrimp mixture over each triangle.
3. In a saucepan, heat oil to 375°. Gently lower 4 to 6

pieces at a time into the oil, shrimp side down. (Filling will not fall off.) After about a minute, when the edges begin to turn brown, turn pieces over and fry a few more seconds. Remove; drain on paper toweling. Keep warm in very low oven until ready to serve.

Note: Shrimp Toast can also be fried, then frozen. When ready to use, heat in a 400° oven for 10 to 12 minutes.

Ebi No Kikka Age (Chrysanthemum-Shaped Shrimp Balls)

Makes 21 small shrimp balls.

1/2 medium-size sweet potato, pared and cubed	and finely chopped *(optional)*
	1 1/2 cups (2 ounces) white crisp Oriental noodles (Harusame; see Note), or Chinese mein (noodles) broken into short lengths
12 ounces shrimp, peeled, deveined and chopped	
2 1/2 teaspoons cornstarch	
1/4 teaspoon salt	Vegetable oil for deep frying
1 egg white, slightly beaten	1 1/2 tablespoons sake (rice wine)
1 teaspoon finely chopped, pared fresh gingerroot	OR: dry sherry
	1 1/2 tablespoons soy sauce
1 green onion, white part only, finely chopped	2 teaspoons sugar
	1/4 cup water
3 canned water chestnuts, drained	

1. Cook the sweet potato in boiling water to cover in a small saucepan just until barely tender, 5 to 10 minutes. Drain.
2. Meanwhile, mash together the shrimp, 1 1/2 teaspoons of the cornstarch and the salt, adding just enough of the egg white to make a paste, in a food processor fitted with a metal blade or with a mortar and pestle. Blend in the gingerroot and green onion. Stir in the water chestnuts, if using.
3. Toss the sweet potato cubes in the remaining 1 teaspoon of cornstarch to coat. Mold the shrimp mixture around each potato cube with moistened hands; shape to the size of a quarter. Roll each in the noodle pieces.
4. Pour the oil into a large saucepan to a depth of 3 to 4 inches. Heat the oil to 350° on a deep-fat frying thermometer. Add several balls with a slotted spoon to the oil; do not crowd the pan. Fry until golden and the noodles curl, about 1 minute. Remove with the slotted spoon to paper toweling to drain. Repeat with the remaining balls.
5. To prepare the dipping sauce: Combine the sake, soy sauce, sugar and water in a small bowl. Serve with the shrimp balls.

Note: Harusame is available in Oriental grocery stores and specialty food shops.

Pickled Shrimp

Makes about 40.

3 cups water
¼ cup mixed pickling spice (tied in cheesecloth bag)
¼ cup chopped celery leaves
2½ teaspoons salt
2 packages (1 pound each) frozen shrimp, shelled and deveined
1 medium-size onion, sliced and separated into rings
6 bay leaves
1 cup olive or vegetable oil
⅔ cup tarragon or white wine vinegar
1 teaspoon celery seeds
2 tablespoons drained capers
Lemon wedges

1. Combine water, pickling spice, celery leaves and 1¼ teaspoons of the salt in a large saucepan. Bring to boiling; add shrimp. Cook following time on label directions; drain.
2. Transfer shrimp to a large shallow nonmetal dish. Add onion and bay leaves.
3. Beat oil, vinegar, celery seeds and remaining salt in a small bowl; add capers; pour over shrimp; toss to coat. Cover with plastic wrap; refrigerate. Let marinate 2 days. (It will keep for a week.)
4. To serve: Drain shrimp with capers and place in glass bowl. Place this bowl in a larger bowl of crushed ice. Garnish with lemon wedges. Serve with wooden picks.

Salmon Mousse

Gently ease aluminum cups away from mousse for super-easy unmolding.

Makes 6 servings.

2 envelopes unflavored gelatin
⅓ cup water
2 tablespoons lemon juice
1 cup boiling water
1 can (15 ½ ounces) pink or red salmon, drained, boned and skinned
½ cup heavy cream
½ cup mayonnaise or salad dressing
1 tablespoon thinly sliced green onion
1 teaspoon dillweed
½ teaspoon salt
½ teaspoon paprika
¼ teaspoon pepper
Marinated Cucumber Slices (recipe follows)
Lemon slices

1. Sprinkle gelatin over water and lemon juice in container of electric blender; let stand 5 minutes. Add boiling water; cover; whirl for 30 seconds or until smooth.
2. Add salmon, heavy cream, mayonnaise, green onion, dillweed, salt, paprika and pepper. Whirl for 1 minute more or until completely smooth.
3. Pour salmon mixture into 6 reusable aluminum 2⅞ × 1¼-inch cupcake cups (about ⅔ cup). Chill, covered with aluminum foil, for 3 hours or until set.
4. Gently ease aluminum cups away from salmon mixture, loosening sides with small spatula. Unmold onto serving platter or individual serving plates. Serve with Marinated Cucumber Slices and garnish with slices of lemon.

Marinated Cucumber Slices

A pretty and tangy-tasting accompaniment to Salmon Mouse.

Makes 6 servings.

2 small or 1 large cucumber, unpeeled, halved lengthwise, seeded and very thinly sliced
1½ teaspoons salt
½ cup white wine vinegar
¼ cup finely chopped fresh parsley
½ teaspoon sugar
¼ teaspoon white pepper

Layer cucumber slices with 1 teaspoon of the salt in a 9-inch pie plate. Let stand for 10 minutes.
2. Press cucumbers into plate and pour off liquid that accumulates.
3. Sprinkle vinegar, parsley, sugar, pepper and remaining salt over cucumbers, tossing gently to mix.
4. Marinate, covered, for at least 30 minutes to let flavors blend before serving.

Dilled Salmon-Topped Cucumber Rounds

Makes about 36 rounds.

1 can (7¾ ounces) red salmon, drained and flaked
1 package (8 ounces) cream cheese, softened
2 teaspoons dillweed
1 teaspoon grated
lemon rind
1 teaspoon lemon juice
1 teaspoon minced onion
2 cucumbers (each about 10 inches long), unpared

1. Combine drained salmon, cream cheese, dillweed, lemon rind and juice and minced onion in a medium-size bowl. Beat on medium speed with electric mixer until well blended. Refrigerate until stiff enough to pipe onto cucumber rounds.
2. While mixture is chilling, score cucumbers with the tines of a fork. Cut each into eighteen ¼-inch slices. Fit a star tip onto a pastry bag; fill with salmon mixture; pipe onto cucumber rounds. Garnish with dill.

Bacon-Wrapped Scallops in Dijon Sauce

Broil for 4 to 5 minutes.

Makes 20 servings.

10 slices bacon	halved, or quartered if large
1 papaya, peeled, seeded and cut into 1-inch chunks	3/4 cup heavy cream
6 green onions, cut into 1 1/2-inch lengths	1 tablespoon Dijon-style mustard
1 pound sea scallops,	1 teaspoon finely chopped parsley

1. Broil the bacon in a preheated broiler until partially cooked, but not crisp. Cut the pieces in half.
2. Thread a piece of papaya, green onion and scallop, with the bacon intertwining, onto each of 20 short bamboo skewers. Arrange in a single layer on a rack in a broiler pan.
3. Combine the cream and mustard in a saucepan. Heat gently until slightly thickened, 5 minutes. Add the parsley. Brush on the skewers.
4. Broil 6 inches from the heat until the scallops are firm, 4 to 5 minutes, turning once and brushing with the sauce. Serve hot.

To Make Ahead: The bacon can be partially cooked and the skewers threaded and refrigerated early in the day.

Bay/Sea Scallops: Bay — the tiny, tender, pink- or tan-colored scallop. It is considered more of a delicacy and is usually more expensive.
Sea — the larger, whiter, more common mollusk.

Seviche

Makes about 4 1/2 cups or about 8 appetizer servings.

1 cup fresh lime juice	green chilies, chopped
3 medium-size tomatoes, seeded and chopped (about 3 cups)	3 cloves garlic, finely chopped
1 medium-size onion, chopped (1/2 cup)	1 1/2 teaspoons salt
1/2 green pepper, halved, seeded and chopped (1/2 cup)	1/4 teaspoon freshly ground pepper
2 canned mild or hot	1 pound fresh bay or sea scallops*, washed
	8 lettuce cups

1. Combine lime juice, tomatoes, onion, green pepper, chilies, garlic, salt and pepper in medium-size bowl; mix well.
2. Gently stir in scallops. (If using sea scallops, cut into quarters.)
3. Chill 3 hours or overnight. Serve in lettuce cups.

If fresh scallops are not available in your area, use fresh flounder or halibut fillets, and cut into bite-size pieces.

Creamy Herbed Tuna

This dip tastes infinitely more exotic than its simple ingredients would indicate.

Makes 1 1/3 cups.

1 cup mayonnaise	1 tablespoon drained capers
1 can (3 1/2 ounces) chunk or solid white tuna, drained	1/4 cup parsley sprigs
1 tablespoon finely chopped onion	1/2 teaspoon leaf basil
	1 teaspoon lemon juice

1. Place all ingredients in container of electric blender; cover and whirl on medium speed until fairly smooth, stopping machine often to push down contents.
2. Pour into a serving bowl and serve at once, or cover and refrigerate until serving time.

Dipper Tips: Celery sticks or curls, cucumber slices, cherry tomatoes, black olives, hard-cooked eggs, chunks of crusty bread.

Coquilles St. Jacques Mornay

Makes 4 servings as main dish, 6 to 8 as an appetizer.

1 cup dry white wine	1/2 cup heavy cream
1/2 teaspoon salt	2 teaspoons lemon juice
1 pound fresh or thawed, frozen sea scallops, washed	1/3 cup shredded Swiss cheese
2 tablespoons chopped onion	1 tablespoon chopped fresh parsley
1/4 pound small mushrooms, sliced	1/2 cup fresh bread crumbs (1 slice)
1/4 cup butter or margarine	1 tablespoon melted butter or margarine
1/4 cup all-purpose flour	Parsley
	Lemon wedges

1. Bring wine to boiling in small saucepan. Lower heat; add the salt and scallops; cover. Simmer until just tender, 5 to 6 minutes. Drain, reserving liquid (1 cup).
2. Sauté onion and mushrooms until soft in butter in medium-size saucepan, then remove from heat; stir in the flour until smooth; gradually stir in reserved liquid. Cook, stirring constantly, until sauce thickens and bubbles. Stir in cream and lemon juice. Bring to boiling; remove from heat. If sauce is too thick, add more cream or wine. Taste and add more salt or lemon juice, if necessary.
3. Add scallops, cheese and parsley to sauce; spoon into 4 buttered scallop shells or 1-cup casseroles, dividing evenly.
4. Toss bread crumbs with melted butter; sprinkle crumbs around edge of the shells. Place shells on rack over broiler pan. Broil 4 to 6 inches from heat for 4 minutes or until crumbs are brown and sauce bubbles. Garnish with parsley and lemon wedges.

Beef Roulade and an assortment of Finger Foods make perfect appetizers.

Beef Roulade

Make a day or two ahead.
Bake at 350° for 50 minutes.
Makes 40 servings.

2 eggs, slightly beaten
3/4 cup fresh bread crumbs (2 slices)
1/2 cup catsup
1/3 cup chopped parsley
1/2 teaspoon leaf basil, crumbled
1/4 teaspoon leaf oregano, crumbled
1/4 teaspoon pepper
1 clove garlic, crushed
2 pounds ground round
Plain dry bread crumbs
3 packages (4 ounces each) boiled ham slices
3 cups shredded Swiss cheese (3/4 pound)
Mustard Sauce (recipe follows)

1. Preheat the oven to moderate (350°).
2. Combine eggs, bread crumbs, catsup, parsley, basil, oregano, pepper, garlic and ground round in a large bowl; mix lightly until well blended. Divide into 2 equal portions.
3. Cut two 12 × 12-inch squares of aluminum foil. Sprinkle each with dry bread crumbs. Pat out each half of meat mixture on foil to 9 × 12-inch rectangle. Arrange ham slices on top of each to within 1/2 inch of edges. Sprinkle each with Swiss cheese. Using foil as an aid, roll up meat from long side, jelly-roll fashion. Seal the edges and ends. Place on a foil-lined jelly-roll pan.
4. Bake in a preheated moderate oven (350°) for 50 minutes. Cool to room temperature. Serve sliced with Mustard Sauce.

Mustard Sauce: Combine 1 cup dairy sour cream, 1/4 cup mayonnaise, 2 tablespoons Dijon-style mustard, 1 to 3 teaspoons drained prepared horseradish and 1/4 cup chopped green onion; mix until well blended.

Sugared and Salted Pecans

Give your guests a choice.

Roast nuts at 350° for 20 minutes.

Makes ½ pound sugared pecans and ½ pound salted pecans.

¼ cup (½ stick) butter
  or margarine
1 pound pecan halves
1 teaspoon salt
2 teaspoons 10X
  (confectioners')

sugar
½ teaspoon ground
  cinnamon
10X (confectioners')
  sugar

1. Preheat the oven to moderate (350°).
2. Melt the butter in a 13 x 9 x 2-inch baking pan in the oven. Add the pecans; sprinkle with the salt and mix well. Return to the oven for 20 minutes, stirring the nuts occasionally.
3. Remove half of the nuts to a sheet of aluminum foil to cool.
4. Stir together the 2 teaspoons of 10X sugar and the cinnamon in a small bowl. Sprinkle the mixture over the remaining nuts in the pan. Toss well to coat. Cool the nuts in the pan.
5. Store the pecans separately in two airtight containers at room temperature.
6. Just before serving the sugared pecans, lightly dust with 10X sugar.

Ham and Walnut Appetizers

Bake at 400° for 10 to 15 minutes.

Makes about 36 bite-size balls.

½ pound cooked ham,
  ground or very
  finely chopped
½ cup walnuts,
  ground or very
  finely chopped
½ cup soft bread
  crumbs (1 slice)
⅛ teaspoon ground
  pepper
1 egg, slightly beaten
¼ teaspoon ground
  allspice

Dash ground cloves
2 tablespoons butter
  or margarine
3 tablespoons red
  currant jelly
1 tablespoon prepared
  Dijon mustard
2 tablespoons Madeira
  or sherry
1 tablespoon vinegar
2 tablespoons walnut
  pieces

1. Combine ham, walnuts, bread crumbs, pepper, egg, allspice and cloves in a medium-size bowl; blend well. Shape into 36 balls. Melt butter in 13 × 9 × 2-inch baking pan; roll ham balls in butter to coat.
2. Bake in a hot oven (400°) for 10 minutes or until browned and heated through, turning once. Cool. Place in plastic bag or freezer container; freeze up to 1 week.
3. Last minute touches: Remove ham balls to defrost (about 2 hours). Heat jelly, mustard, wine and vinegar in a small skillet until jelly is melted. Add ham balls and heat, turning often, until glazed, about 5 minutes. Serve hot; garnish with walnut pieces.

Brazil Nut Chips

Bake at 350° for 12 minutes.

Makes about 2 cups.

1½ cups shelled
  Brazil nuts
2 tablespoons butter

or margarine
½ teaspoon seasoned
  salt

1. Cover Brazil nuts with cold water in a medium-size saucepan; cover. Heat slowly to boiling; simmer 2 to 3 minutes; drain. (This softens the nuts so they can be shaved.)
2. While still warm, shave each nut lengthwise into thin slices with a vegetable parer or sharp knife. Spread in a large shallow baking pan; dot with butter.
3. Bake in a moderate oven (350°) for 12 minutes or until crisp and lightly browned, shaking pan often. Sprinkle with seasoned salt. Cool and store in a container with a tight-fitting lid.

Taco Tartlets

Bake at 425° for 7 minutes.

Makes 30 tartlets.

1 pound ground round
2 tablespoons taco
  seasoning mix
2 tablespoons ice
  water
1 container (8 ounces)
  dairy sour cream
2 tablespoons taco
  sauce

⅓ cup chopped pitted
  ripe olives
¾ cup crushed tortilla
  chips
2 ounces Cheddar
  cheese, shredded
  (½ cup)
¼ cup sliced pitted
  ripe olives

1. Preheat oven to 425°.
2. Combine beef, taco seasoning mix and ice water in a medium-size bowl; mix well. Press mixture in even layer on bottoms and sides of 1½-inch miniature muffin-pan cups to make a thin shell.
3. Combine sour cream, taco sauce, chopped olives and tortilla chips in a small bowl; spoon into meat shells, dividing evenly. Sprinkle tops with cheese; place an olive slice in center of each.
4. Bake in a preheated hot oven (425°) for about 7 minutes or until meat is firm and no longer pink. Remove from pans; garnish with parsley sprigs, if you wish. Serve hot.

Nachos

Bake at 350° for 5 minutes.

Makes 24 nachos or 6 to 8 servings.

6 fresh or frozen and thawed corn tortillas
Vegetable oil for frying
Salt
1 can (3¹/₂ ounces) hot jalapeño chile peppers

OR: 1 can (4 ounces) whole mild green chilies
1 cup refried beans
2 ounces longhorn, mild Cheddar or Monterey Jack cheese, shredded (¹/₂ cup)

1. Cut tortillas into quarters to form triangular-shaped wedges. Heat about ¹/₈ inch oil in skillet until hot. Sauté a few at a time, turning occasionally, until crisp and golden brown. Drain on paper toweling. Sprinkle lightly with salt. Preheat oven to 350°.
2. Drain chile peppers or chilies; remove seeds or stem and pith. Cut into ¹/₄-inch strips. Spread each tortilla chip with beans, sprinkle with cheese and top with chile strip. Place nachos on cookie sheet.
3. Bake in a preheated moderate oven (350°) for 5 minutes or until beans are hot and cheese melts. Serve immediately.

Popcorn Party Mix

Bake at 275° for 1 hour.

Makes about 3 ¹/₂ quarts.

³/₄ cup (1¹/₂ sticks) butter or margarine, melted
¹/₂ teaspoon garlic salt
¹/₂ teaspoon onion salt
¹/₄ teaspoon celery salt
1¹/₂ tablespoons Worcestershire sauce

¹/₈ teaspoon liquid hot pepper seasoning
3 quarts popped gourmet popping corn
1 cup pretzel sticks, broken
1¹/₂ cups salted mixed nuts

1. Combine butter, garlic, onion and celery salts, Worcestershire and hot pepper seasoning in 1-cup measure.
2. Spread popcorn, pretzel pieces and nuts in a large roasting pan. Pour melted butter mixture over; toss lightly to mix.
3. Bake in a very slow oven (275°) for 1 hour, stirring 4 or 5 times.

Smoky Bacon Cheese Popcorn

Makes about 4 quarts.

4 quarts popped gourmet popping corn
¹/₃ cup butter or margarine, melted
¹/₂ teaspoon seasoned salt

¹/₂ teaspoon hickory-smoked salt
¹/₃ cup grated Parmesan cheese
¹/₃ cup bacon-flavored vegetable protein chips

Put freshly popped corn into a large bowl. Combine butter with seasoned and hickory-smoked salts; pour over corn, tossing to coat evenly. Sprinkle with cheese and bacon chips; toss again. Serve while warm.

Note: For last-minute assembling, corn may be popped ahead of time and warmed in oven before combining with remaining ingredients.

French Onion Tart

Bake at 425° for 10 minutes, then at 400° for 15 minutes.

Makes two 10-inch tarts.

2¹/₂ cups *sifted* all-purpose flour
¹/₂ teaspoon salt
¹/₂ teaspoon sugar
¹/₂ cup (1 stick) butter or margarine
3 tablespoons vegetable shortening
4 to 5 tablespoons cold water
5 large onions, chopped (5 cups)
2 cloves garlic, crushed
3 tablespoons olive oil

1¹/₄ teaspoons salt
¹/₄ teaspoon pepper
¹/₂ teaspoon leaf thyme, crumbled
¹/₄ cup chopped fresh parsley
¹/₄ cup grated Parmesan cheese
2 to 3 tomatoes, thinly sliced
1 can (2 ounces) flat anchovy fillets, drained
12 to 16 ripe olives, pitted and halved

1. Combine flour, ¹/₂ teaspoon salt and sugar in a large bowl; cut in butter and shortening with pastry blender until mixture is crumbly. Sprinkle with cold water, 1 tablespoon at a time; mix with fork until dough holds together. Knead dough with a few quick strokes; gather into a smooth ball; cover. Refrigerate about 1 hour.
2. Preheat oven to 425°. Divide dough in half; roll each half on lightly floured surface into a 12-inch circle; transfer to a cookie sheet; roll up edges to make a 10-inch round shell with stand-up edge. Prick bottom with fork. Repeat with rest of dough.
3. Bake in a preheated hot oven (425°) for 10 minutes or until set; cool on wire rack. Lower oven temperature to 400°.
4. Sauté onions and garlic in oil in a large skillet or

(continued)

Dutch oven over medium heat until tender but not brown, 20 minutes. Stir in 1¼ teaspoons salt, pepper, thyme and parsley; remove from heat.

5. Sprinkle 2 tablespoons Parmesan cheese in each pastry shell; spread onion mixture over cheese, dividing evenly. Overlap slices of tomatoes over one of the tarts. Arrange anchovies and olives over both tarts; brush lightly with additional oil.

6. Bake in a hot oven (400°) for 15 minutes or until bubbly hot. To serve: Cut into small wedges; arrange on serving plate.

Nutritious Nibbles

Vegetables and fruits make crisp and healthful, yet relatively low-calorie, additions to the hors d'oeuvres platter. Try the following — you could even keep some bagged in plastic in the refrigerator, ready for munching.

Leeks, peeled, split and trimmed
Sweet green pepper, cut into squares
Radishes, halved
Cherry tomatoes, halved
Carrots, peeled and cut in slices or sticks
Cauliflower, separated into flowerets
Pineapple, cut into thin slices
Apples, cut into wedges
Zucchini, cut into spears
Turnip, cut into slices
Celery, cut into 1-inch pieces
Kiwi, peeled, cut into slices
Peas, raw
Endive, separated into leaves
Small whole cooked beets, cut into sticks
Mushroom caps, cooked or raw
Chinese snow peas
Sweet red pepper, cut into squares
Sugar snap peas, blanched
Broccoli, separated into flowerets
Orange slices, whole or halved

Herb-Stuffed Mushrooms

Bake at 350° for 20 minutes.

Makes 8 servings.

16 large mushrooms (about 1½ pounds)
½ cup (1 stick) butter or margarine
3 tablespoons finely chopped shallots or green onions
1 cup fresh bread
crumbs (2 slices)
½ cup chopped fresh parsley
1 teaspoon leaf savory, crumbled
½ teaspoon salt
⅛ teaspoon pepper

1. Wash mushrooms and pat dry; remove stems. Chop stems finely.

2. Melt ¼ cup (½ stick) of the butter in a skillet. Sauté mushroom caps briefly on both sides just until they begin to turn beige in color and are well-coated with the butter. Remove mushroom caps to a jelly-roll pan.

3. Melt remaining butter in same skillet. Sauté mushroom stems and shallots briefly, being careful not to overcook. Remove from heat.

4. Add bread crumbs, parsley, savory, salt and pepper to skillet; toss lightly to mix. Spoon into caps.

5. Bake in moderate oven (350°) 20 minutes or just until mushrooms are tender.

Hot Walnut-Stuffed Mushroom Caps

Bake at 400° for 8 minutes for small mushrooms, 10 minutes for large.

Makes 4 appetizer servings.

16 large mushrooms (about 2 inches in diameter)
OR: 1 package (12 ounces) small mushrooms
1 tablespoon minced onion
1 tablespoon butter or margarine
⅓ cup chopped walnuts
2 tablespoons packaged bread crumbs
1 tablespoon grated Parmesan cheese
1 egg white
Grated Parmesan cheese

1. Wash mushrooms. Drain well on paper toweling, if needed. Remove stems and chop finely. (There should be about 1 cup.)

2. Sauté chopped stems and onion in butter in a small saucepan until soft. Remove from heat; mix with walnuts, bread crumbs and 1 tablespoon Parmesan; cool.

3. Preheat oven to 400°. Beat egg white until frothy; stir into mushroom mixture. Spoon evenly into mushroom caps, mounding high. Place on cookie sheet.

4. Bake in a preheated hot oven (400°) for 8 minutes for small mushrooms and 10 minutes for large mushrooms. Sprinkle with more Parmesan before serving.

Tempura   This Japanese word means to fry in deep fat. Tempura consists of seafood and/or vegetables coated with a batter and deep-fat fried, then served dipped into a sauce. It should be eaten as soon as cooked.

Tempura

Makes 6 appetizer or side-dish servings.

2 cups *sifted* **all-
    purpose flour**
1 teaspoon salt
**1/8 teaspoon baking
    soda**
1 egg yolk
2 cups ice water
Vegetable oil for frying
**2 medium-size
    zucchini, thinly
    sliced**
1 cup cauliflower

**flowerets, sliced
    and parboiled for 3
    minutes**
**1/2 pound whole green
    beans, parboiled for
    3 minutes**
**2 large onions, sliced
    and separated into
    rings**
**1/2 pound medium-size
    mushrooms, sliced**

1. Combine flour, salt and baking soda in a medium-size bowl. Beat egg yolk and water in a small bowl until blended; pour into dry ingredients; beat until batter is smooth. Cover and let stand 10 minutes.
2. Pour oil into a large saucepan to a depth of about 2 inches. Heat to 375° on a deep-fat frying thermometer.
3. Dip vegetables in batter, letting excess drip off. Fry in hot oil, a few at a time, until golden brown. Drain on paper toweling. Keep vegetables warm in a very slow oven (250°) until all are fried.

Spinach-Cheese Appetizer Puffs

Tasty little tidbits of multilayered pastry enclosing a savory filling.
Bake at 400° for 10 minutes.

Makes 3 1/2 dozen appetizers.

**1 package (10 ounces)
    frozen chopped
    spinach, thawed**
1 egg, slightly beaten
1/2 cup ricotta cheese
**2 tablespoons grated
    Parmesan cheese**
**2 ounces feta cheese,
    crumbled (1/2 cup)**
**1 tablespoon chopped
    fresh dill
    OR: 1 teaspoon**

dillweed
**2 tablespoons
    chopped green
    onion**
**1/2 of a 16-ounce
    package frozen
    phyllo or strudel
    pastry leaves (about
    14 leaves), thawed**
**1/2 cup (1 stick butter,
    melted**

1. Squeeze spinach with hands to remove as much liquid as possible. Combine egg, ricotta, Parmesan and feta cheese in a medium-size bowl. Stir in spinach, dill and green onion; refrigerate 1 hour.
2. Remove phyllo from refrigerator; leave in package and let warm to room temperature until the leaves can be unfolded easily. Unwrap leaves; unroll; place on a sheet of wax paper and cover with a damp towel to prevent drying. Place one phyllo leaf on work surface; brush lightly with melted butter. Cover with second leaf. Cut into 6 strips, each about 2-inches wide. Place

a rounded teaspoonful of the filling at one end of one of the strips. Fold one corner to the opposite side, forming a triangle. Continue folding, keeping triangular shape, to the other end of the strip. This makes one pastry; repeat filling and folding with remaining 5 strips.
3. Preheat oven to 400°. Using 2 phyllo leaves for every 6 pastries, continue using all the filling and the phyllo. Arrange triangles on ungreased jelly-roll pan or rimmed cookie sheet. Brush tops lightly with butter.
4. Bake in a preheated hot oven (400°) for 10 minutes or until golden brown. Remove to wire rack to cool.
To freeze: Place pastries in sealed plastic container; label; freeze.
To reheat: Place frozen puffs on cookie sheet and heat in a preheated hot oven (400°) for 12 minutes.

Cheesy Tomato and Garlic Loaf

A pizza-like appetizer that's sure to please.
Bake at 400° for 15 minutes.

Makes about 18 to 20 appetizer servings.

**1/4 cup (1/2 stick) butter
    or margarine**
**6 medium-size
    tomatoes, coarsely
    chopped (about
    6 cups)**
**3 medium-size onions,
    chopped (1 1/2 cups)**
**6 cloves garlic, finely
    chopped**
**1/4 cup chopped fresh
    parsley**
**1 1/2 teaspoons leaf
    oregano, crumbled**
1 teaspoon salt

1/4 teaspoon pepper
**1 package (8 ounces)
    mozzarella cheese,
    shredded**
**1/2 cup freshly grated
    Parmesan cheese**
**1 loaf unsliced Italian
    bread (about 14 to
    16 inches long)**
**Sliced cherry
    tomatoes,
    anchovies or sliced,
    pitted olives for
    garnish** *(optional)*

1. Melt butter in large skillet; add chopped tomatoes, onions, garlic, 2 tablespoons of the parsley, oregano, salt and pepper. Cook, stirring frequently, over high heat until sauce thickens and most of the liquid is evaporated (about 15 to 20 minutes).
2. Combine mozzarella and Parmesan cheeses with remaining parsley in a small bowl.
3. Preheat oven to 400°. Cut bread in half horizontally. Place bread on cookie sheet. Spread bread halves with tomato mixture; sprinkle with cheese mixture.
4. Bake in a preheated hot oven (400°) for 15 minutes or until the cheese is golden brown or bubbly. Cut each bread half crosswise into 9 or 10 slices. Garnish each slice with cherry tomato slices, anchovies or olive slices, if you wish. Serve these appetizers or snacks warm.

Tomato Eye Opener, page 71; American Caviar Sampler, page 48; Cheese and Blueberry Crêpe Triangles, page 360; Golden Coffee Bread, page 90.

American Caviar Sampler

Makes 8 servings.

Arrange about 2 ounces each, black lumpfish caviar, salmon caviar and golden whitefish caviar (or caviar of your choice) on a serving plate. Garnish with chopped hard-cooked egg white and yolk, chopped green onion and lemon wedges. Chill. Accompany with toast points.

Rumaki

An appetizer for a very special party.

Makes 2 dozen.

12 chicken livers, halved	**cut in half**
24 thin slivers water chestnut	**1¹/₂ cups soy sauce**
12 bacon slices,	**1 clove garlic, minced**
	1 cup firmly packed light brown sugar

1. Make a small incision in center of each piece of chicken liver and insert a sliver of water chestnut. Wrap each with a half-strip of bacon; secure with a wooden pick.
2. Mix soy sauce and garlic; add livers; cover and marinate in the refrigerator several hours.

3. Remove livers from marinade, roll lightly in brown sugar and place on broiler pan.
4. Broil 4 inches from heat for 5 minutes or until bacon is crisp. Serve hot.

Sherried Chicken Livers

This canapé spread is excellent on melba toast or pumpernickel bread rounds.

Makes 8 servings.

1 large onion, chopped (1 cup)	**halved**
2 tablespoons butter or margarine	**2/3 cup dry sherry**
1 pound chicken livers, trimmed and	**3 tablespoons brandy**
	1 teaspoon salt
	1/4 teaspoon pepper
	Boston lettuce

1. Sauté onion in butter in a large skillet until soft. Stir in livers and sherry. Simmer, uncovered, 20 minutes.
2. Place half the mixture in container of electric blender. Cover. Whirl until smooth; remove to a small bowl. Repeat with remaining mixture. Stir in brandy, salt and pepper. Cover and chill.
3. To serve: Pipe or spoon about 1/4 cup of the mixture onto a leaf of lettuce for each serving. Garnish with thin slivers of truffle, cocktail onions, thin tomato slices and parsley, if you wish.

Barbecued Chicken Wing Appetizer

Bake at 375° for 45 minutes.

Makes 6 servings.

**3 pounds chicken
 wings, wing tips
 removed (about 20)**
³/₄ cup catsup
**1 tablespoon
 Worcestershire
 sauce**
**1¹/₂ teaspoons
 distilled white
 vinegar**
¹/₂ teaspoon dry

mustard
**¹/₂ teaspoon onion
 powder**
**¹/₂ teaspoon garlic
 powder**
¹/₄ teaspoon pepper
**5 to 6 drops liquid red-
 pepper seasoning**
Lettuce leaves
Orange slices

1. Preheat the oven to moderate (375°). Line a
13 × 9 × 2-inch baking dish with aluminum foil. Pat
wings dry with paper toweling.
2. To prepare barbecue sauce, combine catsup,
Worcestershire sauce, vinegar, dry mustard, onion
powder, garlic powder, pepper and liquid red-pepper
seasoning in a small bowl.
3. Brush wings all over with half (about 6
tablespoons) of the barbecue sauce. Arrange wings
in one layer in an aluminum foil–lined baking dish.
4. Bake in the preheated moderate over (375°) for 25
minutes. Brush chicken with remaining sauce.
Continue to bake another 20 minutes or until tender.
Arrange chicken wings on a lettuce-lined platter.
Garnish with orange slices.

Chicken-Filled Pastry Boats

*A zesty chicken mixture fills these crispy make-ahead
pastry shells.*
Bake at 400° for 8 minutes.

Makes about 2 dozen.

**¹/₂ package piecrust
 mix**
**³/₄ cup finely diced
 cooked chicken**
**3 tablespoons finely
 chopped celery**
**2 tablespoons
 chopped green
 onions**
1¹/₂ teaspoons finely

**chopped canned hot
 chile pepper**
**¹/₂ teaspoon lime or
 lemon juice**
¹/₂ teaspoon salt
**¹/₄ cup dairy sour
 cream**
**2 hard-cooked egg
 yolks, sieved**
Parsley

1. Prepare piecrust mix following label directions. Roll
out, half at a time, to a ¹/₈-inch thickness on lightly
floured surface. Preheat oven to 400°.
2. Using 3-inch barquette pans or tin tart pans, invert
pans onto pastry and cut pastry ¹/₂-inch wider than
pans. Press pastry into pans and trim edges even with
pans. Arrange pans on cookie sheets; prick pastry
with a fork.
3. Bake in a preheated hot oven (400°) for 8 minutes
or until golden. Cool in pans on wire rack 5 minutes.
Ease out of pans; cool completely.
4. Place in foil or plastic boxes; cover, label and
freeze.
5. To serve: Combine chicken, celery, onion, chile

(continued)

Barbecued Chicken Wings.

pepper, lime juice, salt and sour cream in small bowl; toss to mix well; spoon into shells. Garnish with sieved egg yolks and small sprigs of parsley. Cover; refrigerate until serving time.

Sesame Chicken Wings

Miniature "drumsticks" in a cream and crumb coating "fry" with ease in the oven. Delicious hot or cold.

Bake at 375° for 40 minutes.

Makes about 36 appetizers.

3 pounds chicken wings (about 18)	**1 teaspoon paprika**
2 tablespoons toasted sesame seeds*	**1/2 teaspoon salt**
	1/3 cup heavy cream
3/4 cup packaged bread crumbs	**1/2 cup (1 stick) butter**
	Bottled duck sauce

1. Remove tips of chicken wings; save for making soup. Cut each wing into two sections.
2. Combine sesame seeds, bread crumbs, paprika and salt in shallow dish.
3. Dip chicken pieces in cream, using brush to coat completely; roll in crumb mixture. Refrigerate 1 hour.
4. Place butter in a 13 × 9 × 2-inch baking pan. Melt in oven while oven preheats to 375°. Remove from oven; turn chicken pieces in butter to coat completely.
5. Bake in a moderate oven (375°) for 40 minutes. Serve with duck sauce.

*Shake sesame seeds in small skillet over low heat until golden.

Chicken Pillows

These crisp and garlicky chicken pastries can be put together way ahead of time and frozen, unbaked. Remove from the freezer just before baking.

Bake at 400° for 15 minutes.

Makes about 24 pastries.

2 whole chicken breasts, skinned, boned and halved (about 1 pound)	**chopped**
	1 teaspoon leaf oregano, crumbled
3 tablespoons lemon juice	**1/2 teaspoon salt**
2 tablespoons olive or vegetable oil	**1/2 cup (1 stick) butter**
	1/2 package (16-ounce size) phyllo or strudel pastry leaves
1 clove garlic, finely	

1. Cut the chicken into 1-inch cubes.
2. Combine lemon juice, oil, garlic, oregano and salt in a small bowl; mix well. Add the chicken pieces and coat with marinade. Cover and refrigerate overnight.
3. Melt butter over low heat. Unwrap phyllo and place on a piece of wax paper. Keep phyllo covered with another piece of wax paper at all times to prevent drying out. Halve pastry lengthwise with scissors, forming 2 long strips, about 6 inches wide. Take one strip of phyllo, fold in half crosswise and brush with butter. Place 2 pieces of chicken at one short end and roll up in pastry to the midpoint. Fold left and right edges toward the center over filling and continue rolling, forming a neat package. Brush all over with butter and place seam-side down on a jelly-roll pan. Repeat with remaining chicken and phyllo. Preheat oven to 400°.
4. Bake in a preheated hot oven (400°) for 15 minutes or until golden brown.

To Freeze Ahead: Place filled and buttered phyllo rolls on a large baking sheet and freeze. When frozen, transfer to large plastic bags and seal. To bake: Place rolls in a single layer in 2 jelly-roll pans; brush with additional melted butter. Bake in a preheated hot oven (400°) for 20 minutes or until golden brown.

Chicken Walnut Strips

Bake at 425° for 15 minutes.

Makes 6 to 8 appetizer servings.

2 whole chicken breasts, skinned, boned and halved (about 1 pound)	**1/4 teaspoon pepper**
	1 cup packaged bread crumbs
2 eggs	**1 cup very finely chopped walnuts**
Peanut or vegetable oil	**Mustard Mayonnaise Dip (recipe follows)**
1/2 teaspoon salt	

1. Cut the chicken breasts into 1/2 × 3-inch strips with a very sharp knife.
2. Beat the eggs with 1 tablespoon of the oil, salt and pepper in a shallow bowl. Mix the crumbs and nuts on a plate. Preheat oven to 425°.
3. Dip the strips, 1 at a time, in the egg mixture and then coat with the crumbs. Arrange half the strips in a single layer in a jelly-roll pan and pour 1/4 cup oil around, not over, them. Repeat with the remaining chicken, arranging in a second pan.
4. Place one pan in center and one in upper third of preheated hot oven (425°); bake for 15 minutes, reversing pan positions after 8 minutes.
5. Turn out on serving plate; serve with Mustard Mayonnaise Dip.

Mustard Mayonnaise Dip: Stir 2 tablespoons Dijon mustard into 1 cup mayonnaise or salad dressing. Cover and chill at least 1 hour before serving.

Herring-Stuffed Beets

Make herring stuffing and scoop out beets early in the day. Stuff just before serving.

Makes about 8 appetizer servings.

2 cans (16 ounces each) whole small beets, drained
1 jar (8 ounces) pickled herring, well drained, onions discarded and herring

chopped
1 hard-cooked egg, chopped
2 tablespoons minced green onion
2 tablespoons dairy sour cream

1. Scoop out center of each beet, using a melon ball scoop or a small spoon, leaving a 1/4-inch-thick shell. (Use beet centers in salads.)
2. Combine herring, egg, green onion and sour cream in a small bowl. Spoon into hollowed-out beets, mounding high. Serve immediately.

Fresh Corn Dollars

These tiny golden pancakes can be served as appetizers—or make them larger for breakfast.

Makes about 2 1/2 dozen small pancakes.

2 eggs, lightly beaten
2 cups whole-kernel corn (from 4 ears)
2 tablespoons flour
1 teaspoon baking

powder
1/2 teaspoon salt
Pinch black pepper
Vegetable oil

1. Combine eggs, corn, flour, baking powder, salt and pepper in medium-size bowl. Stir to blend well.
2. Heat griddle or skillet slowly. Add enough oil to coat lightly. Test temperature by sprinkling a few drops of water on hot surface. When drops bounce, temperature is right.
3. Measure batter, a scant tablespoon for each pancake, onto griddle. Cook until little holes appear on top; turn and cook briefly until bottoms brown. Remove to warm platter; repeat with remaining batter, stirring frequently.

Benne Sticks

Bake at 325° for 30 minutes.

Makes 16 sticks.

1/3 cup sesame seeds
1 cup *sifted* all-purpose flour
1/8 teaspoon salt
Dash cayenne

3 tablespoons butter or margarine
3 tablespoons shortening
Ice water

1. Spread the sesame seeds on a shallow baking pan.
2. Bake in a slow oven (325°) for 15 minutes or until golden, stirring twice. Cool seeds.
3. Combine the flour, salt and cayenne in a bowl. With a pastry blender or the fingertips, work the butter and shortening in until the mixture resembles coarse crumbs.
4. Add the cooled sesame seeds. While stirring with a fork, add 2 to 3 tablespoons ice water or enough to make a dough. Gather into a ball.
5. Roll out the dough on a lightly floured board into a rectangle 1/8-inch thick. Cut into sticks 4 inches by 1/2 inch. Transfer sticks to a cookie sheet.
6. Bake sticks in a preheated slow oven (325°) for 15 minutes or until golden. Cool on a wire rack. Store in a tightly covered container.

Chile Cheese Squares

The custardy cheese mixture can also be baked in a 9-inch pie plate and served in wedges like a Southwestern quiche.

Bake at 375° for 30 minutes.

Makes about 16 two-inch squares.

1 can (4 ounces) diced, mild green chilies, drained
8 ounces Monterey Jack or sharp Cheddar cheese, shredded (2 cups)
1 cup buttermilk

baking mix
1 cup light cream or half-and-half
4 eggs
1/4 teaspoon salt
1/4 cup sliced pimiento-stuffed olives

1. Sprinkle green chilies and shredded cheese in the bottom of a lightly greased 9-inch square baking pan. Preheat oven to 375°.
2. Combine buttermilk baking mix, cream, eggs and salt in a medium-size bowl; beat until thoroughly blended. Pour over chile-cheese mixture; spread evenly.
3. Bake in a preheated moderate oven (375°) for 30 minutes or until puffed, golden and a skewer inserted in center comes out clean. Let stand 10 minutes before cutting into squares to serve. Garnish squares with olive slices.

To Freeze Ahead: Freeze squares in a single layer on a jelly-roll pan or large baking sheet. Transfer to a plastic bag when frozen. To reheat: Arrange squares in a single layer on a large baking sheet and bake in a moderate oven (350°) for 15 minutes. Garnish as above with pimiento-stuffed olives.

Overleaf (from left): Carnitas con Salsa, page 54; Bambini, page 55; Chile Cheese Squares, page 51; Chicken Walnut Strips, page 50; Chinese Pork and Ginger Balls, page 54; Toasted Tartare, page 54; Chicken Pillows, page 50.

Toasted Tartare

All the piquant accompaniments to steak tartare season this broiled beef topping.

Makes 24 canapés.

24 slices party-size rye bread	sour cream or heavy cream
Butter	2 tablespoons drained capers, mashed
1 pound ground round	1/2 teaspoon salt
1 small onion, minced (1/4 cup)	1/4 teaspoon pepper
2 egg yolks	Chopped fresh parsley
2 tablespoons dairy	

1. Lightly toast bread, on one side only, under broiler. Spread untoasted sides with butter.
2. Combine remaining ingredients, except parsley, in a medium-size bowl and blend well.
3. Mound a generous tablespoonful of the meat mixture on the buttered side of each bread slice. Make sure meat mixture completely covers the bread to prevent burning. Arrange bread on broiler pan.
4. Broil 3 inches from heat for 3 to 4 minutes. Sprinkle with parsley.

Note: Bread can be toasted and buttered and meat mixture can be made ahead of time and refrigerated. Assemble and broil just before serving.

Chinese Pork and Ginger Balls

Makes about 36 meatballs.

1 pound ground pork	OR: 1 teaspoon ground ginger
1 can (8 ounces) water chestnuts, drained and finely chopped	1 tablespoon soy sauce
1 tablespoon finely chopped fresh ginger	1 egg
	Peanut or vegetable oil

1. Combine pork, water chestnuts, ginger, soy sauce and egg in medium bowl; blend thoroughly. Shape mixture with wet hands into 1-inch balls.
2. Cover the bottom of a large skillet with oil; heat over medium heat.
3. Place as many meatballs in skillet as will fit without crowding. Cook 5 to 8 minutes, turning often, until crisp and brown and no trace of pink remains on the inside. Transfer meatballs to a serving platter with a slotted spoon; serve immediately.

To Freeze Ahead: Brown meatballs in skillet without cooking all the way through. Freeze in a single layer on baking sheets. When frozen solid, place in a plastic bag; seal. To reheat: Place meatballs in a large baking pan; heat, covered, in a moderate oven (350°) for 30 minutes or until hot and cooked through.

Carnitas Con Salsa

"Carnitas" is Spanish for "little meats." "Salsa" is a spicy fresh tomato sauce. Together, they're terrific!
Bake at 200° for 2 hours.

Makes 10 to 12 appetizer servings.

2 pounds boneless pork shoulder	1 cup finely chopped peeled, fresh tomatoes
1/2 teaspoon salt	1/4 cup finely chopped red onion
1/4 teaspoon pepper	1/4 cup chopped fresh parsley
Salsa:	
1 jar or can (8 ounces) mild taco sauce	

1. Trim as much of the fat from the meat as possible with a very sharp knife; cut meat into 1-inch cubes. Arrange in a single layer in a jelly-roll pan; sprinkle with the salt and pepper.
2. Bake in a slow oven (200°) for 2 hours or until crisp and brown.
3. Make Salsa: Combine taco sauce, tomatoes, onion and parsley in a small bowl. Cover and refrigerate.
4. To serve: Center bowl of Salsa on a serving platter and surround with pork cubes for dipping.

Miniature Sausage-Crêpe Quiches

Bake at 425° for 5 minutes, then at 350° for 15 minutes.

Makes about 48 miniature quiches.

Crêpes:	5 sweet Italian sausages (5 ounces)
3 eggs	2 ounces Swiss cheese, shredded (1/2 cup)
1/4 teaspoon salt	2 eggs, slightly beaten
2 cups *sifted* all-purpose flour	1/2 cup milk
2 cups milk	1/4 cup light cream or half-and-half
1/4 cup (1/2 stick) butter, melted	2 tablespoons grated Parmesan cheese
Filling:	1/4 teaspoon salt
2 cups shredded zucchini (about 2 medium-size, or 1/2 pound)	1/8 teaspoon white pepper
2 tablespoons butter	

1. Prepare Crêpes: Beat eggs with salt in a small bowl until foamy. Gradually add flour alternately with milk; beat until smooth. Beat in melted butter; cover; refrigerate 1 hour or more.
2. Make crêpes in a lightly buttered 6- to 7-inch skillet, using 1 tablespoon batter for each crêpe. Cook one side of crêpe until golden brown; turn and lightly cook underside. Keep crêpes warm between sheets of wax paper. (Crêpes may be stacked with plastic wrap or foil, overwrapped with freezer-weight plastic wrap and frozen for up to 2 weeks.)
3. Prepare Filling: Sauté zucchini in butter in a large

skillet until tender, about 5 minutes. Remove to a medium-size bowl. Remove casing from sausages. Cook sausage over low heat in same skillet, breaking up with a spoon, until no pink remains. Drain on paper toweling. Add sausage, Swiss cheese, eggs, milk, cream, Parmesan, salt and pepper to zucchini; mix well.

4. Preheat oven to 425°. Press crêpes, browned side out, into well-greased 1³/₄-inch miniature muffin pan cups. Spoon sausage filling into crêpe-lined cups.

5. Bake in a preheated hot oven (425°) for 5 minutes. Lower heat to moderate (350°) and bake an additional 15 minutes or until tops of quiches are lightly golden. Remove to heated serving dish; serve warm.

Chinese Egg Rolls

These crunchy and flavorful Chinese egg rolls are superb when dipped into two pungent sauces.

Makes 12 servings.

¹/₄ cup chopped green onions	**bean sprouts, drained**
1 small clove garlic, minced	**2 tablespoons soy sauce**
4 mushrooms, coarsely chopped (¹/₂ cup)	**¹/₄ teaspoon salt**
¹/₄ cup diced celery	**¹/₄ teaspoon sugar**
1 tablespoon vegetable oil	**¹/₄ teaspoon ground ginger**
¹/₂ cup fresh or frozen shelled and deveined shrimp, diced	**1¹/₂ teaspoons cornstarch**
	Egg Roll Wrappers (recipe follows)
¹/₂ package (10 ounces) frozen leaf spinach, thawed and well drained	**1 egg, beaten**
	Peanut or vegetable oil
1 can (16 ounces)	**Bottled duck sauce**
	Hot Mustard (recipe follows)

1. Sauté onions, garlic, mushrooms and celery in hot oil in large skillet for 5 minutes; add shrimp; sauté 1 minute just until shrimp turn pink.

2. Stir in well-drained spinach and bean sprouts. Combine soy sauce, salt, sugar, ginger and cornstarch in small cup or bowl. Add to skillet; cook, stirring constantly, until thickened, about 1 minute. Turn mixture into a bowl and cool completely.

3. Prepare Egg Roll Wrappers.

4. When ready to fill, spoon about 1 rounded teaspoonful or 1 level tablespoonful of filling on center of each wrapper. Brush edges with beaten egg. Bring 1 corner up and over filling, then bring each of the adjacent corners, 1 at a time, up and over enclosed filling, pressing points down firmly; roll into a neat package. Place filled rolls on cookie sheet; cover with plastic wrap.

5. Heat a 1¹/₂-inch depth of oil in electric or deep heavy skillet to 375°. Drop in rolls 8 to 10 at a time;

deep-fry 2 to 3 minutes or until golden brown and crisp. Drain on paper toweling. Serve with bottled duck sauce and Hot Mustard.

To freeze rolls: Cool completely, then arrange in single layer on jelly-roll pans or cookie sheets. Place in freezer. When solid, place in plastic bags or layer in plastic boxes.

To reheat: Place egg rolls in single layer on large cookie sheet. Heat at 400° for 8 to 10 minutes.

Hot Mustard: Mix ¹/₄ cup dry mustard with 1¹/₂ teaspoons vinegar and ¹/₃ cup cold water.

Egg Roll Wrappers

Makes 24.

2 cups *sifted* all-purpose flour	**1 egg**
1 teaspoon salt	**¹/₂ cup ice water**
	Cornstarch

1. Sift flour and salt into large bowl. Make a well in center and add egg and water. Stir with fork until dough holds together and leaves sides of bowl clean. Turn out onto lightly floured surface; knead until smooth and elastic, 5 minutes. Cover dough with bowl; allow dough to rest at least 30 minutes.

2. Divide dough in fourths. Dust pastry board lightly with cornstarch; roll each piece of dough to a 14 × 11-inch rectangle. Cut into 3¹/₂-inch squares. Stack on a plate (cornstarch will prevent them from sticking together).

Bambini

This is a two-bite version of those giant pizzeria cheese and meat turnovers called calzone.

Bake at 350° for 20 minutes.

Makes 20 turnovers.

1 cup ricotta cheese	**large flaky refrigerator biscuits**
¹/₂ cup shredded mozzarella cheese	**20 very thin slices pepperoni (half of a 3¹/₂-ounce package)**
¹/₄ cup grated Parmesan cheese	
1 package (10 ounces)	

1. Combine ricotta, mozzarella and Parmesan cheeses in a small bowl. Preheat oven to 350°.

2. Halve each biscuit horizontally, forming 20 thin biscuits. If kitchen is hot, refrigerate half the dough while filling the remainder. Gently shape one piece of dough into an oval about 2¹/₂ × 4 inches. Place a slice of pepperoni slightly off center on dough. Top with about 1 level tablespoon of cheese mixture. Moisten edges; fold dough over to enclose filling, pinching edges carefully to seal. Transfer to a lightly-greased cookie sheet and repeat with the remaining dough, pepperoni and filling.

3. Bake in a preheated moderate oven (350°) for 20 minutes. Serve warm.

BEVERAGES

Cucumber Smoothie

Tangy, smooth and refreshing.

Makes about 3 cups or 2 servings.

1¹/₂ cups (12 ounces) vanilla yogurt	cucumber, halved, seeded and cut into chunks
1 tablespoon honey or to taste	3 eggs
1 medium-size	

Combine yogurt, honey, cucumber and eggs in container of electric blender. Cover; whirl on medium speed until smooth.

Pineapple Nog

Tropical in taste, an invigorating way to start the day.

Makes about 4 cups or 2 servings.

1 can (8 ounces) crushed pineapple in pineapple juice	coconut cream
	1 cup skim milk
4 eggs	¹/₈ teaspoon ground nutmeg
¹/₂ can (8³/₄ ounces)	

1. Combine pineapple, eggs, coconut cream, milk and nutmeg in container of electric blender. Cover; whirl on medium speed until smooth.
2. Pour into 2 large glasses; sprinkle each with additional nutmeg.

Buttermilk Swirl

Makes about 3 cups or 2 servings.

2 cups buttermilk	4 teaspoons honey
2 large bananas, peeled	Strawberry preserves OR: Partially thawed frozen strawberries
¹/₂ cup wheat germ	

1. Combine buttermilk, bananas, wheat germ and honey in container of electric blender. Cover. Whirl until smooth.
2. Pour a small amount into 2 large glasses, alternating with spoonfuls of preserves or strawberries to swirl.

Pictured opposite (left to right): Pineapple Nog, page 57; Cucumber Smoothie, page 57; Buttermilk Swirl, page 57.

Apricot Yogurt Fizz

The apricot yogurt mixture can be blended ahead and refrigerated.

Makes about 3¹/₂ cups or 2 servings.

1 can (16 ounces) apricot halves, drained	2 eggs
	¹/₃ cup instant nonfat dry milk powder
1 container (8 ounces) plain yogurt	¹/₂ cup club soda

1. Combine apricot halves, yogurt, eggs and dry milk powder in container of electric blender. Cover; whirl on medium speed until smooth.
2. Pour into 2 large glasses; add club soda to fill glass. Serve immediately.

Cranberry-Orange Cooler

Makes 3 servings.

1 cup cranberry juice cocktail	1 cup water
	Orange slices
1 cup orange juice	

Combine cranberry juice cocktail, orange juice and water in a small pitcher. Stir to mix; chill. Pour into 3 tall ice-filled glasses. Garnish with orange slice.

Indian Yogurt Drink

Makes 1 quart.

1 container (8 ounces) plain yogurt	3 tablespoons honey
	Cold plain or bottled water
¹/₄ cup lime juice	

1. Put yogurt, lime juice and honey in container of electric blender. Whirl until smooth.
2. Pour into quart container; fill with cold water. Chill; stir before serving.

Seltzer
A mineral water originating from Nieder Selters in the Wiesbaden district of Germany. The water is now artificially prepared and bottled. It contains a great deal of carbon dioxide.

Apricot-Apple Quencher

Makes 3 servings.

1 can (12 ounces) apricot nectar	½ cup apple juice
1 cup water	Apple wedges

Combine apricot nectar, water and apple juice in small pitcher. Stir to mix. Chill until ready to serve. Pour into 3 tall ice-filled glasses. Garnish with apple wedges.

Orange Juice Sparkler

Makes 1 serving.

¾ cup orange juice	¼ cup quinine water
Ice cubes	Orange slice

Pour orange juice over ice cubes in a glass. Stir in quinine water. Serve with orange slice.

Grape Cooler

Makes 3 servings.

1 cup peach nectar	1 bottle (8 ounces) carbonated water
1 cup white grape juice	

Combine peach nectar, grape juice and carbonated water in a pitcher. Stir to mix; pour into ice-filled glasses.

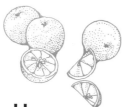

Pacific Sparkler

A fruity and cooling punch.

Makes 50 4-ounce servings.

2 quarts orange juice, chilled	2 bottles (28 ounces each) lemon-lime carbonated beverage or ginger ale, chilled
2 cans (46 ounces each) unsweetened pineapple juice, chilled	Ice block or cubes
2 cans (6 ounces each) frozen limeade concentrate	Lime slices
	Halved strawberries *(optional)*

1. Combine orange juice, pineapple juice and limeade concentrate in large punch bowl; stir to dissolve concentrate.

2. Just before serving, add lemon-lime carbonated beverage or ginger ale. Add ice and garnish with lime slices and halved strawberries.

Note: For 12 servings, use 2 cups orange juice, 3 cups pineapple juice, ⅓ cup frozen limeade concentrate and 1 bottle (12 ounces) lemon-lime carbonated beverage or ginger ale.

Cranberry Orange Punch

Makes 6½ cups.

1 can (6 ounces) frozen orange juice concentrate, reconstituted (3 cups)	1¾ cups cranberry juice cocktail, chilled
	1 bottle (12 ounces) ginger ale, chilled

Combine orange juice and cranberry juice cocktail in a large pitcher or small punch bowl with ice. Stir in ginger ale just before serving.

Tomato Sunrise

An eye-opener for tomato juice lovers.

Makes about 3½ cups or 2 servings.

2 cups tomato juice	3 eggs
1 cup canned beef broth	⅛ teaspoon liquid hot pepper seasoning

1. Combine tomato juice, beef broth and eggs in container of electric blender. Cover; whirl on medium speed until frothy.
2. Add hot pepper seasoning to taste. Serve immediately.

Pink Tomato Drink

Makes 1 serving.

1 cup tomato juice, chilled	Worcestershire sauce
¼ cup plain yogurt	Dash garlic powder
3 drops	Salt to taste

Whirl all ingredients in container of electric blender just until blended. Serve with cucumber stick.

Fresh Lemonade; Lemon Leaf Cookies, page 206.

Summertime Lemonade

Nothing like a pitcher of cool homemade lemonade to quench a thirst.

Makes about 2 quarts.

6 cups water
2 cups sugar

2¹/₂ cups fresh lemon juice

1. Heat water and sugar to boiling in a medium-size saucepan, stirring constantly. Boil 5 minutes without stirring; cool; chill.
2. Just before serving, combine sugar syrup and lemon juice. Pour over ice in tall glasses. Garnish with strawberries and lemon slices, if you wish.

Fresh Lemonade

Make the lemon syrup ahead and refrigerate. When ready for a glass of lemonade, simply combine water and ice with a little syrup; make it as lemony as you wish.

Makes 6 servings.

1 teaspoon grated lemon rind
1 cup lemon juice (4 to 5 lemons)
³/₄ to 1 cup sugar
4¹/₂ cups water

1 lemon, sliced
Ice cubes
Fresh mint leaves or lemon slices for garnish (optional)

1. Prepare the lemon syrup: Combine the lemon rind, lemon juice and sugar in a 4-cup glass measure; stir

to dissolve the sugar. Chill, covered, until ready to use.
2. Lemonade by the pitcher: Combine the lemon syrup, the 4¹/₂ cups water and the lemon slices in a large pitcher. Stir to mix. Add the ice cubes just before serving. Garnish with the mint leaves or lemon slices, if you wish.
3. Lemonade by the glass: Measure 3 tablespoons lemon syrup (or more or less according to taste) into a tall 10- or 12-ounce glass. Add ice cubes and water; stir to mix. Garnish with the mint or lemon slices, if you wish.

Lemon Spritzer: Measure 2 to 3 tablespoons lemon syrup into a 10-ounce stemmed glass. Add chilled club soda and garnish with a lemon wedge.

Frosty Lemonade

Makes about 1 quart.

1 cup fresh lemon juice (4 to 6 lemons)
³/₄ to 1 cup sugar

3 cups cold water
Ice cubes

Combine juice and sugar in a large pitcher; stir with long-handled spoon until sugar dissolves. Just before serving add cold water and ice cubes. Garnish with lemon slices, if you wish.

Apple Iced Tea

Makes 4 servings.

2 cups boiling water
3 tea bags

1 cup apple juice
¹/₄ cup lemon juice

Pour boiling water over tea bags; steep 3 minutes; remove tea bags; let stand at room temperature until ready to serve. Combine tea, apple juice and lemon juice in pitcher. Pour into ice-filled glasses. Sweeten to taste; garnish with mint leaves, if you wish.

Sun Tea

Makes about 1 quart.

12 tea bags
1 quart tepid water

Ice cubes

1. Place tea bags and water in jar. Seal tightly.
2. Set jar in a sunny window or backyard and leave until liquid is dark--how long this will take varies with the intensity of the sun, but allow anywhere from 4 to 8 hours. Turn jar several times as tea brews.
3. Remove tea bags; store sun tea in the refrigerator.
4. *To serve:* Pour sun tea over ice cubes in tall glasses until half-full. Add cold water to fill. Serve with lemon wedges and sprigs of mint, if you wish.

Tropical Tea

Makes about 12 servings.

4 cups boiling water	chilled
4 tea bags	2 bottles (28 ounces
1/2 cup sugar	each) ginger ale,
8 limes	chilled
4 cups unsweetened	Strawberries
pineapple juice,	

1. Pour boiling water over tea bags in a 1-gallon container. Let steep 3 to 5 minutes; remove and discard tea bags. Stir in sugar.
2. Cut limes in half; squeeze juice (about 1 cup) and reserve juice and shells. Stir pineapple juice into tea. (Can be prepared ahead up to this point.)
3. Just before serving, add lime juice and ginger ale.
4. Serve over ice cubes with straws in 10-ounce highball glasses or pour over an ice ring in a punch bowl. Place strawberry in center of each lime shell; use to garnish servings.

Fruit Smoothie

Makes 5 servings (8 ounces each)

1 can (6 ounces) frozen orange juice concentrate	OR: 1 1/2 cups fresh, frozen dry-pack or drained canned peaches
1 large ripe banana, sliced (1 cup)	1 cup skim milk
OR: 1 1/2 cups fresh or frozen dry-pack strawberries	1 cup water
	2 tablespoons honey
	5 ice cubes

1. Combine orange juice concentrate, banana or other fruit, skim milk, water and honey in container of electric blender. Cover; whirl at high speed until thick and smooth, about 1 minute.
2. Add ice cubes, one at a time, and blend until smooth and frothy. Garnish with a whole strawberry, if you wish. Serve.

Spiced Coffee Vienna

Makes 6 servings.

3 cups extra-strong hot coffee	4 whole cloves
2 3-inch pieces stick cinnamon	4 whole allspice
	Softly whipped cream
	Ground nutmeg

1. Pour coffee into chafing dish with a flame underneath. Add cinnamon, cloves and allspice. Steep the mixture over very low heat for 10 to 15 minutes. Strain.
2. Pour into heatproof wine glasses or cups; top with cream and nutmeg. Serve with sugar.

Espresso   Robust, dark, Italian-style coffee brewed under steam pressure. Espresso is traditionally served in small cups and, in this country, though usually not in Italy, is accompanied by a twist of lemon rind.

Cappucino

A sophisticated Italian after-dinner coffee. The name comes from the color of the coffee—that of the robe of a Capuchin monk.

Makes 8 servings.

3 cups hot espresso coffee	Ground cinnamon
3 cups scalded milk	Ground nutmeg

Combine coffee and milk, Pour into heated demitasse cups; sprinkle with cinnamon and nutmeg. Add some sugar to taste, if you wish.

Fruit Smoothie.

Café Brûlot

A New Orleans classic flamed just before serving.

Makes 8 servings.

5 lumps sugar	**cinnamon**
1 cup brandy	**6 whole cloves**
4 cups very strong hot coffee	**1 piece vanilla bean**
1 3-inch piece stick	**1 3-inch strip orange rind**

1. Soak a sugar lump in brandy, remove and set aside. Add remaining 4 sugar lumps to brandy.
2. Pour coffee into chafing dish or metal bowl with a flame underneath it. Add cinnamon stick, cloves, vanilla bean and orange rind. Stir together. Add brandy.
3. Place the brandy-soaked lump of sugar on a serving ladle and ignite. Add, flaming, to the Café Brûlot and serve immediately.

Café au Lait

The French way to serve coffee.

Pour equal parts of freshly brewed, double-strength coffee and scalded milk or light cream into heated coffee cups. Serve at once. Make a cup at a time, or in quantity.

Frozen Irish Coffee

Makes 6 servings.

4 cups freshly brewed hot espresso or very strong regular coffee	**2 teaspoons 10X (confectioners') sugar**
1/2 cup granulated sugar	**1/4 teaspoon vanilla**
3/4 cup Irish whiskey	**1 square (1 ounce) semisweet chocolate, coarsely grated**
1/2 cup heavy cream	

1. Combine the coffee, granulated sugar and whiskey in a 6-quart pitcher. Cool.
2. Pour the coffee into ice cube trays or a 13 × 9 × 2-inch pan. Freeze until firm.
3. Unmold the coffee cubes. If using a baking pan, cut into 2-inch chunks. Place one-quarter of the chunks in a food processor fitted with a metal blade. Process until smooth.
4. With the motor running, add another quarter of the cubes; process until smooth. Spoon into the freezer container. Repeat with the remaining cubes. Freeze until firm.
5. Several hours before serving, return the frozen coffee to the food processor. Process just until

smooth. Scoop into serving dishes. Freeze until ready to serve.
6. Beat the cream, 10X sugar and vanilla until stiff. Refrigerate until ready to serve.
7. To serve, top with the whipped cream and sprinkle with the grated chocolate.

To Make Ahead: Frozen coffee can be made several days ahead through step 4. Scoop into dishes several hours before serving.

Irish Coffee

Makes 8 servings.

8 teaspoons sugar	**8 jiggers Irish whiskey**
6 cups strong hot coffee	**1/2 cup heavy cream, whipped**

1. Heat each goblet or mug by putting a metal spoon in the empty goblet and pouring hot water onto the spoon and then into the goblet. Pour out water.
2. Put a teaspoon of sugar in each goblet. Add enough coffee to dissolve the sugar; stir. Add a jigger of Irish whiskey to each goblet, then fill goblet to within an inch of the brim with more coffee.
3. Add whipped cream by sliding each spoonful over the back of a teaspoon held over the goblet of coffee. Do not stir. Serve at once.

Dublin Irish Coffee

Makes 1 serving.

Boiling water	**Irish whiskey**
1 teaspoon granulated sugar	**Hot coffee**
1 ounce (2 tablespoons)	**Softly whipped heavy cream**

Heat a heavy stemmed glass with boiling water; pour out. Combine sugar and whiskey in the glass; stir in coffee to within 1 inch of the top. Pour whipped cream over the back of a spoon onto coffee. Serve without stirring.

Overleaf (clockwise from left): Winter Fruit Salad with Honey-Lemon Dressing, page 699; Savory Cream Puffs, page 91; Nutty Maple-Honey Buns, page 108; Hot Herbed Tomato Juice, page 64; Overnight Seed Bread, page 108; Frozen Irish Coffee, page 61.

Frozen Coffee 'n' Cream

Makes 2 servings.

1 pint coffee ice cream	**Club soda**
1/2 cup coffee-flavored liqueur	**Chocolate curls (optional)**

1. Prechill the container of an electric blender and 2 large glasses.
2. Make 2 small scoops of the ice cream; place on a cookie sheet in the freezer. Soften the remainder of the ice cream in the refrigerator for 15 minutes.
3. Combine the softened ice cream and liqueur in a blender. Cover; whirl until smooth. Pour into the chilled glasses. Add a splash of the club soda. Place a scoop of the ice cream in each glass and garnish with chocolate curls, if you wish.

Homemade Tomato Juice

Makes 1 quart.

3 to 3 1/2 pounds tomatoes, cored	**and cut up** **Salt**

1. Simmer tomatoes in large saucepan or Dutch oven, stirring often, just until juice is running freely and tomatoes are soft, about 30 minutes.
2. Press through food mill or sieve. Add salt to taste. Refrigerate and use within a day. To can tomato juice, reheat tomato juice to boiling. Ladle into a hot, sterilized 32-ounce preserving jar. Add 1 teaspoon salt. Wipe rim; seal jar.
3. Process 15 minutes in boiling water bath. Cool; check seal. Label and store in a cool, dark, dry place.

Hot Herbed Tomato Juice

Makes 6 servings.

6 small green onions	**Worcestershire**
2 cans (18 ounces each) tomato juice	**sauce**
2 tablespoons lemon juice	**1/2 teaspoon dried dillweed, crumbled**
1 tablespoon	**1/2 teaspoon leaf chervil, crumbled**

1. Slice a 1- to 2-inch piece from the bulb end of the green onions. Chop the pieces; reserve. To curl the onion, make thin, lengthwise cuts through the top of the green ends, leaving enough stalk uncut so the onion doesn't separate.
2. Combine the tomato juice, lemon juice, Worcestershire, dillweed, chervil and chopped white portion of the onion in a medium-size saucepan. Bring to boiling.
3. Pour the tomato mixture into a blender or food processor fitted with a metal blade. Blend until smooth. Pour into heatproof glasses or mugs. Garnish with the onion curls.

Curried Clam Cocktail

Curry and lemon give a fresh flavor lift to this jiffy-fix special.

Makes 4 servings.

2 bottles (8 ounces each) clam juice	**juice**
1 can (8 ounces) tomato sauce	**1/2 teaspoon curry powder**
1 tablespoon lemon	**Crushed ice**

1. Combine clam juice, tomato sauce, lemon juice and curry powder in a 4-cup shaker; shake to mix well.
2. Pour over crushed ice in glasses; serve plain or garnish with a slice of lemon, if you wish.

Tropical Refresher

Makes 2 servings.

1/2 cup chopped fresh pineapple	**1 tablespoon lemon juice**
1/4 cup orange juice	**Lemon-lime soda**
1/4 cup pineapple juice	**2 lemon slices for garnish**
1/4 to 1/2 cup crushed ice	**Fresh mint (optional)**

1. Prechill the container of an electric blender and 2 large glasses.
2. Combine the chopped pineapple, orange juice, pineapple juice, crushed ice and lemon juice in the chilled blender container. Cover; whirl until smooth.
3. Pour half of the juice mixture into each glass. Fill with the lemon-lime soda. Garnish each glass with a lemon slice, and mint, if you wish.

Cocoa

Makes 4 to 6 servings.

3 tablespoons unsweetened cocoa powder	**1 quart milk**
	1/4 teaspoon vanilla
1/4 cup sugar	**4 to 6 marshmallows**

1. Blend cocoa and sugar.
2. Heat milk to scalding; mix a little hot milk into cocoa mixture, then add to hot milk and stir until well blended. Add vanilla; pour into cups or mugs and float a marshmallow in each.

Top: Frozen Coffee 'n'
Cream, page 64; Tropical
Refresher, page 64;
Grapefruit Campari,
page 71.

Mexican Hot Chocolate

Makes 6 servings.

4 cups milk	**1 teaspoon ground**
3 squares semisweet	**cinnamon**
chocolate	**2 eggs**
(3 ounces)	

1. Heat milk just to scalding in a large saucepan. Stir in chocolate and cinnamon until chocolate melts, then beat with a rotary beater until smooth.
2. Beat eggs well in a small bowl; slowly beat in about 1 cup of the hot chocolate mixture, then beat back into remaining chocolate mixture in pan. Heat slowly 1 minute, stirring constantly; beat again until frothy.
3. Ladle into heated mugs or glasses; place a cinnamon stick in each mug for a stirrer, if you wish. Serve warm.

Low-Calorie Strawberry Nog

Makes one 18-ounce serving at 250 calories.

Ice cubes	**½ cup instant nonfat**
Water	**dry milk**
6 whole strawberries,	**½ teaspoon vanilla**
hulled	**Sugar substitute to**
OR: 6 unsweetened	**equal 2 tablespoons**
frozen strawberries	**sugar**
1 egg	

1. Fill a 1-cup measure with ice cubes; add cold water to fill cup. Pour into electric blender container. Add strawberries, egg, nonfat dry milk powder, vanilla and sugar substitute.
2. Cover; whirl at high speed until thick and frothy. Pour into a tall glass. Serve immediately.

Aperitif   A mild alcoholic drink sipped before meals to sharpen the appetite. It is usually a wine or wine-based drink served chilled, on the rocks, straight or with soda water. The word aperitif comes from the Latin meaning "to open". With an aperitif like dry vermouth or dry sherry, you'll open the taste buds for the meal that follows.

Daiquiri

Makes 1 serving.

1½ teaspoons lime	**1 jigger (1½ fluid**
juice	**ounces) light rum**
1 teaspoon sugar	**Ice cubes**

Place lime juice, sugar, rum and ice in a shaker. Cover and shake well. Strain into a stemmed glass.
Frozen Daiquiri: Prepare daiquiri but use cracked ice and whirl in an electric blender.

Strawberry Daiquiri: Whirl 6 hulled, fresh strawberries, 1 tablespoon lime juice, 1 teaspoon sugar, 1 jigger rum and ½ cup crushed ice in electric blender.

Daiquiri Liqueur

Makes about 1 quart.

4 limes	**1½ cups superfine**
3 cups light rum	**granulated sugar**

1. Pare very thinly the bright-colored rind from the limes (no white). Blot rind on paper toweling to remove any excess oil. Place rind in a 4-cup screw-top jar. Add 2 cups of the rum. Close jar. Store in a cool, dark place for 2 days or until rum has absorbed the flavor and color of the rind.
2. Remove rind; add sugar; shake vigorously until sugar dissolves. Add remaining 1 cup rum and stir until liquid becomes clear. Close jar and store in cool, dark place at least 1 week to age.

Cranberry-Orange Liqueur

Makes about 1¼ quarts.

1 package (12 ounces)	**1 bottle (750 ml) vodka**
cranberries	**1½ cups sugar**
1 orange	**¾ cup water**

1. Chop cranberries coarsely. Pare orange with vegetable parer; using only the thin orange rind, no white.
2. Combine cranberries, orange rind and vodka in a glass or plastic one-gallon container. Cover, let steep at room temperature 3 to 4 weeks.
3. Strain into a clean container; filter or siphon off clear liquid, if cloudy.
4. Combine sugar and water in a medium-size saucepan; bring to boiling; boil 1 minute; cool.
5. Stir sugar syrup into cranberry-orange liquid. Taste. For a sweeter liqueur, more sugar syrup may be prepared and added.

Julep   A sweet alcoholic drink flavored with an aromatic plant such as mint leaves. The word is derived from the Arab *julab* or rosewater. Juleps are widely known but the Mint Julep made with bourbon is the most famous.

Sake   A Japanese liquor made from rice which is cleansed, steamed and fermented. Sake is colorless and sweet with a bitter aftertaste. Usually served warm in porcelain cups. It is 12 to 16 percent alcohol by volume.

How to Dress Drinks for a Party

Sugar-coated Grapes
Break off dainty bunches and dip into an egg white beaten slightly with about a half teaspoon of water, then into granulated sugar, turning to coat well. Set aside on paper toweling until dry. Drape over rim of a glass.

Fruit Kebabs
Thread any combination of fruits on drinking straws or stirrer sticks. Make them long or short to fit into a pitcher or glass. Combinations shown here: Watermelon and honeydew balls; cut-up kumquats and chunks of banana rolled in lemon juice and coconut; marshmallows on a candy stick; orange slices and whole strawberries; and raspberries, pear rounds, and blueberries.

Citrus Cartwheel
Notch orange and lemon or lime slices around the edge, and thread with a maraschino cherry onto a cocktail or short drinking straw.

Colorful Cubes
Place a berry; cherry; wedge of orange, lemon, or lime; or a thin strip of peel in each compartment of an ice-cube tray. Fill with water and freeze as usual.

Orange Cup
Just plain, or simply decorated with a sprig of mint, a scooped-out orange makes a colorful cup. Save the fruit to dice and add to salad or dessert.

Eggnog This traditional winter holiday beverage, usually served cold, is an American drink derived from the English. Basically, it's a sweet milk and egg drink, often fortified with an alcoholic spirit.

A "nog" in England is the shortened word for "noggin," a drinking cup with an upright handle that was used for ale. The English did have a milk and egg drink made with ale or sack, a dry wine from Spain and the Canary Islands.

The earliest American eggnogs were probably made with rum. Today, spirits such as brandy or whiskey are also used.

Eggnog

Makes about twenty 1/2-cup servings.

9 eggs, at room temperature	**brandy**
1 cup sugar	**1 quart milk**
2 cups bourbon	**1 cup heavy cream**
1/2 cup Cognac or	**Ground nutmeg**

1. Beat eggs in a large bowl with electric mixer until foamy. Gradually beat in sugar until fluffy-thick. Stir in bourbon, Cognac and milk. Chill until serving time.
2. Just before serving, beat cream in a small bowl until stiff. Fold into egg mixture. Pour into a punch bowl. Sprinkle with nutmeg.

Eggnog Brasilia

Makes about 16 four-ounce servings.

4 eggs, separated	**crystals**
3 cups milk	**1/2 cup light corn**
2 cups light cream or half-and-half	**syrup**
3 tablespoons instant coffee powder or	**1/2 cup brandy**
	1/4 cup water
	Ground nutmeg

1. Beat egg yolks slightly in a large saucepan; stir in milk, cream, instant coffee and 1/4 cup of the corn syrup. Heat slowly, stirring often, to scalding; remove from heat. Stir in brandy.
2. Heat remaining 1/4 cup corn syrup with water to boiling in a small saucepan; simmer 5 minutes. Beat egg whites until foamy in a large bowl; slowly beat in hot syrup until meringue forms soft peaks; fold in egg-yolk mixture.
3. Pour or ladle into a punch bowl; sprinkle with nutmeg. Serve warm in punch or demitasse cups.

Punch

An alcoholic beverage introduced to England from India, made with five ingredients -- a spirit, lime, sugar, spices and water. The word is derived from the Hindi word *panch*, meaning five. Nowadays a punch may be made of any number of ingredients, served hot or cold and contain no alcohol or spirit.

Blazing Spiced Wine Punch

Makes about 24 four-ounce servings.

1/4 cup sugar	**2 cups ruby port wine**
2 4-inch pieces stick cinnamon, broken	**1 cup raisins**
8 whole cardamom seed pods, crushed	**1 cup whole blanched almonds**
8 whole cloves	**1 orange, sliced**
4 whole allspice	**20 tiny sugar cubes (1/2-inch size)**
Thin rind from 1 orange (no white)	**1 2-inch piece lemon rind stuck with 2 whole cloves**
1/2 cup water	**1 cup brandy, warmed**
1/2 gallon (8 cups) dry red wine	

1. Combine sugar, cinnamon, cardamom, cloves, allspice, orange rind and water in a small saucepan; bring to boiling. Cover; simmer over low heat 5 minutes. Let stand several hours or until ready to make punch. Strain, discarding spices and orange rind.
2. Just before serving, combine wine, port, raisins and almonds in a large saucepan; add strained spice mixture. Bring just to boiling. Pour into a warm, heat-proof punch bowl; float orange slices on top.
3. Place sugar cubes and lemon rind in a large ladle; add about 1/4 cup of the warm brandy; carefully pour remaining brandy over surface of punch. Hold the ladle over punch bowl. Ignite the mixture in ladle; rotate and shake ladle until sugar is almost dissolved.
4. Lower ladle into punch to ignite brandy floating on top; stir slowly a few times. When flames have died, serve in small mugs or punch cups with a few raisins and almonds in each serving. Give each guest a spoon to eat raisins and almonds.

Holiday Punch

Our versatile holiday punch, with or without champagne.

Makes 20 servings (10 cups).

1 cup crème de cassis (black currant liqueur)	**1 bottle (750 ml.) champagne, chilled***
2 tablespoons lime juice	**1 bottle or can (12 ounces) carbonated water (seltzer or soda water), chilled**
3 to 4 tablespoons honey	
1 quart cranberry juice, chilled	**Ice cubes** *(optional)*

1. Stir together the cassis, lime juice and honey in a punch bowl or large pitcher until blended. Add the cranberry juice. Chill until ready to serve.
2. Just before serving, add the champagne and carbonated water. Add the ice, if you wish.

*One quart of carbonated water may be substituted for the champagne.

Pictured opposite: Low-Calorie Strawberry Nog, page 66.

Champagne Punch

Makes about 30 four-ounce servings.

1/4 **cup sugar**	2 **bottles (750 ml.**
1 **tablespoon aromatic**	**each) dry**
bitters	**champagne, chilled**
1/2 **cup fresh or frozen**	2 **bottles (28 ounces**
lemon juice	**each) club soda,**
1 **cup Cognac or**	**chilled**
brandy	1 **large block ice***
1 **cup orange-flavored**	**Lemon and orange**
liqueur	**slices**

1. Combine sugar, bitters and lemon juice in large punch bowl; stir to dissolve sugar. Add Cognac and liqueur.
2. Just before serving, pour in champagne and club soda; stir to blend. Add block of ice, lemon and orange slices.

To make ice block: A day or so ahead of time, fill a 1 1/2-quart bowl or decorative mold with cold water; place in freezer until frozen solid. To unmold, run cold water over mold to loosen; slide ice block into punch.

Fruited Champagne Punch

Makes about 3 quarts.

2 **large peaches,**	**Moselle wine**
peeled and sliced	1 **bottle (750 ml.)**
1 **pint strawberries,**	**Rhine wine, chilled**
washed and hulled	1 **bottle (750 ml.)**
1/2 **cup sugar**	**champagne, chilled**
1 **bottle (750 ml.)**	

1. Place peaches and strawberries in large punch bowl; prick fruit with fork in several places so it will absorb wine; sprinkle with sugar.
2. Pour Moselle wine over fruit. Let stand at room temperature for 2 hours.
3. Just before serving, pour chilled Rhine wine and champagne over fruit. Add an ice ring, if you wish.

Pink Champagne Punch

Makes about 32 four-ounce servings.

Green Grape Ice Block	1 **bottle (28 ounces)**
(recipe below)	**ginger ale, chilled**
1 **can (6 ounces)**	1 **bottle (28 ounces)**
frozen lemonade	**club soda, chilled**
concentrate, thawed	2 **bottles (750 ml.**
2 **cups brandy**	**each) pink**
1/4 **cup bottled**	**champagne, chilled**
grenadine syrup	

1. Prepare Green Grape Ice Block.
2. Combine frozen lemonade concentrate, brandy and grenadine syrup in large punch bowl. Stir in ginger

ale, club soda and champagne. Top with Green Grape Ice Block or several trays of ice cubes.

Green Grape Ice Block: Half-fill a ring mold, 2-quart rectangular plastic container or metal mixing bowl, whichever fits your punch bowl best, with water. Partially freeze. Add small clusters of green grapes in decorative design. Freeze to anchor fruit; fill with ice water and freeze until firm. To unmold, quickly dip in and out of warm water.

Strawberry-Lemon Punch

Makes thirty-six 1/2-cup servings.

2 **packages (10 ounces**	2 **tablespoons**
each) frozen	**grenadine**
strawberries,	2 **bottles (1 liter each)**
thawed	**ginger ale, chilled**
1 **can (12 ounces)**	1 **bottle (1 liter) seltzer,**
frozen lemonade	**chilled**
concentrate, thawed	**Ice cubes**
1 **can (12 ounces)**	**Lemon and lime slices**
frozen limeade	**for garnish**
concentrate, thawed	

1. Puree the strawberries in a blender or food processor until smooth. Pour into a large pitcher. Stir in the juice concentrates and grenadine. Refrigerate.
2. Just before serving, pour the strawberry mixture into a large punch bowl. Pour in the ginger ale and seltzer. Add the ice cubes. Garnish with the lemon and lime slices.

Darjeeling Punch

Makes about 12 four-ounce servings.

4 **cups boiling water**	1 **tablespoon grated**
6 **tea bags**	**lemon rind**
6 **egg yolks**	2 **cups rum, warmed**
1/2 **cup sugar**	

1. Pour boiling water over tea bags; let steep 3 to 5 minutes.
2. Beat egg yolks and sugar in a large bowl with electric mixer at high speed until fluffy. Beat in lemon rind.
3. Remove tea bags. Gradually add hot tea to egg-yolk mixture; stir in rum.
4. Serve in warmed punch cups or small mugs. Sprinkle with additional grated lemon rind, if you wish.

Double Apple Punch

Makes 20 four-ounce servings.

²/₃ cup firmly packed light brown sugar	¹/₂ teaspoon ground cinnamon
¹/₄ cup (¹/₂ stick) butter or margarine	¹/₄ teaspoon ground nutmeg
1 tablespoon grated orange rind	¹/₂ gallon (8 cups) apple cider
1 tablespoon grated lemon rind	¹/₂ cup applejack (apple brandy)

1. Combine brown sugar, butter, orange and lemon rinds, cinnamon, nutmeg and apple cider in a large saucepan. Heat slowly, stirring until mixture just comes to boiling, but do not boil.
2. Carefully pour into a heat-proof punch bowl; stir in applejack. Garnish with orange or lemon slices, if you wish.
3. Serve in warmed punch cups or mugs with a cinnamon stick as a stirrer.

Grapefruit Campari

Makes 1 serving.

1 orange slice	3 ounces (6 tablespoons) grapefruit juice
Granulated sugar	
Ice cubes	
3 ounces (6 tablespoons) Campari	Club Soda
	Half orange slice (optional)

1. Rub the rim of one tall 14-ounce glass with 1 orange slice. Dip the rim into the granulated sugar and place in the freezer for 1 hour.
2. Place several ice cubes in a chilled glass. Add the Campari and grapefruit juice. Fill the glass with the club soda; stir thoroughly. Garnish with the orange slice, if you wish.

Hawaiian Sunrise

Makes 1 serving.

2 teaspoons grenadine syrup	¹/₄ cup fresh orange juice
Ice cubes	2 tablespoons fresh lime juice
¹/₄ cup light rum	
1 tablespoon orange-flavored liqueur	1 tablespoon fresh lemon juice
¹/₄ cup unsweetened pineapple juice	Lemon slice and strawberry

1. Pour grenadine syrup in bottom of a large, round, footed (about 16-ounce) glass. Fill glass with ice.
2. Combine rum, orange liqueur and pineapple, orange, lime and lemon juices in a small pitcher; mix well. Carefully pour over ice. Stir slightly, if necessary, to give sunrise effect. Garnish with lemon and strawberry.

Tomato Eye-Opener

Makes about 8 servings.

6 cups tomato juice	pepper sauce
¹/₃ cup lime juice	1 teaspoon salt, or to taste
4 to 5 teaspoons bottled horseradish	Frozen Spirits (optional; recipe follows)
1 teaspoon Worcestershire sauce	Celery sticks
6 to 8 drops red hot	Lime wedges

1. Combine tomato juice, lime juice, horseradish, Worcestershire sauce, pepper sauce and salt in a large pitcher. Chill.
2. To serve, let each guest who wishes add Frozen Spirits to taste (provide a shot glass for measuring). Stir with a celery stick; garnish with a lime wedge. Add ice cubes, if you wish.

Frozen Spirits

Place a bottle, fifth or quart, of American vodka or Aquavit in an empty ¹/₂-gallon milk carton or plastic container or large juice can, allowing about 1-inch space all around the bottle; add cold water to fill the container. Place upright in the freezer overnight or until the water is frozen solid (alcohol will not freeze). Remove to room temperature for 20 to 30 minutes to loosen the container. Remove the container and return the block of ice with bottle to the freezer until ready to serve. Place on a folded napkin or towel on a deep plate or in a shallow bowl to catch the melting ice.

Sangria

A red wine punch of Spanish origin traditionally mixed in a pitcher. A cool and refreshing summer drink, sangria is made by pouring a light red wine into a pitcher with sliced oranges, sliced lemon, a bit of sugar, a splash of brandy or other liqueur, and finally soda water and ice. It is mixed with a wooden spoon and served by the glassful. White wine may also be used for sangria but red wine is the favorite.

Overleaf (clockwise from bottom left): Huevos Rancheros, page 353; Orange Avocado Salad, page 698; Mexican Hot Chocolate, page 66; Margaritas, page 74; Buñuelos, page 120.

Sangria

Makes about 3 quarts.

2 bottles (750 ml.
  each) red wine
1 cup orange juice
¼ cup lime juice
⅔ cup sugar
½ cup orange-
  flavored liqueur

2 bottles (12 ounces
  each) club soda,
  chilled
Ice cubes
Orange slices
Lime slices

1. Combine wine, orange and lime juices and sugar in
a very large pitcher or punch bowl; stir until sugar is
dissolved; add liqueur; chill.
2. Just before serving, add club soda, ice cubes and
orange and lime slices.

Summer Sangria

Makes about 2 quarts.

1 cup sugar
1½ cups water
1 cup orange juice
½ cup brandy
1 large orange, sliced
  and quartered

1 lime, sliced
1 cup honeydew
  melon balls
Ice cubes
1 bottle (750 ml.) dry
  white wine, chilled

1. Combine sugar and water in large pitcher; stir until
sugar dissolves. Add orange juice, brandy, orange,
lime and honeydew. Chill 2 hours.
2. Just before serving, add ice cubes and stir in chilled
wine.

Margaritas

Makes 6 servings.

7 slices lime
Coarse salt
⅓ cup fresh lime juice
1 cup Tequila

⅓ cup orange-
  flavored liqueur
2 cups crushed ice

1. Rub rims of 6 cocktail glasses with one of the lime
slices; dip rims in coarse salt. Refrigerate to chill
glasses and let salt rim set.
2. Combine lime juice, Tequila, orange liqueur and
crushed ice in cocktail shaker; shake well; strain and
pour into prepared glasses; or whirl in container of
electric blender for 30 seconds. Garnish each glass
with lime slice.

Scorpion

*Very exotic and a great favorite in Polynesian
restaurants.*

Makes 1 serving.

¼ cup dark rum
2 tablespoons brandy
¼ cup fresh orange
  juice
3 tablespoons fresh
  lemon juice

1 tablespoon orgeat
  syrup or amaretto
  liqueur
1 cup crushed ice
Gardenia

Combine rum, brandy, orange and lemon juices,
orgeat and ice in container of electric blender; whirl 30
seconds. Serve over ice cubes in large footed
champagne-type glass. Garnish with gardenia.

Guava Fruit Punch

Makes 9 cups or 18 four-ounce punch-cup servings.

2 cans (7.1 ounces
  each) guava juice
  (about 2 cups)
1½ cups unsweetened
  pineapple juice
1 cup fresh orange
  juice
¾ cup fresh lemon

  juice
¼ cup sugar
3 tablespoons
  grenadine syrup
1 bottle (28 ounces)
  ginger ale, chilled
Assorted fresh fruit for
  garnish

Combine guava, pineapple, orange and lemon juices,
sugar and grenadine syrup in 2½-quart container; stir
until sugar is dissolved. (Can be prepared ahead to
this point.) Just before serving, add ginger ale. Pour
over an ice ring in a punch bowl. Garnish individual
glasses with skewers of assorted fresh fruit.

Banana Cow

Creamy and cool — kids will love it!

Makes 2 servings.

1 medium-size
  banana, peeled and
  cut into chunks
½ cup milk

1 tablespoon honey
⅛ teaspoon vanilla
1 cup crushed ice
Lime wedges

Combine banana, milk, honey, vanilla and ice in
container of electric blender; whirl until smooth. Pour
into two 10-ounce highball glasses. Garnish with lime
wedges.

Pictured opposite (from top): Scorpion, page 74; Guava Fruit
Punch, page 74; Mai Tai, page 76; Piña Colada, page 76; Banana
Cow, page 74; Pineapple-Mint Cooler, page 76.

Mai Tai

This has many versions throughout the islands, but is considered the classic Hawaiian drink.

Makes 1 serving.

3 tablespoons light rum	lime juice
2 tablespoons dark rum	1 teaspoon sugar
1 tablespoon orange-flavored liqueur	2 dashes aromatic bitters
1 tablespoon fresh	Crushed ice
	Fresh mint sprigs

Combine light and dark rums, liqueur, lime juice, sugar and bitters in a cocktail shaker; shake well. Pour over crushed ice in a 6-ounce old-fashioned glass. Or, serve in a scooped out small pineapple. Garnish with mint; serve with straws.

Piña Colada

Smooth and mellow, one of the big favorites borrowed from the Caribbean.

Makes 2 servings.

1/3 cup light rum	heavy cream
1/2 cup unsweetened pineapple juice	1 cup crushed ice
1/4 cup cream of coconut (from a 15 1/2-ounce can)	Fresh coconut (optional)
2 tablespoons	Pineapple slices or sticks
	Fresh mint sprigs

Combine rum, pineapple juice, cream of coconut, cream and crushed ice in container of electric blender. Whirl until smooth. Pour over crushed ice in two 10-ounce highball glasses. Or, serve the drinks in a coconut half. Garnish with pineapple and mint; serve with straws.

Pineapple-Mint Cooler

Sparkling pineapple juice with the cool zip of mint.

Makes about 12 servings.

4 cups unsweetened pineapple juice, chilled	1 bottle (28 ounces) lemon-lime carbonated beverage
1/2 cup lemon juice	Canned or fresh pineapple slices
1/4 cup green crème de menthe	

1. Combine pineapple and lemon juices and crème de menthe in a 2 1/2-quart container; mix well. (Can be prepared ahead to this point.)
2. Add carbonated beverage just before serving. Serve over ice cubes in 8-ounce highball glasses; or pour over an ice ring in a punch bowl. Garnish each serving with a quarter pineapple slice.

Cassis Punch Royale

Makes about 24 servings.

Red and green grapes for ice block	wine, chilled
1/2 cup crème de cassis (black currant liqueur)	2 bottles champagne, chilled
1 bottle (750 ml.) white	Whole fresh or frozen strawberries (optional)

1. Prepare the ice block: Fill a fancy mold that will fit inside a punch bowl with ice cubes. Add cold water to almost fill. Arrange clusters of the grapes in the mold, half in the ice and water and half out. Place in the freezer until firm enough to unmold. Unmold, dipping in warm water to loosen, if necessary; be careful not to break the grapes. Return to the freezer until ready to use.
2. Just before serving, pour the cassis and wine into the punch bowl. Add the ice block with the grapes on top. Slowly pour in champagne. Add a strawberry to each glass, if you wish.

To Make Ahead: Make the ice block several days ahead.

Kir

Makes 6 servings.

1 tablespoon crème de cassis	2 1/2 cups chilled dry white wine

1. Combine crème de cassis and wine; stir. Pour into chilled wine glasses; serve immediately. Or serve over ice in tall glass, if you wish.

Strawberry Kir

This is a twist on the summertime Continental cooler. Strawberry liqueur replaces crème de cassis.

Makes 1 serving.

1 ounce strawberry liqueur	4 ounces dry white wine

1. Pour the strawberry liqueur into the bottom of a chilled stemmed glass. Carefully pour the chilled white wine down the side of the glass. Serve with a stirrer to blend both of the layers before drinking.

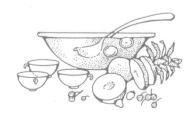

Minted Lemon and Lime

A new drink for the warm weather. Crème de menthe combines with lemon-lime soda.

Makes 1 serving.

1½ ounces crème de menthe	soda
	2 lemon wedges
6 ounces lemon-lime	1 maraschino cherry

1. Fill a glass with ice cubes. Pour the crème de menthe down the side and add lemon-lime soda. Garnish with a kabob of lemon wedges and maraschino cherry, if you wish.

Sangria Spritzer

Red wine and orange juice plus club soda and fruits is such a refreshing combo.

Makes 1 serving.

2 ounces red wine	Fruit kabob of orange
1 ounce orange juice	and lime wedges
Club soda, chilled	

1. Fill a tall glass with ice; stir in the red wine and orange juice until blended. Fill with the club soda and stir in the kabob.

Margaritas

This version is mixed in the blender.

Makes 2 servings.

Coarse salt	1½ ounces tequila
Lime wedge	4 ounces Margarita
1½ cups ice cubes	mixer

1. Pour the salt into a shallow saucer; moisten the rim of two 4-ounce stem glasses with the lime wedge; dip glasses into salt to coat evenly. Allow to dry.
2. Place the ice cubes in the container of an electric blender; add tequila and Margarita mixer. Cover the blender; process on high speed for 10 seconds, or until the mixture is smooth; strain into prepared glasses, dividing evenly.

Rose Spritzer

Mineral water, rather than club soda, adds a new touch.

Makes 1 serving.

4 ounces rosé wine	water, chilled
4 ounces mineral	Lemon slice

Fill a glass with ice and add the rosé wine, then the mineral water; garnish the glass with a lemon slice.

Wine

Wine can be served with meals, before them and after, or even enjoyed alone, just like any other beverage. Before a meal, many people prefer a dry to medium-sweet wine such as sherry, vermouth of any of the aperitif wines known by such brand names as Campari. All of these wines should be served chilled, on the rocks or with soda. Champagne and other not-too-sweet sparkling wines also make excellent pre-dinner drinks. The reason for not choosing very sweet wines is that the pre-dinner drink should lead into the first course, which is not sweet. Thus, a very sweet pre-dinner drink is like starting the meal with dessert.

A glass of table wine, preferably white and well chilled, is becoming an increasingly popular drink before meals. In summer, a splash of soda combined with the wine turns it into a "spritzer," a most refreshing drink.

Wine is most often enjoyed with meals since food and wine complement each other.

Everyday meals are suitable accompaniments for the modest, inexpensive wines which the two major wine-drinking countries in the world, France and Italy, call *vin ordinaire* and *vino da tavola* (meaning "plain" and "table" wine). Serve a white, rosé or red wine throughout the meal, choosing the kind that goes best with your main dish. Finer wines, and the *unusually* fine wines called "great" ones, are for company and special occasions. On more formal occasions, some people like to serve several different wines in different glasses, usually a white wine with a first dish of fish or seafood and a red one with the meat. But, more and more, even people who entertain a good deal are serving one wine only throughout the meal.

Which Wine with Which Food?

What kind of wines to serve with certain foods is a subject about which many contradictory words have been written. You can serve any wine you like with any food you like--provided the people who eat and drink with you share the same taste. However, a little experimenting with the more traditional food and wine combinations will soon persuade you that there are good reasons to mate certain wines with certain foods simply because both taste better.

Here are the most widely accepted guidelines, but bear these reservations in mind: Do not serve wine with highly spiced foods like curry or with vinegary ones like salads; they make the wine taste sour. If you serve cheese with wine, a favorite combination, do not

(continued)

Overleaf (from left to right): Strawberry Kir, page 76; Minted Lemon and Lime, page 77; Sangria Spritzer, page 77; Mexican Margaritas, page 77; Rosé Spritzer, page 77.

select a cheese that is very strong because it will overwhelm the wine.

Hors d'Oeuvres and Soup: For your first course, serve the wine you have chosen for your entrée.

Fish: Dry white wine, or dry sherry.

Shellfish: Dry or medium-dry (not sweet) white wine or a light red wine.

Chicken and Other Fowl: Light or full red, or white wine, depending on the way the fowl is cooked and on its richness. The richer the food, the fuller flavored the wine should be. Cold chicken takes a light white wine; roast chicken a fuller one or a light red wine; *coq au vin* (chicken in wine) is cooked in, and also served with, red wine; chicken with a cream sauce takes a full white wine; roast duck, a full white or medium-full red wine, and the same goes for goose. If the dish is cooked with a certain wine, the same wine should be served at the meal.

Veal and Pork: Full white wine, light red wine, rosé.

Beef and Lamb: Full red wine.

Ham: Full white or medium-full red wine, or a good-quality rosé.

Venison and Game: Full red wine is right with venison. For the more delicate gamebirds, such as pheasant, dove and quail--use a full white wine. For wild duck--a medium-full red.

Dessert: Sweet wine for cakes, puddings and fruits, except acid citrus fruits. Another choice is champagne, not the bone-dry variety but one that is a little sweet.

Nuts and Cheese: Port or sweet sherry or Madeira.

How to Serve Wine

Temperature: The classic rule says that in order to bring out their full flavor, white wines should be drunk cool and red ones at room temperature. But this needs some clarification. "Cool" means cool in the mouth--slightly chilled, but not icy, a temperature of around 45° to 50°. If you chill a white wine too much, or freeze it, you destroy the flavor. You can properly chill your white wines, including champagnes and rosé, by putting them into the refrigerator, not the freezer, for one to two hours. (White aperitif or dessert wines are another matter, as they can be served on the rocks.) If you are in a hurry, fill an ice bucket or a large pot with water and ice, and leave the bottle in it for about 20 minutes. This is also a good idea to use when serving a crowd.

The room temperature at which red wines should be served refers to the range between 60° and 68°. If the wine is very warm, you can bring down the temperature by standing it near an open window for 10 to 15 minutes, depending on the weather, or by putting it in the refrigerator for five minutes before serving. But never warm up a bottle of red wine which is too cold by heating it; this would ruin the wine. Simply let it stand in a warm room.

A good bottle of red wine should be uncorked one to two hours before it is consumed. This is called "letting the wine breathe." Uncorking in this way allows the full flavor of the wine to develop by permitting the air to touch it.

Needless to say, the wines we choose to serve every day with our meals, especially the excellent--in taste and value--gallon and half-gallon jugs, do not require anything beyond pouring. (Many of these fine wines are made right here in the United States.) But they should be at the right temperature, the one you prefer. Remember that extreme cold or heat destroys the flavor of food and wine.

Which Wines First: White before red and dry before sweet is the basic rule, just as fish comes before the meat, and dessert at the end of a meal. If you are serving two wines of the same kind, serve the lesser one before the superior one. And, of course, you can follow a dry red dinner wine with a sweet white or champagne for dessert.

The Basic Types of Wine

Table Wines: These wines, called "table wines" because they are drunk with meals, may be white, pink (rosé) or red. They may also be dry or sweet. Table wines account for the vast majority of all wines produced in the world and are available in an enormous range of flavors and qualities.

Sparkling Wines: Champagne, which is usually reserved for festive occasions, is the best known of these wines, but there are many others—sparkling Burgundy, to name one.

Fortified Wines: These wines have been made stronger and longer-lasting by the addition of brandy. Sherry, port and Madeira are the best known. Fortified wines can be sweet or dry; the sweet ones are generally served as dessert wines and the dry ones as before-dinner drinks.

Aromatized Wines: These wines are fortified and flavored with herbs, seeds and/or spices. They may be white or red. Vermouth is the best known. Aromatic wines are often combined with liquor for cocktails, or they can be served alone as *aperitifs* (before-dinner drinks).

How Much Wine to Buy: Remember that liquor stores now sell in new liter sizes, so keep these measurements in mind when shopping: One liter = 33.8 ounces, which yields a little more than a quart-size; 750 milliliters = 25.4 ounces (3¼ cups), which yields a little more than a fifth-size. Also, if serving wine with dinner, figure on fewer glasses to the bottle: 5 to 6 for a liter; 3 to 4 for 750 milliliters.

Table wines (red, white, rosé—4- to 5-ounce servings): 6 to 8 servings per liter; 5 to 6 servings per 750 milliliters.

Sherry (3-ounce servings): 11 servings per liter; 8 servings per 750 milliliters.

Champagne, sparkling wine (4- to 5-ounce servings): 6 to 8 servings per liter; 5 to 6 servings per 750 milliliters.

How to Store Wine

Always store wine lying down on its side; the bottle must never stand up. The reason for this is that the cork must stay moist. If it dries out, air will get into the bottle and spoil the wine.

Wine should be stored in a cool, dark place. The

ideal temperature is about 55° to 60°. It is important that the temperature be steady all year round, never varying more than a few degrees. In days past, spacious houses used to have wine cellars with the ideal temperature, where wine could live and mature in peace and quiet. Most of today's houses, and all of today's apartments, are hotter in winter and summer than is good for wine, even when there is sufficient storage space. Therefore, unless you have good wine-storage conditions, do not buy more wine at a time than you will drink within a reasonable period of time. Your wine will not keep well.

How to Cook with Wine

Wine, in the kitchen, should be considered a flavoring like other flavorings. In cooking, the alcohol in all wine spirits evaporates when the boiling point is reached, so that only the flavor remains. But the flavoring, wine or other, of a dish must not be too strong; it should blend in with the other flavors. If a dish tastes noticeably of salt, pepper or cloves, you have put in too much. The same goes for wine; the chief flavor of a dish to which wine has been added should be that of the fish, the bird or the meat on which the dish is based. Most people use far more wine than is necessary to round out the flavor of what they are cooking.

In cooking main dishes or dishes that are not sweet, use a dry wine, preferably the wine you are going to drink with the meal--that is, use a good ordinary wine. But don't cook with rare, exquisite wines or expensive wines. These are far too good for the purpose and should be drunk and enjoyed.

The standard rule of white wines for white meats and red wines for red meats does not have to be followed in the kitchen any more than at the table. Poultry, veal, beef, pork, lamb and sauces are excellent with either white or red wine; the flavor of the dish will depend on the wine used. The one exception is fish, which generally tastes better when cooked with white wine, though some famous French dishes call for red.

When cooking with wine, bring the dish to the boiling point to let the alcohol evaporate. Do not cover the pan; cook at the boiling point for a few minutes. The time depends on the amount of wine used; a cupful of wine in a stew will take longer to evaporate than two tablespoons in a sauce. Then lower the heat and continue cooking according to the recipe.

Wine is an excellent tenderizer of meats, before and during cooking. Meats, and all foods which have been marinated or soaked in wine to tenderize them, must be thoroughly dried before cooking. A strained wine marinade can become the base of a sauce or gravy. Or you may simply add some dry wine to the pan juices of roasted meat or poultry, let the mixture cook down to reduce it slightly, and pour it over the meat to serve as a sauce.

When wine is not part of a recipe, but you feel you would like to add some to it, add a very little wine at one time, a tablespoon or so, and taste before you add more.

Sherry is an excellent cooking aid. Dry sherry goes well with all nonsweet dishes, especially seafood. Sweet sherry takes to fruit, creams and puddings. But remember that a little goes a very long way and use it sparingly. The same goes for the sweet Marsala, Madeira and Malaga wines.

All dishes cooked with wine can be reheated successfully.

BREADS

YEAST AND QUICK BREADS

Bread   The story of breadmaking parallels the history of civilization. Bread made during the Stone Age was flat or unleavened with a tough texture. It was made of crushed grains mixed with water and probably spread on stones to "bake" or dry in the sun. Later, these breads were baked in the hot ashes of a fire.

The first leavened breads were made by the Egyptians, probably by accident. One theory is that dough was left in the sun too long and began to bubble and rise because of wild yeast spores. The "soured" dough was mixed with fresh dough which upon baking produced gases that raised it to make a lighter loaf.

Excavations show that in ancient Egypt there was a community bakery in every village; a wealthy family would have its own bakery.

Breads were so highly prized that they were placed in the tombs of the dead to provide food for afterlife. Breads dating back over 3500 years have been excavated from Egyptian tombs.

The Greeks had public bakeries that produced over fifty kinds of bread. In Rome, around 100 B.C., there were over 250 bakeries. Each baker stamped the loaves he made with his own identifying mark.

In the Middle Ages, town guilds (associations of people with similar interests) formed. The bakers' guild, which actually formed during the Roman Empire, was a powerful group. Laws were enacted that protected the consumer from dishonest bakers and protected the bakers from unfair competition. The "baker's dozen" came into being during this time as bakers, in an effort to insure their business practices were beyond reproach, would add an extra loaf of bread with an order of twelve.

In Europe, the type of bread eaten was often an indication of status or wealth. During the era of William and Mary, for example, people in the rural areas ate a coarse type of barley bread or oat cakes while the upper class ate white breads made from wheat.

Bread is made of ground grain. The first grains to be used for bread were probably millet and buckwheat. Wheat and rye are the most commonly used today, but oats, barley and corn are also used. American Indians made a flat bread of maize or Indian corn long before the earliest settlers arrived. But these settlers introduced wheat to the Colonies. Breadmaking was most often done at home rather than in bakeries, unlike so much of the rest of the world.

Many countries produce breads which are special to them. For example, the French baton-like baguettes; German and Austrian black breads; Scandinavian dark breads and crisp flat breads; Irish soda bread; the British cottage loaf; Middle Eastern pita or pocket bread. Unleavened bread is eaten by Jewish people during Passover. American breads include Boston brown bread, Anadama bread (made of cornmeal and whole wheat flour) and cornbread.

Homemade breads are of two types: yeast or quick. Yeast breads, in which yeast is the leavening agent, can be either plain, savory or sweet. Quick breads, in which the leavening agent is baking soda or powder, include biscuits, loaves, muffins, doughnuts, and even pancakes.

The Making of Yeast Breads

Know Your Ingredients: *Yeast* causes dough to rise and gives bread its porous texture. Yeast is actually a small plant or cell that "grows" or multiplies under the proper temperature conditions. Yeast feeds on the sugar and produces carbon dioxide; it is this gas that causes dough to rise. It is yeast that is primarily responsible for the marvelous aromas and flavors of breads. Yeast is available as compressed cakes which must be dissolved before using or the dry granular form which can, in some recipes, be mixed directly with the dry ingredients.

Compressed yeast is moist, creamy white, and firm in texture. It is perishable and must be kept refrigerated. Look for it in the supermarket dairy case packaged in foil. It is best when used within a few days from purchase or it can be wrapped in heavy-duty aluminum foil and frozen. It keeps up to 6 months stored at 0°F. Defrost it overnight in the refrigerator before using. Compressed yeast must be dissolved in lukewarm liquid (80° to 90°) before using.

Dry yeast is a strain of yeast that has been dried and packaged in envelopes or jars. Two level teaspoons dry yeast equal a single $1/4$-ounce envelope or a $5/8$-ounce cake. Dry yeast can be stored over 6 months unrefrigerated. In areas of the country with high temperatures, refrigeration will help keep it

Pictured opposite (counterclockwise, from upper left): Cinnamon Nut Coffee Ring, page 132; Georgian Cheese Bread, page 112; Golden Orange Rolls, page 112; Lemon Cheese Braid, page 111; Cheese Puffs, page 32; Meat Piroshki, page 468.

fresh. Dry yeast is activated by dissolving in warm liquid (110° to 115°) but can also be blended first with dry ingredients and liquid of higher temperature (120° to 130°). Dry yeast should be used before the expiration date which is stamped on the envelope.

Flour is the most essential ingredient in breadmaking. Wheat flour is the most widely used. Different varieties of wheat grain are milled and blended into flour. Wheat, especially hard wheat, is most suitable for breads because of its high gluten content. Gluten is a substance that forms an elastic network through the dough, trapping the carbon dioxide gases produced by the yeast as it feeds on and digests the sugar. Soft wheat contains less gluten and is best for quick breads, cakes and pastries. It is used primarily for cake flour.

Wheat flours are ground either from the whole kernel or from the endosperm, which is the central portion of the kernel. Flour labeled all-purpose is ground from the endosperm with the bran and germ of the kernel removed before milling. All-purpose flour is a blend of both soft and hard wheats. Most bread recipes offer a range in the amount of flour to use since the results of a recipe will be affected by the type and brand of flour to be used, the amount of moisture in the flour, the time of year it is used, and variables such as the size of eggs.

Bread flour, now currently available in some markets, is also ground from the endosperm of the wheat kernel. Similar to all-purpose flour, it has a higher gluten content than regular all-purpose flour and therefore gives excellent results in breadmaking.

Whole wheat flour is a coarse-textured flour ground from the entire wheat kernel (endosperm, bran and germ). Because whole wheat flour has a lower gluten content, baked products tend to be more dense and, therefore, heavier than those made with all-purpose flour. A lighter bread loaf is achieved when all-purpose flour is used as part of the flour in a given recipe. Stone-ground whole wheat flour is milled by coarsely crushing the wheat kernels between heavy, rotating stones. The advantages of stone grinding the wheat are that the oil in the germ is more evenly distributed and, because the grain is kept cooler during milling, rancidity is reduced. Graham flour is a whole wheat flour and can be used interchangeably in recipes calling for whole wheat flour.

Flour is also milled from other grains. Rye flour is ground from the endosperm of the rye kernel. Medium rye refers to the color of the flour. Pumpernickel rye flour is ground from the entire rye kernel and is more coarse-textured. Outside of wheat and rye, no other cereal grain contains sufficient gluten to make a satisfactory loaf of bread. Corn, bran, barley, buckwheat, soy or oats can be added to a wheat dough, but are unsatisfactory used exclusively in yeast breads.

All flour should be stored in air-tight containers in the refrigerator or freezer, if possible.

Whole wheat or graham flour can be substituted for all-purpose flour in bread recipes in a ratio of 60 percent to 40 percent all-purpose flour. But the general rule when substituting flour is that the more all-purpose flour in a dough, the easier it is to knead. Whole wheat and rye breads made with whole wheat and rye flour are firmer and heavier than white breads. Rye dough requires less kneading; kneading too long increases the stickiness and makes it difficult to handle. A slightly soft, sticky dough is typical of rye flour.

Liquid, usually water or a combination of water and milk, is needed to dissolve the yeast and bind the flour. Other liquids may be used such as buttermilk, eggs, and even molasses or honey. Liquids should be at room temperature before using.

Water makes a crisp crust. Milk gives a softer crumb. Do not use milk to dissolve yeast, since the milk fat coats the yeast cells, preventing them from dissolving. (Some old-style recipes may dissolve yeast in milk.) Potato water can be used, yielding a coarser textured loaf. ·

Fat, added to bread dough, flavors and tenderizes the bread. Fat coats the gluten strands and shortens them to form a more tender cell structure. Fats used in bread are butter, margarine, vegetable oil or shortening. Butter or margarine are interchangeable but use only the stick form, not whipped or diet varieties. Do not substitute vegetable oil for shortening or vice versa.

Flavoring ingredients include salt, sugar, herbs, spices, raisins, nuts, berries and cheese. Although small amounts of sugar are necessary in activating the yeast, too large an amount inhibits yeast growth. Salt inhibits yeast growth so it should not be used in water in which yeast is dissolved. Raisins, nuts, berries (such as wheat berries or wheat kernels), bean or grain sprouts can be added for extra crunch just before shaping the bread loaves. If these types of flavorings are added to the dough before it has proofed the first time, the dough will be heavier, and the bread will take longer to rise.

Coarse grains like cracked wheat (the whole kernel is broken into bits) can be used to add a nutty flavor and crunchy texture. Use only a small amount of coarse grains or cook to tenderize before adding to bread dough since the sharp pieces will cut the gluten strands, resulting in a smaller loaf.

How to Mix, Knead and Shape Yeast Bread: Successful yeast baking depends on the temperature of water used to dissolve the type of yeast, the temperature at which the dough rises and the baking temperature.

When mixing the ingredients in a large bowl, use either an electric mixer or a wooden spoon. Vigorous beating causes the gluten to form more rapidly. Use only enough flour to form a soft dough that no longer clings to sides of the bowl.

Kneading is a rhythmic procedure that completes the mixing of the dough. Yeast doughs are proofed, i.e., allowed to rise and fall one or more times to improve the texture. Dough is properly proofed when double in volume. A simple test to see if the dough is proofed sufficiently is to press two fingertips lightly (1/2 inch) into the dough. If the dough springs back, proofing is complete. Overproofed dough will cause the baked bread to have large holes throughout. Proofed doughs are punched down after they have risen by pushing a fist into the center of the dough to deflate it. Batter breads are not kneaded. The dough is beaten until it leaves the sides of the bowl, covered and allowed to rise.

Bake breads in a preheated oven. The final rising of the dough takes place during the first 10 to 15 minutes of baking time. When baking two loaves, place them on the center rack in the oven; for four loaves, use two racks, placed in the bottom and next to the highest positions.

Breads should be checked for doneness near the end of suggested baking time. Breads are done when nicely browned and hollow sounding when tapped lightly on top. Remove loaves from pans so they do not become soggy. Cool completely on wire racks.

The Making of Quick Breads

Quick breads are made with fast-acting leavening agents, most often baking powder or soda. Air, steam and a combination of baking soda and an acid liquid, such as buttermilk or sour milk, can also cause the leavening action during baking.

Quick breads include loaves, muffins, biscuits, doughnuts, scones, shortcakes, dumplings, pancakes, waffles, popovers and spoon breads. Each differs in appearance and flavor but all are considered quick breads because they have similar leavening action, are easy to make, fast-rising and light and porous.

Quick bread batters are of three types: soft dough, drop batters or pourable batters. Soft doughs can be rolled and shaped by hand. Biscuits, scones and doughnuts are examples of soft doughs. Examples of drop batters are muffins, cornbread, loaves and dumplings. These thick batters need only be spooned into a baking pan and take the shape of the pan utensil. Pourable batters include waffles, pancakes, Yorkshire pudding and popovers, which are made with a thin batter.

Know Your Ingredients: *Baking powder* was first made in the 1850's. Prior to that time, baked goods were leavened either by beating air into the dough or

beating eggs and folding them into the dough. Another leavening agent was sourdough yeast starter. In the 1790's, a substance called pearlash was discovered which produced carbon dioxide during baking. That discovery changed breadmaking! Baking powder can be derived from a number of substances. A phosphate baking powder was the first type to be produced.

Another type is composed of soda and tartaric acid. The tartrate baking powders begin reacting upon being mixed with batter or dough and liquid. When using this type of baking powder, work quickly mixing the batter and bake in a preheated oven.

A third type of baking powder is a combination of ingredients which causes two rising actions instead of one as occurs in the other types of baking soda. The first rising begins in the bowl as the liquid is added. The second rising occurs when exposed to heat during baking or cooking. This double action enables you to mix the batter, yet delay baking or cooking.

All baking powders contain baking soda and an acid and are activated when mixed with a liquid. The chemical reaction produces carbon dioxide bubbles, which, when heat is applied, cause the dough to expand and the heat sets the dough at this point.

Baking soda (bicarbonate of soda) works only when combined with an acid substance (such as in baking powder mixtures) or when an acidic liquid—buttermilk, sour milk, chocolate, honey, corn syrup or molasses— is used.

Some recipes use both baking powder and baking soda. The baking soda neutralizes an acidic ingredient while the baking powder provides the leavening action.

Flour forms the framework of quick breads. All-purpose flour is most often used. Flour with a low gluten content is desirable for making quick breads.

Fats such as shortening, vegetable oil, butter or margarine are used to add flavor, richness, tenderness and moisture to quick breads. Use the type of fat specified in the recipe.

Liquid ingredients bind the dry ingredients. Milk, buttermilk, sour cream or yogurt add moisture to the bread.

Eggs add flavor, a golden color, and tenderness to bread. Unless otherwise specified, recipes calling for eggs refer to eggs graded large.

Flavoring ingredients include sugar, which gives dough tenderness, flavor and aids in browning. Herbs, spices, bacon bits, nuts, shredded vegetables, mashed bananas, chocolate, raisins or grated peel are frequently added to quick breads, helping to give each bread its distinct flavor.

How to Mix Quick Breads:

Biscuit method: Soft dough quick breads are made using the following method. First the dry ingredients are stirred together. The fat is then cut into the dry ingredients with a pastry blender or two knives until the mixture resembles coarse crumbs. Today's food processors make quick work of this. Liquid is added and stirred lightly just to make a soft dough. The dough is then gently kneaded 8 to 10 *times* (not minutes). The kneaded dough is ready to be cut or shaped.

Muffin method: Drop batters are made using the following method. The dry ingredients are stirred together, and in a separate bowl the liquid ingredients are stirred together. The liquid ingredients are gradually added to the dry ingredients and mixed just until the dry ingredients are moistened. Overmixing will result in peaked muffins with large holes inside.

The Effects of High Altitudes

High altitudes, i.e., over 5,000 feet, cause breads to rise faster and higher. If a recipe calls for two envelopes or cakes of yeast, use only one. Watch the proofing closely. Punch dough down and bake, even if not yet double in volume as long as finger indentation remains in dough. In quick breads, the amount of baking powder and baking soda needs to be decreased also. For best results, use recipes designed for high altitudes.

Hints for Better Breads

• Use the specified pan size called for in the recipe. A pan that is too large will yield a flat bread. Too small a pan will cause the dough to overflow.

• The material the pan is made of can affect the baking time. Uncoated metal pans need longer baking. Glass and enamel pans need a lower oven temperature. Reduce the oven temperature called for in the recipe by 25 degrees.

• For shiny crust on a loaf of yeast bread, brush it with an egg beaten with a little water. For a soft crust, rub with softened butter or margarine just after the bread is removed from the pan to cool.

Storing Bread

Completely cooled yeast breads, when properly wrapped in freezer paper, heavy foil or heavy plastic bags, can be frozen for up to 6 months. If bread is to be used for sandwiches, slice it before freezing. The frozen slices will pull apart easily and thaw quickly.

Quick breads are better if allowed to stand overnight. When completely cool, wrap in foil or plastic wrap and store at room temperature.

Keep Your Flour Fresh

Regular all-purpose flour can be stored in an airtight container at room temperature. Whole-wheat flour and rye flour should be stored in the freezer in an airtight freezer bag or container if you will not be using them right away.

Flour Range in Bread Recipes   Most bread recipes offer a range in the amount of flour to use since the results of a recipe will be affected by the type and brand of flour to be used, the amount of moisture in the flour, the time of year it is used and such variables as the size of eggs.

Sesame Potato Twist Loaf

Bake at 400° for 10 minutes, then at 350° for 35 minutes.

Makes two loaves.

¹/₂ **cup (1 stick) butter or margarine**	**dry yeast**
¹/₂ **cup sieved hot cooked potatoes or prepared instant potatoes**	¹/₃ **cup very warm water**
2 tablespoons sugar	**5¹/₂ cups all-purpose flour**
2 teaspoons salt	**1 egg white slightly beaten with 1 tablespoon water**
1 cup milk, scalded	**Sesame seeds**
2 envelopes active	

1. Combine butter and potatoes in a large bowl; stir until melted. Add sugar, salt and milk; stir until mixture is smooth. Cool to lukewarm.

2. Dissolve yeast in very warm water ("very warm water" should feel comfortably warm when dropped on wrist); stir into potato mixture. Stir in 3 cups of the flour, beating with a spoon until smooth. Gradually stir in enough of the remaining flour to make a moderately firm dough which does not stick to sides of bowl. Turn out on a lightly floured board and knead until smooth and elastic, about 10 minutes, working in only as much additional flour as needed (about 1 cup) to prevent dough from sticking.

3. Place dough in a large buttered bowl; turn dough to bring buttered side up. Cover and let rise in a warm draft-free place until double in bulk, about 50 minutes.

4. Punch dough down and turn out onto lightly floured surface. Divide into four parts. Roll each part between buttered palms to form a strand about 15 inches long. Spiral-wrap two strands to form a twisted loaf; tuck ends under. Place in a buttered 9 × 5 × 3-inch loaf pan. Repeat with remaining strands. Cover and let rise in a warm place until almost double in bulk, about 20 to 30 minutes.

5. Preheat oven to 400°. Gently brush tops of loaves with egg white mixture; sprinkle on sesame seeds.

6. Bake in a preheated hot oven (400°) for 10 minutes. Lower heat to moderate (350°) and bake for 35 minutes or until golden brown. Turn loaves out to cool on wire racks.

Sesame Potato Twist Loaf, page 86; Steamed Ginger Brown Bread, page 116; Honey Wheat Bread, page 89.

How to Knead and Shape Bread

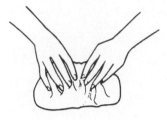

1. Turn soft dough out on floured board. Flour hands lightly, then pat dough to flatten slightly. Begin to knead this way. Pick up edge of dough with fingers and fold over toward you.

2. Push the dough away from you with the heels of both hands. If the dough sticks to the board, have a metal spatula handy to scrape the board clean; then re-flour and continue on.

3. Give dough a quarter turn, then repeat folding, pushing, turning. As you knead, you will develop your own speed. You'll find well-kneaded bread dough is satiny, elastic and smooth.

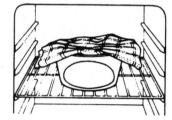

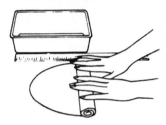

4. For an easy way to determine when dough has doubled in bulk: Press the dough flat in bowl, mark level, then remove dough. Fill bowl with water to double the first mark; mark level.

5. For warm, draft-free place to let dough rise, use oven with door closed. If the oven is electric, warm to 200°, then turn off and let cool for 5 minutes. If gas, pilot light will keep dough warm.

6. To shape a handsome loaf of bread: Roll or pat dough out to a rectangle with short side equal to length of a bread pan. Roll up the dough, in jelly-roll style, pressing the turns firmly.

7. When loaf has been shaped, make sure dough is even on both ends. Then, with fingers, pinch long seam firmly—to seal and keep from unrolling. Put in pans, with seam on bottom.

8. How to smooth ends of loaves: Press the dough down on each end of loaf with sides of hands. Tuck the thin strips formed under the loaf. Lift the loaf to the pan without stretching.

9. For shaping long loaves of bread: Roll up, in jelly-roll style, pinching seam, as in Figure 7. Then, with the palms of your hands, taper the ends by rolling loaf back and forth on board.

Honey Wheat Bread

Bake at 400° for 15 minutes, then at 350° for 30 minutes.

Makes 3 medium-size loaves.

2 envelopes active dry yeast	**vegetable oil**
4 cups very warm water	**2 teaspoons salt**
3 tablespoons honey	**5 cups unbleached all-purpose flour**
1 tablespoon	**5 cups whole wheat flour**

1. Sprinkle yeast over very warm water in a large bowl ("very warm water" should feel comfortably warm when dropped on wrist); stir to dissolve. Stir in honey and oil. Let stand 10 minutes, until bubbly.
2. Stir in salt, 1 cup white flour and 1 cup whole wheat flour; stir well. Continue adding flour until 8 cups have been incorporated. Turn out onto lightly floured surface. Knead in enough of the remaining flour to make a smooth ball. Knead 10 minutes, until smooth and elastic.
3. Place in large greased bowl, turning to bring greased side up. Let it rise 45 minutes to an hour in a warm place away from drafts. Punch down. Divide into 3 parts.
4. Pat out each part to make a 12 × 8-inch rectangle; roll up from short end; place in greased 8 × 4 × 3-inch pans. Cut slashes 1-inch deep on tops of loaves. Preheat oven to 400°. Let loaves rise in warm place about 10 minutes.
5. Bake in a preheated hot oven (400°) for 15 minutes. Lower heat to moderate (350°) and bake 30 minutes longer or until bread sounds hollow when tapped. Remove from pans to wire racks to cool completely.

Old-fashioned Rye Bread

Bake at 400° for 35 minutes.

Makes 2 loaves.

2 envelopes active dry yeast	**shortening**
2¹/₂ cups very warm water	**2¹/₂ cups rye flour**
¹/₄ cup light molasses	**1 tablespoon caraway seeds, crushed**
4 teaspoons salt	**5¹/₂ to 6 cups *sifted* all-purpose flour**
2 tablespoons vegetable	**Cornmeal**

1. Sprinkle yeast into ¹/₂ cup of the very warm water; stir in 1 teaspoon of the molasses. ("Very warm water" should feel comfortably warm when dropped on wrist.) Stir until yeast dissolves. Let stand to proof, undisturbed, until bubbly and double in volume, about 10 minutes.
2. Combine remaining water and molasses with salt and shortening in a large bowl; stir in yeast mixture, rye flour and caraway seeds; add enough all-purpose flour to make a soft dough.
3. Turn out onto lightly floured surface. Knead until smooth and elastic, about 10 minutes, using enough of the remaining flour to keep dough from sticking.
4. Place in buttered large bowl; turn dough to bring buttered side up. Cover with towel. Let rise in a warm, draft-free place, 1 hour or until double in bulk.
5. Butter a large cookie sheet. Sprinkle lightly with cornmeal.
6. Punch dough down; turn out onto lightly floured surface; knead 3 to 4 times; invert bowl over dough; let rest 10 minutes. Divide dough in half and knead each half 3 to 4 times. Shape into 2 loaves. Place loaves at least 4 inches apart on prepared cookie sheet.
7. Let rise again in a warm place, away from draft, 45 minutes or until double in bulk. Preheat oven to 400°. Brush tops with water.
8. Bake in a preheated hot oven (400°) for 35 minutes or until browned and loaves sound hollow when tapped. Remove from cookie sheet to wire rack; cool completely.

Granola-Yogurt Loaves

Bake at 375° for 35 minutes to 40 minutes.

Makes 2 round loaves.

2 envelopes active dry yeast	**5 to 5¹/₂ cups *sifted* unbleached all-purpose flour**
1¹/₂ cups very warm water	**2 cups natural cereal with fruits and nuts**
1 teaspoon honey	**1 egg white slightly beaten with 1 tablespoon water**
1 container (8 ounces) plain yogurt	
3 teaspoons salt	

1. Sprinkle yeast into ¹/₂ cup of the very warm water in a 1-cup measure; stir in honey. ("Very warm water" should feel comfortably warm when dropped on wrist.) Stir until yeast dissolves. Let stand, undisturbed, to proof until bubbly and double in volume, about 10 minutes.
2. Combine remaining water, yogurt and salt in large bowl; stir in yeast mixture. Beat in 4 cups of the flour with electric mixer at medium speed for 2 minutes. Stir in cereal. Gradually stir in remaining flour to make a stiff dough.
3. Turn out onto lightly floured surface; knead until smooth and elastic using only enough flour to keep dough from sticking, about 10 minutes.
4. Place in buttered large bowl; turn to bring buttered side up. Cover with a towel or wax paper. Let rise in a warm place, away from draft, 1 hour or until double in bulk.
5. Punch dough down; turn out onto lightly floured board; knead a few times; invert bowl over dough; allow to rest 10 minutes. Divide dough in half and

(continued)

knead each half a few times; shape into two round loaves. Place on a large greased cookie sheet, 5 inches apart.

6. Let rise in a warm place, away from draft, 40 minutes or until double in bulk. Preheat oven to 375°. Cut a ¹/₂-inch deep cross in the top of each with a sharp knife. Brush with beaten egg white.

7. Bake in preheated moderate oven (375°) for 35 minutes or until golden brown and loaves sound hollow when tapped. Remove from cookie sheet to wire racks; cool completely.

Golden Coffee Bread

Bake at 350° for 50 to 60 minutes.

Makes one 7-inch round loaf (8 servings).

1 envelope active dry yeast	**4¹/₂ to 5 cups** *unsifted* **all-purpose flour**
¹/₄ cup very warm water (105° to 115°F.)	**10 tablespons butter or margarine**
¹/₂ cup sugar	**¹/₂ cup golden raisins**
³/₄ cup milk	**¹/₂ cup coarsely chopped candied fruits**
¹/₄ teaspooon saffron threads	
OR: **1¹/₂ teaspoons ground cinnamon**	**¹/₂ cup chopped blanched almonds**
3 eggs	**Sliced almonds** *(optional)*

1. Sprinkle yeast into very warm water in a 1-cup measure. ("Very warm water" should feel comfortably warm when dropped on wrist.) Add 1 teaspoon of the sugar. Stir until yeast and sugar are dissolved. Let stand until bubbly, 10 minutes.

2. Heat milk with remaining sugar in a saucepan until lukewarm; pour into a large mixing bowl. Add saffron, 2 eggs and one egg yolk (reserve remaining egg white), yeast mixture and 3 cups of the flour. Beat until smooth and elastic, 4 minutes. Beat in butter gradually, about 4 minutes. Add remaining flour; beat 2 minutes. Stir in raisins, fruits and almonds. Smooth top.

3. Cover bowl with wax paper, then a clean towel. Let rise in a warm place 1 hour or until doubled in bulk. Grease a straight-sided ovenproof bowl or soufflé dish, 7¹/₄ × 3¹/₂-inches.

4. Stir dough down; turn out onto lightly floured surface. Knead lightly several times, using only enough flour to keep dough from sticking; shape into ball. Press gently into prepared bowl. Cover. Let rise again in a warm place until doubled in bulk, about 1 hour. Brush with slightly beaten reserved egg white; decorate top with sliced almonds if you wish.

5. Bake in a preheated moderate oven (350°) for 50 to 60 minutes or until loaf sounds hollow when tapped. If loaf browns too quickly, cover loosely with foil. Cool in bowl on a wire rack 10 minutes. Turn out onto wire rack; cool completely. To serve, cut into quarters; slice each quarter crosswise.

Cracked Wheat Bread

A tender, crunchy loaf that makes delicious toast.
Bake at 350° for 45 minutes.
Makes 2 loaves.

1¹/₂ cups boiling water	**water**
³/₄ cup cracked wheat	**¹/₂ teaspoon sugar or honey**
1 cup buttermilk	
¹/₄ cup unsulphured molasses	**2 to 3 cups unbleached all-purpose flour**
2 tablespoons honey	
¹/₄ cup (¹/₂ stick) unsalted butter	**2 cups whole wheat flour**
2 teaspoons salt	**2 tablespoons butter, melted**
2 envelopes active dry yeast	**Egg Glaze** *(recipe follows)*
¹/₄ cup very warm	

1. Pour water over wheat in large bowl. Let stand 1 hour.

2. Heat buttermilk, molasses, honey, butter and salt in small saucepan just until butter is melted. Stir to mix; cool to lukewarm.

3. Sprinkle yeast over very warm water in large bowl. ("Very warm water" should feel comfortably warm when dropped on wrist.) Stir in sugar. Let stand 10 minutes or until bubbly.

4. Add buttermilk mixture and 2 cups of the all-purpose flour to yeast. Beat with electric mixer for 2 minutes or 200 strokes by hand. Stir in wheat mixture.

5. Gradually add the whole wheat flour and enough of the remaining all-purpose flour to make a dough that holds together and pulls away from bowl.

6. Turn dough out onto floured surface and knead 10 minutes, adding more flour, if necessary. Dough will be slightly sticky. Place in greased large bowl, turning to bring greased side up. Cover; let rise in a warm draft-free place until double in volume, about 1 hour.

7. Punch dough down; turn out onto lightly floured surface; knead a few times to press out air bubbles. Let rest 10 minutes.

8. Divide dough in half; shape each half into a loaf and place in 2 greased 8¹/₂ × 4¹/₂ × 2¹/₂-inch loaf pans. Brush with melted butter; cover and let rise again until almost doubled.

9. Bake in a preheated moderate oven (350°) for 45 miniutes or until loaves sound hollow when tapped with fingers. If you like a glossy crust, brush loaves with Egg Glaze 10 minutes before end of baking time. Remove loaves from pans to wire racks and cool.

Egg Glaze: Beat 1 egg with 1 tablespoon water in small cup until foamy.

Savory Cream Puffs

Bake at 400° for 40 minutes.

Makes 6 servings.

Cream Puffs:
1 cup water
1/2 cup (1 stick) unsalted butter or margarine
1/8 teaspoon salt
1/4 teaspoon leaf marjoram, crumbled
1/4 teaspoon leaf thyme, crumbled
1 cup *sifted* all-purpose flour
4 eggs

Filling:
1/2 pound medium-size mushrooms, coarsely chopped
1 small onion, finely chopped
1/4 teaspoon leaf thyme, crumbled
2 teaspoons unsalted butter or margarine
1/2 pound chicken breast cutlets, cut into 1/2-inch dice
1 1/4 cups dry white wine
2 tablespoons all-purpose flour
1/2 pound 1/2-inch-thick boiled ham, cut into 1/2-inch dice
3/4 cup frozen small peas

1. Lightly grease a cookie sheet. Preheat the oven to hot (400°).
2. Prepare the Cream Puffs: Combine the water, butter, salt, marjoram and thyme in a saucepan. Bring to a full rolling boil. Add the flour all at once. Stir vigorously with a wooden spoon to form a thick, smooth ball that leaves the sides of the pan clean. Remove from the heat. Cool for 2 or 3 minutes.
3. Add the eggs, one at a time, beating well after each addition until the dough is shiny and smooth.
4. Spoon the dough into a large pastry bag fitted with a large star tip. Pipe onto the prepared cookie sheet in a solid 3-inch circle. Make a small circle of dough on top, ending in a point at the center. Repeat to make 5 more cream puffs.
5. Bake in the preheated hot oven (400°) for 40 minutes or until puffed and golden brown. Cool on a rack. Slice in half horizontally, three-quarters through. Remove any filaments of soft dough that remain.
6. Prepare the Filling: Sauté the mushrooms, onion and thyme in the butter in a large skillet until just tender and golden brown. Add the chicken and 1 cup of the white wine. Simmer until the chicken is just cooked through, 5 to 8 minutes.
7. Stir the flour into the remaining 1/4 cup of wine until smooth. Add to the simmering mixture. Cook, stirring, until thickened. Fold in the ham and peas; simmer for 1 minute. Spoon into the puffs.

To Make Ahead: The filling and the puffs may be made up to 24 hours ahead. Store the puffs in an airtight container in a cool, dry place; refrigerate the filling. To serve, spoon the filling into the puffs. Place on a cookie sheet. Bake in a preheated hot oven (400°) for 15 to 20 minutes or until heated through.

Microwave Directions
650 Watt Variable Power Microwave Oven

Ingredient Changes: Reduce the amount of wine from 1 1/4 cups to 3/4 cup.
Directions: Prepare the puffs as directed above. To prepare the filling, combine the mushrooms, onion, thyme and butter in a 2-quart microwave-safe casserole. Microwave at full power for 4 minutes, stirring once. Add the chicken and 1/2 cup of the wine. Cover. Microwave at full power for 4 minutes, stirring once. Stir together the remaining 1/4 cup of wine and the flour in a small cup until smooth. Stir into the casserole along with the ham and peas. Microwave at full power for 5 minutes, stirring once. Serve as directed above.

Mushroom Bread Magnifique

Bake at 350° for 45 minutes.

Makes 2 loaves (12 slices each).

Mushroom Filling:
2 pounds mushrooms, sliced
1 small onion, chopped (1/4 cup)
3 tablespoons vegetable oil
1 package (8 ounces) cream cheese
1 cup dry fine bread crumbs
1/2 cup plain yogurt
1/2 cup dairy sour cream
1/3 cup chopped parsley
2 cloves garlic, finely chopped
2 teaspoons lemon juice
1/2 teaspoon caraway seeds
1/2 teaspoon pepper

Dough:
10 cups *unsifted* all-purpose flour
1/3 cup instant nonfat dry milk powder
1 tablespoon sugar
1 tablespoon salt
2 envelopes fast-rising dry yeast
2 1/2 cups water
1/4 cup vegetable oil
2 eggs, slightly beaten
1 tablespoon butter or margarine, melted

1. To prepare the Mushroom filling: Sauté the mushrooms and onion in oil in a large skillet until the mushrooms give off their liquid. Continue cooking, stirring occasionally, until liquid evaporates. Add the cream cheese; stir until melted. Stir in the bread crumbs, yogurt, sour cream, parsley, garlic, lemon juice, caraway seeds and pepper. Set aside.
2. To prepare the Dough: Set aside 1 cup of the flour. Mix together the remaining 9 cups flour, dry milk powder, sugar, salt and yeast in a large bowl.
3. Combine the water and oil in a saucepan. Heat to 130° (mixture should feel comfortably hot to the touch). Mix into the dry ingredients. Mix in the eggs. Mix in enough reserved 1 cup flour to make a soft dough.
4. Turn out onto a floured surface. Knead until smooth and elastic, 8 to 10 minutes. Cover; let rest for 10 minutes.
5. Divide the dough in half. Roll out each half on a lightly floured surface into a 15 × 12-inch rectangle.

(continued)

Clockwise from bottom right: Crunch-Topped Hamburger Rolls, page 101; Caramelized Carrot Swirl, page 103; Saffron Raisin Loaf, page 103; Whole-Wheat "Yamadamia" Bread, page 92; Apricot-Yogurt Chestnut Bread, page 112; Mushroom Bread Magnifique, page 91.

Spread each with half the Mushroom Filling to within 1/2 inch of the edges. Starting at a long side, roll each up jelly-roll fashion; pinch along the seams to seal. Place seam-sides down on greased cookie sheets. Make cuts in the top of each loaf, three-quarters of the way through and at 1 1/2-inch intervals. Twist every other slice to opposite side. Cover with buttered wax paper and a towel. Let rise in a warm place, away from drafts, until doubled in volume, about 45 minutes.
6. Meanwhile, preheat the oven to moderate (350°).
7. Bake in the preheated moderate oven (350°) for 45 minutes or until the loaves are browned and sound hollow when tapped with fingers. Remove the breads from the cookie sheets to wire racks to cool; brush with the butter. Serve warm or at room temperature. Store in the refrigerator

Whole-Wheat "Yamadamia" Bread

Bake at 350° for 60 minutes.

Makes 2 loaves (8 slices each).

9 1/2 cups whole-wheat flour
1 cup mashed cooked yams
2/3 cup macadamia nuts, chopped
1 tablespoon salt
1 envelope fast-rising dry yeast
3 cups milk
1/3 cup water
1 tablespoon honey
1 tablespoon molasses
3 tablespoons butter or margarine
Confectioners' Glaze (recipe follows; optional)

1. Set aside 1 cup of the flour. Mix together the remaining 8 1/2 cups flour, yams, macadamia nuts, salt and yeast in a large bowl.
2. Combine the milk, water, honey, molasses and 1 tablespoon of the butter in a medium-size saucepan. Heat to 130° (mixture should feel comfortably hot to the touch). Stir into the dry ingredients. Stir in just enough of the reserved 1 cup flour to make a stiff dough.
3. Turn the dough out onto a lightly floured surface. Knead until smooth and elastic, 6 to 8 minutes. Cover; let rest for 10 minutes.

4. Divide the dough in half. Shape into 2 loaves. Place in 2 greased 8½ × 4½ × 2½-inch baking pans or other 6-cup baking pans or molds. Cover with buttered wax paper and a towel. Let rise in a warm place, away from drafts, until doubled in volume, 45 to 55 minutes.

5. Meanwhile, preheat the oven to moderate (350°).

6. Bake in the preheated moderate oven (350°) for 60 minutes or until the loaves are browned and sound hollow when tapped with fingers. Remove the breads from the pans to wire racks to cool.

7. Spread the Confectioners' Glaze over the top of the bread, if you wish, allowing the glaze to run down the sides. Sprinkle tops with chopped macadamia nuts, if you wish.

Confectioners' Glaze: Combine 1 cup 10X (confectioners') sugar, 1 to 1½ tablespoons milk and ¼ teaspoon vanilla in a small bowl, stirring until smooth and good of spreading consistency.

Cream Cheese Loaf

Bake at 325° for 40 minutes.

Makes 2 loaves (15 slices each).

6 cups *unsifted* **all-purpose flour**	**margarine**
2 tablespoons sugar	**4 ounces (half an 8-ounce package) cream cheese, at room temperature**
1 teaspoon salt	
1 envelope fast-rising dry yeast	
1 cup water	**1 egg yolk mixed with 1 tablespoon water**
1 cup milk	
2 tablespoons	**4 teaspoons instant onion flakes**

1. Combine 3½ cups of the flour, the sugar, salt and yeast in a large bowl; stir to mix.

2. Combine the water, milk and margarine in a small saucepan. Heat to 130° (mixture should feel comfortably hot to the touch). Add to the flour mixture; add the cheese. Beat at low speed until blended; then beat at medium speed for 3 minutes. Mix in 1½ cups of the remaining flour, ½ cup at a time, scraping down the sides with a spatula.

3. Turn the dough out onto a lightly floured surface. Knead until smooth and elastic, about 5 minutes, using up to 1 cup of the remaining flour.

4. Shape the dough into a ball. Place in a large oiled bowl, turning to bring the oiled side up. Cover with buttered wax paper and a towel. Let rise in a warm place, away from drafts, until doubled in volume, about 30 minutes. Press finger into the dough; you'll know dough has doubled when the finger indentation remains in the dough.

5. Grease 2 loaf pans (8½ × 4½ × 2½-inches).

6. After the dough has risen, punch down. Knead briefly. Divide in half. Roll out each half into a rectangle, about 12 × 8½ inches. Roll up from the short end; pinch the edges together. Place in the prepared pans, seam-side down. Cover with buttered wax paper and a towel. Let rise in a warm place, away from drafts, until doubled in bulk, about 30 minutes.

7. Meanwhile, preheat the oven to slow (325°).

8. Bake in the preheated slow oven (325°) for 30 minutes. Brush with the egg yolk mixture; sprinkle with the onion flakes. Bake for 10 minutes more or until the loaves are golden brown and sound hollow when tapped with fingers. Remove the bread from pans to racks to cool.

Mincemeat Braid

Bake at 350° for 45 minutes.

Makes 2 braids (16 slices each).

4 cups *unsifted* **all-purpose flour**	**¼ cup water**
¼ cup firmly packed brown sugar	**2 tablespoons butter or margarine**
1 teaspoon salt	**1 egg**
1 envelope fast-rising dry yeast	**1½ cups bottled mincemeat**
1 cup milk	**Sugar Glaze** *(recipe follows)*

1. Combine 2 cups of the flour, the sugar, salt and yeast in a large bowl; stir to mix.

2. Combine the milk, water and butter in a small saucepan. Heat to 130° (mixture should feel comfortably hot to the touch). Add to the flour mixture; add the egg. Beat at low speed until blended; then beat at medium speed for 3 minutes. Mix in 1 cup of the remaining flour, ½ cup at a time, scraping down the sides with a spatula.

3. Turn the dough out onto a lightly floured surface. Knead until smooth and elastic, about 5 minutes, using up to 1 cup of the remaing flour.

4. Shape the dough into a ball. Place in a large oiled bowl, turning to bring the oiled side up. Cover with buttered wax paper and a towel. Let rise in a warm place, away from drafts, until doubled in volume, about 30 minutes. Press a finger into the dough; you'll know the dough has doubled when the finger indentation remains in the dough.

5. After the dough has risen, punch down. Divide into 6 equal pieces. Roll each piece between the palms into a "sausage," about 10 inches long. Flatten each piece with a rolling pin until 3 inches wide. Spoon ¼ cup of mincemeat lengthwise down the center of each piece.

6. Bring the long sides up over the filling and pinch edges closed to seal. Braid the 3 mincemeat "sausages" together to make 1 loaf. Pinch the ends

(continued)

Overleaf: Cream Cheese Loaf, page 93;
Mincemeat Braid, page 93.

together to seal. Transfer the braid to a greased cookie sheet. Repeat to make a second braid.

7. Cover the braids with buttered wax paper and a towel. Let rise in a warm place, away from drafts, until doubled in volume, about 30 minutes.

8. Meanwhile, preheat the oven to moderate (350°).

9. Bake in the preheated moderate oven (350°) for 45 minutes, or until the braids are browned and sound hollow when tapped with fingers. Cool on wire racks.

10. Drizzle Sugar Glaze over the bread.

Sugar Glaze: Place 1 cup sifted 10X (confectioners') sugar in a small bowl. Gradually stir in 1 to 2 tablespoons milk until thin enough to drizzle over the braids.

Herbed Garlic and Onion Bread

You can make the herb butter ahead of time and refrigerate.

Grill about 15 minutes.

Makes 8 servings.

1/2 cup (1 stick) butter or margarine	**marjoram, crumbled**
1 clove garlic, finely chopped	**1/4 teaspoon leaf thyme, crumbled**
2 tablespoons instant minced onion	**1 loaf French or Italian bread, 12 to 14 inches long**
1/4 teaspoon leaf	

1. Combine butter, garlic, onion, marjoram and thyme in bowl until well mixed.

2. Cut bread into 1-inch-thick slices, but don't cut all the way through bottom crust. Spread herb butter on cut surface of slices. Wrap loaf in heavy-duty or double-thick regular aluminum foil.

3. Place bread on grill; grill until heated through, about 15 minutes. Unwrap and break into slices to serve.

Note: Bread can be heated in an oven. Bake bread in a preheated hot oven (400°) for 15 minutes.

Nut and Raisin Bread

Bake at 375° for 50 minutes.

Makes 1 loaf.

2 envelopes active dry yeast	**2 cups very warm milk**
1/3 cup nonfat dry milk powder	**1 1/2 cups whole wheat flour**
2 tablespoons honey	**1 1/2 cups all-purpose flour**
2 tablespoons molasses	**1/2 cup raisins**
1 teaspoon salt	**1/2 cup walnuts, chopped**
1/4 cup vegetable oil	

1. Combine yeast, dry milk, honey, molasses, salt and oil in a large bowl. Stir in the very warm milk. ("Very warm," about 120° to 130°, should feel very warm to the hand.) Beat mixture until well blended, about 30 seconds.

2. Blend the whole wheat and all-purpose flours in a medium-size bowl. Stir 1 1/2 cups of the flour mixture into the yeast mixture. Beat with electric mixer at medium speed for 2 minutes. Stir in another 1/2 cup of flour; beat 1 minute. Beat in raisins, walnuts and remaining flour by hand until a heavy, sticky dough forms. If dough seems too stiff, beat in 2 extra tablespoons of vegetable oil while adding the last of the flour.

3. Preheat oven to 375°. Turn dough into a well-greased 9 × 5 × 3-inch loaf pan. Cover with a clean cloth and let rise in a warm place, away from drafts, about 20 minutes.

4. Bake in a preheated moderate oven (375°) for 50 minutes or until loaf sounds hollow when tapped with fingers. Remove from pan; cool.

Basil Breads

Two unusual breads from one recipe--a coiled loaf and rolls.

Bake loaf at 375° for 30 to 35 minutes; bake rolls at 375° for 20 to 25 minutes.

Makes 1 loaf (8 servings) and 8 rolls.

7 1/2 cups *unsifted* all-purpose flour	**juice**
1 tablespoon sugar	**3 teaspoons sesame seeds *(optional)***
2 teaspoons salt	**2 tablespoons finely chopped walnuts**
1 envelope fast-rising dry yeast	**2 tablespoons grated Parmesan cheese**
2 1/2 cups water	**1 egg yolk**
1 cup finely chopped fresh basil leaves	**1 teaspoon water**
1 tablespoon lemon	

1. Set aside 1 cup of the flour. Combine remaining flour, sugar, salt and yeast in large bowl; stir to mix well.

2. Heat water in small saucepan to 130° (water should feel comfortably hot to the touch). Add to flour mixture. Beat with a wooden spoon until smooth. Gradually stir in enough of the remaining flour to make a soft dough.

3. Turn out on lightly floured surface. Knead until smooth and elastic, 8 to 10 minutes, adding more flour as needed to prevent sticking. Form into ball. Place in an oiled bowl. Turn dough, oil side up. Cover with plastic wrap. Refrigerate 12 to 24 hours.

4. Punch dough down; turn out onto lightly floured surface. Knead a few times. Invert bowl over dough. Let rest 10 minutes.

5. Combine 1/2 cup of the chopped basil, the lemon juice and 2 teaspoons of the sesame seeds, if using, in a small bowl. Combine the remaining basil, the walnuts and Parmesan cheese in another small bowl. Reserve 1 tablespoon of this mixture.

6. Divide dough in half. Keep one half under the bowl.

Basil Breads, page 96;
Quick Basil Biscuits, and
Basil Cheese Straws,
page 97.

Roll the other half into a 16 x 12-inch rectangle. Spread with basil-lemon mixture. Roll up from long side, jelly-roll fashion, into a 16-inch long roll.

7. Lightly oil a solid 8-inch circle on baking sheet no larger than 15 x 12 inches. Coil roll into a 6-inch circle on the oiled section. With remaining section of the roll, coil a 4-inch circle on top. Tuck end of roll into center of top circle. The bread should look like a flattened cone. Cover; let rise in a warm place away from drafts until doubled in bulk, about 45 minutes.

8. Meanwhile, divide remaining half of dough into 8 equal pieces. Roll each piece into a 5-inch circle. Place about 1 1/2 tablespoons of the basil-Parmesan mixture in center of each. Pinch dough together over top of filling. Arrange rolls on lightly oiled baking sheet, three pairs in a row, all touching. Place 1 roll at each end of the row. Cover; let rise in warm place away from drafts until doubled in bulk, about 45 minutes.

9. Preheat the oven to moderate (375°). Arrange one oven shelf in bottom third of oven, second shelf in top third; shelves should be at least 7 inches apart.

10. Beat egg yolk with 1 teaspoon water. Brush coiled loaf with egg wash. Sprinkle with reserved 1 teaspoon sesame seeds, if using. Brush rolls with plain water. Sprinkle with reserved 1 tablespoon basil-Parmesan mixture.

11. Bake loaf on bottom shelf in preheated moderate oven (375°) for 30 to 35 minutes, and rolls on top shelf for 20 to 25 minutes or until bottoms sound hollow when tapped with fingers. Transfer to wire rack. Let stand at least 10 minutes before cutting loaf or tearing rolls apart.

Quick Basil Biscuits

Add 3 tablespoons finely chopped, fresh basil to every 2 cups biscuit mix. Make biscuits following label directions.

Basil Cheese Straws

Add 2 tablespoons finely chopped fresh basil leaves to 1 package (11 ounces) pie crust mix or to any pastry for a double crust pie. Prepare the pastry as you would normally. Roll out into a 12-inch square. Sprinkle with 2 tablespoons grated Parmesan cheese. Fold into quarters to make a 6-inch square. Roll pastry out to make a square 1/8-inch thick. Cut into 1/2-inch wide strips. Twist the strips and place on cookie sheets. Bake in a preheated moderate oven (375°) for about 8 minutes or until golden.

Flaky Croissants

Bake at 400° for 20 minutes.
Makes 1 1/2 dozen.

7 cups *unsifted* **all-purpose flour**	**milk**
1 envelope active dry yeast	**1 teaspoon salt**
1/4 cup very warm water	**1/2 cup sugar**
2 cups lukewarm	**1 cup (2 sticks) butter, softened**
	1 egg
	1 tablespoon milk

1. Measure 2 cups of the flour into a large bowl; make a well in the center.
2. Sprinkle the yeast over the very warm water in a

(continued)

cup; stir to dissolve. ("Very warm water" should feel comfortably warm when dropped on the wrist.) Pour into well in flour; let stand until yeast mixture is bubbly, about 5 minutes.

3. Add milk, salt and sugar; beat until smooth. Beat in enough of the remaining flour, 1/2 cup at a time, to form a soft dough.

4. Turn dough out onto lightly floured surface. Knead about 3 minutes, using only enough flour to keep dough from sticking.

5. Press dough into a large, lightly greased bowl; cover with plastic wrap. Let rise at room temperature for 1 1/2 hours.

6. While dough is rising, knead the 2 sticks of butter with a dough scraper or stiff-bladed putty knife until soft but not melted. Shape into a 8 × 6-inch rectangle, 1/2-inch thick.

7. Roll the dough to a 12 × 10-inch rectangle on a lightly floured surface; let it rest for 10 minutes.

8. Place the butter on top of dough so that the 8-inch edge is parallel to the 10-inch edge, leaving a 1-inch margin on 3 sides and 5 inches on remaining side. Fold the 5 inches of dough over to cover half the butter. Lift the uncovered butter and dough layer up and fold over the covered butter as for a letter. (The layers will be dough, butter, dough, butter, dough.) Press dough firmly to seal. Turn dough so folds are at right angles to lower edge of work surface.

9. Lightly flour the work surface. Roll the dough to a 14 × 8-inch rectangle about 1-inch thick. Fold in thirds as for a letter. Let rest 10 minutes.

10. Give the dough a quarter turn so that the folds will be at right angles to the front edge of the work surface. Roll to a 14 × 8-inch rectangle. Fold in thirds again. Repeat rolling and folding once again.

11. Wrap dough in moist cloth; refrigerate about 1 1/2 hours. If refrigerating overnight, over-wrap with wax paper.

12. For shaping, roll dough on a lightly floured surface to a 25 × 10-inch rectangle, about 1/4-inch thick. Divide dough into 2 long strips, each 5 inches wide. Let dough "relax" about 5 minutes. Mark each strip lightly into 5 even divisions. Mark and cut each of these fifths diagonally to make 2 triangles each. Shape each croissant: Roll each from base to point with rolling pin, pressing a little to make a larger and thinner elongated triangle. Roll up from the base of the triangle to the point.

13. Place croissants on baking sheets 1 1/2 inches apart. Curve ends slightly to form crescent shape. Beat egg and milk in cup; brush over croissants.

14. Let croissants rise, at room temperature, 30 minutes. Brush again; let rise 30 minutes longer or until double in volume.

15. Preheat oven to 400°. When oven is ready, brush croissants for the third time.

16. Bake in a preheated hot oven (400°) for 20 minutes or until golden brown. Cool on wire rack. If croissants are to be frozen, take from oven when just a light brown. To bake, thaw, then bake in a hot oven (400°) for 8 minutes or until golden brown.

Roll Also called bun, a roll is an individual bread made in the shape of a small oval or round. It can be made from either a yeast or quick dough.

Cinnamon Buns

Bake at 375° for 25 minutes.

Makes 1 1/2 dozen buns.

2 envelopes active dry yeast	**Filling:**
1/2 cup very warm water	**1/2 cup (1 stick) butter or margarine, softened**
1 teaspoon sugar	**1 cup firmly packed light brown sugar**
1/2 cup milk	
1/2 cup sugar	**1 cup raisins**
1 1/2 teaspoons salt	**1/2 cup chopped walnuts**
1/4 cup (1/2 stick) butter or margarine	**1 teaspoon ground cinnamon**
2 eggs	
4 1/2 cups *sifted* **all-purpose flour**	

1. Sprinkle yeast into very warm water in a 1-cup measure. ("Very warm water" should feel comfortably warm when dropped on wrist.) Stir in 1 teaspoon sugar and allow to stand 10 minutes or until mixture begins to foam.

2. Heat milk, remaining sugar, salt and butter in a medium-size saucepan, just until butter melts; pour into a large bowl; allow to cool slightly. Beat in eggs with a wire whisk until well blended. (Test temperature of liquid at this time. It should be no warmer than water used with yeast.) Stir in foaming yeast.

3. Beat in 2 cups of the flour until smooth; stir in enough of the remaining flour to make a soft dough.

4. Turn dough out onto a lightly floured pastry board; knead until smooth and elastic, about 5 minutes, using only as much flour as needed to keep dough from sticking.

5. Place dough in a large greased bowl; turn over to bring greased side up. Cover. Let rise in warm place 1 1/2 hours or until double in bulk.

6. Punch dough down; knead a few times; let rest 5 minutes.

7. Make Filling: Combine softened butter and brown sugar until well blended; stir in raisins, nuts and cinnamon.

8. Divide dough in half; roll out to a 15 × 9-inch rectangle on a lightly floured pastry board. Spread half the raisin and nut mixture over dough. Roll up, jelly-roll fashion, starting with short end. Cut into 9 equal slices.

9. Place, cut-side down, in buttered 8 × 8 × 2-inch baking pan. Repeat with remaining dough and filling to make a second pan of buns.

10. Cover pans; let rise in a warm place 45 minutes or until double in bulk. Preheat oven to 375°.

11. Bake in a preheated moderate oven (375°) for 25 minutes or until golden-brown. Invert pans immediately onto wire racks over wax paper.

How to Shape Yeast Rolls

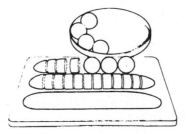

Pan Rolls: Divide dough into three equal parts and shape each into a fat roll, 12 inches long. Slice each roll crosswise every inch; roll slices into balls; place 1/4 inch apart in greased 9-inch layer-cake pans.

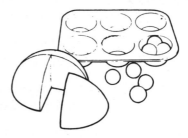

Cloverleaf Rolls: Divide dough into four equal parts, then working with one part at a time, pinch off small pieces of dough; shape into balls about the size of marbles. Place three balls of dough in each cup of greased muffin pans, forming "three-leaf clovers."

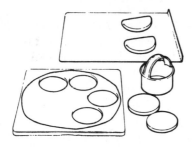

Parker House Rolls: Divide dough in three equal parts; roll, one part at a time, on a floured board into a circle 9 inches across. Cut into rounds with a lightly floured, 2½-inch biscuit cutter; brush each round with softened butter or margarine, make crease across each slightly to one side of center, then fold smaller "half" over the larger, forming half-moons, and place on greased baking sheets 1-inch apart. Pinch edges lightly to seal.

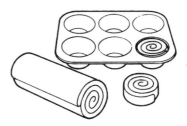

Pinwheels: Divide the dough into three equal parts and roll, one part at a time, on a floured board into a 16 × 8-inch rectangle. Spread with softened butter or margarine and, if you like, cinnamon-sugar, jam or other filling. Roll up from the long side, jelly-roll fashion; slice 1-inch thick. Place, cut-sides up, in greased muffin-pan cups.

Quick Cloverleafs: Pinch off pieces of the dough and shape into balls slightly larger than golf balls. Place in greased muffin-pan cups, then with kitchen shears, snip a cross into the top of each roll, forming "four-leaf clovers."

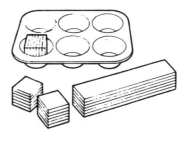

Fan-Tans: Divide dough into three equal parts and roll each part on a floured board into a 15 × 9-inch rectangle; cut crosswise into strips 1½ inches wide, then make a stack by piling 6 strips on top of one another. Cut stack crosswise into squares and place, cut-sides down, in greased muffin-pan cups.

Basic Yeast Roll

Bake at 400° for 15 minutes.

Makes 3 dozen rolls.

1 envelope active dry yeast	shortening
¼ cup very warm water	¼ cup sugar
⅓ cup butter, margarine or vegetable	1 tablespoon salt
	2¼ cups milk, scalded
	1 egg, slightly beaten
	7 to 8 cups *sifted* all-purpose flour

1. Sprinkle yeast into very warm water in a small bowl. ("Very warm water" should feel comfortably warm when dropped on wrist.) Stir until yeast dissolves.
2. Place butter, margarine or shortening, sugar and salt in a large mixing bowl; add scalded milk and stir until fat melts and sugar and salt dissolve. Let mixture cool to lukewarm.
3. Stir yeast mixture into lukewarm milk mixture; add egg and beat until well mixed.
4. Add about half the flour and beat vigorously until smooth; beat in enough of the remaining flour, about ½ cup at a time, to make a soft dough.
5. Turn dough out onto a lightly floured pastry board or cloth; invert the bowl over it and let rest for 10 minutes; knead dough, adding enough flour to keep it from sticking, about 10 minutes or until it becomes smooth and elastic in your hands.
6. Shape dough into a ball and place in a greased mixing bowl, turning to coat all over with shortening; cover with a clean towel and let rise in a warm place, away from draft, about 1 hour or until double in bulk.
7. Punch dough down, then shape into rolls, as desired, and place on greased baking sheets; cover rolls with towels; let rise again in warm place, away from draft, about 30 minutes or until dough is double in bulk. Preheat oven to 400°.
8. Bake in a preheated hot oven (400°) for 15 minutes or until golden. Brush tops with butter or margarine, if you wish. Serve hot.

Glazed Orange Rolls

Bake at 350° for 20 minutes.

Makes 2 dozen rolls.

1 envelope active dry yeast	½ cup (1 stick) butter or margarine, melted
¼ cup very warm water	3½ cups *sifted* all-purpose flour
1 cup sugar	2 tablespoons grated orange rind
1 teaspoon salt	Glaze *(recipe follows)*
2 eggs	
½ cup dairy sour cream	

1. Dissolve yeast in very warm water in a large mixing bowl. ("Very warm water" should feel comfortably warm when dropped on wrist.) Beat in ¼ cup of the sugar, salt, eggs, sour cream and 6 tablespoons of the melted butter with electric mixer. Gradually add 2 cups flour. Beat until smooth. Stir in enough of the remaining flour to make a soft dough.
2. Turn dough out onto a lightly floured surface. Knead dough, adding enough flour to keep from sticking, about 10 minutes or until it becomes smooth and elastic. Shape dough into a ball. Place in a greased bowl; grease top of dough. Cover with a towel.
3. Let dough rise in a warm place away from draft until double in bulk, about 2 hours. Knead dough on well-floured surface about 15 times.
4. Roll one half of the dough to a 12-inch circle. Combine ¾ cup of the sugar and the orange rind. Brush dough with 1 tablespoon melted butter and sprinkle with one half of the orange-sugar mixture. Cut into 12 wedges. Roll up, starting with the wide end. Repeat with remaining dough.
5. Place, point-side down, in three rows in a greased 13 × 9 × 2-inch baking pan. Cover and let rise in warm place, about 1 hour. Preheat oven to 350°.
6. Bake in a preheated moderate oven (350°) for 20 minutes or until golden-brown. Pour Glaze over rolls.

Glaze: Combine ¾ cup sugar, ½ cup dairy sour cream, 2 tablespoons orange juice and ½ cup (1 stick) butter or margarine in a saucepan. Bring to boiling; boil 3 minutes, stirring.

Herb-Onion Rolls

Bake at 375° for 20 minutes.

Makes 1½ dozen rolls.

2 envelopes active dry yeast	oregano, crumbled
⅓ cup nonfat dry milk powder	½ teaspoon leaf tarragon, crumbled
2 tablespoons honey	¼ cup vegetable oil
1 tablespoon salt	1 cup milk, heated until very warm
1 small onion, minced (¼ cup)	1 cup very warm water
1 teaspoon leaf basil, crumbled	2 cups whole wheat flour
1 teaspoon leaf	1½ cups unbleached all-purpose flour

1. Combine yeast, dry milk, honey, salt, onion, basil, oregano, tarragon and oil in a large bowl. Stir in the very warm milk and water. ("Very warm," about 120° to 130°, should feel very warm to the hand.) Beat mixture until well blended, about 30 seconds.
2. Blend the whole wheat and all-purpose flours in a medium-size bowl. Stir 2 cups of the mixture into the yeast mixture. Beat with electric mixer at medium

speed for 2 minutes. Stir in another cup of the flour mixture; beat 1 minute. Beat in remaining flour mixture by hand until a heavy sticky dough forms, about 2 minutes. If dough seems too stiff, beat in 2 extra tablespoons of oil while adding the last of the flour.

3. Fill 18 well-greased muffin-pan cups, using a wet tablespoon or ice cream scoop. Push dough down, smoothing tops slightly. Cover with a clean cloth, and let rise in a warm place, away from drafts, no longer than 20 minutes.

4. Bake in a preheated moderate oven (375°) for 20 minutes or until rolls sound hollow when lightly tapped with fingers. Remove from pans; cool on wire racks.

Sour Cream Sunrise Rolls

Bake at 350° for 25 minutes.

Makes 1½ dozen rolls.

7 cups *unsifted* all-purpose flour	or margarine
½ cup sugar	½ cup thawed, frozen pineapple-orange juice concentrate
½ cup instant, nonfat dry milk powder	1 tablespoon grated orange rind
2 teaspoons salt	
2 envelopes fast-rising dry yeast	2 eggs
1 cup water	Cinnamon Filling (recipe follows)
1 cup dairy sour cream	Sunrise Icing (recipe follows)
½ cup (1 stick) butter	

1. Combine 4 cups of the flour, the sugar, milk powder, salt and yeast in a large bowl; stir to mix.
2. Combine the water, sour cream, butter, juice concentrate and orange rind in a small saucepan. Heat to 130° (the mixture should feel comfortably hot to the touch). Add to the flour mixture. Add the eggs. Blend with an electric mixer at low speed; then beat at medium speed for 3 minutes. Gradually stir in 2 cups of the remaining flour to make a soft dough.
3. Turn the dough out onto a well-floured surface. Knead for about 5 minutes, adding up to 1 cup of the remaining flour, until smooth and elastic. Place the dough in an oiled large bowl; turn to coat. Cover and let rise in a warm place, away from drafts, until doubled in volume, about 30 minutes.
4. Grease a 15 × 10-inch jelly-roll pan.
5. Punch the dough down; knead briefly. Divide the dough into 2 equal parts. Roll out each part on a lightly floured surface into a 13 × 9-inch rectangle. Spread one rectangle with half of the Cinnamon Filling. Beginning with a short side, roll up, jelly-roll fashion. Cut crosswise into 1-inch-thick slices. Place the slices, cut-side down, in the prepared pan. Repeat with the remaining dough and filling. Cover and let rise until doubled in volume, about 30 minutes.
6. Meanwhile, preheat the oven to moderate (350°).
7. Bake the rolls in the preheated moderate oven (350°) for 25 minutes or until golden on top. Remove

from the oven. Drizzle the Sunrise Icing over the warm rolls. Serve warm or at room temperature.

Cinnamon Filling: Combine ⅓ cup sugar, ½ teaspoon ground cinnamon and 2 tablespoons melted butter in a small bowl.

Sunrise Icing: Combine 1 cup *unsifted* 10X (confectioners') sugar, 3 tablespoons thawed, frozen pineapple-orange juice concentrate, ½ teaspoon vanilla and 1 tablespoon softened butter in a small bowl. Mix together until well blended.

Crunch-Topped Hamburger Rolls

Bake at 350° for 20 to 25 minutes.

Makes 12 buns.

4 cups *unsifted* unbleached flour	whole-grain mustard
2½ cups whole-wheat flour	⅓ cup butter or margarine
⅓ cup instant nonfat dry milk powder	¼ cup honey
2 teaspoons salt	1 tablespoon butter or margarine, melted
2 envelopes fast-rising dry yeast	Instant chopped onion, sesame seeds and poppy seeds for topping
1¼ cups water	
⅔ cup Dijon-style or	

1. Set aside 1 cup of the unbleached flour. Mix together the remaining 3 cups of unbleached flour, whole-wheat flour, milk powder, salt and yeast in a large bowl.
2. Combine the water, mustard, the ⅓ cup of butter and honey in a medium-size saucepan. Heat to 130° (the mixture should feel comfortably hot to the touch). Mix into the dry ingredients. Stir in enough of the reserved 1 cup flour to make a fairly stiff dough.
3. Turn the dough out onto a lightly floured surface. Knead until smooth and elastic, 8 to 10 minutes. Cover; let rest for 10 minutes.
4. Divide the dough into 12 equal pieces. Form each into a smooth ball. Place about 2 inches apart on greased cookie sheets; press to flatten slightly. Cover with buttered wax paper and a towel. Let rise in warm place, away from drafts, until doubled in volume, for 45 minutes.
5. Meanwhile preheat the oven to moderate (350°).
6. Brush the tops of the rolls with the melted butter. Sprinkle with instant chopped onion. Sprinkle half the rolls with sesame seeds and half with poppy seeds.
7. Bake in the preheated moderate oven (350°) for 20 to 25 minutes or until rolls are browned and sound hollow when tapped with the fingers. Remove to wire racks to cool.

Cardamon Rolls.

Cardamom Rolls

For a sweet breakfast treat, pour a thin sugar glaze over the tops.

Bake at 375° for 10 to 15 minutes.

Makes about 2¹/₂ dozen rolls.

1 envelope active dry yeast	**crushed cardamom seeds**
¹/₂ cup sugar	**¹/₂ teaspoon salt**
¹/₄ cup warm water	**4 to 4¹/₂ cups *unsifted***
1 cup evaporated milk	**all-purpose flour**
¹/₄ cup (¹/₂ stick) butter	**2 eggs, slightly beaten**
1 teaspoon coarsely	

1. Sprinkle the yeast and ¹/₂ teaspoon of the sugar over them warm water in a small cup; stir to dissolve the yeast. Let stand until bubbly, 10 minutes.
2. Combine the remaining sugar, milk, butter, cardamom and salt in a small saucepan. Heat just until the butter melts. Pour into a large bowl. Cool to lukewarm. Stir in the yeast mixture.
3. Beat in 3 cups of the flour until smooth. Beat in the eggs, one at a time, until well blended. Gradually stir in enough of the remaining flour to make a soft dough.
4. Turn out onto a lightly floured surface. Knead until smooth and elastic, about 8 minutes. Press into a buttered bowl; bring the buttered-side up. Cover with buttered wax paper and a towel. Let rise in a warm place, away from drafts, until doubled in volume, about 1 hour.
5. Punch down dough; knead a few times.
6. Roll the dough into "knots" or "snail-shaped" rolls: Pinch off about 2 tablespoons of dough for each roll. Roll each into a 9-inch-long rope. For "knots," tie each rope into a knot; tuck ends under and place on greased cookie sheets. For "snails," hold one end of the rope down on the greased cookie sheet; wind the

other end around and around in a tight spiral, and tuck the end under. Arrange the rolls about 2½ inches apart on the sheets. Cover with buttered wax paper and a towel. Let rise in a warm place, away from drafts, until doubled in volume, about 45 minutes.
7. Meanwhile, preheat the oven to moderate (375°). Bake in the preheated moderate oven (375°) for 10 to 15 minutes, or until golden brown. Transfer to wire racks to cool. Serve warm.

Caramelized Carrot Swirl

Bake at 400° for 20 to 25 minutes.

Makes 4 loaves (6 servings each).

Carrot Filling:
6 cups shredded carrots (about 2 pounds)
½ cup firmly packed brown sugar
½ cup granulated sugar
½ cup Cognac
½ teaspoon ground cinnamon
¼ teaspoon ground ginger

Dough:
8 cups *unsifted* all-purpose flour
½ cup granulated sugar
1 tablespoon salt
½ teaspoon ground ginger
2 envelopes fast-rising dry yeast
1½ cups buttermilk
6 tablespoons butter or margarine
¼ cup plain yogurt
4 eggs, slightly beaten
1 egg white
1 tablespoon water

1. Prepare Carrot Filling: Combine carrots, brown and granulated sugars, Cognac, cinnamon and ginger in large skillet. Bring to boiling, stirring constantly. Lower heat; cook, stirring constantly, until liquid has evaporated and carrots are caramelized, slightly darkened, about 20 minutes. Reserve.
2. To prepare Dough: Set aside 1 cup of the flour. Mix remaining 7 cups flour, sugar, salt, ginger and yeast in large bowl.
3. Combine buttermilk, butter and yogurt in medium-size saucepan. Heat to 130° (mixture should feel comfortably hot to the touch). Mix into dry ingredients. Mix in eggs. Stir in enough of the reserved 1 cup flour to make soft dough.
4. Turn dough out onto lightly floured surface. Knead until smooth and elastic, 8 to 10 minutes. Cover; let rest 10 minutes.
5. Divide dough into 4 equal pieces. Roll out each piece into 12 × 9-inch rectangle. Spread each with one quarter of the filling to within ½-inch of the edges. Starting at a long end, roll up each jelly-roll fashion. Pinch along seams to seal. Shape each roll into a ring; pinch ends together to make unbroken circle. Place rings seam-side down on greased cookie sheets. With kitchen scissors, make 12 evenly spaced cuts around outer edge, cutting about three quarters toward center. Twist each slice, turning cut-side up to show pinwheel. Cover; let rise in warm place, away

from drafts, until doubled in volume, 35 to 45 minutes.
6. Beat egg white with water in small cup. Brush on loaves.
7. Bake in preheated hot oven (400°) for 20 to 25 minutes or until loaves are browned and sound hollow when tapped with fingers. Remove cookie sheets to wire racks to cool. Serve warm or at room temperature. Store in refrigerator.

Saffron Raisin Loaf

Since it takes about 75,000 flower blossoms to yield about 1 pound of saffron, this orange, pungent spice is very expensive. But a little goes a long way.

Bake at 350° for 30 to 35 minutes.

Makes 2 loaves (8 servings each).

6 cups *unsifted* all-purpose flour
½ cup currants
½ cup raisins
½ cup pecans, chopped
1 tablespoon grated grapefruit rind
1 tablespoon grated orange rind
1 teaspoon grated lemon rind
1 teaspoon salt
½ teaspoon ground nutmeg
2 envelopes fast-rising dry yeast
¾ cup water
½ cup honey
½ cup (1 stick) butter or margarine
⅓ cup milk
⅛ teaspoon saffron threads
2 eggs, slightly beaten

1. Set aside 1 cup of the all-purpose flour. Mix together remaining 5 cups flour, currants, raisins, pecans, grated grapefruit, orange and lemon rinds, salt, nutmeg and yeast in large bowl.
2. Combine water, honey, butter, milk and saffron in medium-size saucepan. Heat to 130° (mixture should feel comfortably hot to the touch.) Stir into dry ingredients. Mix in eggs. Mix in just enough of the reserved flour to make soft dough.
3. Turn dough out onto lightly floured surface. Knead until smooth and elastic, 6 to 8 minutes. Cover; let rest 10 minutes.
4. Divide dough in half. Shape into loaves. Place in 2 greased 8½ × 4½ × 2½-inch baking pans. Cover; let rise in warm place, away from drafts, until doubled in volume, about 2 hours.
5. Bake in preheated moderate oven (350°) for 30 to 35 minutes or until loaves are browned and sound hollow when tapped with fingers. Remove breads from pans to wire racks to cool.

Cruller

A long, twisted yeast doughnut. The name comes from the Dutch word *krulle,* "twisted cake." French crullers are different in that they are made from a cream puff dough which is piped into a ring shape, fried and glazed or iced.

Doughnut

Doughnuts are made of either a yeast or baking powder dough, and fried in hot oil until crisp and browned. Traditionally, they are ring-shaped, but variations give rise to twisted or filled round cakes.

Doughnuts once existed as plain, fried cakes and were made by prehistoric American Indians. The holes are a later addition (or should we say subtraction). According to a popular story, in the 1800's, a sea captain became dissatisfied with the fried cakes his mother had made because the centers were uncooked. To rid the cakes of the uncooked dough, he poked holes in the centers and, hence, what we now call doughnuts.

Doughnuts can easily be made at home. With our recipes for yeast-raised, cake-style baking powder and cream puff doughs, homemade doughnuts are just minutes away.

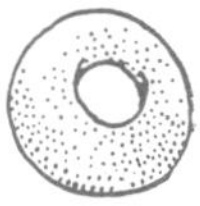

Yeast-Raised Doughnuts
(Basic recipe)

This recipe can also be made into popular Bismarcks, Twists or French Market doughnuts.

Makes about 2 dozen doughnuts.

1¼ cups milk	½ cup sugar
⅓ cup butter or margarine, cut up	1 teaspoon salt
5 cups *unsifted* all-purpose flour	1 teaspoon ground nutmeg
2 envelopes active dry yeast	2 eggs
	Vegetable oil for frying

1. Heat milk and butter in a small saucepan over low heat until very warm. ("Very warm" should feel comfortably warm when dropped on wrist.) Butter does not have to melt.
2. Combine 2 cups of the flour, yeast, sugar, salt and nutmeg in a large bowl. With electric mixer on low speed, stir in warm milk mixture until smooth.
3. Beat on medium speed 2 minutes, occasionally scraping bowl. Beat in ½ cup more flour and the eggs.
4. Stir in about 1½ cups more flour with spoon to make a soft dough. Turn out onto lightly floured surface; knead until smooth and elastic, about 8 minutes, adding only enough of remaining cup of flour to keep dough from sticking.
5. Place dough in oiled bowl, turning dough over to grease top. Cover bowl with a towel; let rise in a warm, draft-free place, 1 to 1½ hours or until double in volume.
6. Punch dough down; knead 8 to 10 times to remove

any large bubbles; cover with bowl; let rest 15 minutes. Meanwhile, oil 2 large cookie sheets.
7. Roll dough ¼-inch thick; cut with floured 3- to 3½-inch doughnut cutter. Lift off trimmings and doughnut centers. Press trimmings together; re-roll and cut. Transfer doughnuts to cookie sheets; brush top with oil to prevent a skin from forming. Cover with plastic wrap. Let rise in a warm place 45 minutes or until double in volume.
8. Fry as for French Crullers (recipe in this chapter).

Old-fashioned Cake Doughnuts
(Basic recipe)

Makes about 2 dozen doughnuts.

4 cups *sifted* all-purpose flour	¼ cup (½ stick) butter, softened
5 teaspoons baking powder	¾ cup sugar
½ teaspoon salt	2 eggs
½ teaspoon ground nutmeg or mace	¾ cup milk
	1 teaspoon vanilla
	Vegetable oil for frying

1. Sift flour, baking powder, salt and nutmeg onto wax paper.
2. Beat butter, sugar and eggs in a large bowl with electric mixer until well mixed. Beat in milk and vanilla. Beat in about 1¼ cups of the flour mixture.
3. Stir in remaining flour mixture with spoon until mixture forms soft dough. If dough is too sticky to handle, sprinkle with flour.
4. Wrap dough in plastic wrap; chill at least 2 hours or overnight.
5. Roll dough on lightly floured surface to a ⅓-inch thickness; cut out with lightly floured 3-inch doughnut cutter. Lift off dough around doughnuts and in center. Doughnut "holes" can be fried separately, if you wish. Re-roll and cut out trimmings.
6. Fill a large saucepan or Dutch oven ⅓ full with oil. Heat to 370° on a deep-fat thermometer.
7. Transfer doughnuts to hot oil with a flexible spatula or pancake turner, frying 2 or 3 at a time. Fry, turning once, 3 minutes or until golden. Drain on paper toweling. Cool.

French Crullers

Makes about 1 dozen crullers.

1 cup water	purpose flour
¼ cup (½ stick) butter or margarine	3 eggs
¼ cup sugar	Vegetable oil for frying
½ teaspoon salt	Honey Glaze *(recipe under Glazes)*
1 cup *sifted* all-	

1. Combine water, butter, sugar and salt in a large saucepan; bring to boiling.
2. Add flour all at once. Stir vigorously just until mixture leaves side of pan. Remove from heat. Add

eggs, 1 at a time, beating well after each addition. Refrigerate mixture 15 minutes.

3. Cut 12 three-inch squares of foil; oil each. Fit pastry bag with a ½-inch star tube; fill with dough. Press a 3-inch ring of dough onto each square.

4. Fill a large saucepan half full with vegetable oil. Heat to 370° on a deep-fat thermometer. Hold ring of dough close to surface of oil; carefully slip from foil into oil. Or, drop dough and foil into hot oil. Crullers will slip off foil as they cook; remove foil with tongs. Fry 3 at a time, turning once, about 3 to 5 minutes or until golden and puffed. Drain on paper toweling; cool.

5. Dip top half of cruellers into Honey Glaze, letting excess drip back into bowl. Place, glazed side up, on wire rack over wax paper; let crullers stand until dry.

Orange Beignets

Scrumptious and fast to make, these airy dropped doughnuts are prepared from cream-puff dough.

Makes about 2½ dozen puffs.

French Crullers (recipe in this chapter)

1 teaspoon grated orange rind
Superfine sugar

Prepare batter for French Crullers as directed and stir in orange rind. Drop batter by teaspoonfuls into hot oil heated to 370° as for French Crullers. Fry 6 at a time, until golden and puffed, about 5 minutes. Puffs should turn themselves as they cook; if not, turn once. Drain on paper toweling. Cool; toss with superfine sugar in a plastic or paper bag.

Glazed Jelly Doughnuts

Makes about 2 dozen doughnuts.

Yeast-Raised Doughnuts (recipe in this chapter)
Vanilla Glaze or Orange Glaze

(recipes under Glazes)
1 cup red currant or other flavor jelly

1. Prepare dough and let rise as directed for Yeast-Raised Doughnuts. Roll out, but cut with a 3-inch round cutter; let rise. Fry, drain and cool as for Yeast-Raised Doughnuts.

2. Hollow out center of each doughnut about ¼-inch deep. Dip top half of doughnut into Vanilla Glaze; let dry. Fill center with jelly.

Bismarcks

Makes about 2 dozen doughnuts.

Yeast-Raised Doughnuts (recipe in this chapter)
1 cup red currant or

other flavor jelly
10X (confectioners') sugar

1. Prepare dough and let rise as directed for Yeast-Raised Doughnuts. Roll out, but cut with a 3-inch round cutter; let rise. Fry, drain and cool as for Yeast-Raised Doughnuts.

2. Cut a slit in one side of each doughnut. Fit a pastry bag with a small plain tube; fill with jelly; fill each doughnut. Dust lightly with 10X sugar.

Maple-Glazed Twists

Makes about 2 dozen twists.

Yeast-Raised Doughnuts (recipe in this chapter)

Maple Glaze (recipe under Glazes)

1. Prepare dough and let rise as directed for Yeast-Raised Doughnuts. Divide dough into quarters. Cut one quarter into 6 pieces; cover others.

2. Roll each piece on floured surface into a rope about 14 inches long. Bring ends together and press to seal into a ring. Twist ring a few times. Place on oiled cookie sheet; let rise; fry and drain as for Yeast-Raised Doughnuts.

3. Brush Maple Glaze over twists; let stand until dry.

Chocolate Cake Doughnuts

Makes about 2 dozen doughnuts.

Old-fashioned Cake Doughnuts (recipe in this chapter)
1 cup unsweetened cocoa
½ teaspoon baking

soda
Mint or Vanilla Glaze (recipes under Glazes)
Crumb Topping (recipe follows)

1. Prepare recipe for doughnuts as directed, except in step 1 use only 3½ cups of flour. Add cocoa and baking soda to sifter with other dry ingredients. And in step 2 increase sugar to 1 cup; increase milk to 1 cup.

2. Roll out; cut and fry as for Old-fashioned Cake Doughnuts.

3. Dip top half of doughnuts into Mint or Vanilla Glaze. While glaze is still wet, dip into Crumb Topping; let dry. Sprinkle with 10X (confectioners') sugar, if you wish.

Crumb Topping: Combine 1 cup chocolate doughnut crumbs (2 or 3 doughnuts crumbed in blender), ¼ cup finely chopped walnuts and 2 tablespoons light brown sugar in small bowl until well mixed.

French Market Doughnuts

Makes about 2 dozen doughnuts.

Yeast-Raised Doughnuts *(recipe in this chapter)*	**1 cup heavy cream 10X (confectioners') sugar**

1. Prepare recipe for Yeast-Raised Doughnuts but add only ½ cup of the milk. Omit butter. Heat the ½ cup milk and the cream as in step 1.
2. Let dough rise; roll out and cut into 3-inch squares; let rise. Fry and drain as for Yeast-Raised Doughnuts; dust lightly with 10X sugar. Serve warm.

Zucchini-Nut Cake Doughnuts

Makes about 2 dozen doughnuts.

Old-fashioned Cake Doughnuts *(recipe in this chapter)* **2 small zucchini, shredded 1 cup finely chopped**	**walnuts 1 teaspoon grated lemon rind Lemon Glaze** *(recipe under Glazes)*

1. Prepare recipe for doughnuts as directed, except in step 2 add shredded zucchini, walnuts and rind.
2. Roll out; cut and fry as for Old-fashioned Cake Doughnuts.
3. Dip top half of doughnuts into Lemon Glaze; let dry.

Whole Wheat Cake Doughnuts

Makes about 2 dozen doughnuts.

Old-fashioned Cake Doughnuts *(recipe in this chapter)* **2 cups** *unsifted* **whole**	**wheat flour 10X (confectioners') sugar**

1. Prepare recipe for doughnuts as directed but use only 2 cups sifted all-purpose flour and add the whole wheat flour.
2. Roll out; cut and fry as for Old-fashioned Cake Doughnuts.
3. Toss doughnuts with 10X sugar in a paper or plastic bag.

Carrot-Raisin Cake Doughnuts

Makes about 2 dozen doughnuts.

Old-fashioned Cake Doughnuts *(recipe in this chapter)* **3 small carrots, finely shredded (1½ cups)**	**½ cup raisins, cut up ½ teaspoon ground cinnamon Orange Glaze** *(recipe under Glazes)*

1. Prepare recipe for doughnuts as directed, except in

Pictured opposite: (top) French Crullers, page 104; Orange Beignets, page 105; (second row) Glazed Jelly Doughnuts, page 105; Bismarcks, page 105; Maple-glazed Twists, page 105; French Marked Doughnuts, page 106; (third row) Chocolate Cake Doughnuts, page 105; Zucchini-Nut Cake Doughnuts, page 106; Whole Wheat Cake Doughnuts, page 106; Banana-Spice Cake Doughnuts, page 106; Carrot-Raisin Cake Doughnuts, page 106.

step 2 add shredded carrots, raisins and cinnamon.
2. Roll out; cut and fry as for Old-fashioned Cake Doughnuts.
3. Dip top half of doughnuts into Orange Glaze; let dry.

Banana-Spice Cake Doughnuts

Makes about 2 dozen doughnuts.

Old-Fashioned Cake Doughnuts *(recipe in this chapter)* **½ teaspoon baking soda 1 teaspoon ground cinnamon ½ teaspoon ground**	**cloves 1 cup mashed ripe bananas (2 or 3) Chocolate Glaze** *(recipe under Glazes)* **Chopped almonds or flaked coconut**

1. Prepare recipe for doughnuts as directed, except in step 1 add baking soda, cinnamon and cloves to sifter with other dry ingredients. And in step 2 add only ⅓ cup of milk along with the mashed banana.
2. Roll out; cut and fry as for Old-fashioned Cake Doughnuts.
3. Dip top half of doughnuts into Chocolate Glaze. While glaze is still wet, dip into almonds or coconut; let dry.

Challah (Sabbath Night Braided Bread)

This bread is delicious toasted and makes beautiful puffy French toast. For orthodox Jews, it is for either a meat or a dairy meal.

Bake at 375° for 30 minutes.

Makes 2 loaves.

2 envelopes active dry yeast 1 tablespoon sugar 2 cups very warm water 1 tablespoon salt	**4 eggs, lightly beaten 8 to 8½ cups** *sifted* **all-purpose flour 1 egg 1 tablespoon water**

1. Sprinkle yeast and sugar into very warm water in a large bowl; stir to dissolve. ("Very warm water" should

(continued)

feel warm when dropped on wrist.) Stir in salt, 4 eggs and 4 cups of the flour; beat until well mixed. Stir in enough remaining flour to form a soft dough.

2. Turn dough out onto floured surface. Knead about 5 minutes or until smooth and elastic, using as much of the remaining flour as necessary. Press dough into an oiled large bowl; turn to bring oiled side up; cover. Let rise in a warm place, away from draft, until double in volume, about 1 hour. Turn dough out onto lightly floured surface and knead to distribute gas bubbles.

3. Cut dough evenly into 6 pieces. Roll each piece with floured hands into a 15-inch rope, making the rope fat in the middle and thin at the ends. Braid 3 of the ropes together for 1 loaf, pinching ends together; repeat. Place loaves on greased cookie sheet; cover. Let rise in a warm place until double in volume, about 30 minutes.. Brush gently with a mixture of remaining egg and water. Preheat oven to 375°.

4. Bake in a preheated moderate oven (375°) for 30 minutes or until loaves sound hollow when thumped with fingers. Cool on wire racks.

Fast-Rising Yeast Breads

For the old-fashioned flavor of homemade yeast breads in a lot less time, use fast-rising dry yeast.

TIPS FOR USING FAST-RISING DRY YEAST

Follow these pointers for using the new yeast in our delicious breads, as well as in your own favorite recipes.

• Always include water in the ingredients. If your recipe calls for all milk or liquid other than water, decrease the amount of liquid by 1/4 cup per envelope of fast-rising yeast used and substitute an equal amount of water.

• Combine the yeast with about two-thirds of the flour and the other dry ingredients in a large bowl. No need to dissolve the yeast in a liquid first. See Note, below.

• Heat the liquids and solid or liquid fats, but not the eggs, in a saucepan until hot to the touch, 130°. This is hotter than the 110° to 115° usually required if the yeast is being dissolved directly in a liquid.

• Stir the hot liquids into the dry ingredients; add the eggs, if using. Blend at low speed with an electric mixer; then beat at medium speed for 3 minutes. Stir in enough remaining flour to make a soft dough.

• Follow the recipe directions for kneading and rising (the rising time is reduced by one-half to one-third). Start checking the dough halfway through the suggested rising time in a recipe calling for regular yeast.

SUBSTITUTING REGULAR ACTIVE DRY YEAST FOR FAST-RISING

Note: When combining the yeast with a portion of the flour and other dry ingredients, combine with about one-third of the flour (instead of two-thirds as with the fast-rising) and other dry ingredients. Also increase the rising times by one-third to one-half.

Pictured opposite: Glazed Orange Rolls, page 100.

Overnight Seed Bread and Nutty Maple-Honey Buns

Bake at 350° for 20 to 25 minutes.

Makes 1 loaf bread (12 servings) and 36 miniature sticky buns (12 servings).

7 cups *sifted* all-purpose flour	1/2 cup currants
2 tablespoons sugar	3/4 cup chopped pecans
1 teaspoon salt	2 tablespoons poppy seeds
2 packages fast-rising dry yeast	2 tablespoons sesame seeds
2 cups hot water (125° to 130°)	2 tablespoons wheat germ
2 tablespoons butter, softened	1 egg white
1/2 cup honey	1 teaspoon water
1/4 cup maple syrup	3/4 teaspoon ground ginger
3 tablespoons chopped candied ginger	2 tablespoons light brown sugar

1. Set aside 1/2 cup of flour. Combine the remaining flour, sugar, salt and yeast in a bowl. Stir in the water and butter. Beat until smooth. Gradually stir in enough reserved flour to make a soft dough.

2. Knead on a floured surface until smooth and elastic, 3 to 5 minutes. Invert a bowl over the dough; let rise for 15 minutes.

3. Grease and flour a 9-inch-round layer-cake pan. Combine the honey and maple syrup. Pour into thirty-six 1-inch cupcake cups or a 13 × 9 × 2-inch baking pan. Combine the candied ginger, 1/4 cup of the currants and 1/2 cup of the pecans. Sprinkle equally over the cupcake cups or over the pan.

4. Divide the dough in half. Set half aside, under the inverted bowl. Divide the remaining dough into 3 equal pieces. Roll each piece into a 16-inch-long rope.

5. Cut 3 lengths of wax paper, each 18 inches long. Spread the poppy seeds on one, the sesame seeds on another, the wheat germ on the third. Beat the egg white with the 1 teaspoon of water in a bowl.

6. Brush one rope with the egg wash; roll in the poppy seeds. Brush another rope with the wash; roll in the sesame seeds. Brush the third with the wash; roll in the wheat germ. Reserve the remaining seeds and wheat germ.

7. Lay the ropes, side by side, on a flat surface. Braid together gently, trying not to shake off the seeds. Coil the braid into the prepared layer-cake pan. Carefully spoon any excess seeds and wheat germ into the seedless areas on the braid. Cover loosely; refrigerate overnight.

8. Roll out the remaining dough into a 20 × 10-inch

(continued)

rectangle. Combine the remaining currants and pecans, the ground ginger and brown sugar. Sprinkle over the dough; gently press into the dough.

9. Roll the dough up from a long side. Slice into 36 pieces. Place 1 piece, cut-side up, in each cupcake cup or arrange in rows in the pan. Cover loosely; refrigerate overnight.

10. Preheat the oven to moderate (350°).

11. Bake the bread and the buns in the preheated moderate oven (350°) for 20 to 25 minutes or until firm to the touch and golden brown. Turn the buns out onto wax paper immediately, sticky-side up. Cool the bread in the pan on a rack for 10 minutes. Turn out onto the rack to cool.

Dark Rye Bread

Use this bread as a base for hors d'oeuvres, especially smoked ham.

Bake at 375° for 35 to 40 minutes.

Makes one large round (12 slices).

2 cups rye flour
1/2 cup cocoa powder (not a mix)
1 tablespoon instant coffee powder
2 envelopes fast-rising dry yeast
1 1/2 cups very warm water
1 1/2 cups molasses
2 tablespoons brown sugar

2 tablespoons caraway seeds
2 teaspoons salt
2 tablespoons butter or margarine, melted
2 1/2 cups whole-wheat blend flour
1 egg, lightly beaten with 1 teaspoon water
Caraway seeds

1. Combine the rye flour, cocoa and instant coffee in a small bowl. Dissolve the yeast in 1/2 cup of the very warm water in a cup. ("Very warm water" should feel comfortably warm when a few drops are sprinkled on your wrist.)

2. Combine the molasses, sugar, caraway seeds and salt with the remaining 1 cup very warm water in a large bowl; stir with a wooden spoon to blend.

3. Stir in the rye flour mixture, yeast mixture, melted butter or margarine and 1 cup of the whole-wheat flour. Beat until the batter is smooth.

4. Sprinkle the remaining 1 1/2 cups whole-wheat flour on a bread board or work surface. Scrape the dough out of the bowl onto the flour. Work in the flour, adding more flour, if necessary, to form a dough that doesn't stick to the surface. Knead the dough until smooth and elastic, about 10 minutes. Place in a greased large bowl; turn to coat dough all over. Cover with buttered wax paper and a towel.

5. Let rise until doubled in volume, about 30 minutes. Shape into a large round on a cookie sheet. Brush the top with the egg beaten with 1 teaspoon water; sprinkle with additional caraway seeds.

6. Meanwhile, preheat the oven to moderate (375°).

7. Bake in the preheated moderate oven (375°) for 35

to 40 minutes, or until the loaf sounds hollow when lightly tapped.

Whole Wheat Bread

Perfect for sandwiches, if it's not all eaten while still warm!

Bake at 400° for 10 minutes, then at 350° for 40 minutes.

Makes 2 loaves (12 slices each).

2 envelopes fast-rising dry yeast
1 cup very warm water
2 cups milk
1/2 cup firmly packed brown sugar
2 teaspoons salt
7 cups whole-wheat

blend flour
1/4 cup butter-flavor vegetable shortening
Butter or margarine, melted
Coarse salt (optional)

1. Dissolve the yeast in the very warm water in a large bowl. ("Very warm water" should feel comfortably warm when a few drops are sprinkled on your wrist.) Let stand for 5 minutes.

2. Scald, but do not boil, the milk in a medium-size saucepan. Remove from the heat; stir in the brown sugar and salt until dissolved. Cool slightly.

3. Add the milk mixture to the yeast mixture in the bowl, stirring constantly with a large wooden spoon. Add 3 cups of the flour and the melted shortening, still stirring constantly. Gradually beat in the remaining flour, adding more flour if necessary, to form a dough that doesn't stick to the bowl.

4. Turn out the dough onto a lightly floured bread board. Knead for 10 minutes, or until smooth and elastic. Shape into a ball; place in a greased bowl; turn to coat the dough all over. Cover with buttered wax paper and a towel.

5. Let rise in a warm place, away from drafts, until doubled in volume, about 45 minutes. Punch down the dough; turn out onto a floured board. Let rest for 5 minutes.

6. Cut the dough in half; roll each half into a 12 × 9-inch rectangle; roll up tightly from a short end; place seam-side down in a greased 9 × 5 × 3-inch loaf pan. Brush with the melted butter or margarine; sprinkle with coarse salt, if desired. Cover with buttered wax paper and a towel. Let rise until doubled in volume, about 30 minutes.

7. Meanwhile, preheat the oven to hot (400°).

8. Bake in the preheated hot oven (400°) for 10 minutes. Lower the oven temperature to moderate (350°). Bake for 40 minutes longer, or until the tops are golden brown. Cool on wire racks.

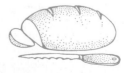

Easy Yeast Breads

If you love warm, fresh bread, but don't have time to knead and wait for the dough to rise twice, try these easy mix-and-bake breads. The electric mixer does much of the work for you. The results are delicious—their flavor and fragrance may have you baking your own bread regularly.

Pumpernickel Raisin Bread

Bake at 375° for 40 minutes.

Makes 1 loaf.

2 packages active dry yeast	**milk powder**
1 cup whole wheat flour	**2 teaspoons salt**
1 cup rye flour	**1½ cups very warm water**
1½ cups *sifted* **all-purpose flour**	**¼ cup molasses**
½ cup instant dry	**2 tablespoons vegetable oil**
	½ cup raisins

1. Mix yeast, whole wheat flour, rye flour, ½ cup of the all-purpose flour, dry milk and salt in a large bowl.
2. Add water, molasses and oil ("very warm water" should feel comfortably warm when dropped on wrist); beat with electric mixer at medium speed, 3 minutes. Stir in remaining flour to make a stiff dough. Stir in raisins.
3. Cover bowl with a towel. Let dough rise in a warm place, away from drafts, 45 minutes or until double in volume.
4. Stir dough down. Spoon into greased 9 × 5 × 3-inch loaf pan, pushing dough well into corners.
5. Let rise again in a warm draft-free place, 35 minutes or until double in volume. Preheat oven to 375°.
6. Bake in a preheated hot oven (375°) for 40 minutes or until bread sounds hollow when tapped. Cool on wire rack.

Alfalfa Wheat Bread

A nutty, moist casserole bread that's nutritious and easy to prepare.
Bake at 375° for 30 to 35 minutes.

Makes one round loaf.

1 cup water	**yeast**
½ cup plain yogurt	**2 teaspoons salt**
2 tablespoons molasses	**1½ to 2 cups** *unsifted* **whole wheat flour**
1 cup *unsifted* **all-purpose flour**	**1 cup alfalfa sprouts, coarsely chopped**
1 envelope active dry	**Cornmeal**

1. Heat water, yogurt and molasses in a small saucepan over low heat just until very warm, about 120°. (Mixture will appear curdled.)
2. Combine flour, yeast and salt in a large bowl. Gradually beat in yogurt mixture with electric mixer on low speed until mixed. Beat in 1½ cups whole wheat flour slowly. Beat batter on medium speed 2 minutes; increase speed to medium-high; beat 2 minutes more.
3. With spoon, stir in sprouts and enough of the remaining whole wheat flour to make a soft dough that will stay in a mound. Cover bowl with a towel. Let rise in a warm place, away from draft, until double in volume, about 45 minutes.
4. Grease a 1½-quart casserole dish; sprinkle bottom and side with cornmeal or packaged bread crumbs. Stir dough and turn into prepared dish. Sprinkle top with more alfalfa sprouts, if you wish. Cover with towel. Let rise in a warm place, away from draft, until almost double in volume, 45 minutes.
5. Bake in a moderate oven (375°) for 30 minutes or until golden brown and bread sounds hollow when lightly tapped with fingertips.
6. Loosen bread around edge with metal spatula; remove to wire rack; cool completely. Wrap in foil or plastic; store in refrigerator.

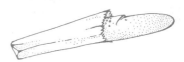

Frozen Bread Dough

Bread dough, commercially frozen and ready for you to thaw and use, is a miracle worker. It can be turned into all kinds of wonderful breads and coffee cakes. You can buy plain, frozen bread dough or sweet dough.

Lemon Cheese Braid

Bake at 350° for 30 minutes.

Makes 1 braid.

1 loaf (14 ounces) frozen sweet dough, thawed overnight in refrigerator	**(8 ounces) cream cheese, softened**
OR: 1 loaf (1 pound) frozen plain dough, thawed overnight in refrigerator	**1 egg yolk**
	2 tablespoons sugar
	½ teaspoon vanilla
	1 teaspoon grated lemon rind
1 package	**1 egg, beaten with 1 teaspoon water**

1. Allow dough to stand at room temperature on a lightly floured surface for 1 hour. Roll and push to a 16 × 8-inch rectangle. Let rest while making filling.
2. Beat cheese, egg yolk, sugar and vanilla in small bowl with electric mixer. Stir in lemon rind.
3. Place dough on large greased cookie sheet; spread cheese down center third of dough. Cut dough from

(continued)

outside to filling, spacing cuts 1 inch apart. Overlap dough strips alternately from left and right to cover cheese mixture.

4. Brush braid with egg mixture; let stand in warm place 30 minutes. Preheat oven to 350°.

5. Bake in a preheated moderate oven (350°) for 30 minutes. Remove to rack. Serve warm.

Georgian Cheese Bread

Bake at 375° for 35 minutes.

Makes 8 servings.

1 loaf (1 pound) frozen plain bread dough, thawed overnight in refrigerator	2 eggs
	$1/2$ teaspoon salt
	$1/2$ cup dairy sour cream
16 ounces Muenster cheese	1 tablespoon butter or margarine

1. Allow dough to stand at room temperature on a lightly floured surface for 1 hour. Roll dough into 9-inch circle. Continue to roll and pat dough to make larger circle 18 to 20 inches in diameter. Let rest while making the cheese filling.

2. Shred Muenster cheese into large bowl. Beat eggs in small bowl; measure out 2 tablespoons; reserve; stir remaining eggs, the salt and sour cream into cheese in bowl, mixing thoroughly.

3. Generously butter a 9-inch pie plate. Place dough loosely in pan, draping excess over sides. Spoon in filling, making a flat circle. Gather the dough loosely to the center of the filling, turning pan as you go, pleating the folds. Twist ends into a topknot in center of the pie. Let rest 30 minutes, Preheat oven to 375°. Brush top of dough with reserved egg.

4. Bake in a preheated moderate oven (375°) for 35 minutes. If crust is browning too fast, lower temperature to 350°. Let cool slightly and cut into wedges.

Golden Orange Rolls

Bake at 350° for 25 minutes.

Makes 16 rolls.

1 loaf (14 ounces) frozen sweet dough, thawed	2 tablespoons butter, softened
OR: 1 loaf plain dough, thawed overnight in refrigerator	1 orange
	$1/4$ cup slivered almonds
	$1/4$ cup granulated sugar
$1/3$ cup firmly packed brown sugar	$1/3$ cup golden raisins

1. Allow dough to stand at room temperature on a lightly floured surface for 1 hour. Roll and push dough to a 20 × 9-inch rectangle. Let rest while making filling.

2. Combine brown sugar and butter in small bowl. Grate rind from orange (1 tablespoon) and reserve. squeeze juice from orange; stir 2 tablespoons into brown sugar mixture. Spread in bottom of 9 × 9 × 2-inch baking pan. Sprinkle with almonds.

3. Mix orange rind and granulated sugar. Stir in raisins; sprinkle over dough.

4. Roll jelly-roll fashion from long side. Cut into $1^1/4$-inch slices. Place in prepared pan; cover with cloth and let rise 45 minutes, until double in volume. Preheat oven to 350°.

5. Bake in a preheated moderate oven (350°) for 25 minutes. Invert onto serving platter. Serve warm.

Apricot-Yogurt Chestnut Bread

Bake at 375° for 35 minutes.

Makes 2 loaves (6 slices each).

3 cups *unsifted* unbleached flour	1 cup apricot yogurt
1 cup cooked or shelled chestnuts, chopped	$1/3$ cup apricot nectar
	$1/4$ cup water
OR: 1 cup walnuts, chopped	$1/4$ cup milk
	3 tablespoons butter or margarine
$1/3$ cup dried apricots, chopped	1 egg
$3/4$ teaspoon salt	
$1/2$ teaspoon baking soda	Garnish (*optional*):
	Apricot preserves, strained
1 envelope fast-rising dry yeast	Cooked shelled chestnuts
	Dried apricot halves

1. Set aside 1 cup flour. Mix together the remaining flour, chestnuts, apricots, salt, baking soda and yeast in a large bowl.

2. Combine the apricot yogurt, apricot nectar, water, milk and butter in a medium-size saucepan. Heat to 130° (mixture should feel comfortably hot to the touch). Stir into the dry ingredients. Mix in the egg. Mix in just enough of the reserved 1 cup flour to make a very thick batter. Cover the bowl; let rest for 10 minutes.

3. Divide the batter evenly into two greased $8^1/2 \times 4^1/2 \times 2^1/2$-inch baking pans or other 6-cup baking pans. Cover with buttered wax paper and a towel. Let rise in warm place, away from drafts, until doubled in volume, about 45 minutes.

4. Meanwhile, preheat the oven to moderate (375°).

5. Bake in the preheated moderate oven (375°) for 35 minutes or until the centers spring back when lightly pressed with fingertip and the bottom sounds hollow when tapped with fingers. Remove the breads to a wire rack to cool.

6. Prepare the optional Garnish: Brush the loaves with strained apricot preserves. Garnish the top of the loaves with a chestnut placed on each dried apricot half. Arrange the apricots down the center of the loaves.

Honey Raisin Bread, page 114.

Preheated Ovens for Baking Bread

Bake breads in a preheated oven. The final rising of the dough takes place during the first 10 to 15 minutes of baking time.

Bridie's Irish Soda Bread

Bake at 400° for 40 minutes.

Makes 1 loaf.

4 cups *sifted* all-purpose flour
1 tablespoon sugar
1½ teaspoons salt

1 teaspoon baking soda
1 cup dried currants
1½ cups buttermilk

1. Preheat oven to 400°. Sift flour, sugar, salt and baking soda into a large bowl; stir in currants to coat with flour.
2. Stir in buttermilk, just until flour is moistened. Knead dough 10 times in bowl with lightly-floured hands.
3. Turn dough out onto lightly floured cookie sheet and shape into an 8-inch round. Cut a cross into the top with a floured knife.
4. Bake in a preheated hot oven (400°) for 40 minutes or until loaf turns golden and sounds hollow when tapped. Cool completely on wire rack before slicing.

Steamed Boston Brown Bread

A true New England contribution to our cooking. Its favorite companion is baked beans.

Steam 3 hours.

Bake at 325° for 10 minutes.

Makes two 1-pound loaves.

1 cup cornmeal
1 cup whole-wheat or graham flour
1 cup rye flour
1 teaspoon salt
1 teaspoon baking soda
1 tablespoon water

½ cup molasses
2 tablespoons vinegar or lemon juice
Milk
1 cup raisins
2 tablespoons all-purpose flour

1. Combine cornmeal, whole-wheat flour, rye flour and salt in a large mixing bowl.
2. Stir baking soda into water in a medium-size bowl; add molasses.
3. Put vinegar in a 2-cup measure. Add milk to make 2 cups. Combine with molasses mixture. Stir liquids into dry ingredients until well mixed.
4. Combine raisins and flour in a small bowl; add to batter.
5. Pour batter into two greased 1-quart molds or clean coffee cans. Cover tightly with a double-thickness of aluminum foil.
6. Place molds on rack in kettle. Add boiling water to

(continued)

haltway up sides of molds. Cover kettle. Steam 3 hours, adding more boiling water as necessary to keep proper level. Unmold loaves; place on cookie sheet.

7. Bake in a slow oven (325°) for 10 minutes to dry. Cool loaves.

8. To serve: Purists say to slice bread with a string, never a knife.

Honey Raisin Bread

Bake at 325° for 1 hour, 10 minutes.

Makes 1 loaf (12 slices).

2³/₄ cups *sifted* all-purpose flour	2 tablespoons shortening
1 teaspoon baking powder	¹/₂ cup honey
¹/₂ teaspoon baking soda	³/₄ cup milk
¹/₂ teaspoon salt	¹/₄ cup buttermilk
1 egg	1 cup raisins
	1 cup chopped pecans

1. Preheat the oven to slow (325°). Grease a 9 × 5 × 3-inch loaf pan.

2. Sift together the flour, baking powder, baking soda and salt into a medium-size bowl.

3. Beat together the egg, shortening and honey in a large bowl. Stir in the flour mixture alternately with the milk and buttermilk, just until the dry ingredients are moistened. Stir in the raisins and pecans. Spoon into the prepared pan.

4. Bake in preheated slow oven (325°) for 1 hour and 10 minutes, or until a wooden pick inserted in the center tests clean. If it browns too fast, cover with foil. Remove the bread from the pan to a wire rack. Let stand overnight before slicing.

Country Corn Bread

Bake at 450° for 25 minutes.

Makes two 8 × 8 × 2-inch breads.

1¹/₂ cups yellow cornmeal	1 teaspoon salt
2 cups *sifted* all-purpose flour	2 eggs
2 tablespoons sugar	2 cups milk
4 teaspoon baking powder	¹/₄ cup bacon drippings or shortening, melted

1. Preheat oven to 450°. Combine cornmeal, flour, sugar, baking powder and salt in a large bowl. Add eggs and milk. Stir to make a smooth batter; stir in bacon drippings.

2. Pour into 2 greased 8 × 8 × 2-inch baking pans.

3. Bake in a preheated very hot oven (450°) for 25 minutes or until crusty and golden brown. Cool slightly in pans on wire racks; serve warm.

Corn Bread

Bake at 425° for 40 minutes.

Makes 1 large loaf.

1²/₃ cups *sifted* all-purpose flour	1²/₃ cups yellow cornmeal
²/₃ cup sugar	2 eggs, beaten
5 teaspoons baking powder	1²/₃ cups milk
1 teaspoon salt	¹/₃ cup butter or margarine, melted

1. Sift flour, sugar, baking powder and salt into a large bowl; stir in cornmeal until well blended. Preheat oven to 425°.

2. Add eggs and milk; stir to make a smooth batter; stir in melted butter or margarine, just until blended. (Do not overstir.)

3. Pour into a well-buttered 9 × 5 × 3-inch loaf pan.

4. Bake in a preheated hot oven (425°) for 40 minutes or until golden and a wooden pick inserted in center comes out clean.

5. Cool in pan on wire rack 10 minutes. Loosen around edges with a knife; turn out onto rack. Cool.

Banana Nut Bread

Bake at 325° for 1 hour, 20 minutes.

Makes 1 loaf.

2¹/₂ cups *sifted* all-purpose flour	3 eggs
3 teaspoons baking powder	3 medium-size ripe bananas, peeled and mashed (1 cup)
¹/₂ teaspoon salt	¹/₄ cup wheat germ
¹/₄ teaspoon baking soda	¹/₂ cup finely chopped walnuts
¹/₂ cup (1 stick) butter or margarine	¹/₂ cup raisins, chopped
1 cup sugar	

1. Sift flour, baking powder, salt and baking soda onto wax paper. Grease a 9 × 5 × 3-inch loaf pan; line bottom with wax paper; grease paper.

2. Beat butter, sugar and eggs in a large bowl until light and fluffy; stir in bananas. Preheat oven to 325°.

3. Stir in flour mixture; fold in wheat germ, walnuts and raisins. Pour into prepared pan.

4. Bake in a preheated slow oven (325°) for 1 hour and 20 minutes, or until a wooden pick inserted near the center comes out clean. Cool in pan on a wire rack 10 minutes. Loosen around edges with knife; turn out onto rack; peel off wax paper. Let cool completely. Wrap in aluminum foil and store overnight for easier slicing.

Pictured opposite: Banana Nut Bread.

Corn Bread Sticks

Bake at 450° for 10 minutes.

Makes 14 sticks.

Vegetable oil
1 cup yellow cornmeal
1 teaspoon baking
  soda
1/2 teaspoon salt

1 3/4 cups buttermilk
1 egg, slightly beaten
4 teaspoons butter,
  melted

1. Preheat oven to 450°. Brush cornstick pans with vegetable oil. Put pans in oven, while oven is heating to temperature, just until they are hot.
2. Combine cornmeal, baking soda and salt in a medium-size bowl. Stir in buttermilk, egg and melted butter until batter is smooth.
3. Remove heated cornstick pans from oven; pour in cornmeal batter, filling about 2/3 full.
4. Bake in a preheated very hot oven (450°) for 10 minutes or until browned and have pulled away from sides of pan. Remove from pans; serve warm with butterballs, if you wish.

Apricot-Wheat Germ-Corn Bread

Bake at 375° for 40 minutes.

Makes 2 small loaves.

2/3 cup *sifted* all-
  purpose flour
1/3 cup sugar
3 1/2 teaspoons baking
  powder
1 teaspoon salt
2/3 cup wheat germ

2/3 cup yellow
  cornmeal
3/4 cup chopped dried
  apricots
2 eggs
1 cup milk
1/4 cup vegetable oil

1. Sift flour, sugar, baking powder and salt into a medium-size bowl. Stir in wheat germ, cornmeal and apricots. Preheat oven to 375°.
2. Beat eggs slightly in a small bowl. Stir in milk and oil.
3. Pour liquid ingredients into dry and stir just until flour is evenly moist. Spoon batter into 2 greased 7 3/8 × 3 5/8 × 2 1/4-inch loaf pans.
4. Bake in a preheated moderate oven (375°) for 40 minutes or until wooden pick inserted in the centers comes out clean. Cool in pans on wire rack 10 minutes. Remove from pans; cool completely. Wrap in foil or plastic when cool; store overnight for easier slicing.

Carrot-Walnut Bread

Bake at 350° for 1 hour.

Makes 1 loaf.

1 cup vegetable oil
3/4 cup sugar
2 eggs
1 teaspoon vanilla
1 1/2 cups *sifted* all-
  purpose flour
1 1/2 teaspoons baking
  soda
1 1/2 teaspoons

ground cinnamon
1/2 teaspoon salt
3 large carrots, grated
  (1 1/2 cups)
1 1/2 cups ground
  walnuts
Lemon Glaze (recipe
  follows)

1. Preheat oven to 350°. Grease and flour a 9 × 5 × 3-inch loaf pan.
2. Combine vegetable oil, sugar, eggs and vanilla in a large bowl.
3. Sift flour, baking soda, cinnamon and salt onto wax paper; add to sugar mixture; stir in carrots and walnuts; mix until just blended. Turn into prepared pan.
4. Bake in a preheated moderate oven (350°) for 1 hour or until center springs back when lightly pressed with fingertip. Cool bread in pan 10 minutes. Turn out onto wire rack; cool completely. Spread top with Lemon Glaze.

Lemon Glaze: Combine 1/2 cup 10X (confectioners') sugar, 1 teaspoon grated lemon rind and 1 tablespoon lemon juice in a small bowl; stir until smooth; drizzle over top and sides of Carrot-Walnut Bread.

Steamed Ginger Brown Bread

Makes 2 loaves.

1 package gingerbread
  mix
1/4 cup yellow
  cornmeal

1 teaspoon salt
1 1/2 cups milk
1 cup raisins

1. Combine gingerbread mix, cornmeal and salt in a large bowl; stir in milk until mixture is evenly moist; beat at medium speed with electric mixer 2 minutes, or 300 vigorous strokes by hand; stir in raisins.
2. Pour batter into 2 greased 1-pound coffee cans; cover with foil; fasten with string to hold tightly.
3. Place cans on a rack or trivet in a kettle or steamer (or make a rack by crumpling foil in a doughnut shape to fit bottom of kettle); pour in boiling water to half the depth of cans; cover.
4. Steam 3 hours or until bread is firm and a long skewer inserted in center comes out clean. (Keep water boiling gently during entire cooking time, adding more boiling water, if needed.)
5. Cool bread in cans on a wire rack 5 minutes. Loosen around edges with a knife; turn out onto rack; cool. Slice and serve warm or cold.

Orange Whole-Wheat Bread

Bake at 350° for 1 hour.

Makes 1 loaf.

2 cups *sifted* all-purpose flour	nut-like cereal nuggets
1 cup sugar	1 egg
3¹/₂ teaspoons baking powder	4 teaspoons grated orange rind
1 teaspoon salt	³/₄ cup orange juice
1 cup whole wheat flour	³/₄ cup milk
³/₄ cup crunchy	¹/₄ cup (¹/₂ stick) butter, melted

1. Sift all-purpose flour, sugar, baking powder and salt into a large bowl. Stir in whole wheat flour and cereal nuggets. Preheat oven to 350°.
2. Beat egg slightly in small bowl. Stir in orange rind and juice, milk and butter.
3. Pour liquid ingredients into dry and stir just until flour is evenly moist. Spoon batter into greased 9 × 5 × 3-inch loaf pan.
4. Bake in a preheated moderate oven (350°) for 1 hour or until a wooden pick inserted in the center comes out clean. Cool in pan on wire rack 10 minutes. Remove from pan; cool completely. Wrap in foil or plastic when cool; store overnight.

Pumpkin 'n' Spice Tea Bread

The American Indians were already growing crops of pumpkin, squash and corn when the colonists arrived. The colonists used pumpkin not only for pies but also for delicious breads like this one.

Bake at 350° for 1 hour or for 40 minutes.

Makes two 9 × 5 × 3-inch loaves or four 6 × 3¹/₂ × 2-inch loaves.

2 cups sugar	powder
1 cup vegetable oil	1 teaspoon ground cinnamon
3 eggs, lightly beaten	¹/₂ teaspoon ground nutmeg
1 can (16 ounces) pumpkin	¹/₂ teaspoon ground cloves
3 cups *sifted* all-purpose flour	³/₄ teaspoon salt
1 teaspoon baking soda	10X (confectioners') sugar
³/₄ teaspoon baking	

1. Preheat oven to 350°. Combine sugar and oil with electric mixer in a large bowl. Beat in eggs, 1 at a time, and continue beating until light. Beat in pumpkin, blending well.
2. Sift flour, baking soda, baking powder, cinnamon, nutmeg, cloves and salt into creamed mixture. Beat at low speed until blended.
3. Pour batter into 2 greased 9 × 5 × 3-inch loaf pans, or 4 greased 6 × 3 ¹/₂ × 2-inch loaf pans.*
4. Bake large loaves in a preheated moderate oven

(350°) for 1 hour or small loaves for 40 minutes. Cool in pans on wire rack for 15 minutes. Remove from pans; cool completely. Sprinkle with 10X sugar.
Aluminum disposable pans of this size are sold in supermarkets.

Zucchini Bread

Bake at 350° for 50 minutes.

Makes 2 loaves.

3 cups *sifted* all-purpose flour	1 cup vegetable oil
1 teaspoon salt	2 medium-size zucchini, washed and shredded (2 cups)
1 teaspoon baking powder	
1 teaspoon baking soda	1 tablespoon grated lemon rind
1 tablespoon ground cinnamon	2 teaspoons vanilla
3 eggs	¹/₂ cup coarsely chopped walnuts
1³/₄ cups sugar	

1. Preheat oven to 350°. Sift flour, salt, baking powder, baking soda and cinnamon onto wax paper.
2. Beat eggs lightly in a large bowl; stir in sugar, oil, zucchini, lemon rind and vanilla. Add flour mixture, blending thoroughly; stir in walnuts. Spoon batter into two well-greased 8¹/₂ × 4¹/₂ × 2¹/₂-inch loaf pans.
3. Bake in a preheated moderate oven (350°) for 50 minutes or until centers spring back when lightly pressed with fingertip. Cool in pans on wire rack 10 minutes. Remove from pans and cool thoroughly.

Spoon Bread

Bake at 350° for 40 minutes.

Makes 4 to 6 servings.

5 eggs	¹/₂ teaspoon salt
4 teaspoons baking powder	2 cups milk
¹/₄ cup white cornmeal	2 tablespoons butter or margarine, melted
1 tablespoon sugar	

1. Preheat oven to 350°. Beat eggs with baking powder until foamy in a medium-size bowl.
2. Stir in cornmeal, sugar, salt, milk and melted butter. Pour into a greased 6-cup baking dish.
3. Bake in a preheated moderate oven (350°) for 40 minutes or until puffed and golden. Serve hot in place of potatoes or bread.

From left: Kilkenny Corned Beef, page 434; Bantry Brown Bread, page 118; Shannon Vegetable Platter, page 762.

Bantry Brown Bread

South of Cork lies Bantry Bay, a land of seafaring men who keep warm with large mugs of strong tea and wedges of soda bread.

Bake at 375° for 45 minutes.

Makes 1 seven-inch round (12 generous slices).

1 cup *unsifted* all-purpose flour	2 cups *unsifted* whole wheat flour
1/4 cup sugar	1/4 cup currants
2 teaspoons baking powder	1/4 cup vegetable shortening
1 teaspoon baking soda	1 1/4 cups buttermilk
1 teaspoon salt	2 tablespoons sugar
	1 tablespoon water

1. Preheat the oven to moderate (375°).
2. Sift together the flour, 1/4 cup sugar, baking powder, baking soda and salt into a medium-size bowl. Stir in the whole-wheat flour and currants. Cut in the shortening with a pastry blender or fork until the mixture resembles small peas. Stir in the buttermilk.
3. Turn the dough out onto a lightly floured pastry cloth or board. Knead 10 times.. Shape into a 7-inch round loaf. Place on a cookie sheet. Cut a cross in the top of the dough.
4. Bake in the preheated moderate oven (375°) for 40 minutes; remove from the oven.
5. Combine the 2 tablespoons of sugar and the water in a saucepan; bring to boiling. Brush over the hot loaf. Return to the oven and bake for 5 minutes or until golden.

Onion Rounds

Bake at 400° for 15 minutes.

Makes 10 rolls.

1/3 cup instant minced onion	buttermilk or country-style biscuits
1/3 cup water	(10 biscuits)
1 package (7.5 ounces) refrigerated	1 egg

1. Combine onion and water in a bowl. Let stand 10 minutes. Preheat oven to 400°.

2. Flatten each biscuit into a 3-inch round with a rolling pin; place on lightly buttered cookie sheet.
3. Beat egg in small bowl. Brush on each roll with a pastry brush.
4. Drain water from onion; blot onion between paper toweling; sprinkle evenly over all rolls.
5. Bake in a preheated hot oven (400°) for 15 minutes or until golden brown. Serve warm.

Onion and Bacon Bread

Bake at 425° for 25 minutes.

Makes one 8-inch round loaf.

3 bacon slices	baking mix
2 large onions, sliced (2 cups)	1/2 cup milk
2 tablespoons chopped fresh parsley	1 container (8 ounces) dairy sour cream
2 cups buttermilk	1 egg, slightly beaten
	1/2 teaspoon salt

1. Cook bacon until crisp in large skillet; remove bacon; drain on paper toweling; crumble and reserve.
2. Sauté onions in bacon drippings just until soft but not brown. Remove from heat; stir in parsley.
3. Mix baking mix and milk in a medium-size bowl; stir with fork just until blended. Spread in lightly greased 8 × 1 1/2-inch layer-cake pan. Spoon onion mixture on top. Preheat oven to 425°.
4. Blend sour cream, egg and salt in small bowl. Spoon over onion layer. Sprinkle with reserved bacon; mix partially into cream with fork.
5. Bake in a preheated hot oven (425°) for 25 minutes or until the topping is set and begins to brown. Cool on a wire rack. Cut into wedges and serve warm.

Buckwheat Cakes

Serve these piping hot with lots of butter and maple syrup.

Makes about 40 3-inch cakes.

1 cup light buckwheat flour	2 teaspoons sugar
1 cup *sifted* all-purpose flour	1 teaspoon salt
2 teaspoons baking powder	2 eggs, separated
1 teaspoon baking soda	1/4 cup (1/2 stick) butter, melted
	2 cups buttermilk
	Butter
	Maple syrup

1. Combine buckwheat and all-purpose flours, baking powder, baking soda, sugar and salt on wax paper.
2. Beat egg yolks lightly in medium-size bowl. Stir in flour mixture alternately with melted butter and buttermilk until mixture is smooth.

3. Beat egg whites in a small bowl with electric mixer until soft peaks form. Fold into batter.
4. Drop batter by tablespoonsful onto lightly greased hot griddle; spread to 3-inch rounds. Cook on 1 side until edges begin to brown and bubbles form on surface; turn to brown second side. Serve with butter and maple syrup.

Rice Cakes (Calas)

Makes 18 cakes

1 1/4 cups *sifted* all-purpose flour	1/4 teaspoon salt
1/4 cup sugar	2 eggs, slightly beaten
1 1/2 teaspoons baking powder	1/4 cup milk
1 teaspoon ground cinnamon	1 1/2 cups cold cooked rice
1/2 teaspoon ground nutmeg	Vegetable oil for frying
	10X (confectioners') sugar

1. Combine all ingredients except oil and 10X sugar.
2. Heat 1 1/2 inches oil in a large heavy saucepan to 360° on a deep-fat frying thermometer.
3. Drop batter by tablespoonfuls into hot oil, 4 or 5 at a time. Fry, turning several times, until golden brown, about 5 minutes. Drain cakes on paper toweling. Sprinkle with sugar; serve for breakfast with coffee.

Shredded-Wheat Prune Bread

A wholesome spicy dark bread.

Bake at 350° for 1 hour.

Makes one medium-size loaf.

1 3/4 cups *sifted* all-purpose flour	2/3 cup sugar
2 teaspoons baking powder	2 eggs
1 teaspoon ground cinnamon	1 teaspoon grated lemon rind
1/2 teaspoon salt	1/2 cup milk
1/3 cup butter or margarine	1 cup crumbled shredded wheat
	1 cup chopped pitted prunes

1. Sift flour, baking powder, cinnamon and salt onto wax paper. Preheat oven to 350°.
2. Beat butter, sugar and eggs in a large bowl with electric mixer at high speed until light and fluffy. Stir in lemon rind.
3. Stir in flour mixture alternately with milk until batter is smooth. Stir in shredded wheat and prunes. Spoon into a greased 8 1/2 × 4 1/2 × 2 1/2-inch loaf pan.
4. Bake in a preheated moderate oven (350°) for 1 hour or until a wooden pick inserted in the center comes out clean. Cool in pan on wire rack 10 minutes. Remove from pan; cool completely. Wrap in foil or plastic when cool; store overnight.

Buñuelos
(Mexican Fritters)

Makes 32 fritters.

2 cups *sifted* all-
  purpose flour
2 tablespoons sugar
½ teaspoon baking
  powder
½ teaspoon salt
¼ teaspoon anise
  seeds, crushed (use
  a hammer)
1 teaspoon grated
  lemon rind

1 egg, slightly beaten
3 tablespoons butter
  or margarine,
  melted
3 to 4 tablespoons
  milk
Vegetable oil
⅔ cup honey
¼ cup (½ stick) butter
  or margarine

1. Combine flour, sugar, baking powder, salt, anise seeds and lemon rind in a large bowl.
2. Stir in egg, butter and just enough milk to make the dough hold together.
3. Turn out on lightly-floured surface and knead 3 to 5 minutes or just until dough becomes smooth. Let rest 10 minutes.
4. Divide dough into 32 equal-size pieces. Roll each out on a lightly floured surface with a lightly floured rolling pin to a 5-inch circle (edges will be irregular). Keep between pieces of wax paper until all have been rolled out.
5. Heat about 1 inch oil in a heavy skillet to 375° on a deep-fat frying thermometer. Fry rounds, a few at a time, about 30 seconds on each side. (Buñuelos will puff up when frying.) Drain on paper toweling.
Do-ahead Tip: Buñuelos can be stored at this point between clean paper toweling in a metal tin, or frozen in single layers on a jelly-roll pan. To serve, place on a jelly-roll pan or cookie sheet in a 325° oven for 1 minute; then glaze with honey butter.
6. Just before serving, heat honey and butter in a medium-size saucepan until mixture bubbles 1 minute. Cool slightly. With a spoon, drizzle mixture over each buñuelo; let set.

Oatmeal Bannocks

Makes 8 bannocks.

1 cup lightly spooned
  all-purpose flour
1 teaspoon baking
  soda
1 teaspoon cream of
  tartar

½ teaspoon salt
1 cup quick oats
2 eggs
1 tablespoon honey
1½ cups milk

1. Sift the flour, baking soda and cream of tartar into a medium-size bowl. Stir in the salt and oats.
2. Beat the eggs, honey and milk in a small bowl until well mixed. Make a well in the center of the dry ingredients and add the liquids. Beat until smooth. Grease a griddle lightly; heat over low to medium heat. When griddle is hot, drop batter by spoonfuls without crowding. When bubbles form, turn and cook the other side for 2 to 3 minutes. Serve warm with butter and honey.

Cranberry Bread

Bake at 350° for 50 minutes.
Makes 1 loaf.

2 cups *sifted* all-
  purpose flour
¾ cup sugar
1½ teaspoons baking
  powder
½ teaspoon baking
  soda
½ teaspoon salt
1 egg
2 tablespoons grated
  orange rind

½ cup orange juice
3 tablespoons melted
  butter or margarine
2 tablespoons hot
  water
1½ cups fresh or
  frozen cranberries,
  halved (thawed if
  frozen)
¾ cup chopped
  walnuts

1. Sift flour, sugar, baking powder, baking soda and salt into a large bowl.
2. Beat egg lightly in a small bowl; stir in orange rind and juice, butter and hot water. Add to dry ingredients; mix thoroughly. Fold in cranberries and nuts. Turn batter into a well-greased 9 × 5 × 3-inch loaf pan.
3. Bake in a moderate oven (350°) for 50 minutes or until cake tester inserted in center comes out clean. Remove from pan; cool on wire rack.

Hush Puppy   Deep-fried cornmeal fritters supposedly named at Southern fish fries. To quiet the barking dogs, the extra pieces of fried batter were tossed to the dogs with the admonition to "hush, puppies."

Hush Puppies

Makes 2 dozen.

1¾ cups white
  cornmeal
¾ teaspoons salt
1½ teaspoons baking
  powder

1 cup milk
1 egg
¼ cup chopped green
  onion
Vegetable oil for frying

1. Combine cornmeal, salt and baking powder in a medium-size bowl. Stir in milk, egg and onion.
2. Pour oil to a 3- or 4-inch depth in a medium-size saucepan. Heat to 350° on a deep-fat frying thermometer.
3. Drop batter by the spoonfuls onto hot oil. Fry until golden brown. Drain.

Pictured opposite: Cranberry Bread, page 120.

Garlic Bread Sticks

Bake at 400° for 11 to 15 minutes.

Makes 1½ dozen.

1 loaf unsliced French or Italian bread (about 20 to 22 inches long)	margarine, melted
	2 cloves garlic, crushed
1 cup (2 sticks) butter or	¼ cup chopped fresh parsley

1. Cut bread into 3 equal crosswise pieces. Cut each piece into 6 equal lengthwise sticks.
2. Combine melted butter, garlic and parsley. Brush on bread sticks.
3. Wrap sticks in foil securely. Bread sticks may be refrigerated at this point and heated just before serving.
4. Bake in a hot oven (400°) for 8 to 10 minutes or until heated thoroughly. Unwrap foil and bake an additional 3 to 5 minutes or until bread sticks are golden. Serve warm.

Herb-Cheese Filled Bread

An unusual bread for brunch or supper.

Bake at 350° for 50 minutes.

Makes 1 nine-inch loaf.

1 cup milk	*unsifted* all-purpose flour
6 tablespoons (¾ stick) butter or margarine	2 eggs
1 tablespoon sugar	½ teaspoon ground coriander
2 teaspoons salt	¼ teaspoon pepper
1 envelope active dry yeast	¼ cup chopped parsley
Pinch sugar	1½ pounds Muenster cheese, shredded
¼ cup very warm water	1 tablespoon sesame seeds
3¼ to 3½ cups	

1. Combine milk, 3 tablespoons of the butter sugar and salt in a small saucepan; heat until butter melts. Cool to lukewarm.
2. Sprinkle yeast and the pinch sugar into very warm water in a large bowl. ("Very warm water" should feel comfortably warm when dropped on wrist.) Stir until yeast dissolves. Let stand until bubbly, about 5 minutes.
3. Stir milk into yeast mixture. Gradually stir in 3 cups of the flour; turn out onto lightly floured surface. Knead until smooth and elastic, about 8 minutes, using only as much remaining flour as needed to keep dough from sticking.
4. Place dough in buttered large bowl; turn to bring buttered side up. Cover with a towel. Let rise in a warm place, away from drafts, 1 hour or until double in volume.
5. Soften remaining 3 tablespoons butter in large bowl. Beat eggs slightly in a small bowl, reserving 1 tablespoon for glaze. Add remaining eggs, coriander, pepper and parsley to butter. Stir in cheese; toss well. Grease a 9 × 1½-inch layer pan; sprinkle with half of the sesame seeds.
6. Punch dough down; turn out onto very lightly floured surface; roll or stretch to a 16-inch round. Center dough over prepared pan; fill with cheese mixture. Gather edges of dough up and over filling into center, pleating the dough into large folds; hold the ends of the dough that meet in center between fingers; pinch together, then twist into a little knob.
7. Let rise again in a warm place, away from drafts, 45 minutes or until almost double in volume. Preheat oven to 350°. Brush bread with reserved egg. Sprinkle with remaining seeds.
8. Bake in a preheated moderate oven (350°) for 50 minutes or until loaf is golden and sounds hollow when tapped. Remove from pan to wire rack to cool. Serve slightly warm or at room temperature.

Popover A quick bread made by preparing a batter from flour, milk, eggs and salt. The batter is poured into individual well-greased cups and quickly baked in a hot oven in order to form steam which causes them to pop over the cups.

Popovers

Bake at 425° for 40 minutes.

Makes 8 popovers.

2 eggs	1 cup *sifted* all-purpose flour
1 cup milk	
1 tablespoon butter, melted	½ teaspoon salt

1. Preheat oven to 425°. Butter eight 5-ounce custard cups generously; place on a jelly-roll pan. Place in oven to heat while preparing batter.
2. Beat eggs in large bowl; add milk and butter. Beat until blended. Add flour and salt; beat until batter is quite smooth. Ladle into prepared cups to fill about half-full.
3. Bake in a preheated hot oven (425°) for 35 minutes. Cut slit in side of each popover to allow steam to escape. Bake for 5 minutes longer or until popovers are a deep brown and very crisp. Serve at once.

Scone Triangular or diamond-shaped biscuit-like tea cake of Scottish origin. Pronounced SKAHN, it is baked on a griddle or in a hot oven.

Bridie's Irish Scones

Bake at 450° for 10 minutes.
Makes about 12 scones.

2 cups buttermilk baking mix	**¹/₄ cup sugar**
¹/₂ cup golden raisins	**¹/₂ cup water**
¹/₂ cup dried currants	**Sugar**

1. Preheat oven to 450°. Combine baking mix, raisins, dried currants and sugar in large bowl with wooden spoon.
2. Stir in water until dough is well mixed and sticks together.
3. Scoop up tablespoonfuls of mixture and drop onto buttered cookie sheet. Sprinkle with sugar.
4. Bake in a preheated very hot oven (450°) for 10 minutes or until golden brown.

Griddle Scones

Makes 8 scones.

1¹/₂ cups lightly spooned all-purpose flour	**tartar**
	¹/₄ cup sugar
¹/₂ teaspoon salt	**¹/₄ cup (¹/₂ stick) butter or margarine**
¹/₂ teaspoon baking soda	**1 egg**
¹/₂ teaspoon cream of	**¹/₄ cup buttermilk**

1. Sift the flour, salt, baking soda, cream of tartar and sugar into a medium-size bowl. Cut in the butter with a pastry blender until mixture forms crumbs.
2. Beat the egg with the buttermilk in a small bowl and add to the flour mixture, stirring to make a soft dough. Turn dough onto a floured surface and roll or pat out into a ¹/₂-inch-thick round. Cut into 8 triangles.
3. Heat griddle over low to medium heat; sprinkle lightly with flour. Bake triangles about 5 minutes or until the underside is golden brown; turn over and finish baking 4 to 5 minutes longer. Split; spread with butter and jam.

Fruit Scones: Follow recipe for Griddle Scones, adding ¹/₄ teaspoon ground cinnamon with flour, and ¹/₂ cup raisins with buttermilk.

Cheese Scones: Follow recipe for Griddle Scones but using only 2 tablespoons sugar and adding ¹/₄ teaspoon pepper, ¹/₄ teaspoon dry mustard, and ¹/₄ to ¹/₂ cup shredded Cheddar cheese to dry ingredients.

Whole Wheat Scones: Follow recipe for Griddle Scones but using ³/₄ cup whole wheat flour and ³/₄ cup all-purpose flour in place of all white flour. Increase baking soda to 1 teaspoon.

Biscuit   In the United States, the word "biscuit" is used to describe a small, soft, unsweetened cake, considered a quick bread, made from baking powder

or soda-leavened dough and served as a hot bread. It was in the late 1700's that these little cakes first appeared here in place of traditional yeast breads. They became popular because they were so quick and easy to make.

Our biscuits are not found in other parts of the world. In fact, the word is French in origin for flour-made cakes that were baked twice to dry them out for use on long trips. The English call sweet biscuits, cream biscuits or water biscuits what Americans term cookies or crackers.

To make tender, flaky biscuits, handle the dough as little as possible. If you want biscuits with soft sides, bake them in a small round pan with the sides of the biscuits touching. Refrigerated ready-to-bake biscuits and packaged heat-and-serve biscuits are readily available today.

Baking Powder Biscuits

Bake at 450° for 12 minutes.

Makes 12 biscuits.

2 cups sifted all-purpose flour	**¹/₂ teaspoon salt**
	¹/₄ cup vegetable shortening
3 teaspoons baking powder	**³/₄ cup milk**

1. Sift flour, baking powder and salt into a large bowl.
2. Cut in shortening with a pastry blender until mixture resembles cornmeal. Preheat oven to 450°.
3. Add milk; stir lightly with a fork until a soft, puffy dough forms.
4. Turn out onto a lightly floured surface. Knead lightly about 20 times.
5. Roll or pat dough to ¹/₂-inch thickness. Cut into 2-inch rounds with a floured biscuit cutter, working neatly from rim to middle so there will be few scraps to reroll. Place biscuits, 1 inch apart, on an ungreased cookie sheet.
6. Bake in a preheated very hot oven (450°) for 12 minutes or until golden brown. Serve immediately.

Drop Biscuits: Prepare Baking Powder Biscuits, increasing the milk to 1 cup. Drop by spoonfuls, 1 inch apart, on ungreased cookie sheet. Bake following Biscuit directions.

Sesame Butter Fingers: Heat oven to very hot (450°). Melt ¹/₄ cup (¹/₂ stick) butter or margarine in a 9 × 9 × 2-inch pan. Put ¹/₂ cup sesame seeds on a large plate. Prepare Baking Powder Biscuits. Roll or

(continued)

pat dough to an 8-inch square on a lightly floured surface. Cut square in half. Cut each half into nine 4-inch strips. Dip each strip into the melted butter, then dip one side into sesame seeds. Arrange strips in 2 rows in the baking pan. Bake 15 minutes or until golden brown.

Scones: Prepare Baking Powder Biscuits, but do not add the 3/4 cup milk. Instead, add 3 tablespoons sugar, 1 teaspoon grated orange rind and 1/2 cup raisins to dry mix. Beat 1 egg with 1/3 cup milk; pour into dry ingredients. Stir and knead as in Biscuits. Divide dough in half. Pat each half to an 8-inch circle. Cut each circle into 6 wedges. Brush tops with milk; sprinkle with sugar. Place wedges, 1 inch apart, on ungreased cookie sheet. Bake in a very hot oven (450°) for 10 minutes or until golden brown.

Cheddar Biscuits: Prepare Baking Powder Biscuits and roll dough out to a 12 × 8-inch rectangle. Place twelve 1/2-inch cubes of Cheddar cheese about 1 1/2 inches apart in 3 rows of 4 each, on half of the dough. Fold other half of dough over to make a second layer. Cut between cubes of cheese into twelve (about 2-inch) squares. Place on greased cookie sheet. Bake following Biscuit directions.

Mini-Herb Biscuits: Prepare Baking Powder Biscuits but stir 1 teaspoon dry mustard and 1 teaspoon Italian herb seasoning mix into flour-shortening mixture. Add milk; knead and roll dough into a 10 × 6-inch rectangle. Cut into 1-inch squares. Place on ungreased cookie sheet. Bake following Biscuit directions.

Raleigh Buttermilk Ham Biscuits

Bake at 450° for 10 minutes.

Makes 22 biscuits.

1 1/2 cups lightly spooned all-purpose flour	mustard
	1/8 teaspoon salt
2 teaspoons baking powder	4 ounces peppered ham luncheon meat, finely chopped
1/2 teaspoon baking soda	7 tablespoons butter, melted and cooled
1/4 teaspoon dry	3/4 cup buttermilk

1. Preheat oven to 450°. Combine flour, baking powder, baking soda, mustard, salt and ham in a medium-size bowl. Stir in 4 tablespoons of the melted butter and the buttermilk with a fork until the dough is moistened and clings together. Knead the dough on lightly floured surface 8 to 10 times.
2. Roll out dough to 1/2-inch thickness. Cut with a 2-inch floured biscuit cutter. Place on ungreased cookie sheet, 1 inch apart.
3. Bake in a preheated very hot oven (450°) for 10

Pictured opposite: Baking Powder Biscuits, page 123.

minutes or until biscuits are well risen and golden brown. Remove from oven to wire rack; brush tops with remaining melted butter.

Buttermilk Biscuit Squares

Bake at 450° for 20 minutes.

Makes 24 biscuits.

3 cups *sifted* all-purpose flour	soda
	1 1/2 teaspoons salt
3 teaspoons baking powder	3/4 cup vegetable shortening
1/2 teaspoon baking	1 1/3 cups buttermilk

1. Sift flour, baking powder, baking soda and salt into a large bowl.
2. Cut in shortening with a pastry blender until mixture resembles cornmeal. Preheat oven to 450°.
3. Add buttermilk; stir lightly with fork until a soft puffy dough forms.
4. Turn out onto a lightly floured surface. Knead lightly about 20 times.
5. Transfer dough to a large, ungreased cookie sheet. Roll out to a 12 × 8-inch rectangle. Cut into 2-inch squares. Separate slightly, about 1/4 inch apart.
6. Bake in a preheated very hot oven (450°) for 20 minutes. Dust lightly with flour. Serve hot or at room temperature.

Yorkshire Pudding   A quick bread of

English origin which traditionally was baked under the meat or roast, which is on a wire rack in the roasting pan. It was served before the meat. Now it is baked and served separately.

Its name comes from Yorkshire, a county in the north of England. Yorkshire pudding is made from a batter of eggs, flour and milk, baked in beef drippings until puffy and golden brown.

Yorkshire Pudding

Bake at 450° for 15 minutes, then at 350° for 20 minutes.

Makes 12 servings.

4 tablespoons beef drippings	1 cup *sifted* all-purpose flour
2 eggs	1/2 teaspoon salt
1 cup milk	

1. Measure 2 tablespoons beef drippings from beef roast into each of two 8-inch round fluted baking pans or two 8-inch round layer-cake pans. Place in the oven as it heats to 450°.

(continued)

2. Beat eggs lightly in a medium-size bowl with electric or rotary beater. Beat in milk.
3. Sift flour and salt onto wax paper; add all at once to egg mixture. Beat until batter is smooth. Remove pans from oven; pour batter evenly into the 2 pans.
4. Bake in a preheated very hot oven (450°) for 15 minutes. Lower oven temperature to 350°; bake 20 minutes longer or until puddings are puffed and brown. Cut into wedge-shaped pieces and serve with beef roast.

Muffin

Muffin   A quick bread made with a drop batter, or a yeast-leavened unsweetened bread. The round and flat yeast muffins used to be sold by street vendors in England. We call them English muffins. The quick muffins are leavened with baking powder or baking soda.

Mixing Muffins: Three Important Tips

- Add the beaten liquid ingredients to the combined dry ingredients with a few, quick stirring strokes to just moisten the dry ingredients.
- The batter should be lumpy; if it pours smoothly from the spoon, you are guilty of overbeating.
- You can recognize overbeaten muffins by the coarse texture and the tunneling throughout.

Apple-Spice Granola Muffins

Bake at 400° for 15 to 20 minutes.

Makes 12 muffins.

2 cups Homemade Granola Crunch (see recipe in chapter Sandwiches and Snacks)
1 cup *sifted* **all-purpose flour**
1/4 cup firmly packed light brown sugar
2 teaspoons baking powder
1/2 teaspoon ground cinnamon
1/4 teaspoon ground
nutmeg
1/4 teaspoon salt
1 cup finely chopped pared cooking apples, such as Granny Smith (1 medium-size)
1/2 cup milk
1/3 cup margarine, melted and cooled to room temperature
1 egg, slightly beaten
1 teaspoon vanilla

1. Preheat the oven to hot (400°). Grease twelve 2½-inch muffin tins.
2. Combine the granola, flour, sugar, baking powder, cinnamon, nutmeg and salt in a large bowl. Mix well. Stir in the apples. Make a well in center.
3. Beat together the milk, margarine, egg and vanilla in a small bowl. Pour into the well of granola mixture; stir just to combine. Spoon the batter into the prepared muffin tins.

Apple-Spice Granola Muffins.

Pecan Corn Muffins.

4. Bake in the preheated hot oven (400°) for 15 to 20 minutes, or until a wooden pick inserted in the centers comes out clean. Cool the muffins in the pan on a wire rack for 5 minutes. Turn out the muffins. Serve warm or cool completely on the wire rack.

Pecan Corn Muffins

Bake at 350° for 20 minutes.

Makes 18 muffins.

3¹/₂ cups whole-wheat flour
1 cup yellow cornmeal
1 envelope active dry yeast
1 teaspoon baking powder
1 teaspoon salt

1 cup milk
¹/₂ cup (1 stick) butter
¹/₂ cup water
¹/₃ cup honey
2 eggs
1 cup coarsely chopped pecans

1. Grease 18 medium-size muffin-pan cups. Sprinkle each with cornmeal. Preheat oven to moderate (350°).
2. Combine 1 cup flour, the cornmeal, yeast, baking powder and salt in large bowl.
3. Heat milk, butter, water and honey in small saucepan until butter melts; cool to lukewarm. Pour into flour mixture. Beat at medium speed with electric mixer 2 minutes. Beat in eggs. Stir in remaining flour. Add pecans.

4. Shape dough in prepared muffin cups, filling each three-quarters full. Smooth tops slightly. Cover; let rise in a warm place away from drafts until muffins come close to top of muffin cups, about 45 minutes.
5. Bake in a preheated moderate oven (350°) for 20 minutes or until golden. Turn out onto a wire rack. Serve warm.

Blueberry Muffins

Bake at 425° for 20 minutes.

Makes 12 muffins.

2 cups *sifted* all-purpose flour
¹/₃ cup sugar
3 teaspoons baking powder
1 teaspoon salt
1 egg, well beaten
1 cup milk
¹/₄ cup (¹/₂ stick) butter

or margarine, melted and cooled
1 cup fresh or slightly thawed dry-pack frozen blueberries
1 tablespoon sugar
1 teaspoon grated lemon rind

1. Preheat oven to 425°. Sift flour, the ¹/₃ cup sugar, baking powder and salt into a large bowl. Mix egg, milk and melted, cooled butter in a small bowl; add all at once to flour mixture; stir lightly with a fork just until

(continued)

liquid is absorbed. (Batter will be lumpy.) Fold in blueberries.
2. Spoon into greased medium-size muffin-pan cups, filling each 2/3 full. Sprinkle with a mixture of the 1 tablespoon sugar and lemon rind.
3. Bake in a preheated hot oven (425°) for 20 minutes or until golden; remove from cups. Serve hot.

Favorite Muffins

Light, tender, melt-in-your-mouth muffins—delicious plain, super with cheese or bacon. Either way, simple to make.

Bake at 400° for 25 minutes.

Makes 12 medium-size muffins.

2 cups *sifted* all-purpose flour
2 tablespoons sugar
2 teaspoons baking powder
1 teaspoon salt
1 egg, beaten
1 cup milk
1/4 cup (1/2 stick) butter or margarine, melted and cooled

1. Sift flour, sugar, baking powder and salt into a medium-size bowl. Make a well in the center of dry ingredients. Preheat oven to 400°.
2. Combine egg, milk and melted, cooled butter in a small bowl; add all at once to flour mixture; stir lightly, just until liquid is absorbed. (Batter will be lumpy.)
3. Spoon into 12 greased medium-size muffin-pan cups, filling each 2/3 full.
4. Bake in a preheated hot oven (400°) for 25 minutes or until golden brown. Serve hot with plenty of butter.

Jelly Muffins: Spoon part of batter into cups; add a dab of jelly; top with remaining batter.

Cheese Muffins: Add 1/2 cup shredded Cheddar cheese to dry ingredients.

Bacon Muffins: Add 4 slices of crumbled, crisp-cooked bacon to dry ingredients.

Corn Muffins

Bake at 400° for 20 minutes.

Makes 12 medium-size muffins.

1 cup *sifted* all-purpose flour
3 tablespoons sugar
1 1/2 teaspoons baking powder
1/2 teaspoon baking soda
1/2 teaspoon salt
1 cup yellow or white cornmeal
1 egg, well beaten
2/3 cup buttermilk
1/4 cup vegetable shortening, melted and cooled

1. Sift flour, sugar, baking powder, baking soda and salt into a large bowl; stir in cornmeal. Preheat oven to 400°.
2. Mix egg, buttermilk and melted, cooled shortening in a 1-cup measure; add all at once to flour mixture; stir lightly with a fork just until liquid is absorbed. (Batter will be lumpy.)
3. Spoon into greased medium-size muffin-pan cups, filling each 2/3 full.
4. Bake in a preheated hot oven (400°) for 20 minutes or until golden. Serve hot.

Whole Wheat Muffins

Vitamin-rich whole wheat gives these tasty muffins a nutrition boost.

Bake at 400° for 25 minutes.

Makes 12 medium-size muffins.

1 cup *sifted* all-purpose flour
2 teaspoons baking powder
1 teaspoon salt
1 cup *unsifted* whole wheat flour
1/4 cup molasses
1 egg, beaten
1 cup milk
1/4 cup (1/2 stick) butter or margarine, melted and cooled

1. Sift all-purpose flour, baking powder and salt into a medium-size bowl; stir in whole wheat flour; make a well in center. Preheat oven to 400°.
2. Combine molasses, egg, milk and melted, cooled butter in a small bowl; add all at once to flour mixture; stir lightly just until liquid is absorbed. (Batter will be lumpy.)
3. Spoon into 12 greased medium-size muffin-pan cups, filling each 2/3 full.
4. Bake in a preheated hot oven (400°) for 25 minutes or until golden brown and springy to the touch.

Pumpkin-Nut Muffins

Bake at 350° for 20 minutes.

Makes 2 dozen muffins.

2 cups *sifted* all-purpose flour
1 teaspoon baking soda
1/2 teaspoon baking powder
1/2 teaspoon ground cinnamon
1/2 teaspoon ground nutmeg
1/4 teaspoon ground ginger
2 eggs, slightly beaten
1/3 cup buttermilk
1/3 cup butter or margarine, melted
1 tablespoon molasses
1/2 teaspoon vanilla
1 cup sugar
1 cup canned pumpkin
1/2 cup chopped pecans
1/2 cup raisins

1. Preheat the oven to moderate (350°). Grease 24 muffin-pan cups, 2 1/4 inches in diameter.

2. Sift together the flour, baking soda, baking powder, cinnamon, nutmeg and ginger onto wax paper.

3. Beat together the eggs, buttermilk, melted butter, molasses, vanilla, sugar and pumpkin in a large bowl. Stir in the dry ingredients, all at once, just until moistened. Fold in the nuts and raisins. Spoon into the prepared muffin-pan cups, filling almost to the top.

4. Bake in the preheated moderate oven (350°) for 20 to 25 minutes or until a wooden pick inserted in the centers comes out clean. Remove the muffins from the cups and cool on wire racks. Serve warm.

Microwave Directions

650 Watt Variable Power Microwave Oven

Directions: Place two 2¹/₂-inch paper cupcake liners into each of 18 microwave-safe muffin cups. Prepare the muffin batter as above. Divide the batter equally among the lined cups. Microwave 6 at a time at full power for 4¹/₂ minutes. Remove the muffins from the pans, peel off the outer paper liners and cool on wire racks. Makes 1¹/₂ dozen large muffins.

Note: Uncooked batter-filled cups can be frozen. To bake, place 6 frozen filled paper liners in microwave-safe muffin cups. Microwave at full power for 6 minutes.

Blueberry-Bran Muffins

Nutritious bran fortifies these tender, cake-like muffins.

Bake at 425° for 23 minutes.

Makes 12 muffins.

¹/₃ **cup unsalted butter or margarine, softened**	**powder**
	¹/₂ **teaspoon salt**
¹/₂ **cup sugar**	¹/₄ **cup unprocessed bran**
1 **egg**	
³/₄ **cup milk**	1 **generous cup fresh blueberries**
¹/₄ **teaspoon vanilla**	OR: **1 generous cup unsweetened frozen blueberries, slightly thawed**
1²/₃ **cups** *sifted* **all-purpose flour plus 1 tablespoon**	
2¹/₂ **teaspoons baking**	

1. Preheat the oven to hot (425°). Grease the bottoms only of twelve 2¹/₂-inch muffin-pan cups.

2. Beat together the butter and sugar in a large mixing bowl until light and fluffy. Beat in the egg, then the milk and vanilla; mix well (the mixture may look separated).

3. Sift together the 1²/₃ cups of flour, the baking powder and salt into a medium-size bowl. Stir in the bran. Add to the butter mixture. Stir briskly with a fork, just until the dry ingredients are moistened; do not overstir. The batter will not be smooth.

4. Toss the berries with 1 tablespoon of the flour in a small bowl. Fold into the batter.

5. Fill each prepared muffin-pan cup two-thirds full with batter, using a large spoon and rubber spatula.

6. Bake in the preheated hot (425°) oven for 23 minutes or until golden brown. Remove the pan to a wire rack. Loosen the muffins with a spatula and remove from the pan at once to prevent steaming. Serve piping hot.

Wheat Germ Muffins

Doubly rich with old-fashioned molasses and nut-sweet wheat germ — and good for you, too!

Bake at 400° for 30 minutes.

Makes 12 medium-size muffins.

1¹/₂ **cups** *sifted* **all-purpose flour**	1 **egg, well beaten**
	³/₄ **cup milk**
¹/₄ **cup sugar**	¹/₄ **cup (¹/₂ stick) butter or margarine, melted and cooled**
2 **teaspoons baking powder**	
1 **teaspoon salt**	¹/₄ **cup molasses**
1 **cup wheat germ**	

1. Sift flour, sugar, baking powder and salt into a medium-size bowl; stir in wheat germ. Preheat oven to 400°.

2. Combine egg, milk, melted and cooled butter and molasses in a small bowl; add all at once to flour mixture; stir lightly just until liquid is absorbed. (Batter will be lumpy.)

3. Spoon into 12 greased medium-size muffin-pan cups, filling each ²/₃ full.

4. Bake in a preheated hot oven (400°) for 30 minutes or until richly browned; remove from pans at once.

Ginger-Apricot Muffins

Delicious for breakfast, these muffins are also good with lunch or afternoon tea.

Bake at 400° for 25 muffins.

Makes 12 muffins.

1³/₄ **cups** *sifted* **all-purpose flour**	³/₄ **cup milk**
	¹/₃ **cup unsalted butter or margarine, melted**
3 **tablespoons sugar**	
2¹/₂ **teaspoons baking powder**	³/₄ **cup finely cut-up dried apricots**
1¹/₂ **teaspoons ground ginger**	
¹/₂ **teaspoon salt**	1¹/₂ **teaspoons grated fresh lemon rind (1 lemon)**
1 **egg**	

1. Preheat the oven to hot (400°). Grease the bottoms only of twelve 2¹/₂-inch muffin-pan cups.

(continued)

2. Sift together the flour, sugar, baking powder, ginger and salt into a large bowl.

3. Lightly beat the egg in a small bowl. Beat in the milk and butter; stir in the apricots and lemon rind. Pour all at once into the flour mixture. Stir briskly with a fork, just until all the ingredients are moistened; do not overstir. The batter will look lumpy.

4. Fill each prepared muffin-pan cup two-thirds full with batter, using a large spoon and rubber spatula.

5. Bake in the preheated hot oven (400°) for 25 minutes or until golden brown. Remove the pan to a wire rack. Loosen the muffins with the spatula and remove from the pan at once to prevent steaming. Garnish with additional cut-up dried apricots, if you wish. Serve piping hot.

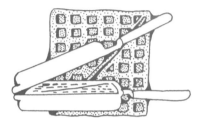

Waffle
A quick bread made from a pourable batter and baked in a special utensil or waffle iron. Europe has a long history of waffle making. The word "waffle" comes from a German word, *wabe,* meaning honeycomb.

Waffles are traditionally served for breakfast or brunch topped with a syrup, fruit or sugar. They may also be served topped with eggs or creamed chicken or seafood for a luncheon meal. Ready-made frozen waffles make quick dishes.

Waffles

Makes 6 waffles.

2 cups *sifted* all-purpose flour	½ teaspoon salt
3 tablespoons sugar	2 eggs, separated
2 teaspoons baking powder	1¼ cups milk
	⅓ cup vegetable oil

1. Sift flour with sugar, baking powder and salt onto a large piece of wax paper.

2. Beat egg whites until stiff but not dry in a small bowl; set aside.

3. Beat the egg yolks well in a medium-size bowl and stir in milk.

4. Add sifted dry ingredients and mix just enough to blend; add vegetable oil. Fold in egg whites.

5. Bake in a moderately hot waffle iron, 4 to 5 minutes, until crisp and brown, or as iron manufacturer directs. Serve hot with butter and syrup or honey.

Sour Cream Waffles with Brown Sugar Syrup

Makes 16 four-inch waffles.

1¾ cups *sifted* all-purpose flour	1 cup milk
3 teaspoons baking powder	1 container (8 ounces) dairy sour cream
½ teaspoon baking soda	1 tablespoon grated lemon rind
½ teaspoon salt	Brown Sugar Syrup (*recipe follows*)
3 eggs	

1. Sift flour, baking powder, baking soda and salt onto wax paper.

2. Beat eggs, milk, sour cream and lemon rind together in a large bowl. Beat in flour mixture until smooth.

3. For each waffle, pour about 1 cup waffle mixture into center of hot waffle iron. Cook following manufacturer's directions. Serve with Brown Sugar Syrup.

Brown Sugar Syrup: Combine 2 cups firmly packed light brown sugar with 2 cups water in a medium-size saucepan. Bring to boiling. Lower heat and simmer 20 minutes or just until mixture thickens. Stir in 1 teaspoon maple extract. Cool slightly. Makes 2 cups.

Belgian Waffles

Here's our basic recipe for crisp and puffy Belgian waffles, and ideas for transforming them into festive desserts.

1¾ cups *sifted* all-purpose flour	1 cup milk
2 teaspoons baking powder	1 cup heavy cream
¼ teaspoon salt	1 tablespoon plus 1 teaspoon grated lemon rind
2 tablespoons sugar	3 tablespoons melted butter
3 eggs, separated	

1. Sift together flour, baking powder, salt and sugar into large bowl.

2. Beat egg yolks slightly in small bowl. Stir in milk and cream. Blend in flour mixture until smooth. Stir in lemon rind and melted butter.

3. Beat egg whites in medium-size bowl until stiff but not dry peaks form. Fold gently into batter.

4. Bake in waffle iron following manufacturer's instructions. Serve hot, sprinkled with 10X

(continued)

Pictured opposite: Sour Cream Waffles with Brown Sugar Syrup, page 130.

(confectioners') sugar and garnished with sliced fresh fruit. Or, serve with one of the following toppings.

Red, White and Blue Waffle Shortcake

For each serving, cut large square or round waffles into triangles or wedges. Layer with whipped cream or thawed frozen whipped topping, strawberries and fresh or frozen blueberries. Garnish with whipped cream and fresh mint leaves.

Maple-Blueberry Topping

Combine 1/4 cup brown sugar and 1 tablespoon cornstarch in saucepan. Gradually blend in 1/2 cup maple syrup and 1/2 cup water. Cook, stirring, until thick and bubbly, 1 minute. Stir in 2 cups fresh or frozen blueberries, 1 tablespoon lemon juice and 1/8 teaspoon nutmeg. Cool slightly. Serve over waffles with dollop of sour cream.

Banana Split Waffles

For each serving, cut square waffles in half into triangles and place in dish. Slice or split small banana lengthwise; arrange over waffles. Add small scoops vanilla, strawberry and chocolate ice cream. Spoon prepared strawberry, pineapple and chocolate toppings over top. Garnish with whipped cream and chopped nuts.

Black Forest Waffles

Cherry Sauce: Drain 8³/₄-ounce can dark sweet pitted cherries, reserving syrup. Place 2 teaspoons cornstarch in small saucepan. Blend in reserved syrup and 2 tablespoons port wine. Bring to boiling, stirring; cook 1 minute. Stir in cherries. Cool slightly. Spoon 3 to 4 tablespoons sauce over each serving of waffles. Top with whipped cream, shaved semisweet chocolate and maraschino cherry.

Peach & Chocolate Shortcake

For each serving, stack 2 small waffles on serving plate with drained, canned, sliced peaches and whipped cream or thawed frozen whipped topping. Top with dollop of whipped cream and peach slices. Serve with warm chocolate fudge sauce.

Cherry-Cheese Waffles

Ricotta-Cheese Topping: Beat 1 cup ricotta cheese with 4 tablespoons sugar, 2 teaspoons amaretto liqueur and 1/2 teaspoon grated lemon rind. For each serving, spoon 1/4 cup cherry pie filling over 2 overlapped small waffles. Garnish with 2 to 3 tablespoons ricotta topping and grated lemon rind.

Soy-Flour Waffles

Makes 6 waffles.

1³/₄ cups all-purpose flour	1¹/₂ teaspoons baking powder
1/4 cup low-fat soy flour	2 eggs, separated
1/4 teaspoon baking soda	1³/₄ cups buttermilk
	5 tablespoons melted butter or margarine

1. Sift dry ingredients together into bowl.
2. Beat egg yolks in a separate bowl until light. Add buttermilk and butter to egg yolks; beat; add to dry ingredients, combining with a few strokes.
3. Beat egg whites until stiff; fold into batter. Cook in a nonstick waffle iron.

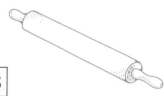

COFFEE CAKES

Coffee Cake   There's nothing quite as satisfying as a slice of homemade coffee cake enjoyed with your morning coffee or favorite hot beverage. Of course, coffee cakes are great for brunch or afternoon snacks, too. Coffee cakes can be made from either a cake batter or a sweet quick or yeast bread dough.

Cinnamon-Nut Coffee Ring

Bake at 350° for 25 minutes.

Makes 1 coffee cake.

1 loaf (14 ounces) frozen sweet dough, thawed overnight in refrigerator OR: 1 loaf (1 pound) frozen plain dough, thawed overnight in refrigerator	softened 1/2 cup chopped walnuts 1/2 cup sugar 2 teaspoons ground cinnamon Confectioners' Glaze (recipe follows)
1/2 cup (1 stick) butter,	

1. Allow dough to stand at room temperature on a lightly floured surface for 1 hour. Roll and push dough to a 14 × 8-inch rectangle.
2. Spread 2/3 of the dough with all but 2 tablespoons of the butter; fold entire rectangle in thirds. Tap gently with rolling pin. Turn dough so open edge faces you and roll out again. Fold in thirds again. Let rest 15 minutes while making filling.
3. Combine nuts, sugar and cinnamon in small bowl. Roll dough to 14 × 8-inch rectangle. Spread remainig 2 tablespoons butter over surface; sprinkle with cinnamon-sugar mixture almost to edges. Roll jelly-roll fashion from long side. Place seam-side down on greased jelly-roll pan and shape into a circle, pinching seam well to seal.
4. Using scissors, make deep cuts from outside almost to center, 1 inch apart. Turn each section cut-side up so filling shows. Cover; let rise until double in volume, about 1 hour. Preheat oven to 350°.
5. Bake in a preheated moderate oven (350°) for 25 minutes. Remove to wire rack. Cool. Drizzle with Confectioners' Glaze.

Confectioners' Glaze: Blend 1/2 cup 10X (confectioners') sugar with 1 tablespoon milk in a small bowl.

Old-fashioned Crumb Cake

Bake at 375° for 30 minutes.

Makes one 8-inch cakes.

Crumb Topping:

1/3 cup firmly packed brown sugar	cinnamon
1 cup *sifted* all-purpose flour	1/2 cup (1 stick) butter or margarine, softened
1/2 teaspoon ground	

Cake:

1 1/2 cups *sifted* all-purpose flour	3/4 cup firmly packed brown sugar
1/2 teaspoon ground cinnamon	1/4 cup (1/2 stick) butter or margarine, softened
1/2 teaspoon salt	
2 1/2 teaspoons baking powder	1 egg
	3/4 cup milk

1. Make Crumb Topping: Combine sugar, flour, cinnamon and butter in small bowl; mix until crumbly.
2. Make Cake: Sift flour, cinnamon, salt and baking powder onto wax paper. Preheat oven to 375°.
3. Beat sugar, butter and egg in medium-size bowl until smooth. Add milk alternately with flour, stirring well after each addition. Spread in greased 8 × 8 × 2-inch pan. Sprinkle with Crumb Topping.
4. Bake in a preheated moderate oven (375°) for 30 minutes or until top springs back when lightly pressed with fingertip. Serve warm.

Date Tea Bread

Bake at 350° for 1 hour 10 minutes.

Makes 1 loaf.

1 package (8 ounces) pitted dates, cut in small pieces	(3/4 stick) butter
	1 egg, beaten
1 1/4 cups boiling water	2 1/4 cups *sifted* all-purpose flour
1 1/2 cups firmly packed brown sugar	1 1/2 teaspoons baking soda
6 tablespoons	1 1/2 teaspoons salt

1. Place dates in medium-size bowl; pour boiling water over. Stir in sugar and butter or margarine until butter melts; cool. Stir in beaten egg.
2. Sift flour, soda and salt onto wax paper; stir into date mixture just until blended. Pour into a greased 9 × 5 × 3-inch loaf pan; let stand 15 minutes. Preheat oven to 350°.
3. Bake in a preheated moderate oven (350°) for 1 hour 10 minutes or until a wooden pick inserted into loaf comes out clean. Cool 5 minutes; turn out on rack; cool completely.
4. Wrap in wax paper, foil or plastic wrap; store at least 1 day before slicing.

Raisin Spice Coffee Cake

Bake at 350° for 40 minutes.

Makes one 9-inch square cake.

2 cups *sifted* all-purpose flour	or margarine, softened
3 teaspoons baking powder	1 cup firmly packed brown sugar
1/4 teaspoon salt	1 egg
1/2 teaspoon ground cloves	3/4 cup cooled coffee
1 teaspoon ground cinnamon	1 cup raisins
1 teaspoon ground nutmeg	1/4 cup 10X (confectioners') sugar
1/2 cup (1 stick) butter	1 tablespoon lemon juice

1. Preheat oven to 350°. Sift flour, baking powder, salt, cloves, cinnamon and nutmeg onto wax paper.
2. Combine butter, brown sugar and egg in a large bowl with electric mixer at medium-high speed until well blended and fluffy.
3. Lower mixer speed to very low; add sifted dry ingredients alternately with coffee. Mix just until blended. Stir in raisins. Turn batter into a buttered 9 × 9 × 2-inch baking pan.
4. Bake in preheated moderate oven (350°) for 40 minutes or until center of cake springs back when lightly pressed with fingertip. Cool in pan on wire rack. Combine 10X sugar and lemon juice in a small bowl; add a few drops of water, if necessary, to achieve a spreading consistency. Spread over top of cake while still warm. Frosting will form a thin glaze. Cut cake into squares to serve.

Orange-Honey Bubble Loaf

Bake at 350° for 30 minutes.

Makes 20 rolls.

1 package (13 3/4 ounces) hot roll mix	orange rind
	1/4 cup golden raisins
3/4 cup very warm water	1/3 cup orange juice
	2 tablespoons butter
2 eggs	1/4 cup honey
1/4 teaspoon ground mace	Pecan halves
1 tablespoon grated	3/4 cup chopped pecans

1. Sprinkle yeast from roll mix over very warm water in large bowl. ("Very warm water" should feel comfortably warm when dropped on wrist.) Stir to dissolve.

(continued)

2. Beat in eggs, mace, orange rind and raisins; blend thoroughly. Stir in flour from roll mix. Place in greased medium-size bowl. Let rise in warm place until double in volume, about 45 minutes. (Dough will be soft.)
3. While dough is rising, heat orange juice, butter and honey in small saucepan until butter is melted. Reserve.
4. Butter a 9-inch ring mold or tube pan; place 2 tablespoons of the orange juice syrup in bottom of mold. Arrange pecan halves, top-sides down, in the syrup.
5. Punch dough down. Knead on well-floured surface; add more flour, if necessary, until dough is no longer sticky. Shape into 20 rolls.
6. Dip each roll into syrup to coat completely; roll in chopped pecans. Arrange, rounded-side down, in 2 layers in prepared pan; let rise in warm place until double, about 45 minutes. Preheat oven to 350°.
7. Bake in a preheated moderate oven (350°) for 30 minutes or until loaf sounds hollow when tapped. (Cover with foil if top is browning too quickly.) Loosen around edges with spatula; invert onto serving plate; remove mold. Spoon remaining syrup over hot rolls. Break the loaf apart with 2 forks to serve.

Hot Cross Buns

Bake at 350° for 30 minutes.

Makes 32 buns.

2 envelopes active dry yeast
1/2 cup sugar
1/2 cup very warm water
1/2 cup (1 stick) butter or margarine
2/3 cup (1 small can) evaporated milk
1 teaspoon salt
2 eggs
1/2 cup currants
1 container (4 ounces) candied citron, chopped (1/2 cup)
4 to 4 1/2 cups sifted all-purpose flour
1/4 teaspoon ground cinnamon
1/4 teaspoon ground nutmeg
Sugar Icing (recipe with Swedish Tea Ring)

1. Sprinkle yeast and 1 teaspoon of the sugar over very warm water in small bowl. ("Very warm water" should feel comfortably warm when dropped on wrist.) Stir to dissolve. Let stand until bubbly, 10 minutes.
2. Heat butter, the remaining sugar, evaporated milk and salt in small saucepan just until butter is melted. Cool to lukewarm.
3. Beat eggs in large bowl; measure out and reserve 2 tablespoons. Stir cooled milk mixture into remaining

eggs; add yeast mixture, currants, citron, 2 cups of the flour, cinnamon and nutmeg. Beat until smooth. Stir in 2 more cups flour to make a soft dough.
4. Turn out onto lightly floured surface; knead until smooth and elastic, about 8 minutes; place in greased bowl; let rise in warm, draft-free place, about 2 hours or until double in volume.
5. Punch dough down; turn out onto lightly floured surface. Divide in half.
6. Grease two 8 × 8 × 2-inch pans. Divide each piece of dough into 16 pieces; shape each piece into a smooth round. Arrange, almost touching, in prepared pans.
7. Cover; let rise in a warm, draft-free place until doubled, about 45 minutes. Preheat oven to 350°. Brush tops with reserved egg.
8. Bake in a preheated moderate oven (350°) for 30 minutes or until buns are brown and sound hollow when tapped. Remove from pans; cool on wire racks.
9. When cool, drizzle Sugar Icing from tip of teaspoon on top of buns to make crosses.

Swedish Tea Ring

Bake at 375° for 25 minutes.

Makes 2 tea rings.

1 envelope active dry yeast
1/3 cup sugar
1/4 cup very warm water
1/3 cup milk
1/4 cup (1/2 stick) butter or margarine
1 teaspoon salt
2 eggs, beaten
3 cups unsifted all-purpose flour
1/2 teaspoon ground
cardamom
1/4 cup (1/2 stick) butter or margarine, softened
1/2 cup firmly packed brown sugar
1 teaspoon ground cinnamon
1/3 cup raisins
1/3 cup chopped walnuts
Sugar Icing (recipe follows)

1. Sprinkle yeast and 1/2 teaspoon of the sugar over very warm water in a 1-cup measure. ("Very warm water" should feel comfortably warm when dropped on wrist.) Stir to dissolve; let stand until bubbly, about 10 minutes.
2. Heat milk, 1/4 cup butter, salt and the remaining sugar in small saucepan just until butter is melted. Pour into large bowl; cool to lukewarm.
3. Add eggs and yeast mixture to milk mixture; beat until blended. Add 1 1/2 cups of the flour mixed with cardamom; beat 2 minutes. Stir in just enough remaining flour to make a soft dough.
4. Turn out onto lightly floured surface. Knead until smooth and elastic, about 8 minutes. Place dough in greased medium-size bowl, turning to bring greased side up. Cover; let rise in a warm, draft-free place, 1 1/2 hours or until double in volume. Punch dough down; let rest 5 minutes.

(continued)

5. Divide dough in half; roll to make two 12 × 9-inch rectangles. Spread each rectangle with 2 tablespoons soft butter.

6. Combine brown sugar, cinnamon, raisins and walnuts in a small bowl; sprinkle half the mixture over each dough rectangle. Roll up each tightly, jelly-roll fashion, from long side, pinching seam to seal.

7. Place each, seam-side down, on greased cookie sheet and shape into a circle; pinch ends to seal.

8. Make cuts 2/3 of the way from outside edge through the dough and 1 inch apart with scissors or sharp knife. Turn each section, cut-side up, so filling shows. Cover; let rise until double in volume, about 45 minutes.

9. Preheat oven to 375°. Bake in a moderate oven (375°) for 25 minutes or until golden brown and tea ring sounds hollow when tapped. (Cover with foil if tops are browning too quickly.) Remove to wire rack. Cool. Drizzle with Sugar Icing.

Sugar Icing: Blend 1 cup *unsifted* 10X (confectioners') sugar with 2 tablespoons milk until smooth in small bowl. Makes 1/2 cup.

Lemon Cheese Babka

Freeze one for later.

Bake at 350° for 40 minutes.

Makes two 8-inch cakes.

1 envelope active dry yeast	**2 teaspoons grated lemon rind**
1/4 cup sugar	**2 eggs plus 2 egg yolks**
1/4 cup very warm water	**1/3 cup warm milk**
3 1/2 to 4 cups *unsifted* all-purpose flour	**6 tablespoons (3/4 stick) butter, softened**
3/4 teaspoon salt	

Cheese filling:	
1 package (8 ounces) cream cheese	**1 egg yolk**
1/2 cup cottage cheese	**1/4 cup sugar**
	1 teaspoon grated lemon rind

Crumb Topping:	
1/3 cup chopped nuts	**sugar**
3 tablespoons flour	**1/4 teaspoon ground cinnamon**
3 tablespoons butter, softened	**1/2 cup raisins**
3 tablespoons	**10X (confectioners') sugar**

1. Sprinkle yeast and 1/2 teaspoon of the sugar over very warm water in a 1-cup measure. ("Very warm water" should feel comfortably warm when dropped on wrist.) Stir to dissolve. Let stand until bubbly, about 10 minutes.

2. Combine 2 cups of the flour, salt, lemon rind and the remaining sugar in large bowl; make a well in middle. Beat the eggs and egg yolks in a small bowl just to mix. Pour eggs, yeast mixture and warm milk into well. Stir liquids into flour until smooth. Beat well.

3. Gradually add softened butter, beating well. Stir in 1 more cup of the flour. Beat until dough leaves side of bowl.

4. Turn out onto lightly floured surface; knead until smooth and elastic, about 10 minutes, adding more flour.

5. Place dough in buttered bowl, turning to bring buttered side up; cover. Let rise in warm, draft-free place, 1 1/2 to 2 hours until double in volume.

6. While dough is rising, make Cheese Filling: Beat cream cheese and cottage cheese in small bowl with electric mixer until smooth; beat in egg yolk and sugar. Stir in grated lemon rind.

7. Make Crumb Topping: Combine nuts, flour, butter, sugar and cinnamon in small bowl. Grease two 8 × 1 1/2-inch layer pans.

8. When dough has doubled, punch down; knead in raisins; divide dough into 4 equal parts; press 2 parts into the bottoms and about 1/2 inch up the sides of each of the layer pans; spread each with about 1 cup of the cheese filling.

9. Shape remaining dough into 8-inch circles; place on top of cheese filling. Press spoon handle into dough around edges to seal.

10. Sprinkle half the crumb topping over each Babka. Let rise in warm place until dough reaches top of pans, about 1 hour. Preheat oven to 350°.

11. Bake in a preheated moderate oven (350°) for 40 minutes or until cakes sound hollow when tapped. Turn out onto wire rack to cool. (Place foil loosely over crumb topping; invert onto rack, then turn right-side up.) Let cool at least 30 minutes before serving. Sprinkle with 10X sugar.

Kuchen   A German word for coffee cake made from a yeast or baking powder dough, usually topped or filled with fruit.

Plum and Peach Kuchen

Bake at 400° for 35 minutes.

Makes 8 servings.

1 1/2 cups *sifted* all-purpose flour	**half-and-half**
1/2 cup sugar	**1 tablespoon grated lemon rind**
2 teaspoons baking powder	**6 large plums, cut into quarters (about 1 pound)**
1/2 teaspoon salt	
1/4 teaspoon ground cardamom	**1 large peach, cut into 6 equal pieces (about 1/4 pound)**
1/2 cup (1 stick) butter or margarine	**1 tablespoon light cream**
2 eggs	
1/4 cup light cream or	**2 tablespoons sugar**

1. Sift flour, the 1/2 cup sugar, baking powder, salt and cardamom into large bowl. Cut in butter with a pastry blender or two knives until evenly mixed and crumbly.

Pictured above (clockwise from top left): Fresh Coconut Layer Cake, page 182; Pecan Candy Cake, page 182; Christmas Stollen, page 138; Cranberry Nut Cheesecake, page 167.

2. Beat eggs, light cream and lemon rind together in a small bowl; add all at once to flour mixture; stir just until batter is thoroughly moistened. Spread mixture into a lightly buttered 9 x 1½-inch layer-cake pan. Preheat oven to 400°.

3. Arrange plum quarters on batter around edge of pan; arrange peach slices in center. Brush with the remaining 1 tablespoon light cream; sprinkle with 2 tablespoons sugar.

4. Bake in a preheated hot oven (400°) for 35 minutes or until a wooden pick inserted near center comes out clean.

Plum Kuchen

Bake at 375° for 30 to 40 minutes.

Makes 4 servings.

½ **cup (1 stick) butter or margarine**	½ **teaspoon ground cinnamon**
¾ **cup firmly packed brown sugar**	1 **can (17 ounces) purple plums, drained, halved, pitted**
1 **cup** *sifted* **all-purpose flour**	
½ **teaspoon salt**	1 **egg, slightly beaten**
¼ **teaspoon baking powder**	1 **cup light cream or half-and-half**

1. Beat butter and sugar in a small bowl until smooth. Sift flour, salt, baking powder and cinnamon onto wax

(continued)

paper. Blend into sugar mixture. Press evenly on bottom and about 1 inch up sides of 9-inch pie plate or 8 x 8 x 2-inch baking pan. Preheat oven to 375°.

2. Arrange plum halves on shell.

3. Combine egg and cream; pour over plums.

4. Bake in a preheated moderate oven (375°) for 30 to 40 minutes or until custard is set. Serve warm.

Christmas Stollen

Bake at 350° for 30 to 35 minutes.
Makes 2 stollens (about 12 slices each).

³/₄ **cup milk**	¹/₂ **teaspoon ground mace**
¹/₂ **cup water**	
¹/₂ **cup (1 stick) unsalted butter, at room temperature**	2 **tablespoons brandy**
	³/₄ **cup chopped mixed candied fruits**
4 to 4¹/₄ **cups** *unsifted* **all-purpose flour**	²/₃ **cup coarsely chopped blanched almonds**
¹/₂ **cup sugar**	
1³/₄ **teaspoons salt**	2 **tablespoons unsalted butter, melted**
2 **envelopes active dry yeast**	
1 **egg, at room temperature**	10X **(confectioners') sugar**
¹/₂ **cup golden raisins**	

Combine the milk, water and the ¹/₂ cup of butter in a small saucepan. Heat over low heat until warm (120° to 130°) and the butter is melted. Remove from the heat.

2. Combine 1¹/₄ cups of the flour, sugar, salt and yeast in a large bowl. Gradually beat in the milk mixture. Beat for 2 minutes at medium speed, scraping down the sides of the bowl occasionally with a rubber spatula. Beat in the egg and ³/₄ cup of the flour. Beat at high speed for 2 minutes. Stir in 2 cups of the flour or enough to make a stiff batter. Transfer to a lightly oiled bowl; turn to bring the oiled-side up. Cover tightly with plastic wrap. Refrigerate for 2 to 3 hours.

3. When ready to shape, remove the dough from the refrigerator. Combine the raisins, mace and brandy in a small saucepan. Heat gently over very low heat just until the brandy begins to simmer. Cool to lukewarm. Add the candied fruits and almonds. Set aside.

4. Grease 2 cookie sheets. Turn out the dough onto a lightly floured surface. Knead in the fruits and nuts. Divide the dough in half. Roll each half into a 12 × 6-inch oval. Fold each in half lengthwise. Transfer to the prepared cookie sheets. Curve the ends of each slightly to form a crescent shape. Cover with buttered wax paper and a towel. Let rise in a warm place, away from drafts, until doubled in volume, about 1 hour. Meanwhile, preheat the oven to moderate (350°). Bake in a preheated moderate oven (350°) for 30 to 35 minutes until golden brown and the undersides sound hollow when tapped with the fingers. Remove to wire racks to cool. Brush with the melted butter while still warm. Sprinkle evenly with the 10X sugar.

BREAD LEFTOVERS

Bread Leftover   Ready-made leftover bread can be put to many other uses. So, don't throw that heel away! It can be cubed for a stuffing or bread pudding, added to soup or gravy as a thickener, made into bread crumbs or cubes for croutons. Bread can also be used to make "stratas," an inexpensive baked egg custard main dish.

To Make Cubes and Croutons

Soft Bread Cubes Stack 2 or 3 slices of bread on a cutting board and cut into strips of desired width; then cut across the strips to form even-size cubes. Trim crusts off bread slices before cutting into cubes, if you wish.

Toasted Bread Cubes Spread soft bread cubes in a jelly-roll pan and place in a slow oven (300°). Toast, shaking occasionally, until golden brown on all sides.

Croutons Brown soft bread cubes, about 1 cup at a time, in 2 tablespoons olive or vegetable oil in a large, heavy skillet over moderately high heat, stirring and turning often until evenly golden brown.

Garlic Croutons Sauté 1 clove garlic, crushed, in 2 tablespoons olive or vegetable oil in a large skillet over moderate heat until golden. Discard the garlic. Add 1 cup soft bread cubes to garlic-flavored oil. Sauté, stirring and turning often until cubes are evenly golden brown. Drain on paper toweling.

To Make Bread Crumbs

Fresh Bread Crumbs Tear slices of bread into small pieces with your fingers. Or, place one slice at a time, quartered, in the container of an electric blender or food processor; cover; whirl at high speed 15 seconds.

Dry Bread Crumbs Put dry bread slices through a food chopper fitted with a fine blade. (A neat trick is to tie a plastic bag on the blade end of the grinder so that the crumbs will drop directly into the bag as they are ground—no mess.) Or, place slices of dry bread in a plastic bag and seal; crush with a rolling pin. Or, fastest trick of all, whirl dry bread pieces in the container of an electric blender or food processor.

For fine crumbs: Sift the ground crumbs through a fine sieve. Store the fine crumbs and the coarse (those left behind in the sieve) separately in covered containers.

Buttered Bread Crumbs Melt 2 tablespoons butter or margarine in a skillet; add 1 cup of dry bread crumbs and stir-fry until crumbs are golden brown. Makes 1 cup.

Seasoned Bread Crumbs Prepare Buttered Bread Crumbs and remove from heat. Stir in 2 tablespoons chopped fresh parsley, 2 tablespoons grated Parmesan cheese, ¹/₂ teaspoon leaf basil, crumbled, ¹/₂ teaspoon leaf oregano, crumbled and dash of pepper.

Freezer Orange French Toast

Bake at 500° for 13 to 18 minutes.

Makes 4 to 6 servings.

4 eggs	ground nutmeg
1 cup milk	8 to 10 slices day-old
2 tablespoons sugar	French bread,
1 teaspoon vanilla	3/4 inch thick
1 teaspoon grated	Butter or margarine,
orange rind	melted
1/4 cup orange juice	10X (confectioners')
1/4 teaspoon freshly	sugar

1. Beat eggs, milk, sugar, vanilla, orange rind and juice and nutmeg. Place bread on a jelly-roll pan. Pour egg mixture over bread and let stand a few minutes; turn slices over and let stand until all egg mixture is absorbed. Place in freezer, uncovered, until firm; transfer to freezer bag and return to freezer.
2. To serve: Preheat oven to 500°. Place frozen slices on greased jelly-roll pan. Brush each with melted butter or margarine.
3. Bake in a preheated very hot oven (500°) for 8 minutes. Turn slices, brush again and bake 5 to 10 minutes longer.or until lightly browned. Serve with confectioners' sugar, honey or maple syrup, if you wish.

Curried Egg Strata

For a pleasant flavor combination, serve with chutney or pickled melon rind.

Bake at 375° for 45 minutes.

Makes 4 servings.

1/4 cup mayonnaise	3 hard-cooked eggs
1 teaspoon curry	1/4 cup chopped green
powder	onions
4 slices firm whole	2 ounces Swiss
wheat bread, lightly	cheese, shredded
toasted	(1/2 cup)
4 slices firm white	3 eggs
bread, lightly	2 1/2 cups milk
toasted	1 teaspoon salt

1. Combine mayonnaise and curry powder in small bowl. Spread on two slices of the whole wheat and two slices of the white bread. Cut slices into quarters. Place in bottom of buttered 6-cup shallow baking pan.
2. Slice hard-cooked eggs and place on top of bread. Sprinkle with green onions and the cheese.
3. Cut remaining 4 slices bread into quarters. Arrange in checkerboard design over the cheese.
4. Beat eggs slightly in medium-size bowl; stir in milk and salt. Pour over bread slices.
5. Cover and chill at least 1 hour or overnight.
6. Bake uncovered in a moderate oven (375°) for 45 minutes or until puffed and golden. Remove to wire rack. Let stand 10 minutes before serving.

Apple-Bread Pudding

Bake at 350° for 40 minutes.

Makes 6 servings.

1/4 cup dried currants	1 3/4 cups milk
or raisins	1/2 cup heavy cream
2 tablespoons apple	1/2 cup sugar
cider or juice	1/2 teaspoon vanilla
1 large tart cooking	2 cups *unseasoned*
apple (Rome Beauty	croutons
or Granny Smith)	1/3 cup slivered
1/4 cup (1/2 stick) butter	almonds
or margarine,	2 tablespoons brown
melted	sugar
4 eggs, beaten	

1. Soak currants in the apple cider while preparing other ingredients.
2. Peel, core and cut apple into very thin slices. Cook slices in 2 tablespoons of butter in a small skillet just until soft and translucent; spoon into a 1 1/2 -quart casserole.
3. Beat eggs in a medium-size bowl. Add milk, cream, sugar and vanilla and stir to blend well.
4. Add croutons, remaining butter and currant mixture to casserole; stir gently to mix with apples.
5. Pour custard mixture into casserole and let stand 20 minutes until croutons are soaked with custard. Sprinkle with almonds and sugar.
6. Place casserole in a large, shallow baking pan; place on oven shelf. Pour boiling water into pan to come 1 to 2 inches up sides of casserole.
7. Bake in a moderate oven (350°) for 40 minutes or until a thin-bladed knife comes out clean when inserted 1 inch from edge. Serve warm or cold with heavy cream, if you wish.

Bread Pudding

Bake at 325° for 1 hour.

Makes 10 servings.

3/4 cup granulated	raisins
sugar	10 slices firm white
3 eggs	bread, crusts
1/8 teaspoon salt	removed
1 tablespoon vanilla	1/3 cup strawberry or
3 cups milk	red raspberry
1/4 cup (1/2 stick)	preserves
butter, melted	Fresh strawberries,
1/2 cup seedless	sliced

1. Reserve 1 teaspoon of the sugar. Combine the remaining sugar with eggs, salt and vanilla in a large bowl. Gradually beat in milk until well combined.
2. Brush bottom and sides of 11 3/4 x 7 1/2 x 1 3/4-inch baking dish with some of the melted butter. Reserve 1 tablespoon of the raisins. Sprinkle the remaining raisins over the bottom of the baking dish. Pour milk mixture over raisins.

(continued)

3. Cut bread slices in half diagonally. Brush both sides of the bread triangles with butter.

4. Arrange bread, slightly overlapping, on top of the milk mixture. Sprinkle with the reserved raisins and reserved sugar. Set the baking dish in a larger pan; place on oven shelf. Pour boiling water into the larger pan to come halfway up side of baking dish. Preheat oven to slow (325°).

5. Bake in the preheated slow oven (325°) for 1 hour or until a knife blade inserted 1 inch from the edge comes out clean. Let stand for 15 minutes before serving.

6. Force preserves through a sieve with the back of spoon. Drizzle over pudding. Serve with strawberries.

Microwave Directions: 650 Watt Variable Power Microwave Oven

Ingredient Changes: Reduce butter from 1/4 cup to 1/2 teaspoon.

Directions: Place 1/2 teaspoon butter in an 11 3/4 × 7 1/2 × 1 3/4-inch microwave-safe baking dish. Microwave at full power for 30 seconds or until butter is melted. Brush over bottom of the dish. Place milk in a microwave-safe bowl. Microwave at full power for 3 minutes, stirring once. Assemble bread pudding according to the recipe (above), without brushing bread with butter. Microwave, uncovered, at full power for 12 minutes, turning twice, or until the center feels set. Let stand for 10 minutes.

Chili Pie Casserole

Bake at 375° for 45 minutes.

Makes 8 servings.

Cornbread (recipe follows)	powder
3/4 pound ground chuck	1 can (6 ounces) tomato paste
1 medium-size onion, chopped	2 cups water
2 teaspoons salt	4 ounces Cheddar cheese, shredded (1 cup)
1 tablespoon plus 1 teaspoon chili	4 eggs, slightly beaten
	3 cups milk

1. Make Cornbread. Remove cooled cornbread from pan; carefully split cooled cornbread crosswise to make 2 thin layers. Cut bottom layer into nine 2 1/2-inch squares. Cut each square to make 2 triangles. Crumble remaining layer and place in bottom of well buttered 11 3/4 × 7 1/2 × 1 3/4-inch baking pan.

2. Sauté meat and onion in heavy skillet 5 minutes. Stir in 1 teaspoon of the salt, the chili powder, tomato paste and water. Cook, uncovered, stirring occasionally, 15 minutes. Spread over cornbread in pan. Sprinkle with 1/2 cup of the cheese.

3. Arrange cornbread triangles on top. Combine eggs with milk and remaining teaspoon of salt. Pour over cornbread. Sprinkle with remaining 1/2 cup cheese. Cover and chill at least 1 hour or overnight.

4. Bake uncovered in a moderate oven (375°) for 45

minutes or until puffed and golden. Remove to wire rack. Let stand 10 minutes before serving.

Note: Cover tips of cornbread with foil if they are browning too rapidly.

Cornbread: Preheat oven to 425°. Combine 1 cup cornmeal, 1 cup sifted all-purpose flour, 4 teaspoons baking powder and 1/2 teaspoon salt in a large bowl. Stir in 1 cup milk, 1 egg and 1/4 cup vegetable shortening. Beat until fairly smooth, 1 minute. Pour into greased 8 × 8 × 2-inch pan. Bake in a preheated hot oven (425°) for 20 minutes or until top springs back when lightly touched with fingertip; cool in pan on wire rack.

Spinach Cheese Strata

The flavor of this convenient dish is similar to a spinach quiche.

Bake at 375° for 45 minutes.

Makes 6 servings.

1 loaf French bread (day-old is best)	chopped spinach, thawed
1 large onion, chopped (1 cup)	1 teaspoon dillweed
2 tablespoons butter	1 teaspoon salt
3/4 cup cooked, chopped spinach (8 cups fresh)	Pinch pepper
	6 ounces Swiss cheese, shredded (1 1/2 cups)
OR: 1 package (10 ounces) frozen	3 eggs
	2 1/2 cups milk

1. Cut bread into thin slices; line bottom of buttered shallow 6-cup baking dish with half the slices.

2. Sauté onion in butter in large skillet 5 minutes. Squeeze spinach dry and add to pan with dill, 1/4 teaspoon of the salt and the pepper. Stir just to combine.

3. Spread spinach over bread in pan; sprinkle with 1 cup of the cheese. Arrange remaining bread overlapping on top.

4. Beat eggs in medium-size bowl; stir in milk and remaining 3/4 teaspoon salt. Pour over bread. Sprinkle with remaining cheese. Cover and chill at least 1 hour or overnight.

5. Bake uncovered in a moderate oven (375°) for 45 minutes or until puffed and golden. If bread is browning too quickly, cover with foil. Remove to wire rack. Let stand 10 minutes before serving.

Pictured opposite (clockwise from upper right): Spinach Cheese Strata, page 140; Chili Pie Casserole, page 140; Curried Egg Strata, page 139.

CAKES and TORTES

Cake Cake baking is not only an art, but also a science—the proper ingredients in the proper proportions are needed to chemically transform a wet batter into a light, airy product. There are two types of cakes: butter and foam.

Butter cakes, such as pound cakes, fruitcakes, chocolate or spice cakes, are made of butter or vegetable shortening, sugar, flour and a leavening agent and can be shaped into round layers, loaves or cupcakes. Some tortes, usually made of many layers and a rich filling or frosting, are also considered butter cakes.

Foam cakes rely on air beaten into egg whites as the leavening agent, although some baking powder may also be added. Angel food cakes, for example, are made with only egg whites, sugar, cake flour and a flavoring. No butter or oil or additional leavening agent is used. Chiffon cakes on the other hand, are made with egg yolks and oil mixed into the batter; then the batter is folded into beaten egg whites. Sponge cakes, which include jelly-roll cakes, are made by beating the whole eggs with sugar until thick, then gradually folding in a mixture of cake flour, baking powder and salt.

How to Frost a Cake

1. Place the cake plate on something you can turn—a lazy susan, if you have one. Or, set plate on a large, inverted bowl or a sugar canister. Then rotate the plate as you frost the cake.
2. Before frosting the cake, brush off all loose crumbs.
3. When frosting layer cakes, put flat bottoms of cake together, facing one another. This way the cake will be steady and level.
4. Frost the entire outside of the assembled cake with a *very thin layer of frosting;* let it set about 20 minutes. The thin coating holds the crumbs in place and keeps them from mixing with the final coat of frosting.
5. Frost the sides of the cake first from bottom up, then top, swirling frosting into soft peaks.

Torte A very rich, multilayered cake made with eggs and often grated nuts. Usually it is filled and left unfrosted.

Pictured opposite (clockwise from the top): Peanut Butter Cake, page 143, Mississippi Mud Cake, page 144; Colonial Seed Cake, page 144; Bourbon Applesauce Cake, page 144.

Cake Storage

● Cakes with a butter cream frosting can be left at room temperature. Cover the cut surface of the cake with plastic wrap and place it in a cake keeper, or invert a large bowl over the cake plate. The cake will keep for 2 or 3 days this way. (In hot weather, it is still best to refrigerate the cake.)
● Cakes with a cream frosting or filling should be refrigerated, with plastic wrap over the cut part.
● Unfrosted cakes freeze best—for up to 4 months. Wrap in aluminum foil, plastic wrap or large plastic bags; thaw at room temperature for 1 hour.
● Frosted cakes should be frozen on a piece of cardboard or a cookie sheet until firm, then wrapped in aluminum foil, plastic wrap or very large plastic bags; freeze cakes for up to 3 months and thaw at room temperature for 2 hours.

Peanut Butter Cake

Bake at 350° for 45 minutes, then at 325° for 20 minutes.

Makes one 12-cup Bundt cake.

³/₄ cup (1¹/₂ sticks) butter	powder
¹/₄ cup creamy peanut butter	3 cups *sifted* all-purpose flour
4 eggs	1 teaspoon vanilla
¹/₂ cup buttermilk	¹/₂ cup water
2 cups sugar	Peanut Butter Topping *(recipe follows)*
3 teaspoons baking	

1. Let butter, peanut butter, eggs and buttermilk warm to room temperature for easy mixing. (Butter should be very soft.) Grease and flour a 12-cup Bundt pan or a 10-inch tube pan. Preheat oven to 350°.
2. Combine room temperature ingredients with sugar, baking powder, flour, vanilla and water in a large bowl. Beat at slow speed with electric mixer for 30 seconds, then at medium speed for 2 minutes, scraping side of bowl. Pour into prepared pan.
3. Bake in a preheated moderate oven (350°) for 45 minutes, then lower heat to 325° and bake 20 minutes longer or until top springs back when lightly pressed with fingertip. Cool on wire rack 10 minutes. Turn out; cool completely before frosting.

Peanut Butter Topping: Combine ¹/₄ cup creamy peanut butter, 1 cup 10X (confectioners') sugar and 4 to 5 tablespoons buttermilk in small bowl until smooth. Spoon over cake.

Colonial Seed Cake

Bake at 350° for 1 hour, 15 minutes.

Makes one loaf cake.

1 jar (2 ounces) poppy seeds (1/2 cup)	**1 teaspoon vanilla**
3/4 cup milk	**2 teaspoons baking powder**
3/4 cup (1 1/2 sticks) soft butter	**2 cups** *sifted* **all-purpose flour**
3 eggs	**10X (confectioners') sugar**
1 1/4 cups sugar	

1. Combine poppy seeds and milk in a large bowl. Let stand at room temperature 3 to 4 hours. Let butter and eggs warm to room temperature for easy mixing. (Butter should be very soft.) Grease and flour an 8 1/2 × 4 1/2 × 2 1/2 -inch loaf pan. Preheat oven to 350°.
2. Add butter, eggs, sugar, vanilla, baking powder and flour to poppy seeds and milk. Beat at medium speed with electric mixer for 1 minute, scraping side of bowl with plastic spatula. Pour into prepared pan.
3. Bake in a preheated moderate oven (350°) for 1 hour, 15 minutes or until center springs back when lightly pressed with fingertip. Cool in pan on wire rack 5 minutes. Loosen around edges; turn out to cool. Sprinkle with 10X sugar. Serve plain or with whipped cream, if you wish.

Mississippi Mud Cake

Candy bars frost this easy cake.
Bake at 350° for 40 minutes.

Makes one 11 3/4 × 7 1/2-inch cake.

3/4 cup (1 1/2 sticks) butter	**purpose flour**
1/2 cup heavy cream	**2 teaspoons baking powder**
1/2 cup brewed coffee	**1/2 teaspoon salt**
4 eggs	**1 teaspoon vanilla**
1 1/2 cups sugar	**4 bars (1.2 ounces each) milk chocolate candy**
1/2 cup cocoa	
1 3/4 cups *sifted* **all-**	

1. Let butter, cream, coffee and eggs warm to room temperature for easy mixing. (Butter should be very soft.) Grease and flour an 11 3/4 × 7 1/2 × 1 3/4-inch baking pan. Preheat oven to 350°.
2. Combine room temperature ingredients with remaining ingredients, except candy bars, in a large bowl. Beat at medium speed with electric mixer for 1 minute, scraping side of bowl with plastic spatula. Pour into prepared pan.
3. Bake in a preheated moderate oven (350°) for 40 minutes or until center springs back when lightly pressed with fingertip. Place on wire rack.

4. Break chocolate bars into pieces; place on hot cake; let stand 1 minute, then spread softened chocolate with spatula to frost cake. Cool before serving.

Bourbon Applesauce Cake

Moist and delicious, this cake keeps very well.
Bake at 325° for 1 hour, 30 minutes.

Makes one loaf cake.

1/2 cup (1 stick) butter	**1/4 cup wheat germ**
2 eggs	**2 cups sweetened applesauce**
1 cup firmly packed brown sugar	**1/4 cup bourbon or apple cider**
2 1/2 cups *sifted* **all-purpose flour**	**3/4 cup finely chopped walnuts**
2 teaspoons baking soda	**10X (confectioners') sugar**
1/4 teaspoon salt	

1. Let butter and eggs warm to room temperature for easy mixing. (Butter should be very soft.) Grease and flour a 9 × 5 × 3-inch loaf pan. Preheat oven to 325°.
2. Combine room temperature ingredients with brown sugar, flour, baking soda, salt, wheat germ, applesauce and bourbon or cider in a large bowl. Beat at medium speed with electric mixer for 3 minutes, scraping down side of bowl with plastic spatula. Stir in nuts. Pour into prepared pan.
3. Bake in a preheated slow oven (325°) for 1 hour, 30 minutes or until center springs back when lightly pressed with fingertip. Cool in pan on wire rack 10 minutes. Loosen around edges with metal spatula; remove from pan. Cool completely. Sprinkle with 10X sugar.

Note: Spoon an additional 1/4 cup bourbon or apple cider over cake while it is still warm, if you wish.

Apricot Cake Roll

Bake at 375° for 12 to 15 minutes.

Makes 1 jelly roll.

1 cup *sifted* **cake flour**	**1/3 cup water**
1 teaspoon baking powder	**1 teaspoon vanilla**
1/4 teaspoon salt	**10X (confectioners') sugar**
3 eggs	**3/4 cup apricot preserves**
3/4 cup sugar	

1. Grease a 15 1/2 × 10 1/2 × 1-inch jelly-roll pan; line bottom with wax paper; grease paper.
2. Sift flour, baking powder and salt. Preheat oven to 375°.

3. Beat eggs in a medium-size bowl with electric mixer until thick and creamy. Gradually add sugar, beating constantly until mixture is very thick. (This will take at least 5 minutes.) Blend in water and vanilla on low speed. Add flour mixture, beating (on low speed) just until batter is smooth. Pour into prepared pan, spreading evenly into corners.

4. Bake in a preheated moderate oven (375°) for 12 minutes or until center of cake springs back when lightly pressed with fingertip.

5. Loosen cake around edges with a small knife; invert onto a clean towel dusted with 10X sugar; peel off wax paper. Starting at short end, roll up cake and towel together. Cool on wire rack. When cool, unroll carefully; spread evenly with preserves. Reroll cake. Place seam side down on platter or small cookie sheet until ready to slice and serve.

Devil's Food Cake

So wickedly delicious, someone called it "the devil's own food." This kind of ultra-chocolatey cake has pleased generations of Americans.

Bake at 350° for 35 minutes.

Makes one 9-inch cake.

3 squares unsweetened chocolate	3 large eggs
2¼ cups *sifted* cake flour	2 teaspoons vanilla
2 teaspoons baking soda	1 container (8 ounces) dairy sour cream
½ teaspoon salt	1 cup boiling water
½ cup (1 stick) butter or margarine	Fluffy 7-Minute Frosting (*recipe follows*)
1¾ cups firmly packed light brown sugar	1 square unsweetened chocolate
	1 tablespoon butter or margarine

1. Melt chocolate in small bowl over hot, not boiling, water; cool.

2. Grease and flour two 9 × 1½- inch layer cake pans or one 13 × 9 × 2-inch baking pan; tap out excess flour.

3. Sift flour, baking soda and salt onto wax paper.

4. Beat butter until soft in large bowl. Add brown sugar and eggs; beat with electric mixer at high speed until light and fluffy, 5 minutes. Beat in vanilla and cooled melted chocolate. Preheat oven to 350°.

5. Stir in dry ingredients with spoon alternately with sour cream after each addition until batter is smooth. Stir in boiling water. (Batter will be thin.) Pour at once into prepared pans.

6. Bake in a preheated moderate oven (350°) for 35 minutes or until centers spring back when lightly pressed with fingertip.

7. Cool cake in pans on wire rack 10 minutes; loosen around edges with a small knife or spatula; turn out onto wire racks; cool completely. If using 13 × 9 × 2-inch pan, split cooled cake to make 2 layers.

8. Make Fluffy 7-Minute Frosting. Place one cake layer on a serving plate; spread with about ¼ of the frosting; place second layer over. Gently brush off loose crumbs. Frost sides and top, swirling frosting with spatula.

9. Melt chocolate square with the butter in a cup over hot water; stir until smooth. Drizzle over top of cake, letting mixture drip down side.

Deep Dark Devil's Food Cake

Bake at 350° for 40 minutes.

Makes one 9-inch cake.

2 cups *sifted* cake flour	3 large eggs
⅔ cup unsweetened cocoa powder	2 teaspoons vanilla
¾ teaspoon baking powder	1¼ cups water
1¼ teaspoons baking soda	Fluffy 7-Minute Frosting (*recipe follows*)
1 teaspoon salt	1 square unsweetened chocolate
⅔ cup vegetable shortening	1 tablespoon butter or margarine
1⅓ cups sugar	

1. Sift flour, cocoa, baking powder, baking soda and salt onto wax paper. Preheat oven to 350°.

2. Beat shortening, sugar, eggs and vanilla in a large bowl with electric mixer at high speed until fluffy-light, about 5 minutes. Beat in flour mixture alternately with water on low speed. Do not overbeat. Pour into two greased 9 × 1½-inch layer-cake pans.

3. Bake in a preheated moderate oven (350°) for 40 minutes or until centers spring back when lightly pressed with fingertip. Cool in pans on wire rack for 10 minutes. Remove from pans; cool.

4. Make Fluffy 7-Minute Frosting. Place 1 cake layer on a serving plate; spread with about ¼ of the frosting; place second layer over. Gently brush off loose crumbs and spread a thin coat of frosting over top and sides; let set. Spread remaining frosting, making swirls with spatula.

5. Melt chocolate square with the butter in a cup over hot water; stir until smooth. Drizzle over top of cake, letting mixture drip down side, if you wish.

Overleaf (counterclockwise from top center): Deep Dark Devil's Food Cake, page 145; Chocolate Meringue Torte, page 148; Chocolate Fudge Cake, page 148; Brazilian Chocolate Roll, page 149.

Fluffy 7-Minute Frosting

Makes enough to fill and frost two 8- or 9-inch cake layers or one 13 × 9 × 2-inch cake.

1½ cups sugar
¼ cup water
2 egg whites
2 tablespoons light

corn syrup
¼ teaspoon salt
1 teaspoon vanilla

1. Combine sugar, water, egg whites, corn syrup and salt in top of double boiler; beat mixture until well blended.
2. Place over simmering water; cook, beating constantly at high speed with electric hand mixer or rotary beater about 7 minutes, or until mixture triples in volume and holds firm peaks. Remove from heat; beat in vanilla. Spread on cooled cake while still warm.

Chocolate Meringue Torte

Bake at 300° for 30 minutes.

Makes 10 servings.

Meringue Layers:
3 egg whites, at room
temperature
⅛ teaspoon cream of
tartar
¾ cup superfine sugar
Chocolate Curls
(recipe follows)

Chocolate Filling:
1 cup heavy cream
5 squares

semisweet
chocolate
2 squares
unsweetened
chocolate
2 tablespoons butter
or margarine
¾ cup superfine sugar
3 egg whites
10X (confectioners')
sugar

1. Prepare Layers: Grease 1 large and 1 small cookie sheet; dust with flour, tapping off excess. Using an 8-inch layer-cake pan as a guide, draw two 8-inch circles on large cookie sheet and one on small one. Preheat oven to 300°.
2. Beat the 3 egg whites with cream of tartar until foamy-white and double in volume in large bowl with electric mixer. Sprinkle in ¾ cup sugar, 1 tablespoon at a time, beating all the time until sugar dissolves completely and meringue stands in firm peaks. (Beating will take about 15 minutes in all with an electric mixer.) Spoon mixture evenly onto the 3 circles; spread out to edge.
3. Bake in a preheated slow oven (300°) for 30 minutes or until layers are firm and lightly golden. Cool 5 minutes on cookie sheets on wire racks, then loosen meringue layers carefully with a wide spatula and slide onto racks; cool.
4. Make Chocolate Curls.
5. Prepare Filling: Heat cream in top of double boiler; add semisweet and unsweetened chocolate. Stir often with a wooden spoon until chocolate is completely melted. Stir in butter and ¼ cup of remaining sugar.

6. Beat remaining 3 egg whites until foamy-white in large bowl with electric mixer; gradually add remaining ½ cup sugar, beating well after each addition; continue beating until meringue is glossy and stands in firm peaks.
7. Partly fill bottom of double boiler with ice and water; set top of boiler with chocolate mixture in ice water. Beat chocolate mixture at high speed with electric mixer or rotary hand beater until light and fluffy and almost double in volume; scrape down sides of double boiler often. Fold chocolate into meringue until no streaks of white or brown remain.
8. Place 1 meringue layer on a serving plate; spread with about 1 cup chocolate filling; repeat with another layer and 1 cup filling. Place third layer on top. Frost sides and top with remaining filling. Arrange prepared Chocolate Curls on top of cake; chill. Thirty minutes before serving, remove cake from refrigerator for ease in serving; sprinkle lightly with 10X sugar. Cut in wedges with sharp serrated knife.

Chocolate Curls: Melt 6 squares semisweet chocolate in a small bowl over hot water, stirring often. Turn out onto cold cookie sheet. It will spread naturally to about ¼-inch thick. Cool until set. Pull a long metal spatula at a 45-degree angle across chocolate, letting the chocolate curl up in front of the spatula. Place curls on wax paper. It takes a little practice, so count on a few to be less than perfect; put these on the cake first. Makes enough curls to decorate an 8- or 9-inch cake.

Chocolate Fudge Cake

Bake at 350° for 35 minutes.

Makes one 9-inch cake.

3 squares
unsweetened
chocolate
2¼ cups *sifted* cake
flour
2 teaspoons baking
soda
½ teaspoon salt
½ cup (1 stick) butter
or margarine
2¼ cups firmly

packed light brown
sugar
3 large eggs
1½ teaspoons vanilla
1 cup dairy sour
cream
1 cup boiling water
Chocolate Fudge
Frosting (recipe
follows)

1. Melt chocolate in a small bowl over hot, not boiling, water; cool.
2. Grease and flour two 9 × 1½-inch layer-cake pans; tap out excess flour. (Or, use cocoa in place of flour to keep cake dark on outside.)
3. Sift flour, baking soda and salt onto wax paper. Preheat oven to 350°.
4. Beat butter until soft in large bowl. Add brown sugar

and eggs; beat with electric mixer at high speed until light and fluffy, 5 minutes. Beat in vanilla and cooled melted chocolate.

5. Stir in dry ingredients alternately with sour cream, beating well with a wooden spoon after each addition until batter is smooth. Stir in boiling water. (Batter will be thin.) Pour at once into prepared pans.

6. Bake in a preheated moderate oven (350°) for 35 minutes or until centers spring back when lightly pressed with fingertip.

7. Cool layers in pans on wire rack, 10 minutes; loosen around edges with a small knife or spatula; turn out onto wire racks; cool completely.

8. Prepare Chocolate Fudge Frosting. Place one cake layer on a serving plate; spread with about one-quarter of frosting; place second layer over. Gently brush off loose crumbs and spread a thin coat of frosting over top and sides; let set. Spread remaining frosting, making swirls with spatula.

Chocolate Fudge Frosting

Makes enough to fill and frost two 9-inch layers.

4 squares unsweetened chocolate	**1 package (1 pound) 10X (confectioners') sugar**
1/2 cup (1 stick) butter or margarine	**1/2 cup milk**
	2 teaspoons vanilla

1. Combine chocolate and butter in small heavy saucepan. Cook over low heat just until melted; remove.

2. Combine 10X sugar, milk and vanilla in medium-size bowl; stir until smooth; add chocolate mixture.

3. Set bowl in pan of ice and water; beat with wooden spoon until frosting is thick enough to spread and hold its shape.

Brazilian Chocolate Roll

Bake at 375° for 12 minutes.

Makes one 10-inch roll.

3/4 cup *sifted* cake flour	**coffee**
1/4 cup unsweetened cocoa powder	**1 teaspoon vanilla**
1 teaspoon baking powder	**10X (confectioners') sugar**
1/4 teaspoon salt	**Coffee Cream Filling (*recipe follows*)**
3 eggs	**Chocolate Glaze (*recipe follows*)**
1 cup granulated sugar	**Chopped pistachio nuts**
1/3 cup strong cold	

1. Grease a 15 1/2 × 10 1/2 1-inch jelly-roll pan; line bottom with wax paper; grease paper. Preheat oven to 375°.

2. Sift flour, cocoa, baking powder and salt onto a piece of wax paper.

3. Beat eggs in a medium-size bowl with an electric mixer until thick and creamy. Gradually add sugar while continuing to beat until mixture is very thick and light. Stir in coffee and vanilla. Fold in flour mixture. Spread batter evenly in prepared pan.

4. Bake in a preheated moderate oven (375°) for 12 minutes or until center springs back when lightly pressed with fingertip.

5. Loosen cake around edges; invert onto clean towel which has been liberally sprinkled with 10X sugar. Peel off wax paper. Trim 1/4 inch from all 4 sides for easy rolling. Starting at short end, roll up cake and towel together. Place, seam-side down, on wire rack; cool completely.

6. Prepare Coffee Cream Filling.

7. Unroll cake carefully; spread evenly with filling. Reroll cake and filling by lifting towel at short end and tucking under first turn, then letting cake roll over on itself. Place, seamside down, on serving plate.

8. Prepare Chocolate Glaze: Reserve 1 tablespoon of the glaze for decorating; spread remaining glaze evenly over cake. Drizzle reserved glaze over; sprinkle with pistachio nuts; refrigerate until serving time.

Coffee Cream Filling: Combine 1 cup heavy cream, 2 teaspoons instant coffee and 1/4 cup 10X sugar in a medium-size bowl. Beat with electric mixer until stiff. Makes 2 cups.

Chocolate Glaze: Melt 1 square unsweetened chocolate and 1 tablespoon butter or margarine in a small saucepan over low heat. Remove from heat; stir in 1/2 cup 10X sugar and 2 tablespoons boiling water until smooth. Spread on cooled cake while still warm. Makes 1/3 cup.

Fudgies

Devilishly dark and rich.

Makes 24 cupcakes.

Devil's Food Cupcakes (*recipe follows*)	**(*recipe follows*)**
	Chocolate Glaze (*recipe follows*)
Creamy Vanilla Filling	**Walnuts**

1 Prepare, bake and cool Devil's Food Cupcakes. Prepare Creamy Vanilla Filling.

2. Remove paper cupcake liners from cooled cupcakes. With a sharp knife cut off a 1/8-inch slice from bottom of cupcake; reserve. Cut a cone shape piece from bottom, 1/8-inch from sides and almost to the top of the cupcake. Fill with about 2 teaspoons Creamy Vanilla Filling; press reserved slice back onto cupcake.

3. Place cupcakes top down on wire rack set over a piece of wax paper. Coat with Chocolate Glaze. Let set. Garnish with remaining cream filling and walnuts.

Devil's Food Cupcakes

Bake at 350° for 20 minutes.

Makes 24 to 26 cupcakes.

1³/₄ cups *sifted* cake flour	cocoa powder
1¹/₄ cups sugar	¹/₂ cup vegetable shortening
1¹/₄ teaspoons baking soda	1 cup milk
¹/₂ teaspoon salt	3 eggs
¹/₂ cup unsweetened	1¹/₂ teaspoons vanilla

1 Combine flour, sugar, baking soda, salt and cocoa in a large bowl. Add shortening and ³/₄ cup of the milk. Beat at low speed with electric mixer ¹/₂ minute to combine ingredients, then at high speed for 2 minutes.
2. Preheat oven to 350°. Add remaining milk, eggs and vanilla and continue to beat an additional 2 minutes. Fill paper-lined muffin cups half full.
3. Bake in a preheated moderate oven (350°) for 20 minutes or until tops spring back when lightly pressed with fingertip. Remove from pans; cool on wire racks.

Creamy Vanilla Filling

Makes 1 cup.

6 tablespoons vegetable shortening	¹/₂ teaspoon vanilla
1 egg white	1¹/₂ cups 10X (confectioners') sugar

Beat shortening with egg white, vanilla and ¹/₂ cup of the 10X sugar until blended. Beat in remaining sugar until thick.

Chocolate Glaze

Makes 2¹/₂ cups (enough to frost 24 to 26 cupcakes).

4 squares unsweetened chocolate	4 cups 10X (confectioners') sugar
8 teaspoons vegetable shortening	¹/₂ cup water

Melt chocolate and shortening in a medium-size bowl over simmering water in a saucepan. Remove from heat; beat in confectioners' sugar and water with a wire whisk to make smooth mixture. Keep warm over simmering water.

Pictured opposite: Spicy Oatmeal Cupcakes, page 151.

Cupcake

These individual cakes are baked in special pans, or they can be baked in custard cups. For convenience, pans can be lined with small, fluted paper cups. Cupcakes are perfect in lunch boxes or for coffee breaks. Bake a batch for a fund-raising bazaar.

Spicy Oatmeal Cupcakes

Bake at 375° for 20 minutes.

Makes 24 to 26 cupcakes.

1¹/₂ cups *sifted* cake flour	¹/₄ teaspoon ground cloves
1 cup quick oats	¹/₄ teaspoon ground allspice
³/₄ cup firmly packed light brown sugar	¹/₂ cup vegetable shortening
¹/₂ cup granulated sugar	1 cup milk
1 teaspoon baking soda	2 eggs
¹/₂ teaspoon salt	Honey Cream Cheese Frosting (recipe under Frostings)
¹/₂ teaspoon ground cinnamon	

1. Combine flour, oats, sugars, baking soda, salt, cinnamon, cloves and allspice in large bowl. Add shortening and ³/₄ cup of the milk. Beat at low speed with electric mixer ¹/₂ minute to combine ingredients, then at high speed for 2 minutes. Preheat oven to 375°.
2. Add remaining ¹/₄ cup milk and eggs and continue to beat an additional 2 minutes. Fill paper-lined muffin cups half full.
3. Bake in a preheated moderate oven (375°) for 20 minutes or until tops spring back when lightly pressed with fingertip. Remove from pans; cool on wire racks. Frost with Honey Cream Cheese Frosting.

Bourbon Street Pecan Cake

Bake at 325° for 1 hour and 15 minutes.

Makes one 10-inch tube cake.

¹/₂ cup bourbon	1 cup (2 sticks) butter or margarine
1 cup raisins	2¹/₄ cups sugar
3¹/₄ cups *sifted* all-purpose flour	5 eggs
1¹/₂ teaspoons ground nutmeg	1 cup buttermilk
1 teaspoon baking powder	2 cups coarsely chopped pecans
¹/₂ teaspoon baking soda	Praline Glaze (recipe follows)

1. Pour bourbon over raisins; soak at least 1 hour. Sift flour, nutmeg, baking powder and baking soda onto wax paper. Grease a 10-inch tube pan.

(continued)

2. Beat butter, sugar and eggs in a large bowl with electric mixer at high speed 5 minutes or until light and fluffy. Preheat oven to 325°.

3. Stir in flour mixture alternately with buttermilk, beating with a wooden spoon after each addition. Stir in raisins with any remaining bourbon and the pecans. Pour batter into prepared pan; set aside.

4. Bake in a preheated slow oven (325°) for 1 hour and 15 minutes or until center springs back when lightly touched with fingertip.

5. Cool in pan on wire rack 10 minutes; loosen cake around tube and outside edge with knife; turn out onto wire rack; cool completely. Spoon Praline Glaze over top, letting glaze dribble down the side.

Praline Glaze: Combine 1/2 cup firmly packed light brown sugar, 1/4 cup granulated sugar and 1/4 cup (1/2 stick) butter or margarine in small sauce pan. Heat until sugar melts and mixture is bubbly; stir in 1/4 cup heavy cream. Heat 1 minute; add 1/2 cup pecan halves and heat just until bubbly. Remove from heat; cool slightly.

Swiss Almond Meringue Torte

A famous Swiss cake with alternating layers of nutted meringue, butter cream, sponge cake and cherry preserves.

Bake at 275° for 30 minutes.

Makes 12 to 16 servings.

4 egg whites	**1/4 cup cherry brandy**
1/8 teaspoon cream of tartar	**or dry sherry**
1 cup granulated sugar	**Almond Butter Cream (recipe follows)**
1/3 cup ground blanched almonds	**1/2 cup cherry preserves**
1 tablespoon cornstarch	**1/2 cup sliced blanched almonds, toasted**
16 ladyfingers, split	**10X (confectioners') sugar**

1. Butter and flour 2 cookie sheets. Outline an 8-inch circle on each.

2. Beat egg whites with cream of tartar in a small bowl with electric mixer on high speed until foamy. Beat in 1/3 cup sugar, 1 tablespoon at a time, until meringue forms soft peaks. Gradually beat in another 1/3 cup sugar, until meringue is very stiff and dull. Preheat oven to 275°.

3. Mix remaining sugar, almonds and cornstarch; fold into meringue. Spoon into pastry bag with large plain tip (about 1/2-inch opening), or no tip. Starting in center, pipe small puffs touching each other in neat circles with the last circle just inside outline. This will be the top layer. For second layer, pipe remaining meringue in a continuing spiral until outline is filled in. Or use spatula to spread meringue 1/2-inch thick.

4. Bake in a preheated slow oven (275°) for 30 minutes or until crisp and a light golden color. Turn off

oven and let meringues cool in oven. Loosen from cookie sheets.

5. Sprinkle split ladyfingers with cherry brandy.

6. Cover plain meringue layer with about 1/3 of Almond Butter Cream. Arrange half of ladyfingers, cut-side up, on butter cream, cutting to fit, if necessary. Spoon cherry preserves over; top with remaining ladyfingers. Spread half of remaining butter cream over ladyfingers. Gently place second meringue layer on top. Smooth remaining butter cream around side of torte. Press toasted almonds onto side. Chill overnight. Sprinkle top with 10X sugar.

Almond Butter Cream

Makes about 3 cups.

3/4 cup sugar	**or margarine**
1/2 cup water	**2 egg yolks**
1/4 cup light corn syrup	**1/2 teaspoon almond extract**
1 cup (2 sticks) butter	

1. Bring sugar, water and corn syrup to boiling in a small saucepan; lower heat; cook, covered, 5 minutes. Uncover and boil 5 minutes longer without stirring. There should be about 3/4 cup. Cool.

2. Beat butter until soft in a medium-size bowl with electric mixer on medium speed; beat in egg yolks. Gradually beat in cooled syrup until light and fluffy. Beat in almond extract. Chill briefly if mixture is too soft to hold its shape.

Family Circle's Big Burger Cake

Bake at 350° for 25 to 30 minutes.

Makes 12 servings.

1 package any yellow cake mix for 2-layer cake	**2 tablespoons unsweetened cocoa powder**
2 recipes Decorator Frosting (recipe in this chapter)	**3 tablespoons warm water**
Orange and red paste food coloring	**2 tablespoons instant coffee powder**
Red, yellow and green liquid food coloring	**1 can (8 ounces) almond paste**
1/4 cup finely chopped walnuts or pecans	**1 tablespoon sunflower kernels, toasted**
2/3 cup plus	

1. Preheat the oven to moderate (350°). Grease and flour three 8-inch-round layer-cake pans.

2. Prepare the cake mix according to the package directions. Divide evenly between the 3 pans. Bake according to the package directions, but only for 25 to 30 minutes or until the tops spring back when lightly pressed with a fingertip. Cool according to the

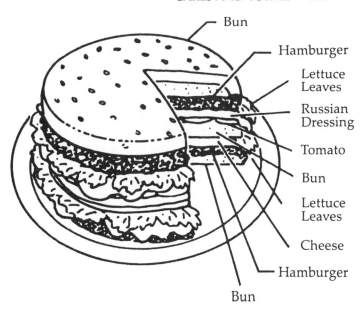

Family Circle's Big Burger Cake, page 152.

package directions. Set all 3 layers, right-side up, on cooling racks.

3. Prepare 2 recipes of the Decorator Frosting. Spoon ½ cup into each of 3 small bowls. Color one light orange, to resemble cheese. Color another with red and yellow liquid coloring, to resemble Russian dressing. Fold in the chopped nuts. Color the third with the red paste food coloring, to resemble tomato.

4. Spoon 1½ cups of the white frosting into a medium-size bowl. Set aside the 2 tablespoons of cocoa. Stir the remaining cocoa and 2 tablespoons of the warm water into the 1½ cups of frosting until smooth and evenly colored to make cocoa frosting for the hamburgers. Add the reserved 2 tablespoons of cocoa and the instant coffee, stirred into 1 tablespoon of the warm water, to the remaining frosting to make mocha frosting for the buns.

5. Knead several drops of the green and 1 drop of yellow food coloring into the almond paste. Divide into 12 pieces. Roll out the pieces between wax paper to form uneven shapes resembling lettuce leaves.

6. Frost halfway up the side of the first cake layer with the mocha frosting. Place the layer, unfrosted-side up, on a cake plate. Thickly frost the top half of the side of the layer with a little less than half the cocoa frosting. Round the edges and rough with a fork to resemble a hamburger. Frost the top of the layer with the cocoa frosting.

7. Spoon all of the orange frosting on top of the layer. Spread with a spatula to cover the top and extend over the sides at places to resemble melted cheese. Top with 6 almond paste lettuce leaves.

8. Turn the second cake layer over on a cooling rack. Frost the bottom and halfway down the side with the mocha frosting. Turn, right-side up, on top of the almond paste leaves on the first layer. To make the tomato, spread a thin layer of the red frosting with a

spatula around the unfrosted half of the side of the cake and over the top of the cake.

9. Spoon all of the frosting which resembles Russian dressing on top of the red frosting. Spread with a spatula to cover the top of the cake and extend partway down the sides in some places to resemble the dressing. Top with the remaining 6 almond paste lettuce leaves.

10. Turn the remaining cake layer over on a cooling rack. Thickly frost halfway down the side of the layer with the cocoa frosting. Round the edges and rough with a fork to resemble a hamburger. Frost the bottom of the cake with the remaining cocoa frosting.

11. Turn the cake layer, right-side up, onto the almond paste leaves on the cake. Frost the unfrosted top half of the side and top of the cake with the remaining mocha frosting, rounding the top to look like the hamburger bun. Sprinkle with the sunflower kernels.

Sweetheart Cakes

Bake yellow cakes at 350° for 20 to 22 minutes; bake chocolate cakes at 325° for 22 to 25 minutes.

Makes 12 Frosted Yellow Cakes or 13 Cream-Filled Chocolate Cakes.

Frosted Yellow Cakes: Prepare 1 package (1 pound) pound cake mix following package directions. Preheat the oven to slow (325°). Grease and flour 4-ounce (½ cup) heart-shaped tart pans. Measure ⅓ cup batter into each pan. If making 4 cakes at a time, cover remaining batter and refrigerate until ready to use. Bake in the preheated slow oven (325°) for 20 to 22 minutes or until tops are browned and edges start to shrink from sides of pan. Let cakes cool in pans on

(continued)

wire rack for 5 minutes. Remove cakes from pans and cool completely on rack.

Pink-and-White Frosted Hearts: Frost tops and sides of cakes with half of a 1-pound tub prepared vanilla frosting. Tint two-thirds of remaining frosting pale pink and remaining dark pink with red food coloring. Spoon into pastry bags fitted with fancy tips and decorate.

White-on-White Frosted Hearts: Frost tops and sides of cakes with about half of a 1-pound tub prepared vanilla frosting. Fill pastry bag fitted with fancy tip with remaining frosting. Pipe a white ruffle around top and bottom edges. Garnish with chocolate heart, icing rose and silver dragees, if you wish.

Cream-Filled Chocolate Cakes: Melt ¹/₂ cup semisweet chocolate pieces in small saucepan over very low heat. Prepare 1 package (1 pound) pound cake mix following package directions. Stir in melted chocolate. Preheat the oven to slow (325°). Grease and flour 4-ounce (¹/₂ cup) heart-shaped tart pans. Measure ¹/₃ cup batter into each pan. If making 4 cakes at a time, cover remaining batter and refrigerate until ready to use. Bake in the preheated slow oven (325°) for 22 to 25 minutes or until tops are browned and edges start to shrink from sides of pan. Let cakes cool in pans on wire rack for 5 minutes. Remove cakes from pans and cool completely on rack. Beat 1 cup heavy cream in small bowl until stiff. Carefully cut cakes in half horizontally. Spread bottom halves with whipped cream. Frost top halves with about one-third of a 1-pound tub prepared chocolate frosting. Set on top of cream. Place a heart-shaped cookie cutter on frosting. Sprinkle red decorating sugar or colored sprinkles into center. Carefully lift off cutter. Outline sugar heart with silver dragees, if you wish.

Pink and white Frosted Heart.

Preparing Pans for Baking: Spray baking pans with vegetable spray-on, following label directions. Grease pans with vegetable shortening and sprinkle with flour; turn and pat pan to coat evenly, tap out excess. (Note: Use shortening — butter or margarine can make cake stick.)

Dad's Golden Car Cake

Bake according to the package directions.
Makes 10 servings.

1 package pound cake mix	**water**
Firm cardboard	**Chocolate sprinkles**
Aluminum foil	**6 chocolate cookies (1¹/₂ inches)**
Wooden picks	**Silver dragees**
2 recipes Decorator Frosting *(recipe in this chapter)*	**4 square cherry-flavored hard candies**
Green and yellow food coloring	**4 small white gumdrops**
¹/₄ cup unsweetened cocoa powder	**2 small red gumdrops**
1 tablespoon warm	**8 small red cinnamon candies**

1. Prepare, bake and cool the cake mix, following the label directions for a 9 × 5 × 3-inch loaf pan.
2. Cut an 11 × 5-inch rectangle from firm cardboard. Round off the corners. Cover with foil.
3. To make the back of the car: Cut across the cake's width (A) on top, starting 1 inch from the top left edge and slanting to a point ³/₄ inch from the left end and 1 inch below the top of the cake. Cut in from the left side to remove a piece of the cake.
4. To make the front of the car: Cut across the cake's width (B) on top, starting 4 inches from the top right edge and slanting to a point 3¹/₂ inches from the right end and 1 inch below the top of the cake. Cut in from the right side to remove a piece of the cake.
5. Set the large remaining cake on the cardboard so the back end is even with one end of the cardboard. From the larger of 2 removed pieces, cut a 1-inch-wide piece (C) across the width from the outside baked end; this piece should match the piece removed from the back. These will be the 2 axles (A and C) for underneath the car. Trim the remainder of the large removed piece (B) so it fits snugly in front of the car and covers the remaining cardboard base. Fasten to the front of the cake with 2 wooden picks.
6. Prepare the 2 recipes of the Decorator Frosting. Spoon ¹/₂ cup of the white frosting into a pastry bag fitted with an adapter and writing tip. Spoon ³/₄ cup of the white frosting in a small bowl and reserve. Measure 1 tablespoon of the white frosting into a small cup. Spoon ¹/₂ cup of the frosting into a small bowl and color green. Place the green frosting in a small pastry bag fitted with a leaf tip. Spoon 1 cup of the white frosting into a small bowl; stir in the cocoa and the 1 tablespoon of warm water until smooth and

Dad's Golden Car Cake, page 154.

Car

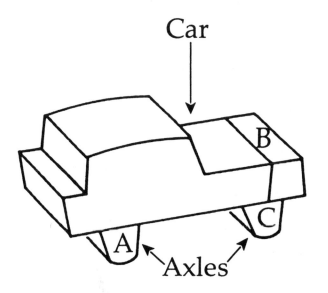

easy to spread. Measure 1 tablespoon of the cocoa frosting and add to the 1 tablespoon of white frosting to make a light cocoa frosting. Color the remaining unmeasured white frosting yellow.

7. Using the green frosting, outline a 12 × 6-inch oval on a serving platter, tray or board to make a grass border. Fill in the oval with the chocolate sprinkles to make a driveway.

8. Frost the 2 pieces of cake reserved for the axles with the cocoa frosting. Place on the chocolate driveway so they are 3 inches apart.

9. With a small spatula, frost window areas on the car cake with the $3/4$ cup of white frosting, reserving some for the wheels and bumpers; press gently and in only one direction over the cut areas. Frost the rest of the car yellow, reserving some of the yellow frosting.

10. Carefully set the car on the axles so the rear axle is $1^{1}/_{2}$ inches from the rear of the car.

11. Frost a $1/_{2}$-inch circle of white onto 5 of the chocolate cookies. Press 7 silver dragees into the frosting on each wheel to make the hubcaps. Fill any areas where the cake axles do not extend to the edge of the cardboard base with the cocoa frosting. Press the cookie wheel at the end of each axle.

12. Using the white frosting and the writing tip, pipe the grill onto the front of the car. Pipe a double row of dots around the silver dragees on the remaining frosted cookie. Pipe some of the white frosting on the back of the unfrosted cookie; press the back of the frosted cookie onto it. Press the double cookie into place on the back of the car for the spare tire.

13. Spoon the remaining yellow frosting into a pastry bag fitted with a small star tip. Pipe a star border along all the edges of the car, outlining and dividing

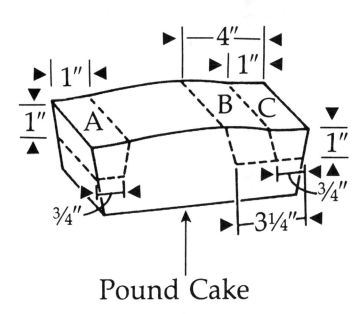

Pound Cake

the windows. Pipe a series of stars outlining the fenders and covering the tops of the cookie wheels. Pipe stars to fill in and build up the fender areas. Fill in the area between the front fender and the grill with flat stars.

14. Frost a $1/_{2}$-inch band of white along the front and back of the car for bumpers. Press 2 square red candies in the center of each for the license plates. Press 2 white gumdrops on either side of the front grill for headlights, and 1 red gumdrop on either side in the back for the taillights.

15. Change from the writing tip to a small star tip on the pastry bag of white frosting. Outline the headlights with small white stars. Press 2 small red candies into

(continued)

the frosting at either side for the running lights on the front and back of the car.

16. If you wish, press silver dragees in rows on any white bumper areas still visible, and on the front of the hood for ornaments.

17. Mix together 1 tablespoon of the remaining cocoa frosting and 1 tablespoon of the remaining white frosting in a small cup. Clean the writing tip. Fill the tip with the light cocoa frosting and place in the adapter on the bag of the white frosting. Pipe the windshield wipers onto the front of the car. If the frosting begins to flow white, clean the tip and refill with the light cocoa frosting.

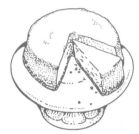

Family Circle's Carrot Cake

For a rich ending to a family dinner or for a wonderful have-on-hand winter snack, this super carrot cake fills the bill.

Bake at 325° for 1 hour, 20 minutes.

Makes 12 servings (one 10-inch tube cake).

3¹⁄₃ **cups** *sifted* **all-purpose flour**	**cinnamon**
2 cups sugar	**4 eggs**
1 teaspoon baking powder	**1¹⁄₂ cups vegetable oil**
1 teaspoon baking soda	**2 teaspoons vanilla**
1 teaspoon salt	**2 cups coarsely shredded carrots**
1 teaspoon ground nutmeg	**1 cup chopped walnuts**
1 teaspoons ground	**Confectioners' Frosting** *(recipe follows)*

1. Preheat the oven to slow (325°). Grease a 10-inch Bundt or angel-cake tube pan.

2. Sift together the flour, sugar, baking powder, baking soda, salt, nutmeg and cinnamon into a large bowl. Make a well in the center. Add the eggs, oil and vanilla; beat with a wooden spoon until smooth. Stir in the carrots and walnuts. Turn the mixture into the prepared pan.

3. Bake in the preheated slow oven (325°) for 1 hour and 20 minutes, or until the top springs back when lightly pressed with a fingertip.

4. Cool the cake in the baking pan on a wire rack for 10 minutes. Remove the cake from the pan. Cool completely before frosting.

5. Drizzle with the Confectioners' Frosting.

Confectioners' Frosting: Place 1 cup of *sifted* 10X (confectioners') sugar in a small bowl. Gradually stir in 1 to 2 tablespoons of milk, whisking constantly, until the mixture is of a good drizzling consistency.

Chocolate Heart Cake

Bake according to directions on package.
Makes 12 servings.

1 package any flavor cake mix for 2-layer cake	**3 tablespoons unsweetened cocoa powder**
2 cups heavy cream	**1 bag (6 ounces) semisweet chocolate pieces**
¹⁄₂ teaspoon vanilla	**Gold ribbon bow** *(optional)*
¹⁄₄ cup 10X (confectioners') sugar	

1. Grease and flour two 8-inch heart-shaped cake pans. Prepare, bake and cool the cake, following the package directions for two 8-inch layers.

2. Combine the cream, vanilla, 10X sugar and cocoa in a bowl. Refrigerate.

3. Melt the chocolate pieces in a double boiler over hot, not boiling, water. Line the bottom of one heart-shaped pan with foil. Spread the chocolate evenly over the bottom. Place in the freezer until firm.

4. When the cakes are completely cool, beat the refrigerated cream mixture just until stiff. Spoon 1¹⁄₂ cups into a pastry bag fitted with a large star tip. Spoon ¹⁄₂ cup into a pastry bag fitted with an adapter and small star tip.

5. Fill and frost the cake layers on a serving plate with the remaining cocoa cream, swirling cream on the top and sides.

6. Using the pastry bag with the large star tip, pipe a shell border around the base of the cake. Pipe a line down the center of the cake.

7. Remove the chocolate heart from the cake pan. Carefully heat the blade of a sharp knife. Cut the heart in half. Return to the freezer for 1 minute to reset the chocolate. When the chocolate is firm again, peel off the aluminum foil and separate the halves. Using the pastry bag with the small star tip, pipe a border of small stars around the outer edge on the smooth side of each half of the chocolate heart.

8. Set half of the chocolate heart into a row of cream in the center of the cake top. Using the large star tip, pipe a puff of cream under the heart to prop it at an angle so the outer edge is about 1 inch above the edge of the cake. Repeat with the other half.

9. Change the small star tip on the adapter to a medium rose tip.

10. Press the gold bow into the cream at the bottom point of the heart, if you wish.

11. Pipe a row of rosebuds down the seam of the heart. Extend the bud over the edge to cover the center of the bow, if using. Refrigerate until ready to serve.

Pictured opposite: Chocolate Heart Cake.

Minted Pineapple Cake

Makes 10 to 12 servings.

Pineapple Chiffon Cake *(recipe follows)*	mint OR: 2 tablespoons dried mint
1³/₄ cups unsweetened pineapple juice	1 medium-size ripe pineapple
³/₄ cup sugar	1 pint strawberries
¹/₂ cup coarsely chopped fresh	Sprigs of mint Green grapes

1. Prepare Pineapple Chiffon Cake. Place cake on serving plate.
2. Combine pineapple juice and sugar in medium-size saucepan; bring to boiling, stirring often, until sugar is dissolved; boil, uncovered, 5 minutes. Remove from heat; stir in mint and let stand 5 to 10 minutes for mint flavor to develop as strong as you like it. Strain syrup into a small bowl. Measure out ¹/₂ cup. Reserve.
3. Gradually brush remaining warm syrup over cake until all is absorbed.
4. Pare, quarter and core pineapple; cut each quarter crosswise into thin slices. Place slices in large bowl; add ²/₃ of reserved syrup. Hull strawberries and cut in half; place in medium-size bowl; add remaining syrup. Let both fruits stand at room temperature to macerate 30 minutes.
5. Just before serving, fill center of cake with fruits; serve any extra fruit mixture and juice in a separate bowl.
6. Garnish with sprigs of mint and small bunches of green grapes.

Pineapple Chiffon Cake

Bake at 325° for 35 minutes.

Makes one 9-inch ring cake.

1 cup *sifted* cake flour	¹/₄ cup vegetable oil
³/₄ cup sugar	2 eggs, separated
1 teaspoon baking powder	¹/₃ cup unsweetened pineapple juice
¹/₄ teaspoon salt	

1. Grease and flour 8-cup ring mold or 9-inch Bundt pan.
2. Sift flour, ¹/₂ cup of the sugar, baking powder and salt into large bowl. Add oil, egg yolks and pineapple juice; beat with wooden spoon until smooth. Preheat oven to 325°.
3. Beat egg whites in medium-size bowl until foamy-white and double in volume. Gradually beat in the remaining sugar until meringue stands in soft peaks. Add to yolk mixture; fold in gently. Spoon into pan.
4. Bake in a preheated slow oven (325°) for 35 minutes or until top springs back when lightly pressed with fingertip.
5. Cool on wire rack 10 minutes; loosen around edge with small spatula; unmold; cool completely.

Sour Cream Walnut Cake

A delicate old-fashioned layer cake that will please the whole family.

Bake at 350° for 30 minutes.

Makes 8 servings.

2¹/₂ cups *sifted* cake flour	orange rind
1 teaspoon baking soda	³/₄ cup dairy sour cream
1 teaspoon baking powder	¹/₄ cup milk
¹/₂ cup (1 stick) butter or margarine	1 cup finely chopped walnuts
¹/₄ cup vegetable shortening	Rum Butter Frosting *(recipe follows)*
1¹/₄ cups sugar	Coarsely chopped walnuts
3 eggs	Kumquats and leaves *(optional)*
2 teaspoons grated	

1. Preheat the oven to moderate (350°). Grease two 9 × 1¹/₂-inch round layer-cake pans; dust the pans lightly with flour; tap out the excess flour.
2. Sift together flour, baking soda and baking powder onto wax paper.
3. Combine butter, shortening, sugar and eggs in a large bowl. Beat with an electric mixer at high speed for 3 minutes or until the mixture is light and fluffy. Beat in the orange rind.
4. Combine sour cream and milk. Stir flour mixture into batter, alternating with sour cream mixture, beginning and ending with the flour. Stir in finely chopped nuts. Scrape batter into the prepared pans, dividing evenly.
5. Bake in the preheated moderate oven (350°) for 30 minutes or until tops spring back when lightly pressed with fingertip.
6. Cool layers in pans on wire racks for 10 minutes; loosen around edges with small spatula; turn out onto wire racks; cool completely.
7. Prepare Rum Butter Frosting.
8. Fill and frost layers with Rum Butter Frosting. Cover side with coarsely chopped walnuts; garnish with kumquats and leaves, if you wish.

Rum Butter Frosting: Beat ¹/₂ cup (1 stick) butter or margarine in a bowl until soft. Beat in 1 package (1 pound) 10X (confectioners') sugar alternately with 3 tablespoons rum and 1 tablespoon milk until the mixture is smooth and spreadable.

Gingerbread

In the Middle Ages, gingerbread was a heavy, spicy bread. it was not the tender, brown, flat square cake we know today but was made into fancy shapes and highly decorated. Some shapes represented people, birds, animals and letters of the alphabet. Gingerbread was often given as gifts on special occasions. When Europeans settled in America, they brought along their gingerbread molds.

Nowadays, gingerbread is a cake made of flour,

spices, a leavening agent, sugar, molasses, eggs and water. The cake is usually served warm. Or, gingerbread can be made as a cookie. The dough is cut into fancy shapes which are favorites during the winter holidays.

Gingerbread

Bake at 350° for 30 minutes.

Makes one cake.

3 cups *sifted* all-purpose flour	1/2 cup firmly packed brown sugar
1 teaspoon cream of tartar	3 eggs
2 tablespoons ground ginger	1/2 cup milk
1 teaspoon ground cinnamon	1 cup molasses
1 teaspoon ground mace	1 teaspoon grated orange rind
1 teaspoon ground nutmeg	3/4 cup orange juice
1/2 cup (1 stick) butter, softened	1 teaspoon baking soda
	1 tablespoon warm water
	1 cup raisins

1. Grease and flour a 13 x 9 x 2-inch baking pan. Sift flour, cream of tartar, ginger, cinnamon, mace and nutmeg onto wax paper. Preheat oven to 350°.
2. Beat butter, sugar and eggs in a large bowl with electric mixer at high speed until fluffy.
3. Heat milk in a small saucepan just enough to take the chill off. Stir in molasses, orange rind and juice.
4. Add flour mixture alternately with the milk mixture to the butter, sugar and eggs. Beat with a wooden spoon after each addition until batter is smooth.
5. Stir baking soda into warm water in a small cup. Quickly stir into batter. Stir in raisins. Pour batter into prepared pan.
6. Bake in a preheated moderate oven (350°) for 30 minutes or until center springs back when lightly pressed with fingertip. Cool in pan on wire rack. Cut in squares to serve.

Ginger Pound Cake

Bake at 350° for 1 hour.

Makes one large tube cake.

3 cups *sifted* all-purpose flour	8 eggs, separated
1 teaspoon baking powder	1 tablespoon grated orange rind
1/2 teaspoon salt	1 tablespoon vanilla
2 cups (4 sticks) butter	1/4 cup shredded preserved or crystallized ginger
1 3/4 cups sugar	

1. Grease and flour 10-inch tube pan.
2. Sift flour, baking powder and salt onto wax paper. Preheat oven to 350°.

3. Beat butter in large bowl with electric mixer until creamy. Beat in 3/4 cup of the sugar. Add egg yolks, one at a time, beating well after each. Stir in orange rind, vanilla and flour mixture until smooth and well blended.
4. Beat egg whites in large bowl with electric mixer until foamy, using clean beaters. Beat in remaining 1 cup sugar, slowly, until meringue holds soft peaks. Fold into batter until no streaks remain.
5. Spoon half the batter into pan. Sprinkle 2 tablespoons of the ginger over batter; spoon in remaining batter; top with remaining ginger.
6. Bake in a preheated moderate oven (350°) for 1 hour or until top springs back when lightly pressed with fingertip. Let cool in pan on wire rack 10 minutes. Loosen around edges with spatula; lift out onto wire rack; cool completely. Wrap in foil and keep at room temperature overnight. Store in refrigerator.

Great-grandma's Soft Ginger Cake

Bake at 350° for 30 minutes.

Makes one 13 x 9-inch cake.

2 1/2 cups *sifted* all-purpose flour	cloves
1 3/4 teaspoons baking soda	1/4 teaspoon salt
1 teaspoon ground ginger	1 cup sugar
1 teaspoon ground cinnamon	1/2 cup vegetable shortening
1/4 teaspoon ground	1 cup molasses
	1 cup boiling water
	2 eggs, well beaten

1. Sift together flour, soda, ginger, cinnamon, cloves and salt; set aside.
2. Cream sugar with shortening and molasses until well blended. Preheat oven to 350°.
3. Add sifted dry ingredients to creamed mixture alternately with boiling water, beginning and ending with dry ingredients. Stir in eggs.
4. Pour into a well-greased 13 x 9 x 2-inch baking pan.
5. Bake in a preheated moderate oven (350°) for 30 minutes or until center springs back when lightly pressed with fingertip. Cool in pan on wire rack to room temperature. Cut in large squares.

Upside-Down Cake
An American original, this popular cake is baked with the fruit or topping in the bottom of the pan. After baking, it is turned right-side up to show off the buttery glazed fruit, nuts or preserves. It is easy to make and can be served hot or cold for a perfect dessert or snack. Europeans have upside-down pastries such as the *Tarte Tatin*, an upside-down apple tart.

Prune Upside-Down Cake

Bake at 350° for 50 to 55 minutes.

Makes 9 servings.

1 package (12 ounces) pitted prunes	2 teaspoons baking powder
1/4 cup (1/2 stick) butter or margarine	1/4 teaspoon salt
1/3 cup firmly packed brown sugar	1/4 teaspoon ground cinnamon
1/2 cup pecan halves	1/2 cup vegetable shortening
1 1/2 cups *sifted* all-purpose flour	3/4 cup milk
1 cup granulated sugar	1 teaspoon vanilla
	1 egg
	Whipped cream

1. Cook prunes following label directions; drain. Preheat oven to 350°.
2. Melt butter in a 9 × 9 × 2-inch baking pan in the oven; sprinkle brown sugar over. Arrange cooked prunes and pecans in butter-sugar mixture in baking pan.
3. Sift flour, sugar, baking powder, salt and cinnamon into large bowl. Add shortening, milk and vanilla. Beat 2 minutes with electric mixer at medium speed. Add egg; beat 2 minutes more. Pour over prunes.
4. Bake in a preheated moderate oven (350°) for 50 to 55 minutes or until top springs back when lightly touched with fingertip. Loosen edges with spatula.
5. Invert pan onto serving plate; leave in place 2 minutes; lift off pan. Replace any of the fruit and nuts left in pan. Cool slightly. Serve warm with whipped cream.

Piña Colada Down-Up Cake

Bake at 350° for 50 minutes.

Makes 12 servings.

1/3 cup butter or margarine	purpose flour
1/2 cup firmly packed light brown sugar	1 3/4 cups granulated sugar
1 can (20 ounces) sliced pineapple in juice, well drained	1 tablespoon baking powder
4 maraschino cherries, halved	1/2 teaspoon salt
	3 eggs
3 1/2 ounces flaked coconut (half of 7-ounce package)	1 1/4 cups milk
	3/4 cup golden Jamaican rum
3 cups *sifted* all-	1/2 cup vegetable oil
	1 teaspoon vanilla

1. Place the butter in a 13 × 9 × 2-inch metal baking pan. Place the pan over low heat until the butter melts, stirring occasionally. Remove from the heat. Sprinkle the brown sugar evenly over the bottom. Arrange the pineapple slices in an attractive pattern over the butter-sugar mixture; cut 1 or 2 slices into quarters or halves for a neat fit, if necessary. Place

the cherry halves in the center of the pineapple rings. Sprinkle with the coconut. Set aside.
2. Preheat the oven to moderate (350°).
3. Sift together the flour, sugar, baking powder and salt into a large mixer bowl.
4. Beat the eggs slightly in a medium-size bowl. Mix in the milk, rum, oil and vanilla. Pour into the dry ingredients. Beat at low speed until blended. Increase speed to medium; beat for 2 minutes. Carefully pour over the mixture in the pan.
5. Bake in the preheated moderate oven (350°) for 50 minutes or until the center of the cake springs back when lightly touched with a fingertip. Remove to a wire rack. Let stand for 5 minutes. Loosen the sides; invert the cake carefully onto a large serving platter. Cool to room temperature.

Rhubarb Upside-Down Cake

Serve cake warm with vanilla ice cream for a special treat.

Bake at 350° for 35 minutes.

Makes 9 servings.

1 1/4 cups *sifted* all-purpose flour	cut into 1/2-inch slices (3 cups)
1 1/2 teaspoons baking powder	1/3 cup vegetable shortening
1 1/2 cups sugar	1 egg
1 pound fresh rhubarb, leaves discarded, ends trimmed, and stalks	1 teaspoon vanilla
	1/2 cup milk
	Ice cream

1. Preheat the oven to moderate (350°). Grease an 8 × 8 × 2-inch square baking pan.
2. Sift together flour and baking powder onto wax paper.
3. Combine 1 cup of the sugar and the rhubarb in a large saucepan. Cook over medium-low heat, stirring constantly, until sugar is completely melted and rhubarb just begins to soften, 5 to 8 minutes. Scrape into the prepared baking pan, spreading evenly.
4. Beat shortening with the remaining 1/2 cup sugar in large bowl until fluffy. Beat in egg and vanilla. Beat in flour mixture, alternately with milk, starting and ending with dry ingredients, until well blended. Spoon batter into mounds over rhubarb; spread out as evenly as possible.
5. Bake in the preheated moderate oven (350°) for 35 minutes or until a wooden pick inserted in the center comes out clean. Cool the cake in the pan on a wire rack for 5 minutes.
6. Loosen edges of the cake from the pan with a small knife. Cover the pan with an inverted high-rimmed serving dish. Invert pan and dish; shake gently. Lift off pan. Cut into 9 squares. Spoon any syrup that runs onto the dish over cake. Serve with ice cream.

Note: The cake can also be served directly from the pan, if you wish.

Pineapple-Apricot Upside-Down Cake

Bake at 350° for 45 minutes.

Makes 9 servings.

1/4 cup (1/2 stick) butter or margarine
1/4 cup firmly packed brown sugar
6 pineapple slices in pineapple juice (from a 20-ounce can), drained
1 can (8 ounces) apricot halves, drained
Walnut halves or pieces
1 1/4 cups *sifted* all-purpose flour
2 teaspoons baking powder
1/4 teaspoon salt
1 cup sugar
1/4 cup vegetable shortening
3/4 cup milk
1 teaspoon vanilla
1 egg

1. Preheat oven to 350°. Melt butter in a 9 x 9 x 2-inch baking pan in oven while oven is heating. Sprinkle brown sugar over butter. Arrange pineapple slices and apricot halves in butter-sugar mixture; fill centers of pineapple slices with walnuts.
2. Sift flour, baking powder, salt and sugar into large bowl. Add shortening and milk. Beat 2 minutes at medium speed with electric mixer, scraping sides of bowl several times. Add vanilla and egg; beat 2 minutes longer. Pour over fruit in baking pan.
3. Bake in a preheated moderate oven (350°) for 45 minutes or until center springs back when lightly touched with fingertip.
4. Invert cake on serving plate; leave pan in place 2 minutes. Lift off pan.

Chocolate Nut Upside-Down Cake

Bake at 350° for 45 minutes.

Makes one 10-inch tube cake.

10 tablespoons butter or margarine
1/4 cup firmly packed light brown sugar
2/3 cup light corn syrup
1/4 cup heavy cream
1 cup walnut pieces
1 3/4 cups *sifted* cake flour
2 teaspoons baking powder
1/4 teaspoon salt
1 1/2 cups granulated sugar
2 eggs, separated
3 squares unsweetened chocolate, melted and cooled
1 teaspoon vanilla
1 cup milk

1. Melt 4 tablespoons of the butter in a small saucepan; stir in brown sugar; heat until bubbly. Stir in corn syrup and cream; heat, stirring constantly, just to

(continued)

Rhubarb Upside-Down Cake, page 160.

boiling. Add nuts; pour into a generously buttered 10-inch Bundt pan. (Mixture will be thin.)

2. Sift flour, baking powder and salt onto wax paper. Preheat oven to 350°.

3. Beat remaining butter until soft in a large bowl. Gradually beat in granulated sugar until well mixed. Beat in egg yolks, chocolate and vanilla.

4. Add flour mixture alternately with milk, beginning and ending with flour. Beat egg whites until stiff in a small bowl; fold into cake batter. Spoon batter over nut mixture.

5. Bake in a preheated moderate oven (350°) for 45 minutes or until cake tester inserted in center comes out clean.

6. Loosen cake from edges with a small knife; cover pan with plate; invert; shake gently; lift off pan.

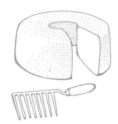

Pound Cake   A rich butter cake of British origin in which the ingredients at one time were weighed. It was made with a pound of sugar, a pound of butter, a pound of flour and a pound of eggs.

Lemon Pound Cake

Lemony and refreshing.

Bake at 350° for 1 hour, 5 minutes.

Makes one loaf cake.

2¹/₃ **cups** *sifted* **cake flour**	3 **eggs**
1 **teaspoon baking powder**	³/₄ **cup milk**
¹/₂ **teaspoon salt**	1 **teaspoon grated lemon rind**
²/₃ **cup vegetable shortening**	1 **tablespoon lemon juice**
1¹/₃ **cups sugar**	10X **(confectioners') sugar**

1. Grease and flour a 9 × 5 × 3-inch loaf pan.

2. Sift flour, baking powder and salt onto wax paper. Preheat oven to 350°.

3. Beat shortening, sugar and eggs in a large bowl with electric mixer at high speed for 3 minutes or until light and fluffy.

4. Add flour mixture alternately with milk on low speed. Stir in lemon rind and juice. Turn into prepared pan.

5. Bake in a preheated moderate oven (350°) for 1 hour and 5 minutes or until top springs back when lightly touched with fingertip.

6. Cool in pan on wire rack 10 minutes; loosen edge with spatula; turn out onto wire rack; cool completely. Dust lightly with 10X sugar.

Sherried Pound Cake

Bake at 350° for 1 hour, 20 minutes.

Makes one 12-cup Bundt cake.

3¹/₂ **cups** *sifted* **all-purpose flour**	3 **cups firmly packed brown sugar**
1¹/₂ **teaspoons baking powder**	5 **eggs**
¹/₂ **teaspoon ground nutmeg**	1 **tablespoon vanilla**
1¹/₂ **cups (3 sticks) butter**	¹/₂ **cup milk**
	¹/₂ **cup cream sherry**
	Sugar Glaze *(recipe follows)*

1. Grease and flour a heavy 12-cup Bundt pan.

2. Sift flour, baking powder and nutmeg onto wax paper. Preheat oven to 350°.

3. Beat butter in a large bowl with electric mixer until creamy. Beat in sugar gradually until well mixed. Add eggs, 1 at a time, beating well after each addition. Beat in vanilla.

4. Combine milk and sherry in a 1-cup measure. Stir dry ingredients alternately with milk and sherry into butter mixture just until smooth. Pour into prepared pan.

5. Bake in a preheated moderate oven (350°) for 1 hour and 20 minutes, or until top springs back when lightly pressed with fingertip. Cool in pan on wire rack 10 minutes; loosen around edge with spatula; turn out onto wire rack; cool completely. Wrap in foil and keep at room temperature overnight. Store in refrigerator.

6. Just before serving, drizzle with Sugar Glaze. Garnish with sliced almonds, if you wish.

Sugar Glaze: Combine 1 cup sifted 10X (confectioners') sugar and 1 tablespoon milk until smooth in a small bowl. Stir in more milk until glaze is thin enough to pour from a spoon.

Sour Cream Pound Cake

This fine-textured cake has a lovely flavor and keeps well.

Bake at 325° for 1 hour, 30 minutes.

Makes 1 ten-inch tube cake.

1 **cup (2 sticks) butter, softened**	¹/₄ **teaspoon baking soda**
3 **cups sugar**	1 **container (8 ounces) dairy sour cream**
6 **eggs, separated**	3¹/₃ **cups** *sifted* **all-purpose flour**
1 **teaspoon lemon extract**	
1 **teaspoon vanilla**	

1. Grease and flour a 10 × 4-inch angel-cake tube pan. Preheat oven to 325°.

2. Beat butter and 2¹/₂ cups of the sugar in a large bowl with electric mixer until well blended. Add egg yolks, 1 at a time, and continue beating until mixture is creamy-light; add lemon extract and vanilla.

3. Beat egg whites in a medium-size bowl until foamy-

white. Add remaining $1/2$ cup sugar, 1 tablespoon at a time, beating until mixture forms soft, glossy peaks.
4. Stir baking soda into sour cream. Add flour alternately with sour cream mixture to butter mixture, blending well after each addition. Fold in beaten egg white mixture until no streaks of white remain. Pour into prepared pan.
5. Bake in a preheated slow oven (325°) for 1 hour and 30 minutes or until cake tester or wooden pick inserted near center comes out clean. Cool in pan on wire rack 10 minutes. Loosen around edge and tube; remove from pan; cool completely.

Sour Cream Marble Pound Cake

Rich chocolate swirls through this sour cream pound cake.

Bake at 350° for 1 hour, 30 minutes.

Makes one 9-inch tube cake.

3 cups *sifted* all-purpose flour	extract
	6 eggs
1 teaspoons baking soda	1 container (8 ounces) dairy sour cream
$1/2$ teaspoon salt	2 squares unsweetened chocolate, melted and cooled
1 cup (2 sticks) butter	
3 cups sugar	
$1/2$ teaspoon almond	

1. Grease and flour a 9-inch tube pan.
2. Sift flour, baking soda and salt onto wax paper. Preheat oven to 350°.
3. Beat butter and sugar in a large bowl with electric mixer until well mixed. Beat in almond extract. Add eggs, one at a time, beating at high speed until mixture is light and fluffy.
4. Stir in $1/3$ of the flour mixture, then half the sour cream; repeat, ending with flour. Divide batter in half. Mix one part with the melted chocolate.
5. Spoon half the plain batter into prepared pan. Pour chocolate batter over, then top with remaining plain batter. Pull a spatula in a zigzag motion through batter to marbleize. Do not overmix.
6. Bake in a preheated moderate oven (350°) for 1 hour, 30 minutes or until top springs back when touched lightly with fingertip.
7. Cool in pan on wire rack 10 minutes. Loosen cake around the side with spatula. Remove side of pan by lifting cake out with tube; let cake cool completely on wire rack. Remove cake from tube and bottom; wrap in foil and let stand at room temperature overnight before slicing.

Overleaf (from the top): Strawberry Cheesecake Deluxe, page 163; Chocolate Espresso Cheesecake, page 166; Cheddar and Beer Cheesecake; page 166.

Cheesecake

Who can resist a luscious strawberry-topped cheesecake? This dessert rivals apple pie in popularity and has become a standard dessert on restaurant menus. More cheesecake is consumed in this country than anywhere else. Today you can find everything from tofu cheesecakes to "no cheese" cheesecakes.

Just about every country that produces cheese has a sweet cheese dessert similar to cheesecake. Some are made like custard pies, some are chilled and molded in a special shape. Italy's *Torta di Ricotta* and *Cassata alla Siciliana* are popular cheese desserts. Greece has *melopita,* a honey-sweetened cheese mixture in pastry. No matter where a cheesecake is made, its basis is usually a fresh, soft, unripened cheese like cream cheese, ricotta, cottage or pot cheese.

Strawberry Cheesecake Deluxe

Bake at 475° for 12 minutes, then at 250° for $1 1/2$ hours.

Makes 16 to 20 servings.

5 packages (8 ounces each) cream cheese	2 egg yolks
Sweet Pastry *(recipe follows)*	1 tablespoon grated lemon rind
$1 3/4$ cups sugar	$1/4$ cup heavy cream
3 tablespoons flour	Strawberry Topping *(recipe follows)*
5 eggs	

1. Let the cream cheese soften to room temperature in a large bowl while preparing the Sweet Pastry. Preheat oven to 400°.
2. Roll $1/3$ of chilled Sweet Pastry between two pieces of wax paper to a circle 9 inches in diameter. Remove top sheet of wax paper. Invert dough onto bottom of a 9-inch springform pan. Carefully remove remaining wax paper. Press dough to fit inside rim.
3. Bake in a preheated hot oven (400°) for 6 minutes or until lightly browned; cool. Butter side of springform pan; fit over cooled bottom. Roll remaining dough into a rectangle, 4 inches wide and 15 inches long, between two pieces of wax paper; remove top sheet of wax paper and cut dough in half lengthwise through bottom paper; press on side of pan; remove remaining wax paper; press firmly to bottom. Refrigerate. Raise oven temperature to 475°.
4. Beat cheese with electric mixer at medium speed just until smooth. Add sugar gradually, beating just

(continued)

until light and fluffy; sprinkle flour over mixture; blend thoroughly. Add eggs and egg yolks, one at a time. beating well after each addition. Beat in lemon rind and heavy cream on low speed. Pour into prepared pan.

5. Bake in a preheated very hot oven (475°) for 12 minutes; lower temperature to 250° and bake 1½ hours. Turn off oven heat and let cake remain in oven, with door ajar, 30 minutes longer.

6. Remove cake from oven; let cake cool completely on wire rack.

7. Decorate top with Strawberry Topping. Refrigerate several hours or overnight.

8. To serve: Loosen cake around edge with metal spatula; then remove side of springform pan. Serve at room temperature. Keep leftover cake in refrigerator.

Sweet Pastry: Combine 1 cup *sifted* all-purpose flour with ¼ cup sugar in a medium-size bowl; cut in 6 tablespoons butter with knife or pastry blender until mixture is crumbly. Add 1 egg yolk, slightly beaten, and ½ teaspoon vanilla; mix lightly with fork just until pastry is moistened; shape into ball with fingers. Wrap in wax paper; chill 1 hour.

Strawberry Topping: Wash, pat dry and hull 4 cups (2 pints) strawberries. Combine ½ cup red currant jelly and 1 tablespoon sugar in a small saucepan; bring to boiling over low heat, stirring constantly; boil 1 minute; remove from heat; cool slightly. Dip strawberries into jelly to coat. Transfer to wax paper-lined wire rack with stem-side down; let set. When glaze has set, arrange strawberries on top of cheesecake.

Cheddar and Beer Cheesecake

Bake at 300° for 2 hours.

Makes 16 to 20 servings.

4 packages (8 ounces each) cream cheese	**¼ cup sugar**
6 ounces extra sharp Cheddar cheese, finely shredded (1½ cups)	**¼ cup (½ stick) butter or margarine, melted**
1 box (6 ounces) zwieback crackers, crushed (1½ cups)	**1¾ cups sugar**
	4 eggs
	2 egg yolks
	⅓ cup beer
	¼ cup heavy cream

1. Let the cream cheese and grated Cheddar soften to room temperature in a large bowl. Preheat oven to 300°.

2. Combine zwieback crumbs, ¼ cup sugar and butter in a medium-size bowl. Press firmly over the bottom and halfway up the side of a lightly buttered 9-inch springform pan. Chill briefly before filling.

3. Beat cheeses with electric mixer at medium speed just until smooth. Add 1¾ cups sugar gradually, beating just until light and fluffy. Add eggs and egg yolks, one at a time, beating well after each addition.

Beat in beer and heavy cream at low speed. Pour into prepared pan.

4. Bake in a preheated slow oven (300°) for 2 hours. Turn off oven heat and let cake remain in oven, with door ajar, 30 minutes longer.

5. Remove cake from oven; let cool completely on wire rack. Refrigerate several hours or overnight.

6. To serve: Loosen cake around edge with metal spatula; remove side of springform pan. Serve at room temperature, but keep leftover cake in refrigerator. Garnish with frosted green grapes, if you wish.

To Frost Grapes: Dip small clusters of green grapes in slightly beaten egg white; sprinkle with granulated sugar. Let dry on wire rack.

Chocolate Espresso Cheesecake

Bake at 350° for 1 hour.

Makes 16 to 20 servings.

3 packages (8 ounces each) cream cheese	**chocolate pieces**
26 packaged chocolate wafers, crushed (1½ cups)	**2 tablespoons instant espresso coffee**
2 tablespoons sugar	**2 tablespoons hot water**
¼ cup (½ stick) butter or margarine, melted	**1 cup sugar**
	3 tablespoons flour
1 package (12 ounces) semisweet	**3 eggs**
	2 egg yolks
	1 cup heavy cream

1. Let the cream cheese soften to room temperature in a large bowl.

2. Blend crumbs, 2 tablespoons sugar and butter in a medium-size bowl. Press firmly over the bottom and halfway up the side of a lightly buttered 9-inch springform pan. Chill before filling. Preheat oven to 350°.

3. Melt chocolate in top of double boiler over hot, not boiling, water. Dissolve espresso in 2 tablespoons hot water.

4. Beat cream cheese with electric mixer at medium speed just until smooth. Add 1 cup sugar gradually, beating just until light and fluffy; sprinkle flour over mixture; blend thoroughly. Add eggs and egg yolks, one at a time; beat well after each.

5. Beat in melted chocolate, dissolved espresso and cream at low speed. Pour into prepared pan.

6. Bake in a preheated moderate oven (350°) for 1 hour. Turn off oven heat and let cake remain in oven, with door closed, 40 minutes longer.

7. Remove cake from oven; let cake cool completely on wire rack. Refrigerate several hours or overnight.

8. To serve: Loosen cake around edge with metal spatula; remove side of springform pan. Serve at room temperature, but keep leftover cake in refrigerator. Garnish with whipped cream rosettes and chocolate curls, if you wish.

Slim Cheesecake (Low-Cal)

If you love cheesecake but can't afford the calories, try this stingy-on-the-calories version.

Bake at 250° for 1 hour, 10 minutes.

Makes 12 servings at 224 calories each.

1 tablespoon butter or margarine	sugar
1/2 cup graham cracker crumbs	1 1/2 tablespoons flour
3 packages (8 ounces each) Neufchâtel cheese, softened	3/4 teaspoon grated orange rind
	1 teaspoon vanilla
1/3 cup sugar	3 eggs
Sugar substitute to equal 6 tablespoons	1 egg yolk
	2 tablespoons skim milk

1. Butter bottom and side of 8-inch springform pan. Sprinkle with graham cracker crumbs; press firmly into place. Refrigerate 1 hour.
2. Preheat oven to 250°. Place cheese, sugar, sugar substitute, flour, orange rind, vanilla, eggs, egg yolk and milk in the container of an electric blender. Cover. Whirl 2 minutes or until mixture is the consistency of heavy cream. Spoon carefully into prepared pan with graham cracker crust.
3. Bake in a preheated very slow oven (250°) for 1 hour, 10 minutes. Turn oven off; open door and allow cheesecake to cool gradually. Refrigerate at least 4 hours before serving.

Cranberry-Nut Cheesecake

Bake crust at 400° for 10 minutes. Bake cake at 475° for 10 minutes, then at 200° for 1 hour.

Makes 16 servings.

Crust:	1 3/4 cups sugar
1 cup *sifted* all-purpose flour	3 tablespoons all-purpose flour
1 teaspoon sugar	1/8 teaspoon salt
1/4 teaspoon ground cinnamon	5 eggs, at room temperature
1/2 cup (1 stick) butter, at room temperature	2 egg yolks, at room temperature
1 egg yolk, slightly beaten	1/4 cup dairy sour cream
1/4 teaspoon vanilla	1 teaspoon grated lime rind
1/2 cup finely ground walnuts (2 ounces)	1/2 teaspoon grated lemon rind
	2 tablespoons fresh lime juice
Cheese Filling:	1 teaspoon vanilla
5 packages (8 ounces each) cream cheese, softened	Cranberry Topping *(recipe follows)*

1. Preheat the oven to hot (400°). Butter the sides of a 9 × 3-inch springform pan; set aside.

2. Prepare the Crust: Combine the flour, sugar and cinnamon in a medium-size bowl; mix well. Cut in the butter with pastry blender until the mixture resembles coarse crumbs. Add the egg yolk and vanilla; mix just until dough holds together. Set aside two-thirds of the dough. Mix the walnuts into the remaining third.
3. Press the walnut dough evenly into the bottom of the prepared pan. Press the remaining dough evenly over the sides to a height of 2 inches. If the crust becomes soft, refrigerate for 10 minutes.
4. Bake in the preheated hot oven (400°) for 10 minutes, or until lightly golden. (Crust may shrink on the sides.) Cool on a wire rack. Increase the oven temperature to very hot (475°).
5. Prepare the Cheese Filling: Beat the cream cheese in a large bowl until smooth. Combine the sugar, flour and salt in a small bowl. Gradually beat into the cheese. Beat in the eggs and yolks, one at a time, beating well after each addition.
6. Combine the sour cream, lime and lemon rinds, lime juice and vanilla in a small bowl. Blend into the cheese mixture.
7. Place the prepared pan on a foil-lined jelly-roll pan. Pour the cheese mixture into the pan.
8. Bake in the preheated very hot oven (475°) for 10 minutes. Lower the heat to slow (200°). Bake for 1 hour longer or until the cake is set. Turn the oven off. Let the cake sit in the oven with the door ajar for 1/2 hour. Transfer to a wire rack to cool completely. Cover and refrigerate until thoroughly chilled.
9. Remove the sides of the pan. Spread the top of the cheesecake with the Cranberry Topping. Chill for at least 1/2 hour before serving. Garnish with walnut halves and frosted cranberries, if you wish.

Cranberry Topping: Combine 2 cups fresh or frozen cranberries (about 7 1/2 ounces) 3/4 cup sugar, 1/4 teaspoon ground cinnamon, 1/8 teaspoon salt and 2/3 cup water in a medium-size saucepan. Cook over medium heat, stirring occasionally, until the berries begin to pop, about 7 minutes. Reduce the heat to low; cook 6 minutes longer. Force the mixture through a strainer. Stir in 1 tablespoon of fresh lime juice. Cool.

Matzo Honey Cake

This cake has the texture of a sponge cake but the flavor of a dense honey cake.

Bake at 350° for 45 minutes.

Makes 16 servings.

6 eggs, separated	juice
2/3 cup sugar	1/2 cup matzo cake flour (see Note)
1/4 cup honey	1/2 cup potato flour (starch)
1/4 cup orange juice	
1 tablespoon grated lemon rind	1/4 teaspoon salt
1 tablespoon lemon	Honey *(optional)*

1. Preheat the oven to moderate (350°). Line the

(continued)

bottom of a 9 × 9 × 2-inch-square baking pan with wax paper.

2. Beat the egg yolks in a large bowl until thick and lemon-colored. Add the sugar, 2 tablespoons at a time, beating well after each addition. Beat in the honey, orange juice, lemon rind and juice. Fold in the matzo cake flour, then the potato flour.

3. Beat the egg whites and salt in a large, clean bowl until stiff, but not dry, peaks form. Gently fold the whites into the batter. Pour into the prepared pan.

4. Bake in the preheated moderate oven (350°) for 45 minutes or until a cake tester comes out clean. Cool on a wire rack. (The center of the cake will sink slightly.) When cooled, turn the cake out of the pan; remove the wax paper from the bottom. Place the cake, top-side up, on a serving plate. Drizzle with the honey, if you wish.

Note: If matzo cake flour is not available, process matzo meal in a blender on high speed until the texture of flour is attained.

Chocolate-Pecan Chess Tart

Bake at 425° for 10 minutes; then at 325° for 35 minutes.

Makes 8 servings.

1¹/₃ cups piecrust mix	or margarine,
1 egg yolk	melted
1 tablespoon water	2 tablespoons
3 eggs	cornstarch
1 cup sugar	1 cup pecan halves
¹/₂ cup firmly packed	¹/₂ cup heavy cream,
light brown sugar	whipped
¹/₂ cup chocolate-	Chocolate cutouts and
flavored syrup	green grapes
¹/₄ cup milk	dipped in melted
¹/₄ cup (¹/₂ stick) butter	chocolate (optional)

1. Combine piecrust mix, egg yolk and the 1 tablespoon water. Prepare the crust following label directions. Pat into a 9-inch fluted tart pan with removable bottom.

2. Beat eggs slightly in a medium-size bowl. Stir in sugars, chocolate syrup, milk, butter and cornstarch. Pour into the prepared tart shell. Arrange pecan halves on top.

3. Bake in a preheated hot oven (425°) for 10 minutes. Lower the oven temperature to slow (325°). Continue baking for 35 minutes, or until the center is almost set but still soft; do not overbake. Cool on wire rack.

4. Remove tart from the pan. Decorate with whipped cream rosettes. Add chocolate cutouts and green grapes dipped in melted chocolate, if you wish.

Individual Birthday Cakes

The bonus with these minicakes is that everyone gets their own.

Bake at 325° for 25 to 30 minutes.

Makes 14 minicakes.

3 cups *sifted* cake flour	2 eggs
2 teaspoons baking powder	2 teaspoons vanilla
¹/₄ teaspoon salt	1¹/₄ cups milk
²/₃ cup butter or margarine, softened	Chocolate Cream Frosting (*recipe follows*)
1³/₄ cups sugar	Sliced blanched almonds for garnish

1. Preheat oven to slow (325°). Butter fourteen 4-ounce (¹/₂ cup) soufflé dishes.

2. Combine flour, baking powder and salt in medium-size bowl.

3. Beat together butter, sugar, eggs and vanilla in large bowl until light and fluffy. Mix in flour mixture alternately with milk, beginning and ending with flour mixture. Spoon a scant ¹/₂ cup batter into prepared dishes. Place on cookie sheet.

4. Bake in preheated slow oven (325°) for 25 to 30 minutes or until wooden pick inserted in center comes out clean. Cool cakes in soufflé dishes on wire racks for 10 minutes.

5. Run knife around edges of cakes to loosen. Remove from dishes. Turn cakes upside down; trim edges to form a neat cylinder. Slice into two layers. Frost middle, sides and top of cakes with Chocolate Cream Frosting. Garnish with almonds.

Note: These cakes can be baked in batches. Cover and refrigerate unused batter while baking first batch.

Chocolate-Pecan Chess Tart.

Bottom right: Individual Birthday Cake with Chocolate Cream Frosting, page 168. On server, clockwise from top left: Mini Cheesecake, page 170; Carrot Cake with Cream Cheese Hard Sauce, page 169; Baby Brownie Cake, page 170; Mini Cheesecake, page 170; Chocolate Cheesecake, page 171; Chocolate Cream Cheese Cupcakes, page 172. At center: Spice Cake with Banana Cream Filling, page 171.

Chocolate Cream Frosting: Combine 2¹/₂ cups heavy cream, ³/₄ cup sugar, ¹/₂ cup *sifted* unsweetened cocoa powder and 2 teaspoons vanilla in large bowl. Beat until stiff.

Carrot Cakes with Cream Cheese Hard Sauce

Bake at 350° for 20 to 25 minutes.

Makes 24 minicakes.

1¹/₂ cups *unsifted* **all-purpose flour**	**1 cup vegetable oil**
2¹/₄ teaspoons ground cinnamon	**2 eggs**
1 teaspoon baking soda	**3 cups grated carrots (about 1 pound)**
³/₄ teaspoon baking powder	**1 cup coarsely chopped walnuts**
³/₄ teaspoon ground nutmeg	**Cream Cheese Hard Sauce** *(recipe follows)*
¹/₂ teaspoon salt	**Shredded carrot for garnish** *(optional)*
1¹/₃ cups sugar	

1. Preheat oven to moderate (350°). Line twenty-four 2¹/₂-inch muffin-pan cups with foil or paper baking cups.

2. Combine flour, cinnamon, baking soda, baking powder, nutmeg and salt in small bowl; stir to mix. Set aside.

3. Beat together sugar, oil and eggs in large bowl. Stir in grated carrot. Add dry ingredients, stirring until just combined. Stir in nuts. Spoon batter into lined muffin-pan cups, dividing equally.

4. Bake in preheated moderate oven (350°) for 20 to 25 minutes or until wooden pick inserted in centers comes out clean. Remove cakes from pans to wire racks to cool.

5. Prepare Cream Cheese Hard Sauce.

6. Frost cakes with Hard Sauce. Garnish with shredded carrot, if you wish.

Cream Cheese Hard Sauce: Beat ¹/₄ cup (¹/₂ stick) softened butter or margarine, 1 package (3 ounces) softened cream cheese and 1 teaspoon vanilla in bowl until well blended. Gradually beat in 1¹/₂ cups *sifted* 10X sugar until smooth and creamy.

Mini Cheesecakes

Individual creamy cheesecakes with a graham cracker crust and topped with a sour cream glaze.

Bake cake at 325° for 15 to 17 minutes; bake with glaze at 400° for 3 minutes.

Makes 18 minicakes.

Sour Cream Lemon Glaze *(recipe follows)*

Crumb Crust:
1¹/₃ **cups fine graham cracker crumbs**
OR: ²/₃ **cup fine gingersnap crumbs and ²/₃ cup fine graham cracker crumbs**
2 **tablespoons sugar**
¹/₄ **teaspoon ground cinnamon**
4 **tablespoons**

(¹/₂ **stick) butter or margarine, melted**

Cheese Filling:
2 **packages (3 ounces each) cream cheese, softened**
1 **container (16 ounces) dairy sour cream**
1 **egg**
¹/₂ **cup sugar**
2 **teaspoons vanilla**
Raspberries and mint leaves for garnish *(optional)*

1. Prepare Sour Cream Lemon Glaze. Set aside.
2. Line eighteen 2¹/₂-inch muffin-pan cups with foil or paper baking cups.
3. Prepare Crumb Crust: Combine crumbs, sugar and cinnamon in small bowl. Stir in melted butter until well mixed. Spoon a rounded tablespoon of crumb mixture into each cup; press evenly and firmly in bottom. Set aside.
4. Preheat oven to slow (325°).
5. Prepare Filling: Beat cream cheese in medium-size bowl until creamy. Beat in sour cream, egg, sugar and vanilla until well blended. Spoon scant ¹/₄ cup filling into each muffin-pan cup.
6. Bake in preheated slow oven (325°) for 15 to 17 minutes or until tops are set but centers are still creamy; do not overbake.(Cheesecakes will firm up as they chill.) Remove cups from oven. Increase oven temperature to hot (400°).
7. Gently spread top of each cake with 1 tablespoon Sour Cream Lemon Glaze. Bake in hot oven (400°) for 3 minutes.
8. Remove pans with cheesecakes to wire rack to cool to room temperature. Remove cakes from pans; refrigerate until cold. Garnish with raspberries and mint leaves, if you wish.

Sour Cream Lemon Glaze: Mix together 1 cup dairy sour cream, 2 tablespoons sugar, ¹/₂ teaspoon grated lemon rind and ¹/₄ teaspoon vanilla in small bowl.

Microwave Oven Directions for Mini Cheesecakes
650 Watt Variable Power Microwave Oven

Directions: Place butter in 1-cup microwave-safe measure. Microwave, uncovered, at full power for 30 to 45 seconds to melt. Combine crumb crust as in Step 3 above. Place paper baking cups in microwave-safe muffin-pan cups. Spoon a rounded tablespoon crumb mixture into each; press into even layer on bottom. Place cold cream cheese in medium-size microwave-safe bowl. Microwave, uncovered, at full power for 30 seconds to soften. Prepare cheese filling as in Step 5 above. Spoon scant ¹/₄ cup filling into each crumb-lined cup. Microwave 6 cheesecakes at a time, uncovered, at half power for 2 minutes, turning once. Remove from microwave; spread scant 1 tablespoon Glaze over each. Microwave, uncovered, at full power for 30 seconds. Let stand in cups 5 minutes. Carefully transfer to other regular muffin cups to cool completely so cakes hold their shape. Cover and refrigerate to chill. Repeat twice more to make 18 cakes.

Baby Brownie Cakes

They're as scrumptious as full-size cakes, and these mini versions are fun (and festive) for special occasions.

Bake at 350° for 20 to 25 minutes.

Makes 18 cakes.

³/₄ **cup butter or margarine**
4 **squares (1 ounce each) unsweetened chocolate**
3 **eggs**
¹/₄ **teaspoon salt**
1¹/₂ **cups sugar**

2 **teaspoons vanilla**
1 **cup all-purpose flour**
1 **cup chopped walnuts or pecans**
Chocolate Glaze *(recipe follows)*
White chocolate, melted *(optional)*

1. Preheat oven to moderate (350°). Line eighteen 2¹/₂-inch muffin-pan cups with paper or foil baking cups.
2. Melt together butter and chocolate in top of double boiler over hot water. Let cool slightly.
3. Beat together eggs and salt in large bowl until foamy. Gradually add sugar and beat until thick and pale yellow, about 3 to 5 minutes. Beat in vanilla. Blend in melted chocolate mixture. Add flour, stirring just until combined. Stir in nuts. Spoon into lined cups, dividing batter equally.
4. Bake in preheated moderate oven (350°) for 20 to 25 minutes or until wooden pick inserted in centers comes out slightly moist. Remove cakes to wire rack to cool.
5. Frost tops with Chocolate Glaze. Drizzle with melted white chocolate, if you wish.

Chocolate Glaze for Baby Brownie Cakes: Melt together 1 package (4 ounces) sweet cooking chocolate, coarsely chopped, and ¹/₃ cup heavy cream in top of double boiler over hot water, stirring until smooth. Remove from heat.

Chocolate Cheesecakes

Bake at 325° for 15 to 17 minutes.

Makes 16 minicakes.

Crust:
1¼ cups fine chocolate wafer crumbs (about 26 wafers)
¼ cup (½ stick) butter or margarine, melted

Filling:
1 package (8 ounces) cream cheese, softened
¼ cup sugar
½ cup heavy cream

½ teaspoon vanilla
¼ teaspoon salt
3 eggs
1 package (6 ounces) semisweet chocolate pieces, melted over low heat
Whipped Cream Topping (recipe follows)
Chocolate Hearts (optional; recipe follows)

1. Preheat oven to slow (325°). Line sixteen 2½-inch muffin-pan cups with foil or paper baking cups.
2. Prepare Crust: Combine crumbs and butter in small bowl. Press into bottoms of lined muffin-pan cups.
3. Prepare Filling: Beat cream cheese in small bowl until smooth. Beat in sugar, cream, vanilla and salt. Add eggs, one at a time, beating well after each. Blend in melted chocolate. Spoon into muffin-pan cups, dividing equally.
4. Bake in preheated slow oven (325°) for 15 to 17 minutes, or until tops are just set. Remove cheesecakes from oven to wire rack; cool in pans to room temperature. Remove from pans and refrigerate until cold.
5. Spoon or pipe Whipped Cream Topping onto cheesecakes. Garnish with Chocolate Hearts, if you wish.

Whipped Cream Topping: Beat ½ cup heavy cream and 2 teaspoons sugar in small bowl until stiff.

Chocolate Hearts: Melt ½ cup semisweet chocolate pieces in top of double boiler set over hot water. Let cool slightly. Spoon into pastry bag fitted with small writing tip. Pipe heart shapes onto wax paper-lined cookie sheets. Chill until firm.

Microwave Oven Directions for Chocolate Cheesecakes

650 Watt Variable Power Microwave Oven

Dirctions: Line microwave-safe muffin-pan cups with paper baking cups. Place butter in 1-cup microwave-safe measure. Microwave, uncovered, at full power for 30 to 45 seconds to melt. Combine melted butter with wafer crumbs. Press a rounded tablespoonful into bottom of each prepared muffin cup. Place chocolate pieces in 2-cup microwave-safe measure. Microwave, uncovered, at half power for 4 minutes to melt; set aside. Place cream cheese in large microwave-safe bowl. Microwave, uncovered, at full power 30 seconds to soften. Prepare cheese filling as in Step 3 above. Spoon about 3 tablespoons cheese mixture into each prepared muffin cup. Microwave 6 cakes at a time, uncovered, at half power for 2½ minutes until set around edges, rotating muffin pan one-quarter turn twice. Or, microwave 4 cakes at a time for 1 minute and 45 seconds, turning once. Let cakes cool in pan on wire rack 5 minutes. Remove cakes from pans; place in other regular muffin cups to cool so cakes hold their shape. Cover and refrigerate to chill. Serve with Whipped Cream Topping, and Chocolate Hearts, if you wish.

Spice Cakes with Banana Cream Filling

Bake at 325° for 20 to 25 minutes.

Makes 8 minicakes.

1½ cups *sifted* cake flour
½ teaspoon baking soda
½ teaspoon ground cinnamon
¼ teaspoon salt
¼ teaspoon ground allspice
¼ teaspoon ground cloves
½ cup (1 stick) butter or margarine,

softened
¾ cup firmly packed light brown sugar
2 eggs
½ cup buttermilk
Maple Cream (recipe follows)
1 or 2 small bananas, peeled and thinly sliced
½ cup flaked coconut, toasted

1. Preheat oven to slow (325°). Butter eight 4-ounce (½ cup) soufflé dishes.
2. Combine flour, baking soda, cinnamon, salt, allspice and cloves in small bowl; set aside.
3. Beat butter and brown sugar in large bowl until light and fluffy, 3 to 5 minutes. Add eggs, one at a time, beating well after each addition. Mix in flour mixture alternately with buttermilk, beginning and ending with flour mixture. Spoon about ⅓ cup batter into each prepared dish. Place on a cookie sheet.
4. Bake in preheated slow oven (325°) for 20 to 25 minutes or until wooden pick inserted in centers comes out clean. Cool cakes in soufflé dishes on wire racks. Run knife around edges of cakes to loosen. Remove from dishes. Trim rounded tops with serrated knife. Turn cakes cut-side down; slice horizontally into two layers.
5. Spread bottom layers with Maple Cream. Top with banana slices. Cover with top layers of cakes. Spread with Maple Cream, leaving sides unfrosted. Sprinkle with toasted coconut.

Note: These cakes can be baked in 2 batches. Cover and refrigerate unused batter while baking first batch.

Maple Cream: Beat 1 cup heavy cream with 2 tablespoons maple syrup in small bowl until stiff.

Chocolate–Cream Cheese Cupcakes

Bake at 350° for 25 to 30 minutes.

Makes 18 minicakes.

Cream Cheese Filling
(recipe follows)
1 1/2 cups *unsifted* all-
purpose flour
1 cup sugar
1/4 cup unsweetened
cocoa powder
1 teaspoon baking

soda
1/2 teaspoon salt
1 cup water
1/3 cup vegetable oil
1 tablespoon distilled
white vinegar
1 teaspoon vanilla

1. Preheat oven to moderate (350°). Line eighteen 2 1/2-inch muffin-pan cups with foil or paper baking cups.
2. Prepare Cream Cheese Filling. Set aside.
3. Sift together flour, sugar, cocoa powder, baking soda and salt into large bowl.
4. Combine water, oil, vinegar and vanilla in small bowl. Stir into flour mixture until blended.
5. Half fill each lined muffin-pan cup with batter. Place spoonful of Cream Cheese Filling into center of batter in each cup.
6. Bake in preheated moderate oven (350°) for 25 to 30 minutes or until wooden pick inserted into chocolate part comes out clean. Remove from pans to wire racks to cool completely.

Cream Cheese Filling: Beat 1 package (8 ounces) cream cheese, softened, 1 egg and 1/4 cup sugar in bowl until smooth. Stir in 1 cup (6-ounce package) semisweet chocolate pieces.

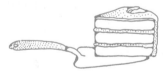

Carrot-Pineapple Cake

Recipes for carrot cakes are popping up all over. Their popularity is well deserved, as they are moist, flavorful, and very good keepers.

Bake at 350° for 1 hour, 15 minutes.

Makes one 10-inch tube cake.

4 eggs
1 1/2 cups sugar
1 1/2 cups vegetable oil
3 1/4 cups whole wheat
flour
2 teaspoons baking
powder
2 teaspoons baking
soda
1/2 teaspoon salt

1 teaspoon ground
cinnamon
1 can (8 ounces)
crushed pineapple
in pineapple juice,
drained
2 cups shredded
carrots
1 cup chopped pecans
1 cup chopped dates

1. Grease a 10-inch tube pan; line bottom with wax paper. Preheat oven to 350°.
2. Beat eggs in large mixing bowl. Gradually beat in sugar. Stir in oil.

3. Combine 3 cups of the whole wheat flour with baking powder, baking soda, salt and cinnamon. Stir into egg mixture. Add drained pineapple and carrots; mix well.
4. Toss pecans and dates with remaining 1/4 cup whole wheat flour; stir into batter. Turn into prepared pan.
5. Bake in a preheated moderate oven (350°) for 1 hour, 15 minutes or until top of cake springs back when lightly pressed with fingertip. Cool cake in pan on wire rack about 15 minutes. Remove cake from pan; peel off wax paper. Cool completely before cutting. Wrap tightly in foil or plastic wrap to store. Cake keeps well.

Coconut Marmalade Cake

Bake at 375° for 25 minutes.

Makes one three-layer 8-inch cake.

1 1/2 cups *sifted* cake
flour
1 teaspoon baking
powder
1/2 teaspoon salt
6 eggs, separated
1/2 teaspoon cream of
tartar
1 1/2 cups sugar
1/3 cup water
1 teaspoon vanilla

10X (confectioners')
sugar
1 jar (18 ounces)
orange marmalade
or peach jam
White Mountain
Frosting *(recipe
follows)*
1 can (3 1/2 or 4
ounces) coconut

1. Grease bottoms of a 15 1/2 × 10 1/2 × 1-inch jelly-roll pan and two 8 × 1 1/2-inch layer pans; line with wax paper; grease again. Flour all pans lightly, tapping out excess. Preheat oven to 375°.
2. Sift the flour, baking powder and salt onto wax paper.
3. Beat egg whites and cream of tartar in large bowl with electric mixer at high speed until foamy white and doubled in volume. Beat in 1/2 cup of the sugar, slowly, until meringue stands in soft peaks.
4. Beat egg yolks in small bowl with mixer at high speed until thick and lemon-colored. Beat in the remaining 1 cup sugar, gradually, until mixture is very thick and fluffy. Beat in the water and vanilla at low speed.
5. Fold flour mixture into egg yolk mixture until completely blended.
6. Fold yolk mixture into meringue until no white streaks remain.
7. Measure 4 cups batter into prepared jelly-roll pan, spreading evenly into corners; divide remaining batter evenly into layer-cake pans. Place jelly-roll pan on lower shelf in oven, cake layers on middle shelf.
8. Bake in a preheated moderate oven (375°) for 15 minutes. Reverse pans in oven and continue baking for 10 minutes or until tops spring back when lightly pressed with fingertip.
9. As soon as cakes are done, loosen around sides of

Coconut Marmalade Cake, page 172.

pans with knife; invert oblong cake onto a clean towel dusted with 10X (confectioners') sugar; peel off wax paper. Roll up with towel; let cool 10 minutes. Invert cake layers onto racks. Peel off wax paper; cool layers.

10. Unroll oblong cake; spread with 1 cup of the jam. Divide remaining jam between the tops of the round cake layers.

11. Place one cake layer, jam-side up, on serving plate. Cut oblong cake lengthwise into 8 strips, each 1¼-inches wide. (Measure with ruler so strips will be even.) Roll up one strip, jelly-roll fashion; lay flat on center of cake layer on serving plate. Matching ends, wind remaining strips, one at a time, around roll to make a big pinwheel. Place second cake layer, jam-side down, on the pinwheel to make three layers.

12. Prepare frosting. Frost sides, then top of cake. Press coconut onto sides and top of cake while still moist. Chill several hours. Cut with sharp knife dipped in hot water.

(continued)

White Mountain Frosting

Makes enough to frost two or three 8-inch cake layers.

1/2 **cup sugar**	**2 egg whites**
1/4 **cup light corn syrup**	1/8 **teaspoon cream of tartar**
2 tablespoons water	1/2 **teaspoon vanilla**

1. Combine sugar, corn syrup and water in a small saucepan; cover. Heat to boiling; uncover; boil gently, without stirring, until mixture registers 242° on a candy thermometer or until a small amount of the hot syrup falls, threadlike, from spoon.
2. While syrup cooks, beat egg whites with cream of tartar in a large bowl with electric mixer until stiff peaks form when beaters are removed. Pour hot syrup into egg whites in a very thin stream, beating all the time at high speed, until frosting is stiff and glossy. Beat in the vanilla.

Sidewalk Sundae Cake

Bake according to the package directions.

Makes 12 servings.

1 package any flavor cake mix for 2-layer cake	**unsweetened cocoa powder**
6 cups *unsifted* **10X (confectioners') sugar**	**1 tablespoon instant coffee powder**
12 tablespoons (3/4 cup) vegetable shortening	**4 to 6 medium-size fresh strawberries, washed, hulled and sliced**
1/4 **teaspoon almond extract**	**1 tablespoon chopped walnuts**
4 tablespoons warm water	**1 large strawberry, washed, with stem left on**
1 tablespoon	

1. Grease and flour one 9-inch-round layer-cake pan and one 8-inch heart-shaped cake pan. Prepare, bake and cool the cake, following the package directions.
2. Prepare the white frosting: Combine 2 cups of the 10X (confectioners') sugar, 4 tablespoons of the shortening, the almond extract and 2 tablespoons of the warm water in a medium-size bowl. Beat until smooth.
3. Prepare the mocha frosting: Combine 2 cups of the 10X (confectioners') sugar, 4 tablespoons of the shortening, the cocoa and the instant coffee stirred into the remaining 2 tablespoons of warm water, in a medium-size bowl. Beat until smooth.
4. Prepare the strawberry frosting: Combine the remaining 2 cups of 10X (confectioners') sugar, 4 tablespoons of vegetable shortening and 4 sliced strawberries in a medium-size bowl. Beat until smooth. If the frosting is too stiff, beat in more strawberries until the consistency matches the other frostings.

5. Place a round cake layer at one end of a 19 × 11-inch, or larger, tray or board. Fit the heart-shaped cake tightly against the round layer.* Trim the heart cake so the sides are in a straight line with the sides of the round layer; these will be the sides of the cone. Trim any scraps to fit into the hollows on either side of the areas where the cakes meet.
6. Frost the trimmed heart cake, the trimmings fitted into the hollows on either side of the cake and the lower one-quarter of the round layer with the mocha frosting to make the cone. Be very careful to frost gently and in one direction over the cut edges. Score as pictured, to resemble a cone.
7. Frost the remaining part of the round cake with the strawberry frosting to resemble the ice cream. Swirl half of the white frosting over the top center of the strawberry frosting. Sprinkle with the nuts. Place the remaining white frosting in a pastry bag fitted with a medium star tip. Tuck doilies, cut in half, under the edges of the cake, if you wish. Pipe a shell border around the base of the cake, starting at the bottom point of the cone, and working up one side to the top, and then up the other side. Place the large strawberry at the top of the cake; fasten with a wooden pick to hold in place, if necessary.

*Instead of using a platter on which to serve the cake, cut a piece of cardboard 1/2 inch larger than the cake, using the unfrosted cakes fitted together as a guide. Cover the cardboard with aluminum foil and doilies.

Happy Birthday Teddy Bear Cake

Bake according to directions on package.

Makes 12 servings.

1 package any flavor cake mix for 2-layer cake	**Miniature marshmallows**
2 recipes Decorator Frosting *(recipe follows)*	**Wooden picks**
	Green and yellow food coloring
4 teaspoons instant coffee powder	1/4 **teaspoon unsweetened cocoa powder**
1 teaspoon warm water	**Birthday candles**

1. Prepare, bake and cool the cake mix, following the label directions for a 13 × 9 × 2-inch baking pan.
2. Prepare 2 recipes of the Decorator Frosting. Spoon 1 1/2 cups into a pastry bag fitted with a medium star tip. Measure 1 cup into a small bowl, 1/4 cup into a custard cup, 2 tablespoons into a second custard cup and 1 tablespoon into a third custard cup.
3. Place the cake, upside down, on a 14 × 10-inch or larger serving tray or board. Frost with the remaining unmeasured white frosting. Using a bag with a medium star tip, pipe a reverse shell border around the top edge of the cake. Pipe a shell border around the bottom edge of the cake.

(continued)

Happy Birthday Teddy
Bear Cake, page 174.

Sidewalk Sundae Cake,
page 174.

4. Stir the instant coffee into the 1 teaspoon of warm water. Beat into the 1 cup of frosting in a small bowl until evenly colored. Spoon into a pastry bag fitted with a small star tip.

5. To make the sitting teddy bears on top of the cake: Push 2 miniature marshmallows onto a wooden pick, allowing 1/4 inch of the pick to extend beyond the marshmallows at one end and about 1 inch on the other. Pipe small stars to completely cover the sides of the marshmallows. Holding the top 1/4 inch of the wooden pick, push the long end of the pick into the cake until the teddy bear body is sitting on the cake. Insert straight into the cake for the sitting teddy bears and at an angle for resting teddy bears. Press a quarter of a marshmallow on the end of the pick for the head; cover completely with piped stars. Pipe on ears, the arms and legs as pictured. Pipe small white stars on the faces for eyes.

6. To make the teddy bears on the sides of the cake: Pipe a 3/4-inch puff of frosting onto the side of the cake for the body. Pipe a large star above it for the head; cover both completely with small stars. Pipe on the ears, arms and legs. Pipe small white stars on the faces for the eyes.

7. To make the teddy bears standing on their heads: Push 2 wooden picks through a stack of 2 marshmallows to form an X with the center inside the marshmallows. Insert one wooden pick end into the star tip on the pastry bag filled with the coffee frosting so that the tip touches the marshmallow. Gently pull back the tip, piping the coating of frosting on the pick, extending 1/2 inch from the marshmallow. Repeat on the other wooden pick on the same end of the marshmallows. Pipe small stars to cover the marshmallows. Push the frosted wooden picks into the cake until the teddy bear is stable. Pipe the paws at the end of the arms. Pipe the head on the body just above the arms.

8. Using the piping technique described in Step 7, coat the top 2 wooden picks with frosting. Pipe the paws at the end of the legs.

9. Pipe a message on the cake with remaining light brown frosting, if you wish.

10. Color the 1/4 cup of frosting green. Spoon into a small pastry bag fitted with a leaf tip. Pipe leaves around the bears.

11. Color the 2 tablespoons of frosting yellow. Spoon into a small pastry bag fitted with a small star tip. Pipe small stars for flowers on the leaves.

12. Stir the cocoa into the 1 tablespoon of frosting. Spoon into a small parchment bag with a small hole cut in the end. Pipe, or apply with a wooden pick, noses and centers of eyes on the bears. Pipe clusters of dots on the leaves for flowers. Insert birthday candles into the leaves and into the bears' arms just before serving.

Decorator Frosting

Makes about 2 1/4 cups.

1/2 cup vegetable shortening
1 box (1 pound) 10X (confectioners') sugar
1/4 teaspoon almond extract
3 to 4 tablespoons warm water

Combine the shortening, sugar, almond extract and 3 tablespoons of water in a large bowl. Beat until smooth and easy to spread. If necessary, add more water.

Dobos Cake Ah La Holiday

Bake at 350° for 20 minutes.
Makes 12 servings.

6 eggs, separated
1 1/4 cups sugar
2 tablespoons lemon juice
1 cup *sifted* all-purpose flour
1/4 cup cornstarch
1/2 teaspoon salt
Chocolate Frosting (*recipe follows*)
1 cup ground walnuts
Walnuts and glacé fruit for garnish (*optional*)

1. Preheat the oven to moderate (350°). Grease two 9-inch-round layer-cake pans. Line the bottoms with wax paper; grease the paper with vegetable shortening.

2. Beat the egg yolks in a medium-size bowl until thick and pale yellow. Gradually beat in the sugar until the yolks are thick and fluffy. Beat in the lemon juice.

3. Sift together the flour, cornstarch and salt over the yolk mixture all at once; fold into the yolk mixture with a rubber spatula.

4. Beat the egg whites in a medium-size bowl until stiff peaks form. Stir one-quarter of the beaten whites into the yolk mixture to lighten. Fold in the remaining whites until no streaks remain. Spread the batter into the prepared pans, dividing equally.

5. Bake in the preheated moderate oven (350°) for 20 minutes or until the tops spring back when lightly touched with a fingertip. Cool the cakes in the pans on wire racks for 10 minutes. Turn the cakes out onto the racks; remove the wax paper and let cool. Cut each layer in half horizontally with a serrated knife.

6. Fill and stack the layers with the Chocolate Frosting. Frost the top layer. Make a design with a decorating comb, if you wish. Cover the sides with the ground walnuts. Garnish the top with the walnuts and the glacé fruit, if you wish.

Chocolate Frosting: Melt 4 1/2 squares (1 ounce each) of semisweet chocolate in the top of a double boiler or in a small bowl over hot water. Beat 6 egg yolks and 1/2 cup of sugar in a medium-size bowl until pale yellow. Stir in 3/4 cup of heavy cream and 1/8 teaspoon of salt. Stir into the melted chocolate. Cook

Dobos Cake Ah La Holiday, page 176.

over hot water, stirring occasionally, until thick. Remove from the heat. Beat in 1½ cups (3 sticks) of softened butter, 1 tablespoon at a time. If the frosting cools too rapidly to incorporate the butter, place over hot water for a minute or two. Cool the frosting in the refrigerator or over ice water until it reaches a good spreading consistency.

Sour Cream Cake with Coconut Topping

So quick to whip up when you're expecting a neighbor to stop by.

Bake at 350° for 35 minutes.

Makes one 8-inch square cake.

1 container (8 ounces) dairy sour cream	2 teaspoons baking powder
2 eggs	½ to 1 teaspoon almond extract
¾ cup sugar	Coconut Topping *(recipe follows)*
1½ cups *sifted* all-purpose flour	

1. Let sour cream and eggs warm to room temperature for easy mixing. Remove 2 tablespoons sour cream to small bowl; reserve for Coconut Topping. Grease and flour an 8 × 8 × 2-inch baking pan. Preheat oven to 350°.
2. Combine remaining sour cream, eggs, sugar, flour, baking powder and almond extract in a large bowl. Beat at medium speed with electric mixer for 1 minute, scraping down side of bowl with plastic spatula. Pour into prepared pan.
3. Bake in a preheated moderate oven (350°) for 25 minutes or until the center springs back when lightly pressed with fingertip.
4. Remove baked cake from oven. Spread Coconut Topping evenly over top. Return to oven. Bake 10 minutes longer. Cool in pan on wire rack.

Coconut Topping: Combine reserved sour cream, 2 tablespoons soft butter, ½ cup firmly packed brown sugar and ½ cup flaked coconut until well mixed.

Sparkling Cookie Cake

Bake cake at 375° for 40 minutes. Bake cookies at 375° for 9 to 10 minutes.

Makes 8 cake servings and about 33 cookies.

1 recipe Christmas
   Tree Cookies dough
   *(recipe in chapter
   Cookies and
   Candies)*
1 unused, clean clay
   flowerpot
   (7¼ inches across
   inside top, and
   6¾ inches, or more,
   deep) or see
   Editor's Note
   (follows recipe)
Extra-wide, heavy-duty
   aluminum foil
1 box (14.5 ounces)
   angel food cake
   mix*

1 container
   (16 ounces) vanilla-
   flavored frosting
Yellow food color
   paste**
Green food color
   paste
Silver candy decorator
   balls
1 container
   (16 ounces) frozen
   non-dairy whipped
   topping, thawed
   OR: 1 box (2.8
   ounces) whipped
   topping mix
Sugar fruit candies***
   (optional)

Sparkling Cookie Cake.

1. Prepare Christmas Tree Cookies dough, following recipe directions through Step 2. Refrigerate and reserve.
2. Remove top oven rack and place bottom rack at lowest position. Center 10-inch square of aluminum foil on rack to catch any spills. Preheat oven to moderate (375°).
3. Prepare flowerpot: Turn flowerpot, bottom-end up, on counter. Center 26 × 18-inch piece of extra-wide, heavy-duty aluminum foil over bottom of pot. Press foil gently to outside of pot to shape foil. Remove foil. Invert pot and place shaped foil inside pot, gently easing foil into pot. Be careful not to tear foil. Gently press foil against sides of pot to flatten all creases. Fold excess foil over top and press firmly to outside of pot, anchoring under flowerpot rim.
4. Prepare angel food cake batter following package directions. Remove 1 generous cup batter and discard. (The full amount of batter will overflow pot during baking; see *Editor's Note.* Pour remaining batter into prepared flowerpot, being careful not to create air pockets. Smooth top gently with spatula.
5. Place in preheated moderate oven (375°) on aluminum foil square. Bake for 40 minutes or until cake tester inserted in center of cake comes out clean. Check cake after 25 minutes. If top is becoming too brown, gently lay 8-inch square of foil on top. Open and close oven door carefully so as not to disturb cake.
6. When cake is done, remove from oven and cool, inverted, resting edges of flowerpot on edges of three 8- or 9-inch-round cake pans.
7. Make patterns for tree cookies. For large tree: Use a ruler to draw a rectangle, 2½ × 4¼ inches. Label one 2½-inch side TOP. Make a mark to indicate center 1¼ inches from either side on TOP. Draw a

line connecting mark at center TOP with bottom right corner. Draw a line connecting mark at TOP with bottom left corner. You should have a tree-shaped triangle. Cut out.
8. For small tree cookies: Draw a rectangle 2½ x 3½ inches and proceed as in Step 7.
9. Divide reserved cookie dough in half. Roll out, half at a time, on floured surface to ⅜-inch thickness: Cut out star cookie, using 3-inch star cookie cutter. Lightly flour tree patterns and place on dough. Cut out equal numbers of small and large trees with a small sharp knife. Place trees 1 inch apart on greased cookie sheets. Repeat with remaining dough. Reroll and use all scraps. You should have about 16 large trees, 16 small trees and 1 star cookie.
10. Bake cookies in preheated moderate oven (375°) for 9 to 10 minutes or until lightly browned around edges. Remove cookies to wire racks to cool.
11. Remove 1 tablespoon vanilla-flavored frosting from container to small bowl. Stir in yellow food color paste and use to frost star.
12. Stir small amount of green food color paste into container with remaining frosting, to tint a pale green. Frost one-third of cookies. Stir additional green food color paste into pale green to tint medium green. Use to frost another third of the cookies. Add more green food color paste to the medium green frosting to make dark green frosting. Frost remaining cookies. Decorate cookies with silver candy decorator balls. Reserve cookies.

13. When cake is completely cooled, lift foil with cake from pot. Place cake, top-side down, on serving plate. Trim if cake does not sit evenly. Carefully peel off and discard foil.

14. Frost sides and top of cake with frozen nondairy whipped topping. Or, prepare whipped topping mix following package directions and use to frost cake. Top cake with star cookie. Arrange some of the trees around base of cake. Pass remaining cookies when you serve cake. Garnish plate around base of cake with sugar fruit candies, if you wish. Store in refrigerator.

15. To serve, remove cookies and pass. Cut cake with serrated knife.

Do not use any cake mix except the angel food cake mix specified in the recipe.

**Food color pastes produce deeper shades than regular food coloring. They are available wherever cake decorating supplies are sold.*

***We used 1 pound assorted fruit-shaped hard candies.*

Editor's Note: If you wish, use the whole angel food cake mix and bake in a 10-inch tube pan as directed on package. You may then proceed with the recipe as directed. The tube cake will yield a shorter, fuller centerpiece.

Valentine Cheesecake

The best way to anyone's heart is with this love of a cheesecake! Topped with a luscious maraschino cherry glaze, it has an easy-to-prepare graham cracker crust and cream cheese filling—and will make any dinner special.

Bake crust at 350° for 5 minutes; bake cheesecake at 350° for 1 hour, 10 minutes.

Makes 10 servings.

Crumb Crust:
1 cup graham cracker
  crumbs
2 tablespoons sugar
2 tablespoons butter
  or margarine,
  softened

Filling:
2 pounds cream

cheese, at room
  temperature
1 cup sugar
Grated rind of
  1 orange
4 eggs
Cherry Glaze *(recipe
  follows)*

1. Preheat the oven to moderate (350°). Coat the inside of a heart-shaped cake pan (8¹⁄₂ × 1³⁄₄ inches) with nonstick vegetable cooking spray.

2. Prepare Crumb Crust: Thoroughly blend together the graham cracker crumbs, the 2 tablespoons of

(continued)

Valentine Cheesecake.

sugar and butter in a small bowl. Press firmly in an even layer over bottom of the prepared pan.

3. Bake in preheated moderate oven (350°) for 5 minutes. Remove the pan to a wire rack. Leave the oven on.

4. Prepare the filling: Combine the cream cheese, the 1 cup of sugar and orange rind in a large bowl. Beat just until the mixture is smooth. Add the eggs, one at a time, beating just until the eggs are incorporated. Pour over the crumb crust. Place the pan in a larger pan. Pour in enough water to come 1 inch up the sides of the heart pan.

5. Bake in preheated moderate oven (350°) for 1 hour and 10 minutes, or until a small knife inserted in the center comes out clean. Remove the heart pan from the water bath to a wire rack to cool to room temperature.

6. Run small sharp knife around the sides of the cake. Cover the top with wax paper. Place a wire rack over the top of cake; carefully invert the pan and rack. Carefully remove the pan. Place the serving plate, upside down, over the crumb bottom of the cake; invert the plate, cake and rack. Remove the rack and wax paper. Cover the cake loosely and refrigerate until chilled.

7. Cover the top of the cheesecake with the Cherry Glaze. Refrigerate until serving time.

Cherry Glaze: Drain 2/3 cup of maraschino cherry syrup (from a 16-ounce jar of maraschino cherries) into a glass measure; pour into small saucepan. Whisk in 2 teaspoons of cornstarch until smooth. Cook over low heat, stirring constantly, until the mixture thickens and bubbles; cook for 1 more minute. Set aside. Arrange 2 1/4 cups of the drained maraschino cherries (about one and a half 16-ounce jars) over top of cheesecake.. Carefully spoon the thickened cherry syrup over cherries.

Note: If you prefer, use canned cherry pie filling to top the cheesecake.

Golden Honey Gingerbread

Bake at 350° for 35 minutes.
Makes one 13 × 9 × 2-inch cake.

2 1/2 cups *sifted* all-purpose flour	allspice
1 1/2 teaspoons baking soda	1/2 cup vegetable shortening
1/4 teaspoon salt	1/2 cup sugar
3/4 teaspoon ground cinnamon	3/4 cup honey
1/2 teaspoon ground nutmeg	1 egg
1/4 teaspoon ground	1 cup hot water
	Honey Whipped Cream *(recipe follows)*

1. Sift flour, baking soda, salt, cinnamon, nutmeg and allspice onto wax paper.

2. Preheat oven to 350°. Beat shortening with sugar in a large bowl until fluffy; beat in honey and egg.

3. Stir in flour mixture, half at a time, just until blended; beat in hot water until smooth. Pour into a greased 13 × 9 × 2-inch baking pan.

4. Bake in preheated moderate oven (350°) for 35 minutes or until center springs back when lightly pressed with fingertip. Cut into rectangles. Top with Honey Whipped Cream and orange slices, if you wish.

Honey Whipped Cream: Beat 1 cup heavy cream until soft peaks form; fold in 2 tablespoons honey.

Norwegian Honey Cake

Bake at 325° for 1 hour, 15 minutes.
Makes 12 servings.

4 cups *sifted* all-purpose flour	cinnamon
1 cup raisins	3 eggs
1 teaspoon baking soda	2 1/3 cups sugar
1/2 teaspoon ground cloves	1 1/2 cups dairy sour cream
1/2 teaspoon ground	2 tablespoons honey
	3 tablespoons grated orange rind

1. Sprinkle 1 tablespoon flour over raisins in a bowl; toss to coat. Sift together the remaining flour, baking soda, cloves and cinnamon.

2. Beat eggs and sugar in a bowl until fluffy. Beat in sour cream and honey. Stir in flour mixture just until blended. Add raisins and orange rind. Pour into a greased and floured 10-inch angel-cake tube pan.

3. Bake in preheated slow oven (325°) for 1 hour and 15 minutes or until the cake pulls away from the sides of the pan and the top springs back when lightly pressed. Cool in pan on a wire rack 5 minutes. Run knife around inner and outer edges of cake. Turn out onto wire rack; cool completely.

4. Store covered at room temperature overnight before cutting. Sprinkle top with 10X (confectioners') sugar, if you wish.

Coconut Cream Cake

Bake at 350° for 30 minutes.
Makes 12 servings.

1 package (18 3/4 ounces) yellow cake with pudding mix	1 1/2 cups heavy cream
3 eggs	3 tablespoons 10X (confectioners') sugar
1 cup water	Coconut Cream Filling *(recipe follows)*
1/3 cup vegetable oil	Flaked coconut
2 tablespoons grated orange rind	

1. Preheat oven to 350°. Prepare cake mix with eggs, water and oil, adding orange rind, following label directions. Divide batter into 2 greased and floured round 9 × 1 1/2-inch cake pans.

2. Bake in a preheated moderate oven (350°) for 30

Norwegian Honey Cake, page 180.

minutes or until centers spring back when lightly touched with fingertip.

3. Cool in pans on wire racks 10 minutes; turn out onto racks, cool completely. Split each layer in half to make 4 thin layers.

4. Beat cream with confectioners' sugar in a small bowl until stiff.

5. Put layers together with Coconut Cream Filling. Frost side and top with whipped cream. Sprinkle generously with flaked coconut.

Coconut Cream Filling

Makes 2¹/₂ cups.

¹/₄ **cup sugar**
2 tablespoons cornstarch
¹/₈ **teaspoon salt**
2 egg yolks

1¹/₄ **cups milk**
1 tablespoon butter or margarine
¹/₂ **cup flaked coconut**
¹/₂ **cup heavy cream**

1. Combine sugar, cornstarch and salt in small saucepan; beat in egg yolks, then gradually blend in milk.

2. Cook, stirring constantly, until mixture thickens and bubbles 1 minute. Remove from heat.

3. Stir in butter and coconut. Place a piece of plastic wrap directly on filling. Cool completely. Beat cream until stiff; fold into filling.

Sacher Torte
A rich chocolate cake, split and spread with apricot preserves, then sandwiched and iced with a bittersweet chocolate coating. One of Vienna's most famous desserts, Sacher torte was created in 1832 by Franz Sacher, chef to Prince von Metternich.

Sacher Torte

This classic cake from the Hotel Sacher in Vienna is shipped all over the world in little wooden boxes. Serve it with whipped cream.

Bake at 325° for 1 hour, 15 minutes.

Makes one 8-inch cake.

Almond Praline *(recipe follows)*
6 eggs, separated
¹/₂ **cup sugar**
¹/₂ **cup (1 stick) butter or margarine, softened**
1 package (6 ounces) semisweet chocolate pieces,

melted and cooled
³/₄ **cup** *sifted* **cake flour**
1 teaspoon baking powder
1 jar (12 ounces) apricot preserves
Chocolate Glaze *(recipe follows)*

1. Make Almond Praline. Grease an 8 × 3-inch springform pan. Preheat oven to 325°.

2. Beat egg whites in a large bowl with electric mixer at high speed until foamy-white. Sprinkle in ¹/₃ cup of the sugar, 1 tablespoon at a time, beating all the time until meringue forms soft peaks.

3. With same beaters, beat butter until soft in a small bowl; add remaining sugar and egg yolks; beat until light and fluffy, about 3 minutes. Beat in chocolate and ¹/₂ cup Almond Praline at low speed; gently fold into egg whites. Sift flour and baking powder over bowl; fold in just until blended. Pour into prepared pan.

4. Bake in a preheated slow oven (325°) for 1 hour and 15 minutes or until cake tester inserted into center comes out clean. Cool 10 minutes in pan on wire rack. Loosen around edge; remove ring from pan; cool completely.

5. Even off top, then split cake horizontally into 2

(continued)

layers. Spread about ¹/₂ of the preserves on bottom layer; replace top. Brush or spread remaining preserves on top and side of cake. Let stand at least 2 hours for preserves to soak in and partially dry.

6. Prepare Chocolate Glaze and pour over top of cake, letting it drip down side, smoothing with a warm spatula. Reserve about 2 tablespoons glaze to drizzle over top. Sprinkle top with reserved praline powder. Drizzle reserved glaze from a wax paper cone over praline. Serve with whipped cream, if you wish.

Almond Praline: Heat ¹/₃ cup sugar in small skillet just until melted and starting to turn golden in color. Add ¹/₃ cup slivered almonds. Continue heating over medium heat until almonds start to "pop" and mixture is deep golden. Pour onto buttered cookie sheet. Cool completely. Break into smaller pieces and crush finely in blender or with rolling pin. Makes about ³/₄ cup.

Chocolate Glaze: Blend 2 tablespoons water, 2 tablespoons light corn syrup and 1¹/₂ cups 10X (confectioners') sugar in medium-size bowl; stir in 1¹/₂ squares unsweetened chocolate. Set bowl over hot, not boiling, water; heat, stirring often, until chocolate melts and glaze is thin enough to pour over the cake. Makes about 1 cup.

Pecan Candy Cake

Serve this rich, fruitcake-like confection sparingly. Make at least 2 weeks ahead so flavors can mellow.
Bake at 250° for 1¹/₂ hours.

Makes one 9-inch cake (32 thin slices).

¹/₂ **pound candied red cherries, cut in quarters (1¹/₃ cups)**	**all-purpose flour**
¹/₂ **pound candied pineapple, coarsely chopped (1 cup)**	**4¹/₃ cups coarsely chopped pecans (1 pound, shelled)**
¹/₂ **pound pitted dates, coarsely snipped (1¹/₂ cups)**	**4 ounces flaked coconut (about 1¹/₄ cups)**
1 tablespoon	**1 can (14 ounces) sweetened condensed milk**

1. Preheat oven to slow (250°). Grease and flour 9 × 3-inch tube pan with removable bottom; set pan aside.
2. Combine cherries, pineapple and dates in very large bowl. Sprinkle with flour; toss to coat well. Add pecans and coconut; toss to mix. Add sweetened condensed milk; stir to mix well. Spoon evenly into prepared pan, smoothing top.
3. Bake in preheated slow oven (250°) for 1¹/₂ hours. Cool in pan on rack. Remove from pan. Wrap tightly in foil. Refrigerate at least 2 weeks. Cake cuts best when cold. Slice very thin with serrated knife.

Fresh Coconut Layer Cake

Bake at 350° for 20 to 25 minutes.

Makes 12 servings.

Cake:
2¹/₂ cups *unsifted* cake flour
2¹/₂ teaspoons baking powder
1 teaspoon salt
1 cup milk
¹/₄ cup cold water
1¹/₂ teaspoons vanilla
4 egg whites, at room temperature
1¹/₂ cups sugar
¹/₂ cup vegetable shortening
¹/₄ cup (¹/₂ stick) butter, softened

Lemon Filling:
²/₃ cup sugar
2 tablespoons cornstarch
¹/₈ teaspoon salt
³/₄ cup water
¹/₃ cup strained fresh lemon juice
1 tablespoon butter
3 egg yolks, slightly beaten
1 tablespoon grated lemon rind

Fluffy White Frosting:
1 cup sugar
¹/₈ teaspoon cream of tartar
¹/₈ teaspoon salt
2 egg whites
¹/₄ cup cold water
1¹/₂ teaspoons vanilla
2 to 3 cups grated fresh (see Note) or canned coconut

1. Preheat the oven to moderate (350°). Grease and flour three 9-inch-round layer-cake pans; set aside.
2. Prepare the Cake: Sift together the cake flour, baking powder and salt onto a sheet of wax paper; set aside. Combine the milk, water and vanilla in a 2-cup glass measure or small bowl; set aside.
3. Beat the egg whites in a medium-size bowl until frothy. Gradually beat in ¹/₄ cup of the sugar until soft peaks form; set aside.
4. Combine the shortening, butter and remaining sugar in a large bowl. Beat on medium-high speed until light, 2 to 3 minutes. Reduce the speed to low; beat in the dry ingredients alternately with the milk mixture, beginning and ending with the dry ingredients. Fold in the beaten whites, half at a time. Divide the batter among the prepared pans, spreading evenly to the edges.
5. Bake in the preheated moderate oven (350°) for 20 to 25 minutes, or until the edges start to pull away from the sides of the pan. Cool the cakes in the pans on wire racks for 10 minutes. Turn the cakes out onto wire racks to cool completely.
6. Prepare the Filling: Combine the sugar, cornstarch and salt in a small saucepan. Stir in the water, lemon juice and butter. Cook, stirring, over medium heat until the mixture comes to boiling, 3 to 4 minutes. Lower the heat; cook 1 minute, stirring constantly. Stir ¹/₄ cup of the hot mixture into the yolks in a small bowl.

(continued)

Quickly stir the yolk mixture into the saucepan. Cook, stirring, 1 minute. Do not boil.

7. Remove the saucepan from the heat. Add the lemon rind. Cool for 10 minutes, stirring once or twice. Cover; refrigerate until chilled.

8. Prepare the Frosting: Combine the sugar, cream of tartar, salt, egg whites and water in the top of a double boiler. Beat for 1 minute. Then beat over simmering water, for 5 to 7 minutes, or until the frosting is thick, shiny and holds firm peaks. Remove from the simmering water. Beat a little longer until cool. Beat in the vanilla; set aside.

9. Stir the Lemon Filling to soften. Place the cake layer on a serving plate. Spread with half the filling. Top with the second layer. Spread with the remaining filling. Top with the remaining layer. Frost the top and sides with frosting. Sprinkle the top and sides with the coconut.

Note: For grated fresh coconut, pierce the "eyes" of a coconut with a screwdriver; drain off the liquid. Heat the coconut on a baking sheet for 20 minutes in 400° oven. Tap all over to loosen the meat; crack open with a hammer. Pry the chunks of white meat from the shell; peel off the brown skin. Grate the meat on a hand grater or in a food processor.

Fruitcake

Christmas just wouldn't be the same without fruitcakes. They are some of the easiest food gifts to make and most should be made ahead so they can mellow for several weeks before cutting. A fruitcake can be chock-full of dried fruits or nuts or be more cake than fruit. It can be baked in a tube pan, in a round cake pan or a loaf pan.

Golden Light Fruitcake

Bake at 300°, small cake for 1½ hours, loaf cake for 2 hours or miniature cakes 30 minutes.

Makes 2 small fruitcakes or 1 loaf fruitcake or 8 dozen miniature fruitcakes.

1 container (8 ounces) candied red cherries, chopped	**½ teaspoon salt**
1 package (15 ounces) golden raisins	**1 cup (2 sticks) butter or margarine**
1 can (3½ ounces) sliced almonds	**1 cup sugar**
½ cup light rum	**5 eggs**
2 cups *sifted* **all-purpose flour**	**1 teaspoon vanilla**
	½ cup apricot preserves
	2 tablespoons light rum or orange juice

1. Grease two 4-cup molds or one 9 × 5 × 3-inch loaf pan. Dust lightly with flour; tap out excess. For miniatures you will need 8 dozen small paper baking cups (petits fours or baking cases—1 tablespoon capacity) set in miniature muffin tins.

2. Combine cherries, raisins, nuts and the ½ cup rum in large bowl. Allow to stand 1 hour.

3. Preheat oven to 300°. Sift flour and salt onto wax paper. Sprinkle ¼ cup of mixture over fruits and nuts; toss to coat well.

4. Beat butter, sugar, eggs and vanilla in a large bowl of an electric mixer at high speed for 3 minutes, until fluffy.

5. Stir in remaining flour mixture until batter is quite smooth. Pour over prepared fruit and nuts and fold just until well blended. Spoon batter into prepared pans. For miniatures, drop batter by heaping tablespoonfuls into paper baking cups.

6. Bake all cakes in a preheated slow oven (300°). Bake large loaf for 2 hours, small cakes for 1½ hours or until centers spring back when lightly pressed with fingertip. Cool in pans on wire racks 15 minutes. Loosen around edges of pans with a knife; turn out. Cool completely. Bake miniatures for 30 minutes; remove from tins; cool on wire racks.

7. To decorate: Heat apricot preserves with 2 tablespoons light rum or orange juice until bubbly in a small saucepan. Press through a sieve. Brush hot mixture on fruitcakes.

Note: Cakes may be kept at room temperature for 1 week, in the refrigerator for 1 month, and in the freezer 3 months.

Macadamia-Nut Fruitcake

Bake at 300° for 2 hours.

Makes 2 medium-size loaves.

1 cup golden raisins	**macadamia nuts, chopped**
1 container (4 ounces) candied red cherries, quartered	**1 cup** *sifted* **all-purpose flour**
1 container (4 ounces) candied green cherries, quartered	**1½ teaspoons baking powder**
2 containers (4 ounces each) candied citron	**½ teaspoon ground mace**
2 containers (4 ounces each) candied pineapple, chopped	**4 eggs**
	1 cup sugar
1 package (6 ounces) dried apricots, chopped	**¼ cup light corn syrup**
1 can (5 ounces)	**Candied red and green cherries, halved (for garnish)**
	Macadamia nuts

1. Combine fruits and nuts in bowl.

2. Sift flour, baking powder and mace over fruits. Toss. Preheat oven to 300°.

3. Beat eggs and sugar together in small bowl with electric mixer. Pour over fruits, stirring to coat well.

4. Pour into 2 greased 7⅜ × 3⅜ × 2¼-inch loaf pans.

5. Bake in a preheated slow oven (300°) for 2 hours or until centers spring back when lightly pressed with fingertip.

6. Cool cakes in pans on wire racks 10 minutes; loosen around edges with a spatula. Turn out onto wire racks; cool completely.

Chocolate Ice Cream Linzer Torte, page 190.

7. To decorate: Heat corn syrup in small saucepan until bubbly; brush over cakes. Garnish cakes with halved candied cherries and nuts.

8. To store: Cake keeps well. Wrap in foil; refrigerate for up to 3 weeks.

Pineapple Coconut Cheesecake

A delicious no-bake dessert.

Makes 16 servings.

2 packages (8 ounces each) cream cheese	**1 can (15¹/₂ ounces) cream of coconut**
2 cans (8 ounces each) crushed pineapple in pineapple juice	**1 cup zwieback cracker crumbs**
	¹/₂ cup flaked coconut
3 teaspoons unflavored gelatin (1¹/₂ envelopes)	**¹/₄ cup (¹/₂ stick) butter or margarine, melted**
3 eggs, separated	**2 tablespoons sugar**

1. Let the cream cheese soften to room temperature in a large bowl.

2. Drain juice from pineapple into a glass measure; reserve ³/₄ cup drained pineapple juice and the crushed pineapple.

3. Sprinkle gelatin over pineapple juice in a medium-size saucepan; let stand 5 minutes to soften. Beat egg yolks slightly in a small bowl; stir in cream of coconut, then add mixture to gelatin. Cook over medium heat, stirring constantly, just until mixture comes to boiling, but do not allow to boil. Cool.

4. Combine zwieback crumbs, flaked coconut and butter in a medium-size bowl. Sprinkle ¹/₄ cup mixture around sides of a lightly buttered 9-inch springform pan; press remaining mixture onto bottom. Chill briefly before filling.

5. Beat cream cheese just until smooth with electric mixer at medium speed. Beat in the cooled gelatin mixture.

6. Place pan in a bowl of ice and water to speed set; chill, stirring often, until mixture mounds lightly when dropped from a spoon.

7. While gelatin mixture chills, beat egg whites in small bowl with electric mixer until foamy; slowly beat in sugar until meringue stands in firm peaks.

8. Fold meringue and crushed pineapple into chilled

(continued)

gelatin mixture. Turn into prepared pan. Chill several hours, preferably overnight, until firm. Loosen cake around side with a spatula, then release and remove side.

Plantation Fruitcake

Bake at 300°, the tube cake for 2 hours or the miniature cakes for 30 minutes.

Makes one 9-inch tube cake or 8 dozen miniature fruitcakes.

2 cups raisins
1 can (16 ounces)
cling peaches,
drained and
chopped
1 cup vegetable
shortening
1 cup firmly packed
brown sugar
¹/₂ cup cream sherry
or orange juice
1 jar (16 ounces)
mixed candied
fruits, chopped

2 cups chopped
walnuts
4 eggs, beaten
2¹/₂ cups *sifted* **all-**
purpose flour
1 teaspoon baking
powder
1¹/₂ teaspoons salt
1 teaspoon ground
cinnamon
¹/₂ teaspoon ground
cloves
¹/₄ cup light corn
syrup

1. Grease a 9-inch Bundt pan. Dust with flour; tap out excess. For miniatures, you will need 8 dozen small baking cups (petits fours or baking cases—1 tablespoon capacity) set in miniature muffin tins.
2. Combine chopped raisins, peaches, shortening, brown sugar and sherry or orange juice in a medium-size saucepan. Heat just to boiling. Remove from heat; cool.
3. Add candied fruits and nuts to cooled mixture; stir in beaten eggs.
4. Preheat oven to 300°. Sift flour, baking powder, salt, cinnamon and cloves together on wax paper; stir into fruit mixture. Turn into prepared pan. For miniatures, drop by heaping tablespoonfuls into paper baking cups.
5. Bake all cakes in a preheated slow oven (300°). Bake tube cake for 2 hours or until center springs back when lightly pressed with fingertip. Cool in pan on wire rack 15 minutes; turn out of pan; cool completely. Bake miniatures for 30 minutes; remove from tins; cool on wire racks.
6. Heat corn syrup just until bubbly in a small saucepan. Brush syrup over cake. Decorate with additional candied fruit and nuts, if you wish.
Note: Cakes may be kept at room temperature for 1 week or in the refrigerator for 1 month. Glaze just before serving.

Whiskey Cake

Bake at 325° for 1 hour.

Makes one 10-inch tube cake.

3 eggs, separated
³/₄ cup granulated
sugar
¹/₂ cup (1 stick) butter
¹/₄ cup firmly packed
dark brown sugar
1¹/₂ cups *sifted*
unbleached all-
purpose flour
1 can (8 ounces)
pecans, chopped

(2 cups)
1 cup raisins
1 teaspoon baking
powder
2 teaspoons ground
nutmeg
Dash salt
¹/₂ cup bourbon
Pecan halves for
decoration

1. Grease and flour a 10 × 4-inch tube pan.
2. Beat egg whites in small bowl with electric mixer until foamy-white. Beat in ¹/₄ cup of the granulated sugar slowly until meringue forms stiff peaks; reserve.
3. Beat butter, brown sugar, remaining granulated sugar and egg yolks in large bowl with electric mixer until light and fluffy.
4. Mix ¹/₄ cup of the flour with pecans and raisins in small bowl, stirring until nuts and fruit are coated. Preheat oven to 325°.
5. Sift remaining 1¹/₄ cups flour with baking powder, nutmeg and salt onto wax paper. Beat into batter alternately with bourbon until well blended. Stir in pecans and raisins. Fold in reserved meringue until no streaks of white remain.
6. Spoon batter into prepared pan, pressing down with spoon to pack pan. Decorate top with pecan halves.
7. Bake in a preheated slow oven (325°) for 1 hour or until top springs back when lightly pressed with fingertip. Cool in pan on wire rack for 1 hour. Remove from pan; cool completely. Wrap cake with cheesecloth soaked with bourbon. Store in tightly covered container several days.

Hazelnut Torte

Bake at 375° for 25 minutes.

Makes 12 servings.

7 eggs, separated
¹/₄ teaspoon salt
³/₄ cup granulated
sugar
2 teaspoons grated
lemon rind
1 teaspoon vanilla
2 cups ground
hazelnuts
¹/₃ cup packaged
bread crumbs

1 teaspoon baking
powder
1 cup heavy cream
¹/₄ cup 10X
(confectioners')
sugar
Mocha Butter Cream
(recipe follows)
2 tablespoons
unsweetened cocoa
powder

1. Line three 8 x 1¹/₂-inch round layer pans with wax paper.

2. Beat egg whites with salt in a large bowl with electric mixer at high speed until foamy-white. Beat in 1/2 cup of the sugar, 1 tablespoon at a time, until meringue forms soft peaks.

3. Preheat oven to 375°. With the same beaters, beat egg yolks with the remaining sugar until very thick and fluffy. Beat in lemon rind and vanilla. Fold yolk mixture into meringue. Combine nuts, bread crumbs and baking powder; gently fold into egg mixture. Pour into prepared pans, dividing evenly; smooth tops.

4. Bake in preheated moderate oven (375°) for 25 minutes or until center springs back when lightly touched with fingertip. Turn pans upside down on wire rack; cool.

5. Loosen edges of cakes with knife; turn out of pans; peel off wax paper.

6. Beat cream and sugar in medium-size bowl until stiff. Stack layers on serving plate with whipped cream between each layer. Refrigerate while making Mocha Butter Cream.

7. Spread butter cream on side and top of torte, reserving about 1 cup. Add 2 tablespoons cocoa to reserved butter cream. Pipe onto top and around base of cake. Refrigerate 3 hours before serving.

Mocha Butter Cream

Makes about 1 1/2 cups.

1/2 cup (1 stick) butter or margarine	**3 tablespoons unsweetened cocoa powder**
1 egg yolk	**3 teaspoons instant coffee powder**
2 3/4 cups 10X (confectioners') sugar	**1/3 cup cold water**

Beat butter in medium-size bowl until soft; beat in egg yolk, 1 cup of the sugar and the cocoa. Dissolve coffee in water. Beat in alternately with remaining sugar until smooth.

Nectarine Cream Torte

Bake at 350° for 35 minutes.
Makes 8 servings.

2 cups *sifted* cake flour	**extract**
2 teaspoons baking powder	**1/3 cup milk**
1/2 teaspoon salt	**3/4 cup sliced almonds**
4 eggs, separated	**4 cups sliced, peeled nectarines**
2 cups sugar	**1 tablespoon lemon juice**
1/2 cup (1 stick) butter or margarine	**1 pint heavy cream**
1 teaspoon vanilla	**2 tablespoons 10X (confectioners') sugar**
1/2 teaspoon almond	

1. Sift flour, baking powder and salt onto wax paper.
2. Beat egg whites in small bowl with electric mixer at

high speed until foamy-white and double in volume. Beat in 1/2 cup of the sugar, 1 tablespoon at a time, until meringue stands in firm peaks. Preheat oven to 350°.

3. Beat 1 cup of the sugar, the butter, egg yolks, vanilla and almond extract in large bowl with electric mixer at high speed for 2 minutes.

4. Stir in flour mixture alternately with milk, beating after each addition, until batter is smooth. Spread batter in two greased and floured 9 × 9 × 2-inch pans. Carefully spread meringue over cake batter; sprinkle with all but 2 tablespoons of the sliced almonds.

5. Bake in a preheated moderate oven (350°) for 35 minutes or until meringue is golden brown; remove pans to wire racks to cool. Put reserved 2 tablespoons almonds in a pie plate; bake for 2 minutes; remove.

6. When cake layers are cool enough to handle, loosen around edges with a knife; turn out onto your hand, then gently place, meringue-side up, on wire racks to cool completely.

7. Combine nectarines with lemon juice and 1/2 cup sugar in a large bowl; let stand 30 minutes; drain and discard syrup.

8. Beat cream with 10X sugar in a bowl; reserve 1/2 cup. Fold remaining cream into 2 cups fruit.

9. To assemble: Place one cake layer, meringue-side down, on serving plate; spread with nectarine-cream filling; top with remaining cake layer, meringue-side up. Arrange reserved fruit slices and whipped cream on top. Sprinkle with toasted almonds.

Chocolate Orange Torte

This delicate tube cake is split into layers and spread with luscious whipped cream and preserved kumquats.

Bake at 325° for 45 minutes.

Makes one 10-inch tube cake.

1 jar (9 to 10 ounces) kumquats in syrup	**juice**
6 eggs, separated	**1 cup *sifted* cake flour**
1/4 teaspoon salt	**1 square semisweet chocolate, grated**
1 cup granulated sugar	**2 cups heavy cream**
1 teaspoon grated orange rind	**3 tablespoons 10X (confectioners') sugar**
1 tablespoon orange	**Mint leaves**

1. Drain kumquats, reserving syrup. Halve and pit about 6 kumquats for decorating cake; pit and chop remainder.

2. Grease bottom only of 10-inch tube pan. Preheat oven to 325°.

3. Beat egg whites with salt in large bowl with electric

(continued)

Chocolate Orange Torte,
page 187.

mixer until foamy. Gradually beat in ¹/₂ cup of the granulated sugar until meringue forms soft, glossy peaks.

4. Beat egg yolks in small bowl with electric mixer on high speed 5 minutes or until thick and light. Gradually beat in remaining ¹/₂ cup of the sugar or until mixture is pale and thick enough to form a ribbon when beater is lifted from batter, about 3 minutes. Stir in orange rind and juice.

5. Sprinkle ¹/₄ cup of the flour over egg yolk mixture. Fold in gently using rubber spatula. Repeat with remaining flour. Stir in grated chocolate. (Do not overmix.)

6. Fold meringue into chocolate mixture gently until no streaks of white remain.

7. Pour batter gently into prepared pan. Cut through batter with spatula to remove air pockets.

8. Bake in lower third of a preheated slow oven (325°) for 45 minutes or until top is golden and springs back when lightly pressed.

9. Invert pan; let stand until completely cold. Loosen around edges with knife; remove from pan. Slice horizontally to make three even layers. Place one layer, cut-side up, on serving plate.

10. Drizzle 2 tablespoons syrup from kumquats over cake layer. Beat cream in small bowl with electric mixer on medium speed until soft peaks form. Sprinkle 10X sugar in gradually, beating until firm peaks form. Spread cake layer with 1 cup of the cream.

11. Sprinkle half the chopped kumquats over cream.

Cover with second cake layer. Drizzle 2 tablespoons syrup over cake. Spread with 1 cup of cream and remaining chopped kumquats. Cover, cut-side down, with third layer of cake. Drizzle with remaining syrup. Spread sides and top with remaining cream. Refrigerate several hours. Garnish with reserved kumquat halves and mint leaves before serving.

Cranberry Linzer Torte

Bake at 350° for 40 minutes.
Makes 8 servings.

2³/₄ cups granulated sugar	¹/₄ teaspoon ground cloves
¹/₂ cup orange juice	1 cup finely ground almonds
1 package (12 ounces) fresh or frozen cranberries (3 cups)	³/₄ cup (1¹/₂ sticks) butter or margarine
1 small to medium-size apple, pared, cored and chopped	1 tablespoon grated orange rind
1³/₄ cups *sifted* all-purpose flour	2 egg yolks 1 teaspoon vanilla
¹/₂ teaspoon ground cinnamon	10X (confectioners') sugar

1. Heat 2 cups of the sugar and the orange juice in a large saucepan until the sugar dissolves. Add the cranberries and apple. Bring to boiling. Lower the heat; simmer, uncovered, for 20 minutes or until slightly thickened. Cool completely.
2. Sift together the flour, cinnamon and cloves into a large bowl. Add the remaining ³/₄ cup of sugar and the almonds. Cut in the butter with a pastry blender until crumbly. Blend in the orange rind, egg yolks and vanilla. Knead the dough a few times until smooth. Chill for 1 hour.
3. Roll half of the dough between 2 sheets of wax paper to a 10-inch round, using a tart pan with removable bottom as a guide. Remove the top sheet of paper; turn the dough out onto a cookie sheet; remove the paper. Trim the edges evenly. Trace and cut 2 stars in the dough, one 10 inches with the points touching the outer rim of the dough, and one 4- to 5-inches in the center, lined up with the larger star. Remove the dough between two cuts, leaving the center star and outer pieces on the cookie sheet. Place the cookie sheet in the freezer for a few minutes, until the dough is firm.
4. Preheat the oven to moderate (350°).
5. Combine the trimmings with the remaining dough. Press evenly over the bottom and up the sides of a 10-inch tart pan with a removable bottom. Spread 1 cup of the cranberry mixture over the dough. Place a star on the cranberry mixture in the center. Arrange the corresponding outer pieces along the edge of the pan, so the cutout lines up with the star in the center. Press the edge down together with the side all around to form an even rim.

6. Bake in the preheated moderate oven (350°) for 40 minutes, or until lightly browned. Cool in the pan for 15 minutes. Remove the outer rim of the pan. Cool the torte completely.
7. Fill in the open space with ¹/₃ to ¹/₂ cup cranberry filling.* Sprinkle the center star with 10X sugar. Garnish with fresh cranberries and strips of orange peel, if you wish.
*Extra cranberry filling can be served as a condiment with roast turkey or chicken.

Cake à L'Orange

Fragrant with fresh oranges, this cake needs no frosting.

Bake at 350° for 50 minutes.

Makes one 9-inch tube cake.

2 cups *sifted* all-purpose flour	dairy sour cream
1 teaspoon baking powder	1 tablespoon grated orange rind
1 teaspoon baking soda	¹/₂ cup chopped walnuts or pecans
1 cup (2 sticks) butter or margarine, softened	¹/₄ cup orange juice
1¹/₂ cups sugar	¹/₃ cup Grand Marnier or other orange-flavored liqueur
3 eggs, separated	2 tablespoons chopped nuts
1 container (8 ounces)	

1. Sift flour, baking powder and baking soda onto wax paper.
2. Preheat oven to 350°. Beat butter, 1 cup of the sugar and egg yolks in a large bowl until light and fluffy.
3. Add flour mixture alternately with sour cream, starting and ending with flour. Stir in orange rind and the ¹/₂ cup chopped walnuts or pecans.
4. Beat egg whites in a small bowl with electric mixer until stiff but not dry; fold into batter. Spoon batter into a greased 9-inch tube pan.
5. Bake in a preheated moderate oven (350°) for 50 minutes or until a wooden pick inserted in top comes out clean.
6. Combine orange juice and remaining ¹/₂ cup sugar in a small saucepan. Heat, stirring constantly, over low heat just until sugar is dissolved. Remove from heat and stir in Grand Marnier. Spoon mixture over hot cake. Sprinkle with 2 tablespoons nuts. Cool in pan on wire rack 15 minutes; loosen around edge and tube with knife; turn out onto wire rack; cool completely.

Chocolate Ice Cream Linzer Torte

Chocolate ice cream is sandwiched between layers of chocolate meringue, then covered with whipped cream and toasted almonds.

Bake meringue at 300° for 45 minutes.

Makes 12 servings.

1/2 **cup egg whites (about 5 eggs)**	**1 jar (12 ounces) raspberry preserves**
1/2 **cup granulated sugar**	**1 quart chocolate ice cream, softened**
1 cup *sifted* **10X (confectioners') sugar**	**2 cups (1 pint) heavy cream**
1 tablespoon cornstarch	2/3 **cup toasted ground almonds**
1/4 **cup unsweetened cocoa powder**	**1 package (12 ounces) frozen dry-pack whole raspberries**
1/2 **cup toasted ground almonds**	OR: **3 cups fresh raspberries**

1. Preheat the oven to slow (300°). Cut three 9-inch circles from plain brown paper. Place the circles on cookie sheets.
2. Beat the egg whites in a large bowl with an electric mixer until soft peaks form. Slowly beat in the granulated sugar, 1 tablespoon at a time, until the meringue forms stiff shiny peaks.
3. Sift together the 10X sugar, cornstarch and cocoa onto wax paper. Gradually beat into the meringue, 1 tablespoon at a time, beating just until blended. Fold in the 1/2 cup of toasted ground almonds.
4. Spread the meringue evenly over the brown paper circles on the cookie sheets; spread to the edge of the circles.
5. Bake in the preheated slow oven (300°) for 45 minutes. Turn off the oven; let the meringues cool completely in the oven with the oven door closed.
6. Carefully remove the cooled meringues from the brown paper, being careful not to break or crack them.*
7. To assemble: Place 1 meringue layer on a plate. Carefully spread one-third of the raspberry preserves over the meringue. Spread with half the ice cream, smoothing the sides. Repeat with the second meringue layer and the other half of the ice cream. Top with the remaining meringue layer. Press down gently to secure the layers. Freeze until firm, about 3 hours.
8. To decorate: Beat the heavy cream in a medium-size bowl until stiff. Frost the top and sides of the torte with about two-thirds of the whipped cream. Press the 2/3 cup toasted ground almonds into the sides of the torte. Spoon remaining whipped cream into a pastry bag fitted with a star tip; pipe rosettes around the outer top edge of the torte. Arrange the raspberries in the center. Top the berries with the remaining preserves.

The meringue layers can be made several days ahead and stored in a tin with a tight-fitting cover at room temperature.

Linzer Torte

A lovely, spicy almond pastry that holds a generous filling of tart raspberry preserves.

Bake at 350° for 50 minutes.

Makes one 9-inch torte.

1 3/4 **cups** *sifted* **all-purpose flour**	**butter or margarine**
1 teaspoon ground cinnamon	1 1/2 **teaspoons grated lemon rind**
1/4 **teaspoon ground cloves**	**2 egg yolks**
3/4 **cup sugar**	**1 teaspoon vanilla**
1 can (4 1/2 **ounces) whole almonds, ground (1 cup)**	**1 jar (10 ounces) red raspberry preserves**
3/4 **cup (1** 1/2 **sticks)**	**Whole blanched almonds** *(optional)*
	10X (confectioners') sugar

1. Sift flour, cinnamon and cloves into a large bowl; add sugar and almonds. Cut in butter with pastry blender until crumbly. Blend in lemon rind, egg yolks and vanilla; knead a few times until smooth. Chill dough about 1 hour.
2. Press 2/3 of dough evenly on bottom and 1 inch up the side of a 9-inch cake pan with a removable bottom. Spread 3/4 of the jam over dough.
3. Preheat oven to 350°. Roll remaining pastry between 2 sheets of wax paper to 9 × 6-inch rectangle; cut lengthwise into 6 strips. Arrange strips over jam to form a lattice top. Press edge down all around to form a rim. Arrange whole almonds on rim, if you wish.
4. Bake in a preheated moderate oven (350°) for 50 minutes or until browned. Cool 10 minutes on wire rack. Remove outer rim of pan; cool completely. Fill lattices with remaining jam; sprinkle with 10X sugar before serving.

Chocolate Chestnut Torte

Ribbons of smooth, chestnut-flavored cream between tender sponge layers.

Bake at 375° for 12 minutes.

Makes 10 servings.

2/3 **cup** *sifted* **cake flour**	3/4 **cup sugar**
1/3 **cup unsweetened cocoa powder**	**1 teaspoon vanilla**
1 teaspoon baking powder	**10X (confectioners') sugar**
4 eggs	**Chestnut Butter Filling** *(recipe follows)*
	1 cup heavy cream

1. Grease a 15 1/2 × 10 1/2 × 1-inch jelly-roll pan; line bottom with wax paper; grease paper.
2. Sift flour, cocoa and baking powder onto a piece of wax paper.
3. Preheat oven to 375°. Beat eggs in a medium-size bowl with an electric mixer until thick and creamy.

Gradually add sugar, beating constantly until mixture is very thick (about 10 minutes). Add vanilla. Fold in flour mixture just until smooth. Pour batter into prepared pan, spreading evenly.
4. Bake in a preheated moderate oven (375°) for 12 minutes or until center of cake springs back when lightly pressed with fingertip.
5. Loosen cake around edges with a small knife; invert onto a towel dusted with 10X sugar. Cool on wire rack.
6. Prepare Chestnut Butter Filling.
7. Cut cake crosswise into 4 strips. Stack the strips on a serving plate with Chestnut Butter Filling between each layer. (This can be done several days ahead. Cover and refrigerate until ready to frost and decorate.)
8. Whip cream until stiff; spread a smooth layer over sides and top of cake. Pipe rosettes of cream along top edges and bottom of cake. Garnish top with glacéed chestnuts, if you wish.

Chestnut Butter Filling: Drain 2 jars (10 ounces each) glacéed chestnuts in syrup. Reserve 6 for garnish, if you wish. Press remainder through a food mill or sieve into a medium-size bowl. Add ³/₄ cup (1¹/₂ sticks) unsalted butter, 1 tablespoon at a time, while beating with electric mixer, until all butter has been absorbed and mixture is smooth and spreadable. Makes about 1¹/₂ cups.

Shortcake
An original American favorite, shortcake with strawberries can only be topped by whipped cream. Although the shortcake can be a sponge cake baked in a MaryAnne shape, the classic is a biscuitlike cake.

Old-fashioned Strawberry Shortcake

Bake at 450° for 15 minutes.
Makes 6 servings.

2 cups sifted all-purpose flour	¹/₂ cup (1 stick) butter or margarine, chilled
1 tablespoon sugar	
3 teaspoons baking powder	1 egg
¹/₄ teaspoon salt	1²/₃ cups heavy cream
Pinch ground nutmeg	2 pints strawberries
	1 tablespoon sugar

1. Preheat oven to 450°.
2. Combine flour, sugar, baking powder, salt and nutmeg in a medium-size bowl. Cut in butter with a pastry blender or two knives until mixture forms coarse crumbs. Stir in egg and ²/₃ cup of the heavy cream until mixture comes together in a ball. Pat into a lightly greased and floured 8-inch round layer-cake pan.
3. Bake in a preheated very hot oven (450°) for 15 minutes or until lightly browned. Remove from pan and place on a wire rack to cool slightly.

4. Whip remaining 1 cup cream in a small bowl. Cut cake in half horizontally while cake is still warm. Wash and hull berries. Crush enough to make 1 cup. Stir in 1 tablespoon sugar. Slice remaining berries. Spread bottom layer with crushed berries, half of the whipped cream and some of the sliced berries. Add top layer of cake and spread with remaining cream. Arrange berries on top and serve immediately.

Raspberry Chocolate Torte

Makes 12 servings.

2 packages (10 ounces each) frozen raspberries	¹/₄ cup (¹/₂ stick) butter, melted and cooled slightly
1 envelope unflavored gelatin	1 package (10 ounces) frozen pound cake, thawed
¹/₂ of a 12¹/₂-ounce package fudge-covered graham crackers, finely crumbled	¹/₃ cup crème de cacao liqueur
	2¹/₂ cups heavy cream

1. Thaw berries; drain syrup into a medium-size saucepan. Puree half the berries in container of electric blender or food processor; strain through a fine sieve into saucepan. (Reserve remaining berries.)
2. Sprinkle gelatin over raspberries in saucepan; let stand to soften 5 minutes. Heat, stirring constantly, until gelatin dissolves. Cool; refrigerate 45 minutes or until mixture is consistency of unbeaten egg whites.
3. Meanwhile, thoroughly blend crumbs and butter in a bowl with a fork. Carefully pat the mixture around the side (but not bottom) of a buttered 8-inch springform pan.
4. Cut pound cake crosswise into 10 slices; then, holding slices together, cut loaf lengthwise into thirds; separate pieces of cake (30 pieces). Brush each piece with crème de cacao. Place half of the pieces on the bottom of the springform pan. Top with reserved berries.
5. Whip 2 cups of the cream in a medium-size bowl with an electric mixer at high speed until soft peaks form. Fold thickened raspberry mixture into whipped cream until no streaks of white remain. Pour half the mixture over cake and berries in pan; top with remaining cake pieces, then remaining whipped cream mixture. Refrigerate 6 hours or overnight.
6. At serving time, carefully remove side of pan; place cake on serving plate. Whip remaining cream in a small bowl until stiff. Garnish cake with whipped cream.

Chocolate–Peanut Butter Torte

Who could resist this sinfully rich dessert? It's layered with chocolate and peanut butter fillings and slathered with chocolate-flavored cream cheese frosting and whipped cream. And it requires no baking!

Makes 12 servings.

24 ladyfingers (two 3-ounce packages), split in half lengthwise	liqueur
	4 eggs
	¹/₂ cup extra-chunky peanut butter
³/₄ cup (1¹/₂ sticks) butter, softened	2 squares (1 ounce each) unsweetened chocolate, melted and cooled
4 cups *sifted* 10X (confectioners') sugar	Chocolate–Peanut Butter Frosting *(recipe follows)*
1 tablespoon vanilla	
1 tablespoon amaretto	

1. Line a 9 x 5 x 3-inch metal loaf pan with 2 sheets of aluminum foil, 1 laid crosswise and 1 laid lengthwise; allow the foil to extend several inches beyond the rim.
2. Arrange 7 ladyfinger halves, flat-side up, in the bottom of the pan, parallel to the short end of the pan. Line each long side with 7 ladyfinger halves, standing upright and flat-side in. Line each short end with 3 ladyfinger halves.
3. Beat together the butter, 10X sugar, vanilla and amaretto in a large bowl until well blended. Add the eggs, one at a time, beating well after each addition, until smooth and fluffy.
4. Transfer 2 cups of the butter mixture to a small bowl. Add the extra-chunky peanut butter; mix well. Spoon evenly over the bottom of the ladyfinger-lined pan. Tap the pan on the counter to settle the filling. Smooth evenly with a spatula. Arrange 7 ladyfinger halves, parallel to the short end of the pan, over the peanut butter mixture. Wedge 3 ladyfinger halves lengthwise, down one long side of the pan.

Chocolate-Peanut Butter Torte.

5. Stir the melted chocolate into the remaining butter mixture in the large bowl. Spoon over the ladyfingers; spread evenly. Arrange 10 ladyfinger halves as in Step 4. Crumble the remaining ladyfinger half over the top, filling the spaces between the ladyfingers.
6. Fold the overhanging foil over the top; wrap securely. freeze for at least 6 hours or overnight.
7. Fold back the foil. Invert the torte onto the serving platter. Remove the pan; carefully remove the foil. Frost the sides and top with Chocolate–Peanut Butter Frosting.＊Freeze, uncovered, for 1 hour until the frosting is firm.
8. To serve, cut into thin slices with a thin-bladed sharp knife. Garnish with whipped cream, if you wish.

Chocolate–Peanut Butter Frosting: Beat together 4 packages (3 ounces each) softened cream cheese, 2 cups *sifted* 10X (confectioners') sugar and 1 tablespoon milk in a medium-size bowl until fluffy. Beat in ¹/₃ cup smooth peanut butter and ¹/₃ cup unsweetened cocoa powder until well mixed.

＊If the ladyfingers begin to crumble when applying the frosting, carefully cover the cake with a very thin layer of frosting. Place in the freezer until firm. Spread evenly with the remaining frosting.

Sponge Cake
A foam-type of cake that is leavened with air beaten into eggs and sometimes with the addition of baking powder. A sponge cake is light and delicate, usually made with eggs, flour and sugar. No fat is used. When a sponge cake is dressed up a bit, it turns into a glorious dessert. In France, sponge cake is known as *genoise* and in Italy it's *genovese*. It is said to have originated in Genoa.

To make the best sponge cake, just follow our step-by-step tips.

Strawberries 'n' Cream Sponge Cake

Bake at 350° for 25 minutes.

Makes 8 servings.

1 cup *sifted* all-purpose flour	or margarine
	3 eggs
1 teaspoon baking powder	1 cup sugar
	1 teaspoon vanilla
¹/₄ teaspoon salt	2 pints strawberries
¹/₃ cup milk	¹/₂ cup sugar
2 tablespoons butter	1 cup heavy cream

1. Grease and flour two 8 x 1¹/₂-inch layer-cake pans. Preheat oven to 350°.
2. Sift flour, baking powder and salt onto wax paper. Heat milk and butter just until small bubbles appear around edge (scalding); do not boil; cool slightly.
3. Beat eggs until foamy in a small bowl with electric mixer on high speed. Gradually add 1 cup sugar while continuing to beat until very thick and fluffy; beat in vanilla and cooled milk.
4. Fold flour mixture gently into eggs just until well

Strawberries 'n' Cream Sponge Cake, page 192.

blended. (Don't overmix.) Pour batter into prepared pans.

5. Bake in a preheated moderate oven (350°) for 25 minutes or until tops spring back when lightly touched with fingertip. Cool layers on wire racks 10 minutes. Loosen cakes around edges with spatula; remove from pans. Cool completely on wire racks.

6. Wash, hull and slice strawberries into a bowl.

Sprinkle with $1/2$ cup sugar. Let stand at least 30 minutes to allow juice to form. Beat cream in small bowl until firm peaks form.

7. Place one cake layer on serving plate. Spread with half of whipped cream and top with half of the sliced strawberries. Top with remaining cake layer. Top with remaining whipped cream and strawberries. Garnish with mint sprigs, if you wish.

Step-by-Step to the Perfect Sponge Cake

The secret to a feathery-light sponge cake is beaten eggs, sometimes separated and other times whole. While beating the eggs or egg yolks, combine slowly with sugar to form a thick, pale yellow mixture that is creamy smooth. This should fall from the beaters in a narrow ribbon which stays on the surface of the batter for a while. (Step 1). *Note:* Thorough beating is essential at this stage in order to produce a good sponge cake.

Next, sprinkle sifted dry ingredients over the surface of the egg-sugar mixture (Step 2), and gently fold in with a rubber spatula.

If you are using separated eggs, beat the whites in a clean, grease-free metal or ceramic bowl until they form soft, glossy peaks (Step 3). *Caution:* Do not overbeat. This reduces the volume and makes the whites dry and difficult to fold in.

Then, gently fold the whites into the batter, using a rubber spatula in a down-across-and-up motion (Step 4).

Sherry Bavarian Cream with Sponge Cake

A super-special dessert with a satin smooth sherry bavarian crowning a tender sponge cake split and layered with raspberry jam and whipped cream.

Makes 12 servings.

1 envelope unflavored gelatin	2 cups heavy cream
1/2 cup sugar	1/4 cup 10X (confectioners') sugar
1/2 cup half-and-half or light cream	
4 eggs, separated	1 jar (12 ounces) raspberry jam
2/3 cup cream sherry	1 pint strawberries, hulled
Dash ground nutmeg	
Lemony Sponge Cake (recipe follows)	Chopped pistachio nuts

1. Mix gelatin and 1/4 cup sugar in small saucepan; blend in half-and-half; let stand 5 minutes. Separate eggs, placing whites in a large bowl and adding yolks to gelatin mixture. Beat gelatin mixture with rotary beater until blended.
2. Cook over medium heat, stirring constantly, until mixture is lightly thickened and gelatin is dissolved. Remove from heat; stir in 1/4 cup of the sherry and the nutmeg.
3. Place saucepan in larger pan of ice and water to speed thickening. Chill, stirring often, until mixture is thick enough to mound when spooned.
4. While mixture chills, beat egg whites in a large bowl until foamy-white and double in volume. Beat in remaining sugar gradually until meringue stands in soft peaks.
5. Beat about 1/4 of the meringue into thickened

gelatin mixture, then fold this mixture into remaining meringue until no streaks of white remain. Spoon into a 5-cup star-shape mold if you have it or use any 5-cup mold that will fit over a 9- or 10-inch cake. Chill until firm, about 3 hours.
6. Prepare, bake and cool Lemony Sponge Cake. Split sponge cake into 4 layers with a long thin-bladed knife.
7. Beat cream with the 10X sugar in a medium-size bowl until stiff.
8. Place bottom layer on serving plate; sprinkle with 1/4 of remaining sherry; spread with 1/3 cup of raspberry jam; top with second layer; sprinkle with sherry; spread with 1 cup of the whipped cream. Top with third layer; sprinkle with sherry; spread with 1/3 cup jam. Top with fourth layer; sprinkle with remaining sherry. Spread a thin coating of cream on side and top of cake.
9. Loosen gelatin mold around edge with tip of a knife; invert mold over cake. Place a hot damp towel over mold to release. Pipe remaining cream through a pastry bag onto side of cake and on top of mold. Fill in top of star with halved strawberries and garnish with remaining berries.
10. Press remaining jam through a sieve to remove seeds; brush over berries on top of mold. Garnish with pistachio nuts. Chill until ready to serve.

Lemony Sponge Cake

Bake at 350° for 25 minutes.

Makes one 9- or 10-inch cake.

3/4 cup *sifted* cake flour	3/4 cup sugar
1/2 teaspoon baking powder	2 tablespoons lemon juice
1/4 teaspoon salt	2 tablespoons water
4 eggs, separated	1 teaspoon vanilla

1. Sift flour, baking powder and salt onto wax paper. Preheat oven to 350°.
2. Beat egg whites in large bowl with electric mixer on high speed until foamy-white and double in volume. Gradually beat in half of the sugar until meringue stands in firm peaks when beaters are slowly raised.
3. With same beaters, beat egg yolks with remaining sugar in small bowl for 5 minutes or until light and fluffy; beat in lemon juice, water and vanilla.
4. Stir in flour mixture on low speed until completely blended. Fold into meringue until no streaks of white remain. Pour into ungreased 9- or 10-inch springform pan; smooth top.
5. Bake in a preheated moderate oven (350°) for 25 minutes or until top springs back when gently pressed

with fingertip. Invert pan over a wire rack to cool completely, upside down. If cake top is higher than top rim of pan, balance edge of pan on custard cups so it hangs free. Loosen around edge with small spatula; release and remove side; loosen and remove from bottom.

Applesauce Sponge Roll

Bake at 375° for 12 minutes.

Makes 1 roll.

1 cup *sifted* cake flour	sugar
1 teaspoon baking powder	1 jar (16 ounces) applesauce
1/4 teaspoon salt	1 tablespoon lemon juice
1 1/4 teaspoons ground cinnamon	10X (confectioners') sugar
1/2 teaspoon ground nutmeg	1/2 cup heavy cream
1/4 teaspoon ground ginger	1 tablespoon 10X (confectioners') sugar
3 eggs	
3/4 cup granulated	

1. Grease a 15 1/2 x 1 1/2 x 1-inch jellyroll pan; line with wax paper; grease paper. Preheat oven to 375°.
2. Sift flour, baking powder, salt, 1 teaspoon of the cinnamon, nutmeg and ginger onto wax paper.
3. Beat eggs in large bowl with electric mixer on high speed 5 minutes or until thick. Gradually beat in granulated sugar, about 3 minutes or until mixture is pale and thick enough to form a ribbon when beater is lifted from batter. Stir in 2/3 cup of the applesauce and lemon juice.
4. Sprinkle 1/3 of the dry ingredients over egg mixture. Fold in gently using rubber spatula. Repeat with remaining flour. Spread in prepared pan.
5. Bake in a preheated moderate oven (375°) for 12 minutes or until top is golden brown and springs back when lightly pressed with fingertip.
6. Sift 10X sugar over a clean towel on work surface. Loosen cake around edges. Turn out onto towel. Peel off paper. Starting at 10-inch side, roll up cake and towel together. Cool completely, seam-side down, on rack.
7. Beat cream in small chilled bowl with electric mixer on medium speed until soft peaks form. Add 1 tablespoon 10X sugar, beating until firm peaks form. Stir in remaining 1 cup applesauce and remaining 1/4 teaspoon cinnamon. Unroll cake; spread with whipped cream mixture. Re-roll gently. Place on serving platter. Chill.

Walnut Sponge Cake

Bake at 325° for 45 minutes.

Makes one tube cake.

1 cup *sifted* cake flour	1 teaspoon vanilla
1 teaspoon baking powder	1/2 cup finely chopped black walnuts or English walnuts
1/4 teaspoon salt	
3 eggs	1/2 cup sugar
1 cup sugar	1/4 cup water
1/4 cup milk, scalded	1/4 cup cream sherry

1. Grease and flour a 12-cup Bundt pan. Preheat oven to 325°.
2. Sift flour, baking powder and salt onto wax paper.
3. Beat eggs in large bowl with electric mixer on high speed for 5 minutes or until thick and light. Gradually add 1 cup sugar; beat 3 minutes or until mixture is pale and thick enough to form a ribbon when beater is lifted from batter. Stir in hot milk and vanilla.
4. Sprinkle 1/3 of the flour over egg mixture. Fold in gently using rubber spatula. Repeat with remaining flour. Stir in walnuts. Do not overmix. Pour into prepared pan.
5. Bake in lower third of a preheated oven (325°) for 45 minutes until top is golden and springs back when lightly pressed with fingertip.
6. Cool in pan on wire rack 10 minutes. Loosen around edge with knife. Remove from pan to wire rack. Punch holes in top of cake with a skewer.
7. Heat sugar and water in small saucepan until boiling; lower heat. Simmer 10 minutes; remove from heat; stir in sherry. Place cake and rack on shallow tray to catch glaze. Spoon hot glaze slowly over warm cake until it is absorbed.

Peach-filled Cheese Tart

Love cheesecake? Try our low-calorie version.
Bake at 350° for 45 minutes.

Makes 10 servings.

4 eggs, separated	yogurt
1 egg white	4 ripe peaches
1/8 teaspoon salt	2 teaspoons lemon juice
1 1/2 cups low-fat cottage cheese	1/3 cup low-sugar strawberry spread
1/2 cup low-fat vanilla	

1. Preheat oven to moderate (350°). Generously spray bottom and sides of 9-inch springform pan, 2 1/2- to 3-inches deep, with nonstick cooking spray.
2. Beat together the 5 egg whites and salt in large bowl until soft peaks form.
3. Combine the 4 egg yolks, cottage cheese and yogurt in container of electric blender or food processor. Cover; whirl until smooth. Transfer to large bowl.

(continued)

4. Gently fold beaten egg whites into cottage cheese mixture until no streaks of white remain. Spoon batter into prepared pan.

5. Bake in preheated moderate oven (350°) for 45 minutes or until puffed and golden. Remove to wire rack. Cool completely, away from drafts. (Cake will fall considerably as it cools.) Run sharp knife around edge. Loosen and remove side of pan. Cover and refrigerate.

6. Just before serving, peel, pit and thinly slice peaches. Toss slices gently with lemon juice in large bowl. Arrange slices, overlapping, in circles on top of cake.

7. Heat strawberry spread in small saucepan just until it becomes liquid. Strain; discard fruit bits. Brush liquid over peach slices. Garnish center of tart with mint leaves, if you wish.

No-Bake Black Forest Refrigerator Cake

Prepare this easy-to-put-together cake, with store-bought ladyfingers and a no-bake chocolate filling, a day ahead. Unmold just before serving.

Makes 10 servings.

10 ladyfingers, split in half	1 envelope unflavored gelatin
1/3 cup evaporated milk	2/3 cup strong coffee
1/2 teaspoon lemon juice	4 ice cubes
2 egg whites	3 packages (.75 ounces each) chocolate reduced-calorie dairy drink mix
1/8 teaspoon salt	
2 tablespoons cold water	
2 tablespoons cherry-flavored liqueur OR: water	2 teaspoons vanilla
	1 cup fresh or frozen cherries, thawed

1. Line bottom and long sides of 8 1/2 x 4 1/2 x 2-inch glass loaf pan with one long sheet of wax paper, extending the ends of the paper several inches beyond the rims. Arrange 6 ladyfinger halves, flat side up, across the bottom, parallel to the short ends of the dish. Line each long side of the pan with 7 ladyfinger halves, standing up with flat sides facing in. Set aside.

2. Place medium-size bowl in freezer along with mixer beaters. Pour evaporated milk into ice cube tray. Place in freezer until ice crystals form around the edge, about 25 minutes.

3. Scoop out the evaporated milk into the chilled bowl.

Add lemon juice. Beat with chilled beaters until stiff. Reserve.

4. Beat egg whites and salt in second bowl until stiff peaks form. Reserve.

5. Combine cold water and cherry-flavored liqueur in container of electric blender. Sprinkle gelatin over liquid; allow to soften about 1 minute.

6. Meanwhile, heat coffee to boiling in small saucepan. Pour over softened gelatin. Cover container; whirl until gelatin is dissolved. Add ice cubes, chocolate dairy drink mix and vanilla. Cover; whirl until well mixed. Transfer to large bowl. If mixture has not begun to set, chill just until it does.

7. Fold whipped evaporated milk and beaten egg whites into chocolate mixture. Spoon the chocolate filling into the ladyfinger-lined baking dish.

8. With a serrated knife, carefully trim ends of ladyfingers even with top of filling. Sprinkle trimmed pieces evenly over top of filling. Bring ends of wax paper over top; cover entire top lightly with plastic wrap. Refrigerate overnight.

9. To unmold, carefully invert dish onto serving plate. Remove dish and wax paper. Garnish top of cake with whole cherries. Serve immediately.

Romanoff Roll

This sugar-free sponge cake roll can be filled with a variety of fruits. Sweeten the cake with a low-calorie sugar substitute after baking, or let the filling sweeten the cake.

Bake at 400° for 5 minutes.

Makes 10 servings.

3/4 cup *sifted* all-purpose flour	ounce package) imitation low-calorie cream cheese
1 teaspoon baking powder	2 tablespoons orange flavored liqueur
5 eggs, separated	
1/8 teaspoon salt	1/8 teaspoon ground cinnamon
1/4 cup orange juice	
1/8 teaspoon grated orange rind	1/8 teaspoon ground allspice
Sugar substitute equal to 14 teaspoons sugar *(optional)*	2 cups pressurized light whipped cream topping
Creamy Romanoff Filling:	1 cup coarsely chopped strawberries
4 ounces (half of 8-	

1. Preheat oven to hot (400°). Spray 15 x 10 x 1-inch jelly-roll pan with non-stick vegetable cooking spray. Line only the bottom with wax paper; do not let paper come up sides of pan.
Generously spray paper with non-stick vegetable spray.

2. Sift together flour and baking powder onto clean piece of wax paper. Reserve.

3. Beat together egg whites and salt in large bowl until soft peaks form.

Clockwise from center: Peach-Filled Cheese Tart, page 195; No-Bake Black Forest Refrigerator Cake, page 196; Romanoff Roll, page 156.

4. Beat egg yolks with orange juice and orange rind in large bowl until light and fluffy. Beat in reserved flour mixture. Gently fold in beaten egg whites until no streaks of white remain. Turn batter into prepared jelly-roll pan, spreading evenly.

5. Bake in preheated hot oven (400°) for 5 to 7 minutes or until top springs back when lightly pressed with fingertip and wooden pick inserted in center comes out clean. Cake should not be brown.

6. Loosen cake around edges with tip of knife. Invert onto clean towel. Very carefully peel off paper. (Use knife to help peel off wax paper, if necessary.) Sprinkle cake with sugar substitute, if using. Starting at short end, roll up cake and towel together. Place roll, seam-side down, on rack. Cool completely.

7. Meanwhile, prepare Creamy Romanoff Filling: Combine cream cheese, liqueur, cinnamon and allspice in container of electric blender or food processor. Cover; whirl until smooth. Transfer to medium-size bowl. Gently fold in cream topping. If filling is not firm enough to spread, refrigerate.

8. When jelly roll is cool, unroll carefully. Spread roll evenly with filling; sprinkle with strawberries. Reroll, without the towel. Place roll, seam-side down, on serving plate. Refrigerate, covered, until ready to serve. Garnish with additional strawberries, if you wish.

Raspberry Cream Roll

Bake at 400° for 8 to 10 minutes.

Makes 10 servings.

1 recipe Basic Cake Batter *(see index for recipe)*
¼ cup 10X (confectioners') sugar
1 recipe Basic Cream Pudding Filling *(recipe follows)*

⅓ cup seedless raspberry preserves
Raspberry Whipped Cream *(recipe follows)*
½ recipe Deep Chocolate Glaze

1. Preheat oven to hot (400°). Grease bottom and sides of 15½ × 10½ ×1-inch jelly-roll pan. Line with wax paper; grease paper.
2. Prepare Basic Cake Batter as directed. Pour into pan.
3. Bake in preheated hot oven (400°) for 8 to 10 minutes or until wooden pick inserted in center comes out clean.
4. Sprinkle top of cake with 10X sugar. Place dish towel over cake. Invert cake and towel onto counter. Peel off wax paper. Trim ¼ inch from edges. Starting at short end, roll up cake with towel. Cool on wire rack.
5. Prepare Basic Cream Pudding Filling.
6. Unroll cake slowly and carefully on flat surface. Spread preserves over cake. Spread Basic Cream Pudding Filling over cake, leaving a ½-inch border around edges. Reroll cake using towel as aid. Place on serving platter, seam-side down.
7. Prepare Raspberry Whipped Cream. Frost sides and top with cream.
8. Prepare Deep Chocolate Glaze. Drizzle glaze with spoon over cake in back-and-forth motion to create lines. Refrigerate until ready to serve.

Raspberry Whipped Cream: Beat 1 cup heavy cream, 2 teaspoons 10X sugar and ½ teaspoon vanilla in small chilled mixer bowl until stiff. Fold in ⅓ cup seedless raspberry preserves.

English Toffee Cake

Bake at 325° for 40 to 45 minutes.

Makes 14 servings.

1 recipe Basic Cake Batter *(recipe follows)*
1 recipe Butterscotch-Pecan Cream Pudding Filling *(recipe follows)*
1 recipe Deep Chocolate Glaze

(see recipe in chapter Sauces, Glazes, Frostings and Stuffings)
Toffee Whipped Cream *(recipe follows)*
Pecan halves for garnish *(optional)*

1. Preheat the oven to slow (325°). Grease bottom of

Raspberry Cream Roll.

English Toffee Cake,
page 198.

9-inch angel-cake tube pan. Line bottom with wax paper.
2. Prepare Basic Cake Batter as directed. Pour into prepared pan.
3. Bake in the preheated slow oven (325°) for 40 to 45 minutes or until wooden pick inserted in center comes out clean. Invert pan on bottle or wire rack. Let cake cool completely.
4. Loosen cake with knife around edge and tube. Remove cake from pan; peel off wax paper.
5. Prepare Butterscotch-Pecan Cream Pudding Filling.
6. Prepare Deep Chocolate Glaze.
7. Cut cake horizontally into 3 equal layers. Place top layer, cut-side up, on serving platter. Spread with half of the glaze and half of the pudding filling. Place middle layer on top of filling, pressing down gently. Spread with remaining glaze and pudding filling. Place third layer, cut-side down, on top. Gently press down to seal layers together.
8. Frost sides and top with Toffee Whipped Cream. Garnish with pecan halves, if you wish. Refrigerate until ready to serve.

Toffee Whipped Cream: Beat 1¹/₂ cups heavy cream, ¹/₂ teaspoon instant coffee granules and 3 tablespoons brown sugar in chilled bowl until stiff.

Basic Cream Pudding Filling

Makes 2 cups.

1 package (4 ounces) vanilla-flavor instant pudding and pie filling	**1 cup cold milk** **¹/₂ cup cold heavy cream**

1. Blend together the pudding mix and milk in a small mixer bowl with the mixer on low speed. Add the heavy cream; beat for about 1 minute at medium speed.
2. Chill for 10 minutes before folding in any additional ingredients.

Orange Cream Pudding Filling: Prepare as directed above. After chilling for 10 minutes, fold in 2 tablespoons Triple Sec or other orange-flavored liqueur and ¹/₄ cup finely chopped mixed candied fruit. Makes 2 cups.

Butterscotch-Pecan Cream Pudding Filling: Prepare as directed above, using 1 package (3¹/₂ ounces) butterscotch-flavor instant pudding and pie filling. After chilling for 10 minutes, fold in ¹/₂ cup chopped pecans. Makes 2 cups.

Orange Chiffon Cake

Truly an all-American variety, the chiffon cake is one of the best of the sponge-type cakes to come along in this century. It was created in the 1930's following the development of the angel food cake.

Bake at 325° for 1 hour, 10 minutes.

Makes one 10-inch cake.

1½ cups *sifted* cake flour	2 tablespoons grated orange rind
1⅓ cups sugar	¼ cup orange juice
3 teaspoons baking powder	7 to 8 egg whites (1 cup)
¼ teaspoon salt	½ teaspoon cream of tartar
½ cup vegetable oil	
5 egg yolks	Orange Glaze *(recipe follows)*
½ cup water	

1. Sift flour, 1 cup of the sugar, baking powder and salt into a medium-size bowl. Make a well in center and add in order: oil, egg yolks, water, orange rind and orange juice; beat with a spoon until smooth. Preheat oven to 325°.
2. Beat egg whites and cream of tartar in a large bowl with electric mixer on high speed until foamy white and doubled in volume. Gradually beat in remaining sugar until meringue stands in firm peaks.
3. Pour egg yolk mixture over beaten egg white mixture; fold mixture gently until no streaks of white remain. Pour batter into an ungreased 10-inch tube pan.
4. Bake in a preheated slow oven (325°) for 1 hour, 10 minutes or until top springs back when lightly pressed with fingertip.
5. Invert pan on funnel or soda bottle to keep top of cake off countertop; let cake cool completely upside down. When cool, loosen cake around the tube and down the side with spatula. Remove from pan. Drizzle with Orange Glaze or sprinkle with 10X sugar and serve with fresh fruits, if you wish.

Orange Glaze: Combine 1 cup 10X (confectioners') sugar with 2 tablespoons orange juice in a small bowl until smooth.

Coconut Raspberry Gems

Flaked coconut and raspberry glaze top these favorites.

Makes 24 cakes.

Golden Yellow Cupcakes *(recipe follows)*	*(recipe follows)*
Raspberry Glaze	2 cans (4 ounces each) flaked coconut

1. Prepare, bake and cool Golden Yellow Cupcakes. Prepare Raspberry Glaze.

2. Remove paper liners from cooled cupcakes. Spread warm glaze on sides and bottoms of cupcakes; sprinkle with coconut, pressing lightly. Place on wire rack to set.

Raspberry Glaze: Combine 1 cup sieved raspberry jam or preserves and ¼ cup sugar in a small skillet. Cook over moderate heat, stirring constantly, until mixture comes to boiling; boil 1 minute.

Orange-Glazed Lemon Cups

Bake at 375° for 15 minutes.

Makes 16 shortcakes.

Golden Yellow Cupcakes *(recipe follows)*	*follows)*
	Lemon Filling *(recipe follows)*
Orange Marmalade Glaze *(recipe*	Whipped cream Lemon slices

1. Grease and flour 8 MaryAnne pans*. Set on cookie sheet. Preheat oven to 375°. Prepare Golden Yellow Cupcake batter. Fill each pan with ¼ cup batter.
2. Bake in a preheated moderate oven (375°) for 15 minutes or until tops spring back when lightly pressed with fingertips. Cool on wire racks 10 minutes. Turn out; cool completely. Wash pans; grease and flour; repeat with remaining batter.
3. To assemble: Brush sides and centers of cakes with Orange Marmalade Glaze; let set. Fill with Lemon Filling; top with whipped cream and a thin wedge of lemon.

Orange Marmalade Glaze: Combine 1 cup orange marmalade with ¼ cup sugar in a small skillet. Cook over moderate heat, stirring constantly, until mixture comes to boiling; boil 1 minute.

* Pans are available at many department stores and specialty shops.

Golden Yellow Cupcakes

Bake at 375° for 25 minutes.

Makes 24 to 26 cupcakes.

3 cups *sifted* cake flour	1 teaspoon vanilla
2½ teaspoons baking powder	1¼ cups milk
½ teaspoon salt	Lemon or Orange Butter Cream Frosting *(recipe under Frostings)*
¾ cup (1½ sticks) butter or margarine, softened	
1½ cups sugar	OR: Honey-Cream Cheese Frosting *(recipe under Frostings)*
2 eggs	

1. Sift flour, baking powder and salt onto wax paper. Preheat oven to 375°.
2. Beat butter, sugar, eggs and vanilla in a large bowl with electric mixer at high speed 2 minutes.
3. Add flour mixture alternately with milk, beating after

each addition until batter is smooth. Fill paper-lined muffin cups half full.

4. Bake in a preheated moderate oven (375°) for 25 mintues or until tops spring back when lightly pressed with fingertips. Remove from pans; cool. Frost with Lemon Butter Cream.

Lemon Filling

Makes 2 cups (enough to fill 16 Lemon Cups).

1 cup sugar	**2 tablespoons butter**
6 tablespoons	**or margarine**
cornstarch	**1 tablespoon grated**
1½ cups water	**lemon rind**
2 egg yolks, slightly	**6 tablespoons lemon**
beaten	**juice**

1. Combine sugar and cornstarch in a small saucepan. Stir in water.
2. Cook, stirring constantly, until mixture thickens and bubbles, 1 minute. Remove from heat.
3. Beat half of the hot mixture into beaten egg yolks; stir back into saucepan. Cook 1 minute longer.
4. Stir in butter, lemon rind and juice. Place a piece of plastic wrap directly on filling to prevent skin from forming. Chill until ready to use.

Poppy Seed Cake

Bake at 350° for 30 minutes.

Makes one two-layer 9-inch square cake.

1 cup poppy seeds	**1½ cups sugar**
1½ cups milk	**¾ cup (1½ sticks)**
3 cups *sifted* cake	**butter**
flour	**1 teaspoon vanilla**
3 teaspoons baking	**Lemon Butter Cream**
powder	**Frosting *(recipe**
1 teaspoon salt	**follows)***
4 egg whites	

1. Combine poppy seeds and ¾ cup of the milk in a small saucepan. Heat to boiling. Remove from heat; cover saucepan. Allow to stand until milk is absorbed, about 1 hour.
2. Grease two 9 × 9 × 2-inch baking pans; dust lightly with flour; tap out any excess.

3. Sift flour, baking powder and salt onto wax paper; reserve. Preheat oven to 350°.
4. Beat egg whites until foamy-white and double in volume in a medium-size bowl; beat in ½ cup of the sugar, 1 tablespoon at a time, until meringue forms soft peaks; reserve.
5. Beat butter and remaining 1 cup sugar in large bowl of mixer at high speed for 3 minutes; blend in poppy seed mixture.
6. Stir in flour mixture alternately with the remaining ¾ cup milk and vanilla, beating after each addition until batter is smooth.
7. Fold meringue into batter until no streaks of white remain; pour into prepared pans.
8. Bake in a preheated moderate oven (350°) for 30 minutes or until centers spring back when lightly pressed with fingertip.
9. Cool layers in pans on wire racks 10 minutes; loosen around edges with a knife; turn out onto wire racks; cool completely.
10. Put layers together with Lemon Butter Cream Frosting; frost sides and top with remaining frosting.

Lemon Butter Cream Frosting

Makes enough to fill and frost two 9-inch square layers.

½ cup (1 stick) butter	**lemon rind**
or margarine	**Dash salt**
1 package (1 pound)	**3 tablespoons lemon**
10X (confectioners')	**juice**
sugar, sifted	**1 tablespoon milk**
½ teaspoon grated	

Beat butter until soft in a medium-size bowl. Beat in 10X sugar alternately with lemon rind, salt, lemon juice and milk. Continue beating until smooth and spreadable.

Hazelnut Roll

Bake at 400° for 8 to 10 minutes.

Makes 10 servings.

1 recipe Hazelnut Cake	***(recipe follows)***
Batter (*recipe	**1 recipe Silky**
follows*)	**Chocolate Mocha**
¼ cup 10X	**Frosting (*recipe**
(confectioners')	**follows*)**
sugar	**Whole and ground**
Rum Whipped Cream	**hazelnuts**

1. Preheat the oven to hot (400°). Grease the bottom and sides of a 15½ × 10½ × 1-inch jelly-roll pan. Line with wax paper; grease the paper.

(continued)

Hazelnut Roll, page 201.

2. Prepare the Hazelnut Cake Batter as directed. Pour into the prepared jelly-roll pan.

3. Bake in the preheated hot oven (400°) for 8 to 10 minutes, or until a wooden pick inserted in the center comes out clean.

4. Sprinkle the top of the cake with the 10X sugar. Place a dish towel over the cake. Invert the cake and towel. Peel off the wax paper. Trim 1/4 inch from the edges. Starting at the short end, roll up the cake with the towel. Cool completely on a wire rack.

5. Prepare the Rum Whipped Cream.

6. Prepare the Silky Chocolate Mocha Frosting.

7. Unroll the cake slowly and carefully on a flat surface. Spread the Rum Whipped Cream over the cake, leaving a 1/2-inch border around the edges. Reroll the cake using the towel as an aid. Place on a platter, seam-side down.

8. Frost the sides and top with the Silky Chocolate Mocha Frosting. Garnish with whole and ground hazelnuts. Store in the refrigerator.

Rum Whipped Cream: Beat 1 cup heavy cream, 1 tablespoon 10X (confectioners') sugar and 1 tablespoon rum in a small chilled mixer bowl until stiff.

Basic Cake Batter

1 cup *unsifted* cake flour
11/2 teaspoons baking powder
1/4 teaspoon salt

5 eggs, separated
1/4 cup water
1 cup granulated sugar
1$^{1}/_{2}$ teaspoons vanilla

1. Prepare the pan(s) and preheat the oven as directed in the individual cake recipe.
2. Sift together the flour, baking powder and salt onto a piece of wax paper.
3. Beat egg whites in large mixer bowl with the electric mixer at high speed until soft peaks form. Set aside.
4. Beat together the egg yolks and water in a second large bowl until foamy. Gradually beat in the sugar and vanilla; beat until thickened and light in color. Fold in the flour mixture just until all flour is incorporated. Gently fold in the beaten egg whites with a whisk or rubber spatula just until no streaks remain.
5. Pour the batter into the prepared pan(s). Bake and cool as directed in the individual recipe.

Chocolate Cake: Reduce the sugar to $^{1}/_{2}$ cup. Melt and cool 1 package (6 ounces) semisweet chocolate pieces. Fold into the flour-egg-yolk mixture before adding the beaten egg whites.

Lemon Cake: Add 2 teaspoons grated lemon rind when adding the vanilla.

Almond Cake: Reduce the flour to $^{1}/_{2}$ cup and the baking powder to $^{3}/_{4}$ teaspoon. Fold 1 cup finely ground almonds into the flour-egg-yolk mixture.

Hazelnut Cake: Reduce the flour to $^{1}/_{2}$ cup and baking powder to $^{3}/_{4}$ teaspoon. Fold 1 cup finely ground hazelnuts into the flour-egg-yolk mixture.

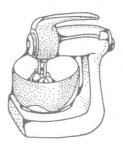

Silky Chocolate Mocha Frosting

Makes 1$^{1}/_{2}$ cups.

1 package (6 ounces) semisweet chocolate pieces
$^{1}/_{4}$ cup hot, strong

black coffee
$^{1}/_{2}$ cup (1 stick) unsalted butter, cut into small pieces

1. Melt chocolate, stirring constantly, in small saucepan over low heat.
2. Pour chocolate into small mixer bowl. Beat in hot coffee at low speed. When mixture is smooth, beat in butter, 1 piece at a time; beat until smooth.
3. Refrigerate frosting until slightly thickened, about 30 minutes.

COOKIES and CANDIES

Cookie   An American term which covers a wide variety of small, sweet, filled or unfilled cakes. The word is derived from the Dutch "koekie," meaning small cake. Cookies can be divided into six basic categories: drop, shaped or molded, cookie-press or spritz, rolled and cut, refrigerator and bar.

Drop cookies are one of the easiest to make, since the dough is simply dropped by spoonfuls onto the cookie sheet.

Shaped or molded cookies are made from a dough that is worked with the hands and rolled into balls, logs or crescents or pressed into small molds.

Spritz (a German word meaning "to squirt") cookies are made from a soft dough that is forced through a cookie press, gun or machine.

Rolled and cut cookies, such as sugar cookies, are made as simply as it sounds; the dough is rolled out and cut into the desired shape. They are usually rolled in sugar before baking or frosted after baking.

Refrigerator cookies are made by shaping the dough into a long roll, chilling or freezing until firm and slicing before baking.

Bar cookies are often a variation of a cookie dough in which the dough is baked in a shallow pan, then cut into bars or squares.

The cookie recipes that follow include some from each of the basic categories.

Date 'n' Oat Bar Cookies

Bake at 375° for 30 minutes.

Makes 16 squares.

1 large orange	unbleached all-purpose flour
1 cup chopped pitted dates	1/4 cup sugar
1/2 cup water	1 cup rolled oats
1/2 teaspoon ground cinnamon	1/2 cup (1 stick) unsalted butter, softened
1 cup *sifted*	

1. Grate a tablepoon of rind from orange; reserve. Squeeze 1/4 cup of juice.
2. Mix dates, water and orange juice in a small saucepan. Cook, stirring until thickened. Remove from heat and stir in reserved rind and cinnamon. Cool.
3. Sift flour into a large bowl. Stir in sugar and oats. Cut in butter with pastry blender until coarse crumbs form.
4. Preheat oven to 375°. Pat half of crumb mixture firmly into buttered 8 × 8 × 2-inch baking pan. Spread cooled filling evenly over top; sprinkle remaining crumb mixture over filling. Sprinkle with additional sugar.
5. Bake in a preheated moderate oven (375°) for 30 minutes or until top is very lightly browned. Cool; cut into squares.

Brandy Snaps

Originally made as a French gaufrette (small wafer) on a hot griddle, this recipe evolved to the baked cookies below. The snaps are similar to the German hippen, *which are rolled and filled with buttercream.*

Bake at 300° for 10 to 15 minutes.

Makes about 4 dozen cookies.

1 1/2 cups *sifted* all-purpose flour	3/4 cup (1 1/2 sticks) unsalted butter or margarine, melted
Pinch salt	
2 teaspoons ground ginger	1 cup firmly packed brown sugar
1 teaspoon ground nutmeg	1/2 cup dark molasses
	2 tablespoons brandy

1. Preheat oven to 300°. Sift flour, salt, ginger and nutmeg into a large bowl. Combine melted butter, sugar, molasses and brandy in a small bowl; stir into dry ingredients.
2. Drop by teaspoonfuls onto a lightly buttered cookie sheet, leaving 2 1/2 inches between cookies.
3. Bake in a preheated slow oven (300°) for 10 to 15 minutes. Let cool only until cookies can be handled. While still warm, roll each cookie around the handle of a wooden mixing spoon to form "cigarettes." If cookies harden before being rolled, reheat in a slow oven. Cool completely; store in airtight container. Cookies can also be shaped into cones, which may be filled with a mixture of whipped cream and chopped crystallized ginger just before serving.

Little Party Cakes

Bake at 350° for 25 minutes.

Makes about 50 servings (96 cakes or 1 plus per serving).

2 packages yellow or white cake mix	lemon rind
Water	Apricot Glaze *(recipe follows)*
Eggs	Easy Fondant Frosting *(recipe follows)*
2 tablespoons grated	

1. Grease a 15 1/2 × 10 1/2 × 1-inch jelly-roll pan. Line

(continued)

Pictured opposite: Brandy Snaps.

bottom and sides with wax paper; grease paper. Preheat oven to 350°.

2. Prepare 1 cake mix, following label directions using the water and the eggs. Stir in 1 tablespoon lemon rind. Pour batter into prepared pan.

3. Bake in a preheated moderate oven (350°) for 25 minutes or until center springs back when lightly pressed with fingertip. Cool in pan on wire rack 10 minutes. Remove from pan; cool completely. Repeat with remaining package of cake mix and remaining lemon rind.

4. Cut each cake lengthwise into 6 strips (do not separate strips). Then cut strips diagonally to make diamond-shaped cakes (48 cakes from each pan).

5. Prepare Apricot Glaze.

6. Spear each cake from the bottom with a 2-tined fork; dip in glaze, then place right side up on wire rack over a sheet of wax paper to catch drippings. Let stand until glaze is set. (Cakes can be frozen at this point.)

7. Day before serving: Prepare Easy Fondant Frosting. Pour frosting over each cake, letting excess drip down onto paper. (Drippings can be scraped into the double boiler. reheated and used). Or, spear each cake from the bottom with a 2-tined fork; quickly dip in and out of frosting; place cakes on wire rack. Let frosting set; decorate cake with contrasting frosting, if you wish.

8. Place cakes on a tray and cover loosely with wax paper. Store in a cool place.

Note: For 12 servings, use 1/2 package cake mix, with water and egg as label directs. Add 1 teaspoon lemon rind. Bake in a prepared 9 × 9 × 2-inch pan.

Easy Fondant Frosting

Make this recipe *twice* to frost 96 cakes.

8 cups 10X (confectioners') sugar	**syrup**
1/2 cup water	**1 teaspoon brandy or rum extract**
1/2 cup light corn	**Red and green food colorings**

1. Combine confectioners' sugar, water and corn syrup in top of double boiler. Set over barely simmering water. (Don't let water boil, as steam will dull frosting.) Heat, stirring often, until frosting is fluid and pourable. Remove from heat; stir in brandy.

2. Frost some of the cakes with the white uncolored frosting, then tint remainder with red food coloring and frost some of the cakes. With second batch of frosting, frost more cakes with white, then tint remainder with green food coloring.

Note: For 12 servings, use 4 cups sugar, 1/4 cup water, 1/4 cup corn syrup and 1/2 teaspoon brandy extract.

Apricot Glaze

Makes enough for 96 little cakes.

3 cups apricot preserves	**2/3 cup water**
	6 tablespoons sugar

Combine preserves, water and sugar in a medium-size saucepan. Cook over medium heat until bubbly; continue to cook 3 to 5 minutes, stirring occasionally. Pour through a fine sieve to remove any small particles.

Note: For 12 servings, use 1 jar (12 ounces) apricot preserves, 3 tablespoons water and 2 tablespoons sugar.

Lemon Leaf Cookies

Bake at 350° for 10 minutes.

Makes 3 dozen cookies.

2 cups *sifted* all-purpose flour	**sour cream**
1/2 teaspoon baking powder	**1 tablespoon grated lemon rind (2 medium-size lemons)**
1/4 teaspoon baking soda	**Lemon Icing (*recipe follows*)**
1/2 cup (1 stick) butter or margarine	**1 cup semisweet chocolate bits, melted**
2/3 cup sugar	
1 egg	
3 tablespoons dairy	

1. Sift together the flour, baking powder and baking soda onto wax paper.

2. Beat the butter in a large bowl until soft. Add sugar and egg; beat with an electric mixer until light and fluffy. Beat in the sour cream and lemon rind.

3. Gradually stir in sifted dry ingredients until blended and smooth. Form dough into a ball with a rubber spatula. Wrap in wax paper. Chill several hours or overnight.

4. To bake the cookies, preheat the oven to moderate (350°).

5. Divide the dough in quarters. Roll out the dough, a quarter at a time, on lightly floured surface to slightly less than 1/4-inch thickness. Cut out cookies with 3-inch cookie cutter. Arrange on cookie sheets, 1 1/2 inches apart.

6. Bake in the preheated moderate oven (350°) for 10 minutes or until golden around edges; do not let cookies brown. Remove to wire racks to cool completely. Store in airtight tin.

7. Decorate cookies as pictured on opposite page. Spread Lemon Icing over half of each cookie. Spread melted chocolate over other half. Using a pastry bag fitted with small writing tips, pipe "veins" of chocolate over the lemon half and veins of Lemon Icing over the chocolate half.

Lemon Icing: Combine 1 1/2 cups 10X (confectioners'

sugar and 2 teaspoons lemon juice in small bowl. Add just enough water to make smooth, spreadable icing. Add 1 to 2 drops yellow food coloring to tint pale yellow.

Chocolate Chip Cookies

In 1940, the owner of a Massachusetts restaurant, the Toll House, dropped chopped chocolate pieces into her cookie dough when she ran out of raisins—and thus, the birth of the chocolate chip cookie! Today there are hundreds of variations; ours includes nuts as well as chocolate.

Bake at 350° for 8 minutes.

Makes about 4 dozen cookies.

1³/₄ cups *sifted* **all-purpose flour**	**¹/₄ cup firmly packed light or dark brown sugar**
¹/₂ teaspoon baking soda	**1 egg**
¹/₄ teaspoon salt	**1 teaspoon vanilla**
³/₄ cup (1¹/₂ sticks) butter or margarine, softened	**1 cup chopped walnuts or pecans**
¹/₂ cup granulated sugar	**1 package (6 ounces) semi-sweet chocolate pieces**

1. Sift flour, baking soda and salt onto wax paper.
2. Beat butter, granulated and brown sugars, egg and vanilla in a large bowl with electric mixer until fluffy. Preheat oven to 350°.
3. Stir in flour mixture by hand until mixed. Stir in nuts and chocolate.
4. Drop dough by rounded teaspoonsful, 1 inch apart, onto greased cookie sheets.
5. Bake in a preheated moderate oven (350°) for 8 minutes or until cookies are golden brown. Remove from cookie sheets; cool on wire racks. When thoroughly cool, store in covered containers.
Note: For larger cookies, drop dough by rounded tablespoonsful onto greased cookie sheets. Increase baking time to 10 to 12 minutes.

Apricot-Coconut Cookie Bars

Bake at 350° for 25 minutes, and then for 35 minutes.

Makes about 40 bars.

¹/₂ cup (1 stick) butter, softened	**1 can (15 ounces) sweetened condensed milk**
¹/₄ cup sugar	
1¹/₃ cups *sifted* **all-purpose flour**	**1 can (3¹/₂ ounces) flaked coconut**
¹/₂ teaspoon baking powder	**1 package (6 ounces) dried apricots, finely chopped**
¹/₄ teaspoon salt	
2 eggs, well beaten	

1. Preheat oven to 350°. Place the butter, sugar and 1 cup of the flour in a medium-size bowl. Cut in butter with pastry blender until coarse crumbs form.
2. Press crumbs firmly onto the bottom of a buttered 9-inch square baking pan to make a bottom crust.
3. Bake in a preheated moderate oven (350°) for 25 minutes. Remove from oven to wire rack.
4. Combine remaining ¹/₃ cup flour, baking powder, salt, eggs, condensed milk, coconut and apricots in a medium-size bowl; mix until well blended. Spread mixture evenly over baked cookie layer.
5. Bake in a preheated moderate oven (350°) for 35 minutes or until top is firm to the touch. Cool in pan on wire rack. Cut into 2 × 1-inch bars.

Brownies
Children love them and so do adults. A truly American concoction, according to legend, the first brownies were a fallen chocolate cake. Whatever their beginnings, these bar cookies are favorites for snacks, picnics and lunchboxes.

Double Chocolate Walnut Brownies

Bake at 350° for 35 minutes.

Makes about 24 bars.

1 cup (2 sticks) butter or margarine	**1 teaspoon vanilla**
4 squares unsweetened chocolate (4 ounces)	**1 cup** *sifted* **all-purpose flour**
	1¹/₂ cups coarsely chopped walnuts
2 cups sugar	**1 package (6 ounces) semisweet chocolate pieces**
3 eggs	

1. Melt butter and chocolate in a medium-size saucepan over moderate heat. Remove from heat. Preheat oven to 350°.
2. Beat in sugar gradually with a wooden spoon until thoroughly combined. Add eggs, 1 at a time, beating well after each addition; stir in vanilla. Stir in flour until thoroughly combined. Stir in 1 cup of the walnuts. Spread into a greased 13 × 9 × 2-inch pan. Combine remaining ¹/₂ cup walnuts with chocolate pieces; sprinkle over top of brownie mixture, pressing down lightly.
3. Bake in a preheated moderate oven (350°) for 35 minutes or until top springs back when lightly pressed with fingertip. Cool completely in pan on wire rack. Cut into bars or squares.

Cream Cheese Brownies

Bake at 350° for 40 minutes.

Makes 16 squares.

3 tablespoons butter
4 squares semisweet
    chocolate
    (4 ounces)
2 tablespoon butter,
    softened
1 package (3 ounces)
    cream cheese,
    softened
1 cup sugar
3 eggs

1 tablespoon flour
2 teaspoons vanilla
1/2 cup *unsifted* all-
    purpose flour
1/2 teaspoon baking
    powder
1/2 teaspoon salt
1/2 cup chopped
    walnuts
1/4 teaspoon almond
    extract

1. Melt the 3 tablespoons butter with the chocolate in top of double boiler over hot water. Remove and cool.
2. Grease a 9 × 9 × 2-inch baking pan.
3. Blend remaining 2 tablespoons butter with the cream cheese in medium-size bowl with electric mixer until fluffy. Beat in 1/4 cup of the sugar, 1 egg, the 1 tablespoon flour and 1 teaspoon of the vanilla. Preheat oven to 350°.
4. Beat remaining 2 eggs in large bowl with electric mixer until foamy. Slowly add 3/4 cup sugar, beating until blended. Stir in the 1/2 cup flour, the baking powder and salt until smooth. Add chocolate mixture, walnuts, 1 teaspoon vanilla and almond extract.
5. Spread half of chocolate mixture evenly in prepared pan. Spread cream cheese mixture on top. Drop spoonfuls of remaining chocolate mixture on top of cream cheese. Swirl top of batter.
6. Bake in a preheated moderate oven (350°) for 40 minutes. Cool in pan on wire rack.

Deluxe Orange-Frosted Brownies

Bake at 350° for 30 minutes.

Makes about 36 squares.

3/4 cup *sifted* all-
    purpose flour
1/4 teaspoon baking
    soda
1/4 teaspoon salt
1/2 cup sugar
1/3 cup vegetable
    shortening
2 tablespoons water
1 package (6 ounces)
    semisweet

chocolate pieces
1 teaspoon vanilla
2 eggs
1 1/2 cups coarsely
    chopped walnuts
1/4 cup golden rum or
    orange juice
Orange Frosting
    (recipe follows)
Chocolate Icing
    (recipe follows)

1. Sift flour, baking soda and salt onto wax paper. Preheat oven to 350°.

Pictured opposite:
Double Chocolate Walnut Brownies, page 207.

2. Combine sugar, shortening and water in a medium-size saucepan. Heat, stirring constantly, until sugar melts and mixture comes to boiling. Remove from heat; stir in chocolate pieces and vanilla until smooth.
3. Beat in eggs, 1 at a time. Stir in flour mixture and walnuts. Spread evenly in a greased 9 × 9 × 2-inch pan.
4. Bake in a preheated moderate oven (350°) for 30 minutes or until shiny and firm on top. Remove from oven; sprinkle rum over top; cool completely.
5. Spread Orange Frosting smoothly over top; chill until firm. Spread Chocolate Icing over frosting; chill. Remove from refrigerator about 1 hour before serving; cut into squares.

Orange Frosting: Beat 1/3 cup softened butter or margarine and 1 teaspoon grated orange rind in a small bowl until creamy. Gradually beat in 2 cups 10X (confectioners') sugar alternately with 1 to 2 tablespoons orange juice until of spreading consistency.

Chocolate Icing: Combine 1 package (6 ounces) semisweet chocolate pieces and 1 tablespoon vegetable shortening in the top of a double boiler. Set over hot, not boiling, water until melted.

Southern-Style Butterscotch Brownies

Bake at 350° for 30 minutes, then at 550° for 3 minutes.

Makes 16 squares.

3/4 cup *sifted* all-
    purpose flour
1 teaspoon baking
    powder
1/2 teaspoon salt
1/4 cup (1/2 stick) butter
    or margarine
3/4 cup firmly

packed light brown
    sugar
2 eggs
1 teaspoon vanilla
1/2 cup coarsely
    chopped walnuts
Coconut Topping
    (recipe follows)

1. Preheat oven to 350°. Sift flour, baking powder and salt onto wax paper.
2. Melt butter in a medium-size saucepan over moderate heat. Remove from heat; stir in brown sugar with a spoon until blended; beat in eggs and vanilla.
3. Stir in flour mixture and walnuts until thoroughly combined. Pour into a greased 8 × 8 × 2-inch pan.
4. Bake in preheated moderate oven (350°) for 30 minutes or until top springs back when lightly pressed with fingertip. Remove from oven; raise temperature to broil (550°). Prepare Coconut Topping and spread evenly on warm cookies. Place pan of cookies with tops 3 inches from broiler heat; broil for 3 minutes or just until sugar is melted and top is a light golden brown. Cut into squares. Serve warm or at room temperature.

Coconut Topping: Combine 1/4 cup (1/2 stick) butter or margarine, 1/2 cup firmly packed light brown sugar and 1 cup shredded coconut in a small bowl.

Carrot Brownies

Bake at 350° for 30 minutes.

Makes 32 squares.

1/2 cup (1 stick) butter	**2 cups finely grated**
1 1/2 cups firmly	**carrots**
packed light brown	**1/2 cup chopped**
sugar	**walnuts**
2 cups *unsifted* all-	**Cream Cheese**
purpose flour	**Frosting *(recipe***
2 teaspoons baking	***follows)***
powder	**Walnut halves**
1/2 teaspoon salt	***(optional)***
2 eggs	

1. Melt butter in large saucepan. Add brown sugar; stir until blended. Remove from heat; cool slightly.
2. Sift flour, baking powder and salt onto wax paper. Preheat oven to 350°.
3. Beat eggs into cooled butter mixture 1 at a time. Stir in flour mixture, blending well. Add carrots and walnuts, mixing well. Pour into 2 greased 8 × 8 × 2-inch baking pans.
4. Bake in a preheated moderate oven (350°) for 30 minutes or until centers spring back when lightly pressed with fingertip. Cool 10 minutes in pans on wire rack; remove from pans; cool completely.
5. Frost tops with Cream Cheese Frosting. Cut into squares and top each square with a walnut half, if you wish.

Cream Cheese Frosting: Combine 2 ounces (2/3 of a 3-ounce package) softened cream cheese with 1/3 cup softened butter in a small bowl; beat until smooth. Stir in 1 teaspoon vanilla and 1 1/2 cups 10X (confectioners') sugar until fluffy and smooth. Makes 1 cup.

Sesame Seed Bars

Bake at 375° for 25 minutes.

Makes 18 bars.

1/2 cup sesame seeds	**1 cup firmly packed**
1/2 cup (1 stick) butter	**brown sugar**
1 1/4 cups *sifted* all-	**2 eggs**
purpose flour	**1 teaspoon vanilla**
1 teaspoon baking	**Honey-Butter Frosting**
powder	***(recipe follows)***
1/2 teaspoon salt	

1. Toast sesame seeds in a medium-size saucepan over very low heat, stirring frequently, until a light golden brown, about 10 mintues; remove from heat. Measure and reserve 1 tablespoon of the toasted sesame seeds for top. Add butter to seeds in saucepan and stir to melt. Cool.

2. Sift flour, baking powder and salt onto wax paper. Preheat oven to 375°.
3. Beat sugar, eggs and vanilla into butter mixture with a wooden spoon until smooth. Stir in flour mixture; beat until thoroughly combined. Pour into a greased 9 × 9 × 2-inch pan.
4. Bake in a preheated moderate oven (375°) for 25 minutes or until top springs back when lightly touched with fingertip. Cool completely in pan on wire rack. Frost with Honey-Butter Frosting. Sprinkle with reserved sesame seeds. Cut into bars.

Honey-Butter Frosting: Whip 2 tablespoons butter or margarine with 2 tablespoons honey in a medium-size bowl. Stir in 1 1/2 cups 10X (confectioners') sugar, 1 tablespoon milk, and a pinch of salt.

Apple Squares

Bake at 350° for 30 minutes.

Makes 16 squares.

1 cup *sifted* all-	**brown sugar**
purpose flour	**1/2 cup granulated**
1 teaspoon baking	**sugar**
powder	**1 egg**
1/4 teaspoon salt	**1 teaspoon vanilla**
1/4 teaspoon ground	**1/2 cup chopped pared**
cinnamon	**cooking apple**
1/4 cup (1/2 stick) butter	**1/2 cup finely chopped**
or margarine	**walnuts**
1/2 cup firmly packed	**Cinnamon Sugar**
light	***(recipe follows)***

1. Preheat oven to 350°. Sift flour, baking powder and salt onto wax paper.
2. Melt butter in a medium-size saucepan over moderate heat. Remove from heat. Beat in sugars, egg and vanilla with a wooden spoon until smooth.
3. Stir in flour mixture, apple and walnuts until thoroughly combined. Spread into a greased 8 × 8 × 2-inch pan. Sprinkle with 1 tablespoon of the Cinnamon Sugar mixture.
4. Bake in a preheated moderate oven (350°) for 30 minutes or until top springs back when lightly pressed with fingertip. Cool completely in pan on wire rack. Cut into squares.

Cinnamon Sugar: Combine 1/2 cup granulated sugar with 1 1/2 teaspoons ground cinnamon in a small jar with a screw-top lid. Cover; shake thoroughly. Store remainder for future use (for French toast, pancakes, fruit-topped desserts, etc.).

Pictured opposite (clockwise from the top): Peanut Butter Bars, page 212; Southern-Style Butterscotch Brownies, page 209; Danish Spice Cookies, page 212; Sesame Seed Bars, page 210; Apple Squares, page 210.

Peanut Butter Bars

Bake at 375° for 25 minutes.

Makes 18 bars.

1½ cups *sifted* all-purpose flour
½ teaspoon baking soda
½ teaspoon salt
½ cup (1 stick) butter or margarine
½ cup granulated sugar
½ cup firmly

packed brown sugar
½ cup peanut butter
1 egg
¼ cup milk
½ teaspoon vanilla
Orange Frosting
   (*recipe follows*)
Chocolate Icing
   (*recipe follows*)

1. Preheat oven to 375°. Sift flour, baking soda and salt onto wax paper.
2. Melt butter in a medium-size saucepan over moderate heat. Remove from heat. Add sugars and peanut butter; beat with wooden spoon until thoroughly combined. Blend in egg, milk and vanilla until thick and creamy.
3. Stir in flour mixture until thoroughly combined. Spread into a greased 9 × 9 × 2-inch pan.
4. Bake in a preheated moderate oven (375°) for 25 minutes or until top springs back when lightly touched with fingertip. Cool completely in pan on wire rack. Spread with Orange Frosting; drizzle Chocolate Icing across frosting in lines about 1 inch apart. Draw edge of spatula across lines. Cut into bars.

Orange Frosting: Beat 3 tablespoons butter with 1 teaspoon grated orange rind in a small bowl until creamy. Gradually beat in 2 cups 10X (confectioners') sugar with 1 or 2 tablespoons orange juice to make it spreadable.

Chocolate Icing: Melt ½ square unsweetened chocolate with ¼ teaspoon vegetable shortening in a small bowl over hot, not boiling, water.

Danish Spice Cookies

Bake at 350° for 30 minutes.

Makes about 4 dozen.

2 cups *sifted* all-purpose flour
½ teaspoon salt
¼ teaspoon baking soda
1 teaspoon ground cinnamon
¼ teaspoon ground cloves
½ cup (1 stick) butter

OR margarine
1 cup firmly packed brown sugar
½ cup dairy sour cream
1 egg
1 teaspoon vanilla
1 cup chopped dates
½ cup finely chopped walnuts

1. Preheat oven to 350°. Sift flour, salt, baking soda, cinnamon and cloves onto wax paper.
2. Melt butter in a medium-size saucepan over moderate heat. Remove from heat. Add sugar and

beat with a wooden spoon until combined. Beat in sour cream, egg and vanilla until smooth.
3. Stir in flour mixture until thoroughly combined; stir in dates and nuts. Spread evenly into a greased 15 × 10 × 1-inch pan.
4. Bake in a preheated moderate oven (350°) for 30 minutes or until top springs back when lightly touched with fingertip. Cool in pan on wire rack. Cut into diamond shapes.

Master Plan for Making 20 Cookies from One Kind of Dough

General Directions

1. Read the recipes and master plan carefully and completely; then decide which of the 20 cookie varieties you want to bake. All 20 can be made from our Basic Cookie Dough recipe, but we suggest picking out your four favorite recipes and making 3 to 4 dozen of each (the exact quantity varies with the variety). Therefore, all recipes are based on ¼ of the amount of Basic Cookie Dough.
2. Once you've decided on the cookies you want, make the Basic Cookie Dough, then the fillings and frostings. Perhaps you'd like to begin by baking those cookies that require a soft dough (those that are spread in a pan, baked and cut into slices or squares). Dough should be the consistency of heavy frosting. Next, make those cookies that require a softer or *cool* dough that is chilled for one hour. These include cookies that are pressed through a pastry tube and drop cookies. Third, go on to cookies that call for a colder, firmer *cold* dough which is chilled for three hours. These would include those that are rolled out and cut. Last, make cookies that are shaped with your hands. These also require dough that has been chilled for 3 hours.

Baking Hints

1. Prepare pans by very lightly greasing with unsalted vegetable shortening or spraying with non-stick vegetable spray, or using non-stick silicone cookie papers (unless otherwise specified). The last are available in baking specialty shops and are excellent because they are reusable and save on cleanup time.
2. Check temperature and baking time carefully; they vary with each recipe. DO NOT OVERBAKE.

Storing Tips

1. For storing up to six months, pack cookies in freezer boxes between wax paper or in light

cardboard boxes, overwrapped in large plastic bags. Seal for airtight storage. Keep at 0° in the freezer.
2. To keep cookies for just a day or two, pack crisp cookies between wax paper in container that is *loosely* covered. Store soft cookies separately, packed between wax paper in a tightly closed container, such as a cookie jar or large pan with a cover. Keep containers in a cool dry place.

Defrosting Pointers
1. Thaw frozen cookies in their sealed containers. This prevents condensation from forming, which makes them go limp.
2. If using just a few cookies, defrost in a covered bowl or baking pan or place on a plate in a securely closed plastic bag.

Basic Cookie Dough

(Basic Recipe for all cookies)

Makes about 8³/₄ cups dough (enough for 4 cookie recipes).

3¹/₃ cups *sifted* all-purpose flour	1 pound (4 sticks) butter or margarine, softened
2³/₄ cups *sifted* cake flour	2 cups sugar
1¹/₄ teaspoons salt	4 eggs
2 cans or packages (8 ounces each) almond paste (not marzipan)	1¹/₂ teaspoons vanilla or ¹/₂ teaspoon almond extract

1. Sift the 2 flours and the salt onto wax paper.
2. Crumble almond paste thoroughly with fingers into a large bowl to eliminate any lumps before adding other ingredients. Add butter; mix with hands until thoroughly blended and smooth.
3. Beat in sugar, eggs and vanilla with electric mixer on medium, until mixture is light and fluffy.
4. Add flour mixture, ¹/₃ at a time, beating well after each addition. (Use a wooden spoon if dough is too heavy for mixer.) Divide dough in 4 equal parts. Wrap each part separately in plastic wrap; refrigerate dough at least 1 hour.

1. Bon Bon Slices

Tender almond layers sandwiched with raspberry jam or frosting and rimmed with dark chocolate.

Makes 36 slices.

Preheat oven to 375°. Grease the bottom and sides of a 13 × 9 × 2-inch pan; line bottom with wax paper. Spread 1 part dough evenly in pan. Bake in a preheated moderate oven (375°) for 12 minutes or until firm and golden brown. Remove from oven; loosen around edges with a knife. Turn out onto a wire rack; peel off paper. Cool completely. Cut crosswise in half, then cut each half crosswise in thirds. Spread 3 of the strips evenly with a thin layer of jam or frosting; top with 3 remaining pieces. Wrap each stacked sandwich tightly with plastic wrap. Put a cutting board or heavy flat pan on top of the sandwiches to weight down. Let stand several hours or overnight. Unwrap sandwiches; place on wire rack over wax paper. Spread top and sides with Chocolate Coating *(recipe under Fancy Fingers)*; sprinkle with chocolate sprinkles, if you wish. Let coating harden, then cut into ¹/₂-inch slices.

Freezer Tip: Store after coating is completely firm and dry. Freeze, uncovered, then wrap in plastic wrap and store in freezer box. Slice as needed or slice the entire bar and layer with wax paper between slices. Defrost, covered, to keep soft.

2. Chocolate Almond Squares

Makes 24 two-inch squares.

Preheat oven to 350°. Grease a 13 × 9 × 2-inch pan; line bottom with wax paper. Combine 1 part dough with ¹/₂ cup Chocolate Coating *(recipe under Fancy Fingers)*; blend well. Work in 1¹/₃ cups chopped nuts. Spread evenly in pan. Bake in preheated moderate oven (350°) for 25 minutes or just until dough is firm and lightly golden. (Do not overbake.) Remove from oven; loosen around edges with a knife. Turn out onto wire rack; peel off paper; cool. Frost with Light Chocolate Cream Cheese Frosting *(recipe follows)*. Refrigerate or freeze briefly until frosting is firm. Cut into 2-inch squares with sharp knife dipped in hot water. Decorate with additional frosting, chopped nuts or cake decorettes.

Light Chocolate Cream Cheese Frosting

Makes about 1¹/₂ cups.

Combine 2 tablespoons softened butter or margarine and ¹/₄ cup 10X (confectioners') sugar in a small bowl; blend well. Add ¹/₂ cup Chocolate Cream Cheese Filling *(recipe under Chocolate Go 'Rounds)*, 1 teaspoon vanilla, dash salt and 1¹/₂ to 2 cups additional 10X sugar to make frosting of good spreading consistency. For darker frosting, add a little more Chocolate Coating. This frosting can also be used to sandwich double cookies.

3. Spritz Rosettes

Makes about 42 cookies.

Preheat oven to 375°. Fit a large pastry bag or cookie press with a large star tip. Fill bag with 1 part of the *cool* dough (chilled 1 hour). Press out in half-dollar size rosettes onto lightly greased cookie sheets, about 1 inch apart. Press indentation in center of each with finger dipped in water. Bake in a preheated moderate oven (375°) for 7 minutes or until firm and lightly golden. Remove from sheets to wire racks; cool. Fill centers with tinted Confectioners' Glaze *(recipe follows)* or candied red or green cherry halves.

Freezer Tip: Pack as suggested in General Directions.

Confectioners' Glaze

Makes about 1 cup.

2 cups *sifted* 10X (confectioners') sugar	warm milk or water
2 to 2¹/₂ tablespoons	¹/₄ teaspoon vanilla Red and green food coloring

Put sugar in a small bowl. Stir in milk and vanilla until glaze is smooth. Divide into 3 small bowls; tint 1 portion pink, 1 pale green and leave 1 white. Cover bowls with damp towels while working, to keep them from hardening. Store, covered, and rewarm over hot tap water when needed.

4. Paillettes

Makes about 44 cookies.

Preheat oven to 375°. Fit large pastry bag or cookie press with a large star tip. Fill bag with 1 part *cool* dough (chilled 1 hour). Press out in slim fingers about 2¹/₂ inches long on lightly greased cookie sheets, about 1 inch apart. Bake in a preheated moderate oven (375°) for 7 minutes or until firm and lightly golden. Remove from sheets to wire racks; cool. Dip 1 end in tinted Confectioners' Glaze *(recipe under Spritz Rosettes),* then in your choice of chopped nuts, confetti candy decorations or chocolate sprinkles.

Freezer Tip: Omit decorations before freezing and follow directions for Spritz Rosettes *(recipe above).*

5. Fancy Fingers

Makes about 42 sandwich cookies.

Preheat oven to 375°. Fit large pastry bag or cookie press with large ribbon tip (notched on one side, flat on the other). Fill bag with 1 part of the *cool* dough

(chilled 1 hour). Press out in strips ¹/₂ inch wide and 3 inches long, on lightly greased cookie sheets. Bake in a preheated moderate oven (375°) for 6 minutes or until firm and lightly golden. Remove from sheets to wire racks; cool. Sandwich together with seedless raspberry jam or any ready-to-spread frosting. Dip ends in Chocolate Coating *(recipe follows),* then in chocolate sprinkles or chopped nuts.

Freezer Tip: When chocolate is completely dry, pack cookies in freezer boxes in a single layer until frozen, then follow General Directions.

Chocolate Coating

This chocolate is used for coating, dipping and as an ingredient in the cookie recipes.

Makes about 2 cups.

Melt 1 package (12 ounces) semi-sweet chocolate pieces with 4 tablespoons vegetable shortening in top of double boiler, set over hot, not boiling, water. Stir until very smooth. May be prepared, stored in a covered container in the refrigerator and heated when needed.

6. Party Pretties

These are glorified cookie rounds, crisp and delicious.

Makes about 56 cookies.

Preheat oven to 375°. Shape 1 part *cool* dough (chilled 1 hour) into 1-inch balls between palms of hands. Place on lightly greased cookie sheets, about 1 inch apart. Use a glass wrapped in plastic wrap to press cookies down to make a thin flat round. Finish in any of the following ways: Brush unbaked cookies with slightly beaten egg; sprinkle with chopped nuts, chocolate sprinkles or candied fruit pieces before baking. Bake cookies in a preheated moderate oven (375°) for 6 minutes or until firm and lightly golden.

(continued)

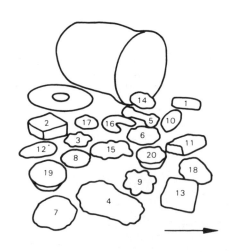

Remove from cookie sheets to wire racks; cool. Dip in tinted Confectioners' Glaze *(recipe under Spritz Rosettes)*, roll edges in colored sugars or dip tops in Chocolate Coating *(recipe under Fancy Fingers)*, sprinkle with chocolate sprinkles.

Freezer Tip: See Fancy Fingers.

7. Boutons

Makes 48 sandwich cookies.

Preheat oven to 375°. Fit large pastry bag or cookie press with ¼-inch plain round tip. Fill bag with 1 part of the *cool* dough (chilled 1 hour). Press out in rounds about the size of a quarter on lightly greased baking sheets, about 1 inch apart. Flatten slightly with fingers. Bake in a preheated moderate oven (375°) for 6 minutes or until firm and lightly golden. Remove from cookie sheets to wire racks; cool. Sandwich 2 together with Chocolate Coating *(recipe under Fancy Fingers)* or any frosting or jam. Place filled cookies on a wire rack; drizzle with Chocolate Coating.

Freezer Tip: See Fancy Fingers.

8. Goodie Drops

Chock-full of dried fruit and nuts.

Makes 64 cookies.

Preheat oven to 375°. Combine 1 part Basic Dough with 2 cups of any of the following or combination: chopped candied fruit, raisins, chopped nuts or semisweet chocolate pieces. (Chill mixture 1 hour.) Drop by teaspoonfuls or form into 1-inch balls; place on lightly greased cookie sheets, 1 inch apart. Or, mixture can be pressed through a pastry bag without a tip. Flatten shapes slightly. Bake in a preheated moderate oven (375°) for 10 minutes or until firm and lightly golden.

Freezer Tip: Pack in container with wax paper between layers; cover; overwrap with plastic wrap. Defrost in closed container.

9. Chocolate Rosettes

A spritz variation in deep chocolate. It's rich and buttery.

Makes about 76 cookies.

Blend ¼ cup Chocolate Coating *(recipe under Fancy Fingers)* with 1 part *cool* dough in a small bowl. (Chill mixture 1 hour.) Shape and bake as Spritz Rosettes.

Freezer Tip: Follow general freezing and thawing directions.

10. French Sables

Delectable round sandwich cookies with bright jelly peeking through.

Makes about 27 double cookies.

Preheat oven to 375°. Mix 1 part Basic Dough with ¼ cup sifted all-purpose flour in a medium-size bowl until smooth. (Chill mixture 3 hours.) Divide dough in half; roll one half between 2 sheets of wax paper to a ⅛-inch thickness. Slide paper and dough onto a small cookie sheet; freeze for 10 minutes. Peel off top sheet of paper, then replace loosely. Flip dough and paper over; peel off second sheet. Cut out rounds with a fluted or plain 2-inch cutter, dipping cutter frequently in flour. Roll out remaining half of dough; cut out the same number of rounds as the first half. Cut out centers of these rounds with a thimble or ½-inch decorating tip. Leave cookies in place on wax paper; return to freezer for 15 minutes so they are easy to handle. Lift to lightly greased cookie sheets with a flexible pancake turner, placing ½ inch apart. Bake in a preheated moderate oven (375°) for 5 minutes or until firm and lightly golden. Remove from oven to wire rack; cool. Spread the bottoms of solid rounds with seedless raspberry jam or preserves. Dust the tops of cut-out rounds with 10X (confectioners') sugar; place on top of jam-spread rounds.

Freezer Tip: Do not assemble before freezing. Pack in single layers with wax paper between. Defrost in closed containers.

11. Gold-Filled Pockets

To keep shapes neat, follow directions for putting dough in freezer for easy handling.

Makes about 36 cookies.

Preheat oven to 375°. Mix 1 part *cool* dough (chilled 1 hour) with ¼ cup all-purpose flour in a medium-size bowl until smooth. (Chill mixture 3 hours.) Roll one half of the dough to a 15 × 7½-inch rectangle between 2 sheets of wax paper. Measure with a ruler and keep edges square. Slide paper with dough onto a small cookie sheet; place in freezer for 10 minutes. Peel off top sheet of paper, then replace loosely. Flip dough and paper over; carefully peel off second sheet. (If dough softens, return to freezer.) Cut dough into 2½-inch squares; leave squares in place on paper; return to freezer until partially frozen. Lift squares onto lightly greased cookie sheets with spatula, placing ½ inch apart. Put a scant teaspoonful of apricot jam or preserves in center; pinch opposite corners together. Brush tops with lightly beaten egg. Bake in a preheated moderate oven (375°) for 7 minutes or until firm and lightly golden. Remove from cookie sheet to wire rack; cool. Repeat with remaining half of dough. Before serving, dust lightly with 10X (confectioners') sugar, if you wish.

Freezer Tip: Follow general directions for crisp-type cookies. It's very important to cool these cookies on a rack to prevent softening.

12. Chocolate Go'Rounds

Creamy dark filling goes 'round and 'round in this pretty pinwheel.

Makes about 64 cookies.

Preheat oven to 375°. Mix 1 part *cool* dough (chilled 1 hour) with 1/4 cup all-purpose flour in a medium-size bowl until smooth. (Chill mixture 3 hours.) Roll to a 14 × 8-inch rectangle between 2 sheets of wax paper. Slide onto small cookie sheet; freeze for 10 minutes. Remove from freezer; peel off top sheet and replace it loosely. Flip dough and paper over. Peel off second sheet. Spread 1/4 cup of the Chocolate Cream Cheese Filling *(recipe follows)* over the entire surface; return to freezer for 10 minutes. Carefully roll up dough and filling, starting with one short side, easing off wax paper as you roll. Roll will be about 2 inches in diameter. Wrap in plastic wrap; freeze until solid. Repeat with second half. Cut roll into 1/4-inch slices. Place slices on lightly greased cookie sheet, about 1 inch apart. Bake in a preheated moderate oven (375°) for 5 minutes or until firm and lightly golden. Remove from cookie sheets to wire rack; cool the cookies completely.

Freezer Tip: Follow instructions for crisp-type cookies. It's very important to cool these cookies on a rack to prevent softening.

Chocolate Cream Cheese Filling

Makes about 3 cups.

4 packages (3 ounces each) cream cheese, softened	**1 teaspoon vanilla**
3/4 cup sugar	**1/2 cup Chocolate Coating (recipe under Fancy Fingers)**
2 eggs	

Beat softened cream cheese and sugar in a medium-size bowl until smooth and fluffy. Stir in eggs, vanilla and Chocolate Coating; blend well; refrigerate until ready to use.

13. Linzer Squares

Raspberry jam shines through the criss-cross tops of these little squares.

Makes about 36 cookies.

Preheat oven to 375°. Mix 1 part *cool* dough (chilled 1 hour) with 1/4 cup all-purpose flour in a medium-size

bowl until smooth. (Chill mixture 3 hours.) Roll about 2/3 cup of the dough to a 9-inch square between 2 sheets of wax paper. Slide onto small cookie sheet; freeze 15 minutes. Remove from freezer; peel off top sheet of paper, and replace loosely. Flip dough and paper over; peel off second sheet. Cut strips about 3/8-inch wide; return to freezer. Spread remaining dough in a lightly greased 9 × 9 × 2-inch baking pan lined with wax paper. (Use floured fingertips to pat dough evenly.) Spread 1/2 cup raspberry jam or preserves to within 1/4 inch of edges of dough. Arrange semi-frozen dough strips criss-cross over jam. Brush lattice with slightly beaten egg. Bake in a preheated moderate oven (375°) for about 7 minutes or until top is golden brown. Remove from oven; cool 2 minutes. Loosen around edges of pan with a small knife. Carefully turn out of pan onto wire rack; remove and discard wax paper. Turn right-side up; cool cookie on wire rack completely. Cut into 36 squares.

Freezer Tip: Pack as for crisp-type cookies. Defrost, covered.

14. Nut Crisps

Crispy, crunchy cookie rounds.

Makes about 50 cookies.

Preheat oven to 375°. Spread 1 3/4 cups finely chopped nuts on a piece of wax paper. Drop 1 part *cold* dough (chilled 3 hours) by teaspoonfuls into the nuts. Form nut-coated dough into balls. Place on lightly greased cookie sheets, about 2 inches apart. Press to a 1/8-inch thickness with bottom of a glass wrapped in plastic wrap. Bake in a preheated moderate oven (375°) for 7 minutes or until firm and lightly golden. Remove from sheets to wire racks; cool.

15. Chocolate Pretzels

Handsome cookie pretzels coated with shiny dark chocolate.

Makes about 42 cookies.

Preheat oven to 375°. Mix 1 part Basic Dough with 1/4 cup all-purpose flour in a medium-size bowl until smooth. (Chill mixture 1 hour.) Form into 1-inch balls; chill 3 hours. Roll, 1 ball at a time, into a pencil-shaped length 9 inches long (measure!) with palms of

(continued)

hands on lightly floured surface. Curve into a U-shape directly on lightly greased cookie sheet. Bring one arm over to opposite side; pinch to secure; repeat with second arm to form pretzel shape. Keep cookies about 1 inch apart. Bake in a preheated moderate oven (375°) for 5 minutes, or until firm and lightly golden. Remove from cookie sheets to wire rack; cool. Dip into Chocolate Coating *(recipe under Fancy Fingers);* let dry on rack.

Freezer Tip: Pack in single layer until frozen; store with wax paper between layers.

16. Crescents

Makes about 80 cookies.

Preheat oven to 375°. Shape 1 part *cold* dough (chilled 3 hours) into ³/₄-inch balls. Roll, 1 ball at a time, into pencil-shaped lengths 3 inches long. Curve into crescents (like the letter C) on lightly greased cookie sheets, about ¹/₂ inch apart. Bake in a preheated moderate oven (375°) for 7 minutes or until firm and very lightly golden. Remove from oven to wire rack; cool. Dust heavily with 10X (confectioners') sugar.

Freezer Tip: Freeze cookies unsugared. Defrost in covered container. Dust with 10X sugar.

17. Pushbuttons

Solid chocolate "button" tops a tender cookie.

Makes about 63 cookies.

Preheat oven to 375°. Shape 1 part *cold* dough (chilled 3 hours) into ³/₄-inch balls. Arrange on lightly greased cookie sheets, about 2 inches apart. Top with a chocolate candy "kiss" or wafer, pushing down slightly so cookies spread. Bake in a preheated moderate oven (375°) for 7 minutes or until firm and lightly golden. Remove from cookie sheets to wire racks; cool.

Freezer Tip: Give chocolate pushbuttons time to harden and dry before storing. Defrost in covered container.

18. Jelly Jewels

Makes about 63 cookies.

Preheat oven to 375°. Shape 1 part *cold* dough (chilled 3 hours) into 1-inch balls. Dip balls of dough into slightly beaten egg, then roll in 2 cups finely chopped nuts. Place on lightly greased cookie sheets, 2 inches apart. Flatten to ¹/₂-inch thickness with fingers or bottom of a glass wrapped in plastic wrap. Bake in a preheated moderate oven (375°) for 10

minutes or until firm and lightly golden. Remove cookies and baking sheets to wire racks. While still hot, press an indentation in center of each cookie (use a small measuring spoon or the small end of a melon ball scoop). Let cookies remain on sheet for 5 minutes; remove from sheet to wire racks. Fill indentations with jelly or thick jam or preserves in several colors, if possible.

Freezer Tip: Freeze until firm. Pack with wax paper between layers. Defrost, uncovered.

19. Chocolate Cheesecakes

Little tarts with luscious cheesecake-like filling baked in.

Makes about 60 cookies.

Preheat oven to 375°. Form 1 part *cold* dough (chilled 3 hours) into 1-inch balls. Press balls of dough into generously greased tiny muffin pan cups (1³/₄ inches), pressing against bottom and side with fingers to form cups, keeping dough slightly below rim. (Pastry shells will rise somewhat during baking.) Put 2 level teaspoonfuls of Chocolate Cream Cheese Filling *(recipe under Chocolate Go 'Rounds)* in each cup. Top with candied cherry halves, if you wish. Bake in a preheated oven (375°) for 10 minutes or until firm and lightly golden around edges. Remove from oven; loosen pastry cups with a small knife; remove from pan to wire rack; cool.

Freezer Tip: Freeze with wax paper between layers. Thaw in closed container.

20. Mini Fruit Tarts

Makes about 63 tarts.

Preheat oven to 375°. Shape 1 part *cold* dough (chilled 3 hours) into 1-inch balls; press balls into generously greased tiny muffin pan cups (1³/₄ inches). Bake in a preheated moderate oven (375°) for 7 minutes or until lightly golden around edges. Loosen pastry cups with a small knife; remove cups from pan to wire racks; cool. Fill with cherry pie filling or thick preserves.

Freezer Tip: Freeze baked pastry shells without filling. Defrost in closed container.

At left, Easter Cookies; below, Goblin' Good Cookies.

Goblin' Good Cookies

Your little gremlins will love these treats.

Bake at 375° for 5 minutes.

Makes about 5¹/₂ dozen 3-inch cookies.

3 cups *unsifted* all-purpose flour	**¹/₂ cup vegetable shortening**
2 teaspoons baking soda	**¹/₂ cup sugar**
1¹/₂ teaspoons ground ginger	**1 egg**
¹/₂ teaspoon ground cinnamon	**¹/₂ cup molasses**
¹/₂ teaspoon ground cloves	**1¹/₂ teaspoons cider vinegar**
¹/₄ teaspoon salt	**Orange Decorator Frosting *(recipe follows)***

1. Sift together flour, baking soda, ginger, cinnamon, cloves and salt onto wax paper.
2. Beat together the shortening, sugar and egg in a large bowl with an electric mixer until fluffy, about 3 minutes. Beat in the molasses and cider vinegar. Stir in the flour mixture until blended and smooth. Gather the dough into a ball, wrap and chill for several hours.
3. Preheat the oven to moderate (375°).
4. Divide the dough in half. Roll out one half of the dough, keeping the remainder of the dough refrigerated, on a lightly floured surface to a ¹/₈-inch thickness. Cut out cookies from the dough with Halloween cookie cutters. Reroll the scraps of dough and cut out as many as you can. Arrange on ungreased cookie sheets 2-inches apart.
5. Bake in the preheated moderate oven (375°) for 5 minutes or until firm. Transfer the cookies to wire racks to cool.
6. Repeat with the remaining dough.
7. Decorate and/or frost with melted semisweet chocolate and Orange Decorator Frosting.

Orange Decorator Frosting: Beat together 1 egg

white, ¹/₈ teaspoon cream of tartar and 1¹/₄ cup *sifted* 10X (confectioners') sugar in a small bowl until thick and creamy. Tint with orange food coloring.

Easter Cookies

Bake at 350° for 7 to 8 minutes.

Makes 36 cookies.

2¹/₂ cups *sifted* all-purpose flour	**1 egg**
1 teaspoon baking powder	**1 to 2 teaspoons grated orange rind**
¹/₂ teaspoon salt	**1 tablespoon orange juice**
¹/₂ cup (1 stick) butter, softened	**Decorating Frosting *(recipe follows)***
²/₃ cup sugar	

1. Sift together the flour, baking powder and salt onto wax paper.

(continued)

2. Beat together the butter and sugar in a large bowl until smooth. Beat in the egg, orange rind and juice.

3. Add the flour mixture, a third at a time, stirring well.

4. Shape the dough into a ball; flatten slightly. Wrap in plastic wrap. Refrigerate for several hours or overnight.

5. To bake the cookies, preheat the oven to moderate (350°).

6. Roll out half the dough on a lightly floured surface to a 1/8-inch thickness. Cut into bunny, chick or flower shapes with 3- to 3 1/2-inch cutters. Place on 2 large, lightly greased cookie sheets. Repeat with the other half of the dough.

7. Bake in the preheated moderate oven (350°) for 7 to 8 minutes or until light golden around the edges; the cookies should not brown. Remove to wire racks with a metal spatula. Cool completely. Frost and decorate with the Decorating Frosting.

Decorating Frosting

Makes enough to decorate 36 cookies.

3 egg whites	**sugar**
1/2 teaspoon cream of tartar	**1 tablespoon water**
3 1/2 cups *sifted* **10X (confectioners')**	**Food coloring** *(optional)*

1. Beat the egg whites and cream of tartar in a medium-size bowl until foamy. Slowly beat in the 10X (confectioners') sugar; continue beating until thick and creamy. Measure out 1 1/4 cups of the frosting; cover with damp paper toweling; set aside.

2. Thin the remaining frosting with the 1 tablespoon of water. Tint with the food coloring, if you wish. Spread evenly over the cookies.

3. Place the reserved frosting in a pastry tube fitted with a writing tip. Decorate the cookies as pictured.

Our Best-Ever Brownies

Bake at 350° for 30 minutes.

Makes 16 brownies.

2 squares unsweetened chocolate	**1 teaspoon vanilla**
1/2 cup (1 stick) butter or margarine	**1/2 cup** *sifted* **all-purpose flour**
2 eggs	**1/8 teaspoon salt**
1 cup sugar	**3/4 cup chopped walnuts**

1. Preheat oven to 350°. Melt chocolate and butter in a small saucepan over low heat; cool slightly.

2. Beat eggs in a small bowl with electric mixer; gradually beat in sugar until mixture is fluffy and thick. Gradually stir in chocolate mixture and vanilla.

3. Fold in flour and salt until well-blended; stir in

walnuts. Spread evenly in a greased 8 × 8 × 2-inch baking pan.

4. Bake in a preheated moderate oven (350°) for 30 minutes or until shiny and firm on top. Cool in pan on wire rack.

Chocolate Raisin Cookies

Bake at 350° for 10 to 12 minutes.

Makes about 2 dozen.

1 3/4 cups *sifted* **all-purpose flour**	**1 egg**
1/2 teaspoon baking soda	**1 teaspoon vanilla**
1/4 teaspoon salt	**1/2 cup chopped walnuts**
3/4 cup (1 1/2 sticks) butter or margarine	**1/2 cup raisins**
3/4 cup sugar	**1 package (6 ounces) semisweet chocolate pieces**

1. Preheat oven to 350°. Sift flour, baking soda and salt onto wax paper.

2. Beat butter, sugar, egg and vanilla in a large bowl with electric mixer until fluffy.

3. Stir in flour mixture by hand until well mixed. Stir in walnuts, raisins and chocolate pieces.

4. Drop dough by rounded tablespoonfuls, 1 inch apart, onto greased cookie sheets.

5. Bake in a preheated moderate oven (350°) for 10 to 12 minutes or until cookies are golden brown. Remove from cookie sheets; cool on wire racks. When thoroughly cool, store in covered containers.

Sugared Chocolate Wafers

Bake at 350° for 10 minutes.

Makes 5 dozen.

4 squares unsweetened chocolate	**1/2 teaspoon salt**
2 cups *sifted* **all-purpose flour**	**3/4 cup (1 1/2 sticks) butter or margarine**
1 teaspoon baking powder	**3/4 cup firmly packed brown sugar**
1/4 teaspoon baking soda	**1 egg**
	1 teaspoon vanilla
	Granulated sugar
	Walnuts

1. Preheat oven to 350°. Melt chocolate in a small bowl over hot, not boiling, water; cool.

2. Sift flour, baking powder, baking soda and salt onto wax paper.

(continued)

Pictured opposite (from lower left): Chocolate Almond Snowdrops, page 222; Chocolate Raisin Cookies, page 220; Sugared Chocolate Wafers, page 220; Our Best-Ever Brownies, page 220.

3. Beat butter, sugar, egg, vanilla and cooled chocolate in a large bowl with electric mixer until thoroughly blended. Stir in flour mixture. Chill 2 hours.

4. Form dough into walnut-size balls using about 2 level teaspoons of the dough. Arrange balls on ungreased cookie sheets 1 inch apart. Butter a glass tumbler, dip in sugar and flatten balls into 2-inch rounds. Dip glass frequently for a nicely sugared top. Press a walnut piece into each cookie.

5. Bake in a preheated moderate oven (350°) about 10 minutes or until cookies are set. Remove cookies to wire rack with a spatula. Cool completely. Store in tightly covered container.

Chocolate-Almond Snowdrops

Delicate mounds to serve with tea.

Bake at 325° for 20 minutes.

Makes about 5 dozen.

1 can (4 ounces) slivered, blanched almonds	sugar
	2/3 cup *sifted* all-purpose flour
1/2 cup (1 stick) butter or margarine, softened	1/3 cup unsweetened cocoa powder
3 tablespoons 10X (confectioners')	10X (confectioners') sugar

1. Preheat oven to 325°. Place 1/3 of the almonds in an electric blender. Cover; whirl until smooth; turn out onto wax paper. Repeat until all almonds are blended.

2. Beat butter with the 3 tablespoons 10X sugar in a medium-size bowl until light and fluffy; work flour, cocoa and almonds into dough with a wooden spoon until dough begins to clean sides of bowl. Cover with plastic wrap. Refrigerate at least 2 hours or until firm enough to handle.

3. Shape dough, 1 teaspoonful at a time (use teaspoon from measuring spoon set), into marble-size balls. Place on ungreased cookie sheets 1 inch apart.

4. Bake in a preheated slow oven (325°) 20 minutes or until firm. Remove carefully from cookie sheets. While still warm, roll in 10X sugar to generously coat; cool completely on wire racks. Store with wax paper between layers in tightly covered container.

Jumbo Double Chocolate Chip Cookies

A fun variation of a popular cookie.

Bake at 375° for 12 minutes.

Makes 1 1/2 dozen 4- to 5-inch cookies.

1 recipe Chocolate Chip Cookies *(recipe follows)*	Chocolate Chip Cookies *(recipe follows)*
1 recipe Double	

1. Preheat oven to 375°. For each cookie, drop a rounded tablespoonful of each dough side by side on a greased cookie sheet. Spread each dough to form a 3-inch semicircle joined to form a large two-toned cookie. Space cookies 5 to 6 inches apart.

2. Bake in a preheated moderate oven (375°) for 12 minutes or until golden brown. Remove from cookie sheet to wire rack with wide spatula. Cool completely.

Chocolate Chip Cookies

Bake at 375° for 12 minutes.

Makes 1 1/2 dozen.

1/2 cup *unsifted* all-purpose flour	softened
1/2 teaspoon baking soda	3/4 cup sugar
	1 egg
1/2 cup whole wheat flour	1 teaspoon vanilla
1/2 cup (1 stick) butter or margarine,	1 package (6 ounces) semisweet chocolate pieces
	1/2 cup chopped nuts

1. Sift flour and baking soda onto wax paper. Add whole wheat flour.

2. Preheat oven to 375°. Beat butter, sugar, egg and vanilla in a medium-size bowl until fluffy.

3. Gradually stir in flour mixture until well blended. Stir in chocolate pieces and nuts.

4. Drop by slightly rounded tablespoonfuls onto lightly greased cookie sheets.

5. Bake in a preheated moderate oven (375°) for 12 minutes or until golden brown. Remove from cookie sheets to wire racks; cool completely.

Valentine Cookies

Bake at 325° for 18 to 20 minutes.

Makes six 6-inch heart-shaped cookies.

3/4 cup (1 1/2 sticks) butter or margarine, softened	2 1/2 cups *sifted* all-purpose flour
1/2 cup sugar	Valentine Cookie Glaze *(recipe follows)*
1 egg	

1. To make pattern: Enlarge the heart (see Fig. 1) on folded brown paper. Open, for the full pattern. Or use a 6-inch cookie cutter if you have one.

2. Beat together the butter, sugar and egg in a large bowl until smooth. Gradually beat in the flour to make a firm dough. Shape into a ball. Wrap in wax paper. Refrigerate for 20 minutes.

3. Preheat the oven to slow (325°).

4. Divide the dough in half. Cover half with plastic wrap. Roll out the other half on a lightly floured surface to a 1/4-inch thickness. Cut into three 6-inch hearts around the pattern, or use the cookie cutter. Transfer the cookies with a spatula to an ungreased cookie sheet, spacing 1 inch apart. Repeat with the other half of the dough.

Valentine Cookies,
page 222.

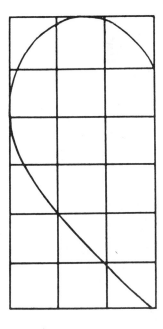

Heart Pattern

FIG. **1**

1 sq. = 1"

5. Bake in the preheated slow oven (325°) for 18 to 20 minutes or just until the edges begin to turn golden; do not let brown. Remove the cookies to a wire rack to cool completely. Frost with the Valentine Cookie Glaze.

Valentine Cookie Glaze

Makes enough frosting for six 6-inch cookies.

1 box (1 pound) 10X (confectioners') sugar
¹/₄ teaspoon cream of tartar

3 egg whites
¹/₂ teaspoon almond extract
Red paste food coloring

1. Combine the 10X sugar, cream of tartar, egg whites and almond extract in a small bowl. Beat with an electric mixer just until smooth and completely combined; the glaze will be very spreadable, rather than stiff.
2. Divide the frosting into 2 bowls. Color one red. Frost the top surfaces of the cookies with red or white glaze. Set aside at room temperature, loosely covered, to dry overnight. Cover the bowls of frosting tightly; refrigerate.
3. The next day, spoon the glazes into pastry bags fitted with small writing tips. Decorate as illustrated.

Chinese Almond Cookies

These crisp cookies, served with sherbet, make a delightful ending to a heavy meal. They also make a delicious between-meal snack.

Bake at 325° for 15 minutes.

Makes 4 dozen cookies.

1/3 cup butter, softened	1/4 teaspoon salt
1/3 cup vegetable shortening	1 tablespoon milk
1/2 cup sugar	1/2 teaspoon almond extract
1 1/2 cups *sifted* all-purpose flour	2 egg whites
1 1/2 teaspoons baking powder	Granulated sugar
	Whole blanched almonds

1. Combine butter, shortening and sugar in a large bowl. Beat until fluffy-light. Preheat oven to 325°.
2. Sift flour, baking powder and salt onto wax paper. Add flour mixture to butter mixture alternately with milk and almond extract.
3. Beat egg whites in a small bowl until soft peaks form; fold into mixture.
4. Measure teaspoon-size pieces of dough and shape into balls. Roll in granulated sugar and place on a greased cookie sheet. Press a whole almond into the center of each.
5. Bake in a preheated slow oven (325°) 15 minutes. Cool on wire rack.

Butterscotch Crispies

Bake at 325° for 5 minutes.

Makes about 3 dozen.

1 egg	1/2 teaspoon vanilla
1/4 cup granulated sugar	1/2 cup finely chopped walnuts
1/4 cup firmly packed brown sugar	1/4 cup finely chopped mixed candied fruits
2 tablespoons flour	
Dash salt	

1. Preheat oven to 325°. Beat egg until light in a small bowl; beat in granulated and brown sugar; stir in flour, salt, vanilla, walnuts and fruits.
2. Drop batter from tip of small spatula about 1 1/2 inches apart, on well-greased cookie sheets.
3. Bake in a preheated slow oven (325°) for 5 minutes, or until golden.
4. Remove from the cookie sheets with a spatula; cool on wire racks.

Double Chocolate Chip Cookies

Bake at 375° for 12 minutes.

Makes 1 1/2 dozen.

1/2 cup *unsifted* all-purpose flour	1 egg
1/2 teaspoon baking soda	2 squares unsweetened chocolate, melted
1/2 cup whole wheat flour	1 teaspoon vanilla
1/2 cup (1 stick) butter or margarine, softened	1 package (6 ounces) semisweet chocolate pieces
3/4 cup sugar	1/2 cup chopped walnuts *(optional)*

1. Sift flour and baking soda onto wax paper. Mix in whole wheat flour.
2. Preheat oven to 375°. Beat butter, sugar, egg, chocolate and vanilla in a large bowl until fluffy.
3. Stir in flour mixture, chocolate pieces and nuts until blended.
4. Drop by slightly rounded tablespoonfuls onto greased cookie sheets.
5. Bake in a preheated moderate oven (375°) for 12 minutes or until cookies feel firm. Remove to wire racks; cool completely.

Gingerbread Cookies

Bake at 350° for 8 minutes.

Makes 6 dozen cookies.

5 1/2 cups *sifted* all-purpose flour	1/2 teaspoon ground nutmeg
1 teaspoon baking soda	1 cup vegetable shortening
1 teaspoon salt	1 cup sugar
2 teaspoons ground cinnamon	1 cup molasses
1 teaspoon ground ginger	1 egg
1 teaspoon cloves	1 teaspoon vanilla
	Royal Frosting *(recipe follows)*

1. Sift flour, baking soda, salt and spices onto wax paper.
2. Beat vegetable shortening with sugar until fluffy-light in a large bowl; beat in molasses, egg and vanilla.
3. Stir in flour mixture, a third at a time, blending well after each addition, to make a soft dough. Wrap dough in foil and chill 4 hours or overnight.
4. Preheat oven to 350°. Roll out dough, 1/4 at a time, to a 1/8-inch thickness on a lightly floured surface. Cut with 3-inch cookie cutters.
5. Place 1 inch apart on ungreased cookie sheets.
6. Bake in a preheated moderate oven (350°) for 8 minutes or until cookies are firm but not too dark. Remove to wire racks with spatula; cool. Decorate with Royal Frosting and allow frosting to harden before storing.

Royal Frosting

Makes about 1 1/2 cups.

**2 egg whites, at room
  temperature
1 teaspoon lemon
  juice**

**3 1/2 cups *sifted* 10X
  (confectioners')
  sugar**

Beat egg white and lemon juice until foamy in a
medium-size bowl. Slowly beat in sugar until frosting
stands in firm peaks and is stiff enough to hold a
sharp line when cut through with a knife. Keep frosting
covered with a damp paper towel to keep from drying.

Currant-Nut Drops

Bake at 400° for 8 minutes.

Makes 4 1/2 dozen cookies.

**2 cups *sifted* all-
  purpose flour
1/2 teaspoon baking
  soda
1/2 teaspoon salt
1 teaspoon ground
  cinnamon
1/2 teaspoon ground
  nutmeg**

**1/2 cup vegetable
  shortening
1 cup firmly packed
  brown sugar
1 egg
1/3 cup cold coffee
1 cup dried currants
1 cup coarsely
  chopped walnuts**

1. Sift flour, baking soda, salt, cinnamon and nutmeg
onto wax paper.
2. Beat shortening, sugar and egg in a large bowl with
an electric mixer until light and fluffy.
3. Alternately add dry ingredients, one third at a time
with coffee, starting and ending with flour mixture.
Fold in currants and walnuts. Refrigerate 1 hour.
Preheat oven to 400°.
4. Drop by teaspoonfuls, 2 inches apart, onto
greased cookie sheets.
5. Bake in a preheated hot oven (400°) 8 minutes or
until firm. Remove to wire racks to cool.

Hanukkahgelt Cookies

Bake at 350° for 10 minutes.

Makes about 5 1/2 dozen.

**1 cup pareve or
  regular margarine
1 cup honey
4 cups *unsifted* all-
  purpose flour
2 teaspoons baking
  soda
1/2 teaspoon ground
  cinnamon**

**1/2 teaspoon ground
  cloves
1/2 teaspoon ground
  allspice
2 cups *sifted* 10X
  (confectioners')
  sugar
Frozen orange juice
  concentrate, thawed**

1. Beat margarine and honey together in a large bowl

until blended. Combine flour with soda, cinnamon,
cloves and allspice on wax paper. Stir into margarine
mixture until soft dough forms. Chill 1 hour.
2. Preheat oven to 350°. Roll dough on a floured
surface to a 1/4-inch thickness. Cut into rounds with a
2-inch cutter. Place rounds on greased cookie sheets.
3. Bake cookies in a preheated moderate oven (350°)
for 10 minutes or until firm to the touch in the center.
Cool on wire racks.
4. Beat 10X sugar with enough of the orange juice
concentrate to make an icing the consistency of heavy
cream. Ice the cookies and let dry.

Raspberry-Almond Cookies

Bake at 350° for 8 minutes.

Makes 1 1/2 dozen cookies.

**1 cup (2 sticks) butter,
  softened
1/2 cup granulated
  sugar
1 egg
1/2 cup almond paste
  (not almond filling
  or marzipan)
2 1/4 cup *sifted***

**all-purpose flour
1 teaspoon grated
  lemon rind
10X (confectioners')
  sugar
1 cup red raspberry
  jam, sieved
Whole blanched
  almonds**

1. Beat butter, sugar and egg in a large bowl with
electric mixer until smooth. Crumble in almond paste;
beat until well blended.
2. Gradually add flour, blending thoroughly; stir in
lemon rind. Wrap dough in foil (mixture will be sticky).
Refrigerate several hours.
3. Preheat oven to 350°. Divide chilled dough in half.
Roll out between sheets of lightly floured wax paper to
an 1/8-inch thickness. (Moisten countertop with water
to hold bottom sheet in place.) Chill briefly if too soft.
Cut out with a 4-inch floured star-shaped cutter. Place
cookies 1 inch apart on an ungreased cookie sheet.
Chill scraps for second rolling.
4. Roll out remaining half of dough. Cut out star
shapes. Cut out centers of stars with a 1/2-inch round
cutter. Save scraps for second rolling. (Be sure you
have enough solid cookies to match the cut-out
cookies.) Reroll the scraps, cutting solids and cut
outs.
5. Bake in a preheated moderate oven (350°) for 8
minutes or until edges of cookies are lightly browned.
Remove from oven; let stand 1 minute. Remove to
wire racks; cool.
6. Sift 10X sugar through a fine strainer over the cut-
out cookies. Spread the solid cookies with a thin layer
of jam. Press together to make a sandwich. Add a bit
more jam in the center; top with a whole almond.

Raspberry-Nut Pinwheels

Bake at 375° for 9 minutes.

Makes 3 dozen cookies.

2 cups *unsifted* all-purpose flour	1 cup sugar
1 teaspoon baking powder	1 egg
½ cup (1 stick) butter or margarine, softened	1 teaspoon vanilla
	¼ cup seedless raspberry jam
	1 cup finely chopped walnuts

1. Sift together flour and baking powder onto wax paper.
2. Beat together butter, sugar and egg in large bowl with electric mixer until fluffy. Stir in vanilla. Gradually add flour mixture, stirring until well combined.
3. Roll out dough between two pieces of wax paper to 12 × 10-inch rectangle. Remove top piece of wax paper. Spread jam evenly over entire surface of dough. Sprinkle evenly with nuts.
4. Firmly roll up dough from a long side, jelly-roll style, removing wax paper as you roll. Wrap roll in wax paper and refrigerate several hours or overnight.
5. When ready to make cookies, preheat oven to moderate (375°).
6. Cut roll into generous ¼-inch-thick slices with thin sharp knife. Transfer slices to ungreased cookie sheet, spacing 2 inches apart.
7. Bake in preheated moderate oven (375°) for 9 minutes or until golden around edges. Cool on wire racks.

Butter Nut Bars

Bake at 350° for 15 minutes.

Makes about 4 dozen.

½ cup chopped blanched almonds	1 teaspoon almond extract
1½ tablespoons granulated sugar	1¾ cups *sifted* all-purpose flour
¾ cup (1½ sticks) butter or margarine, softened	1 egg white, slightly beaten
⅓ cup granulated sugar	10X (confectioners') sugar (*optional*)

1. Preheat oven to moderate (350°).
2. Combine almonds with the 1½ tablespoons sugar in small bowl. Reserve.
3. Beat together butter, ⅓ cup sugar and almond extract in medium-size bowl until smooth. Stir in flour. Gather dough into ball and flatten slightly. Divide in half.
4. Roll out each half on floured surface to rectangle, ¼ inch thick and about 3 inches wide and 12 inches long. Even edges with a ruler to measure 2½ inches wide. Cut crosswise into bars, ¾ inch wide. Brush tops with egg white. Sprinkle evenly with almond-

sugar mixture. Lift bars with spatula to ungreased cookie sheet, spacing 1 inch apart.
5. Bake in preheated moderate oven (350°) for 15 minutes or until golden brown. Transfer to racks to cool. Store in tightly covered container up to 2 weeks. Dust with 10X sugar, if you wish.

Lemon Slice Cookies

Bake at 400° for 6 minutes.

Makes about 7 dozen.

2½ cups *sifted* all-purpose flour	2 teaspoons grated lemon rind
1 teaspoon baking powder	1 teaspoon lemon juice
½ teaspoon salt	Decorator Frosting (*recipe follows*)
¾ cup (1½ sticks) butter or margarine, softened	Yellow food coloring
1 cup sugar	Small white mint candies (½-ounce package)
2 eggs	

1. Sift together flour, baking powder and salt onto wax paper.
2. Beat together butter, sugar and eggs in large bowl until well blended. Stir in lemon rind and juice, then the flour mixture, until dough is smooth.
3. Wrap dough in plastic wrap and refrigerate several hours or overnight.
4. When ready to make cookies, preheat oven to hot (400°).
5. Roll out dough to ⅛-inch thickness on a lightly floured surface. Cut out cookies using 3-inch-round cutter. Cut each cookie in half and place 1 inch apart on ungreased cookie sheet.
6. Bake in preheated hot oven (400°) for 6 minutes or until lightly golden. Remove cookies to wire racks to cool.
7. Tint Decorator Frosting pale yellow with several drops yellow food coloring. Divide frosting in half. Set half aside, covered with damp paper toweling. Use other half to frost tops of cookies. Tint reserved frosting dark yellow. Spoon into pastry bag fitted with plain writing tip. Pipe lemon rind and sections on each cookie as pictured on opposite page. Add 1 or 2 small white mint candies for lemon seeds.

Decorator Frosting: Combine 3 egg whites, at room temperature, 1 box (1 pound) 10X (confectioners') sugar and ½ teaspoon cream of tartar in medium-size bowl. Beat with electric mixer until frosting reaches good spreading consistency.

Pictured opposite: Raspberry-Nut Pinwheels, page 226; Butternut Bars, page 226; Mocha Bar Cookies, page 228; Apricot-Coconut Cookie Squares, page 228; Rainbow Venetians, page 228; Lemon Slice Cookie, page 226.

Apricot-Coconut Cookie Squares

Bake bottom cookie layer at 350° for 25 minutes; bake whole cookie at 350° for 35 minutes.

Makes 36 squares.

1/4 **cup sugar**	1/4 **teaspoon salt**
1 1/3 **cups** *sifted* **all-purpose flour**	2 **eggs, well beaten**
1/2 **cup (1 stick) butter or margarine, softened**	1 **can (15 ounces) sweetened condensed milk**
1 **package (6 ounces) dried apricots**	1 **package (7 ounces) flaked coconut**
1/2 **teaspoon baking powder**	1/3 **cup apricot preserves**

1. Preheat oven to moderate (350°). Butter 9 × 9 × 2-inch-square baking pan.
2. Combine sugar and 1 cup of the flour in medium-size bowl. Cut in butter with pastry blender until coarse crumbs form.
3. Press crumbs firmly over bottom of prepared pan to form bottom crust.
4. Bake in preheated moderate oven (350°) for 25 minutes or until pale golden. Remove pan to wire rack. Leave oven on.
5. Reserve 4 apricots for garnish. Finely chop remaining apricots. Combine with remaining 1/3 cup flour, baking powder, salt, eggs, condensed milk and half the coconut in bowl. Spread evenly over baked cookie layer.
6. Bake in preheated moderate oven (350°) for 35 minutes or until top is firm to the touch. Cool in pan on wire rack.
7. Spread preserves over top and sprinkle with remaining coconut. Cut into 36 squares. Cut reserved apricots into small pieces. Decorate top of each square with apricot piece.

Rainbow Venetians

Bake at 350° for 15 minutes.

Makes about 6 dozen.

1 **can (8 ounces) almond paste (not marzipan)**	**all-purpose flour**
	1/4 **teaspoon salt**
1 1/2 **cups (3 sticks) butter or margarine, softened**	10 **drops green food coloring**
	8 **drops red food coloring**
1 **cup sugar**	
4 **eggs, separated**	1 **jar (12 ounces) apricot preserves**
1 **teaspoon almond extract**	5 **squares (1 ounce each) semisweet chocolate**
2 **cups sifted**	

1. Preheat oven to moderate (350°). Grease three 13 × 9 × 2-inch baking pans; line with wax paper; grease paper.
2. Break up almond paste in large bowl with fork. Add

butter, sugar, egg yolks and almond extract. Beat with electric mixer until light and fluffy, about 5 minutes. Beat in flour and salt.
3. Beat egg whites in medium-size bowl with electric mixer until stiff peaks form. Stir into almond mixture with wooden spoon, using a turning motion similar to folding.
4. Remove 1 1/2 cups batter; spread evenly into one of the prepared pans. Remove another 1 1/2 cups batter to small bowl; tint with green food coloring. Spread evenly into second prepared pan. Add red food coloring to remaining 1 1/2 cups batter and spread into third prepared pan.
5. Bake in preheated moderate oven (350°) for 15 minutes or until edges are lightly golden. (Note: Cake layers will each be 1/4 inch thick.) Immediately remove cakes from pans onto large wire racks. Cool thoroughly.
6. Place green layer on upturned jelly-roll pan. Heat apricot preserves in small saucepan; strain. Spread half the warm preserves over green layer to edges. Place yellow layer on top. Spread with remaining preserves. Place pink layer, top-side up, on yellow layer.
7. Cover with plastic wrap. Weight down with large wooden cutting board or heavy flat tray. Refrigerate overnight.
8. Melt chocolate in top of double boiler over hot water. Trim cake edges even. Cut cake crosswise into 1-inch-wide strips. Frost top (pink layer) with chocolate. Turn strip on side. Frost bottom (green layer). Let chocolate dry. Cut into 1-inch pieces. Repeat with remaining strips.

Mocha Bar Cookies

Bake at 350° for 20 minutes.

Makes 30 diamonds.

1 1/2 **cups** *sifted* **all-purpose flour**	**light brown sugar**
	1 **egg**
1 **teaspoon baking powder**	1/2 **cup strongly brewed coffee**
1/4 **teaspoon baking soda**	1/2 **cup raisins**
1/4 **teaspoon salt**	1 **cup chopped walnuts**
1/2 **teaspoon ground cinnamon**	1/2 **cup semisweet chocolate pieces**
1/4 **cup (1/2 stick) butter, softened**	1 **white chocolate candy bar (3 ounces)**
1 **cup firmly packed**	

1. Preheat oven to moderate (350°). Grease 13 × 9 × 2-inch pan.
2. Sift flour, baking powder and soda, salt and cinnamon onto wax paper.
3. Beat together butter, brown sugar and egg in medium-size bowl until light and fluffy, about 2 minutes. Stir in coffee alternately with flour mixture until batter is smooth. Add raisins and 1/2 cup nuts.

Crispy Bow Tie Cookies.

4. Spread batter evenly into prepared baking pan. Sprinkle remaining nuts and chocolate pieces over batter.

5. Bake in preheated moderate oven (350°) for 20 minutes or until top springs back when lightly touched with fingertip. Cool in pan on wire rack. Cut into 30 diamonds.

6. Melt white chocolate in top of double boiler over hot, not boiling, water. Drizzle over each diamond using a spoon or pastry bag fitted with small writing tip.

Crispy Bow Tie Cookies

Makes about 2 dozen.

2 eggs	**1 teaspoon grated**
2 tablespoons sugar	**lemon rind**
2 cups *sifted* all-	**Vegetable oil for frying**
purpose flour	**10X (confectioners')**
2 tablespoons vanilla	**sugar**

1. Beat together the eggs and sugar in a medium-size bowl until the mixture is light and fluffy. Stir in 1½ cups of the flour, the vanilla and lemon rind until blended. Shape into a ball.

2. Turn the dough out onto a lightly floured surface. Knead until the dough is smooth and elastic, about 8 minutes; add as much of the remaining flour as necessary to prevent sticking. Cover with plastic wrap. Let rest for 5 minutes.

3. Divide the dough into 4 equal portions. Roll one-fourth of the dough to ⅛-inch thickness. Keep the remaining dough covered with plastic wrap while working with the one-fourth. Cut into 5 × 1½-inch strips with a pastry wheel or pizza cutter. Make a lengthwise slit about 1-inch long in center of each strip. Pull one end through the slit to make a bow tie. As you work, keep bow ties covered with plastic wrap. Repeat with the remaining dough.

4. Pour vegetable oil into a large saucepan or Dutch oven to a depth of 4 inches. Heat oil until it registers 375° on a deep-fat frying thermometer, or until a 1-inch cube of white bread turns golden brown in about 50 seconds. Transfer 3 or 4 cookies to the hot oil with a metal spatula. Fry the cookies for a total of 3 minutes or until golden, turning once. Drain on paper toweling; cool. Keep unfried bow ties covered with plastic wrap. Fry the remaining cookies.

5. Store in lightly covered container. Sprinkle with 10X (confectioners') sugar just before serving.

Mocha Lace Roll-Ups

Bake at 325° for 9 minutes.

Makes about 1³/₄ dozen.

½ **cup** *sifted* **all-purpose flour**	**1 square unsweetened chocolate**
½ **cup ground blanched almonds**	½ **teaspoon vanilla**
¼ **cup light corn syrup**	**1 cup heavy cream**
¼ **cup sugar**	**2 tablespoons 10X (confectioners') sugar**
¼ **cup** (½ **stick**) **butter or margarine**	**Chopped pistachio nuts**

1. Combine flour and almonds. Combine corn syrup, sugar, butter and chocolate in a small heavy saucepan. Cook, stirring constantly, until the mixture comes to boiling and the chocolate is melted. Remove from heat; stir in vanilla. Stir in the flour mixture gradually until well blended.

2. Drop the mixture by rounded teaspoonsfuls about 3 inches apart onto ungreased cookie sheets; bake no more than 6 at a time.

3. Bake in a preheated slow oven (325°) for 9 minutes. Remove to a wire rack; cool for 1 to 1½ minutes. Scoop up warm cookies with a large metal spatula; quickly roll around a wooden spoon handle (at least ½-inch in diameter). Hold a few seconds until the cookie stiffens. (If the cookies cool too quickly or are too brittle to work, return to a warm oven briefly to soften.) Slide cookie off the handle onto a wire rack to cool completely.

4. Beat heavy cream with 10X (confectioners') sugar until stiff. Pipe into the ends of cookies. Dip the ends into chopped pistachios.

Poinsettia Cookies

Bake at 350° for 8 to 10 minutes.

Makes 5 dozen.

2½ **cups** *sifted* **all-purpose flour**	**1 egg**
1 teaspoon salt	1½ **teaspoons almond extract**
1 cup (2 **sticks**) **butter**	**1 teaspoon vanilla**
1 cup *sifted* **10X (confectioners') sugar**	**Red decorating sugar**
	Edible silver decorating shot

1. Sift together the flour and salt onto wax paper.

2. Beat the butter in a medium-size bowl until light. Beat in the 10X sugar until light and fluffy. Beat in the

Mocha Lace Roll-Ups.

Macaroon Tartlets.

almond extract and vanilla. Blend in the flour mixture. Shape dough into 2 equal balls. Wrap each in wax paper. Chill for 2 hours or until firm.

3. When ready to make the cookies, preheat the oven to moderate (350°). Grease cookie sheets with vegetable shortening.

4. Roll out the dough, one half at a time, into a 12 × 10-inch rectangle, 1/8 inch thick. (Work in a cool room since the dough is very rich and soft.) Cut into 2-inch squares. Cut each corner of each square diagonally toward the center about 3/4 inch. Turn down the alternate corners, placing the tips in the center to achieve a pinwheel effect. Sprinkle the center of each cookie with red sugar and press a silver ball in the center. Place, 1 inch apart, on the prepared cookie sheets.

5. Bake in the preheated moderate oven (350°) for 8 to 10 minutes; watch carefully so the edges of the cookies do not overbrown. Remove the cookies from sheets to wire racks to cool.

Honey Date-Nut Bars

Bake at 350° for 35 minutes.

Makes 28 bars.

1¹/₂ cups *sifted* all-purpose flour	2 tablespoons chopped crystallized ginger
1 teaspoon baking powder	3 eggs
¹/₂ teaspoon salt	1 cup honey
1 package (8 ounces) pitted dates, snipped into tiny pieces	Cream Cheese Topping (*recipe follows*)
1 cup coarsely chopped walnuts	¹/₃ cup chopped walnuts

1. Sift flour, baking powder and salt onto wax paper.

Combine dates, 1 cup walnuts and ginger in a bowl; coat with 2 tablespoons of the flour mixture. Preheat oven to 350°.

2. Beat eggs in a large bowl until frothy; stir in honey. Stir in flour mixture just until well blended. Fold in date and nut mixture. Pour into a well greased 13 × 9 × 2-inch baking pan.

3. Bake in a preheated moderate oven (350°) for 35 minutes or until center springs back when lightly pressed with fingertip. Cool on wire rack. Cover; let stand overnight.

4. Spread with Cream Cheese Topping; sprinkle with nuts.

Cream Cheese Topping: Beat 1 package (8 ounces) softened cream cheese with 2 tablespoons honey.

Macaroon Tartlets

Bake at 350° for 25 to 30 minutes.

Makes 22 tartlets.

Dough:	sugar
9 tablespoons (1 stick plus 1 tablespoon) butter, at room temperature	²/₃ cup blanched whole almonds, finely ground
4¹/₂ tablespoons sugar	2 egg whites
3 egg yolks	¹/₈ teaspoon almond extract
1¹/₂ cups *sifted* all-purpose flour	¹/₄ teaspoon grated lemon rind (*optional*)
Filling:	White Icing (*recipe follows*)
³/₄ cup 10X (confectioners')	Glacé cherries

1. Prepare Dough: Beat together butter and sugar in small bowl until light and fluffy. Beat in yolks and flour until well blended. Chill in freezer 5 minutes.

(continued)

2. Prepare Filling: Combine 10X sugar, almonds, whites, almond extract and lemon rind, if using, in small bowl.

3. Spray twenty-two 2- to 3½-inch tartlet pans with nonstick vegetable cooking spray. Press about 2 teaspoons of dough into each pan, forming an even layer over bottom and up sides. (If you have less than 22 pans, work in batches). If tart shells become too soft, refrigerate before filling.

4. Spoon about 2 teaspoons of the filling into each shell, so each is about three-quarters full. Arrange on cookie sheets.

5. Bake in preheated moderate oven (350°) for 25 to 30 minutes or until fillings puff and are golden.

6. Remove cookie sheets to wire racks. When cool enough to handle, carefully remove tartlets from pans. Drizzle each with White Icing. Decorate each tartlet with a tiny piece of glacé cherry.

White Icing: Stir together 1 egg white, ¼ teaspoon cream of tartar and 1½ cups *sifted* 10X sugar in small bowl until of a good drizzling consistency.

Meringue

A stiffly beaten mixture of sugar and egg whites that can be used as a topping on pies, cakes and puddings. Meringue can also be shaped into round layers or shells, baked until dry and used for other desserts. Ground nuts, cocoa and flavoring can be added to meringue and then baked into cookies. The word comes from the German town of Meyringen where meringue was first made in the 1700's by a Swiss pastry chef.

Tips for Making Perfect Meringues

• Choose a cool, dry day—humid air tends to soften meringues. Be sure your tools—non-plastic bowl and beater—are clean and dry. The tiniest speck of fat will spoil meringues.

• Egg whites will beat higher if allowed to stand at room temperature to warm slightly.

• Depend on your electric mixer, since long beating is a must to dissolve sugar completely and prevent meringue from "weeping." To test if sugar is completely dissolved: Rub a bit of meringue between your fingers. Meringue should feel smooth.

Giant Cocoa Meringues

Bake at 325° for 10 minutes.

Makes 15 big cookies.

4 egg whites, at room temperature	**2 teaspoons vanilla**
⅛ teaspoon salt	**¾ cup *sifted* unsweetened cocoa powder**
1 package (1 pound) 10X (confectioners') sugar	**1 cup semisweet chocolate pieces**

1. Preheat oven to 325°. Beat egg whites with salt in bowl with electric mixer at high speed until foamy.

Gradually add sugar and beat at low speed until meringue forms soft peaks; beat in vanilla and cocoa. With spoon, stir in chocolate.

2. Drop by large tablespoonfuls onto parchment or wax paper-lined cookie sheets, six to a sheet.

3. Bake in a preheated slow oven (325°) for 10 minutes or until tops of meringues are firm, but centers remain moist. Remove cookies from oven and let cool completely before removing from paper.

Meringue Miniatures

Airy wisps aglitter with colored sugar. They're inexpensive, too, using only two egg whites. No need to worry about leftover yolks—simply mix them into scrambled eggs, custard, gravy or sauce.

Bake at 250° for 25 minutes.

Makes 5 dozen cookies.

2 egg whites	**½ teaspoon vanilla**
1 teaspoon white vinegar	**½ cup granulated sugar**
Dash salt	**Red food coloring**
½ teaspoon almond extract	**Colored decorating sugars**

1. Beat egg whites with vinegar and salt until foamy-white and double in volume in medium-size bowl with electric mixer at high speed; beat in almond extract and vanilla. Preheat oven to 250°.

2. Beat in granulated sugar, 1 tablespoon at a time, until meringue stands in firm peaks.

3. Spoon half of mixture into a second medium-size bowl; blend in a few drops of red food coloring to tint a delicate pink; leave remainder plain.

4. Drop by teaspoonfuls, 1 inch apart, on brown paper-lined cookie sheets; sprinkle with colored decorating sugars.

5. Bake in a preheated very slow oven (250°) for 25 minutes or until crisp. Remove cookies on brown paper to wire rack and cool completely; remove from paper. Keep tightly covered, for they absorb moisture.

Chocolate-Almond Meringues

Crackly-crisp with a light touch of chocolate. Best made on a dry day.

Bake at 275° for 20 minutes.

Makes about 7 dozen.

3 egg whites, at room temperature	**4 squares unsweetened chocolate, coarsely grated**
1 teaspoon vinegar	
½ teaspoon salt	**Chocolate Glaze (recipe follows)**
1 cup sugar	
1 cup finely chopped blanched almonds	**Chopped pistachio nuts**

1. Preheat oven to 275°. Beat egg whites, vinegar and

salt in a large bowl with electric mixer at high speed until foamy. Add sugar, 1 tablespoon at a time, and continue beating until mixture forms stiff glossy peaks, about 8 to 10 minutes. Fold in almonds and chocolate very gently.

2. Spoon mixture by teaspoonsfuls 1 inch apart onto greased cookie sheets.

3. Bake in a preheated very slow oven (375°) for 20 minutes or until just set. Remove from cookie sheets with metal spatula to wire racks. Cool completely. Swirl tops of cooled meringues with Chocolate Glaze; sprinkle with pistachio nuts.

Chocolate Glaze: Melt 2 squares unsweetened chocolate with 3 tablespoons butter or margarine in a small saucepan over very low heat. Watch carefully to prevent scorching. Cool. Combine chocolate mixture with 2 cups sifted 10X (confectioners') sugar and 1/4 cup boiling water in a medium-size bowl. Beat with rotary beater until smooth. Mixture will be thin, but will thicken on standing. Cool until thickened.

Macaroon
Small, sweet, crunchy cookie made of almond paste or ground almonds, sugar, egg whites and vanilla. The French claim to have originated this cookie calling it *macaron*. However, the Italians called little delicacies *ma caroni*, which also refers to macaroni. Today, the Italian version is called amaretti. Over the years, coconut macaroons have evolved from amaretti.

Coconut Macaroons

Bake at 300° for 20 minutes.

Makes 3 dozen.

2 egg whites	**1 cup chopped**
1/4 teaspoon salt	**walnuts**
1/2 cup granulated	**1/2 cup quick-cooking**
sugar	**oats**
1/2 cup firmly packed	**8 maraschino cherries,**
dark brown sugar	**chopped**
1 can (3 1/2 ounces)	**1/2 teaspoon vanilla**
flaked coconut	

1. Beat egg whites and salt with an electric mixer in a medium-size bowl until foamy-white and double in volume, add sugars, 1 tablespoon at a time, beating until stiff peaks form. Preheat oven to 300°.

2. Fold coconut, walnuts, oats, cherries and vanilla into meringue. Drop by teaspoonfuls, 1 inch apart, on well-greased cookie sheets.

3. Bake in a preheated slow oven (300°) for 20 minutes or just until set. Cool on cookie sheets 2 minutes, then remove carefully with spatula to wire rack; cool.

Amaretti

Bake at 325° for 45 minutes.

Makes 3 dozen.

1 can or package	**1 cup *sifted* 10X**
(8 ounces) almond	**(confectioners')**
paste	**sugar**
2 egg whites	**1 tablespoon coarse**
Pinch salt	**sugar crystals**
1 teaspoon vanilla	

1. Grease 2 large cookie sheets; dust with flour; tap off any excess. Preheat oven to 325°.

2. Break up almond paste with fingers in small bowl. Add egg whites, salt and vanilla. Beat with electric mixer at low speed until mixture is smooth. Add confectioners' sugar slowly, beating at low speed until a soft dough forms.

3. Fit a pastry bag with a small round tip. Fill with dough. Pipe dough out in small rounds or drop by teaspoonfuls on prepared cookie sheets.

4. For a cracked top: Dip fingertip into water; pat over tops; sprinkle with coarse sugar crystals.

5. Bake in a preheated slow oven (325°) for 45 minutes or until golden brown. Remove to wire racks with a spatula to cool. Store in an airtight tin.

Pine Nut Macaroons

Lacy and sugary, with nut-covered tops, and so easy to make.

Bake at 375° for 10 minutes.

Makes about 2 1/2 dozen cookies.

1 cup blanched	**1/2 teaspoon almond**
almonds	**extract**
1 cup sugar	**1 jar (8 ounces) pine**
2 egg whites	**nuts (pignoli)**

1. Dry blanched almonds thoroughly by placing them in a warm oven (350°) for 5 to 10 minutes. Grind as fine as possible in an electric blender or food processor until powdery, while still warm.

2. Combine ground almonds and sugar in a medium-size bowl; add unbeaten egg whites and almond extract; beat thoroughly.

3. Drop by teaspoonfuls onto generously buttered and floured cookie sheets, leaving 1 inch between cookies. Smooth into rounds. Top each cookie with approximately 1/2 teaspoon pine nuts, pressing pine nuts into cookie. Let stand 3 hours.

4. Bake in a preheated moderate oven (375°) for 10 minutes. Remove cookies from oven; let stand on cookie sheets for 5 minutes; carefully remove with wide spatula (if cookies stiffen, put back into oven for a few seconds to soften). Store in airtight container when thoroughly cooled.

Blarney Castle Parfait, page 304;
Shamrock Sugar Cookies.

Shamrock Sugar Cookies

Bake at 375° for 7 minutes.

Makes 4 dozen cookies.

1 cup butter-flavored
  vegetable
  shortening
1 cup sugar
1 egg
1/2 teaspoon vanilla
2 1/4 cups all-purpose
  flour

1 teaspoon baking
  powder
1/4 teaspoon ground
  ginger
1/4 teaspoon salt
Green decorating
  sugar

1. Beat butter-flavored vegetable shortening with sugar, egg and vanilla in bowl with an electric mixer at high speed until fluffy.
2. Combine flour, baking powder, ginger and salt in small bowl. Stir into shortening mixture to make a stiff dough. Divide dough in half; shape into two balls. Wrap in wax paper; chill at least 2 hours.
3. Preheat oven to moderate (375°).
4. Roll dough out on lightly floured board to 1/4-inch thickness. Cut cookies out with a 2 1/2- or 3-inch shamrock-shaped cutter. Place 1 inch apart on ungreased cookie sheets. Sprinkle with decorating sugar.
5. Bake in preheated moderate oven (375°) for 7 minutes or until light brown around the edges. Remove to wire racks to cool. Store in tightly covered metal tin.

Carrot-Zucchini Bar Cookies with Cream Cheese Frosting

Bake at 350° for 30 minutes.

Makes 12 bar cookies.

2/3 cup firmly packed
  light brown sugar
1/2 cup (1 stick)
  unsalted butter or
  margarine, at room
  temperature
1 package (3 ounces)
  cream cheese, at
  room temperature
1 egg
1 teaspoon vanilla
1 1/2 cups *unsifted* all-
  purpose flour

1 teaspoon baking
  powder
1/4 teaspoon salt
2/3 cup coarsely grated
  carrot
2/3 cup coarsely grated
  zucchini, excess
  liquid squeezed out
1/2 cup golden raisins
Cream Cheese
  Frosting *(recipe
  follows)*

1. Preheat oven to moderate (350°). Grease 9 × 9 × 2-inch-square baking pan.
2. Beat together brown sugar, butter and cream cheese in large bowl with electric mixer until fluffy. Beat in egg and vanilla. Beat in flour, baking powder and salt until well blended. Stir in carrot, zucchini and raisins. Spoon into prepared pan; spread evenly.
3. Bake in preheated moderate oven (350°) for 30 minutes or until wooden pick inserted in center comes out clean and cake begins to pull away from sides.

Cool in pan on wire rack 10 minutes. Invert cake on wire rack; cool completely.

4. Spread Cream Cheese Frosting over top. Cut into 12 bar cookies.

Cream Cheese Frosting: Beat together 1/4 cup (1/2 stick) butter or margarine, at room temperature, 1 package (3 ounces) cream cheese, at room temperature, and 1 1/2 cups 10X (confectioners') sugar until smooth and fluffy. Beat in 1/2 teaspoon vanilla. Makes about 1 cup.

Microwave Oven Directions for Cookies

650 Watt Variable Power Microwave Oven

Directions: Grease 10-inch microwave-safe pie plate. Prepare batter as in above recipe. Spread batter evenly in prepared pie plate. Place pie plate on inverted saucer in center of microwave oven. Microwave, uncovered, at full power for 7 minutes, rotating pie plate one-quarter turn after 4 minutes. Place pie plate directly on counter to cool.

Peanut Butter Cookies

Bake at 375° for 12 minutes.

Makes about 5 dozen.

2 cups *sifted* all-purpose flour	shortening
3/4 teaspoon baking soda	1/2 cup peanut butter
1/2 teaspoon baking powder	1/2 cup firmly packed brown sugar
1/4 teaspoon salt	1/2 cup granulated sugar
1/2 cup vegetable	1 egg
	1/4 cup orange juice

1. Sift flour, baking soda, baking powder and salt onto wax paper.

2. Beat shortening and peanut butter with brown and granulated sugars in a large bowl until fluffy; beat in egg. Stir in flour mixture alternately with orange juice, blending well to make a stiff dough. Chill until firm enough to handle.

3. Preheat oven to 375°. Shape dough, a teaspoonful at a time, into balls. Place 3 inches apart on ungreased cookie sheets; flatten, criss-cross fashion, with a fork.

4. Bake in a preheated moderate oven (375°) for 12 minutes or until golden. Remove from cookie sheets; cool completely on wire racks.

Carrot-Zucchini Bar Cookies with Cream Cheese Frosting, page 234.

Granola Fruit Squares

Bake at 375° for 25 minutes.

Makes 16 squares.

1 cup chopped dried apricots (6 ounces)	1¼ cups *unsifted* all-purpose flour
1 cup chopped dates (6 ounces)	½ teaspoon baking soda
¾ cup water	½ teaspoon salt
2 teaspoons grated lemon rind	1½ cups quick-cooking oats (not instant)
2 teaspoons lemon juice *(optional)*	¾ cup firmly packed dark brown sugar
1 cup chopped walnuts	¾ cup butter, melted

1. Preheat oven to moderate (375°). Lightly grease 9 × 9 × 2-inch-square baking pan.
2. Combine apricots, dates and water in small saucepan. Bring to boiling. Lower heat; simmer, stirring occasionally, until water is absorbed, about 5 minutes. Let cool.
3. Stir lemon rind and juice and walnuts into apricot mixture.
4. Combine flour, baking soda, salt, oats and brown sugar in large bowl. Stir in melted butter; mixture will be crumbly.
5. Reserve 1 cup crumb mixture. Pat remainder evenly over bottom of prepared pan. Spoon apricot mixture evenly over crumb base. Sprinkle with reserved crumb mixture.
6. Bake in preheated moderate oven (375°) for 25 minutes. Remove to wire rack to cool. Cut into 16 squares. Wrap in foil packets, about 4 to a packet. Refrigerate several hours or overnight to make squares firm.

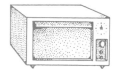

Microwave Oven Directions for Granola Fruit Squares
650 Watt Variable Power Microwave Oven
Ingredient Changes: Do not melt the ¾ cup butter.
Directions: Combine apricots, dates and water in microwave-safe 1½-quart bowl. Microwave, uncovered, at full power for 4 to 5 minutes or until water is absorbed and mixture is fairly smooth, stirring every minute. Stir in lemon rind and juice and walnuts. Combine flour, baking soda, salt, oats, and sugar on wax paper; set aside. Cut butter into 6 pieces; place in 9-inch microwave-safe dish. Microwave, uncovered, at full power for 1 minute or until butter is melted. Pour flour mixture over butter. Mix thoroughly with fork. Remove 1 cup for topping. Press remaining flour mixture into an even layer over bottom of dish. Spread apricot mixture evenly over crust. Sprinkle reserved crust mixture over top. Place baking dish on inverted saucer in microwave oven. Microwave, uncovered, at full power for 6 minutes or until puffed and set, rotating quarter turn every 2 minutes. Place dish directly on countertop to cool.

Shortbread
This rich, pastry-like firm cookie was traditionally served at Hogmanay, the Scottish New Year's Day. Shortbread has been made in Scotland for four centuries. It is made of flour, sugar and butter, formed into a round patty, scored, the edges crimped, and baked until dry in a slow oven. It is then broken into pieces.

Shortbread

Bake at 325° for 25 minutes.

Makes 2 dozen cookies.

1 cup (2 sticks) butter, softened	2½ cups *sifted* all-purpose flour
½ cup sugar	

1. Preheat oven to 325°. Beat butter and sugar in a large bowl until creamy and smooth. Work in flour with a wooden spoon until a stiff dough forms.
2. Divide dough into 3 parts. Working with one part at a time, roll out to about a 5-inch circle on an ungreased cookie sheet. Score circle with knife into 8 equal wedges. Pierce dough along the score lines with tines of fork. Make sure the tines go through the entire thickness to facilitate breaking later. Press back of fork around edge of cookie to decorate. Repeat with remaining dough.
3. Bake in a preheated slow oven (325°) for 25 minutes or until cookies are faintly golden brown. They should be quite pale.
4. Remove from oven to wire rack. While still warm, break along score lines. Remove cookies to racks to cool. Store in covered containers.

Chocolate-Glazed Bars

Brown sugar "brownies" enriched with wheat germ.
Bake at 325° for 20 minutes.

Makes 16 bars.

½ cup (1 stick) butter or margarine, softened	1½ cups *sifted* all-purpose flour
½ cup firmly packed brown sugar	1 cup wheat germ
1 teaspoon vanilla	½ cup semisweet chocolate pieces (from a 6-ounce package)
1 egg	

1. Preheat oven to 325°. Beat butter and brown sugar in a large bowl. Beat in vanilla and egg. Stir in the flour and wheat germ. Press evenly into an 8½ × 8½ × 2-inch baking pan.

2. Bake in a preheated slow oven (325°) for 20 minutes or until lightly browned. Remove from oven.
3. Immediately sprinkle the tops of cookie bars with chocolate pieces. When the chocolate has softened, spread carefully over surface with metal spatula. Cool on wire rack; cut into 16 bars. Store in single layer, covered with foil.

Chocolate Coconut Crisps

Bake at 350° for 12 minutes.
Makes about 7 dozen cookies.

²/₃ cup *sifted* unbleached all-purpose flour	unsalted butter, softened
¹/₃ cup unsweetened cocoa powder	1 cup firmly packed brown sugar
¹/₂ teaspoon baking soda	1 egg
¹/₂ teaspoon salt	¹/₄ cup water
³/₄ cup (1¹/₂ sticks)	3 cups rolled oats
	1 cup flaked coconut

1. Sift flour, cocoa, baking soda and salt onto wax paper. Beat the butter, sugar and egg in large bowl with electric mixer until fluffy; stir in water; blend well.
2. Stir flour mixture into butter mixture, blending well. Stir in oats and coconut.
3. Preheat oven to 350°. Drop by teaspoonfuls onto lightly greased cookie sheet. Dip fingertips in cold water; flatten cookies slightly.
4. Bake in a preheated moderate oven (350°) for 12 minutes. Cool on wire racks.

Oatmeal Raisin Cookies

Bake at 350° for 15 minutes.
Makes about 2¹/₂ dozen cookies.

¹/₂ cup (1 stick) unsalted butter, softened	purpose flour
	1¹/₄ teaspoons ground cinnamon
¹/₂ cup firmly packed light brown sugar	1 cup rolled oats
¹/₄ cup milk	¹/₃ cup raisins
1¹/₄ cups *sifted* unbleached all-	¹/₃ cup chopped walnuts or pecans

1. Beat butter and sugar until fluffy in a bowl with electric mixer; stir in milk.
2. Sift flour and cinnamon onto wax paper. Stir in oats. Stir mixture into butter mixture until blended. Add raisins and nuts; mix well.
3. Preheat oven to 350°. Drop cookies by level tablespoonfuls on ungreased cookie sheets, about 2 inches apart. Dip fingertips in cold water; flatten cookies slightly.
4. Bake in a preheated moderate oven (350°) for 15 minutes or until lightly browned. Cool on wire racks.

Pecan Cookies

Buttery, melt-in-the-mouth confections that can be frozen.
Bake at 300° for 25 minutes.
Makes about 4 dozen.

1 cup (2 sticks) unsalted butter, softened	purpose flour
	2 cups finely chopped pecans
¹/₄ cup sugar	10X (confectioners') sugar
3 tablespoons brandy	
3 cups *sifted* all-	

1. Beat butter, sugar and brandy in a large bowl until smooth. Stir in flour to make a soft dough. Work in pecans until well blended.
2. Preheat oven to 300°. Shape dough by level tablespoonfuls into balls. Place, 1 inch apart, on ungreased cookie sheets.
3. Bake in a preheated slow oven (300°) for 25 minutes or until bottoms are brown and tops are lightly golden. Remove from cookie sheet; roll in 10X sugar. Cool; roll in sugar again. Store in airtight container.

Prune Oatmeal Bars

Bake at 350° for 35 to 40 minutes.
Makes about 18 bars.

1 package (12 ounces) pitted prunes	light brown sugar
	³/₄ cup *sifted* all-purpose flour
¹/₃ cup granulated sugar	¹/₄ teaspoon salt
1 teaspoon grated orange rind	¹/₄ teaspoon ground cloves
1 tablespoon orange juice	¹/₄ teaspoon ground cinnamon
1¹/₂ cups quick oats	¹/₂ cup (1 stick) butter or margarine
¹/₂ cup firmly packed	

1. Cook prunes following label directions; drain; chop and mix with granulated sugar, orange rind and juice in a medium-size heavy saucepan. Cook, stirring constantly, over low heat until thick. Cool. Preheat oven to 350°.
2. Combine oats, brown sugar, flour, salt, cloves and cinnamon in a bowl; blend in butter until mixture is crumbly.
3. Press 1 ¹/₂ cups crumb mixture into bottom of an 8 × 8 × 2-inch baking pan, using spatula. Spread with prune mixture, then sprinkle remaining crumbs over, pressing down lightly.
4. Bake in a preheated moderate oven (350°) for 35 to 40 minutes. Cool completely on wire rack; cut into bars.

Sunflower Oatmeal Cookies

Bake at 350° for 12 minutes.

Makes about 2 dozen jumbo cookies.

1½ cups *sifted* all-purpose flour
½ cup instant nonfat dry milk powder
1 teaspoon baking soda
½ teaspoon salt
1 cup (2 sticks) butter or margarine
1 cup granulated sugar
1 cup firmly packed light brown sugar
2 eggs
1 teaspoon vanilla
3 cups quick oats
¾ cup dry-roasted sunflower seeds

1. Preheat oven to 350°. Sift flour, dry milk powder, baking soda and salt onto wax paper.
2. Beat butter, granulated sugar and brown sugar in a large bowl with electric mixer until light and fluffy; beat in eggs, 1 at a time; add vanilla.
3. Add flour mixture, blending well; fold in oats and sunflower seeds.
4. Measure out cookie mix with a ¼-cup metal measure onto a lightly greased cookie sheet (4 to a cookie sheet). Flatten to a 3 ½-inch round with a fork.*
5. Bake in a preheated moderate oven (350°) for 12 minutes or until golden. Remove from oven; let stand 1 minute on cookie sheet. Remove with wide spatula to wire rack. Cool completely.
Cookies can be dropped by teaspoonfuls onto greased cookie sheets. Bake at 350° for 10 minutes or until golden. Makes about 7 dozen.
Note: Cookie dough can be stored, covered, in the refrigerator up to a week and baked when convenient.

Sugar and Spice Jumbo Cookies

Bake at 400° for 10 minutes.

Makes 2 dozen four-inch cookies.

4 cups *sifted* all-purpose flour
3 teaspoons baking powder
1 teaspoon baking soda
1 teaspoon salt
½ teaspoon ground cinnamon
½ teaspoon ground nutmeg
1 cup (2 sticks) butter or margarine
2 cups sugar
2 eggs
¼ cup milk
2 teaspoons vanilla

1. Sift flour, baking powder, baking soda, salt, cinnamon and nutmeg onto wax paper.
2. Beat butter, sugar and eggs in a large bowl with electric mixer until light and fluffy. Beat in milk and vanilla. Stir in flour mixture until well blended.
3. Turn dough out onto a large piece of wax paper; divide in half and shape into two equal balls; wrap each half in wax paper and chill 3 hours or until firm enough to roll.

4. Preheat oven to 400°. Roll dough, one half at a time, to ¼-inch thickness on a lightly floured surface. Cut into rounds with a 4-inch scalloped cutter. (You can use the top of a 3-pound vegetable shortening can, cutting around with a small sharp knife.)
5. Place cookies on an ungreased large cookie sheet (5 to a sheet).
6. Bake in upper third of a preheated hot oven (400°) for 10 minutes or until lightly browned. Cool on wire racks.

Apricot Bars

Bake at 350° for 30 minutes.

Makes about 10 bars.

1 egg, separated
¼ cup (½ stick) butter, softened
6 tablespoons sugar
⅔ cup *sifted*
all-purpose flour
½ cup apricot preserves
¼ cup finely chopped pecans

1. Mix together egg yolk, butter and ¼ cup of the sugar in a medium-size bowl; then stir in flour until smooth. Pat into bottom of greased aluminum foil pan (8⁵⁄₁₆ × 5 ⁵⁄₁₆ × 1-inch).
2. Bake in toaster oven at moderate (350°) for 15 minutes until firm and slightly browned. Remove from oven; spread with apricot preserves.
3. Beat egg white in small bowl with electric mixer until foamy. Add remaining 2 tablespoons sugar, 1 tablespoon at a time, until soft peaks form. Stir in nuts; spread over preserves.
4. Return to oven and bake 15 more minutes. Lower heat, if meringue gets too brown.

Russian Tea Cakes

Bake at 400° for 12 minutes.

Makes about 50 servings (100 cakes or 2 per serving).

2 cups (4 sticks) butter or margarine
1 cup 10X (confectioners') sugar
2 teaspoons vanilla
½ teaspoon salt
4½ cups *sifted* all-purpose flour
1 cup ground walnuts
10X (confectioners') sugar

1. Beat butter with 1 cup confectioners' sugar in a large bowl until fluffy and light. Beat in vanilla and salt. Gradually blend in flour and walnuts to make a stiff dough. Preheat oven to 400°.
2. Roll dough into 1-inch balls between palms of hands. Place balls 1 inch apart on lightly greased cookie sheets.
3. Bake in a preheated hot oven (400°) for 12 minutes or until firm and lightly brown on edges. Carefully remove from cookie sheets; while still hot, roll in

confectioners' sugar to make a generous white coating before serving. Keeps several weeks in tightly covered box.

Note: For 12 servings, use 1 stick butter, ¼ cup confectioners' sugar, ½ teaspoon vanilla, dash of salt, 1 cup flour and ¼ cup walnuts.

Granola with Raisins

Bake at 300° for 20 minutes.

Makes 6 cups.

3 cups rolled oats	**½ cup walnuts**
⅓ cup firmly packed brown sugar	**⅓ cup shelled sunflower seeds**
½ teaspoon salt	**⅓ cup shelled pumpkin seeds**
½ cup vegetable oil	**2 tablespoons sesame seeds**
1 cup dried apples, cut in half	
1 cup raisins	

1. Combine rolled oats, brown sugar, salt and oil in a large bowl.
2. Add apples, raisins, walnuts, sunflower seeds, pumpkin seeds and sesame seeds to oat mixture, stirring thoroughly. Spread mixture in a jelly-roll pan or other shallow baking pan.
3. Bake in a slow oven (300°) for 20 minutes, turning once. Remove to wire rack. Let cool thoroughly. Store in tightly covered container.

Cookie Tiers

Bake at 350° for 10 to 12 minutes for large cookies, 8 to 10 minutes for small cookies.

Makes 2½ dozen cookie tiers.

¾ cup (1½ sticks) unsalted butter	**2 cups *sifted* all-purpose flour**
¾ cup sugar	**¼ teaspoon salt**
4 hard-cooked egg yolks	**⅓ cup currant jelly**
2 tablespoons white rum	**10X (confectioners') sugar**

1. Beat butter and sugar in large bowl until light and fluffy. Press yolks through strainer into butter mixture. Add rum; mix well. Mix in flour and salt until well blended. Shape dough into a ball; wrap in plastic wrap. Refrigerate overnight.
2. When ready to bake cookies, preheat oven to moderate (350°).
3. Divide dough into thirds. Roll out chilled dough, one-third at a time, between sheets of wax paper to ⅛-inch thickness. Carefully peel off top paper. Cut cookie rounds with plain or scalloped cutters in three sizes (2, 1½ and 1 inch). Place on ungreased cookie sheets, keeping large cookies on one sheet and the two smaller sizes on another sheet.

4. Bake in preheated moderate oven (350°) for 10 to 12 minutes for large cookies, and 8 to 10 minutes for smaller cookies; edges of cookies should be lightly browned. Cool cookies on wire racks.
5. To assemble, spread bottoms of middle-size cookies thinly with jelly. Press onto center of large cookies. Repeat with small cookies to make three-tiered cookies. Dust with *sifted* 10X sugar. Garnish with glacé cherry wedge, if you wish.

Italian Stars

Bake at 350° for 15 to 17 minutes for large stars, 10 to 12 minutes for small stars.

Makes 16 large stars and 30 small stars.

½ cup (1 stick) butter, softened	**1 teaspoon vanilla**
½ cup (1 stick) margarine, softened	**4 cups *sifted* all-purpose flour**
1 cup sugar	**1 egg, slightly beaten**
6 egg yolks	**Colored nonpareils**

1. Beat together butter, margarine and sugar in large bowl until light and fluffy. Beat in egg yolks and vanilla until thoroughly mixed. Stir in flour until well mixed. Shape mixture into a ball. Wrap in wax paper; refrigerate 15 minutes.
2. Preheat oven to moderate (350°). Lightly grease 2 cookie sheets.
3. Divide dough into thirds. Roll out dough, one-third at a time, on lightly floured surface to ¼-inch thickness. Cut out with 3- or 2½-inch star cookie cutters. Transfer cookies to prepared sheets, leaving 2 inches between each. Brush tops with egg. Sprinkle with nonpareils.
4. Bake in preheated moderate oven (350°) for 15 to 17 minutes for large stars, and 10 to 12 minutes for small stars. Remove cookies to wire racks to cool.

Grand Marnier Christmas Wreaths

Bake at 350° for 10 to 12 minutes.

Makes about 3 dozen cookies.

2¼ cups *unsifted* all-purpose flour	**orange rind**
1 teaspoon ground nutmeg	**1 egg**
¼ teaspoon salt	**2 tablespoons Grand Marnier liqueur**
⅔ cup unsalted butter or margarine, softened	**½ cup glacé red cherries, chopped**
⅓ cup sugar	**Glaze (*recipe follows*)**
2 tablespoons grated	**Red and green glacé cherries**

1. Preheat oven to moderate (350°). Grease cookie sheets.

(continued)

2. Sift flour, nutmeg and salt onto wax paper.

3. Beat together butter, sugar and orange rind in large bowl until light and fluffy. Beat in egg and liqueur until smooth. Stir in flour mixture until well blended. Gently stir in cherries. Using 1 tablespoon dough for each cookie, roll dough into 5-inch-long ropes. Shape into wreaths; pinch edges together to seal. Place on prepared cookie sheets, leaving about 2 inches between each.

4. Bake in preheated moderate oven (350°) for 10 to 12 minutes or until lightly browned around edges. Transfer cookies to wire racks to cool. Spread Glaze lightly over each cookie. Decorate with red and green glacé cherries.

Glaze: Combine $1^{1}/_{4}$ cups *sifted* 10X (confectioners') sugar, 1 tablespoon Grand Marnier liqueur, $^{1}/_{8}$ teaspoon ground nutmeg and 1 tablespoon milk in small bowl; mix until smooth and of good spreading consistency. Add additional milk as needed.

Spritz Cookie Sandwiches

Bake at 350° for 10 to 12 minutes.

Makes about $3^{1}/_{2}$ dozen sandwiches.

4 cups *sifted* all-purpose flour	1 egg
1 teaspoon baking powder	1 teaspoon vanilla
1 teaspoon salt	1 tablespoon grated orange rind
$1^{1}/_{2}$ cups (3 sticks) unsalted butter or margarine, softened	2 tablespoons unsweetened cocoa powder
1 cup sugar	Orange Butter Cream (recipe follows)

1. Preheat oven to moderate (350°).

2. Sift together flour, baking powder and salt onto wax paper.

3. Beat together butter and sugar in large bowl until light and fluffy. Beat in egg and vanilla. Stir in flour mixture until well mixed. Remove half of cookie dough to another bowl. Stir orange rind into half; stir cocoa powder into other half of dough.

4. Fill cookie press with orange dough. Press out onto ungreased cookie sheet into desired design, leaving about 2 inches between cookies.

5. Bake in preheated moderate oven (350°) for 10 to 12 minutes or until lightly browned around edges. Transfer cookies to wire racks to cool. Wash cookie press; fill with remaining chocolate dough. Press out as above, using same design. Bake and cool as above.

6. Sandwich an orange cookie together with a chocolate cookie with Orange Butter Cream or Chocolate-Orange Butter Cream. Decorate with a piping of Orange Butter Cream, if you wish.

Orange Butter Cream: Beat together $^{1}/_{4}$ cup ($^{1}/_{2}$ stick) butter and $^{1}/_{2}$ teaspoon grated orange rind in medium-size bowl until light and fluffy. Stir in 2 cups *unsifted* 10X (confectioners') sugar and 1 to 2

tablespoons orange juice until frosting is of good spreading consistency. To make Chocolate-Orange Butter Cream, remove half of frosting to small bowl; stir in 2 teaspoons unsweetened cocoa powder until well mixed. Makes enough to fill $3^{1}/_{2}$ dozen sandwich cookies.

Almond-Raspberry Sandwich Cookies

Bake at 350° for 8 to 10 minutes.

Makes about 2 dozen sandwich cookies.

$^{3}/_{4}$ cup ($1^{1}/_{2}$ sticks) unsalted butter or margarine, softened	1 egg white, slightly beaten
$^{1}/_{4}$ cup sugar	1 tablespoon finely chopped almonds
1 teaspoon almond extract	$1^{1}/_{2}$ teaspoons sugar
2 cups *sifted* all-purpose flour	$^{1}/_{2}$ cup seedless red raspberry preserves

1. Beat together butter, the $^{1}/_{4}$ cup sugar and almond extract in large bowl until well mixed. Stir in flour until well blended. Shape dough into ball. Cover and refrigerate until chilled, about 1 hour.

2. To roll out cookies, slightly dampen cookie sheet. Cover with wax paper; flour paper. Divide dough into thirds. Roll out, one-third at a time, on prepared sheet to $^{1}/_{8}$-inch thickness. Make cutouts in dough with 2-inch hexagonal or round cookie cutter, leaving dough intact on sheet. In center of half the cookies, make cutout for small opening with small cookie cutter (about $^{3}/_{4}$ inch). Place cookie sheet with dough in freezer for 5 minutes to stiffen.

3. Remove cookie sheet from freezer. Remove cookie cutouts from dough with spatula. Place on ungreased cookie sheets, leaving about $1^{1}/_{2}$ inches between cookies. Remove small cutouts from centers of half the cookies to make cookie rings.

4. Preheat oven to moderate (350°).

5. Repeat rolling and cutting with remaining thirds of dough. Press all scraps together and roll and cut as above.

6. Brush rings with egg white. Combine almonds and the $1^{1}/_{2}$ teaspoons sugar; sprinkle over egg white.

7. Bake in preheated moderate oven (350°) for 8 to 10 minutes or until cookies are a light golden brown. Remove cookies to wire rack to cool. Spread bottom of whole cookies with raspberry preserves. Top each with cookie ring.

Pictured opposite: Cookie Tiers, page 239; Italian Star, page 239; Grand Marnier Christmas Wreaths, page 239; Christmas Tree Cookies, page 242; Spritz Cookie Sandwich, page 240; Chocolate Pistachio Meringues, page 242; Almond-Raspberry Sandwich Cookies, page 240; Cottage Cheese Thumbprint, page 241.

Cottage Cheese Thumbprints

Bake at 400° for 12 to 14 minutes.

Makes about 8 dozen cookies.

1 container (16 ounces) cottage cheese
1 pound (4 sticks) unsalted butter or margarine, softened
1 teaspoon vanilla

4 cups *unsifted* all-purpose flour
1/2 teaspoon salt
Granulated sugar
1 cup seedless raspberry preserves

1. Press cottage cheese through wire sieve into large bowl, or puree in food processor. Add butter and vanilla; beat until light and fluffy. Stir in flour and salt until well blended. Shape into ball; refrigerate 30 minutes to firm.

2. Preheat oven to hot (400°). Spray cookie sheets with nonstick vegetable cooking spray.

3. Break off pieces of chilled dough; roll into balls the size of small walnut. Roll in sugar. Place on prepared sheets, leaving about 2 inches between. Make indentation in middle of each cookie with thumb. Fill each center with 1/2 teaspoon preserves.

4. Bake in preheated hot oven (400°) for 12 to 14 minutes or until cookies are lightly browned and crispy. Remove from sheets to wire racks to cool.

Chocolate Pistachio Meringues

Bake at 250° for 30 minutes.

Makes about 3 dozen cookies.

1/3 **cup pistachio nuts**	1/8 **teaspoon cream of**
1/4 **cup semisweet**	**tartar**
chocolate pieces	2/3 **cup superfine sugar**
2 **egg whites**	1/2 **teaspoon vanilla**

1. Preheat oven to slow (250°). Grease and flour 2 cookie sheets.
2. Combine pistachios and chocolate in blender or food processor. Cover; whirl until very finely chopped. Reserve.
3. Beat together egg whites and cream of tartar in small bowl until soft peaks form. Gradually beat in sugar, 1 tablespoon at a time, until mixture forms very stiff peaks. Fold in chocolate mixture and vanilla. Using a teaspoon, drop small mounds of meringue on prepared sheets, leaving 1 inch between.
4. Bake in preheated slow oven (250°) for 30 minutes or until firm but not browned. Let stand several minutes on cookie sheets. Loosen meringues carefully with small knife; transfer to wire rack to cool completely. Store in tightly covered container in a dry place.

Christmas Tree Cookies

Bake at 375° for 9 to 10 minutes.

Makes about 2 1/2 dozen 4-inch cookies.

2 1/2 **cups** *sifted* **all-**	1 **egg**
purpose flour	1 **teaspoon vanilla**
1 **teaspoon baking**	1/2 **teaspoon almond**
powder	**extract**
1/8 **teaspoon salt**	**Decorator Icing** *(recipe*
1/2 **cup (1 stick) butter**	*follows)*
or margarine,	**Silver candy decorator**
softened	**balls**
1 **cup sugar**	

1. Sift flour, baking powder and salt onto wax paper. Grease 2 cookie sheets.
2. Beat together butter and sugar in large bowl until light and fluffy. Beat in egg, vanilla and almond extract. Gradually stir in flour mixture to make a stiff dough. (If mixture is too dry, mix in 1 to 2 tablespoons milk.) Shape into a ball; wrap in wax paper and refrigerate until chilled, about 30 minutes.
3. Preheat oven to moderate (375°).
4. Divide dough into thirds. Roll out, one-third at a time, on floured surface to a 3/8 inch thickness. Cut with floured tree-shape cookie cutter. Place cookies on prepared cookie sheets, leaving about 2 inches between each.
5. Bake in preheated moderate oven (375°) for 9 to 10 minutes or until lightly browned around edges. Remove cookies from sheets to wire racks to cool.
6. Pipe Decorator Icing through a plain or fancy tip

onto cookies. Decorate with silver candy decorator balls.

Decorator Icing: Combine 1 egg white, 1 1/4 cups *sifted* 10X sugar and 1/8 teaspoon cream of tartar in small bowl. Beat at high speed until mixture forms stiff peaks. Tint light green with food coloring, if you wish.

Orangy Sugar Cookies

Bake at 375° for 8 minutes.

Makes 3 dozen large cookies.

2 1/4 **cups** *sifted* **all-**	2 **tablespoons lemon**
purpose flour	**juice**
1 **teaspoon baking**	**Corn syrup for garnish**
powder	*(optional)*
1/4 **teaspoon salt**	**Colored decorating**
1/2 **cup (1 stick) butter,**	**sugar and silver**
softened	**dragees for garnish**
2 **tablespoons grated**	*(optional)*
orange rind	**Decorator Frosting**
1 **cup sugar**	*(recipe follows)*
1/4 **cup orange juice**	

1. Sift together the flour, baking powder and salt onto wax paper.
2. Beat together the butter, orange rind and sugar with an electric mixer until fluffy. Stir in the orange and lemon juices. Stir in the dry ingredients until blended. Chill for several hours or overnight until firm.
3. Preheat the oven to moderate (375°).
4. Roll out the dough, one-third at a time, on a floured surface to a 1/6-inch thickness. Cut out with floured cookie cutters. Arrange, 1 inch apart, on ungreased cookie sheets.
5. Bake in the preheated moderate oven (375°) for 8 minutes or until set and lightly golden. Cool on wire racks.
6. If you wish, brush areas of the cookies with the corn syrup and sprinkle with the colored sugar and silver dragees. Decorate with white or colored Decorator Frosting.

Decorator Frosting: Combine 1 egg white, 1/2 teaspoon of cream of tartar and 1 cup of 10X (confectioners') sugar in a small bowl. Beat with an electric mixer until stiff but of a good spreading consistency. Cover with a damp towel until ready to use. If you wish, stir food coloring into small amounts of the frosting before using. Pipe or spread onto cookies.

Vertical rows from left to right: Orangy Sugar Cookies, page 242; Frozen Chocolate Cookie Cakes, page 243, alternating from top to bottom with Fruit and Nut Cookies, page 243; Brown Molasses Cookies, page 244; Frozen Chocolate Cookie Cakes, alternating with Fruit and Nut Cookies; Orangy Sugar Cookies; Danish Spritz Cookies, page 244.

Frozen Chocolate Cookie Cakes

Bake at 350° for 10 minutes.

Makes 2 dozen cookies.

1 cup *sifted* all-purpose flour	1/3 cup sugar
1/2 teaspoon baking soda	1 teaspoon vanilla
1/8 teaspoon salt	1 egg
1/2 cup (1 stick) butter	1 cup heavy cream
6 squares (1 ounce each) semisweet chocolate	2 tablespoons 10X (confectioners') sugar
1/4 cup light corn syrup	2 tablespoons orange-flavored liqueur
	Candy decorations for garnish *(optional)*

1. Preheat the oven to moderate (350°). Cover 2 large cookie sheets with aluminum foil; grease with vegetable shortening.
2. Sift together the flour, baking soda and salt onto wax paper.
3. Heat the butter, chocolate, corn syrup and sugar in a medium-size saucepan over low heat until the butter and chocolate are melted. Stir until smooth; cool for 5 minutes.
4. Stir the vanilla, egg and flour mixture into the chocolate mixture. Beat until smooth.
5. Drop the mixture by level teaspoons, 2 inches apart, onto the prepared cookie sheets. Spread with a small spatula into an even circle, 1 1/2 inches in diameter.
6. Bake in the preheated moderate oven (350°) for 10 minutes or until the cookies have flattened and become firm. Cool completely on foil on a wire rack.
7. Remove the cookies from the foil and match into stacks of three cookies each.
8. Beat the cream with the 10X sugar and liqueur in a small bowl until stiff. Spoon into a pastry bag fitted with a large star tip. Pipe a star onto each cookie in each of the stacks. Reassemble the stacks, pushing the cookies together until they are about 1/4 inch apart. Sprinkle the top star with the candy decorations, if you wish.
9. Place the cookies in a deep dish or pan. Cover tightly; freeze until ready to serve.

Fruit and Nut Cookies

Bake at 350° for 15 minutes.

Makes 4 1/2 dozen cookies.

1/2 cup dried apricots, diced	1 tablespoon lemon juice
1 cup boiling water	1/2 cup dairy sour cream
2 cups *sifted* all-purpose flour	1/4 cup diced candied orange peel
1 teaspoon baking powder	3/4 cup diced candied pineapple
1/2 teaspoon baking soda	2/3 cup chopped walnuts
2/3 cup butter, softened	Frosting *(recipe follows)*
1 cup sugar	Apricots, candied pineapple and walnuts for garnish *(optional)*
1 teaspoon grated orange rind	
1 teaspoon grated lemon rind	
2 eggs	

1. Combine the apricots and the 1 cup of boiling water in a small bowl. Set aside for 10 minutes. Drain well. Reserve.

(continued)

2. Preheat the oven to moderate (350°). Lightly grease 2 large cookie sheets with vegetable shortening.

3. Sift together the flour, baking powder and baking soda onto wax paper.

4. Beat together the butter, sugar, orange and lemon rinds, eggs and lemon juice in a large bowl with an electric mixer until fluffy.

5. Stir in the flour mixture and sour cream until blended. Fold in the apricots, candied orange and pineapple, and walnuts. Drop by tablespoonfuls, 1½ inches apart, onto the prepared cookie sheets.

6. Bake in the preheated moderate oven (350°) for 15 minutes or until the edges are golden and the centers feel firm to the touch. Remove to racks to cool completely.

7. Spread the cookies with the Frosting and garnish with more apricots, pineapple and walnuts, if you wish.

Frosting: Blend in a small bowl 1¼ cups 10X (confectioners') sugar, 1 tablespoon light corn syrup, ¼ teaspoon vanilla and 1½ hot water until blended and of a good spreading consistency.

Brown Molasses Cookies

Bake at 375° for 10 to 12 minutes.

Makes 6 dozen cookies.

4 cups *sifted* all-purpose flour	1 cup granulated sugar
1 teaspoon baking soda	1 egg
1 teaspoon baking powder	1 cup light molasses
⅓ cup butter, softened	Vanilla Decorating Icing *(recipe follows)*
2 tablespoons grated orange rind	Silver dragees for garnish

1. Sift together the flour, baking soda and baking powder onto wax paper.

2. Beat together the butter and orange rind in a large bowl with an electric mixer until creamy. Add the sugar and egg. Beat until light and fluffy. Beat in the molasses. Add the flour mixture and beat on low speed just until well blended.

3. Divide the dough in half, wrap in wax paper and refrigerate overnight.

4. When ready to make the cookies, preheat oven to moderate (375°). Lightly grease cookie sheets with vegetable shortening.

5. Roll out the dough on a lightly floured board to a ⅛-inch thickness. Cut out the cookies with floured cookie cutters. Arrange, 1½ inches apart, on the prepared cookie sheets.

6. Bake in the preheated moderate oven (375°) for 10 to 12 minutes or until firm. Remove the cookies from the cookie sheets to wire racks; cool completely.

7. Spoon the Vanilla Decorating Icing into a pastry bag fitted with the writing tip. Pipe decorations onto the cooled cookies. Decorate with the silver dragees.

Vanilla Decorating Icing: Blend in a bowl 1 box (1 pound) of 10X (confectioners') sugar with ½ teaspoon of salt, 1 teaspoon vanilla and 3 to 4 tablespoons milk to make a smooth, firm frosting.

Danish Spritz Cookies

Bake at 350° for 8 to 10 minutes.

Makes 4 dozen cookies.

1 cup (2 sticks) butter, softened	purpose flour
⅔ cup sugar	1 egg white, slightly beaten *(optional)*
3 egg yolks	Chocolate shot and colored decorating sugar for garnish *(optional)*
½ teaspoon almond extract	
2½ cups *sifted* all-	

1. Preheat oven to moderate (350°).

2. Beat together the butter, sugar, egg yolks and almond extract in a large bowl with an electric mixer until fluffy. Stir in the flour, blending well.

3. Spoon the dough into a pastry bag fitted with a star tip, or into a cookie press with a star plate. Press out the dough into 3-inch lengths, 1 inch apart, on ungreased cookie sheets. Gently push into wreaths, "S" shapes, candy canes or leave straight.

4. Bake in the preheated moderate oven (350°) for 8 to 10 minutes or until the edges are lightly browned.

5. If you wish, brush the warm cookies with egg white and sprinkle with the chocolate shot or colored sugar. Cool on wire racks.

Almond Tartlets

Bake at 325° for 20 to 25 minutes.

Makes 7 dozen cookies.

1 cup blanched almonds	⅔ cup sugar
1 cup (2 sticks) butter, softened	2 egg yolks
½ teaspoon almond extract	2 cups sifted all-purpose flour
½ teaspoon lemon extract	1 jar (12 ounces) currant jelly or apricot preserves

1. Grind the almonds in a food processor or blender to a fine powder.

2. Beat together the butter, almond extract, lemon extract, sugar and egg yolks in a large bowl with an electric mixer until light and fluffy. Add the ground almonds and flour. Beat at low speed until firm dough forms.

3. Preheat the oven to slow (325°).

4. Place small cupcake papers in 1-inch muffin pans (gem pans). Divide the dough into ¾-inch balls. Press one ball into each cupcake paper to cover the sides

Vertical rows from left to right: Pecan Wafers, page 246; Coconut Flake Cookies, page 246; Almond Tartlets, page 244; Almond Macaroons, page 246; Almond Tartlets; Coconut Flake Cookies; Small Sand Cookies, page 247.

Vertical rows from left to right: Frozen Chocolate Cookie Cakes, page 243, alternating from top to bottom with Fruit and Nut Cookies, page 243; Almond Macaroons, page 246; Brown Molasses Cookies, page 244; Almond Macaroons; Danish Spritz Cookies, page 244.

and bottom, hollowing out the center to form the tartlet.

5. Bake in the preheated slow oven (325°) for 20 to 25 minutes or until the edges are golden. Remove from the pans and cool completely on wire racks.

6. Spoon about ½ teaspoon the jelly or preserves into each tart. If the tartlets are to be stored for several days, do not fill them until ready to serve.

Microwave Directions

650 Watt Variable Power Microwave Oven

Directions: Prepare the tartlets as directed above, placing the papers in a 1-inch muffin pan to form the tartlets. Remove from the pan and arrange, just in papers, 12 at a time, in a circle with 3 in the center, on

(continued)

a microwave-safe baking sheet. Microwave, uncovered, at full power for 1 minute, 40 seconds. Remove to a cooling rack. Cool and fill as directed above. If you wish, the unbaked, formed tartlets may be frozen. Microwave, unthawed, as directed above when ready to use. Do not increase the time.

Almond Macaroons

Bake at 300° for 15 minutes.

Makes 2½ dozen cookies.

1½ cups blanched almonds, toasted	**Icing** *(recipe follows)*
1 cup sugar	**Red and green candied pineapple, sliced unblanched almonds for garnish** *(optional)*
2 large egg whites	
½ teaspoon almond extract	

1. Preheat the oven to slow (300°).
2. Grind the nuts to a fine powder in a food processor. Add the sugar; process just to combine.
3. Beat the whites until stiff, not dry. Fold in the almond mixture and extract until the mixture forms a smooth paste.
4. Cut 30 rectangles, 3½ × 1½ inches, from brown paper. Divide the dough into 30 pieces. Shape each into a 2-inch-long roll. Flatten onto the paper to make a 2½ × 1-inch oval. Place the papers on a cookie sheet.
5. Bake in the preheated slow oven (300°) for 15 minutes or until firm and dry on the surface. Cool completely on racks.
6. Frost the cookies with the Icing. Return to the cool oven just until the surface of the frosting is firm. Decorate with the optional garnishes.

Icing: Beat 1 egg white in a bowl until stiff. Add 1 cup 10X (confectioners') sugar, and 1 teaspoon lemon juice. Beat to a good spreading consistency.

Pecan Wafers

Bake at 350° for 12 to 15 minutes.

Makes 5 dozen cookies.

3 egg whites	**2 tablespoons** *unsifted* **all-purpose flour**
⅛ teaspoon salt	
1¼ cups firmly packed light brown sugar	**1 cup finely chopped pecans**
3 tablespoons melted butter	**Corn syrup, red and green sugar for garnish** *(optional)*
1 teaspoon vanilla	

1. Cover 2 large cookie sheets with aluminum foil; grease with vegetable shortening. Preheat the oven to moderate (350°).

2. Beat the egg whites with salt in a medium-size bowl with an electric mixer until stiff.
3. Combine the sugar, butter, vanilla and flour in a medium-size bowl. Fold the mixture into the egg whites just until uniformly combined. Fold in the nuts.
4. Drop by slightly rounded teaspoonfuls, 3 inches apart, on the prepared cookie sheets.
5. Bake in the preheated moderate oven (350°) for 12 to 15 minutes or until the centers and edges are evenly colored. Cool on foil. If not crisp when cooled, return to the oven for 2 to 3 minutes. Store in an airtight container.
6. If you wish, brush two parallel lines of the syrup in each direction on the cookies while warm. Sprinkle red sugar over one line in each direction, and green over the others.

Coconut Flake Cookies

Bake at 325° for 15 minutes.

Makes 5 dozen cookies.

1 cup *sifted* **all-purpose flour**	**extract**
⅛ teaspoon salt	**2 teaspoons grated orange rind**
⅛ teaspoon ground cinnamon	**2 teaspoons grated lemon rind**
⅛ teaspoon ground nutmeg	**2 egg whites, slightly beaten**
½ cup (1 stick) butter, softened	**2 cans (3½ ounces each) flaked coconut**
¼ cup firmly packed dark brown sugar	**Red and green candied pineapple, cut into ¼-inch cubes, for garnish**
1 egg yolk	
½ teaspoon vanilla	
¼ teaspoon almond	

1. Preheat the oven to slow (325°). Grease 2 large cookie sheets with vegetable shortening.
2. Sift together the flour, salt, cinnamon and nutmeg onto wax paper.
3. Beat together the butter, brown sugar, egg yolk, vanilla, almond extract, orange and lemon rinds in a medium-size bowl with an electric mixer until fluffy. Add the flour mixture; beat at low speed until smooth.
4. Drop the dough by half teaspoonfuls into the beaten whites; toss in the coconut to coat evenly. Place, 1 inch apart, on the prepared cookie sheets. Press 1 candied pineapple cube into the center of each cookie.
5. Bake in the preheated slow oven (325°) for 15 minutes or until the coconut is golden. Transfer to wire racks to cool.

Small Sand Cookies

Bake at 375° for 8 to 10 minutes.

Makes 4 dozen cookies.

1⅓ cups firmly packed dark brown sugar	all-purpose flour
	3 squares (1 ounce each) semisweet chocolate, melted
1 cup (2 sticks) butter, softened	Candy decorations for garnish (optional)
2 egg yolks	
2 cups sifted	

1. Beat together the brown sugar, butter and egg yolks in a large bowl with an electric mixer until fluffy. Gradually beat in the flour until smooth. Chill for several hours or overnight until firm.
2. Preheat the oven to moderate (375°). Grease 2 large cookie sheets with vegetable shortening.
3. Roll out the dough on a floured surface to a ⅙-inch thickness. Cut out with a floured 2-inch-round cookie cutter. Arrange, 1½ inches apart, on the prepared cookie sheets.
4. Bake in the preheated moderate oven (375°) for 8 to 10 minutes. Transfer from the cookie sheets to wire racks to cool.
5. When completely cool, drizzle the cookies with the melted chocolate. Sprinkle with the candy decorations, if you wish.

Candy

The first sweets ever made were probably dried fruits, nuts, seeds and spices mixed with a bit of honey. Egyptians, Arabs and Chinese all made confections with those ingredients. The word candy derives from the Persian word, qand. The Persians are also credited with spreading their knowledge of growing, refining and processing sugar cane.

It wasn't until the 14th century that sugar came into wide use in European confections. Only the wealthy could afford candy. Now that sugar is plentiful, you can make and enjoy candy in any of hundreds of variations. Making candy at home is not difficult. Just follow our helpful tips and enjoy the recipes for quick and easy candies.

Helpful Hints for Making Candy
● Don't attempt to make candies on a hot or humid day. Cool, dry days are best.
● Use a heavy saucepan for more even heat.

Remember that the candy might bubble up, so use a pan that's 2 to 3 times larger than the mixture.
● Don't substitute ingredients.
● Don't stir sugar mixture after it comes to a boil, unless it has butter, milk or molasses in it—then stir, or it might burn or boil over.
● To prevent sticky counters, have a bowl of hot water next to the stove to plunge utensils into as they are used.
● To clean saucepan and equipment, boil all together in a larger pot of water—hardened syrup will boil away in a few minutes.
● Sugar cooks in definite stages. It must be watched carefully and removed from heat at the right time. A candy thermometer is a must if you want perfect candy every time, although experienced cooks can tell when candy is done by observing a teaspoon of syrup dropped into cold water.

Brittle   A type of candy that is so hard it must be broken into small pieces for serving. Brittle is generally made with sugar, syrup and nuts which are boiled to a very high temperature and then poured onto a surface to cool and harden.

Almond Brittle

Makes about ¾ pound.

1 cup sugar	margarine
½ cup light corn syrup	1 cup whole unblanched almonds or peanuts
½ cup water	
¼ teaspoon salt	1 teaspoon baking soda
1 tablespoon butter or	

1. Butter a large cookie sheet.
2. Combine sugar, corn syrup, water, salt and butter in a large saucepan. Cook, stirring constantly, until sugar dissolves. Cover pan for 1 minute to allow the steam to wash down the sugar crystals that cling to side of pan, or wipe down the crystals with a damp cloth.
3. Uncover pan; insert candy thermometer. Cook, without stirring, until candy thermometer reaches 270° (soft crack stage, where syrup, when dropped into very cold water, separates into hard, but not brittle, threads).
4. Remove from heat; stir in almonds; return to heat. Continue cooking until candy thermometer reaches 300° (hard crack stage, where syrup, when dropped into very cold water, separates into threads that are hard and brittle).
5. Remove from heat; stir in baking soda. Let foaming syrup settle slightly, then quickly pour onto prepared cookie sheet and stretch out as thinly as possible with the aid of 2 forks. Cool completely, then break in pieces. Store up to 3 weeks in tightly-covered containers, separating the layers with foil or plastic wrap.

Temperatures for Candy

Type of Candy	Temperature on Candy Thermometer (at Sea Level) Degrees F.	Test	Description of Test
Sugar Syrup	230° to 234°	Thread	Syrup spins a 2-inch thread when dropped from fork or spoon.
Fondant, Fudge	234° to 240°	Soft ball	Syrup, when dropped into very cold water, forms a soft ball that flattens on removal from water.
Caramels	244° to 248°	Firm ball	Syrup, when dropped into very cold water, forms a firm ball that does not flatten on removal from water.
Divinity, Marshmallows, some Taffy	250° to 266°	Hard ball	Syrup, when dropped into very cold water, forms a ball that is hard enough to hold its shape, yet is still plastic.
Taffy	270° to 290°	Soft crack	Syrup, when dropped into very cold water, separates into threads that are hard but not brittle.
Brittle, Glacé	300° to 310°	Hard crack	Syrup, when dropped into very cold water, separates into threads that are hard and brittle.

Ginger Sesame Brittle

Makes 1 1/2 pounds.

1 1/2 cups sesame seeds (about 3 jars, 2 3/4 ounces each)
1 cup sugar
1 cup dark corn syrup
1/4 cup water
2 tablespoon butter or margarine
1 teaspoon baking soda
1/4 cup finely chopped crystallized ginger

1. Toast sesame seeds in a skillet over moderate heat, stirring occasionally.
2. Butter a jelly-roll pan or other rimmed baking sheet.
3. Combine sugar, corn syrup, water and butter in a large saucepan. Bring to boiling, stirring constantly. Lower heat and cook, without stirring, until mixture reaches 300° on a candy thermometer or until a small amount of syrup, when dropped into very cold water, separates into threads that are hard and brittle.
4. Remove from heat; stir in sesame seeds, baking soda and ginger. Pour into prepared pan, spreading quickly with spatula to fill pan. Cool, then break into pieces. Store in tightly-covered containers with foil or plastic wrap between layers.

Peanut Brittle

Makes 2 3/4 pounds.

3 cups sugar
1 1/4 cups water
1/2 cup light corn syrup
3 tablespoons butter or margarine
1 pound Spanish peanuts
1 teaspoon baking soda
1 tablespoon water
1 1/2 teaspoons vanilla

1. Butter 2 large cookie sheets.
2. Combine sugar, water and corn syrup in a large, heavy saucepan. Bring to boiling over medium heat, stirring constantly.
3. Boil mixture, without stirring, until candy thermometer registers 270° (soft crack stage). Remove from heat. Add butter and peanuts.
4. Continue cooking until candy thermometer registers 300°. (A teaspoonful of syrup will separate into brittle threads when dropped in cold water.) Remove from heat. Mix baking soda with the 1 tablespoon water; add to hot candy with vanilla.
5. When bubbles subside, pour candy onto the prepared cookie sheets as thinly as possible. Cool;

break into pieces. Store in airtight container with wax paper between the layers.

Bourbon Balls

Makes 3 dozen confections.

1 package (6 ounces) semisweet chocolate pieces	vanilla wafer cookies (about 36)
3 tablespoons light corn syrup	1 cup finely chopped pecans
1/4 cup bourbon	1 container (4 ounces) chocolate sprinkles or jimmies
1/2 cup sugar	
1 1/4 cups crushed	

1. Melt chocolate pieces in top of a double boiler over simmering water; remove from heat. Blend in corn syrup and bourbon; stir in sugar, crushed vanilla wafers and pecans.
2. Use hands to roll mixture in balls, 1 rounded teaspoonful at a time. Roll balls in chocolate sprinkles to generously coat, pressing firmly as you roll. Place in a jelly-roll pan; cover; chill several hours.

Butterscotch
Flavoring made from cooking brown sugar with butter. It's also the name of a popular hard candy, possibly of Scottish origin.

Butterscotch Patties

Little wafers of golden butterscotch.

Makes 8 dozen 1-inch patties.

2 cups sugar	1/4 cup milk
3/4 cup dark corn syrup	1/3 cup butter or margarine
1/4 cup water	

1. Lightly butter 3 large cookie sheets.
2. Combine sugar, corn syrup, water and milk in a medium-size heavy saucepan. Bring to boiling over medium heat, stirring constantly. Cook, stirring often, to 260° on a candy thermometer; add butter.
3. Cook, stirring constantly, to 280° on a candy thermometer. (A teaspoonful of syrup will separate into threads that are hard but not brittle when dropped in cold water.) Remove from heat.
4. Drop hot syrup from tip of teaspoon onto cookie sheets to form 1-inch patties; or pour into a 9 × 9 × 2-inch pan and, when almost set, mark into small squares. When firm, turn out and break apart.

Marshmallows

Candy-pan magic! Simple ingredients unfold before your eyes into fluffy white confections.

Makes about 4 dozen.

1/2 cup cornstarch	1/2 cup granulated sugar
1/2 cup *sifted* 10X (confectioners') sugar	1/3 cup water
2 envelopes unflavored gelatin	2/3 cup light corn syrup
	1/2 teaspoon vanilla

1. Combine cornstarch and 10X sugar in a small bowl. Butter an 8 × 8 × 2-inch baking pan; sprinkle with some of the cornstarch mixture. (You will be using all the mixture eventually.)
2. Combine gelatin and granulated sugar in a small saucepan; stir in the water. Heat mixture over low heat, stirring constantly, until sugar and gelatin are dissolved.
3. Pour gelatin mixture into a large bowl; add corn syrup and vanilla. Beat with electric mixer on high speed for 15 minutes or until mixture is thick and fluffy. (A stand-up mixer, if you have one, makes the job easier.)
4. Pour marshmallow mixture into prepared pan; smooth top surface with a spatula. Refrigerate overnight to firm.
5. Sieve some cornstarch mixture over the chilled marshmallow mixture. Loosen mixture from sides of pan and turn out onto a cookie sheet sprinkled with cornstarch mixture. Marshmallows will be sticky until thoroughly coated.
6. Cut marshmallow mixture into 1-inch squares with a large sharp knife. Cut straight down in one motion rather than pulling the knife through. Roll each marshmallow in remaining cornstarch mix; dry on wire racks. Will stay moist in a tightly covered container about 3 weeks.

Orange Sugared Pecans

Makes 2 dozen pecan clusters.

1 1/2 cups sugar	concentrate
1/4 cup water	1/2 teaspoon grated orange rind
3 tablespoons thawed, frozen orange-juice	2 cups pecan halves

1. Combine sugar, water and orange-juice concentrate in a medium-size saucepan. Bring to boiling over medium heat, stirring constantly.
2. Boil slowly, without stirring, to 240° on a candy thermometer or until a small amount of mixture dropped into cold water forms a semi-firm ball. Remove from heat.
3. Add orange rind and pecans. Stir until syrup begins to look cloudy. Drop by teaspoonsfuls into clusters on wax paper. Cool. Store in airtight container.

Orange Candied Nuts

Bake at 250° for 5 minutes, then for 1 hour.

Makes 3 cups.

3 cups walnut or pecan halves	¼ cup grated orange rind
2 tablespoons butter or margarine	1 teaspoon grated lemon rind
3 tablespoons orange juice	½ cup light corn syrup
½ cup sugar	

1. Place nuts in a 13 × 9 × 2-inch baking pan. Heat in a slow oven (250°) for 5 minutes.
2. Melt butter in a medium-size saucepan. Stir in orange juice, ¼ cup of the sugar, orange and lemon rinds and corn syrup, stirring constantly. Bring to boiling over medium heat. Boil, without stirring, for 5 minutes. Pour syrup over nuts, stirring constantly, to coat evenly.
3. Bake in a slow oven (250°) for 1 hour, stirring several times. Sprinkle with the remaining ¼ cup sugar; do not stir. Immediately spread out onto greased cookie sheets and separate into individual nuts with two forks; cool. Store in a tightly covered container for up to 3 weeks.

Easy Chocolate Peanut Clusters

Makes about 2 dozen.

2 packages (4 ounces each) sweet cooking chocolate	condensed milk
⅔ cup sweetened	1 cup unsalted peanuts, lightly toasted

1. Melt chocolate in top of double boiler over hot, not boiling, water; stir until smooth. Remove from heat; blend in condensed milk and peanuts.
2. Drop by teaspoonfuls onto cookie sheet. Let stand at room temperature until firm, about 2 hours. Store in tightly covered container.

Rocky Roads

Simple and delicious.

Makes about 1½ pounds.

1 pound rich milk chocolate, coarsely chopped	pecans or walnuts
1 cup broken	1 cup miniature marshmallows

1. Melt chocolate in top of double boiler over hot, not boiling, water. Stir mixture until smooth. Remove from heat; spoon half the mixture into an 8 × 8 × 2-inch foil-lined pan; spread to edges. Return remaining chocolate to the heat.

2. Sprinkle nuts and marshmallows over chocolate in pan. Spoon the remaining chocolate over top. Let stand at room temperature until firm.
3. Turn out onto cutting board; remove foil. Cut candy into pieces. Candy will stay fresh several weeks if left in one piece and wrapped in foil.

Basket of "Fruit" Candies

Makes 1 pound.

1 packages (3 ounces) cream cheese, softened	3 drops almond extract
3 to 3½ cups *sifted* 10X (confectioners') sugar	Red and yellow food coloring
	Whole cloves and green gumdrops

Mix cream cheese and sugar in medium-size bowl with wooden spoon until well blended. Stir in almond extract. Divide in thirds. Color one part pink, one part yellow. Mix yellow and red coloring to make the third part orange. Shape into strawberries, bananas and oranges. Roll oranges and strawberries on smallest holes of a grater for texture. Insert a clove into each orange; slice gum drops and use as tops for strawberries. Refrigerate.

French Chocolate Truffles

A classic French sweet, and a specialty in northern Italy, where they are served in little fluted cups with pungent espresso.

Makes about 2 dozen.

3 squares unsweetened chocolate	(confectioners') sugar
⅓ cup butter or margarine, softened	4 egg yolks
1¼ cups *sifted* 10X	1 teaspoon vanilla Cocoa, coconut or ground nuts

1. Melt chocolate in top of double boiler over hot, not boiling, water; cool slightly.
2. Combine butter and 10X sugar in medium-size bowl; beat until smooth. Beat in egg yolks, one at a time. Stir in the cooled chocolate and the vanilla. Chill until mixture is firm enough to handle.
3. Shape into 1-inch balls. Roll in cocoa, coconut or nuts. Place on cookie sheet to set. Store in tightly covered container in refrigerator for not more than 1 week.

Caramel
This can either be a chewy candy or simply sugar that has been heated until it melts into a brown syrup. Caramel syrup is used to coat molds for custards or flans. Caramel candy is made of sugar, cream, butter and flavoring.

Peanutty Caramel Corn, page 592.

Glazed Walnuts

A thin crackly candy coats the nuts, making them such good nibbles.

Makes 5 cups.

2 cups sugar
1 cup water

1 package (1 pound)
shelled walnuts

1. Combine sugar and water in a small, heavy saucepan. Heat slowly, stirring constantly, until sugar dissolves, then cook rapidly, without stirring, to 300° on a candy thermometer. (Or until a spoonful of syrup poured into a cup of cold water forms hard, brittle threads that break when pressed.)
2. Remove saucepan from heat. Add walnuts to syrup, $1/2$ cup at a time, and toss to coat well. (If syrup begins to harden, return saucepan to a very low heat.)
3. Remove nuts from syrup with two forks and place on wire racks lined with wax paper or foil. Cool until glaze is firm. Store in airtight metal tins or containers.

Marzipan   One of the oldest European

confections, marzipan is made from almond paste. Blanched almonds are very finely ground and refined with the addition of sugar or a sweetener and water. Then 10X (confectioners') sugar is added with flavoring and coloring. Traditionally, marzipan is molded into various fruit and vegetable shapes or it can be shaped into animals or flowers.

Fondant   A simple candy made by cooking sugar

with water, flavoring it, then cooling and kneading until it solidifies. Of French origin, fondant can be shaped, used as a coating or as the center of dipped candies. No-cook fondants are shortcut versions of such candies.

Basic Cooked Fondant

Makes 1 pound.

2 cups sugar
$1/8$ teaspoon salt
2 tablespoons light

corn syrup
$1^1/4$ cups water

1. Combine sugar, salt, corn syrup and water in a large heavy saucepan. Heat, stirring constantly, until sugar dissolves and mixture comes to boiling. Wrap a fork with damp paper toweling; wipe sugar crystals from side of pan as mixture cooks.
2. Reduce heat to medium and cook, without stirring, to 240° on a candy thermometer. (Syrup forms a soft ball when dropped in cold water.)
3. Pour syrup onto a dampened, large platter or marble slab, if you have one. Do not scrape pan. Cool to 110° or until mixture feels lukewarm.
4. Beat mixture with a broad-bladed spatula or a new stiff-bladed putty knife (from a paint store), until white and creamy, scraping and lifting mixture from the

(continued)

edge toward the center, turning the platter occasionally. Continue beating until fondant becomes very white and stiffens.

5. Knead fondant until it softens and is smooth; do not overknead. Pack into a plastic refrigerator container; cover. Refrigerate 2 days to ripen. Shape as follows.

Peppermint Patties: Let ripened fondant warm to room temperature. Knead $1/2$ teaspoon peppermint extract and 4 drops red food coloring into the fondant until the color is evenly pink. Shape into small balls; place on wax paper, 2 inches apart and flatten with the back of a glass to form patties. Let dry about 1 hour. Store in layers, separated by wax paper, in a tightly covered container. Makes about 4 dozen.

Fondant Logs: Let the ripened fondant warm to room temperature. Then knead $1/4$ cup very finely chopped walnuts or almonds into fondant; flavor with 1 teaspoon vanilla or rum flavoring or extract. Shape into $11/2 \times 3/4$-inch logs. Let dry 1 hour on wax paper. Store in layers, separated by wax paper, in a tightly covered container. Makes about 4 dozen.

Bonbons: Melt fondant in top of a double boiler over hot, not boiling, water. Divide into 3 portions, tinting green, pink and yellow. Prepare Maple Nut Creams *(recipe follows)*, rolling mixture into $1/2$-inch balls. Dip in melted fondant; place on wax paper to set. Store in tightly covered container. Makes about 2 pounds.

Maple Nut Creams: Prepare Basic Fondant, working 1 teaspoon maple flavoring and $1/2$ cup finely chopped walnuts into the ripened fondant. Roll mixture into $1/2$-inch balls. Store in tightly covered container. Makes about 1 pound.

Stuffed Fruits: Stuff pitted dates or dried apricots with a small ball of Basic Fondant.

No-Cook Fondant Confections

Here's an easy fondant that can be flavored and shaped in numerous ways.

Makes about $11/4$ pounds.

$1/4$ **cup ($1/2$ stick) butter, softened**	**mint extract**
$1/4$ **cup light corn syrup**	**OR: 2 teaspoons grated orange rind plus 2 tablespoons**
$1/4$ **teaspoon salt**	**orange juice**
$11/4$ **to $11/2$ packages (1 pound each) 10X (confectioners') sugar, *sifted***	**OR: two teaspoons grated lemon rind plus 2 tablespoons lemon juice**
1 teaspoon vanilla OR: $1/2$ teaspoon	**Assorted food coloring**

1. Combine butter, corn syrup and salt in a medium-size bowl. Stir in 2 cups of the 10X sugar, vanilla or other flavoring. Tint with drops of desired food coloring. Stir in enough of the remaining sugar to make the fondant stiff yet firm enough to knead without crumbling.

2. Knead in enough additional sugar by hand until smooth and firm enough to hold its shape. Shape into balls or patties or follow variations below. (When shaping, keep unused portions covered with plastic wrap to keep moist.) Place shaped fondant on cookie sheet to dry and become firm. Store in airtight container in refrigerator or at cool room temperature.

Mint Pinwheels: Prepare fondant with mint extract but do not add coloring yet. Divide fondant in half. Into half, knead in green food coloring. With rolling pin, roll each half separately between two pieces of wax paper to an 8-inch square. Remove top paper. Place white layer over green. Press firmly together. Cut square in half to form two 8×4-inch rectangles. Starting from long edge, roll up fondant, jelly-roll style. Wrap rolls in wax paper; chill until firm. Remove paper; cut each crosswise into $1/4$-inch slices. Reshape into perfect rounds; let dry.

Miniature Oranges: Prepare fondant with orange rind and juice. Tint with yellow and red food coloring to get orange color. Toast about 1 cup ($41/2$ ounces) shelled small hazelnuts in a moderate oven (350°) for 15 minutes or until golden; cool; rub off skins. Wrap a small amount of fondant around each nut to form a 1-inch orange. When dry, dip toothpick into green food coloring and make stem ends on them.

Orange Fondant Dates: Prepare fondant with orange rind and juice. Tint with yellow and red food coloring to get orange color. From 2 cartons (10 ounces each) pitted dates, cut each date lengthwise halfway. Form small pieces of fondant into logs; insert into each date. Let dry and store in a single layer.

Miniature Lemons: Prepare fondant with lemon rind and juice. Tint yellow. Toast 1 cup (5 ounces) shelled blanched whole almonds in a moderate oven (350°) for 15 minutes or until golden; cool. Wrap a small amount of fondant over each almond; mold into lemon shape. When dry, dip toothpick into green food coloring and make stem ends on them.

Molasses Chips

Makes about $13/4$ pounds.

2 cups sugar	**1 tablespoon butter or margarine**
$3/4$ **cup light corn syrup**	$3/4$ **cup water**
$1/4$ **cup molasses**	

1. Combine sugar, corn syrup, molasses, butter and water in a large saucepan. Cook, stirring constantly, until sugar dissolves. Cover pan for 1 minute to allow the steam to wash down the sugar crystals that cling to side of pan or wipe down the crystals with a damp cloth.

2. Uncover pan; insert candy thermometer. Cook, without stirring, until candy thermometer reaches 266° (hard ball stage, where syrup, when dripped into very cold water, forms a ball in the fingers that is hard enough to hold a shape, yet still plastic).

3. Remove from heat; pour syrup onto two well-buttered jelly-roll pans or a very large platter. Cool candy for 5 minutes, then fold edges to center.
4. When candy is cool enough to handle, butter hands and pull candy into a rope. Pull rope, folding it back on itself as you pull, 25 times. When candy loses its transparent appearance but is still "plastic," knead it like bread dough on a well-buttered surface. Flatten candy, then stretch it from one side into a long ribbon-like strip. Cut the ribbon into 1 1/2-inch pieces.
5. Wrap each piece of candy separately in foil or plastic wrap. Store 2 to 3 weeks in a tightly covered container.

Molasses Coconut Chews

Tender little nuggets bursting with coconut, coated with chocolate.

Makes 2 1/2 pounds.

1 1/4 cups sugar	3 cans (4 ounces
2/3 cup light corn	each) shredded
syrup	coconut (about
1/3 cup molasses	4 cups)
2 tablespoons butter	Chocolate Coating
or margarine	(*recipe follows*)

1. Combine sugar, corn syrup, molasses and butter in a large saucepan. Cook, stirring constantly, until sugar dissolves. Cover pan for 1 minute to allow the steam to wash down the sugar crystals that cling to side of pan or wipe crystals with damp cloth.
2. Uncover pan; insert candy thermometer. Cook, without stirring, until candy thermometer reaches 266° (hard ball stage, where syrup, when dropped in very cold water, forms a ball in the fingers that is hard enough to hold a shape, yet still plastic).
3. Remove from heat; stir in the coconut. Pour mixture into a well-buttered 13 × 9 × 2-inch pan. Cool until lukewarm or comfortable to handle.
4. Form candy into 1/2-inch balls, then cool completely before coating.
Chocolate Coating: Melt 1 large package (12 ounces) semisweet chocolate pieces in top of double boiler over hot, *not boiling*, water. Dip each ball in chocolate with a fork; tap off excess on edge of pan. Cool on wax paper until firm. Store up to 2 to 3 weeks in refrigerator.

Chocolate Rum Raisin Mounds

Makes 4 dozen.

1 box (15 ounces)	semisweet
seedless raisins	chocolate pieces
(3 cups)	1 tablespoon light
1 cup light or dark rum	corn syrup
1 package (12 ounces)	

1. Place raisins in a large plastic food bag; add rum;
secure bag. Let raisins soak for 3 hours. Drain raisins by placing in a sieve; do not press. Use liquid in fruit compote or spoon over ice cream.
2. Combine chocolate pieces and corn syrup in top of double boiler. Place over hot, not boiling, water until chocolate melts; stir occasionally. Remove from heat.
3. Fold raisins into melted chocolate, coating well. Drop by heating teaspoonfuls onto wax paper. Chill until firm. Store in refrigerator. When packing for gift giving, place wax paper between layers to prevent sticking.

Sesame Crunch

These candies are easy to make using honey, sesame seeds and brown sugar.

Makes 1 pound (52 pieces).

2 cups sesame seeds	1/2 teaspoon ground
(about 12 ounces)	ginger
1/2 cup honey	1/2 teaspoon ground
1/2 cup firmly packed	cinnamon
light brown sugar	1/4 teaspoon salt

1. Heat sesame seeds in a large skillet over medium heat until lightly browned, stirring frequently. Remove to a bowl; wipe skillet clean.
2. Combine honey, sugar, ginger, cinnamon and salt in same skillet. Heat to boiling over medium heat, stirring constantly. Boil 2 minutes.
3. Butter or coat a 10 3/4 × 7-inch pan with vegetable cooking spray. Stir seeds into syrup; pour into pan. Spread candy to an even layer with buttered metal spatula. Cool on wire rack 15 minutes. Lift out of pan to board.
4. Cut candy with a large knife into 4 lengthwise strips. Cut each strip crosswise into thirteen 3/4-inch pieces. When pieces are firm, wrap individually in plastic wrap or store in single layer in airtight container.

Taffy
Candy made by boiling sugar with water and molasses or corn syrup until the proper consistency is reached, then pulling the mixture until it is light and airy.

Vanilla Taffy

Makes 1/2 pound.

1 cup sugar	tartar
2/3 cup light corn	1 teaspoon vanilla
syrup	1 tablespoon butter or
1/2 cup water	margarine
1/4 teaspoon cream of	

1. Butter a large platter or jelly-roll pan.

(continued)

2. Combine sugar, corn syrup, water and cream of tartar in medium-size heavy saucepan. Bring to boiling over medium heat, stirring constantly.

3. Boil mixture, without stirring, until candy thermometer registers 266°. (A teaspoonful of syrup will form a hard ball when dropped in cold water.) Remove from heat; stir in vanilla and butter.

4. Pour onto prepared platter or jelly-roll pan. Let candy stand until cool enough to handle.

5. Butter hands. Gather up candy; pull between hands until it becomes satiny and light in color. Pull into long strips; twist. Cut into 1-inch pieces with scissors. To store, wrap each candy in plastic wrap and place in an airtight container.

Praline

Praline   A candy made of either almonds or pecans coated with a sugar mixture. It is made by boiling the nuts with sugar until brown and then pouring the mixture onto an oiled surface where it is allowed to cool and harden. It is then crushed to a powder and used as a topping or to flavor other desserts. Originally, praline was an almond candy made in France. When French colonists settled in Louisiana in the 1700's, they used native pecans (in place of almonds) and brown sugar, then spooned the candy into patties.

Almond Praline

Makes 1½ cups.

½ **cup whole blanched almonds**	2 **tablespoons water**
½ **cup sugar**	⅛ **teaspoon cream of tartar**

1. Spread almonds on a cookie sheet. Toast in a moderate oven (350°) for 10 minutes or until golden.

2. Combine sugar, water and cream of tartar in small skillet; heat to boiling, stirring constantly. Cook over medium heat until sugar begins to caramelize and turn deep amber. Stir in almonds. Turn out onto lightly buttered cookie sheet. Cool completely.

3. Break praline into small pieces. Whirl in electric blender, half at a time, until finely pulverized. Store in tightly covered jar.

New Orleans Pralines

Makes about 1⅓ pounds (24 pieces).

2 **cups sugar**	¼ **teaspoon salt**
⅔ **cup milk**	½ **teaspoon vanilla**
⅓ **cup dark corn syrup**	1 **cup pecan pieces (about 4 ounces)**

1. Combine sugar, milk, corn syrup and salt in a medium-size heavy saucepan. Heat to boiling over medium heat, stirring constantly.

2. Continue cooking without stirring until candy thermometer registers 238°F. (A teaspoonful of syrup dropped into cold water forms a soft ball which flattens on removal.)

3. Remove pan from heat. Let stand on wire rack until temperature cools to 110°. Add vanilla. Beat with a clean wooden spoon until mixture begins to thicken.

4. Stir in pecans. Drop by teaspoonfuls onto waxed paper to 2-inch flat patties. Let set; remove; store in airtight container with paper between layers.

Neapolitan Jellies

Jewel-bright colors in this easy, tender tri-layered confection.

Makes about 8 dozen.

6 **envelopes unflavored gelatin**	**Marshmallows** (*recipe follows*)
4 **cups sugar**	⅓ **cup green crème de menthe liqueur**
2⅓ **cups water**	**Granulated sugar**
⅓ **cup red cinnamon candies**	

1. Combine 3 envelopes of the gelatin and 2 cups of the sugar in a large saucepan. Stir in 1⅓ cups of the water. Cook mixture over medium heat, stirring constantly, until mixture comes to boiling. Stir in cinnamon candies until they dissolve. Simmer over low heat 20 minutes. Remove from heat.

2. Spoon off foam from surface. Pour jelly into a well-oiled 13 × 9 × 2-inch pan. Chill until firm, about 2 hours.

3. Prepare Marshmallows recipe following *only* steps 2 and 3. Wipe off any excess oil from surface of jelly layer with paper toweling; spread marshmallow evenly over jelly layer. Chill until firm, about 2 hours.

4. Combine the remaining 3 envelopes gelatin and 2 cups sugar in large saucepan. Stir in 1 cup water. Cook mixture over medium heat, stirring constantly, until mixture boils. Stir in crème de menthe. Simmer over low heat 20 minutes. Skim off any foam; cool jelly long enough so that it can be spooned carefully over marshmallow layer without melting it completely. You will get some blending in of the layers. Chill until firm.

5. Run spatula around sides of candy to loosen. Sprinkle top with sugar to coat evenly. Place inverted cookie sheet over pan; holding pan and sheet, turn to unmold candy. Cut into 4 strips lengthwise by pressing knife down through candy but do not pull or draw knife. Cut strips crosswise into ½-inch pieces, wiping knife clean occasionally. Roll candies in sugar. Place on wire rack over wax paper to dry overnight. When dry, store in tightly covered container.

Pictured opposite: Jelly Candies (in lower section of glass), page 256; Neapolitan Jellies, page 254; Quick and Easy Fudge, page 256.

Jelly Candies

Pretty, light-textured candies with a tart-sweet flavor.

Makes 40 candies.

3 envelopes unflavored gelatin	grated orange rind
2 cups sugar	1 tablespoon grated lemon rind
1 cup water	1/4 cup orange juice
8 drops yellow food coloring	2 tablespoons lemon juice
2 tablespoons	Sugar for coating

1. Combine gelatin and sugar in a large saucepan; stir in water. Heat to boiling over medium heat, stirring constantly. Lower heat; boil mixture slowly for 20 minutes.
2. Remove pan from heat; add food coloring, orange and lemon rinds and juices. Stir for 2 to 3 minutes, then strain into a well-oiled 9 × 5 × 3-inch pan. Refrigerate until firm, about 4 hours.
3. Loosen around sides with a spatula; turn out onto lightly oiled cookie sheet. Cut into 1-inch cubes by pressing a large sharp knife down through jelly—do not draw through.
4. Toss jelly squares in granulated sugar to coat. Dry overnight on wire racks. Store in tightly covered container. Will stay moist for approximately two weeks at room temperature.

Fudge

A popular creamy candy. Chocolate is the favorite flavor, but fudge can be light-colored and vanilla-flavored. *Penuche* is a fudge made with brown sugar.

Quick and Easy Fudge

A foolproof fudge that turns out right in any kind of weather.

Makes about 2 1/2 pounds.

3 1/3 cups sugar	3 cups miniature marshmallows
1 1/3 cups evaporated milk	1 cup chopped walnuts
1 package (12 ounces) semisweet chocolate pieces	1 cup candied red cherries, quartered

1. Line an 8 × 8 × 2-inch pan with foil; butter foil.
2. Combine sugar and milk in a medium-size saucepan. Cook over medium heat, stirring constantly, until sugar is dissolved and mixture comes to boiling. Boil, stirring constantly, 5 minutes.
3. Remove from heat; beat in chocolate and marshmallows with wooden spoon. Stir until mixture thickens; stir in nuts and cherries. Pour into prepared pan; let stand until cool and firm.
4. Turn out onto cutting board; remove foil; cut fudge into 1-inch squares. Store in tightly covered container.

Peanut Butter and Chocolate Layered Fudge

Makes about 2 pounds.

1 package (8 ounces) semisweet chocolate squares	chopped peanuts (dry roasted or cocktail peanuts)
1 can (14 ounces) sweetened condensed milk (not evaporated)	1 cup peanut butter chips (1/2 of a 12-ounce bag)
1/2 cup coarsely	1 teaspoon butter

1. Melt 7 squares of the chocolate with half of the sweetened condensed milk (about 2/3 cup) over low heat in small saucepan; stir in peanuts. Quickly spread on bottom of wax paper-lined 8-inch square pan.
2. Melt peanut butter chips with remaining sweetened condensed milk over low heat in another small saucepan; spread over chocolate mixture.
3. Melt remaining 1 square of chocolate with the butter and quickly drizzle over the peanut butter layer with spoon or wax paper cone. Chill 2 hours or until firm. Turn out onto cutting board; peel off wax paper. Cut into squares. Store tightly covered in refrigerator for up to 3 weeks.

Fabulous Fudge

Makes about 1 1/4 pounds.

2 cups sugar	(2/3 cup)
1/8 teaspoon salt	2 tablespoons light corn syrup
2 squares unsweetened chocolate	2 tablespoons butter or margarine
1 small can evaporated milk	1/2 teaspoon vanilla

1. Combine sugar, salt, chocolate, evaporated milk and corn syrup in a heavy saucepan. Heat and stir just until the sugar dissolves and chocolate melts. Remove spoon; insert candy thermometer.
2. Cook mixture rapidly, without stirring, to 238°. (Syrup forms a soft ball when dropped in cold water.) Remove from heat. Add butter or margarine and vanilla (no stirring yet), then let cool on a wire rack to 110°. Bottom of the pan should feel lukewarm.
3. Beat 10 to 15 minutes or until fudge starts to thicken and lose its glossiness; pour the fudge into a buttered 8 × 8 × 2-inch pan. Let stand until set—only 2 to 3 minutes; cut at once in smooth neat squares. Store in tightly covered container.

Old-fashioned Chocolate Fudge

A marvelous, melt-in-your-mouth chocolate fudge recipe.

Makes about 2 pounds.

1¹/₂ cups milk	3 tablespoons light
4 squares	corn syrup
unsweetened	¹/₄ teaspoon salt
chocolate	1¹/₄ teaspoons vanilla
(4 ounces)	3 tablespoons butter
4 cups sugar	or margarine

1. Combine milk and chocolate in medium-size heavy saucepan; cook over low heat until chocolate is melted. Add sugar, corn syrup and salt and cook, stirring constantly, to boiling.
2. Cook without stirring to 234° on a candy thermometer. (A teaspoonful of syrup will form a soft ball when dropped in cold water.) Remove from heat at once. Add vanilla and butter, but do not stir in.
3. Leave thermometer in pan while fudge is cooling. Let mixture cool to 110°. When cool enough, you can rest bottom of pan comfortably on hand. Beat with wooden spoon until mixture thickens and just begins to lose its gloss. Mixture will lighten in color as you beat. Beating will take about 15 minutes.
4. Spread in a buttered 8 × 8 × 2-inch pan. Let stand until set and cool; cut into squares.

Golden Fudge

Makes about 1¹/₂ pounds.

3 cups sugar	1 cup evaporated milk
¹/₄ cup light corn	1¹/₂ cup water
syrup	2 teaspoons vanilla
3 tablespoons butter	Candied green and red
or margarine	cherries, slivered
¹/₂ teaspoon salt	

1. Combine sugar, corn syrup, butter or margarine, salt, evaporated milk and water in a medium-size heavy saucepan.

2. Heat, stirring constantly, to boiling, then cook rapidly, stirring several times, to 238° on a candy thermometer. (Syrup forms a soft ball when dropped in cold water.) Remove from heat at once. Add vanilla, but do not stir in.
3. Let mixture cool in pan on rack to 110° or until bottom of pan feels lukewarm; beat 10 to 15 minutes or just until fudge starts to thicken and lose its glossiness.
4. Spread in a buttered 8 × 8 × 2-inch pan. Let stand 2 to 3 minutes or just until set; cut into squares. Decorate each with the slivered cherries. Let stand until firm.

Creamy Penuche

Makes about 2 pounds.

2 cups firmly packed	2 tablespoons butter
light brown sugar	or margarine
1 cup granulated	³/₄ cup milk
sugar	¹/₈ teaspoon salt
¹/₄ cup dark corn	1 teaspoon vanilla
syrup	

1. Combine sugars, corn syrup, butter or margarine, milk and salt in a medium-size heavy saucepan.
2. Heat, stirring constantly, to boiling, then cook, stirring several times, to 238° on a candy thermometer. (A teaspoonful of syrup will form a soft ball when dropped in cold water.) Remove from heat at once. Add vanilla, but do not stir in.
3. Cool mixture in pan to 110° or until lukewarm; beat with wooden spoon until mixture thickens and begins to lose its gloss. (This will take about 15 minutes.)
4. Spread in buttered 9 × 5 × 3-inch loaf pan. Let stand until set and cool; cut into squares.

DESSERTS

Dessert   Some find this final course an almost indispensable part of a meal. Dessert can be as elaborate as a Viennese or French pastry or as simple as fresh fruit. The word "dessert" is based on the French word *desservir*, "to remove or clear away." It was first used in reference to clearing a table.

Desserts are an integral part of a menu and as such should be given some consideration. Think of them not just as something sweet to be tacked onto the end of the meal, but as a way to round out—fill in—the day's nutritional needs. Not enough fruit in a day's meals? Then include a fruit dessert. Insufficient milk or eggs? Then plan to serve ice cream or custard or a milk-rich chocolate pudding. The day's diet short on cereal? A bread or rice pudding will help fill in the gaps.

The choice of a dessert is as important as the meal it will follow. A canned fruit would be an inappropriate end to a fine steak dinner just as flaming crêpes would be after soup and sandwiches. It's a matter of common sense—of creating variety, sustaining interest and adding a final, well-chosen touch so that the tone of a meal carries through to the end. A heavy meal, thus, is best followed by something light and tart; a bland one by something fairly substantial. Aim, too, for a contrast of flavors, colors and textures so that the meal, from start to finish, is delicately balanced.

Desserts cover a variety of items. There are pastries, pies, tarts, cream puffs, cakes, tortes, fruitcakes, cookies, brownies—all considered baked items. Dairy-based desserts include custards, flans, puddings, ice cream, bombes and cheesecake. Fruit desserts abound for spring, summer, autumn and winter. There are quick-to-prepare desserts and intricate company desserts. Truly there's a large repertoire!

Frozen Soufflé Amaretto

Makes 8 to 10 servings.

5 egg yolks	**1 cup finely crushed**
3 eggs	**almond macaroons**
1/2 cup superfine sugar	**2 cups heavy cream,**
1/3 cup Amaretto	**whipped**
liqueur	

1. Prepare a 5-cup soufflé or other straight-sided dish with foil collar 2 inches higher than rim of dish. Fasten foil with tape. Put dish in freezer.

Pictured opposite:
Apricot Charlotte Bombe, page 260.

2. Combine egg yolks, eggs and sugar in a large bowl. Beat with electric mixer at high speed until very thick and light. (This takes 10 to 12 minutes.) Turn mixer to low speed; add Amaretto and macaroons.
3. Fold in whipped cream with a rubber spatula until no streaks of white remain. Pour into prepared dish; freeze overnight. Remove collar from soufflé.

Cold Cranberry Soufflé

Makes 8 servings.

1 envelope plus 1 teaspoon unflavored gelatin	**1 1/4 cups sugar**
	5 egg whites
2 1/4 cups cranberry juice	**1/2 teaspoon salt**
	1 1/2 cups heavy cream
1 1/2 cups fresh or frozen cranberries	**2 tablespoons 10X (confectioners') sugar**

1. Soften the gelatin in 1/2 cup of the cranberry juice, about 5 minutes.
2. Wash and pick over the berries. Combine berries with 3/4 cup of the sugar and the remaining cranberry juice in a large saucepan. Bring to boiling; lower heat. Simmer 4 minutes or until sugar is dissolved and cranberry skins have "popped." Remove from heat; stir in softened gelatin. Strain mixture into large bowl. Reserve 16 cranberries; chop remainder. Cool gelatin mixture; chill until syrupy.
3. Beat egg whites and salt in a large bowl with electric mixer until frothy. Add remaining sugar gradually, beating until meringue forms soft peaks. Whip 3/4 cup of the heavy cream in a small bowl until stiff. Fold meringue and cream together.
4. Pour the meringue-cream mixture over the thickened cranberry mixture and fold together until no trace of white remains. Fold in the chopped berries. Pour into a 6-cup soufflé dish with a high collar of wax paper. Chill until firm, about 4 hours.
5. To serve, whip remaining heavy cream with the confectioners' sugar in a small bowl until stiff. Pipe 16 rosettes on soufflé with a pastry bag. Place a cranberry in center of each.

Bombe   A festive frozen dessert with a French name for the tall, cylindrical mold which originally resembled a bomb. Bombes range from very simple to very elaborate, but all have two things in common: they are made with ice cream and they are frozen in decorative molds. We've shortcut the original, more complicated version by using good quality commercial ice creams.

Apricot Charlotte Bombe

A spectacular dessert with five ingredients that go together like a breeze.

Makes 6 servings.

1 can (16 ounces) whole apricots	or your favorite flavor)
1/3 cup apricot preserves	7 to 8 ladyfingers, split
1 pint ice cream (vanilla, chocolate	Thawed, frozen whipped topping or whipped cream

1. Drain apricots, reserving 1 tablespoon syrup. Heat preserves with syrup in small saucepan until melted.
2. Unmold ice cream from carton in one piece onto a chilled serving plate. Press ladyfingers onto side and top of ice cream to cover completely, cutting to fit where necessary. Brush melted preserve mixture over ladyfingers until absorbed. Return to freezer.
3. Just before serving, arrange apricots on plate and decorate with whipped topping.

Cranberry-Pistachio Bombe with Pineapple Galliano Sauce

Here's a festive bombe for your holiday table. It's a bit fussy to make, but worth the effort.

Makes 12 servings.

1 cup water	1 tablespoon lemon juice
1 1/4 cups sugar	2 pints pistachio ice cream, softened
3/4 cup light corn syrup	2 egg whites
4 cups fresh or frozen cranberries (16 ounces)	Pineapple Galliano Sauce *(recipe follows)*
1 can (13 ounces) evaporated milk	

1. Combine water and sugar in a large saucepan. Heat until sugar is dissolved. Add corn syrup and cranberries. Cook over medium heat until cranberries pop, about 10 minutes. Cool 10 minutes.
2. Puree cranberries in container of electric blender. Add milk and lemon juice; blend well.
3. Strain mixture into a 13 × 9 × 2-inch baking pan. Cover with aluminum foil. Freeze until firm.
4. Line a 6-cup mold evenly with pistachio ice cream. Cover with aluminum foil. Freeze until firm.
5. Beat egg whites in a small bowl with an electric mixer until stiff. Turn cranberry mixture into a bowl, breaking up the lumps with a wooden spoon. Beat with same electric mixer until mixture is smooth.
6. Fold in beaten egg whites. Gently spoon mixture into lined mold. Cover with aluminum foil. Freeze until solid. To serve, unmold onto serving plate about 1 hour before serving; return to freezer to refreeze. Serve with Pineapple Galliano Sauce.

Pineapple Galliano Sauce: Combine a 20-ounce can of crushed pineapple in pineapple juice, 3/4 cup sugar and 2 teaspoons cornstarch in a medium-size saucepan. Cook, stirring constantly, until sauce thickens and clears. Stir in 1/3 cup Liquore Galliano; refrigerate. Makes 3 1/4 cups.

Chocolate-Raspberry Bombe

Pretty, colorful and an easy make-ahead dessert.

Makes 8 servings.

2 packages ladyfingers, split	1 tablespoon seedless raspberry or currant jelly *(optional)*
1 1/2 pints chocolate ice cream	
1 pint frozen raspberry yogurt	Raspberry Sauce *(recipe follows)*

1. Line a 9 × 5 × 3-inch loaf pan with wax paper. Arrange the ladyfingers around the edges and bottom of the pan. Place in freezer to chill.
2. Soften 1 pint chocolate ice cream in a medium-size bowl in refrigerator for 30 minutes.
3. Spread the softened ice cream along the bottom and up the long side of the chilled pan with the back of a spoon to a 1/2-inch thickness. Return to freezer until firm.
4. Soften yogurt and remaining chocolate ice cream in separate medium-size bowls in refrigerator. Spread yogurt into center of ice cream-lined pan, leveling top. Gently spread the remaining chocolate ice cream over the entire top. Return to freezer until solid, at least 3 hours.
5. Melt jelly in a small saucepan over low heat; cool slightly. Unmold bombe; peel off wax paper. Gently brush ladyfingers with jelly. Serve with Raspberry Sauce.

Raspberry Sauce

Makes about 1 cup.

1 package (10 ounces) frozen raspberries, thawed	1 teaspoon cornstarch
	1 tablespoon kirsch

1. Puree raspberries in container of electric blender. Strain puree to remove seeds.
2. Blend cornstarch and puree in a saucepan; bring to boiling; lower heat; simmer 1 minute, stirring constantly, until thickened and clear.
3. Remove from heat; stir in kirsch. Refrigerate until cold.

Bombe Glacé

Prepare this French ice cream dessert up to 2 months ahead.

Makes 8 to 10 servings.

1/2 cup chopped
mixed candied
fruits
2 tablespoons apricot
liqueur or brandy
1 quart chocolate ice
cream, slightly
softened

1 pint strawberry ice
cream, slightly
softened
1 cup heavy cream
1/4 cup superfine
granulated sugar
Whipped cream

1. Combine candied fruits and liqueur; let stand while preparing remainder of recipe.
2. Rinse a 6-cup fluted mold with cold water. Spread chocolate ice cream evenly around bottom and side of mold with a large spoon; freeze 30 minutes. Spread strawberry ice cream evenly over chocolate; freeze 30 minutes.
3. Beat cream in a small bowl until stiff; fold in sugar and fruits with any liqueur not absorbed. Spoon into center of mold; level off with spatula.
4. Cover mold with a piece of wax paper, then cover tightly with lid of mold or heavy-duty foil. Freeze until solid, about 3 hours.
5. Remove mold from freezer 30 minutes before serving. Run a spatula around top edge; hold a hot, wet towel around mold for 3 to 4 seconds; turn out onto chilled serving dish. Return to freezer until softened outside has refrozen.
6. Just before serving, garnish outside of bombe with whipped cream. Cut into wedges to serve.

Note: Bombe can be frosted with whipped cream and garnished with candied red cherries.

Strawberry Ice-Cream Brownie Bombe

A brownie mix makes this spectacular dessert even easier.

Bake at 350° for 30 minutes.

Makes 12 servings.

1 package (23 ounces)
double-fudge
brownie mix
1/2 cup walnuts,
chopped
1/2 cup strawberry
preserves
1 quart strawberry ice
cream, softened
2 cups (1 pint) heavy

cream
Few drops red food
coloring
1/4 cup 10X
(confectioners')
sugar
Chocolate-covered
strawberries for
garnish *(optional)*

1. Preheat the oven to moderate (350°).
Grease two 8-inch-round layer-cake pans.
Line the bottoms with wax paper; grease the paper.
Place a 1 1/2-quart bowl in the refrigerator to chill.

2. Prepare the brownie mix, following the package directions for cake-like brownies. Stir the walnuts into the batter. Pour into the prepared pans, dividing equally.
3. Bake in the preheated moderate oven (350°) for 30 minutes or just until the cakes begin to pull away from the sides of the pans. Cool the cakes in the pans on a wire rack to room temperature. Remove the cakes from the pans.
4. Line the chilled bowl with aluminum foil. Cut and fit one brownie layer to evenly line the inside of the bowl. Spread the strawberry preserves over the brownie layer. Place in the freezer until cold. Wrap the second layer in plastic wrap; refrigerate.
5. Spoon the ice cream into the lined bowl, packing down firmly. Smooth the top. Cover with plastic wrap; freeze until firm.
6. To assemble: Unwrap the refrigerated brownie layer; place on a serving plate. Remove the plastic wrap from the ice-cream bombe top and unmold the ice-cream bombe onto the brownie layer. Remove the foil. Return to the freezer while preparing the cream, or for up to 3 days. Beat the cream with a few drops of the red food coloring in a medium-size bowl until slightly thickened. Beat in the 10X sugar until stiff. Spoon about 1 1/2 cups of the whipped cream into a pastry bag fitted with a star tip. Refrigerate. Frost the bombe with the remaining cream. Pipe the cream in lines decoratively up the side and around the base of the bombe. Return to the freezer until the cream is hard.
7. Garnish the bombe with the chocolate-dipped strawberries, if you wish.

Apricot Ice-Cream and Chablis-Ice Bombe

A delicately flavored white wine ice is the hidden treat in this cooling dessert.

Makes 12 servings.

1 can (17 ounces)
unpeeled apricot
halves, chilled and
drained
1 quart vanilla ice
cream, softened
1 1/2 cups water
1/2 cup sugar
Outer yellow peel from
1 lemon, cut in
single strip

1 1/2 teaspoons gelatin
1 cup Chablis wine
2 tablespoons lemon
juice
Whipped cream,
chopped pistachio
nuts, apricot halves
and fresh mint
leaves for garnish
(optional)

1. Chill an 8-cup bombe mold.
2. Puree the drained apricots in a blender or food

(continued)

processor. Stir the pureed apricots into the softened ice cream in a medium-size bowl. Place in the freezer to stiffen to a spreading consistency.

3. Line the mold with the apricot ice cream to within 1/4 inch of the top edge, leaving a hollow center. Cover with plastic wrap and freeze until firm.

4. Combine the water, sugar and lemon peel in a medium-size saucepan. Bring to boiling, stirring to dissolve the sugar. Lower the heat; simmer for 15 minutes without stirring.

5. Sprinkle the gelatin over 1/4 cup of the wine in a small bowl. Let stand to soften for about 5 minutes. Stir into the hot sugar syrup until dissolved. Stir in the remaining 3/4 cup of wine and the lemon juice. Remove the lemon peel. Cool to room temperature. Chill.

6. Pour the chilled wine mixture into the ice-cream-lined mold. Cover with plastic wrap and freeze overnight or for up to 3 days.

7. To serve, unmold on a chilled serving plate. Garnish with the whipped cream, chopped pistachio nuts, apricot halves and mint, if you wish. Serve immediately.

Removing an Ice-Cream Mold: To serve, place a towel wrung out in hot water over the bottom of the mold and turn out onto a chilled serving platter.

Bavarian Cream
Originally called *bavarois* or *fromage bavarois*, Bavarian cream is basically a gelatin dessert blended with egg custard and whipped cream. It can be flavored in a number of ways: with fruits, such as strawberries, peaches or lemons or with chocolate, vanilla or a liqueur. Bavarian creams are usually molded in fancy shapes, then served with a sauce.

Rainbow Bavarian Cream

Yellow, green and white layers create such a showy effect for so little effort.

Makes 6 to 8 servings.

4 eggs, separated	1/4 cup lemon juice
3/4 cup sugar	1 teaspoon vanilla
1 cup water	1 cup heavy cream
1 envelope unflavored gelatin	Yellow and green food coloring

1. Beat egg yolks slightly in the top of a double boiler; stir in 1/4 cup of the sugar and water; sprinkle gelatin over top; let stand several minutes to soften gelatin.

2. Cook, stirring constantly, over simmering water 10 minutes, or until gelatin dissolves and mixture coats a spoon; remove from heat. Stir in lemon juice and vanilla. Strain into a large bowl.

3. Set bowl in a pan of ice and water to speed setting. Chill, stirring often, just until mixture is as thick as unbeaten egg white.

4. While gelatin mixture chills, beat egg whites in a large bowl until foamy-white and double in volume; beat in remaining 1/2 cup sugar, 1 tablespoon at a time, until sugar dissolves completely and meringue forms stiff peaks. Beat cream until stiff in a small bowl.

5. Fold whipped cream, then meringue into thickened gelatin mixture until no streaks of white remain; remove from ice and water. Spoon 1 cup into a deep 6-cup mold; set mold in ice and water; chill until not quite firm. Tint remaining mixture in bowl pale yellow with food coloring; spoon 2 cups into mold; chill again. Tint remaining mixture pale green with food coloring; spoon over yellow layer; remove from ice and water. Chill at least 4 hours or overnight.

6. When ready to serve, run a sharp thin-blade knife around top of dessert, then dip mold *very quickly* in and out of a pan of hot water. Cover with a serving plate; turn upside down; gently lift off mold. Cut in wedges; serve with your favorite lemon sauce, if you wish.

Strawberry Yogurt Bavarian

Chill this innovative version of the popular Bavarian cream in a large, pretty mold and serve at a luncheon or dinner party.

Makes 10 to 12 servings.

2 envelopes unflavored gelatin	frozen sliced strawberries, thawed
1/2 cup cold water	
8 tablespoons sugar	2 tablespoons lemon juice
4 eggs, separated	
1/4 teaspoon salt	2 containers (8 ounces each) plain yogurt
2 packages (10 ounces each)	

1. Sprinkle gelatin over water in a medium-size saucepan to soften. Add 6 tablespoons of the sugar, egg yolks, which have been lightly beaten, salt and strawberries.

2. Cook over low heat, stirring constantly, until gelatin is dissolved and mixture coats a spoon, about 8 minutes.

3. Remove from heat and add lemon juice and yogurt. Mix well and turn into a large bowl; chill until mixture begins to thicken.

4. Beat egg whites in a large bowl until foamy. Add remaining 2 tablespoons sugar and beat until stiff. Fold into strawberry-yogurt mixture and spoon into a 2-quart mold.

5. Cover; chill until firm, at least 4 hours, or overnight.

6. When ready to serve, loosen edges of mold with a knife, dip mold in hot water, turn out on a chilled serving plate. Garnish with whipped cream or fresh strawberries and toasted almonds, if you wish.

Pictured opposite:
Bombe Glacé, page 261.

Apricot Cream

Makes 2 1/2 cups.

1 cup dried apricots, chopped coarsely	**1 container (16 ounces) dairy sour cream (2 cups)**
1 cup water	
1/3 cup honey	**Toasted slivered almonds**
1/2 teaspoon salt	

1. Cook apricots in water in a small saucepan until tender, about 10 minutes. Drain well; cool.
2. Combine honey, salt and sour cream in bowl; stir in cooled apricots. Chill before serving. Garnish with almonds.

Pineapple Cream

A quickie—makes a creamy dessert.

Makes about 6 servings.

2 envelopes unflavored gelatin	**heavy syrup**
1/3 cup sugar	**1 can (6 ounces) frozen lemonade concentrate**
1 can (8 1/4 ounces) crushed pineapple in	**1 cup heavy cream**
	1 cup crushed ice

1. Combine gelatin and sugar in container of electric blender. Heat pineapple with syrup to boiling; add to blender all at once. Cover. Blend on high until smooth.
2. Add frozen concentrate, cream, then crushed ice. Blend until completely smooth. Pour into 6 serving glasses. Chill until ready to serve, about 15 minutes.

Café Cream Royale

Such a lusciously rich way to enjoy coffee and cream.

Makes 8 to 10 servings.

6 eggs, separated	**2 envelopes unflavored gelatin**
3/4 cup sugar	
Dash salt	**3 tablespoons light rum**
2 cups warm freshly brewed coffee	**1 cup heavy cream**

1. Beat egg yolks slightly in the top of a double boiler; stir in 1/4 cup of the sugar, salt and coffee; sprinkle gelatin over top; let stand several minutes to soften gelatin.
2. Cook, stirring constantly, over simmering water 10 minutes, or until gelatin dissolves and mixture coats a

spoon; remove from heat. Strain into a large bowl; stir in rum.
3. Place bowl in a pan of ice and water to speed setting. Chill, stirring often, just until as thick as unbeaten egg white.
4. While gelatin mixture chills, beat egg whites in a large bowl until foamy-white and double in volume; beat in remaining 1/2 cup sugar, 1 tablespoon at a time, until sugar dissolves completely and meringue forms stiff peaks. Beat cream until stiff in a small bowl.
5. Fold whipped cream, then meringue into thickened gelatin mixture until no streaks of white remain. Spoon into a 2-quart mold. Chill at least 6 hours, or overnight.
6. When ready to serve, run a sharp, thin knife blade around top of dessert, then dip mold very quickly in and out of a pan of hot water. Cover with a serving plate; turn upside down; gently lift off mold.

Meringue Creams

Bake at 250° for 1 hour.

Makes 4 dozen.

2 egg whites	**crystals**
1 teaspoon lemon juice	**1 cup heavy cream**
1/2 cup sugar (for meringue shells)	**2 tablespoons sugar (for filling)**
1 teaspoon vanilla	**1 teaspoon brandy extract**
1 teaspoon instant coffee powder or	**Red food coloring**

1. Line two large cookie sheets with brown paper; draw twenty-four 1 1/2-inch rounds, 2 inches apart, on each paper. Preheat oven to 250°.
2. Beat egg whites with lemon juice until foamy-white and double in volume with electric mixer at high speed in a small bowl. Beat in the 1/2 cup sugar, 1 tablespoon at a time, until meringue stands in firm peaks; beat in vanilla and instant coffee.
3. Attach a fancy tip to a pastry bag; fill bag with meringue. Starting at center of each circle on paper, press out meringue to form tiny shells. (If you do not have a pastry bag, spread 1 tablespoonful of meringue into each circle, building up edge slightly.)
4. Bake in a preheated very slow oven (250°) for 1 hour or until delicately golden. Cool on cookie sheets 5 minutes; loosen carefully from paper with a spatula; cool completely on wire racks. (If shells are made ahead, store in a single layer in a cool dry place.)
6. About an hour before serving, beat cream with the 2 tablespoons sugar until stiff in a medium-size bowl; stir in brandy extract and a few drops red food coloring to tint pink. Spoon about 2 teaspoonfuls into each shell, swirling top to a peak. Chill before serving.

Orange Egg Cream

This is especially good when the ice cream is just melted.

Makes about 4 cups or 2 servings.

2 cups orange juice
²/₃ cup instant nonfat dry milk powder

2 eggs
1 pint vanilla ice cream

1. Combine orange juice, dry milk powder and eggs in container of electric blender. Cover; whirl on medium speed until smooth.
2. Add ice cream; whirl just until blended. Pour into 2 large glasses. Serve immediately.

Avocado Whip

Especially refreshing. Serve as a party dessert with thin butter cookies.

Makes 4 servings.

1 large avocado
2 tablespoons lemon juice
2 tablespoons

sugar
¹/₂ pint (1 cup) vanilla ice cream, softened

1. Halve avocado; pit and peel. Cut into small pieces, then mash in a medium-size bowl with a fork until smooth, sprinkling with the lemon juice to prevent darkening. Stir in sugar. (You should have 1 cup of avocado mixture.)
2. Spoon softened ice cream into avocado mixture. Beat with electric mixer until well mixed, but do not let ice cream melt.
3. Spoon into stemmed glasses and serve at once or spoon into a shallow pan and place in freezer until semi-firm, but not hard-frozen, about 2 hours. If frozen in pan, spoon into serving dishes. Garnish with lemon twists, if you wish.

Banana Dessert Crêpes

Try this recipe on your family first, then put it on the menu for your next dinner party.

Makes 6 servings.

Crêpes:
¹/₂ cup *sifted* all-purpose flour
1 tablespoon sugar
¹/₈ teaspoon salt
2 eggs
³/₄ cup milk
1 tablespoon butter, melted

Orange Sauce:
¹/₄ cup (¹/₂ stick) butter or margarine
¹/₃ cup sugar
2 teaspoons grated orange rind
¹/₃ cup orange juice
3 small bananas
2 tablespoons rum

1. Make Crêpes: Combine flour, sugar, salt, eggs and milk in a medium-size bowl; beat with rotary beater until smooth. Beat in the 1 tablespoon butter. Let stand 20 minutes.
2. Slowly heat 7-inch skillet or crêpe pan until a drop of water sizzles when dropped on surface. Butter skillet lightly for the first few crêpes.
3. Pour batter, 2 tablespoons for each crêpe, into heated skillet; quickly rotate skillet to spread batter evenly. Cook over medium heat until lightly browned; turn and brown other side. Remove to plate. Cool, then fold in quarters.
4. Make Sauce: Combine butter, sugar, orange rind and orange juice in a large chafing dish or skillet; bring to boiling. Peel bananas; cut in quarters lengthwise; add to skillet; heat 1 minute. Add crêpes and heat, spooning sauce over. Heat rum in a small saucepan; ignite; pour over crêpes. Serve 2 crêpes and 2 pieces of banana per serving.

Blackberry Buckle

A coffee-cake-style dessert dappled with soft blackberries and covered with a thin crunch of sugar.

Bake at 350° for 45 minutes.

Makes 6 servings.

1²/₃ cups *sifted* all-purpose flour
1³/₄ teaspoons baking powder
¹/₂ teaspoon salt
¹/₂ teaspoon ground cardamom
¹/₄ cup (¹/₂ stick) butter, softened
³/₄ cup sugar

1 egg
¹/₂ teaspoon vanilla
²/₃ cup milk
2 cups frozen unsweetened blackberries (from a 1-pound bag), thawed and drained
2 tablespoons sugar
Whipped cream

1. Sift flour, baking powder, salt and cardamom onto wax paper.
2. Beat butter and the ³/₄ cup sugar in a medium-size bowl until creamy. Beat in egg and vanilla until smooth and light. Preheat oven to 350°.
3. Add milk alternately with flour mixture to the butter and sugar, beating just to blend thoroughly.
4. Spread less than half the batter in a buttered 9 × 1¹/₂-inch layer cake pan. Sprinkle with half the berries. Spoon remaining batter evenly over the berries; smooth with a spatula. Sprinkle with remaining berries, then top with the 2 tablespoons sugar.
5. Bake in a preheated moderate oven (350°) for 45 minutes or until center springs back when lightly pressed with fingertip. Cool slightly on wire rack Serve warm with whipped cream.

Zabaglione

An Italian dessert originating in the Piedmont region, prepared from egg yolks, sugar and wine, which is barely cooked. It is prepared in a double boiler to keep the heat low. It is a delicate custard, and if overcooked the yolks will scramble. Frothy and rich, zabaglione may be served warm or cold in stemmed glasses with cookies. Often, zabaglione is used as a sauce over fruit.

Zabaglione

Makes 6 to 8 servings.

3 egg yolks	**$^1/_3$ cup Marsala wine**
$^1/_4$ cup sugar	

1. Beat egg yolks with portable electric mixer in the top of a double boiler (glass is best) until thick and lemon-colored.
2. Beat in sugar gradually until mixture is very thick and light in color. Beat in wine slowly.
3. Place top of double boiler over simmering water. (If using a metal double boiler, do not allow the water to touch the bottom of the pan.)
4. Beat at high speed for 5 minutes or until mixture has thickened and becomes very fluffy. Serve warm.

Zabaglione Sauce with Fruit

Prepare the fruit ahead of time and make this elegant topping just before serving.

Makes 5 cups sauce.

4 egg yolks	**peaches or any**
$^1/_4$ cup sugar	**other fresh fruits,**
$^3/_4$ cup Marsala wine	**cut up**
Strawberries, melon,	

1. Combine egg yolks and sugar in top of double boiler over simmering, not boiling, water. Beat with electric hand mixer until fluffy-light.
2. Gradually add wine; continue beating on high speed for 10 minutes, until very thick and light and mixture holds its shape in a spoon. (Do not overbeat.) Spoon warm zabaglione over fresh fruit.

Frozen Maple Sabayon

Makes 8 servings.

$^3/_4$ cup maple syrup or	**$^1/_2$ cup sugar**
maple-blended	**$^1/_4$ cup orange**
syrup	**marmalade**
8 egg yolks	**$^1/_4$ cup chopped**
1$^1/_2$ cups heavy cream	**pecans**
1$^1/_2$ cups cranberries	

1. Heat maple syrup in top of double boiler over direct heat just until syrup starts to boil.

2. Beat egg yolks in a medium-size bowl until light; gradually beat in hot syrup. Return to double boiler.
3. Cook over simmering water, beating constantly, until very thick and fluffy and mixture has more than doubled in volume, about 8 minutes. Remove from hot water and continue to beat until slightly cooled. Chill, beating often.
4. Beat cream in a medium-size bowl until stiff. Fold in maple mixture. Pour into individual dessert glasses or an 8-cup serving dish. Freeze until firm. Cover with plastic wrap.
5. Prepare cranberry sauce a few hours befor serving: Chop cranberries; transfer to small bowl; stir in sugar, orange marmalade and nuts. Let stand at room temperature, stirring often, until sugar is dissolved. Chill until serving time. Spoon sauce over Frozen Maple Sabayon.

Chocolate Blancmange

Makes 6 servings.

1 cup sugar	**unsweetened**
$^1/_3$ cup cornstarch	**chocolate, cut up**
$^1/_4$ teaspoon salt	**3 cups milk**
3 squares	**1$^1/_2$ teaspoons vanilla**

1. Combine sugar, cornstarch, salt and chocolate in a medium-size saucepan; gradually stir in milk.
2. Cook over medium heat, stirring constantly, until chocolate melts and mixture comes to boiling and is thickened. Boil 1 minute. Remove from heat; stir in vanilla. Pour into a 3-cup mold. Cover with plastic wrap; refrigerate until cold, about 3 hours.
3. When ready to serve, run a knife around top; dip mold *very quickly* in and out of hot water. Cover with serving plate; turn upside down; shake gently; lift off mold. Garnish with whipped cream and maraschino cherries, if you wish.

Clafouti

Traditionally made with just-picked, unpitted cherries (the seeds contain the perfume, according to the French), clafouti is just as good baked with peach wedges or apricot halves.

Bake at 400° for 45 minutes.

Makes 6 servings.

1 pound fresh sweet	**$^2/_3$ cup sugar**
cherries, or 1 can	**Pinch salt**
(17 ounces) dark	**3 eggs, slightly beaten**
sweet cherries	**1$^1/_2$ cups milk**
$^1/_2$ cup *sifted*	**3 tablespoons butter**
unbleached all-	**or margarine,**
purpose flour	**melted and cooled**

1. Wash and dry fresh cherries, or thoroughly drain canned cherries. Preheat oven to 400°.
2. In a large bowl, combine flour, $^1/_2$ cup of the sugar

At right, Apricot Ice-Cream and Chablis-Ice Bombe, page 261.

Below, Strawberry Ice-Cream Brownie Bombe, page 261.

and salt. Add eggs, blending thoroughly with a wire whisk or wooden spoon. Add milk and melted butter, stirring until mixture is quite smooth. (Do not beat.)

3. Butter a 9 × 9 × 2-inch baking pan. Sprinkle in 1 tablespoon of the remaining sugar. Spread cherries on bottom; pour into batter.

4. Bake in a preheated hot oven (400°) for 30 minutes. Sprinkle top with remaining sugar. Continue baking for 15 minutes or until the custard is firm and a knife inserted near center comes out clean.

Pots de Crème au Chocolat

Bake at 325° for 20 minutes.

Makes 4 to 6 servings.

4 squares semisweet chocolate	**3 egg yolks**
1¼ cups light or heavy cream	**2 tablespoons light brown sugar**

1. Place four 4-ounce or six 3-ounce pots de crème cups, custard cups or individual soufflé dishes in shallow baking dish. Preheat oven to 325°.

2. Chop the chocolate coarsely. Place in small, heavy

(continued)

saucepan; add cream. Cook, stirring constantly, over medium-high heat, until chocolate melts and mixture comes to boiling.

3. Beat egg yolks and sugar with wire whisk in medium-size bowl until blended; gradually beat in hot cream mixture. Strain into 4-cup measure; pour into cups.

4. Set shallow baking pan on oven rack. Pour boiling water into pan, about halfway up the sides of cups.

5. Bake in a preheated slow oven (325°) for 20 minutes or just until mixture begins to set around edges. Remove cups from water to a wire rack; let cool 30 minutes. Cover with lids or plastic wrap; refrigerate at least 4 hours. Decorate with rosettes of whipped cream and candied violets, if you wish.

Blueberry Fool

Makes 6 servings.

2 cups (1 pint) fresh blueberries	1 package (3 ounces) cream cheese
1/4 cup sugar	1/4 cup 10X (confectioners') sugar
1 1/2 teaspoons cornstarch	
1 teaspoon grated lemon rind	1 teaspoon vanilla
	1 cup heavy cream

1. Cook blueberries, sugar and cornstarch over medium heat, stirring until mixture thickens and bubbles 1 minute. Stir in lemon rind. Pour into a 5-cup glass bowl; cover and chill.

2. To serve: Beat cream cheese, 10X sugar and vanilla until smooth; add cream and beat until fluffy. Spoon mixture on top of blueberries; fold in.

Cheese Blintzes

We like these little packages of cheese as a dessert, although they can be served with cinnamon and sugar (instead of cherry sauce) as a main dish.

Makes 12 blintzes.

2 eggs	uncreamed (dry) cottage or pot cheese
1 1/4 cups milk	
1 cup *sifted* all-purpose flour	1 egg
1/2 teaspoon salt	2 tablespoons sugar
2 tablespoons butter or margarine, melted	1 teaspoon grated lemon rind
	Butter or margarine
2 packages (3 ounces each) cream cheese	1 can (21 ounces) cherry pie filling
1 container (12 ounces)	Dairy sour cream

1. Beat eggs and milk just until blended in a medium-size bowl; add flour and salt; beat just until smooth. Stir in butter; chill at least 1 hour.

2. Meanwhile, beat cream cheese and cottage cheese in a small bowl until smooth. Stir in egg, sugar and

lemon rind until well blended; refrigerate while preparing blintz wrappers or pancakes.

3. Heat a 7-inch skillet over medium heat. Grease lightly with butter. Pour in 3 tablespoons batter, rotating pan quickly to spread batter evenly. Cook until lightly browned on underside and dry on top. Remove from pan to a plate. Repeat with remaining batter to make 12 blintzes; stack on plate.

4. Place about 3 tablespoons filling on browned side of each blintz. Fold opposite sides over filling; then overlap ends envelope-style to cover filling completely.

5. Melt 2 tablespoons butter in a large skillet; add 5 or 6 blintzes, seam-side down. Cook over low to medium heat about 5 minutes, until lightly browned on underside; carefully turn and brown other side, about 5 minutes. Keep warm in a low oven until all blintzes are browned.

6. Heat cherry pie filling in a small saucepan. Serve heated pie filling and sour cream with blintzes.

Note: To freeze blintzes, fill and fold. Place seam-side down on cookie sheet or in foil pans; cover tightly with freezer wrap. To cook, follow Step 5, cooking 10 minutes on each side or until heated through.

Cream Puff
A simple French pastry, cream puffs are made from pâté a choux, a soft dough made of flour, butter and water, with eggs beaten into the cooked dough, causing it to puff during baking. Cream puffs can be filled either with a sweet or savory mixture. The dough is dropped by spoonfuls onto greased baking sheets and baked.

Profiteroles with Espresso Sauce

Bake at 400° for 35 to 40 minutes.
Makes 12 servings.

Basic Cream Puff Paste (*recipe follows*)	espresso coffee
	1/4 cup light corn syrup
1 quart vanilla, butter pecan or chocolate ice cream	1/2 cup water
	2 tablespoons butter or margarine
1 1/4 cups firmly packed light brown sugar	1 to 2 tablespoons brandy or whiskey (*optional*)
1 tablespoon instant	

1. Prepare Basic Cream Puff Paste. Preheat oven to 400°.

2. Drop by slightly rounded teaspoonfuls into 36 even mounds, 1 inch apart, on ungreased large cookie sheet.

3. Bake in a preheated hot oven (400°) for 35 minutes

or until puffed and golden brown. Remove to wire rack; cool completely.
4. Cut a slice from top of each puff; remove any filaments of soft dough. Fill puffs with small scoops of ice cream of your choice; replace tops. Freeze until serving time. (To keep puffs frozen over 4 hours, wrap in plastic or foil.)
5. For Espresso Sauce: Combine sugar, coffee, corn syrup and water in large saucepan. Heat to boiling, stirring constantly. Cook over low heat 5 minutes, stirring often. Remove from heat; stir in butter until melted. Stir in brandy or whiskey. Cool, stirring several times.
6. To serve, mound filled profiteroles in compote dish or deep serving plate. Spoon Espresso Sauce over and serve.

Basic Cream Puff Paste (Choux Paste)

Makes 12 large cream puffs or 12 eclairs or 36 profiteroles.

1 cup water	1/4 teaspoon salt
1/2 cup (1 stick) butter or margarine	1 cup *sifted* all-purpose flour
1 teaspoon sugar	4 eggs

1. Heat water, butter, sugar and salt to a full rolling boil in large saucepan.
2. Add flour all at once. Stir vigorously with a wooden spoon until mixture forms a thick, smooth ball that leaves the sides of pan clean, about 1 minute. Remove from heat.
3. Add eggs, 1 at a time, beating well after each addition with wooden spoon or electric hand mixer until paste is shiny and smooth. Shape and bake, following particular recipe instructions.

Strawberry Cream Puffs

Cloud-light puffs filled with glistening berries and snowy cream.
Bake at 400° for 40 minutes.
Makes 12 cream puffs.

Basic Cream Puff Paste *(recipe, above)*	4 tablespoons 10X (confectioners') sugar
2 pints strawberries	2 cups heavy cream

1. Prepare Cream Puff Paste. Drop by rounded tablespoonsfuls into 12 even mounds, 2 inches apart, on ungreased large cookie sheet.
2. Bake in a preheated hot oven (400°) for 40 minutes, or until puffed and golden brown. Remove to wire rack; cool completely.
3. Wash strawberries; let dry on paper toweling. Reserve a few for garnish; hull remainder. Slice into a medium-size bowl; stir in 2 tablespoons 10X sugar. Chill 30 minutes.

4. Beat cream with remaining 2 tablespoons sugar in medium-size bowl until stiff. Chill.
5. Just before serving, cut slice from top of each puff; remove any filaments of soft dough. Fold berries into cream; spoon into puffs, dividing evenly; replace tops. Sieve extra 10X sugar over tops. Arrange on serving plate; garnish with reserved strawberries and green leaves, if you wish.
Note: Below are recipes for alternate fillings for cream puffs. Recipes for puffs and filling will halve evenly to make 6 puffs.
Banana Honey Cream Filling: Combine 2 tablespoons honey and 1/2 teaspoon ground cinnamon in medium-size bowl; gradually blend in 1 cup heavy cream. Beat until stiff; fold in 1 banana, diced. Makes about 2 cups; enough to fill 6 puffs.
Cocoa Cream Filling: Combine 1 cup heavy cream, 2 tablespoons dry cocoa, 1/4 cup 10X sugar and 1 teaspoon vanilla in medium-size bowl. Beat until stiff. Makes about 2 cups, enough to fill 6 puffs.

Instant Cherry Crisp

Bake at 350° for 10 to 15 minutes.
Makes 8 servings.

2 1/2 cups ready-to-eat granola-type cereal with raisins and dates	1 can (21 ounces) cherry pie filling
	2 tablespoons butter or margarine

1. Preheat oven to 350°. Sprinkle 1 cup of the cereal in an 8 x 8 x 2-inch baking dish; spoon pie filling over, then sprinkle remaining cereal over top; press down slightly into filling. Dot with butter.
2. Bake in a preheated moderate oven (350°) for 10 to 15 minutes or just until heated through. Serve with softened vanilla ice cream, if you wish.

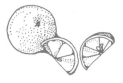

Eggs in Snow

Makes 6 servings.

Soft Custard:	OR: 2 tablespoons frozen orange juice concentrate
1 large navel orange	
2 cups milk	
3 egg yolks	
2 whole eggs	
1/4 cup sugar	Meringue:
1 teaspoon vanilla	3 egg whites
2 tablespoons Grand Marnier	6 tablespoons sugar
	Candied Orange Rind *(recipe follows)*

1. To make Soft Custard: Pare orange thinly with

(continued)

vegetable parer, cutting only the bright orange part and none of the white. Reserve rind and the orange.

2. Scald milk with a 3-inch piece of rind in top of a double-boiler placed over direct heat. Beat egg yolks, eggs, and 1/4 cup sugar with wire whisk or rotary beater until light and fluffy; gradually stir in scalded milk; pour mixture back into top of double-boiler.

3. Cook, stirring constantly, over simmering water 10 minutes or until custard thickens slightly. Remove from heat; strain into a small bowl; stir in vanilla and Grand Marnier. Cover; chill.

4. To make Meringue: Heat 1 quart lightly salted water just to simmering in large skillet.

5. Beat egg whites in medium-size bowl with electric mixer until foamy-white and double in volume. Beat in 6 tablespoons sugar, 1 at a time, until meringue stands in firm peaks.

6. Scoop meringue with large spoon into 6 large egg-shaped puffs. Float, not touching, on simmering water; cover skillet. Cook over very low heat 5 minutes. Lift from water with slotted spoon; drain on cookie sheet covered with paper toweling; chill.

Frozen Eggnog Charlotte, page 271.

7. To serve: Pare all white from reserved orange and cut orange into thin slices. Press slices against sides of shallow glass bowl; carefully pour in custard sauce. Float meringue islands gently on top; spoon a little candied orange rind and syrup over each.

Candied Orange Rind: Cut the remaining rind removed from the orange into match-like strips. Simmer in water 5 minutes; drain. Combine 1/2 cup sugar and 1/4 water in small saucepan; bring to boiling, stirring constantly until sugar is melted. Boil 2 minutes; add orange rind; continue cooking 5 minutes. Cool completely. When covered, will keep in refrigerator several weeks.

Butterscotch Brownie Cake

Bake at 325° for 30 minutes.

Makes 8 servings.

1 tablespoon butter	brownies
1 1/2 cups walnuts, coarsely chopped	2 pints coffee ice cream
1 package (20 ounces) refrigerated fudge	1/4 cup bottled butterscotch sauce

1. Preheat oven to 325°. Butter a 9-inch springform pan; sprinkle bottom with 1/4 cup walnuts. Slice brownie dough as directed on label and gently press on bottom of pan.
2. Bake in a preheated slow oven (325°) for 30 minutes. Remove from oven and cool in pan.
3. Soften ice cream in a large bowl in refrigerator for about 30 minutes.
4. Combine remaining 1 1/4 cups walnuts with butterscotch sauce in a small bowl. Blend 2/3 of this mixture into the softened ice cream. Reserve the remaining sauce.
5. Smooth ice cream over cooled brownie layer. Spoon remaining walnut mixture evenly over top.
6. Return to freezer until firmly frozen, at least 3 hours. Remove from freezer to refrigerator to soften about 30 minutes before serving.

Frozen Eggnog Charlotte

Makes 10 servings.

Apricot Roll (recipe follows)	1/4 teaspoon ground nutmeg
1/2 cup sugar	4 egg whites
1 envelope unflavored gelatin	1 cup heavy cream, whipped
2 teaspoons cornstarch	Whole canned apricots, whipped cream, candied angelica for garnish
6 egg yolks	
1 cup milk	
3 teaspoons vanilla	

1. Cut 10 to 12 slices from Apricot Roll. Arrange slices against side and bottom of an 8-inch springform pan.

2. Combine 1/3 cup of the sugar, gelatin and cornstarch in medium-size heavy saucepan; add egg yolks; beat until well blended. Gradually stir in milk. Cook, stirring constantly, over medium heat, just until mixture is slightly thickened. Remove from heat; stir in vanilla and nutmeg.
3. Set pan in a larger pan filled with ice and water. Chill, stirring often, until mixture mounds when spooned.
4. While mixture chills, beat egg whites until foamy and double in volume. Beat in remaining sugar gradually, until meringue stands in soft peaks.
5. Fold whipped cream, then meringue, into gelatin mixture until no streaks of white remain. Pour into prepared pan; smooth top. Wrap with foil or plastic wrap and freeze overnight or until firm. May be frozen up to 1 week.
6. To serve: Remove from freezer; loosen around edge with small spatula; release spring and remove side of pan. Garnish center with drained apricots, whipped cream and angelica. Or, use green candied cherries.

Apricot Roll

Bake at 375° for 12 to 15 minutes.

Makes 1 jelly roll.

1 cup *sifted* cake flour	1/3 cup water
1 teaspoon baking powder	1 teaspoon vanilla
1/4 teaspoon salt	10X (confectioners') sugar
3 eggs	3/4 cup apricot preserves
3/4 cup sugar	

1. Grease a 15 1/2 × 10 1/2 × 1-inch jelly-roll pan; line bottom with wax paper; grease paper. Preheat oven to 375°.
2. Sift flour, baking powder and salt onto wax paper.
3. Beat eggs in a medium-size bowl with electric mixer until thick and creamy. Gradually add sugar, beating constantly until mixture is *very* thick. (This will take at least 5 minutes.) Blend in water and vanilla on low speed. Add flour mixture, beating (on low speed) just until batter is smooth. Pour into prepared pan, spreading evenly into corners.
4. Bake in a preheated moderate oven (375°) for 12 minutes or until center of cake springs back when lightly pressed with fingertip.
5. Loosen cake around edges with a small knife; invert onto a clean towel dusted with 10X sugar; peel off wax paper. Starting at short end, roll up cake and towel together. Cool on wire rack. When cool, unroll carefully; spread evenly with preserves. Reroll cake. Place, seam-side down, on platter or small cookie sheet until ready to prepare charlotte.

Hot Apple Spice Sundae

Like pie à la mode without the pastry.

Makes 8 servings.

2 tablespoons butter
  or margarine
¹/₂ cup firmly packed
  brown sugar
¹/₂ teaspoon ground
  cinnamon

1 can (20 ounces)
  unsweetened apple
  slices, drained
¹/₄ cup walnut pieces
1 quart vanilla ice
  cream

Melt butter in a small skillet; add sugar, cinnamon and apple slices. Heat just until bubbly hot. Remove from heat. Stir in nuts. Serve warm over ice cream.

Sunshine Sundae

Makes 2 servings.

1 container (8 ounces)
  plain yogurt
1 tablespoon orange

marmalade
3 tablespoons granola
Fresh fruit

1. Combine the yogurt and marmalade in a small mixing bowl. Place 1 tablespoon of the granola in

Sunshine Sundae.

each of two sundae glasses. Spoon half of the yogurt mixture into each dish. Sprinkle the remaining 1 tablespoon granola over the yogurt, dividing evenly.
2. Garnish with fresh fruit.

Double Banana-Split Cake

An ice cream parlor classic in a cake.

Makes 8 servings.

1 package
  (13³/₄ ounces)
  frozen banana cake
3 ripe bananas
1 pint vanilla or
  strawberry ice
  cream

2 tablespoons bottled
  chocolate fudge
  sauce
2 tablespoons walnut
  pieces
Whipped topping

1. Remove frozen cake from package; split horizontally into 2 layers. Place bottom layer on serving plate.
2. Peel and split 2 bananas; arrange over cake. Spoon ice cream over in an even layer; top with frosted cake layer.
3. Peel and slice remaining banana; arrange slices on top. Drizzle with fudge sauce; sprinkle with nuts; decorate with whipped topping.

Chocolate Supreme

Bake at 350° for 25 minutes.
Makes 12 servings.

³/₄ cup boiling water
³/₄ cup unsweetened
  cocoa powder
1 cup buttermilk
2¹/₂ cups *unsifted* all-
  purpose flour
1¹/₂ teaspoons baking
  soda
¹/₂ teaspoon baking
  powder

¹/₂ teaspoon salt
³/₄ cup (1¹/₂ sticks)
  butter, softened
2 cups sugar
4 eggs
1¹/₂ teaspoons vanilla
Frosting (*recipe
  follows*)
Chocolate Curls
  (*recipe follows*)

1. Preheat the oven to moderate (350°). Grease and flour three 9-inch-round layer-cake pans.
2. Pour the boiling water over the cocoa powder in a medium-size bowl; stir to dissolve the cocoa. Stir in the buttermilk; the mixture should be cool. Set aside.
3. Sift together the flour, baking soda, baking powder and salt onto wax paper.
4. Beat together the butter and sugar in a large bowl with an electric mixer at medium speed until light and fluffy. Add the eggs, one at a time, beating well after each addition. Stir in the vanilla.
5. Beat the dry ingredients into the butter mixture, alternating with the cocoa mixture, beginning and ending with the dry ingredients. Pour into the prepared pans, dividing the batter equally.

Chocolate Supreme, page 272.

6. Bake in the preheated moderate oven (350°) for 25 minutes or until the centers spring back when lightly pressed with a fingertip. Cool the cakes in the pans on wire racks for 10 minutes. Turn the cakes out of the pans onto the racks to cool completely.

7. Place one cake layer on a serving plate. Spread the top with one-third of the Frosting. Stack the second layer on top and spread with another third of the Frosting. Repeat with the remaining layer and Frosting. Top with the Chocolate Curls. Refrigerate until ready to serve.

Frosting: Beat 2 cups of heavy cream with $^1/_4$ cup *sifted* 10X (confectioners') sugar and 1 teaspoon vanilla in a large bowl with an electric mixer at high speed until stiff.

Chocolate Curls: Draw a swivel-bladed vegetable peeler across the flat side of an 8-ounce chocolate candy bar (at room temperature), letting the chocolate curl. Lift the curls with a wooden pick and place on the cake.

Frozen Strawberry Yogurt

Makes about $1^1/_2$ quarts.

1 envelope unflavored gelatin
$^1/_4$ cup orange juice
$^1/_2$ cup grenadine syrup
1 pint (2 cups) strawberries, washed and hulled
OR: 2 cups

unsweetened frozen strawberries
2 containers (8 ounces each) plain yogurt
$^1/_2$ cup dairy sour cream
2 egg whites
$^1/_4$ cup sugar

1. Sprinkle gelatin over orange juice in a small cup to soften, 5 minutes. Set cup in simmering water, stirring occasionally, until gelatin is completely dissolved. Cool.

2. Combine grenadine, strawberries, yogurt and sour

(continued)

cream in container of an electric blender; blend on medium speed until smooth. Blend in gelatin. Pour into a 9 x 9 x 2-inch pan. Freeze, stirring occasionally, until partially frozen, 2 to 3 hours.

3. Beat egg whites until foamy and double in volume in a small bowl. Beat in sugar, 1 tablespoon at a time, until meringue forms soft peaks.

4. Spoon partially frozen mixture into a chilled large bowl. Beat with electric mixer until smooth. Fold in meringue. Spoon into freezer container; freeze until softly frozen, about 2 hours.

Frozen Vanilla Yogurt

Makes about 7 cups.

1 cup sugar	**cream cheese**
1/3 cup water	**3 containers (8 ounces**
3 egg whites	**each) plain yogurt**
1/8 teaspoon cream of	**1 tablespoon vanilla**
tartar	**1 teaspoon grated**
1 package (3 ounces)	**lemon rind**

1. Combine sugar and water in a small saucepan; bring to boiling, stirring until sugar dissolves. Boil rapidly, without stirring, 5 to 8 minutes or until syrup registers 236° on candy thermometer.

2. Beat egg whites with cream of tartar in small bowl with electric mixer until soft peaks form; pour hot syrup in a thin stream over egg whites while beating constantly. Continue beating until very stiff peaks form and mixture cools.

3. Soften cream cheese in large bowl; gradually blend in yogurt; stir in vanilla and lemon rind. Add 1/4 of meringue to yogurt mixture; stir to combine well. Fold in remaining meringue.

4. Pack in freezer containers and freeze until firm, 4 to 6 hours.

Crème Brûlée

A classic dessert made of a rich egg custard with a caramelized sugar glaze on top which was originated in New Orleans by French cooks. The words translate literally as "burnt cream." Before broilers were used, the sugar topping was caramelized or burnt by passing a hot, round shovel, called a salamander, over the top.

Crème Brûlée

Makes 6 servings.

7 egg yolks	**cream, heated**
2 tablespoons	**1 tablespoon vanilla**
cornstarch	**1/2 cup firmly packed**
1/4 cup sugar	**light brown sugar**
3 cups heavy or light	

1. Beat egg yolks, cornstarch and sugar in small bowl

with electric mixer until mixture is thick and pale. Gradually beat in the heated heavy or light cream.

2. Return cream to saucepan and cook over moderate heat, stirring constantly and taking care to reach entire bottom and sides of the pan, until custard thickens and bubbles 1 minute. Remove immediately from heat, while still mixing. Stir in vanilla.

3. Pour into a 6-cup heatproof serving bowl; cover; chill overnight.

4. To serve, preheat broiler and cover the surface of the cream with the brown sugar. Surround the bowl with aluminum foil and place 3 inches from broiler heat. Broil for 2 to 3 minutes or until brown sugar is melted and caramelized. Refrigerate until ready to serve.

Mincemeat   A finely chopped mixture of fruit and spices with or without meat. Over the years, meatless versions have become more popular. Commercially prepared mincemeat is easy to use and available in jars, or dried, condensed and sold in packages. Dried, condensed mincemeat can be reconstituted with water and used to make pies, sauces or other desserts.

Mincemeat Roll with Hard Sauce

Bake at 350° for 35 minutes.

Makes 8 servings.

3 1/4 cups _sifted_ all-	**2 tablespoons lemon**
purpose flour	**juice**
1 teaspoon salt	**1 1/2 cups prepared**
1 tablespoon sugar	**mincemeat (from a**
1/4 teaspoon baking	**28-ounce jar)**
soda	**2 tablespoons brandy**
1 cup vegetable	**(_optional_)**
shortening	**1 egg yolk**
1 egg	**1 tablespoon water**
2 tablespoons ice	**Hard Sauce (_recipe_**
water	**_follows_)**

1. Sift flour, salt, sugar and baking soda into a medium-size bowl. Cut in shortening with a pastry blender until mixture is crumbly.

2. Beat egg with the 2 tablespoons water and lemon juice in a small bowl. Add to flour mixture; mix lightly with fork just until pastry holds together. Gather into a ball; wrap in wax paper. Chill at least 30 minutes.

3. Preheat oven to 350°. Roll pastry out on a lightly floured surface to a 17 x 10-inch rectangle, about 1/8-inch thick. Trim edges evenly.

4. Combine mincemeat and brandy. Spread evenly over pastry. Roll lengthwise, jelly-roll fashion. Place

roll, seam-side down, on cookie sheet. Cut 4 gashes on top to allow steam to escape. Beat yolk and water; brush over roll.

5. Bake in a preheated moderate oven (350°) for 35 minutes or until crust is golden brown. Slice and serve with Hard Sauce.

Hard Sauce: Blend ½ cup (1 stick) softened unsalted butter with 1 cup sifted 10X (confectioners') sugar in a medium-size bowl. Add 1 teaspoon lemon juice and 2 tablespoons brandy. Beat until fluffy.

Trifle

The whimsical name for this updated version of the classic Christmas dessert from England will intrigue even the most dessert-resistant guests.

Makes 12 servings.

2 packages (3³/₄ ounces each) vanilla-flavored instant pudding and pie filling
2¹/₄ cups milk
1 pint (2 cups) heavy cream
¹/₄ cup orange-flavored liqueur or orange juice
1 package (10 ounces) frozen raspberries, thawed and drained, syrup reserved
¹/₄ cup raspberry preserves
¹/₃ cup sweet sherry
3 packages (3 ounces each) ladyfingers (36 double ladyfingers)
2 tablespoons 10X (confectioners') sugar
2 teaspoons vanilla
¹/₂ cup whole unblanched almonds

1. Prepare instant pudding with milk, 1¹/₂ cups of the heavy cream and the liqueur to make 4 cups liquid, following label directions.
2. Combine 3 tablespoons of the reserved raspberry syrup, the raspberry preserves and the sherry in a small bowl; mix well. Separate ladyfingers. Brush mixture over flat side of half the ladyfingers; arrange against side of a 2-quart glass or crystal bowl, rounded sides out, lining bowl completely.
3. Spoon in half the pudding and top with remaining ladyfingers. Top with drained raspberries and remaining pudding. Cover; refrigerate several hours or overnight until completely chilled.
4. Just before serving, beat remaining ¹/₂ cup cream with 10X sugar and vanilla in a small bowl until stiff. Spoon cream into a pastry bag fitted with a star tip. Pipe cream in a lattice pattern on top of custard. Garnish with almonds.

Cassata alla Siciliana

Makes 8 servings.

1 package (10³/₄ ounces) frozen pound cake
¹/₄ cup orange marmalade
2 tablespoons rum or orange juice
1 container (15 ounces) ricotta cheese
2 tablespoons orange-flavored liqueur or orange juice
3 tablespoons sugar
1 tablespoon grated
orange rind
¹/₄ cup chopped mixed candied fruits or raisins
1 square (1 ounce) semisweet chocolate, coarsely chopped
1 can (16.5 ounces) chocolate ready-to-spread frosting
Candied pineapple slices, candied red cherries, candied angelica

1. Line an 8¹/₂ × 4¹/₂ × 2¹/₂-inch loaf pan with a long sheet of plastic wrap or foil cut to fit, with ends extending up and over the short sides of the pan.
2. Slice pound cake horizontally into 4 even layers.
3. Blend marmalade and rum in a cup. Combine ricotta, liqueur, sugar, orange rind, candied fruits and chocolate in a medium-size bowl; mix well.
4. Place top cake layer, smooth side down, in bottom of pan; spread evenly with a third of the marmalade mixture. Spread this layer with a third of the ricotta mixture; top with second layer. Repeat with remaining layers, marmalade and ricotta mixtures, ending with cake. Wrap loaf and pan in plastic wrap or foil; freeze several hours or overnight.
5. About 1 hour before serving, unmold cake onto serving platter. Frost cake thinly with chocolate frosting. Spoon remaining frosting into a pastry bag fitted with a star tip. Pipe frosting in decorative pattern on loaf. Garnish top of loaf with candied pineapple slices, cherries and angelica. Keep cake in refrigerator to soften until ready to serve. Any leftover cake can be wrapped and stored in freezer for up to 2 weeks.

Honey Almond Crunch Ice Cream

Makes 1 quart.

1 cup honey
2 cups heavy cream
2 cups milk
1 tablespoon vanilla
3 eggs, separated
¹/₂ cup Almond Crunch (recipe follows)

1. Combine honey, cream and milk in a medium-size saucepan. Cook over medium heat, stirring, until mixture just begins to bubble. Remove from heat; stir in vanilla.
2. Set pan in a bowl of ice water to chill, stirring occasionally, until mixture is cold.
3. Beat egg yolks until frothy; stir in chilled honey-cream mixture.

(continued)

4. Beat egg whites in a medium-size bowl just until soft peaks form; fold into honey mixture with a wire whisk or rubber spatula.

5. Pour mixture into a 4- to 6-quart ice cream freezer can; freeze, following manufacturer's directions.

6. Fold Almond Crunch quickly into soft ice cream. Pack in plastic containers; freeze until firm.

Almond Crunch: Toast $1/2$ cup chopped almonds on cookie sheet in a moderate oven (350°) for 10 minutes until lightly browned. Combine $1/4$ cup ($1/2$ stick) butter or margarine, 3 tablespoons honey, 3 tablespoons sugar and 1 tablespoon water in a small saucepan. Cook over medium heat, stirring constantly, until mixture reaches 300° on candy thermometer (hard crack). Remove from heat; stir in almonds; pour immediately onto a buttered cookie sheet, spreading as thin as possible with a spatula. Let cool completely, then crush with a hammer. Store leftover amount in a screw-top jar; it will make a delicious topping for ice cream, pudding, fruit desserts or cakes. Makes $1 1/2$ cups.

Peach Praline Ice Cream

Makes 2 quarts.

2 packages (1 pound each) frozen peach slices	3 cups milk, scalded
1 cup sugar	1 cup sugar
2 tablespoons lemon juice	$1/4$ teaspoon salt
2 envelopes unflavored gelatin	3 cups heavy cream
$1/4$ cup water	1 teaspoon almond extract
	$1/2$ teaspoon vanilla
	Praline *(recipe follows)*

1. Combine peaches, 1 cup sugar and lemon juice in a large bowl; toss gently. Let stand 15 minutes.

2. Soften gelatin in water in a 1-cup measure. Place over hot water in a small saucepan until gelatin is dissolved.

3. Stir gelatin mixture into scalded milk in a large bowl. Stir in remaining 1 cup sugar and the salt until sugar is dissolved; cool.

4. Place half the peaches into container of electric blender; cover. Puree until smooth. Chop remaining peaches. Combine chopped and pureed peaches, $1 1/2$ cups of the heavy cream, almond extract and vanilla with gelatin mixture; chill about 2 hours.

5. Pour mixture into a 13 x 9 x 2-inch metal baking pan. Freeze until mixture is partly frozen, 1 hour or more. Whip remaining cream in a medium-size bowl until stiff. Beat frozen mixture in a chilled large bowl with electric mixer until smooth.

6. Quickly fold Praline and whipped cream into ice cream. Pour back into metal pan; cover. Freeze until firm, stirring once or twice, about 4 hours.

Praline: Combine $1/4$ cup ($1/2$ stick) butter or margarine, 6 tablespoons firmly packed light brown sugar, $1/2$ cup light corn syrup, 1 tablespoon water and

$1/3$ cup pecans in a small saucepan. Heat to 300° (hard crack) on candy thermometer or cook 15 minutes until a little bit of syrup dropped into very cold water separates into threads which are hard but not brittle. Remove from heat; pour immediately onto a buttered cookie sheet, spreading as thin as possible with a metal spatula. Let cool completely, then crush coarsely. Makes 1 cup.

One-Step Strawberry Ice Cream

You don't need to have an ice cream freezer for this very rich and creamy ice cream. Simply mix three ingredients together, freeze and scoop out to make your favorite ice cream dessert. Good over ripe bananas with strawberry and chocolate toppings, whipped cream and toasted chopped almonds.

Makes $1 1/2$ quarts.

1 pint strawberries	*(not evaporated milk)*
1 can (14 ounces) sweetened condensed milk	2 cups heavy cream, whipped

1. Line a $9 \times 5 \times 3$-inch loaf pan with aluminum foil. Wash, hull and pat strawberries dry. Puree in the container of an electric blender or food processor.

2. Combine strawberry puree with condensed milk in a large bowl. Fold in whipped cream; pour into foil-lined pan. Cover with aluminum foil and freeze 6 hours or until firm.

3. To serve: Either peel off foil and slice ice cream with a large sharp knife or scoop from pan and serve in sundae dishes.

All-American Vanilla Ice Cream

Makes about 2 quarts.

$1 1/2$ cups sugar	4 eggs, slightly beaten
$1/4$ cup all-purpose flour	1 quart (4 cups) heavy cream
Dash salt	2 tablespoons vanilla
2 cups milk	

1. Combine sugar, flour and salt in a large saucepan; stir in milk. Cook, stirring constantly, over medium heat, until mixture thickens and bubbles 1 minute.

2. Stir half the hot mixture slowly into beaten eggs in a medium-size bowl; stir back into remaining mixture in saucepan. Cook, stirring, 1 minute.

3. Pour into a large bowl; stir in cream and vanilla. Chill at least 2 hours.

4. Pour mixture into a 4- to 6-quart freezer can; freeze.

5. Pack in plastic containers; freeze until firm.

Pictured opposite: Frozen Honey Mousse, page 288; Honey Almond Crunch Ice Cream, page 275; Golden Honey Gingerbread, page 180.

Chocolate Burnt Almond Ice Cream

A heavenly rich chocolate ice cream, crunchy with sugary almonds and nuggets of dark chocolate.

Makes about 3 quarts.

1¹/₂ **cups sugar**	4 **eggs, slightly beaten**
¹/₄ **teaspoon salt**	1 **quart (4 cups) heavy**
3 **tablespoons flour**	**cream**
2 **cups milk**	1 **tablespoon vanilla**
6 **squares**	**Burnt Almonds** (*recipe*
unsweetened	*follows*)
chocolate	

1. Combine sugar, salt and flour in a large saucepan; gradually stir in milk with 4 of the squares of chocolate. Cook over medium heat, stirring constantly, until mixture thickens and chocolate is melted. Remove from heat.
2. Slowly stir half of the mixture into beaten eggs; stir back into remaining mixture in saucepan. Cook over low heat, stirring constantly, 1 minute. Remove from heat; pour into a large bowl; cool. Stir in 2 cups of the cream and the vanilla; chill about 2 hours.
3. Pour mixture into a 13 x 9 x 2-inch metal baking pan. Freeze until mixture is partly frozen, 1 hour or more.
4. Coarsely chop the remaining 2 squares of chocolate.
5. Whip the remaining cream in a medium-size bowl until stiff. Beat frozen mixture in a chilled large bowl with electric mixer until smooth. Quickly fold in whipped cream, chocolate and almonds. Pour back into metal pan; cover. Return to freezer; freeze until firm, stirring once or twice, about 4 hours.

Burnt Almonds: Combine ¹/₄ cup water, ¹/₄ cup sugar and ¹/₃ cup whole unblanched almonds in a small heavy skillet. Heat to boiling, stirring constantly over medium heat; continue simmering, without stirring, until almonds start to make a popping sound, 10 to 15 minutes; remove from heat. Stir with wooden spoon until syrup crystallizes and mixture looks dry. Return skillet to heat; heat and stir over medium heat until sugar melts slightly and begins to cling to almonds. Turn out onto buttered cookie sheet; separate with fork; cool completely. When almonds are cooled completely, chop coarsely. Store in tightly covered container until ready to use. Makes 1 cup.

Strawberry Ice Cream

Makes 3 quarts.

1¹/₂ **cups sugar**	3 **eggs, slightly beaten**
¹/₄ **teaspoon salt**	2 **pints (4 cups)**
3 **tablespoons flour**	**strawberries**
2 **cups milk**	3 **cups heavy cream**

1. Combine 1 cup of the sugar, salt and flour in a medium-size saucepan; gradually stir in milk. Cook

Chocolate Burnt Almond Ice Cream.

over medium heat, stirring, until mixture thickens and bubbles. Remove from heat.
2. Stir half of the mixture slowly into beaten eggs in a medium-size bowl; stir back into the remaining mixture in saucepan. Cook, stirring constantly, 1 minute. Remove from heat; pour into a large bowl; cool.
3. Wash, hull, dry and halve strawberries into a large bowl. Toss with the remaining ¹/₂ cup sugar. Let stand 10 minutes. Remove 1 cup of the strawberries and chop coarsely. Place remainder in the container of an electric blender or food processor. Cover; whirl until pureed. Add chopped strawberries, pureed strawberries and 1¹/₂ cups of the heavy cream to custard mixture. Chill about 2 hours.
4. Pour mixture into a 13 x 9 x 2-inch metal baking pan. Freeze until mixture is partly frozen, 1 hour or more.
5. Whip the remaining cream in a medium-size bowl until stiff. Beat frozen mixture in a chilled large bowl with electric mixer until smooth. Quickly return to freezer; freeze until firm, stirring once or twice, about 4 hours.

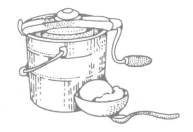

Low-Cal Vanilla Ice Cream

Makes 8 servings at 71 calories each.

1 tall can (13 ounces)
  evaporated skim
  milk
1¼ teaspoons
  unflavored gelatin
  (½ envelope)
¼ cup sugar
⅓ cup cold water

Granulated sugar
  substitute to equal
  16 teaspoons sugar
4 teaspoons vanilla
½ teaspoon butter
  flavoring
2 egg whites
¼ teaspoon salt

1. Pour evaporated skim milk into a deep bowl. Place bowl and beaters from electric mixer in freezer for 1 hour or until milk has begun to freeze.
2. Combine gelatin and sugar in a small saucepan. Add water; let stand 1 minute. Heat slowly, stirring constantly, until gelatin and sugar are dissolved. Stir in sugar substitute, vanilla and butter flavoring; cool.
3. Beat frozen milk at high speed until the consistency of whipped cream. Beat egg whites and salt until stiff in a small bowl. Fold gelatin mixture and beaten egg whites into whipped milk until well blended.
4. Pour into a 9 x 9 x 2-inch pan. Freeze until almost firm. Beat mixture in a bowl with electric mixer until smooth. Refreeze, 30 minutes. Beat again.
5. Spoon into container and freeze firm. Let soften slightly before serving.

Coffee Butterscotch Swirl Ice Cream

Makes about 2 quarts.

1½ cups sugar
¼ teaspoon salt
3 tablespoons flour
¼ cup instant coffee
  powder
3 cups milk

4 eggs, slightly beaten
3 cups heavy cream
1 tablespoon vanilla
1 jar (12 ounces)
  butterscotch
  topping

1. Combine sugar, salt, flour and coffee in a large saucepan; stir in milk gradually. Cook over medium heat, stirring constantly, until mixture thickens and coffee is dissolved. Remove from heat.
2. Stir half the mixture slowly into beaten eggs; stir back into remaining mixture in saucepan. Cook, stirring constantly, 1 minute. Remove from heat; pour into a large bowl; cool. Stir in 1½ cups of the cream and the vanilla; chill 2 hours.
3. Pour mixture into a 13 x 9 x 2-inch metal baking pan. Freeze until mixture is partly frozen, 1 hour or more. Whip remining cream in a medium-size bowl until stiff. Beat frozen mixture in a chilled large bowl with electric mixer until smooth. Fold in cream quickly. Return to freezer for 1 hour or until just firm enough to spoon.
4. Working very quickly, spoon about one-fifth of the ice cream into large plastic container; drizzle butterscotch sauce over. Continue to layer the ice cream and sauce. Freeze until firm.

Walnut Crunch Ice Cream

Makes 1 quart.

¼ cup (½ stick)
  butter or margarine
6 tablespoons sugar
½ teaspoon light corn
  syrup
1 tablespoon water

Dash salt
¼ cup chopped
  walnuts
All-American Vanilla
  Ice Cream (recipe
  above)

1. Combine butter, sugar, corn syrup, water and salt in a small heavy saucepan. Cook over medium heat, stirring constantly, until a candy thermometer reaches 305°. Add nuts; mix well.
2. Pour immediately onto a buttered cookie sheet. Cool.
3. When candy is hardened, chop into small pieces.
4. Stir candy pieces into freshly made All-American Vanilla Ice Cream.
5. Pack in plastic containers; freeze until firm.

Plum Ice Cream Sandwiches

Makes 15 sandwiches.

2 pounds ripe red
  plums
1 cup sugar
¼ cup water
1 tablespoon lemon
  juice
1½ teaspoons

unflavored gelatin
Pinch salt
1 cup light cream or
  half-and-half
1 cup heavy cream
Chocolate Wafers
  (recipe follows)

1. Wash, pit and dice plums (you should have about 4 cups).
2. Combine plums, sugar, water, lemon juice, gelatin and salt in large saucepan. Bring to boiling, stirring constantly, until sugar is dissolved; lower heat. Cook, stirring occasionally, until plums are a sauce-like consistency. Cool.
3. Stir light cream into plum mixture; pour into 13 x 9 x 2-inch pan. Freeze mixture until firm, about 3 hours. Chill a large bowl and beaters.
4. Whip heavy cream in a small bowl until soft peaks form.
5. Break frozen plum mixture into chunks into chilled bowl. Beat with electric mixer until very fluffy. Fold in whipped cream, working quickly so mixture does not melt.
6. Quickly line same pan with foil so that it extends up the sides. Spoon mixture into pan; spread to an even thickness; cover surface with plastic wrap. Return to freezer; freeze until firm.

(continued)

7. Prepare Chocolate Wafers.
8. Lift plum ice cream from pan with foil to cutting board; cut into 3 long strips, then cut each strip crosswise into 5 pieces to form rectangles that will fit the chocolate wafers. Transfer ice cream onto half of wafers with broad spatula; top with other half of wafers. Wrap each sandwich in plastic wrap; freeze until serving time.

Chocolate Wafers

Bake at 350° for 10 minutes.

Makes about 30 wafers or enough for 15 sandwiches.

3 squares unsweetened chocolate (3 ounces)	**1/2 cup (1 stick) butter or margarine, softened**
2 1/4 cups *sifted* all-purpose flour	**3/4 cup firmly packed brown sugar**
1 teaspoon baking powder	**1 egg**
1/2 teaspoon salt	**1 teaspoon vanilla**
	1/2 cup milk

1. Melt chocolate in a small bowl over hot, not boiling, water; cool.
2. Sift flour, baking powder and salt onto wax paper.
3. Beat butter, sugar, egg, vanilla and cooled chocolate in a large bowl with electric mixer until thoroughly blended. Stir in flour mixture alternately with milk until stiff dough forms. Add more flour if needed. Wrap the dough in plastic wrap; chill in refrigerator for 2 hours or overnight.
4. Divide dough in half. Roll one half between a sheet of foil and wax paper into a 13 × 9-inch rectangle, lifting off wax paper often to dust with flour and turning dough over for even rolling.
5. Peel off wax paper; with floured pastry wheel, cut dough into a perfect 12 1/2 × 8 1/2-inch rectangle. Remove trimmings. Cut rectangle, still on foil, into 3 strips lengthwise, each about 2 3/4-inches wide. Cut strips crosswise into five 2 1/2-inch pieces. Place wafers, still on foil, on cookie sheet. Preheat oven to 350°.
6. Repeat for other half of dough. (Bake trimmings, if you wish.)
7. Bake in a preheated moderate oven (350°) for 10 minutes or until cookies are set. Remove cookie sheet to wire rack; re-cut cookies with wheel. Cool cookies completely. Remove from foil; store in tightly covered container until ready for filling.

Mint Chocolate Chip Ice Cream

Mint-cool and speckled with little nuggets of chocolate.

Makes 2 quarts.

1 1/2 cups sugar	**3/4 teaspoon green food coloring**
1/4 cup all-purpose flour	**2 teaspoons peppermint extract**
Dash salt	**1 square semisweet chocolate, finely chopped**
2 cups milk	
4 eggs, slightly beaten	
1 quart (4 cups) heavy cream	

1. Combine sugar, flour and salt in a medium saucepan; gradually add milk. Cook over medium heat, stirring constantly, until mixture thickens and bubbles. Remove from heat.
2. Stir half of the mixture slowly into beaten eggs in a medium bowl; stir back into remaining mixture in saucepan. Cook, stirring constantly, 1 minute. Remove from heat; pour into a large bowl; cool. Stir in cream, food coloring and peppermint extract; chill at least 2 hours
3. Pour into a 4- to 6-quart freezer can; freeze.
4. Fold chocolate into soft ice cream.
5. Pack in plastic containers; freeze until firm.

Baked Alaska

President Thomas Jefferson served a version at a White House dinner in 1802. Now, see how simple it is to serve this show-stopper.

Bake at 425° for 3 minutes.

Makes 8 servings.

3 cups mint-chocolate chip ice cream, slightly softened	**(recipe follows)** **4 egg whites**
3 cups strawberry ice cream, slightly softened	**3/4 cup sifted sugar** **Cherries Jubilee Amandine (*recipe follows*)**
Lemon Loaf Cake	

1. Line a 9 × 5 × 3-inch loaf pan with a sheet of heavy-duty aluminum foil long enough to seal pan.
2. With the back of a spoon, firmly pack mint-chocolate chip ice cream onto bottom of foil-lined pan, spreading evenly. Repeat, making a second layer, with strawberry ice cream. Cover and seal with overlapping edges of foil; freeze for 2 hours, or until firm.
3. Slice Lemon Loaf Cake in half horizontally. Place on foil-wrapped wooden board. (Use second half to make another Baked Alaska or save for snacking.)
4. Unmold ice cream layers onto cake. Remove aluminum foil from ice cream. Freeze layers while making meringue topping.
5. Beat egg whites until foamy white in large bowl of

electric mixer at high speed. Beat in sifted sugar, 1 tablespoon at a time, until meringue forms firm peaks.
6. Spread meringue over ice cream and cake to coat completely, making deep swirls on top with spatula. Freeze until meringue is firm, then cover with plastic wrap. (Meringue-covered cake can be wrapped and frozen up to one week.)
7. Just before serving, bake in a preheated hot oven (425°) for 3 minutes, or just until meringue peaks turn golden. Slide onto serving platter and serve immediately with Cherries Jubilee Amandine. Return any remaining dessert to freezer.
Cherries Jubilee Amandine: Makes 4 cups. Drain syrup from 1 can (1 pound, 13 ounces) pitted sweet dark cherries into a 2-cup measure. Add water to make 2 cups. Combine ¼ cup sugar and 2 tablespoons cornstarch in a large heavy saucepan; stir in cherry liquid. Cook, stirring constantly, until sauce thickens and bubbles, 1 minute; stir in cherries and ¼ cup almond-flavored liqueur or brandy. Simmer 5 minutes. Sprinkle with sliced almonds.
Note: Sauce may be made ahead; cool to room temperature; refrigerate. Reheat before serving.

Lemon Loaf Cake

Use as the base for Baked Alaska or cut into slices, toast and top with a scoop of ice cream and sweetened strawberry slices.

Bake at 325° for 1 hour, 15 minutes.

Makes one 9 × 5 × 3-inch loaf (12 slices).

2½ cups all-purpose flour	**1½ cups sugar**
2 teaspoons baking powder	**1 tablespoon grated lemon rind**
½ teaspoon salt	**4 eggs**
1 cup (2 sticks) butter or margarine, softened	**¼ cup milk**
	2 teaspoons vanilla
	Vegetable spray

1. Sift the flour, baking powder and salt onto wax paper.
2. Preheat the oven to slow (325°).
3. Beat the butter or margarine, sugar and lemon rind until light and fluffy in a large bowl with an electric mixer at high speed.
Beat in the eggs, one at a time, until well blended.
4. Stir in the dry ingredients, alternately with the milk and vanilla, beginning and ending with the dry ingredients, to make a smooth batter.
5. Line a 9 × 5 × 3-inch loaf pan with two thicknesses of wax paper; spray generously with vegetable spray-on. Pour the batter into the prepared pan and smooth the batter into the corners.
6. Bake in the preheated slow oven (325°) for 1 hour, 15 minutes, or until a wooden pick inserted near the center comes out clean; cool in the pan on a wire rack

for 15 minutes; loosen the cake around the edges with a sharp knife. Invert onto the wire rack; cool completely. Place in a large plastic bag and tie to seal.

Double Peach Baked Alaska

Bake at 500° for 3 minutes.

Makes 6 servings.

1½ pints peach ice cream	**cake dessert shells**
1 can (16 ounces) peach slices	**5 egg whites, at room temperature**
6 tablespoons orange-flavored liqueur	**¼ teaspoon cream of tartar**
6 individual sponge	**10 tablespoons sugar**
	½ teaspoon vanilla

1. Scoop ice cream into 6 portions; return to freezer until frozen *very hard,* about 3 hours.
2. Drain peaches; select 12 thick slices. Combine slices with orange liqueur in small bowl; let stand at room temperature until ice cream is frozen hard.
3. To assemble: Place 2 peach slices in well of each sponge shell. Spoon about 1 tablespoon of liqueur from peaches in center of each shell. Place a scoop of ice cream on top. Return to freezer.
4. Preheat oven to 500°.
5. Beat egg whites with cream of tartar in a medium-size bowl with electric mixer at high speed until foamy-white. Sprinkle in sugar, a tablespoon at a time; continue beating until meringue forms soft peaks. Add vanilla; beat until meringue forms stiff peaks.
6. Arrange shells, 2 inches apart, on a breadboard. Working quickly, spread meringue in a thick layer over ice cream and shell. Place in middle of preheated oven.
7. Bake in a preheated extremely hot oven (500°) about 3 minutes or until meringue is lightly golden. Place on dishes and serve immediately.

Peach Ice Cream

Makes about 1½ pints.

5 large peaches	**juice**
¾ cup sugar	**¼ teaspoon almond extract**
1 teaspoon unflavored gelatin	**Dash salt**
2 teaspoons lemon	**1 cup heavy cream**

1. Dip peaches into boiling water 30 seconds, then into ice water 1 minute. Peel, halve, pit and slice. Puree enough peaches in the container of an electric blender or food processor to measure ¾ cup. Finely chop remaining peaches.
2. Combine pureed peaches, sugar and gelatin in small saucepan. Heat, stirring often, until mixture bubbles and is very hot. Remove from heat. Add

(continued)

Apricot-Banana Ice Cream.

Lemon Cream Ice Cream.

chopped peaches, lemon juice, extract and salt. Pour into 9 x 9 x 2-inch baking pan. Freeze until mixture is firm throughout, but not hard, about 1 1/2 hours.
3. Beat cream in small bowl with electric mixer until soft peaks form. Scoop peach mixture into large bowl. Beat with electric mixer until all frozen lumps are gone, but do not allow it to become watery. Add whipped cream; continue to beat until mixture is fluffy and well blended. Return to baking pan. Freeze overnight until firm.

Macaroon Ice Cream

A delicate, almondy variation of vanilla ice cream.

Makes about 1 1/2 quarts.

1/2 cup sugar	**2 cups light cream**
2 tablespoons cornstarch	**1/4 cup almond-flavored liqueur**
1/2 teaspoon salt	**3/4 cup crushed macaroon cookies**
2 cups milk	
1/2 cup light corn syrup	**1/4 cup toasted almonds, chopped**
2 eggs, slightly beaten	

1. Combine sugar, cornstarch and salt in a large saucepan; gradually stir in milk and corn syrup. Cook over medium heat, stirring constantly, until mixture comes to boiling; boil 1 minute; remove from heat.
2. Stir 1 cup of the mixture slowly into beaten eggs;

stir back into remaining mixture in saucepan. Cook over low heat, stirring constantly, until mixture thickens and coats a metal spoon. (Do not boil.) Remove from heat; pour into a large bowl; cover surface with plastic wrap or wax paper to prevent skin from forming; chill about 2 hours.
3. Stir in light cream and almond-flavored liqueur. Pour mixture into a 13 x 9 x 2-inch metal baking pan. Freeze until mixture is partly frozen, 1 hour or more.
4. Beat frozen mixture in a chilled large bowl with electric mixer until smooth. Quickly fold in macaroon crumbs and almonds. Pour back into metal pan; cover. Return to freezer; freeze until firm, stirring once or twice, about 4 hours.

Fresh Strawberry Ice Cream

Juicy red strawberries are deep-frozen in this creamy custard mixture.

Makes about 2 quarts.

1 1/4 cups sugar	**1 pint (2 cups) strawberries, washed and hulled**
Dash salt	
3 tablespoons flour	
1 1/2 cups milk	**Few drops red food coloring (*optional*)**
3 eggs, slightly beaten	
3 cups heavy cream	

1. Combine 1 cup of the sugar, salt and flour in a medium-size saucepan; add milk gradually. Cook over

Macaroon Ice Cream.

Fresh Strawberry Ice Cream.

medium heat, stirring, until mixture thickens and bubbles. Remove from heat.
2. Stir half of the mixture slowly into beaten eggs in a medium-size bowl; stir back into remaining mixture in saucepan. Cook, stirring constantly, 1 minute. Remove from heat; pour into a large bowl; cool; stir in cream. Chill at least 2 hours.
3. Mash strawberries with a potato masher or a fork in a large bowl; stir in the remaining ¼ cup sugar. Blend strawberries into chilled mixture; add food coloring for a deeper pink, if you wish.
4. Pour mixture into a 4- to 6-quart freezer can; freeze.
5. Pack in plastic containers; freeze until firm.

Lemon Cream Ice Cream

Lemony-light and silky-smooth.

Makes about 2 quarts.

1½ cups sugar	beaten
¼ teaspoon salt	2 tablespoons grated
2 tablespoons	lemon rind
cornstarch	½ cup lemon juice
3 cups half-and half	2 cups heavy cream
6 egg yolks, slightly	

1. Combine sugar, salt and cornstarch in a large saucepan; gradually stir in half-and-half. Cook over medium heat, stirring constantly, until mixture thickens

and bubbles. Remove from heat.
2. Stir half of the mixture slowly into beaten egg yolk; stir back into remaining mixture in saucepan. Cook, stirring constantly, 1 minute. Remove from heat; pour into a large bowl; cool. Add lemon rind and lemon juice. Stir in 1 cup of the cream; chill about 2 hours.
3. Pour mixture into a 13 x 9 x 2-inch metal baking pan. Freeze until mixture is partly frozen, 1 hour or more.
4. Whip the remaining cream in a small bowl until stiff. Beat frozen mixture in a chilled large bowl with electric mixer until smooth. Quickly fold in whipped cream. Pour mixture back into metal pan; cover. Return to freezer; freeze until firm, stirring once or twice, about 4 hours.

Apricot-Banana Ice Cream

Makes about 1½ quarts.

1 package (6 ounces)	3 small)
dried apricots	1 cup sugar
1¾ cups water	4 egg whites
1 cup mashed	¼ teaspoon salt
bananas (about	2 cups heavy cream

1. Cover apricots with 1 cup of the water in a small saucepan. Heat to boiling. Cover saucepan and remove from heat. Allow to stand 1 hour or until

(continued)

almost all of the water has been absorbed. Pour apricots and their liquid into the container of an electric blender. Cover; whirl until pureed. Turn out into a large bowl; add bananas.

2. Combine remaining ¾ cup water with sugar in a small saucepan. Heat to boiling; boil 5 minutes or until mixture is syrupy.

3. Beat egg whites with salt in large bowl with electric mixer until soft peaks form. Pour hot sugar syrup over in a slow steady stream while beating. Beat until mixture stands in firm peaks.

4. Wash beaters. Whip 1 cup of the heavy cream in small bowl with electric mixer until soft peaks form.

5. Fold meringue mixture, then whipped heavy cream, into apricots and bananas until no streaks of white remain.

6. Pour mixture into a 13 x 9 x 2-inch metal baking pan. Freeze until mixture is partly frozen, 1 hour or more. Whip the remaining cream in a small bowl until stiff. Beat frozen mixture in a chilled large bowl with electric mixer until smooth. Fold in whipped cream quickly. Pour back into metal pan; cover. Return to freezer; freeze until firm, stirring once or twice, about 4 hours.

Chestnut Ice Cream Log

Honeyed chestnut-vanilla ice cream curled around green-cherry-dotted strawberry ice cream.

Makes 10 servings.

1 can (15½ ounces) chestnut puree	**1 quart strawberry ice cream**
½ cup honey	**½ cup candied green cherries, halved**
1 quart vanilla ice cream, softened	

1. Line a 15½ × 10½ × 1-inch jelly-roll pan with plastic wrap.

2. Beat chestnut and honey in a large bowl with electric mixer at medium speed until smooth. Gradually beat in vanilla ice cream until no streaks of white remain. Spoon evenly into prepared pan. Freeze until firm to the touch, several hours or overnight.

3. Soften strawberry ice cream in a large bowl; spoon dollops over surface of chestnut layer; spread in an even layer; sprinkle with cherries. Roll up, beginning with short side, by lifting up plastic wrap. (If chestnut layer cracks on rolling, wait until it softens.) Cover with plastic wrap; refreeze until very firm.

4. Transfer log to serving plate. Smooth outer surface with metal spatula. Use serrated knife or tip of fork to score surface to give rough textured look. Garnish with whipped cream, candied chestnuts, candied cherries and citron, if you wish.

Icebox Cake

The first icebox cake was probably created during the Twenties when an enterprising cook sandwiched cookies together with whipped cream and stuck it in the icebox. We've come a long way since then. But what hasn't changed is that icebox cakes are quick and easy to put together and can be made ahead for terrific desserts or snacks! Store leftovers in the refrigerator and they'll keep a few days longer.

Peppermint Icebox Cake

Makes 8 servings.

1½ cups heavy cream	**ounce package)**
½ cup after-dinner mints	**2 tablespoons semisweet chocolate pieces**
10 drops green food coloring (*optional*)	**½ teaspoon vegetable shortening**
24 chocolate wafer cookies (from 8½-	

1. Beat cream until stiff in medium-size bowl; divide in half into two bowls; refrigerate one half.

2. Crush mints finely with rolling pin, or blend, half at a time, in the container of an electric food processor or blender until almost pulverized. Fold into one bowl of whippped cream with food coloring.

3. Frost each chocolate wafer with about 1 tablespoon of the mint mixture, making 3 stacks end to end on a serving plate, joining with mint mixture to make a long roll. Frost with reserved uncolored whipped cream. Chill at least 3 hours before serving.

4. Melt chocolate and shortening in a small pan over *very* low heat. Drizzle chocolate mixture from the tip of a spoon over frosted cake. To serve: Cut diagonally into ½-inch thick slices with a sharp knife.

Chocolate Rum Icebox Cake

An Updated version of an old favorite that is still easy to make ahead for a special occasion.

Makes 10 servings.

2 cups heavy cream	**Dash salt**
6 tablespoons unsweetened cocoa powder	**32 chocolate wafer cookies (from an 8½-ounce package)**
6 tablespoons sugar	**Rum Cream (*recipe follows*)**
2 tablespoons rum	

1. Combine cream, cocoa powder, sugar, rum and salt in a small deep bowl; refrigerate 2 hours.

2. Beat chilled mixture with electric mixer at high speed until stiff peaks form.

3. Frost each wafer with about 1 tablespoon cocoa-cream mixture, making 4 stacks of 8 cookies each. Set aside remaining cocoa mixture. Place 1 stack on its side on a serving plate. Press another stack of

wafers onto the frosted end of the first stack to make a long roll.

4. Arrange remaining 2 stacks, end to end, to make another long roll. Place second roll adjacent to first roll on plate.

5. Frost rolls together with remaining cocoa mixture to make one cake, swirling top in a decorative pattern. Refrigerate at least 4 hours or overnight before serving.

6. When ready to serve, prepare Rum Cream. Decorate cake with rosettes of cream; garnish with chocolate curls, if you wish. To serve: Cut icebox cake in 1/2-inch slices on the diagonal.

Rum Cream: Combine 1/2 cup heavy cream, 1 tablespoon sugar and 2 teaspoons rum in small bowl. Beat with electric mixer at high speed until soft peaks form. Makes 1 cup.

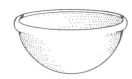

Honey Bubbles

Makes about 4 cups.

3 cups *sifted* all-purpose flour
1 tablespoon sugar
1/2 teaspoon salt
4 eggs
1/4 cup (1/2 stick) butter or margarine, softened
Vegetable oil for frying

Honey Syrup (*recipe follows*)
1/2 cup diced citron
1/4 cup toasted pine nuts (*optional*)
1 to 2 tablespoons multicolored sprinkles

1. Sift flour, sugar and salt into a large bowl; make a well in center of flour; add eggs and butter. Stir with a fork to mix flour gradually into eggs. When dough is stiff enough to handle, turn out onto lightly floured surface and knead with hands until very smooth and no longer sticky, about 5 minutes. Cover dough; refrigerate at least 1 hour.

2. Divide dough into 10 pieces; roll each piece into a rope about 18 inches long; cut each into about 36 small pieces.

3. Pour oil in large heavy saucepan to 3-inch depth. Heat to 375° on a deep-fat frying thermometer. Drop enough dough pieces into hot oil from a broad spatula to just cover the surface. Stir with a slotted spoon to separate. Cook until evenly golden, 2 to 3 minutes. Lift out with slotted spoon; drain on paper toweling.

4. Make Honey Syrup. Add the "bubbles" to Honey Syrup and stir with rubber spatula or wooden spoon until syrup is absorbed and "bubbles" stick together. Add citron and pine nuts. Pile onto serving plate into a cone or ring or dome shape. Sprinkle with multicolored sprinkles.

Honey Syrup: Combine 3/4 cup honey, 1/3 cup sugar, 1/3 cup water and 1 tablespoon lemon juice in a large

saucepan; bring to boiling, stirring constantly, until sugar dissolves. Continue cooking, uncovered, without stirring, 15 minutes or until slightly thickened. Add yellow rind or zest from 1 lemon, cut into julienne strips.

Cannoli

Cannoli shells are filled with creamy ricotta cheese and chocolate bits.

Makes 16 to 18 pastries.

1 3/4 cups *sifted* all-purpose flour
1 tablespoon sugar
1/4 teaspoon salt
1 teaspoon ground cinnamon
3 tablespoons wine vinegar
3 tablespoons water
1 egg
2 tablespoons butter or margarine, softened
1 container (3 pounds) ricotta cheese
1 1/2 cups sifted 10X (confectioners') sugar

1 teaspoon vanilla
1/3 cup finely chopped candied orange peel
3 squares semisweet chocolate, coarsely chopped
1/3 cup orange-flavored liqueur
1 teaspoon ground cinnamon (*optional*)
1 egg white
Vegetable oil for deep frying
1/4 cup chopped pistachio nuts
1 tablespoon 10X (confectioners') sugar

1. Combine 1 cup of the flour, sugar, salt and cinnamon in medium-size bowl. Make a well in center of dry ingredients; add vinegar (it makes dough tender) and water; blend well. Beat in egg and butter.

2. Add remaining flour, 1/4 cup at a time, until dough becomes a solid mass that can be easily lifted out of the bowl.

3. Knead dough on a lightly floured surface until it is soft and smooth, about 8 minutes, adding flour, if necessary, to prevent dough from sticking.

4. Wrap dough in plastic wrap. Chill in refrigerator for at least 1 hour.

5. Combine ricotta cheese, 10X sugar, vanilla, orange peel, chocolate, liqueur and cinnamon, if using, in a large bowl; blend well. Chill until shells have been prepared.

6. Divide dough into 16 equal-size pieces. Roll each piece on a lightly floured surface to a round about 1/16-inch thick. *Hint:* If dough pulls back, allow it to relax for 2 minutes, then roll again.

7. Cut 4 1/2-inch diameter circles from each piece using a saucer or lid for a pattern. When circles are all rolled, roll each again just before they are placed on cannoli tubes to give each circle an oval shape, about 5 inches long and 4 1/2 inches wide.

8. Using metal cannoli tubes, place dough lengthwise on tube. Brush edges of dough with egg white, then press firmly to seal. *Note:* If cannoli forms are

(continued)

unavailable, tear 18-inch wide heavy-duty aluminum foil into 16 six-inch lengths. Roll each piece, starting with the 6-inch side, around a 1-inch diameter broom handle or other similar form to shape into tubes. Wrap dough around foil tubes as directed above.

9. Heat 3 inches oil in deep-fat fryer or heavy kettle to 375° on deep-fat frying thermometer. Fry 2 or 3 cannoli shells at a time, depending on the size of the fryer or kettle, until golden brown, turning once. Remove with tongs or slotted spoon to paper toweling. Gently remove cannoli from forms; cool completely.

10. Fill each shell with $1/3$ cup filling using a small spoon or pastry bag fitted with a large plain tip. Dip ends into nuts. Sprinkle with 10X sugar.

Frozen Raspberry Cream Cheesecake

Makes 12 servings.

1 cup graham cracker crumbs	2 packages (8 ounces each) cream cheese
3 tablespoons sugar	1 quart vanilla ice cream
$1/2$ teaspoon ground cinnamon	$3/4$ cup red raspberry preserves
3 tablespoons butter or margarine, melted	$1/2$ cup heavy cream

1. Combine crumbs, sugar, cinnamon and butter in small bowl; blend well. Press firmly over bottom and sides of a buttered 8-inch springform pan; chill.

2. Beat cream cheese in large bowl until soft. Soften ice cream in a chilled large bowl; beat into cream cheese just until blended.

3. Spoon about $1/4$ of the ice cream-cheese mixture into prepared pan; drizzle part of raspberry preserves over (use $1/2$ cup of preserves for layering). Repeat until all of the cheese mixture and preserves are used; smooth top. Cover with plastic wrap. Freeze overnight or until firm.

4. Remove cake from freezer about $1/2$ hour before serving. Spread the remaining $1/4$ cup of raspberry preserves over top. Whip cream in small bowl. Pipe cream in a lattice design over preserves.

Orange Charlotte

Makes 8 servings.

1 package (3 ounces) ladyfingers	4 eggs, separated
3 tablespoons orange-flavored liqueur	1 can (6 ounces) frozen orange juice concentrate, thawed, undiluted
2 envelopes unflavored gelatin	$1 1/4$ cups water
$1/2$ cup sugar	1 cup heavy cream

1. Separate ladyfingers; place on a cookie sheet; drizzle part of the liqueur over; let stand while making the orange filling.

2. Combine gelatine and $1/4$ cup of the sugar in a heavy saucepan; beat in egg yolks, juice concentrate and water.

3. Cook over medium heat, stirring constantly, until mixture thickens and just coats spoon. Pour mixture into a large bowl; stir in the remaining liqueur. Chill 30 minutes in refrigerator or until mixture is slightly thickened.

4. While gelatin chills, stand ladyfingers around edge of an 8-inch springform pan; arrange remaining ladyfingers in the bottom.

5. Beat egg whites until foamy-white and double in volume in a medium-size bowl; beat in remaining $1/4$ cup sugar, 1 tablespoon at a time, until meringue forms soft peaks. Beat heavy cream until stiff in a small bowl.

6. Fold whipped cream, then meringue, into thickened gelatin mixture until no streaks of white remain. Spoon mixture into prepared pan. Chill 4 hours in refrigerator or until firm.

7. To serve: Remove side of pan; slide dessert, on its metal base, onto a plate.

Chocolate-filled Mimosa Lemon Roll

Looking for a special summer dessert? This easy and delicious lemon roll is it.

Bake at 375° for 12 minutes.

Makes 8 servings.

1 cup *sifted* cake flour	10X (confectioners') sugar
1 teaspoon baking powder	Rich Chocolate Filling *(recipe follows)*
$1/4$ teaspoon salt	Mimosa-Lemon Frosting *(recipe follows)*
3 eggs	
$3/4$ cup granulated sugar	
$1/3$ cup water	Green and yellow food coloring
2 teaspoons grated lemon rind	

1. Preheat the oven to moderate (375°). Grease a $15 \times 10 \times 1$-inch jelly-roll pan. Line the bottom with wax paper; grease the paper; sprinkle lightly with flour.

2. Sift together the cake flour, baking powder and salt onto a second piece of wax paper.

3. Beat the eggs in a medium-size bowl with an electric mixer until fluffy. Gradually add the granulated sugar, beating constantly, until the mixture is very thick and forms ribbons when the beaters are raised. Gently stir in the water and lemon rind until well mixed.

4. Fold in the flour mixture. Spread the batter evenly in the prepared pan.

5. Bake in the preheated moderate oven (375°) for 12 minutes or until the cake is golden and the center springs back when lightly touched with the fingertip.

6. Loosen the cake around the edges with a small spatula. Invert the pan carefully onto a clean towel

Chocolate-filled Mimosa
Lemon Roll, page 286.

dusted with 10X sugar. Peel off the wax paper. Trim
1/4 inch from the sides of the cake. Roll up the cake
and towel together, starting at a short end. Place
seam-side down on a wire rack to cool completely.
7. Prepare the Rich Chocolate Filling.
8. Unroll the cooled cake and towel. Spread the cake
evenly with the Rich Chocolate Filling. Reroll from the
short end, using the towel as a guide. Refrigerate
while making the Mimosa-Lemon Frosting.
9. Place 2 tablespoons of the Mimosa-Lemon Frosting
in a small cup and 3 tablespoons in a second small
cup. Tint the 2 tablespoons of frosting light green, and
the 3 tablespoons bright yellow. Spoon the tinted
frosting into 2 small wax paper cones with the ends
snipped off.
10. Spread the remaining Mimosa-Lemon Frosting
over the cake roll. Pipe green mimosa stems with
yellow flowers over the cake. Refrigerate until ready to
serve.

Rich Chocolate Filling: Combine 1 package (3$\frac{1}{2}$
ounces) chocolate-flavored pudding mix, 1$\frac{2}{3}$ cups
milk and 2 tablespoons butter in a small saucepan.
Cook over medium heat, stirring constantly, until the
mixture comes to a full rolling boil. Cool completely.

Mimosa-Lemon Frosting: Beat 1/4 cup (1/2 stick

butter or margarine in a small bowl until creamed.
Beat in 1 cup 10X (confectioners') sugar and 1
tablespoon lemon juice until well blended. Beat in
another 1 cup 10X (confectioners') sugar and enough
water or milk, about 1 tablespoon, until the frosting is
smooth and spreadable.

Peach Coupes

Makes 6 servings.

1 can (16 ounces)	**juice**
freestone peach	**1 quart vanilla ice**
slices	**cream**
1 tablespoon brandy	**Sliced almonds**
1 tablespoon lemon	

1. Drain syrup from peaches and reserve for another
use. Place peaches, brandy and lemon juice in
container of electric blender; cover; puree until
smooth. Place blender container in refrigerator until
ready to use.
2. To serve: Scoop ice cream into six individual
serving dishes. Pour sauce over. Garnish with
almonds.

Mousse

Mousse A rich, creamy dish which may be hot or cold, sweet or savory. As a dessert or a main dish, mousse is rich with cream and bound with eggs or gelatin. *Mousse* is the French word for froth and this is the criterion for such a dish. It must be light and frothy, accomplished by folding beaten egg whites or whipped cream into the mixture.

Frozen Honey Mousse

Makes 8 servings.

4 eggs, separated	**lemon juice**
3/4 cup honey	**1/8 teaspoon cream of**
2 teaspoons grated	**tartar**
lemon rind	**1 1/2 cups heavy cream**
2 tablespoons	

1. Prepare a 4-cup soufflé or straight-sided dish with wax paper collar: Measure a length of wax paper long enough to encircle dish. Fold in half lengthwise. (Wax paper should be about 2 inches higher than the rim of the dish.) Fasten collar with tape.
2. Beat egg yolks in top of double boiler; stir in honey. Cook over simmering water, stirring frequently for 20 minutes until mixture is slightly thickened. Remove from heat. Stir in lemon rind and juice.
3. Set top part of double boiler in a bowl of ice water to chill; stir until mixture mounds slightly.
4. While honey mixture chills, beat egg whites and cream of tartar in small bowl with electric mixer just until soft peaks form. Whip cream in a large bowl until soft peaks form.
5. Gently fold whipped cream, then egg whites, into honey mixture until no streaks of white remain.
6. Turn into prepared soufflé dish; freeze overnight. When ready to serve, remove collar gently, freeing mousse from wax paper, if necessary, with a small paring knife. Garnish with additional whipped cream, apricots and mint, if you wish.

Apple Mousse with Raspberry-Apple Sauce

Makes 8 servings.

5 medium-size cooking apples (McIntosh), pared, quartered, cored and sliced (5 cups)	**1 teaspoon grated lemon rind**
	2 tablespoons lemon juice
3/4 cup sugar	**2 egg whites**
2 envelopes unflavored gelatin	**1 cup heavy cream, whipped**
1 cup unsweetened apple juice	**Raspberry-Apple Sauce (recipe follows)**

1. Combine apples and 1/2 cup of the sugar in a medium-size saucepan. Bring to boiling; lower heat; cover; simmer 20 minutes or until apples are tender.

Puree through food mill or press through sieve over a large bowl. Return to saucepan. Cook over high heat, stirring constantly, until thick, about 5 minutes. Pour the mixture into a large bowl.
2. Soften the gelatin in the apple juice in a small saucepan, 5 minutes. Heat, stirring constantly, over low heat, until gelatin dissolves. Stir into applesauce along with lemon rind and lemon juice. Chill over ice and water, stirring often, until the mixture mounds when spooned.
3. While mixture chills, beat egg whites in small bowl with electric mixer until foamy-white and double in volume. Add remaining 1/4 cup sugar, 1 tablespoon at a time, until egg whites stand in soft peaks.
4. Fold meringue and whipped cream into apple mixture until no streaks of white remain. Turn into a 6-cup mold.
5. Refrigerate several hours or until firm; unmold on serving plate. Serve with Raspberry-Apple Sauce.

Raspberry-Applesauce

Makes 1 1/2 cups.

1 package (10 ounces) frozen raspberries in quick-thaw pouch, thawed	**2 tablespoons sugar**
	2 teaspoons cornstarch
1/2 cup unsweetened apple juice	**1 tablespoon lemon juice**

1. Combine raspberries and apple juice in container of electric blender; cover. Whirl until smooth. Force mixture through sieve to remove seeds.
2. Combine sugar and cornstarch in medium-size saucepan; stir in raspberry mixture. Cook, stirring constantly, until mixture thickens and clears. Remove from heat; add lemon juice. Pour into small bowl. Refrigerate until cold.

Strawberry Mousse

Makes 8 servings.

2 pints (4 cups) strawberries OR: 1 package (1 pound) frozen unsugared strawberries, thawed	**1 envelope unflavored gelatin**
	1/2 cup sugar
	1/2 cup water
	2 egg whites
	Pinch cream of tartar
	1 cup heavy cream

1. Prepare a collar for a 5-cup soufflé dish: Measure wax paper long enough to encircle dish. Fold lengthwise in half (wax paper should be about 2 inches higher than rim of dish). Fasten collar with tape or string.
2. Wash, hull and pat strawberries dry on paper toweling. Puree berries, a cup at a time, in container

of electric blender. Pour into bowl. Repeat until all are pureed.

3. Combine gelatin and 1/4 cup of the sugar in a small saucepan; stir in water. Place over very low heat and stir constantly until gelatin and sugar are dissolved. Cool mixture.

4. Stir cooled gelatin mixture into pureed strawberries. Place bowl in pan partly filled with ice and water to speed setting.

5. Beat egg whites with cream of tartar in small bowl with electric mixer until foamy white. Beat in the remaining 1/4 cup sugar, 1 tablespoon at a time, until meringue stands in soft peaks. Beat cream in another small bowl until soft peaks form.

6. Fold meringue and whipped cream into strawberry mixture until no streaks of white remain. Pour into prepared dish. Refrigerate 4 hours or until set. Remove collar gently, freeing soufflé from wax paper, if necessary, with a small knife. Garnish with additional whipped cream and strawberries, if you wish.

Chocolate Zabaglione Mousse

Makes 8 servings.

1/3 **cup plus 1 tablespoon sugar**	2 **egg whites**
3/4 **cup sweet Marsala wine**	**Pinch salt**
1 1/2 **teaspoons unflavored gelatin**	1/8 **teaspoon cream of tartar**
4 **large egg yolks**	1 1/2 **cups heavy cream, whipped**
3 **squares semisweet chocolate, melted**	2 **squares semisweet chocolate, coarsely chopped**
1 **teaspoon vanilla**	

1. Combine the 1/3 cup sugar, Marsala, gelatin and egg yolks in a medium-size saucepan. Beat over low heat 2 to 3 minutes until mixture is foamy and hot and gelatin is dissolved. *Do not boil or yolks will curdle.*

2. Remove from heat and continue beating 2 minutes to cool.

3. Stir in melted chocolate and vanilla. Set saucepan in bowl of water and ice to speed cooling.

4. Meanwhile, beat egg whites with the remaining tablespoon sugar, the salt and cream of tartar in a small bowl until soft peaks form.

5. Fold whites and all but 1 cup of the whipped cream into the chocolate mixture. Refrigerate remaining cream until later for garnish. Spoon mousse into 8 demitasse or teacups or small wine glasses. Cover and chill at least 2 hours.

6. Just before serving, garnish each serving with the reserved whipped cream and the chopped chocolate.

Note: Dessert is best prepared up to, but no more than, 8 hours in advance.

Espresso Mousse

Makes 12 servings.

1 **envelope unflavored gelatin**	1 **teaspoon grated lemon rind**
1 1/4 **cups water**	3 **egg whites**
2 **tablespoons instant espresso coffee**	1/4 **teaspoon salt**
1 **cup sugar**	2 **cups heavy cream**
3 **tablespoons brandy**	1/3 **cup toasted slivered almonds**

1. Sprinkle gelatin over water in a medium-size saucepan to soften, about 5 minutes. Stir in espresso coffee and 3/4 cup of the sugar. Heat, stirring constantly, over low heat until gelatin and sugar are dissolved. Pour into a large bowl. Cool; stir in brandy and lemon rind. Chill over ice and water, or in refrigerator, until slightly thickened.

2. Beat egg whites and salt in a medium-size bowl with electric mixer until foamy. Beat in the remaining 1/4 cup sugar gradually until meringue forms stiff peaks. In a small bowl, beat 1 1/2 cups of the cream until stiff.

3. Fold cream, then meringue, into gelatin until no streaks of white remain. Pour into serving bowl. Refrigerate 4 hours.

4. To serve: Whip the remaining 1/2 cup cream until stiff. Decorate top of mousse; sprinkle with almonds.

"Instant" Mousse au Chocolat

It's just as smooth and velvety as the longer version.

Makes 8 servings.

1 **package (6 ounces) semisweet chocolate pieces**	**apricot brandy or other fruit-flavored brandy**
1/3 **cup hot brewed coffee**	4 **egg whites, at room temperature**
4 **egg yolks**	3 **tablespoons sugar**
2 **tablespoons**	

1. Combine chocolate pieces and hot coffee in the container of an electric blender; cover. Whirl at high speed for 30 seconds or until smooth.

2. Add egg yolks and brandy; cover. Whirl at high speed for 30 seconds.

3. Beat egg whites in a small bowl with an electric mixer until foamy and double in volume; beat in sugar, 1 tablespoon at a time, until meringue stands in firm peaks. Gently fold in chocolate mixture until no streaks of white remain. Spoon into 8 parfait glasses or a serving bowl.

4. Chill at least 1 hour. To serve: Garnish with whipped cream, if you wish.

Yogurt Lime Parfaits.

Yogurt Lime Parfaits

Mixed fruits and strawberries are spooned into individual dessert glasses, and then topped with a frothy lime-yogurt gelatin. Make several hours ahead.

Makes 6 servings.

1 envelope unflavored gelatin	**1 cup heavy cream, whipped**
1/4 cup cold water	**1 package (10 ounces) quick-thaw frozen mixed fruits, partly thawed**
1 1/2 cups unflavored yogurt	
2/3 cup sugar	
2 teaspoons grated lime rind	**9 fresh or frozen strawberries**
1/4 cup lime juice (about 2 limes)	**6 thin lime slices, halved and seeded**

1. Sprinkle gelatin over cold water in a small bowl; let stand to soften for 5 minutes. Set bowl in simmering water; stir gelatin until completely dissolved.
2. Combine dissolved gelatin, yogurt, sugar, lime rind and juice in bowl. Place bowl in pan of ice water; stir often until slightly thickened. Fold in whipped cream.
3. Divide mixed fruits with their juice among six 8-ounce dessert glasses.
4. Reserve 3 strawberries for garnish; refrigerate. Slice remaining strawberries and divide among the glasses. Spoon lime mixture over fruits. Refrigerate for several hours or until ready to serve.
5. Halve reserved strawberries. Garnish each parfait with strawberry half and 2 lime slices.

Granola Parfait

Makes 4 servings.

2 cups granola	**ounces each) frozen mixed fruit, partially thawed and drained**
2 containers (8 ounces each) vanilla yogurt	
2 packages (10	

In each of 4 tall parfait glasses, place 1/8 of the

granola, $^1/_8$ of the yogurt and $^1/_8$ of the fruit. Repeat layering. Serve immediately or refrigerate to serve later.

Pink Grapefruit Snow with Warm Orange Sauce

Makes 6 servings.

1 envelope unflavored gelatin	juice
	3 egg whites
$^1/_4$ cup cold water	Orange Sauce (recipe
$^2/_3$ cup sugar	follows)
$^1/_2$ teaspoon grated lemon rind	Pink grapefruit sections (optional)
1 cup pink grapefruit	

1. Sprinkle gelatin over cold water in small bowl; let soften for 5 minutes. Set bowl in hot water; stir gelatin to dissolve.
2. Combine dissolved gelatin, $^1/_3$ cup of the sugar, the lemon rind and grapefruit juice in large bowl. Set bowl in pan of ice and water; stir often just until mixture begins to set, 15 to 20 minutes.
3. Beat egg whites in medium-size bowl with electric mixer until soft peaks form. Gradually beat in remaining sugar; continue beating until stiff peaks form.
4. Beat gelatin mixture on high speed until light and frothy. Fold in egg whites until well blended. Turn into 1-quart mold. Refrigerate until firm, at least 3 hours.
5. To serve, run small, thin spatula around edge of mold. Dip mold quickly in pan of hot water. Cover mold with plate; invert plate and mold together. Shake gently to release snow. Carefully lift off mold.

Pink Grapefruit Snow with Warm Orange Sauce.

6. Prepare Orange Sauce.
7. Spoon warm Orange Sauce around base of snow. Garnish with pink grapefruit sections, if you wish. Pass additional warm Orange Sauce.

Orange Sauce

Grate rinds before squeezing juice.

Makes about $1^3/_4$ cups.

3 eggs	margarine, cut into
$^1/_2$ cup sugar	small pieces
$^3/_4$ cup orange juice (2 oranges)	1 tablespoon grated orange rind
1 tablespoon lemon juice (1 lemon)	$^1/_4$ teaspoon grated lemon rind
$^1/_4$ cup butter or	

1. Beat together lightly eggs and sugar in top of double boiler. Stir in orange juice, lemon juice and butter.
2. Place over barely simmering water. Cook, stirring constantly, until sauce thickens slightly and coats back of spoon, 10 to 15 minutes. Stir in grated rinds.
3. Remove from heat. Serve warm or cold.

Spumoni   An Italian frozen dessert, shaped in a mold, consisting of an outer layer of ice cream with chopped almonds and an inner layer of cream with candied mixed fruit.

Instant Spumoni

Makes 8 servings.

1 pint vanilla ice cream	$^1/_4$ cup chopped mixed candied fruits
1 tablespoon rum	

1. Soften ice cream in a bowl. Stir in rum and candied fruits.
2. Spoon in muffin-pan cups lined with 8 paper baking cups. Freeze just until firm, about 2 hours.

Ices   A frozen dessert made of sweetened fruit juices or fruit puree usually diluted with water. Some people think ices and sherbets are the same, but sherbet is made with cream or milk added to sweetened fruit juice or puree; ices contain no dairy products. Ices can also be made from coffee or a wine such as champagne. They are sometimes called "Italian water ice" or "sorbet" in French.

Ices must be stirred often during the freezing process to produce a smooth product or made in an ice cream freezer. Sometimes gelatin or egg whites are used as a stabilizer to keep the ice crystals small.

(continued)

Ices can be molded in a variety of shapes or simply served attractively in hollowed fruit such as lemons, oranges and melons.

A *frappé* is similar to an ice but it is served in a mushy consistency. *Granité* is an ice which is stirred infrequently during freezing, giving a gritty texture.

A *popsicle* is an ice which originally was called "epsicle" for a man named Epperson, who, in 1926, accidentally left a glass of lemonade with a spoon in it on a cold windowsill where the lemonade froze. Epperson subsequently made more and sold them as popsicles.

Pink Lemonade Ice

Makes 6 cones.

1 can (6 ounces) frozen pink lemonade concentrate	3 cups finely crushed ice 6 3-ounce paper cups

Defrost lemonade just until slushy. Quickly mix with crushed ice in small bowl. Pack into paper cups, mounding slightly. Place in freezer; freeze until firm. To serve: Allow to defrost slightly; squeeze paper cup from bottom to bring flavored ice up to top.

Banana Popsicles

Makes 6 popsicles.

2 large firm-ripe bananas 6 long flat wooden skewers 6 5-ounce paper cups	2 cups fruit juice (apple, orange, grape or cranberry juice cocktail)

Peel bananas; cut each into 3 equal pieces; insert a skewer halfway into each. Place, skewer up, in center of paper cups. Pour 1/3 cup juice into each paper cup. Freeze until firm. To serve; Remove paper cups. Slip small paper doily or napkin onto handle of each popsicle before serving.

Cranberry Ice

Makes 2 1/2 quarts.

1 envelope unflavored gelatin 2 tablespoons grated orange rind 1/2 cup orange juice 1 tablespoon grated lemon rind	1/4 cup lemon juice 1 pound fresh or frozen cranberries, washed and stemmed 2 1/4 cups sugar 3 cups cold water

1. Combine gelatin with orange and lemon rinds and juices.
2. Simmer cranberries with sugar and water about 5 minutes over moderate heat, stirring now and then, until skins pop. Set a food mill or large fine sieve over a large heatproof bowl and pour in cranberries and all liquid. Puree cranberries in the food mill or by forcing as much pulp as possible through the sieve. Stir gelatin mixture into hot cranberry puree; if it does not dissolve completely, empty mixture into a large heavy saucepan and heat and stir over low heat until gelating does dissolve, 2 to 3 minutes. Cool.
3. Pour mixture into a 13 x 9 x 2-inch pan and freeze 2 hours until mushy-firm. Break up semifrozen mixture; beat in a chilled large bowl with electric mixer until fluffy.
4. Pack into freezer containers and store in the freezer. Soften the cranberry ice slightly before serving.

Orange Ice

Makes 6 servings.

3 cups water 2 cups sugar 4 to 6 juice oranges	1/4 cup fresh lemon juice

1. Combine water and sugar in a heavy saucepan. Bring to boiling; cover; simmer 5 to 8 minutes. Remove from heat; cool.
2. Grate 1 tablespoon rind from the oranges before squeezing; reserve rind. Squeeze enough oranges to get 2 cups juice. Stir orange and lemon juices and grated orange rind into sugar mixture; mix thoroughly; pour into a 9 x 9 x 2-inch pan. Place in freezer until frozen.
3. Scoop half of orange mixture into container of electric food processor fitted with metal chopping blade. Cover and process until smooth but still frozen. Serve in individual sherbet glasses. Repeat with other half of mixture.

Grapefruit Ice

For best results, use pink or naturally sweet grapefruit for making this recipe. You can, of course, substitute canned or bottled grapefruit juice for the fresh, but it will have a more bitter, acid flavor.

Makes 1 1/4 quarts.

1 envelope unflavored gelatin 1 1/4 cups sugar 1 cup water 2 teaspoons finely grated grapefruit	rind 3 cups strained fresh grapefruit juice (about 3 large grapefruit)

1. Combine gelatin, sugar and water in a small heavy saucepan. Heat and stir over low heat until gelatin and sugar are both completely dissolved, about 5 minutes. Stir in rind and let steep 2 to 3 minutes. Mix with grapefruit juice.
2. Pour into a 13 x 9 x 2-inch pan and freeze 2 hours

or until mushy-firm. Break up semi-frozen mixture; beat in a chilled large bowl with electric mixer until fluffy.
3. Pack in freezer containers and store in the freezer. Soften ever so slightly before serving.

Honeydew Ice

Makes about 1¹/₂ quarts.

1 cup sugar	**melon**
1¹/₂ teaspoons	**4 to 5 tablespoons**
unflavored gelatin	**lemon juice**
1¹/₂ cups water	**Green and yellow food**
1 large honeydew	**coloring**

1. Combine sugar and gelatin in small suacepan. Stir in water. Bring to boiling, stirring until sugar is dissolved; lower heat. Cook, uncovered, 5 minutes. Cool completely.
2. Cut honeydew in half; scoop out and discard seeds. Scoop out pulp and puree in the container of an electric blender or food processor.
3. Pour pureed honeydew, sugar and gelatin mixture and 4 tablespoons lemon juice (taste and add more if you like) into ice cream freezer can or a 13 × 9 × 2-inch pan. Tint a pale green with food coloring.
4. If using ice cream freezer, adjust dasher and top of can. Freeze following manufacturer's directions.
5. Without ice cream freezer, place pan in freezer. Freeze mixture, stirring several times, until firm, about 4 hours. Chill a large bowl and beaters. Break frozen honeydew into chunks into chilled bowl; beat with electric mixer until very smooth.
6. Spoon ice from can of ice cream freezer or bowl of mixer into plastic container; cover. Freeze until firm, at least 6 hours or overnight.

Watermelon Ice

Makes 4 servings.

3 cups small pieces watermelon, seeded	**¹/₂ cup sugar**
2 tablespoons lemon juice	**1 envelope unflavored gelatin**
	¹/₂ cup water

1. Place watermelon, about half at a time, in an electric blender container; cover. Whirl until smooth and liquid. (You should have about 2 cups.) Pour into medium-size bowl; stir in lemon juice. (If you do not have a blender, press the melon through a sieve into a bowl.)
2. Mix sugar and gelatin in a small saucepan; stir in the water. Heat slowly, stirring constantly, until gelatin dissolves. Cool slightly; stir into watermelon mixture. Pour into a 9 × 9 × 2-inch pan.
3. Freeze about 1¹/₂ hours or until firm around edges.
4. Spoon into a large bowl; beat until smooth; return to pan. Freeze several hours longer or until firm.

Sherbet   Along with ice cream, sherbet is a favorite frozen dessert. Sherbet is made of a fruit puree or juice, a sweetener, water and milk. Egg white or gelatin is sometimes added. Some people think of sherbet and ice as the same but they differ. Ice is considered a nondairy product because it's made of fruit or juice, a sweetener and water.

Lemon Sherbet

Makes 1¹/₂ quarts.

1¹/₄ cups sugar	**lemon rind**
1 envelope unflavored gelatin	**¹/₂ cup lemon juice**
2¹/₄ cups water	**1¹/₂ cups milk**
1 tablespoon grated	**2 egg whites**
	¹/₄ cup sugar

1. Combine the 1¹/₄ cups sugar and unflavored gelatin in a medium-size saucepan; stir in water and lemon rind.
2. Heat, stirring often, until mixture comes to boiling; *lower heat and simmer 5 minutes;* remove saucepan from heat; stir in lemon juice. Strain mixture into a 13 x 9 x 2-inch metal pan.
3. Cool at room temperature 30 minutes. Stir in milk until well blended. Freeze mixture, stirring several times so that sherbet freezes evenly, until almost frozen, about 4 hours.
4. Beat egg whites until foamy and double in volume in a small bowl. Beat in the ¹/₄ cup sugar, 1 tablespoon at a time, until meringue forms soft peaks.
5. Spoon frozen mixture into a chilled large bowl. Beat with an electric mixer until mixture is very smooth.
6. Fold in meringue quickly. Spoon into a 6-cup mold or bowl; cover with foil or plastic wrap.
7. Freeze at least 6 hours or overnight. Unmold or scoop directly from bowl to serve.

Buttermilk-Lime Sherbet

A tangy, fixed-in-a-wink refresher, perfect for a summertime dessert.

Makes 6 to 8 servings.

4 cups buttermilk	**lime rind**
1 cup sugar	**1¹/₂ teaspoons grated lemon rind**
1¹/₂ cups light corn syrup	**¹/₂ cup lime juice**
1¹/₂ teaspoons grated	

1. Combine buttermilk and sugar in a large bowl; stir until sugar is completely dissolved. Blend in corn syrup, lime and lemon rinds and lime juice.
2. Pour into 2 dry freezer trays; freeze until firm around edges.
3. Spoon into large bowl; beat until smooth; return to freezer trays; freeze until firm.

Pineapple Yogurt Sherbet

This easy-to-make and refreshing dessert can be served alone or with fresh berries.

Makes about 1 quart.

2 cans (8 ounces each) crushed pineapple in pineapple juice	1 container (16 ounces) plain yogurt
1/2 cup honey	1 teaspoon vanilla
	1/8 teaspoon salt

1. Drain juice from pineapple (about 1/2 cup) into small saucepan; add honey. Bring to boiling, stirring until honey is dissolved. Boil, uncovered, over low heat 5 minutes. Pour into large bowl; cool. Stir in pineapple, yogurt, vanilla and salt.
2. Spoon mixture into a 9 × 9 × 2-inch pan. Freeze, stirring several times, until mushy, about 3 hours.
3. Turn partially frozen mixture into chilled bowl; beat with electric mixer until smooth. Return to pan and freeze until firm, at least 6 hours. Leave at room temperature 15 to 30 minutes before serving. Scoop into sherbet glasses; garnish with fresh mint or fresh berries, if you wish.

Strawberry Sherbet

A delightfully smooth, fresh berry frozen dessert, this sherbet can be made in either an ice cream freezer or in the freezer section of refrigerator.

Makes about 1 quart.

1 cup sugar	(20 ounces) frozen
1/4 cup light corn syrup	unsweetened strawberries, thawed
3/4 cup water	
1/2 cup orange juice	*For Refrigerator-*
1/4 cup lemon juice	*Freezer Method.*
2 pints strawberries OR: 1 bag	2 egg whites
	2 tablespoons sugar

Method for Ice Cream Freezer:
1. Combine sugar, syrup and water in small saucepan; bring to boiling; stirring constantly, until sugar is dissolved. Cook 5 minutes over low heat. Remove from heat; stir in orange and lemon juices; cool completely.
2. Wash and hull strawberries; puree in container of electric blender, adding about 1/2 cup of the sugar syrup. Stir in the remaining syrup.
3. Pour mixture into freezer can; adjust dasher and top. Freeze, using recommended amounts of ice and salt and following manufacturer's directions. Spoon

mixture into plastic containers; cover. Return to freezer until firm.

Method for Refrigerator-Freezer:
Before you begin, make sure freezer section will maintain 0°.
3. Follow recipe through Step 2. Pour strawberry mixture into a 9 × 9 × 2-inch pan. Place in freezer with the pan touching one of the freezing surfaces. Freeze mixture, stirring several times for even freezing, until frozen to a mush, about 4 hours.
4. Beat 2 egg whites until foamy-white in a small bowl. Beat in 2 tablespoons of sugar slowly until meringue forms soft peaks.
5. Break up frozen mixture and spoon into chilled large bowl. Beat with electric mixer until very smooth. Fold in meringue, working quickly so mixture does not melt. Spoon into plastic containers; cover. Return to freezer for at least 6 hours or until firm.

Mint-Pineapple Lemon Sherbet

Fragrant fresh pineapple makes a natural container for refreshing sherbets.

Makes 8 servings.

2 pints lemon sherbet	crème de menthe
2 tablespoons green	1 fresh pineapple

1. Spoon 1 pint sherbet into a chilled medium-size bowl; beat until smooth but not melted. Stir in creme de menthe. Spoon back into sherbet container; refreeze overnight or until firm.
2. Cut pineapple in half through top. Carefully cut flesh away from rind, leaving a shell about 1/2-inch thick. Wrap and refrigerate shells. Remove core from pineapple. Puree about half of the pineapple in an electric blender or food processor to make 1 cup. Slice remaining pineapple thinly; refrigerate.
3. Spoon remaining pint of sherbet into chilled medium-size bowl; beat until soft but not melted; stir in puréed pineapple. Spoon into 3-cup freezer container. Freeze overnight or until firm.
4. To serve: Arrange scoops of mint and pineapple sherbets and sliced pineapple in chilled pineapple shells. Garnish with fresh mint, if you wish.

Lime Sherbet

Makes 1 1/2 quarts.

1 1/4 cups sugar	1/2 cup lime juice
1 envelope unflavored gelatin	1 1/2 cups milk
2 1/4 cups water	2 egg whites
1 tablespoon grated lime rind	1/4 cup sugar
	Green food coloring (*optional*)

1. Combine the 1 1/4 cups sugar and gelatin in a medium-size saucepan; stir in water and lime rind.

2. Heat, stirring often, until mixture comes to boiling; lower heat and simmer 5 minutes. Remove saucepan from heat; stir in lime juice. Strain mixture into a 13 x 9 x 2-inch metal pan.

3. Cool at room temperature 30 minutes. Stir in milk until well blended. Freeze mixture, stirring several times so that sherbet freezes evenly, until almost frozen, about 4 hours.

4. Beat egg whites until foamy and double in volume in a small bowl. Beat in the ¼ cup sugar, 1 tablespoon at a time, until meringue forms soft peaks.

5. Spoon frozen mixture into a chilled large bowl. Beat with an electric mixer until mixture is very smooth.

6. Fold in meringue quickly. Tint mixture a pale green with a few drops green food coloring, if you wish. Spoon into a 6-cup mold or bowl; cover with foil or plastic wrap.

7. Freeze at least 6 hours or overnight. Unmold and serve immediately or scoop directly from bowl.

Plum Sherbet

This sherbet can be made in either an ice cream maker or the freezer section of your refrigerator.

Makes about 2 quarts.

2 pounds red or purple plums	**juice**
1⅓ cups sugar	**Refrigerator-Freezer Method:**
1¼ cups water	**2 egg whites**
2 tablespoons lemon	**2 tablespoons sugar**

Method for Ice Cream Freezer:

1. Wash, pit and slice plums (you should have about 5 cups).

2. Combine sugar and water in large saucepan; bring to boiling, stirring constantly, until sugar is dissolved. Cook, uncovered, over low heat 5 minutes. Add plums; bring to boiling, stirring often. Remove from heat; stir in lemon juice; cover; cool completely.

3. Lift plums from juice with slotted spoon to container of electric blender or food processor. Puree until smooth; return puree to juice.

4. Pour mixture into freezer can; adjust dasher and top. Freeze, using recommended amounts of ice and salt and following manufacturer's directions. Spoon sherbet into plastic containers; cover. Freeze until firm.

Method for Refrigerator-Freezer:

Before you begin, make sure freezer is at and will maintain 0°.

1. Follow above recipe through step 3. Pour plum mixture into 9 × 9 × 2-inch pan. Place in freezer with the pan touching one of the freezer surfaces. Freeze mixture, stirring several times, until frozen to a mush, about 4 hours. Chill a large bowl.

2. Beat egg whites until foamy-white in small bowl; beat in the 2 tablespoons sugar until meringue forms soft peaks.

3. Turn partially frozen mixture into chilled bowl. Beat with electric mixer until very smooth. Fold in meringue, working quickly so mixture does not melt. Spoon into plastic containers; cover. Return to freezer for at least 6 hours.

Peachy Sherbet

No need to wait for the peach season to make this sherbet. Frozen sliced peaches work perfectly.

Makes 2 quarts.

2 packages (10 or 12 ounces each) frozen sliced peaches, slightly thawed	**¼ cup lemon juice**
	¼ teaspoon almond extract
	2 cups milk
1 can (14 ounces) sweetened condensed milk	**1 envelope unflavored gelatin**

1. Puree peaches, half at a time, in container of electric blender or put through a food mill. Combine peach puree with sweetened condensed milk, lemon juice and almond extract.

2. Combine milk and gelatin in a small saucepan. Heat and stir over low heat until gelatin is dissolved, about 5 minutes; cool. Combine with puree mixture.

3. Pour into a 13 × 9 × 2-inch pan, set in the freezer and freeze 2 hours or until mushy-firm. Break up semi-frozen mixture; beat in a chilled large bowl with electric mixer until fluffy.

4. Pack in freezer containers and store in the freezer. Allow the sherbet to soften somewhat before serving.

Orange Sherbet in Orange Cups

A most appealing and attractive dessert.

Makes 6 servings.

8 navel or Valencia oranges	**blanched almonds**
1 envelope unflavored gelatin	**3 tablespoons orange-flavored liqueur**
1¼ cups sugar	**1 teaspoon almond extract**
1 cup milk	**2 egg whites**
¼ cup ground	

1. Cut oranges in half; squeeze and strain juice. Measure and reserve 2¾ cups of the juice. Remove crushed pulp from 8 or the orange shells for serving cups; scallop edges with a paring knife. Wrap in foil or plastic; refrigerate.

2. Combine gelatin and 1 cup of the sugar in a medium-size saucepan. Stir in 1½ cups of the orange

(continued)

juice. Heat, stirring constantly, until mixture just comes to boiling. Lower heat; simmer, stirring occasionally, 5 minutes.

3. Remove from heat; cool. Stir in remaining orange juice and the milk, almonds, orange liqueur and almond extract. (Mixture will look curdled.) Pour into a 13 × 9 × 2-inch metal pan. Freeze until mixture is almost solidly frozen, about 4 hours.

4. Beat egg whites in a small bowl with electric mixer until foamy. Gradually beat in remaining ¼ cup sugar until meringue forms soft peaks.

5. Break up frozen mixture into chunks; turn into chilled large bowl. Beat with electric mixer until smooth. Quickly fold in meringue. Cover with foil; freeze overnight.

6. To serve: Spoon frozen sherbet into reserved orange shells.

Café Granité

Serve this coffee-flavored ice for a refreshing dessert.

Makes 4 servings.

⅓ **cup cold water**	**instant espresso**
⅓ **cup granulated or**	**coffee**
firmly packed light	**12 ice cubes (regular**
brown sugar	**size)**
2 tablespoons	**4 strips lemon rind**

1. Measure water, sugar and coffee in the container of an electric blender; whirl on low speed until sugar is dissolved. Chill 4 sherbet glasses.

2. Just before serving, turn blender to high and add ice cubes to mixture, one at a time. Keep blending until mixture is a complete mush. Spoon into chilled glasses. Add a twist of lemon rind.

Lemon Granité

Makes 1½ quarts.

1 envelope unflavored	**2 tablespoons grated**
gelatin	**lemon rind**
2 cups sugar	¾ **cup lemon juice**
3½ **cups water**	

1. Combine gelatin, sugar and water in a medium-size saucepan. Stir over low heat until sugar and gelatin are dissolved, about 5 minutes. Remove from heat; stir in lemon rind and juice. Cool.

2. Pour mixture into a 13 x 9 x 2-inch pan and freeze 3 hours or until mushy-firm.

3. Break up semifrozen mixture; beat in a chilled large bowl with electric mixer until fluffy.

4. Spoon into freezer containers; cover; freeze until firm. To serve: Scape across granité with a large spoon and serve in stemmed goblets or paper cups.

Golden Peach Floating Island

An old-time favorite--floating island--is transformed into a handsome dessert with yogurt sauce and peaches.

Bake at 275° for 25 minutes.

Makes 6 to 8 servings.

4 egg yolks	½ **teaspoon vanilla**
⅓ **cup honey**	**4 egg whites**
⅛ **teaspoon salt**	½ **cup sugar**
1 container	**1 package (10 ounces)**
(16 ounces) plain	**frozen peaches in**
yogurt	**quick-thaw pouch**

1. Beat egg yolks with honey and salt in top of double boiler; gradually beat in yogurt. Cook, stirring constantly, over simmering water, 15 to 20 minutes or until a soft custard forms, coating a metal spoon. Remove from heat; stir in vanilla; cool; chill.

2. Butter a 6-cup ovenproof mixing bowl or deep baking dish; sprinkle with sugar; tap out any excess.

3. Beat egg whites in a medium-size bowl until foamy and double in volume. Sprinkle in the ½ cup sugar, 1 tablespoon at a time, beating constantly until sugar completely dissolves and meringue stands in firm peaks. Spoon the meringue into prepared bowl, smoothing carefully against the side.

4. Bake in very slow oven (275°) for 25 minutes or until firm and golden. Cool in bowl on wire rack; chill. (Meringue will shrink while cooling.)

5. When ready to serve, partially thaw, then drain peaches; turn meringue into compote or shallow dish. Pour yogurt custard around meringue. Garnish with peaches. Sprinkle top with toasted, sliced almonds, if you wish.

Frozen Papaya Cream

Makes 4 servings.

2 papayas	⅓ **cup sugar**
4 tablepoons lime	½ **cup heavy cream**
juice	**Lime wedges**

1. Cut papayas in half lengthwise; scoop out and discard seeds. Scoop out 4 small balls with a melon baller, reserving for garnish. Carefully scoop out remaining pulp, reserving papaya shells. Puree papaya with lime juice and sugar in the container of an electric blender until smooth or beat with a fork or rotary beater.

2. Beat the cream until stiff; quickly but gently fold papaya into cream (do not overmix). Pour mixture into a shallow 8-inch cake pan. Place in freezer 1 hour or until frozen 1 inch around edge. Stir with a spoon.

Pictured opposite: Café Granité.

Return to freezer another 30 minutes to 1 hour or until soft-frozen.

3. To serve: Spoon mixture into reserved papaya shells, dividing evenly (or spoon into sherbet glasses). Garnish with a wedge of lime and reserved papaya balls.

Regal Peach Crown

A frozen charlotte-like dessert with a peach-flavored ricotta cheese filling.

Makes 8 servings.

10 plain ladyfingers*, split	cinnamon
1 bag (20 ounces) frozen peach slices OR: 3 cups fresh peach slices	1 container (15 ounces) part-skim ricotta cheese
4 tablespoons sugar	1/2 cup dairy sour cream
3/4 cup peach preserves	2 teaspoons lemon juice
1/8 teaspoon ground	Whipped cream for garnish

1. Line the bottom of a 5 1/2-cup brioche mold or 1 1/2-quart bowl with aluminum foil. Arrange 3 to 4 ladyfinger halves on the bottom, cutting to fit exactly in a single layer. Line the sides with the ladyfinger halves slightly overlapping. (The brioche mold needs 17 halves; the bowl may require more.)
2. Combine 1 cup of the peach slices, 2 tablespoons of the sugar, the preserves and cinnamon in the container of an electric blender or food processor. Cover; whirl until smooth. Transfer to a clean bowl. Stir in the ricotta cheese and sour cream. Pour into the prepared mold. Cover with plastic wrap. Freeze for at least 8 hours or overnight.
3. Prepare the peach sauce up to 1 hour before serving: Set aside 6 or 7 peach slices for garnish. Combine the remaining peaches, the remaining 2 tablespoons of the sugar and the lemon juice in the container of the blender or food processor. Cover; whirl until pureed. Set aside in the refrigerator.
4. Turn the mold out onto a serving platter. Let stand at room temperature for 20 minutes before serving. Garnish the top with the reserved peach slices and whipped cream. Serve with the peach sauce on side.

Make sure the ladyfingers are very fresh, or they will "float."

Ladyfinger   A small, finger-shaped piece of sponge cake, often used as a basis for other desserts. Some are commercially made and sold in packages or they can easily be made at home. Lady Finger is also a green variety of grapes.

Ladyfingers

Bake at 300 for 20 minutes.

Makes about 30 ladyfingers.

3 eggs, separated	1 teaspoon grated lemon rind
1/8 teaspoon salt	
3 tablespoons plus 1/3 cup sugar	10X (confectioners') sugar
2/3 cup *sifted* cake flour	Strawberry jam

1. Grease and flour 2 cookie sheets. Preheat oven to 300°.
2. Beat egg whites with salt in a small bowl with electric mixer until foamy. Gradually beat in the 3 tablespoons sugar until meringue forms soft peaks.
3. With same beaters, beat egg yolks in a large bowl with electric mixer at high speed until thick, about 5 minutes. Gradually beat in 1/3 cup sugar until yolks are pale and very thick, about 3 minutes.
4. Sprinkle 1/3 of the sifted flour over the egg-yolk mixture. Fold in gently, using rubber spatula. Repeat with remaining flour just until blended.
5. Stir 1/4 of the meringue into the batter to loosen it a little. Fold in lemon rind and remaining meringue gently until no streaks of white remain.
6. Fit pastry bag with a 1/2-inch plain round tip; fill bag with batter. Press batter out onto prepared cookie sheets to form strips about 3 inches long and spaced 1 inch apart. Sprinkle lightly with 10X sugar.
7. Bake in upper third of a preheated slow oven (300°) for 20 minutes or until a delicate brown. Remove to wire racks with spatula; cool. Store in container with tight-fitting cover. Before serving, sandwich in pairs with strawberry jam and sprinkle generously with 10X sugar. May also be served singly.

Peach Brown Betty

Bake at 375° for 30 minutes.

Makes about 4 servings.

8 slices whole wheat bread	1/4 teaspoon salt
1/4 cup (1/2 stick) butter or margarine	1/8 teaspoon almond extract
1 can (29 ounces) cling peach slices	1/2 teaspoon grated lemon rind
1/2 teaspoon vanilla	2 tablespoons lemon juice
1/4 teaspoon ground cinnamon	1 tablespoon sugar

1. Place bread slices on a cookie sheet. Toast in a moderate oven (350°) for 20 minutes to dry out; cool.

Pictured opposite: Regal Peach Crown, page 298; Tomatoes Stuffed with Ham Salad, page 783.

Crush into crumbs with rolling pin or whirl in blender. Melt butter in a small saucepan; stir in crumbs.

2. Drain syrup from peaches into a small saucepan. Simmer until syrup has reduced to about 1/2 cup.

3. Combine peaches, vanilla, cinnamon, salt, almond extract, lemon rind and juice with the 1/2 cup syrup.

4. Spread 1/3 of the buttered crumbs in a buttered 1-quart baking dish. Spoon in half the peach mixture. Repeat with crumbs and remaining peach mixture. topping with remaining crumbs. Sprinkle crumbs with sugar. Cover with foil.

5. Bake in a moderate oven (375°) for 15 minutes. Uncover; bake 15 minutes longer or until top is browned.

Flan

Flan This word applies to three desserts: a pastry shell filled with fruit, custard or cream; an egg custard baked in a mold, usually with a caramel sauce; and a sponge cake baked in a shallow round pan, served filled with fruit and/or a custard.

Blueberry/Strawberry-Topped Sponge Flan

Bake at 350° for 25 minutes.

Makes 12 servings.

1 cup *sifted* all-purpose flour	1 teaspoon vanilla
1 teaspoon baking powder	1/2 cup strawberry jelly
1/4 teaspoon salt	1 tablespoon water
1/3 cup milk	Pastry Cream *(recipe follows)*
2 tablespoons butter	7 to 8 large strawberries, hulled
3 eggs	2 cups (1 pint) fresh blueberries
1 cup sugar	

1. Sift flour, baking powder and salt onto wax paper. Preheat oven to 350°.

2. Heat milk with butter just to scalding; cool slightly.

3. Beat eggs, sugar and vanilla in a medium-size bowl with electric mixer until thick and creamy. Add flour mixture alternately with milk mixture, beating after each addition. Pour into greased and floured 10-inch sponge flan pan.

4. Bake in a preheated moderate oven (350°) for 25 minutes or until top springs back when lightly pressed with fingertip.

5. Cool layer in pan on wire rack 10 minutes; loosen around edges with a knife; turn out onto wire rack; cool.

6. Heat strawberry jelly and water in a small saucepan until melted and bubbly. Brush over interior of shell and sides of cake; allow to set for 5 minutes.

7. To assemble: Fill center of sponge flan with Pastry Cream. Arrange 7 or 8 strawberries in center, stem ends down; arrange blueberries around top. Glaze berries with additional melted strawberry jelly, if desired.

Pastry Cream

Makes 1 1/3 cups.

1 cup milk	purpose flour
4 egg yolks	1/8 teaspoon salt
1/3 cup sugar	1 teaspoon vanilla
1/4 cup *sifted* all-	

1. Heat milk to scalding in a medium-size saucepan.

2. Beat egg yolks with sugar in a medium-size bowl with wire whisk or electric beater until thick and creamy. Beat in flour and salt; gradually beat in scalded milk until smooth.

3. Pour mixture back into saucepan; cook, stirring constantly, until mixture thickens. (Mixture may become lumpy; if this occurs, beat with either a wire whisk or electric mixer until it becomes smooth.)

4. Lower heat and continue to cook 2 to 3 minutes, stirring constantly until mixture is very thick. Remove from heat; add vanilla; pour into small bowl. Cover with plastic wrap to keep skin from forming; chill.

Spanish Custard Flan

Bake at 325° for 30 minutes.

Makes 6 to 8 servings.

2/3 cup sugar	1 four-inch piece stick cinnamon
1 cup light cream or half-and-half	4 eggs
1 1/2 cups milk	2 tablespoons vanilla

1. Preheat oven to 325°; place an 8 × 1/2-inch layer-cake pan or a 4- to 5-cup ring mold in the oven to warm. (Caramelized sugar coats a warm mold more evenly.)

2. Heat 1/3 cup of the sugar in a large skillet over medium heat until sugar melts and turns golden. Remove pan or mold from oven; immediately pour caramelized sugar into pan. Hold pan with pot holder and tilt from side to side to cover bottom and side of pan with the sugar.

3. Combine cream, milk, remaining sugar and the cinnamon in a medium-size saucepan; heat just until bubbles form around edge.

4. Beat eggs slightly with vanilla in medium-size bowl; gradually pour in hot milk mixture, stirring constantly; strain into prepared pan. Place pan in large shallow pan; place on oven shelf; pour boiling water into larger pan to depth of about 1/2 inch.

5. Bake in a preheated slow oven (325°) for 30 minutes or until center is almost set. Remove from pan of water; cool, then chill several hours or overnight.

6. To unmold, loosen custard around edge with small

spatula. Cover pan with serving dish or plate; turn upside down, shaking gently to release custard; lift off mold. Spoon onto serving dishes with a little of the caramel syrup spooned over each serving.

Peach and Banana Flan

Makes 10 servings.

1 package (3³/₄ ounces) instant vanilla-flavored pudding and pie filling mix	1 10-inch flan layer (see Golden Sponge Layers, *recipe follows*)
1 cup milk	1 can (16 ounces) peach slices, drained
1 container (8 ounces) dairy sour cream	1 banana, sliced
1 cup apricot preserves	Lemon juice

1. Combine pudding mix with milk and sour cream in bowl. Beat with electric mixer on low speed until smooth; chill 15 minutes.
2. Heat apricot preserves until melted and bubbly in a small saucepan; press through sieve. Brush ¹/₃ cup over interior and sides of flan. Let stand 5 minutes.
3. Spread pudding mixture evenly in center of flan. Arrange peach and banana slices on top. (Brush bananas with lemon juice to keep from discoloring.) Spoon remaining apricot glaze over fruit. Refrigerate until serving.

Golden Sponge Layers

Bake at 350° for 20 minutes.

Makes one 10-inch flan layer and one 8 × 8 × 2-inch layer.

1¹/₂ cups *sifted* cake flour	6 egg yolks
2 teaspoons baking powder	1 cup sugar
¹/₄ teaspoon salt	¹/₃ cup boiling water
	1¹/₂ teaspoons vanilla

1. Grease and flour one 10-inch flan pan and one 8 × 8 × 2-inch baking pan. Preheat oven to 350°.
2. Sift flour with baking powder and salt onto wax paper.
3. Beat egg yolks in large bowl with electric mixer on high speed, 5 minutes, until thick and light. Add sugar gradually, beating until mixture is pale and thick enough to form a ribbon when beater is lifted, about 3 minutes. Stir in boiling water and vanilla.
4. Sprinkle ¹/₃ of the flour mixture over the egg-yolk mixture. Fold in gently using rubber spatula. Repeat with the remaining flour. Pour 2 cups of the batter into each prepared pan.
5. Bake layers in a preheated moderate oven (350°) for 20 minutes or until tops are golden brown and

centers spring back when lightly touched with fingertip.
6. Cool in pans on wire racks 10 minutes; loosen around edges with a knife. Turn onto wire rack; cool.

Caramel Coconut Flan

Bake at 350° for 1 hour.

Makes 8 servings.

1¹/₂ cups sugar	milk, undiluted
8 large eggs	¹/₈ teaspoon salt
2 cans (13 ounces each) evaporated	¹/₂ cup flaked coconut

1. Place a 6-cup mold in a large shallow baking pan filled with 1 inch of hot water. Place in a moderate oven (350°) for 10 minutes to warm.
2. While mold is warming, heat 1 cup of the sugar in a small saucepan, stirring constantly until melted and golden. Remove mold from water with pot holder. Pour melted sugar into mold and swirl to coat bottom and sides with the caramel; cool slightly.
3. Beat eggs until foamy in a large bowl. Beat in the remaining sugar, milk and salt until blended; stir in coconut. Pour mixture into caramel-lined mold. Replace mold in water bath.
4. Bake in a preheated moderate oven (350°) for 1 hour or until knife inserted 1 inch from edge comes out clean. (Center will still be soft.) Remove from water bath; cool on wire rack 10 minutes.
5. Refrigerate until cold. To serve: Loosen flan around edge with knife. Place rimmed serving dish upside-down over mold. Holding mold and dish, turn dish upright and lift off mold. Caramel will flow out to form sauce.

Triple Fruit Flan

Bake at 375° for 15 minutes.

Makes 8 to 10 servings.

1 package piecrust mix	2 tablespoons lemon juice
1 egg, beaten	8 fresh plums, halved and pitted
2 tablespoons sugar (for pastry)	3 cups sliced fresh peaches
1 package (8 ounces) cream cheese	1¹/₂ cups seedless green grapes (about 1 pound)
¹/₄ cup sugar (for filling)	¹/₂ cup strawberry jelly
1 teaspoon grated lemon rind	

1. To make the flan pastry: Fold a 30-inch length of

(continued)

18-inch-wide heavy-duty foil in half lengthwise, then in half crosswise, to make a 15 × 9-inch rectangle.

2. Blend piecrust mix, egg and the 2 tablespoons sugar until mixture leaves side of bowl clean.

3. Pat pastry onto foil rectangle to cover evenly. Turn up edges of foil with pastry to make a 1-inch rim on all sides, squaring off corners and pressing the extra pastry into corners to make a smooth edge. Prick well with fork. Freeze flan crust 2 hours. Preheat oven to 375°.

4. Bake in a preheated moderate oven (375°) for 15 minutes or until golden. Cool completely in foil pan, then remove from foil to serving plate.

5. Blend cream cheese and the 1/4 cup sugar until smooth in a small bowl; stir in lemon rind and juice. Spread mixture in bottom of pastry.

6. Arrange fruits in a pretty pattern over cheese layer. Melt jelly in a small saucepan. Brush over fruits. Chill.

Grape and Sour Cream "High Hats"

Refrigerated ready-to-make biscuits are the secret shortcut for these crowd-pleasing shortcakes.

Makes 10 small servings.

1 tube (10 ounces) refrigerated ready-to-bake flaky biscuits	cream
	4 tablespoons dark brown sugar
1 cup dairy sour	2 cups seedless green grapes

1. Bake biscuits following package directions.

2. Split biscuits in half. Lightly toast cut sides.

3. To serve, place bottom halves of biscuits on small dessert plates. Spoon about 2/3 cup of the sour cream onto the biscuit bottoms. Sprinkle with a total of 3 tablespoons of the brown sugar, dividing equally.

4. Reserve 10 grapes for garnish. Divide the remaining grapes over sour cream-topped biscuits. Cover with tops. Garnish each with the remaining sour cream, brown sugar and grapes. Serve immediately.

Waffles Suzette

A take-off on the popular Crêpes Suzette.

Makes 8 servings.

1 package (11 ounces) frozen round waffles (8 to a package)	1/4 cup (1/2 stick) butter or margarine
	4 teaspoons sugar
2 large oranges	1/2 cup Grand Marnier

1. Toast waffles following label directions. Cut each into four wedges. Place in a large chafing dish or skillet.

2. Pare the *thin* orange rind (no white part) from one orange with a vegetable parer; cut into julienne strips. Cut and squeeze oranges to extract 2/3 cup juice.

3. Melt butter in a small saucepan over low heat. Add

sugar, orange juice and julienned rind. Simmer 3 minutes. Stir in 1/4 cup Grand Marnier. Pour mixture over waffles.

4. Gently heat remaining 1/4 cup Grand Marnier in the same saucepan 2 minutes. Pour over waffles. Ignite; serve when flame subsides.

Frozen Semi-Freddo

This rich dessert, inspired by the original from Italy, is similar to a frozen mousse.

Makes 8 servings.

2 ounces milk chocolate, finely chopped	1 cup heavy cream
1/3 cup crushed amaretti cookies	Garnish *(optional):*
1/4 cup chopped almonds	2 tablespoons chopped almonds
1 tablespoon brandy	2 tablespoons crushed amaretti cookies
3 eggs, separated	1 ounce milk chocolate, finely chopped
1/3 cup superfine sugar	
1 teaspoon vanilla	

1. Line 8 1/2 × 4 1/2 × 2 5/8-inch pan with aluminum foil or plastic wrap. Set aside in freezer while preparing filling.

2. Toss chocolate, cookie crumbs, almonds and brandy in bowl. Reserve.

3. Beat egg whites in medium-size bowl until soft peaks form. Gradually add half the sugar and 1/4

Grape and Sour Cream "High Hats".

Frozen Semi-Freddo,
page 302.

teaspoon of the vanilla, beating until stiff, but not dry, peaks form.

4. Beat egg yolks in small bowl until foamy. Gradually add remaining sugar and ¹/₄ teaspoon of the vanilla, beating until almost white, about 3 minutes. Set aside.

5. Beat cream and remaining ¹/₂ teaspoon vanilla in clean medium-size bowl until stiff peaks form. Gently fold in beaten yolks and beaten whites just until mixed. Layer one-third of the mixture in bottom of prepared pan. Sprinkle on half of the cookie mixture. Spoon on another third of the cream mixture. Sprinkle on remaining cookie mixture. Spoon remaining cream mixture on top. Tap pan lightly on counter to settle.

6. Cover pan with aluminum foil or plastic wrap. Freeze at least 8 hours or overnight.

7. To serve, remove top wrapping. Invert onto serving platter. Remove pan. Peel off foil or plastic wrap. Garnish top with stripes of chopped almonds, crushed cookies and chopped chocolate, if you wish.

Jelly Roll
A sponge cake baked in a very shallow pan, called a jelly-roll pan. The cake is spread with jelly or jam and rolled. The top is dusted with 10X (confectioners') sugar, then sliced to serve.

Old-fashioned Jelly Roll

Bake at 375° for 12 minutes.
Makes 8 servings.

1 cup *sifted* cake flour
1 teaspoon baking powder
¹/₄ teaspoon salt
3 eggs
¹/₂ cup sugar
¹/₂ teaspoon orange extract
¹/₄ teaspoon lemon extract
3 tablespoons 10X (confectioners') sugar
³/₄ cup fruit jelly (any flavor)

1. Grease a 15¹/₂ x 10¹/₂ x1-inch jelly-roll pan; line bottom with wax paper; grease paper.

2. Sift flour, baking powder and salt onto wax paper; reserve.

3. Beat eggs in large bowl with electric mixer at high speed until foamy and double in volume. Beat in sugar, 1 tablespoon at a time, until eggs are thick and pale yellow. Beat in the orange and lemon extracts.

4. Preheat oven to 375°. Fold flour mixture, ¹/₃ at a time, into egg mixture with a wire whisk or rubber spatula until completely blended. Spread evenly in prepared pan.

(continued)

5. Bake in a preheated moderate oven (375°) for 12 minutes or until top springs back when pressed with fingertip.

6. Loosen cake around edges with a knife; invert onto a clean towel sprinkled with 1 tablespoon 10X sugar; peel off wax paper. Trim $1/4$ inch from all 4 sides for easier rolling. Starting at the short end, roll up cake and towel together. Place roll, seamside down, on wire rack, cool completely.

7. When cool, unroll cake carefully. Spoon jelly over cake, spreading to make an even layer. Reroll cake and place, seam-side down, on serving plate. Dust with remaining 10X sugar. Cut into slices to serve.

Strawberry Charlotte with Strawberry Sauce

Makes 8 servings.

2 pints strawberries, washed and hulled
2 envelopes unflavored gelatin
$1/4$ cup water
2 egg whites
$1/4$ cup sugar
$1/2$ cup heavy cream,
whipped
1 package (3 ounces) ladyfingers
Strawberry Sauce (recipe follows)
Whipped cream (optional)

1. Puree 2 cups of the berries in the container of an electric blender or food processor; pour into a large bowl. Slice remaining berries.

2. Sprinkle gelatin over water in a small saucepan; let stand 5 minutes to soften. Heat over very low heat, stirring constantly, until gelatin dissolves. Stir into pureed berries; chill until mixture is almost set.

3. Beat egg whites with an electric mixer at high speed until soft peaks form. Gradually add sugar, beating constantly until whites are stiff and glossy. Fold whites and whipped cream into strawberry mixture.

4. Lightly oil the bottom of a 2-quart soufflé dish and line the sides with 18 ladyfinger halves. Pour in about $1/3$ of the strawberry mixture and sprinkle with $1/2$ of the sliced berries. Repeat layering and top with remaining strawberry mixture. Arrange remaining ladyfinger halves on top; chill 6 hours or until very firm.

5. To serve: Dip soufflé dish in and out of warm water for a few seconds. Invert onto serving plate to unmold. Pour some of the Strawberry Sauce over the top of the Charlotte, letting some drip down sides and onto dish. Pipe small rosettes of whipped cream around top edge of Charlotte to garnish, if you wish. Serve with remaining sauce.

Strawberry Sauce: Wash and hull 1 pint strawberries. Puree in the container of an electric blender or food processor with 3 tablespoons sugar and 1 tablespoon brandy. Makes about $1^3/4$ cups.

Orange Cheese Parfaits

Makes 8 servings.

1 package (10$3/4$ ounces) cheesecake mix
2 tablespoons sugar
2 tablespoons butter
or margarine, melted
1 orange
2 cups milk

1. Mix crumbs from cheesecake mix with sugar and butter. Spoon about half into eight parfait glasses, dividing evenly. Reserve remaining.

2. Grate 2 teaspoons rind from orange. Remove white membrane from orange with a sharp knife; section orange; halve each section.

3. Prepare cheesecake mix from package with milk. Stir in orange rind and orange. Layer with reserved crumb mixture in glasses.

Blarney Castle Parfaits

Makes 12 servings.

$1/2$ gallon vanilla ice cream
1 bottle (12 ounces) green crème de menthe
OR: $1^1/2$ cups light
corn syrup combined with few drops green food coloring and 2 teaspoons peppermint extract

Scoop ice cream into 12 parfait or sherbet glasses. Top with crème de menthe or corn syrup mixture.

Fruit Molded in Sherry Jelly

This shimmering jewel of a gelatin dessert is refreshing and cool.

Makes 8 servings.

2 envelopes unflavored gelatin
1 cup water
$3/4$ medium dry sherry
1 can (12 ounces) peach nectar
$1/4$ cup sugar
3 large peaches
1 large banana
$1/2$ pint strawberries
1 cup heavy cream

1. Sprinkle gelatin over water in a medium-size saucepan. Let stand 5 minutes to soften. Heat saucepan over low heat until gelatin dissolves. Remove from heat; stir in sherry, nectar and sugar. Chill mixture until syrupy or it has consistency of unbeaten egg whites, about 1 hour.

2. Dip peaches into boiling water 30 seconds, then into ice water 1 minute. Peel, halve, pit and slice. Peel and slice banana; wash, hull and quarter strawberries.

3. Pour about $1/2$-inch layer of gelatin in bottom of a 6-cup mold. Leave remaining gelatin at room temperature. Set mold in bowl of ice and water. Swirl mold until gelatin is thickened and coats bottom of

mold. Arrange pieces of fruit against bottom and halfway up side of mold. Leave mold in ice water until fruit is set in gelatin.

4. Add a third of remaining gelatin to mold. Add a third of remaining fruit. Repeat layering until mold is filled. Chill mold 4 hours or overnight.

5. To serve: Unmold by dipping mold in warm water, then inverting onto platter. Beat cream until soft peaks form; serve with mold. Garnish with additional peach slices and sprigs of mint, if you wish.

Strawberry Shortcakes

Bake at 450° for 10 minutes.

Makes 6 servings.

$1/2$ **cup granulated sugar**	**granulated sugar**
2 pints strawberries, washed, hulled and sliced	$1/2$ **cup vegetable shortening**
	1 cup milk
3 cups *sifted* **all-purpose flour**	$1/4$ **cup ($1/2$ stick) butter, softened**
$3^{1}/2$ **teaspoons baking powder**	**1 cup heavy cream**
	2 tablespoons 10X (confectioners') sugar
$1/2$ **teaspoon salt**	
3 tablespoons	

1. Sprinkle the $1/2$ cup granulated sugar over strawberries in large bowl. Let stand 1 hour.

2. Preheat oven to 450°. Combine flour, baking powder, salt and 3 tablespoons granulated sugar in large bowl; cut in shortening with pastry blender until mixture forms fine crumbs.

3. Add milk; stir in with fork just until blended. Turn out onto lightly floured surface; knead about 20 times.

4. Roll to about $1/4$-inch thickness; fold dough in half, then cut 6 double biscuits with 3- or $3^{1}/2$-inch floured round cutter. Place the double biscuits 1 inch apart on an ungreased cookie sheet.

5. Bake in a preheated very hot oven (450°) for 10 minutes or until golden brown. Pull the 2 layers apart to split; spread bottom layer with softened butter.

6. Beat heavy cream with 10X sugar in a small bowl until soft peaks form. Fill and top biscuits with strawberries and cream.

Creamy Tapioca with Strawberry-Wine Sauce

Makes 6 servings.

$1/4$ **cup quick-cooking tapioca**	**2 cups milk**
	1 teaspoon vanilla
$1/2$ **cup sugar**	**Strawberry-Wine Sauce (recipe follows)**
$1/8$ **teaspoon salt**	
2 eggs, separated	

1. Combine tapioca, $1/4$ cup of the sugar, salt and egg yolks in a medium-size saucepan. Stir in milk. Let stand 5 minutes to soften tapioca.

2. Cook tapioca mixture over medium heat, stirring constantly, about 6 minutes or until thickened and bubbly. Remove from heat, stir in vanilla; cover surface with plastic wrap. Chill until cold.

3. Prepare Strawberry-Wine Sauce.

4. Just before serving, beat egg whites in small bowl until foamy. Gradually beat in remaining $1/4$ cup sugar, 1 tablespoon at a time, until meringue forms soft peaks.

5. Stir chilled tapioca until softened; fold in meringue until no streaks of white remain. Spoon into stemmed wine glasses; top with sauce.

Strawberry-Wine Sauce

Makes about 3 cups.

2 tablespoons quick-cooking tapioca	$3/4$ **cup water**
	1 pint strawberries
$1/4$ **cup sugar**	$1/2$ **cup ruby port wine**

1. Combine tapioca, sugar and water in small saucepan. Let stand 5 minutes. Cook until thickened, stirring constantly. Remove from heat. Cool.

2. Wash, hull and pat berries dry on paper toweling. Halve or slice, if large, into tapioca mixture. Stir in wine. Cover and chill until cold.

Syllabub
A frothy, drinkable milk or cream and wine dessert of English origin. The word is derived from two words--*Sill* or *Sille*, a wine from the Champagne district of France and once the best known wine name in England, and *bub*, which meant a bubbling drink.

Syllabub

Makes fourteen $1/2$-cup servings.

1 bottle (750 ml) Madeira or cream sherry	**3 egg whites**
	$1/2$ **cup heavy cream**
1 tablespoon grated lemon rind	**3 cups ($1^{1}/2$ pints) light cream or half-and-half**
$1/3$ **cup lemon juice**	**Shredded lemon rind**
$1^{1}/2$ **cups sugar**	**Ground nutmeg**

1. Combine Madeira, the grated lemon rind, and $1^{1}/4$ cups of the sugar in a large punch bowl. Stir until sugar is dissolved.

(continued)

Overleaf (from top to right): Fresh Apple Brûlées, page 309; Open Fresh Fruit Pie, page 308; Poached Pears with Hot Caramel Sauce, page 308; Danish Apple Dessert, page 309.

2. Beat egg whites with remaining ¼ cup sugar until stiff peaks form. Whip heavy cream until soft peaks form; fold into beaten egg whites.

3. Just before serving, stir light cream into Madeira mixture; spoon whipped cream mixture on top. Sprinkle with rind and nutmeg.

Strawberries with Brandied Syllabub

Makes 4 servings.

1 tablespoon sugar	½ cup heavy cream
1 tablespoon brandy	½ cup crushed
1½ tablespoons medium-dry sherry	strawberries
¾ teaspoon grated orange rind	1 cup sliced strawberries

1. Combine sugar, brandy, sherry and orange rind in a medium-size bowl; let stand 30 minutes.

2. Add cream to brandy mixture and beat with rotary or hand electric mixer until cream forms stiff peaks.

3. Spoon crushed strawberries evenly into 4 stemmed glasses. Top with brandied cream; cover and refrigerate up to 24 hours. Top with sliced strawberries just before serving.

Poached Pears with Hot Caramel Sauce

An elegant but simple dessert! For the best effect, make sure the pears are well chilled and the sauce is hot.

Makes 6 servings.

6 firm-ripe pears such as Bartlett, Bosc or Comice	**Caramel Sauce:**
	1 cup heavy cream
2 tablespoons lemon juice	1 cup sugar
	1 teaspoon vanilla
4 to 5 cups water	Toasted sliced almonds

1. Core the pears from the bottom. Pare the pears without removing the stems. Brush well with the lemon juice to prevent discoloration.

2. Bring the water to boiling in a large skillet. Place the pears in the skillet. Lower the heat and simmer, turning and basting the pears occasionally, until firm-tender, for 8 to 10 minutes. Transfer the pears and liquid to a deep bowl; make sure the pears are completely submerged. Refrigerate until well chilled.

3. Prepare the Caramel Sauce: Heat the cream in a small saucepan just until bubbles form around the edge; do not let boil.

4. Heat the sugar in a large, heavy skillet over medium-high heat, stirring constantly. When the sugar begins to melt, reduce the heat to low and continue to stir constantly, until the sugar is dissolved and the mixture is light brown.

5. Slowly add the warm cream, stirring constantly until the sauce is smooth. (If some of the sugar crystallizes, cook, stirring constantly, until the crystals dissolve.) Remove from the heat. Stir in the vanilla.

6. To serve, drain the pears thoroughly. Place on individual serving plates. Spoon the hot sauce over the pears. Garnish with the almonds.

Note: For advance preparation, make the Caramel Sauce ahead. Reheat very slowly over low heat, stirring constantly until hot.

Open Fresh Fruit Pie

This dessert, which looks like a fresh fruit pizza, is a chance for the artistic cook to show off. To serve, cut in wedges and pass the Finnish Vanilla Sauce instead of whipped or heavy cream.

Bake crust at 450° for 7 minutes.

Makes 12 servings.

1½ cups packaged piecrust mix	4 large plums, halved, pitted and thinly sliced (2 cups)
1 egg yolk	
1 tablespoon water	1 tablespoon lemon juice
¾ cup apricot preserves	½ cup seeded red grapes
1 to 2 large pears, halved, cored and thinly sliced (2 cups)	Finnish Vanilla Sauce *(recipe follows)*

1. Preheat the oven to very hot (450°). Lightly grease a 12-inch pizza pan.

2. Prepare the piecrust, following the directions for a single-crust pie. Roll out the dough on a lightly floured surface into a circle 13 to 13½ inches in diameter. Gently fold the dough over into quarters to form a triangle. Transfer to the prepared pan. Unfold and gently press the dough into the pan so it fits evenly. Trim the edges, leaving a ½-inch overhang. Turn the overhang under to make a stand-up edge; flute. Prick holes all over the crust with a fork.

3. Beat together the egg yolk and water in a small bowl. Gently brush the egg wash over the fluted edge.

4. Bake the tart crust in the preheated very hot oven (450°) for 7 minutes or until lightly browned. Remove to a wire rack to cool.

5. Melt the preserves in a small saucepan over low heat. Force through a sieve with the back of a spoon into a small bowl. Brush the pastry with ¼ cup of the strained preserves.

6. Toss the pears and plums with the lemon juice in a large bowl until completely coated. Arrange the pear and plum slices, overlapping, in a circle around the outside edge of the tart. Arrange the grapes in the center.

7. Brush the fruits carefully with the remaining strained preserves. Refrigerate until chilled. Serve with the Finnish Vanilla Sauce.

Finnish Vanilla Sauce: Combine 2 cups milk, 3 tablespoons sugar, 2 egg yolks and 1 tablespoon cornstarch in a medium-size heavy saucepan. Cook, stirring constantly, over medium-high heat until the mixture is thick and bubbly. Remove from the heat; continue to stir for about 1 minute. Stir in 1 teaspoon vanilla. Cover the surface with plastic wrap and cool completely.

Danish Apple Dessert

This classic Scandinavian dessert, layered in a straight-sided glass bowl, makes an attractive buffet dessert centerpiece.

Makes 8 servings.

8 medium-size Golden Delicious apples	light brown sugar
1 tablespoon lemon juice	1/2 cup chopped blanched almonds
1 tablespoon butter or margarine	1 teaspoon ground cinnamon
1 tablespoon granulated sugar	1 cup heavy cream
1/4 cup (1/2 stick) butter or margarine	2 tablespoons 10X (confectioners') sugar
1/4 cup zwieback crumbs (16 toasts)	1 teaspoon vanilla
1/2 cup firmly packed	Red and green apple slices for garnish *(optional)*

1. Pare, core and slice each apple into 12 wedges. Toss the wedges with the lemon juice in a large bowl until completely coated.
2. Melt the 1 tablespoon of butter in a large (12-inch) skillet over medium heat. Add the apples and sprinkle with the granulated sugar. Cook, covered, stirring occasionally, for 15 minutes or until the apples are tender, but not brown.
3. Meanwhile, melt the 1/4 cup of butter in another skillet. Stir in the zwieback crumbs, brown sugar, almonds, and cinnamon until well blended. Toast over low heat, stirring occasionally, 15 minutes or until golden.
4. Sprinkle half of the crumb mixture evenly over the bottom of a 2-quart serving bowl. Layer the apples over the top of the crumb mixture. Sprinkle the remaining crumb mixture over the top. Chill for several hours or serve at room temperature.
5. At serving time, beat together the cream, 10X sugar and vanilla in a small bowl until stiff. Garnish the top with the whipped cream and apple slices, if you wish.

Fresh Apple Brûlées

Individual apple custards with a caramelized sugar topping.

Bake at 350° for 30 minutes, then broil for 2 to 3 minutes.

Makes 8 servings.

2 to 3 large Golden Delicious apples, pared, cored and finely chopped (about 2 2/3 cups)	2 cups heavy cream
	1/4 cup sugar
	1 teaspoon vanilla
	1/2 cup slivered blanched almonds, toasted
1 tablespoon lemon juice	3/4 cup firmly packed brown sugar
6 egg yolks	

1. Preheat the oven to moderate (350°).
2. Toss together the apples and lemon juice in a small bowl until completely coated. Spoon about 1/3 cup of the apples into each of eight 6-ounce baking dishes.
3. Beat the yolks slightly in a large bowl. Stir in the cream, sugar and vanilla. Pour about 1/2 cup of the cream mixture into each baking dish. Place the baking dishes in a large, shallow baking pan and place on oven rack. Pour in boiling water to a depth of about 1/2 inch.
4. Bake in the preheated moderate oven (350°) for 30 minutes or until the custards are almost set. Remove the custards from the pan of water to a wire rack to cool. Refrigerate for several hours or until chilled.
5. To serve, sprinkle about 1 tablespoon almonds over each custard. Sieve the brown sugar over each, dividing equally.
6. Broil about 6 inches from the heat until the sugar caramelizes for about 2 to 3 minutes; watch carefully to prevent burning. Serve immediately.

Chocolate Fondue

Makes 2 1/2 cups.

2 bars (8 ounces each) milk chocolate candy	and apple slices, seedless grapes, banana chunks, tangerine and orange sections, pound cake squares, angel food cake squares
3/4 to 1 cup heavy cream	
3 tablespoons brandy	
For dipping: strawberries, pear	

1. Combine chocolate candy and 3/4 cup heavy cream in a heavy saucepan. Cook over low heat, stirring constantly, until chocolate is melted. Add brandy. Remove from heat.
2. Pour into small fondue pot; surround by fruit and cake. Spear pieces of fruit or cake on fondue forks; twirl into sauce; provide small plates to catch drippings. If mixture becomes too thick, stir in additional cream.

Pudding Although this word usually refers to dessert or sweet foods, a pudding can also be savory such as corn pudding, fish pudding or Yorkshire pudding. A pudding can be baked, boiled or steamed, served hot or cold as a main dish, accompaniment or dessert. The word may have been derived from old Germanic words meaning "sausage" or "swollen." Blood puddings are sausages.

Pear-Ginger Pudding with Two Sauces

Steam for 2¼ hours.
Makes 8 to 10 servings (without sauce).

2 slightly underripe pears	3 tablespoons chopped crystallized ginger
1 tablespoon lemon juice	14 tablespoons (1¾ sticks) butter or margarine
1 tablespoon granulated sugar	¾ cup light brown sugar
2 cups *sifted* all-purpose flour	2 eggs
2 teaspoons ground ginger	1 cup applesauce
1 teaspoon ground cinnamon	¾ cup chopped walnuts or pecans
1 teaspoon baking powder	Nesselrode Sauce *(recipe follows)*
1 teaspoon baking soda	Lemon Sauce *(recipe follows)*

1. Butter an 8-cup steamed-pudding mold or a heatproof bowl.
2. Pare, quarter and core the pears. Cut each quarter crosswise into ⅛- to ¼-inch-thick slices .Toss with the lemon juice and sugar in a heavy medium-size skillet. Cook, stirring often, over medium-high heat until tender, 10 to 15 minutes. Cool completely.
3. Sift together the flour, ginger, cinnamon, baking powder and baking soda onto wax paper; mix in the crystallized ginger.
4. Beat the butter in a large bowl until soft. Add the sugar and eggs. Beat until light and fluffy, 3 to 5 minutes. Stir in the applesauce, then the flour mixture, a third at a time, adding the nuts with the last addition. Fold in the pear mixture. Spoon into the prepared mold or bowl; cover with the lid of the mold or foil. Fasten tightly with string.
5. Place the mold on a rack in a deep kettle. Pour in boiling water to come halfway up the side of the mold. Cover the kettle. Keep the water gently boiling, adding more boiling water if necessary. Steam for 2¼ hours, or until a wooden skewer tests clean.
6. Cool the pudding in the mold for 10 minutes on a

Pictured opposite (clockwise from front left): Frozen Payaya Cream, page 296; Summer Pudding Surprise, page 312; Lemon Meringue Tarts, page 322; Melon in Sabayon Sauce, page 322; Minted Pineapple Cake, page 158.

rack. Turn out onto plate. Serve warm with Lemon Sauce and Nesselrode Sauce.

Note: Pudding can be steamed 2 to 3 days ahead. Cool and unmold as in Step 6. Wrap tightly in foil; refrigerate. Reheat wrapped pudding on a cookie sheet in a slow oven (300°) for 30 minutes.

Microwave Directions for Pudding
650 Watt Variable Power Microwave Oven
Ingredient Changes: Add dry bread crumbs for coating the pan.
Directions: Toss together the pear pieces, lemon juice and 1 tablespoon of the butter in a microwave-safe 9-inch pie plate. Cover. Microwave at full power for 5 minutes, stirring after 3 minutes. Cool. Grease a 2-quart microwave-safe tube pan; sprinkle the sides with the dry bread crumbs. Assemble the pudding as in the above recipe. Spoon the batter into the prepared pan. Cover tightly with plastic wrap. Place the pan on an inverted saucer in the microwave oven. Microwave at half power for 16 to 17 minutes, rotating the pan a quarter turn after 8 minutes. Pudding will pull away slightly from the sides and a wooden pick inserted in the center will come out clean. Let stand for 10 minutes. Loosen the pudding sides with a small knife. Invert onto plate. (Small pieces of pudding may remain in mold; patch on top of pudding. Microwaving saves about 1 hour and 50 minutes.)
To Reheat: Place the unmolded pudding on a microwave-safe plate. Cover loosely with paper toweling. Microwave at half power for 7 minutes. Let stand for 5 minutes.

Lemon Sauce

Makes 1½ cups.

⅔ cup sugar	1 tablespoon butter
1 tablespoon cornstarch	1 tablespoon grated lemon rind
⅔ cup water	¼ cup fresh lemon juice, strained
2 egg yolks, slightly beaten	

1. Combine the sugar and cornstarch in a small saucepan; stir in the water until smooth. Cook, stirring constantly, until the mixture thickens and bubbles, 1 minute. Remove from the heat.
2. Beat half of the cornstarch mixture into the beaten yolks in a small bowl; stir back into the saucepan. Cook, stirring for 1 minute longer. Remove from the heat. Stir in the butter, lemon rind and juice.
3. Pour into a serving bowl. Place a piece of plastic wrap directly on the surface to prevent a skin from forming. Serve warm or cold.

Microwave Directions
650 Watt Variable Power Microwave Oven
Directions: Combine the sugar, cornstarch, water and egg yolks in a 4-cup microwave-safe measure; stir to mix. Microwave, uncovered, at full power for 2 to 3 minutes, stirring well every minute, until thickened and bubbly. Stir in the butter, lemon rind and juice.

Nesselrode Sauce

Makes about 1¹/₄ cups.

3 egg yolks	**¹/₂ cup heavy cream,**
3 tablespoons 10X	**whipped**
(confectioners')	**3 tablespoons**
sugar	**chopped mixed**
2 tablespoons brandy	**candied fruits**

Beat the egg yolks and sugar in a small bowl until thick and fluffy, 3 to 5 minutes. Beat in the brandy. Fold in the whipped cream and candied fruits.

Summer Pudding Surprise

Makes 8 servings.

3 cups sliced fresh	**ounces) frozen**
strawberries	**raspberries,**
1 pint fresh or frozen	**partially thawed**
unsweetened	**10 slices firm white**
blueberries	**bread**
¹/₃ to ¹/₂ cup sugar	**1 cup heavy cream**
1 package (10	

1. Place strawberies and blueberries in large bowl; stir in sugar. Let stand, stirring often, until juicy and sugar is dissolved, about 30 minutes. Stir in raspberries.
2. Meanwhile, remove crusts from bread slices. Line a 1¹/₂-quart deep mixing bowl with 6 or 7 overlapping bread slices. Cut one slice to fit bottom. Fill bowl with berry mixture; cover top completely with remaining bread. Cover with wax paper; set a small flat plate or pie plate on top and place a 3- to 4-pound weight on the plate. (Several large cans of fruit or vegetables will do.) The weighted plate presses on the bread to compact the mixture. Refrigerate overnight.
3. To serve: Invert pudding onto a chilled serving plate. Garnish with a few extra berries, if you wish. Cut pudding in wedges to serve. Beat the cream just until softly whipped. Serve with the pudding.

Queen of Puddings

Bread pudding becomes a regal dessert when topped with meringue.

Bake at 350° for 1 hour.

Makes 6 servings.

4 eggs	**melted**
³/₄ cup sugar	**1 quart milk**
Dash salt	**4 cups soft white**
¹/₄ teaspoon ground	**bread cubes**
cinnamon	**1 cup apricot**
2 teaspoons vanilla	**preserves**
1 tablespoon butter or	**¹/₂ cup strawberry**
margarine,	**preserves**

1. Separate 2 eggs; reserve egg whites. Combine egg yolks, remaining 2 eggs, ¹/₂ cup of sugar, salt,

cinnamon, vanilla and butter in a large bowl; stir in milk. Place bread cubes in a lightly buttered 8-cup baking dish; pour egg mixture over the bread cubes and let stand for 15 minutes. Preheat oven to 350°.
2. Set dish in a baking pan; place on oven rack; pour boiling water into pan to depth of 1 inch.
3. Bake in a preheated moderate oven (350°) for 50 minutes or until knife inserted ¹/₂ inch from edge of pudding comes out clean. (Center will be almost set, but still soft.) Do not overbake.
4. Beat egg whites until foamy-white and double in volume in a small bowl; beat in remaining ¹/₄ cup sugar, 1 tablespoon at a time, until meringue stands in firm peaks.
5. Spoon ¹/₂ cup apricot preserves over hot pudding. Using a pastry bag with a large notched tip, press meringue into puffs on top of pudding, as close together as possible, so no pudding shows through. (This will keep the pudding from overcooking.) Place in same pan of hot water.
6. Bake in a preheated moderate oven (350°) for 10 minutes or just until peaks turn golden; cool pudding.
7. Just before serving, melt remaining apricot and strawberry preserves in separate small saucepans over low heat. Strain separately through a sieve; cool slightly. Carefully drizzle apricot preserves and strawberry preserves over meringue.

Coconut Pudding

Makes 12 servings.

7 tablespoons	**papaya, kiwi, fresh**
cornstarch	**pineapple or**
¹/₂ cup sugar	**canned sliced**
¹/₄ teaspoon salt	**pineapple**
Fresh Coconut Milk	**Orange Syrup** *(recipe*
(recipe follows)	*follows)*
Sliced oranges,	

1. Mix cornstarch, sugar and salt in a medium-size saucepan; gradually stir in Fresh Coconut Milk.
2. Cook over medium heat, stirring constantly, until mixture thickens and bubbles 1 minute. Remove from heat.
3. Pour into a 4- or 5-cup mold. Chill 4 hours or until pudding is firm. Unmold onto serving plate. Arrange cut fresh fruits around it; spoon Orange Syrup over pudding and fruits.

Orange Syrup: Remove zest from 1 navel orange with a vegetable parer or sharp knife; cut into thin strips. Simmer in 1 cup boiling water 5 minutes to blanch; drain; rinse in cold water and reserve. Combine ³/₄ cup orange juice and ¹/₂ cup sugar in small saucepan; bring to boiling, stirring constantly, until sugar is dissolved. Continue cooking without stirring, 5 minutes; add blanched orange peel; cook 2 minutes. Remove from heat. Cool completely. Makes about 1 cup.

Orange Bread Pudding.

Fresh Coconut Milk

Bake at 375° for 20 minutes.

Makes about 4 cups.

2 medium-size coconuts	**or half-and-half Milk**
2 cups light cream	

1. To Open Coconut: Puncture the "eyes" with screwdriver and hammer; drain coconut juice; reserve. Preheat oven to 375°.
2. Bake coconut in a preheated moderate oven (375°) for 20 minutes to loosen meat from shell. Tap shell all over with hammer, then crack open. Pry meat from shell; pare off brown skin.
3. Cut meat into small pieces. (You should have 3$^{1}/_{2}$ to 4 cups.)
4. In a 4-cup measure, combine reserved juice from coconuts, light cream and enough milk to make a total of 3 cups liquid. Heat mixture just to boiling in a medium-size saucepan.
5. Puree one-third of the coconut meat with one-third of the liquid in container of electric blender. Pour into large bowl. Repeat twice with remaining coconut and liquid.
6. Pour puree through large strainer lined with a double layer of cheesecloth into a large bowl. Squeeze cloth hard to remove all milk from coconut. Discard coconut pulp and refrigerate or freeze milk until ready to use. Keeps frozen 2 to 3 weeks; refrigerated, no more than several hours.

Orange Bread Pudding

Just-squeezed orange juice is the secret of this dessert.

Bake at 350° for 45 minutes.

Makes 6 servings.

10 to 12 slices French bread, about $^{3}/_{4}$-inch thick and with crust	**$^{1}/_{2}$ cup sugar**
	2 teaspoons grated orange rind
$^{1}/_{4}$ cup ($^{1}/_{2}$ stick) butter or margarine, softened	**$^{2}/_{3}$ cup orange juice (2 oranges)**
	2$^{3}/_{4}$ cups milk
4 eggs	**$^{1}/_{4}$ cup orange marmalade, melted**

1. Spread bread slices generously on one side with

(continued)

butter. Arrange slices, buttered-side up, overlapping in lightly buttered 2-quart shallow baking dish.

2. Beat eggs, sugar and orange rind in bowl just until blended. Gradually stir in orange juice and milk. Pour evenly over bread. Let stand 15 minutes.

3. Preheat the oven to moderate (350°).

4. Set dish in large baking pan. Place on oven rack. pour boiling water into pan so it comes halfway up sides of bread pudding dish.

5. Bake in the preheated moderate oven (350°) for 45 minutes or until knife inserted in center comes out clean. Center will be almost set but still soft.

6. Remove pudding from water bath. Cool at least 30 minutes.

7. Brush melted marmalade over top. Serve pudding warm or chilled with light cream to pour over, or with whipped cream on the side, if you wish.

Indian Pudding

Bake at 325° for 3 hours.

Makes 6 servings.

5 cups milk	**¼ cup (½ stick) butter**
½ cup yellow	**or margarine**
cornmeal	**1 teaspoon salt**
½ cup sugar	**1 teaspoon pumpkin**
½ cup molasses	**pie spice**

1. Combine 2 cups of the milk with the cornmeal, sugar, molasses, butter, salt and pumpkin pie spice in a large, heavy saucepan. Heat slowly until bubbling, then simmer, stirring often, 5 minutes or until creamy-thick.

2. Pour into a buttered, 8-cup baking dish; stir in 2 more cups milk.

3. Bake in slow oven (325°) 1 hour; stir in remaining 1 cup milk. Bake 2 hours longer or until pudding sets. Serve warm with cream or ice cream, if you wish.

Peach Pudding

Makes 6 servings.

1 can (17 ounces)	**vanilla-flavored**
cling peach slices,	**instant pudding and**
drained	**pie filling**
1 cup milk	**¼ cup firmly packed**
1 container (8 ounces)	**brown sugar**
dairy sour cream	**2 tablespoons broken**
1 package	**pecans**
(3¾ ounces)	

1. Divide peach slices among six dessert dishes.

2. Blend milk into sour cream in medium-size bowl; add pudding mix and beat until smooth and thickened, about 1 minute. Spoon over peaches. Chill.

3. While pudding chills, press sugar through a sieve onto small cookie sheet in a ¼-inch-thick layer. Broil 3 inches from heat for 2 to 4 minutes or until sugar has

melted in a lacy pattern. Cool on cookie sheet. Break into pieces and place on top of puddings. Sprinkle with pecans.

Tropical Queen of Puddings

Bake at 400° for 3 minutes.

Makes 6 servings.

1 package	**1 can (8 ounces)**
(3¾ ounces)	**crushed pineapple**
banana cream-	**in pineapple juice**
flavored instant	**2 egg whites**
pudding and pie	**2 tablespoons sugar**
filling	**2 tablespoons flaked**
2 cups milk	**coconut**
6 slices pound cake	

1. Prepare pudding with milk following label directions.

2. Layer cake, pineapple and pudding in 4-cup ovenproof dish. Chill 30 minutes.

3. Just before serving, preheat oven to 400°. Beat egg whites until foamy; gradually beat in sugar until soft peaks form. Spread over pudding, making swirls with spoon. Sprinkle coconut around edge.

4. Bake in a preheated hot oven (400°) for 3 minutes or just until slightly browned.

Steamed Apple-Date Pudding with Custard Sauce

Makes 6 servings.

3 medium-size Rome	**1 teaspoon baking**
Beauty apples,	**powder**
pared, cored and	**2 teaspoons ground**
diced	**cinnamon**
1 package (8 ounces)	**1 teaspoon ground**
pitted dates,	**nutmeg**
coarsely chopped	**1 teaspoon ground**
(1 cup)	**allspice**
1 cup coarsely	**¾ teaspoon ground**
chopped walnuts	**cloves**
1¼ cups *sifted* all-	**3 eggs**
purpose flour	**¼ cup vegetable oil**
1 cup sugar	**Granulated sugar**
1 teaspoon salt	**Custard Sauce *(recipe***
1½ teaspoons baking	***follows)***
soda	

1. Combine apples, dates and walnuts in large bowl. Combine flour, sugar, salt, baking soda, baking powder, cinnamon, nutmeg, allspice and cloves on wax paper. Sprinkle over fruit and nuts; toss until they are evenly coated.

2. Beat eggs and oil in a small bowl until well blended. Pour over floured fruit mixture. Stir until well blended.

3. Generously butter a 6-cup decorative mold; sprinkle with granulated sugar. Turn pudding into prepared

mold. Cover securely with a double thickness of aluminum foil.

4. Place mold on a wire rack or trivet in a large kettle; pour in boiling water to half the depth of the mold; cover the kettle. Keep water boiling gently, adding more if necessary.

5. Steam pudding for 2 hours. Remove pudding from kettle; let cool 5 minutes; remove foil. Unmold onto heated serving plate and serve with Custard Sauce.

Custard Sauce: Heat 1 cup milk in top of double boiler over direct heat just until bubbles appear around edge. (Do not boil.) Beat 3 egg yolks and 3 tablespoons sugar together in a small bowl until blended. Stir in hot milk slowly. Return mixture to double boiler. Cook over hot, not boiling, water just until mixture coats a metal spoon. Add 1 teaspoon vanilla. Serve warm or chilled.

Date-Apricot Steamed Pudding

Makes 6 servings.

1 package (6 ounces) dried apricots, chopped	**³/4 teaspoon ground cinnamon**
1/2 cup pitted dates, chopped	**1/4 teaspoon ground nutmeg**
2 cups *sifted* all-purpose flour	**1/2 cup vegetable shortening**
1 1/2 teaspoons baking powder	**1 cup firmly packed light brown sugar**
1/2 teaspoon baking soda	**2 eggs**
1/2 teaspoon salt	**1/3 cup orange juice**
	Orange Custard Sauce *(recipe follows)*

1. Grease an 8-cup tube pan or pudding mold; dust with sugar.

2. Simmer apricots in boiling water to cover for 5 minutes; drain. Combine apricots and dates in a small bowl.

3. Sift flour, baking powder, baking soda, salt, cinnamon and nutmeg onto wax paper.

4. Beat shortening, sugar and eggs in a large bowl until fluffy. Stir in flour and orange juice until mixture is smooth. Fold in apricots and dates. Spoon batter into mold and cover with aluminum foil, securing tightly with string.

5. Place mold on a wire cake rack in pot large enough to hold mold. Pour in boiling water to a depth of 2 inches. Cover; simmer for 2 hours or until a wooden skewer inserted near center comes out clean, replenishing water if necessary.

6. Cool in mold on wire rack 5 minutes; remove from mold. Serve with Orange Custard Sauce.

To reheat: Wrap in foil; heat in a preheated moderate oven (350°) for 20 minutes.

Orange Custard Sauce: Combine 1 package (3 ³/4 ounces) vanilla-flavored instant pudding and pie filling, 1/4 cup 10X (confectioners') sugar, 2 cups milk, 1 cup orange juice and 2 tablespoons grated orange rind in a medium-size bowl; beat 1 minute with rotary beater. Beat 1/2 cup heavy cream until stiff; fold into orange mixture; cover; chill 1 hour. Makes about 4 cups.

Chocolate Pecan Pudding

Makes 6 servings.

1 envelope unflavored gelatin	**4 egg whites**
2 tablespoons cold water	**1/8 teaspoon salt**
1/4 cup hot coffee	**1/2 cup sugar**
2 squares unsweetened chocolate	**1 teaspoon vanilla**
	1/2 cup heavy cream
	1/4 cup chopped pecans

1. Sprinkle gelatin over cold water in a small saucepan; let stand 5 minutes to soften; stir in hot coffee. Place over low heat, stirring constantly, until gelatin is dissolved. Remove from heat; cool; chill until mixture is the consistency of unbeaten egg white.

2. Melt chocolate in a small cup placed in saucepan half filled with water and placed over very low heat.

3. Beat egg whites in a small bowl with electric mixer at high speed until frothy. Add salt and sugar, 1 tablespoon at a time, until egg whites form glossy peaks. Add vanilla.

4. Reduce speed of mixer to low. Drizzle syrupy gelatin mixture over egg whites until completely mixed. Drizzle in warm chocolate.

5. Pour into a 1-quart glass bowl or six individual dessert dishes. Cover with plastic wrap. Chill until set softly.

6. Whip cream until stiff in a small bowl. Garnish pudding with whipped cream and sprinkle with pecans.

Prune Pudding

Makes 6 servings.

1 package (12 ounces) pitted prunes	**1/2 cup water**
2 cups water	**1 teaspoon grated lemon rind**
2/3 cup sugar	**1/4 cup lemon juice**
1/2 teaspoon ground cinnamon	**1/2 cup heavy cream**
1/4 cup cornstarch	**Toasted almonds**

1. Cook prunes in 2 cups water in saucepan until very soft, about 15 minutes. Drain; reserve liquid. Measure 1/3 cup liquid; poor remaining into a 1-cup measure.

2. Press prunes and the 1/3 cup liquid through food mill or strainer to puree (do not use blender). Place in saucepan.

3. Combine the remaining prune liquid with enough water to make 1 cup. Stir into prunes; add sugar and

(continued)

cinnamon. Cook over medium heat, stirring occasionally, for 5 minutes or until mixture thickens.
4. Mix cornstarch with $1/2$ cup water; stir into prune mixture. Cook, stirring constantly, until mixture is very thick, about 10 minutes.
5. Remove from heat; stir in lemon rind and juice. Pour into serving bowl. Cool, then chill.
6. Whip cream in a small bowl until soft peaks form; spoon whipped cream onto pudding; sprinkle with toasted almonds.

Rice Custard Pudding

Bake at 350° for 45 minutes.

Makes 8 servings.

3 cups milk	**$3/4$ cup sugar**
1 cup heavy cream	**$1/4$ teaspoon salt**
$1/2$ cup uncooked long-grain rice	**1 teaspoon vanilla**
	Ground nutmeg
3 eggs, separated	

1. Combine milk and cream in the top of a double boiler over simmering water. Stir in rice; cover. Cook, stirring occasionally, until the rice is tender and creamy and all the liquid is absorbed, about $1 1/2$ to 2 hours. Stir occasionally to prevent sticking. Remove from heat.
2. Beat the egg yolks until frothy in a large bowl. Gradually beat in the sugar, salt and vanilla. Stir in the hot rice, a small portion at a time.
3. Beat the egg whites in a small bowl until soft peaks form. Fold into rice mixture. Turn mixture into buttered 2-quart baking dish; sprinkle top with nutmeg. Place baking dish in shallow pan, then put pan on oven shelf. Pour about 2 inches of hot water into pan.
4. Bake in a moderate oven (350°) for 45 minutes. Remove to wire rack; cool; chill.

Meringue Rice Pudding

Get a head start on dessert by making the pudding the day before.

Bake meringue at 425° for 5 minutes.

Makes 10 servings.

$1/2$ cup long-grain white rice	**$1/2$ cup plus 2 tablespoons sugar**
1 cup water	**2 teaspoons vanilla**
$4 1/4$ cups milk	**$1/8$ teaspoon salt**
$1/4$ cup raisins	**$1/2$ cup raspberry preserves**
3 eggs, separated	

1. Combine rice and water in 2-quart saucepan. Bring to boiling; boil for 8 to 10 minutes or until water is absorbed. Stir in milk. Return to boiling. Lower heat and simmer, stirring often, for 25 minutes. Add raisins; cook for 5 to 10 minutes longer or until rice is very tender.

2. Beat egg yolks in small bowl until frothy. (Reserve whites in small bowl.) Beat in $1/4$ cup of the sugar, vanilla and salt. Stir $1/3$ cup hot rice mixture into yolks; return mixture to saucepan. Cook over very low heat for 2 minutes or until mixture thickens slightly; mixture should be very loose and creamy.
3. Pour into $1 1/2$-quart casserole dish. Cover surfaces of pudding and egg whites with plastic wrap. Refrigerate overnight.
4. Bring egg whites to room temperature. Preheat the oven to hot (425°).
5. Beat egg whites until frothy. Gradually beat in at high speed the remaining 6 tablespoons sugar, a tablespoon at a time, until meringue forms firm peaks.
6. Blot any accumulated moisture on top of pudding with paper toweling. Spread layer of preserves over rice pudding. Mound meringue over top. Spread with back of spoon so meringue touches all sides of casserole; swirl to form peaks.
7. Bake in the preheated hot oven (425°) for 5 minutes or until peaks of meringue are golden brown. Serve immediately.

Cinnamon-Raisin Bread Pudding

Bread puddings were invented by our thrifty ancestors to make good use of stale bread. If you can't wait for your bread to become stale, follow our directions for drying fresh bread.

Bake at 350° for 50 minutes.

Makes 6 to 8 servings.

8 to 10 slices firm white bread	**1 teaspoon ground cinnamon**
$1/4$ cup ($1/2$ stick) butter or margarine, melted	**$1/4$ teaspoon salt**
	4 eggs
	4 cups milk
$1/2$ cup golden or dark raisins	**1 teaspoon vanilla**
	$1/4$ cup apple jelly
$3/4$ cup sugar	

1. If bread is very fresh, place in single layer on cookie sheet to dry out for about 1 hour at room temperature. Brush 1 side of each slice with melted butter; cut into quarters. Arrange bread, overlapping, in shallow 2-quart baking dish; sprinkle with raisins. Mix sugar and cinnamon; sprinkle half over bread.
2. Combine remaining sugar-cinnamon mixture, salt and eggs in large bowl; beat with wire whisk or rotary beater, just until combined. Stir in milk and vanilla; ladle over bread. Preheat oven to 350°.
3. Set baking dish in a shallow pan; place pan on oven shelf; pour boiling water into pan to a depth of 1 inch.
4. Bake in a preheated moderate oven (350°) for 50 minutes or until center is almost set, but still soft; remove baking dish from water to a wire rack.
5. Melt apple jelly in small saucepan; brush over top of bread pudding. Serve hot or warm; pass cream to pour over each serving, if you wish.

Cool Lemon Soufflé, page 318.

Meringue Rice Pudding, page 316.

Cool Lemon Soufflé

Makes 8 servings.

2 envelopes unflavored gelatin	1 tablespoon grated lemon rind
1/2 cup water	2/3 cup lemon juice
6 eggs	Lemon slices
1 1/2 cups sugar	Green grapes
2 cups heavy cream	

1. Fold heavy-duty foil, long enough to go around a 4-cup soufflé dish, lengthwise in half. Fasten foil around dish to make a collar 2 inches higher than rim.
2. Sprinkle gelatin over water in a small saucepan; let stand 10 minutes to soften. Stir over very low heat until gelatin is dissolved. Remove from heat; cool.
3. Beat eggs and sugar in a large bowl with electric mixer at high speed, until very thick and light, about 7 minutes.
4. Beat 1 1/2 cups of the cream in a medium-size bowl until stiff; refrigerate.
5. Stir lemon rind and juice into cooled gelatin; pour mixture into egg mixutre. Beat at low speed until well blended.
6. Chill mixture over a bowl of ice water until mixture mounds softly when spooned.
7. Fold in whipped cream until no streaks of white remain. Pour into prepared dish. Refrigerate at least 3 hours or until set. Remove collar gently; whip remaining cream. Garnish soufflé with whipped cream, lemon slices and grapes.

Orange Soufflé

Makes 6 servings.

1 envelope unflavored gelatin	orange rind
1/4 cup water	3/4 cup fresh orange juice
3 eggs, separated	1 tablespoon lemon juice
1/2 cup sugar	1 cup heavy cream
2 tablespoons grated	

1. Prepare a 1-quart soufflé dish with a collar. Sprinkle gelatin over water in a small saucepan; let stand to soften, 10 minutes. Place saucepan over very low heat until gelatin dissolves, 2 or 3 minutes (mixture will be clear). Remove; cool.
2. Beat the egg yolks until light in large bowl of electric mixer. Add sugar, 2 tablespoons at a time, and beat until mixture becomes thick and light. Add orange rind, orange and lemon juices.
3. Combine cooled gelatin with egg yolk mixture. Place bowl in a larger bowl partly filled with ice and water. Stir frequently just until mixture is thick enough to mound.
4. Beat egg whites in a small bowl until firm peaks form. Beat heavy cream in another small bowl until soft peaks form.
5. Fold in egg whites and heavy cream with a rubber

spatula until no streaks of white remain. Pour into prepared dish. Refrigerate 3 hours or until set. Remove collar. Garnish with additional heavy cream and orange slices, if you wish.

Swedish Apple Cake

Here's a cook-saving crowd pleaser.
Bake at 350° for 30 minutes.

Makes 12 servings.

1 package (6 ounces) zwieback	applesauce
1/2 cup (1 stick) butter or margarine, melted	1 package (3 3/4 ounces) vanilla-flavored pudding and pie filling mix
2 teaspoons grated lemon rind	3 cups milk
2 jars (about 16 ounces each)	2 teaspoons vanilla
	1 cup heavy cream

1. Crush zwieback fine. (You will have about 2 1/2 cups.) Toss with melted butter in a large bowl. Measure out 1 cup of the mixture; press into a 9 × 9 × 2-inch baking dish.
2. Stir lemon rind into applesauce in a medium-size bowl; spread half over crumb layer in pan. Sprinkle with half of the remaining crumb mixture; spread with the remaining applesauce mixture; sprinkle with remaining crumb mixture.
3. Bake in a moderate oven (350°) for 30 minutes or until firm and golden. Cool in dish on wire rack.
4. Several hours before serving, prepare pudding mix with milk following label directions; stir in vanilla; chill.
5. Just before serving, beat cream until stiff in a medium-size bowl. Cut cake into squares; place on rimmed serving plates. Spoon custard sauce around cake; top with whipped cream. Garnish each with a small spoonful of red currant jelly, if you wish.

Low-Cal Chocolate Cream Roll

Bake at 375° for 12 minutes.

Makes 12 servings at 89 calories each.

4 egg whites	flour
1/4 teaspoon salt	3/4 teaspoon baking powder
7 tablespoons sugar	10X (confectioners') sugar
3 egg yolks	1 envelope low-calorie whipped topping mix
2 tablespoons skim milk	
3 tablespoons unsweetened cocoa powder	3/4 teaspoon instant coffee powder
1/2 cup *sifted* cake	

1. Preheat oven to 375°. Beat egg whites with salt until soft peaks form. Gradually beat in 3 tablespoons of the sugar; beat until stiff.
2. Beat egg yolks in small bowl until thick and lemon-

colored. Gradually beat in remaining 4 tablespoons sugar. Beat in milk. Fold into beaten egg whites.

3. Sift cocoa, cake flour and baking powder together on wax paper. Fold into egg mixture ⅓ at a time. Turn batter into a wax paper-lined 15½ x10½ x1-inch nonstick jelly-roll pan; spread evenly.

4. Bake in a preheated moderate oven (375°) for 12 minutes or until center springs back when lightly pressed with fingertip.

5. Turn cake out onto a clean kitchen towel dusted with 10X sugar; remove paper. Roll cake, together with towel, starting at short end; cool completely on wire rack.

6. Combine whipped topping mix and instant coffee powder; prepare following directions on package. Unroll cake; spread evenly with topping mixture. Re-roll cake; place on serving plate. Sift a little 10X sugar over top, if you wish. Refrigerate until serving time.

Low-Cal Chocolate-Glazed Eclairs

Baked at 375° for 45 minutes.

Makes 9 eclairs at 115 calories each.

½ cup water	2 cups skim milk
2 tablespoons butter or margarine	⅓ cup 10X (confectioners') sugar
½ cup *sifted* all-purpose flour	1 tablespoon unsweetened cocoa powder
½ teaspoon salt	
2 eggs	1 tablespoon hot black coffee or boiling water
1 envelope (½ package low-calorie vanilla pudding mix	

1. Preheat oven to 375°. Combine water and butter in saucepan. Heat until butter melts and water is boiling. Turn heat very low. Add flour and salt; beat until mixture leaves side of pan. Remove from heat. Beat in eggs 1 at a time.

2. Use a pastry bag fitted with a large plain tip or a spoon to shape nine 3 x 1-inch eclairs on a nonstick cookie sheet. Allow 2½ inches between eclairs.

3. Bake in a preheated moderate oven (375°) for 45 minutes or until eclairs are crisp and golden. Cool on wire rack.

4. While eclairs cool, combine low-calorie pudding mix with skim milk in saucepan. Cook pudding following directions on package. Chill.

5. Slice tops from cooled eclairs with sharp knife; remove any uncooked dough inside. Fill with the chilled vanilla pudding; replace tops.

6. Combine 10X sugar, cocoa and hot black coffee or water in small bowl; mix until smooth. Drizzle over eclairs. Chill before serving.

Vanilla Custard Filling

Makes about 3½ cups filling (enough for 12 eclairs).

2½ cups milk	purpose flour
5 egg yolks	2 tablespoons butter or margarine
¾ cup sugar	1 tablespoon vanilla
⅔ cup *sifted* all-	

1. Heat milk in large, heavy saucepan until bubbles appear around edges.

2. Beat egg yolks and sugar in large bowl with wire whisk or mixer until pale yellow and thick. Beat in flour until well mixed. Gradually beat in hot milk; pour all back into saucepan. Cook, stirring constantly, over moderately high heat until mixture thickens and comes to boiling; lower heat. (Mixture will be lumpy in the beginning, but lumps disappear during cooking and stirring.) Continue cooking 2 to 3 minutes, over low heat, stirring constantly. Mixture will be quite thick. Remove from heat.

3. Stir in butter and vanilla. Place a piece of wax paper directly on surface of filling to prevent skin from forming. Chill at least 2 hours. If filling becomes too stiff after it's chilled, gradually stir in 2 to 4 tablespoons cream or milk, 1 tablespoon at a time.

Chocolate Custard Filling: Follow the directions for Vanilla Custard Filling, adding 3 squares unsweetened chocolate to milk in step 1, stirring often until melted.

Quick Blueberry Cobbler

Bake at 400° for 20 minutes.

Makes 4 servings.

2 containers (9 ounces each) frozen, drypack blueberries	1 teaspoon grated lemon rind (*optional*)
⅓ cup sugar	⅛ teaspoon ground cinnamon
1 tablespoon flour	
1 tablespoon butter or margarine	1¾ cups buttermilk baking mix
1 tablespoon water	⅔ cup half-and-half

1. Preheat oven to 400°. Combine blueberries, sugar, flour, butter, water, lemon rind and cinnamon in a medium-size saucepan. Bring to boiling, stirring, for 5 minutes.

2. Meanwhile, combine baking mix and half-and-half in a medium-size bowl.

3. Pour hot berries into a 9-inch pie plate. Drop heaping tablespoons of batter over top, leaving space between each.

4. Bake in a preheated hot oven (400°) for 20 minutes or until biscuits are lightly browned. Serve warm with ice cream.

Peach Cobbler

Bake at 375° for 30 minutes.

Makes 6 servings.

3 to 4 large peaches	lemon juice
1/2 cup sugar	1/8 teaspoon salt
1 tablespoon cornstarch	1 cup buttermilk baking mix
1 teaspoon grated lemon rind	1 tablespoon sugar
2 tablespoons	1/2 cup light cream or half-and-half

1. Dip peaches into boiling water 30 seconds, then into ice water 1 minute. Peel, halve, pit and slice (about 4 cups). Combine peach slices, sugar, cornstarch, lemon rind and juice and salt in a medium-size saucepan. Bring mixture to boiling, stirring constantly; pour into 1 1/2-quart baking dish.
2. Bake in a moderate oven (375°) for 10 minutes. Meanwhile, combine baking mix and the 1 tablespoon sugar in a medium-size bowl. Stir in cream until a soft dough forms. Remove peaches from oven. Drop dough by teaspoonfuls over peaches so that fruit is completely covered. Return to oven.
3. Bake 20 minutes longer or until crust is golden.

Spicy Pear Cobbler

Bake at 400° for 20 minutes.

Makes 6 servings.

1 can (29 ounces) pear halves	1/2 teaspoon ground ginger
1 teaspoon grated lemon rind	1/4 teaspoon ground cinnamon
3 tablespoons lemon juice	1/4 teaspoon ground allspice
3 tablespoons butter	1/4 teaspoon ground nutmeg
1 cup *sifted* all-purpose flour	1/4 cup molasses
1 teaspoon baking powder	1 container (8 ounces) plain yogurt
1/2 teaspoon baking soda	1 tablespoon milk
1/4 teaspoon salt	1 teaspoon sugar
	1/2 cup heavy cream

1. Drain pears, reserving syrup. Measure 1/2 cup syrup into medium-size saucepan. Stir in lemon rind, lemon juice and 1 tablespoon of the butter. Heat to boiling; lower heat; simmer mixture for 5 minutes.
2. While sauce is heating, cut pears into 1-inch pieces.
3. Sift flour, baking powder, baking soda, salt, ginger, cinnamon, allspice and nutmeg into a medium-size bowl. Cut in remaining 2 tablespoons butter with pastry blender until flour mixture is crumbly.
4. Combine molasses and 1/4 cup of the yogurt in 1-cup measure. Stir into flour mixture just until blended (dough will be very soft).
5. Turn dough out onto well-floured surface; pat into a 5-inch circle. Cut circle into 6 wedges with floured knife. Preheat oven to 400°.

6. When syrup has cooked, gently stir in pear pieces until heated through. Pour pears into buttered 9-inch pie plate. Place pie plate on cookie sheet. Arrange gingerbread wedges evenly over pears. Brush with milk. Sprinkle with sugar.
7. Bake in a preheated hot oven (400°) for 20 minutes or until gingerbread is nicely browned.
8. While the cobbler bakes, whip the heavy cream in small bowl until soft peaks form. Fold in the remaining yogurt. Serve with hot cobbler.

Strawberry-Rhubarb Cobbler

Here's an old-fashioned combination of fruits topped with orange-flavored biscuit pinwheels.

Bake at 400° for 25 minutes.

Makes 8 servings.

1 pound rhubarb OR: 1 package (1 pound) frozen unsugared rhubarb	1/2 cup water
	2 1/2 tablespoons cornstarch
2 pints strawberries OR: 1 package (1 pound) frozen strawberries, thawed	1/2 cup milk
	2 cups buttermilk baking mix
	1 tablespoon grated orange rind
1 1/4 cups sugar	1/3 cup sugar

1. Wash rhubarb; trim ends; cut into 1-inch pieces (you should have 4 cups); wash, hull and halve strawberries (you should have 4 cups).
2. Combine rhubarb, 3/4 cup sugar and 1/4 cup of the water in a large saucepan. Cook over low heat, stirring occasionally, just until rhubarb is tender. (Do not overcook.)
3. Combine remaining 1/4 cup water with cornstarch and remaining 1/2 cup sugar in a 1-cup measure. Stir into the hot rhubarb. Continue cooking, stirring constantly, until mixture thickens and bubbles. Remove from heat. Stir in strawberries; pour into a 2-quart shallow baking dish (11 3/4 × 7 1/2 × 1 3/4-inches).
4. Preheat oven to 400°. Place baking dish in oven while preheating.
5. Stir milk into baking mix in a medium-size bowl until soft dough forms. Turn out onto a lightly floured surface; knead 8 to 10 times. Roll dough to a 12 × 13-inch rectangle.
6. Combine orange rind with 1/3 cup sugar; sprinkle over surface of dough; roll up jelly-roll style. Cut dough into 18 slices approximately 3/4-inch thick.
7. When filling is bubbly hot, arrange biscuit pinwheels over top.
8. Bake in preheated hot oven (400°) for 25 minutes or until biscuits are golden brown.

Pictured opposite: Spicy Pear Cobbler.

Lemon Meringue Tarts

Bake at 250° for 30 minutes.

Makes 12 servings.

Meringues:
3 egg whites, at room temperature
1/8 teaspoon cream of tartar
3/4 cup sugar

Lemon Custard Filling:
3 egg yolks

1 egg
3/4 cup sugar
2 tablespoons grated lemon rind
1/3 cup lemon juice
1/2 cup (1 stick) butter or margarine
Assorted fruits

1. Make Meringues: Line 1 large or 2 small cookie sheets with brown paper. Outline 12 ovals, about 4 × 2 inches, on paper.
2. Beat egg whites with cream of tartar in a large bowl until foamy and double in volume. Sprinkle in sugar, 1 tablespoon at a time, beating constantly with mixer at high speed until sugar is dissolved completely and meringue stands in firm peaks when beater is lifted slowly. (Beating will take 10 to 15 minutes.) Preheat oven to 250°.
3. Spoon meringue into pastry bag fitted with a star tip. Pipe into outlines on paper, building up sides slightly to form a shell or spoon meringue into outline, building up sides with the tip of a spoon.
4. Bake in a very slow oven (250°) for 30 minutes. Turn off heat and leave meringues in oven with door closed at least 1 hour or overnight. When cool, store in container with tightfitting cover. (They will keep several weeks.)
5. Make Lemon Custard Filling: Combine egg yolks, egg and sugar in top of double boiler; mix well. Stir in lemon rind, lemon juice and butter. Cook over simmering water, stirring constantly, 10 to 15 minutes or until mixture thickens. Remove from heat; cool. Spoon into jars; cover tightly. (Can be stored in refrigerator several days, or stored in freezer for weeks.)
6. When ready to fill shells, spoon about 2 tablespoons filling into each meringue shell. Top with fresh berries or sliced fruits of your choice.

Ambrosia
A dessert of assorted sweet fruit and shredded coconut. It can also be a sweet beverage. In Greek mythology, ambrosia was the food of the gods.

Ambrosia

Makes about 12 servings.

2 large pineapples
OR: 3 cans (20 ounces each) pineapple chunks in juice
12 large oranges

3 cups grated fresh coconut
OR: 2 cans (4 ounces each) shredded coconut

1. Pare and core the fresh pineapple; cut the fruit into chunks into a large bowl, saving as much juice as possible. (For canned pineapple, use all the juice.)
2. Remove rind from oranges with a sharp knife, holding fruit over bowl to catch juice. Slice oranges, removing any seeds.
3. Layer pineapple, part of the coconut and oranges in a serving bowl. Sprinkle top with remaining coconut. Cover; chill at least 4 hours before serving.

Melon in Sabayon Sauce

Makes 6 servings.

1/2 teaspoon unflavored gelatin
1/4 cup sugar
1/2 cup orange juice
1/2 cup white port

wine or dry sherry
2 eggs, slightly beaten
1 honeydew melon, chilled

1. Sprinkle gelatin and sugar over orange juice and port wine in large bowl or double boiler; beat in eggs. Set over barely simmering water.
2. Cook, beating constantly with a whisk or rotary hand beater until mixture thickens slightly and is double in volume, about 8 to 12 minutes. Remove from hot water and set in ice water. Beat mixture until cool, then remove from ice water.
3. Scoop enough melon balls from melon with melon baller to fill 6 dessert glasses; keep refrigerated. Just before serving, pour sauce over each serving.

Pineapple Spears in Rum

Serve these citrus- and rum-flavored spears as stirrers in your next rum-flavored beverage or add to a fruit compote.

Makes 4 pints.

2 large ripe pineapples
1 cup sugar
2 cups water

4 thin slices orange
4 thin slices lemon
1/4 cup light rum

1. Cut off leafy crown from pineapple; cut off ring; quarter lengthwise; cut out core; cut each quarter into 4 equal spears. Trim spears, if necessary, to fit wide-mouth pint jars.
2. Combine sugar, water, orange and lemon slices in a large saucepan; bring to boiling; carefully add pineapple spears; bring back to boiling; simmer 5 minutes.
3. Remove spears and place 8 spears and orange and lemon slices into 4 hot sterilized, wide-mouth 16-ounce jars.
4. Drain any syrup that may be in the bottom of the jars back into the saucepan. Boil syrup until reduced to about 1 1/2 cups.
5. Add 1 tablespoon rum to each jar of pineapple spears. Pour in the syrup, leaving 1/4-inch head space. Seal; cool; label; date. Store in refrigerator.

Cheese and Grape Compote

A low-calorie goodie.

Makes 6 servings.

**1 pound seedless
green grapes
2 tablespoons honey
1 tablespoon lemon
juice**

**1 container (12
ounces) low-fat
cottage cheese
2 to 3 tablespoons
light brown sugar**

1. Wash and remove stems from grapes. (You should have about 3 cups.) Mix honey and lemon juice; toss with grapes.
2. Puree cottage cheese in blender until smooth; spoon over grapes; sprinkle brown sugar over cheese.

Frosty Cantaloupe Compotes

Makes 6 servings.

**1 container (8 ounces)
dairy sour cream
1/3 cup firmly packed
light brown sugar
1/4 teaspoon ground
cinnamon
1 medium-size ripe
cantaloupe**

**1 pint fresh
blueberries, rinsed
and drained
1/2 pound seedless
green grapes,
rinsed, drained and
halved**

1. Mix sour cream, brown sugar and cinnamon in a small bowl. Cover; chill until ready to serve.
2. Pare, seed and cut cantaloupe into 6 wedges; place each wedge in a serving bowl. Divide blueberries and grapes evenly among bowls; cover with plastic wrap; chill.
3. To serve: Spoon sour cream topping over fruit, dividing evenly.

Glacéed Oranges

Bright slivers of candied orange peel and a touch of orange-flavored liqueur add zest to this simple dessert.

Makes 6 servings.

**6 large navel oranges
2 cups sugar
1 cup water**

**2 tablespoons orange-
flavored liqueur**

1. Remove thin, bright-colored rind (no white) from each orange with a vegetable parer or sharp knife; cut into thin strips; reserve.
2. Simmer rind in 4 cups boiling water for 8 minutes; drain and reserve the rind.
3. With a sharp knife, cut remaining white membrane from oranges. Remove core from center of orange. Place oranges in a bowl just large enough to hold them.
4. Combine sugar with water in a heavy saucepan;

cook over medium heat, stirring constantly, until sugar is dissolved. Continue cooling without stirring until mixture is syrupy, about 10 minutes. Add blanched orange rind; cook about 5 minutes or until rind becomes translucent. Remove from heat; add orange liqueur. Pour hot syrup with rind over oranges. Cool; chill several hours or overnight. Garnish each orange with candied violets if you wish.

Peaches and Cream Tart

Peach slices baked in a rich custardy cream makes a luscious company dessert. This tart is best made early in the day.

Bake at 400° for 40 minutes.

Makes one 9-inch tart.

**Rich Tart Pastry:
1 1/2 cups *unsifted* all-
purpose flour
2 tablespoons sugar
1 teaspoon baking
powder**

**1/8 teaspoon salt
1/2 cup (1 stick) butter
or margarine
1 egg
1/2 teaspoon grated
lemon rind**

**Filling:
4 to 6 large peaches
1/2 cup sugar
1 tablespoon
cornstarch
1 tablespoon lemon**

**juice
2 eggs
1 cup heavy cream
1/4 teaspoon ground
nutmeg**

1. Prepare Pastry: Combine flour, sugar, baking powder and salt in medium-size bowl. Cut in butter with pastry blender until mixture is crumbly. Beat egg with lemon rind in cup; sprinkle over flour mixture. Toss with fork just until pastry is moist. Work with fingers until pastry holds together.
2. Press dough evenly over bottom and 2 inches up side of a 9-inch springform or removable-bottom fluted tart pan. Preheat oven to 400°.
3. Prepare Filling: Dip peaches into boiling water 30 seconds, then into ice water 1 minute. Peel, halve, pit and slice (you should have about 5 cups). Combine peaches, sugar, cornstarch and lemon juice in medium-size bowl; toss to mix. Arrange peach slices, overlapping, in bottom of pastry-lined pan.
4. Bake in a preheated hot oven (400°) for 20 minutes.
5. Meanwhile, beat eggs, cream and nutmeg in small bowl. Pour over baked peaches. Return tart to oven.
6. Bake 20 minutes more or until cream is firm around the edge but soft-set in the center and top is golden. Cool tart on wire rack at least 2 hours. Remove side of pan. Serve cool but not chilled.

Peaches and Sour Cream Tarts

Juicy ripe peaches and cool green grapes cap an apricot-sour cream filling.

Makes 8 tarts.

1 package (3 ounces) apricot-flavored gelatin	cracker tart shells
	3 to 4 peaches or nectarines
1 cup boiling water	1 cup seedless green grapes, halved
1 container (8 ounces) dairy sour cream	2 tablespoons Marsala wine or cream sherry
8 individual baked pastry or graham	

1. Dissolve gelatin in boiling water. Measure and reserve 1/4 cup of the mixture for glaze. Chill remaining gelatin mixture until slightly thickened. Stir in sour cream; spoon into tart shells. Chill until set, about 30 minutes.
2. Pare and slice peaches; arrange peach slices and grape halves over filling. Add wine to reserved gelatin mixture in small cup; set in ice water; when slightly thickened, brush over peaches. Chill until ready to serve.

Strawberry-Kiwi Tart

Bake at 400° for 10 minutes, then at 350° for 5 minutes.

Makes 10 servings.

1 1/3 cups *sifted* all-purpose flour	1/3 cup milk
1/4 cup sugar	4 egg yolks, lightly beaten
1/2 cup (1 stick) butter or margarine, softened	1 1/2 teaspoons vanilla
	3 tablespoons plus 1/3 cup strawberry ice cream topping
2 egg yolks	
1 cup half-and-half or light cream	1 pint strawberries, washed, hulled and halved
1/3 cup sugar	
3 tablespoons cornstarch	2 kiwi fruit, pared and sliced crosswise

1. Preheat oven to 400°. Mix flour and sugar in a medium-size bowl. Add butter and egg yolks; stir with a fork until mixture clings together in a ball. Press dough into an 11-inch tart pan with removable bottom; chill 15 minutes.
2. Bake shell in a preheated hot oven (400°) for 10 minutes (no need to prick bottom); lower heat to moderate (350°) and bake 5 minutes longer or until shell is lightly browned. Transfer to wire rack to cool completely.
3. Heat cream and sugar in a small saucepan until mixture comes to boiling. Combine cornstarch and milk in a cup; stir into cream mixture and cook a few seconds longer, stirring until thick.
4. Beat a small amount of cream mixture into egg yolks; return mixture to pan and cook over low heat for about 10 minutes longer or until thick. *Do not overcook* or mixture will curdle. Remove from heat; stir in vanilla.
5. Pour filling into a small bowl; press a piece of plastic wrap directly on the surface of the filling to keep film from forming. Chill until very cold.
6. Spread 3 tablespoons strawberry topping over the bottom of the tart shell. Spread chilled custard filling on top. Brush strawberries with remaining strawberry topping and arrange over filling with kiwi slices. Chill until ready to serve, up to 2 hours later.

Cherry-Nut Tarts

These easy-to-make cherry tarts, made with ready-to-use graham cracker tart shells, may be prepared a day ahead and refrigerated.

Save the protective plastic tart shell inserts to use as covers.

Makes 2 servings.

2 ready-to-use graham cracker tart shells (from 4-ounce package; freeze remaining shells in package for another use; or to make 6 tarts, see Note)	brown sugar
	1 tablespoon finely chopped pecans
	1/2 cup prepared cherry pie filling (use remainder of 1-pound can as sauce for ice cream, or for 6 tarts, see Note)
1 teaspoon melted butter	
2 teaspoons dark	1/4 teaspoon grated lemon rind

1. Remove plastic inserts from 2 tart shells; leave shells in foil. Wash inserts and reserve.
2. Combine melted butter, brown sugar and pecans in small bowl.
3. Combine 1/2 cup pie filling with lemon rind in bowl. Spoon into tart shells. Sprinkle half the nut mixture over each.
4. Invert reserved plastic tart inserts and use to cover filled tarts. Secure to foil tart pan with several pieces of tape. Place the tarts in a covered plastic container, if you wish. Refrigerate several hours or overnight.

Note: To prepare 6 tarts, stir 3/4 teaspoon grated lemon rind into 1 can (1 pound) prepared cherry pie filling. Spoon evenly into 6 tart shells (one 4-oz. package). Combine 1 tablespoon melted butter, 2 tablespoons dark brown sugar and 3 tablespoons finely chopped pecans in bowl. Sprinkle over tops of tarts, dividing equally.

Pictured opposite:
Strawberry-Kiwi Tart.

Praline Ice Cream Cake

Makes 20 servings.

Almond Praline *(recipe follows)*
1 quart pistachio ice cream
1 quart lemon sherbet
1 quart orange sherbet
1 quart strawberry ice cream
1¹/₂ cups heavy cream
¹/₂ cup 10X (confectioners') sugar
¹/₂ cup chopped pistachio nuts

1. Prepare Almond Praline. Sprinkle ³/₄ cup of the praline powder over the bottom of a 10 x 2³/₄-inch springform pan.
2. Soften the ice creams and the sherbets, 1 flavor at a time, in a chilled large bowl, starting with pistachio. Layer, in order, pistachio ice cream, lemon and orange sherbets and strawberry ice cream, sprinkling ³/₄ cup praline powder between each layer. Freeze each layer of ice cream about 1 hour before adding praline and next flavor. Freeze layers at least 4 hours or overnight. Remove side of pan.
3. Whip cream with sugar in a medium-size bowl until stiff. Spread side of layers, then decorate top with a ring of whipped cream pressed through a pastry bag. Sprinkle with pistachio nuts and garnish with fresh fruits, if you wish.

Almond Praline: Combine 1 cup sugar, ¹/₄ cup water and ¹/₄ teaspoon cream of tartar in a large skillet. Cook over medium heat until sugar mixture caramelizes to a golden brown; stir in 1 cup toasted blanched almonds. Pour onto a lightly buttered cookie sheet; cool; break up into small pieces; whirl in the container of an electric blender until pulverized. Makes 3 cups.

Glazed Fruit Tarts

Bake at 450° for 10 minutes.

Makes 36 tarts.

2 packages piecrust mix
¹/₄ cup sugar
2 eggs, slightly beaten
Pastry Cream *(recipe follows)*
Fresh fruits for garnish:
strawberries, bananas, grapes, kiwi, mandarin orange, pineapple slices, etc.
²/₃ cup apple jelly
2 teaspoons sugar

1. Combine piecrust mix and sugar in a medium-size bowl; blend in eggs with a fork until pastry is moistened and leaves side of bowl. Press about 1 tablespoon of the dough into tiny 2- to 3-inch fluted

Praline Ice Cream Cake.

Glazed Fruit Tarts, page 326.

tart pans.* Prick shells all over with tines of fork. Place on cookie sheets; chill 15 minutes. Preheat oven to 450°.

2. Bake in a preheated very hot oven (450°) for 10 minutes or until brown. Cool on wire racks.

3. Spoon a small amount of Pastry Cream into each cooled shell. Decorate with fruits.

4. Melt jelly with sugar in a small skillet over low heat; cool slightly; brush over fruits. Chill.

If you don't have enough tart pans, fill those you have, bake and refill.

Pastry Cream: Prepare 1 package (3³/₄ ounces) French vanilla-flavored instant pudding and pie filling mix with 1 cup milk, following label directions; whip ¹/₂ cup heavy cream until stiff; fold into pudding; cover with plastic wrap; chill.

Baklava   A multi-layered, sweet pastry of honey and nuts from Middle Eastern cuisines. Each layer of phyllo, the paper-thin pastry, is buttered and then sprinkled with sugared-and-spiced ground nuts. The pastry is cut into diamond shapes to serve.

Baklava

Bake nuts at 350° for 10 minutes.

Bake at 325° for 50 minutes.

Makes about 3¹/₂ dozen pieces.

3 cups walnuts (about ³/₄ pound)	**leaves**
¹/₂ cup sugar	**¹/₂ cup (1 stick)**
1¹/₂ teaspoons ground cinnamon	**unsalted butter or margarine, melted**
1 package (16 ounces) phyllo or strudel pastry	**1 tablespoon water**
	Honey Syrup (*recipe follows*)

1. Place walnuts on 15¹/₂ × 10¹/₂ ×1-inch jelly-roll pan; toast in a moderate oven (350°) for 10 minutes. Whirl walnuts, while still warm, ¹/₂ cup at a time, in container of electric blender until finely ground. (You may use a food grinder or food processor, if you wish.) Remove ground walnuts to a medium-size bowl. Repeat this procedure until all of the walnuts are ground. Mix in the sugar and ground cinnamon; set aside.

2. Brush bottom of a 13 × 9 × 2-inch baking pan with melted butter. Fold two phyllo leaves in half; place on the bottom of pan; brush with butter. Place two more

(continued)

folded leaves in pan; brush with butter. (Keep rest of pastry leaves covered with a clean damp kitchen towel to prevent drying out.)

3. Sprinkle top with 1/2 cup nut mixture. Add two more folded leaves; brush with butter.

4. Repeat step 3 five more times. Stack remaining leaves, brushing every other one. Brush top leaf with remaining butter; sprinkle with the 1 tablespoon of water.

5. With a sharp knife, mark off the Baklava. Cut through the top layer of the phyllo only, making 5 lengthwise cuts, 1 1/2-inches apart (you will have 6 equal strips). Then cut diagonally again at 1 1/2-inch intervals, making diamonds (9 strips).

6. Bake in a slow oven (325°) for 50 minutes, or until top is golden. Remove pan to wire rack. Cut all the way through the diamonds, separating slightly. Pour cooled Honey Syrup over. Cool thoroughly in pan on rack. Cover with foil; let stand at room temperature overnight for syrup to be absorbed. Baklava will keep in refrigerator up to 2 weeks.

Honey Syrup

Makes 2 cups.

1 small lemon	2 whole cloves
1 cup sugar	1 cup honey
1 cup water	1 tablespoon brandy
1 two-inch piece stick cinnamon	(optional)

1. Grate the rind from the lemon (the thin, yellow skin only) and reserve. Squeeze out 1 1/2 teaspoons lemon juice into a small cup; set aside.

2. Place lemon rind, sugar, water, cinnamon stick and cloves in a heavy medium-size saucepan. Bring to boiling; lower heat; continue cooking, without stirring, 25 minutes, or until mixture is syrupy (230° on a candy thermometer).

3. Stir in honey; pour through strainer into a 2-cup measure. Stir in reserved lemon juice and brandy. Cool.

Macadamia Nut Tarts

Bake at 400° for 15 minutes.

Makes 16 tarts.

1 package (11 ounces) piecrust mix	1/4 cup honey
1/2 cup (1 stick) butter, softened	4 eggs, beaten
	1 teaspoon vanilla
3/4 cup firmly packed light brown sugar	1 can (5 ounces) macadamia nuts, coarsely chopped
3/4 cup light corn syrup	Whipped cream (optional)

1. Prepare piecrust following label directions; roll out;

cut into sixteen 4 1/2-inch rounds. Fit into 3 1/2 inch tart pans. Preheat oven to 400°.

2. Beat butter and sugar in large bowl with electric mixer until creamy. Beat in com syrup and honey, then eggs and vanilla. Stir in nuts.

3. Place about 1/4 cup filling in each tart shell. Place on cookie sheet.

4. Bake in a preheated hot oven (400°) for 15 minutes or until golden brown. Cool before serving. Decorate with whipped cream, if you wish.

For 9-inch Pie: Use 1/2 package piecrust mix to prepare one 9-inch crust. Proceed as directed with remaining ingredients; pour into pie shell. Bake on bottom rack in a hot oven (425°) for 10 minutes. Lower oven temperature to slow (325°) and continue baking for 25 minutes or until golden.

Note: Tarts or pie may be made ahead and frozen; cool thoroughly and wrap well with aluminum foil before freezing.

Pecan Tart

Bake at 350° for 1 hour.

Makes one 11-inch tart.

1 package piecrust mix	flour
4 eggs	2 cups light or dark corn syrup
1 cup sugar	2 teaspoons vanilla
Pinch salt	2 cups chopped pecans
1/4 cup all-purpose	

1. Prepare piecrust mix following label directions. Roll out to a 13-inch round on a lightly floured surface; fit into an 11-inch fluted tart or quiche pan with removable bottom; trim edge even with top of pan.

2. Preheat oven to 350°. Beat eggs in a large bowl just enough to break up. Stir in sugar, salt, flour, corn syrup and vanilla until mixture is well blended. Stir in pecans. Pour into prepared shell.

3. Bake in a preheated moderate oven (350°) for 1 hour or until center is almost set. (Filling will set as it cools.) Cool on wire rack.

Maple Walnut Tarts

The colonists used maple sugar to sweeten almost everything, as in their version of English chess tarts.

Bake at 425° for 15 minutes.

Makes 1 1/2 dozen 2 1/2 -inch tarts.

1 package piecrust mix	1/2 cup maple syrup
2 eggs	1/3 cup butter, melted and slightly cooled
1/4 cup firmly packed brown sugar	1/2 cup chopped walnuts
1 teaspoon salt	Whipped cream

1. Prepare piecrust mix following label directions. Roll

out pastry slightly larger than a 16 x 12-inch rectangle. Trim to 16 x 12 inches. Using a ruler as a guide, cut into 4-inch squares. Line 2½-inch fluted tart pans with pastry; trim excess pastry and reserve. Reroll trimmings to 12 x 8 inches; cut into 4-inch squares. Line tart pans and trim. Preheat oven to 425°.
2. Beat eggs with brown sugar and salt. Beat in maple syrup and butter until creamy smooth. Stir in walnuts.
3. Fill each tart pan ⅔ full. Place on cookie sheet.
4. Bake in a preheated hot oven (425°) for 15 minutes. (Filling will puff up during baking but will flatten when cooled.) Remove tarts to wire racks to cool. Garnish with whipped cream and additional chopped walnuts, if you wish.

Note: If using 2-inch mini muffin tins, reroll pastry trimmings to 16 x 12 inches; cut into 4-inch squares; line pans and trim. Fill ⅔ full. Bake according to directions above. Remove from tins using small metal spatula or small knife; cool on wire racks. Makes 2 dozen.

Ambrosia Tarts

Easy-to-make crunchy coconut tart shells hold a heavenly fruit and cheese filling.

Makes 8 tarts.

2 eggs	**Shells** *(recipe*
½ cup sugar	*follows)*
1 tablespoon grated	**2 packages (3 ounces**
lemon rind	**each) cream cheese**
¼ cup lemon juice	**1 to 2 bananas**
¼ cup (½ stick) butter	**3 kiwi fruits**
or margarine	**¼ cup orange**
Toasted Coconut Tart	**marmalade**

1. Combine eggs, sugar, lemon rind, lemon juice and butter in top of a double boiler. Cook over simmering water, stirring constantly, until mixture thickens, about 8 minutes. Remove from heat; cool completely.
2. Prepare Toasted Coconut Tart Shells.
3. Soften cream cheese in a small bowl; gradually blend in cooled lemon mixture. Spoon filling into prepared tart shells. Peel and slice banana and kiwi; arrange slices on top of tarts.
4. Melt orange marmalade in small saucepan over low heat; brush over fruits. Refrigerate until ready to serve.

Toasted Coconut Tart Shells: Crush 20 vanilla wafer cookies in plastic bag with rolling pin. Heat ½ cup flaked coconut in a heavy skillet over medium heat, stirring often until golden. Stir in 3 tablespoons butter until melted. Remove from heat; stir in cookie crumbs. Press mixture into 8 individual aluminum foil tart pans, dividing evenly. Chill until firm.

Double Chocolate Tarts

A super velvety chocolate mousse fills quick-made chocolate-crumb crusts.

Makes 6 tarts.

16 chocolate cookie	**chocolate**
wafers	**1 egg**
3 tablespoons butter	**1 teaspoon vanilla**
or margarine,	**3 small navel oranges**
melted	**¼ cup orange**
½ cup heavy cream	**marmalade**
4 squares semisweet	

1. Whirl cookies, a few at a time, in the container of an electric blender or food processor to make crumbs; place in small bowl. Add melted butter; blend well. Press crumb mixture into six individual aluminum foil tart pans, dividing evenly. Chill.
2. Heat cream and chocolate in a small saucepan just until chocolate melts. Remove from heat; beat in egg and vanilla. Set pan in ice water. Beat mixture with electric hand mixer at medium speed, scraping side and bottom of pan often until mixture becomes light and fluffy and starts to hold its shape. Spoon into prepared tart shells; chill.
3. Pare oranges; section; drain well and arrange over chocolate filling. Heat orange marmalade in a small saucepan over low heat until melted. Brush over tops. Sprinkle with pistachio nuts, if you wish. Refrigerate.

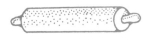

Greek Walnut Cakes

Bake at 350° for 30 minutes.

Makes about 2 dozen squares.

Honey Syrup *(recipe*	**butter or margarine,**
follows)	**softened**
1½ cups *sifted* **all-**	**1 cup sugar**
purpose flour	**4 eggs**
2 teaspoons baking	**1 tablespoon grated**
powder	**orange rind**
1 teaspoon ground	**⅓ cup orange juice**
cinnamon	**2 cups finely chopped**
¼ teaspoon salt	**walnuts**
1 cup (2 sticks)	

1. Prepare and cool Honey Syrup.
2. Sift flour, baking powder, cinnamon and salt onto wax paper. Butter a 13 x 9 x 2-inch pan. Preheat oven to 350°.
3. Beat butter with sugar in a large bowl with electric mixer until well blended. Beat in eggs, 1 at a time, until mixture is light and fluffy. Stir in orange rind.
4. Stir in flour mixture alternately with orange juice,

(continued)

beating after each addition, until batter is smooth. Stir in walnuts. Pour into prepared pan.

5. Bake in a preheated moderate oven (350°) for 30 minutes or until center springs back when lightly pressed with fingertip.

6. Cool cake in pan on wire rack 10 minutes; gradually pour cool syrup over cake, letting syrup soak into cake before adding more. Or, cool cake completely, then pour *hot* syrup over cake.

7. To serve: Cut cake into small squares (about 2 inches each) or in 2-inch diamond shapes. Put each cake into a fluted paper baking cup. Garnish each square or diamond shape with walnut halves, if you wish.

Honey Syrup: Combine one 2-inch piece orange rind (no white), 1/2 cup sugar, 1/2 cup water and one 1-inch piece stick cinnamon. Bring to boiling; lower heat; simmer 25 minutes or to 230° on a candy thermometer. Stir in 1/2 cup honey. Remove rind and cinnamon stick; cool.

Strudel

Strudel   A sweet or savory filled pastry made by wrapping paper-thin dough around the filling. Strudel is considered a specialty of Austrian, Hungarian and Czechoslovakian cuisines. Traditionally, the pastry is made of flour, egg and water, rolled as thinly as possible, then stretched until paper-thin. The filling of apples, cherries, cheese, mushrooms, eggs or fish is placed on the pastry, which is then rolled to enclose the filling. It is transferred to a cookie sheet and baked.

Commercially made strudel dough looks like phyllo, the Greek or Turkish pastry dough. Often, the two doughs are used interchangeably in recipes.

Apple Strudel

Crispy pastry with a buttery apple-nut filling.
Bake at 400° for 35 minutes.

Makes 2 strudels.

1 cup fresh bread crumbs (2 slices bread)	lemon rind
1 cup ground walnuts	1 tablespoon lemon juice
8 medium-size cooking apples (McIntosh, Golden Delicious), pared, quartered, cored and thinly sliced (8 cups)	1 teaspoon ground cinnamon
	16 strudel or phyllo leaves (from a 16-ounce package)
	3/4 cup (1 1/2 sticks) unsalted butter, melted
1 cup sugar	10X (confectioners') sugar
1 cup golden raisins	
1 teaspoon grated	

1. Combine bread crumbs and walnuts in a large skillet and stir over medium-high heat until crumbs

and nuts are golden, about 5 minutes. Remove from heat.

2. Combine apples, sugar, raisins, lemon rind, lemon juice and cinnamon in a large bowl.

3. Place 4 strudel leaves on a clean towel; place another 4 leaves overlapping to form an 18 × 18-inch square of dough.

4. Brush dough completely with some of the melted butter. Sprinkle half of the crumb-nut mixture over entire surface.

5. Spoon half of the apple mixture in an even row down one side of the dough, 2 inches in from edges.

6. Using the towel, lift dough up and over filling. Fold the two adjacent sides of the dough toward center, in order to completely enclose the apple filling.

7. Continue rolling strudel, aided by towel; allow it to roll over and over on itself until completely rolled. (You will have a 15 × 3-inch roll.) Preheat oven to 400°.

8. Carefully ease filled roll onto a jelly-roll pan; repeat for remaining apple strudel.

9. Bake in a preheated hot oven (400°) for 35 minutes, brushing several times with remaining butter.

10. Allow strudel to cool 15 minutes before removing to serving board. Sprinkle with 10X sugar.

Apple Dumplings in Cheese-Walnut Pastry

Whole apples spiced and sugared and enclosed in a Cheddar cheese pastry.

Bake at 425° for 45 minutes.

Makes 6 servings.

3 cups *sifted* all-purpose flour	Granny Smith)
1 1/2 teaspoons salt	1/4 cup (1/2 stick) butter or margarine, softened
3/4 cup vegetable shortening	1/3 cup sugar
2 ounces Cheddar cheese, shredded (1/2 cup)	1/2 teaspoon apple pie spice
1/4 cup ground or very finely chopped walnuts	OR: A combination of ground cinnamon, nutmeg and cloves
10 to 12 tablespoons ice water	1 egg yolk, slightly beaten
6 medium-size baking apples (Rome Beauty,	Custard Sauce (*recipe follows*)

1. Sift flour and salt into a medium-size bowl; cut in shortening with a fork or pastry blender until mixture is crumbly; stir in cheese and walnuts.

2. Sprinkle water over mixture; mix lightly with a fork

(continued)

Pictured opposite: Apple Strudel; Apple Mousse with Raspberry-Apple Sauce, page 288; Apple dumplings in Cheese-Walnut Pastry, page 331.

just until pastry holds together and leaves side of bowl clean.

3. Pare apples and core 2/3 way down. Remove any remaining seeds. Combine butter, sugar and apple pie spice in a small bowl until smooth and paste-like. Spoon into centers of apples, dividing evenly.

4. Roll out pastry on a lightly floured surface to a 21 × 14-inch rectangle; trim excess. Cut into six 7-inch squares; place apple in center of each square. Press pastry firmly around apple. Brush with part of the beaten egg yolk. Place in a 13 × 9 × 2-inch baking pan. Preheat oven to 425°.

5. Roll out pastry trimmings; cut out leaf shapes with hors d'ouevre cutter or knife. Cut out six 1 × 1/4-inch wide strips. Press 1 strip on center top of dumpling and arrange leaves around "stem." Brush with remaining beaten egg yolk.

6. Bake in a preheated hot oven (425°) for 45 minutes or until apples are tender and pastry is golden. Serve warm with Custard Sauce.

Custard Sauce

Makes 2 1/2 cups.

4 egg yolks	cornstarch
1/4 cup sugar	2 cups milk, scalded
2 teaspoons	1 teaspoon vanilla

Beat egg yolks with sugar and cornstarch in a medium-size bowl; gradually stir in milk. Pour into medium-size saucepan; cook over moderate heat, stirring constantly, until custard thickens slightly and coats a spoon. Remove from heat; pour into a small bowl; stir in vanilla; cover. Chill.

Apple-Nut Strudel

It's always impressive--tissue-thin strudel dough twirled around a buttery apple-nut filling.

Bake at 400° for 50 minutes.

Makes 8 servings.

3 cups *sifted* all-purpose flour	1 can (20 ounces) sliced apples, drained
1/4 teaspoon salt	3/4 cup raisins
1 egg	1/2 cup chopped walnuts
3/4 cup lukewarm water	3/4 cup granulated sugar
2 tablespoons vegetable oil	1 teaspoon ground cinnamon
1/2 cup (1 stick) butter or margarine, melted	10X (confectioners') sugar
3 cups fresh white bread crumbs (6 slices)	

1. Sift flour and salt into a large bowl. Make a well in center of flour and add egg, water and vegetable oil. Stir to make a sticky dough.

2. Place dough on a lightly floured pastry board or cloth. Slap dough down onto board; pick up; slap down again for 10 minutes to develop the gluten (as in bread), which gives the elasticity necessary for stretching dough. Cover dough with a bowl and allow to rest 30 minutes.

3. Place a clean fabric cloth or sheet on a kitchen or card table about 30 inches square. Sprinkle cloth with flour and rub in.

4. Roll out dough to as large a square as possible on a floured cloth. Place hands, palm-sides down, under the dough and begin, gently, to stretch dough, moving around table until the dough has stretched over all corners of the table. (*Tip:* Remove rings and your watch to prevent making holes in the dough.)

5. Sprinkle dough with about 2 tablespoons of the melted butter. Measure 2 more tablespoons of the melted butter into a large skillet. Add bread crumbs and stir until crumbs are crisp and golden-brown. Sprinkle crumbs over the entire surface of the dough. Preheat oven to 400°.

6. Combine apples, raisins, nuts, sugar and cinnamon in a large bowl. Spoon apple mixture in an even row down one end of dough, 2 inches in from the end of table.

7. Trim off thick parts of dough on all four overhanging sides with kitchen scissors.

8. Using the overhanging cloth to lift dough, roll dough just over filling. Fold the two parallel sides of dough toward center to enclose the filling completely.

9. Lift the cloth at filling end to allow dough to roll over and over on itself until completely rolled.

10. Line a large cookie sheet with a double thickness of heavy-duty aluminum foil. Ease filled roll onto cookie sheet, shaping roll into horseshoe shape. Turn up the ends of foil 1 inch all around cookie sheet to keep oven clean in case of spill-over.

11. Bake in a preheated hot oven (400°) for 50 minutes, brushing several times with remaining butter or until pastry is golden.

12. Allow pastry to cool 15 minutes and then slide onto serving board. Sprinkle with 10X sugar.

Fruit-Filled Melon

Makes about 8 servings.

1 large ripe honeydew melon	1/2 pint strawberries, hulled and halved
4 large peaches, peeled and sliced	1/4 cup sugar or according to taste
1/2 pint blueberries, washed	1/4 cup dry white wine

1. Cut a 1-inch lengthwise slice from honeydew; discard seeds. Scoop pulp into balls with melon-ball

(continued)

Pictured oposite: Fruit-Filled Melon.

cutter; place in large bowl. Cut a very thin slice off bottom of honeydew shell, so melon will stand up.

2. Combine peach slices, berries, sugar and wine with melon in bowl. Place fruit mixture in melon shell. Place shell on a serving plate. Cover with plastic wrap. Chill.

Glazed Apple Turnovers

Bake at 400° for 20 minutes.

Makes 12 turnovers.

3 cups *sifted* **all-purpose flour**
3 tablespoons sugar
1 cup (2 sticks) butter or margarine, softened
1 container (8 ounces) dairy sour cream
3 medium-size apples (Mcintosh, Golden Delicious, Granny Smith), pared, cored and coarsely chopped (3 cups)
1/3 cup firmly packed

light brown sugar
3/4 teaspoon ground cinnamon
1/8 teaspoon ground nutmeg
2 teaspoons grated lemon rind
2 tablespoons raisins
Water
1 cup 10X (confectioners') sugar
3 1/2 teaspoons lemon juice

1. Measure flour and sugar in a medium-size bowl; cut in butter with a pastry blender or fork until mixture is crumbly; add sour cream.

2. Mix lightly with a fork until dough clings together and starts to leave side of bowl; gather dough together with hands and shape into a ball. Wrap dough in plastic wrap or wax paper; chill overnight.

3. Divide dough in half. Keep one half refrigerated until ready to use. Roll out other half on a lightly floured surface to an 18 × 12-inch rectangle; trim edges evenly with a sharp knife. Cut into six 6-inch squares. Place between wax paper to keep dough from drying out; refrigerate. Repeat with other half of dough.

4. Combine apples, brown sugar, cinnamon, nutmeg, lemon rind and raisins in a medium-size bowl; toss with fork to mix well. Preheat oven to 400°.

5. Place 4 pastry squares on a large ungreased cookie sheet. (Keep remainder refrigerated.) Place 2 tablespoons filling on each square; moisten edges with water; fold over to make triangles. Press down securely around apple filling. Crimp edges with fork to seal; press tines of fork 1 or 2 times in top of each turnover to let steam escape. Refrigerate. Repeat with remaining pastry squares and filling.

6. Bake in a preheated hot oven (400°) for 20 minutes or until golden brown; remove to wire rack to cool. Repeat with remaining turnovers.

7. Combine 10X sugar and lemon juice in a small bowl. Drizzle over each turnover. Serve turnovers warm or completely cooled. Can be frozen and reheated.

Danish Pastry Dough

Makes enough dough for 24 individual pastries.

2 envelopes active dry yeast
1/2 cup very warm water
1/3 cup sugar
3/4 cup cold milk
2 eggs

4 1/4 cups *sifted* **all-purpose flour**
1 teaspoon salt
1 pound (4 sticks) butter or margarine
Flour

1. Sprinkle yeast into very warm water in a 1-cup measure. ("Very warm" water should feel comfortably warm when dropped on wrist.) Stir in 1/2 teaspoon of the sugar. Stir until yeast dissolves. Let stand undisturbed until bubbly and double in volume, about 10 minutes. Now you can tell the yeast is working.

2. Combine remaining sugar, milk, eggs, 3 cups of the flour, salt and the yeast mixture in large bowl. Beat with electric mixer at medium speed or with a wooden spoon for 3 minutes. Beat in remaining flour with spoon until dough is shiny and elastic. Dough will be soft. Scrape down side of bowl. Cover with plastic wrap. Refrigerate 30 minutes.

3. Place the sticks of butter or margarine 1 inch apart, between 2 sheets of wax paper; roll out to a 12-inch square. Chill on a cookie sheet until ready to use.

4. Sprinkle working surface heavily with flour, about 1/3 cup; turn dough out onto flour; sprinkle flour on top of dough. Roll out to an 18 × 13-inch rectangle. Brush off excess flour with a soft pastry brush.

5. Peel off top sheet of wax paper from butter; place butter, paper-side up, on one end of dough to cover two-thirds of the dough; peel off remaining sheet of wax paper. For easy folding, carefully score butter lengthwise down center, without cutting into dough. Fold uncovered third of dough over middle third; brush off excess flour; then fold remaining third of dough over middle third to enclose butter completely. Turn dough clockwise so open side is away from you.*

6. Roll out to a 24 × 12-inch rectangle using enough flour to keep dough from sticking. Fold ends in to meet on center; then fold in half to make 4 layers. Turn again so open side is away from you.

*Repeat rolling and folding this way 2 more times. Keep the dough a perfect rectangle by rolling straight up and down and from side to side. When it is necessary, chill the dough between rollings. Clean off the working surface each time and dust lightly with flour. Refrigerate dough 1 hour or more (even overnight, if you wish, to relax dough and firm up butter layers). Cut dough in half. You can see the buttery layers which, when baked, become flaky and crisp. Work with only half the dough at a time. Keep the other half refrigerated.

Prune Danish

Bake at 400°, then 350° for 20 minutes.

Makes 12 individual pastries.

¹/₂ Danish Pastry Dough (*recipe in this chapter*)	**OR: 1 jar (8 ounces) lekvar**
1 can (12 ounces) prune filling*	**Slightly beaten egg** **¹/₂ cup corn syrup**

1. Roll dough and cut into squares as in Almond Crescents. Spoon a rounded tablespoon prune filling onto center of each square; bring 2 opposite corners over filling to overlap about 1 inch. Place on cookie sheet 2 inches apart; let rise in a warm place until double in bulk, about 30 minutes.
2. Preheat oven to 400°. Brush pastries with beaten egg.
3. Place in a preheated hot oven (400°); lower heat to 350° immediately, then bake 20 minutes. Warm corn syrup slightly in a small saucepan; brush over pastries; bake 5 minutes longer. Remove to wire rack; cool.
*Or you may use canned cherry or apple pie filling, or apricot preserves.

Apricot Bow Ties

Bake at 400°, then 350° for 20 minutes.

Makes 12 individual pastries.

¹/₂ Danish Pastry Dough (*recipe in this chapter*)	**Slightly beaten egg** **2 tablespoons chopped walnuts mixed with 2 tablespoons sugar**
¹/₄ cup apricot preserves	

1. Roll and cut dough as in Almond Crescents. Place 1 teaspoon of the apricot preserves along one of the edges of the pastry ¹/₂ inch in from edge. Fold over opposite edge; press edges together to seal. With a sharp knife, make a lengthwise slit in folded pastry to within 1 inch of each end. Slip one end under and pull it through the slit. Place 2 inches apart on cookie sheets. Let rise in a warm place until double in bulk, 30 to 45 minutes.
2. Preheat oven to 400°. Brush pastries with egg; sprinkle on walnuts.
3. Place in a preheated hot oven (400°); lower heat immediately to 350°. Bake 20 minutes or until golden brown. Remove to wire rack; cool.

Almond Crescents

Bake at 400°, then 350° for 20 to 25 minutes.

Makes 12 individual pastries.

¹/₂ Danish Pastry Dough (*recipe in this chapter*)	*follows*) **Slightly beaten egg** **Sugar**
Almond Filling (*recipe*	**Sliced almonds**

1. Roll pastry on floured surface to two 20 × 15-inch rectangles; trim edges even; with a sharp knife, cut into 12 five-inch squares. Spoon filling onto one corner of each square, dividing evenly. Roll each square around filling to opposite corner. Place, point down, 2 inches apart on cookie sheet. Curve into crescent shape. Let rise in warm place until double in volume, about 30 minutes.
2. Preheat oven to 400°. Brush crescents with egg; sprinkle with sugar and almonds.
3. Place in a preheated hot oven (400°); lower heat immediately to 350°, then bake 20 to 25 minutes or until puffed and golden. Cool on wire rack.
Almond Filling: Beat ¹/₂ an 8-ounce package or can almond paste (4 ounces), ¹/₄ cup softened butter or margarine and ¹/₄ cup sugar in a small bowl until smooth and well blended. Makes 1 cup.

Cockscombs

Bake at 400°, then 350° for 20 to 25 minutes.

Makes 12 individual pastries.

¹/₂ Danish Pastry Dough (*recipe in this chapter*)	*above*) **Slightly beaten egg** **Sugar**
Almond Filling (*recipe*	

1. Roll and cut dough as in Almond Crescents. Spoon filling onto center of each square, dividing evenly. Spread filling slightly parallel to one edge; brush edges lightly with egg, then fold opposite edge over; press edges together to seal. Make 4 or 5 slits in sealed edge; place on cookie sheet, curving pastries slightly to resemble a cockscomb. Let rise in a warm place until double in bulk, about 30 minutes.
2. Preheat oven to 400°. Brush cockscombs with egg; sprinkle generously with sugar.
3. Place in a preheated hot oven (400°); lower heat immediately to 350°. Bake 20 to 25 minutes or until puffed and golden brown. Remove to wire rack; cool.

Tips on Making Danish Pastry
1. It is important to keep butter enclosed in dough. If it oozes out, immediately sprinkle with flour. If dough becomes too sticky to handle, butter has probably softened. Just refrigerate 30 minutes or freeze 15 minutes before continuing.

(continued)

2. Use more flour than you normally would to roll out pastries; brush off excess with soft brush before folding or filling; this way flour will not build up in pastry.

3. Since dough is very rich, it is best to let pastries rise at room temperature. Do not try to hasten the rising by using heat; doing so would melt the butter and spoil the texture.

4. If using margarine, which has a softer consistency than butter, refrigerate 20 minutes between each rolling.

5. Have ready a rolling pin, a soft pastry brush, ruler and a working surface large enough to roll dough to 30 inches.

Fruit Empanadas

These crisp, deep-fried turnovers, made here as a dessert, can also be filled with a meat mixture to serve as appetizers.

Makes 16 empanadas.

1½ cups *unsifted* all-purpose flour	vegetable shortening
1 teaspoon baking powder	About ⅓ cup milk
½ teaspoon salt	Pineapple Filling (*recipe follows*)
⅓ cup lard or	Vegetable oil for frying

1. Mix flour, baking powder and salt in bowl. Cut in lard with pastry blender or two knives until mixture resembles cornmeal. Sprinkle with milk; mix with fork until dough clings together. (Add a little more milk, if necessary.)

2. Gather dough into a ball and knead about 10 times until smooth. Roll dough on lightly floured surface to ⅛-inch thickness. Cut into 4-inch circles with floured cookie cutter. Fill each with about 1 tablespoon filling; moisten edge with water. Fold in half and press edges to seal. Press edge with tip of fork. Reroll trimmings; cut and fill.

3. Heat ½ to 1 inch oil in a small skillet to 370°. Lower 4 or 5 empanadas in hot oil. Fry 2 minutes, turning once, until golden brown. Drain on paper toweling. Serve warm or cold. Dust with 10X (confectioners') sugar, if you wish.

Pineapple Filling

Makes about 1 cup.

1 can (8 ounces) crushed pineapple in pineapple juice	cornstarch
	1½ teaspoons butter or margarine
2 tablespoons sugar	1 teaspoon grated lemon rind
1 tablespoon	

Combine pineapple, sugar, cornstarch, butter and lemon rind in small saucepan. Cook over medium heat until mixture is bubbly thick. Cool to room temperature.

Fruit Turnovers

Bake at 400° for 30 minutes.

Makes 8 turnovers.

1 can (8¼ ounces) crushed pineapple, drained	⅛ teaspoon ground cinnamon
1 can (11 ounces) mandarin oranges, drained	1 package (17¼ ounces) pre-rolled frozen puff pastry
1½ teaspoons cornstarch	1 egg white, lightly beaten

1. Combine pineapple, oranges, cornstarch and cinnamon in a small saucepan; heat to boiling, stirring constantly. Cool.

2. Follow steps 2 and 3 of Tuna Turnovers (above) for preparing pastry, dividing fruit mixture evenly among pastry squares.

3. Immediately lower temperature to hot (400°). Bake turnovers for 30 minutes.

Bananas Hawaiian

Makes 8 servings.

¾ cup flaked coconut	¼ teaspoon ground cinnamon
3 tablespoons butter or margarine	6 bananas, peeled and sliced
½ cup firmly packed brown sugar	1 quart vanilla ice cream
1 cup dark rum	

1. Heat coconut in large skillet on grill until toasted; stir to brown evenly. Remove to a sheet of foil; cool.

2. Add butter, sugar, rum and cinnamon to skillet. Heat until bubbly. Add bananas and cook until slices are heated through.

3. Spoon ice cream into serving dishes and spoon hot bananas and juices over. Sprinkle with coconut. Serve at once.

Pineapple, Luau Style

Grill about 15 minutes.

Makes 8 servings.

1 large ripe pineapple	2 tablespoons lime juice
⅓ cup butter or margarine	¼ teaspoon ground ginger
⅓ cup honey	

1. Remove leafy top of pineapple; reserve. Cut pineapple lengthwise into 8 wedges. Cut off core of

each wedge. Slash pineapple vertically 1 inch apart down to but not through skin.

2. Heat butter in small saucepan on grill until melted. Add honey, lime juice and ginger. Brush cut surfaces of pineapple with lime mixture. Place wedges on grill. Grill 15 minutes, turning every 5 minutes and brushing with lime mixture.

3. Line serving platter with lemon leaves; place reserved pineapple top in center. Arrange wedges on leaves. Serve hot with remaining lime mixture. Garnish with lime slices, if you wish.

Watermelon Basket

Makes 18 servings.

1 watermelon (8 to 10 pounds)	1 quart strawberries, rinsed and hulled
2 cantaloupes	1 bunch seedless grapes
1 ripe pineapple	

1. Remove the top third of the watermelon, cutting horizontally across the top of the melon with a long thin knife.

2. Hollow out the bottom and top sections with a melon baller. Place watermelon balls in a large bowl.

3. Cut the edge of the watermelon basket into a zigzag pattern with a sharp knife.

4. Halve and seed the cantaloupes. Scoop out the balls with a melon baller. Add to the watermelon balls.

5. Halve and core the pineapple. Cut the fruit into cubes. Add to the bowl along with the strawberries and grapes. Toss gently to mix. Spoon into the watermelon basket.

6. Cover the basket with plastic wrap, making sure all the fruit and cut surfaces are covered. Refrigerate for up to 2 hours.

Wine Fruit Compote

Makes 6 servings.

1 pound mixed dried fruit	1/2 cup honey
1/2 small lemon, thinly sliced and seeded	3 cups sweetened Concord grape wine
	1 1/2 cups water

Combine dried fruit, lemon, honey, wine and water in a large saucepan. Bring to boiling; lower heat; cover. Simmer 30 to 35 minutes or until fruits are tender. Cool; chill.

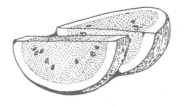

Dried Fruit Compote

Chilled poached dried fruit is served with a cool spiced yogurt topping.

Makes 4 servings.

1 1/2 cups water	OR: 1/2 teaspoon ground allspice
1/4 cup honey	
1 package (8 ounces) mixed dried fruit	1 tablespoon chopped walnuts
1 1-inch piece stick cinnamon	Cinnamon Yogurt Topping (*recipe follows*)
2 whole allspice	

1. Combine water and honey in small saucepan. Heat to boiling; lower heat; simmer 5 minutes.

2. Remove pits from prunes; cut all fruits into bite-size pieces. Add fruits, cinnamon stick and allspice to water.

3. Cover and simmer 10 to 15 minutes, just until fruits are tender but not mushy.

4. Remove from heat. Cool to lukewarm. Remove cinnamon and whole allspice. Spoon into serving dishes or bowl. Cover and chill.

5. Place walnuts on baking sheet in a slow oven (325°) for 15 minutes until golden. Sprinkle over fruit and serve with Cinnamon Yogurt Topping.

Cinnamon Yogurt Topping: Combine 1/2 cup plain yogurt, 1 tablespoon 10X (confectioners') sugar and 1/4 teaspoon ground cinnamon in small bowl. Stir until well blended. Cover and chill before serving.

Greek Apple Pastry

A Greek version of Viennese strudel.

Bake at 350° for 50 minutes to 1 hour.

Makes 10 servings.

1/2 cup walnuts	nutmeg
1/4 cup packaged bread crumbs	3/4 cup (1 1/2 sticks) butter, melted
2 1/2 pounds tart cooking apples, pared and chopped (7 to 8 cups)	1/2 of a 16-ounce package frozen phyllo or strudel pastry leaves, thawed
1/2 cups raisins	1 tablespoon water
1/2 cup sugar	Honeyed Apple Syrup (*recipe follows*)
1 teaspoon ground cinnamon	
1/4 teaspoon ground	

1. Place walnuts on cookie sheets; toast in moderate oven (350°) for 10 minutes. Cool slightly, then whirl in container of electric blender until finely chopped. Mix with bread crumbs in small bowl.

2. Combine apples, raisins, sugar, cinnamon and nutmeg in large bowl.

3. Brush bottom of 13 × 9 × 2-inch baking pan with melted butter. Fold one phyllo leaf in half or to fit

(continued)

bottom of pan; place in bottom of pan; brush lightly with melted butter; sprinkle with a scant tablespoon walnut mixture. Repeat about 6 or 7 times or until half of phyllo leaves are used.

4. Spread apple mixture in pan; top with remaining phyllo leaves, brushing with butter and sprinkling nut mixture between each layer. Brush top leaf with remaining butter. Preheat oven to 400°.

5. With a very sharp knife, make cuts through top 3 or 4 layers to mark pastry, making one cut lengthwise and five across. Sprinkle with water.

6. Place in a very hot oven (400°), then turn heat to 350° and bake 50 minutes to 1 hour or until pastry is golden and apples are tender. Remove pan to wire rack; cut all the way through the markings. Pour cooled Honeyed Apple Syrup over. Cool on wire rack.

Honeyed Apple Syrup: Combine ½ cup apple juice or cider, ½ cup sugar and 3 × 1-inch strip of lemon rind in small saucepan. Bring to boiling; lower heat; simmer 5 minutes. Remove from heat; stir in 2 to 3 tablespoons honey; cool.

Bananas Foster

Makes 4 servings.

½ cup firmly packed brown sugar	**Dash of ground cinnamon**
¼ cup (½ stick) butter or margarine	**½ cup light rum**
4 ripe bananas, peeled and quartered	**¼ cup banana liqueur**
	1 pint vanilla ice cream

1. Melt brown sugar and butter or margarine in a chafing dish or skillet, stirring often.

2. Add bananas and sauté just until soft (don't overcook). Sprinkle cinnamon over bananas.

3. Heat rum and banana liqueur in a small saucepan. Pour over bananas, but do not stir into sauce. Carefully light liquor in chafing dish and keep spooning sauce over bananas till flames die.

4. Scoop ice cream into 4 large dessert dishes. Spoon bananas and sauce over and serve immediately.

Peach Melba-Topped Raspberry Soufflé

Makes 8 servings.

2 packages (10 ounces each) frozen raspberries, thawed	**⅔ cup sugar**
2 envelopes unflavored gelatin	**1 cup heavy cream**
½ cup water	**2 cups peeled, sliced fresh peaches, sweetened with 2 tablespoons sugar**
4 egg whites	
½ teaspoon cream of tartar	**Melba Sauce** *(recipe follows)*

1. To fit a 4-cup soufflé or other straight-sided dish

with a wax paper collar, measure two lengths of wax paper long enough to encircle dish. Fold in half lengthwise (wax paper should be about 2 inches higher than the rim of the dish); fasten collar with tape.

2. Drain syrup from one package of the raspberries into a cup (you should have about ½ cup syrup); reserve for Melba Sauce. Placed drained raspberries and second package of raspberries with syrup into container of electric blender; cover; whirl until thick. To remove seeds, press puree through sieve into large bowl.

3. Sprinkle gelatin over water in a small saucepan to soften; let stand 10 minutes. Place saucepan over very low heat until gelatin dissolves (mixture will be clear). Remove from heat; cool. Stir into raspberry puree; chill until mixture mounds when spooned.

4. With electric mixer, beat egg whites and cream of tartar until foamy-white and double in volume in a large bowl. Beat in the sugar, 1 tablespoon at a time, until stiff peaks form.

5. Whip cream in a small bowl until soft peaks form. Fold heavy cream, then egg whites, into thickened raspberry mixture with a rubber spatula until no streaks of white remain; pour into prepared dish. Refrigerate at least 3 hours or until set.

6. To assemble: Remove collar gently, freeing soufflé from wax paper, if necessary, with a small paring knife. Drain peach slices; garnish top of soufflé. Top with Melba Sauce.

Melba Sauce: Combine 1 teaspoon cornstarch with the reserved ½ cup raspberry juice in a small saucepan. Cook, stirring constantly, until sauce thickens and clears; cool.

Fresh Pineapple Compote

Makes 8 servings.

1 ripe large pineapple	**brandy)**
¼ cup 10X (confectioners') sugar	**2 jars (17 ounces each) pitted dark sweet cherries**
½ cup kirsch (cherry	

1. Cut off leafy top, then cut pineapple lengthwise with a sharp knife. Cut each half into 3 or 4 wedges. Loosen fruit in 1 piece from each wedge; trim core. Cut into ½-inch chunks.

2. Place pineapple in a large bowl; sprinkle with confectioners' sugar; add kirsch and toss gently. Cover with plastic wrap; refrigerate several hours for pineapple to absorb flavor of brandy, tossing once or twice. Chill the cherries.

3. Just before serving, drain juice from cherries. Add cherries to pineapple; toss thoroughly.

Pictured opposite:
Peach Melba-Topped Raspberry Soufflé.

Rhubarb and Raspberry Soufflé

A refreshing light dessert for a spring dinner. There's no last-minute fuss because it's made ahead.

Makes 8 to 10 servings.

4 cups frozen unsweetened cut rhubarb (about a 1-pound package), or fresh rhubarb, if available
3/4 cup sugar
2 tablespoons cornstarch
Dash salt
1 cup water
1/3 cup orange-flavored liqueur
or juice
1 tablespoon lemon juice
2 envelopes unflavored gelatin
1/3 cup cold water
1 package (10 ounces) frozen raspberries
4 large egg whites, at room temperature
1/2 cup sugar
1 cup heavy cream

1. Mix rhubarb, 3/4 cup sugar, cornstarch and salt in a large saucepan; stir in 1 cup water. Cook mixture until rhubarb is tender, stirring often. Stir in orange liqueur and lemon juice; cook 1 minute more.
2. Remove 2 cups rhubarb mixture for sauce; chill. Sprinkle gelatin over the 1/2 cup water; let stand a minute to soften. Stir into rhubarb remaining in pan; stir in raspberries. Cook mixture over low heat just until gelatin is dissolved and raspberries are thawed. Pour mixture into container of electric blender. Cover; whirl until smooth. Strain to remove seeds. Cool slightly.
3. Beat egg whites until foamy in large bowl with electric mixer. Beat in the 1/2 cup sugar, 1 tablespoon at a time, until soft peaks form. Fold rhubarb mixture gently into whites.
4. With same beaters, whip cream in a small bowl until stiff. Fold into rhubarb mixture. Pour into a glass bowl or an 8-cup soufflé dish with a 2-inch foil collar. Chill until firm. Spoon rhubarb sauce on top or serve in bowl along with the soufflé.

Figs Stuffed with Chocolate

A chocolate-almond surprise inside each delicious fig.
Bake at 350° for 16 minutes.

Makes 2 dozen.

2/3 cup whole blanched almonds (60 to 70 almonds)
1 square semisweet chocolate
24 large dried figs

1. Spread the almonds in one layer on a cookie sheet.
2. Toast them in a moderate oven (350°) for about 10 minutes or until they color lightly. Set 24 of the almonds aside and finely pulverize the rest in the container of an electric blender or food processor.
3. Grate the chocolate with the fine side of a hand grater and stir it into the pulverized almonds, mixing or pounding them together to form a fairly dry paste.

4. Cut the stems off the figs with scissors or a small sharp knife. With your fingers or the handle of a small spoon, make a deep depression in the stem end of each fig (be careful not to tear it) and stuff about a teaspoon of the chocolate-almond mixture into it, packing it in tightly. Pinch the openings firmly closed with your fingers. Arrange the figs, pinched-sides up, side by side, on an ungreased baking sheet.
5. Bake in a moderate oven (350°) for 8 minutes. Turn them over and bake for 8 minutes more. Press a toasted whole almond gently but firmly into the outside of each fig and serve warm (not hot) or at room temperature.

Ginger Figs in Port Wine

The zest of ginger enhances the mellow flavor of the figs.

Makes 1 1/2 cups.

2 jars (17 ounces each) whole figs in syrup
1/2 cup sugar
1/2 cup chopped
preserved ginger
1 4-inch strip fresh lemon rind
1/4 cup white port wine
2 lemon slices

1. Drain syrup from figs into measuring cup, reserving 1 cup (use remaining syrup for a fruit punch).
2. Combine the 1 cup fig syrup, sugar, ginger and lemon rind in a medium-size saucepan. Slowly bring to boiling over medium heat; lower heat; simmer 5 minutes or until mixture becomes syrupy. Add figs; simmer an additional 5 minutes. Remove rind; add port.
3. Pack into two small jars; add a lemon slice to each. Store in refrigerator. (Allow flavors to develop for 1 week.)

Pears in White Wine

A lovely, make-ahead dessert, pears are cooked in white wine, chilled and served with fruit sauce.

Makes 8 servings.

8 firm, ripe pears (Bartlett or Anjou)
2 tablespoons lemon juice
3 cups dry white wine
1 1/2 cups sugar
Angelica *(optional)*
Sauce Cardinale *(recipe follows)*

1. Wash pears; pare and core from blossom end but leave stems intact. Brush with lemon juice.
2. Combine wine and sugar in large saucepan; bring to boiling, stirring until sugar dissolves. Lower heat;

add pears; cover. Simmer 10 minutes or until tender but still firm. Let pears cool in syrup. Refrigerate several hours or overnight.
3. Drain pears; arrange on serving dish; garnish with angelica, if you wish. Serve with Sauce Cardinale.

Sauce Cardinale

Makes 1½ cups.

1 package (10 ounces) frozen raspberries, thawed	1 cup strawberries, fresh or frozen
1 teaspoon cornstarch	¼ cup red currant jelly

Drain raspberries, reserving juice. Dissolve cornstarch in a little raspberry juice in a small saucepan; add remaining juice and strawberries, raspberries and jelly. Cook, stirring constantly, until mixture thickens slightly and clears. Force mixture through a sieve to remove seeds. Chill.

Spiced Peaches

Makes 8 servings.

2 cans (29 ounces each) cling peach halves	4 three-inch pieces stick cinnamon
1⅓ cups sugar	2 teaspoons whole cloves
1 cup cider vinegar	

1. Drain syrup from peaches into a large saucepan. Put peach halves in a large bowl.
2. Add sugar, vinegar, cinnamon and cloves to peach syrup. Bring to boiling; lower heat; simmer gently 10 minutes.
3. Pour hot syrup over peach halves; cover and cool thoroughly. Refrigerate several hours or overnight. (This is not a preserve; it will keep in refrigerator about 1 week.)

Glacéed Strawberries

Fresh strawberries with a crackling sugar-glaze coating. Do not make glacéed berries more than 2 to 3 hours before serving; 1 hour if very humid.

Makes 24 glacéed strawberries.

24 strawberries	⅛ teaspoon cream of tartar
1 cup sugar	
¼ cup water	

1. Wash berries carefully, leaving hulls on, and pat dry with paper toweling. Lightly oil a cookie sheet.

2. Heat sugar, water and cream of tartar in a small saucepan over high heat, stirring constantly, until sugar dissolves. Boil 12 to 15 minutes, without stirring, until a candy thermometer registers 295°F. (hard crack stage). Remove pan from heat.
3. Working quickly, dip berries into syrup, one at a time, holding each by the stem. Remove from syrup and place on cookie sheet to let coating harden. Do not let glacéed berries touch each other while drying.

Bananas Baked with Pineapple and Honey

Bake at 375° for 20 minutes.

Makes 6 servings.

6 small firm-ripe bananas	1 tablespoon lemon juice
1 can (8 ounces) crushed pineapple in pineapple juice	2 teaspoons cornstarch
¼ cup honey	2 tablespoons butter or margarine

1. Peel bananas and place in single layer in baking dish just large enough to hold them. Preheat oven to 375°.
2. Combine pineapple with juice, honey, lemon juice and cornstarch in a bowl; pour over bananas. Dot with butter.
3. Bake in a preheated moderate oven (375°) for 20 minutes or just until bananas are softened and sauce is bubbly.

Creamy Cottage Cheese Dessert

Makes 6 servings.

1 container (16 ounces) creamed cottage cheese	(confectioners') sugar
1 package (3 ounces) cream cheese, softened	1½ tablespoons lemon juice
1 cup 10X	½ teaspoon vanilla
	½ cup heavy cream
	Fresh fruit in season

1. Press cottage cheese through a sieve or food mill into a large bowl. Add cream cheese, 10X sugar, lemon juice and vanilla; beat with wire whisk or electric mixer until thoroughly blended.
2. Beat cream in a small bowl until soft peaks form; fold into cottage cheese mixture.
3. Line a heart-shaped basket or medium-size sieve (about 6 inches wide) with 2 layers of damp cheesecloth. Spoon mixture into basket. Level mixture

(continued)

by giving basket a firm tap over the bowl. Fold overhanging ends of the cloth over the mixture. Place basket over bowl to catch draining liquid. Refrigerate 24 hours.

4. When ready to serve, carefully peel back the cheesecloth and invert the cottage cheese dessert gently over serving plate. Surround with strawberries, grapes, peaches or fruit of your choice. Garnish with fresh mint, if you wish.

Peach-Pear Compote

When you have more peaches on hand than you planned, here's a great solution. This compote keeps well for three to four days in the refrigerator.

Makes 9 servings.

6 large peaches	1 cup sugar
3 large ripe pears	1 lemon, thinly sliced
4 cups water	

1. Dip peaches into boiling water 30 seconds, then into ice water 1 minute. Peel, halve and pit, reserving pits. Peel and halve pears; remove core.
2. Heat water, sugar, lemon slices and reserved pits to boiling in large saucepan; lower heat. Keep syrup at a steady simmer. Add fruit, about half at a time; cook until soft on the outside but firm in center, about 10 minutes. Remove fruit to large bowl with slotted spoon as it cooks.
3. Remove pits from syrup. Pour syrup over fruit. Refrigerate until cold.

Tortoni Ice Cream Cake

Makes 12 servings.

1/2 cup boiling water	1/2 cup chopped, toasted, blanched almonds
2 teaspoons instant espresso coffee or regular coffee	
2 tablespoons dark or light rum	1/2 cup chopped red and green candied cherries
1 package (10 3/4 ounces) frozen pound cake	1/2 teaspoon almond extract
1 quart chocolate chip ice cream	1/2 pint heavy cream
	Candied red and green cherries

1. Stir water into coffee in a cup until dissolved; stir in rum.
2. Line a 2-quart bowl with foil or plastic wrap.
3. Cut pound cake into 1/4-inch slices. Cut half the slices diagonally into triangles. Arrange triangles in bottom of lined bowl, pin-wheel fashion, with points toward center. Line side of bowl with whole cake slices. Sprinkle slices with 2/3 of the coffee mixture.
4. Soften ice cream slightly in a chilled large bowl. Work in almonds, the half cup cherries and the

almond extract. Spoon evenly into cake-lined bowl, working quickly so ice cream does not melt. Cover ice cream with remaining cake slices, pressing down firmly; sprinkle slices with remaining coffee mixture. Cover bowl with plastic wrap or foil; freeze overnight or for up to 2 days.
5. Unmold cake onto serving plate about 2 hours before serving. Beat cream in a small bowl until stiff. Spread a thin layer of cream over surface of cake. Spoon remaining cream into a pastry bag fitted with a star tip. Pipe rosettes of cream around bottom of cake and on top and side. Garnish with cherries.

Lemon Curd Charlotte with Blueberry Topping

Bake at 375° for 12 minutes.

Makes 8 servings.

1 cup *sifted* cake flour	cut in small pieces
1 teaspoon baking powder	2 teaspoons grated lemon rind
1/4 teaspoon salt	1/3 cup plus 1/4 cup lemon juice
9 eggs	
1 3/4 cups sugar	2 envelopes unflavored gelatin
1/3 cup water	
1 teaspoon vanilla	1 1/2 cups plain yogurt
10X (confectioners') sugar	2 cups heavy cream
	Blueberry Topping
1/2 cup (1 stick) butter,	*(recipe follows)*

1. Preheat the oven to moderate (375°).
2. Grease a 15 x 10 x 1-inch jelly-roll pan; line with wax paper; grease the paper.
3. Sift the flour, baking powder and salt onto the wax paper.
4. Beat 3 of the eggs in a bowl until very thick and creamy. Gradually add 3/4 cup of the sugar, beating constantly until very thick. Stir in the water and vanilla. Gently fold in the dry ingredients until blended. Spread the batter evenly into the prepared pan.
5. Bake in the preheated moderate oven (375°) for 12 minutes or until the cake springs back when lightly touched with a fingertip. Remove from the oven. Dust a clean kitchen towel with the 10X sugar. Loosen the cake around the edges with a small spatula. Invert onto the towel. Peel off the paper. Roll up the cake with the towel from the short side. Place, seam-side down, on a wire rack to cool thoroughly.
6. Beat together the remaining 6 eggs, 1 cup of sugar, butter, lemon rind and the 1/3 cup of lemon juice in the top of a double boiler. Cook over hot, not boiling, water, stirring constantly, until the mixture thickens, for 15 minutes. Remove the lemon curd from the heat. Cool. Measure out 1 cup; set aside.
7. Sprinkle the gelatin over the remaining 1/4 cup of lemon juice in a small saucepan. Let soften for 3 minutes. Place over low heat; stir to dissolve the gelatin. Stir into the remaining curd, along with the yogurt; blend well.

8. Beat 1 cup of the heavy cream in a small bowl until stiff. Gently fold into the lemon curd-yogurt mixture. Refrigerate.

9. Unroll the cake. Spread evenly with the reserved 1 cup of curd. Reroll from the short side. Cut into 8 equal slices. Line the side of an 8-inch springform pan with the slices. Turn the curd mixture into the cake-lined pan. Smooth the top. Cover; refrigerate for 5 to 6 hours.

10. To serve, place the charlotte on a serving plate. Carefully remove the sides of the pan. Spoon some of the Blueberry Topping over the lemon curd filling. Pass the remainder. Beat the remaining 1 cup of cream until stiff. Pipe around the outer top edge and base. Garnish with mint and strips of lemon rind, if you wish.

To Make Ahead: Make the charlotte and topping the day before. Garnish with whipped cream before serving.

Blueberry Topping: Combine $1/3$ cup sugar, 1 tablespoon cornstarch and $1/4$ cup orange juice in a medium-size saucepan. Cook over medium heat, stirring constantly, for 2 to 3 minutes. Add 1 pint fresh or frozen blueberries. Cook until the mixture thickens and clears, for about 5 minutes. Refrigerate until chilled.

Strawberry Topping Variation: Prepare the recipe as directed through Step 7. Cover and refrigerate the reserved lemon curd. Unroll the cake. Spread with one jar (12 ounces) strawberry preserves. Reroll from the short side. Cut the roll into 8 equal slices, wiping the knife with damp paper toweling after each cut. Line the side of an 8-inch springform pan with the slices. Turn the lemon mixture into the cake-lined pan. Smooth the top. Cover and refrigerate for 5 to 6 hours. To serve, place the charlotte on a serving plate. Carefully remove the sides of the pan. Beat the remaining 1 cup cream until stiff. Spread a very thin layer of whipped cream over the top. Pipe the remaining cream around the outer edge and base. Fill the center and garnish the base with hulled strawberries (about 1 pint). Garnish with mint and strips of lemon rind, if you wish. Serve with the reserved lemon curd as a sauce.

Lemon Curd Charlotte with Blueberry Topping.

Piña Colada Ice Cream Cake

Combine sweet tropical fruits with the zing of rum for a taste that evokes a sunny Caribbean island.

Makes 8 servings.

1 can (8 ounces) crushed pineapple in pineapple juice	1 frozen pound cake (about 1 pound), thawed
1 quart vanilla ice cream	2 tablespoons rum
1 can (8³/4 ounces) cream of coconut	2 cups heavy cream
1 can (3¹/2 ounces) flaked coconut	1 can (8 ounces) pineapple slices, drained
	Maraschino cherries

1. Drain crushed pineapple in sieve, pressing well with spoon to remove juice; reserve juice.
2. Soften ice cream in a chilled large bowl; stir in pineapple and coconut cream. Freeze mixture until firm, several hours or overnight.
3. Toast coconut on cookie sheet in a moderate oven (350°) for about 10 minutes, stirring several times; cool.
4. Cut pound cake lengthwise into 3 thin layers. Blend rum and pineapple juice; sprinkle over layers.
5. Beat ice cream with electric mixer or wooden spoon to soften; spread thickly and evenly on 2 of the layers, stacking the third on top. Freeze cake until firm.
6. To decorate: Even edges of ice cream with cake, if necessary. Beat cream in a medium-size bowl until stiff; spread some over sides and top of cake. Sprinkle cake generously with toasted coconut. Decorate bottom edge and top of cake with whipped cream piped through a pastry bag. Garnish with half slices of pineapple and maraschino cherries. Freeze until 20 minutes before serving.

Strawberry Strips

Tart, juicy strawberries top this ready-to-bake airy pastry.

Bake at 350° for 20 minutes.

Makes 16 pieces.

¹/2 of a 17¹/4-ounce package pre-rolled frozen puff pastry (1 sheet)	*follows)*
	1 pint medium-size strawberries, washed and hulled
Water	¹/4 cup strawberry jelly
3 teaspoons sugar	2 tablespoons chopped pistachio nuts
¹/2 recipe Pastry Cream (*recipe*	

1. Thaw pastry sheet 20 minutes; place on a large cookie sheet; unfold.
2. Preheat oven to 350°. Cut pastry in half lengthwise. Cut a ¹/2-inch lengthwise strip from the 2 long sides of each pastry rectangle; prick pastry well with fork. Brush all 4 narrow strips with water. Press a strip, moistened-side down, along each of the 4 long sides of the 2 pastry rectangles to form "sides" to hold in the filling. Press strips down with tines of fork to make a decorative pattern; brush again with water; sprinkle with 2 teaspoons of the sugar.
3. Bake in a preheated moderate oven (350°) for 20 minutes or until light golden brown. Cool completely on wire rack.
4. Spread ¹/2 cup Pastry Cream down length of each strip. Top with strawberries, pointed ends up, 2 to a row, 8 times.
5. Melt strawberry jelly with the remaining 1 teaspoon sugar in a small skillet over low heat; let bubble ¹/2 minute; cool slightly. Brush over strawberries to glaze; sprinkle nuts down sides of strawberry strips. Chill until serving time. Cut in serving pieces across rows of strawberries.

Pastry Cream: Prepare 1 package (3³/4 ounces) French vanilla-flavored instant pudding and pie filling with 1 cup milk, following label directions; whip ¹/2 cup heavy cream until stiff; fold into pudding; cover with plastic wrap; chill. Makes 2 cups.

Figs with Lemon Cream

When fresh figs are out of season, use the canned variety.

Makes 6 servings.

1 package (3 ounces) cream cheese, softened	1 teaspoon sugar
	1 teaspoon lemon juice
2 tablespoons light cream or half-and-half	12 ripe figs
	Grated lemon rind

1. Blend cream cheese, cream, sugar and lemon juice in a small bowl until thoroughly mixed.
2. Peel and quarter figs; arrange 8 quarters, petal-fashion, on each of 6 dessert dishes. Spoon a generous dollop of the cream cheese mixture on top; garnish with a sprinkling of grated lemon rind.

Oranges in Wine with Honeyed Walnuts

Wine and liqueur-laced oranges make the most refreshing dessert. The honeyed walnuts are a typically Greek addition.

Makes 8 servings.

8 navel oranges, rinsed	flavored liqueur
	¹/3 cup honey
1 cup dry white wine	1 cup walnuts, lightly toasted
3 tablespoons sugar	
¹/4 cup orange-	

1. Pare 4 of the oranges (orange part only) with a

vegetable parer or sharp paring knife in strips as long and wide as possible. Cut strips into julienne slivers.

2. Cut the white membrane off these 4 oranges and the rind and membrane from the 4 remaining oranges. Slice all the oranges thinly into a glass serving bowl.

3. Add the wine, sugar and julienned orange rind and toss gently to mix. Cover and refrigerate up to 24 hours before serving.

4. Just before serving, add the liqueur and mix gently. Combine the honey and walnuts in a separate small serving bowl.

5. Divide oranges among 8 serving bowls and let guests help themselves to the honeyed walnuts, spooning them over the oranges.

Apple-Stuffed Apple

Bake at 350° for 30 to 45 minutes.

Makes 1 serving.

1 small baking apple	**cut in pieces**
1 tablespoon raisins	**1 tablespoon fresh**
1 tablespoon firmly	**bread crumbs**
packed brown	**Dash ground**
sugar	**cinnamon**
1 tablespoon butter,	

1. Cut a thin slice from top of apple; core and hollow out, leaving a 1/2-inch shell. Chop apple pulp finely.

2. Combine chopped apple with remaining ingredients in small bowl; spoon into apple cavity; press filling down firmly; replace top. Place in heat-resistant custard cup or place apple on aluminum foil; fold up edges to enclose; fold foil over on top. Place in small aluminum foil tart pan.

3. Bake in toaster oven at moderate (350°) for 30 to

45 minutes or until tender. (Make sure foil is not touching top heating element.)

Lemon Yogurt Cake

Bake at 350° for 50 minutes.

Makes one 9-inch tube cake or one 9-inch square cake.

$2^3/_4$ cups *sifted* all-purpose flour	**1 cup sugar**
2 teaspoons baking powder	**2 eggs**
1 teaspoon baking soda	**$1^1/_2$ containers (8-ounce size) plain yogurt**
1/2 teaspoon salt	**1 tablespoon grated lemon rind**
1/2 cup (1 stick) butter or margarine, softened	**10X (confectioners') sugar**

1. Grease a 9-inch kugelhopf pan or 9 × 9 × 2-inch baking pan.

2. Sift flour, baking powder, baking soda and salt onto wax paper.

3. Preheat oven to 350°. Beat butter and sugar in large bowl with electric mixer until light and fluffy. Add eggs, one at a time, beating well after each addition.

4. Add flour mixture alternately with yogurt, beating after each addition until batter is smooth. (Use low speed on mixer.) Stir in grated lemon rind. Pour into prepared pan.

5. Bake in a preheated moderate oven (350°) for 50 minutes or until top springs back when lightly pressed with fingertip. Cool in pan on wire rack 5 minutes; loosen around edges with knife; turn out onto rack; cool completely. Sprinkle top with 10X sugar.

EGGS and CHEESE

Egg   Before chickens were domesticated, eggs were gathered from wild birds. Eggs from ducks, quail, geese, pigeons and other birds are still used in various cuisines. Nowadays, when a recipe calls for eggs, use chicken eggs only.

The list of uses for eggs is practically endless: they are a major ingredient in baked goods; a coating agent to bind crumbs to meat or vegetables; an addition to ice cream to reduce ice crystals; a basis for many cold and hot sauces, such as mayonnaise and hollandaise.

Eggs with brown shells may cost more, but are no different nutritionally from eggs with white shells. The color of the shell is simply determined by the breed of chicken. The color of the egg yolk will vary, as well, depending on the chicken's diet.

Eggs are an excellent source of protein. A single large-size egg will provide 6 grams of protein with only 80 calories. Eggs are packaged according to size and weight. When buying, check to see that none are cracked. Keep them refrigerated but keep in mind that the shell of an egg is porous and will absorb strong odors, such as onion. Store them, wide-end up, in a carton or in the egg compartment of the refrigerator.

Leftover egg whites and yolks can be frozen in separate containers and stored at 0°F. for up to a year.

Tips on Using Eggs
● When a recipe requires eggs to be beaten, allow them to come to room temperature first. If only the yolks or whites are to be beaten, separate the yolks from the white while the eggs are cold; then let them warm to room temperature. This will result in a greater volume.
● An egg should be cold before frying or poaching so that it will keep its shape during cooking.

Grading and Storing Eggs   Eggs are graded by the U.S. Department of Agriculture according to appearance. Grade AA or Fresh Fancy Eggs are the highest quality.

Eggs should be stored in the refrigerator large end up (this keeps the yolks centered) in their original carton for up to one week. Soiled eggs should be wiped clean with a dry cloth before storing. A wet cloth would wash off the natural protective film.

Keep eggs away from strong-smelling foods since the shell is porous and will absorb odors.

If you're in doubt about an egg's freshness, break it

into a saucer. A super-fresh egg has a cloudy white and a high-standing yolk. Older eggs will have less cloudy whites and flatter yolks. A "bad" egg will have a definite odor or "chemical" smell when sniffed.

To Hard-Cook Eggs   Place the eggs in a saucepan and add cold water to cover the eggs by about 1 inch. Bring rapidly to boiling, cover, remove from the heat and let stand for 15 minutes. Drain and rinse under cold running water until the eggs are cold. Crack the shells on the countertop for easy peeling.

Separating Eggs   Eggs separate most easily when cold since the whites hold together better. After separating the whites from the yolks, however, the whites should be brought to room temperature for maximum volume when beating. (Avoid getting any of the yolk mixed with the whites since the fat from the yolk will decrease the volume of the beaten whites.)

Optimum Temperature for Separating Eggs   Cold eggs separate more easily than those at room temperature, because the whites hold together better. After separating, however, egg whites should be brought to room temperature for maximum volume with beating. Avoid getting yolks into the egg whites; the fat in them will prevent the whites from beating up.

Beating Egg Whites   Ideally whites should be at room temperature for maximum volume when beating. To warm refrigerator-cold whites, place in a nonplastic (grease-free) bowl and set in a larger bowl of warm water. Stir the whites briefly to remove the chill. Add a pinch of salt to help the whites liquefy to a point where they will begin absorbing air. Then start beating the whites, slowly. If using an electric mixer, set on medium speed. Continue beating until the whites are very white and opaque. Then increase the speed to high and beat until the whites are of the desired consistency, soft peaks or firm. If you are adding sugar, add in a very slow, thin stream when you increase the mixer speed. Be careful not to overbeat the whites or they will separate and become granular.

Pictured opposite:
Puffy Spanish Omelet, page 363.

A Quick Table of Popular Cheeses

KIND	DESCRIPTION	FLAVOR	USES
American	Process cheese of uniform texture made from domestic Cheddar; comes in slices and loaves.	Mild. Very popular with children.	A favorite for sandwiches and casseroles.
Bel Paese	Mellow, semi-soft Italian cheese.	Mildly nutty.	Superb teamed with fresh fruit as dessert. Also good with cocktails.
Blue, Gorgonzola, Roquefort, Stilton	Medium-soft with blue to blue-green veins, crumbles easily.	Mild to tangy, slightly peppery.	These give a gourmet touch to appetizers, salads, dressings, desserts.
Brie, Camembert	Rounds and wedges with an edible gray-white crust; soft inside.	Mild to pungent, depending on age.	Favorites for desserts and appetizers. Serve at room temperature.
Cheddar	Semi-hard, cream to orange color. Sold as wedges, blocks, cubes, slices; also shredded.	Mild to very sharp, depending on aging. Always clearly marked on the package.	America's choice for sandwiches, cooked dishes, salads, snacks, desserts.
Cottage, Ricotta, Cream	Cottage and ricotta are creamy-white curd-like, low-calorie. Cream cheese is smooth and calorie-rich.	All are delicately mild; easily spoonable and spreadable.	Perfect for appetizers, sandwiches, cooked dishes, desserts, cake fillings or frostings.
Edam, Gouda	Creamy orange with red-wax coat. Edam is round; Gouda, flattish.	Mellow, slightly salty, with a nut-like taste.	Excellent for appetizer and dessert trays. Good snack cheeses, too.
Gruyère	Smooth, firm, pale, cream-colored cheese; process Gruyère is often sold in foil-wrapped triangles.	Nut-like, faintly caramel.	An all-purpose cheese, excellent for sauces, toppings. Also good in salads, soufflés and omelets. Delicious eaten out-of-hand.
Liederkranz, Limburger	Soft, bacteria-ripened cheese.	Strong to overpowering; acquired tastes.	Best eaten out-of-hand or on crackers.
Mozzarella	Soft and white with a ball-like shape. Also comes shredded.	Mild and a bit chewy to eat, especially when heated.	Known as the pizza-lasagna cheese. Use in salads or on appetizer platter.
Muenster, Brick	Creamy-yellow to white; semi-soft; tiny holes.	Muenster is mild; Brick, mild to sharp.	Appetizers, sandwiches, salads, desserts.
Parmesan, Romano, Sapsago	The grating cheeses—very hard. White to light green. Sold in blocks, as well as grated.	Parmesan is pungent, but milder than Romano. Sapsago has herb-like flavor.	Topper for casserole dishes and spaghetti. Also popular for sauces and vegetable seasoners.
Port du Salut	Firm, smooth French cheese, the color of cream.	Fairly sharp.	A good cocktail or dessert cheese.
Provolone	Light brown outside; light yellow inside. Sometimes lined with rope marks.	Mellow to sharp, smoky and salty.	Try it in macaroni, spaghetti dishes, for sandwiches, snacks or appetizer trays.
Swiss	Light to creamy-yellow; large uneven holes. Buy sliced or in cuts.	Mild, with nut-like sweetness. One of our most popular cheeses.	Same as Cheddar, but in cooked dishes it may string somewhat.

Cheese

There are literally hundreds of different kinds of cheeses in the world, yet all have the same main ingredient—milk. Milk is curdled by the action of heat or rennet (or other bacteria) or both, then the watery part, called whey, is separated from the curd. The curd, sometimes the whey, is made into cheese.

The origin of cheese-making is lost in antiquity. It was probably discovered by chance. Records show that cheese was known to the Sumerians in 4000 B.C. We do know that cheese existed in Biblical times. Roman conquerors probably introduced cheese to England. Cheese was made by monks during the Middle Ages.

The word "cheese" comes from *cese* or *cyse* in Old English. To the French, cheese is *fromage;* Italians call it *fromaggio.*

Cheese-making begins with milk, usually cow's milk. Goat's or ewe's (sheep) milk is also used in making some cheese. Cow's milk can be whole, skimmed or with more cream added. Milk may be sweet or sour; or cow's milk may be mixed with other types of milk. Cheese differs according to the milk used and the manufacturing process. The method used to curdle milk, what flavors or organisms are added and how the cheese is ripened and aged all give cheeses their distinct characteristics.

Cheese is divided into two categories. The first is *natural cheeses.* The other category is cheese blends, in which natural cheeses are used to make new products.

Natural cheeses may be subdivided by texture or consistency and degree or kind of ripening. The amount of whey drained from the curd generally determines the consistency of the cheese. Examples:
- Very hard—Parmesan, Romano
- Hard—Cheddar, Swiss
- Semi-soft to hard—Colby, Gouda
- Semi-soft—Blue, Brick, Muenster, Roquefort
- Soft—Brie, Camembert, cottage cheese, cream cheese, Limburger, Neufchâtel, ricotta.

Cheese blends can be subdivided into three products:
- Pasteurized process cheese is a blend of shredded fresh and aged natural cheeses heated with water and an emulsifier to a homogeneous mixture. It is shaped into loaves or wheels. Buy it by the piece, or presliced or cut up and packaged. Popular-priced, it is perfect for cooking or making sandwiches. American cheese is an example.
- Pasteurized process cheese food is made the same way as process cheese, but with nonfat dry milk added. The moisture content is higher so it is softer and spreads more easily. It will melt faster than process cheese. It is packaged as loaves, rolls or links.
- Pasteurized process cheese spread is similar to process cheese food but spreads more easily because it contains more moisture. The milk fat content is lower. It's packaged in jars, tubes and pressurized cans. Some may be flavored with pimiento, olives or onions. Cheese spreads can be used for appetizers and sandwiches.

Buying Cheese: Remember that cheese is perishable. Buy often and only what you can use in a short time. Larger pieces or packages are usually your thriftiest buys. Aged cheese is highest in price; save the aged cheeses for the cheese board. For cooking, use less costly, "younger" cheeses, which may be labeled mild. An aged cheese may be labeled sharp.

Storing Cheese: The softer the cheese, the more perishable it is. The harder the cheese, the longer it will keep. Keep cheese chilled, the same as milk. Use soft cheese—cottage, cream, ricotta, Brie—within a week. Hard cheeses will keep for weeks if left in their original wrapper or rewrapped tightly with plastic wrap. Should the surface of a hard cheese get moldy, simply cut off the affected area. Cheese mold is harmless and should not affect the cheese's quality. Some pasteurized cheese products do not need refrigeration, but once they are opened, they should be refrigerated if labels direct. Freeze cheese only if you must. Cheese loses flavor and becomes crumbly when frozen.

Cooking Cheese: Cheese is very heat-sensitive and can curdle or become rubbery with excessive heat. Cook cheese over low or moderate heat. Since it melts quickly, you really don't need much heat. When making a cheese sauce, add the cheese last and cook just to melt it.

Cheese Nutrition: Cheese is a good source of high-quality protein (as that in meat, poultry and eggs). It contains most of the nutrients of milk, including calcium and riboflavin.

Baked Scrambled Eggs

Bake at 350° for 30 minutes.

Makes 4 servings.

6 eggs	**¼ teaspoon pepper**
½ cup heavy cream	**2 tablespoons cooked**
1 teaspoon salt	**chopped onion**

1. Preheat oven to 350°. Beat eggs with cream, salt, pepper and onion in a medium-size bowl.
2. Fill 4 buttered ramekins or custard cups with the mixture. Place ramekins in a shallow baking pan and add a little water to the pan.
3. Bake in a preheated moderate oven (350°) for 30 minutes or until eggs are set.

Baked Creamy Eggs

Bake at 350° for 30 minutes.

Makes 4 servings.

¼ cup (½ stick) butter or margarine	**⅓ cup milk**
¾ cup fresh bread crumbs (from 2 slices bread)	**1 can condensed cream of celery soup**
1 small onion, chopped (¼ cup)	**2 tablespoons fresh lemon juice**
¼ teaspoon leaf tarragon, crumbled	**6 hard-cooked eggs**
	½ pound fresh asparagus, cooked

1. Melt butter in a large skillet; remove 1 tablespoon and combine with bread crumbs in a small bowl; reserve.
2. Sauté onion in remaining butter until soft. Stir in tarragon, milk, soup and lemon juice until well blended. Chop the eggs coarsely; stir into sauce.
3. Arrange asparagus in greased ovenproof baking dish; pour sauce over; sprinkle with reserved bread crumbs.
4. Bake in a moderate oven (350°) for 30 minutes or until bubbly and crumbs are browned.

Eggs with Pink Mayonnaise

An attractive first course.

Makes 8 servings.

½ package unflavored gelatin	**pepper seasoning**
¼ cup water	**8 hard-cooked eggs**
½ cup mayonnaise	**Celery leaves and stems**
2 tablespoons chili sauce	**Mayonnaise**
4 drops liquid hot	**Hard-cooked egg yolk**
	Watercress

1. Sprinkle gelatin over water in a small saucepan. Place over *very low* heat until dissolved.
2. Mix the ½ cup mayonnaise, chili sauce, salt and hot pepper seasoning in small bowl until smooth. Gradually stir in half the dissolved gelatin.
3. Dip eggs, one at a time, in mixture to coat evenly. Arrange in a baking pan; refrigerate just until set. Keep the remaining gelatin at room temperature. Cut celery leaves into blade-like leaf shapes ¼ × 1-inch in size. Cut stems into thin ⅛-inch slivers about 1-inch long. Dip in gelatin in pan. (Reheat if thickened.)
4. To decorate: Arrange leaves and a stem on each egg. Make a small paper cone with wax paper; fill with spoonful of mayonnaise. Cut tip to ⅛-inch opening. Pipe a daisy on each egg at tip of stem. Sprinkle center of daisy with some cooked yolk.
5. Cover top of pan with plastic wrap so that it does not touch eggs. Chill until ready to serve, up to 2 hours. Transfer eggs with broad spatula to watercress-lined plate.

Florentine
Applied to foods served in the style of Florence, Italy. Food is prepared on a bed of spinach, topped with a delicate cheese sauce and then browned in the oven. Fish and eggs are two foods often served Florentine style.

Eggs à La Florentine

Makes 4 servings.

2 packages (9 ounces each) creamed spinach in boilable bag	**spice section of supermarket)**
4 eggs	**4 slices mozzarella cheese (from an 8-ounce package), cut into strips**
Salt blended with herb mixture (in	

1. Remove frozen spinach from plastic bag and place in a large skillet. Cover skillet and heat over low heat 5 minutes. Remove cover and stir and break up bits of frozen spinach until completely thawed and bubbly.
2. Break an egg into a cup. Make a hollow in spinach with the back of a large spoon. Slip egg into hollow.
3. Make 3 more hollows, evenly spaced, and add eggs. Cover skillet.
4. Cook over very low heat 5 minutes or until eggs are done almost as you like them. Sprinkle with salt blended with herbs and cheese strips; cover skillet. Cook 1 minute longer. Serve with crusty bread and thick slices of garden-ripe tomatoes, if you wish.

Onion and Egg Bake

A creamy casserole for onion lovers.

Bake at 350° for 30 minutes.

Makes 6 servings.

2 large Spanish onions (2½ pounds)	**1 teaspoon salt**
¼ cup (½ stick) butter or margarine	**¼ to ½ teaspoon leaf tarragon, crumbled**
1 can condensed cream of mushroom soup, undiluted	**¼ teaspoon pepper**
	8 hard-cooked eggs, sliced
½ cup milk	**¼ cup grated Parmesan cheese**

1. Peel, quarter and thinly slice onions. (You will have about 8 cups.)
2. Melt butter in large skillet; add onions. Sauté, stirring often, until tender but not browned. Stir in soup, milk, salt, tarragon and pepper.
3. Cover the bottom of a 2-quart casserole with a thin layer of onion mixture. Add a layer of egg slices. Repeat layers until all ingredients are used, ending with onion mixture. Sprinkle with cheese.
4. Bake in a moderate oven (350°) for 30 minutes or until hot and bubbly.

Pipérade.

Pipérade

Makes 4 servings.

1 small red or green pepper, halved and seeded
1 small onion, sliced
1 small clove garlic, crushed
¼ cup (½ stick) butter
⅓ cup diced cooked

ham
¼ teaspoon leaf basil, crumbled
½ teaspoon salt
Pinch pepper
6 eggs
1 small tomato, cut into wedges

1. Cut pepper into strips; sauté with onion and garlic in 2 tablespoons of the butter in a medium-size skillet until soft, about 5 minutes.

2. Stir in ham, basil, salt and pepper; cook to heat through. Remove to a small bowl; cover to keep warm.

3. Beat eggs with fork in medium-size bowl until foamy. Melt remaining 2 tablespoons of the butter in same skillet.

4. Pour in eggs; stir quickly with fork until eggs are almost set. Add warm vegetables to top layer of eggs, stirring once or twice. Stop stirring; cook until edges of eggs are set. Garnish with tomato wedges and fresh basil, if you wish. Cut into wedges to serve.

Scotch Eggs

Makes 6 servings.

1 pound bulk pork sausage	6 hard-cooked eggs, well chilled
2 tablespoons finely chopped fresh parsley	1/4 cup all-purpose flour
1/2 teaspoon ground sage	2 eggs, beaten
1/4 teaspoon pepper	1/2 to 3/4 cup packaged bread crumbs
	Vegetable oil for frying

1. Combine sausage, parsley, sage and pepper in a large bowl; mix well. Divide into 6 equal portions.
2. Press meat mixture around eggs with hands, keeping the oval shape. Sprinkle eggs with flour, coating lightly on all sides. Dip into beaten egg and then roll in bread crumbs.
3. Heat 2 to 3 inches oil in deep fryer or deep heavy saucepan to 350° on deep-fat thermometer. Cook 2 eggs at a time for about 4 to 5 minutes or until well browned. Drain on paper toweling; cool; refrigerate.

"Eggspandable" Eggs with Apricot-Glazed Sausages

An easy-to-make dish for a Sunday brunch. Hard-cook the eggs and make the onion sauce the day before.

Bake at 400° for 20 minutes.

3 medium-size onions, thinly sliced	salad dressing
3 tablespoons butter or margarine	1/4 cup packaged unseasoned bread crumbs
1/2 teaspoon dried dillweed	2 tablespoons butter or margarine, melted
1/2 teaspoon salt	2 tablespoons chopped parsley
1/4 teaspoon pepper	
1/4 cup *unsifted* all-purpose flour	1 package (1 pound) breakfast-style sausage links
1 cup chicken broth	
1 cup milk	1 can (5 1/2 ounces) apricot nectar (2/3 cup)
12 hard-cooked eggs, halved	
3 tablespoons prepared mustard	2 tablespoons apricot preserves
2 tablespoons mayonnaise or	

1. Sauté the onions in the butter in a large, heavy skillet over medium heat for 5 minutes. Lower the heat. Cover; cook for 5 minutes.
2. Stir in the dillweed, salt, pepper and flour. Cook over medium heat, stirring constantly, 1 minute. Stir in the broth and milk; cook, stirring constantly, until thickened, about 3 minutes.

3. Preheat the oven to hot (400°).
4. Spoon the onion sauce into each of twelve 3-inch baking dishes, dividing equally. Place 2 egg halves in each dish.
5. Combine the mustard and mayonnaise in a small bowl. Spoon evenly over the eggs. Combine the bread crumbs, butter and parsley in a small bowl; blend well. Sprinkle evenly over each dish.
6. Bake in the preheated hot oven (400°) for 20 minutes or until bubbly and light brown.
7. Meanwhile, combine the sausages and apricot nectar in a large skillet. Bring to simmering over medium heat. Cook the sausages, turning several times, until the sausages are browned and the nectar has evaporated, about 10 minutes. Remove and discard any fat.
8. Add the preserves to the sausages; stir gently to coat the sausages. Cook over medium heat, turning the sausages frequently, until glazed, about 5 minutes. Arrange on a platter and serve with the eggs. Garnish the eggs with parsley sprigs, if you wish.

Chinese Steamed Eggs with Pork

Makes 4 servings.

8 eggs	1/2 cup chicken broth
1/2 pound very lean pork, chopped	3 tablespoons soy sauce
4 green onions, chopped (1/3 cup)	1 1/2 tablespoons peanut oil
2 tablespoons finely chopped water chestnuts	1 1/2 teaspoons sugar
	1/2 teaspoon salt

1. Beat eggs in a large bowl until frothy. Add pork, onions, water chestnuts, chicken broth, soy sauce, oil, sugar and salt. Stir until well mixed.
2. Pour mixture into a bowl deep enough to allow the egg mixture to expand an inch as it cooks.
3. Place bowl on a wire rack in a large pot or Dutch oven. Pour hot water into pot to a 1/2- to 1-inch depth just below bowl. Leave bowl uncovered, but cover pot tightly. Adjust heat to allow water to bubble gently and create steam around bowl. Steam eggs for 30 to 40 minutes or until set.

Eggs Benedict

Makes 6 servings.

1/2 cup (1 stick) butter	12 thin slices cooked ham
2 egg yolks	
1 teaspoon lemon juice	6 eggs
1/3 cup boiling water	6 English muffins, split, toasted and buttered
Dash salt and cayenne	

1. Divide butter into thirds. Beat egg yolks with lemon juice in the top of a double boiler; add 1/3 of the butter.

2. Place pan over simmering, *not boiling,* water; cook, beating constantly, until sauce starts to thicken; add remaining butter, $^1/_3$ at a time.

3. Beat in boiling water slowly; continue stirring until mixture thickens; remove from water. Stir in salt and cayenne.

4. Cook ham in a large skillet until lightly browned; keep warm.

5. Bring 2 inches water *just* to boiling in another large skillet. Break eggs, 1 at a time, into a cup and slip into water; simmer, basting with water, 3 minutes or just until set. Lift out egg with slotted spoon; drain on paper toweling.

6. To serve: Top each muffin half with ham. Place 2 halves on a plate; put egg on top between them; spoon sauce over egg.

Shirred Eggs with Cheese

Bake at 350° for 15 minutes.

Makes 4 servings.

2 tablespoons butter or margarine, melted	4 eggs
	Salt and pepper
	$^1/_2$ cup tomato sauce
4 slices Gruyère or Swiss cheese	1 ounce Swiss cheese, shredded ($^1/_4$ cup)

1. Preheat oven to 350°. Divide butter equally among 4 individual ramekins or baking dishes. Place a slice of cheese in each. Carefully slide an egg on top of cheese. Season to taste with salt and pepper. Top each egg with 2 tablespoons of the tomato sauce; sprinkle each with 1 tablespoon shredded Swiss.

2. Bake in a preheated moderate oven (350°) for 15 minutes or until eggs are set.

Huevos Rancheros
(Ranch-style Eggs)

Makes 6 servings.

$^1/_4$ cup vegetable oil	1 can (4 ounces) whole green chilies, seeded and chopped
6 canned or frozen tortillas	
1 large onion, diced (1 cup)	$^3/_4$ teaspoon liquid hot pepper seasoning
1 medium-size green pepper, seeded and diced ($^1/_2$ cup)	1 teaspoon salt
	6 eggs
1 clove garlic, minced	2 cups shredded Romaine lettuce
3 medium-size tomatoes, peeled, seeded and diced (3 cups)	$^1/_2$ cup shredded sharp Cheddar cheese *(optional)*

1. Heat 2 tablespoons of the oil in a medium-size skillet. Heat tortillas just until limp on each side. Drain on paper toweling; keep warm.

2. In same skillet, cook onion, green pepper and garlic

until tender, about 5 minutes. (Add more oil, if necessary.) Stir in tomatoes, green chilies, hot pepper seasoning and salt. Cook, uncovered, 10 minutes, stirring occasionally.

3. Heat remaining 2 tablespoons oil in a large skillet. Break and slip eggs into skillet. Reduce heat and cook slowly to desired doneness.

4. Line large serving plate with shredded lettuce. Arrange tortillas on lettuce. Slip eggs onto each tortilla; spoon sauce around eggs. Sprinkle with cheese, if using.

Beef Sausage Over Eggs

Makes 4 servings.

1 pound ground chuck	$^1/_4$ teaspoon ground nutmeg
1 small onion, grated	
$^1/_4$ cup cold water	$^1/_8$ teaspoon cayenne
$1^1/_2$ teaspoons salt	8 eggs
$1^1/_2$ teaspoons leaf marjoram, crumbled	$^1/_3$ cup milk
	$^1/_8$ teaspoon pepper
$^1/_2$ teaspoon ground allspice	2 tablespoons butter or margarine

1. Combine beef, onion, water, 1 teaspoon of the salt, marjoram, allspice, nutmeg and cayenne in a medium-size bowl until well mixed. Shape into roll about $2^1/_2$ inches in diameter and 7 inches long. Wrap in wax paper; chill several hours or overnight until firm enough for slicing.

2. Cut sausage roll into $^1/_2$-inch slices with a sharp knife. Cook slices in skillet until well browned, turning often.

3. While sausage cooks, beat eggs, milk, remaining $^1/_2$ teaspoon salt and pepper in medium-size bowl. Melt butter in large skillet. Add beaten eggs; cook until eggs are thickened but still moist. Transfer to platter; arrange sausages on top.

Egg Patty Muffin

Makes 4 servings.

2 tablespoons butter or margarine	split
	1 package (6 ounces) sliced boiled ham
$^1/_2$ small onion, diced	
$^1/_2$ small green pepper, seeded and diced	2 eggs
	4 slices process American cheese
4 English muffins,	

1. Melt 1 tablespoon of the butter in large skillet. Add onion and green pepper; sauté until tender. Remove from heat.

2. Toast muffins and keep warm.

3. Cut ham into matchstick-size strips. Combine

(continued)

sautéed onion, green pepper, ham and eggs in large bowl.

4. Heat remaining butter in same skillet. Spoon egg mixture into 4 mounds; flatten each to make 4-inch patties. Cook until underside is set, reshaping into patty, if necessary. Turn patties; cook until bottoms are set. Place a cheese slice on each patty. Cover skillet and cook until cheese is melted. Serve in muffins.

Deviled Egg Patties

Makes 4 servings.

6 hard-cooked eggs	**crumbs**
6 tablespoons	**¹/₄ cup vegetable oil**
mayonnaise or	**4 ounces Cheddar**
salad dressing	**cheese, shredded**
1 tablespoon prepared	**(1 cup)**
mustard	**2 tablespoons**
¹/₂ cup packaged	**chopped peanuts**
seasoned bread	**(optional)**

1. Mash eggs fairly well with a fork (best done while eggs are warm). Stir in mayonnaise, mustard and bread crumbs.
2. Heat oil in a large skillet. Drop egg mixture in 8 mounds, flattening each to an oval pattie about 1 inch thick. Fry until golden on 1 side, turn and brown other side; drain on paper toweling.
3. Place patties on heatproof serving dish; sprinkle with cheese; heat in broiler, just until cheese melts. Top with peanuts, if using. Serve hot.

Note: Peanuts can be folded into egg mixture before frying, if you wish.

Eggs Divan

Bake at 375° for 10 minutes, then at 400° for 10 minutes.

Makes 4 servings.

¹/₂ cup uncooked long-	**mustard**
grain rice	**¹/₄ teaspoon**
1 package (10 ounces)	**Worcestershire**
frozen broccoli	**sauce**
spears	**Dash cayenne**
1 tablespoon butter or	**³/₄ cup milk**
margarine	**4 ounces Cheddar**
1 tablespoon flour	**cheese, shredded**
¹/₄ teaspoon salt	**(1 cup)**
¹/₄ teaspoon dry	**4 hard-cooked eggs**

1. Cook rice following label directions; reserve. Cook broccoli following label directions; reserve.
2. Melt butter in a small saucepan; blend in flour, salt,

mustard, Worcestershire sauce and cayenne; cook 1 minute. Stir in milk. Cook, stirring constantly, until mixture thickens and bubbles. Remove from heat; add cheese; stir until melted.

3. Spread rice over bottom of 10-inch pie plate or quiche pan. Arrange broccoli over rice. Top with ²/₃ of the cheese sauce. Slice eggs; arrange over sauce; cover dish with foil.

4. Bake in a moderate oven (375°) for 10 minutes. Remove from oven; uncover; top with remaining sauce. Increase temperature to hot (400°); bake 10 minutes longer.

Ziti with Sausage and Eggs

Makes 4 servings.

2 large onions, diced	**3 eggs**
(2 cups)	**1 cup chicken broth**
1 tablespoon olive oil	**¹/₄ teaspoon pepper**
4 sweet or hot Italian	**¹/₂ cup grated**
sausages	**Parmesan cheese**
1 package (1 pound)	**¹/₄ cup chopped fresh**
ziti	**parsley**

1. Sauté onions in oil in a medium-size skillet until soft, about 3 minutes. Remove casings from sausages. Add sausage meat to skillet; cook, breaking up with a spoon until no pink remains.
2. Cook ziti following label directions. While pasta cooks, beat eggs with broth and pepper in a small bowl.
3. Drain pasta; return to kettle. Reheat sausage mixture; add to pasta with the egg mixture, cheese and parsley. Toss gently to mix. Serve with additional cheese, if you wish.

Soufflé
A light, puffy egg dish that is sweet or savory. The classic soufflé is baked and should rise above its dish. It must be served immediately. It can be flavored with cheese, vegetables, seafood, vanilla or chocolate. Nowadays, a cold soufflé is made with gelatin added. In order to have the appearance of having risen, a collar is wrapped around the dish. After the dish is filled and chilled, the collar is removed.

Twin Zabaglione Soufflés

Makes 8 servings.

1 envelope unflavored	**1 tablespoon instant**
gelatin	**espresso powder**
¹/₄ cup water	**4 egg whites**
7 egg yolks	**¹/₂ cup heavy cream,**
³/₄ cup sugar	**whipped**
²/₃ cup Marsala or	**Whipped cream**
sherry	**Chocolate curls**

1. Prepare a 5-cup soufflé dish or straight-sided

glass dish with a collar this way: Fold a 24-inch length of 12-inch-wide foil in thirds lengthwise; wrap around dish to make a 2-inch collar. Fasten with tape or string. To make divider for the two mixtures: Tear off a length of foil that will just fit vertically inside the dish. Fold in thirds and stand it inside dish. Tape to collar at top.

2. Sprinkle gelatin over water in a 1-cup measure. Let stand 5 minutes to soften. Set cup in a saucepan of simmering water, stirring until gelatin is completely dissolved.

3. Beat egg yolks and 1/2 cup of the sugar slightly in top of double boiler. Beat in all but 1 tablespoon of the Marsala. Place over simmering, not boiling, water.

4. Cook, beating constantly with rotary hand mixer or portable electric mixer at medium speed, until mixture thickens slightly and is more than double in volume. This will take about 20 minutes. Remove double boiler top from water; add gelatin and continue beating a few minutes longer. Divide mixture evenly between 2 medium-size bowls.

5. Dissolve espresso in reserved tablespoon of Marsala; beat into mixture in one of the bowls. Chill both bowls until mixture mounds slightly when spooned.

6. Beat egg whites until foamy; gradually beat in remaining sugar and continue beating until meringue stands in soft peaks.

7. Fold half the meringue and half the whipped cream into each bowl of gelatin mixture. Spoon both mixtures simultaneously into prepared dish, placing espresso mixture on one side of the divider and plain mixture on the other. When dish is full, gently pull divider out, scraping off each side. Refrigerate 4 hours.

8. To serve: Remove collar carefully; garnish with additional whipped cream and curls or gratings of semisweet chocolate.

Corn and Cheese Soufflé

Bake at 350° for 50 minutes.

Makes 6 servings.

6 eggs	flour
2 tablespoons	1 teaspoon salt
packaged bread	1/2 teaspoon dry
crumbs	mustard
2 cups whole-kernel	1 3/4 cups milk
corn (from 4 ears)	3 ounces Swiss
6 tablespoons butter	cheese, shredded
1/4 teaspoon pepper	(3/4 cup)
1/3 cup chopped green	Few drops liquid hot
onions	pepper seasoning
1/3 cup all-purpose	

1. Separate eggs, placing yolks in large bowl and whites in medium-size bowl. Reserve.

2. Butter a 2-quart soufflé dish; sprinkle bottom and side with bread crumbs.

3. Sauté corn in 1 tablespoon of the butter in skillet for 5 minutes. Remove from heat. Sprinkle with pepper.

5. Sauté onions in remaining 5 tablespoons butter in medium-size saucepan; stir in flour, salt and mustard; cook and stir until mixture bubbles 1 minute. Gradually stir in 1 1/2 cups of the milk. Cook and stir until mixture thickens and bubbles 3 minutes. Remove from heat. Preheat oven to 350°.

5. Stir 1/3 cup of the sauce and the remaining 1/4 cup milk into the corn. Spoon corn mixture into bottom of prepared dish.

6. Stir cheese and liquid hot pepper into remaining sauce in pan. Beat egg yolks slightly with fork. Gradually beat in the sauce until thoroughly blended.

7. Beat egg whites until they form soft peaks. Stir 1/4 of the whites into the sauce until well mixed. Gently fold remaining whites into sauce until no streaks of white remain. Do not over-mix. Spoon over corn in dish.

8. Bake in a preheated moderate oven (350°) for 50 minutes or until puffy and golden brown.

Cheese Soup Soufflé

Bake at 375° for 35 minutes.

Makes 4 servings.

1 can (10 3/4-ounces)	shredded (1/2 cup)
condensed Cheddar	5 eggs, separated
cheese soup	1 teaspoon Dijon
2 ounces sharp	mustard
Cheddar or	4 drops liquid hot
pasteurized process	pepper seasoning
cheese spread,	1 egg white

1. Preheat oven to 375°. Grease a 2-quart soufflé dish.

2. Bring soup to boiling in a small saucepan, stirring often. Remove pan from heat.

3. Stir in cheese, egg yolks, mustard and hot pepper seasoning.

4. Beat the 6 egg whites in a medium-size bowl until soft peaks form.

5. Stir 1/4 of the whites into the soup mixture. Pour soup mixture slowly into whites; fold until well blended, with some traces of whites remaining. Pour mixture into prepared dish; place in center of oven.

6. Bake in a preheated moderate oven (375°) for 35 minutes or until puffed and golden. Serve at once.

Fresh Apple Nougat Soufflé

Makes 8 servings.

3 to 4 medium-size apples	1/8 teaspoon ground nutmeg
1/2 cup apple juice or water	5 eggs, separated
1 envelope unflavored gelatin	1/2 cup heavy cream, whipped
1/2 cup sugar	1 cup crushed Walnut Nougat (recipe follows)
1/2 teaspoon ground cinnamon	

1. Prepare a 5-cup soufflé or other straight-sided glass dish with a collar this way: Fold a 24-inch length of wax paper in half lengthwise; wrap around dish to make a 2-inch collar. Fasten with tape or string.
2. Pare, quarter, core and slice apples. (You'll have about 4 cups.) Sprinkle with 1/4 cup of the apple juice. Cook, covered, over low heat, just until apples are tender, about 10 minutes.
3. While apples are cooking, sprinkle gelatin over remaining apple juice in a medium-size bowl. Let stand 5 minutes to soften.
4. Beat 1/4 cup of the sugar, the cinnamon, nutmeg and egg yolks into softened gelatin. Beat mixture well; add to apples all at once, beating constantly. Remove from heat; pour into medium-size bowl. Chill, stirring often, just until mixture mounds slightly when spooned.
5. Beat egg whites in a large bowl until foamy-white. Gradually beat in remaining 1/4 cup sugar until meringue stands in soft peaks. Fold meringue, then whipped cream, into chilled apple mixture until no streaks of white remain. Fold in nougat. Pour into prepared dish. Refrigerate until firm, about 4 hours.
6. To serve: Gently remove collar. Garnish with additional whipped cream and apple slices, if you wish. Sprinkle edge with crushed Walnut Nougat.

Walnut Nougat: Combine 5 tablespoons butter, 1/2 cup sugar, 1 tablespoon honey and 1 tablespoon water in small heavy saucepan. Cook, stirring often, over medium-high heat until candy thermometer reaches 300° to 305°, about 5 minutes. Add 1/2 cup coarsely chopped walnuts; mix well. Pour onto buttered cookie sheet. Cool completely. When candy is cooled and hardened, chop or crush into small pieces. Makes about 1 1/2 cups crushed.

Note: Keep any extra Walnut Nougat in tightly covered jar to sprinkle on ice cream or breakfast cereal.

Pictured opposite:
Fresh Apple Nougat Soufflé.

Individual Cheese Soufflés

Bake at 350° for 40 minutes.

Makes 6 servings.

2 tablespoons butter or margarine	mustard
	1 cup milk
1/4 cup all-purpose flour	6 ounces sharp Cheddar cheese, shredded (1 1/2 cups)
1/2 teaspoon salt	
1/4 teaspoon pepper	6 eggs, separated
1/4 teaspoon dry	

1. Butter six 1-cup soufflé dishes or 10-ounce custard cups.
2. Melt butter in a medium-size saucepan; remove from heat. Stir in flour, salt, pepper and mustard; gradually stir in milk until smooth. Return to heat; continue cooking and stirring until mixture thickens and bubbles, 1 minute. Stir in cheese until melted. Remove from heat; let cool while beating eggs.
3. Beat egg whites until stiff in a large bowl. Beat egg yolks well in a small bowl; pour a little cooled cheese mixture into egg yolks, blending thoroughly. Then pour egg yolk mixture into cheese mixture, blending thoroughly.
4. Fold cheese mixture into egg whites until no streaks of white or yellow remain. Pour into prepared dishes, dividing evenly. Cover with plastic wrap; freeze.
5. To bake, place frozen soufflés on cookie sheet for easy handling. Bake in a moderate oven (350°) for 40 minutes or until puffed and golden. Serve immediately.

Never-Fail Cheese Soufflé

Bake at 400°, then at 375° for 30 minutes.

Makes 4 servings.

2 ounces Swiss cheese, shredded (1/2 cup)	margarine
	2 tablespoons flour
6 tablespoons freshly grated Parmesan cheese	1/2 teaspoon salt
	Pinch cayenne
	Pinch ground nutmeg
1 tablespoon butter or margarine	1 cup skim milk or liquefied non-fat dry milk
5 eggs	
2 tablespoons butter or	1/4 teaspoon cream of tartar

1. Combine the Swiss cheese with 4 tablespoons of the Parmesan in a small bowl; reserve. Butter a 2-quart soufflé dish or other straight-sided dish with the 1 tablespoon butter. Sprinkle the remaining 2 tablespoons Parmesan over buttered surface to coat. Preheat oven to 400°.
2. Separate 4 of the eggs, putting the yolks into a cup and the whites in a large bowl. Separate the fifth egg,

(continued)

putting the white with the other whites. Refrigerate the yolk for another use.

3. Melt remaining 2 tablespoons butter in a medium-size saucepan. Add flour, salt, cayenne and nutmeg; cook and stir 1 minute; stir in milk. Cook, stirring constantly, until thickened and bubbly, about 3 minutes. Remove from heat; stir in yolks, 1 at a time, until mixture is smooth. Stir in cheese mixture.

4. Beat whites with cream of tartar in a large bowl with electric mixer until soft peaks form. Stir ¼ of the beaten whites into the cheese sauce to lighten; gently fold in remaining whites. Turn into prepared dish. Scoop a trough around the mixture about an inch in from the edge to give a "high hat" effect. Place soufflé in center of preheated oven; lower heat to moderate (375°).

5. Bake for 30 minutes or until soufflé is risen and nicely browned.

Individual Orange Soufflés

Fragrant and fragile, yet easy to make, these tiny orange dessert soufflés are a pure pleasure to eat.
Bake at 375° for 18 minutes.

Makes 6 servings.

¼ cup (½ stick) sweet butter	2 large navel oranges
½ cup all-purpose flour	5 egg yolks
⅓ cup plus 1½ tablespoons sugar	2 tablespoons Grand Marnier
1½ cups milk, scalded	6 egg whites
	10X (confectioners') sugar

1. Butter 8 small individual soufflé dishes or 6 slightly larger ones. Dust lightly with sugar; shake out the excess.

2. Melt the butter in a saucepan. Blend in the flour; cook, stirring constantly, 1 to 2 minutes. Cool slightly.

3. Add the sugar to milk; stir to dissolve. Whisk milk mixture rapidly into the *roux* until smooth. Cook, stirring constantly, until mixture thickens and comes to a boil. Remove from heat.

4. Grate rind from oranges; then peel and section. Preheat oven to 375°.

5. Whisk egg yolks, grated orange rind and Grand Marnier into hot mixture. Beat egg whites until stiff but not dry; fold into hot mixture.

6. Fill prepared soufflé dishes ⅓ full with soufflé mixture. Divide the orange sections among the dishes. Add enough soufflé mixture to ¾ fill each dish. Smooth surfaces.

7. Bake in a preheated moderate oven (375°) for 18

minutes or until souflés are puffed and golden brown. Sprinkle tops with 10X sugar and *serve at once,* while puffed and perfect. Any extra soufflé mixture can be warmed in a double boiler over hot, not boiling, water, thinned down with orange juice; serve as a sauce.

Note: The same mixture can, of course, be baked in a single large souflé dish (filled 3/4 full). Bake at 325° for 20 minutes, increase oven temperature to 350° and bake 10 minutes longer or until soufflé is well-puffed and golden brown.

Hot Chocolate Soufflé

Bake at 350° for 50 minutes.

Makes 6 servings.

½ cup sugar	2 tablespoons butter or margarine
3 tablespoons flour	1 teaspoon vanilla
¼ teaspoon salt	4 egg yolks
1 cup milk	6 egg whites, at room temperature
3 squares unsweetened chocolate	Sugar

1. Coat a 6-cup soufflé dish well with soft butter or margarine; sprinkle evenly with sugar, tapping out excess. Fold a 24-inch piece of foil in thirds lengthwise; butter on one side; wrap around dish, buttered-side in, to make a 2-inch collar. Tie with string. Sprinkle paper with sugar.

2. Blend 6 tablespoons of the sugar with the flour and salt in small saucepan. Gradually stir in milk; add chocolate. Cook over medium heat, stirring constantly, until the chocolate is melted and mixture thickens and bubbles 2 minutes. Remove from heat; stir in butter and vanilla. Preheat oven to 350°.

3. Beat egg yolks in small bowl with wire whisk; add slightly cooled chocolate mixture.

4. Beat egg whites in large bowl until soft peaks form when beater is raised. Add remaining 2 tablespoons sugar, 1 tablespoon at a time, beating until shiny and stiff peaks form when beaters are raised.

5. Stir about ¼ of egg white mixture into chocolate mixture, then add to remaining whites and gently fold in. Pour mixture into prepared dish; sprinkle top lightly with sugar. Place dish in baking pan on oven rack; pour boiling water into pan to depth of 1 inch.

6. Bake in a preheated moderate oven (350°) for 50 minutes or until light and puffy. To serve: Remove collar; serve immediately with ice cold whipped cream, a custard sauce or warm chocolate sauce, if you wish.

Broccoli and Ham Soufflé

Bake at 350° for 35 minutes.

Makes 4 servings.

2 tablespoons chopped onion	**frozen chopped broccoli, thawed**
3 tablespoons butter or margarine	**1 cup finely chopped cooked ham (about 4 ounces)**
3 tablespoons flour	**3 tablespoons grated Parmesan cheese**
1/2 teaspoon salt	**1 teaspoon cream of tartar**
1/8 teaspoon pepper	
1 cup milk	
4 eggs, separated	
1 package (10 ounces)	

1. Sauté onion in butter in a medium-size saucepan, stirring occasionally, until tender but not brown, about 2 minutes. Stir in flour, salt and pepper; cook 1 minute. Stir in milk until mixture is smooth. Cook, stirring constantly, until mixture thickens.
2. Beat egg yolks slightly in a small bowl; stir in a little of the hot mixture; return blended mixture to saucepan. Cook over low heat, stirring constantly, 2 minutes. Preheat oven to 350°.
3. Drain broccoli in a colander, pressing with a spoon to remove excess moisture. Stir into sauce along with ham and cheese. Remove from heat.
4. Beat egg whites with cream of tartar in a large bowl until soft peaks form. Gently fold broccoli mixture into whites until no streaks of white remain. Spoon into a lightly greased 1 1/2-quart soufflé or other straight-sided dish.
5. Bake in a preheated moderate oven (350°) for 35 minutes or until browned and puffed and a knife inserted 1 inch from edge comes out clean. Serve at once.

Crêpe   The French word for a very thin pancake. Crêpes are served filled with creamed meats or savory vegetables as a main dish or sweet fillings as a dessert.

With just a little practice, perfect crêpes can be made at home in a small skillet, an electric crêpe maker or upside-down griddle pan.

Crêpes can be cooled, stacked and wrapped in foil or a plastic bag and stored in the refrigerator for 2 to 3 days or in the freezer for 3 months. Foil or plastic wrap placed between crêpes to be frozen will make it easier to separate them to thaw.

Basic Crêpes

Makes 12 to 16 small crêpes (6 to 7 inches in diameter) or 10 to 12 large crêpes (8 to 10 inches in diameter).

3 eggs	**2 tablespoons butter or margarine, melted**
3/4 cup all-purpose flour	**Butter**
1/4 teaspoon salt	
1 cup milk	

1. Combine eggs, flour, salt and 1/4 cup of the milk in medium-size bowl; beat with rotary beater until smooth. Beat in melted butter, then remaining milk. Refrigerate, covered, at least 1 hour.
2. Slowly heat skillet until a drop of water sizzles when dropped on surface. Butter skillet lightly for the first few crêpes; after that it will be seasoned and crêpes will not stick. To make small crêpes, use 2 to 3 tablespoons batter for each and a 7- or 8-inch skillet. To make large crêpes, use 3 to 4 tablespoons batter for each and an 8- or 10-inch skillet. Measure amount of batter into a small measuring cup or ladle to make the first crêpe, then scoop up batter and pour into skillet all at once for subsequent ones.
3. Pour batter into hot skillet; quickly rotate skillet to spread batter evenly. Cook over medium heat until lightly browned; turn and brown other side. Remove to plate; when cool, stack with foil or plastic wrap between each.

Sweet Crêpes: Prepare the recipe for Basic Crêpes, adding 2 tablespoons sugar to the batter.

Ham and Cheese Appetizer Crêpes

Makes 32 appetizer crêpes.

Basic Crêpes (see recipe in this chapter)	**1/2 teaspoon leaf basil, crumbled**
	1/4 teaspoon fennel seed, crushed
Filling:	**1/8 teaspoon pepper**
1 medium-size onion, minced	**2 tablespoons chopped parsley**
2 tablespoons butter or margarine	**1 cup shredded Swiss cheese (4 ounces)**
1 cup cooked ham, minced	**1/4 cup (1/2 stick) butter or margarine, melted**
1 large ripe tomato, peeled, seeded and chopped	**1/2 cup grated Parmesan cheese**

1. Prepare Basic Crêpes in a 7- or 8-inch skillet, using 2 to 3 tablespoons batter for each. (Makes about 16.)
2. Prepare Filling: Sauté onion in butter in a large skillet until soft. Stir in ham, tomato, basil, fennel and pepper. Cook and stir over low heat until liquid has almost evaporated. Remove from heat; stir in parsley.
3. Fill crêpes, putting about 2 teaspoons filling and 1

(continued)

tablespoon Swiss cheese near edge. Roll up part way, fold in sides, then roll up completely, envelope fashion. Place crepes on small cookie sheet (crepes can be covered and refrigerated several hours); brush tops with melted butter and sprinkle with Parmesan.
4. Broil about 4 inches from heat for 2 minutes or until lightly browned. Cut each in half diagonally.

Zucchini and Onion-Filled Crêpes Stack

Bake at 350° for 30 minutes.
Makes 6 servings as a main course, 10 to 12 servings as an accompaniment.

Basic Crêpes (see recipe in this chapter)	1¹/₂ teaspoons leaf oregano, crumbled
3 tablespoons butter or margarine	1¹/₂ teaspoons salt
3 tablespoons vegetable oil	¹/₄ teaspoon pepper
4 large onions, sliced (4 cups)	Sauce:
6 zucchini (about 2 pounds)	2 tablespoons butter or margarine
2 tablespoons chopped fresh parsley	3 tablespoons flour
	¹/₂ teaspoon salt
	1¹/₂ cups milk
	2 eggs
	¹/₄ cup grated Parmesan cheese

1. Make crepes in an 8- or 10-inch skillet, using a scant ¹/₄ cup batter for each. (Makes about 10.)
2. Heat 2 tablespoons of the butter and 2 tablespoons of the oil in a large skillet; add onion and sauté until tender, stirring often, about 10 minutes. Remove with slotted spoon to bowl.
3. Meanwhile, shred zucchini on coarsest side of grater. You should have about 5 cups. (If you wish, cut a few slices and save for garnish.) Heat remaining butter and oil in skillet; add zucchini. Sauté over high heat, stirring often, until zucchini is tender and juices have evaporated, 5 to 10 minutes (do not brown). Add zucchini to onion; stir in parsley, oregano, salt and pepper.
4. Prepare Sauce: Melt butter in saucepan; stir in flour and salt. Gradually add milk; cook, stirring constantly, until sauce thickens and bubbles, about 1 minute. Beat eggs in medium-size bowl; gradually beat in half of hot sauce; pour back into saucepan; stir in cheese. Measure and reserve 1 cup of sauce.
5. Assemble crepes in a buttered 10-inch pie plate or shallow baking dish. Place 1 crêpe in dish; spread with a generous ¹/₃ cup of zucchini filling and about 2 tablespoons sauce. Continue stacking and filling, ending with a plain crêpe on top.
6. Arrange a few reserved zucchini slices and onion rings on top. Pour the reserved 1 cup sauce over top, letting it run down the sides. Sprinkle with a little additional cheese.
7. Bake in a moderate oven (350°) for 30 minutes to

heat through and brown top. Cut in pie-shaped wedges to serve.

Note: This dish can be assembled through step 6 several hours ahead; cover and hold in the refrigerator. Allow 5 to 10 minutes extra to heat through.

Cheese and Blueberry Crêpe Triangles

Make the crêpes ahead and freeze for up to 2 weeks. Make the filling the day before.

Makes 8 servings.

Batter:	room temperature
1¹/₂ cups milk	1 egg yolk
3 eggs	2 tablespoons sugar
1 cup sifted all-purpose flour	¹/₄ teaspoon ground cinnamon
¹/₂ teaspoon salt	Butter or margarine
3 tablespoons butter, melted	1 cup fresh or frozen blueberries
	2 tablespoons melted butter or margarine
Filling:	Cinnamon sugar
1 pound creamed cottage cheese	Sour cream
7¹/₂-ounce package farmers cheese, at	Strawberry or cherry preserves

1. Prepare Batter: Place milk, eggs, flour and salt in the container of electric blender; whirl for 1 minute or until smooth. Whirl in butter. Cover. Refrigerate for 30 minutes or until ready to use.
2. Prepare Filling: Beat cottage cheese and farmers cheese in a small bowl until smooth. Beat in egg yolk, sugar and cinnamon. Refrigerate.
3. Heat a 7- or 8-inch skillet over medium-high heat. Grease lightly. Pour 3 tablespoons batter into the pan, rotating quickly to spread batter evenly. Cook over medium heat until lightly browned, about 1 minute. Flip over; cook for 30 seconds. Remove to a plate. Repeat with the remaining batter to make about sixteen 6-inch crêpes; stack with wax paper between them.
4. Spread about 3 tablespoons filling on 8 crêpes; sprinkle 1 tablespoon blueberries over each. Fold in quarters. Arrange on a platter. Fill the remaining crêpes with plain filling; arrange on a platter. Brush lightly with melted butter.
5. To serve, heat crêpes in a preheated moderate oven (350°) for 10 to 15 minutes. Serve with cinnamon sugar, sour cream and preserves.

Pictured opposite (from top right): Flamed Spicy-Nut Crêpes, page 362; Zucchini and Onion-Filled Crêpes Stack, page 360; Ham and Cheese Appetizer Crêpes, page 359.

Flamed Spicy-Nut Crêpes

Makes 6 servings.

Sweet Crêpes (*recipe in this chapter*)

Filling:
1/2 cup firmly packed light brown sugar
6 tablespoons butter or margarine
1 teaspoon ground cinnamon
1/4 teaspoon ground nutmeg
2 tablespoons apple

brandy or applejack
1/2 cup chopped walnuts

Sauce:
2 tablespoons butter or margarine
2 tablespoons honey
1/2 cup orange juice
1 red apple, cored and thinly sliced
1/2 cup apple brandy or applejack

1. Prepare Sweet Crêpes in an 8- or 10-inch skillet, using 3 tablespoons of batter for each. (Makes about 12.)
2. Prepare Filling: Beat sugar, butter, cinnamon and nutmeg until light and fluffy in small bowl; beat in 2 tablespoons apple brandy, 1 at a time. Fold in nuts.
3. Spread each crêpe with butter mixture, dividing evenly. Fold each in half, then in half again. Arrange on plate; cover and refrigerate until ready to serve.
4. Prepare Sauce: Heat shallow chafing dish over an alcohol flame; add butter and honey; heat until bubbly. Add orange juice and sliced apple; bring to boiling and boil 1 minute. Arrange the folded crêpes in sauce and heat through.
5. Pour 1/2 cup apple brandy over crêpes; stand back and ignite with a lighted match; shake chafing dish gently back and forth, spooning the flaming sauce over crêpes until flames die.

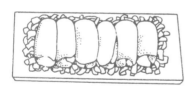

Omelet

(Also (**Omelette**) This popular dish is a combination of eggs beaten with water or milk and seasonings. It is cooked in a small skillet or omelet pan until firm and can be filled with cooked meat, cheese or vegetables. This type of omelet is called a French omelet. A puffy omelet is another type of omelet in which the eggs are separated and the egg whites beaten until stiff. The egg yolks are folded into the egg whites with seasonings and then cooked in a skillet. This type of omelet is light and fluffy.

About Omelet Skillets

● Any skillet with a rounded bottom, whether it's heavy aluminum, cast iron or stainless steel, can be used to make omelets. If it is your everyday skillet you plan to use, do clean it thoroughly with a soapy steel-wool pad, then rinse and dry. **To season** (which you must do each time), heat a 1/4-inch depth of vegetable oil in the skillet over low heat for 10 minutes; pour off the oil, wipe out the skillet.
● You can skip the cleaning process if you use a skillet solely for making omelets or a skillet with a nonstick surface. You need to season only the first time you use the skillet. Simply wipe off—not wash—after each use and it'll be ready for the next omelet.
● Omelets will stick to the skillet if you let the butter brown. If this happens, pour off browned butter, wipe out skillet with paper toweling and start again.

Fines Herbes An herb mixture of minced, fresh or dried parsley, chervil, tarragon and sometimes chives. It is used for seasoning salads, omelets and other dishes. *Fines herbe* are French words which translate simply to "fine herbs." It is sold in jars or you can make your own mixture and keep it on hand.

Fines Herbes

For omelets and scrambled eggs, butter-sauced vegetables, meat and fish sauces, broiled chicken and fish.

Makes 1 cup.

1/4 cup dried parsley flakes
1/4 cup leaf chervil

1/4 cup freeze-dried chives
1/4 cup leaf tarragon

Combine all ingredients. Keep in tightly closed containers.

Potato-Beef Omelet

Prepare the filling in advance, then reheat while preparing the eggs.

Makes 4 omelets.

1/2 pound sliced mushrooms
1 cup chopped onion
2/3 cup chopped sweet red pepper (1 small)
3 tablespoons vegetable oil
1 1/2 cups frozen, unseasoned hash brown potato cubes

1/2 pound ground round
1/4 teaspoon leaf thyme
1 cup grated Fontina cheese (4 ounces)
4 teaspoons butter or margarine
12 eggs

1. Prepare the filling: Sauté the mushrooms, onion and red pepper in the oil in a medium-size skillet until soft, about 5 minutes. Stir in the hash browns. Cook, stirring occasionally, 8 minutes longer or until the potatoes are tender. Stir in the beef and thyme. Cook

until the beef is no longer pink, about 2 minutes. Stir in the cheese. Remove from the heat and reserve; keep warm.

2. Prepare the omelets: Heat 1 teaspoon of the butter in an 8-inch nonstick skillet. Beat 3 eggs lightly in a small cup. Pour into the skillet. Cook, stirring with the flat of a fork and shaking the pan back and forth, until the omelet is firm on the bottom and almost set on top. Spoon about ³/₄ cup of the filling in the center. Fold the omelet over the filling. Slide onto a heated serving plate. Keep warm in a very low oven while making the remaining omelets.

Puffy Spanish Omelet

Bake at 350° for 10 minutes.

Makes 4 servings.

6 eggs, separated	**(¹/₂ cup)**
6 tablespoons milk or water	**¹/₄ teaspoon leaf marjoram, crumbled**
1 teaspoon salt	**¹/₈ teaspoon cayenne**
¹/₄ teaspoon pepper	**3 medium-size tomatoes, peeled and coarsely chopped**
4 tablespoons (¹/₂ stick) butter or margarine	
1 medium-size onion, sliced	**1 cup dairy sour cream**
1 small green pepper, seeded and diced	**2 tablespoons snipped chives**

1. Beat egg whites until stiff in a large bowl with electric mixer.
2. Beat egg yolks slightly in a medium-size bowl with same mixer. Add milk, ¹/₂ teaspoon of the salt and pepper, beating until thick. Fold into egg white mixture thoroughly.
3. Preheat oven to 350°. Heat a 10-inch skillet or omelet pan with an ovenproof handle. Swirl 2 tablespoons of the butter over bottom and side of skillet.
4. Pour in egg mixture. Cook over low heat 5 minutes or until mixture is set on the bottom and is golden brown.
5. Bake in a preheated moderate oven (350°) for 10 minutes or until puffy and golden on the top.
6. While omelet is baking, sauté onion and green pepper in remaining 2 tablespoons butter in a large skillet until soft, about 5 minutes. Add marjoram, remaining salt, cayenne and tomatoes; cook just until hot.
7. Remove omelet from oven. Loosen around edge with a knife, cut a gash down center of omelet; place tomato mixture down one side of omelet; fold over with pancake turner; turn onto heated platter. Serve with sour cream and chives. Garnish with parsley and tomato wedges, if you wish.

Egg Foo Yung

Chinese-style omelets full of crunchy vegetables and pieces of chicken.

Makes 4 servings.

6 eggs	**¹/₂ to 1 cup minced cooked chicken**
1 cup fresh or canned bean sprouts, rinsed and drained on paper toweling	**2 teaspoons soy sauce**
	1 teaspoon salt
1 small onion, chopped (¹/₄ cup)	**Vegetable oil**
	Egg Foo Yung Sauce (recipe follows)
3 to 4 mushrooms, chopped	

1. Beat eggs in large bowl until foamy. Stir in bean sprouts, onion, mushrooms, chicken, soy sauce and salt.
2. Heat an omelet pan or small skillet (about 6 inches). Add 1 tablespoon oil. Pour ¹/₄ of egg mixture (about ¹/₂ cup) into skillet; cook 1 to 2 minutes or until crisp and golden on one side; turn with a wide pancake turner; cook 1 minute longer. Fold in half and arrange on heated serving plate. Keep warm while using the remaining egg mixture to make 3 more "omelets." Serve with Egg Foo Yung Sauce.

Egg Foo Yung Sauce: Mix 1 tablespoon cornstarch and 1 tablespoon soy sauce in small saucepan; gradually stir in 1 cup chicken broth. Cook, stirring constantly, until sauce thickens and bubbles 1 minute. Serve hot over Egg Foo Yung. Makes 1 cup.

French Omelet

Makes 1 serving.

2 eggs	**1 tablespoon butter or margarine**
2 tablespoons water	
Salt and pepper	

1. Beat the eggs with water in a small bowl until blended; season with salt and pepper.
2. Heat a small, heavy skillet slowly until it is very hot. Add butter and swirl pan to coat entire surface. *Do not allow butter to brown.*
3. Pour egg mixture into skillet. As soon as eggs begin to set, start lifting the edge of egg mixture all the way around with a spatula until all the liquid has cooked.
4. To turn omelet out, tip pan, lift edge with a spatula; fold omelet over onto plate.

Toppings for French Omelet: Add just before folding omelet.
1. Sprinkle with chopped fresh parsley, watercress or chives.
2. Spread lightly with jam, jelly or marmalade for a dessert omelet.
3. Top with thinly sliced Gruyère, Swiss or shredded Cheddar cheese.

Pork Omelets

The shape and color of these tiny omelets resemble gold nuggets and are a symbol of wealth for the New Year. This is a simplified version of the traditional dish from the Eastern region of China.

Makes 4 servings.

1 pound Chinese celery cabbage OR: 1 package (10 ounces) frozen green peas	1 tablespoon dry sherry
	1 green onion, finely chopped
	3 to 4 tablespoons vegetable oil
4 eggs	
1/4 pound ground pork or beef	1 cup chicken broth (see Note below)
1 teaspoon cornstarch	1 teaspoon salt
1 tablespoon soy sauce	1/2 teaspoon sugar

1. Cut cabbage into 2 × 1-inch strips (about 4 cups).
2. Beat eggs in large bowl with rotary beater until frothy. Add pork, cornstarch, soy sauce, sherry and onion. Stir with fork to make sure pork is in very small pieces.
3. Heat large skillet; add 1 tablespoon of the oil. Pour egg mixture by tablespoonfuls into skillet to make 2 1/2-inch omelets. Make 4 or 5 at a time. Cook about 2 minutes or just until most of the egg is set. While omelets are still soft, fold in half, using a small spatula. Press lightly, then turn and cook 1 more minute. Remove to platter. Continue with remaining mixture and use as much oil as is necessary. (Makes about 24 omelets.)
4. Wipe skillet clean; reheat and add 2 tablespoons of the oil. Stir-fry cabbage 2 minutes. Add chicken broth, salt and sugar. Stir well.
5. Arrange omelets on top of cabbage. Cover; cook until cabbage is just tender, about 5 minutes. Serve with hot cooked rice, if you wish.

Note: If peas are used, decrease the amount of chicken broth to 1/2 cup.

Avocado Omelet

This is a colorful omelet that makes a most satisfying luncheon entrée.

Makes 2 large omelets (4 servings).

1/4 cup chopped green pepper	herb seasoning mix
1/4 cup chopped green onions	1/4 teaspoon salt
	1 large avocado
5 tablespoons butter or margarine	1 tablespoon lemon juice
1 ripe tomato, peeled, seeded and chopped	8 eggs
	1/2 teaspoon salt
	1/8 teaspoon pepper
1/4 teaspoon Italian	1/4 cup water

1. Sauté pepper and onions in 1 tablespoon of the butter in a small skillet until soft. Stir in tomato, Italian seasoning and 1/4 teaspoon salt. Cook and stir until most of the liquid has evaporated; remove from heat.
2. Halve avocado; pit; peel. Sprinkle with lemon juice, then chop coarsely. Stir into tomato mixture.
3. Beat eggs with salt, pepper and water in a medium-size bowl until foamy. For each omelet: Heat 2 tablespoons of the butter in a large skillet until foamy-hot. Ladle half of the beaten egg mixture into the skillet. Stir the eggs rapidly with the flat of a fork, while shaking the skillet back and forth over the heat. Stir just until liquid sets, then cook 15 seconds longer.
4. Fold 1/3 of omelet toward center, then roll out onto serving plate. Omelet can be filled with 1/2 of the avocado filling just before rolling, or you can slash the rolled omelet lengthwise and spoon the filling into the cavity. Keep omelet warm in a very slow oven (275°) until other is made. Serve at once.

Potato Zucchini Omelet

Bake at 375° for 20 minutes.

Makes 6 servings.

8 eggs	3/4 pound), pared and grated
2 tablespoons milk	2 zucchini, thinly sliced
3/4 teaspoon salt	
1/8 teaspoon pepper	
4 tablespoons vegetable oil	1 tablespoon butter or margarine
1 small onion, chopped (1/4 cup)	1/2 cup grated Parmesan cheese
2 large all-purpose potatoes (about	1 large tomato, sliced

1. Preheat oven to 375°. Beat eggs, milk, salt and pepper in a bowl.
2. Heat 3 tablespoons of the oil in a large skillet with ovenproof handle. Add onion and potatoes and cook, stirring constantly, until potatoes are almost tender, about 3 minutes. Stir into egg mixture. Wipe skillet clean.
3. Add remaining 1 tablespoon oil to skillet and sauté zucchini until tender. Remove to paper toweling.
4. Melt butter in skillet. Add egg-potato mixture; top with half of the cheese, zucchini and then the remaining cheese.
5. Bake in a preheated moderate oven (375°) for 20 minutes or until a knife inserted in the center of the omelet comes out clean. Loosen around edges with metal spatula. Garnish with tomato.

Pictured opposite (clockwise from the top): Glazed Beef, page 435; Stir-Fried Shrimp, page 402; Velvet Sliced Chicken, page 652; Pork Omelets, page 362.

Basic French Omelet

Makes 1 serving.

3 eggs
1 tablespoon water
¹/₄ teaspoon salt
¹/₈ teaspoon white pepper

Sausage and Pepper (recipe follows)
Parsley or celery leaves (optional)

1. Beat the eggs, water, salt and pepper together, in a medium bowl, using a fork.
2. Heat a 9- or 10-inch heavy seasoned skillet with a rounded bottom and sloping sides, or a heavy aluminum pan, with or without a nonstick surface. Swirl a tablespoon of butter over the entire surface of the pan.
3. When the butter stops foaming, pour the egg mixture into the skillet.
4. Cook over moderately high heat until the bottom is set. Using a heatproof spatula, move the cooked mixture to the center and allow the uncooked mixture to flow into the bottom of the pan.
5. When cooked, the omelet should be barely brown on the bottom, soft and moist in the center.
6. Spoon the filling down the center of the omelet.
7. Using the spatula, and starting from the handle side, fold one-third of the omelet over the center.
8. With a heated serving plate in one hand, grasp the skillet in the other, palm up and tilt so the omelet rolls over onto the plate. Garnish with parsley or celery leaves, if you wish.

Sausage and Pepper Filling

Makes 1¹/₂ cups filling (enough for 2 French Omelets).

2 hot or sweet Italian sausages or a combination (about 6 ounces)
1 small sweet green pepper, halved, seeded and thinly sliced (¹/₂ cup)
1 small sweet red

pepper, halved, seeded and thinly sliced (¹/₂ cup)
1 medium-size onion, cut into thin wedges
¹/₄ teaspoon leaf oregano, crumbled
¹/₄ teaspoon leaf basil, crumbled

1. Remove casings from the sausages. Crumble into a large skillet. Cook slowly until sausage is lightly browned; remove sausage with a slotted spoon to paper toweling. Pour sausage fat into a small cup; return 2 tablespoons to the skillet.
2. Sauté peppers and onion in the fat in the skillet just until tender, about 5 minutes. Add cooked sausage, oregano and basil; toss gently to mix. Lower the heat; cover; keep warm.
3. Fill as directed in French Omelet recipe.

Corn Omelet

Bake at 325° for 2 minutes.
Makes 4 servings.

2 large ears of corn
6 bacon slices
4 tablespoons (¹/₂ stick) butter or margarine
1 large onion, thinly sliced

1 cup diced green pepper
6 eggs
1 teaspoon salt
¹/₄ teaspoon pepper
Few drops hot pepper seasoning

1. Scrape corn from cobs (you should have 1 cup). Cook corn in boiling unsalted water to cover in a small saucepan 3 to 5 minutes or until tender; drain; spoon into a large bowl. Preheat oven to 325°.
2. Cook bacon in a large skillet until crisp and brown. Drain on paper toweling; crumble; add to corn. Pour bacon drippings into a cup. Measure and return 1 tablespoon to skillet. Add 2 tablespoons of the butter and heat until melted. Sauté onion and pepper until tender; add to corn.
3. Add eggs, salt, pepper and liquid hot pepper seasoning to bowl with corn mixture; beat until mixed.
4. Wipe the skillet out with paper toweling. Heat the remaining 2 tablespoons butter with 1 tablespoon of the bacon drippings until very hot. Add the egg mixture and cook until bottom is set, but top is still liquid.
5. Bake in a preheated slow oven (325°) for 2 minutes or until top is set.

Normandy Omelet

For a breakfast or supper treat try this puffy omelet with its apple filling.

Bake at 350° for 8 to 10 minutes.

Makes 4 servings as a dessert, or 2 servings as breakfast.

4 tablespoons (¹/₂ stick) butter or margarine
2 tablespoons honey
¹/₄ teaspoon ground cinnamon
1 can (20 ounces) unsweetened apple

slices
¹/₂ teaspoon grated lemon rind
4 eggs, separated
2 tablespoons sugar
¹/₄ cup heavy cream
10X (confectioners') sugar

1. Heat 2 tablespoons of the butter in small skillet; stir in honey and cinnamon; heat until bubbly. Add apples and lemon rind; heat through; keep warm.
2. Beat egg whites with 1 tablespoon of the sugar in a large bowl with rotary beater until stiff peaks form. Using same beaters, beat egg yolks with remaining sugar until light and thick; then beat in cream, 1 tablespoon at a time. Fold egg yolks into whites, using a rubber spatula, until thoroughly blended.
3. Preheat oven to 350°. Heat a 9- or 10-inch heavy

ovenproof skillet over medium heat. Add remaining butter to skillet; tilt pan to cover side with butter. As the butter foams and then subsides (do not allow to brown), pour in egg mixture. Spread mixture evenly in pan; cook over low heat, without stirring, until omelet is golden brown on underside, about 5 minutes.

4. Bake in a preheated moderate oven (350°) for 8 to 10 minutes or until omelet feels firm when pressed with fingertip.

5. To serve: Ease half of omelet onto serving platter. Spoon apple filling over, then fold other half over filling or serve right from skillet. Sprinkle top with 10X sugar.

Rolled Shrimp and Sprout Omelet

This rolled, puffy omelet is really a soufflé mixture baked in a pan instead of a soufflé dish.

Bake at 400° for 25 to 30 minutes.

Makes one 10-inch roll or 6 servings.

Roll:
1/4 cup (1/2 stick) butter or margarine
1/2 cup all-purpose flour
1 teaspoon salt
2 cups milk
6 eggs, separated

Filling:
1 tablespoon vegetable oil
1/2 pound shrimp, shelled, deveined and diced (1 cup)
1/2 pound bean

sprouts, coarsely chopped (3 1/2 cups)
1 bunch green onions, thinly sliced, both green and white parts (1 1/2 cups)
1 tablespoon cornstarch
1 tablespoon dry sherry
1 teaspoon salt
Dash cayenne
1 package (3 ounces) cream cheese, cubed

1. Prepare Roll: Melt butter in a medium-size saucepan. Stir in flour and salt; cook 1 minute. Remove from heat; stir in milk gradually. Cook, stirring constantly, until mixture is thick.

2. Beat egg yolks in a medium-size bowl. Slowly beat one half of hot mixture into yolks until blended. Stir yolk mixture into remaining hot mixture. Cook and stir 1 minute more. Remove from heat. Cover surface of sauce with plastic wrap to prevent skin from forming. Refrigerate until cool.

3. Preheat oven to 400°. Butter a 15 1/2 × 10 1/2 × 1-inch jelly-roll pan; line bottom with wax paper; butter paper; dust with flour.

4. Beat egg whites in a large bowl until soft peaks form. Fold in cooled sauce mixture until no streaks of yellow remain. Spread evenly in pan.

5. Bake in a preheated hot oven (400°) for 25 minutes or until firm and browned.

6. While roll bakes, prepare Filling: Heat oil in large skillet; add shrimp; sauté 1 minute just until shrimp turn pink. Stir in bean sprouts and onions. Cook until onions are just wilted. Combine cornstarch, sherry, salt and cayenne in small cup. Add to skillet; cook,

stirring constantly, until thickened. Stir in cream cheese until blended. Cool slightly.

7. Remove roll from oven. Loosen around edges with spatula; cover with clean towel or foil. Place a large cookie sheet on top; then quickly turn jelly-roll pan upside down. Lift pan; peel off paper.

8. Spread filling over surface of roll. Starting at short end, roll up jelly-roll fashion, lifting away towel or foil. Lift roll onto cutting board with two wide spatulas. Cut into slices to serve.

Pancake One of the oldest forms of bread, a pancake is a flat cake cooked or baked on a griddle. The first pancakes were probably made of ground meal and water and spread on a hot stone to dry. Almost every country has its own version of a pancake. Pancakes can be served as an appetizer, stuffed and served as a main dish or as dessert.

Tips for Perfect Pancakes

1. Make sure your griddle is hot before adding the batter. Here's how to test it: Sprinkle on several drops of water; when they sputter and dance about, grease griddle and pour the pancake batter.

2. For equal-size pancakes, measure batter, using a scant 1/4 cup for a 4-inch round. The batter spreads, so leave space between cakes.

3. When pancakes look puffy and golden on the undersides, flip them over with a wide spatula.

Apple Pancakes

Makes about 24 two-inch pancakes.

1 cup *unsifted* all-purpose flour
1/2 teaspoon baking powder
1/2 cup milk*
2 eggs, lightly beaten

3 small McIntosh apples, pared, quartered, cored and chopped
1 tablespoon vegetable oil

1. Mix flour and baking powder in a medium-size bowl; stir in milk and eggs until batter is smooth. Fold in chopped apples.

2. Heat oil in a large skillet. For each pancake, drop a heaping tablespoon of batter in the skillet. Cook until golden brown on bottom; turn; cook until golden on the other side. Serve with butter and honey or syrup, if you wish.

If batter is too thick, stir in more milk.

Buttermilk Pancakes

Makes about 12 pancakes.

³/₄ **cup** *sifted* **unbleached all-purpose flour**
³/₄ **cup buckwheat or whole wheat flour**
2¹/₂ **to 3 tablespoons sugar** *(see note below)*
1 **teaspoon baking soda**
¹/₂ **teaspoon salt**
2 **eggs, slightly beaten**
1¹/₂ **cups buttermilk**
2 **tablespoons butter or margarine, melted**
Butter or margarine for frying

1. Sift unbleached flour, buckwheat or whole wheat flour, sugar, baking soda and salt in a bowl. (If using whole wheat flour, add any wheat grains that remain in the sifter.)
2. Combine eggs, buttermilk and melted butter in a second bowl; gradually stir into dry ingredients just until blended, but not overmixed.
3. Heat a griddle untile it is hot enough for a drop of water to sizzle. Grease with butter.
4. Using a ladle, pour about 2¹/₂ tablespoons batter onto griddle for each pancake. When edges look dry and bubbly, turn and brown second side. Serve with butter or margarine and syrup, if you wish.

Note: Vary the amount of sugar according to your family's taste.

Variation: These pancakes can be made with all-purpose flour, with or without the addition of ¹/₄ cup wheat germ. In that case, add an extra ¹/₄ cup buttermilk and use only 1¹/₂ tablespoons sugar and 1 tablespoon butter.

Pancakes with Orange-Honey Butter

Makes about 40 three-inch pancakes or 8 servings.

1³/₄ **cups** *sifted* **all-purpose flour**
1 **teaspoon baking powder**
¹/₂ **teaspoon salt**
3 **eggs**
1 **tablespoon honey**
1¹/₂ **cups buttermilk**
1 **teaspoon baking soda**
3 **tablespoons vegetable oil**
Orange-Honey Butter *(recipe follows)*

1. Sift flour, baking powder and salt onto wax paper.
2. Beat eggs and honey in a medium-size bowl; stir in buttermilk and baking soda.
3. Add sifted dry ingredients and oil to the egg mixture and beat until smooth.
4. Drop batter by tablespoonfuls onto a lightly greased, medium-hot griddle. Brown pancakes; turn and cook other side. Serve with Orange-Honey Butter.

Orange-Honey Butter: Beat ¹/₂ cup (1 stick) softened butter or margarine, ¹/₃ cup honey and 2 tablespoons thawed, undiluted, frozen orange juice concentrate in a medium-size bowl until mixture is light and fluffy. Makes about 1 cup.

Cheese Pancakes with Pear Sauce

Makes about 9 four-inch pancakes or 3 servings.

1 **can (16 ounces) pear slices**
1 **tablespoon minced crystallized ginger**
1 **teaspoon cornstarch**
1 **tablespoon butter or margarine**
1 **container (8 ounces)** cottage cheese
1 **cup water**
1¹/₄ **cups complete pancake mix**
Melted butter or vegetable oil for frying

Drain pears, reserving ¹/₄ cup syrup. Combine pears, syrup, ginger and cornstarch in a medium-size saucepan. Cook over medium heat until thickened and bubbly. Stir in butter; keep warm.
2. Combine cottage cheese and water in container of electric blender or food processor. Cover; whirl until smooth. Stir in pancake mix.
3. Heat griddle or large skillet. Brush generously with butter or oil. Pour batter until 4-inch pancake forms. Cook until golden brown; turn and cook until firm. Serve with sauce.

Sour Cream Potato Pancakes

Makes about 2¹/₂ dozen pancakes.

2 **pounds baking potatoes (about 3 large)**
2 **eggs**
1 **small onion, grated (¹/₄ cup)**
1 **container (8 ounces) dairy sour cream**
¹/₂ **cup** *sifted* **all-purpose flour**
¹/₄ **teaspoon baking powder**
1 **teaspoon salt**
¹/₄ **teaspoon white pepper**
Vegetable oil for frying

1. Pare potatoes; shred coarsely into a large bowl of cold water. Drain, then rinse in cold running water. Squeeze firmly in clean linen toweling or cheesecloth to remove as much water as possible.
2. Beat eggs in a large bowl until frothy. Add potatoes, onion, sour cream, flour, baking powder, salt and pepper; stir.
3. Heat a ¹/₄-inch depth of oil in a large skillet. Drop potato mixture by tablespoonfuls into hot oil (add more oil as needed); flatten with pancake turner to make an even thickness. Brown on one side (about 5 to 6 minutes); turn and brown other side. Drain on paper toweling. Serve warm.

Pictured opposite:
Dilled Creamed Eggs in a
Puffy Pancake, page 370.

Low-Cal Pancakes

Makes 26 three-inch pancakes at 27 calories each.

1¼ **cups** *sifted* **all-purpose flour**	½ **teaspoon salt**
2½ **teaspoons baking powder**	1 **egg, slightly beaten**
	1¼ **cups milk**

1. Sift flour, baking powder and salt into a mixing bowl.
2. Combine egg and milk; add to flour mixture. Stir only until ingredients are moistened. Batter will be lumpy.
3. Heat a nonstick skillet or griddle until a drop of water dances on the surface. Use a measuring tablespoon to drop level tablespoons of batter on heated griddle. Bake over low heat until the surfaces of the pancakes are bubbled. Turn and bake other side.

Whole Wheat Cakes: Substitute whole wheat flour (*unsifted*) for the all-purpose flour. Makes 20 three-inch pancakes at 35 calories each.

Dilled Creamed Eggs in a Puffy Pancake

Bake at 500° for 5 minutes, then at 450° for 10 minutes.

Makes 4 servings.

10 eggs	½ **teaspoon salt**
8 bacon slices	½ **teaspoon dry mustard**
¼ **cup** (½ **stick**) **butter or margarine**	½ **teaspoon dillweed**
¾ **cup milk**	OR: 1½ **teaspoons chopped fresh dill**
¾ **cup** *unsifted* **all-purpose flour**	1½ **cups milk**
¼ **teaspoon salt**	**Dash liquid hot pepper seasoning**
2 tablespoons flour	

1. Cover 8 of the eggs with cold water in a saucepan. Bring to boiling. Remove from heat. Cover; let stand 15 minutes. Drain; rinse with cold water and peel.
2. Cook bacon until crisp in a large skillet. Drain on paper toweling and, while still warm, roll up 2 slices together into a roll that resembles a rose; make 3 more.
3. Melt butter in a medium-size saucepan. Remove from heat. Pour half of butter into 9-inch pie plate; swirl to coat bottom and side. Preheat oven to 500°. Beat the remaining 2 eggs in a small bowl with mixer at high speed until light and fluffy. Beat in ¾ cup milk, ¾ cup flour and ¼ teaspoon salt on low speed. Pour into buttered pie plate.
4. Bake in a preheated very hot oven (500°) for 5 minutes. Lower oven temperature to 450° and bake 10 minutes longer or until pancake is puffy around edges and golden brown. Keep warm in oven.
5. Stir 2 tablespoons flour, ½ teaspoon salt, mustard and dillweed into butter remaining in saucepan. Cook until bubbly. Gradually stir in 1½ cups milk. Cook until thickened and bubbly, stirring constantly. Stir in hot pepper seasoning. Remove from heat.
6. Cut 2 hard-cooked eggs into quarters; coarsely chop remainder and add to dill sauce. Spoon egg mixture into center of pancake; top with bacon roses and quartered eggs. Garnish with fresh dill, if you wish.

Fondue
The French word for "melted," fondue can be a dish of melted cheese into which cubes of bread are dipped or a dish of melted chocolate with cubes of cake and fruit. Cheese fondue is a Swiss dish which now has many variations. Fondue Bourguignonne is a misnomer, since nothing is actually melted in that recipe. Instead, cubes of steak are dunked into hot oil to cook at the table, then dipped into sauces to serve.

Cheese and Wine Fondue

Makes 6 servings.

1¼ **pounds Jarlsberg or Swiss cheese, shredded (5 cups)**	**2 whole cloves**
1 **tablespoon dry mustard**	**2 tablespoons aquavit, kirsch or vodka**
½ **teaspoon cornstarch**	1 **loaf Italian or rye bread**
½ **teaspoon ground coriander**	**Blanched vegetables such as firm flowerettes of broccoli and cauliflower**
½ **teaspoon caraway seeds, crushed**	
⅛ **teaspoon salt**	**Cubed cooked chicken breast, ham, frankfurters, etc.**
2 cups dry white wine	
1 **clove garlic**	

1. Toss shredded cheese with mustard, cornstarch, coriander, caraway seeds and salt in a large bowl.
2. Heat wine with garlic and cloves in fondue dish or flameproof casserole until bubbles start to rise from bottom. Remove garlic and cloves with slotted spoon.
3. Gradually add cheese mixture, stirring constantly with a wooden spoon after each addition, until cheese melts. Do not boil. Stir in aquavit, kirsch or vodka. Set dish over alcohol burner to keep hot while serving.
4. Cut bread into bite-size pieces. (Mix 2 or 3 different kinds of breads.) Place in a basket or on serving plates. Arrange blanched vegetables and cooked

meat on plates. Set out fondue or regular forks so everyone can spear a piece of bread, vegetable or meat, then twirl in hot cheese sauce.

Mexican Fondue

Makes 8 servings.

16 ounces Cheddar cheese, shredded (4 cups)	taste)
	1 large green pepper
16 ounces Monterey Jack cheese, shredded (4 cups)	1 large red pepper
	1 loaf sourdough or French bread
¼ cup all-purpose flour	1 clove garlic, halved
	1 can (12 ounces) beer
2 teaspoons chili powder (or more to	1 can (4 ounces) diced green chilies, drained

1. Combine Cheddar and Monterey Jack cheeses with flour and chili powder in a large bowl until well blended.
2. Halve and seed green and red peppers; cut into thin strips. Cut bread into 1-inch cubes, leaving some crust on each piece.
3. When ready to serve, rub the garlic along the inside of a ceramic fondue pot or flameproof ceramic baking dish; add beer and heat slowly, just until beer stops foaming and begins to bubble.
4. Gradually add cheese mixture, a handful at a time, stirring constantly, until cheese is melted and smooth; add green chilies. Place pan over a candle warmer and serve on a tray with pepper strips and bread chunks.

Kasha-Cheese Skillet

Broil 3 to 5 minutes.

Makes 4 to 6 servings.

1 large onion, chopped (1 cup)	1 teaspoon salt
	1 cup cottage cheese
¼ cup (½ stick) butter or margarine	1 cup frozen whole-kernel corn
1 egg, slightly beaten	4 ounces Cheddar cheese, shredded (1 cup)
1 cup medium kasha (cracked buckwheat)	2 or 3 tomatoes, cut into wedges
2 cups water	

1. Sauté onion in butter in skillet with heatproof handle, about 10 minutes.
2. Stir egg into kasha in small bowl; add to onion, stirring constantly until each grain separates. Stir in water and salt; bring to boiling. Lower heat; cover and cook 5 minutes. Remove from heat.
3. Mix in cottage cheese and corn. Sprinkle with Cheddar cheese.
4. Broil 3 to 5 minutes until cheese melts. Garnish with tomato wedges.

Herbed Cheese

A savory, easy-to-prepare cottage cheese spread.
Makes 1¼ cups.

1 container (8 ounces) cottage cheese	¼ teaspoon salt
	¾ teaspoon fresh thyme
1 package (3 ounces) cream cheese, softened	OR: ¼ teaspoon leaf basil, crumbled
1 tablespoon chopped fresh parsley	¾ teaspoon minced fresh savory
1 tablespoon chopped fresh chives	OR: ¼ teaspoon leaf savory, crumbled

Press cottage cheese through a food mill or large strainer into a medium-size bowl. Beat in cream cheese until smooth. Stir in parsley, chives, salt, thyme, basil and savory. Spoon into serving dish; cover. Refrigerate several hours or until ready to serve. Garnish with parsley sprigs and serve with crackers, if you wish.

Rarebit   Also known as Welsh rabbit, this cheese and toast dish was devised by a Welsh cook from whatever foodstuff he had on hand when he ran out of game. He may have named it "rare-bite." Whatever its name, this dish has been made for a long time in England, Scotland and Wales. Each has its own version but all agree that it's made with Cheddar cheese.

Welsh Rarebit

The cheese mixture can be prepared ahead and refrigerated for 1 to 2 days. Reheat in double boiler.

Makes 4 servings.

8 ounces shredded sharp Cheddar cheese (2 cups)	or margarine
	⅛ to ¼ teaspoon liquid hot pepper seasoning
1 tablespoon flour	
½ teaspoon dry mustard	¼ cup beer or ale
	8 slices white bread
1 tablespoon butter	

1. Combine cheese, flour, mustard, butter and pepper seasoning in a medium-size saucepan. Stir in beer. Cook over low heat, stirring constantly, until cheese is melted.
2. Trim crusts from bread. Cut bread into triangles. Toast bread on one side only.
3. Pour the melted cheese over the toasted side; serve immediately.

Frittata

A frittata is a mixture of eggs, grated cheese, cooked meat, herbs and vegetables, cooked in a skillet over very low heat. It is sometimes called an open-faced Italian omelet, although it resembles a quiche without a crust. Since a frittata is brown only on the bottom, it can be placed under the broiler to brown the top. In Italy, a frittata is served for supper, preceded by a light soup or cold cuts. It makes a delicious light lunch, accompanied by a salad and bread.

Frittata with Ham and Mozzarella

Versions of this home-style omelet abound, since any number of vegetables, cheeses and meats taste wonderful with eggs. The amounts of the additions depend entirely on what remains in your refrigerator. The method is always the same—very slow pan-cooking and a quick run under the broiler at the end.

Makes 4 servings.

6 eggs	**or margarine**
1 teaspoon salt	**4 thick slices**
1/4 teaspoon freshly	**mozzarella cheese**
ground pepper	**(from an 8-ounce**
1/2 to 1 cup freshly	**package), cut into**
grated Parmesan	**strips**
cheese	**4 slices cooked ham,**
3 tablespoons butter	**cut in strips**

1. Beat eggs in a large bowl; stir in salt, pepper and most of the grated Parmesan.
2. Melt butter in a 9-inch skillet with an ovenproof handle. When foaming subsides, add eggs and turn heat as low as possible. (Meantime, preheat the broiler.)

Ratatouille Frittata.

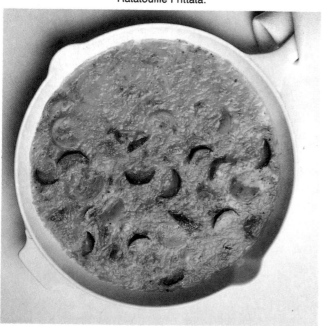

3. When eggs are partially cooked, in about 8 to 10 minutes, add mozzarella cheese strips and ham. Sprinkle remaining Parmesan over all.
4. When eggs are almost firm but not dry, slide pan under the broiler for just a minute until cheese starts to bubble. Cut into wedges and serve with hot Italian bread and a salad of sliced tomatoes, cucumber and red onions, if you wish.

Ratatouille Frittata

Makes 4 servings.

8 eggs	**frozen ratatouille,**
1/4 teaspoon salt	**thawed**
1 tablespoon butter or	**1/4 cup grated Cheddar**
margarine	**cheese**
1 package (10 ounces)	

1. Beat eggs with salt in large bowl until foamy. Set aside.
2. Melt butter in heavy ovenproof 10-inch skillet. Add ratatouille, cook until bubbly.
3. Preheat broiler.
4. Add beaten eggs to ratatouille. Cook, stirring, until eggs are almost set on top. Sprinkle with cheese.
5. Place under broiler until cheese melts, about 30 seconds. Cut into wedges.

Zucchini Frittata

A quiche-like dish without a crust that's prepared and served from one pan. Add a mixed green salad and crisp bread sticks for a light meal.

Bake at 350° for 10 minutes.

Makes 6 servings.

3 tablespoons butter	**10 eggs**
or margarine	**1/2 cup heavy cream**
1 small onion,	**1 1/4 teaspoons salt**
chopped (1/4 cup)	**1/8 teaspoon pepper**
2 small zucchini,	**1 cup diced cooked**
sliced (2 cups)	**ham**
1/2 teaspoon Italian	**1 large tomato, peeled**
herb seasoning mix	**and thinly sliced**

1. Heat butter in ovenproof 10-inch omelet pan or cast iron skillet. Add onion, zucchini and Italian seasoning. Sauté over high heat, stirring often, until zucchini is lightly browned. Remove with slotted spoon to bowl, leaving fat in pan.
2. Beat eggs, cream, salt and pepper together until blended. Pour into pan. Scatter zucchini and ham over
(continued)

eggs. Cover; cook over low heat 20 minutes or until eggs are partially set.
3. While eggs are cooking, heat oven to moderate (350°). Arrange tomato slices over frittata in single layer.
4. Bake frittata 10 minutes or until center is firm but creamy on top. Loosen frittata around sides of pan with spatula. Cut into wedges.

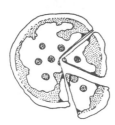

Quiche　An open-face savory baked custard tart or pie. The best known is Quiche Lorraine, which originated in Lorraine, a French province.

Quiche Lorraine

A marvelously mellow pie made with cheese, eggs, bacon and onion.

Bake crust at 425° for 5 minutes. Bake at 450° for 15 minutes, then at 350° for 15 minutes.

Makes 6 servings.

- 1/2 **package piecrust mix**
- 6 **bacon slices**
- 1 **medium-size onion, chopped (1/2 cup)**
- 8 **ounces Swiss cheese, shredded**
- **(2 cups)**
- 4 **eggs**
- 2 **cups milk**
- 1 **teaspoon salt**
- 1/4 **teaspoon ground nutmeg**
- 1/8 **teaspoon pepper**

1. Preheat oven to 425°. Prepare piecrust mix following label directions or make your own single-crust pastry recipe. Roll out to a 12-inch round on a lightly floured pastry board; fit into a 9-inch pie plate or fluted quiche dish. Trim overhang to 1/2 inch; turn under, flush with rim; flute to make a stand-up edge. Prick shell all over with fork. (For quiche dish, level pastry even with rim.)
2. Bake in a preheated hot oven (425°) for 5 minutes; remove to rack; cool slightly. Increase temperature to 450°.
3. Cook bacon in small skillet until crisp; drain on paper toweling; crumble bacon; reserve.
4. Drain off all but 1 tablespoon drippings from skillet. Sauté onion in drippings until soft. Sprinkle cheese in pastry shell; add bacon and onion.
5. Beat eggs slightly in a medium-size bowl; beat in milk, salt, nutmeg and pepper; pour into shell.
6. Bake in a preheated hot oven (450°) for 15 minutes.

Lower oven temperatures to moderate (350°); bake for 15 minutes or until center is almost set but soft. (Do not overbake; custard will set as it cools.) Let stand 15 minutes.

California Quiche

Bake at 425° for 15 minutes, then at 350° for 20 minutes.

Makes 6 servings.

- 1 **nine-inch unbaked pastry shell**
- 1 **jar (6 ounces) marinated artichoke hearts**
- 1 **small zucchini, cut in 1 × 1/4-inch sticks**
- 1 **small onion, sliced**
- 4 **eggs**
- 1 **cup heavy cream**
- 1/2 **cup milk**
- 1/2 **teaspoon leaf savory, crumbled**
- 1/2 **teaspoon salt**
- 1/4 **teaspoon pepper**
- 4 **ounces Monterey Jack cheese, shredded (1 cup)**

1. Prepare pastry shell; chill. Preheat oven to 425°. Drain artichokes, reserving 2 tablespoons of the marinade; cut artichoke hearts in half.
2. Sauté zucchini and onion in the 2 tablespoons reserved marinade in a large skillet until tender, about 5 minutes.
3. Beat eggs in a medium-size bowl until foamy. Stir in cream, milk, savory, salt and pepper.
4. Spoon zucchini mixture into pastry shell; add artichokes; then sprinkle with cheese. Pour egg and cream mixture over vegetables.
5. Bake in a preheated hot oven (425°) for 15 minutes; lower heat to moderate (350°) and bake 20 minutes longer or until the tip of a knife inserted 1 inch from edge comes out clean. Cool 15 minutes before serving.

Tomato-Broccoli Quiche

Bake at 375° for 1 hour.

Makes 8 main-dish servings or 20 appetizer servings.

- 1/2 **package piecrust mix**
- 4 **cups chopped fresh broccoli**
- 1 **medium-size onion, chopped (1/2 cup)**
- 2 **tablespoons butter or margarine**
- 2 **tablespoons water**
- 1 **cup light cream or half-and-half**
- 2 **eggs**
- 2 **ounces Swiss**
- **cheese, shredded (1/2 cup)**
- 1 **teaspoon salt**
- 1/8 **teaspoon pepper**
- 1/4 **teaspoon ground nutmeg**
- 1 **cup freshly grated Parmesan cheese**
- 1/2 **cup packaged bread crumbs**
- 3 **medium-size firm tomatoes, thinly sliced**

1. Prepare piecrust mix following label directions or

(continued)

make your own single-crust pastry recipe. Roll out to a 15 × 11-inch rectangle on a lightly floured surface; fit into an 11 × 7-inch baking dish. Turn edges under and press to sides.

2. Cook broccoli and onion, covered, in large skillet over medium heat with butter and water just until tender, about 5 minutes. Remove from heat.

3. Beat cream and eggs together in a medium-size bowl; stir in Swiss cheese, salt, pepper and nutmeg. Add broccoli mixture.

4. Combine Parmesan and bread crumbs in a small bowl.

5. Preheat oven to 375°. To assemble quiche: Sprinkle 1/3 cup Parmesan mixture on bottom of crust. Dip tomato slices on both sides in Parmesan mixture and arrange half in a layer in the crust. Pour broccoli mixture over tomatoes. Arrange remaining tomatoes, overlapping, along the long edges of quiche. Sprinkle any remaining cheese mixture on top.

6. Bake in preheated moderate oven (375°) for 1 hour or until top is puffy and knife comes out clean when inserted near center. Cool 20 minutes before cutting.

Collard Greens Quiche

Bake crust at 425° for 5 minutes, then quiche at 350° for 40 minutes.

Makes 6 servings.

1 unbaked, 9-inch, homemade pie shell OR: 9-inch, store-bought frozen, deep-dish pie shell	1/4 teaspoon leaf tarragon, crumbled
1 package (10 ounces) frozen chopped collard greens	1 1/4 cups half-and-half (half cream, half milk)
1 medium-size onion, chopped (1/2 cup)	4 eggs
1/2 cup chopped sweet green pepper	1/2 teaspoon salt
2 tablespoons butter or margarine	1/4 teaspoon pepper
	4 ounces Swiss cheese, grated (1 cup)
	1/4 teaspoon ground nutmeg

1. Preheat the oven to hot (425°).
2. Bake the pie shell in the preheated hot oven (425°) for 5 minutes. Remove to a wire rack. Lower the oven temperature to moderate (350°).
3. Cook the collard greens following the package directions. Drain well. Squeeze out the excess liquid.
4. Sauté the onion and green pepper in the butter in a large skillet until tender. Remove from the heat. Stir in the collard greens and tarragon.

5. Combine the half-and-half, eggs, salt and pepper in the container of an electric blender. Whirl until mixed.
6. Spread the collard greens mixture into the bottom of the pie shell. Sprinkle with the cheese. Stir lightly to mix. Pour the egg mixture over. Sprinkle with the nutmeg.
7. Bake in the preheated moderate oven (350°) for 40 minutes or until the mixture is set and the quiche is lightly browned on top. Let stand for 5 minutes before slicing.

Sloppy Joe Quiche

A tangy yogurt and cream custard tops the juicy Sloppy Joe filling. The filling and the pastry can be made a day ahead.

Bake crust at 400° for 15 minutes; bake pie at 375° for 30 to 40 minutes.

Makes 6 servings.

1 Pastry Shell (recipe follows)*	thyme, crumbled
1 cup finely chopped onion (1 large onion)	1/2 pound lean ground beef
1 cup finely chopped celery	1 can (8 ounces) tomato sauce
1 tablespoon vegetable oil	1 tablespoon cider vinegar
2 cloves garlic, finely chopped	1/2 teaspoon salt
3 teaspoons paprika	1/2 teaspoon pepper
1 teaspoon leaf basil, crumbled	1 cup coarsely shredded Cheddar cheese (4 ounces)
1/2 teaspoon leaf	2 eggs
	3/4 cup heavy cream
	1/2 cup plain yogurt

1. Prepare Pastry Shell dough at least 1 hour ahead or day before.
2. Preheat oven to hot (400°).
3. Roll out chilled dough on a lightly floured surface to 12-inch round. Fit into a 9-inch pie plate. Fold edge under to make stand-up edge; flute. Line crust with aluminum foil. Fill with pie weights or dried beans.
4. Bake in preheated hot oven (400°) for 10 minutes. Remove foil and weights. Bake 5 minutes longer. Remove from oven. If any bubbles have formed, flatten gently with wooden spoon. Lower oven temperature to moderate (375°).
5. Sauté onion and celery in oil in a medium-size skillet, stirring, 5 minutes. Add garlic, 2 teaspoons of the paprika, basil and thyme. Cook 1 minute. Crumble ground beef into skillet; cook until no longer pink. Drain off excess fat. Add tomato sauce. Simmer, stirring occasionally, 10 minutes. Stir in vinegar, salt and pepper.
6. Sprinkle cheese over bottom crust. Spoon meat mixture over evenly.
7. Combine the eggs, cream and yogurt in medium-size bowl. Beat with wire whisk until smooth. Pour gently over meat filling in the crust.

8. Bake quiche on baking sheet in preheated moderate oven (375°) for 30 to 40 minutes or until set and golden.

9. Cool on a wire rack 30 minutes before cutting. Sprinkle top with remaining paprika. Or, if you wish, cut a waxed paper stencil and sprinkle paprika over it to make a design on the quiche; do not let wax paper touch surface of quiche.

A pie crust mix may be substituted for the Pastry Shell. Follow package directions for single crust 9-inch pie.

Pastry Shell: Stir together 1¼ cups unsifted all-purpose flour and ½ teaspoon salt in a medium-size bowl. Cut in ¼ cup chilled unsalted butter and 2 tablespoons chilled vegetable shortening with pastry blender until mixture resembles coarse crumbs. Drizzle 3 tablespoons ice water over mixture, tossing lightly with a fork just until dough forms a ball. Flatten into a 5-inch round. Wrap tightly. Refrigerate 1 hour or overnight.

Microwave Directions:
650 Watt Variable Power Microwave Oven
Ingredient Changes: Reduce vegetable oil from 1 tablespoon to 1 teaspoon, tomato sauce from 1 can to 2/3 cup and vinegar from 1 tablespoon to 2 teaspoons.
Directions: Prepare a 9-inch pastry shell in a microwave-safe pie plate, from half of an 11-ounce box pie crust mix, following label directions. Chill. Prick bottom and sides with fork. Microwave, uncovered, at full power 4 minutes. Combine the 1 teaspoon oil, onion, celery, garlic and crumbled beef in an 11¾ × 7½ × 1¾-inch microwave-safe baking dish. Cover. Microwave at full power 6 minutes, rotating half turn after 3 minutes. Drain meat mixture well. Stir in 2 teaspoons paprika, basil, thyme, the 2/3 cup tomato sauce, the 2 teaspoons vinegar and salt and pepper. Assemble quiche as directed in steps above. Microwave, uncovered, at full power about 14 minutes, rotating quarter turn twice. Center should be almost set. Let stand at room temperature 15 minutes to set center of quiche.

Cheese Lentil Loaf

Bake at 350° for 25 minutes.

Makes 4 servings.

1 package (8 ounces) process cheese spread (loaf)	thyme, crumbled
2 cups cooked drained lentils (¾ cup raw)	½ teaspoon salt
½ small onion, finely chopped	¼ teaspoon pepper
¼ teaspoon leaf	1 cup fresh bread crumbs (2 slices)
	1 egg, slightly beaten
	1 tablespoon margarine, softened

1. Cut half the cheese into 3 slices. Cut each slice in half to make 6 strips. Shred the remaining cheese.
2. Mash the hot lentils with the back of a wooden spoon or potato masher. Cool. Combine lentils with onion, thyme, salt, pepper, bread crumbs, egg, margarine and shredded cheese. Mix well. Spread evenly in a well-greased 9-inch pie plate.
3. Bake in a moderate oven (350°) for 20 minutes.
4. Arrange cheese strips on top of the lentil mixture in a spoke pattern and bake 5 minutes more.

Italian Bean and Provolone Bake

Bake at 350° for 35 minutes.

Makes 8 servings.

½ pound piece salami, diced	¼ cup wine vinegar
1 large onion, chopped (1 cup)	2 cans (about 20 ounces each) white (cannellini) or red kidney beans, drained
2 cloves garlic, minced	
1 teaspoon leaf basil, crumbled	1 package (6 ounces) sliced Provolone cheese
1 teaspoon salt	
½ teaspoon pepper	

1. Sauté salami in a large skillet; remove with slotted spoon; drain on paper toweling. Sauté onion and garlic in pan drippings.
2. Stir in basil, salt, pepper and wine vinegar; cook 2 minutes. Stir in beans and salami; heat to bubbling. Spoon into 10-cup baking dish.
3. Bake in a moderate oven (350°) for 30 minutes; top with cheese; bake until cheese melts.

Baked Lentils with Cheese

Bake at 375° for 1 hour, 15 minutes.

Makes 8 servings.

1¾ cups dried lentils, washed	½ cup chopped green pepper
2½ quarts water (10 cups)	1 can (16 ounces) tomatoes, drained
1 bay leaf	1 tablespoon salt
2 large onions, finely chopped (2 cups)	½ teaspoon pepper
2 cloves garlic, minced	¼ teapoon leaf marjoram, crumbled
2 tablespoons vegetable oil	¼ teaspoon ground sage
2 large carrots, thinly sliced (1 cup)	¼ teaspoon leaf thyme, crumbled
½ cup thinly sliced celery	1 package (8 ounces) process cheese spread (loaf)

1. Combine lentils, water and bay leaf in a large

(continued)

suacepan; bring to boiling. Lower heat; cover; simmer 30 minutes or until lentils are tender. Drain; reserve liquid for another use. Put lentils in a shallow 13 x 9 x 2-inch baking dish.

2. Sauté onions and garlic in oil in a medium-size skillet until soft, about 5 minutes. Add to lentils with carrots, celery, green pepper, tomatoes, salt, pepper, marjoram, sage and thyme. Stir to mix. Cover with aluminum foil.

3. Bake in a moderate oven (375°) for 1 hour. Uncover. Slice cheese; layer evenly over top. Bake 15 minutes longer or until cheese melts and begins to brown. Let stand 15 minutes before serving.

Reuben Brunch Casserole

Bake at 350° for 55 minutes.

Makes 10 servings.

10 slices rye bread, cut into 3/4-inch cubes	**Swiss cheese (10 ounces)**
1 1/2 pounds cooked corned beef	**6 eggs, lightly beaten**
2 1/2 cups shredded	**3 cups milk**
	1/4 teaspoon pepper

1. Grease a 13 × 9 × 2-inch glass baking dish. Arrange the bread cubes on the bottom of the dish.

2. Coarsely shred the corned beef with a knife. Layer the meat over the bread. Sprinkle with the cheese.

3. Beat the eggs, milk and pepper in a bowl until well blended. Pour over the corned beef mixture. Cover with foil. Refrigerate overnight.

4. When ready to bake, preheat the oven to moderate (350°).

5. Bake the casserole, covered, in the preheated moderate oven (350°) for 45 minutes, then uncovered for 10 minutes, or until bubbly and puffed. Serve immediately.

Low-Calorie Reuben Brunch Casserole

We've lowered calories by using a reduced-calorie sausage, less cheese and skim milk.

Bake at 350° for 55 minutes.

Makes 10 servings.

1 pound Light Breakfast Pork and Rice Bulk Sausage, thawed and crumbled	**cubes**
	2 cups shredded Swiss cheese (8 ounces)
10 slices rye bread, cut into 3/4-inch	**6 eggs, lightly beaten**
	3 cups skim milk
	1/4 teaspoon pepper

1. Panfry the sausage in a medium-size nonstick skillet, without adding oil, for 4 minutes. Drain. Reserve.

2. Spray a 13 1/2 × 8 1/2 × 2-inch glass baking dish with nonstick vegetable cooking spray. Arrange the bread

cubes in the bottom of the prepared dish. Sprinkle the sausage over the top; sprinkle with the cheese.

3. Beat together the eggs, milk and pepper in a medium-size bowl until well blended. Pour over the sausage mixture. Cover with aluminum foil; refrigerate overnight.

4. Bake, covered, in a preheated moderate oven (350°) for 45 minutes. Uncover and bake another 10 minutes, or until puffed and bubbly. Serve immediately.

Apple Cheese Toast

Bake at 450° for 10 minutes.

Makes 2 servings.

1/4 cup (1/2 stick) butter or margarine	**softened**
2 eggs	**1 red cooking apple**
2 tablespoons milk	**1 tablespoon brown sugar**
4 slices raisin bread	**1/2 teaspoon lemon juice**
1 package (3 ounces) cream cheese,	

1. Heat butter until bubbly in jelly-roll pan while preheating oven to 450°. Spread butter evenly in pan. Remove from oven.

2. Beat 1 whole egg and 1 egg white with milk in pie plate. Dip bread slices on both sides in egg mixture until well coated. Place in buttered pan.

3. Bake in a preheated very hot oven (450°) for 5 minutes.

4. Meanwhile, combine cream cheese and remaining egg yolk in small bowl. Cut apple into quarters; remove core and cut each quarter into 4 wedges. Toss with brown sugar and lemon juice in small bowl.

5. Remove bread from oven; turn and top center of each slice with cheese mixture. Arrange apple slices on top. Bake 5 minutes more or until cheese is just set. Serve with maple-flavored syrup, if you wish.

Swiss Puff

Bake at 375° for 40 minutes.

Makes 6 servings.

4 eggs, separated	**2 tablespoons chopped fresh parsley**
4 cups hot, seasoned mashed potatoes	
8 ounces Swiss cheese, shredded (2 cups)	**2 tablespoons diced canned pimiento**
2 tablespoons finely chopped chives	**Few drops liquid hot pepper seasoning**

1. Preheat oven to 375°. Beat egg whites just until they form soft peaks in a large bowl.

2. Beat egg yolks, 1 at a time, into hot mashed potatoes in a second large bowl; stir in the cheese,

Reuben Brunch Casserole, page 378.

chives, parsley, pimiento and pepper seasoning. Fold in beaten egg whites until no streaks of white remain, spoon into a buttered, 6-cup baking dish.
3. Bake in a preheated moderate oven (375°) for 40 minutes.

Orange French Toast

Makes 3 servings.

2 eggs
1 cup buttermilk
1½ tablespoons sugar
⅛ teaspoon salt
¼ teaspoon baking soda

¼ teaspoon ground cinnamon
1 teaspoon grated orange rind
6 slices very dry bread
Butter

1. Beat eggs in a small bowl. Stir in buttermilk, sugar, salt, baking soda, cinnamon and orange rind; pour into shallow pan large enough to hold bread.
2. Soak bread for 20 minutes in egg mixture, turning once.
3. Melt some butter on griddle or skillet over medium high heat and cook bread *quickly* until lightly brown.

Turn bread over and brown other side. Serve with maple-flavored syrup, if you wish.

Cheese Strata

Bake at 325° for 1 hour.

Makes 6 servings.

8 slices sandwich-style white bread
8 ounces Cheddar cheese, shredded

(2 cups)
2 cups milk
4 eggs

1. Cut each slice of bread into 4 triangles. Arrange half of the bread triangles, points up and slightly overlapping, in a 9-inch square baking pan; sprinkle with half the cheese; top with remaining bread triangles and cheese.
2. Beat milk with eggs in a medium-size bowl. Pour over bread mixture. Cover and refrigerate overnight.
3. Bake, uncovered, in a slow oven (325°) for 1 hour or until mixture is puffy and a light golden brown. Serve immediately.

Cheese and Bean Enchiladas

Bake at 350° for 20 minutes.

Makes 4 servings.

3 tablespoons
   vegetable oil or lard
1¹/₂ tablespoons chili
   powder
1¹/₂ tablespoons flour
1¹/₂ cups water
1 teaspoon vinegar
¹/₂ teaspoon garlic
   powder
¹/₂ teaspoon onion
   powder
¹/₂ teaspoon salt
¹/₄ teaspoon leaf
   oregano, crumbled
Vegetable oil or lard

8 corn tortillas
³/₄ cup refried beans
   (from a 16-ounce
   can)
4 ounces Monterey
   Jack or Cheddar
   cheese, shredded
   (1 cup)
¹/₂ cup cottage cheese
1 medium-size onion,
   finely chopped
   (¹/₂ cup)
¹/₂ cup chopped pitted
   ripe olives

1. Heat 3 tablespoons oil, chili powder and flour in a small saucepan to make a paste. Add water gradually to make a smooth sauce; add vinegar, garlic powder, onion powder, salt and oregano. Bring to boiling; lower heat; simmer, uncovered, 3 minutes.
2. Pour vegetable oil or melt lard to depth of ¹/₄ inch in a small skillet. Holding each tortilla with tongs, quickly dip into hot fat just long enough to soften, 3 to 4 seconds. Drain on paper toweling.
3. To assemble: Place 1 tablespoon each refried beans, Jack cheese, cottage cheese, onion and olives down center of each tortilla; roll up; place, seam-side down, in shallow baking dish just large enough to hold enchiladas (13 × 9 × 2-inch). Pour sauce over enchiladas. Sprinkle with remaining cheese.
4. Bake in a moderate oven (350°) for 20 minutes or until bubbly.

Mexican Cheese Enchiladas with Beans

Bake at 375° for 20 minutes.

Makes 6 servings.

1 container (8 ounces)
   cottage cheese
¹/₂ cup dairy sour
   cream
8 ounces Monterey
   Jack cheese,
   shredded (2 cups)
¹/₄ teaspoon salt
¹/₈ teaspoon pepper
8 corn tortillas
2 cans (10 ounces
   each) mild

enchilada sauce
1 can (4 ounces)
   whole, mild green
   chilies, seeded and
   cut into long strips
1 can (20 ounces)
   white kidney
   (cannellini) beans,
   rinsed and drained
1 can (16 ounces)
   pinto beans, rinsed
   and drained

1. Mix cottage cheese with sour cream, 1 cup of the Monterey Jack cheese, the salt and pepper.

2. Steam tortillas over boiling water for 30 seconds until hot and pliable, or wrap in plastic wrap and microwave for 30 seconds on high power.
3. Pour enchilada sauce into a 2-quart rectangular casserole dish. Dip tortillas into sauce, one at a time, and place on baking sheet. Top tortillas with cheese mixture and green chilies. (You are the best judge of how many chilies to use.) Fold tortillas in half to enclose filling.
4. Add kidney and pinto beans to remaining sauce in dish. Stir to mix and top with filled tortillas. Sprinkle with remaining cheese.
5. Bake in a moderate oven (375°) for 20 minutes until bean mixture is hot and bubbly. Garnish with avocado and onion slices, if you wish.

Swiss Enchilada Casserole

Bake at 375° for 45 minutes.

Makes 6 to 8 servings.

2 cans (5 ounces
   each) chunk
   chicken
¹/₂ of a 4-ounce can
   whole green chilies,
   drained and
   coarsely chopped*
1 can (13 ounces)
   evaporated milk
1 can (8 ounces) taco
   or tomato sauce

1 dozen fresh or
   frozen corn tortillas
   (if frozen, thaw
   enough to separate)
8 ounces sharp
   Cheddar or
   pasteurized process
   cheese spread,
   shredded (2 cups)
Chopped fresh parsley
   (optional)

1. Preheat oven to 375°. Grease a 2-quart baking dish.
2. Blend the chicken with the chilies and 1 cup of the evaporated milk in a small bowl.
3. Heat taco sauce in a small skillet. Dip 3 tortillas in sauce until slightly softened and arrange in the bottom of baking dish. Spoon over a third of the chicken mixture and ¹/₂ cup of the cheese.
4. Make 2 more layers of tortillas, filling and cheese and cover the last layer with the 3 remaining tortillas. Pour over any remaining sauce and evaporated milk; sprinkle with remaining cheese; cover.
5. Bake in a preheated moderate oven (375°) for 30 minutes. Uncover; bake 15 minutes longer or until bubbly hot and browned.
6. Remove baking dish from oven; let stand 10 minutes before serving. Garnish with chopped parsley, if you wish.
For spicy food lovers, go ahead and use the whole can of chilies!

Pictured opposite:
Mexican Cheese Enchiladas with Beans.

FISH and SHELLFISH

Fish   These cold-blooded water animals can be divided into two groups: saltwater and freshwater. Saltwater fish include striped or sea bass, cod, haddock, halibut, herring, mackerel, pompano, salmon, shad, sole, sturgeon, swordfish and tuna. Freshwater fish include large- or small-mouth bass, catfish, perch, pike and trout. Fish is low-caloried and contains high-quality protein. It is also a good source of vitamin B and fluorine, iron and calcium. Saltwater fish also provides iodine.

Fish is universally used as food. Some cuisines use fish raw, while others salt and dry or smoke it. Fish roe is a prized delicacy of the sea. Caviar is the roe of sturgeon; red caviar is the roe of salmon. Shad roe is a seasonal favorite.

Wherever you live, you'll find fresh, frozen or canned fish year-round in varieties to suit every palate and pocketbook. Since many fish are, in fact, quite costly, knowing the different varieties and how to choose and prepare them can result in considerable savings.

Buying and Storing: Whenever you buy fresh fish, choose those that are clear-eyed, red-gilled, bright-skinned and sweet-smelling.

The forms of fresh fish available:

Whole Fish: This is, of course, the entire fish, no different than it was when just pulled from the water. Hence, the most work has to be done with this form before it is cooked. It must be cleaned, dressed, scaled and finned.

Drawn Fish: This form of fish has already been eviscerated, but it still must be scaled and finned before it is cooked.

Pan-dressed Fish: This is completely cleaned and dressed fish, so all you have to do is cook it.

Fish Fillets: These are sides of fish, skinned and boned, that are ready to cook.

Fish Steaks: Crosscut slices of large fish containing the backbone and vertebrae; ready to cook.

How much to buy? As a general rule, allow 1 pound whole or drawn fish for 1 serving or $1/2$ pound pan-dressed fish, fillets or steaks for 1 serving.

Fresh fish is highly perishable. It should be used within one day. Keep it refrigerated. For freezing, wrap fish in moisture-proof paper and store it up to 6 months at 0°F. Store-bought frozen fish should be solidly frozen when purchased. If thawed, use immediately. Do not refreeze.

In addition to fresh fish, there are dozens of varieties of frozen, canned and dried fish. Among the most popular: dried salt cod; canned tuna, salmon, sardines, anchovies; frozen fish fillets and sticks, frozen fish patties and fish dinners.

To Cook: Fresh or frozen fish may be cooked in a number of ways. But whichever way you choose, keep in mind that it takes little time to cook. Most often, people overcook fish. You need only cook it until the flesh is firm and has lost its translucent appearance.

To test for doneness, insert a fork into the thickest part and gently separate the flesh. It should fall into thick flakes or layers; with whole fish, the flesh should easily be freed from the backbone.

Most fresh or frozen fish can be baked, pan-fried, broiled, grilled, poached or steamed. For more information, see specific fish.

Shellfish   Divided into two categories, shellfish are either mollusks or crustaceans. Mollusks have a soft body and are partially or wholly enclosed in a single or two-part shell. Single-shelled (univalve) mollusks include the abalone, conch and periwinkle. Two-part, shelled (bivalve) mollusks are clams, mussels, oysters and scallops. Crustaceans have thin shells and segmented bodies. They include lobsters, crabs and shrimp.

In general, shellfish are low in calories, contain high-quality protein and are a good source of vitamins and minerals.

Uncooked fresh shellfish should be purchased live. Bivalve mollusks, except for scallops, should be tightly closed. Shucked mollusks should be fresh-smelling and plump with little or no liquor. Crabs and lobsters should be lively when picked up.

Keep fresh shellfish loosely wrapped and refrigerated. Cook or use shellfish within 1 day after purchase.

Orange Salmon Patties

Makes 4 servings.

1 small orange	**³/₄ teaspoon salt**
1 can (15 ¹/₂ ounces) salmon	**¹/₄ teaspoon pepper**
1 medium-size onion, minced (¹/₂ cup)	**¹/₄ cup vegetable oil**
	¹/₄ cup mayonnaise or salad dressing
1 egg	**¹/₄ cup plain yogurt**
1 cup packaged bread crumbs	**2 tablespoons orange juice**

1. Pare skin from orange (no white); section, seed and cut orange into small pieces; place in large bowl.
2. Remove bones and skin from salmon and flake into bowl with orange pieces; add onion, egg, bread

(continued)

Pictured opposite:
Flounder and Salmon Roulade, page 384.

crumbs, salt and pepper; mix lightly. (It's quickest with your hands.) Shape into 8 patties.

3. Sauté patties in hot oil in a large skillet until golden brown, turning once.

4. Combine mayonnaise, yogurt and orange juice in a small bowl; serve with patties.

Flounder and Salmon Roulade

Makes 8 servings.

1 fresh or thawed frozen salmon steak (about 1 pound)	**¹/₂ cup water**
4 fresh or thawed frozen fillets of flounder or sole (about 8 ounces each)	**¹/₂ cup dry white wine**
	2 shallots, thinly sliced
	¹/₂ teaspoon salt
	1 teaspoon leaf tarragon
2 teaspoons lemon juice	**Lobster or Crab Sauce (recipe follows)**
¹/₄ teaspoon pepper	**Fresh dill sprigs**

1. Skin and bone salmon; halve crosswise; cut each half into 4 strips.

2. Halve each flounder fillet lengthwise; sprinkle with lemon juice and pepper. Place a strip of salmon on each fillet. Roll up; secure with wooden picks.

3. Combine water, wine, shallots and salt in a large skillet. Tie tarragon in a small piece of cheesecloth; drop into skillet. Stand fish rolls in skillet.

4. Heat to boiling; lower heat; cover; simmer 5 minutes or until fish loses its translucency, becomes white and feels firm. Remove to a platter; keep warm. Cook pan liquid rapidly until reduced to ¹/₂ cup; reserve.

5. Prepare Lobster or Crab Sauce; spoon over fish; garnish with dill.

Lobster or Crab Sauce: Cook 1¹/₂ cups heavy cream rapidly in a large saucepan until reduced to 1 cup. Add reserved fish liquid, ¹/₄ teaspoon salt, ¹/₈ teaspoon paprika and 1 can (6 ¹/₂ ounces) drained, boned and coarsely shredded lobster or crab meat. Heat, stirring until hot.

Fish Bonne Femme

Makes 4 servings.

¹/₄ pound mushrooms, sliced	**butter or margarine**
2 shallots or 1 green onion, minced	**1 pound fresh or thawed, frozen flounder, perch or haddock fillets**
1 teaspoon minced parsley	
¹/₃ cup dry white wine	**¹/₂ teaspoon salt**
1¹/₂ tablespoons	**¹/₄ teaspoon pepper**

1. Combine mushrooms, shallots, parsley, wine and butter in a large skillet.

2. Cut fillets in half if they are large. Arrange on mushroom layer.

3. Sprinkle salt and pepper over fillets. Bring to boiling; lower heat; cover. Simmer 3 minutes or until fish flakes easily with a fork.

Cod Creole

Bake at 350° for 40 minutes.

Makes 6 servings.

1¹/₂ pounds frozen cod fillets, thawed	**¹/₂ teaspoon salt**
1 green pepper, seeded and chopped	**¹/₄ cup chopped pimiento-stuffed green olives**
1 medium-size onion, chopped (¹/₂ cup)	**1 can (16 ounces) tomatoes, drained; reserve juice**
¹/₂ cup sliced celery	**1 tablespoon cornstarch**
¹/₈ to ¹/₄ teaspoon cayenne	

1. Cut cod fillets into 1¹/₂-inch pieces; place in a shallow 8-cup baking dish. Spread green pepper, onion and celery in a layer over fish. Sprinkle with cayenne, salt and chopped olives.

2. Cut up tomatoes over fish. Combine cornstarch with reserved tomato juice; pour over fish in dish.

3. Bake in a moderate oven (350°) for 40 minutes or until fish flakes easily with a fork.

Codfish Cakes

Although most recipes for this New England favorite call for a higher proportion of potatoes to fish, this recipe favors a more marked texture of fish.

Makes 4 servings.

1¹/₂ pounds dried salt codfish	**or margarine**
1 small onion, sliced	**3 tablespoons heavy cream**
1 celery stalk with leaves	**¹/₂ teaspoon white pepper**
6 peppercorns	**¹/₄ teaspoon ground nutmeg (optional)**
6 medium-size potatoes	**Vegetable oil for frying**
2 eggs	**Tartar Sauce (recipe follows)**
3 tablespoons butter	

1. Cut codfish into convenient-size pieces and soak 24 hours in several changes of cold water. (Extremely salty fish must be soaked longer, up to 48 hours. It is

a good idea, therefore, to allow 2 days when planning to serve the fish cakes. After fish has soaked 24 hours, taste with the tip of your tongue and if it is still extremely salty, continue soaking until it is mild enough.)

2. Place soaked fish in an enameled or stainless steel pot with water to cover. Add onion slices, celery and peppercorns. Simmer for about 25 minutes or until fish is tender.

3. Drain well and flake fish with a fork. If fish has not been boned, do so as you flake it. If possible, buy it already boned.

4. While fish cooks, peel and boil potatoes until tender. Drain, return to empty pot and shake gently over low heat until potatoes are dry and floury. Puree with a food mill or mash finely.

5. Combine potatoes and flaked fish. Add eggs, butter, cut into small pieces, heavy cream, pepper and nutmeg. Beat with a wooden spoon until smooth and well amalgamated. Taste and add salt, if necessary.

6. Shape into 10 to 12 small cakes or 30 cocktail-size fish balls. (To shape patties without using flour or having to chill mixture, drop spoonfuls of potato-fish mixture onto wax paper and shape into patties with a spatula. Slide a broad pancake turner under patty to transfer to hot fat. Shake pancake turner several times in hot fat to remove patty from pancake turner.)

7. Fill a deep-fat fryer to a depth of 3 inches with oil. Heat oil to 375° (or until a 1-inch cube of bread browns in 25 seconds).

8. Add a few cakes at a time. Turn once so that both sides are golden brown. Total frying time should be about 4 to 5 minutes. Drain on paper towels. Serve with Tartar Sauce.

Notes: Fish cakes can be shaped in advance, but they should be fried at room temperature so that the inside will be hot before the outside has burned. Dried salt codfish is available in all Italian and Latin American neighborhoods and in many other areas as well. There is also a packaged shredded salt codfish in most supermarkets that can be soaked according to directions. Mix one 2-ounce package shredded salt cod with 1 1/2 cups mashed potatoes, 1 egg, 1 tablespoon butter or margarine and 2 teaspoons cream. Season and fry as above. Fresh cod can also be used, but the fish cakes will have less flavor and texture.

Variations: In some parts of New England, 1 teaspoon dry mustard and 1 tablespoon Worcestershire sauce are added to the mixture. In the South, minced green pepper, grated onion and minced chile peppers are added along with the mustard, and the results are like deviled crab cakes.

Tartar Sauce

Makes about 1 1/2 cups.

1 cup mayonnaise
1 hard-cooked egg, chopped
2 teaspoons minced parsley
2 teaspoons minced chives
2 teaspoons minced tarragon
1 tablespoon very finely minced onion
5 or 6 chopped pickled gherkins (preferably sour instead of sweet)
Pinch of dry mustard
Lemon juice, if necessary

1. Combine all ingredients. Thin, if necessary, with a little lemon juice.

Coulibiac   Of Russian origin, coulibiac is a fish pie often made with rice or cabbage and cooked eggs. In this country ground meat sometimes replaces the fish.

Coulibiac

Bake at 400° for 30 minutes.

Makes 10 servings.

Brioche Dough (recipe follows)
Crêpes (recipe follows)
1 large onion, chopped (1 cup)
3 tablespoons butter
1/2 pound mushrooms, sliced
2 tablespoons lemon juice
1/4 cup snipped dill
2 tablespoons chopped parsley
3 cups cooked rice (3/4 cup uncooked)
1/2 teaspoon salt
1/4 teaspoon pepper
2 salmon steaks, weighing 1 1/2 pounds, poached (see Note)
OR: 1 can (15 1/2 ounces) red salmon
5 hard-cooked eggs
1 egg white, slightly beaten
Dill
1 lemon, sliced
Sauce Mousseline (recipe follows)

1. Day before serving, make Brioche Dough. Prepare Crêpes. Chill.
2. The next day prepare filling: Sauté onion in butter 5 minutes in large skillet. Toss mushrooms with lemon juice; add to skillet, sauté 5 minutes. Remove from heat. Stir in dill, parsley, rice, salt and pepper; cool.
3. Drain salmon, remove bones and skin; break meat into small chunks. Peel eggs; cut in half lengthwise.

(continued)

4. Remove Brioche Dough from refrigerator. Turn out onto lightly floured pastry cloth; knead a few times. Roll to an 18 × 14-inch rectangle. Trim 1¹/₂ to 2 inches dough from end and reserve for decoration.

5. Overlap 4 or 5 crêpes lengthwise down center of dough; spread half of rice mixture over crêpes; arrange egg halves, then salmon on top. Spread remaining rice mixture over salmon. Top with remaining crêpes. Brush edges of pastry with lightly beaten egg white. Bring long sides over filling, 1 at a time, press edges together to seal; pinch ends together. Roll over onto lightly greased cookie sheet, sealed-side down. Form into even shape with hands; tuck ends under. Make V-shaped slits at each end of loaf for steam to escape.

6. Cut ovals or leaf shapes from reserved dough strip; decorate top of loaf. (If you wish, prepare up to this point early in the day. Cover with wax paper and a damp towel; refrigerate until about 2 hours before serving.) Cover with towel; let rise in a warm draft-free place until dough doubles in volume, 30 to 45 minutes (slightly longer if refrigerated). Preheat oven to 400°. Gently brush loaf with beaten egg white.

7. Bake in a preheated very hot oven (400°) for 30 minutes or until golden brown. Check after 20 minutes; if browning too fast, cover loosely with foil. Cool 10 to 20 minutes before slicing. Transfer to a serving platter or tray covered with a napkin. Garnish with dill and lemon. Serve with Sauce Mousseline or melted butter with lemon juice.

Note: To poach salmon, combine 1¹/₂ cups water (or half water and half white wine), 1 teaspoon salt, 1 small onion, sliced, and 1 slice lemon in a small skillet. Bring to boiling; add salmon steaks. Cover; simmer over low heat just until fish flakes easily, about 15 to 20 minutes.

Brioche Dough

¹/₂ cup very warm water	temperature
1 envelope active dry yeast	³/₄ cup (1¹/₂ sticks) very soft butter or margarine
2 tablespoon sugar	4 cups *sifted* all-purpose flour
1 teaspoon salt	
4 eggs, at room	

1. Measure very warm water into a large bowl; sprinkle in yeast. ("Very warm water" should feel comfortably warm when dropped on wrist.) Stir until yeast dissolves.

2. Add sugar, salt, eggs, butter and 2¹/₂ cups of the flour. Beat with mixer on medium speed 3 minutes, scraping sides of bowl often. Gradually beat in about ¹/₂ cup flour on low speed for 2 minutes. Stir in remaining flour, by hand, until smooth.

3. Cover bowl with wax paper, then a towel. Let rise in a warm place, away from draft, for about 1 hour or until it has doubled in volume. Refrigerate, covered, overnight.

Sauce Mousseline

Makes about 3 cups.

1 cup (2 sticks) butter or margarine	lemon juice
5 egg yolks	¹/₂ teaspoon salt
¹/₃ cup water	¹/₂ cup heavy cream, whipped
3 to 4 tablespoons	

1. Cut each stick of butter into 8 pieces.

2. Beat egg yolks in top of double boiler until smooth with a small wire whisk or rotary beater; blend in water and lemon juice. Cook over simmering, not boiling, water, stirring constantly, until mixture begins to thicken slightly, about 1 minute.

3. Add butter, 1 piece at a time, stirring constantly with wire whisk, and letting 1 piece almost melt before adding the next. After last piece is melted and sauce is smooth and thickened, remove top from double boiler; stir in salt. Taste and add more salt and lemon juice if needed.

4. Fold whipped cream into sauce. Serve immediately.

Crêpes

Makes 8 to 10 crêpes.

2 eggs	¹/₃ cup milk
¹/₂ cup all-purpose flour	1 tablespoon butter or margarine, melted
¹/₄ teaspoon salt	

1. Combine eggs, flour, salt and milk in small bowl; beat with rotary beater until smooth. Beat in butter.

2. Slowly heat 7- or 8-inch skillet until a drop of water sizzles when dropped on surface. Butter skillet lightly for the first few crêpes.

3. Pour batter, 2 to 3 tablespoons for each crêpe, into heated skillet; quickly rotate skillet to spread batter evenly. Cook over medium heat until lightly browned; turn and brown other side. Remove to plate; when cool, stack with wax paper between each.

Canned Tuna Guide

Light meat tuna—from the yellowfin, skipjack or small bluefin tuna.

White meat tuna—from the albacore tuna. Use the light meat in mayonnaise-dressed salads, casseroles or any other dish where appearance is not important. The more expensive white tuna is more attractively suited for antipasto platters and vinaigrette salads.

Three styles of canned tuna—solid-packed has large pieces of tuna; chunk tuna has about 3 chunks, filled in with small bits; and flake tuna is entirely small bits or fragments.

Nutrition—Tuna packed in water has about half the calories of tuna packed in oil. But even packed-in-oil tuna has only 200 to 300 calories per 3¹/₂ ounce

Fluffy Tuna Pâté.

serving, while providing 1/3 to 1/2 of the suggested daily protein requirement. Also available are some reduced-sodium brands which have 60% less sodium.

Fluffy Tuna Pâté

Serve as an attractive centerpiece for a luncheon buffet.

Makes 12 servings.

**5 slices bacon
2 packages (8 ounces each) cream cheese, softened and cut into pieces
2 cans (7 ounces each) tuna packed in water, drained and flaked
2 tablespoons dry white wine**

**2 tablespoons lemon juice
1 tablespoon soy sauce
1 teaspoon dillweed
2 tablespoons parsley
Lettuce leaves
Olive slice
Crackers and/or raw vegetables for dipping**

1. Fry bacon in a small skillet until crisp. Drain on paper toweling. Reserve 1 piece for garnish. Crumble the remaining 4 pieces.
2. Beat together the cream cheese, tuna, wine, lemon juice, soy sauce and dillweed in a medium-size bowl until smooth. Stir in parsley and crumbled bacon.

3. Generously oil a 3-cup fish mold or 3-cup bowl. Allow a slight pool of oil to run to the bottom of the mold. Pack fish mixture into the prepared mold; unmold immediately onto a lettuce-lined plate.
4. Use an olive slice for the eye; cut up reserved bacon slice for scales. Serve with crackers and/or raw vegetables.

Hot Tuna Bake

A wonderful combination of tuna and mozzarella cheese, accented with onion and green pepper.

Bake at 375° for 45 minutes.

Makes 4 servings.

**8 slices firm whole wheat or white bread, lightly toasted
1 can (7 ounces) tuna, drained
1/4 cup chopped green pepper
1 small onion, diced**

**(1/4 cup)
3/4 teaspoon salt
4 ounces mozzarella cheese, shredded (1 cup)
2 eggs
2 cups milk
1/2 teaspoon leaf oregano, crumbled**

1. Place 4 slices bread in buttered 6-cup shallow baking dish.

(continued)

2. Combine tuna, green pepper, onion and $1/4$ teaspoon of the salt in a small bowl. Stir in half the shredded cheese. Spread over bread. Top with remaining 4 slices bread.

3. Beat eggs in medium-size bowl. Stir in milk, remaining $1/2$ teaspoon salt and oregano. Pour milk mixture over bread; sprinkle with remaining cheese. Cover and refrigerate at least 1 hour or overnight. Press bread down into milk before baking.

4. Bake in a moderate oven (375°) for 45 minutes or until puffed and golden. Remove from oven. Let stand 10 minutes before serving.

Tuna and Cheese Beanburgers

Makes 6 servings.

5 tablespoons butter or margarine	$1/2$ cup chopped sweet gherkins
1 medium-size onion, chopped ($1/2$ cup)	1 can ($6^1/2$ or 7 ounces) tuna, drained and flaked
1 can (16 ounces) red kidney beans, drained	Salt Pepper Flour
2 cups fresh bread crumbs (4 slices)	6 slices process American cheese
1 egg, well beaten	

1. Melt 1 tablespoon butter in a saucepan over low heat; add onion and cook until tender.

2. Mash kidney beans in a large bowl; add onion, bread crumbs, egg, gherkins, tuna, salt and pepper; mix well. Shape tuna mixture into 6 patties and dredge with flour.

3. Melt the remaining butter in skillet. Add patties and cook on both sides until browned. Place 1 slice cheese over each pattie; cover and cook until cheese is melted.

Tuna Croquettes à l'Indienne

Makes 4 servings.

$1/4$ cup ($1/2$ stick) butter or margarine	cheese, shredded (1 cup)
1 medium-size onion, chopped ($1/2$ cup)	2 eggs, slightly beaten 2 tablespoons chopped parsley
$1/2$ cup chopped green pepper	$1/2$ teaspoon salt
2 teaspoons curry powder	$1/4$ teaspoon pepper $1/4$ cup all-purpose flour
2 cans (7 ounces each) tuna, drained and flaked	$1/2$ cup packaged bread crumbs
2 cups fresh bread crumbs (about 4 slices)	1 egg 1 tablespoon water $1/4$ cup melted butter or vegetable oil
4 ounces Cheddar	

1. Melt butter in a medium-size skillet; add onion, green pepper and curry powder; sauté until onion is

transparent, about 5 minutes. Turn into a large mixing bowl.

2. Add tuna, fresh bread crumbs, cheese, eggs, parsley, salt and pepper; mix thoroughly.

3. Divide tuna mixture into 8 equal portions; shape each portion into an oblong shape.

4. Place flour and bread crumbs on 2 pieces of wax paper. Beat egg and 1 tablespoon water in a pie plate.

5. Roll each croquette in flour; coat evenly with egg; roll in bread crumbs. Place each finished croquette on a plate or cookie sheet. Cover with wax paper. Refrigerate until ready to cook.

6. To cook, sauté the croquettes in hot butter or vegetable oil until nicely browned on all sides. Serve on a bed of cooked rice with mushroom, Mornay or curry sauce, and garnished with lemon slices and fresh parsley, if you wish.

Tuna Aioli

Makes 4 servings.

1 cup mayonnaise	each) tuna, drained
2 large cloves garlic, minced	1 can (20 ounces) chick-peas, drained
1 tablespoon lemon juice	1 can (16 ounces) sliced beets, drained
$1/4$ teaspoon dry mustard	4 carrots, pared and sliced
1 package (9 ounces) frozen Italian green beans	1 red or white onion, thinly sliced
2 cans (7 ounces	

1. Blend mayonnaise with garlic, lemon juice and mustard. If possible, cover sauce; refrigerate 30 minutes before serving. Cook green beans following label directions; cool.

2. Arrange tuna and vegetables (vegetables can be heated, chilled or served at room temperature) on a serving platter and serve with garlic (aioli) sauce.

Tuna Rarebit Pie

Bake at 350° for 40 minutes.

Makes 6 servings.

$1/2$ package piecrust mix	4 eggs, beaten 1 cup milk
4 ounces sharp Cheddar cheese, shredded (1 cup)	$1/2$ teaspoon Worcestershire sauce
1 can ($6^1/2$ ounces) chunk-style tuna, drained and flaked	$1/4$ teaspoon dry mustard
$1/3$ cup thinly sliced green onions	$1/4$ teaspoon paprika Dash liquid hot pepper seasoning

1. Prepare piecrust mix following label directions. Roll out to an 11-inch round. Line a 9-inch foil pie plate with pastry. Pinch to form a standing edge; flute.

2. Preheat oven to 350°. Place cheese, tuna and green onions in prepared pastry shell.

3. Combine eggs, milk, Worcestershire, mustard, paprika and liquid hot pepper seasoning in a small bowl. Pour into shell.

4. Bake in a preheated moderate oven (350°) for 40 minutes or until knife inserted near center comes out clean. Let stand 10 minutes before cutting.

Note: May be reheated in a moderate oven (350°) for 10 minutes.

Sarasota Fish Steaks

Broil or grill for 8 minutes.

Makes 4 to 6 servings.

¹/₄ **cup lime juice**	¹/₂ **teaspoon salt**
3 **tablespoons vegetable oil**	¹/₄ **teaspoon pepper**
1 **teaspoon instant minced onion**	2 **packages (12 ounces each) frozen halibut or cod steaks,**
1 **teaspoon dillweed**	**thawed**

1. Combine lime juice, oil, onion, dillweed, salt and pepper in a small cup; allow to stand 15 minutes.

2. Place steaks on broiler pan. Brush fish generously on both sides with lime-juice mixture.

3. Broil or grill for 8 minutes or just until fish flakes easily, turning once and brushing with remaining sauce.

Fillets of Sole in Cucumber Sauce

This unusual sauce is also excellent served with baked whole fish.

Makes 6 servings.

2 **large cucumbers (1¹/₂ pounds)**	1¹/₂ **pounds fillet of sole**
4 **tablespoons (¹/₂ stick) butter**	¹/₂ **teaspoon salt**
³/₄ **cup heavy cream**	¹/₈ **teaspoon fresh ground pepper**
¹/₂ **teaspoon salt**	**Flour**
¹/₈ **teaspoon pepper**	2 **tablespoons minced fresh parsley**
2 **tablespoons lemon juice**	

1. Pare cucumbers; halve lengthwise and scoop out seeds with tip of teaspoon. Cut crosswise into ¹/₄-inch slices.

2. Sauté cucumber in 2 tablespoons of the butter in a large skillet until lightly browned, about 2 minutes. Stir in the cream, ¹/₂ teaspoon salt, ¹/₈ teaspoon pepper and lemon juice. Cook mixture, stirring constantly, until it is reduced and coats the spoon heavily.

3. Sprinkle the fish with the remaining salt and pepper. Dredge lightly in flour, shaking off the excess.

4. Heat remaining butter in a large skillet. Sauté fish 2 to 3 minutes on each side, turning carefully with a large spatula. Transfer fish to a warm serving platter.

5. Reheat cucumber sauce. Spoon sauce over fish; garnish with parsley.

Napa Valley Kabobs

Broil or grill 10 minutes.

Makes 4 servings.

2 **small zucchini**	2 **tablespoons vegetable oil**
¹/₂ **teaspoon leaf basil, crumbled**	1 **package (1 pound) frozen cod, haddock or turbot fillets**
3 **tablespoons dry red wine**	
¹/₄ **cup bottled barbecue sauce**	4 **cherry tomatoes**

1. Wash zucchini; cut each into 1-inch-thick slices. Cook in boiling salted water 5 to 8 minutes or just until tender. Drain.

2. Soak basil in wine in a cup for 5 minutes; stir in barbecue sauce and oil until well blended.

3. Cut frozen fish into 8 cubes with a large sharp knife. (If fish is too hard, let stand at room temperature just until it begins to thaw.)

4. Thread frozen fish cubes and zucchini onto 4 medium-size skewers. Brush well with barbecue sauce. Place on broiler pan.

5. Broil or grill, turning and basting once, 10 minutes; thread a cherry tomato onto each before serving.

Broiled Saucy Fish Fillets

Makes 6 to 8 servings.

2 **pounds fresh or thawed frozen flounder or sole fillets**	2 **tablespoons lemon juice**
	3 **tablespoons grated Parmesan cheese**
2 **tablespoons drained prepared horseradish**	¹/₃ **cup plain yogurt**
	2 **tablespoons unsalted butter or margarine, melted**
2 **tablespoons Dijon mustard**	

1. Arrange the fish in a single layer in a foil-lined broiler pan.

2. Combine horseradish, mustard, lemon juice, Parmesan cheese and yogurt in a small bowl. Add butter; stir until smooth. (Mixture should be firm, but spreadable.) Spread the mixture over the fillets in a thin even layer.

3. Broil for about 4 minutes or until the fish is just cooked through and the sauce is bubbly and slightly glazed. (Timing depends on the thickness of the fillets. Do not overcook.)

Steamed Fish

Makes 4 servings.

1 package (1 pound)
  frozen flounder
  fillets, thawed
  OR: 2 packages
  (10 ounces each)
  frozen trout (2 to a
  package), thawed
4 medium-size
  mushrooms, sliced
1 bacon slice, cooked
  and crumbled
4 green onions,
  chopped
1 small celery stalk,
  chopped
1 thin slice fresh
  ginger, chopped
  OR: 1/2 teaspoon
  ground ginger
1 tablespoon dry white
  wine
1 teaspoon soy sauce
1 teaspoon
  Worcestershire
  sauce
Dash liquid hot pepper
  seasoning

1. Place the fillets or trout on a large heatproof plate that will fit inside a steamer.
2. Combine mushrooms, bacon, onions, celery and ginger in a small bowl. Sprinkle mixture over the fillets or trout.
3. Combine wine, soy sauce, Worcestershire and hot pepper seasoning in a cup. Spoon over fish.
4. To make a steamer, put 3 custard cups with a wire rack on top inside a large pot. Add 1 inch water. Cover; bring to boiling.
5. Place plate of fish on rack. Cover and steam over low heat for 15 minutes or until fish flakes easily.

Tuna Peppers

Makes 4 servings.

4 medium-size sweet
  green or red
  peppers
1 can (7 ounces) tuna
  packed in olive oil,
  drained and flaked
2 hard-cooked eggs,
  chopped
1/2 cup chopped fresh
  parsley
1/2 teaspoon leaf basil,
  crumbled
1/4 teaspoon pepper
3 tablespoons lemon
  juice
8 thin slices
  mozzarella cheese

1. Wash and dry peppers; place on foil-lined broiler pan.
2. Broil 5 inches from heat for 8 minutes, turning until all sides are charred. Remove from broiler and wrap in a clean towel to steam for 1 minute. Mix tuna, eggs, parsley, basil, pepper and juice in a bowl.
3. Cut peppers in half lengthwise; remove and discard seeds. Stuff peppers with tuna mixture, mounding high. Top each with 1 slice cheese.
4. Broil 5 inches from heat for 2 minutes or until cheese melts.

Skillet Tuna Chowder

Makes 4 servings.

1 can condensed New
  England-style clam
  chowder
1 1/2 cups light cream
1 package (10 ounces)
frozen peas with
  sliced mushrooms
1 can (7 ounces) tuna,
  undrained

Combine clam chowder with light cream in a large skillet; stir in peas with mushrooms. Heat slowly, stirring occasionally, 5 minutes. Add tuna in chunks; heat thoroughly.

Tuna Turnovers with Mushroom Cheese Sauce

Bake at 400° for 20 minutes.

Makes 8 turnovers.

1 medium-size onion,
  finely chopped
  (1/2 cup)
2 tablespoons butter
1 can (9 1/4 ounces)
  tuna, drained
1 egg yolk, lightly
  beaten
1 can (3 to 4 ounces)
  chopped
  mushrooms,
  drained
1/4 cup chopped
  pimiento-stuffed
  olives
2 ounces Swiss
cheese, shredded
  (1/2 cup)
1/4 teaspoon salt
1/8 teaspoon pepper
1 package (17 1/4
  ounces) pre-rolled
  frozen puff pastry
1 egg white, lightly
  beated
Mushroom Cheese
  Sauce (*recipe
  follows*)
1/4 cup sliced
  pimiento-stuffed
  olives

1. Sauté onion in butter in a small skillet until tender, about 3 minutes. Cool to room temperature. Flake tuna into a medium-size bowl. Stir in onion, egg yolk, mushrooms, chopped olives, cheese, salt and pepper. Blend mixture well. Refrigerate until cold.
2. Thaw frozen pastry sheets 20 minutes at room temperature or until pliable, but still very cold. Roll out each sheet on a lightly floured surface to a 13-inch square; divide into 4 equal quarters; repeat with second sheet.
3. Divide filling equally among the 8 pastry squares, leaving a 1-inch border of uncovered pastry on all sides. Brush borders generously with some of the beaten egg white. Fold squares diagonally in half to form triangles. Press edges firmly together, then press with tines of fork to seal securely. Brush tops with egg white. Pierce each top in center with small paring knife to allow steam to escape. Arrange pies 1 inch apart on cookie sheets. Place in freezer while oven heats. Preheat oven to 450°.
4. Immediately lower temperature to hot (400°). Bake turnovers for 20 minutes.

(continued)

From top: Tuna Aioli, page 388; Hot Nachos Salad, page 696; Swiss Enchilada Casserole, page 380.

5. Spoon Mushroom Cheese Sauce over each; garnish with olives.

Mushroom Cheese Sauce: Combine 1 can condensed cream of mushroom soup, 1/2 cup shredded Swiss cheese, 2 dashes liquid hot pepper seasoning and 1/4 cup dry white wine in a medium-size saucepan. Cook, stirring, until cheese melts.

Oven-Fried Fish

Bake at 475° for 8 minutes.

Makes 4 servings.

2 tablespoons plain yogurt	**1 package (1 pound) frozen flounder or sole fillets, thawed**
1 tablespoon vegetable oil	**1 teaspoon seasoned salt**
1 1/2 teaspoons lemon juice	**1/2 teaspoon pepper**
1/4 cup packaged bread crumbs	**Paprika**

1. Spray a nonstick cookie sheet or shallow baking pan liberally with vegetable cooking spray (or wipe with vegetable oil).
2. Preheat oven to 475°. Combine yogurt, oil and juice in a shallow dish; mix well. Sprinkle bread crumbs on wax paper.
3 Dip fillets in the yogurt mixture, then press into the crumbs, lightly coating both sides.
4. Arrange fish in a single layer on the cookie sheet. Sprinkle with salt, pepper and paprika.
5. Bake, uncovered, in a preheated very hot oven (475°) for 8 minutes or longer depending on thickness of the fillets. Do not turn fillets. Fish is done when coating is golden and fish flakes easily.

Salmon Timbales

Bake at 325° for 30 minutes.

Makes 4 servings.

1 can (15 1/2 or 16 ounces) red salmon, drained and flaked	**1/2 cup chopped celery**
	1/2 cup plain dry bread crumbs
1 medium-size onion, chopped (1/2 cup)	**1/4 cup plain yogurt**
	1/4 cup mayonnaise
1 small sweet green pepper, halved, seeded and chopped (1/2 cup)	**1 egg, slightly beaten**
	1/4 teaspoon pepper
	Cucumber-Dill Sauce (recipe follows)

1. Preheat the oven to slow (325°). Generously grease four 6-ounce custard cups.
2. Combine salmon, onion, green pepper, celery, bread crumbs, yogurt, mayonnaise, egg and pepper in bowl. Stir until well blended. Divide mixture evenly among prepared custard cups; pack well. Arrange on a small cookie sheet.

3. Bake in the preheated slow oven (325°) for 30 minutes or until salmon mixture begins to pull away from sides of cups.
4. Meanwhile, prepare Cucumber-Dill Sauce.
5. To unmold timbales, run small knife around edge of each cup. Invert onto serving dish. Spoon Cucumber-Dill Sauce over tops. Garnish with sprigs of dill, if you wish.

Cucumber-Dill Sauce: Stir together 1/2 cup mayonnaise, 1/4 cup dairy sour cream, 1/4 cup plain yogurt, 3/4 cup finely chopped seeded cucumber, 1/4 cup finely chopped onion and 1 tablespoon chopped fresh dill, or 1 teaspoon dillweed in saucepan. Heat over very low heat just until warmed through.

Microwave Directions for Salmon Timbales: 650 Watt Variable Power Microwave Oven

Directions: Assemble the salmon mixture as directed in the recipe. Pack into 4 well-greased 6-ounce microwave-safe custard cups. Place on microwave-safe plate. Cover each with plastic wrap; cut slits for vents. Microwave at full power 2 minutes. Rotate plate a quarter turn. Microwave at full power 2 more minutes or until top feels firm to the touch. Let stand, covered, 5 minutes. Combine sauce ingredients in small microwave-safe bowl or 2-cup glass measure. Microwave at full power 2 minutes, stirring once. Unmold timbales and serve as directed in recipe.

Grilled Alaska Salmon

Here's an easy and flavorful way to prepare salmon.
Grill for 10 minutes.

Makes 6 servings.

6 salmon steaks (about 7 ounces each), cut 1 inch thick	**onion**
	1 teaspoon grated lemon rind
	1/2 teaspoon liquid red-pepper seasoning
Salt and pepper	
6 tablespoons butter or margarine, melted	**Fresh dill sprigs (optional)**
	Lemon wedges (optional)
1/4 cup lemon juice	
1 tablespoon grated	

1. Build a hot fire, or set an electric or a gas grill to high, following the manufacturer's directions.
2. Rinse the salmon steaks and pat dry with paper toweling. Season lightly with the salt and pepper. Place the steaks on a sheet of greased heavy-duty aluminum foil on the grill rack.

3. Combine the melted butter or margarine, lemon juice, onion, lemon rind and red pepper sauce in a small bowl; brush the steaks with some of the butter mixture.

4. Grill, 4 inches from the heat, 5 minutes on each side or until the fish flakes easily when tested with a fork, basting often. Garnish with the fresh dill and the lemon wedges, if you wish.

Baked Salmon and Green Bean Puff

Bake at 375° for 50 minutes.

Makes 4 servings.

1 package (9 ounces) frozen cut green beans	mustard
2 tablespoons water	1 tablespoon minced drained capers
1 can (15 1/2 ounces) salmon	1 tablespoon caper juice
1 can condensed Cheddar cheese soup	1/8 teaspoon pepper
2 tablespoons flour	**Soufflé Topping:**
1 tablespoon grated Parmesan cheese	4 eggs, separated
1/2 teaspoon dillweed	1/4 teaspoon salt
1 tablespoon prepared spicy brown	1/4 teaspoon dillweed
	Pinch pepper
	2 tablespoons grated Parmesan cheese

1. Cook beans in water in a small covered saucepan over moderate heat, about 5 minutes until tender but still crisp.

2. Meanwhile, drain and flake the salmon, discarding any large bones or pieces of skin. Blend 1/4 cup of the soup with the flour, then combine with the remaining soup; mix in grated Parmesan, dillweed, mustard, minced capers, caper juice and pepper.

3. Drain beans well and place in an 8-cup soufflé dish. Add salmon and cheese soup mixture; stir well to mix. Bake, uncovered, in a moderate oven (375°) for 20 minutes.

4. When casserole has baked almost 20 minutes, prepare Soufflé Topping. Beat egg whites with salt to soft peaks; beat yolks with dillweed and pepper until smooth, then stir in grated Parmesan. Spoon a little beaten whites into yolk mixture, then pour yolks over whites and fold in gently until no streaks of white or yellow show. Spoon quickly on top of hot beans and salmon, return to oven and bake 30 minutes longer until puffy and touched with brown. Serve immediately.

Baked Salmon with Sour Cream Dill Sauce

Bake at 375° for about 1 hour.

Makes 8 servings.

1 center-cut fresh salmon steak (3 1/2 to 4 pounds)	1/2 teaspoon leaf tarragon, crumbled, OR: 6 sprigs fresh tarragon
2 tablespoons chopped shallots	1 teaspoon salt
2 stalks fresh dill	Sour Cream Dill Sauce (recipe follows)
1/4 cup dry white wine	

1. Preheat oven to 375°. Rinse fish in cold water; pat dry with paper toweling. Tear off piece of heavy-duty aluminum foil large enough to enclose fish. Place fish in center of foil; fold up sides. Place 1 tablespoon of the shallots and 1 stalk of the dill on fish.

2. Combine wine, tarragon, salt, remaining shallots and dill in a small saucepan. Simmer until reduced by half; pour over the fish. Close the foil tightly. Place fish packet in a baking pan.

3. Bake in a preheated oven (375°) for 20 to 25 minutes per pound. Serve with Sour Cream Dill Sauce.

Sour Cream Dill Sauce: Combine 1 cup dairy sour cream, 1/4 cup mayonnaise, 2 tablespoons chopped fresh dill, 1 tablespoon drained capers, 1 teaspoon lemon juice, 1/2 teaspoon salt and 1/4 teaspoon freshly ground pepper in a small bowl. Refrigerate until serving time. Makes 1 1/4 cups.

Poached Salmon Steaks

Makes 4 servings.

1 large lemon, cut in 6 slices	1/2 teaspoon salt
2 slices onion	3 peppercorns
1 bay leaf	4 salmon steaks, each cut 1-inch thick

1. Fill a large skillet half full with water; season with 2 of the lemon slices, onion slices, bay leaf, salt and peppercorns; bring to boiling.

2. Place salmon steaks in the pan; cover. Simmer over low heat for 15 minutes or until fish just flakes. Drain.

3. Transfer to warm plates. Serve with hollandaise sauce, if you wish. Garnish with remaining lemon slices.

Salmon Mousse with Cucumber Dressing

Makes 4 servings.

1 can (15½ ounces) red salmon
2 tablespoons white wine vinegar
2 envelopes unflavored gelatin
½ cup boiling water
1 small onion, quartered

½ cup mayonnaise
1 container (8 ounces) plain yogurt
¼ cup coarsely cut fresh dill
¾ teaspoon salt
¼ teaspoon cayenne
Cucumber Dressing (recipe follows)

1. Combine juice from salmon, vinegar and gelatin in the container of a food processor; add boiling water. Process 40 seconds.
2. Add onion, mayonnaise, yogurt, dill, salt, cayenne and salmon. (Remove and discard any dark skin from salmon.) Process until smooth, about 30 seconds.
3. Pour mixture into an 8 × 8 × 2-inch pan or a 4-cup shallow mold. Place pan or mold in coldest part of your freezer to chill quickly, 20 to 30 minutes, depending on how cold the freezer is. If you have more time, refrigerate 2 to 3 hours or until firm. Slice and serve on bed of crisp lettuce with Cucumber Dressing.

Cucumber Dressing: Combine ½ cup plain yogurt, ¼ cup sour cream, ¼ cup chopped green onion, ½ teaspoon salt and 1 small cucumber, peeled, seeded and diced (1 cup), in small bowl. Makes 1 cup.

Baked Red Snapper

Bake at 350° for 35 minutes.

Makes 8 servings.

1 whole red snapper (about 4 pounds), cleaned and ready to cook
2 teaspoons salt
1 cup chopped green onions
2 tablespoons vegetable oil
¼ cup chopped fresh parsley
1 teaspoon grated lemon rind
½ teaspoon leaf

oregano, crumbled
⅛ teaspoon pepper
2 tablespoons lemon juice
½ cup saltine cracker crumbs
¼ cup (½ stick) butter or margarine
¾ cup dry white wine
1 lemon, sliced
1 medium-size onion, sliced
2 small tomatoes, sliced

1. Wash fish; pat dry with paper toweling. Sprinkle fish inside and out with salt. Preheat oven to 350°.
2. Sauté green onions in oil in small skillet for 2 minutes; stir in parsley, rind, oregano, pepper and juice.
3. Spread half of onion mixture in bottom of baking pan which holds fish snugly. Place fish on onion mixture; spread remaining mixture on top. Sprinkle with cracker crumbs; dot with butter. Pour wine into pan.
4. Bake in preheated moderate oven (350°) for 15 minutes. Arrange lemon and onion slices alternately on top of fish and tomato slices on both sides; brush with pan juices. Bake 20 minutes longer or until fish flakes easily.

Wine-Marinated Halibut

Firm fish, such as halibut, is excellent for grilling whole or as kabobs.

Grill for 16 minutes.

Makes 6 servings.

6 halibut steaks, cut about 1 inch thick
½ cup dry white wine
¼ cup olive or vegetable oil
1 tablespoon white wine vinegar
1 tablespoon lime juice
1 tablespoon minced

green onion
1 tablespoon minced parsley
1 clove garlic, crushed
½ teaspoon salt
½ teaspoon leaf oregano, crumbled
⅛ teaspoon freshly ground pepper

1. Place the halibut steaks in a single layer in a large, shallow glass dish.
2. Combine the wine, oil, vinegar, lime juice, green onion, parsley, garlic, salt, oregano and pepper in a small bowl. Pour over the halibut; cover with plastic wrap; refrigerate for several hours or overnight. Drain and reserve the marinade.
3. Build a medium-hot fire, or set an electric or a gas grill to medium-hot following the manufacturer's directions.
4. Grill, 3 inches from the heat, basting often, for 8 minutes per side or until the fish flakes easily when tested with a fork.

Note: You may substitute another firm fish, such as red snapper or cod, for the halibut in this recipe.

Suggested Variation: Halibut Kabobs—Makes 6 servings. Cut the halibut into chunks; discard the skin and bones. Proceed with the recipe above. Just before grilling, thread the halibut on six long metal skewers, alternating with cherry tomatoes, green pepper squares and fresh mushrooms. Grill over medium-hot coals for 8 to 10 minutes, turning once and basting frequently with the marinade.

Grill Fish by the Thickness
For perfectly cooked salmon or any other firm fish, grill 10 minutes per inch of thickness measured at its thickest part.

Grilled Whole Fish

Makes 12 servings.

2 whole dressed red
  snappers, striped
  bass or haddock
  (each weighing 3 to
  4 pounds)
1/3 cup soy sauce
1/3 cup dry sherry
1/4 cup lemon juice
2 tablespoons

vegetable oil
1 tablespoon finely
  chopped fresh
  ginger
1 tablespoon sugar
6 green onions, sliced
Lemon slices
Green onions, cut into
  1-inch pieces

1. Make several diagonal incisions in both sides of
fish. Place in shallow dish.
2. Combine soy sauce, sherry, lemon juice, oil,
ginger, sugar and onions; pour over fish. Marinate,
turning fish several times, 1 hour at room
temperature; insert pieces of lemon and green onion
in slits on both sides. Place fish in a greased hinged
broiler.
3. Grill fish over hot coals 4 inches from heat 10 to
15 minutes on each side, brushing several times with
marinade or until fish flakes when pierced with a
fork. (Fish can be broiled, using a greased broiler
pan.) Transfer to heated serving platter. Serve with
rice, if you wish.

Italian Fish Stew

*Five kinds of fish and shellfish simmer together in a
smooth tomato-wine sauce for this Italian provincial
stew. Serve it with crispy buttered bread.*

Makes 8 servings.

1/2 cup olive oil
1 clove garlic,
  chopped
1 tablespoon leaf
  basil, crumbled
1 medium-size onion,
  chopped (1/2 cup)
1/2 teaspoon crushed
  red pepper
1/2 cup dry white wine
1 can (35 ounces)
  plum tomatoes
2 tablespoons tomato
  paste
1 bottle (8 ounces)
  clam broth or juice
2 teaspoons salt
1 package (1 pound)
  frozen cod fillets,
  thawed

1 package (1 pound)
  frozen haddock
  fillets, thawed
1 package (12 ounces)
  halibut steak,
  thawed
1/2 pound scallops
1/2 pound fresh or
  frozen shrimp,
  shelled and
  deveined
2 tablespoons
  tubettini or other
  small pasta
2 tablespoons finely
  chopped fresh
  parsley
1 tablespoon grated
  lemon rind

1. Heat oil in a heavy kettle or Dutch oven; sauté
garlic, basil, onion and crushed red pepper until
onion is tender. Add wine; simmer about 5 minutes
or until liquid is somewhat reduced. Add tomatoes,
tomato paste, clam broth and salt; simmer,
uncovered, for 20 to 30 minutes to thicken sauce.
2. Leave fish fillets in blocks, cut into large pieces.
Cut halibut steak into 4 pieces, through bones. If
scallops are large, cut in half. Add all fish and
shellfish to sauce. Cover; simmer 10 minutes or until
fish is just done (it will look opaque).
3. Remove fish to serving dish; keep warm. Add
pasta to sauce. Cover; simmer 10 minutes longer or
until pasta is tender. Pour over fish in serving dish;
garnish with chopped parsley and grated lemon rind.
Stew may be ladled over slices of Italian bread
rubbed with garlic for a heartier dish.

Broiled Paprika Halibut

Makes 6 servings.

6 halibut steaks,
  (about 2 pounds)
  cut about 3/4-inch
  thick
3 tablespoons butter
  or margarine,

melted
Paprika
Salt and pepper
1 lemon, cut in
  wedges

1. Place the halibut steaks in a single layer on
buttered broiler pan; brush with about half the melted
butter; sprinkle with paprika, salt and pepper.
2. Broil about 6 inches from heat for 8 to 10 minutes;
turn; brush with remaining butter. Sprinkle again with
paprika, salt and pepper. Broil 8 to 10 minutes longer
or until halibut flakes easily. Serve with lemon.

Halibut Steaks Meunière

*A handy sauce mix does double-duty in this quick fish
sauté.*

Makes 4 servings.

1 1/2 pounds fresh or
  frozen halibut
  steaks, partially
  thawed
1 envelope
  (1 1/2 ounces) white

sauce mix
1/4 cup butter or
  margarine
1/4 cup lemon juice
2 tablespoons sliced
  almonds, toasted

1. Sprinkle halibut steaks with white sauce mix.
2. Melt 2 tablespoons of the butter or margarine in a
large skillet; sauté halibut steaks 3 minutes on each
side or until they flake easily.
3. Add the remaining butter or margarine to skillet; stir
in lemon juice. Heat a few minutes. Sprinkle with
almonds.

Marjoram Poached Halibut

A tasty marjoram-flavored sauce transforms and enhances the fish flavor; even fish-haters will like this dish.

Makes 4 servings.

2 leeks, chopped
  OR: 2 large onions, chopped (2 cups)
2 cloves garlic, minced
¼ cup (½ stick) butter or margarine
1 can (35 ounces) plum tomatoes

1 tablespoon chopped fresh marjoram
  OR: 1 teaspoon leaf marjoram, crumbled
1 teaspoon salt
¼ teaspoon pepper
4 halibut steaks (4 ounces each)

1. Sauté leeks and garlic in butter in a large skillet until soft. Drain liquid from tomatoes into skillet; cook, stirring often, until liquid is reduced by half.
2. Stir in tomatoes, marjoram, salt and pepper, breaking up tomatoes with the back of a wooden spoon.
3. Place fish on tomato mixture, spooning part of the sauce over fish; lower heat. Cover skillet; simmer 10 minutes or until fish flakes easily. Serve with boiled potatoes, if you wish.

Gumbo

A Creole stew made with chicken, ham or seafood, tomatoes and okra. Filé powder is sometimes used as a last-minute gumbo thickener. The word gumbo is a Creole corruption of the African word for okra.

Seafood Gumbo

Makes 8 servings.

¼ cup (½ stick) butter or margarine
3 tablespoons flour
2 large onions, chopped (2 cups)
1 clove garlic, minced
1 can (28 ounces) tomatoes
1 can condensed chicken broth
2 cups water
1 teaspoon salt

1 tablespoon Worcestershire sauce
¼ teaspoon liquid hot pepper seasoning
1 pound shelled and deveined shrimp
1 pint shucked oysters with liquor
2 tablespoons filé powder
Hot cooked rice

1. Melt butter in a heavy kettle; stir in flour. Cook, stirring constantly, over low heat, until flour turns a rich brown, about 15 minutes.

2. Stir in onions and garlic. Cook until soft. Add tomatoes, broth, water, salt, Worcestershire and pepper seasoning. Cover.
3. Simmer 15 minutes. Add shrimp and oysters with their liquor. Cook until oysters are curled. Remove from heat.
4. Stir in filé powder to thicken broth. Serve in deep bowls over rice, if you wish.

Note: Reheating gumbo with filé powder will make it stringy, so always add the powder at the last minute.

Okra with Fish

Makes 6 servings.

1½ pounds fresh okra, trimmed and finely diced
1½ pounds fresh (or frozen) whiting, boned and cut into

thin strips
1 medium onion, diced (½ cup)
½ teaspoon salt
¼ teaspoon pepper

Combine all ingredients in a large saucepan. Add enough cold water to barely cover mixture. Bring to boiling; lower heat. Cook, uncovered, for 3 to 5 minutes. Okra should be slightly crunchy and green.

Gourmet Sole Véronique

Simply elegant--sole in a silky, grape-garnished sauce.

Bake at 350° for 25 minutes.

Makes 4 servings.

1 can condensed chicken broth
1 soup can water
⅛ teaspoon salt
Dash white pepper
⅛ teaspoon bouquet garni for fish
12 seedless green grapes, halved

1 package (1 pound) frozen fillets of sole, thawed
¼ cup (½ stick) butter or margarine
¼ cup all-purpose flour
2 tablespoons dry white wine

1. Combine chicken broth, water, salt, pepper, bouquet garni and grapes in a large skillet; bring to boiling.
2. Separate the fillets; place in pan; cover. Simmer 5 to 8 minutes.
3. Lift the fillets from liquid with a pancake turner; place in a shallow baking dish. Pour liquid into a 2-cup measure; add water, if necessary, to make 2 cups.
4. Melt butter in a medium-size saucepan; stir in the flour. Cook slowly, stirring constantly, until bubbly. Stir in the 2 cups liquid; continue cooking and stirring until the sauce thickens and bubbles for 3 minutes. Stir in wine; pour over fish.
5. Bake in moderate oven (350°) for 25 minutes or until fish flakes easily.

Pictured opposite:
Poached Salmon Steaks, page 393.

Sherried Sole

Bake at 450° for 10 minutes.

Makes 4 servings.

1 pound fresh or frozen fillets of sole, thawed	1/2 teaspoon salt
1 can (3 or 4 ounces) sliced mushrooms	Pinch of white pepper
2 tablespoons instant minced onion	1 tablespoon dried parsley flakes
1/2 cup dry sherry	1/2 cup milk
	1 tablespoon flour
	Paprika

1. Dry the fillets. Pour mushrooms with their liquid into a shallow, 6-cup, flameproof dish. Sprinkle with the onion. Place the fillets over the mushrooms, folding to fit. Pour the sherry over fish; sprinkle with salt, pepper and parsley flakes.
2. Bake in very hot oven (450°) for 10 minutes.
3. Carefully drain the liquid from the fish into a small saucepan. Cook quickly over high heat until liquid is reduced by half. Combine milk with flour; stir into liquid. Cook, stirring constantly, until the sauce thickens and bubbles. Pour over fish; sprinkle with paprika. Broil 4 inches from heat, about 3 minutes or until top is lightly browned and bubbly.

Colorado Rainbow Trout Fillets in Mustard Dill Sauce

Makes 6 servings.

3 pan-dressed rainbow trout, each about 12 ounces	chopped fresh dill
OR: 3 packages (8 to 10 ounces each) frozen trout, thawed	OR: 2 teaspoons dillweed
	1/8 teaspoon salt
2 to 3 cups dry white wine	1/8 teaspoon white pepper
1/4 cup Dijon mustard	3 tablespoons olive or vegetable oil
1/4 cup prepared mustard	2 tablespoons lime juice
1 tablespoon sugar	1 tablespoon white wine vinegar
2 tablespoons	Boston lettuce leaves

1. Fillet the large trout, leaving skin on for poaching. Since the frozen trout will be smaller, fillet them if you wish or poach whole.
2. Heat wine to boiling in large skillet. Lower heat. Add fillets or whole fish. Cover and simmer gently about 3 minutes for fillets or 5 minutes for whole fish, turning whole fish once. Lift out of wine with broad spatula. Drain on paper toweling. Carefully lift off skin of fish with knife.
3. Combine mustards, sugar, dill, salt, pepper, oil, lime juice and vinegar in small bowl until creamy.

Place fish in glass dish in single layer. Pour mustard sauce over. Cover with plastic wrap. Refrigerate overnight or at least 6 hours. Serve on lettuce-lined platter.

Trout Meunière

Makes 4 servings.

2 packages (8 to 10 ounces each) frozen trout, thawed	1 cup vegetable oil
	1/2 cup (1 stick) butter or margarine
2 eggs	1 teaspoon chopped fresh parsley
3/4 teaspoon salt	1/2 clove garlic, chopped
1/2 teaspoon pepper	
1/4 cup all-purpose flour	

1. Cut heads from trout; split each trout lengthwise.
2. Beat eggs with 1/2 teaspoon of the salt and 1/4 teaspoon of the pepper in a pie plate; sprinkle flour on wax paper. Dip trout in egg mixture, then in flour to coat well.
3. Heat vegetable oil until hot in a large skillet. Add trout, 2 pieces at a time, and fry, turning once, until firm; lift out with a slotted pancake turner; drain on paper toweling.
4. While trout cooks, melt butter in a small skillet; stir in parsley, garlic and remaining salt and pepper. Heat slowly just until hot.
5. Place trout on a warm serving platter; pour sauce over.

Sole-Almond Bake

Bake at 375° for 15 minutes.

Makes 6 servings.

2 packages (1 pound each) frozen fillets of sole	1/4 teaspoon pepper
	2 eggs
1/2 cup all-purpose flour	2 tablespoons dry white wine or milk
2 teaspoons salt	3/4 cup chopped blanched almonds
1 teaspoon paprika	2 tablespoons melted butter or margarine
1/2 teaspoon leaf thyme, crumbled	

1. Defrost fish following label directions. Pat dry on paper toweling.
2. Combine flour, salt, paprika, thyme and pepper on wax paper.
3. In shallow dish, stir together eggs and wine.
4. Coat fish with flour then dip into egg mixture; roll in almonds.
5. Place fish in well-greased baking pan. Drizzle melted butter over.
6. Bake in a moderate oven (375°) for 15 minutes or until fish flakes easily. Thicker pieces will take longer.

Fillet of Flounder with Lobster.

Fillet of Flounder with Lobster

Bake at 500° for 10 minutes.

Makes 4 servings.

**4 flounder fillets
(1¼ to 1½ pounds)
1 medium-size carrot,
pared
1 medium-size leek
1 stalk fennel or celery
Vegetable oil
½ teaspoon salt**

**⅛ teaspoon pepper
¼ teaspoon leaf
tarragon, crumbled
1 package (6½
ounces) frozen
lobster Newburg in
boilable bag,
partially thawed**

1. Cut out four 12-inch squares of aluminum foil. Preheat oven to very hot (500°).
2. Rinse flounder fillets; dry on paper toweling.
3. Cut carrot, leek and fennel or celery into julienne strips, 2½ × ¼-inch.
4. Brush lower half of each aluminum foil square with a little oil. Place a flounder fillet on each, folding fillet to fit. Spread vegetables equally over each fillet. Sprinkle with salt, pepper and tarragon. Divide lobster Newburg into 4 equal portions; spread over each fillet.
5. Fold top half of aluminum foil over to meet lower edge. Fold edges all around twice, to seal. Place packages on a hot cookie sheet in the oven, 1 inch apart.
6. Bake in a preheated very hot oven (500°) for 10 minutes. Remove the packages to dinner plates; cut X in top; open up and serve in aluminum foil.

Stuffed Flounder

Makes 4 servings.

**1 package (1 pound)
frozen flounder
fillets, thawed
6 tablespoons
(¾ stick) butter or
margarine
1 cup fresh bread
crumbs (2 slices)
2 tablespoons
chopped fresh
parsley**

**1 teaspoon leaf
tarragon, crumbled
¾ teaspoon salt
Dash plus ¼ teaspoon
pepper
2 cups water
1 tablespoon lemon
juice
Few celery tops
¼ cup all-purpose
flour**

1. Separate fillets carefully; spread flat on wax paper.
2. Melt 2 tablespoons of the butter in a small

(continued)

saucepan; remove from heat. Lightly stir in bread crumbs, parsley, tarragon, 1/4 teaspoon of the salt and a dash of pepper until evenly moist. Spread evenly down center of each fillet; roll up, jelly-roll fashion; fasten with wooden picks.

3. Combine water, lemon juice, celery tops, the remaining 1/2 teaspoon salt and 1/4 teaspoon pepper in a medium-size skillet; heat to boiling. Place fish rolls in skillet; cover. Simmer 15 minutes or until fish flakes easily. Lift rolls from liquid with a slotted spoon and place on a heated deep serving platter. Carefully pull out picks; keep rolls warm. Strain liquid into a 2-cup measure and set aside for next step.

4. Melt the remaining 4 tablespoons butter in a small saucepan; stir in flour. Cook, stirring constantly, until bubbly. Stir in strained liquid; continue cooking and stirring until sauce thickens and boils 1 minute. Spoon over the fish rolls.

Flounder Florentine

Bake at 350° for 1 hour.

Makes 6 servings.

1 package (10 ounces) frozen chopped spinach, thawed and squeezed dry
1 cup cooked rice
1/4 cup thinly sliced green onions
1/4 cup toasted slivered almonds, chopped
1/2 teaspoon salt
1/4 teaspoon pepper
1/8 teaspoon ground nutmeg

6 flounder fillets (about 1 1/2 pounds)
OR: 2 packages (1 pound each) frozen flounder fillets, thawed, drained and separated
1 can condensed cream of mushroom soup
1/4 cup light cream or half-and-half
Paprika

1. Combine spinach, rice, onions, almonds, salt, pepper and nutmeg in a small bowl.
2. Tear off a 26-inch piece of 18-inch-wide heavy-duty foil. Place in center of 12 × 8× 2-inch baking pan. Grease foil lightly.
3. Place fish fillets in single layer on foil. Spread 1/4 cup spinach mixture on each fillet. Roll; secure fish rolls with wooden picks.
4. Combine soup and cream. Pour over fish. Close and seal foil.
5. Bake in a moderate oven (350°) for 1 hour or until fish flakes easily when tested with a fork. Garnish with paprika. Remove wooden picks before serving.

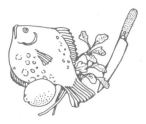

Flounder Fillets North Beach

Bake at 450° for 10 minutes.

Makes 8 servings.

8 flounder fillets
2 tablespoons hot prepared mustard
1/4 cup packaged bread crumbs
1/4 teaspoon leaf thyme, crumbled
1/4 teaspoon fines herbes, crumbled
1/4 teaspoon

seasoned salt
1/8 teaspoon seasoned pepper
2 to 3 tablespoons bottled French or Italian dressing
Lemon slices
8 teaspoons butter or margarine
Chopped fresh parsley

1. Butter or oil a very shallow baking dish big enough to hold fillets in a single layer. Brush fillets on both sides with mustard; arrange in baking dish. Preheat oven to 450°.
2. Mix crumbs, thyme, fines herbes, salt and pepper; spread some of the mixture on each fillet, then sprinkle with salad dressing.
3. Bake in a preheated very hot oven (450°) for 10 minutes. Top each fillet with a thin slice of lemon, 1 teaspoon butter and a generous sprinkle of chopped parsley.

Baked Fish Rolls with Clam Sauce

Bake at 375° for 20 minutes.

Makes 6 servings.

1 1/2 pounds fresh or thawed, frozen flounder or sole fillets
1 teaspoon salt
1/4 teaspoon white pepper
1 small onion, thinly sliced
2 tablespoons butter or margarine
1 can condensed

Manhattan-style clam chowder
1/2 cup milk
1 tablespoon dry sherry
2 tablespoons packaged bread crumbs
2 tablespoons shredded Swiss cheese or grated Parmesan cheese

1. Cut fillets in half lengthwise; sprinkle with salt and pepper. Roll each piece jelly-roll style; fasten with wooden pick.
2. Sauté onion in butter in a large skillet with ovenproof handle 3 minutes or until tender. Arrange fish rolls over onion.
3. Preheat oven to 375°. Combine soup, milk and sherry in a 2-cup measure; pour over fish.
4. Bake in a preheated moderate oven (375°) for 15 minutes or until fish flakes easily. Combine bread crumbs and cheese in a small bowl; sprinkle over fish; bake 5 minutes longer.

Coquilles St. Jacques

A gourmet seafood meal complete in a shell.

Bake at 400° for 15 minutes.
Top-brown 1 to 2 minutes.

Makes 2 servings.

1 cup hot, seasoned mashed potatoes
1/4 cup dry vermouth or white wine
1 tablespoon chopped green onion
1/2 small bay leaf
1/4 teaspoon salt
Dash white pepper
1 can (3 to 4 ounces) sliced mushrooms
1/2 pound fresh or frozen unbreaded scallops*
Milk
2 tablespoons butter
2 tablespoons flour
1 egg yolk
1/4 cup heavy cream
1/2 teaspoon lemon juice
1/2 cup frozen peas
2 teaspoons grated Parmesan cheese

1. Make mashed potatoes; keep warm over hot water while preparing scallops.
2. Simmer vermouth, onion, bay leaf, salt, pepper and liquid from mushrooms in large skillet for 5 minutes.
3. Add scallops to wine mixture. Simmer, covered, 5 minutes. Remove scallops and onion to a small bowl with a slotted spoon; discard bay leaf. Pour skillet liquid into a 1-cup measure. Add enough milk to make 3/4 cup.
4. Melt butter in medium-size saucepan; stir in flour; cook 2 minutes. Remove from heat. Stir milk-wine mixture into saucepan. Cook over low heat, stirring constantly, until thickened and bubbly.
5. Beat egg yolk and cream lightly in medium-size bowl. Gradually stir in hot sauce; return mixture to saucepan. Cook over low heat; stir in lemon juice, frozen peas, mushrooms and scallops. If sauce is too thick, stir in a tablespoon more heavy cream to thin slightly.
6. Butter 2 scallop shells; spoon mixture into shells. Spoon mashed potatoes around edges or pipe with pastry bag. Sprinkle each with Parmesan cheese.
7. Bake in a toaster oven at hot (400°) for 15 minutes until bubbly-hot. Top-brown 1 to 2 minutes.
Or use half a 1-pound package frozen turbot fillets and cut into 1-inch pieces. Return other half of fish to freezer.

Cocquilles St. Jacques.

Stir-Fried Shrimp

A hot and spicy Szechuan dish typical of cooking in western China.

Makes 4 servings.

1 pound medium-size shrimp, shelled and deveined
OR: ¹/₂ pound frozen shelled and deveined shrimp, thawed
1 egg white
2 teaspoons cornstarch
¹/₂ teaspoon salt
2 cups peanut or corn oil
Sherry Sauce *(recipe follows)*
2 teaspoons minced fresh ginger
OR: ¹/₂ teaspoon ground ginger
1 clove garlic, minced (¹/₂ teaspoon)
¹/₄ to ¹/₂ teaspoon crushed red pepper

1. Split shrimp in half lengthwise; rinse; dry on paper toweling. Combine egg white, cornstarch and salt in medium-size bowl. Add shrimp and toss until coated. Refrigerate 1 to 24 hours.
2. Heat oil in wok or deep skillet until temperature is 300° on deep-fat frying thermometer. Add shrimp; stir-fry 1 to 2 minutes or until shrimp changes color and pieces separate. Pour shrimp and oil into strainer placed over a bowl. (May be prepared an hour ahead of time to this point.)
3. Prepare Sherry Sauce.
4. Reheat wok; return 2 tablespoons of the drained oil to the wok. Add ginger; stir-fry 5 seconds. Add garlic and pepper; stir-fry 5 seconds. Add shrimp; stir-fry until heated throughout, about 1 minute.
5. Stir Sherry Sauce to combine; pour into wok, stirring until sauce thickens and coats shrimp with a clear glaze. Serve with hot cooked rice, if you wish.

Sherry Sauce: Combine 1 teaspoon sugar, 1 teaspoon cornstarch, 2 tablespoons soy sauce, 1 tablespoon dry sherry, 1 tablespoon water and 1 teaspoon vinegar in a cup. Stir well.

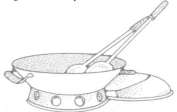

Skewered Shrimp with Vegetables

Makes 6 servings.

1 large zucchini, halved lengthwise
18 large shrimp (about 1¹/₂ pounds), peeled and deveined
18 cherry tomatoes
12 strips bacon
¹/₄ cup honey
4 teaspoons grated orange rind

1. Slice each zucchini half into 6 equal pieces.
2. Thread 3 shrimp onto each of 6 long skewers, alternating with 2 zucchini pieces, 3 cherry tomatoes and 2 strips of bacon; spiral bacon around shrimp and vegetables as you thread it.
3. Combine honey and orange rind in a bowl. Brush over skewers.
4. Grill 6 inches from the coals, turning often and basting frequently with honey mixture, 8 to 10 minutes or until shrimp is bright pink, bacon is golden and vegetables are tender. Use a small fork to slide the shrimp and vegetables onto serving plates.

Dilled Shrimp in Aspic

Makes 6 servings.

1 package (1 pound) frozen shelled, deveined shrimp
1 medium-size cucumber
2 tablespoons chopped fresh dill
1 tablespoon minced onion
2 tablespoons lemon juice
¹/₂ teaspoon salt
¹/₈ teaspoon pepper
2 cans (13³/₄ ounces each) chicken broth
2 envelopes unflavored gelatin
2 tablespoons lemon juice
Canned pimiento
Fresh dill sprigs
Creamy Dressing (*recipe follows*)

1. Cook shrimp, following package directions; drain; cool. Pick out several even-size shrimp; reserve for decoration. Cut remaining shrimp into ¹/₄-inch pieces; place in a medium-size bowl.
2. Cut half the cucumber into very thin slices; reserve for decoration. Pare and seed remaining half of cucumber; cut into ¹/₂-inch pieces; place in bowl with diced shrimp. Stir in chopped dill, onion, 2 tablespoons of the lemon juice, salt, and pepper. Let stand 1 hour to season. Drain well.
3. Skim fat from chicken broth; discard. Soften gelatin in 1 cup of the broth about 5 minutes in a small saucepan. Heat, stirring constantly, until gelatin dissolves; stir into remaining chicken broth in a medium-size bowl. Add remaining 2 tablespoons lemon juice. Cut out decorative shapes from pimiento.
4. Pour ¹/₂ cup of the gelatin mixture into bottom of a 6-cup ring mold; place in a large bowl filled with mixture of ice and water until mixture is sticky-firm. Quickly arrange reserved shrimp, cucumber slices, pimiento cutouts and sprigs of dill in aspic in bottom of mold; spoon several tablespoons of liquid aspic over decorations. Chill again until sticky-firm.
5. Chill remaining gelatin mixture until as thick as unbeaten egg white in bowl of ice and water to speed setting. Stir in drained shrimp and cucumber mixture; gently spoon over decorated layer in ring mold; chill until firm, at least 4 hours or overnight.
6. Just before serving, loosen salad around edge with a knife; dip mold very quickly in and out of hot water; wipe off water. Cover pan with serving plate; turn upside-down; shake gently; lift off mold. Border with

reserved cucumber slices, halved. Top with Creamy Dressing.

Creamy Dressing: Combine ¹/₂ cup dairy sour cream; ¹/₂ cup mayonnaise or salad dressing; ¹/₂ teaspoon salt; ¹/₄ teaspoon celery seeds, crushed; and ¹/₄ teaspoon dry mustard in a small bowl; stir to blend well. Cover; refrigerate at least 1 hour to blend flavors. Makes about 1 cup.

Shrimp Curry

A delightful, not-too-hot curry that is colorful and unusual.

Makes 6 servings.

2 tablespoons butter or margarine	shelled and deveined shrimp
1 tablespoon vegetable oil	2 tablespoons cornstarch
1 cup frozen chopped onion	¹/₂ teaspoon ground ginger
4 teaspoons curry powder	2 tablespoons water
1 can condensed chicken broth	1 tablespoon lime juice
¹/₂ teaspoon salt	1 tomato, cut into wedges
1 package (1¹/₂ pounds) frozen,	1 cup shredded lettuce
	Hot cooked rice

1. Heat butter and oil in large skillet; sauté onion until soft, about 5 minutes. Stir in curry powder; cook, stirring constantly, 2 minutes longer. Add chicken broth, salt and shrimp. Bring to boiling; simmer for 6 minutes.
2. Blend cornstarch, ginger, water and lime juice in a small bowl. Stir into shrimp mixture; continue cooking and stirring until mixture thickens and bubbles 1 minute. Stir in tomato wedges and shredded lettuce. Cover; simmer 3 minutes longer or until tomatoes are hot, but still firm. Serve over hot cooked rice. Serve with chutney, shredded coconut and peanuts, if you wish.

Shrimp Scampi

Makes 4 servings.

1 pound large raw shrimp (see *Note*)	¹/₄ cup olive or vegetable oil
¹/₂ cup (1 stick) butter or margarine	1 tablespoon finely chopped garlic

1. Cut shrimp down the back lengthwise with kitchen shears, being careful not to cut through the shrimp. With shells intact, remove black vein; rinse and pat dry.

2. Melt butter with oil in a large skillet. Add garlic; cook until garlic just begins to brown.
3. Add shrimp; sauté, shaking skillet and stirring, 2 to 3 minutes or just until shrimp is pink and firm. Garnish with chopped parsley and lemon wedges, if you wish.

Note: If using frozen, shelled, deveined shrimp, defrost, then begin recipe at Step 2.

Shrimp and Sausage Jambalaya

Makes 8 servings.

1 medium-size onion, chopped (¹/₂ cup)	1 can (13³/₄ ounces) chicken broth
¹/₂ cup chopped green pepper	1 teaspoon salt
¹/₂ cup chopped celery	¹/₂ teaspoon leaf savory, crumbled
¹/₄ pound chaurice (chorizo) sausage or other hot sausage, sliced ¹/₄-inch thick	¹/₂ teaspoon liquid hot pepper seasoning
	1 pound frozen shelled and deveined shrimp
2 tablespoons butter or margarine	¹/₂ pound cooked ham, diced
1¹/₂ cups uncooked long-grain rice	¹/₂ cup chopped green onions
2 cups tomato juice	Chopped fresh parsley

1. Sauté onion, pepper, celery and sausage in butter in large, heavy Dutch oven 5 minutes. Add rice; cook and stir 1 minute. Add tomato juice, chicken broth, salt, savory and hot pepper seasoning. Heat to boiling; lower heat; cover. Simmer, stirring occasionally, 20 minutes.
2. Stir in shrimp and ham; cook 15 minutes or until rice and shrimp are tender. Stir in green onions. Serve sprinkled with parsley.

Shrimp with Feta Cheese

Makes 6 servings.

2 cans (16 ounces each) stewed tomatoes	crumbled
	4 cups cooked brown rice (1¹/₃ cups uncooked)
1 package (1 pound) frozen shelled and deveined shrimp	¹/₄ cup chopped fresh parsley
¹/₄ pound feta cheese,	

1. Simmer tomatoes in a large skillet for 10 to 15 minutes or until tomato liquid is reduced by about half.
2. Add shrimp; simmer just until they begin to turn pink; sprinkle with cheese. Cover skillet; simmer about 5 minutes longer or until shrimp are cooked and cheese is hot.
3. Spoon rice onto a large serving platter; top with shrimp mixture. Sprinkle with parsley.

Shrimp Creole

Makes 8 to 10 servings.

3 pounds sweet green
   peppers, seeded
   and chopped
1 pound onions,
   chopped
2 celery stalks, thinly
   sliced
1/2 cup (1 stick) butter
   or margarine
1/4 cup olive or
   vegetable oil
Flavorful Broth (recipe
   follows)
1/2 cup tomato puree
1/3 cup Worcestershire
   sauce
1/3 cup dry white wine
1 1/2 to 2 tablespoons
   liquid red-pepper
   seasoning
1 teaspoon salt
3 pounds large
   shrimp, shelled and
   deveined

1. Sauté the peppers, onions and celery in the butter and oil in a large pot until tender, for 10 minutes. Stir in the Flavorful Broth and tomato puree. Bring to boiling. Lower the heat; simmer, uncovered, for 15 minutes.
2. Add the Worcestershire, wine, red-pepper seasoning and salt; simmer for 5 minutes. Add the shrimp; simmer for 10 minutes more. Serve with rice and sprinkle with chopped parsley, if you wish.

To Make Ahead: Chop the green peppers and onions, and slice the celery; place in a large bowl, cover and refrigerate. Shell, devein and place the shrimp in a plastic bag. Tie the bag securely and refrigerate. When ready to serve the shrimp, proceed with the recipe.

Flavorful Broth: Combine 2 1/2 cups water, 1 tablespoon vinegar, 2 bay leaves and 2 whole cloves in a saucepan. Bring to boiling. Lower the heat; simmer for 5 minutes. Remove the bay leaves and cloves.

Shrimp Remoulade

Makes 6 servings.

1/4 cup prepared
   mustard with
   horseradish
1 tablespoon paprika
1 teaspoon salt
1/4 teaspoon cayenne
1/2 cup tarragon-
   flavored vinegar
3/4 cup vegetable oil
1 bunch green onions
   including tops,
   coarsely chopped
   (1 cup)
2 celery stalks, finely
   chopped
1/2 cup coarsely
   chopped fresh
   parsley
2 pounds frozen
   shelled and
   deveined shrimp
1 medium-size head
   iceberg lettuce,
   shredded

1. Combine mustard-horseradish, paprika, salt and cayenne in small deep mixing bowl. Beat in vinegar with a rotary beater until well mixed.
2. Continue beating, pouring in oil in a slow steady stream, until sauce is thick and smooth. Stir in green onions, celery and parsley. Cover; refrigerate while preparing shrimp.
3. Cook shrimp following label directions; drain; cool slightly.
4. Pour sauce over shrimp; toss gently to coat shrimp with sauce. Cover; refrigerate several hours or overnight.
5. Spoon shrimp and sauce over bed of shredded lettuce.

Caldeirada

Makes 8 servings.

1 pound small
   mussels in the shell
2 tablespoons olive oil
4 tablespoons butter
   or margarine
1 large onion,
   chopped (1 cup)
1/2 medium-size green
   pepper, halved,
   seeded and minced
1 clove garlic, minced
2 teaspoons salt
Freshly ground pepper
2 large ripe tomatoes,
   peeled, cored and
   coarsely chopped
   (reserve juice)
3 pounds inexpensive,`
cleaned, fresh or
   frozen fish (1 pound
   each of 3 of the
   following: cod,
   scrod, mackerel,
   haddock, hake, sea
   bass or squid), cut
   in 1 1/2-inch chunks
1/4 cup minced fresh
   parsley
1 cup dry white wine
   or 1/2 cup each dry
   white wine and
   water
8 slices (about 1-inch
   thick) Italian bread,
   toasted

1. Scrub mussels under cool running water with a stiff brush; cut off beards with a sharp knife and scrape the shells clean. Soak mussels in cool water 1 hour to purge them of grit. Discard any that float or whose shells are not tightly shut.
2. Heat 1 tablespoon each of the oil and butter in a heavy kettle over moderate heat; add the onion, green pepper and garlic and stir-fry 5 to 8 minutes or until golden. Remove and set aside. Mix 1/2 teaspoon salt and a pinch pepper into tomatoes and their juice and set aside also.
3. Add remaining 1 tablespoon oil and 1 more tablespoon butter or margarine to kettle; rinse mussels and arrange over bottom. Scatter one-third of the onion mixture on top, then one-third of the tomatoes. Top with half of the fish and sprinkle generously with some of the salt, pepper and minced parsley. Add another one-third each of onion mixture and tomatoes, top with the remaining fish, sprinkle with more salt, pepper and parsley. Finally, top with

(continued)

Pictured opposite (clockwise from top left):
Collard Green Quiche, page 376; Piña Colada Down-Up Cake,
page 160; Shrimp Creole, page 404.

remaining onion mixture and tomatoes; sprinkle with parsley.

4. Pour in wine, bring mixture to a boil, reduce heat, cover and simmer 30 minutes. Dot with remaining 2 tablespoons butter or margarine; recover; simmer 10 minutes.

5. To serve: Place toasted rounds of bread in soup plates; ladle fish on top.

Bouillabaisse

This classic French seafood stew was created centuries ago by the fishermen on the Mediterranean coast. Each recipe differed from cook to cook, as it was simply a mixture of whatever fish were caught that day. The classic included not only fish but also eel and langoustine, a lobster-shrimp-like crustacean.

A good bouillabaisse must contain a rich fish stock, dry white wine, tomatoes and saffron. The best fish combination is of fat fish, such as mackerel, salmon or swordfish and lean fish, such as flounder, sole, halibut, cod, sea bass, snapper, sea trout or rockfish. For shellfish, use lobster, shrimp and mussels or clams. Plan to include a variety of seafood for different textures and flavors.

Traditionally the seafood is removed from the broth and served separately on a platter. The broth is then spooned over slices of French bread rubbed with garlic. More often the stew is served, fish and all, in a shallow bowl, accompanied with crusty, sliced French bread.

Creole Bouillabaisse

This Creole version of the French classic makes good use of the bounty of the rivers, bays and Gulf waters.

Makes 8 servings.

3 tablespoons vegetable oil	1 cup dry white wine
2 tablespoons flour	2 to 2¹/₂ pounds fish fillets (red snapper and/or bass), cut into 1¹/₂-inch pieces
1 large onion, chopped (1 cup)	
2 cloves garlic, chopped	
1 can (28 ounces) tomatoes	¹/₂ pound scallops
1¹/₂ teaspoons salt	2 lobster tails, cut into chunks
1 bay leaf	OR: ¹/₂ pound shelled and deveined fresh or frozen shrimp
1 teaspoon leaf thyme, crumbled	
¹/₂ teaspoon ground allspice	¹/₂ cup sliced green onions
¹/₄ teaspoon crumbled saffron	French bread, sliced and toasted
¹/₄ teaspoon cayenne	Fresh parsley (optional)
¹/₂ cup water	

1. Heat oil in large Dutch oven or deep skillet; stir in flour. Cook, stirring constantly, over low to medium heat until flour turns a rich brown, about 5 minutes. Stir in onion and garlic. Cook, stirring, until soft, about 5 minutes. Add tomatoes, salt, bay leaf, thyme, allspice, saffron, cayenne and water. Bring to boiling, crushing tomatoes. Cover kettle.

2. Simmer 15 minutes; stir in wine. Add fish fillets, scallops, lobster or shrimp, and green onions; cover. Cook 5 to 10 minutes longer or just until fish is tender and flakes easily.

3. Serve in deep plates or bowls over toasted French bread. Sprinkle with chopped parsley, if you wish.

Note: Substitute any firm white fish (halibut, cod or haddock) or substitute frozen fish cut into chunks and allow 5 to 10 minutes longer cooking time.

Shrimp on Chinese Cabbage

Makes 4 servings.

1 pound raw shrimp, shelled and deveined OR: 1 package (1 pound) frozen, shelled and deveined shrimp, thawed	3 tablespoons vegetable oil
	¹/₂ teaspoon salt
	¹/₂ teaspoon sugar
	1 tablespoon soy sauce
	1 clove garlic, minced
1 small head Chinese celery cabbage	2 tablespoons dry sherry
3 green onions	4 to 6 dried small whole red peppers
¹/₄ cup water	¹/₂ cup unsalted shelled roasted peanuts
1 tablespoon cornstarch	

1. Rinse shrimp; pat dry with paper toweling. Cut cabbage into 1 × 2-inch pieces. (You should have about 8 cups.) Cut onions into 1-inch lengths. Mix water and cornstarch in 1-cup measure.

2. Heat large deep skillet, Dutch oven or wok over high heat. Add 1 tablespoon of the oil; swirl to coat bottom and side. Add cabbage; stir-fry until coated with oil. Add salt, sugar and soy sauce. Stir-fry until just tender-crisp. Restir cornstarch mixture; remove 1 tablespoon and add to cabbage. Stir until juices are thickened. Remove cabbage to platter; keep warm.

3. Reheat pan with remaining oil. Add shrimp and garlic. Stir-fry just until shrimp turn firm and pink. Add sherry and peppers. Stir-fry to loosen browned bits in pan. Restir cornstarch mixture; pour over shrimp. Cook until sauce is thick and coats shrimp. Stir in green onions and peanuts. Taste for salt; add, if needed. Spoon shrimp over cabbage. Serve with hot fluffy rice, if you wish.

Pictured opposite: Shrimp on Chinese Cabbage.

Tempura

This deep-fried seafood and vegetable dish, introduced into Japan by Jesuit missionaries late in the 16th century, has become a classic of Japanese cuisine—and a favorite of many Americans. The secret of good tempura is to use ice water in preparing the batter.

Makes 4 servings.

1 cup *sifted* all-purpose flour	shrimp in shells
1 teaspoon salt	1 large sweet potato
1 teaspoon sugar	1/2 bunch large green onions
1 teaspoon ground ginger	6 large mushrooms
1 egg yolk	1/2 small eggplant
1 cup ice-cold water	Vegetable oil for frying
1 pound large raw	Soy Dipping Sauce *(recipe follows)*

1. Combine the flour, salt, sugar, ginger and egg yolk in a medium-size bowl; beat until smooth; stir in water (batter will be medium-thin). Chill at least 2 hours.
2. Shell shrimp carefully, leaving on tails; remove vein down back; dry shrimp on paper toweling.
3. Pare sweet potato; cut in half lengthwise; cut into 1/4 -inch slices. Trim onion of roots; cut onions into 2-inch pieces. Slice mushrooms. Cut eggplant in slices like the sweet potato.
4. Pour enough oil into a large, heavy skillet or a deep-fat fryer to make a depth of 2 inches; heat to 380°.
5. Holding each shrimp by the tail, dip in batter, then drop into hot fat; fry, turning once, about 1 minute or until golden-brown; drain on paper toweling-lined cookie sheet. Keep hot in a very, very slow oven (250°) while frying vegetables. Fry no more than 6 to 8 pieces at a time.
6. Skim the surface of the oil to remove any excess pieces of batter; check temperature.
7. Give each diner an individual bowl of Soy Dipping Sauce. Serve Tempura hot, either on individual plates or a platter from which each diner will serve himself.

Note: For frozen shrimp, thaw 1 bag (12 ounces) frozen, shelled, deveined, raw shrimp. Dip into batter with tongs and drop into hot fat.

Soy Dipping Sauce: Combine 1/2 cup sake or dry sherry, 1/4 cup soy sauce, 1 teaspoon sugar, 1/2 teaspoon prepared horseradish and 1/2 teaspoon ground ginger in small saucepan. Bring to boiling; remove from heat at once and cool. Place 2 tablespoons of grated fresh white radishes in small bowl, slowly pour in sauce. Makes about 3/4 cup.

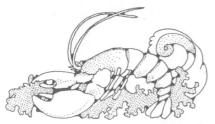

Lobster Iolani

Grill about 15 minutes.

Makes 4 servings.

4 frozen lobster tails (3/4 to 1 pound each), thawed	4 cloves garlic, minced
1 cup butter, melted	1 tablespoon chopped fresh parsley
2 tablespoons Hawaiian or golden rum	1/4 teaspoon leaf oregano, crumbled

1. Slit undersides of tails lengthwise and bend backwards to crack shells to prevent tails curling during cooking. Brush undersides with melted butter.
2. Grill, shell-side down, about 3 inches from hot coals for 10 to 15 minutes, brushing often with melted butter.
3. Add rum to remaining butter; give tails a final brushing with the buttered rum mixture and turn shell-side up. Grill for 5 minutes longer or until shell turns red.
4. Add garlic, parsley and oregano to remaining buttered rum mixture, Set on side of grill so butter will heat and blend gradually with the other ingredients. Do not let sauce boil. Serve sauce spooned over the lobster tails. Garnish with parsley sprigs, if you wish.

Note: To broil lobster tails, place shell-side up, on rack over broiler pan. Broil 3 inches from heat for 10 minutes, brushing often with melted butter. Turn tails over; brush with buttered rum mixture; broil. Serve with sauce.

Baked Parsley-Stuffed Lobster

If you can buy ready-cooked lobsters, the preparation is speedy.

Bake at 425° for 15 minutes.

Makes 4 servings.

4 small live lobsters (about 1 1/4 pounds each)	soda-cracker crumbs (32 crackers)
1 cup (2 sticks) butter or margarine, melted	1 cup chopped fresh parsley
2 2/3 cups unsalted	2 teaspoons paprika
	1 teaspoon salt

1. Drop live lobsters into a very large kettle of boiling salted water; cover. Lower heat; simmer 10 minutes or until lobsters turn red. Remove at once with tongs; drain; let cool enough to handle.
2. Place each lobster on its back and cut down middle with scissors, being careful not to cut through hard shell of back. Press lobster open so it will lie flat. (If necessary, crack shell of back in a few places.)
3. Lift out the pink coral (roe) if any, and green tomalley (liver).* Discard stomach sac or "lady" from back of head, black vein running from head to tail and

spongy gray tissue. Brush meat with some of the melted butter or margarine. Place lobsters on cookie sheets. Preheat oven to 425°.

4. Mix cracker crumbs, parsley, paprika and salt in a medium-size bowl; drizzle with the remaining melted butter or margarine; toss lightly to mix. Pack into opened lobsters, dividing evenly.

5. Bake in a preheated hot oven (425°) for 15 minutes or until meat is hot and topping is golden. Place on individual, large platters.

Add pink coral and tomalley to cracker mixture or serve separately on Pilot crackers.

Deviled Crab

Bake at 400° for 15 minutes.
Makes 6 servings.

1/2 **green pepper, seeded and diced**	1 **tablespoon parsley flakes**
3 **green onions, minced (include some green tops)**	1/2 **teaspoon salt**
	1/8 **teaspoon lemon pepper seasoning**
3 **tablespoons butter or margarine**	2 **packages (6 ounces each) Alaska king crab, thawed by package directions and flaked**
1 **cup herbed poultry stuffing mix, crushed**	
1 **teaspoon dry mustard**	1 **cup mayonnaise**

1. Stir-fry pepper and onion in butter in a large skillet until tender and golden, about 3 minutes; add stuffing mix and toss lightly. Stir in mustard, parsley, salt, lemon pepper seasoning, crab and mayonnaise.

2. Spoon into well buttered scallop shells or small ramekins. (Recipe may be prepared ahead up to this point—simply place filled shells or ramekins on a cookie sheet, cover and refrigerate until ready to bake.) Preheat oven to 400°.

3. Bake, uncovered, in a preheated hot oven (400°) for about 15 minutes or until sizzling and touched with brown.

Oyster Stew

Makes 4 servings.

2 **cups milk**	**with liquor**
2 **cups light cream or half-and-half**	OR: 2 **cans (8 ounces each) oysters**
1/2 **teaspoon salt**	
1/4 **teaspoon paprika**	1/4 **cup (1/2 stick) butter or margarine**
1 **pint (about 24) shucked oysters**	

1. Scald milk with cream in medium-size saucepan over low heat, but do not boil; stir in salt and paprika.

2. Heat oysters and their liquor in butter in medium-size saucepan until edges of oysters begin to curl; stir in milk mixture.

3. Ladle into soup bowls. Serve with oyster crackers, if you wish.

New England Oyster Scallop

Oysters bake plump and moist between layers of buttery crumbs.

Bake at 350° for 30 minutes.

Makes 4 to 6 servings.

1/4 **cup (1/2 stick) butter or margarine**	**shucked oysters with liquor**
2 **cups coarse soda-cracker crumbs (about 24 crackers)**	OR: 2 **cans (8 ounces each) oysters**
1/2 **cup chopped fresh parsley**	1/2 **cup light cream**
1 **teaspoon salt**	1 **teaspoon Worcestershire sauce**
1/4 **teaspoon pepper**	
1 **pint (about 24)**	

1. Melt the butter in a saucepan; remove from heat; stir in crumbs, parsley, salt and pepper.

2. Drain and save 1/4 cup liquor from oysters. Sprinkle 1/3 of crumb mixture into a 9-inch pie plate; layer half of the oysters on top, then half of remaining crumbs and rest of oysters.

3. Combine reserved oyster liquor, cream and Worcestershire sauce; pour over the top; sprinkle with remaining crumbs.

4. Bake in a moderate oven (350°) for 30 minutes or until top is golden. Serve hot, plain or with chili sauce.

Herb-Baked Scallops

Bake at 350° for 25 minutes.

Makes 6 servings.

2 **pounds fresh or thawed, frozen sea scallops**	**chopped fresh parsley**
	1 1/2 **teaspoons leaf basil, crumbled**
1/2 **cup (1 stick) butter or margarine**	1 **teaspoon salt**
3 **tablespoons**	1/4 **teaspoon pepper**

1. Preheat oven to 350°. Wash the scallops in cold water and drain thoroughly between sheets of paper toweling.

2. Place the scallops in a single layer in a large, shallow baking dish; dot with the butter; sprinkle with parsley, basil, salt and pepper.

3. Bake in a preheated moderate oven (350°) for 5 minutes. Stir scallops to coat well with butter mixture. Bake 20 minutes longer or until tender. Serve the buttery sauce from dish over mashed or baked potatoes, if you wish.

Scallop Kabobs

Bake at 425° for 20 minutes.

Makes 6 servings.

2 packages (7 ounces each) batter-fried scallops
12 cherry tomatoes
2 medium-size zucchini, each cut into 6 chunks
12 medium-size mushrooms
1 large green pepper, seeded and cut into

12 chunks
1/2 cup (1 stick) butter, melted
1/2 teaspoon whole fennel seeds, crushed
1/2 teaspoon grated lemon rind
1 tablespoon lemon juice

1. Alternate scallops, tomatoes, zucchini, mushrooms and green peppers on 12 skewers. Preheat oven to 425°.
2. Combine melted butter, fennel seeds, lemon rind and juice. Brush some over kabobs. Place skewers on rack in baking pan.
3. Bake in a preheated hot oven (425°) for 20 minutes or until vegetables are tender, basting frequently with lemon butter. Heat remaining lemon butter and serve with kabobs.

Sweet and Sour Scallop Kebobs

Bake at 400° for 22 minutes.

Makes 6 servings.

1 package (6 1/4 ounces) fried rice mix with vermicelli and almonds
OR: 1 package (7 ounces) instant fried rice mix
1 package (10 ounces) frozen Brussels sprouts, partially thawed and each halved
1 can (16 ounces) whole carrots, drained

1 tablespoon vegetable oil
2 packages (8 ounces each) frozen batter-fried scallops, partially thawed
3/4 cup apricot or peach preserves
3 tablespoons sweet and spicy bottled French dressing
2 tablespoons prepared mustard
1/2 teaspoon ground ginger

1. Cook rice mix following label directions; keep warm. Preheat oven to 400°.
2. Gently toss Brussels sprouts and carrots with oil in large bowl. Thread scallops, sprouts and carrots alternately on six 15-inch metal skewers. Place on foil-lined jelly-roll pan, allowing the skewers to rest on the edge of pan so that the ingredients do not touch bottom of pan.
3. Bake in a preheated hot oven (400°) for 20 minutes.
4. Combine preserves, French dressing, mustard and ginger in a small saucepan; bring to boiling. Brush some of the sauce over kebobs; bake 2 minutes more or until glazed.
5. Spoon rice on warm platter; arrange kebobs on top. Pass remaining sauce.

Shrimp and Scallops in Wine Sauce

Delicately pink and temptingly tender, this shellfish combination tastes as good as it looks.

Makes 8 servings.

1 1/2 cups dry white wine
1/2 cup clam juice or water
1 bay leaf
1 pound fresh or thawed, frozen shelled and deveined shrimp, washed
1 pound fresh or thawed, frozen scallops, washed (large sea scallops should be quartered)

1 small onion, finely chopped (1/4 cup)
3 tablespoons butter or margarine
1/4 cup all-purpose flour
1/2 teaspoon salt
2 tablespoons tomato paste*
1 cup light cream or half-and-half
1 package (10 ounces) frozen puff pastry shells, baked following label directions

1. Combine wine, clam juice and bay leaf in large saucepan; bring to boiling; add shrimp and scallops. After mixture comes to the boil again, lower heat; simmer 3 minutes or just until shrimp and scallops are firm-tender. Drain, reserving cooking liquid.
2. Sauté onion in butter in a large saucepan just until tender but not browned; stir in flour and salt until mixture is smooth. Gradually stir in reserved cooking liquid and tomato paste. Cook, stirring constantly, until mixture thickens and bubbles. Lower heat; simmer 5 minutes.
3. Add cream, shrimp and scallops; place over low heat just until heated through. Serve in pastry shells. Garnish with lemon and watercress, if you wish.
To keep opened tomato paste for a future use, measure paste by tablespoonfuls onto a small sheet of foil; freeze. When solid, store pieces in plastic bag and keep frozen.

Pictured opposite:
Shrimp and Scallops in Wine Sauce.

MEAT

BEEF AND VEAL

Beef The wide variety of fresh beef cuts offers almost unlimited selection for any meal and menu. Beef supplies complete protein with 8 essential amino acids. One serving of cooked ground beef (3 ounces) provides 21.8 grams of protein, or 50 per cent of the recommended daily amount, along with 225 calories, .15 milligrams of riboflavin, 4.8 milligrams niacin and 1.1 micrograms of vitamin B_{12}. Beef is also a good source of iron and zinc.

Buying Beef: All meat sold must, by law, pass an inspection for wholesomeness. Meat which is to cross state lines must be inspected by the United States Department of Agriculture (USDA). Meat sold in the state in which it is produced must pass state and city inspections.

USDA inspectors examine beef before and after slaughter to see that it comes from healthy animals and is processed under sanitary conditions. Beef which passes federal inspection is stamped with a round, purple mark made with an edible vegetable dye. The mark is stamped on wholesale cuts, so you may not see it on small, retail cuts.

Quality: The USDA has also developed a grading system which indicates the meat's quality. The top three grades are U.S. Prime, U.S. Choice, and U.S. Good. Meat marked with these grades is from young animals (usually less than two years old). Beef marked with the lower five grades (Standard, Commercial, Utility, Cutter and Canner) is from more mature, less tender animals. These grades are usually processed into sausage and canned meats, but are just as wholesome and nutritious as the meat of the higher grades.

Prime beef—the top grade—is beef which is well-marbled. Marbling refers to the small flecks of fat interspersed with the lean muscle which contributes to tenderness and flavor. Most prime beef is sold to top restaurants and meat stores.

The grades generally sold at supermarkets are Choice or Good. Choice beef contains sufficient marbling for taste and tenderness, but is less costly than prime meat. Lower-priced Good beef has less marbling (and fewer calories). It is just as tasty and nutritious, but not as tender as the higher grades.

Color: The color of fresh beef should be bright to deep red. When beef is first cut, it is dark, purplish-red. After exposure to air, the cut surface turns bright red due to a reaction with oxygen in the air. That is why ground beef is often red on the outside, while the middle is darker. The middle will also redden when it is exposed to the air.

Cost: The most accurate way to determine meat cost is to base your calculations on price per serving, rather than price per pound. Cuts which contain a large amount of bone and fat may not be as economical as higher priced cuts which contain less waste.

The following chart shows how many servings per pound you can expect from each cut of beef. Remember, do not confuse number of servings with number of people you can serve. A hearty eater can consume 3 servings at a meal!

To find the cost per serving, divide the price per pound by the number of servings per pound the cut will provide. For example, if a roast costs $1.79 a pound and that cut gives you $2\frac{1}{2}$ servings a pound, your cost per serving would be 71¢.

Cut: "Which cut should I buy?" It's a tricky question with no set answers. In general, the cut to buy depends on how the meat is to be prepared. If your recipe calls for the meat to be cooked quickly or by dry heat (as in stir-frying or broiled kabobs), use a tender cut of beef. For slow, moist-heat cooking (stew, for example), a less tender cut will do.

Tender cuts come from muscles which are not used in movement and which have the least connective tissue. These muscles are found along the back of the animal and are called rib, loin or sirloin. The remaining muscles are used in movement and are less tender.

Many stores use a standardized meat-labeling system on their pre-packaged meats. The label tells you the kind of meat (beef, pork lamb, etc.), the primal or wholesale cut (chuck, rib, loin, round, etc.) which is where the cut comes from on the animal, and the retail cut (blade, arm, short rib, etc.) which tells you from what part of the primal cut the meat comes.

Since ground beef can come from several primal cuts, it is usually labeled according to the ratio of lean to fat. Again, your selection will depend on how you plan to use the meat. Ground beef or hamburger contains not less than 70% lean. Use it for burgers, chili, sloppy joes and casseroles. Lean ground beef or ground chuck has not less than 77% lean. Use it for meat loaf, meat balls and steaks. Extra lean ground beef, or ground round or sirloin, has not less than 85% lean. Use it as you would ground chuck, or when you're watching calorie and fat consumption.

Storing Beef: Fresh beef should be kept in the coldest part of the refrigerator or the compartment designed for meat storage. Pre-packaged meat can be stored as purchased in the refrigerator for 2 days or in the freezer for 1 to 2 weeks. For longer freezer

(continued)

Pictured opposite:
Hearty Beef Stew, page 319.

storage, wrap with proper freezer wrapping materials. Beef which has been wrapped in butcher paper should be loosely rewrapped in plastic or foil and stored for up to 2 days.

Cooked beef should be wrapped or covered and stored in the refrigerator within 1 or 2 hours after cooking. Cooked beef will keep better if left in larger pieces and not cut until ready to use.

COOKING BEEF
DRY HEAT METHODS FOR TENDER CUTS:

To Panbroil: For small, tender pieces cut 1-inch thick or less. Place steak or patty in heavy frying pan. Don't add fat or water and do not cover pan. Cook slowly, turning often; pour off any fat as it collects. Brown or cook to desired degree; season and serve.

To Panfry: For very thin, tender cuts or cuts made tender by pounding or cubing. They may be dusted with flour or crumbs. Heat a small amount of fat in frying pan. Add beef and brown on both sides over high heat, turning occasionally. Stir-frying is a form of panfrying used in Oriental-style cooking. A wok, large pan or electric skillet can be used. Ingredients must be cut into uniform sizes before cooking. Sautéing is a French term for panfrying.

To Broil: For tender steaks or patties at least 1-inch thick. Place meat on broiler rack over a pan. Broil meat which is 1-inch thick 2 to 3 inches from preheated heat source. Broil thicker cuts 3 to 5 inches from heat. Turn meat with tongs rather than a fork as a fork will pierce the meat, releasing juices. A charcoal, electric or gas grill can be used for broiling.

To Roast: For large, tender roasts. Season with salt, pepper or herbs. Place beef, fat side up, on a rack in an open, shallow pan. The fat on top bastes the meat and the rack holds it out of the drippings. Insert a meat thermometer in the center of the largest muscle; do not let it touch bone or rest in fat. Do not add water or cover meat. Roast in a slow oven (300 to 325°F.). When thermometer reads 5°F. below desired degree of doneness, remove beef roast from oven and let stand 15 minutes for easier carving. Rotisserie cooking is a form of roasting. Use large, uniformly-shaped cuts. Insert rotisserie rod lengthwise through center of roast; fasten securely. Place a drip pan under the turning beef to prevent flare-ups.

To Microwave: For tender beef roasts that are compact and uniform in shape. Boneless roasts are ideal. Place roast on a rack and cover with wax paper. Use a low power setting for a longer cooking time to get the most uniform doneness. If a roast is irregular in shape and a portion is cooking too fast, cover that piece with a bit of foil to retard cooking. To assure even cooking, turn roast or rotate the dish at intervals during the cooking time. To enhance the appearance of beef cooked by microwave, try brushing the surface with soy sauce, Worcestershire or a browning sauce.

Or coat surface with bread crumbs or glaze. You can also pre-brown the roast in a frying pan or use the browning dish of the microwave. The cooking time will vary depending on the shape and size of the meat.

MOIST HEAT METHODS FOR LESS TENDER CUTS:

To Braise: Brown beef, which may be coated with flour, in its own rendered fat or in a small amount of added fat in a heavy pan. Brown on all sides slowly; add onion, herbs and about 1/4 to 1/2 cup liquid such as water, broth, vegetable juice or a marinade. Cover and cook over low heat until tender. Braising can be done on top of the range or in a slow oven (300 to 325°F.).

To Cook in Liquid: Coat beef with flour and brown on all sides in its own fat or added fat in a heavy pan. Or, omit the step above; cover beef with liquid; cover pan. Cook over low heat until beef is just tender. If you like, add vegetables and cook along with the beef until tender.

To Pressure Cook: Follow manufacturer's directions.

To Slow Cook: Follow manufacturer's or recipe directions.

APPROXIMATE TIME FOR BRAISING LESS TENDER BEEF		
Cut	Approximate Weight or Thickness	Approximate Total Cooking time in hours
CHUCK BLADE ROAST	3 to 5 lbs.	2 to 2 1/2
CHUCK ARM POT ROAST	3 to 5 lbs.	2 1/2 to 3 1/2
CHUCK SHOULDER ROAST, BONELESS	3 to 5 lbs.	2 1/2 to 3 1/2
ROUND STEAK	3/4 to 1 inch	1 to 1 3/4
CHUCK OR ROUND CUBES (1 1/2-inch)	1 1/2 lbs.	1 1/2 to 2 1/2
SHORT RIBS (2 × 2 × 4-inch pieces)	3 lbs.	1 1/2 to 2 1/2

APPROXIMATE TIME FOR COOKING LESS TENDER BEEF IN LIQUID		
Cut	Approximate Weight	Approximate Total Cooking time in hours
FRESH OR CORNED BEEF	4 to 6 lbs.	3 to 4
SHANK CROSS CUTS	3/4 to 1 1/4 lbs.	2 to 3

How to Pare Your Beef Bills

You can save a substantial amount of money by buying large cuts of beef and cutting and wrapping them yourself. Larger beef cuts cost less per pound since they require less handling by the butcher. All you need is a clean, sharp knife, foil or freezing paper, and tape plus a marker to identify the packages. You can divide the cut into meal-size portions such as steaks to broil or panfry; strips to stir-fry, chunks to stew and trimmings to grind. Save the bones for soup stock.

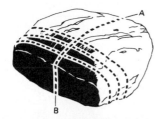

BONELESS BEEF TOP ROUND

With the fat side up, use a sharp knife to first split the Top Round in half. Cut with the grain, from A to B. From either half, 2 or 3 steaks can be cut across the grain, 1 to 1½ inches thick. The remaining portions can be used as roasts. If you would like cubes for braising, cut them from the tapered end of the roasts.

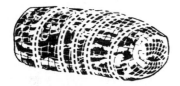

BONELESS BEEF CHUCK ROLL

If steaks for braising are a favorite, cut them with a sharp knife from the center portion. Since slicing thin steaks that hold together is difficult, for best results slice steaks about 1 inch thick. LEAVE THE NETTING OR STRINGS INTACT DURING CUTTING AND COOKING both roasts and steaks. For a roast section cut in half, tie strings to help hold shape during cooking.

Any part of the Chuck Roll is an excellent choice if you want cubes for braising or cooking in liquid or for ground beef.

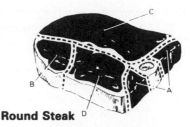

Round Steak

ROUND STEAK
(1¼ to 1½ Inches Thick)

Cut across bone end of steak following natural seams, removing bone and small pieces of meat A attached. Remove eye section B. Cut meat from A and B into small pieces and use for stew or soup (including bone if desired), or grind.

Separate top round C from bottom round D by cutting along natural seams. The larger top round is the most tender part of the round steak. Score if desired, marinate and broil to rare or medium. Carve in thin slices across the grain.

The bottom round D can be chilled and cut into thin strips for braising or marinating and stir-frying. Or it can be sliced into two thin steaks, pounded and braised as for Swiss steak.

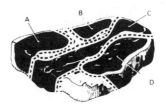

7-BONE POT-ROAST
(2 to 2¼ Inches Thick)

Cut around blade bone and remove sections A and B. Section A is the top blade and the most tender part of this cut. Remove membrane separating section A into two pieces; cut each into slices one-half inch thick. Panfry to rare or medium.

Divide remaining meat by cutting along natural seam between sections C and D. Remove bone from D. Cut meat from D and B into cubes; cook in liquid for stew or soup or grind.

Braise section C as pot-roast. Or chill and cut into thin strips to stir-fry or into four thin steaks to marinate and broil.

TENDERIZING BEEF

Less tender cuts may be tenderized, then cooked using dry heat methods. Tenderize by pounding meat with a meat mallet, or by using a marinade or commercial tenderizing mixture.

Manually pounding cuts such as round steak with a meat mallet tenderizes by breaking down the fibers and tissue. Cube steak is round steak that a butcher has put through a special machine which tears the fiber structure and creates a flattened steak.

Marinades are usually made of an acidic liquid such as vinegar, wine, citrus or tomato juice. The acid helps soften the meat fibers and connective tissue and adds flavor. Marinades also often contain flavoring ingredients, such as garlic, pepper, etc.

Commercial tenderizing mixtures are sold in various forms and contain enzymes which break down the connective tissue. Enzymes such as papain from papaya and bromelain from pineapple are usually used in these tenderizers.

TEMPERATURE AND TIME FOR ROASTING BEEF

Cut	Approximate Pound Weight	Oven Temperature	Internal Meat Temperature When Done	Minutes Per Pound Roasting Time
STANDING RIB (Ribs 6 to 7 inches long)	6 to 8	300° to 325°F.	140°F. (rare)	23 to 25
			160°F. (med.)	27 to 30
			170°F. (well)	32 to 35
	4 to 6	300° to 325°F.	140° F. (rare)	26 to 32
			160°F. (med.)	34 to 38
			170°F. (well)	40 to 42
ROLLED RIB	5 to 7	300° to 325°F.	140°F (rare)	32
			160°F. (med.)	38
			170°F. (well)	48
DELMONICO (Rib Eye)	4 to 6	350°F.	140°F. (rare)	18 to 20
			160°F. (med.)	20 to 22
			170°F. (well)	22 to 24
TENDERLOIN Whole	4 to 6	425°F.	140°F. (rare)	45 to 60*
TENDERLOIN Half	2 to 3	425°F	140°F. (rare)	45 to 50*
ROLLED RUMP (U.S. Prime and Choice)	4 to 6	300° to 325°F.	140° to 170°F.	25 to 30
SIRLOIN TIP (U.S. Prime and Choice)	3½ to 4	300° to 325°F.	140° to 170°F.	35 to 40
	4 to 6	300° to 325°F.	140° to 170°F.	30 to 35

*Total roasting time.

APPROXIMATE TIME FOR BROILING BEEF

Cut	Approximate Weight	Approximate Thickness	Approximate Total Cooking Time in Minutes	
			RARE	MEDIUM
CHUCK BLADE STEAK (U.S. Prime and Choice)	1¼ to 1¾ lbs.	¾ in.	14	20
	1½ to 2½ lbs.	1 in.	20	25
	2 to 4 lbs.	1½ in.	35	40
RIB EYE STEAK	8 to 10 ozs.	1 in.	15	20
	12 to 14 ozs.	1½ in.	25	30
	16 to 20 ozs.	2 in.	35	45
RIB STEAK	1 to 1½ lbs.	1 in.	15	20
	1½ to 2 lbs.	1½ in.	25	30
	2 to 2½ lbs.	2 in.	35	45

APPROXIMATE TIME FOR BROILING BEEF (continued)

Cut	Approximate Weight	Approximate Thickness	Approximate Total Cooking Time in Minutes	
			RARE	MEDIUM
PORTERHOUSE STEAK	1¼ to 2 lbs.	1 in.	20	25
	2 to 3 lbs.	1½ in.	30	35
	2½ to 3½ lbs.	2 in.	40	45
TENDERLOIN STEAK	4 to 6 oz.	1 in.	10	15
	6 to 8 oz.	1½ in.	15	20
TOP LOIN STEAK	1 to 1½ lbs.	1 in.	15	20
	1½ to 2 lbs.	1½ in.	25	30
	2 to 2½ lbs.	2 in.	35	45
SIRLOIN STEAK	1½ to 3 lbs.	1 in.	20	25
	2¼ to 4 lbs.	1½ in.	30	45
	3 to 5 lbs.	2 in.	40	35
TOP ROUND STEAK	1¼ to 1¾ lbs.	1 in.	20	30
	1½ to 2 lbs.	1½ in.	30	35
FLANK STEAK	1 to 1½ lbs.	—	12	14
GROUND BEEF PATTY	4 ozs.	1 in.	8	12

Number of Cooked Servings (3-3½ Ounces) Per Pound from Various Beef Cuts

Roasts
Rib Eye Roast 3
Rib Roast 2
Rump Roast 2
Rump Roast, Boneless 3
Tip Roast 3
Rop Round 3

Braising Steaks
Arm Steak 2
Blade Steak 2
Flank Steak 3
Round Steak 3
Tip Steak 3

Other Cuts
Beef for Stew 4
Brisket 3
Ground Beef 4
Short Ribs 2
Beef Variety Meats (liver, heart, tongue, kidney) 4

Broiling Steaks
Cubed Steak 4
Flank Steak 4
Porterhouse Steak 2
Sirloin Steak 2½
Rib Eye Steak 3
Rib Steak 2
Rib Steak, Boneless 2½
T-Bone 2
Tenderloin (Filet Mignon) Steak 3
Top Loin Steak 2
Top Loin Steak, Boneless 2½

Pot-Roasts
Arm Pot-Roast 2
Blade Roast 2
Bottom Round Roast 3
Cross Rib Pot-Roast 2
Eye Round Roast.................................3
Heel of Round 2
Shoulder Pot-Roast, Boneless 2½

Roast Ribs of Beef

Makes 12 servings.

Rub surface of a *3-rib (seven-inch cut) standing rib roast* with *1 teaspoon salt* and *¼ teaspoon pepper*. Place, fat side up, in shallow roasting pan. Do not cover; do not add water. No rack is necessary. Insert meat thermometer into thickest part of roast, with bulb not touching bone or resting in fat. Roast in a slow oven (325°) 20 minutes per pound for rare (140°), 22 to 25 minutes for medium (160°) and 27 to 30 minutes for well-done (170°). Let meat rest in a warm place 30 minutes before carving.

How to Carve a Standing Rib Roast

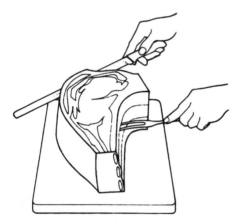

Place roast, broad-side down, on a large platter so that it stands firmly. Trim off any excess fat. Anchor roast with a fork; cut down along rib bones with a carving knife to free roast from the bones.

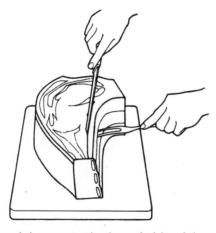

Slice straight across the broad side of the roast, making the slices as thick or thin as you like, cutting from the outer curved edge in to rib bones. The point of placing the roast on its broad side for carving, instead of standing it on its ribs, is that the juices will remain in the meat instead of running out on the platter.

How to Carve a Rolled Roast

Beef: If the shape of the roast permits, place broadside down on platter and slice it horizontally, straight across the face of the meat, making the cuts as thick or thin as you like. The reason for this placement is to keep juices in the roast. However, if roast is long and narrow, it's best to put it on its side and carve straight down.

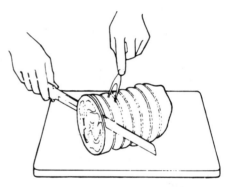

Pork, veal and lamb roasts: These are less juicy than beef roasts, and can rest on their sides. Simply carve straight down and through, from the top to the bottom.

Marinated Filet of Beef

Other cuts can also be used in this recipe.
Roast at 425° for 45 minutes.

Makes 12 servings.

1 filet of beef (about 4 pounds) or 1 rolled boned rib roast of beef, or eye-round roast, or sirloin tip roast (about 4 pounds)
1 cup soy sauce

½ cup medium or dry sherry
⅓ cup olive oil
3 cloves garlic, minced
2 teaspoons ground ginger

1. Trim filet if needed. In a large bowl (not aluminum), mix soy sauce, sherry, olive oil, garlic and ginger.

Place roast in mixture in bowl. Refrigerate 4 hours or overnight, turning roast several times, to season.

2. Remove roast from refrigerator 1 hour before cooking and let stand at room temperature.

3. Place roast on a rack in a roasting pan. Insert meat thermometer into center of thickest part.

4. Roast in a hot oven (425°), brushing with soy mixture 3 or 4 times, 45 to 50 minutes, or until thermometer registers 140° for rare. For medium rare, continue roasting to 150°. Do not overcook.

5. Remove roast to a deep platter; pour pan juices over top. Slice and serve.

Savory Grilled Short Ribs

Grill for about 1 hour.

Makes 6 servings.

4 pounds beef short ribs, cut into serving-size pieces	pepper
	1/2 cup catsup
	1 cup beer
1 teaspoon salt	1/4 cup bottled steak sauce
1/2 teaspoon	

1. Rub meat with salt and pepper. Roast ribs 6 inches from grayed coals 30 minutes, turning often.

2. Combine catsup, beer and steak sauce in a small saucepan; bring to boiling. Brush part over ribs; continue to roast and brush often with beer baste 30 minutes more or until meat is medium rare or done to your taste. Serve ribs with any remaining baste as a sauce.

Hearty Beef Stew

A savory stew with an abundance of spring vegetables.

Makes 8 servings.

3 tablespoons olive or vegetable oil	1/2 teaspoon leaf thyme, crumbled
3 pounds lean chuck or round, cut into 1 1/2- to 2-inch cubes	12 small white onions, peeled
3 tablespoons finely chopped shallots	4 small turnips, pared and quartered
1 clove garlic, minced	3 to 4 carrots, pared and cut into 2-inch lengths
3 tablespoons flour	
1 can condensed beef broth	12 small new potatoes, peeled (1 pound)
1 can (16 ounces) tomatoes or 1 cup peeled and chopped fresh tomatoes	1 package (10 ounces) frozen peas
	2 tablespoons chopped parsley
1 1/2 teaspoons salt	

1. Heat oil in a large kettle or Dutch oven; brown beef, a few pieces at a time. Remove pieces as they brown to a bowl.

2. Remove all but 1 tablespoon fat from kettle; add shallots and garlic; sauté, stirring often, 2 minutes, or until golden-brown. Sprinkle flour over shallots; cook over moderate heat, stirring.

3. Stir in beef broth and tomatoes; bring to boiling, stirring constantly to loosen browned bits. Return beef to kettle. Stir in salt and thyme. Bring to boiling; lower heat, cover. Simmer 1 hour. Skim off fat, if any.

4. Add onions, turnips, carrots and potatoes to beef, pushing them down under liquid; cover; simmer 45 minutes longer, or until beef and vegetables are tender. Stir in peas; cover; simmer 5 to 10 minutes longer. Sprinkle with parsley. Taste, and add more salt, if necessary.

Belgian Beef Stew

Makes 6 servings.

1/4 pound lean bacon, diced	cubes
	2 tablespoons flour
20 small white onions, peeled	2 teaspoons salt
	1/4 teaspoon pepper
1 large clove garlic, minced	1 can or bottle (12 ounces) dark beer
2 pounds boneless chuck or round, cut into 1 1/2-inch	1 tablespoon lemon juice

1. Pour boiling water over bacon in a large skillet and let stand 1 minute. Drain. Cook bacon until limp and transparent. Add onions and garlic. Cook, stirring frequently, until they are golden.

2. Transfer bacon and onions to a Dutch oven or flameproof casserole. Add beef cubes, a few pieces at a time, to the fat in the skillet and brown over high heat. As the cubes brown, transfer to casserole.

3. Add flour, salt, pepper and beer to casserole. Bring to boiling. Lower heat. Cover and simmer 1 1/2 hours or until meat is tender. Check for moisture and, if necessary, add a little more beer.

4. Taste for seasoning and add more salt and pepper. Remove from heat. Stir in lemon juice. Serve with noodles, if you wish.

Oven-Barbecued Brisket of Beef

One of the simplest and easiest ways to cook beef for flavor and tender eating.

Bake at 350° for 3 hours.

Makes 8 servings.

1 lean brisket of beef (4 to 5 pounds)	1/2 recipe Texas Barbecue Sauce (2 cups) (*recipe follows*)
Liquid smoke (*optional*)	

1. Center a 24-inch length of 18-inch heavy-duty foil in a 13×9×2-inch baking pan.

(continued)

2. Place brisket on center of foil. Add liquid smoke to sauce if you wish; pour sauce over meat. Bring ends of foil together evenly; fold over and continue folding down to top of meat. Fold sides up to make a neat sealed package.

3. Bake package in the pan in a moderate oven (350°) for 3 hours or until meat is tender.

4. Remove from oven. Carefully open foil; lift meat to heated serving platter. Pour sauce from foil into sauce dish. Skim off excess fat. Serve sauce with meat.

Texas Barbecue Sauce

Here's a real winner you'll want to make again and again. Stored in clean jars in the refrigerator, it will keep for months.

Makes about 4 1/2 cups.

2 medium-size onions, finely chopped (1 cup)	1/4 cup Worcestershire sauce
1 clove garlic, finely chopped	1/3 cup firmly packed brown sugar
1/4 cup vegetable oil	2 tablespoons prepared mustard
2 tablespoons chili powder	1 tablespoon celery seeds
2 cups catsup	2 teaspoons cumin seeds, crushed
1 cup cider or white vinegar	2 tablespoons butter or margarine
1/2 cup lemon juice	

1. Sauté onions and garlic in oil in a large saucepan until golden and tender, 10 minutes; stir in chili powder and cook 1 minute.

2. Add all remaining ingredients except butter; bring to boiling. Lower heat; simmer uncovered, stirring often, for 30 minutes. Stir in butter.

Ranch-Style Chili

A really fine chili, cooked the way Texans like it. Serve with beans, if you like, but never add them to the chili.

Makes 8 servings.

4 tablespoons vegetable oil	2 tablespoons flour
3 pounds beef chuck or round, cut into 1/4- to 1/2-inch cubes	3 teaspoons cumin seeds, crushed
	2 teaspoons leaf oregano, crumbled
2 large onions, chopped (2 cups)	2 teaspoons salt
3 cloves garlic, finely minced	1/8 to 1/4 teaspoon cayenne
2 tablespoons ground red chile	1 can condensed beef broth
OR: 4 tablespoons chili powder	1 1/2 cups water
	1 to 2 tablespoons cornmeal

1. Heat 2 tablespoons of the oil in a heavy Dutch oven; add meat to brown lightly, 1/3 at a time; remove as it browns. Add onions and garlic to pan, adding more oil as needed; sauté until tender and lightly browned, 10 minutes. Return all meat to pan.

2. Combine ground chile, flour and cumin; sprinkle mixture over meat; stir with wooden spoon over low heat until meat is evenly coated, 1 to 2 minutes. Stir in oregano, salt, cayenne, beef broth and water. Bring to boiling, stirring often. Lower heat; simmer slowly, covered, 1 1/2 to 2 hours or until meat is very tender.

3. Sprinkle in the cornmeal, stirring constantly; cook until slightly thickened, 5 to 10 minutes. Serve with freshly cooked hot rice and cooked pinto beans, if you wish.

Braciole

(Also **braciola**) Pronounced *bra-CHOH-lah*, this Italian word means steak. Braciole is a braised meat roll stuffed with seasonings or vegetables, usually made with very thinly pounded round steak.

Braciole

Makes 8 servings.

2 1/2 pounds round steak	pepper seasoning
	2 tablespoons olive oil
1/2 pound Italian sausage	1 large onion, chopped (1 cup)
1/2 cup chopped fresh parsley	1/2 cup chopped carrot
1/4 cup grated Parmesan cheese	1 1/2 cups dry red wine
	1 can (16 ounces) plum tomatoes
1 clove garlic, minced	1 can (6 ounces) tomato paste
1 teaspoon Italian herb seasoning mix	1 teaspoon salt
1 teaspoon salt	1 bay leaf
1/2 teaspoon lemon-	

1. Trim all fat from steak; cut meat into 8 equal pieces; then pound until very thin with a wooden mallet.

2. Remove casing from Italian sausage. Break up in a medium-size bowl; add parsley, Parmesan cheese, garlic, Italian seasoning, 1 teaspoon salt and the lemon-pepper seasoning; mix thoroughly. Spread each steak with 2 heaping tablespoons of the sausage mixture; roll up, jelly-roll fashion; fasten with wooden picks or tie with string.

3. Brown beef rolls, 3 or 4 at a time, in hot oil in a Dutch oven; remove rolls and place on plate or wax paper. Add onion and carrot to pot; cook until vegetables are soft, about 5 minutes. Stir in wine, tomatoes, tomato paste, remaining 1 teaspoon salt and bay leaf; bring mixture to boiling; lower heat. Add beef rolls; cover and simmer for 1 hour. Remove from heat.

4. Remove the picks or string from braciole before serving.

Roast Beef.

Roast Beef

Serve with baked yams and broccoli.
Roast at 325° for 1 hour and 10 minutes.

Makes 12 servings.

1 boneless beef rump roast (3½ pounds)
1 teaspoon salt
¼ teaspoon pepper
Beef Pan Gravy (*recipe follows*)

1. Rub roast with salt and pepper; place, fat side up, on rack in roasting pan. Do not add water or cover pan. If using a meat thermometer, insert bulb into center of meat.
2. Roast in a slow oven (325°), allowing 20 minutes per pound or about 1 hour and 10 minutes for rare meat (140°); 30 minutes per pound or about 1 hour and 45 minutes for medium (160°).
3. Place roast on cutting board; allow to stand for 15 minutes for easier carving.
4. Cut roast into thin slices. Serve with Beef Pan Gravy.

Beef Pan Gravy: Skim off all fat from roasting pan into a cup, leaving juices in pan. Return 1 tablespoon fat to pan; blend in 1 tablespoon flour. Cook, stirring, just until mixture bubbles. Stir in 1 cup water slowly; continue cooking and stirring, scraping baked-on juices from bottom of pan, until gravy thickens and bubbles 3 minutes. Taste; season with salt and pepper if needed. Makes 1 cup.

Tulsa Ribs

Remember to replenish the coals in the charcoal grill when barbecuing over a long period of time.

Grill for 1½ to 2 hours.

Makes 6 to 8 servings.

6 pounds meaty beef ribs, cut into 4-to 5-inch-long pieces

Barbecue Sauce:
2 tablespoons unsalted butter or margarine
1 cup chopped onion (1 large onion)
1 clove garlic, finely chopped
1 can (16 ounces) tomato sauce

1 cup cider vinegar
1 cup tomato-vegetable juice
½ cup prune juice
1 generous tablespoon slivered lemon peel (½ lemon)
3 tablespoons lemon juice (1 large lemon)
1 bay leaf
6 crushed juniper berries *(optional)*
½ teaspoon brown sugar or honey

1. Prepare the charcoal for grilling or preheat the gas unit.
2. To precook the ribs, divide the ribs up and wrap in 3 heavy-duty aluminum foil packets. Place on the grid. Cover with the dome. * Cook over high heat for 1 hour. (If cooking over coals, replenish with new charcoal as needed.)
3. Meanwhile, prepare the Barbecue Sauce: Melt the butter in a large saucepan over medium heat. Stir in the onion; cook for 2 minutes. Add the garlic; cook for 1 minute longer. Add the tomato sauce, vinegar, tomato-vegetable juice, prune juice, lemon peel, lemon juice, bay leaf, juniper berries, if using, cayenne and brown sugar. Bring to boiling. Lower the heat and simmer until the sauce has thickened, about 30 minutes.

4. Remove the rib packets from the grid. Carefully open and place the ribs back on the grid. Place the hood on the grill. Cook until tender, 30 minutes to 1 hour, basting with the barbecue sauce and turning, if necessary. Pass the extra barbecue sauce

*To make a barbecue cover or dome, see instructions accompanying this recipe.

Buying Ribs. Pork ribs shrink slightly in cooking, so plan on ¾ to 1 pound per serving.

Beef Sukiyaki

Makes 4 servings.

1 pound boneless sirloin steak, cut 2 inches thick
3 celery stalks, cut into ½-inch lengths
¼ pound mushrooms, sliced
6 green onions, cut into 1-inch pieces
1 can (8 ounces) water chestnuts,

drained and sliced
¼ pound fresh spinach, washed and torn into pieces
2 tablespoons vegetable oil
½ cup canned beef broth
¼ cup soy sauce
¼ cup dry sherry
1 tablespoon sugar

1. Slice beef diagonally across the grain into uniformly thin strips. Arrange meat and vegetables on large plate.
2. Heat oil in a large skillet; brown meat quickly. Push meat to one side and add vegetables except spinach, keeping each type in a separate area of the pan. Stir gently to cook.
3. Combine broth, soy sauce, sherry and sugar in a small bowl. When vegetables are tender but still crisp, pour in soy mixture. Cook 5 more minutes.
4. Add spinach and cook until wilted, about 3 minutes. Stir and serve.

To Make a Grill Cover or Dome for a Barbecue Grill

When the recipe calls for a covered grill, an open-style grill may be used by constructing your own dome from a wire coat hanger frame, and then coverng it with aluminum foil. Snip the hooks off of several hangers and open them out into straight pieces. With pliers, twist together the ends of 2 or 3 hanger pieces to make a ring the size of your grill. Use 5 or

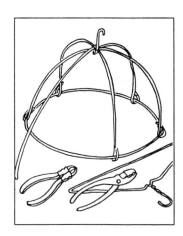

6 more to fashion a dome. Twist the ends of the hangers forming the dome around the ring base *(left).* Then cover the dome with several sheets of overlapping aluminum foil, gathering the foil at the top of the dome and twisting it together to form a topknot for a handle. Cut several flaps for vents near the top *(right).*

Marinated Beef Round

Roast on rotisserie for 1½ hours.

Makes 12 servings.

1 eye-round or top
   round roast (about
   4 pounds and 4
   inches in diameter)
1 cup red wine
⅓ cup red wine
   vinegar
1 large onion,
   chopped (1 cup)
2 envelopes instant
   beef broth

1 teaspoon Italian herb
   seasoning mix
1 teaspoon salt
½ teaspoon coarse
   black pepper
2 tablespoons butter
   or margarine
¼ cup finely chopped
   parsley
2 cloves garlic, finely
   chopped

1. Pierce meat deeply with a fork for flavors to penetrate. Place in a plastic bag in a large bowl.
2. Combine wine, vinegar, onion, beef broth, herbs, salt and pepper; pour over meat in plastic bag; tie closed. Marinate in refrigerator for 24 to 48 hours, turning occasionally.
3. Remove meat from marinade; make deep incisions in meat with the tip of a knife. Mix butter, parsley and garlic to a smooth paste; push mixture into incisions. Tie roast with string every two inches.
4. Insert spit lengthwise through center of meat. Fasten with holding forks so it won't slip. Insert meat thermometer in thickest part of meat.
5. Roast over grayed coals, basting with marinade every 20 minutes, 1 hour and 30 minutes or until thermometer registers 140° for rare. Remove spit and allow roast to rest 15 minutes, covered loosely with aluminum foil.

Beef and Beans

This hearty meal-in-a-dish is the modern version of one that sustained many a cattle driver along the old Chisholm Trail.

Bake at 325° for 1½ hours.

Makes 8 servings.

½ pound small dried
   lima beans
½ pound dried pinto
   or kidney beans
6 cups water
3 bacon slices
4 cross cuts beef
   shank (3½ to 4
   pounds)
2 tablespoons flour
2 large onions,

chopped (2 cups)
1 can (35 ounces)
   plum tomatoes,
   undrained
3 teaspoons salt
½ teaspoon pepper
¼ teaspoon crushed
   red pepper
1 teaspoon leaf thyme,
   crumbled
1 bay leaf

1. Pick over beans and rinse; place in a large saucepan or kettle and add water. Let stand overnight to soak.
2. Next day, bring beans and liquid slowly to boiling;

cover. Simmer 30 minutes. Drain beans, reserving liquid to use later.
3. Meanwhile, sauté bacon until crisp in a large skillet. Remove bacon and set aside. Coat beef shanks with flour. Brown on all sides in bacon drippings; transfer as they brown to a 12-cup baking dish. Add beans to baking dish.
4. Add onions to skillet; sauté, stirring often, until lightly browned and tender, 10 minutes. Stir in tomatoes, salt, pepper, red pepper, thyme and bay leaf; bring to boiling, stirring and crushing tomatoes. Pour over beans and beef shanks. Cover.
5. Bake in a slow oven (325°) for 1½ to 2 hours or until tender, stirring once or twice and adding some reserved bean liquid if mixture becomes dry. Crumble bacon over top of beans before serving.

Beef and Vegetable Kabobs

Grill 12 to 15 minutes.

Makes 4 servings.

1 chuck steak,
   1½ inches thick
   (about 2 pounds)
½ pint cherry
   tomatoes
½ pound mushrooms
2 green peppers
1 jar (16 ounces)
   whole onions in
   liquid
1 jar (6 ounces)
   marinated artichoke
   hearts
½ cup vegetable oil

¼ cup honey
2 tablespoons vinegar
2 tablespoons soy
   sauce
1 large clove garlic,
   minced
2 tablespoons minced
   parsley
1 teaspoon ground
   ginger
1 teaspoon coarse salt
½ teaspoon cracked
   pepper

1. Cut steak into 1½-inch cubes. Prepare vegetables, leaving tomatoes and mushroom caps whole if small; seed peppers and cut into squares; drain onions and artichoke hearts, reserving liquids.
2. Combine oil, honey, vinegar, soy sauce, garlic, parsley, ginger, salt and pepper with reserved liquids. Pour marinade mixture into a large, shallow nonmetal dish. Add meat cubes.
3. Let marinate for 1 to 24 hours, turning occasionally. Cover dish and refrigerate.
4. Thread vegetables, except peppers, on skewers and brush generously with marinade. Remove meat from marinade. Pat with paper toweling to remove excess marinade. Thread meat and peppers alternately on other skewers.
5. Grill meat 5 inches from hot coals 12 to 15 minutes for rare, turning skewers several times and basting with the marinade. Grill vegetables about 5 to 8 minutes, brushing with marinade and turning several times until tender.

Beef and Vegetable Stew

Makes 8 servings.

3 pounds brisket of beef	pared and cut into cubes (2 cups)
1/2 pound pepperoni (1 sausage)	3 carrots, cut into 2-inch pieces
1 teaspoon salt	4 sweet potatoes or yams, pared and cut into quarters
1/4 teaspoon pepper	
1 clove garlic, chopped	2 large all-purpose potatoes, pared and cut into quarters
1 medium-size onion, chopped (1/2 cup)	
1/2 cup chopped celery	4 medium-size ears corn, cut into 2-inch pieces
2 sprigs parsley	
4 cups boiling water	
1 small rutabaga (yellow turnip),	2 tablespoons flour
	1/4 cup water

1. Cut beef into 1 1/2-inch pieces, trimming away as much fat as possible. Slice sausage.
2. Heat a heavy kettle or Dutch oven. Rub fat from meat over bottom until about 2 tablespoons of fat is melted. Brown beef pieces well on all sides, a few at a time, removing pieces as they brown. Add sausage, salt, pepper, garlic, onion and celery; sauté until vegetables are almost tender. Return beef; add parsley and boiling water. Bring to boiling; lower heat; cover. Simmer 2 hours or until meat is almost tender.
3. Add rutabaga, carrots, sweet potatoes and potatoes; simmer about 50 minutes longer or until meat and vegetables are tender. Add corn; simmer 10 minutes longer.
4. Remove meat and vegetables to a large serving platter. Skim fat from liquid in pan, if necessary. Blend flour and water in a cup. Stir into liquid in pan. Cook, stirring constantly, until sauce thickens. Serve over stew.

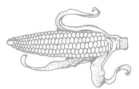

Beef and Lima Bean Stew

Makes 6 servings.

1 1/2 cups dried baby lima beans	2 celery stalks, finely chopped
2 quarts cold water (8 cups)	2 carrots, finely chopped
1 pound beef chuck, cut into 1-inch cubes	1 teaspoon leaf rosemary, crumbled
1/2 cup medium barley	1 can (16 ounces) tomatoes
1 large onion, chopped (1 cup)	4 teaspoons salt
	1/4 teaspoon pepper

1. Pick over and wash beans; drain and combine with 6 cups of the water in Dutch oven or kettle. Bring to boiling; cover. Cook 2 minutes; remove from heat; let stand 1 hour.
2. Add remaining water, chuck, barley, onion, celery, carrots, rosemary and tomatoes. Bring to boiling; lower heat. Simmer, covered, 2 hours or until beef and beans are tender. Stir in salt and pepper.

Chimichangas

A chimichanga is a burrito or rolled, stuffed flour tortilla that has been fried to a golden crispness. The frying changes the flavor and texture of the tortilla. Chimichangas can be made with any type filling, such as chili con carne, refried beans or cheese.

Makes 8 servings.

1 1/2 pounds beef chuck or round, cut into 1 1/2-inch pieces	diced, mild green chilies (about two 4-ounce cans)
1 1/2 pounds boneless pork shoulder, cut into 2-inch chunks	1 clove garlic, minced
	2 tablespoons flour
4 cups water	2 teaspoons salt
2 tablespoons lard or vegetable shortening	1/2 teaspoon ground cumin
	8 large flour tortillas
1 large onion, chopped (1 cup)	Vegetable oil for frying
	Green Chile Salsa (*recipe follows*)
3/4 to 1 cup canned	

1. Heat beef, pork and water to boiling in a large kettle; lower heat; cover. Simmer until meat is fork tender, about 1 1/2 hours. Drain meat and reserve 1 cup broth. Shred meat when cool enough to handle.
2. Heat lard in a large saucepan. Add onion, 3/4 cup chilies and garlic; sauté 1 minute. Add flour, salt and cumin; cook 1 minute. Stir in reserved broth and shredded meat; cook until mixture is moist but quite thick. (Add more chilies if you like it hotter.) Keep meat mixture warm.
3. Heat 1 tortilla on a large griddle or very large skillet over low heat until soft and pliable. Spread about 3/4 cup meat mixture over the lower third of the tortilla in a band about 4 inches long and 1 inch wide. Work quickly so that tortilla does not get crisp. Fold the bottom edge of the tortilla up over filling to cover it almost completely. Then fold the two sides in towards the center over the filling and start rolling the filling into a cylinder. Repeat with remaining tortillas.
4. Heat 1/2 inch oil in a large skillet until very hot. Sauté two chimichangas at a time in hot oil until golden, turning with two broad spatulas. Drain on paper toweling; keep warm while cooking remainder. Serve with Green Chile Salsa. Garnish with shredded lettuce and avocado slices, if you wish.

Pictured opposite:
Beef and Vegetable Stew.

Green Chile Salsa

Makes about 1⅓ cups.

1 can (16-ounces) whole tomatoes, drained
OR 3 fresh tomatoes, peeled, seeded and chopped
1 can (4 ounces) diced
mild, green chilies (½ cup)
½ cup finely chopped green onions
½ teaspoon salt
½ teaspoon leaf oregano, crumbled

Combine all ingredients in a bowl, breaking up canned tomatoes into small pieces. Chill at least 1 hour before serving to blend flavors. Or prepare ahead and store in jar. Refrigerate; use within 1 week.

Texas Chili Beef Stew

Chili adds its own sweet spiciness to this rib-sticking stew with beef and beans for a sturdy winter's meal.

Makes 8 servings.

4 pounds beef short ribs, cut into serving-size pieces
1 large onion, chopped (1 cup)
1 green pepper, halved, seeded and diced
2 cloves garlic, chopped
2 tablespoons chili powder
1 can (16 ounces) tomatoes
1 can (4 ounces) mild whole green chilies,
drained and chopped
1 envelope or teaspoon instant beef broth
1 cup boiling water
1 teaspoon salt
2 tablespoons flour
¼ cup water
2 cans (16 ounces each) kidney beans, drained
1 can (16 ounces) whole-kernel corn, drained

1. Heat heavy kettle or Dutch oven; rub fat edges of short ribs over bottom until about 2 tablespoons of fat melt. Brown short ribs well on all sides; remove. Drain off fat.
2. Sauté onion, green pepper and garlic in same pan. Stir in chili powder; cook, stirring constantly, about 2 minutes. Add tomatoes and green chilies. Dissolve instant beef broth in boiling water; stir into tomato mixture; add salt. Return ribs to pan. Bring to boiling; lower heat; cover. Simmer 2 hours or until meat is very tender and just begins to fall away from the bones.
3. Remove meat to serving bowl; keep warm. Carefully remove bones and skim fat from sauce in pan. Blend flour and water in a cup; mix well. Stir into sauce. Cook, stirring constantly, until sauce bubbles and thickens. Add kidney beans and corn; heat about 5 minutes. Spoon over meat in serving bowl.

Beef Burgundy

Makes 8 servings.

5 bacon slices
3½ pounds beef chuck, cut in 2-inch cubes
½ pound mushrooms, sliced
2 large cloves garlic, crushed
3 teaspoons salt
½ teaspoon pepper
⅓ cup all-purpose flour
4 whole cloves
1 teaspoon leaf thyme,
crumbled
1 bay leaf
1½ cups red Burgundy wine
¼ cup minced fresh parsley
1 pound carrots, pared and cut into 2-inch pieces
12 small white onions, peeled
1 package (10 ounces) frozen peas

1. Cook bacon in open pressure cooker until crisp. Drain on paper toweling. Pour off and reserve bacon drippings. Return 2 tablespoons drippings to cooker.
2. Quickly brown beef cubes on medium-high heat, a small amount at a time (don't crowd). As meat browns, remove with slotted spoon to a bowl. Add more bacon drippings to cooker as needed to brown all the meat.
3. Add mushroom slices to cooker and sauté for just a few minutes. With slotted spoon, remove to small bowl.
4. Add garlic, beef cubes, salt and pepper to cooker; stir well. Then sprinkle flour over meat, stirring to cover and blend well.
5. Tie cloves, thyme and bay leaf in a small piece of cheesecloth; drop into cooker. Add wine and parsley. Mix well. Crumble fried bacon and add to mixture.
6. Close cover securely. Place pressure control on vent pipe (number 10 if your cooker has multi-pressure selections). Turn heat to high until control starts to jiggle or rock, about 5 minutes. Slowly reduce heat to medium-low so control rocks gently; pressure-cook for 20 minutes.
7. Remove from heat immediately; set closed cooker under faucet of running cold water (just a few minutes). Carefully remove control and then the cover.
8. Add carrots and onions. Close cover securely; place pressure control on vent pipe; set on high heat and bring up to pressure again (when control starts to jiggle or rock). Slowly reduce heat to medium-low and pressure-cook for 2 to 3 minutes.
9. Again, reduce pressure by placing cooker under

running cold water. Remove and discard spice and herb bag.

10. Add peas and mushrooms; cook in open cooker until peas are tender.

Pepperpot Stew

Make this hearty stew as hot with pepper as you like. Serve with frosty mugs of beer.

Makes 8 to 10 servings.

4 pounds beef short ribs, cut into 2-inch pieces	**beef broth**
1 teaspoon salt	**¹/₈ teaspoon cayenne**
1 teaspoon freshly ground pepper	**8 whole cloves**
¹/₄ cup vegetable oil	**4 bay leaves**
10 medium-size onions, sliced ¹/₄-inch thick (about 3 pounds)	**1 lemon**
	1¹/₂ cups day-old rye or pumpernickel bread crumbs (about 3 slices)
2 cans (13 ³/₄ ounces)	**2 tablespoons drained capers**

1. Season ribs with salt and pepper. Heat oil in heavy kettle or Dutch oven. Brown ribs, part at a time, removing pieces to a bowl as they brown.
2. Sauté onions in fat remaining in kettle just until tender. Add beef broth and cayenne. Tie cloves and bay leaves together in cheesecloth bag; add to kettle. Return meat to kettle; heat to boiling. Cover. Simmer 2 hours or until meat is very tender.
3. Remove ribs and onions with slotted spoon to deep heated serving dish. Remove bones from ribs; keep warm. Remove and discard cheesecloth bag. Skim off fat from liquid in kettle.
4. Pare the thin yellow rind from the lemon with a vegetable parer and cut into thin strips. Cut lemon. Squeeze 1 teaspoon lemon juice from the lemon.
5. Bring liquid to boiling and stir in bread crumbs, capers, lemon peel and juice; lower heat; simmer, uncovered, about 15 minutes. Taste; season with additional pepper, if necessary.
6. Remove lemon strips and pour sauce over meat. Serve with mashed potatoes, if you wish.

Steak au Poivre

Makes 6 to 8 servings.

1 sirloin steak (about 3 pounds)	**pepper**
Salt	**2 tablespoons olive oil or clarified butter**
Coarsely ground black	**¹/₄ cup brandy or rum**

1. Rub steak on both sides with salt and pepper.
2. Heat oil or butter in a large skillet. Panfry steak over high heat to desired doneness.
3. Remove steak from pan to heated platter. Add brandy or rum to pan. Mix juices; pour over steak. Serve immediately.

Cocido (Spanish Beef Stew)

Frugal Iberian cooks team sausage with beef, chick-peas and cabbage to satisfy appetites and save pesetas.

Makes 6 servings.

2 pounds round steak, cut into 1-inch cubes	**cut into 1-inch cubes**
1 tablespoon salt	**2 cans (20 ounces each) chick-peas, drained**
2 cloves garlic, chopped	**3 tablespoons coarsely chopped fresh parsley**
4 cups water	
1 bay leaf	**3 cups shredded cabbage**
6 peppercorns	
6 whole coriander seeds	**1 large leek, washed and cut into ¹/₄-inch slices (about 1 cup)**
1 large onion, sliced	
4 carrots, pared and cut into 1-inch pieces	**6 pork sausages (¹/₂ pound)**
4 potatoes, pared and	

1. Combine beef, salt, garlic and water in a kettle or Dutch oven. Bring to boiling; lower heat; skim off foam. Tie bay leaf, peppercorns and coriander seeds in a piece of cheesecloth; add to kettle; lower heat; cover, simmer 1 hour.
2. Stir in onion, carrots, potatoes, chick-peas and 2 tablespoons of the parsley. Simmer 45 minutes longer or until meat and vegetables are almost tender. Stir in cabbage and leek.
3. Simmer, stirring several times, for 15 minutes longer or until all is tender. Remove cheesecloth bag. Thicken, if desired, with a little flour mixed with water.
4. Brown sausages in a skillet, 10 to 15 minutes; cut them in half and arrange on top of stew. Sprinkle with remaining parsley.
5. Serve in soup plates or shallow bowls with crusty bread, if you wish.

Goulash   A corruption of the Hungarian word *gulyás*, meaning "shepherd," goulash is a soup-stew which once sustained shepherds. Many versions of this one-dish meal can be found in eastern Europe. The usual ingredients are beef, veal or pork, seasoned with paprika.

Beef Gulyás

The generous use of paprika identifies this hearty beef stew as a native dish in the land of the Magyars.

Makes 8 servings.

4 bacon slices, diced
3 pounds beef round, cut into 1½-inch cubes
1 large onion, chopped (1 cup)
2 cloves garlic, crushed
1½ tablespoons paprika
1 can condensed

beef broth
1½ teaspoons salt
½ teaspoon caraway seeds
1 pound small white onions, peeled
¼ cup all-purpoe flour
6 tablespoons water
Hot cooked egg noodles
Dairy sour cream

1. Sauté bacon until crisp in Dutch oven; remove with slotted spoon to paper toweling to drain; reserve.
2. Brown beef cubes, half at a time, in the bacon drippings; remove to a bowl as they brown.
3. Sauté onion in drippings in pan until soft and golden; stir in garlic and paprika; cook, stirring constantly, 2 minutes.
4. Return browned beef to pan; stir in beef broth, salt and caraway seeds. Heat to boiling; lower heat; cover. Simmer 1½ hours.
5. Add onions and bacon. Simmer 45 to 60 minutes longer or until beef and onions are tender. Mix flour and water to a smooth paste; stir into boiling Gulyás; cook, stirring constantly, until sauce thickens and bubbles 1 minute. Gulyás may now be refrigerated and then reheated just before serving.
6. Spoon Gulyás onto a heated deep platter; arrange egg noodles around edge. Garnish with sautéed green peppers and chopped parsley, if you wish. Pass sour cream at the table.

Chuck Steak Bordeaux

Makes 6 servings.

3½ to 4 pounds boneless chuck, cut 2-inches thick
1 cup dry red wine (Bordeaux) or cider vinegar
½ cup vegetable oil
1 large onion, sliced

2 cloves garlic, halved
1 bay leaf
1 teaspoon leaf thyme, crumbled
3 teaspoons salt
½ teaspoon freshly ground black pepper

1. Place meat in a deep nonmetal dish. Combine remaining ingredients in a 2-cup measure; pour over meat. Marinate meat in refrigerator for 24 to 48 hours, turning occasionally. Drain steak, reserving marinade. Place steak on rack over a broiler pan.
2. Broil meat 6 inches from heat, about 30 minutes for medium rare, turning occasionally and basting with marinade.

Chicken-Fried Steak with Pan Gravy

Sometimes called "country-fried" but always called good eating.

Makes 6 servings.

1¾ pounds round steak, sliced ½-inch thick
OR: 6 cube steaks (about 1¾ pounds)
2 eggs
2 tablespoons water
⅓ cup all-purpose flour
⅓ cup cornmeal
1 teaspoon salt

½ teaspoon pepper
Flour
4 to 6 tablespoons vegetable oil

Pan Gravy:
2 tablespoons flour
1½ cups milk (about)
½ teaspoon salt
⅛ teaspoon pepper

1. Pound steak to ¼-inch thick, or ask butcher to tenderize; cut into 6 pieces.
2. Beat eggs and water together in pie plate. Mix flour, cornmeal, salt and pepper on wax paper. Dip steaks first in plain flour, then in egg mixture. Dip in seasoned flour mixture to coat well.
3. Brown meat, 3 pieces at a time, in hot oil on both sides in a large heavy skillet. Return all meat to skillet; lower heat; cover. Cook 20 minutes or until tender. Remove steaks to heated platter.
4. To prepare Pan Gravy, pour off all but 3 tablespoons of the pan drippings; blend in flour. Stir in milk, salt and pepper. Continue cooking and stirring until gravy thickens and bubbles 1 minute. If gravy is too thick add more milk.

Magyar Beef Paprikash

A Hungarian specialty featuring beef strips, mushrooms and sour cream.

Makes 8 servings.

2 pounds boneless top sirloin or top round, thinly sliced into bite-size pieces
1 teaspoon salt
¼ teaspoon pepper
About 6 tablespoons butter or margarine
12 ounces mushrooms, thickly sliced
2 large onions, thinly sliced
3 tablespoons Dijon-

style mustard
3 tablespoons tomato paste
3 cups beef broth or stock
¼ cup dry sherry
1 tablespoon sweet Hungarian paprika
1 cup dairy sour cream
1 pound wide egg noodles, cooked
Dill sprigs *(optional)*

1. Pat the meat dry with paper toweling. Season with salt and pepper.
2. Heat 2 tablespoons of the butter in a large skillet or wide pot. Quickly sauté the pieces of meat in a single layer until browned on both sides. Transfer to a

Magyar Beef Paprikash, page 428.

platter. Brown the remaining meat, adding more butter as necessary.

3. Sauté the mushrooms in the same skillet over low heat, adding additional butter, if necessary, for about 5 minutes. Transfer to a separate plate.

4. Melt the additional 1 tablespoon of butter in the same skillet. Sauté the onions until tender, but not browned, for about 5 minutes. Add to the mushrooms.

5. Add the mustard and tomato paste to the skillet; stir to mix. Slowly stir in 2 cups of the beef broth to make a smooth sauce, scraping up any browned bits from the bottom of the skillet. Stir in the sherry and paprika. Return the mushrooms and onions to the skillet. Simmer, uncovered, for 10 minutes.

6. Gradually stir the remaining 1 cup of beef broth into the sour cream in a small bowl until the mixture is smooth. Pour into the skillet, stirring constantly. Simmer for 3 minutes.

7. Add the beef and noodles. Gently heat to serving temperature—do not boil. Garnish with the fresh dill sprigs, if you wish. Serve immediately.

To Make Ahead: Prepare through step 5. Cover and refrigerate the meat and the remaining beef broth. Transfer the mushroom-onion mixture to a large bowl, cover and refrigerate. About 30 minutes before serving, remove from the refrigerator and proceed as the recipe directs.

Sautéed Steak with Red Wine

Makes 4 servings.

4 club or shell steaks, cut 1-inch thick (about 2 pounds)*	1/2 cup beef broth
	1/2 cup dry red wine
	1/2 teaspoon Worcestershire sauce
3 tablespoons butter	
1 tablespoon vegetable oil	2 tablespoons brandy

1. Trim any excess fat from steaks. Pat surface dry with paper toweling.

(continued)

2. Heat 2 tablespoons of the butter and the oil in a large skillet until the bubbling subsides. (Do not let the butter get too brown.) Sauté the steaks over medium heat, 3 to 4 minutes on each side, turning once, for rare. Make a small incision with a sharp knife to test for doneness. Remove steaks to hot platter.

3. Pour off fat from skillet. Add broth and wine. Turn heat to high and stir and scrape the browned bits so they dissolve in the broth-wine mixture. Cook rapidly until pan juices are reduced by half, 3 to 4 minutes. Stir in Worcestershire and remaining tablespoon butter. Add salt and pepper to taste.

4. Heat brandy in a large metal kitchen spoon directly over heat. Carefully light with a match and pour into sauce, stirring until flames subside. Pour sauce over each steak. Garnish with watercress, if you wish.

Less tender cuts, chuck or round, can be used. Tenderize first with meat tenderizer.

Swiss Steak

Makes 4 servings.

1 medium-size onion, chopped (1/2 cup)
1/2 cup chopped celery
3 tablespoons bacon drippings or vegetable oil
1 beef round steak, cut 1/2-inch thick
2 tablespoons flour
1 teaspoon salt
Dash pepper
2 cups tomato juice
1/4 teaspoon garlic powder
1 tablespoon Worcestershire sauce

1. Sauté onion and celery in bacon drippings until soft in large skillet or Dutch oven. Remove to small bowl.
2. Trim meat; cut into 4 pieces. Combine flour, salt and pepper; pound into meat on both sides. Brown

Rolled Flank Steak, page 431, with Parsleyed New Potatoes.

meat on all sides, adding 1 more tablespoon drippings, if needed.

3. Add tomato juice, garlic powder, Worcestershire and reserved vegetables to pan. Cover; simmer 1 hour or until meat is fork-tender.

Rolled Flank Steak

The beef is first marinated, then filled with a sweet red pepper and green onion stuffing.

Roast at 450° for 15 minutes; then at 400° for 20 minutes for rare.

Makes 8 servings.

2 flank steaks, about 1¹/₂ pounds each	**1 clove garlic, crushed**
	²/₃ cup chopped sweet red pepper
Marinade:	**²/₃ cup chopped green onion (about 6)**
¹/₂ teaspoon salt	
¹/₄ teaspoon pepper	**¹/₂ cup chopped parsley**
2 tablespoons vegetable oil	**2 tablespoons fresh bread crumbs**
2 tablespoons chopped parsley	**1 clove garlic, crushed**
2 teaspoons leaf basil, crumbled	**2 teaspoons leaf basil, crumbled**
1 teaspoon leaf thyme, crumbled	**¹/₂ teaspoon salt**
	¹/₄ teaspoon pepper

1. Trim excess fat from the meat. Cut a pocket lengthwise into each steak with a long sharp knife to within 1 inch of the edges. (Or ask your butcher to do it for you.)

2. Marinate the steaks: Rub the salt and pepper into only one side of the steaks. Mix together oil, parsley, basil, thyme and garlic in a small bowl. Spread over the same side as the salt and pepper. Place the steaks in a large shallow dish and let stand, covered, at room temperature for ¹/₂ hour or refrigerated for up to 8 hours.

3. Mix the red pepper, green onions, parsley, bread crumbs, garlic, basil and ¹/₄ teaspoon of the salt in a small bowl. Spread the stuffing evenly into each steak pocket.

4. Preheat the oven to very hot (450°).

5. Roll each steak, beginning with the short end, into a tight roll, so the seasoned side (marinated side) is on the inside of the roll. Tie each with string at 1-inch intervals. Sprinkle each with the remaining salt and pepper.

6. Heat lightly an oiled heavy roasting pan in the preheated very hot oven (450°) for 5 minutes. Place the rolls, seam-side down, in the heated pan. Roast for 15 minutes. Lower the oven to hot (400°). Roast for 20 minutes for rare (a meat thermometer inserted in the center of the roll will read 130°), or until desired doneness.

7. Let the meat stand for 20 minutes. Remove the string. Cut into thin slices and arrange on a warmed serving platter.

Beef Pepper Steak

Makes 6 servings.

1 boneless top round steak (about 1 pound), cut 1-inch thick	**peppers, halved, seeded and cut into strips**
¹/₃ cup cornstarch	**3 medium-size onions, sliced**
1 cup uncooked long-grain rice	**2 cloves garlic, crushed**
¹/₂ cup vegetable oil	**¹/₂ cup soy sauce**
3 medium-size green	**1 cup water**

1. Cut meat into ¹/₄-inch thick slices. Toss in a bowl with cornstarch until well coated.

2. Cook rice following label directions.

3. Sauté meat, a few slices at a time, in ¹/₄ cup of the oil in a large skillet until browned, about 3 minutes. Add more oil, if needed. Remove to warm platter.

4. Sauté peppers, onions and garlic in oil remaining in skillet until tender, about 3 minutes. Return meat to skillet.

5. Stir in soy sauce and water. Continue cooking, scraping browned bits in skillet, until sauce thickens and bubbles. Serve over hot cooked rice.

Skillet Steak Meal

Makes 4 servings.

3 celery stalks, sliced (2 cups)	**teaspoon instant beef broth**
1 large onion, sliced	**1 teaspoon dry mustard**
2 tablespoons vegetable oil	**¹/₄ cup chili sauce**
¹/₄ cup all-purpose flour	**¹/₄ teaspoon pepper**
1¹/₂ teaspoons salt	**3 medium-size potatoes, pared and quartered**
2 pounds beef chuck steak, cut 2-inches thick	**3 carrots, quartered**
2 cups hot water	**2 tablespoons chopped fresh parsley**
1 envelope or	

1. Sauté celery and onion in 1 tablespoon of the oil in a large skillet until soft; remove and reserve.

2. Pound mixture of flour and 1 teaspoon of the salt into both sides of the meat. Brown meat on both sides in remaining tablespoon of oil in skillet.

3. Stir 1 cup of the hot water into broth and mustard in 2-cup measure. Add to skillet with chili sauce, pepper and reserved celery and onion; cover.

4. Simmer 1 hour and 15 minutes. Stir in remaining cup of water to thin gravy. Add potatoes and carrots; sprinkle with remaining ¹/₂ teaspoon salt.

5. Continue cooking, covered, 30 to 45 minutes until meat is fork-tender and vegetables are done. Sprinkle with parsley.

Flank Steak with Dill

Makes 6 servings.

1½ pounds trimmed flank steak or skirt steak
¼ cup (½ stick) butter or margarine
1½ cups frozen chopped onions
1 large clove garlic, minced
1 tablespoon flour
1 teaspoon salt
¼ teaspoon pepper
1 container (8 ounces) whole milk yogurt
¼ cup chopped fresh dill
Hot cooked rice

1. Cut flank steak in half lengthwise and slice each half into ¹/₁₆-inch thick slices against the grain.
2. Melt 2 tablespoons of the butter in a large skillet. Add ½ of the meat and cook just until meat loses its red color. Remove with slotted spoon to bowl. Add remaining meat to juices in skillet and cook just until meat loses its red color. Remove with spoon to bowl.
3. Add remaining 2 tablespoons butter to skillet with onions and garlic. Cook over high heat until liquid evaporates from onions, about 1 minute, stirring occasionally.
4. Return meat to skillet. Sprinkle with flour, salt and pepper. Add yogurt and dill, stirring thoroughly. Cover; simmer 10 minutes or until tender. Serve over rice. Garnish with dill, if you wish.

Broiled Steaks Persillade

The persillade is the Provençal seasoning of chopped garlic and parsley. It should always be nicely browned and crisped in butter or olive oil before being used as a seasoning for meats or vegetables.

Makes 6 servings.

6 individual beef steaks, cut ³/₄-inch thick (top loin, club or rib)
¼ cup vegetable oil
1 teaspoon salt
½ teaspoon pepper
2 large green peppers, seeded and cut into ¼-inch strips
2 large red peppers, seeded and cut in ¼-inch strips
2 tablespoons butter or margarine
2 large cloves garlic, minced
½ cup chopped fresh parsley

1. Trim the steaks of fat and gristle. Rub the steaks on both sides with 1 tablespoon of the oil. Put them on a rack over a broiler pan.
2. Broil steaks 3 to 4 inches from heat 3 minutes on the first side; sprinkle with half the salt and pepper;

turn. Broil on second side 4 more minutes; sprinkle with remaining salt and pepper. Remove to a hot platter.
3. While steaks broil, heat 2 tablespoons of the oil in a skillet. Sauté the peppers, stirring often, until they are heated through, about 5 minutes. Remove to platter with steaks.
4. Heat the last tablespoon of oil and butter in the skillet. Sauté garlic and parsley; spoon persillade over steaks.

Cold Marinated Steak

Broil and serve later.

Makes 6 servings.

1 sirloin steak, cut 1½ inches thick (about 3¼ pounds)
½ cup soy sauce
½ cup dry red wine
⅓ cup vegetable oil
⅓ cup thinly sliced green onions
½ teaspoon salt
½ teaspoon dry mustard
½ teaspoon leaf basil
½ teaspoon leaf thyme, crumbled
¼ teaspoon pepper
1 pint cherry tomatoes, halved
½ pound mushrooms, quartered
1 package (10 ounces) frozen artichoke hearts, cooked and drained

1. Place steak in shallow nonmetal dish. Puncture deeply on all sides with a 2-tined fork.
2. Combine soy sauce, red wine, vegetable oil, green onions, salt, dry mustard, basil, thyme and pepper in a small bowl. Pour half of soy mixture over steak. Cover; marinate in refrigerator for at least 2 hours, turning twice.
3. Place tomatoes, mushrooms and cooked artichoke hearts in separate small containers. Pour remaining soy mixture over vegetables, dividing equally. Cover and chill until serving time.
4. Drain steak, reserving marinade. Pat with paper toweling to remove excess marinade. Broil steak 4 to 5 inches from heat, basting several times, about 8 to 12 minutes on each side for rare. Brush cooked steak with any remaining marinade; cool; cover; refrigerate.
5. At serving time: Cut steak into thin slices, holding knife almost parallel to top of steak. Garnish serving platter with tomatoes, mushrooms and artichoke hearts.

Pictured opposite (clockwise from top right): Chicken in a Basket, page 653; Scotch Eggs, page 352; Cold Marinated Steak, page 432; Meat Loaf in Brioche, page 473.

Corned Beef

The term "corned" is derived from an old English word meaning "cured," or preserved with salt. The word corn originally meant any small particle, which described the salt.

Today beef, usually the brisket, is preserved by curing in a brine made of salt, sugar, spices and saltpeter. (Salt preserves the meat; the sugar inhibits the salt from hardening the meat; saltpeter provides a red coloring.)

The origin of canned or pressed corned beef is French. It was called *bouilli* (boiled) beef by the French and used as an army ration during the Franco-Prussian War of 1870. The boiled beef was cured, packed into tins and heated to destroy all organisms—thus making it ideal for long-term shelf storage. The British called it bully beef (a corruption of *bouilli*) during World War I.

Today, canned corned beef is a pantry staple that can be used for sandwiches, salads and casseroles or eaten simply sliced and fried. Corned beef briskets are also available, usually packaged in plastic bags, in the delicatessen section of large supermarkets.

Kilkenny Corned Beef

Bake at 325° for 2 hours; then at 325° for 1 hour.

Makes 12 servings.

1 piece corned beef brisket (about 5 pounds)	⅓ cup prepared mustard
Boiling water	Orange wedges (optional)
1 tablespoon mixed pickling spices	Watercress (optional)
½ cup firmly packed light brown sugar	Killybegs Horseradish Sauce (recipe follows)

1. Preheat the oven to slow (325°).
2. Wash the corned beef brisket. Place in a large roasting pan on the oven rack. Cover meat with boiling water; add pickling spices; cover the pan with aluminum foil.
3. Bake in the preheated slow oven (325°) for 2 hours or until tender when pierced with a two-tined fork. Allow to cool in the cooking liquid. (This can be done the day before; refrigerate.)
4. Prepare Killybegs Horseradish Sauce.
5. About 1 hour before serving, drain the cooked corned beef and place in a roasting pan.
6. Bake in a preheated slow oven (325°) for 30 minutes.
7. Combine brown sugar and mustard in a small bowl and spread over the corned beef. Bake for 30 minutes longer or until well glazed. Place on a platter. Garnish with wedges of orange and sprigs of watercress. Cut into thin slices and serve with Killybegs Horseradish Sauce.

Killybegs Horseradish Sauce: Combine 1 container (8 ounces) dairy sour cream with 2 tablespoons prepared mustard and 2 tablespoons prepared horseradish in a glass or ceramic bowl. Cover with plastic wrap and refrigerate for at least 2 hours to blend the flavors.

Glazed Corned Beef

Makes 10 servings.

2 pieces corned beef brisket, each about 3½ pounds	peppercorns
	6 whole cloves
1 medium-size onion, halved	3 to 4 tablespoons dark corn syrup
1 stalk celery with leaves	2 tablespoons brown sugar
1 bay leaf	2 teaspoons dry mustard
6 whole	

1. Day ahead: Combine corned beef brisket, onion, celery, bay leaf, peppercorns and cloves in large kettle or Dutch oven; add cold water to almost cover meat; cover. Heat to boiling, then simmer 3 to 4 hours, or until meat is tender when pierced with a fork. Cool meat in cooking broth, then remove and refrigerate.
2. To serve: Put beef, fat-side up, in shallow baking pan; spread corn syrup evenly over. Sprinkle with sugar and mustard.
3. Broil, 3 to 4 inches from heat, 5 minutes or until glazed. Serve hot or warm.

Corned Beef-Potato Casserole

Bake at 375° for 40 minutes.

Makes 6 servings.

1 package (10 ounces) frozen mixed vegetables	hash brown potatoes (from a 2-pound bag)
1 can condensed cream of onion soup	¼ cup chopped fresh parsley
1 teaspoon leaf marjoram, crumbled	1 teaspoon seasoned salt
1 can (12 ounces) corned beef, sliced	4 ounces Muenster cheese, shredded (1 cup)
4 cups frozen chopped	

1. Cook frozen vegetables following label directions; drain and turn into a 2-quart casserole. Stir in onion soup and marjoram. Layer corned beef slices over mixture.
2. Combine frozen potatoes, parsley and seasoned salt in a medium-size bowl; spoon over corned beef.
3. Bake in a moderate oven (375°) for 30 minutes; remove foil; top with cheese; bake 10 minutes longer or until casserole is bubbly-hot.

Corned Beef Dinner

Bake at 350° for 3 hours.

Makes 6 servings.

4 pounds corned beef
   brisket
1 can condensed
   onion soup
4 peppercorns
1 clove garlic, minced
1 bay leaf
1/2 teaspoon salt
1/2 teaspoon leaf
   rosemary, crumbled
6 medium-size carrots,
   pared and cut into
   1 1/2-inch pieces

6 medium-size
   potatoes, pared and
   quartered
2 celery stalks, cut
   into 1-inch pieces
1 medium-size head
   cabbage, cut into
   wedges
3 tablespoons flour
3 tablespoons butter
   or margarine,
   softened

1. Tear off a 26-inch length of 18-inch-wide heavy-duty foil and place in center of reusable 11 5/8 × 9 1/4 × 1 1/2-inch aluminum casserole pan.
2. Place beef in center of foil. Pour soup over meat; add peppercorns, garlic, bay leaf, salt and rosemary. Seal up foil.
3. Bake in a moderate oven (350°) for 2 hours.
4. Remove foil container from oven. Carefully open. Arrange carrots, potatoes, celery and cabbage around meat. Re-seal. Return to oven.
5. Bake another hour until meat and potatoes are tender.
6. Remove meat and vegetables to heated serving platter. Strain broth into small saucepan. (You should have abut 1 3/4 cups.) Combine flour and butter; stir into broth bit by bit. Cook over moderate heat, stirring, until thickened and bubbly. Serve with meat.

Italian Beef Rolls

Say good-bye to long cooking when you make this quickie.

Makes 4 servings.

4 minute round steaks,
   or beef for braciole,
   or cube steaks
   (1 pound)
1 teaspoon meat
   tenderizer with
   steak sauce flavor
1 teaspoon leaf
   oregano, crumbled
1/4 pound sliced Genoa
   salami
1/2 an 8-ounce package

mozzarella, cut into
   4 slices
1/4 cup (1/2 stick) butter
   or margarine
1 cup water
1 bar (1 5/16 ounces)
   mushroom
   concentrate for
   gravy
2 tablespoons dry red
   wine

1. Pound meat with a mallet or rolling pin until evenly thinned, 1/8-inch thick, but do not pound through. Sprinkle with meat tenderizer and oregano.
2. Overlap salami slices and 1 slice cheese, cut to fit, on each steak piece. Roll up jelly-roll fashion, tucking ends in to enclose filling; fasten with wooden picks.
3. Melt butter in large skillet. Sauté steak rolls, turning to brown on all sides, until meat is done, about 5 minutes. Remove meat to serving platter; take out the wooden picks.
4. Add water to pan drippings; crumble in mushroom concentrate for gravy; add wine; cook until gravy thickens. Spoon some gravy over rolls. Pour remainder in gravy boat and pass at table. Sprinkle with chopped parsley, if you wish.

Glazed Beef

Makes 4 servings.

3/4 pound boneless
   round steak, cut
   3/4-inch thick
1 egg white
2 tablespoons
   cornstarch
2 tablespoons soy
   sauce
4 cups water
3/4 pound small

zucchini
   (1 1/2- inch diameter)
1 teaspoon cornstarch
1/2 teaspoon sugar
1 tablespoon cold
   water
1 1/2 tablespoons soy
   sauce
3 tablespoons peanut
   or corn oil

1. Cut the beef into 1/4-inch slices, then into 1-inch pieces. (This makes about 1 1/2 cups of 1 × 3/4 × 1/4-inch pieces.)
2. Combine egg white and the 2 tablespoons cornstarch in medium-size bowl with fork. Add beef and the 2 tablespoons soy sauce; mix well, using your hands. Refrigerate 30 minutes.
3. Bring water to boiling in large saucepan. Add the beef and egg white mixture, stirring gently to separate the pieces, about 1 minute Drain immediately; cool in a bowl of cold water. Drain; place on paper toweling. (May be done several hours ahead of time.)
4. Cut zucchini into 1-inch slices, then turn onto flat side; cut into 1/4-inch slices to make about 3 cups of 1 1/2 × 1 × 1/4-inch pieces. Reserve.
5. Make sauce by combining remaining 1 teaspoon cornstarch, 1/2 teaspoon sugar, 1 tablespoon cold water and remaining 1 1/2 tablespoons soy sauce in small cup.
6. Heat a wok or skillet until very hot. Add oil. Place zucchini in oil; stir-fry 1 minute. Increase heat and add drained beef. Mix quickly. Stir in reserved sauce, stirring until the sauce thickens and coats the beef with a clear glaze. Serve with hot cooked rice, if you wish.

Note: Parboiled broccoli or cauliflowerets sliced 2 inches long may be used instead of the zucchini. One teaspoon chopped fresh ginger may be added to oil before the vegetables and meat.

Beefsteak Pie

Bake at 425° for 35 minutes.

Makes 6 servings.

1 large onion, coarsely
  chopped (1 cup)
3 tablespoons butter
  or margarine
2 pounds beef round,
  cut into 1/2-inch
  cubes
3 tablespoons flour
1 can condensed beef
  broth
1/4 cup sherry or dry
  vermouth
1 can (16 ounces)
  whole potatoes,

drained and cubed
1/2 pound mushrooms,
  sliced
1 teaspoon
  Worcestershire
  sauce
1/2 teaspoon leaf
  thyme, crumbled
1/2 teaspoon salt
1/4 teaspoon pepper
1/2 package piecrust
  mix
1 egg yolk
1 tablespoon water

1. Sauté onion in butter in a large saucepan over moderate heat until tender but not browned.
2. Toss beef in flour until lightly coated. Add beef to saucepan, browning on all sides.
3. Pour in beef broth and sherry. Lower heat; cover; simmer 1 hour or until meat is tender, stirring occasionally.
4. Add potatoes, mushrooms, Worcestershire, thyme, salt and pepper, stirring to mix well; cool slightly.
5. Preheat oven to 425°. Prepare piecrust mix following label directions. Roll out to an 11-inch round on a floured surface.
6. Pour beef mixture into a reusable aluminum cake pan, 8 1/2 × 1 5/16-inches (about 3 1/2 cups). Top with pastry. Turn edges under and flute.
7. Beat egg yolk and water. Brush pastry with mixture. Make slits in top of pastry to allow steam to escape.
8. Bake in a preheated hot oven (425°) for 35 minutes or until pastry is golden.

Szechuan Beef

Makes 4 servings.

1 flank steak (about
  1 pound)
1/4 cup chili sauce
2 tablespoons soy
  sauce
1 tablespoon dry
  sherry
1 teaspoon cornstarch
1/2 teaspoon ground
  ginger

1/4 teaspoon crushed
  red pepper
3 tablespoons peanut
  or vegetable oil
1 cloves garlic,
  crushed
1 small bunch green
  onions, cut into
  1-inch pieces

1. Place flank steak on a small cookie sheet; freeze for 15 minutes to "firm up" for easier slicing. Then cut

Pictured opposite: Szechuan Beef.

steak in half lengthwise. Cut each half into 1/8-inch slices.
2. Mix chili sauce, soy sauce, sherry, cornstarch, ginger and red pepper in a small bowl; reserve.
3. Heat 1 tablespoon of the oil in wok or large skillet. Add garlic and green onions; stir-fry 1 minute. Remove to a bowl with slotted spoon.
4. Add remaining oil to wok. Add steak, a third at a time, and stir-fry quickly until meat loses its red color. Place in bowl with green onions.
5. Add chili sauce mixture to wok; heat until bubbly-hot. Stir in meat and onions; cook and stir until sauce coats meat and onions.

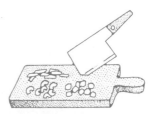

Sirloin of Beef with Sauce Bordelaise

The Bordelaise is easy to make from the pan drippings and yet so much better than ordinary gravy. And here is the serving secret: Always pour the sauce onto the plate and place the beef slices on top.

Roast at 500° for 20 minutes, then at 400° for 15 to 32 minutes.

Makes 6 servings.

3 pounds boneless
  sirloin, cut about
  2 inches thick
Pepper
1/2 cup shallots or
  onion, finely
  chopped
1 cup dry red wine
1 cup Beef Gravy
  (recipe follows)

1/2 teaspoon
  cornstarch
  dissolved in
  1 tablespoon water
2 tablespoons butter
  or margarine,
  softened to room
  temperature
Watercress

1. Sprinkle beef with pepper to taste; place on a rack in a shallow roasting pan. Preheat oven to 500°.
2. Roast in a very hot oven (500°) for 20 minutes; lower heat to hot (400°) and roast for 15 minutes more for rare. (Allow an additional 7 minutes for medium and an additional 10 minutes for well done.)
3. Remove sirloin to a heated serving platter; keep warm. Drain off all but 1 tablespoon fat from roasting pan and add the shallots, wine and Beef Gravy.
4. Bring to boiling; boil 10 minutes or until liquid is reduced by one-quarter. Lower heat; add dissolved cornstarch and stir for about 1 minute or until sauce is thickened. Add butter and mix in lightly.
5. Slice sirloin and serve on heated platter. Serve sauce separately. Garnish platter with watercress.

Beef Gravy: Cook 2 tablespoons flour and 2 tablespoons fat from roasting pan in small saucepan until browned. Gradually stir in 1 cup beef broth with a wire whisk. Cook, stirring constantly, until thickened.

Spicy Szechuan Shredded Beef and Vegetables

Makes 6 servings.

2 tablespoons finely minced fresh ginger root or 1 teaspoon ground ginger
1 clove garlic, crushed
1/4 teaspoon ground cloves
1/4 teaspoon ground cinnamon
1/8 teaspoon fennel seeds, crushed
1/8 teaspoon anise seeds, crushed
1/8 to 1/4 teaspoon crushed red pepper
3 tablespoons soy sauce
3 tablespoons dry sherry
1 tablespoon vegetable oil
1 pound boneless top round
3 tablespoons vegetable oil
3 medium-size carrots, finely shredded
3 medium-size celery stalks, thinly sliced
8 green onions, thinly sliced
Hot cooked rice

1. Combine ginger, garlic, cloves, cinnamon, fennel, anise, crushed pepper, soy, sherry and the 1 tablespoon oil in a jar with a screw-top lid. Shake marinade well to mix.
2. Cut the beef in very thin strips about the size and shape of shoestring potatoes with a sharp knife. (It will make slicing easier if you put the beef in the freezer for an hour.) Put beef strips in large bowl. Shake marinade again and pour over beef; toss; let stand at room temperature for 1 hour, turning once or twice.
3. Heat 2 tablespoons of the remaining oil in a wok or large skillet until a shred of carrot will sizzle, then add the carrots, celery and green onions. Stir-fry about 3 minutes or just until crisp-tender.
4. Quickly add the remaining tablespoon of oil, the beef and any remaining marinade. Stir-fry 3 minutes longer or until beef is no longer bright red. Serve with hot cooked rice.

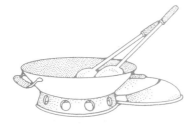

Beer-Braised Short Ribs

Broil about 15 minutes, then bake at 325° for 1 1/2 hours.

Makes 6 servings.

4 pounds beef short ribs, cut into serving-size pieces
1 envelope onion soup mix
2 large onions, sliced
1 can (12 ounces) beer

1. Arrange short ribs in a roasting pan just large enough to hold them. Broil about 6 inches from heat, 8 to 10 minutes or until nicely browned. Turn ribs and broil other side until well browned. Drain off fat. Sprinkle onion soup mix over meat; arrange onion slices over and between ribs; add the beer and cover pan tightly with foil.
2. Bake in a slow oven (325°) for 1 1/2 hours or until meat is very tender. Transfer meat and onions to a heated platter.
3. Skim off excess fat from juices in pan. Serve juices with ribs. If you wish to thicken gravy, combine 2 tablespoons flour with 3 to 4 tablespoons cold water in a cup. Stir until liquid is smooth and free from lumps. Stir into juices in pan; cook over medium heat, stirring constantly, until thickened and bubbly. Serve with boiled or baked potatoes and hot, buttered carrots, if you wish.

Oven Beef Burgundy

Bake at 350° for 1 1/2 hours.

Makes 6 to 8 servings.

2 pounds beef round, cut into 1- to 1 1/2-inch cubes
1/4 cup all-purpose flour
1 teaspoon salt
1/4 teaspoon pepper
2 to 4 tablespoons butter or margarine
2 tablespoons brandy
12 to 18 small white onions, peeled
1/2 pound medium-size mushrooms, halved
1 clove garlic, crushed
2 tablespoons chopped fresh parsley
1/4 teaspoon leaf thyme, crumbled
1 cup condensed beef broth
1 cup red Burgundy wine
1 bay leaf

1. Shake meat with flour, salt and pepper in a plastic bag to coat well; reserve any remaining flour. Preheat oven to 350°.
2. Brown beef, about 1/4 at a time, in hot butter in a large skillet or Dutch oven. Lift out beef as it browns and transfer to a 2 1/2- or 3-quart casserole. Heat brandy in small saucepan; ignite and pour over beef. Add onions and mushrooms. Sprinkle in reserved seasoned flour over the beef and vegetables in casserole.
3. Stir garlic, parsley and thyme into drippings in skillet; cook 1 minute. Add beef broth and wine; heat, stirring to loosen browned bits, until mixture comes to boiling. Pour over beef and vegetables; add bay leaf. Cover.
4. Bake in a preheated moderate oven (350°) for 1 hour, 30 minutes or until meat is tender. Let casserole stand for 20 minutes before serving. Serve with white or wild rice mix, if you wish.

Pictured opposite: Oven Beef Burgundy.

New England Boiled Dinner

Colonists preserved meat by pickling it in brine or drying it. Pickled meat resulted in corned beef. Dried meat was called jerky. Boiled dinners were one-pot colonial meals created for those busy days.

Makes 10 servings.

1 corned beef brisket (about 4 pounds)
3 large yellow turnips, pared and cut into 1/2-inch slices
1 pound carrots, pared and cut into chunks
6 medium-size potatoes, pared and halved
1 bunch beets

without tops
2 medium-size heads of cabbage, each cut into 6 wedges
1/4 cup (1/2 stick) butter or margarine, melted
Chopped parsley
Creamy Horseradish Sauce *(recipe follows)*

1. Simmer corned beef in water to cover in a large kettle for 2 hours. Add the turnips; cook 30 minutes. Add the carrots and potatoes; cook 30 minutes longer or until meat and vegetables are tender.
2. About 1 hour before meat is done, cook beets in water in a large saucepan until tender; skin; keep warm.
3. Start cooking cabbage in a large kettle of water, about 30 minutes before meat is done.
4. Drain meat; arrange on a large warm platter. Spoon hot vegetables around meat; pour melted butter over vegetables; sprinkle with parsley. Serve with Creamy Horseradish Sauce or mustard.

Creamy Horseradish Sauce

Makes 1 1/4 cups.

1/2 cup heavy cream
3 tablespoons prepared horseradish

1 teaspoon sugar
1/4 teaspoon salt
1/8 teaspoon pepper

Beat cream in a small bowl with electric mixer until soft peaks form. Fold in horseradish, sugar, salt and pepper. Refrigerate.

Red Flannel Hash

Makes 4 servings.

1/4 cup (1/2 stick) butter or margarine
1 medium-size onion, chopped (1/2 cup)
2 to 2 1/2 cups diced or cubed leftover roast beef or

corned beef
2 cups chopped cooked potato
1 teaspoon salt
1/4 teaspoon pepper
1 cup drained canned diced beets

1. Heat butter in a large skillet. Add onion; cook, stirring frequently, until golden brown.
2. Add beef and potatoes, patting down firmly with spatula or pancake turner. Cook, uncovered, about 15 minutes or until brown crust forms on bottom.
3. Loosen edge; season with salt and pepper. Add well-drained beets. Turn beef mixture so that top-side becomes browned, about 5 minutes.

New England Boiled Dinner with Creamy Horseradish Sauce.

Old German Sauerbraten,
page 442;
Potato Dumplings,
page 442.

Barbecued Beef Short Ribs

Bake at 450° for 30 minutes.

Makes 6 servings.

**5 to 6 pounds beef
  short ribs**
**1 bottle (12 ounces)
  chili sauce**
1/2 cup water
**1 medium-size onion,
  chopped (1/2 cup)**
1 clove garlic, crushed
**1/4 cup firmly packed
  brown sugar**

**2 tablespoons wine
  vinegar**
2 teaspoons salt
**2 teaspoons prepared
  mustard**
**1 teaspoon liquid hot
  pepper seasoning**
**1/2 teaspoon liquid
  smoke** *(optional)*

1. Preheat oven to 450°. Arrange short ribs on a rack over a large broiler pan or preferably on a disposable foil broiler pan (to save you cleanup). Place pan with short ribs on top rack in oven and bake for 30 minutes.

2. Combine chili sauce and remaining ingredients in medium-size mixing bowl. Add half of chili sauce mixture to 6-quart pressure cooker. Add browned ribs. Pour remainder of sauce over ribs, making sure to coat all pieces. Close cover securely. Place pressure control on vent pipe (number 10 if your control has multipressure selections). Turn heat on high until pressure rises and control starts to jiggle, about 5 minutes.

3. Reduce heat slowly to medium-low so control jiggles or rocks gently; cook for 35 minutes.

4. Turn heat off and let cool about 5 minutes. Then place closed cooker under faucet of running cold water until pressure is reduced and no steam hisses when you test by attempting to lift control. If there are no "hisses," remove control; then carefully lift off

(continued)

cover and remove short ribs to warm serving platter.
5. Skim excess fat from sauce; reheat, if necessary.
Note: Delicious and easy "go-withs" are baked potatoes. Place potatoes in the oven when you start to brown the short ribs. Lower heat to 350° when you remove ribs and let potatoes continue baking. They should be done when ribs are done.

Lemon Sirloin

Grill for 24 minutes.

Makes 10 servings.

1 sirloin steak, 1¹/₂- to 2-inches thick (about 4 pounds)	**1 teaspoon Worcestershire sauce**
2 teaspoons grated lemon rind	**1 teaspoon prepared mustard**
¹/₄ cup lemon juice	**1 clove garlic, minced**
¹/₃ cup vegetable oil	OR: **2 green onion tops, sliced**
1¹/₂ teaspoons salt	
¹/₄ teaspoon pepper	

1. Score fat edges of meat and place in shallow nonmetal dish.
2. Combine remaining ingredients; pour over steak. Cover and marinate at room temperature, turning occasionally, for 3 hours (6 hours if marinated in refrigerator).
3. Remove steak from marinade; pat with paper toweling to remove excess marinade; reserve marinade.
4. Grill 5 inches from hot coals, brushing frequently with remaining marinade, 12 minutes on each side for rare.

Old German Sauerbraten

Makes 10 to 12 servings.

1 boneless round, rump, sirloin tip or chuck roast (5 to 6 pounds), rolled and tied	**chopped (1¹/₂ cups)**
2 cups wine vinegar or cider vinegar	**2 large carrots, pared and diced (1¹/₂ cups)**
2 cups water	**1¹/₂ cups diced celery**
¹/₄ cup firmly packed brown sugar	**2 tablespoons bacon drippings or vegetable shortening (optional)**
1 tablespoon salt	**8 gingersnaps, crumbled**
¹/₂ teaspoon pepper	**Potato Dumplings (recipe follows)**
¹/₂ teaspoon ground cloves	**Parsley sprigs**
1 bay leaf	
3 medium-size onions,	

1. Place meat in a large bowl; add vinegar, water, brown sugar, salt, pepper, cloves, bay leaf, onions, carrots and celery. Cover; store in refrigerator 2 to 3 days, turning meat several times to marinate on all sides.
2. When ready to cook, remove meat from marinade and pat dry; brown in its own fat or in bacon drippings in large, heavy kettle or Dutch oven; add vegetables and marinade. Bring to boiling; cover.
3. Simmer 3 hours or until meat is very tender. Remove to a heated serving platter and keep hot.
4. Strain broth into a 4-cup measure; let stand about 1 minute or until fat rises to top. Skim off fat, returning ¹/₄ cup to kettle.
5. Add water to broth, if needed, to make 2 cups; stir back into kettle; sprinkle crumbled gingersnaps over. Cook and stir until gravy thickens.
6. Arrange Potato Dumplings on platter with meat. Spoon gravy over dumplings. Serve with cooked red cabbage and apple slices, if you wish. Garnish platter with parsley.

Potato Dumplings

Makes 6 servings (12 dumplings).

1 slice white bread	**purpose flour**
1 tablespoon butter or margarine	**¹/₃ cup dry cream of wheat cereal**
3 medium-size potatoes (1¹/₂ pounds)	**1¹/₂ teaspoons salt**
2 eggs, slightly beaten	**¹/₄ teaspoon pepper**
¹/₃ cup sifted all-	**¹/₄ teaspoon ground nutmeg**

1. Cut bread slice into ¹/₂-inch cubes. Melt butter or margarine in small skillet; add bread and sauté until golden brown.
2. Peel potatoes; cook in boiling water in a large saucepan until tender, about 20 minutes. Drain; return to saucepan; toss over low heat for several minutes to dry. Remove from heat.
3. Mash potatoes (there should be about 3 cups); beat in eggs, flour, cream of wheat, salt, pepper and nutmeg until smooth.
4. Heat 3 to 4 quarts water to boiling in a large kettle. Divide potato mixture into 12 equal parts; shape each around 3 or 4 of the bread cubes into a round ball, dusting hands with flour to keep dumplings from sticking.
5. Drop dumplings into boiling water; stir gently once or twice to prevent them from sticking to each other or the bottom of the kettle. Cook, uncovered, until dumplings float to surface of water, about 10 to 15 minutes; remove with slotted spoon to heated platter and spoon a little gravy over each.

Red River Chili

Makes about 10 servings.

3 pounds beef round
  or chuck
1/4 cup vegetable oil
1 large onion, finely
  chopped (1 cup)
1 clove garlic, minced
1 can (35 ounces)
  plum tomatoes
1 can (13 3/4 ounces)
  beef broth
1 can (4 ounces) diced

green chilies
1 teaspoon celery
  seeds, crushed
1 teaspoon cumin
  seeds, crushed
1 tablespoon chili
  powder
1 teaspoon salt
2 cans (16 ounces
  each) red kidney
  beans, drained

1. Cut beef in 1/2 -inch cubes. Brown, part at a time, in 2 tablespoons of the oil in a large kettle or Dutch oven. Remove the pieces of beef to a bowl as they brown.
2. Sauté onion and garlic in remaining 2 tablespoons of the oil until tender, about 3 minutes.
3. Return browned beef to kettle; add tomatoes, beef broth, chilies, celery and cumin seeds, chili powder and salt. Bring to boiling; lower heat. Simmer, stirring occasionally, about 2 1/2 hours or until meat is tender.
4. Add kidney beans; cook 15 minutes longer.

Barbecued Short Ribs

Bake at 450° for 30 minutes.

Makes 4 to 6 servings.

6 pounds beef short
  ribs, cut into
  serving-size pieces
1 bottle (12 ounces)
  chili sauce
1/2 cup water
1/2 cup frozen chopped
  onions
1 clove garlic,

minced
1/4 cup firmly packed
  light brown sugar
2 tablespoons wine
  vinegar
1 tablespoon Dijon
  mustard
2 teaspoons salt

1. Trim excess fat from ribs; place ribs in a single layer on a disposable foil pan or foil-lined jelly-roll pan. Bake in a very hot oven (450°) for 30 minutes, turning once.
2 Combine chili sauce, water, onions, garlic, sugar, vinegar, mustard and salt in a medium-size bowl.
3. Place 1/3 cup of the chili mixture in bottom of a slow cooker; dip ribs, 1 at a time, in remaining chili mixture and place in slow cooker; pour remaining sauce over ribs.

4. Cover slow cooker. Set to low. Cook 8 to 12 hours or until ribs test done.
5. Remove ribs to serving platter. Pour cooking liquid into a 4-cup measure; let fat rise to top; skim off. If desired to thicken, combine 1 tablespoon cornstarch with 1/4 cup water for each cup of the cooking liquid in a small cup. Heat cooking liquid in a medium-size saucepan. Stir in cornstarch mixture. Heat, stirring constantly, until mixture thickens and bubbles. Spoon some gravy over ribs; pour remainder into gravy boat; pass at table.

Ragout   A well-seasoned meat and vegetable stew. The word comes from the French word ragoûter, which means "to stimulate the taste."

Beef Ragout, New Orleans Style

Makes 8 servings.

1/2 pound thickly
  sliced bacon
2 pounds boneless
  beef chuck, cubed
1 large onion,
  chopped (1 cup)
1 cup finely chopped
  carrot
1 cup finely chopped
  celery
2 cloves garlic,
  minced
2 teaspoons salt
1 teaspoon leaf thyme,
  crumbled

1 bay leaf
1/4 teaspoon pepper
2 cups dry red wine
1/4 cup all-purpose
  flour
1 pound mushrooms
1 bunch leeks
1 pound carrots
1/4 cup (1/2 stick) butter
  or margarine
1 envelope or
  teaspoon instant
  chicken broth
1/2 cup water

1. Cut bacon into 1-inch pieces; place in a large kettle; cover with water. Bring to boiling; lower heat and simmer 10 minutes. Dry bacon on paper toweling. Fry bacon until crisp in kettle. Remove bacon and reserve; pour all but 2 tablespoons of the bacon drippings into a cup.
2. Brown beef, a few pieces at a time, in kettle; remove to a bowl. Sauté onion, carrot, celery and garlic in pan drippings, adding more bacon drippings, if needed; stir in salt, thyme, bay leaf and pepper; return beef to kettle; add wine; bring slowly to boiling; lower heat to simmer; cover kettle.
3. Simmer 1 1/2 hours or until beef is very tender; remove bay leaf and discard. Remove beef from liquid with slotted spoon; keep warm.
4. Pour liquid, half at a time, into an electric blender container; add flour, half at a time; cover container; whirl at high speed 1 minute. (Or press liquid through a sieve with a wooden spoon into a bowl; cool slightly; stir in flour until well blended.) Return liquid to kettle; bring to boiling. Cook, stirring constantly, until thickened and bubbly, 3 minutes; return beef to kettle and keep warm.

(continued)

5. While beef cooks, wash mushrooms and drain on paper toweling; cut leeks into 5-inch pieces and halve; wash well to remove all sand; pare and cut carrots into 5-inch pieces.

6. Sauté mushrooms in butter in a large skillet; remove; sauté leeks lightly in skillet; remove; add carrots and sauté 5 minutes; add instant chicken broth and water to skillet; cover and simmer 15 minutes or until carrots are almost tender; spoon to one side. Return mushrooms and leeks to skillet. Cover; simmer 10 minutes or until vegetables are tender.

7. Spoon beef and part of the sauce into a heated serving platter. Surround with vegetables; sprinkle beef with cooked bacon and chopped fresh parsley, if you wish. Stir liquid in skillet into remaining sauce and pass separately in a heated sauce dish.

Beef Roulades

Makes 4 servings.

4 slices beef round steak (about 8 ounces each)	mustard
4 thick strips slab bacon	1 tablespoon tomato paste
4 thick strips dill pickle	1/2 teaspoon salt
2 tablespoons flour	1/4 teaspoon pepper
1/4 cup vegetable oil	1/4 teaspoon leaf thyme, crumbled
2 cloves garlic, minced	1 bay leaf
1 medium-size onion, sliced (1/2 cup)	1 cup stout or beer
1 tablespoon prepared	1/2 cup canned beef gravy
	1/2 cup chopped celery
	1/2 cup chopped carrot

1. Trim any fat from steak. Pound each slice of steak with a mallet or edge of saucer to 1/4-inch thickness.

2. Place 1 strip bacon and pickle in each steak. Roll each steak around filling; fasten with wooden picks.

3. Dredge the rolls in flour, shaking off excess. Brown rolls in oil in a large skillet. Remove from skillet. Pour off all but 2 tablespoons fat.

4. Add garlic and onion; cook for a few minutes until onions are tender. Add mustard, tomato paste, salt, pepper, thyme, bay leaf and beer. Bring to boiling until reduced to half its volume.

5. Stir in beef gravy; arrange beef rolls in sauce. Cover; simmer 30 minutes. Add celery and carrot. Cover; continue to simmer slowly for 45 minutes or until meat is cooked, but firm. Remove picks before serving.

Stroganoff A dish of sautéed beef and mushrooms in a sour-cream sauce created in the late 19th century by the chef to a Russian czar. Beef Stroganoff has become a world-famous dish with many variations.

Beef Stroganoff

Makes 8 servings.

1 boneless sirloin steak, cut 1 1/2 inches thick	sliced mushrooms, drained
1/3 cup butter or margarine	1 can condensed beef broth
2 medium-size onions, sliced	1 teaspoon salt
1/2 pound mushrooms, sliced	2 tablespoons flour
OR: 1 can (6 ounces)	1 container (8 ounces) dairy sour cream
	Hot cooked noodles

1. Trim any excess fat from steak; cut steak into 1/4-inch-thick diagonal slices.

2. Heat a large skillet until very hot; add about 1 tablespoon of the butter and swirl to coat bottom of skillet.

3. Panfry beef strips, a few at a time, 1 minute on each side or until steak is done as you like it and all strips are fried, using more butter as needed; keep warm.

4. Add remaining butter to skillet; stir in onion slices; sauté 5 minutes; push to one side; stir in mushroom slices and sauté 3 minutes. Add beef broth and salt; simmer 5 minutes.

5. Stir flour into sour cream in a small bowl; blend in about 1 cup of the hot mixture. Return sour-cream mixture to skillet and cook, stirring constantly, until mixture thickens and just begins to bubble. (Do not boil.)

6. Add cooked beef strips; stir just until blended. Serve with hot noodles.

Speedy Swiss Steak

Makes 6 servings.

2 tablespoons butter or margarine	1 can (16 ounces) stewed tomatoes, broken up
2 1/2 pounds beef round steak, about 1 1/2 inches thick	1 tablespoon flour
2 teaspoons salt	1 tablespoon Worcestershire sauce
1/4 teaspoon pepper	1 clove garlic, crushed
1 medium-size onion, chopped (1/2 cup)	

1. Heat an open 6-quart pressure cooker until hot; add butter and let sizzle; add steak and brown on both sides. Add salt and pepper. Add onion last few minutes to brown.

(continued)

Pictured opposite:
Spicy Szechuan Shredded Beef
and Vegetables, page 438.

2. Combine stewed tomatoes, flour, Worcestershire and garlic; pour over steak.

3. Close cover securely; place pressure control on vent pipe (number 10 if your unit has multipressure selections); turn heat on high until pressure rises and control starts to jiggle, about 3 to 5 minutes.

4. Reduce heat slowly to medium-low so control jiggles or rocks gently; cook 20 to 30 minutes.

5. Turn heat off and let pressure drop of its own accord about 15 minutes. Remove control and cover carefully. Check tenderness of meat with fork. (If not tender enough, bring pressure back up and cook longer.)

Stir-Fried Beef with Sprouts

Makes 4 servings.

3/4 **pound boneless beef sirloin or round steak**	**vegetable oil**
1 **teaspoon sugar**	1 **medium-size onion, thinly sliced**
1/2 **teaspoon ground ginger**	4 **celery stalks, diagonally sliced**
2 **tablespoons cornstarch**	1 **pound mung or soybean sprouts (6 to 7 cups)**
2 **tablespoons soy sauce**	1 **teaspoon salt**
2 **tablespoons water**	**Coriander leaves** *(optional)*
3 **tablespoons**	

1. Cut beef across the grain into 1/8-inch slices. Place beef in a medium-size bowl; add sugar, ginger, 1 tablespoon cornstarch and soy sauce. Toss until well mixed.

2. Combine remaining 1 tablespoon of the cornstarch and water in a small cup.

3. Heat wok, large deep skillet or Dutch oven over high heat. Add 1 tablespoon of the oil; swirl to coat bottom and side. Add onion and celery. Stir-fry 1 minute or until vegetables are tender-crisp. Remove to medium-size bowl.

4. Reheat pan. Add remaining oil; swirl to coat pan. Add half of the sliced beef. Stir-fry just until well browned. Remove to bowl with vegetables. Stir-fry remaining beef. Return vegetables and beef to pan. Add sprouts and salt; stir-fry beef and sprouts just until sprouts are wilted.

5. Re-stir cornstarch mixture; add to pan; cook until thickened. Garnish with fresh coriander, if you wish.

Note: Sprouts can be used interchangeably in salad, soup and sandwich recipes. However, in cooked dishes and baked goods, use whichever variety the recipe calls for as the moisture content differs from type to type.

Bulgur   Sometimes called parboiled wheat, bulgur is whole wheat that has been cooked, dried, partially debranned and cracked into coarse fragments. A convenient wheat product, bulgur makes delicious salads, soups, and is a good alternate to rice or potatoes in a menu. Bulgur is our oldest recorded use of wheat. This ancient food originated in the Near East. To rehydrate it, soak it in twice its volume of boiling water and let stand until all the water has been absorbed or until the particles are tender. Drain off excess water. Use in salads or cook with other ingredients. Store bulgur in an airtight container in a cool place and use within 6 months.

Beef and Bulgur

Makes 4 servings.

1 **pound ground chuck**	**tomatoes**
1 **large onion, chopped (1 cup)**	1/2 **cup dry sherry**
1 **large clove garlic, mashed**	1 1/2 **teaspoons leaf oregano, crumbled**
8 **medium-size mushrooms (about 2 ounces), sliced**	1 **teaspoon salt**
	1/4 **teaspoon pepper**
3/4 **cup bulgur**	4 **ounces Muenster or Monterey Jack cheese, shredded**
1 **can (3**1/2 **ounces) chopped pitted ripe olives**	2 **tablespoons chopped fresh parsley** *(optional)*
1 **can (16 ounces)**	

1. Cook beef slowly in a large skillet, breaking up with spoon, until beef loses its pink color. Drain off most of the fat from the skillet. Add onion, garlic and mushrooms; cook just until onions begin to soften.

2. Stir in bulgur, olives, tomatoes and their liquid, sherry, oregano, salt and pepper. Cover; simmer until bulgur is soft, about 15 minutes. (If there is not enough liquid to keep the mixture moist, add a little water.)

3. Sprinkle cheese over mixture when bulgur is almost soft. Cover and finish cooking, until cheese is melted, about 2 minutes longer. Sprinkle with parsley, if using.

Beef Teriyaki

The sherry-soy marinade adds flavor as well as tenderizing to a less expensive cut of meat.

Makes about 36 appetizers.

1 **top round steak (about 1**1/2 **pounds), cut 1-inch thick**	**steak sauce**
	2 **tablespoons sugar**
1/2 **cup dry sherry**	2 **cloves garlic, crushed**
3/4 **cup soy sauce**	8-**inch bamboo skewers***
3 **tablespoons bottled**	

1. Pierce steak deeply all over with a fork; place in shallow non-metal dish.

2. Combine sherry, soy sauce, steak sauce, sugar and garlic in small bowl. Pour about 1/3 over steak; cover. (Reserve remaining marinade for dipping.)

Refrigerate several hours or overnight, turning steak once or twice.

3. Cut meat into long, thin slices about 1/8-inch thick; thread accordion-style on bamboo skewers; brush with marinade. Place on rack over pan.

4. Broil, 2 to 3 inches from heat, 1 minute; turn; broil 1 minute longer. Serve with reserved marinade.

Soak in water before using to prevent excess charring.

Stir-Fried Beef with Vegetables

A typical Cantonese stir-fried combination. Thinly slicing meat across the grain allows you to use economical, less tender cuts of beef.

Makes 4 servings.

1 pound boneless beef round steak	**1 medium-size onion**
1 teaspoon sugar	**4 tablespoons vegetable oil**
1 tablespoon cornstarch	**1 can (15 ounces) whole baby corn packed in water**
2 tablespoons dry sherry	OR: **1 can (8 1/2 ounces) sliced bamboo shoots**
3 tablespoons soy sauce	
1 pound green beans	**1 teaspoon salt**

1. Cut beef across the grain into 1/8-inch-thick slices. Place beef in a medium-size bowl; add sugar, cornstarch, sherry and soy sauce; toss until mixed. Cut beans into 2-inch diagonal pieces, discarding ends; slice onion; put vegetables in a large bowl.

2. Heat large deep skillet, Dutch oven or wok over high heat. Add 2 tablespoons of the oil; swirl to coat bottom and side. Add beans and onion. Stir-fry 1 minute or until pieces are coated with oil. Add corn with its liquid; toss; cover. Cook about 5 minutes or until beans are tender-crisp. Remove vegetables to large bowl; discard cooking liquid.

3. Reheat pan. Add remaining oil; swirl to coat bottom. Add half of marinated beef. Stir-fry just until browned. Remove to bowl of vegetables. Stir-fry remaining beef. Return vegetables and beef to pan. Add salt; toss to mix. Spoon onto warm platter. Serve with hot fluffy rice, if you wish.

Braised Beef Rolls

Makes 8 servings.

2 pounds beef round steak, cut about 1/2-inch thick	**1 package (8 ounces) pork sausages**
OR: **2 pounds cubed steaks**	**1 jar (16 ounces) spaghetti sauce**
	3/4 cup water

1. Trim all fat from steak; cut meat into 8 even-size pieces. Pound each slice of beef with a mallet or edge of saucer to 1/4 inch thickness.

2. Brown sausages in a large skillet. Drain on paper toweling. Leave drippings in skillet.

3. Roll each steak around a sausage; fasten with wooden picks.

4. Brown rolls, a few at a time, in the drippings. Drain on paper toweling. Pour off all fat from skillet.

5. Pour spaghetti sauce and water into skillet; bring to boiling, scraping up browned bits; lower heat. Add beef rolls; turn to coat with sauce. Cover; simmer 1 hour or until meat is tender. Remove wooden picks from the steak rolls. Serve with cooked spaghetti, if you wish.

Veal   The most delicate meat of all, veal is bland, thus making it ideal for cooking with sauces. The best veal comes from young milk-fed calves less than 3 months old and the meat shows virtually no pink at all. Veal is fine-grained, with no marbling and only a thin external layer of fat. It has a large amount of connective tissue, which requires cooking at low to moderate temperatures. Veal should not be broiled. It is best panfried, braised or roasted.

Veal scaloppine, sometimes called scallops, are the most expensive cut and come from the leg. They are thin, boneless slices that are pounded to break some of the connective tissue. Scaloppine may also be made from the loin or shoulder. The less expensive cuts include breast of veal, shoulder and shanks. The cuts of veal are similar to beef but smaller in size.

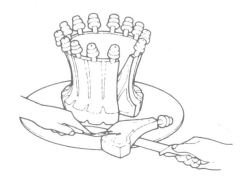

How to Carve a Crown Roast of Veal, Lamb or Pork

Although it looks unusually showy, this is one of the easist of all roasts to carve. Simply steady the roast on the platter with a fork, then use a sharp carving knife to cut down between the ribs, dividing the roast into chops. Serve each person one or two chops and, if the crown roast has been stuffed, a hearty spoonful of the stuffing.

Blanquette

A stew of either veal, lamb or chicken made by boiling cubed meat in a seasoned liquid rather than first browning the meat in fat. The meat is then removed and the cooking liquid is reduced and/or thickened with egg yolks and cream. Small mushrooms and white onions are usually added.

Blanquette de Veau (Creamy Veal Ragout)

Makes 8 servings.

5 pounds breast of veal	quartered
1 onion studded with 6 whole cloves	6 tablespoons flour
1 bay leaf	1 cup heavy cream
1 carrot	½ cup milk
1 celery stalk	½ cup dry white wine
1 parsley sprig	1 teaspoon salt
2 teaspoons salt	¼ teaspoon pepper
¼ teaspoon pepper	2 cups cooked carrots, cut into chunks
8 cups water	16 small white onions, cooked
6 tablespoons butter or margarine	2 tablespoons chopped fresh dill
½ pound fresh mushrooms,	OR: 2 teaspoons dillweed

1. Combine breast of veal, onion studded with cloves, bay leaf, carrot, celery, parsley, the 2 teaspoons salt and ¼ teaspoon pepper in a large kettle. Add water.
2. Heat to boiling; lower heat; cover kettle. Simmer 2 hours or until veal is very tender.
3. Cool veal in broth; then refrigerate until fat rises to top and hardens; discard fat. Remove meat from bones and cut into cubes. (You should have about 4 cups.)
4. Melt butter in a large saucepan; lightly sauté mushrooms.
5. Stir in flour and cook 2 minutes, stirring constantly. Combine 2 cups veal broth (save remaining broth to use in soups or stews), heavy cream, milk and wine in a 4-cup measure; stir into saucepan. Cook, stirring constantly, until mixture thickens and bubbles for 3 mintues. Season with the remaining 1 teaspoon salt and ¼ teaspoon pepper.
6. Add veal, carrots, onions and dill. Heat through.

Veal and Rice Gremolata

Makes 10 servings.

3 pounds boneless veal shoulder, cut into 2-inch cubes	2 carrots, chopped
⅓ cup all-purpose flour for coating, or as needed	2 stalks celery, sliced
	1 cup dry white wine
	1 cup chicken broth
1 teaspoon salt	2 tablespoons tomato paste
¼ teaspoon pepper	1 package (10 ounces) frozen peas
¼ cup olive oil, or as needed	Grated rind of 2 medium-size lemons
2 tablespoons butter or margarine	3 tablespoons finely chopped parsley
1 teaspoon leaf rosemary, crumbled	1 large clove garlic, crushed
2 medium-size onions, chopped	4 cups cooked rice

1. Pat the veal dry with paper toweling. Combine the flour, salt and pepper on wax paper. Lightly coat the veal with the flour mixture, shaking off the excess.
2. Heat 2 tablespoons of the oil and the butter in a large flameproof casserole. Lightly brown the veal in batches, adding more oil as necessary. As the meat browns, remove to a plate. Sprinkle with the rosemary.
3. Sauté the onion, carrot and celery in the oil remaining in the casserole, stirring often, until tender but not browned, about 5 minutes. Stir in the wine and chicken broth, scraping up any browned bits from the bottom of the casserole with a wooden spoon. Stir in the tomato paste.
4. Return the veal to the casserole. Bring to boiling. Lower the heat; cover; simmer 45 minutes to 1 hour, or until the veal is almost tender. Add the peas; cook for 10 minutes.
5. Combine the lemon rind, parsley, and garlic. Stir into the casserole. Serve with rice. Garnish with thin strips of lemon rind, if you wish.

TEMPERATURE AND TIME FOR ROASTING VEAL

Cut	Approximate Pound Weight	Oven Temperature	Internal Meat Temperature When Done	Minutes Per Pound Roasting Time
Leg	5 to 8	300° to 325°F.	170°F.	25 to 35
Loin	4 to 6	300° to 325°F.	170°F.	30 to 35
Rib (Rack)	3 to 5	300° to 325°F.	170°F.	35 to 40
Rolled Shoulder	4 to 6	300° to 325°F.	170°F.	40 to 45

Veal and Rice Gremolata,
page 448.

Veal and Carrot Ragout

Makes 10 servings.

3¹/₂ **pounds boneless
veal shoulder, cut
into 1¹/₂-inch cubes**
5 **cans (13³/₄ ounces
each) chicken broth**
4 **carrots, sliced
(about 2 cups)**
1 **medium-size onion,
studded with 3
cloves**
1 **teaspoon leaf thyme,
crumbled**
1 **teaspoon salt**

1 **bay leaf**
¹/₃ **cup butter**
2 **cups frozen, small
whole onions**
¹/₂ **pound small
mushrooms**
1 **teaspoon lemon
juice**
3 **tablespoons flour
Dash white pepper**
2 **egg yolks**
1 **cup heavy cream**

1. Blanch veal in large kettle or Dutch oven by covering it with cold water, bringing it to boiling and boiling 1 minute. Skim off scum; drain and rinse meat in cold water.
2. Wash pan; return veal and add 6 cups of the chicken broth. Add carrots, the onion with cloves, thyme, salt and bay leaf. Bring to boiling; skim off scum. Lower heat; simmer, partially covered, for 1 hour.

3. Meanwhile, melt 3 tablespoons of the butter in a large skillet; add remaining chicken broth and onions and cook until onions are thawed and tender. Remove with slotted spoon to a bowl.
4. Add mushrooms and lemon juice to skillet; cook 10 minutes. Remove mushrooms to bowl with onions; add skillet liquid to veal liquid.
5. Remove veal and carrots to bowl with onions and mushrooms. Strain broth through fine sieve.
6. Wash pan; add strained broth and boil, uncovered, about 10 minutes. Reserve 3 cups. (Can be made ahead to this point.)
7. Melt remaining butter in a large saucepan; stir in flour and pepper. Cook and stir for 2 minutes, but do not brown. Remove from heat; stir in the 3 cups reserved broth. Place over high heat. Cook and stir constantly until it thickens and bubbles. Lower heat; simmer 10 minutes. Remove the pan from the heat.
8. Beat egg yolks and cream together in a medium-size bowl. Gradually stir in 1 cup of the hot sauce. Return mixture to saucepan, stirring well to blend. Bring just to boiling; lower heat; simmer 30 seconds.
9. Drain veal and vegetables of any liquid that has accumulated in the bowl. Combine veal, vegetables and sauce in large kettle. Reheat until veal is hot, but *do not* boil.

Veal Stew Milanese

Makes 8 servings.

2½ pounds boneless
shoulder, breast or
shank of veal
2 tablespoons flour
1½ teaspoons salt
¼ teaspoon pepper
2 tablespoons
vegetable oil
2 tablespoons butter
1 cup chopped leek or
onion
½ cup finely diced
celery
½ cup finely diced
carrot
¼ cup chopped fresh
parsley
1 teaspoon leaf basil,
crumbled
¾ cup dry white wine
1 can (16 ounces)
plum tomatoes
1 package (10 ounces)
frozen green peas
2 teaspoons chopped
lemon rind (yellow
only)
1 small clove garlic,
chopped
2 tablespoons
chopped fresh
parsley

1. Cut veal into 2-inch cubes. Shake in a mixture of
flour, salt and pepper in a plastic bag to coat evenly.
2. Heat oil and butter in a heavy kettle or Dutch oven.
Brown veal pieces, half at a time, on all sides,
removing pieces as they brown to a bowl.
3. Sauté leek, celery and carrot in same pot until soft,
about 5 minutes. Stir in ¼ cup of parsley, basil and
wine. Bring to boiling; simmer, uncovered, until slightly
reduced, 4 minutes. Add tomatoes with their liquid and
veal; cover.
4. Simmer, stirring occasionally, 2 hours or until meat
is tender. Stir in peas; cook, covered, 5 minutes or just
until peas are tender.
5. Combine lemon rind, garlic and 2 tablespoons
parsley in a cup. Sprinkle over stew just before
serving. Serve with hot cooked rice.

Veal Piccata

Makes 4 servings.

¼ cup all-purpose
flour
1 teaspoon salt
¼ teaspoon pepper
8 thin slices veal for
scaloppine,
pounded thin (about
1 pound)
OR: 4 boned chicken
breasts, pounded
thin
¼ cup (½ stick)
butter
2 tablespoons olive oil
2 lemons
1 tablespoon drained
capers

1. Combine flour, salt and pepper on wax paper; dip
veal on both sides to coat lightly with the flour mixture;
shake off excess.
2. Heat 2 tablespoons of the butter with the oil in a
large skillet. Sauté veal 3 minutes on each side or
until golden brown and tender. Remove to a platter.
3. Squeeze 2 tablespoons juice from one lemon; thinly
slice the other lemon. Add the remaining 2
tablespoons butter, the lemon juice, lemon slices and
capers to pan drippings. Heat and stir, scraping brown
bits from bottom of pan. Return veal to pan; heat,
spooning sauce over, 1 minute. Serve on heated
platter; spoon lemon slices and capers over veal
scaloppine.

Spanish Veal with Almonds

Makes 4 servings.

¼ cup blanched
almonds
2 cloves garlic,
mashed
1 teaspoon plus
1 tablespoon
vegetable oil
1 pound boneless veal
shoulder, cubed
2 tablespoons dry
sherry
⅔ cup canned
condensed beef
broth

1. Toast almonds in a moderate oven (350°) for about
15 minutes or until golden brown.
2. Sauté garlic in 1 teaspoon oil in a large skillet;
remove to a small cup.
3. Add remaining tablespoon oil to skillet. Brown meat,
part at a time, removing cubes to a bowl as they
brown. Return veal to skillet; stir in sherry and all but 1
tablespoon broth. (Add remaining broth to cup with
garlic.) Simmer meat, covered, until tender (about 20
minutes).
4. Meanwhile, grind the toasted almonds in blender;
stir into garlic and broth in cup. When veal is tender,
stir in almond mixture; cook, uncovered, 10 more
minutes. Taste; add salt and pepper, if needed.

Veal Scaloppine Marsala

*Quickly brown the thinly sliced meat, then top with a
delicate wine sauce and serve over rice.*

Makes 8 servings.

½ cup all-purpose
flour
2 pounds veal for
scaloppine
¼ cup (½ stick) butter
or margarine
⅔ cup dry Marsala
½ teaspoon salt
⅛ teaspoon pepper
1 envelope or
teaspoon instant
beef broth

1. Place flour on wax paper. Dip veal slices into flour
to coat lightly.

2. Sauté veal, a few pieces at a time, in part of the butter in a large skillet just until lightly browned. Remove from pan to a plate as they brown; keep warm. Add butter as needed.

3. Stir Marsala into skillet, scraping browned bits from bottom of pan. Stir in salt, pepper and instant beef broth. Simmer 2 minutes.

4. Return veal to skillet; cover. Simmer 5 minutes. Serve with hot cooked rice, if you wish.

Veal Parmigiana

Bake at 400° for 10 minutes.

Makes 4 servings.

1 medium-size onion, chopped (¹/₂ cup)	oregano, crumbled
1 clove garlic, minced	¹/₂ cup packaged bread crumbs
¹/₂ cup vegetable oil	1 pound thin veal for scaloppine
1 can (17 ounces) plum tomatoes	2 eggs, beaten
1 can (6 ounces) tomato paste	4 ounces mozzarella cheese (from an 8-ounce package), sliced
³/₄ teaspoon salt	
2 teaspoons leaf basil, crumbled	¹/₄ cup grated Parmesan cheese
2 teaspoons leaf	

1. Sauté onion and garlic in 2 tablespoons of the oil until soft in a medium-size skillet. Stir in tomatoes, tomato paste, salt, basil and oregano. Simmer, uncovered, stirring frequently, for 45 minutes or until sauce thickens; reserve.

2. Place bread crumbs on wax paper. Dip veal in beaten eggs, then crumbs.

3. Sauté veal, a few pieces at a time, in remaining oil, until golden brown in a large skillet; drain on paper toweling.

4. Layer half the tomato sauce, veal, remaining sauce and sliced mozzarella in a 12-inch baking dish or individual dishes.

5. Bake in a hot oven (400°) for 10 minutes or until cheese is melted and sauce is bubbly-hot. Sprinkle top with Parmesan cheese.

Veal Scallops in Mushroom Sauce

A quick and tasty dish that uses soup as a sauce.

Makes 4 servings.

1 pound veal for scaloppine OR: 1 pound boneless chicken breasts	1 can (7¹/₂ ounces) semi-condensed cream of mushroom soup with wine
2 tablespoons vegetable oil	¹/₂ teaspoon leaf thyme, crumbled

1. Pound veal or chicken between two pieces of wax paper until very thin; pat dry on paper toweling. Heat oil in large skillet; sauté veal quickly until it turns white.

2. Stir in soup and thyme; lower heat; simmer just until heated through, about 10 minutes. Taste; add salt and pepper, if you wish. Serve with buttered spinach noodles, if you wish.

Veal Schnitzel à La Holstein

Makes 4 servings.

¹/₄ cup (¹/₂ stick) butter or margarine	1 small onion, chopped (¹/₄ cup)
4 frozen breaded veal patties (from a 24-ounce package)	¹/₄ cup finely chopped fresh parsley
4 eggs	4 rolled anchovy fillets with capers

1. Melt butter in a large skillet. Sauté veal patties on both sides until golden brown and tender. Remove to platter.

2. Break each egg into a cup, then slide into skillet. Fry eggs to desired firmness. Top each veal pattie with an egg; sprinkle with onion and parsley. Garnish each with rolled anchovy.

Braised Veal Shoulder Roast

Makes 6 servings.

3 pounds boneless veal shoulder, rolled and tied	1 celery stalk, chopped
1 clove garlic	1 carrot, chopped
¹/₂ teaspoon salt	1¹/₄ cups dry white wine or beef broth
¹/₄ teaspoon pepper	
¹/₄ teaspoon leaf thyme, crumbled	6 carrots, pared and cut in half
1 tablespoon butter or margarine	8 red potatoes with strip peeled from center
1 small onion, chopped (¹/₄ cup)	1 pound green beans, tipped

1. Rub veal shoulder roast with cut end of garlic. (If you like highly seasoned meat, make slits in roast and insert slivers of garlic.) Season with salt, pepper and thyme.

2. Melt butter in open 6-quart pressure cooker; brown veal roast on all sides. Let butter get brown to make a tasty sauce. Remove roast to platter.

3. Add onion, chopped celery and carrot to cooker and sauté for a few minutes, just until onion is soft.

(continued)

4. Add wine to cooker; place browned roast on chopped vegetables, basting with sauce. Close cover securely. Place pressure control on vent pipe (number 10 if your control has multipressure selections). Turn heat to high until control starts to jiggle or rock, about 5 minutes. Reduce heat slowly to medium-low so control jiggles only gently; pressure-cook for 30 minutes.

5. Turn heat off and let cool 5 minutes. Then place closed cooker under faucet of running cold water until pressure is reduced and no steam hisses when you attempt to lift control. Carefully remove control and then the cover.

6. Add carrots, potatoes and green beans. Taste cooking liquid; adjust seasonings, if necessary. Close cover securely, place pressure control on vent pipe (number 15 if control has multipressure selections). Turn heat to high until control starts to jiggle or rock, about 5 minutes. Reduce heat to medium-low; pressure-cook 8 minutes.

7. Immediately lower the pressure by placing cooker under running cold water for a few minutes. Carefully remove control, then the cover. Lift roast and vegetables to a serving platter; keep warm.

8. Reheat sauce; taste again. Add additional seasonings, if you wish. Pour into warm sauce boat and pass to serve with veal roast and vegetables.

Note: Sauce will be light and delicate. If you wish, thicken sauce with 2 tablespoons flour blended smoothly with 1/2 cup of water or beef broth. Heat sauce until it thickens and bubbles 1 minute.

Cold Stuffed Breast of Veal

Makes 8 servings.

1 boned breast of veal
3 slices firm-textured white bread, crusts removed
1/2 cup milk
1 medium-size onion, finely chopped (1/2 cup)
2 tablespoons butter or margarine
1 pound lean ground veal
1/3 cup grated Parmesan cheese
1 package (10 ounces) frozen peas, thawed
1/2 cup shelled pistachio nuts
1 egg, slightly beaten
2 teaspoons salt

1 teaspoon grated lemon rind
1/2 teaspoon leaf thyme, crumbled
1/2 teaspoon leaf marjoram, crumbled
1/2 teaspoon ground allspice
1/2 teaspoon pepper
1 carrot, pared and cut into thirds
1 onion, peeled and cut in half
3 garlic cloves
1 bay leaf
8 cups water
4 envelopes or teaspoons instant chicken broth

1. Trim excess fat from breast of veal and place on large cutting board. Keeping meat flat with one hand, cut into meat lengthwise with small sharp paring knife to make pocket for stuffing. Lift top section of veal and cut deeper into meat, keeping knife horizontal. Push your hand inside cavity to loosen top section, making a deep pocket, but do not cut through to other side.

2. Soak bread in milk for 5 minutes.

3. Sauté onion in butter in small skillet until tender but not browned.

4. Combine onion, soaked bread, ground veal, Parmesan cheese, peas, nuts, eggs, salt, lemon rind, thyme, marjoram, allspice and pepper in a large bowl.

5. Spoon stuffing into meat pocket, spreading evenly to make sure corners are filled.

6. Sew the opening of pocket or skewer pocket and lace with cord.

7. Place carrot, onion, garlic, bay leaf and breast of veal in large soup pot or kettle or Dutch oven. Combine water and instant broth; pour over meat. Bring to boiling; lower heat; cover. Simmer for 1 1/4 hours or until meat is tender when tested with tip of sharp knife.

8. Transfer meat to large shallow baking dish and let cool to room temperature. Cover; refrigerate several hours or overnight. Serve cold, cut into slices.

Stuffed Braised Breast of Veal

Makes 10 servings.

4 long thin carrots
1/2 pound spinach, washed
1/2 pound bulk pork sausage
1/2 cup fresh rye or white bread crumbs (1 slice)
1 egg
1 boned breast of veal (about 4 pounds)

2 tablespoons olive or vegetable oil
1 large onion, sliced
1 1/3 cups dry vermouth
1 can (16 ounces) stewed tomatoes
1/2 teaspoon salt
1/2 teaspoon leaf basil, crumbled
1/2 cup pitted green olives, drained

1. Parboil carrots in boiling water in a medium-size saucepan 10 minutes; drain. Cool. Cook spinach in water clinging to leaves, just until wilted, about 3 minutes. Drain very well, then squeeze dry with hands.

2. Combine sausage, bread crumbs and egg in small bowl; beat with a wooden spoon or fork until mixture is smooth.

3. Spread veal flat, skin-side down, on a board. Spread sausage mixture evenly over veal to within 1 inch from edges. Spread spinach over sausage, then arrange carrots, evenly spaced, crosswise over meat.

4. Roll up, jelly-roll fashion, starting at one of the shorter sides. (Carrots go lengthwise through roll.)

(continued)

Pictured opposite:
Stuffed Braised Breast of Veal.

Fasten edge with poultry pins or skewers. Tie with string at 1½-inch intervals.

5. Brown roll in oil in a Dutch oven or large deep skillet about 10 minutes. Add onion; sauté 5 minutes. Stir in vermouth, tomatoes, salt and basil. Bring to boiling; lower heat; cover. Simmer, basting and turning meat several times, 2½ hours or until meat is very tender. (Recipe may be prepared ahead to this point.) Lift roll to heated serving platter; keep warm.

6. Add olives to sauce; simmer 10 minutes.

7. Remove string and skewers from veal; slice about ½-inch thick. Serve with saffron rice, if you wish.

Veal Cutlets and Apples

By flaming the apple brandy in the sauce you cook away the calories but the delightful taste remains.

Makes 6 servings.

Nonstick vegetable cooking spray	1 teaspoon finely chopped, peeled fresh gingerroot
1½ pounds veal cutlets	1 Red Delicious apple, peeled, cored and thinly sliced
1 tablespoon all-purpose flour	1½ teaspoons sugar
Salt and pepper, to taste	¾ cup dry white wine
3 tablespoons apple brandy	¾ cup chicken broth

1. Spray a large skillet with the nonstick vegetable cooking spray. Dredge the veal in the flour; shake off the excess and season with the salt and pepper to taste.

2. Cook the veal in the prepared skillet for 3 minutes on each side or until golden. Remove the veal from the skillet.

3. Add the apple brandy to the skillet. Carefully light the mixture with a long kitchen match. When the flames subside, add the ginger, sliced apple, sugar, wine and broth.

4. Cook the mixture over high heat for 10 minutes or until the apples are tender and the sauce thickens slightly. Return the veal to the skillet. Cover and cook until the veal is heated through.

GROUND AND VARIETY MEATS

Hamburger   The origin of the word "hamburger" is not certain but seems to be based on the German seaport of Hamburg. Hamburg enjoyed trade with Russian provinces where raw ground meat, called "steak tartare," was eaten. As a result, Hamburg residents developed an appreciation of ground meat or "hamburger," but it was an American who first served the hamburger patty on a bun at the St. Louis Exposition in 1904.

All-American Burgers

The first broiled hamburgers were served in 1904 at the St. Louis Exposition; they've been America's #1 favorite ever since. Try this home-style version of the "big stacked" burger.

Makes 6 burgers.

½ cup mayonnaise or salad dressing	or margarine
¼ cup chili sauce	6 crisp, washed lettuce leaves
¼ cup sweet pickle relish	6 hamburger rolls, halved
1½ pounds ground round or chuck	6 tomato slices
1 teaspoon salt	6 slices process American cheese
⅛ teaspoon pepper	6 thin slices sweet Bermuda onion
2 tablespoons butter	

1. Combine mayonnaise, chili sauce and sweet pickle relish in a small bowl; mix until well blended; cover. Refrigerate sauce until ready to use.

2. Mix beef lightly with salt and pepper; shape into 6 patties.

3. Melt butter in a large skillet. Panfry hamburgers over medium heat 2 minutes on each side, or until done as you like them.

4. To assemble: Put lettuce leaf on bottom half of roll; top with hamburger, a spoonful of the sauce, a tomato slice, cheese slice, more sauce and onion slice; top with remaining half of roll.

All-American Superburgers

Make the home-style version of America's #1 favorite — the big stacked hamburger.

Makes 6 double burgers.

Jumbo Burger Rolls (*recipe follows*)	¼ teaspoon pepper
½ cup mayonnaise or salad dressing	2 tablespoons butter or margarine
¼ cup chili sauce	6 crisp, washed lettuce leaves
¼ cup sweet pickle relish	6 tomato slices
1½ pounds ground round or chuck	6 slices process American cheese
1½ teaspoons salt	6 thin slices sweet Bermuda onion

1. Prepare Rolls. Combine mayonnaise, chili sauce and sweet pickle relish in a small bowl; mix until well blended; cover. Refrigerate until ready to use.

2. Mix beef lightly with salt and pepper; shape into 12 very thin patties.

3. Melt butter or margarine in a large skillet. Panfry hamburgers over medium heat for 2 minutes on each side or until desired doneness.

4. To assemble hamburgers: Cut a roll evenly into 3 layers; place a lettuce leaf on bottom layer, then a hamburger, tomato slice, sauce, middle roll layer, another burger, cheese slice, onion slice, more sauce and top of roll.

Jumbo Burger Rolls

Bake at 325° for 25 minutes.

Makes 6 large rolls.

1 package hot roll mix	**2 eggs**
³/₄ cup very warm water	**2 tablespoons sesame seeds**

1. Prepare hot roll mix with water and 1 egg and let rise, following label directions.

2. Turn dough out onto a lightly floured pastry board; knead 8 to 10 times. Divide into 6 even pieces; shape each into a smooth ball, then flatten to make about a 4-inch round. Place on a greased cookie sheet.

3. Cover with a towel; let rise 30 minutes or until double in bulk. Beat the remaining egg, brush over rolls; sprinkle with sesame seeds. Preheat oven to 325°.

4. Bake in a preheated slow oven (325°) for 25 minutes or until rolls are golden and sound hollow when lightly tapped. Let cool on wire rack.

Deviled Hamburgers

Makes 2 servings.

¹/₂ pound ground chuck	**¹/₂ teaspoon minced onion**
3 tablespoons bottled chili sauce	**³/₄ teaspoon Worcestershire sauce**
1 teaspoon prepared mustard	**¹/₄ teaspoon salt**
³/₄ teaspoon bottled horseradish	**2 hamburger buns Melted butter**

1. Combine beef, chili sauce, mustard, horseradish, onion, Worcestershire and salt in a medium-size bowl; mix well.

2. Cut buns in half and spread with meat mixture; brush with melted butter. Broil with tops about 5 inches from heat about 10 minutes or until cooked.

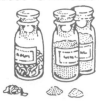

Welsh Burgers

Makes 4 servings.

8 ounces Cheddar cheese, shredded (2 cups)	**1 pound ground round or chuck**
2 teaspoons flour	**1 teaspoon salt**
¹/₄ cup beer	**¹/₈ teaspoon pepper**
1 teaspoon Worcestershire sauce	**2 tablespoons butter or margarine**
¹/₄ teaspoon dry mustard	**4 hamburger rolls, split, toasted and buttered**

1. Toss cheese with flour. Heat beer in a medium-size saucepan over very low heat. Add Worcestershire sauce, mustard and cheese mixture; stir until cheese melts.

2. Season beef with salt and pepper; shape ground beef into 4 equal patties, about the size of the rolls.

3. Melt butter in a large skillet. Panfry hamburgers over medium heat for 4 minutes on each side or until desired doneness. Place on bottom halves of buttered rolls.

4. Spoon cheese mixture over burgers. Top each with remaining halves of rolls.

Dill Burgers

Makes 4 servings.

¹/₂ cup dairy sour cream	**¹/₄ teaspoon ground allspice**
1 tablespoon chopped fresh dill	**¹/₂ teaspoon salt**
OR: 1 teaspoon dillweed	**¹/₄ teaspoon pepper**
	1 pound ground chuck or round

1. Combine sour cream, dill, allspice, salt and pepper in a medium-size bowl; blend well. Add ground chuck and blend lightly with a fork. Shape into 4 patties.

2. Grill over gray coals, 6 inches from heat, about 4 minutes on each side, turning once.

Sour Cream and Horseradish Burgers

Makes 4 servings.

¹/₂ cup dairy sour cream	**¹/₂ teaspoon salt**
3 tablespoons prepared horseradish	**¹/₄ teaspoon pepper**
	1 pound ground chuck or round

1. Combine sour cream, horseradish, salt and pepper in a medium-size bowl; blend well. Add ground chuck and mix lightly with a fork. Shape into 4 equal-size patties. Place on rack over broiler pan.

2. Broil 3 inches from heat about 4 minutes on each side, turning once.

Bacon Burgers

Makes 4 servings.

8 bacon slices
1 small onion, minced
 (¼ cup)
1 pound ground round
 or chuck
½ teaspoon salt
⅛ teaspoon pepper
4 onion rolls
Lettuce leaves
Dill pickle spears

1. Cook bacon in a large skillet until limp. Remove 4 slices; roll up and fasten with wooden picks; return to skillet; cook with remaining bacon until crisp; drain. Remove picks from bacon curls; crumble remaining 4 slices bacon. Drain all but 1 tablespoon bacon drippings from skillet.
2. Sauté onion in drippings until golden. Lightly mix the crumbled bacon, onion, ground round, salt and pepper; shape into 4 equal patties.
3. Panfry burgers over medium heat for 4 minutes on each side or until desired doneness. Split, toast and butter onion rolls. Place burger on lettuce-lined bottom halves of rolls; add top halves. Garnish with bacon curls and dill pickle.

Chile Burgers

Makes 4 servings.

½ cup diced tomato
2 tablespoons
 chopped green
 onion
2 tablespoons
 chopped green
 pepper
2 canned hot green
 chilies, seeded and
 chopped
¼ teaspoon leaf
 oregano, crumbled
⅛ teaspoon salt
1 pound ground round
 or chuck
1 tablespoon
packaged bread
 crumbs
1 egg
1 teaspoon salt
⅛ teaspoon pepper
½ teaspoon chili
 powder
1 tablespoon
 vegetable oil
4 canned or frozen
 corn tortillas,
 thawed, if frozen
Shredded romaine
 lettuce
Green pepper rings
Refried beans

1. Combine tomato, green onion, green pepper, half of the green chilies, oregano and salt in a small bowl. Lightly mix ground round with the remaining green chilies, bread crumbs, egg, salt, pepper and chili powder. Shape into 4 equal patties.
2. Heat oil in a large skillet. Panfry burgers over medium heat for 4 minutes on each side or until done

as you like them; or, broil or grill 5 to 6 inches from heat, turning once. Heat tortillas following label directions. Top each with shredded romaine, a hamburger, green pepper ring and spoon tomato mixture on top. Serve with refried beans.

Nut Burgers

Makes 4 servings.

1 pound ground round
 or chuck
½ cup finely chopped
 walnuts
2 tablespoons finely
 chopped green
 onion
1 egg
2 tablespoons soy
 sauce
¼ teaspoon salt
¼ teaspoon pepper
1 tablespoon
 vegetable oil
4 poppy seed rolls
Unpared cucumber
 slices
Dairy sour cream
Chopped green onions
 or walnuts

1. Lightly mix ground round with walnuts, green onion, egg, soy sauce, salt and pepper in a large bowl. Shape into 4 equal patties.
2. Heat oil in a large skillet. Panfry patties over medium heat for 4 minutes on each side or until desired doneness; or, broil or grill 5 to 6 inches from heat, turning once.
3. Split, toast and butter rolls. Place hamburgers on bottom halves of rolls. Top each with cucumber, sour cream, green onions or walnuts and tops of rolls.

Hamburgers au Poivre

Makes 4 servings.

1 pound ground round
 or chuck
½ teaspoon salt
1 to 2 teaspoons
 freshly ground
 black pepper
1 tablespoon
vegetable oil
2 tablespoons water,
 red wine or beef
 broth
4 slices white bread,
 toasted and
 buttered

1. Shape ground round into 4 equal patties. Sprinkle with salt; press pepper into both sides of patties.
2. Heat oil in large skillet. Panfry hamburgers over medium heat for 4 minutes on each side or until desired doneness. Remove and keep warm. Drain fat from pan; add water to pan drippings; swirl around to deglaze pan.
3. Place each hamburger on toast; pour some pan juices over each of the burgers.

Pictured opposite (from bottom):
Chile Burgers; Bacon Burgers;
Nut Burgers.

Cantonese Burgers

Makes 4 servings.

1 clove garlic, crushed
1 medium-size carrot, thinly sliced
1/2 cup cubed green pepper
1 medium-size onion, chopped (1/2 cup)
2 tablespoons vegetable oil
1 tablespoon cornstarch
1/2 cup water
3 tablespoons cider vinegar
1/4 cup firmly packed light brown sugar
1/2 cup sweet mixed pickles, drained
1 pound ground round or chuck
1 teaspoon salt
1/8 teaspoon pepper
1 tablespoon butter or margarine
4 hamburger rolls, split, toasted and buttered

1. Sauté garlic, carrot, green pepper and onion in oil in a medium-size saucepan 2 to 3 minutes or until vegetables are crisp-tender.
2. Mix cornstarch with 2 tablespoons of the water in a cup. Add remaining water, vinegar, sugar and pickles to saucepan; bring to boiling; stir in cornstarch mixture; bring to boiling, stirring constantly. Cook just until thickened and bubbly, about 1 minute. Cover; keep warm.
3. Mix beef lightly with salt and pepper; shape into 4 equal-size patties about the size of the rolls.
4. Heat butter in a large skillet. Panfry hamburgers over medium heat for 4 minutes on each side or until desired doneness.
5. Place each hamburger on bottom half of roll; spoon some sauce over each. Top each with remaining half of roll. Serve sauce with burgers. Garnish with green onions and green pepper strips, if you wish.

Caesar Burgers

Makes 4 servings.

1 pound ground chuck or round
1/4 cup grated Parmesan cheese
1 tablespoon minced anchovy fillets
1 egg
2 teaspoons lemon juice
1 teaspoon
Worcestershire sauce
1/4 cup olive oil
2 cloves garlic, crushed
4 hamburger rolls, split
Romaine or iceberg lettuce leaves

1. Combine beef, cheese, anchovies, egg, lemon juice and Worcestershire; shape into 4 equal patties.
2. Heat oil and garlic in a large skillet until garlic is golden. Discard garlic; remove half of the oil and reserve.
3. Brown cut sides of 2 rolls in oil; remove. Add the remaining oil and brown the remaining rolls. Place lettuce on bottom halves of rolls.
4. Panfry patties in the same skillet over medium heat

for 4 minutes on each side or until desired doneness. Place over lettuce; cover with tops of rolls.

California Burgers

Makes 4 servings.

1 pound ground round or chuck
1 teaspoon salt
1/8 teaspoon pepper
2 tablespoons butter or margarine
Lettuce leaves
4 hamburger rolls, split, toasted and
buttered
8 thin dill pickle slices
4 thin tomato slices
4 thin red onion slices
Pickle relish
Mayonnaise or salad dressing
Prepared mustard

1. Season beef with salt and pepper; shape into 4 equal patties about the size of the rolls.
2. Melt butter in a skillet. Panfry hamburgers over medium heat for 4 minutes on each side or until desired doneness. Place lettuce, then hamburgers, on bottom halves of buttered rolls.
3. Top each burger with 2 pickle slices, a slice each of tomato and onion, a spoonful each of relish and mayonnaise and a little mustard. Top each with remaining half of roll. Garnish with carrot curls and parsley, if you wish.

Aztec Burgers

Blend buttery avocado with tomato and pepper and you have an easy guacamole topping for your burger.

Makes 4 servings.

1 small tomato, chopped
1 canned mild green chile, seeded and chopped
2 tablespoons minced green onion
1/2 teaspoon salt
4 bacon slices
1 pound ground round
or chuck
1 teaspoon salt
1/4 teaspoon pepper
4 hamburger rolls, split, toasted and buttered
1 small avocado, halved, pitted and sliced

1. Combine tomato, green chile, onion and the 1/2 teaspoon salt in a small bowl.
2. In a large skillet, cook bacon until done but still pliable. Roll up with a fork to make curls; secure with wooden picks. Drain bacon curls on paper toweling. Pour off all but 1 tablespoon drippings.
3. Mix beef lightly with the 1 teaspoon salt and pepper. Shape into 4 equal patties, about the size of the rolls. Panfry hamburgers in drippings over medium heat for 4 minutes on each side or until done.
4. Place a burger on bottom half of each roll. Arrange 3 or 4 slices of avocado on each. Top with tomato mixture; garnish with bacon curl. Top each with remaining half of roll. Serve with pickled peppers, if you wish.

From top: Cantonese Burgers, page 458; Aztec
Burgers, page 458; California Burgers, page 458.

4 Ways to Shape Meat Loaves

Most Popular Loaf A jiffy—that's all this shaping trick takes. Press meat into standard 9 × 5 × 3-inch loaf pan, then invert into a shallow pan for baking.

Bowl-'Em-Over Round Use a casserole or mixing bowl to mold the meat mixture. Then, turn it upside down into pan; lift off bowl. To serve, divide loaf into quarters; slice each quarter.

Casserole Easy A shallow baking dish—round, square or oblong—makes an ideal mold for meat loaves. Most are attractive enough to carry right to the table. For a subtle flavor touch, top loaf with a bay leaf before baking.

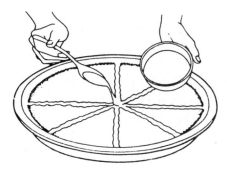

Easy-As-Pie A pie plate serves as baker for this inviting loaf. After pressing meat into the plate, mark it into wedges and outline each with catsup. Cut between marks after baking; lift out each sauce-topped wedge with a spatula.

Country Meat Loaf

Bake at 350° for 1 hour in loaf pan or 45 minutes in ring mold.

Makes 6 to 8 servings.

2 pounds ground chuck	**cream**
1 large onion, finely chopped (1 cup)	**2 tablespoons catsup**
1 tablespoon Dijon mustard	
¹/₂ cup packaged bread crumbs	**¹/₄ cup chopped fresh parsley**
2 eggs	**1¹/₂ teaspoons salt**
¹/₂ cup dairy sour	**¹/₂ teaspoon pepper**

1. Combine chuck, onion, bread crumbs, eggs, sour cream, catsup, mustard, parsley, salt and pepper in a large bowl; mix well.
2. Spoon mixture into a lightly greased 9 × 5 × 3-inch loaf pan or a 6 ¹/₂-cup ring mold. Spread evenly and press down firmly.
3. Bake in a moderate oven (350°) for 1 hour for the loaf pan or 45 minutes for ring mold or until meat loaf shrinks from sides. Remove from oven; pour off any juices. Unmold onto serving platter; cool. Wrap with plastic wrap and refrigerate until ready to tote. Wrap meat loaf with foil for toting.

Rolled Meat Loaf

Bake at 350° for 55 minutes.

Makes 6 servings.

¹/₂ pound sweet Italian sausages	**1 medium-size onion, finely chopped (¹/₂ cup)**
2 slices white bread	
Water	**1 egg**
2 tablespoons catsup	**³/₄ teaspoon salt**
1 pound ground chuck	**¹/₄ teaspoon pepper**

1. Brown sausages in small skillet, turning often (about 20 minutes).

2. While sausages are cooking, cover bread with water in small bowl; let stand until water is absorbed.

3. When sausages are cooked, remove from skillet; add ¼ cup water and catsup to skillet, scraping and stirring up browned bits; reserve.

4. Place the chuck, onion, egg, salt and pepper in a medium-size bowl; squeeze bread and add to meat mixture. Combine thoroughly.

5. Spread meat mixture on foil rectangle to make an 8-inch square about ½-inch thick. Place sausages at one end of mixture. Roll as you would a jelly roll, lifting foil to start the rolling. Lift roll in foil and transfer to a 9 × 5 × 3-inch loaf pan.

6. Bake in a moderate oven (350°) for 45 minutes. Combine ⅓ cup drippings from loaf pan with catsup mixture from skillet. Brush sauce over meat loaf; return to oven for 10 more minutes. Remove from pan; let rest 15 minutes before slicing.

Apple Pork Loaf

Bake at 350° for 1¼ hours.

Makes 8 servings.

2 slices whole-wheat bread	**2 tablespoons chopped fresh parsley**
½ cup milk	**1 teaspoon salt**
1½ pounds lean ground pork	**½ teaspoon pepper**
½ pound pork sausage	**¼ teaspoon leaf basil, crumbled**
1 egg, lightly beaten	**Pinch leaf thyme**
½ cup finely diced baking apple	**Pinch ground nutmeg**
½ cup finely diced celery	**Stir-Fried Apples and Celery (recipe follows)**
¼ cup wheat germ	

1. Crumble bread into milk in a large bowl. Add pork, sausage, egg, apple, celery, wheat germ, parsley, salt, pepper, basil, thyme and nutmeg; stir until well-blended. Shape into a loaf in shallow baking pan.

2. Bake in a moderate oven (350°) for 1¼ hours. Serve with Stir-Fried Apples and Celery.

Stir-Fried Apples and Celery

2 tablespoons butter or margarine	**celery**
2 tablespoons vegetable oil	**2 medium-size cooking apples, quartered, cored and sliced (2 cups)**
1 tablespoon lemon juice	**½ teaspoon salt**
2 cups thinly sliced	**¼ teaspoon pepper**

1. Heat butter and oil in a large skillet. Add lemon juice and celery; stir-fry over high heat for 5 minutes or until almost tender.

2. Add apples; continue cooking and stirring for 5 minutes or until tender. Sprinkle with salt and pepper.

Herbed Beef Loaf with Pastry Crust

Bake at 350° for 1 hour, then at 425° for 15 minutes.

Makes 8 servings .

2 pounds ground round or chuck	**marjoram, crumbled**
½ cup tomato juice	**2 tablespoons chopped fresh parsley**
2 eggs	**1½ teaspoons salt**
1 medium-size onion, minced (½ cup)	**½ teaspoon pepper**
½ cup packaged bread crumbs	**1 package piecrust mix**
1 tablespoon minced fresh marjoram or: 1 teaspoon leaf	**1 egg yolk**
	1 tablespoon water

1. Combine meat, tomato juice, eggs, onion, bread crumbs, marjoram, parsley, salt and pepper in a large bowl; mix well. Press mixture into a lightly greased 9 × 5 × 3-inch loaf pan.

2. Bake in a moderate oven (350°) for 1 hour or until loaf shrinks from sides of pan. Remove from oven; pour off drippings. Unmold loaf onto a jelly-roll pan; cool until easy to handle.

3. Preheat oven to 425°. Prepare piecrust mix following label directions. Roll pastry to a 16 × 14-inch rectangle on a lightly floured surface. Place cooled loaf in center of pastry. Fold pastry around loaf; seal edges with water. Turn loaf upright; cut decorative slits for escape of steam; transfer to jelly-roll pan. Beat egg yolk with water; brush over pastry.

4. Bake in a preheated hot oven (425°) for 15 minutes or until pastry is golden brown.

Beef Loaf with Mushrooms and Sour Cream

Bake at 350° for 1 hour.

Makes 8 servings.

1 pound mushrooms, sliced	**1 tablespoon Worcestershire sauce**
¼ cup (½ stick) butter or margarine	**2 pounds ground round**
2 tablespoons flour	**1 medium-size onion, finely chopped (½ cup)**
¼ teaspoon ground nutmeg	**2 tablespoons chopped fresh dill**
1 carton (8 ounces) dairy sour cream	**OR: 1 teaspoon dillweed**
1 cup fresh bread crumbs (2 slices)	**1½ teaspoons salt**
½ cup grapefruit juice	**½ teaspoon pepper**
¼ cup catsup	
2 eggs	

1. Sauté mushrooms in butter in a large skillet just until tender, about 4 minutes. Sprinkle with flour and nutmeg. Cook, stirring constantly, 1 minute; remove from heat; stir in sour cream. *(continued)*

2. Combine bread crumbs, grapefruit juice, catsup, eggs, Worcestershire sauce, ground meat, onion, dill, salt and pepper in a large bowl; mix thoroughly.

3. Spoon half the meat mixture into a lightly greased 9 × 5 × 3-inch loaf pan. Make a wide and shallow indentation down center of mixture. Spoon about 1/3 of the mushroom mixture into indentation, spreading evenly. Spoon remaining meat mixture over filling, covering completely.

4. Bake in a moderate oven (350°) for 1 hour or until loaf shrinks from sides of pan. Remove from oven; pour off juices. Invert onto warm serving platter. Thin remaining mushroom mixture with a little milk, if necessary. Heat gently over very low heat and serve as a sauce with meat loaf. Garnish with fluted mushroom caps, cherry tomatoes and fresh dill, if you wish.

Burgundy Beef Loaf

The robust flavor of deep red wine gives this meat loaf a classic French touch.

Bake at 350° for 1 hour, 10 minutes.

Makes 8 to 10 servings.

1 cup Burgundy wine	rosemary, crumbled
1/4 cup finely chopped celery	1/4 teaspoon leaf thyme, crumbled
1 clove garlic	1/4 teaspoon pepper
1 bay leaf	2 eggs
2 1/2 pounds ground round or chuck	1 can condensed beef broth
2 1/2 cups fresh bread crumbs (5 slices)	1 teaspoon Worcestershire sauce
1 large onion, finely chopped (1 cup)	1/4 cup water
1 tablespoon chopped fresh parsley	Burgundy Sauce (recipe follows)
2 teaspoons salt	Chopped parsley
1/4 teaspoon leaf	

1. Combine wine, celery, garlic and bay leaf in a small saucepan; bring to boiling; lower heat; simmer, uncovered, until volume is reduced to half, about 10 minutes. Remove and discard garlic and bay leaf; cool wine mixture completely.

2. Combine beef, bread crumbs, onion, parsley, salt, rosemary, thyme and pepper in a large bowl; add the wine mixture, eggs, 1/2 cup of the beef broth (reserve remaining broth for sauce) and Worcestershire. Mix until well blended. Shape into an oval loaf on a lightly oiled shallow baking pan.

3. Bake in a moderate oven (350°) for 1 hour 10 minutes or until loaf is a rich brown. Remove with 2 wide spatulas to a heated serving platter; keep warm. Add reserved broth and 1/4 cup water to drippings in baking pan; bring to boiling, stirring constantly to loosen browned bits. Strain into a 1-cup measure. (Add water to make 1 cup.)

4. Make Burgundy Sauce.

5. Arrange small buttered whole carrots, onions and sautéed mushrooms on platter with loaf, if you wish; sprinkle with chopped parsley. Serve with Burgundy Sauce.

Burgundy Sauce: Sauté 1 tablespoon chopped shallots or green onion in 2 tablespoons butter or margarine in a medium-size saucepan, about 2 minutes. Stir in 3 tablespoons flour; gradually add the reserved broth and 1/2 cup Burgundy wine. Cook, stirring constantly, until sauce thickens and bubbles 2 minutes. Stir in 1 teaspoon chopped fresh parsley. Makes about 1 1/2 cups.

Glazed Meat Loaf

Bake at 350° for 1 hour, 10 minutes.

Makes 6 servings.

1 1/2 pounds ground chuck	1 teaspoon prepared red beet horseradish
3/4 cup packaged seasoned bread crumbs	1 tablespoon plus 1/4 cup water
2 eggs, slightly beaten	Glaze (recipe follows)
1/4 cup catsup	

1. Combine beef, bread crumbs, eggs, catsup, horseradish and 1 tablespoon water in a large bowl. Mix well. Shape into a loaf on a well-greased jelly-roll pan or shallow baking pan.

2. Bake in a moderate oven (350°) for 30 minutes. Baste with half the Glaze. Continue baking for 30 minutes longer. Dilute remaining Glaze with 1/4 cup water. Pour over loaf for a nice gravy. Bake 10 minutes longer.

Glaze: Combine 2 tablespoons catsup with 1 tablespoon soy sauce or teriyaki sauce or meat sauce or Worcestershire sauce.

Meat Loaf and Baked Potato Meal

Bake at 350° for 40 minutes.

Makes 2 servings.

2 baking potatoes (each 4 inches long, 2 inches wide)	pepper
	1/2 cup fresh bread crumbs (1 slice)
3/4 pound ground round	1/4 cup tomato juice
2 tablespoons finely chopped onion	1 egg, slightly beaten
	1/2 teaspoon salt
2 tablespoons finely chopped green	Dash pepper
	2 tablespoons chili sauce

1. Simmer potatoes in water to cover in a covered saucepan for 30 minutes until tender.

(continued)

Pictured opposite: Beef Loaf with Mushrooms and Sour Cream, page 461.

2. Combine meat, onion, green pepper, bread crumbs, tomato juice, egg, salt and pepper in a medium-size bowl. Spoon into 2 small $4\frac{1}{2} \times 2\frac{1}{2} \times 1\frac{1}{2}$-inch loaf pans; smooth mixture with spatula. Place in oven with potatoes.

3. Bake in toaster oven at moderate (350°) for 35 minutes. (Remove pan liquid as it forms with bulb baster or pour off.) Remove from oven; spread each loaf with 1 tablespoon chili sauce; return to oven. Bake 5 more minutes.

Crunchy Meat Loaves

Bake at 375° for 30 minutes.

Makes 6 servings .

2 eggs
$\frac{1}{4}$ cup packaged bread crumbs
1 can (8 ounces) water chestnuts, drained and finely chopped
1 teaspoon salt
$\frac{1}{8}$ teaspoon pepper
$\frac{1}{4}$ teaspoon garlic salt
1 pound ground round
$\frac{1}{2}$ pound lean ground pork
1 cup chicken broth
1 tablespoon

cornstarch
1 tablespoon brown sugar
2 tablespoons soy sauce
2 tablespoons chopped green onion
1 can (11 ounces) mandarin oranges, drained
1 tablespoon toasted sesame seeds

1. Beat eggs until frothy in a medium-size bowl with bread crumbs, water chestnuts, salt, pepper and garlic salt. Add ground meats; mix well. Form into 6 oval-shaped loaves. Place loaves in a $13 \times 9 \times 2$-inch pan.

2. Bake in a moderate oven (375°) for 20 minutes.

3. While loaves are baking, stir chicken broth into cornstarch in a small saucepan. Add brown sugar, soy sauce and green onion. Cook, stirring constantly, until slightly thickened. Add mandarin oranges.

4. Remove pan of meat loaves from oven after 20 minutes baking. Spoon sauce over partially cooked meat loaves in pan. Return to oven. Continue baking another 10 minutes.

5. At serving time, arrange loaves on deep platter; sprinkle with sesame seeds.

Savory Sausage Loaf

Bake at 350° for 1 hour, 15 minutes.

Makes 8 servings.

2 pounds bulk pork sausage
4 medium-size carrots, minced (1 cup)
1 green pepper, seeded and minced (1 cup)
1 can (8 ounces) tomato sauce
1 egg
1 cup packaged bread crumbs

3 tablespoons finely chopped fresh parsley
$1\frac{1}{2}$ teaspoons salt
$\frac{1}{2}$ teaspoon pepper
1 medium-size onion, minced ($\frac{1}{2}$ cup)
1 tablespoon butter or margarine
2 cups packaged seasoned stuffing mix

1. Combine sausage, carrots, green pepper, tomato sauce, egg, bread crumbs, parsley, salt and pepper in a large bowl; mix well.

2. Sauté onion in butter in a large skillet until soft. Add stuffing; blend well.

3. Press half the sausage mixture into a lightly greased 8-cup ring mold or a $9 \times 5 \times 3$-inch loaf pan. Spread stuffing mixture evenly over sausage. Spoon in remaining sausage mixture, pressing down firmly.

4. Bake in a moderate oven (350°) for $1\frac{1}{4}$ hours or until loaf shrinks from side of mold. Remove from oven; pour off any juices. Unmold onto serving platter. Garnish with buttered cooked carrots, green pepper strips and watercress, if you wish.

Individual Pork Loaves with Orange Sauce

Bake at 350° for 50 minutes.

Makes 8 servings.

$1\frac{1}{2}$ pounds ground pork
$\frac{1}{2}$ pound ground round
$\frac{1}{2}$ cup packaged bread crumbs
$\frac{1}{3}$ cup orange juice
2 eggs
1 tablespoon instant minced onion
1 teaspoon dried parsley flakes
$\frac{1}{2}$ teaspoon celery salt

1 teaspoon grated lemon rind
1 tablespoon lemon juice
$1\frac{1}{2}$ teaspoons salt
$\frac{1}{2}$ teaspoon pepper
1 can (11 ounces) mandarin oranges, undrained
1 tablespoon orange juice
1 tablespoon cornstarch

1. Combine pork, beef, crumbs, orange juice, eggs, onion, parsley, celery salt, lemon rind and juice, salt and pepper in a large bowl; mix well. Divide into 8 parts; press into 8 lightly greased 5-ounce custard cups.

2. Bake in a moderate oven (350°) for 50 minutes. Remove cups from oven; pour off any drippings.

3. Combine mandarin oranges and their juice with orange juice and cornstarch in a small saucepan. Cook over medium heat, stirring constantly, until sauce is thickened and clear.

4. Remove meat from cups; arrange on warm platter. Serve with sauce.

Lamb, Beef and Rice Loaf

Bake at 350° for 1 hour.

Makes 8 servings.

1½ pounds lean ground lamb	powder
½ pound ground round or chuck	½ teaspoon salt
1½ cups cooked rice	½ teaspoon pepper
1 large onion, minced (1 cup)	1 small green pepper, seeded and minced
2 cloves garlic, crushed	2 tablespoons vegetable oil
2 eggs	1 can (8 ounces) tomato sauce
2 teaspoons curry	1 teaspoon leaf oregano, crumbled

1. Combine lamb, beef, rice, ½ cup of the onion, garlic, eggs, curry powder, salt and pepper in a large bowl; mix well. Press mixture into a lightly greased 9 × 5 × 3-inch loaf pan.

2. Bake in a moderate oven (350°) for 1 hour or until loaf shrinks from sides of pan. Pour off juices from pan. Unmold loaf onto platter. Let stand 10 minutes while preparing sauce.

3. For sauce: Sauté remaining ½ cup onion and the green pepper in oil in a medium-size saucepan until tender. Stir in tomato sauce and oregano. Cook, uncovered, over low heat, stirring occasionally, for 10 minutes.

Meatballs in Lemon Sauce with Mashed Potatoes

Makes 6 servings.

1 egg	2 envelopes instant beef broth
1½ pounds ground chuck	2 pounds boiling potatoes (about 6)
1 cup fresh bread crumbs (2 slices)	2 tablespoons margarine
1½ teaspoons salt	¼ cup milk
¼ teaspoon pepper	3 tablespoons flour
2 teaspoons grated lemon rind	½ cup water
2 tablespoons lemon juice	1 package (10 ounces) frozen peas
3 cups water	

1. Beat egg slightly in large bowl; add beef, crumbs, salt, pepper, lemon rind and 1 tablespoon of the lemon juice. Combine gently; form into 24 balls.

2. Heat 3 cups of water to boiling with beef broth in Dutch oven; add meatballs, using a large spoon. Lower heat; poach gently 15 minutes, turning once.

3. While meat is cooking, pare potatoes; quarter and cook in boiling salted water to cover until tender. Drain, reserving liquid. Mash potatoes with the margarine and milk. (Use some of the reserved liquid to make creamier potatoes.)

4. Stir flour with water to make a smooth liquid. Remove meatballs to heated platter; skim off any fat. Add flour mixture slowly to broth, stirring with a wire whisk until sauce thickens. (Sauce is thin.) Stir in remaining 1 tablespoon lemon juice; simmer 5 minutes.

5. Cook peas following package directions. Drain and arrange on platter with meat and potatoes. Spoon sauce over meat. Serve.

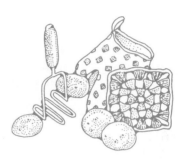

Tiny Meatballs with Nectarines

Makes about 6 dozen ¾-inch meatballs.

1 pound ground round	1 cup orange juice
½ cup packaged bread crumbs	2 tablespoons soy sauce
½ teaspoon salt	½ cup cider vinegar
¼ teaspoon pepper	¼ cup firmly packed light brown sugar
1 teaspoon soy sauce	2 tablespoons cornstarch
⅓ cup milk	½ cup cold water
1 medium-size onion, chopped (½ cup)	3 ripe nectarines, peeled, pitted and sliced
2 tablespoons butter or margarine	
2 tablespoons vegetable oil	

1. Combine ground round, bread crumbs, salt, pepper, soy sauce, milk and onion in a bowl. Shape into ¾-inch balls.

2. Heat butter and oil in a large skillet. Sauté meatballs part at a time, turning frequently, until browned and thoroughly cooked, about 10 minutes. Remove meatballs as they brown to a bowl; keep warm.

3. Pour orange juice, soy sauce and vinegar into skillet, stirring to dislodge browned bits. Stir in brown sugar. Dissolve cornstarch in cold water; add to skillet.

4. Cook over medium heat, stirring constantly, until mixture thickens and clears. Return meatballs to skillet; add nectarine slices; heat until piping hot, stirring gently.

Chili Meatball Stew

Makes 6 servings.

1 pound ground chuck
1 cup fresh bread
   crumbs (2 slices)
2 envelopes instant
   onion soup (2 one-
   cup portions)
1 teaspoon dried
   parsley flakes
1/2 cup milk
2 tablespoons butter
   or margarine
3 medium-size onions,
   chopped (1 1/2 cups)
1 clove garlic, minced

1 green pepper,
   seeded and diced
   (1 cup)
1 1/2 to 2 tablespoons
   chili powder
1 can (28 ounces)
   tomatoes
1 teaspoon salt
1/4 teaspoon cumin
   seeds, crushed
1 can (16 ounces) red
   kidney beans,
   drained

1. Combine beef, bread crumbs, instant soup, parsley flakes and milk in medium-size bowl. Mix lightly but thoroughly with a fork. Shape mixture into 24 balls.
2. Heat butter or margarine in heavy Dutch oven. Add meatballs, about half at a time; sauté until evenly browned. Remove meatballs to a bowl as they brown.
3. Stir onions and garlic into drippings; sauté until soft, 5 minutes; stir in green pepper and chili powder; cook 1 minute. Add tomatoes, salt and cumin; bring to boiling. Return meatballs; cover. Simmer 30 minutes. Add beans; cook 5 to 10 minutes.

Freeze-ahead Tip: A perfect make-ahead — freeze in single portions in heat-sealed, boilable bags. Spoon individual servings into boilable bags. Seal, label, date and freeze (2 months maximum). Great for last-minute meals! To reheat: Plunge bag into boiling water in a large saucepan; boil 20 minutes. Or spoon chili into individual foil containers; label, date and freeze. To reheat: Place covered foil container in moderate oven (350°) for 35 minutes or until chili is bubbly-hot.

Spicy "Sloppy Joes"

Beef, barbecue sauce and pinto beans team up for this South-of-the-Border quickie.

Makes 6 servings.

1 pound ground chuck
1 can (1 pound) pinto
   beans in sugar and
   spice sauce
1/2 cup bottled

barbecue or hot
   barbecue sauce
1/2 cup frozen cut
   sweet red and green
   peppers

1. Brown beef in a large skillet; pour off fat.
2. Add beans, barbecue sauce and peppers. Cook, stirring frequently, until bubbly-hot. Serve over warmed hamburger buns, if you wish.

Pictured opposite:
Savory Sausage Loaf, page 464.

Meatball Stroganoff

Makes 6 servings .

1 1/2 pounds ground
   round
1 envelope
   mushroom-onion
   soup mix
1 can (4 ounces)

sliced mushrooms
1/4 cup (1/2 stick) butter
   or margarine
1 carton (8 ounces)
   dairy sour cream, at
   room temperature

1. Mix meat lightly with 4 teaspoons of the soup mix in a large bowl. Shape into 24 walnut-size meatballs (about 1 level measuring tablespoon each).
2. Drain liquid from mushrooms into a 1-cup measure; add water to make 3/4 cup liquid; stir in remaining soup mix; let stand while browning meatballs.
3. Brown meatballs in butter in a large skillet; transfer to medium-size bowl; pour off all drippings.
4. Add reconstituted soup mixture to skillet; bring to boiling, scraping up browned bits. Return meatballs to skillet; lower heat; cover; simmer 10 minutes or until meatballs are done.
5. Add reserved mushroom slices; slowly stir in sour cream and heat thoroughly, but do not boil. Sprinkle with chopped parsley, if you wish.

Deviled Beef Turnovers

Ground beef holds a spirited onion stuffing.

Makes 4 servings.

1 large onion, halved
   and thinly sliced
1/4 cup (1/2 stick) butter
   or margarine
1 can (12 ounces) beer
1 1/2 teaspoons salt
1 1/2 pounds ground
   chuck or round
1 tablespoon

vegetable oil
1 tablespoon flour
1 tablespoon brown
   sugar
2 tablespoons bottled
   steak sauce
1 tablespoon prepared
   mustard

1. Combine onion, butter, 1/2 cup of the beer and 1/2 teaspoon of the salt in a large skillet. Heat to boiling, stirring frequently. Cook until beer has evaporated and onions are golden. Remove with slotted spoon to bowl, leaving drippings in pan; cool.
2. Divide chuck into 4 balls; roll out each between wax paper to a 6-inch circle. Dust lightly with flour if meat sticks to paper.
3. Place a quarter of the sautéed onions in the center of each circle; fold pattie in half enclosing the filling. Crimp edges firmly to seal.
4. Add oil to drippings in skillet; heat over medium heat. Pan-fry turnovers 4 minutes on each side or until done as you like them. Place on serving platter; keep warm.
5. Stir flour into pan drippings in skillet. Stir in remaining 1 cup of the beer until sauce thickens and boils 1 minute. Stir in remaining 1 teaspoon salt,

(continued)

brown sugar, steak sauce and mustard until well blended. Spoon sauce over turnovers. Garnish platter with watercress, if you wish.

Olé Chili Pie

Bake at 375° for 18 minutes.

Makes 4 to 6 servings.

1 package
  (8¹/₂ ounces) corn
  muffin mix
1 pound ground beef
1 package
  (1¹/₈ ounces) taco
  seasoning mix
3 ounces natural
  Colby or Cheddar

cheese, shredded
  (³/₄ cup)
1 cup shredded lettuce
1 small tomato,
  seeded and
  chopped
¹/₄ cup sliced pitted
  ripe olives

1. Preheat oven to 375°. Prepare corn muffin mix following label directions. Spread batter evenly in bottom of a greased 9-inch pie plate.
2. Bake in a preheated moderate oven (375°) for 18 minutes or until golden brown.
3. Meanwhile, prepare ground beef with taco seasoning mix, following label directions; spoon over hot cornbread. Sprinkle with about half the cheese. Arrange lettuce, tomato, remaining cheese and the olives on top of pie.

Meat Piroshki

Bake at 400° for 30 minutes.

Makes 6 servings.

1 loaf (1 pound) frozen
  plain bread dough,
  thawed overnight in
  refrigerator
1 large onion,
  chopped (1 cup)
2 tablespoons butter
  or margarine
1 pound lean ground
  round or chuck
4 hard-cooked eggs,
  finely chopped

1 teaspoon dried
  dillweed
  OR: 1 tablespoon
  fresh dill, snipped
1 teaspoon salt
¹/₄ teaspoon pepper
¹/₄ cup dairy sour
  cream
1 egg yolk, beaten
  with 1 teaspoon
  water

1. Allow dough to stand at room temperature on a lightly floured surface for 1 hour. Roll ²/₃ of the dough to a 12-inch circle and remaining ¹/₃ to a 9-inch circle. Let dough rest; prepare filling.
2. Sauté onions in butter in large skillet until soft, about 5 minutes. Stir in meat, cooking until pink color is gone.
3. Add eggs, dillweed, salt, pepper and sour cream to meat mixture. Let cool slightly.
4. Line a greased 9-inch pie plate with the 12-inch circle of dough. Spoon in filling, mounding slightly in center; brush edge of dough with egg mixture. Top

with remaining dough circle. Gently fold edge toward center, firmly pressing edges together. Decorate with scraps of dough. Let rise for 30 minutes. Preheat oven to 400°. Brush again with egg.
5. Bake in a preheated hot oven (400°) for 30 minutes. If dough is browning too fast, lower temperature to 375° and cover top with foil.
6. Remove to wire rack to cool slightly; serve warm.

Potato-Frosted Meat Loaf

Bake at 350° for 1 hour, then at 400° for 20 minutes.

Makes 8 servings.

2 pounds meat loaf
  mixture (beef, veal
  and pork) or all beef
¹/₂ cup canned beef
  broth
¹/₃ cup catsup
2 eggs
1 cup packaged
  seasoned bread
  crumbs
¹/₂ cup minced celery
1 tablespoon instant
  minced onion

3 tablespoons finely
  chopped fresh
  parsley
1¹/₂ teaspoons salt
¹/₂ teaspoon pepper
2 cups hot seasoned
  mashed potatoes
¹/₃ cup grated
  Parmesan cheese
2 tablespoons butter
  or margarine,
  melted

1. Combine meat, broth, catsup, eggs, bread crumbs, celery, onion, parsley, salt and pepper in a large bowl; mix well. Press mixture into a lightly greased 6-cup mold or a 9 × 5 × 3-inch loaf pan.
2. Bake in a moderate oven (350°) for 1 hour or until loaf shrinks from side of pan. Remove from oven; pour off drippings. Unmold loaf onto cookie sheet.
3. Combine mashed potatoes with cheese in a medium-size bowl; frost meat loaf with mixture. Brush potatoes with melted butter.
4. Bake in a hot oven (400°) for 20 minutes or until potato topping is golden.

Stuffed Cabbage with Avgojemono Sauce

Bake at 375° for 1 hour, 20 minutes.

Makes 8 servings.

1 head (3¹/₄ pounds)
  savoy or green
  cabbage
2 teaspoons salt
1 package (7 ounces)
  beef-flavored rice
  mix with vermicelli
1 pound ground round
5 eggs
3 tablespoons lemon

juice
¹/₂ cup dry white wine
¹/₂ cup water
1 bay leaf
3 sprigs parsley
2 teaspoons
  cornstarch
Salt
White pepper

1. Rinse cabbage under cold water; remove and discard damaged leaves. Put cabbage in a large

Potato-Frosted Meat Loaf,
page 468.

saucepan; add 2 teaspoons salt and water to cover; simmer 15 minutes or until tender. Drain cabbage, reserving 1 cup broth; let stand until cool enough to handle, about 20 minutes. Prepare rice mix, following label directions. Let cool slightly; stir in ground beef, 2 of the eggs and 1 tablespoon of the lemon juice, mixing thoroughly.

2. Preheat oven to 350°. Place cabbage, stem-end down, on a flat surface and gently pull 12 to 14 leaves away from center, one at a time, being careful not to tear them. Using a small, sharp knife, cut out firm heart of inner leaves from the stem. (Inner leaves may be sliced, tossed with a sweet-sour dressing, refrigerated and used as a salad.) Mound 2¹/₂ cups of the meat mixture in center of cabbage leaves, shaping

into a round ball. Fold 3 or 4 of the leaves up and over meat to enclose, pressing firmly together. Spoon remaining meat mixture around and on top of center leaves, pressing firmly. Gently fold all the remaining leaves back into place, overlapping them to give the cabbage its original rounded shape. (Meat stuffing may show through at top.) Place cabbage, stem-end down, in the center of a large square of cheesecloth; bring edges of cloth together above cabbage and tie tightly. Place in a large deep baking dish that will just fit cabbage. Add white wine, ¹/₂ cup water, bay leaf and parsley. Cover baking dish with aluminum foil.

3. Bake in a preheated moderate oven (375°) for 1 hour, 20 minutes, basting after 30 minutes. Remove

(continued)

cabbage from baking dish. Pour juices into a 2-cup measure. (Discard bay leaf and parsley.) Add enough of reserved cabbage broth to measure 1½ cups; pour into a small saucepan; bring to boiling.

4. Beat the remaining 3 eggs, the remaining 2 tablespoons lemon juice and cornstarch in a medium-size bowl. Pour in boiling hot liquid, beating constantly, until thoroughly combined. Return to saucepan and cook over low heat, 5 minutes, stirring constantly, until thickened. (Be careful not to overcook or eggs will curdle.) Remove from heat; taste and add salt and white pepper, if needed.

5. To serve: Unwrap cabbage, cut into wedges; pour some of the sauce over cabbage wedges and pass the rest in a heated gravy boat. Garnish serving platter with cooked carrot sticks, if you wish.

Baked Meatballs and Spinach Gnocchi

This is a complete-meal-in-a-dish specialty that originated in the northern part of Italy.

Bake at 400° for 30 minutes.

Makes 6 to 8 servings.

1½ **pounds ground chuck**	1 **clove garlic, crushed**
2 **sweet Italian sausages (½ pound)**	2 **tablespoons olive or vegetable oil**
1 **cup fresh bread crumbs (2 slices)**	1 **large onion, chopped (1 cup)**
½ **cup milk**	½ **cup chopped carrot**
1 **egg**	½ **cup chopped celery**
2 **teaspoons salt**	1 **cup tomato or vegetable juice**
¼ **teaspoon pepper**	**Béchamel Sauce (recipe follows)**
3 **tablespoons chopped parsley**	**Spinach Gnocchi (recipe follows)**
½ **teaspoon crumbled leaf basil**	**Grated Parmesan cheese**

1. Combine beef, sausages (casings removed), bread crumbs, milk, egg, 1½ teaspoons of the salt, pepper, parsley, basil and garlic in a large bowl; mix lightly until well blended. Shape mixture into 32 meatballs.

2. Brown meatballs, half at a time, in hot oil in a large skillet or Dutch oven; remove with slotted spoon as they brown. Add onion, carrot and celery to drippings in skillet; sauté, stirring often, until soft, 8 to 10 minutes. Stir in tomato juice and remaining ½ teaspoon salt. Add meatballs. Bring to boiling; lower heat; cover. Simmer 30 minutes. Spoon meatballs and vegetables into 10-cup shallow baking dish.

3. While meatballs cook, make Béchamel Sauce; spoon over meatballs. Cut gnocchi into 2-inch squares; arrange around edge. Sprinkle top with Parmesan cheese.

4. Bake in a hot oven (400°) for 30 minutes or until bubbling hot and top is lightly browned.

Hostess Tip: Prepare through step 2 and freeze several days ahead of time. Or, prepare through step 3 several hours ahead; cover and bake just before serving.

Béchamel Sauce: Melt ¼ cup (½ stick) butter or margarine in a medium size saucepan; stir in ¼ cup flour. Cook and stir 1 minute. Gradually add 2 cups milk. Cook, stirring constantly, until sauce thickens and bubbles 1 minute. Stir in ½ teaspoon salt and ¼ teaspoon pepper.

Spinach Gnocchi

Gnocchi gets its name from the Italian word gnoco, *meaning lump. The dumplings are lumpy in appearance but are light and delicious.*

Makes 6 to 8 servings.

1 **package (10 ounces) frozen chopped spinach**	1 **teaspoon salt**
	⅛ **teaspoon ground nutmeg**
1 **cup milk**	1 **egg**
1¼ **cups water**	¼ **cup freshly grated Parmesan cheese**
½ **cup farina (not instant)**	

1. Cook spinach, following label directions. Drain in colander, pressing spinach to remove as much water as possible.

2. Heat milk and water to boiling in a large saucepan. Sprinkle in farina, stirring constantly. Cook, stirring often, 5 minutes; remove from heat.

3. Add salt, nutmeg, egg and cheese; beat until smooth. Stir in spinach. Spread mixture evenly on a small buttered cookie sheet to an 8 × 10-inch rectangle. Refrigerate until firm, about 3 hours.

Stuffed Peppers, Italian-Style

Chick-peas are the stretcher here instead of the usual rice.

Bake at 350° for 20 minutes.

Makes 6 servings.

6 **medium-size green peppers**	**drained**
	1 **egg**
1 **pound ground round or chuck**	1 **teaspoon leaf oregano, crumbled**
1 **large onion, chopped (1 cup)**	¼ **cup minced fresh parsley**
1 **teaspoon salt**	1 **package (8 ounces) mozzarella cheese, diced**
½ **teaspoon fennel seeds, crushed**	
1 **can (16 ounces) chick-peas (garbanzo beans),**	1 **can (15 ounces) tomato sauce**

1. Cut a slice from top of each pepper; scoop out seeds and membranes. Parboil peppers in a small amount of boiling water 10 minutes; drain well. Stand in a greased shallow baking pan that just fits them. Preheat oven to 350°.

2. Brown beef with onion, salt and fennel in a large skillet, stirring often to break up beef. Spoon off all fat. Remove from heat.

3. Add chick-peas, egg, oregano, parsley and cheese; toss gently to mix. Spoon into pepper cups. Drizzle tomato sauce over and around stuffed peppers. Cover pan with foil.

4. Bake in a preheated moderate oven (350°) for 20 minutes or until bubbly and hot.

Baked Stuffed Zucchini

Bake at 400° for 1 hour.

Makes 6 servings.

6 medium-size zucchini (about 2½ pounds)	finely chopped (½ cup)
1½ pounds ground round	1 egg, slightly beaten
1 can condensed tomato bisque soup	1 teaspoon leaf oregano, crumbled
½ cup packaged bread crumbs	1 teaspoon garlic salt
1 medium-size onion,	¼ teaspoon pepper
	¼ cup grated Parmesan cheese

1. Cut lengthwise slice from top of each zucchini; scoop out seeds and pulp, leaving ¼-inch shell. Put shells in large saucepan with boiling salted water to cover; par-cook 5 minutes. Drain well.

2. Pull off two 20-inch lengths of 18-inch heavy-duty foil and place in center of 2 reusable aluminum toaster oven trays, 9⅞ × 4¾ × ¾-inches (about 2 cups).

3. Combine meat, soup, crumbs, onions, egg, oregano, garlic salt and pepper in a small bowl. Spoon into shells.

4. Place on foil. Sprinkle with cheese. Close and seal foil.

5. Bake in a hot oven (400°) for 1 hour or until zucchini is tender.

Meat-Stuffed Eggplant

Bake at 375° for 20 minutes, then for 25 minutes.

Makes 4 servings.

2 small eggplants (1 pound each)	1½ teaspoons salt
¾ pound ground chuck	1 teaspoon leaf thyme, crumbled
½ cup chopped green pepper	¼ teaspoon liquid hot pepper seasoning
½ cup chopped celery	1 can (8 ounces) tomatoes
½ cup chopped green onion	2 cups fresh bread crumbs (4 slices)
½ cup chopped fresh parsley	1 tablespoon butter or margarine, melted

1. Cut eggplants in half lengthwise; arrange, cut-side down, on lightly oiled jelly-roll pan.

2. Bake in a moderate oven (375°) for 20 minutes or just until tender. Remove from oven. When cool enough to handle, scoop out, leaving a shell about ¼-inch thick. Arrange shells in shallow baking dish. Dice scooped-out eggplant.

3. Heat a large skillet. Add ground chuck, cooking it in its own fat until lightly browned. Stir in green pepper, celery, onion, parsley, salt, thyme, and hot pepper seasoning; cook, stirring often, 5 minutes. Add tomatoes and diced eggplant. Cover; simmer 10 minutes.

4. Remove meat mixture from heat; stir in 1 cup of the bread crumbs; spoon into reserved shells, dividing evenly. Toss the remaining bread crumbs with butter; spoon on top.

5. Bake in a moderate oven (375°) for 25 minutes or until bread crumbs are browned slightly. Sprinkle with additional parsley, if you wish.

Cold Confetti Meatloaf

Serve in a hard-roll sandwich, if you wish.
Bake at 375° for 50 minutes.

Makes 4 servings.

1 tablespoon vegetable oil	¾ pound lean ground beef
¾ cup chopped carrot	½ pound lean ground pork
¼ cup chopped sweet red pepper	1 egg, slightly beaten
¼ cup chopped sweet green pepper	⅓ cup prepared chili sauce
½ cup chopped onion (1 medium-size onion)	1 cup fresh bread crumbs
1 teaspoon chopped fresh sage OR: ¼ teaspoon leaf sage, crumbled	¼ teaspoon salt
	Dash pepper
	½ cup cubed (¼ inch) Cheddar cheese (about 4 ounces)

1. Heat the oil in a medium-size skillet over very low heat. Add the carrot, red and green peppers, onion and sage. Cover and cook over very low heat for 10 minutes; the mixture should be tender, but not browned.

2. Preheat the oven to moderate (375°). Lightly grease an 8½ × 4 ×2⅝-inch. Fold a piece of aluminum foil to line the long sides and bottom of the pan, but not the short ends, leaving a 1-inch overhang on each side. Lightly grease the foil.

3. Combine the beef, pork, egg, chili sauce, bread crumbs, salt and pepper in a large bowl. Gently stir in the vegetables and cheese. Spoon into the prepared pan; pack lightly and smooth the top.

4. Bake in the preheated moderate oven (375°) for 50 minutes or until the juices run clear when pierced with a fork. Remove the pan to a wire rack to cool for 10 minutes.

5. Grasp the foil overhang and gently lift the loaf from

(continued)

the pan, allowing the juices to drain back into the pan. Place the loaf on a plate; refrigerate.

6. When the loaf is cold, carefully peel off the foil. Cut into ¼-inch-thick slices and serve. If planning for a picnic, reform the loaf and wrap tightly in aluminum foil. Refrigerate overnight or until serving time.

7. To pack for a picnic, place in an insulated bag with a frozen ice pack.

Skillet Cumin Meatloaf

Makes 6 servings.

1 pound ground round
1 pound pork sausage meat
¾ cup coarsely chopped celery
¾ cup raisins
¼ teaspoon salt
¼ teaspoon pepper
¼ cup water
1 small tomato, diced

1 small onion, diced
1 small sweet green pepper, halved, seeded and diced
1 large clove garlic
½ teaspoon whole cumin seeds
Celery leaves
Tomato

1. Mix together lightly the beef and pork sausage in a large bowl. Add celery, raisins, salt and pepper.
2. Combine water, tomato, onion, green pepper, garlic and cumin in the container of an electric blender. Whirl until smooth. Pour over meat. Mix well.

3. Pack meat into an ungreased 10-inch cast iron skillet; smooth top so it mounds.
4. Cook, covered, over low heat on top of the stove for 55 minutes or until meat is done. Drain fat. Turn loaf out onto a celery leaf-lined board. Garnish with additional leaves and a tomato, if you wish.

Baked Meat-Stuffed Spanish Onions

Bake at 375° for 1 hour.

Makes 4 servings.

4 large Spanish onions (each about 4 inches in diameter), peeled
1 tablespoon butter or margarine
1 can (13¾ ounces) beef broth
1 package (8 ounces) herb-seasoned

stuffing mix
¾ pound ground round
¼ cup grated Parmesan cheese
¼ teaspoon ground nutmeg
2 eggs
⅓ cup dry white wine

1. Cut off a thin slice from the top of each onion. Scoop out insides with a spoon or melon baller, leaving a ¼-inch thick shell. Chop enough of the onion to measure ½ cup. (Use remaining onion for another recipe.)
2. Sauté onion in butter in a medium-size saucepan

Skillet Cumin Meatloaf.

until soft but not brown. Add $1/2$ cup of the beef broth and bring to boiling. Remove from heat and stir in stuffing mix. Add beef, cheese, nutmeg and eggs; mix thoroughly. Spoon beef mixture evenly into onion shells, mounding high. Place onions in a shallow baking dish and add remaining $1^1/4$ cups beef broth and wine; cover dish with foil.

3. Bake in a moderate oven (375°) for 1 hour, basting after 30 minutes. Serve onions with pan juices.

Meat Loaf in Brioche

Bake at 350° for $1^1/2$ hours.

Makes 8 servings.

Brioche:
1 package hot roll mix
$1/4$ cup very warm water
4 eggs, at room temperature
$1/2$ cup (1 stick) butter or margarine, softened
Flour

Meat Loaf:
1 pound ground round or chuck
$3/4$ pound lean ground pork
$3/4$ pound lean ground veal
$1/2$ cup dry red wine or canned beef broth

$1/2$ cup packaged bread crumbs
2 eggs, slightly beaten
1 can (3 ounces) sliced mushrooms, drained
2 tablespoons finely chopped fresh parsley
2 tablespoons finely chopped chives
$1^1/2$ teaspoons salt
1 teaspoon leaf marjoram, crumbled
$1/2$ teaspoom leaf thyme, crumbled
$1/2$ teaspoon leaf rosemary, crumbled
$1/2$ teaspoon pepper
1 egg, beaten

1. Prepare Brioche. Sprinkle yeast from hot roll mix into very warm water in large bowl; stir until yeast dissolves. ("Very warm water" should feel comfortably warm when dropped on wrist.) Beat eggs slightly and add to yeast.
2. Stir in hot roll mix until smooth. Beat in 5 tablespoons of the butter, 1 tablespoon at a time, with electric mixer at medium speed, beating until buttter is absorbed.
3. Cover bowl with towel; let rise in warm place, away from draft, 1 hour or until double in volume.
4. Stir dough down. Beat in remaining butter, 1 tablespoon at a time, until butter is absorbed. Turn onto lightly floured surface; knead a few times, using only enough flour (up to $1/2$ cup) to keep dough from sticking. Place in greased large bowl. Let rise again in warm place 1 hour or until doubled.
5. Prepare Meat Loaf: Combine ground round, pork, veal, wine, bread crumbs, eggs, mushrooms, parsley, chives, salt, marjoram, thyme, rosemary and pepper in large bowl; mix well. Cover; refrigerate until dough is ready.
6. Roll out $2/3$ of dough on lightly floured board, using only enough flour to keep dough from sticking. Roll out to a 17 x 12-inch rectangle.

7. Line a 9 x 5 x 3-inch pan with dough, letting excess hang over the side. Pack meat mixture loosely into pan. Fold overhanging dough back over meat; trim excess dough where it overlaps. Preheat oven to 350°.
8. Roll out remaining $1/3$ of the dough to a 9 x 5-inch rectangle. Reroll dough from trimmings in step 7 and cut scraps for decorating top. Place small rectangle of dough on top of meat mixture, tucking ends down into sides of pan for a smooth top that will hide seams of the dough underneath. Brush top with beaten egg; top with decorative scraps.
9. Bake in a preheated moderate oven (350°) for $1^1/2$ hours or until meat thermometer in center registers 175°. It top browns too quickly, cover with foil. Cool on wire rack. Use small spatula to loosen edges; carefully remove from pan. Cover with foil and chill until serving time. Cut into $1/4$-inch slices with serrated knife.

Picadillo Tamales

Picadillo is the Mexican version of hash. This savory meat filling with raisins and almonds can also be used to fill tacos. Traditionally, tamales are wrapped in corn husks, but you can use aluminum foil.

Makes 12 tamales.

12 large dry corn husks, or aluminum foil
$1/2$ pound lean ground pork
$1/2$ pound ground round
2 tablespoons vegetable oil
1 large onion, chopped (1 cup)
$1/2$ cup chopped green pepper
1 clove garlic, minced
1 can (16 ounces) plum tomatoes,

drained
1 can (4 ounces) green chilies, seeded and chopped
1 teaspoon salt
$1/4$ teaspoon black pepper
$1/4$ teaspoon ground cinnamon
$1/4$ teaspoon ground cloves
$1/2$ cup raisins
$1/4$ cup slivered blanched almonds
Tamale Dough (*recipe follows*)

1. Soak corn husks in hot water several hours or overnight to soften. Keep in water until ready to use. If husks are not available, use 8-inch squares of aluminum foil.
2. Brown pork and beef in oil in a large skillet, about 5 minutes. Add onion, green pepper and garlic; sauté until vegetables are soft, about 5 minutes. Add drained tomatoes, green chilies, salt, pepper, cinnamon and cloves. Cook, stirring occasionally, 15 minutes or until liquid is absorbed. Stir in raisins and almonds.
3. Prepare Tamale Dough.
4. For each tamale, place a wide, pliable corn husk on work surface horizontally. Husk should measure 8 inches at the wide end; if not, overlap several pieces.

(continued)

Using a metal spatula dipped in cold water, spread $1/3$ cup of the tamale dough, 6-inches long, along edge of corn husk or aluminum foil square. Spread dough 4-inches wide. (You will have a 6 × 4-inch rectangle.)
5. Spoon $1/4$ cup meat filling in a row across the tamale dough. Roll up, jelly-roll fashion, starting at edge nearest filling. Fold ends under or tie ends with a strip of corn husk. If using foil, twist ends to seal.
6. To steam cook: Arrange tamales flat against sides of colander (half at a time, if necessary). Place colander in a large kettle with about 1 inch of boiling water, making sure water level is below bottom of colander. Cover. Steam tamales over medium heat for $1 1/2$ hours or until tamale is firm and falls away from the husk when tested. (Tamales in aluminum foil will be firmer than corn-husk-steamed tamales.) These are traditionally served unwrapped and without sauce. Serve with Salsa (*recipe under Sauces*), if you wish.

Tamale Dough: Combine 3 cups instant corn masa*, $1 1/2$ teaspoons salt and 1 teaspoon baking powder on wax paper. Pour 1 can ($13^3/4$ ounces) beef broth into a glass measure; add water to the 2-cup line; pour into a medium-size saucepan and heat to lukewarm. Beat $3/4$ cup lard until fluffy in a large bowl of electric mixer. Add instant masa mixture alternately with warmed beef broth to make a soft, sticky dough. Let stand 15 minutes.

Can be purchased in ethnic sections of most supermarkets.

To Freeze: Freeze before steaming. Place tamales in a single layer on cookie sheet. Freeze until firm. Store in plastic bag. Steam as above, allowing an additional 30 minutes to thaw during cooking process.

Lamb-Stuffed Zucchini

Bake at 375° for 45 minutes.

Makes 6 servings.

6 medium-size zucchini	**8 flat anchovy fillets**
3 medium-size onions, chopped ($1 1/2$ cups)	**$1/4$ cup chopped pitted ripe olives**
1 sweet red pepper, halved, seeded and chopped	**$1/4$ cup capers, chopped (*optional*)**
2 cloves garlic, finely chopped	**$1 1/2$ cups cooked rice**
4 tablespoons olive or vegetable oil	**1 teaspoon salt**
	$1/4$ teaspoon freshly ground black pepper
1 cup cooked lamb, trimmed of fat	**$1 1/2$ cups plain yogurt**
	3 tablespoons canned tomato sauce

1. Wash zucchini; trim stem end. Cut thin slice off lengthwise and scoop out the pulp, leaving an unbroken shell about $1/4$-inch thick. Reserve the pulp.
2. Sauté onions, pepper and garlic in 2 tablespoons of the oil in a large skillet until soft. Chop the removed zucchini pulp; add to the skillet. Cook until most of the liquid has evaporated and the pulp is soft.

3. Grind lamb with anchovy fillets in a meat grinder with the finest disk, or chop very finely. (Meat grinder gives better texture to the stuffing.)
4. Add lamb mixture to the skillet; cook and stir 1 minute. Remove skillet from heat and stir in olives, capers, cooked rice, salt, pepper and $1/2$ cup of the yogurt.
5. Brush zucchini shells inside and out with remaining oil. Place shells side by side in baking dish large enough to hold them snugly together. Fill shells with stuffing, dividing it evenly among them. Pour about $1/2$ inch of hot water into the baking dish.
6. Bake in moderate oven (375°) for 45 minutes or until the filling is lightly browned and the shells are cooked but still firm. Transfer filled shells to warm serving dish.
7. Combine tomato sauce with the remaining 1 cup yogurt. Serve cold sauce with stuffed zucchini. Or heat gently, but do not allow to boil, and spoon over stuffed zucchini before serving.

Thailand Stuffed Oranges

Bake at 300° for 30 minutes.

Makes 6 servings.

6 large navel oranges	**$1/2$ teaspoon crushed red pepper**
2 tablespoons vegetable oil	**$1/4$ teaspoon ground coriander**
1 clove garlic, minced	**2 teaspoons anchovy paste**
$1 1/2$ pounds lean ground pork	**2 tablespoons flour**
$1/3$ cup chopped unsalted peanuts	**Watercress**
1 teaspoon salt	

1. Cut off top of each orange $1/3$ of the way down; cut a thin slice off the bottom of each orange so that it will stand firmly.
2. With a sharp paring knife or grapefruit knife and holding over a pie plate, cut inside about $1/8$ inch from orange shell and down, rotating knife so that the inside pulp comes out in a cone-shaped piece. Cut off a $1/2$-inch thick piece for garnish; reserve. With a spoon, scrape out excess juice, but do not scrape out remaining orange. Pour juice through strainer into a 2-cup liquid measuring cup; squeeze enough of the pulp into the cup to equal $1 1/2$ cups. Coarsely chop remaining orange pulp; reserve both.
3. Heat oil in large skillet; add garlic and cook just until brown. Add pork, peanuts, salt, red pepper, coriander and anchovy paste, mixing thoroughly. Cook over medium heat for 15 minutes, stirring frequently.

(continued)

Pictured opposite (clockwise from top right): Glacéed Oranges, page 323; Orange Soufflé, page 318; Curried Orange Rice, page 614; Cornish Game Hens, French-Style, page 668; Thailand Stuffed Oranges, page 474.

4. Drain off any fat. Stir in flour to coat meat. Add orange juice; cook, stirring constantly, until mixture thickens; add coarsely chopped orange pulp.
5. Fill orange shells with meat mixture, mounding slightly. Place stuffed oranges in a shallow baking pan.
6. Bake in a slow oven (300°) for 30 minutes or until stuffing is piping hot. Transfer to heated serving platter and garnish with reserved orange pieces and watercress.

Moussaka
This casserole, made primarily of eggplant layered with meat sauce, has many versions. Greeks are credited with creating the dish but a version can be found in other Middle Eastern cuisines.

Moussaka

Bake at 350° for 1 hour.

Makes 8 servings.

1 pound ground lamb or beef	**¹/₂ cup packaged bread crumbs**
2 large onions, diced (2 cups)	**2 small eggplants (1 pound each)**
1 clove garlic, minced	**¹/₃ cup olive or vegetable oil**
1 can (15 ounces) tomato sauce	**2 tablespoons butter or margarine**
1 teaspoon dried parsley flakes	**2 tablespoons flour**
1 teaspoon salt	**¹/₂ teaspoon salt**
¹/₂ teaspoon leaf oregano, crumbled	**¹/₈ teaspoon pepper**
¹/₂ teaspoon ground cinnamon	**1¹/₂ cups milk**
	2 eggs

1. Sauté meat, onions and garlic in a skillet, about 5 minutes; drain fat.
2. Add tomato sauce, parsley, salt, oregano and cinnamon; stir thoroughly; cover; simmer 30 minutes. Cool. Add bread crumbs and set aside.
3. Cut eggplant into ¹/₂-inch slices. Brush both sides with oil. Place in bottom of broiler pan. Broil 4 minutes on each side or until just tender.
4. Melt butter in a medium-size saucepan; remove from heat; stir in flour, salt and pepper. Gradually stir in milk. Return to heat and slowly bring to boiling, stirring constantly, until thickened. Remove from heat.
5. Beat eggs in a small bowl. Beat in ¹/₄ of hot cream sauce into eggs; then return egg mixture to saucepan; cook 1 minute; remove from heat.
6. Place half of the eggplant slices in the bottom of a lightly greased 8-cup shallow baking dish. Spoon

meat mixture evenly over top; cover with remaining eggplant slices. Pour sauce on top.
7. Bake in a moderate oven (350°) for 1 hour. Let stand 15 minutes before serving.

Skillet Moussaka

All the delicious ingredients of the fabled moussaka are together in this quick-to-fix skillet dish.

Makes 6 servings.

1 medium-size eggplant	**¹/₂ teaspoon leaf oregano, crumbled**
2 tablespoons flour	**2 tablespoons butter or margarine**
1 pound lean ground lamb or beef	**2 tablespoons flour**
1 medium-size onion, chopped (¹/₂ cup)	**1 egg yolk, lightly beaten**
1 clove garlic, crushed	**1 cup milk**
1 can (8 ounces) tomato sauce	**4 ounces Monterey Jack cheese, shredded (1 cup)**
¹/₂ teaspoon salt	**Chopped fresh parsley**
¹/₈ teaspoon pepper	

1. Pare eggplant; cut into ¹/₂-inch cubes. Coat with 2 tablespoons of flour.
2. Cook meat slowly in a large skillet until no pink remains. Add onion, garlic and cubed eggplant. Cook and stir over moderate heat several minutes or until eggplant begins to soften. Stir in tomato sauce, salt, pepper and oregano. Simmer for 5 minutes.
3. Melt butter in a small saucepan; stir in remaining 2 tablespoons of flour.
4. Combine beaten egg yolk with milk in a small bowl. Add to butter mixture. Cook and stir over low heat until sauce is slightly thickened.
5. Stir hot sauce into meat mixture; sprinkle with shredded cheese. Cook over low heat just until cheese melts. Sprinkle with chopped parsley. Serve with a tossed salad and feta cheese, if you wish.

Pork Balls in Sour Cream Sauce

Makes 4 servings.

3 slices white bread	**1 cup dry white wine**
¹/₄ cup milk	**2 bay leaves**
1 medium-size onion, very finely chopped (¹/₂ cup)	**¹/₄ teaspoon leaf thyme, crumbled**
2 teaspoons lemon juice	**1 container (8 ounces) dairy sour cream**
¹/₂ teaspoon salt	**¹/₂ cup water**
¹/₈ teaspoon pepper	**1 tablespoon flour**
1 egg, beaten	**1 package (8 ounces) medium noodles, cooked, drained and buttered**
1 pound ground pork	
3 tablespoons butter or margarine	**Chopped fresh parsley**

1. Crumble bread slices into milk in a large bowl. Let

stand until milk is absorbed, about 5 minutes. Stir in onion, lemon juice, salt, pepper and egg. Add ground pork; mix thoroughly. (Mixture will be soft.) Shape mixture into 12 balls of equal size.

2. Heat butter in large skillet. Brown pork balls evenly, about 15 minutes. Add wine, bay leaves and thyme. Bring to boiling; lower heat; cover; simmer 30 minutes. Discard leaves.

3. Remove pork with slotted spoon to heated platter. Combine sour cream, water and flour; stir into pan liquid. Cook, stirring constantly, until sauce is thickened and bubbly. Spoon pork balls into sauce; heat gently until thoroughly hot. Serve over hot buttered noodles; sprinkle with parsley.

Pioneer Sausage Burger Stew

Makes 6 servings.

- 1/4 pound (1/2 cup) liver sausage
- 1 pound ground chuck or round
- 1/2 cup packaged bread crumbs
- 1 small onion, finely chopped (1/4 cup)
- 1 egg, beaten
- 3 tablespoons vegetable oil
- 2 tablespoons flour
- 1/2 teaspoon salt
- 2 envelopes or teaspoons instant beef broth
- 2 cups hot water
- 4 cups thinly sliced zucchini
- 3 cups seasoned hot mashed potatoes
- 1 medium-size tomato, cut in thin wedges
- Paprika

1. Mash liver sausage with fork in a large bowl. Add beef, crumbs, onion and egg; mix well. Divide mixture and shape into 12 balls, using about 1/4 cup for each. Brown meatballs in oil in a large skillet; remove and keep warm.

2. Pour off all but 2 tablespoons of drippings from skillet. Stir in flour and salt; cook 1 minute. Combine instant broth and water in a 2-cup measure; pour into skillet. Cook, stirring constantly, until sauce is slightly thickened. Return meatballs to skillet. Cover; cook slowly for 10 minutes. Add zucchini; cook 10 minutes longer, stirring gently once or twice.

3. Spoon or pipe mashed potatoes around edge of skillet and arrange tomato wedges on top. Sprinkle potatoes with paprika. If skillet isn't flameproof, wrap handle with foil. Place skillet under broiler to heat and brown potatoes lightly, about 5 minutes.

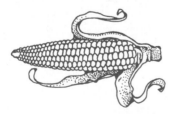

Tostada A corn tortilla fried flat until crisp, then served topped with beans or meat and vegetable garnishes.

Beef Tostadas

A variation of an old favorite.

Makes 6 servings.

- 1 pound ground round or chuck
- 1 medium-size onion, chopped (1/2 cup)
- 1 clove garlic, minced
- 1 can (4 ounces) diced mild green chilies
- 1 teaspoon salt
- 1/2 teaspoon leaf oregano, crumbled
- 1/8 teaspoon pepper
- 2 tablespoons flour
- 1 cup water or beef
- broth
- 6 tostada shells or 6 corn tortillas, fried in oil until crisp
- 4 ounces Monterey Jack cheese, shredded (1 cup)
- 2 cups shredded iceberg lettuce
- 1/2 an avocado, peeled and sliced
- 1 container (8 ounces) dairy sour cream

1. Cook beef, onion and garlic in a large skillet until beef is well browned, stirring often. Drain off any fat.

2. Stir in chilies, salt, oregano and pepper. Stir flour and water or broth in cup until smooth. Stir into meat mixture. Cook until thickened.

3. Divide meat mixture among tostada shells. Sprinkle with cheese; top with lettuce and avocado slices. Serve with sour cream.

Crescent Lamb Triangles

Serve these lamb- and spinach-filled Middle-Eastern pastry triangles with a green salad.

Bake at 350° for 20 minutes.

Makes 8 servings.

- 1 pound ground lamb
- 1 medium-size onion, chopped
- 1 can (16 ounces) mixed vegetables, drained
- 1 can (8 ounces) tomato sauce
- 1 teaspoon garlic powder
- 1 teaspoon ground cumin
- 1/2 teaspoon ground cloves
- 1/2 teaspoon ground ginger
- 1/2 teaspoon ground coriander
- 1/4 teaspoon cayenne pepper
- 1/4 teaspoon salt
- 1/8 teaspoon ground cinnamon
- 2 cans (8 ounces each) refrigerated crescent dinner rolls
- 1 can (15 ounces) spinach, drained
- 12 ounces Cheddar cheese, shredded (3 cups)
- 2 egg yolks, lightly beaten with 2 teaspoons water for egg wash

1. Brown the lamb in a large skillet over medium heat until no longer pink, about 5 minutes. Drain off the fat. Add the onion; cook for 5 minutes. Add the mixed vegetables, tomato sauce, garlic powder, cumin, cloves, ginger, coriander, cayenne, salt and cinnamon. Simmer for 5 minutes.

(continued)

2. Separate 1 can of the crescent rolls into 8 individual crescents. Roll out each on a lightly floured surface into an 11 × 7 × 7-inch triangle. Transfer to ungreased cookie sheets.

3. When cool enough to handle, divide the lamb filling equally among the 8 triangles, about 1/2 cup for each. Spread evenly over the dough, leaving a 1/2-inch border around the edges. Place a mound of spinach in the center of each triangle; mound the shredded cheese on top of the spinach. Spread evenly over the lamb, leaving a 1/2-inch border.

4. Preheat the oven to moderate (350°).

5. Separate the second package of rolls into 8 individual crescents. Roll each out on a lightly floured surface into triangles slightly larger than the first batch. Top each of the filled smaller triangles with a larger one. Press the edges together firmly to form a tight seal. Brush the tops with the egg wash. Cut 1 or 2 steam vents into the top of each triangle.

6. Bake in the preheated moderate oven (350°) for 20 minutes or until golden brown.

Cabbage Bundles in Paprika Cream Sauce

Delicious little packages filled with inexpensive ground beef plus rice, other ingredients, and bathed in a tasty sour cream sauce.

Makes 6 to 8 servings.

1 head green cabbage (3 to 3 1/2 pounds)	2 carrots, sliced (1 cup)
2 cups fresh bread crumbs (4 slices)	1 tablespoon paprika
1 teaspoon seasoned salt	1 teaspoon salt
1/2 cup cold water	1 can condensed beef broth`
1 pound ground chuck	1 can (8 ounces) tomato sauce
2 eggs	1 tablespoon all-purpose flour
1 cup cooked rice	1 container (8 ounces) dairy sour cream, at room temperature
1/4 cup (1/2 stick) butter or margarine	
1 medium-size onion, chopped (1/2 cup)	Fresh dill or parsley

1. In a large kettle heat to boiling enough water to cover cabbage. Trim damaged outer leaves from cabbage. Stick a large fork deep into core. Lower the cabbage into boiling water, holding on to fork. With a small sharp knife, loosen and remove 12 to 16 outer leaves as they become soft and pliable; drain. Chop remaining cabbage coarsely (to make 6 cups).

2. Combine crumbs, salt and water in a large bowl; add beef, eggs and rice; mix well. Place about 1/4 cup meat mixture on each leaf; fold sides of leaf over stuffing; roll up from thick end of leaf.

3. Heat butter in large Dutch oven. Add onion; sauté a few minutes; stir in carrots and chopped cabbage; sauté, stirring often, until soft, about 10 minutes. Stir in paprika, salt, broth and tomato sauce. Arrange stuffed cabbage bundles, seam-side down and close together, over cabbage mixture in Dutch oven; cover. Cook over low heat, basting, 50 minutes to 1 hour.

4. Carefully remove cabbage bundles and keep warm. Stir flour into sour cream; add to Dutch oven. Bring slowly to boiling, stirring constantly; boil 1 minute. Layer cabbage mixture and cabbage bundles in heated serving dish. Garnish with fresh dill or parsley.

Cottage Pie

Similar to a shepherd's pie, but made with only 1/2 pound of ground beef.

Bake at 375° for 45 minutes.

Makes 6 servings.

2 pounds potatoes, pared and cut into eighths	beef
2 teaspoons salt	2 tablespoons all-purpose flour
4 tablespoons (1/2 stick) unsalted butter	1 cup beef broth
	1/2 teaspoon pepper
1 tablespoon vegetable oil	3 tablespoons tomato paste
2 cups chopped onion (2 large onions)	1 package (10 ounces) frozen peas, partially thawed
1 cup finely chopped carrots	1/4 cup heavy cream
1 clove garlic, finely chopped	1/4 teaspoon freshly grated nutmeg
1 teaspoon leaf sage, crumbled	OR: 1/2 teaspoon ground nutmeg
1/2 pound lean ground	2 eggs
	Ground nutmeg *(optional)*

1. Cook potatoes in boiling water with 1/2 teaspoon of the salt in a medium-size saucepan for 15 to 20 minutes or until tender; drain well; keep warm.

2. Meanwhile, melt 1 tablespoon of the butter with the oil in a large heavy skillet over medium heat. Stir in onion and carrot; sauté, stirring, until lightly browned, about 10 minutes. Add garlic and sage; sauté 1 minute longer.

3. Crumble beef into the skillet; cook until no longer pink. Drain off excess fat. Stir in flour until well combined. Add broth, 3/4 teaspoon of the salt, 1/4 teaspoon of the pepper and the tomato paste; stir until well blended. Fold in partially thawed peas; cook, stirring occasionally, until thickened. Pour into an ungreased 8 × 8 × 2-inch square baking dish, spreading evenly.

4. Preheat the oven to moderate (375°).

(continued)

5. Mash the potatoes. Beat in cream, nutmeg and remaining butter, salt and pepper until smooth and fluffy. Beat in eggs, one at a time. Spoon over meat filling, spreading evenly; make sure potato touches all sides of pan. If you wish, decorate by drawing tines of fork from center to edges.

6. Bake in the preheated moderate over (375°) for 45 minutes or until top is puffed and golden. Sprinkle with ground nutmeg, if you wish.

Skillet Lamb à La Grecque

Makes 8 servings.

2 pounds ground lamb	**2 teaspoons salt**
1 medium-size onion, chopped (1/2 cup)	**1/8 teaspoon pepper**
1 clove garlic, minced	**1 teaspoon leaf basil, crumbled**
1 large eggplant, pared and cubed (about 8 cups)	**1 package (6 ounces) mozzarella cheese slices**
1 jar (16 ounces) spaghetti sauce	**Pitted ripe olives, sliced (about 6)**

1. Brown lamb in a large skillet, 5 minutes on each side. Break up into chunks with spoon as it cooks; push to one side.

2. Sauté onion and garlic in drippings just until tender. Stir in eggplant, spaghetti sauce, salt, pepper and basil.

3. Cover; bring to boiling; lower heat. Simmer 20 minutes or until eggplant is tender. Uncover.

4. Cut mozzarella cheese into strips; arrange cheese in lattice pattern on top of eggplant-lamb mixture. Place 1 or 2 slices of olive in each space between cheese strips.

5. Cover; simmer 3 minutes longer or just until cheese begins to melt.

Javanese Curried Noodles and Beef

Makes 4 servings.

3 quarts water	**2 to 3 teaspoons curry powder**
1/4 teaspoon salt	**1/2 cup chopped green onions**
3 1/2 teaspoons vegetable oil	**1 pound ground chuck**
2 1/2 cups curly broad noodles	**1 cup fresh bean sprouts**
1/2 cup catsup	**OR: 2 cups finely shredded romaine lettuce**
2 tablespoons soy sauce	
1/4 teaspoon pepper	
1/4 cup water	

1. Heat water to boiling in large covered kettle; add salt and 1/2 teaspoon of the oil. Add noodles slowly so that water continues to boil. Boil about 5 minutes until noodles are still slightly firm. Drain; place in large bowl; toss with 1 teaspoon of the oil. Keep warm.

2. Combine catsup, soy sauce, pepper and water in small bowl. Reserve.

3. Place wok or skillet over low heat; add curry; heat until fragrant, about 1 minute. Add remaining 2 teaspoons oil. Increase heat; add onions, stir-fry 1 minute. Add meat; stir-fry until no pink remains.

4. Stir in reserved catsup mixture; heat to boiling. Add noodles and bean sprouts. Stir and mix until hot. Garnish with green onion ruffles, if you wish.

Low-Calorie Cheesearoni Beef Casserole

The perfect casserole to keep in your freezer for unexpected guests or when you just don't have time to cook.

Bake at 325° for 1 hour.

Makes 8 servings at 286 calories each.

1 pound lean ground round	**crumbled**
1 1/2 teaspoons garlic salt	**1 1/2 teaspoons chili powder**
1 medium-size onion, sliced	**6 ounces large macaroni**
1 can (28 ounces) tomatoes	**1 carton (16 ounces) low-fat cottage cheese**
1 can (6 ounces) tomato paste	**4 ounces part-skim mozzarella cheese, shredded (1 cup)**
1/2 teaspoon leaf oregano, crumbled	**3 tablespoons grated Romano cheese**
1/2 teaspoon leaf basil,	

1. Season ground round with garlic salt. Spread in a shallow layer in a nonstick baking pan or use a broiler pan with perforated rack.

2. Broil meat about 2 inches from heat just until surface is brown. Drain off any accumulated fat.

3. Combine browned meat, onion, tomatoes, tomato paste, oregano, basil and chili powder in a large saucepan or kettle. Bring to boiling; cover. Lower heat; simmer 1 hour, stirring frequently, until sauce is thick.

4. Cook macaroni in boiling salted water 15 minutes or until tender. Drain; rinse with cold water. Toss macaroni with cottage cheege.

5. Spread cottage cheese-macaroni mixture in bottom of a shallow 12-cup baking dish (or divide into two shallow 6-cup baking dishes). Sprinkle with mozzarella cheese; spoon over sauce. Top with Romano cheese. Casserole may be wrapped tightly in foil and frozen at this point for future use or baked immediately.

6. Bake in a slow oven (325°) for 1 hour or until bubbly.

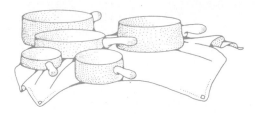

Variety Meat

In Europe, variety meats are considered to be as choice as steaks or chops are in the U.S. because, when properly prepared, these cuts are equally delicious. Americans, for some reason, have not developed a taste for variety meats--the liver, kidney, tongue, heart, tripe, sweetbreads and brain of beef, veal, lamb and pork. The one exception is calf's liver.

By avoiding the variety meats, you're missing not only some elegant recipes, but also some of the most nutritious and, with the exception of calf's liver, economical meats available.

Variety meats are an excellent source of many essential nutrients such as proteins, B vitamins, iron and phosphorus. Liver is an excellent source of iron and vitamin A.

The major differences between variety meats among different animals are size and flavor. Beef variety meats are the largest; those from lamb are the smallest.

Buying, Storing and Cooking: Variety meats are more perishable than other meats, so they should be refrigerated and cooked as soon as possible.

Liver—Of all variety meats, liver is unquestionably the most popular, particularly calf's liver. Because of its popularity, however, calf's liver has become a luxury meat. Far better buys are beef, lamb and pork liver. What most people dislike about beef and pork liver is the strong flavor. Lamb's liver is nearly as delicate as calf's liver although it is not as readily available. Proper cooking will make strong-flavored beef and pork liver taste less pungent. They may be braised or sautéed. Sometimes they are ground and baked into pâté loaves. Calf's or lamb's liver are more tender, so either may be broiled or panfried.

When buying liver, look for moist appearance. Calf's liver has a rosy-red hue, lamb or beef liver will be deep red and pork liver will be brownish-red. Allow $1/4$ to $1/3$ pound per serving.

Kidney—Lamb and veal kidneys are the choicest. Beef and pork kidneys are tougher and have a stronger flavor. They must be braised or stewed to tenderize them. Lamb and veal kidneys may be broiled or skewered and grilled.

Choose kidneys of even dark red or red to brown color and of good, sweet aroma. Allow 2 to 3 lamb kidneys or veal kidneys per serving. Allow about $1/3$ pound pork or beef kidney per serving.

Heart—One of the most economical and nutritious meats available today is heart. Few Americans cook heart, but it is popular in Europe and South America. Because it is a muscle, it is not tender. It should, therefore, be braised or cooked in liquid for several hours. Most heart that is available comes from beef or veal. It can be stuffed or diced and added to a stew. It can also be ground. Choose only hearts that are plump, firm and clear, dark red. Plan on about $1/3$ to $1/2$ pound heart per serving. A beef heart weighs about 3 pounds; veal heart $3/4$ to 1 pound; pork about $1/2$ pound; lamb $1/4$ to $1/2$ pound.

Tongue—Next to calf's liver, this is the most popular of the variety meats. Most familiar of all is beef tongue, which is available fresh, pickled or corned, smoked, or canned. Fresh tongue needs long, slow cooking in liquid. Smoked or pickled tongue may require soaking before cooking. After a tongue is cooked, the skin and any cartilage or gristle from the thick end are removed. The tongue may be sliced and served hot or cold. Cooked tongue is delicious in casseroles or salads. Veal tongue is usually sold fresh; lamb and pork tongue is generally precooked and ready-to-eat.

Choose tongue that is rosy and pink, plump and fresh-looking. Allow $1/3$ to $1/2$ pound per serving.

Tripe—Plain, honeycomb and pocket tripe, all the inner stomach lining of beef, are available fresh, frozen, pickled or canned. Honeycomb is considered the best. Fresh or frozen tripe is usually partially cooked and needs additional cooking in salted water to make it tender. Tripe may be served with a well-seasoned sauce, buttered and broiled or added to soups. Pickled tripe is thoroughly cooked and needs only to be soaked before using. Plan on $1/4$ pound per serving.

Sweetbreads—The thymus gland of veal, calf or young beef which disappears as the animal matures. Sweetbreads are tender and considered a delicacy. They should be soaked and peeled before cooking, then broiled, sautéed, braised or cooked in liquid. If cooked in liquid, they may be peeled afterwards. To soak, which will whiten them, place them in a bowl of cold water, changing the water several times, for $1 1/2$ to 2 hours. Remove from water and peel off the membrane. Soak again in cold water with a tablespoon of vinegar per quart of water. Soak $1 1/2$ to 2 hours longer, changing water frequently. Sweetbreads may be partially cooked for 30 minutes in water with lemon juice or vinegar added (1 tablespoon per quart of water). Precooked sweetbreads may be added to scrambled eggs, sauces, breaded and fried or broiled. Plan on $1/4$ pound per serving.

Brains—From beef, veal, pork or lamb, brains are tender and delicately flavored. They should be soaked and peeled similar to sweetbreads (above). They may be precooked and used in the same way sweetbreads are used. Allow $1/4$ pound per serving.

Oxtail—The tail of beef usually sold cut into its sections. Oxtail requires long, slow cooking. It is often used for soup or stews. A tail weighs $1 1/2$ to 2 pounds. For this bony cut, allow $1/2$ to $3/4$ pound for a serving.

Peppers 'n' Beef Liver

Makes 6 servings.

1 pound beef liver	**cut into large pieces**
¼ cup all-purpose flour	**2 large onions, cut into rings**
1 teaspoon salt	**2 cups water**
¼ teaspoon pepper	**2 envelopes or teaspoons instant beef broth**
3 tablespoons vegetable oil	**1 tablespoon Worcestershire sauce**
2 large peppers (one red and one green), halved, seeded and	

1. Cut liver into 2-inch pieces, discarding any membrane and veins. Coat liver with a mixture of flour, salt and pepper on wax paper.
2. Heat oil in a large skillet; sauté peppers and onion rings until both are soft, but peppers are still bright; remove with a slotted spoon; reserve.
3. Cook liver quickly, part at a time, in oil in skillet; remove and reserve; stir the water, instant beef broth and Worcestershire sauce in skillet; bring to bubbling, stirring constantly; return onion rings, peppers and liver, and heat slowly 2 minutes. Sprinkle with chopped parsley, if you wish.

Swiss Calf's Liver

This dish is a favorite in Switzerland. Watch carefully how you cook the shallots, for if they burn, the dish will be bitter. If you have no shallots, replace them with the finely chopped white part of green onions.

Makes 6 servings.

6 slices calf's liver (4 × ⅓ inches)	**1 teaspoon salt**
2 teaspoons leaf tarragon	**¼ teaspoon pepper**
6 tablespoons butter or margarine	**2½ cups chicken broth**
1 small onion, minced (¼ cup)	**1 tablespoon vegetable oil**
1¼ cups uncooked long-grain rice	**1 tablespoons finely chopped shallot**
	Chopped fresh parsley

1. Remove the membrane surrounding the slices of liver; cut the liver into 2 × ⅓-inch strips. Crumble 1 teaspoon of tarragon very finely and sprinkle it over the liver. Toss and let stand while you prepare the rice.
2. Heat 4 tablespoons butter in a heavy saucepan. Add the onion and cook until translucent. Add the rice and toss until it is well coated with butter and feels very hot to the tip of your finger. Add ½ teaspoon of the salt, ⅛ teaspoon of the pepper, remaining

Pictured opposite:
Low-Calorie Cheesearoni Beef Casserole, page 480.

tarragon and chicken broth. Cover; cook on medium-low heat for 20 to 25 minutes or until tender.
3. When the rice is tender, heat the remaining butter and 1 tablespoon oil in a large skillet. Add the shallots and toss 1 minute. Add the liver strips and toss on high heat until the liver is uniformly gray. This requires no more than 2 minutes, since the liver should remain pink at the center. Add remaining salt and pepper.
4. Make a bed of rice on a serving platter; top it with the liver strips and then sprinkle with chopped parsley and serve immediately.

Liver Teriyaki

This is a tasty dish, cooked with slightly sweetened soy sauce and served on rice.

Makes 4 servings.

1 pound beef liver	**3 tablespoons vegetable oil**
¼ cup all-purpose flour	**1 large onion, sliced**
¼ cup soy sauce	**Dash pepper**
¼ cup water	**Dash garlic salt**
2 tablespoons sugar	**Hot cooked rice**

1. Cut liver into small strips, discarding any membrane and veins. Coat liver with flour on wax paper.
2. Combine soy sauce, water and sugar in a 1-cup measure. Heat oil in large skillet; add onion; sauté 1 minute. Add liver strips; brown quickly, stirring constantly.
3. Lower heat; stir in soy sauce mixture. Cook until thickened. Add pepper and garlic salt. Serve over rice.

Knish This baked or fried stuffed pastry is a Jewish specialty. A knish (the "k" is pronounced) is to Jewish people what the pizza is to the Italians, the egg roll to the Chinese, the hot dog to Americans.

Chicken-Liver Knishes

Makes 24 knishes.

½ pound chicken livers	**pared and thinly sliced**
¼ cup vegetable oil	**1 egg**
2 large onions, thinly sliced	**⅛ teaspoon pepper**
3 teaspoons salt	**1 cup matzo meal**
5 large potatoes,	**Vegetable oil for frying**

1. Sauté livers in the ¼ cup oil in a large skillet 5 minutes or until they lose their pink color; lift out with slotted spoon; place in bowl.
2. Stir the onions into drippings in skillet; sauté until soft; combine with livers. Put livers and onions through a food grinder, using the coarse blade; return to bowl. Stir in 1 teaspoon of the salt. Chill.
3. Cook potatoes, covered, in boiling salted water in a

(continued)

large saucepan 15 minutes or until tender; drain well. Mash, then beat in egg, remaining salt, pepper and 2 tablespoons of the matzo meal. Chill.

4. Spread remaining matzo meal on wax paper. Drop potato mixture, 2 tablespoons at a time, onto meal and flatten into a 4-inch round; place 2 level teaspoons of liver mixture in center. Shape the round of potato mixture up and over filling to cover. Roll in matzo meal to coat lightly.

5. Pour ⅛ inch oil in a large skillet. Fry potato cakes, a few at a time, until golden.

Chicken Livers with Bacon and Green Beans

A tasty way to use economical and nutritious chicken livers.

Makes 4 servings.

1 pound chicken livers	**1 package (9 ounces)**
4 bacon slices	**frozen Italian green**
2 tablespoons flour	**beans**
½ cup water	

1. Trim livers of any connective tissue or fat. Cook bacon in large skillet; remove to paper toweling; crumble and reserve. Pour bacon drippings into a cup; measure and return 2 tablespoons to skillet.
2. Roll chicken livers in flour to coat. Brown on all sides in drippings (5 to 10 minutes). Stir in water, scraping up brown bits from skillet. Add beans; cover and cook 10 minutes until beans are tender. Livers should be brown outside and slightly pink inside. Taste; add salt and pepper, if you wish. Sprinkle with crumbled bacon. Serve with fried rice, if you wish.

Steak and Kidney Pie

Bake at 425° for 30 minutes.

Makes 6 servings.

1 beef kidney (about 1 pound)	**1 medium-size onion, sliced**
2 tablespoons lemon juice	**1 tablespoon prepared mustard**
¾ pound lean chuck steak	**1 cup dry white wine**
¼ cup all-purpose flour	**½ cup water**
1½ teaspoons salt	**1½ cups *sifted* all-purpose flour**
¼ teaspoon pepper	**½ cup vegetable shortening**
½ teaspoon paprika	**4 tablespoons water**
2 tablespoons vegetable oil	**1 egg**

1. Rinse kidney. Soak in lemon juice 30 minutes; drain and dry well. Trim away all fat. Cut kidney in ¼-inch slices. Slice steak in same manner.
2. Combine the ¼ cup flour with 1 teaspoon of the salt, pepper and paprika; dredge sliced kidney and steak.
3. Heat oil in a Dutch oven. Brown steak and kidney, a few pieces at a time. Add onion; sauté a few minutes. Sprinkle with remaining flour mixture.
4. Combine mustard, wine and the ½ cup water; stir into meat in Dutch oven. Bring to boiling; cover. Lower heat; simmer 1½ hours or until kidney and steak are very tender.
5. Combine the remaining 1½ cups flour and remaining salt; cut in shortening until mixture is crumbly. Stir in 3 tablespoons of the water, 1 tablespoon at a time, until mixture forms a ball (add extra water, if needed). Preheat oven to 425°.
6. Roll out half of pastry on a lightly floured pastry cloth or board to a 10-inch circle; fit into 8-inch pie plate. Turn meat mixture into pastry-lined pie plate. Roll out remaining pastry to an 11-inch circle; place over filling. Turn under and flute edge. Slash top to allow steam to escape. Combine egg and remaining tablespoon water; mix well. Brush over top of pastry.
7. Bake in a preheated hot oven (425°) for 30 minutes or until pastry is a deep golden brown.

LAMB

Lamb   Meat of young sheep under 1 year in age, usually 6 months. Lamb is tender, lean meat with a delicate but distinctive flavor. Mutton is the meat from mature sheep.

Sheep and its products go back to antiquity, some 8,000 years ago. In the Middle East and southern Europe, the sheep was valued as an animal that matured quickly and could exist in almost any kind of climate or terrain.

Buying Lamb: Lamb is available fresh or frozen. Frozen lamb is usually imported from New Zealand. Fresh lamb is pink to light red in color with firm, fine-textured flesh. Some cuts of lamb have a thin, papery skin, called "fell," surrounding the fat. If it has not been removed, pull it off steaks and chops before cooking; leave it on roasts to help hold their shape during cooking.

Mutton is more popular in Europe than in the United States. When it is available in our markets, it is likely to be less expensive than lamb. Cuts of mutton are similar to lamb but they are larger in size and dark red in color. The meat is less tender with more fat and stronger flavor.

Some cuts of lamb, such as rib or loin chops, have given lamb an expensive reputation, but there are many other cuts that are economical and excellent to use in everyday meals. For example, buy cuts from the shoulder, such as a shoulder arm roast or shoulder steaks.

Cooking Lamb: Most cuts of lamb are tender and can be cooked by one of the dry heat methods. Some cuts should be braised or cooked in liquid.

Temperature and Time for Roasting Lamb

Cut	Approximate Pound Weight	Oven Temperature	Internal Meat Temperature When Done	Minutes Per Pound Roasting Time
Leg	5 to 9	300° to 325° F.	140° F. (rare)	20 to 25
			160° F. (medium)	25 to 30
			170° F.-180° F. (well)	30 to 35
Leg, Shank	3 to 4	300° to 325°F.	140° F. (rare)	25 to 30
			160° F. (medium)	30 to 35
Half			170° F.-180° F. (well)	35 to 40
Rib	2 to 3	375° F.	140° F. (rare)	25 to 30
			160° F. (medium)	30 to 35
			170° F.-180° F. (well)	35 to 40

Roast Lamb, Middle-Eastern Style

Roast at 425° for 15 minutes, then 325° for 1 hour, 45 minutes.

Makes 10 servings.

1 leg of lamb (about 7 pounds)
1 bunch green onions
1 large lemon
1 small bunch fresh mint
1½ teaspoons salt
¼ teaspoon freshly ground pepper
3 cups boiling water
¼ cup all-purpose flour
½ cup cold water

1. Trim all but a thin layer of fat from lamb. Place lamb, round-side up, on rack in shallow roasting pan.
2. Chop onions, whole lemon and mint leaves until very fine; blend with 1 teaspoon of the salt and the pepper.
3. Press all but ¼ cup of mixture on surface of lamb. Place roasting pan on rack in oven; pour the 3 cups boiling water into pan.
4. Roast in a hot oven (425°) for 15 minutes; reduce heat to slow (325°) and roast for 1 hour, 45 minutes, basting several times with water in pan, for rare lamb. Roast 30 minutes longer for medium lamb. Remove the roast from pan to heated serving platter and sprinkle with reserved green onion mixture. Keep warm.
5. Strain liquid in roasting pan into 4-cup measure; let stand 5 minutes; skim fat. Return liquid to roasting pan; heat to boiling. Blend flour with ½ cup cold water to make smooth paste; stir into bubbling liquid. Cook, stirring constantly, until mixture thickens and bubbles 3 minutes. Season with remaining salt. Serve.

How to Carve a Leg of Lamb

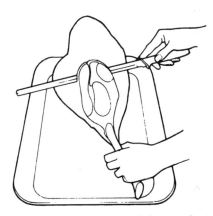

The French have the best—and the easiest—technique. Simply lift the leg bone with your hand, then slice down along (parallel to) the bone in thin slices.

Roast Herbed Leg of Lamb

Roast at 325° for 2 hours.

Makes 8 to 10 servings.

1½ teaspoons salt
2 cloves garlic
1 cup dry white wine
½ cup water
1 cup olive oil
1 tablespoon lemon juice
1 medium-size onion, chopped
1 teaspoon tarragon-
flavored vinegar
1 teaspoon leaf marjoram, crumbled
1 teaspoon leaf rosemary, crumbled
8 peppercorns, cracked
1 leg of lamb (about 6 pounds)

1. Sprinkle salt over garlic on cutting board, then chop very finely.

(continued)

2. Combine garlic, wine, water, oil, lemon juice, onion, vinegar and herbs in a shallow glass or ceramic dish.
3. Pull fell (thin covering membrane), if any, from lamb. Place lamb in marinade. Let marinate several hours in refrigerator, turning occasionally.
4. Pour off marinade; reserve. Place lamb on rack in roasting pan. Insert meat thermometer into thickest part of meat, not touching bone or fat.
5. Roast, uncovered, in a slow oven (325°) for 2 hours or until thermometer reads 140° for rare lamb. Baste occasionally with reserved marinade. Remove lamb to heated platter. Let stand 15 minutes before carving.

Buy a Whole Leg of Lamb

When they are on sale, buy a whole leg of lamb and ask the butcher to cut it into 1-inch-thick chops. You will get about 10 tender chops for broiling and shank meat for braising.

Braised Lamb Chops with Vegetables

A quick, delicious version of lamb stew.

Makes 4 servings.

4 shoulder lamb chops, cut ¹/₂-inch thick (about 1³/₄ pounds)	soup
	1 package (1 pound, 8 ounces) frozen stew vegetables
1 can condensed cream of celery	¹/₂ teaspoon leaf rosemary, crumbled

1. Place lamb chops in a large skillet over low heat. (Do not add fat.) Cook chops slowly in their own melting fat until brown; turn and brown other side; remove.
2. Add soup to skillet, scraping up browned bits on bottom of pan. Stir in stew vegetables and rosemary. (Do not add water.)
3. Arrange lamb chops over vegetables. Cover. Simmer, stirring occasionally, 30 minutes or until lamb chops are tender.

Lamb Chops Provençale

Bake at 350° for 40 minutes.

Makes 6 servings.

2 packages (10 ounces each) frozen ratatouille	³/₄ cup white wine
	6 pitted black olives
	Fresh watercress *(optional)*
6 shoulder lamb chops (2¹/₂ to 3 pounds)	Cooked rice *(optional)*

1. Preheat the oven to moderate (350°).
2. Place pouches of ratatouille in hot water to thaw slightly.
3. Heat a large heavy skillet over medium-high heat. Rub small piece of fat from lamb over bottom of skillet. Brown chops, a few at a time, in skillet in their own fat.

Remove chops as they brown to a shallow ovenproof casserole just large enough to hold chops in a single layer.
4. Add wine to skillet. Cook, scraping up browned bits from bottom and side of the skillet, about 2 minutes. Add slightly thawed ratatouille. Bring to boiling. Spoon over lamb chops. Cover the casserole with aluminum foil.
5. Bake in the preheated moderate oven (350°) for 30 minutes. Uncover; baste chops. Add olives. Bake, uncovered, for 10 minutes longer. Garnish with watercress and serve with rice, if you wish.

Greek-Style Lamb Chops

Less expensive shoulder chops make this an economy meal.

Makes 4 servings.

4 shoulder lamb chops (about 1¹/₂ pounds), cut ¹/₂-inch thick	1 box (6 ounces) Greek-style rice pilaf
	2 cups water
2 tablespoons olive or vegetable oil	¹/₄ cup raisins
	4 thin slices lemon

1. Brown chops slowly in oil in a large skillet, turning once and removing chops to a plate as they brown. Drain off all but 1 tablespoon pan drippings.
2. Add contents of rice packet to skillet; sauté 3 minutes; add water, seasoning mixture and raisins; bring to boiling.
3. Arrange lamb chops over rice with lemon slices. Cover; lower heat; simmer 30 minutes or until liquid is absorbed and lamb chops are tender. Fluff up rice. Transfer to heated serving platter. Garnish with pine nuts and chopped fresh mint, if you wish.

South Seas Lamb Supper

Makes 6 serivngs.

³/₄ cup uncooked long-grain rice	celery
	³/₄ cup mayonnaise
2 tablespoons chopped fresh parsley	2 tablespoons chopped chutney
¹/₄ cup bottled oil-and-vinegar salad dressing	1 tablespoon minced onion
	2 teaspoons curry powder
3 cups diced roast lamb	Lemon juice
1 cup thinly sliced	1 red apple

1. Cook rice following label directions; place in a large

bowl. Sprinkle parsley and oil-and-vinegar dressing over top; toss lightly to mix. Chill while preparing remaining ingredients.

2. Combine lamb and celery in a large bowl. Blend mayonnaise, chutney, onion, curry powder and $1/2$ teaspoon lemon juice in a cup; spoon over lamb mixture; toss to mix.

3. When ready to serve, quarter apple, core and slice thin crosswise. Dip slices in lemon juice to prevent darkening.

4. Spoon rice mixture in a ring on a large serving platter; spoon lamb mixture in center. Overlap apple slices around edge. Garnish with several slices of hard-cooked egg and parsley, if you wish.

Irish Stew

Makes 6 servings.

2$1/2$ pounds lamb neck or shoulder (or lamb combination special)	3 teaspoons salt
	$1/2$ teaspoon pepper
	1$1/2$ teaspoons leaf thyme, crumbled
2 pounds onions	1 clove garlic, peeled
2 pounds potatoes	Chopped fresh parsley

1. Cut the meat into chunks including the bone. Cut off and discard excess fat. Peel the onions and cut into $1/4$-inch thick slices. Pare the potatoes and cut into $1/4$-inch thick slices.

2. Arrange a layer of potatoes and a layer of onions in a Dutch oven or 8-cup flameproof casserole with 1 teaspoon salt, part of the pepper and $1/2$ teaspoon thyme.

3. Add the remaining onion slices and top with the remaining potato slices. Sprinkle with the remaining salt, pepper and thyme. Tuck the peeled garlic down the side.

4. Add water to about three-fourths the way up the meat and vegetables (2 to 4 cups). Bring to boiling, lower heat, cover and simmer for 1 hour or until meat and vegetables are tender. Sprinkle with chopped parsley.

Low-Calorie Irish Stew

Makes 8 servings.

2 pounds boneless leg of lamb, fat-trimmed and cut in cubes	make 3 cups
	2 large onions, sliced
1 bay leaf	1 pound white turnips, pared and sliced
1 teaspoon salt	1 pound carrots, pared and sliced
Pinch pepper	3 tablespoons flour
1 can condensed beef broth plus water to	$1/3$ cup water

1. Combine lamb, bay leaf, salt, pepper and beef broth mixture in a large saucepan or kettle. Heat to boiling. Lower heat; cover; simmer 50 minutes or until

meat is almost tender. Remove from heat; refrigerate several hours or overnight.

2. About 45 minutes before serving time, skim off all surface fat from stew; remove bay leaf. Reheat to boiling; add onions, turnips and carrots. Cover; simmer 30 minutes or until vegetables are tender.

3. Combine the flour and water to make a smooth paste; stir into simmering stew. Cook, stirring constantly, until sauce thickens and bubbles 3 minutes. Garnish with chopped parsley, if you wish.

Deviled Lamb Riblets

Makes 6 servings.

$1/3$ cup all-purpose flour	(1 cup)
	1 clove garlic, minced
1 teaspoon leaf thyme, crumbled	1 can (20 ounces) pineapple chunks in pineapple juice
1 teaspoon salt	
$1/4$ teaspoon pepper	1 bottle (18 ounces) hot barbecue sauce
3 pounds lamb riblets, cut into serving-size pieces	2 tablespoons Dijon mustard
	1 lemon, sliced
$1/3$ cup vegetable oil	Hot cooked rice
1 large onion, diced	

1. Combine flour, thyme, salt and pepper in a large plastic bag. Shake riblets, a few at a time, in seasoned flour to coat. Reserve remaining seasoned flour.

2. Heat oil in a large Dutch oven. Brown riblets, a few at a time on both sides. Remove riblets to platter as they become browned.

3. Drain all but 2 tablespoons drippings from pan. Sauté onion and garlic in drippings until lightly browned, about 5 minutes.

4. Drain juice from pineapple into a 1-cup liquid measure. Reserve.

5. Stir barbecue sauce, $1/2$ cup of the pineapple juice and mustard into the browned onions.

6. Add lamb riblets, coating thoroughly in the barbecue sauce; add lemon slices. Cover. Cook over low heat for 1 hour or until riblets are tender.

7. Skim off fat that may have accumulated during cooking. Add pineapple; cook 1 minute. Thicken gravy, if you wish, with 1 tablespoon reserved seasoned flour mixed with remaining $1/4$ cup pineapple juice. Serve with rice.

Braised Twin Shoulders of Lamb

Bake at 325° for 1 hour, 30 minutes.

Makes 8 servings.

2 tablespoons butter or margarine	2 cloves garlic, minced
2 tablespoons vegetable oil	1½ teaspoons salt
2 boned and tied lamb shoulders (about 3 pounds each)	¼ teaspoon pepper
	1 teaspoon leaf rosemary, crumbled
2 large onions, chopped (2 cups)	½ teaspoon leaf thyme, crumbled
1 cup chopped celery with leaves	½ cup water or white wine

1. Heat butter and oil in a Dutch oven or heatproof casserole; brown lamb on all sides. Remove when browned.
2. Stir onion, celery and garlic into pan drippings; sauté until soft, about 5 minutes.
3. Return lamb to Dutch oven; add salt, pepper, rosemary, thyme and water; cover.
4. Bake in a slow oven (325°) for 1½ hours. Transfer meat to a heated serving platter and keep warm.
5. Pour liquid into a 4-cup measure; allow to stand 5 minutes; skim off all fat. Puree liquid, part at a time, in the container of an electric blender. (You should have 3 cups.) Pour into a medium-size saucepan; heat thoroughly. (If you wish, gravy can be served as is or thickened by mixing 2 tablespoons cornstarch with ¼ cup water to make a smooth paste; stir into mixture. cook, stirring constantly until mixture thickens and begins to bubble.) Pour into gravy boat.
6. Carve part of lamb into slices, removing strings as you carve. Arrange lamb and slices on heated platter. Garnish with mint jelly-filled peach halves, if you wish. Pass gravy.

Stuffed Zucchini

Bake at 375° for 45 minutes.

Makes 6 servings.

6 medium-size zucchini	lamb, trimmed of fat
3 medium-size onions, chopped (1½ cups)	3 flat anchovy fillets
	¼ cup chopped pitted ripe olives
1 sweet red pepper, halved, seeded and chopped	¼ cup capers, chopped (optional)
2 cloves garlic, finely chopped	1½ cups cooked rice
	1 teaspoon salt
4 tablespoons olive or vegetable oil	¼ teaspoon pepper
	1½ cups plain yogurt
1 cup cubed cooked	3 tablespoons canned tomato sauce

1. Wash zucchini; trim stem end. Cut thin slice off lengthwise and scoop out the pulp, leaving shell about ¼-inch thick.
2. Sauté onions, pepper and garlic in 2 tablespoons of the oil in a large skillet until soft. Chop the removed zucchini pulp; add to the skillet. Cook until most of the liquid has evaporated and the pulp is soft.
3. Grind lamb with anchovy fillets in a meat grinder with the finest disc, or chop very finely. (Meat grinder gives better texture to the stuffing.)
4. Add lamb mixture to the skillet; cook and stir 1 minute. Remove skillet from heat and stir in olives, capers, cooked rice, salt, pepper and ½ cup of the yogurt.
5. Brush zucchini shells inside and out with remaining oil. Place shells side by side in baking dish large enough to hold them snugly together. Fill shells with stuffing, dividing it evenly among them. Pour about ½ inch of hot water into the baking dish.
6. Bake in moderate oven (375°) for 45 minutes or until the filling is lightly browned and the shells are cooked but still firm. Transfer filled shells to warm serving dish.
7. Combine tomato sauce with the remaining 1 cup yogurt. Serve cold sauce with hot vegetable or heat gently, but do not allow to boil, and spoon over zucchini to serve. Garnish with olives and parsley, if you wish.

Shish Kebob
Originally, a dish of lamb skewered with other foods and grilled or broiled. The word is derived from the Turkish *shish*, skewered, and *kebap*, roast meat. It was a convenient method of cooking food over a fire devised by the nomadic people of the Near East. Nowadays, any type of meat, poultry or even seafood is skewered.

Shish Kebob

Makes 6 servings.

1 medium-size onion, sliced	½ leg of lamb (butt end), about 2½ pounds
3 cloves garlic, crushed	
1 cup chopped celery	2 large onions, cut in 1½-inch pieces
¼ teaspoon cumin seeds	6 medium-size mushroom caps
1 cup red wine vinegar	
1 cup lemon juice	6 green peppers, halved, seeded and quartered
½ cup vegetable oil	
1 teaspoon salt	Hot cooked rice
¼ teaspoon pepper	

1. Combine sliced onion, garlic, celery, cumin, vinegar, lemon juice, oil, salt and pepper in a medium-size bowl.
2. Bone the lamb; cut meat into 1-inch cubes. Place in a glass or ceramic dish. Pour marinade over lamb; cover; refrigerate 24 hours.
3. Blanch onion pieces in boiling water 5 minutes; drain.
4. Thread a mushroom, pepper and onion piece on

Lamb Kabobs with Vegetables.

long skewers alternately with pieces of the marinated lamb. Place skewers on rack over broiler pan.

5. Broil kebobs 4 inches from heat for 5 minutes. Turn; baste with marinade; broil 5 minutes; turn; broil 5 minutes longer. Serve kebobs on rice.

Lamb Kabobs with Vegetables

Makes 6 servings.

- 1/2 cup vegetable oil
- 1/2 cup lemon juice
- 1 small onion, minced (1/4 cup)
- 1 teaspoon leaf oregano, crumbled
- 2 teaspoons leaf marjoram, crumbled
- 1/4 cup minced fresh parsley
- 1 clove garlic, chopped
- 2 pounds boneless lamb (leg or shoulder), cut in

- 1 1/2-inch cubes
- 2 medium-size green peppers, seeded and cut in squares
- OR: 2 medium-size red peppers, seeded and cut in squares
- 1 pound large mushrooms, stems removed
- 2 summer squash, cut in chunks
- 1 small eggplant, cubed

1. Combine oil, lemon juice, onion, oregano,

marjoram, parsley and garlic in a large deep bowl. Stir in lamb; cover; refrigerate overnight.

2. Thread lamb on 6 metal skewers. Grill or broil, 6 inches from heat, for 15 minutes, turning and basting frequently with marinade. Thread vegetables on separate skewers and continue grilling lamb and vegetables, turning and basting, for about 15 minutes longer or until meat is done. Or, thread lamb and vegetables on the same skewers.

Lamb Ragout with Apricots

Makes 4 servings.

- 1 pound boneless lamb shoulder, trimmed
- 2 tablespoons butter or margarine
- 1 can (17 ounces) plum tomatoes with juice

- 1/2 cup dried apricots
- 1/2 teaspoon leaf rosemary, crumbled
- 2 tablespoons dry sherry
- 1 1/2 teaspoons cornstarch

1. Cut meat into 1-inch cubes; pat dry on paper toweling.

2. Heat butter in a large skillet. Brown lamb cubes. Stir in tomatoes, apricots and rosemary. *(continued)*

3. Bring to boiling; lower heat; simmer, covered, for 45 minutes. If too much liquid, uncover last 15 minutes.
4. To thicken, mix sherry with cornstarch. Stir into lamb mixture. Cook until bubbly. Taste; add salt and pepper, if needed. Serve with kasha or brown rice, if you wish.

Lamb Burgundy

The French favorite with a twist—chunks of lamb, instead of beef, simmer in a deep red wine sauce.
Bake at 375° for 30 minutes.

Makes 6 servings.

1¹/₂ **pounds lean lamb shoulder, cubed**	**broth**
3 tablespoons butter or margarine	**1 cup red Burgundy wine**
¹/₃ **cup all-purpose flour**	**2 large yellow squash**
¹/₂ **teaspoon salt**	**1 bunch leeks**
1 can condensed beef	**1 package (10 ounces) frozen snow peas**

1. Brown the lamb cubes, one-third at a time, in the

butter or margarine in a medium-size skillet; remove with a slotted spoon to an 8-cup casserole.
2. Blend the flour and salt into the drippings in the skillet; stir in the beef broth until smooth, then the wine; bring to boiling, stirring constantly.
3. Tip the yellow squash; cut into ¹/₂-inch-thick slices on the diagonal. Wash the leeks in a bowl of warm salted water.
4. Cook the squash, leeks and snow peas separately, part at a time, in boiling water in a large skillet for 3 minutes, or just until crisp-tender; drain. Spoon into the casserole with lamb. Pour the wine sauce over the lamb and vegetables.
5. Bake in a moderate oven (375°) for 30 minutes, or until bubbly-hot. Serve with French bread, if you wish.

Suggested Variation: For Chicken Burgundy, substitute 1¹/₂ pounds chicken fillets cut into cubes and use white Burgundy wine.

Lamb Burgundy (left), page 490;
Paella Valenciana, page 612.

Savory Lamb Ragout

Makes 8 servings.

1/4 cup all-purpose flour	2 teaspoons leaf thyme, crumbled
3 pounds boneless lean lamb shoulder, cut into 1 1/2-inch cubes	1/2 teaspoon freshly ground pepper
1/4 cup vegetable oil	12 small new potatoes, pared (about 3 pounds)
6 medium-size onions, sliced (about 8 cups)	2 pound carrots, pared and cut into 2-inch pieces
2 cloves garlic, finely chopped	1 can (28 ounces) tomatoes, drained
1 cup beef broth	1 tablespoon flour
2 teaspoons salt	2 tablespoons water

1. Place 1/4 cup flour and the meat in plastic bag; shake to coat thoroughly.
2. Heat oil in heavy kettle or Dutch oven; brown meat, part at a time, removing pieces to bowl as they brown.
3. Add onions and garlic; cook slightly. Stir in broth, salt, thyme and pepper; heat to boiling. Return lamb to kettle. Cover; simmer 45 minutes.
4. Add potatoes and carrots; cover and cook 45 minutes longer or until vegetables are done. Stir in tomatoes. Blend remaining tablespoon of flour with water in cup. Bring stew to boiling; stir in flour mixture. Continue to cook and stir until the sauce is thickened and bubbly.

Rosemary-Braised Lamb Shanks

Makes 4 servings.

4 lamb shanks	leaf rosemary, crumbled
2 tablespoons vegetable oil	1 envelope or teaspoon instant chicken broth
1 package (1 pound) carrots, pared and cut into 2-inch pieces	1 teaspoon salt
8 small yellow onions, peeled	1/4 teaspoon pepper
1 clove garlic, minced	2 1/2 cups water
4 1/2 teaspoons chopped fresh rosemary	4 medium-size boiling potatoes, pared and quartered
OR: 1 1/2 teaspoons	1/4 cup all-purpose flour

1. Brown lamb shanks in oil in a large kettle; remove and reserve. Brown carrots and onions in drippings;

(continued)

Lamb and Mushroom Kabobs

Cook on hibachi 12 to 15 minutes.

Makes 8 servings.

1/3 cup catsup	1/2 cup olive or vegetable oil
1/4 cup lemon juice	2 pounds lean lamb, cut into 1- to 1 1/2-inch cubes
2 tablespoons soy sauce	
1 tablespoon leaf rosemary, crumbled	1 1/2 pounds large mushrooms
1/2 teaspoon salt	

1. Combine catsup, lemon juice, soy sauce, rosemary, salt and oil in a small bowl; mix with fork until well blended.
2. Pour marinade over lamb cubes in large bowl; cover. Refrigerate overnight.
3. Halve or quarter mushrooms; thread onto metal skewers alternating with cubes of meat. Wrap skewers in foil; pour marinade into jar with tight-fitting lid.
4. Cook kabobs over grayed coals, turning and brushing often with marinade, 12 to 15 minutes for pink lamb.

remove and reserve. Sauté garlic in drippings until soft; stir in 3 teaspoons of the fresh or 1 teaspoon dried rosemary, chicken broth, salt, pepper and 2 cups of the water. Return lamb shanks to the kettle; lower heat; cover kettle.

2. Simmer 30 minutes; return browned carrots and onions and add potatoes. Cover kettle and simmer 30 minutes or until meat and vegetables are tender.

3. Combine flour and the remaining 1/2 cup water in a cup until smooth; stir into bubbling liquid. Add the remaining 1 1/2 teaspoons fresh or 1/2 teaspoon dried rosemary; cook, stirring constantly, until mixture thickens and bubbles, 3 minutes.

Barbecued Lamb Shanks

Serve with buttered noodles and a salad.
Bake at 325° for 1 hour, 45 minutes.

Makes 4 servings.

4 lamb shanks (about 1 pound each)	1 tablespoon brown sugar
1/8 teaspoon paprika	1 large onion, sliced
1 teaspoon salt	1 tablespoon vinegar
1/4 teaspoon pepper	1/2 teaspoon dry mustard
2 tablespoons vegetable oil	Dash Worcestershire sauce
1/2 cup catsup	
1/2 cup water	

1. Sprinkle lamb shanks with paprika, salt and pepper. pBrown shanks in hot oil in a Dutch oven.
2. Drain off oil. Stir in catsup, water, brown sugar, onion, vinegar, mustard and Worcestershire. Cover.
3. Bake in a slow oven (325°) for 1 hour, 45 minutes or until meat is tender. Serve immediately.

Springtime Lamb Ragout

Makes 8 servings.

2 1/2 pounds boneless lamb shoulder, cubed	1 large onion, chopped (1 cup)
1/4 cup all-purpose flour	1 cup dry white wine
1 teaspoon leaf rosemary, crumbled	1 can (13 ounces) madrilene
1 teaspoon salt	24 small white onions, peeled
1/4 teaspoon pepper	16 small carrots (1 pound), scraped
4 tablespoons (1/2 stick) butter or margarine	1 cup fresh or frozen peas

1. Shake lamb in plastic bag with flour, rosemary, salt and pepper until well coated. Heat 3 tablespoons of the butter in a large skillet. Add lamb to brown, about half at a time, turning often, until browned on all sides. Transfer pieces to a Dutch oven as they brown. Sprinkle any remaining flour mixture over lamb.

2. Add remaining butter and the onion to same skillet; sauté 5 minutes, stirring often. Stir in wine; cook, stirring and scraping browned bits from bottom of pan, 5 minutes or until reduced by half. Pour over meat.
3. Add madrilene; bring to boiling; cover. Simmer 30 minutes; add onions and carrots; simmer 1 hour longer or until meat and vegetables are tender. Remove from heat; cool. Chill overnight.
4. Last-minute touches: Remove any fat from top of stew; heat just to boiling; add peas. Cover; simmer 5 minutes longer.

Deviled Lamb Shanks

Makes 4 servings.

4 lamb shanks (about 3 1/2 pounds)	soup
1 can condensed cream of onion	1/4 cup water
	2 tablespoons Dijon mustard

1. Trim excess fat from lamb shanks. Melt trimmed fat over low heat in a Dutch oven. (If there is not enough fat on lamb, add 2 tablespoons oil.) Brown lamb shanks, 2 at a time. Remove lamb shanks to platter when browned. Pour off all fat.
2. Add onion soup, water and mustard to drippings in pan. Stir up browned bits in pan. Return lamb shanks to kettle, turning to coat with cream mixture; lower heat and cover Dutch oven.
3. Simmer 1 1/2 hours or until meat is done, turning lamb shanks 2 or 3 times during cooking. If mixture becomes too thick, add a little boiling water. Serve with rice; sprinkle with chopped parsley, if you wish.

Braised Lamb Shanks à La Grecque

Bake at 350° for 1 hour, 30 minutes.

Makes 6 servings.

4 lamb shanks (about 3 pounds)	2 large onions, finely chopped
2 large cloves garlic, crushed	1 can (28 ounces) plum tomatoes, drained and chopped (reserve the juice)
1/2 teaspoon leaf rosemary, crumbled	
1/2 teaspoon salt	1 tablespoon tomato paste
1/8 teaspoon pepper	
3 medium-size eggplants, pared and cut into 1 1/2-inch cubes	1/2 teaspoon ground cumin
	1 teaspoon chili powder
2 tablespoons salt	1/2 teaspoon tumeric
1/2 to 3/4 cup olive oil	
1 cup cubed salt pork	

1. Cut deep gashes in several places in lamb shanks and insert bits of the crushed garlic and crumbled rosemary. Sprinkle shanks with 1/2 teaspoon salt and the pepper; let stand while preparing remaining ingredients.

Chicken-Filled Pastry Boats, page 47; Ham and Walnut Appetizers, page 44; Springtime Lamb Ragout, page 492; Shrimp Curry, Parsleyed Rice and Condiments, page 403.

2. Place the eggplant cubes in a colander and sprinkle with 2 tablespoons salt. Let stand for 2 hours. Dry thoroughly on paper toweling.

3. In a flame-proof casserole or Dutch oven heat ¼ cup of the oil. Add just enough eggplant to cover bottom of skillet and brown evenly on all sides. Remove to paper toweling to drain. Continue browning eggplant, adding more oil as you need it, until all cubes are browned.

4. Blanch the salt pork 5 minutes in boiling salted water; drain well.

5. Heat 2 tablespoons of the oil in the casserole; add the salt pork and cook it until it is almost crisp.

Remove with a slotted spoon to a side dish. Discard all but 3 tablespoons of fat from the casserole.

6. Brown the lamb shanks two at a time, then remove and reserve. Add the onions and cook, stirring occasionally, until nicely browned. Add the tomatoes, tomato paste, cumin, chili powder and turmeric.

7. Return lamb shanks to casserole; add the salt pork and eggplant. Cover casserole; place in center of oven.

8. Bake in a moderate oven (350°) for 1½ hours or until very tender. Check for pan juices from time to time. If liquid is needed, add reserved juice from

(continued)

tomatoes. When lamb is tender, taste. Add additional seasonings, if you wish. Remove lamb to serving platter. Degrease pan juices and pour over lamb. Sprinkle with parsley or basil and serve with curry-flavored rice, if you wish.

Note: This dish is good prepared a day ahead and reheated in a slow oven. As a variation, serve a side dish of yogurt flavored with a sprig of fresh mint and a large clove of garlic, both finely chopped.

Moroccan Lamb Stew

An exotic but simple platter of mixed appetizers would be an exciting way to start an evening of Moroccan fare: Stuffed grape leaves skewered with a sliver of lemon; pita bread quarters filled with eggplant salad or seasoned chick-pea puree; wedges of feta cheese drizzled with olive oil and sprinkled with pepper; and olives, sweet green pepper rings and cherry tomatoes. For dessert, offer baked apples, served with cinnamon and honey-sweetened yogurt.

Makes 10 servings.

3 pounds boneless leg of lamb, cut into large cubes
1 teaspoon salt
1/4 teaspoon pepper
1/4 cup *unsifted* all-purpose flour for coating, or as needed
1/4 cup olive or vegetable oil, or as needed
3 large sweet green peppers, halved, seeded and cut into thin strips
2 large onions, sliced
1 teaspoon finely chopped garlic
1/2 teaspoon ground

cinnamon
1/4 teaspoon ground cardamom
1/4 teaspoon ground coriander
1/4 teaspoon ground cumin
1/4 teaspoon ground ginger
1/8 teaspoon cayenne pepper
2 cups beef broth
2 tablespoons tomato paste
1 cup golden raisins
4 cups hot cooked saffron or white rice
1/2 cup slivered almonds

1. Pat the lamb dry with paper toweling. Season with the salt and pepper. Coat lightly with the flour, shaking off the excess.
2. Heat 2 tablespoons of the oil in a large flameproof casserole. Brown the lamb in batches, adding more oil as necessary. As the meat browns, remove to a plate.
3. Sauté the green peppers in the oil remaining in the casserole, stirring often, for 2 minutes. Remove; reserve.
4. Sauté the onions and garlic in the same casserole until tender, but not browned, about 5 minutes. Add the cinnamon, cardamom, coriander, cumin, ginger and cayenne; cook for 30 seconds, stirring constantly.

Pictured opposite: Greek-Style Lamb Chops, page 486.

5. Add the beef broth, scraping up any browned bits from the bottom of the casserole with a wooden spoon. Stir in the tomato paste. Return the lamb and a third of the peppers to the casserole. Bring to boiling. Lower the heat; cover; simmer 1 hour.
6. Add the raisins; continue cooking, covered, 30 minutes or until the lamb is tender. Stir in the remaining peppers.
7. Serve with the rice, sprinkled with the almonds.

To Make Ahead: Prepare the stew as the recipe directs through Step 5. Cool the stew and transfer to a bowl. Cover and refrigerate the stew and remaining peppers. When ready to serve, remove from the refrigerator, bring to room temperature, transfer to a flameproof casserole and proceed with Step 6.

Pueblo Lamb and Peppers

American Indians gave the world some of its favorite foods, among them corn and peppers, both sweet and hot.

Makes 6 to 8 servings.

1 lamb breast (about 2 pounds)
12 juniper berries (available at spice sections of many supermarkets)
1/2 teaspoon coriander seeds
1/4 teaspoon crushed red peppers
1/8 teaspoon black pepper
2 teaspoons salt
3 tablespoons all-purpose flour
2 tablespoons bacon drippings or

vegetable oil
2 medium-size onions, peeled and coarsely chopped (1 cup)
1 clove garlic, crushed
1 quart cold water
2 tablespoons minced fresh parsley
1 can (16 ounces) whole-kernel hominy (do not drain)
3 medium-size green peppers, cored, seeded and cut in slim wedges

1. With a sharp knife, divide lamb breast into riblets by cutting down between ribs; trim off excess fat. With a mortar and pestle or back of a heavy spoon, crush 6 of the juniper berries and 1/4 teaspoon of the coriander seeds; mix with the red peppers, 1/8 teaspoon of the black pepper and the 2 teaspoons salt. Rub mixture well over lamb, then let lamb stand at room temperature for 1 hour; sprinkle flour over lamb and toss well to coat.
2. Heat bacon drippings in a large heavy kettle over high heat and brown lamb on all sides; drain on paper toweling. Pour off all but 2 tablespoons of the fat. Lower heat to moderate; add onions and garlic and brown lightly, about 5 to 8 minutes. Return lamb to kettle; add water, parsley, the remaining whole juniper berries and the remaining 1/4 teaspoon coriander seeds, crushed. Adjust heat so liquid simmers; cover and cook 1 hour or until lamb is almost tender.

(continued)

Remove from heat; cool, then refrigerate until fat congeals and rises to top of stew. Lift off fat; then add hominy and simmer, uncovered, stirring now and then, for 30 minutes. Add peppers, simmer 45 minutes longer. Add additional salt and pepper, if needed.

3. To serve: Spoon into soup plates, including lots of the liquid and accompany with chunks of fresh-baked corn bread and a crisp green lettuce salad.

Spicy Lamb with Green Peppers

A Chinese-style lamb dish you can make with a minimum of effort.

Makes 4 servings.

1 pound lean boneless leg of lamb	2 medium-size green peppers, seeded
1/2 teaspoon sugar	3 small onions
1 tablespoon cornstarch	1/2 pint cherry tomatoes
1 tablespoon dry sherry	1/4 cup vegetable oil
2 tablespoons soy sauce	1 clove garlic, minced
	1/2 teaspoon crushed red pepper

1. Cut lamb into 1-inch cubes. Place in bowl; add sugar, cornstarch, sherry and soy sauce; toss to mix. Cut green peppers into 1/4 -inch slivers; cut onions into wedges; place in bowl. Cut tomatoes into halves.
2. Heat large deep skillet, Dutch oven or wok over high heat. Add 2 tablespoons oil; swirl to coat bottom and side. Add peppers and onions; stir-fry with slotted spoon until tender-crisp; remove to bowl.
3. Heat remaining oil in pan. Add garlic, red pepper and lamb. Stir-fry until lamb is browned. Return peppers and onions; add tomatoes. Stir-fry just until heated through. Serve with hot fluffy rice, if you wish.

French Marrow Bean Casserole

A hearty French-provincial casserole.
Bake at 325° for 3 hours.
Makes 8 servings.

1 package (1 pound) dried marrow or Great Northern beans	vegetable oil
8 cups water	2 cloves garlic, minced
2 large onions, chopped (2 cups)	1 cup dry vermouth or white wine
3 teaspoons salt	2 envelopes or teaspoons instant beef broth
1 pound boneless lamb shoulder, cubed	1 teaspoon leaf thyme, crumbled
2 tablespoons	1/2 teaspoon pepper
	1 bay leaf

1. Pick over beans and rinse under running water. Combine beans and water in a large kettle. Bring to boiling; cover kettle. Boil 2 minutes; remove from heat; let stand 1 hour. Return kettle to heat; bring to boiling;

add onions and salt; lower heat and simmer 1 hour or until beans are firm-tender.
2. Brown lamb cubes in oil in a large skillet; push to one side; add garlic and sauté 3 minutes; stir in vermouth, instant beef broth, thyme, pepper and bay leaf; bring to boiling.
3 Drain beans, reserving liquid. Combine beans and lamb mixture in a 12-cup baking dish; add enough reserved liquid to just cover the beans; cover dish.
4. Bake in a slow oven (325°) for 2 1/2 hours, adding more reserved liquid, if needed, to prevent beans from drying. Uncover; bake 30 minutes longer or until beans are very tender.

PORK, HAM AND SAUSAGES

Pork The fresh meat of domesticated swine. Cooked pork is delicate, tender, juicy and nutritious and considerably leaner than the pork of our grandparents' day.

There is a wide selection of pork cuts that can add variety to your family's meals. Pork is available fresh or cured and/or smoked. The most tender pork cuts are from the rib, the loin and the leg. (In butcher's terms, a leg is a ham and a fresh ham is simply one that has not been cured or smoked.) These tender cuts require nothing more than a gentle, slow roasting or pan-frying. They can be cooked by one of the dry heat methods. Pork must always be thoroughly cooked.

The not-so-tender cuts -- those from the shoulder -- are better when braised, that is, browned and then cooked in a covered pot on the range or in the oven with vegetables and liquid added.

Cured and/or smoked pork include ham, bacon, smoked pork shoulder rolls and picnics.

Pork contains high-quality proteins, which are proteins with all the essential amino acids. Pork is an excellent source of thiamin, riboflavin, niacin and vitamins B_6 and B_{12}. A 3-ounce serving of cooked lean pork contains 24 grams of protein and 206 calories.

Buying and Storing: There are pork roasts to fit every menu and budget. The loin offers blade end, center and sirloin end roasts. From the pork shoulder, choose either the blade Boston (butt) or arm picnic. From the pork leg, you can buy a fresh, whole or half ham or ham steaks. Chops and steaks include loin, rib, sirloin and blade chops. There are also shoulder steaks. Pork ribs -- spareribs, back ribs and country style -- and fresh or smoked hocks offer more menu variety.

Fresh pork should be stored in the coldest part of the refrigerator or in the compartment designed for meat storage. Pork prepacked for self-service should be stored in the original wrapping no longer than 2 to 3 days. Pork not prepackaged should be loosely rewrapped in wax paper or aluminum foil. For freezer storage, wrap pork in freezer wrap or aluminum foil.

Cuts of Pork

1. Jowl
2. Lard
3. Blade Roast
4. Lard, Fat Back
5. Blade Chop, Country-Style Ribs, Loin Roast, Blade Loin
6. Rib, Butterfly, Loin Chop, Back Ribs, Loin Roast, Center Loin, Tenderloin

7. Sirloin Cutlet, Canadian-Style Bacon, Sirloin
8. Tenderloin
9. 15. Pig's Feet
10. Arm Picnic
11. Arm Picnic, Arm Roast, Neck Bones, Arm Steak, Hock
12. Spareribs, Salt Pork
13. Bacon
14. Ham

Temperature and Time for Roasting Cured and Smoked Pork

Cut	Approximate Pound Weight	Oven Temperature	Internal Meat Temperature When Done	Total Roasting Time
Ham (cook before eating) Bone in, half	5 to 7	325°F	160°F.	2½ to 3 hours
Ham (fully cooked) Bone in, half	5 to 7 lbs.	325°F.	140°F.	1½ to 2¼ hours
Boneless, half	3 to 4 lbs.	325°F.	140°F.	1¼ to 1¾ hours
Arm Picnic Shoulder Bone in	5 to 8 lbs.	325°F.	170°F.	2½ to 4 hours
Shoulder Boneless roll	2 to 3 lbs.	325°F.	170°F.	1½ to 1¾ hours

Temperature and Time for Roasting Pork

Cut	Approx. Pound Weight	Oven Temp.	Internal Meat Temp. When Done	Minutes Per Pound Roasting Time
Loin				
Center	3 to 5	325° to 350° F.	170° F.	30 to 35
Half	5 to 7	325° to 350° F.	170° F.	35 to 40
Blade Loin or Sirloin	3 to 4	325° to 350° F.	170° F.	40 to 45
Rolled	3 to 5	325° to 350° F.	170° F.	35 to 45
Picnic Shoulder	5 to 8	325° to 350° F.	170° F.	30 to 35
Rolled	3 to 5	325° to 350° F.	170° F.	35 to 40
Cushion Style	3 to 5	325° to 350° F.	170° F.	30 to 35
Boston Shoulder	4 to 6	325° to 350° F.	170° F.	40 to 45
Leg (Fresh ham)				
Whole (Bone in)	12 to 16	325° to 350° F.	170° F.	22 to 26
Whole (Rolled)	10 to 14	325° to 350° F.	170° F.	24 to 28
Half (Bone in)	5 to 8	325° to 350° F.	170° F.	35 to 40
Spareribs	3	325° to 350° F.	Well done	1½ to 2½ hrs. (total)

Roast Pork with Basil and Mushroom Stuffing

Bake at 325° for about 2½ hours.

Makes 10 servings.

½ **pound medium-size mushrooms**
½ **cup finely chopped fresh basil leaves**
1 small onion, finely chopped (¼ cup)
½ **teaspoon salt**
¼ **teaspoon pepper**
1 rolled boneless pork

loin (about 3¼ pounds)
1 can (13¾ ounces) chicken broth
1 teaspoon butter
2 tablespoons all-purpose flour
Fresh basil leaves for garnish

1. Select a few nice mushrooms for garnish. Trim stems. Wash, and flute tops, if you wish, reserving scraps. Set aside.
2. Wash, trim and chop remaining mushrooms. Add the scraps if you fluted the mushrooms for garnish.
3. Reserve 2 tablespoons of the chopped basil. Combine the remaining chopped basil, chopped mushrooms, onion, ¼ teaspoon of the salt and pepper in a bowl.
4. Preheat the oven to slow (325°).
5. Unroll the pork roast; lay flat on the counter. Starting in the center of the meat and holding a knife parallel to the counter, cut thick part of the loin through the center and almost in half. Fold the piece back like a book to increase size of the loin by ⅓.
6. Spread the basil-mushroom mixture over the meat. Reroll. Tie at 3-inch intervals with string. Place in a shallow roasting pan. Sprinkle remaining salt over top. Pour ¼ cup of the chicken broth around roast. Refrigerate remaining broth.
7. Roast pork in the preheated slow oven (325°) for 2½ hours or until a meat thermometer registers 170°.
8. Just before the roast is done, sauté reserved mushrooms for garnish in the butter in a heavy saucepan until golden. Remove mushrooms; set aside.
9. Reserve ½ cup of the refrigerated chicken broth. Pour remaining broth into the saucepan in which mushrooms were sautéed. Bring to boiling.
10. Remove roast to a warmed serving platter; keep warm. Pour off fat from the roasting pan. Add hot chicken broth to the pan. Stir, scraping up browned bits from the roasting pan. Bring to boiling on top of stove.
11. Meanwhile, stir flour into remaining ½ cup chilled chicken broth until smooth. Gradually add to boiling broth in the roasting pan, stirring rapidly with a wire whisk. Cook until smooth and thickened. Fold in reserved 2 tablespoons chopped basil. Spoon some gravy over roast. Pour the remainder into sauce boat. Garnish roast with reserved mushrooms and fresh basil leaves.

Microwave Directions
650 Watt Variable Power Microwave Oven.
Ingredient Changes: Omit 1 teaspoon butter.

Increase flour from 2 to 3 tablespoons. Brush pork with browning liquid, if you wish.
Directions: Prepare and roll roast as directed, using all the mushrooms in the filling. Place roast, fat-side down, in an 11½ × 7× 2-inch microwave-safe baking dish. Do not sprinkle with salt or add chicken broth. Microwave, uncovered, at full power for 15 minutes. Turn roast over; brush with browning liquid, if using. Sprinkle with the ½ teaspoon salt. Microwave at full power for 20 minutes or until meat thermometer inserted in center of roast registers 165°. Remove roast to serving platter; cover loosely with foil and set aside until it reaches an internal temperature of 170°, about 5 minutes. Drain fat. Add all but ½ cup broth to baking dish. Microwave at full power for 3 minutes. Stir 3 tablespoons flour into reserved ½ cup broth. Whisk into broth in baking dish. Microwave at full power for 3 to 4 minutes, stirring once, until mixture comes to boiling. Fold in reserved basil. Serve as above.

Saucy Loin of Pork with Baked Apples

Cooking time will vary with the temperature of the fire and the weight of the meat. If using charcoal, replenish it periodically.

Makes 6 to 8 servings (with leftovers).

1 boneless loin of pork, rolled and tied (4 to 6 pounds)
1 clove garlic, crushed
½ **cup Dijon-style mustard**
¼ **cup honey**
1 tablespoon lemon juice (½ lemon)
½ **teaspoon chopped fresh marjoram**
OR: ¼ teaspoon leaf marjoram, crumbled
¼ **cup applejack or apple brandy**

1 tablespoon cider vinegar
Dash liquid red-pepper seasoning
½ **teaspoon freshly ground pepper**
6 to 8 red baking apples
4 to 5 tablespoons unsalted butter or margarine, softened
Ground cinnamon
6 to 8 teaspoons brown sugar

1. Wipe the pork with damp paper toweling. Rub the pork well with the garlic.
2. Combine the mustard, honey, lemon juice, marjoram, applejack, vinegar, red-pepper seasoning and pepper in a medium-size bowl; mix well.
3. Coat the pork with ½ cup of the mustard mixture. Let stand at room temperature, lightly covered, for 3 hours. Cover and reserve the remaining basting mixture.
4. Prepare charcoal for grilling with a drip pan in the center under a grid, or preheat a gas unit with a drip pan.
5. Place the pork on the grid or a rotisserie. Cover the

(continued)

Roast Pork with Basil and Mushroom Stuffing, page 498.

grill with dome.* Cook over high heat for 20 to 22 minutes per pound, basting often with the remaining mustard mixture, until the meat thermometer inserted in thickest part of the meat registers 170°. (If cooking over coals, replenish with new charcoal as needed.) Let the roast stand for 10 to 15 minutes before carving.

6. About 30 minutes before serving, rub each apple with 1 teaspoon of the softened butter. Sprinkle each lightly with cinnamon and 1 teaspoon brown sugar. Enclose each apple in a packet of heavy-duty aluminum foil. Place the packets around the pork on the grill. Cook, with grill covered, until tender, 25 to 30 minutes; the apples will give slightly when gently pressed.

7. To serve, remove the apples from the foil. Place upright on a serving dish. Make a cross with a sharp knife in the top of each apple, about 3/4 inch deep. Pour any liquid in foil packets over the apples. Top each with 1 teaspoon of the softened butter.

To construct a barbecue cover or dome, see illustration following Tulsa Ribs in this chapter.

Tangy Glazed Pork Loin

Roast at 325° for 4 hours.

Makes 12 servings.

1 boneless loin of pork (6 to 7 pounds)	**1/2 cup lemon juice**
2 tablespoons vegetable oil	**1/3 cup molasses**
1 large onion, finely chopped (1 cup)	**3 tablespoons Dijon mustard**
2 cloves garlic, finely chopped	**1 tablespoon Worcestershire sauce**
1 cup chili sauce	**1/4 cup dark rum**

1. Place pork on a rack in a large shallow roasting pan. Do not add water or cover.
2. Roast in a slow oven (325°) for 3 hours.
3. Heat oil in a medium-size saucepan; add onion and garlic. Sauté 5 minutes until onion is tender but not brown.
4. Stir in chili sauce, lemon juice, molasses, mustard and Worcestershire; bring to boiling; lower heat; cover; simmer 20 minutes. Stir in rum.
5. Brush pork with glaze. Continue roasting for 1 hour or until pork registers 170° on meat thermometer, basting frequently with additional glaze.
6. Garnish with sugared grapes, spiced crabapples, whole canned apricots and chicory, if you wish.

How to Carve a Pork Loin Roast

Before placing roast on platter, remove backbone, leaving as little meat on it as possible.

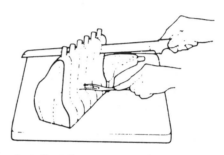

Place roast so that the concave rib side faces carver. The carver can easily cut straight down between ribs, dividing roast into chops.

Orange-Glazed Loin of Pork

Roast at 325° for 2 hours.

Makes 4 servings.

1 loin of pork (about 3 1/2 pounds)	**1 tablespoon grated orange rind**
1 1/2 teaspoons salt	**1 cup orange juice**
1/2 teaspoon pepper	**1/4 cup firmly packed brown sugar**
1/2 teaspoon leaf thyme, crumbled	**1 1/2 tablespoons soy sauce**
1/2 teaspoon ground ginger	**1 tablespoon cornstarch**
2 cloves garlic, sliced	
2 cups water	

1. Rub meat with salt, pepper, thyme and ginger. Make several incisions between the ribs with a sharp knife. Insert a piece of garlic in each cut.
2. Place pork on a rack in a roasting pan. Insert meat thermometer into meaty part of roast, so it is not touching bone or resting in fat. Pour 1 1/3 cups of the water into roasting pan.
3. Roast in a slow oven (325°) for 1 hour.
4. While meat is roasting, prepare orange glaze: Combine orange rind and juice, brown sugar and soy sauce in a small bowl; blend well. Remove and reserve 2/3 cup for orange sauce.

5. Brush pork with remaining glaze. Continue roasting, brushing occasionally with glaze until meat is nicely glazed and meat thermometer registers 170° or about 1 hour longer. Remove roast from oven to heated platter.

6. For orange sauce: Combine reserved glaze with remaining ²/₃ cup water and the cornstarch in a small saucepan. Heat, stirring constantly, until mixture thickens and bubbles; cook 1 minute. Slice loin; serve with orange sauce.

Crown Roast of Pork with Wild Rice Stuffing

This succulent pièce de résistance is an unforgettable combination of tastes.

Bake at 400° for 10 minutes then at 325° for 3 to 3¹/₂ hours.

Makes 8 servings.

1 crown roast of pork (6 to 7 pounds)*
2 packages (6 ounces each) wild rice mix
¹/₂ cup chopped onion (1 medium-size)
¹/₃ cup chopped celery
1 clove garlic, finely chopped
¹/₄ cup (¹/₂ stick) butter or margarine
¹/₂ cup pine nuts
1 package (8 ounces) dried apricots,
chopped
6 tablespoons chopped, drained, preserved ginger**
¹/₂ teaspoon ground allspice
6 whole cloves
2 bay leaves
³/₄ cup to 1 cup Madeira wine
1 can (13³/₄ ounces) beef broth
Kumquats (optional)

1. Preheat the oven to hot (400°). Place the roast on a rack in a large, shallow roasting pan.
2. Cook the rice according to label directions.
3. Sauté the onion, celery and garlic in butter in a skillet just until tender, about 5 minutes.
4. Combine the sautéed vegetables, rice, pine nuts, ginger and allspice in a bowl; mix well. Spoon lightly into the center of the roast. (Spoon any extra stuffing into a buttered, shallow baking dish; bake during the last 20 minutes of roasting.) Cover the ends of bones and top of the stuffing with foil.
5. Roast in the preheated hot oven (400°) for 10 minutes. Lower the oven temperature to slow (325°). Roast for 30 minutes per pound of meat, 3 to 3¹/₂ hours, or until a meat thermometer registers 170° when inserted in the thickest part of the roast; do not let the thermometer touch bone or fat.
6. Remove the roast to a heated serving platter. Keep warm while preparing the gravy.
7. To prepare the gravy: Skim off and discard the fat from the pan drippings. Add the cloves, bay leaves, Madeira and broth to the juices in the pan. Cook over medium heat, scraping up any browned bits from the pan. Increase the heat to high; cook until the gravy is reduced by a third. Strain into a sauce boat. Serve

with the roast and any extra stuffing. Garnish the rib ends with the kumquats, if you wish.

To Make Ahead: The stuffing can be made early in the day.

*Order the roast several days ahead and ask your butcher to assemble and tip the crown roast.

**Preserved ginger is packed in syrup under the Raffeto label and can be found in the gourmet section of the supermarket.

Crown Roast of Pork with Apple-Herb Stuffing

A festive roast with a tangy-sweet apple stuffing. You can order a crown roast in advance from the supermarket meat department when pork is the special for the week, or you can follow our directions for preparing a crown roast at home.

Roast at 325° for 3 to 3¹/₂ hours.

Makes 8 to 10 servings.

1 sixteen-chop crown roast of pork* (about 7 pounds)
1 teaspoon salt
¹/₄ teaspoon pepper
¹/₄ teaspoon leaf sage, crumbled
Apple-Herb
Stuffing (recipe follows)
2 tablespoons light molasses (optional)
2 tablespoons apple or orange juice (optional)
3 tablespoons flour

1. Place roast, rib ends up, in shallow roasting pan; rub well with mixture of salt, pepper and sage. Insert meat thermometer into meaty portion without touching bone or fat.
2. Roast in a slow oven (325°) for 1¹/₂ hours. (Total roasting time based on weight of roast × 35 minutes per pound.) Meanwhile, prepare Apple-Herb Stuffing.
3. Remove roast from oven. Pack stuffing lightly into hollow in the roast, mounding it slightly. Cover stuffing loosely with foil.
4. Return roast to oven; roast 1¹/₂ hours longer or until thermometer registers 170°. If you wish, brush roast with mixture of molasses and apple or orange juice several times during last 15 minutes to glaze.
5. Lift roast carefully onto carving board or heated platter with 2 wide spatulas. Keep warm while making gravy.
6. Pour drippings into a 2-cup measure. Let fat rise to top, then skim off. Measure 2 tablespoons of the fat into a small saucepan. Blend in flour; heat until bubbly. Add water to drippings remaining in cup to make 1³/₄ cups; gradually stir into flour mixture. Cook,

(continued)

Overleaf: Crown Roast of Pork with Wild Rice Stuffing, page 501; Green Beans and Herbed Walnut, Mushroom and Orange Salad, page 689.

stirring constantly until gravy thickens and bubbles 2 minutes. Taste and season with salt and pepper. Serve with Crown Roast. To serve: Slip paper frills over ends of chop bones. Garnish platter with watercress. Carve into chops between ribs, serving a portion of stuffing with each serving.

To make crown roast yourself, buy 2 rib roasts of pork, 8 ribs on each; have butcher crack backbone so it will be flexible. Trim meat from rib ends 3/4- to 1-inch down; place roasts end to end and tie last bone from each together with string at top and bottom. Curve roast to make a ring shape and tie opposite ends together. Tie a string all the way around roast.

Apple-Herb Stuffing

This versatile stuffing is excellent with roast chicken, baked ham or braised sausage.

Makes about 5 cups.

3 medium-size onions, chopped (1 1/2 cups)	1/2 teaspoon leaf sage, crumbled
1/2 cup sliced celery	1/2 teaspoon leaf thyme, crumbled
6 tablespoons butter or margarine	1/4 teaspoon ground nutmeg
3 cups finely diced baking apples	2 envelopes or teaspoons instant chicken broth
3 cups whole-wheat bread cubes	1/2 cup hot water
1/4 cup chopped fresh parsley	

1. Sauté onions and celery in butter in skillet until soft, 5 minutes. Stir in apples; continue cooking and stirring 3 to 5 minutes. Remove from heat.
2. Combine with bread, parsley, sage, thyme, nutmeg, instant chicken broth and water in a large bowl. Toss until evenly moist.

Savory Stuffed Pork Chops

Makes 4 servings.

1 medium-size onion, finely chopped (1/2 cup)	crumbled
	1/2 teaspoon leaf thyme, crumbled
1/2 cup chopped celery	1/4 teaspoon pepper
3 tablespoons butter or margarine	1 egg, slightly beaten
4 slices raisin bread, crumbled (1 1/2 cups)	4 pork chops, each cut about 1 3/4 inches thick
1 small apple, pared, cored and chopped	1/4 cup (1/2 stick) butter or margarine
1/4 cup chopped fresh parsley	1/3 cup water
1 teaspoon salt	2 tablespoons flour
1/2 teaspoon leaf sage,	1 cup chicken broth

1. Sauté onion and celery in the 3 tablespoons butter in a large skillet, about 4 minutes or until tender. Remove from heat. Add bread crumbs, apple, parsley,

salt, sage, thyme and pepper; toss lightly. Add egg and mix well.
2. Cut a deep pocket in the fatty side of each chop with a sharp knife. Fill pockets loosely with stuffing; fasten openings with wooden picks.
3. Melt remaining 1/4 cup butter in a large skillet. Brown chops, about 4 minutes on each side. Add water to skillet; bring to boiling; lower heat; cover. Simmer 40 minutes or until chops are tender. Transfer to heated platter.
4. Stir flour into drippings in skillet; cook 1 minute. Stir in chicken broth. Cook, stirring constantly, until gravy thickens. Serve with chops.

Cornbread-Stuffed Pork Chops

Bake at 350° for 1 hour.

Makes 6 servings.

1/4 cup (1/2 stick) butter or margarine	1 3/4-inches thick
1 small onion, chopped (1/4 cup)	2 tablespoons vegetable oil
1/2 cup chopped celery	1 1/4 cups canned chicken broth
1 package (6 ounces) cornbread stuffing mix	Sautéed Apples (recipe follows)
1 1/2 cups water	1 tablespoon cornstarch
6 thick rib pork chops each cut about	1/2 teaspoon salt
	1/4 teaspoon pepper

1. Melt butter in a medium-size saucepan; sauté onion and celery just until tender. Add seasoning packet from stuffing mix and water; bring to boiling. Cover and simmer 5 minutes. Remove from heat; stir in stuffing mix.
2. Cut a pocket into the fatty side of each pork chop with a sharp knife. Lightly pack stuffing into each pocket; secure with wooden picks to hold in stuffing.
3. Heat oil in a large skillet. Brown chops on each side. Place in a 12 × 8 × 2-inch pan, stuffed-side up. Cover with aluminum foil.
4. Bake in a moderate oven (350°) for 30 minutes; remove foil. Add 3/4 cup of the chicken broth. Bake 30 minutes longer or until chops are fork-tender.
5. While chops bake, prepare Sautéed Apples. Spoon onto platter. Arrange chops over apples; keep warm. Garnish platter with celery leaves, if you wish.
6. To make gravy: Combine cornstarch with remaining 1/2 cup chicken broth. Stir into juices remaining in baking pan. Cook, stirring to loosen any brown bits, until thickened and bubbly. Stir in salt and pepper. Skim off any fat from gravy. Spoon some gravy over chops; serve remainder in gravy boat.

Pictured opposite: Cornbread-Stuffed Pork Chops with Sautéed Apples, page 504, 506.

Sautéed Apples

Makes 6 servings.

2 tablespoons butter
 or margarine
3 red cooking apples,
 quartered, cored
 and sliced
2 tablespoons brown

sugar
1 tablespoon lemon
 juice
1/4 teaspoon ground
 cinnamon

Melt butter in a large skillet. Add apples, sugar, lemon juice and cinnamon. Sauté, stirring gently, just until apples are tender.

Herb-Stuffed Pork Chops

Bake at 350° for 1 hour.

Makes 4 servings.

1/2 pound medium-size
 mushrooms
1/3 cup chopped onion
1/3 cup chopped celery
1/4 cup (1/2 stick) butter
 or margarine
1 cup packaged bread
 crumbs
1/4 teaspoon ground
 sage
1/2 cup chopped

fresh parsley
1/2 cup dried apricots
4 double-ribbed center
 loin pork chops
 with pockets
1/2 teaspoon salt
1/4 teaspoon pepper
1 cup dry white wine
Sweet-Sour Red
 Cabbage (recipe
 follows)

1. Reserve 4 mushrooms for garnish; thinly slice remainder. Sauté sliced mushrooms, onion and celery in 2 tablespoons of the butter in a large flame-proof baking dish or skillet with an ovenproof handle until tender about 3 minutes. Add bread crumbs, sage and parsley.
2. Reserve 4 apricots; chop remainder; add to skillet mixture. Sprinkle pork chops inside and out with salt and pepper. Stuff pork chop pockets loosely with mixture. Secure openings with wooden picks. Wipe out dish.
3. Brown chops on both sides in remaining 2 tablespoons butter in same oven-proof dish. Pour wine around chops; cover dish.
4. Bake in a moderate oven (350°) for 1 hour or until chops are tender. Garnish with reserved mushrooms and apricots, and add a few crisp celery tops for color. Serve with Sweet-Sour Red Cabbage.

Sweet-Sour Red Cabbage: Sauté 1 small chopped onion in 3 tablespoons butter in a Dutch oven or large skillet until tender, about 3 minutes. Shred 1 medium-size head red cabbage; add to pan with 1/2 cup orange juice and 1/2 teaspoon salt. Cover; simmer 10 minutes. Stir in 1 cup cranberries, 1/4 cup water and 1/2 cup sugar; re-cover; simmer 5 minutes longer. Combine 2 teaspoons cornstarch with 3 tablespoons vinegar; add to pan; cook and stir until thickened.

Braised Pork Chops with Cabbage

Makes 4 servings.

4 to 6 thin pork chops
 (about 1 1/4 pounds)
1 tablespoon butter
1 small red cabbage
 (about 1 pound),
 shredded
1 apple, red or green,
 halved, cored and
 sliced
2 tablespoons brown
 sugar
1 teaspoon salt

1/2 teaspoon caraway
 seeds
1/8 teaspoon ground
 pepper
3 tablespoons cider
 vinegar
Frozen fried potato
 rounds, cooked
 according to label
 directions
Watercress (optional)

1. Brown pork chops on both sides in a large heavy skillet over medium-high heat. Remove chops from the skillet.
2. Add butter, cabbage, apple, sugar, salt, caraway seeds, pepper and vinegar to skillet. Cook over low heat, stirring, until well mixed.
3. Return chops to the skillet. Cover; cook over low heat for 15 to 20 minutes, or until pork and cabbage are tender. Arrange on a platter with potato rounds. Garnish with watercress, if you wish.

Pork Chop and Scalloped Potato Casserole

Bake at 350° for 1 hour, 10 minutes.

Makes 4 servings.

4 pork chops, each cut
 about 3/4-inch thick
2 tablespoons
 vegetable oil
1 large onion, sliced
 and separated into
 rings
3 tablespoons butter
3 tablespoons flour
1 teaspoon salt

1/4 teaspoon pepper
1 cup milk
1 cup chicken broth
4 medium-size
 potatoes, pared and
 thinly sliced
 (4 cups)
1 tablespoon chopped
 fresh parsley

1. Brown chops in oil in a large skillet, about 3 minutes on each side. Remove to plate. Add onion rings to skillet; sauté until tender, about 3 minutes. Remove from heat; reserve.
2. Melt butter in a medium-size saucepan. Stir in flour, salt and pepper; cook 1 minute. Add milk and broth slowly. Cook, stirring constantly, until sauce thickens and bubbles. Remove from heat.
3. Arrange sliced potatoes in buttered 11 × 7 × 2-inch baking dish. Top with the reserved onion rings. Pour sauce evenly over potatoes and onions. Top with chops. Cover baking dish tightly with aluminum foil.
4. Bake in a moderate oven (350°) for 1 hour. Uncover; bake 10 minutes longer or until chops and potatoes are tender. Sprinkle with parsley. Garnish with tomato roses, if you wish.

Pork Chops with Scalloped Potato Casserole, page 506.

Pork Chops with Red Cabbage

Makes 4 servings.

**4 loin pork chops, cut
1-inch thick
(1³/₄ pounds)**
**1 large onion,
chopped (1 cup)**
1 jar (15 ounces)

**sweet/sour red
cabbage**
**1 small red apple,
quartered, cored
and sliced**

1. Place pork chops in a large skillet over low heat.

(Do not add fat.) Cook chops slowly in their own fat until brown; turn; brown other side. Remove.
2. Add onion to fat in skillet; sauté 5 minutes. Arrange pork chops over onions. Lower heat; cover. Cook 30 minutes, turning once. Remove cover; cook, turning chops once or twice until glazed and most of the liquid has evaporated. Remove chops; keep warm.
3. Drain liquid from cabbage; stir cabbage into skillet with apple slices; cook until heated thoroughly. Arrange pork chops over mixture.

Braised Stuffed Pork Chops

Makes 4 servings.

4 double-thick loin
  pork chops (about
  6 ounces each)
1 small tart apple,
  peeled, cored and
  diced
1 small onion, finely
  chopped (¼ cup)
2 tablespoons butter
  or margarine
1¾ cups soft bread
  crumbs

¼ cup raisins,
  chopped
½ teaspoon salt
¼ teaspoon powdered
  sage
⅛ teaspoon pepper
All-purpose flour
2 tablespoons
  vegetable oil
¼ cup chicken broth
Apple slices and
  parsley for garnish

1. Cut a pocket in each chop. Set aside.
2. Sauté the apple and onion in the butter in a medium-size skillet until soft, 4 minutes. Mix in the crumbs, raisins, salt, sage and pepper. Spoon the stuffing in the chop pockets. Close the openings with wooden picks. Dredge the chops in the flour.
3. Brown the chops on both sides in the oil in a heavy skillet. Pour off the drippings. Add the broth to the skillet. Cover; cook over medium-low heat for about 45 minutes or until the chops are tender. Remove the wooden picks before serving. Garnish with the apple slices and parsley.

To Make Ahead: Cut the pockets in the chops; wrap the chops in aluminum foil and refrigerate until ready to stuff and cook. Prepare the stuffing mixture, place it in a medium-size bowl, cover and refrigerate until ready to stuff and cook the chops. When ready to stuff and cook, proceed as the recipe directs.

Plum Good Pork Chops

Bake at 375° for 1 hour.

Makes 8 servings.

8 pork chops, each cut
  about 1-inch thick
1 large onion,
  chopped (1 cup)
3 cups fresh bread
  crumbs (6 slices)
8 purple plums,
  halved, pitted and
  quartered

1 teaspoon salt
1 teaspoon pumpkin
  pie spice
1 can (6 ounces)
  frozen limeade
  concentrate, thawed
2 tablespoons soy
  sauce

1. Render a 1-inch piece of trimmed fat from pork chops in a large skillet. Brown chops in skillet; remove chops; reserve.

2. To make a stuffing: Add onion to drippings in skillet and sauté until soft. Stir in bread crumbs, plums, salt, pumpkin pie spice and ⅓ cup of the undiluted limeade concentrate. Toss lightly to blend.
3. Alternately overlap reserved pork chops and stuffing in a shallow 10-cup baking dish; cover with aluminum foil.
4. Bake in a moderate oven (375°) for 45 minutes. Combine remaining limeade and soy sauce in a cup. Uncover dish; brush chops and stuffing with half of the mixture.
5. Bake 15 minutes longer or until chops are well glazed, brushing halfway with remaining limeade mixture.

Country Pork and Blackeyed Peas

Makes 4 to 6 servings, plus meat for another meal.

1 pound dried
  blackeyed peas
1 smoked pork

picnic shoulder
  (about 7 pounds)
Salt and pepper

1. Pick over peas and rinse under running water; place in a medium-size bowl. Add water to cover; let stand overnight; drain. To quick soak: Combine peas and water in a large kettle. Bring to boiling; cover kettle; boil 2 minutes; remove from heat; let stand 1 hour. Drain.
2. Place pork in a kettle; add water to cover. Heat to boiling; cover. Simmer 1½ hours.
3. Add peas to kettle; cover. Simmer 1½ hours longer or until pork and peas are tender. Remove pork from kettle; trim off skin and fat; slice about half of the pork ¼ inch thick.
4. Season peas to taste with salt and pepper; spoon onto a deep large platter; arrange pork slices over top. Wrap remaining pork and chill for another use.

Mu Shu Pork
(Shredded Pork and Eggs)

Makes 8 servings.

½ pound lean
  boneless pork
½ bunch green onions
5 tablespoons
  vegetable oil
2 cups thinly sliced or
  shredded Chinese
  cabbage
1 cup fresh mung
  bean sprouts
1 can (8½ ounces

sliced bamboo
  shoots, drained
4 eggs, beaten
1 tablespoon sesame
  seeds
2 tablespoons soy
  sauce
½ teaspoon salt
½ teaspoon sugar
Mandarin Pancakes
  (recipe follows)

1. Cut pork into match-size strips. Cut onions into 2-inch lengths, then cut lengthwise pieces into shreds.
2. Heat large, deep skillet, Dutch oven or wok over high heat. Add 1 tablespoon of the oil; swirl to coat

bottom and sides. Add onions, cabbage, sprouts and bamboo shoots, Stir-fry with large metal spoon just until vegetables are wilted; remove to large bowl.

3. Reheat pan; add 2 more tablespoons oil. Add eggs, swirling pan to spread eggs into a thin layer. Cook until firm, breaking eggs into small pieces. Remove to bowl with vegetables.

4. Reheat pan; add sesame seeds and remaining oil. Add pork; stir-fry until browned and thoroughly cooked. Add soy sauce, salt and sugar. Return vegetable-egg mixture to pan. Stir-fry until heated. Serve as filling for Mandarin Pancakes.

5. Have each person fill his own pancakes. Place rounded spoonful of pork mixture in center of pancake, fold 1 side over and then fold over other side, envelope-style. Roll pancake over filling and eat with fingers, keeping open side of pancake up.

Mandarin Pancakes

Makes 16 servings.

2 cups *unsifted* all-purpose flour
¼ teaspoon salt

¾ cup boiling water
Vegetable oil

1. Mix flour and salt in a large bowl. Stir in boiling water with fork until mixture is moist. Gather into a ball. Turn out onto floured surface; knead until dough is smooth and soft, about 3 minutes. Let dough rest 10 minutes.

2. Shape dough into a roll about 16 inches long. Cut crosswise into 16 pieces. Keep pieces covered with plastic wrap while shaping.

3. Flatten 2 pieces with fingers into two 3-inch patties. Brush tops with oil, then sandwich patties with oiled tops together. Roll patties with lightly floured rolling pin from center to edges to form a thin pancake 7 inches in diameter, turning it frequently to roll both sides evenly. (Be sure not to roll edges too thinly, because you'll have to be able to separate the pancake into 2 thin layers.)

4. Repeat rolling until half is shaped. Keep pancakes stacked with wax paper between.

5. Heat a large griddle or skillet over medium heat. Cook pancakes, 1 at a time, for 1 minute on each side or until puffed in center and firm but not browned. While warm, separate each into 2 thin pancakes. Keep in plastic bag while shaping and baking remainder.

6. To make ahead, wrap in aluminum foil and refrigerate or freeze. To reheat, place in pie plate set on rack over boiling water in kettle. Cover and steam 10 minutes or until soft and hot.

Chinese Roast Pork

Bake at 350° for 35 minutes, then at 450° for 15 minutes.

Makes 12 servings as an appetizer or 6 servings as a main dish.

3 pounds lean pork butt or pork shoulder
⅓ cup dry sherry
2 cloves garlic, crushed
3 tablespoons dark soy sauce

½ cup catsup
3 tablespoons dark brown sugar
1 teaspoon salt
8 drops red food coloring
¼ cup honey

1. Cut pork into strips about 5 × 1 × 1 inches.

2. Combine remaining ingredients, except honey, in a large flat pan. Marinate pork in sauce for at least 4 hours in the refrigerator, turning occasionally.

3. After marinating, preheat oven to 350°. Drain pork and brush each piece with honey. Arrange on wire rack over foil-lined roasting pan.

4. Bake in a preheated moderate oven (350°) for 35 minutes. Turn heat to very hot (450°); bake 15 to 20 minutes longer, brushing occasionally with reserved marinade. Cool pork and slice.

Sweet and Sour Pork with Noodles

Makes 4 servings.

3 quarts water
1½ pounds lean loin pork chops
1 egg, beaten
¼ cup all-purpose flour
2 tablespoons water
1½ teaspoons salt
1 can (8 ounces) pineapple chunks in pineapple juice
1 tablespoon cornstarch
3 tablespoons distilled white vinegar

1 tablespoon sugar
2 tablespoons soy sauce
¼ cup dry sherry
¼ cup vegetable oil
1 package (8 ounces) small curly noodles
2 green peppers, halved, seeded and cut into strips
½ cup chopped green onions
2 tomatoes, cut in wedges

1. Heat water to boiling in a large covered kettle.

2. While water heats, remove pork meat from bones; cut into ½-inch pieces.

3. Combine egg, flour, water and ½ teaspoon salt in small bowl. Stir in pork to coat well.

4. Drain pineapple juice into a small bowl; add

(continued)

cornstarch, vinegar, sugar, soy sauce and sherry. Reserve.

5. Add ¹/₂ teaspoon of the oil and remaining 1 teaspoon of the salt to boiling water. Add noodles slowly so that water continues to boil. Cook about 5 minutes or until noodles are tender. Drain; keep warm.

6. Heat remaining oil in wok or skillet. Stir-fry pork until brown, about 5 minutes. Stir in green pepper, onions and reserved sauce from step 4; cover; cook 5 minutes longer.

7. Stir in pineapple chunks and tomato wedges. Serve hot over noodles.

Polynesian Roast Pork

Roast at 325° for about 2 hours.

Makes 6 servings.

1 center cut loin of pork (about 4 pounds)	**concentrate**
	¹/₃ cup soy sauce
	¹/₃ cup chopped green onions
1 can (6 ounces) frozen pineapple-orange juice	**1 orange**

1. Place pork in shallow bowl or baking dish. Combine juice concentrate and soy sauce; pour over pork to marinate, turning often, 2 hours at room temperature or several hours in the refrigerator.

2. Remove pork from dish; reserve marinade. Place pork, fat-side up, on rack in roasting pan. Make deep cuts (about 2 inches) with the tip of a knife into meat between each chop; fill each cut with onions, dividing evenly. If using a meat thermometer, insert bulb into center of meat without touching bone.

3. Roast in a slow oven (325°) for 1¹/₂ hours. Brush pork with part of marinade. Continue roasting 30 minutes, brushing several times with marinade until thermometer registers 170° and pork is richly glazed.

4. Heat remaining marinade in small saucepan; skim fat from drippings in pan and add any drippings to saucepan. Add ¹/₂ cup diced fresh orange. Garnish roast with remaining orange cut into wedges. Carve roast between ribs into serving-size pieces. Serve with hot rice and buttered green beans, if you wish.

Sparerib   The finger-licking cut of pork consisting of long rib bones with a thin covering of meat on the outside and between the ribs. It is obtained from the lower portion of the rib cage. The upper portion is where pork chops are cut from. Country-style ribs are meatier than spareribs. They are made by splitting the blade end pork loin into halves lengthwise. Country-style ribs contain part of the loin eye muscle and either rib bones or backbones. Pork back ribs are cut from the blade and center section of the loin. They contain the upper rib bones and a layer of meat from the loin eye muscle. Pork back ribs are usually obtained when pork loins are boned for roasts.

Because of the amount of bone, allow ³/₄ to 1 pound per serving.

Plum-Glazed Spareribs

Grill for 30 minutes.

Makes 8 servings.

6 pounds spareribs, cut into 2-rib sections	**¹/₃ cup cider vinegar**
Water	**¹/₃ cup prepared horseradish**
2 teaspoons salt	**1 small onion, finely chopped**
1¹/₂ pounds fresh red plums	**1 clove garlic, crushed**
1 cup sugar	**1 tablespoon salt**

1. Put ribs in large Dutch oven. Add water to cover ribs plus the 2 teaspoons salt. Bring to boiling; lower heat; cover. Simmer 30 minutes or until ribs are almost tender.

2. While ribs are cooking, prepare glaze. Halve, pit and slice plums. Combine with sugar, vinegar, horseradish, onion, garlic and the 1 tablespoon salt in medium-size saucepan. Bring to boiling, stirring often; lower heat. Simmer 5 minutes or until plums are tender.

3. Pour half the plum mixture into container of electric blender; puree until smooth; pour puree into bowl. Repeat with other half. Reserve 1 cup plum mixture in small bowl; chill to serve as dipping sauce.

4. Drain ribs and pat dry with paper toweling. Place in shallow glass or enamel dish. Pour remaining plum mixture over ribs. Let ribs marinate 2 hours at room temperature or in refrigerator overnight.

5. Drain ribs, reserving plum mixture. Place ribs on grill. Grill ribs 30 minutes, turning often and brushing generously with mixture until ribs are browned and evenly glazed. Arrange ribs on platter lined with lemon leaves and garnish with plum halves and canned lychees stuffed with maraschino cherries, if you wish. Serve ribs with reserved plum mixture as a dipping sauce.

Note: If fresh plums are not available, use recipe for Polynesian Glaze instead of the glaze above.

Polynesian Glaze

Makes about 3 cups.

1 jar (12 ounces) apricot preserves	**2 tablespoons Worcestershire sauce**
1 can (8 ounces) crushed pineapple	**1 teaspoon ground ginger**
¹/₂ cup catsup	**1 teaspoon dry mustard**
¹/₄ cup cider or wine vinegar	

Combine all ingredients in small saucepan; heat to boiling, stirring constantly. Lower heat; simmer 1 minute. Use to glaze pork or ham.

Plum-Glazed Spareribs, page 510; Buttered Sweet Potatoes, page 776; Pineapple Luau Style, page 336; Bananas Hawaiian, page 336.

Polynesian Spareribs

Cook these luscious, gooey spareribs over charcoal or in the oven. We also give you two different methods for precooking.

Bake at 300° for 1 hour, or grill for 45 minutes to 1 hour.

Makes 6 servings.

5 to 6 pounds pork spareribs, cut into 2-rib sections	**juice concentrate, thawed**
Polynesian Sauce:	**¹/₂ cup apricot nectar**
2 teaspoons cornstarch	**3 tablespoons soy sauce**
1 can (6 ounces) frozen pineapple	**1 tablespoon distilled white or cider vinegar**

1. Precook the ribs using one of the following methods: (a) Place the ribs in a Dutch oven or large pot. Cover with cold water. Bring to boiling. Lower the heat and simmer, partially covered, for 45 minutes. Drain. Or (b), place the ribs in a large, shallow baking pan, curved-side up. Add 2 cups of water. Bake in a preheated very hot oven (450°) for 30 minutes. Drain.
2. Meanwhile, prepare the Polynesian sauce: Place the cornstarch in a small saucepan. Gradually stir in the juice concentrate until smooth. Stir in the apricot nectar, soy sauce and vinegar. Cook over medium heat, stirring constantly, until thickened and bubbly. Remove from the heat.
3. To Bake Ribs: Preheat the oven to slow (300°). Place the precooked ribs in a large, shallow baking pan. Brush with the sauce. Bake in the preheated slow oven (300°), for about 1 hour or until the meat is very tender, basting occasionally with the sauce. Or, grill for 45 minutes to 1 hour or until the meat is very tender, turning the ribs often and brushing with the sauce.

Note: For the photograph, we precooked an uncut rack of spareribs in the oven, then finished baking the rack in the oven, brushing often with the sauce.

Ribs Tip   Home-cooked ribs taste best if precooked, either by oven roasting or parboiling, before saucing and baking.

Know Your Ribs   Baby backs, cut from a porker's back, include the rib bone and meat from the eye of a loin. They are generally meatier but more expensive.

Spareribs are the larger variety and include the breast bone, rib bones and rib cartilage.

Spareribs Kun Koki

Grill 20 minutes.

Makes 4 servings.

4 pounds spareribs
1/2 cup catsup
1/4 cup lime juice
1/4 cup soy sauce
1/4 cup honey

1. Simmer spareribs, covered, in enough boiling water to cover in a kettle for 1 hour or just until tender; drain.
2. Mix catsup, lime juice and soy sauce in a small saucepan; brush part over one side of ribs. Place ribs, sauce-side down, on grill about 6 inches above hot coals; brush other side with sauce.
3. Grill 10 minutes, turning once. Blend honey into remaining sauce; brush over ribs. Grill, turning and brushing once or twice with remaining honey mixture, 10 minutes or until meat is tender and richly glazed.
4. Remove to a carving board; cut into serving-size pieces of 1 or 2 ribs each.

Sweet and Pungent Pork

A popular and uniquely Chinese concoction of pork and vegetables.

Makes 4 servings.

1 pound boneless lean pork
1/2 cup all-purpose flour
1 1/4 teaspoons salt
1/2 teaspoon baking powder
1/2 cup cold water
1 can (20 ounces) pineapple chunks in pineapple juice
1 tablespoon cornstarch
2 tablespoons distilled white vinegar
1 medium-size green pepper, halved and seeded
2 carrots, pared
Vegetable oil for frying
1/4 cup sugar

1. Cut pork into 1-inch cubes. Combine flour, 1 teaspoon of the salt and the baking powder in a medium-size bowl; add water, stirring until smooth. Add pork cubes; stir until coated with mixture.
2. Drain juice from pineapple into a 1-cup measure; stir in cornstarch, vinegar and remaining salt. Cut green pepper into 1-inch squares. Cut carrots into paper-thin diagonal slices.
3. Heat 1 inch of oil in a 4-quart saucepan or Dutch oven to 370°. Fry pork cubes until golden brown, removing browned pieces with slotted spoon to paper toweling to drain. Cut one cube to make sure pork is thoroughly cooked.
4. Carefully pour off all oil from pan (you can

refrigerate the oil and reuse it in other recipes). Return 1 tablespoon oil to pan. Add carrots; stir-fry 1 minute. Add green peppers; stir-fry 2 minutes; remove to small bowl. Add sugar to pan. Heat until melted and amber in color, watching carefully so that it does not burn. Remove pan from heat.
5. Restir cornstarch mixture; pour over melted sugar. It will sizzle, but stir until smooth. Cook over medium heat until thickened and bubbly. Return vegetables; cook until carrots are tender. Add pineapple and pork cubes; spoon onto platter.

Sweet and Sour Ribs

Grill 20 to 30 minutes.

Makes 6 to 8 servings.

6 pounds spareribs
1/2 cup vinegar
1 cup catsup
1/2 cup water
1/2 cup soy sauce
1/2 cup honey
2 or 3 cloves garlic, minced
1/2 teaspoon seasoned salt

1. Cut ribs into serving-size portions. Simmer, covered, in vinegar and enough water to cover in a kettle for 1 hour or just until tender; drain.
2. While ribs are cooking, combine catsup, water, soy sauce, honey, garlic and seasoned salt in a large saucepan. Cook over very low heat, stirring occasionally, for 45 minutes or until thick.
3. Arrange ribs in single layer on grill about 6 to 8 inches above hot coals; grill for 20 to 30 minutes, basting with the sauce and turning often until ribs are glazed.

Shortcut Pork Saté

Makes 6 servings.

6 thin pork chops (1 1/4 pounds)
1 tablespoon vegetable oil
1/2 cup peanuts
1 tablespoon honey
2 tablespoons soy sauce
1 clove garlic
1/2 teaspoon coriander seeds
1/4 teaspoon crushed red pepper
1/2 cup chicken broth
1 large orange, peeled and sliced

1. Cook chops slowly on both sides in hot oil in a large skillet, allowing about 8 minutes on each side. Pour off fat.
2. Combine peanuts, honey, soy sauce, garlic, coriander seeds, red pepper and chicken broth in container of electric blender; cover. Whirl until almost smooth.
3. Pour blended sauce over browned chops in skillet. Cover and simmer over low heat for 15 minutes or until tender.
4. To serve: Spoon sauce over chops; top each with slice of orange. Serve with cooked rice, if you wish.

Pictured opposite:
Tangy Glazed Pork Loin, page 500.

Pork Saté

Makes 4 servings.

1/4 cup peanut butter	1/8 teaspoon cayenne
1/4 cup grated onion	2 tablespoons water
1 clove garlic, minced	1 tablespoon soy
1 1/2 teaspoons light	sauce
brown sugar	1 tablespoon lemon
3/4 teaspoon ground	juice
coriander	1 pound boneless
1/2 teaspoon ground	pork, cut into
cumin	3/4-inch cubes

1. Line the broiler pan with a sheet of aluminum foil.
2. Combine peanut butter, onion, garlic, sugar, coriander, cumin, cayenne, water, soy and lemon juice in a medium-size bowl; add pork cubes and toss to coat. Place in a single layer on prepared pan.
3. Broil 4 inches from heat for 5 minutes; turn with large cooking spoon; broil 5 minutes longer or until done.

Note: Pork cubes can be placed on skewers and broiled. If you wish, pork can be marinated in peanut butter mixture overnight in the refrigerator.

Barbecued Country-Style Spareribs

Grill 20 to 30 minutes.

Makes 4 servings.

3 to 4 pounds country-	1/2 cup orange juice
style spareribs	1 tablespoon grated
1/2 cup firmly packed	onion
brown sugar	1/2 teaspoon garlic
1 tablespoon dry	powder
mustard	1 tablespoon
1 teaspoon salt	Worcestershire
1/8 teaspoon pepper	sauce
1 teaspoon ground	Fresh pineapple slices
ginger	(optional)
1/2 cup tomato sauce	

1. Simmer ribs, covered, in enough boiling water to cover in a kettle for 30 minutes. Drain and arrange in a shallow, nonmetal dish.
2. Combine sugar, mustard, salt, pepper, ginger, tomato sauce, orange juice, onion, garlic powder and Worcestershire in a bowl. Let stand for 15 minutes, then pour over ribs, turning ribs to coat. Marinate in refrigerator for at least 2 hours.
3. Grill ribs about 6 inches from hot coals for 10 to 15 minutes, basting occasionally with remaining sauce. Turn ribs, baste and cook for 10 to 15 minutes longer or until glazed and tender. A few minutes before ribs are done, dip the pineapple slices in the remaining sauce; place on the grill and serve with the ribs, if you wish.

Choucroute à L'Alsacienne

A classic dinner of sauerkraut, pork-shoulder roll and sausages.

Bake at 350° for 2 hours, 20 minutes.

Makes 8 servings.

2 cans (27 ounces each) sauerkraut	1 can condensed beef broth
1 smoked pork shoulder roll (about 2 pounds)	1 pound knockwursts or frankfurters
2 carrots, finely chopped (1 cup)	6 parsley sprigs
	4 whole peppercorns
1 large onion, chopped (1 cup)	1 bay leaf
	2 tart cooking apples,
1 can (12 ounces) light beer	quartered, cored and sliced
	Boiled red potatoes

1. Soak sauerkraut for 5 minutes in a large pan of cold water; change the water twice; drain well.
2. Remove casing from pork shoulder. Brown in a 12-cup flameproof baking dish. Remove from dish. Sauté carrot and onion until soft in pan drippings. Stir in drained sauerkraut; toss to blend well.
3. Return browned pork shoulder to dish. Pour beer and beef broth over. Score sausages; place over sauerkraut.
4. Tie parsley, peppercorns and bay leaf in a piece of cheesecloth. Push under liquid in dish; cover.
5. Bake in a moderate oven (350°) for 2 hours; toss in apple slices. Bake 20 minutes longer or until pork is tender and liquid absorbed. Discard herb bag.
6. Remove pork shoulder and cut into thick slices. Spoon sauerkraut, apples and sausages into heated serving dish. Arrange pork slices and a few boiled potatoes on top. Pass remaining potatoes, along with sharp mustard and chunks of pumpernickel bread.

Easy "Choucroute Garni"

Not the classic recipe, but a hearty and satisfying substitute.

Makes 6 to 8 servings.

1 package (3/4 ounce) brown gravy mix	2 knockwursts
	1 package (1 pound)
1/3 cup firmly packed dark brown sugar	chicken frankfurters, halved
1 teaspoon caraway seeds	2 packages (16 ounces each) fresh
1/2 cup beer	sauerkraut
1 medium-size onion, thinly sliced	1 can (20 ounces) sliced apples,
2 bratwursts	drained

Combine gravy mix, brown sugar, caraway seeds and beer in large skillet. Add onion, bratwursts, knockwursts and franks. Simmer, stirring and turning meats for about 20 minutes. Add sauerkraut; mix well. Cook over medium heat 10 minutes. Add sliced apples. Cook until thoroughly heated.

Saucy Loin of Pork with Baked Apples, page 498; Fanned Roast
Potatoes, page 772; Drunken Sauerkraut, page 766.

Pork Stew San Francisco

It's surprising how closely pork can resemble veal when prepared this way.

Makes 6 servings.

2 pounds boneless lean pork shoulder, cubed	3 teaspoons salt
2 tablespoons olive or vegetable oil	2 teaspoons Italian herb seasoning mix
1 large onion, chopped (1 cup)	1/2 teaspoon pepper
2 cloves garlic, minced	1 bay leaf
1 can (35 ounces) plum tomatoes	1 1/2 cups dry red wine
	1 medium-size zucchini, cut into 1-inch pieces
	1/4 cup all-purpose flour

1. Brown pork, a few pieces at a time, in oil in a large kettle or Dutch oven; remove to a bowl. Sauté onion and garlic in pan drippings; return pork to pan; add tomatoes, salt, herb seasoning, pepper, bay leaf and 1 cup of the wine.
2. Bring slowly to boiling; lower heat; cover kettle; simmer 1 hour. Add zucchini; cook 30 minutes longer or until meat and vegetables are tender. Remove bay leaf.
3. Stir flour into remaining 1/2 cup wine in a cup until smooth; stir into bubbling liquid. Cook, stirring gently, until thickened and bubbly, 3 minutes. Serve over hot spaghetti and top with grated Parmesan cheese, if you wish.

Key West Pork Stew

Makes 6 servings.

2 pounds pork shoulder, cubed	1 package (9 ounces) frozen artichoke hearts
2 tablespoons vegetable oil	1 teaspoon grated lime or lemon rind
1 large onion, chopped (1 cup)	1 tablespoon lime juice
1 can condensed chicken broth	1 can (13 1/4 ounces) pineapple chunks
1 1/4 cups water	3 tablespoons cornstarch
2 teaspoons salt	1/4 cup firmly packed brown sugar
2 acorn squash, cut into 1/2-inch slices, pared and seeded	

1. Brown pork cubes, a few at a time, in oil in a large kettle or Dutch oven; remove; reserve. Sauté onion in pan drippings until soft; return browned pork to kettle; add chicken broth, water and salt; bring slowly to boiling; lower heat; cover kettle.
2. Simmer 1 hour or until pork is almost tender; add acorn squash slices and cook 15 minutes; add artichoke hearts and cook 15 minutes longer or until meat and vegetables are tender; stir in lime rind and juice.

3. Drain liquid from pineapple into a cup; blend in cornstarch and brown sugar. Add pineapple chunks to kettle.
4. Stir cornstarch mixture into bubbling liquid in kettle; cook, stirring gently, until thickened and bubbly, 1 minute.

Hong Kong Stir-Fry

Makes 4 to 6 servings.

5 to 6 pork chops (about 1 1/2 pounds)	1 1/2 cups chicken broth
3 tablespoons vegetable oil	1 can (8 ounces) water chestnuts, drained and sliced
1 Bermuda onion, thinly sliced	1 package (10 ounces) frozen broccoli spears, cut in pieces, not chopped
1 clove garlic, minced	
1 cup sliced mushrooms	1/4 cup soy sauce
1 package (7 ounces) frozen snow peas, thawed	2 tablespoons cornstarch

1. Trim fat and bones from pork chops; cut meat into thin strips. Cook pork in hot oil in large skillet or wok; push to one side.
2. Add onion, garlic, mushrooms and snow peas; stir-fry 2 minutes. Add chicken broth, water chestnuts and broccoli; cover and steam 4 minutes.
3. Mix soy sauce and cornstarch to make a smooth paste; stir into hot mixture and cook until it thickens and bubbles, about 3 minutes. Serve with soft Chinese noodles (lo mein), if you wish.

New Mexican Pork Chili (Hot)

Serve beans on the side with this chunky pork chili, along with sour cream and chopped onions for garnish, if you wish. For a "hot" chili, add the maximum number of jalapeño peppers indicated in the recipe.

Makes 6 servings.

2 tablespoons vegetable oil	1 tablespoon)
4 strips bacon, cut into small dice (1/4 cup)	3 tablespoons chili powder
2 pounds stewing pork (shoulder or butt), cut into 1/2-inch cubes	1 to 3 pickled jalapeño peppers, stemmed, seeded and finely chopped
1/2 cup all-purpose flour	2 cups chicken broth
1 medium-size onion, finely chopped (about 1 cup)	1/4 teaspoon salt
	3 1/2 cups cooked pinto beans
3 cloves garlic, finely chopped (about	OR: 2 cans (15 1/4 ounces each) pinto beans, drained and rinsed

1. Heat the oil in a 10-inch skillet over medium-high

heat. Add the bacon; cook until crisp, about 5 minutes. Remove with a slotted spoon to paper toweling to drain; set aside. Reserve the skillet with the drippings.
2. Shake the pork with the flour in a paper bag until coated. Remove the pork and shake off any excess flour.
3. Working in batches, sauté the pork in the bacon drippings in the skillet until evenly browned, about 5 minutes; remove the pork to a plate as it browns.
4. Lower the heat to medium. Return all the pork and bacon to pan. Add the onion and garlic; cook until the onion is softened and transparent, about 8 minutes. Add the chili powder, jalapeño peppers and chicken broth. Bring to boiling. Lower the heat; simmer, uncovered, stirring occasionally, for 2 hours, or until the meat is very tender and the sauce is thickened. If the sauce becomes too thick, thin with a little water. Stir in the salt.
5. To serve, heat the beans in a little water in a medium-size saucepan. Drain. Serve separately. Each person can spoon chili over his own beans.

Portuguese Pork Stew

A splendid, hearty stew.

Makes 8 servings.

2 pounds boneless lean pork shoulder
1 tablespoon flour
1½ teaspoons salt
2 tablespoons olive or vegetable oil
2 medium-size onions, sliced
1 teaspoon paprika
1 clove garlic, chopped
⅛ teaspoon crushed red pepper
2 large ripe tomatoes OR: 1 can (8 ounces) tomatoes
1 cup dry white wine
1 large red or green pepper, halved, seeded and cut into chunks
¼ cup chopped fresh parsley
16 small hard-shell clams (littleneck or cherrystone)

1. Trim excess fat from pork; cut into 1-inch cubes. Toss with flour and salt in a large bowl.

New Mexican Pork Chili (Hot), page 516.

2. Heat oil in Dutch oven or deep skillet. Brown pork, removing it as it browns. Add onions to skillet; sauté 5 minutes or until soft but not brown. Stir in paprika, garlic and crushed red pepper; cook, stirring often, 2 to 3 minutes. Stir in tomatoes and wine; bring to boiling; add pork and pepper. Lower heat; cover. Simmer 1¼ hours or until meat is just tender. Stir in parsley.

3. While pork simmers, scrub clams under running cold water. Then leave them in cold water, changing water often.

4. Add clams to boiling stew. Cover skillet tightly and cook over medium heat for 5 minutes or until clams open. (Do not overcook; discard any clams that have not opened.) Sprinkle with additional parsley and garnish with lemon wedges.

Pork and Chicken Tablecloth Stainer

This Mexican classic has a quaint name and is said to result from the invariable spilling of some of the sauce on the tablecloth during eating. The combination of flavors is intriguing.

Makes 8 servings.

2 pounds boneless lean pork loin, cut into 1-inch pieces	**parsley**
2 tablespoons vegetable oil	**1 can (16 ounces) plum tomatoes**
1 broiler-fryer (2½ pounds), cut up	**½ cup chicken stock or water**
1 large onion, chopped (1 cup)	**2 medium-size sweet potatoes or yams (about ¾ pound), pared, cut in half lengthwise, and cut into ¼-inch slices**
1 clove garlic, minced	
1 cup chopped walnuts	**2 medium-size zucchini (about ¾ pound), cut into ¼-inch rounds**
2 tablespoons sesame seeds	
2 teaspoons salt	**2 small apples, quartered, cored and sliced**
2 teaspoons chili powder	
¼ teaspoon ground cinnamon	**1 can (8 ounces) pineapple chunks, drained**
¼ teaspoon ground cloves	**2 small bananas, peeled and sliced**
¼ cup chopped fresh	

1. Brown pork slowly in oil in a large Dutch oven; remove with slotted spoon to bowl. Brown chicken; remove to bowl. Drain drippings into a glass measure; return 2 tablespoons to Dutch oven. Sauté onion, garlic, walnuts and sesame seeds in Dutch oven until onion is transparent, about 5 minutes. Add salt, chili powder, cinnamon and cloves. Cook and stir 1 minute. Add parsley, tomatoes with their liquid and ½ cup chicken stock. Heat thoroughly.

2. Puree sauce, part at a time, in the container of an electric blender. Return walnut sauce to Dutch oven. Place pork in sauce; arrange chicken over top. Bring

sauce to boiling; cover. Cook over medium-low heat, 45 minutes or until pork is just about fork-tender. Stir mixture occasionally, adding ½ cup additional chicken stock or water, if necessary.

3. Add sweet potatoes and zucchini to Dutch oven; cook, covered, 15 minutes or until sweet potatoes are firm-tender. Add apple slices to Dutch oven; cook 5 minutes longer.

4. Spoon meat and vegetable mixture into deep serving dish. Top with pineapple chunks and banana slices. Serve in soup bowls.

Pork, Yam and Apple Skillet

Makes 4 servings.

2 tablespoons vegetable oil	**1 medium-size onion, sliced**
4 thin loin pork chops, (each cut ½-inch thick)	**1 can (about 16 ounces) yams, drained and halved**
¾ teaspoon salt	**1 red apple, cored and cut into wedges**
¼ teaspoon pepper	
¼ teaspoon ground nutmeg	**¼ cup apple juice or chicken broth**

1. Heat oil in a large skillet. Season chops with salt, pepper and nutmeg. Brown well on one side.

2. Turn chops; add onion, yams, apple wedges and apple juice. Cover; cook until chops are browned and tender, about 15 minutes.

Spanish Pork Shoulder

Makes 6 to 8 servings.

4 pounds boneless pork shoulder	**2 cups cubed pared butternut squash (1 pound) or thickly sliced unpeeled zucchini**
2 teaspoons salt	
½ teaspoon pepper	
1 clove garlic, mashed	
½ teaspoon leaf thyme, crumbled	**2 tablespoons cornstarch**
2 tablespoons vegetable oil	**2 tablespoons water**
2 large onions, sliced	**1 can (20 ounces) chick-peas, drained**
1 can (16 ounces) tomatoes	**1 green pepper, seeded and sliced**
½ cup dry vermouth	

1. Rub pork with mixture of salt, pepper, garlic and thyme. Brown in oil in Dutch oven. Spread onions around and over top of pork. Add tomatoes and vermouth. Bring to boiling; lower heat; cover; simmer 2 hours.

2. Stir in squash; continue cooking 20 minutes or until squash is tender.

3. Remove pork to carving board. Skim fat from liquid. Combine cornstarch and water in 1-cup measure. Stir into liquid in Dutch oven. Cook until thickened.

4. Add chick-peas and pepper slices. Heat 10 minutes; meanwhile, slice pork. Return pork to pan and serve.

Canadian Pork Pie

Bake at 425° for 25 minutes.

Makes 6 servings.

Flaky Pastry (*recipe follows*)
4 bacon slices, coarsely chopped
1¹/₂ pounds boneless lean pork, cut in 1-inch cubes
3 celery stalks, chopped
3 medium-size onions, chopped (1¹/₂ cups)
2 cloves garlic, minced
1 small bay leaf
¹/₂ teaspoon salt
¹/₄ teaspoon leaf thyme, crumbled
¹/₄ teaspoon pepper
¹/₈ teaspoon ground nutmeg
2¹/₂ tablespoons flour
1 can (13³/₄ ounces) beef broth
1 pound turnips, pared and cut in ¹/₂-inch cubes
1 egg yolk
3 tablespoons light cream or milk

1. Prepare Flaky Pastry; refrigerate.
2. Partially cook bacon in a large skillet, about 3 minutes. Add pork cubes, part at a time, if pan is crowded; sauté until brown.
3. Add celery, onions, garlic, bay leaf, salt, thyme, pepper and nutmeg; cook and stir 5 minutes. Sprinkle flour over mixture; stir to coat ingredients. Stir in broth gradually; cover; simmer 20 minutes.
4. Stir in turnips; simmer 25 minutes more or until pork is tender. Taste; add additional seasoning, if needed. Remove and discard bay leaf. Remove skillet from heat; cool 15 minutes on wire rack.
5. Preheat oven to 425°. Roll ²/₃ of the pastry on a floured surface to a 14-inch round; fit into a 10-inch pie plate. Spoon in cooled filling.
6. Roll out remaining pastry to a 13-inch round; cut several slits for steam vents. Cover pie; seal edge; flute. Beat egg yolk with cream; brush over pastry.
7. Bake in a preheated hot oven (425°) for 25 minutes or until golden brown. Cool pie on wire rack about 10 minutes before cutting into wedges to serve.

Flaky Pastry: Combine 3 cups *sifted* all-purpose flour and 1 teaspoon salt in a medium-size bowl. Cut in 1 cup vegetable shortening with a pastry blender or two knives until mixture is crumbly and texture is size of peas. Sprinkle ¹/₂ cup ice water over mixture, stirring with a fork just until it holds together and leaves side of bowl clean. Gather into a ball.

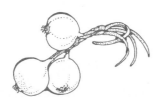

Pork and Eggplant Fricassee

A colorful addition to any party. This dish has a Middle Eastern accent.

Makes 8 servings.

¹/₄ cup all-purpose flour
3 pounds pork, cut into 1¹/₂-inch cubes
3 tablespoons peanut or vegetable oil
1 cup chicken broth
2 teaspoons salt
1 teaspoon leaf oregano, crumbled
1 teaspoon leaf thyme, crumbled
¹/₄ teaspoon leaf sage, crumbled
¹/₄ teaspoon freshly ground pepper
2 medium-size eggplants, cubed (about 3 pounds)
2 green peppers, seeded and cut into chunks
1 jar (7 ounces) pimiento, drained and cut into squares

1. Place flour and pork in a plastic bag; shake to coat thoroughly.
2. Heat oil in heavy kettle or Dutch oven. Brown pork, part at a time, removing pieces to a bowl with slotted spoon as they brown. Pour off remaining oil.
3. Add broth, salt, oregano, thyme, sage and pepper; return pork to kettle. Heat to boiling; lower heat; simmer, covered, 2 hours.
4. Add eggplant and green pepper. Cook 15 minutes or until eggplant is done. Add pimiento the last 5 minutes of cooking time.

Country Picnic Pâté

A handsome make-ahead with rounds of yellow and white hard-cooked egg centered in the pork and ham mixture -- ideal for picnicking in the park or lunching at the beach.

Bake at 350° for 2 hours.

Makes 12 servings.

2 pounds boneless lean pork shoulder or leg of pork, cut into ¹/₄-inch cubes
1 pound fully cooked ham, cut into ¹/₄-inch cubes
1 medium-size onion, finely chopped (¹/₂ cup)
2 small cloves garlic, finely chopped
3 tablespoons chopped fresh parsley
1 teaspoon leaf thyme,
crumbled
¹/₂ teaspoon leaf marjoram, crumbled
1¹/₂ teaspoons salt
¹/₄ teaspoon pepper
¹/₄ teaspoon ground nutmeg
1¹/₂ packages piecrust mix
6 hard-cooked eggs, peeled
1 egg, beaten
1 envelope unflavored gelatin
1 can (13³/₄ ounces) chicken broth

1. Combine pork, ham, onion, garlic, parsley, thyme,

(continued)

marjoram, salt, pepper and nutmeg in a large bowl; blend well. Cover; reserve.

2. Prepare piecrust mix following label directions. Roll out ⅔ of the pastry on a floured surface to a 15-inch circle; fit into an 8- or 9-inch springform pan, pressing pastry against side and bottom of pan with pastry extending about ¼ inch above edge.

3. Spread about ½ of the pork mixture over bottom of pastry-lined pan. Arrange hard-cooked eggs in a circle in pan with pointed ends toward center. Cover eggs with remaining pork mixture. Preheat oven to 350°.

4. Roll out remaining pastry to a 10- or 11-inch circle; cut out a round hole in center for a steam vent. Adjust pastry over filling; trim excess pastry. Press edges together to seal well and pinch to form a sharp fluted edge. Brush pastry with beaten egg. Roll out trimmings; cut into leaf shapes. Arrange leaf shapes on top of loaf. Brush with beaten egg.

5. Bake in a preheated moderate oven (350°) for 2 hours or until golden brown. Place pan on wire rack; cool 30 minutes.

6. Sprinkle gelatin over ½ cup of chicken broth in small saucepan; let stand 5 minutes to soften. Heat over low heat, stirring often, until gelatin is dissolved and mixture is clear. Add remaining broth. Slowly spoon gelatin mixture through hole in center of pie. Let cool at least 2 hours longer, then refrigerate overnight.

7. To serve: Loosen pâté around edge with small knife; remove side of pan. Place pâté on serving plate or cutting board; cut into wedges for serving. Garnish with cherry tomatoes and lettuce, if you wish.

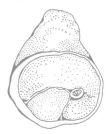

Ham
Ham is cut from the rear leg of a pig. It is available fresh, cured and smoked, or cured and canned.

Fresh ham: Uncooked and uncured; makes a delectable roast.

Cured ham: Fresh ham treated by curing, one of the oldest methods of preserving meat. The ham is soaked in a brine of water, salt, sugar and sodium or potassium nitrite (which gives the characteristic color and flavor and insures safety from botulism) before smoke-cooking or before can-cooking, in the case of canned hams.

During the cooking process, some of the moisture from the ham may be lost. If the cured, cooked ham returns to its original weight before curing, it is simply labeled "ham." If, after cooking, it weighs 10 per cent more than the original weight, it is labeled "ham, water added." Any added moisture cannot exceed 10 per cent of the weight of the fresh, uncured ham.

- *Fully cooked ham* has been cured and smoke-cooked and can be served as is. If served hot, heat to an internal temperature of 130°. Fully cooked hams comprise more than 90 per cent of the hams sold in the supermarket today.

- *Cook-before-eating ham* has been cured and partially smoke-cooked to a lower temperature than fully cooked ham. It should always be cooked to an internal temperature of 160°. Read labels carefully. If there is no label, assume that the ham is the cook-before-eating variety. Smithfield or country-type hams are cook-before-eating hams.

Forms of Cured Ham
- *Smoked bone-in* is available as whole or half leg, shank or butt portion, or as center slices.

- *Smoked semi-boneless* usually has the round leg bone left in and is easier to carve than smoked bone-in ham.

- *Smoked boneless* has all bones removed and most of the fat trimmed. It is usually pressed into either a round or rectangular shape before processing and is very easy to carve.

- *Canned* is boneless, cured ham vacuum-sealed in the can, then fully cooked. A small quantity of dry gelatin is added to absorb natural juices of the ham.

- *Boiled ham* is fully cooked, boneless, cured ham, sold by the piece or sliced.

Related Pork Products
Cook-before-eating or fully cooked smoked picnics, boneless butts or pork shoulder rolls taste much like ham but are often cheaper. The cook-before-eating picnics should be simmered in water until tender. They can be drained, baked and glazed.

Specialty Hams
- *Smithfield, Virginia, Kentucky or Country Cured* hams are dry cured, heavily salted, slow smoked and aged for more than a year. They require thorough scrubbing (to remove mold and coarse pepper) and soaking (to reduce saltiness) before cooking and should be cooked to an internal temperature of 160°. The preferred method of cooking is simmering slowly until tender in water to cover, skinning, glazing and baking. These are rich and flavorful hams and best served in very thin slices.

- *Westphalian* is a very firm ham with the characteristic flavor of the juniper bush used in the smoking process. It needs no further cooking. This type of ham is originally from Germany, but is made in this country, also.

- *Prosciutto* is a delicious dry-cured ham originating in Italy and now made in the United States also. It is ready-to-eat thinly sliced, and especially delicious served with ripe melon as a first course.

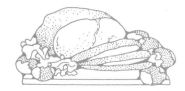

Temperature and Time for Roasting Ham and Smoked Pork

Cut	Approx. Pound Weight	Oven Temp.	Internal Temp.	Minutes Per Pound Roasting Time
Cook-before-eating Ham				
Whole	10 to 14	300° to 325°F.	160°F.	18 to 20
Half	5 to 7	300° to 325°F.	160°F.	22 to 25
Shank or Butt portion	3 to 4	300° to 325°F.	160°F.	35 to 40
Fully cooked Ham				
Whole	12 to 14	325°F.	130°F.	15
Half	5 to 7	325°F.	130°F.	18 to 24
Picnic Shoulder	5 to 8	300° to 325°F.	170°F.	35
Shoulder Roll	2 to 3	300° to 325°F.	170°F.	35 to 40

Glorious Ham

Perfect for a spring buffet, this boneless ham is easily sliced with an electric knife.

Bake at 350° for 1³/₄ hours.

Makes 24 servings.

1 pound fresh
  mushrooms
¹/₄ cup finely chopped
  shallots
  OR: white part of
  green onions
¹/₄ cup (¹/₂ stick)
  unsalted butter or
  margarine
¹/₂ teaspoon salt
Dash white pepper
1 tablespoon lemon
  juice
1 tablespoon all-
  purpose flour
¹/₃ cup milk
1 egg, separated

1 package (1 pound)
  phyllo or strudel
  pastry leaves,
  thawed if frozen
  (see Note)
1 cup (2 sticks)
  unsalted butter,
  melted
1 fully cooked smoked
  boneless ham
  (about 8 pounds)
Sugar-frosted green
  seedless grapes
  and lemon leaves
  for garnish
  (optional)

1. Finely chop mushrooms, half at a time, in a food processor, or by hand; set aside. Sauté shallots in the ¹/₄ cup butter in a large skillet for 1 minute. Stir in chopped mushrooms, salt, pepper and lemon juice. Cook over medium-high heat until tender and most of the liquid has evaporated, about 7 minutes. Stir in flour, then milk, until smooth. Cook until bubbly and thickened. Remove from heat; cool slightly. Refrigerate until cold. (Mushroom mixture can be cooked a day ahead.)
2. Stir egg yolk into the mushroom mixture.

3. Tear off four 18-inch lengths of wax paper. Overlap the long edge of two pieces of wax paper on the counter or table top. Unwrap the phyllo and place on wax paper. Cover the top with slightly dampened paper toweling to keep the phyllo from drying out. Overlap the other two pieces of wax paper on the counter. Lift 1 sheet of phyllo from the stack and place on wax paper. Brush phyllo with melted butter. Place another sheet of phyllo on top; repeat buttering and stacking phyllo. When all sheets are buttered, cut off the corners of phyllo stack to form 4- to 5-inch triangles, thus removing excess pastry when you wrap the ham.
4. Preheat the oven to moderate (350°).
5. Place the ham on a rack in a large open shallow roasting pan. Brush with slightly beaten egg white. Cover top of the ham with the mushroom mixture. Place the stack of phyllo over ham so that the length of the ham is covered by the length of the phyllo. Tuck phyllo along two long sides under the ham. Tuck short ends of the phyllo under the ham. Brush the entire surface of the phyllo with egg white.
6. With the 4 phyllo triangles, cut out decorative pieces using fluted cookie cutters or scissors. Arrange on top of the ham. Brush the pieces with egg white.
7. Bake ham in the preheated moderate oven (350°) for 1³/₄ hours, turning the pan around midway through baking time for even browning. If phyllo browns too quickly on top, cover with a tent of aluminum foil. Transfer ham to a platter using 2 wide pancake turners. Garnish the platter with frosted grapes and lemon leaves, if you wish.

Note: Phyllo or strudel leaves can be found in the refrigerated or frozen foods section of your supermarket.

How to Carve a Whole Ham

Place the ham on platter with the decorated-fat-side up and shank bone to the carver's right (if he is right-handed; the reverse if he is left-handed).

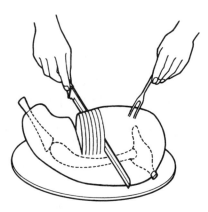

Cut straight down through the boneless cushion in thin slices.

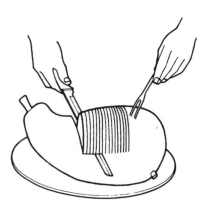

Cut straight down from the top of the ham to the leg bone in thin, even slices, then release slices by cutting along the bone.

How to Carve a Shank Half of Ham

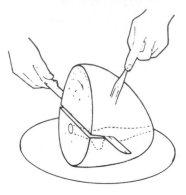

Place ham on platter with shank end at carver's left (the reverse if the carver is left-handed). The thick cushion side of the ham should be on top. Cut along leg bone and lift off chunky cushion.

Cut two or three slices off the thin side of the ham, which contains the kneecap.

To carve the shank portion containing the bone, cut around the leg bone with the tip of a carving knife to free meat from the bone. Turn meat so that thickest part is down, then slice straight down, making thin, even cuts.

Baked Orange Ham with Mustard Fruits

Bake at 325° for 2 1/2 hours.

Makes 16 servings.

**1 fully cooked ham
   (about 10 pounds)
Whole cloves
1 can (6 ounces)
   frozen orange
   juice**

**concentrate,
   thawed
3/4 cup orange
   marmalade
Mustard Fruits
   (recipe follows)**

1. Place ham, fat-side up, on a rack in a large shallow baking dish. (Do not add water or cover pan.)
2. Bake in a slow oven (325°) for 1 1/2 hours. Trim off skin, if any.
3. Score ham; stud with whole cloves. Mix orange juice concentrate and marmalade in a small bowl; brush over ham.
4. Continue baking, brushing several times with remaining marmalade mixture, 1 hour or until richly glazed. Place ham on a heated large serving platter. Serve with Mustard Fruits.

Mustard Fruits: Drain juice from 1 can (8 1/4 ounces) sliced pineapple into a 1-cup measure; add enough juice from 1 can (30 ounces) cling peach halves to make 3/4 cup. Drain peaches and 1 can (30 ounces) pear halves. Combine fruits in a 13 × 9 × 2-inch baking dish. Add 1/2 cup light corn syrup, 1 tablespoon dry mustard, 1/2 teaspoon ground ginger and 1/4 teaspoon ground cardamom to pineapple juice; stir to mix; pour over fruits. Bake, uncovered, along with ham for 30 minutes, basting fruits often with the juices. Lift fruits out of dish to a serving bowl; pour juices into saucepan; cook over heat until reduced by about half. Stir in 1 slice lime or lemon. Spoon over fruits.

Roast Fresh Ham

Roast at 325° for 25 minutes per pound.

Makes 12 to 16 servings.

**1 leg of pork (fresh
   ham) (about 10 to
   15 pounds)*
2 teaspoons salt
1/2 teaspoon pepper
1 large onion, sliced**

**6 medium-size
   baking potatoes,
   quartered
   lengthwise
Cumberland Sauce
   (recipe follows)**

1. *Order roast from butcher with skin (rind) left on (when roasted, the skin will be crackly and brown). Score skin in small diamond pattern. Rub skin with salt and pepper.
2. Place meat in roasting pan. If using roast thermometer, insert into thickest part of meat so bulb is not touching bone or resting in fat.
3. One hour before end of roasting time, pour off all drippings from pan; measure and return 1/4 cup to pan; reserve all remaining drippings for sauce. Remove rack from pan. Add onion and potatoes; continue roasting, turning potatoes once or twice until roast and potatoes are done. Meanwhile, make Cumberland Sauce to serve with roast. Serve potatoes with roast and garnish platter with watercress and orange slices, if you wish.

Cumberland Sauce

Makes 1 2/3 cups.

**Roast Fresh Ham
   pan drippings
2 oranges
2 tablespoons
   cornstarch
1 cup ruby port**

**1/2 cup currant
   jelly
5 drops liquid hot
   pepper
   seasoning**

1. Skim fat from reserved drippings; discard fat. Measure pan juices and add water, if necessary, to equal 1 cup.
2. Pare orange rind thinly from both oranges; parboil rind for 5 minutes; cut into thin shreds. Squeeze oranges; measure 1/3 cup juice.
3. Stir cornstarch into orange juice in medium-size saucepan. Stir in port, currant jelly and pepper seasoning. Bring to boiling, stirring constantly; cook until bubbly, then cook 1 minute longer. Stir in orange rind. Serve with Roast Fresh Ham.

Crumb-Topped Baked Ham

Bake at 325° for 3 hours.

Makes 12 servings.

**1 fully-cooked ham
   (about 10 to 12
   pounds)
1/3 cup Dijon mustard
1/2 cup packed light
   brown sugar
1/2 cup sherry
1 3/4 cups fresh bread
   crumbs (about
   4 slices)**

**2/3 cup finely
   ground pecans
   (about 8 ounces)
1/4 cup chopped
   fresh parsley
Parsley sprigs
Sherried Mustard
   Sauce (recipe
   follows)**

1. Place ham on rack in large roasting pan. Trim off rind, if any, and trim fat to a 1/4-inch thickness.
2. Bake in a slow oven (325°) for 1 1/2 hours. Score ham into 1-inch wide strips; brush with mustard and sprinkle with brown sugar. Return to oven; continue baking for 1 hour.
3. While ham is baking, prepare crumb topping: Combine sherry, bread crumbs, pecans and parsley in a medium-size bowl; mix well. Gently pat crumb mixture onto alternate strips of scored ham. Ham may be refrigerated at this point, if making ahead. Or ham may be completely baked and served at room

(continued)

temperature. Return to oven and continue to bake for 1/2 hour. Garnish with parsley. Serve with Sherried Mustard Sauce.

Sherried Mustard Sauce: Melt 2 tablespoons butter in saucepan. Stir in 3 tablespoons flour. Cook over medium heat, stirring constantly, 1 minute. Gradually stir in 1 1/2 cups beef broth, 2 bay leaves and 6 tablespoons sherry while continuing to cook over medium heat until sauce thickens and is smooth; lower heat; simmer 5 minutes. Heat 3/4 cup sherry in saucepan until reduced to half. Stir in 6 tablespoons Dijon mustard. Gradually stir in mustard sauce. Cook over low heat for 5 minutes. Remove bay leaves and serve with baked ham.

Stuffed Baked Ham, Maryland-Style

A mixture of garden greens tucked into little pockets add a marvelous flavor to baked ham.

Bake at 325° for 2 1/2 hours.

Makes 12 servings.

1 fully cooked ham (about 10 to 12 pounds)	watercress
1 package (10 ounces) frozen chopped kale	1/2 cup finely chopped celery tops
1 cup finely chopped fresh spinach	1/2 teaspoon salt
1 large onion, finely chopped (1 cup)	1/4 teaspoon pepper
3/4 cup finely chopped	1/2 cup honey
	2 tablespoons cider vinegar
	2 teaspoons dry mustard

1. Trim rind, if any, from ham. Trim fat to a 1/4-inch thickness. Make X-shaped cuts with a small paring knife, 2 inches deep and 1 inch apart, staggering rows, all over fat side.
2. Cook kale in boiling salted water to cover, following directions on package; drain; cool; squeeze out excess water with hands.
3. Combine kale, spinach, onion, watercress, celery tops, salt and pepper in a medium-size bowl.
4. Press greens mixture into ham pockets, packing down well with fingertips. Place ham, fat-side up, in a large shallow baking pan.
5. Bake in a slow oven (325°) for 2 hours.
6. Stir honey with vinegar and dry mustard; brush part over ham. Continue baking and brushing with the remaining honey mixture, 30 minutes or until top is richly glazed. Remove ham from pan and let stand about 20 minutes for easier carving.
7. Carve ham carefully, holding slices together to keep filling intact. Garnish platter with cooked carrots and watercress, if you wish.

Skillet Honey-Glazed Ham Steak

Makes 6 servings.

3- to 4-pound fully cooked ham steak, cut 1 1/2- to 2 inches thick	cloves
	1/4 teaspoon ground allspice
1 tablespoon butter or margarine	12 small white onions (about 1 pound)
1/3 cup honey	6 large carrots, sliced (3 cups)
1 lemon, sliced	
1/4 teaspoon ground	

1. Score edge of ham steak to prevent it from curling during cooking. Heat butter in large heavy skillet; add ham steak and brown on both sides.
2. Add honey, lemon slices, cloves and allspice; cover. Cook over medium heat, basting often with honey glaze, for 30 minutes.
3. Meanwhile, parboil onions in boiling salted water, 5 minutes; drain. Add onions and carrots to skillet; cover. Cook 15 minutes longer, basting ham and vegetables once or twice. Remove cover and cook, stirring often, 5 minutes longer or until vegetables are richly glazed. Arrange ham and vegetables on serving platter.

Ham Steak Barbecue

Good-quality ham makes this recipe a sheer success.

Grill 40 to 50 minutes.

Makes 4 servings.

1 cup orange juice	1/4 teaspoon salt
1 tablespoon brown sugar	1 center-cut ham steak, cut 1 1/4-inches thick (2 pounds)
1 tablespoon honey	
1 teaspoon prepared mustard	4 orange slices
1 teaspoon soy sauce	

1. Combine orange juice, brown sugar, honey, mustard, soy sauce and salt in a small saucepan.
2. Slash edges of ham to keep it from curling. Brush sauce liberally on ham.
3. Grill ham about 5 inches above hot coals for 20 minutes; turn; brush again liberally with sauce and grill another 20 to 30 minutes or until ham is glazed and heated through. Meanwhile, heat sauce on side of grill.
4. Remove ham from grill, cut into serving pieces. Spoon some of the hot sauce over each serving and top with a fresh orange slice.

Note: To broil, place ham steak on rack over broiler pan. Broil about 5 inches from heat for 30 to 40 minutes, turning and brushing with sauce frequently.

Pictured opposite: Stuffed Baked Ham, Maryland-Style.

Baked Ham Steak with Sweet Potatoes

Bake at 375° for 30 minutes.

Makes 4 servings.

1 center-cut ham steak (about 1¼ pounds)	**1 cup firmly packed light brown sugar**
8 whole cloves	**1 can (17 ounces) sweet potatoes, drained**
1 can (5½ ounces) apple juice	

1. Stud ham steak with whole cloves. Place in shallow baking dish. Pour apple juice over meat. Sprinkle with brown sugar.
2. Bake in a moderate oven (375°) for 15 minutes. Arrange sweet potatoes around outer edge of baking dish. Spoon baking liquid over meat and potatoes.
3. Bake 15 minutes longer or until glazed.

Hoppin' John 'n' Ham

Cook 35 minutes in a pressure cooker.

Makes 8 servings.

1 pound dried blackeyed peas	**2 teaspoons salt**
1 shank-end smoked ham (about 4½ pounds)	**¼ teaspoon pepper**
	3 cups water
1 medium-size onion, diced (½ cup)	**2 cups uncooked long-grain rice**
	1 bunch green onions, trimmed and sliced

1. Pick over peas and rinse under running water. Soak peas overnight in water to generously cover (about 6 cups); drain. To quick soak: Combine peas and water in a large kettle. Bring to boiling; cover kettle; boil 2 minutes; remove from heat; let stand 1 hour. Drain.
2. Combine peas, ham, onion, salt and pepper in a 6-quart pressure cooker; add the 3 cups water, being sure all peas are covered.
3. Secure cover, following manufacturer's directions; cook at 15 pounds pressure for 35 minutes, following manufacturer's directions. Remove cooker from heat and allow pressure to drop of its own accord (about 10 to 15 minutes).
4. Meanwhile, cook rice, following label directions.
5. When pressure has dropped, remove cover. Place ham on carving board and cut off skin and fat. Cut into thick slices.
6. Add cooked rice to peas, tossing to mix well; spoon onto a heated deep platter; top with ham slices; sprinkle onions over top.

Croquette   Traditionally cone-shaped, a croquette can also be shaped like a log. Croquettes are made of minced or ground, usually leftover, meats, bound with a thick white sauce, shaped, breaded and fried in oil. Croquettes are usually served with a sauce. The word is French in origin, from *croquer,* "to crunch."

Ham Croquettes with Mornay Sauce

Makes 12 croquettes (4 servings).

3 tablespoons butter or margarine	**Salt**
2 tablespoons chopped celery	**Dash liquid hot pepper seasoning**
2 tablespoons chopped onion	**¼ cup all-purpose flour**
⅓ cup all-purpose flour	**½ cup packaged bread crumbs**
1 cup milk	**1 egg**
2½ cups finely ground or minced cooked ham	**1 tablespoon water**
	Vegetable oil for frying
	Mornay Sauce (recipe follows)

1. Melt butter in a medium-size skillet; sauté celery and onion until tender. Stir in ⅓ cup flour; cook 1 minute.
2. Remove from heat; gradually stir in milk until mixture is blended. Cook over low heat, stirring constantly until thick and bubbly; remove from heat. Stir in ham. Taste; add salt and hot pepper seasoning, if needed. Spread evenly in same pan; cover. Chill until cold, preferably overnight.
3. Divide ham mixture into 12 equal portions; form each to make a cone or cylinder shape. Place ¼ cup flour and crumbs on separate pieces of wax paper. Beat egg and water in a bowl.
4. Roll each croquette in flour, coat evenly with egg and roll in crumbs. Place each finished croquette on wax paper. Let dry 30 minutes or refrigerate until ready to cook.
5. Meanwhile, make Mornay Sauce.
6. To cook croquettes: Heat 1 inch oil in large saucepan to 375°. Fry croquettes, 2 or 3 at a time, turning frequently with slotted spoon until golden brown on all sides. Drain on paper toweling. Keep warm while cooking rest. Serve with Mornay Sauce.

Mornay Sauce

Makes about 1½ cups.

3 tablespoons butter or margarine	**Dash cayenne**
3 tablespoons flour	**1½ cups milk**
¼ teaspoon salt	**¼ cup grated Parmesan cheese**

Melt butter in a medium-size saucepan. Stir in flour, salt and cayenne. Cook 1 minute. Remove from heat; gradually stir in milk until mixture is smooth. Cook over low heat, stirring constantly, until thickened and bubbly. Stir in cheese.

Ham 'n' Cheese Puff

Bake at 325° for 1 hour.
Makes 6 servings.

1/2 loaf (8 ounces) Italian or French bread	mustard
1/4 cup (1/2 stick) butter or margarine	6 ounces Muenster cheese, diced (1 1/2 cups)
1 small onion, chopped (1/4 cup)	1/2 cup diced cooked ham
2 tablespoons prepared	4 eggs
	2 cups milk

1. Cut bread into small chunks.
2. Melt butter in a small saucepan; sauté onion in butter until soft; stir in prepared mustard.
3. Layer one-third of the bread chunks in a 10-cup casserole; drizzle one-third of the mustard mixture over; top with half the cheese and ham. Repeat layering, ending with bread chunks and mustard mixture.
4. Beat eggs in a medium-size bowl with a wire whisk; beat in milk; pour over bread in casserole, pushing down bread to soak in custard. Cover casserole and refrigerate overnight.
5. Bake, uncovered, in a slow oven (325°) for 1 hour or until golden and puffed. Serve immediately.

Ham and Swiss in Pastry

Creamy ham, cheese and mushrooms fill this flaky pastry rectangle — a delicious main-dish pie.
Bake at 375° for 35 minutes.
Makes 6 servings.

Pastry:	green onions
1 1/4 cups *unsifted* all-purpose flour	1/2 pound fresh mushrooms, sliced
1/4 teaspoon salt	2 tablespoons flour
1/2 cup (1 stick) butter or margarine	1/2 cup heavy cream
1/2 of an 8-ounce package cream cheese	2 1/2 cups diced cooked ham (about 1 pound)
3 tablespoons milk	4 ounces Swiss cheese, diced (1 cup)
Filling:	1 egg yolk
2 tablespoons butter or margarine	1 tablespoon water
1/2 cup chopped	

1. To make Pastry: Combine flour and salt in a large bowl; cut in butter and cream cheese with pastry blender until mixture is crumbly. Add milk; mix lightly with a fork until dough clings together and starts to leave sides of bowl. Gather dough together with hands and knead a few times.
2. Roll pastry out on floured surface to a 10 × 18-inch rectangle. Fold pastry in thirds starting from short side; bring one-third to center then opposite third over center. Turn dough so that one of the open edges faces you. Roll again to 10 × 18-inch rectangle. Fold into thirds as above. Roll and fold dough one more time. Wrap folded pastry in plastic wrap. Chill pastry for several hours or overnight.
3. To make Filling: Heat butter in large skillet. Add onion and mushrooms. Cook, stirring frequently, 2 to 3 minutes or just until mushrooms are tender. Sprinkle with flour; cook 1 minute. Stir in cream. Cook and stir until mixture is thickened. Cool. Stir in ham and Swiss cheese.
4. Preheat oven to 375°. Roll pastry on lightly floured surface to a 14-inch square. Place square on lightly greased cookie sheet. Mound filling on half of dough about 1 inch from edges. Beat egg yolk and water in a cup; brush along sides. Bring unfilled half of pastry over filling; press edges with fork to seal. Trim edges, if necessary, to form a neat rectangle. Make cut-out designs or slash top crust to allow steam to escape. Brush top with egg yolk and water mixture.
5. Bake in preheated moderate oven (375°) for 35 minutes or until pastry is golden-brown.

Ham Rolls with Curried Rice

Flavored rice mix and packaged ham slices make a quick dinner for four.
Bake at 400° for 20 minutes.
Makes 4 servings .

1 package (6 ounces) curried rice mix	thick
2 packages (9 ounces each) frozen whole green beans	1 envelope (1 1/2 ounces) white sauce mix
8 slices (about 1 pound) cooked ham, each cut 1/8-inch	3 wedges processed Gruyère cheese (from a 6-ounce package), cut up

1. Prepare rice mix following label directions; spread in a shallow 8-cup baking dish.
2. Cook green beans following label directions; drain. Divide beans among ham slices; roll up slices. Place rolls, seam-side down, on rice in baking dish.
3. Prepare sauce mix following label directions. Add cheese; stir until melted.. Pour over ham rolls.
4. Bake in a hot oven (400°) for 20 minutes or until sauce is bubbly. Sprinkle casserole with chopped parsley, if you wish.

Overleaf (clockwise from top left): Italian Sausages with Vegetables, page 539; Chicken Risotto, page 652; Ham and Potatoes au Gratin, page 530; Pork Chops with Red Cabbage, page 507.

Ham and Potatoes au Gratin

No need to pare potatoes to make a sauce for this creamy, convenient dish.

Makes 6 servings.

1 ham steak, cut about 1/2-inch thick (about 1³/4 pounds)	1 package (5.5 ounces) au gratin potatoes
1 medium-size onion, sliced	2¹/4 cups boiling water
	²/3 cup milk

1. Trim fat from ham; heat fat in skillet to render about 2 tablespoons of fat drippings. Remove fat pieces; discard. Sauté onion in drippings until soft.
2. Stir in potato slices, sauce mix, boiling water and the milk. Cut ham into bite-size pieces; add to potatoes. Bring to boiling, stirring frequently; lower heat; cover. Simmer 30 minutes or until potatoes are tender and ham is piping hot. Garnish with parsley, if you wish.

Ham Loaf with Mustard Sauce

Bake in the cool of the morning, then refrigerate until dinner.

Bake at 350° for 1 hour.

Makes 8 servings .

1¹/4 pounds ground cured ham	1 tablespoon prepared spicy brown mustard
³/4 pound ground lean pork	1 teaspoon leaf marjoram, crumbled
1 cup sandwich spread	¹/4 teaspoon leaf rosemary, crumbled
1 package (8 ounces) herbed stuffing mix	¹/4 teaspoon ground allspice
1 envelope (2 to a package) onion soup mix	¹/8 teaspoon ground ginger
2 eggs	1 cup apple juice or cider
¹/4 cup dried parsley flakes	Mustard Sauce (*recipe follows*)
2 tablespoons prepared horseradish	

1. Line bottom and sides of a 9 × 5 × 3-inch loaf pan with foil; grease foil.
2. Combine ham, pork, sandwich spread, stuffing mix, soup mix, eggs, parsley, horseradish, mustard, marjoram, rosemary, allspice, ginger and apple juice in a large bowl; mix well. Press firmly into prepared pan, smoothing top.
3. Bake in a moderate oven (350°) for 1 hour or until loaf begins to pull from sides of pan and is firm. Remove loaf to wire rack. Loosen around edges with a spatula; cool to room temperature. Drain off any juices from pan. Invert loaf onto a sheet of heavy-duty foil; remove foil lining; wrap; chill. Slice and serve with

Mustard Sauce. Garnish with celery leaves, cherry tomatoes and sweet pickles, if you wish.

Mustard Sauce: Combine 1 cup dairy sour cream, 2 tablespoons Dijon mustard, 2 tablespoons sandwich spread, ¹/4 teaspoon dillweed, pinch leaf marjoram and 3 tablespoons milk in a small bowl. Stir until well blended. Cover; chill until ready to serve. Stir well again, adding a little more milk, if needed. Makes 1¹/2 cups.

Creole-Style Ham and Rice

Makes 6 servings.

2 tablespoons bacon drippings or vegetable oil	long-grain rice
6 slices cooked ham (about 3 × 4 inches)	1 can (16 ounces) peeled whole tomatoes
1 medium-size onion, chopped (¹/2 cup)	1 can (13³/4 ounces) chicken broth
1 medium-size green pepper, halved, seeded and cut into strips	1 bay leaf
	¹/2 teaspoon salt
	¹/2 teaspoon leaf thyme, crumbled
1 clove garlic, minced	4 drops liquid hot pepper seasoning
1¹/2 cups uncooked	

1. Heat drippings in a large skillet. Add ham; cook until lightly browned. Remove to plate. Add onion, green pepper, garlic and rice to drippings left in pan. Sauté, stirring often until vegetables are just wilted.
2. Stir in tomatoes with their liquid, broth, bay leaf, salt, thyme and hot pepper seasoning, breaking up tomatoes with spoon. Bring to boiling; lower heat; cover. Simmer 15 minutes. Uncover and arrange ham on top of rice. Cover and continue to cook until rice is tender and liquid is absorbed.

Lentils with Ham, Mushrooms and Dill

Bake at 350° for 25 minutes; then at 400° for 15 minutes.

Makes 8 servings.

1 pound dried lentils	2 carrots, chopped (1 cup)
5 cups water	2 tablespoons flour
6 tablespoons (³/4 stick) butter or margarine	3 cups chicken broth or stock
¹/2 pound small mushrooms, thickly sliced	2 teaspoons dillweed
	2 teaspoons salt
¹/2 pound cooked ham, cut into ¹/2-inch cubes	¹/4 teaspoon pepper
	1 cup fresh bread crumbs (2 slices)
1 large onion, chopped (1 cup)	2 tablespoons chopped parsley

1. Pick over lentils; wash under running water.

Combine lentils and water in a large heavy saucepan. bring to boiling; cover; lower heat and simmer 20 minutes or until lentils are almost tender.

2. Meanwhile, melt 3 tablespoons of the butter in a large skillet. Add mushrooms and ham. Cook until lightly browned. Remove to a 2½-quart baking dish.

3. Add 2 more tablespoons butter to skillet; add onion and carrots; sauté until soft, about 3 minutes. Add flour and stir 2 minutes. Add broth, dillweed, salt and pepper. Bring to boiling, stirring constantly. Boil 1 minute.

4. Drain lentils. Combine lentils and sauce with mushrooms and ham in baking dish. Stir gently.

5. Bake, covered, in a moderate oven (350°) for 25 minutes. Uncover. Sprinkle with crumbs and parsley and dot with the remaining tablespoon of butter. Move casserole to the top oven rack. Raise heat to hot (400°); bake 15 minutes longer or until top is lightly browned.

Ham Mousse with Fruit Salad Platter

This is a delicate, smooth and rich ham salad, surrounded with fresh fruit in season. Ideal for special luncheons or a light dinner.

Makes 6 servings.

2½ cups finely ground cooked ham	lemon juice
1 package (8 ounces) cream cheese	1 tablespoon honey
⅓ cup mayonnaise	2 teaspoons prepared mustard
1 tablespoon minced green onion	3 papayas or large avocados, peeled, halved and seeded
1½ teaspoons dry mustard	
¼ teaspoon white pepper	Lettuce leaves
Salt	Any other fruit in season (grapes, pineapple spears, pear or apple slices)
½ cup heavy cream	
2 tablespoons milk	
2 tablespoons	

1. Beat ham, half of the cream cheese, mayonnaise, onion, dry mustard and pepper in a large bowl with electric mixer until fluffy. Taste; season with salt, if needed. Whip cream in a small bowl until stiff; fold into ham mixture. Cover. Chill at least 1 hour or overnight.

2. To make mustard dressing, beat remaining cream cheese and milk until fluffy. Stir in lemon juice, honey, mustard and a dash of salt until creamy. Chill until serving time.

3. Before serving, spoon ham into cavity of papaya or avocado halves; arrange on lettuce-lined platter. Place other fruit around and garnish with lime wedges, if you wish. Serve with the mustard dressing.

Ham and Cheese Mold

Makes 8 servings.

2 envelopes unflavored gelatin	(about ½ pound) 8 ounces Swiss cheese, finely diced (2 cups)
1 cup water	
2 cans (13¾ ounces each) beef broth, heated	1 cup dairy sour cream
1 can (4 ounces) pitted ripe olives, drained	½ teaspoon dry mustard
2 cups finely diced cooked ham	Salad greens

1. Sprinkle gelatin over water in large mixing bowl; let stand 5 minutes. Bring beef broth to boiling in a large saucepan; pour over softened gelatin; stir to dissolve.

2. Pour ⅓ cup gelatin mixture into each of 4 small foil loaf pans, 5¹¹/₁₆ × 3¼ × 2 inches (about 2 cups each).

3. Cut olives in half lengthwise. Cut into fancy shapes with sharp knife or small hors d'oeuvre cutters. Arrange in gelatin in aluminum pans. Chill until almost set, about ½ hour.

4. Combine remaining gelatin with ham, cheese, sour cream and dry mustard, mixing well. Divide among molds.

5. Chill about 3 hours or until completely set. Gently ease mold away from ham mixture. Unmold. Serve on salad greens.

Bacon   Keep bacon in its original wrapper in the refrigerator. Freezing bacon is not recommended for long periods of time because the salt draws out the moisture and affects the flavor. Tip: bacon slices tear easily when cold, so take bacon out of the refrigerator 10 minutes before cooking. If you forget, try this trick: Place a rubber spatula under one end of a slice then run it slowly between slices to separate.

How to Cook: Perfectly cooked bacon should be crisp, not brittle. You can pan-fry, bake, broil or microwave bacon. To pan fry, place slices in a cold skillet. No need to separate them; they'll fall apart as they cook. Cook slowly, turning often until crisp and brown. Drain on paper toweling. To bake, place slices on a rack in a shallow pan with fat edge of one slice overlapping lean of next. Bake in a hot oven (400°) 12 to 15 minutes or until crisp. No need to turn slices; the perfect way to cook bacon for a crowd. To broil, arrange slices as for baking, but use rack in broiler pan. Broil about 4 inches from heat, turning once, 2 to 3 minutes on each side or until crisp. To microwave, place several layers of paper toweling on oven floor, paper or microwave-proof plate. Place up to 6 bacon slices on toweling; cover with more toweling. Microwave on high power 45 seconds to 1 minute per slice. Let stand 5 minutes. For more than 6 slices, microwave 30 to 45 seconds per slice. Bacon will appear underdone when first removed from oven but upon standing it will be brown and crisp.

Sausage

Sausage Ground meat usually enclosed in a casing. Sausages have been made since antiquity and many countries are noted for their own special sausages. Some are named for the city of origin, such as the frankfurter for Frankfurt, Germany, and the bologna for Bologna, Italy.

Frankfurter

Frankfurter Although we think of a frankfurter as being as American as baseball, it isn't. In fact, the frankfurter is a German sausage originally concocted in the region of Frankfurt—hence the name. However, it was indeed an American who started selling frankfurters in buns and a *New Yorker* cartoonist, T. A. Dorgan, who dubbed this popular sandwich "hot dog" when he described it as a dachshund on a bun.

Frankfurters may be made from a mixture of pork and beef or veal or beef only. Some are made from chicken or turkey. All are seasoned with salt and a variety of spices, then smoked. Most are skinless, but some may have a natural casing. Their sizes range from the jumbo-fat links to the foot-long ones, to the cocktail-size bites.

Although all frankfurters are fully cooked and ready to eat, most people prefer them hot. A quick heating in boiling water is all that's necessary to bring out their flavor.

Knockwurst, sometimes spelled knackwurst, is a German favorite which looks like a plump hot dog. It's made of finely chopped pork and beef and is seasoned similarly to a frankfurter except that a touch of garlic is always added.

Corn Doggies

Makes 8 servings.

1 pound frankfurters (8 to 10)	1/2 teaspoon salt
4 cups vegetable oil	1/2 teaspoon sugar
1/2 cup *sifted* all-purpose flour	1 tablespoon vegetable shortening
1/3 cup yellow cornmeal	1/3 cup milk
1 teaspoon baking powder	1 egg
	8 to 10 wooden skewers

1. Bring 3 cups of water to boiling in a large saucepan. Add frankfurters and return water to boiling. Remove from heat; cover; let stand 20 minutes.
2. Pour vegetable oil into a large skillet or saucepan to a 2-inch depth. Heat to 425° on deep-fat frying thermometer.
3. Combine flour, cornmeal, baking powder, salt and sugar in a medium-size bowl; blend with fork. Add shortening and cut in with fork until the size of small peas.
4. Combine milk and egg in a 1-cup measure. Stir into flour-cornmeal mixture. Pour mixture into a tall glass.
5. Remove frankfurters from water; dry on paper toweling. Insert skewer into 1 end of frankfurter, centering and leaving about 1 inch of stick for a handle.
6. Twirl frankfurter into batter to coat thoroughly; let excess batter drip back into glass. Drop into hot fat; fry 2 minutes or until golden brown. Remove with tongs to paper toweling to drain. If batter becomes too thick, add milk, 1 teaspoon at a time. To eat, dip into mustard or ketchup, then into chopped onion or relish.

Little Dogs

A thin crisp batter covers these bite-size appetizers.

Makes about 3 1/2 dozen appetizers.

3/4 cup *unsifted* all-purpose flour	cocktail frankfurters
2/3 cup flat beer	Vegetable oil for frying
1 package (1 pound)	Spicy brown prepared mustard

1. Combine flour and beer in a medium-size mixing bowl; let stand 1 hour, mixing once or twice. Separate frankfurters into links if attached.
2. Pour 2 inches oil in a medium-size saucepan. Heat to 375° on a deep-fat frying thermometer.
3. Dip franks into batter, letting excess batter drip back into bowl. (If mixture seems too thin add 1 or 2 tablespoons flour, if too thick add more beer.)
4. Fry, a few at a time, until golden brown. Drain on paper toweling. Serve hot, dipped in mustard.

All-American Dogs

Makes 4 to 5 servings.

8 to 10 split frankfurter rolls	1 package (1 pound) frankfurters (8 to 10)
4 bacon slices	8 to 10 thin dill pickle strips
16 to 20 slices American cheese	

1. Cook bacon until crisp in a large skillet; remove and drain on paper toweling; crumble. Reserve.
2. Line each frankfurter roll with 2 slices of the cheese. Place one frankfurter in the center of each roll. Place the rolls on a cookie sheet.
3. Broil, 6 to 8 inches from heat, until frankfurter is hot and cheese is melted. Top with pickle and bacon.

Reuben Dogs

Makes 4 to 5 servings.

Spicy brown prepared mustard	sauerkraut, drained
8 to 10 slices Swiss cheese	1 package (1 pound) frankfurters (8 to 10)
1 can (8 ounces)	8 to 10 split frankfurter buns

1. Spread mustard lightly on one side of Swiss cheese

slices; divide sauerkraut equally over cheese slices. Put frankfurter at one end of cheese; roll up. Place, seam-side down, on split frankfurter roll. Arrange on cookie sheet.

2. Broil, 6 to 8 inches from heat, until cheese is melted and frankfurter is hot. Garnish with olives and cocktail onions, if you wish.

Mediterranean Dogs

Shredded romaine lettuce in a bun, topped with a hot frankfurter and a crisp dill-flavored cucumber salad.

Makes 4 to 5 servings.

2 large cucumbers	**1 package (1 pound)**
¹/₄ cup sliced green	**frankfurters (8 to**
onion	**10)**
¹/₄ teaspoon salt	**1¹/₂ cups shredded**
¹/₈ teaspoon pepper	**romaine lettuce**
¹/₈ teaspoon dillweed	**8 to 10 split frankfurter**
¹/₄ teaspoon sugar	**buns, toasted**
2 tablespoons white	**Plain yogurt** *(optional)*
vinegar	

1. Pare and halve cucumbers; scoop out seeds with spoon; cut cucumbers into thin slices. (You should have 2 cups.)
2. Combine cucumber, onion, salt, pepper, dillweed, sugar and vinegar in a medium-size bowl. Cover. Refrigerate 2 to 3 hours.
3. Drop frankfurters in boiling water in a medium-size saucepan for 5 minutes; drain.
4. To assemble: Layer lettuce, frankfurter and cucumber topping on warm rolls. Garnish with a dollop of yogurt, if you wish.

Frankfurter and Potato Omelet

This is a variation on the Spanish omelet, called a "tortilla" (not bo be confused with the cornmeal variety).

Makes 6 servings.

6 tablespoons olive or	**potatoes, pared,**
vegetable oil	**cooked and diced**
1 large onion,	**1 cup frozen peas,**
chopped (1 cup)	**thawed (from a**
¹/₂ pound (4 to 5)	**10-ounce package)**
frankfurters, sliced	**8 eggs**
¹/₄-inch thick	**1 teaspoon salt**
2 medium-size	**¹/₄ teaspoon pepper**

1. Heat 2 tablespoons of the oil in a large skillet; add onion; cook, stirring occasionally, until onion begins to brown, about 5 minutes. Remove to large bowl; add frankfurters, potatoes and peas.
2. Beat eggs with salt and pepper in another bowl; stir into frankfurter and potato mixture.
3. Add remaining oil to skillet; heat. Pour frankfurter-potato mixture into skillet. As the edges set, draw toward the center to allow uncooked egg to flow

under. When eggs have set and a golden crust has formed underneath, place under broiler for 3 to 5 minutes to set top of eggs. Let stand 5 minutes before cutting into wedges to serve.

Pepper and Onion Dogs

Makes 4 to 5 servings.

2 medium-size red	**vegetable oil**
peppers, halved,	**¹/₂ teaspoon salt**
seeded and cut in	**¹/₂ teaspoon leaf**
thin strips	**oregano, crumbled**
2 medium-size green	**¹/₂ teaspoon leaf basil,**
peppers, halved,	**crumbled**
seeded and cut in	**1 package (1 pound)**
thin strips	**frankfurters (8 to 10)**
1 large onion, cut into	**8 to 10 split frankfurter**
thin rounds	**buns, toasted**
¹/₄ cup olive or	

1. Sauté peppers and onion in oil until crisp-tender; drain off any excess oil. Add salt, oregano and basil; toss gently; heat 1 minute longer.
2. Drop frankfurters in boiling water in a medium-size saucepan for 5 minutes; drain. Place frankfurter in toasted roll; top with pepper-onion mixture.

Frankfurter and Macaroni Bake

Bake at 350° for 35 minutes.

Makes 8 servings.

2 cups uncooked	**¹/₄ teaspoon pepper**
elbow macaroni	**2¹/₂ cups milk**
³/₄ cup diced onion	**8 ounces mild**
³/₄ cup diced carrot	**Cheddar cheese,**
³/₄ cup diced celery	**shredded (2 cups)**
¹/₂ cup (1 stick) butter	**1 package (1 pound)**
or margarine	**frankfurters (8 to**
6 tablespoons flour	**10), sliced ¹/₄-inch**
2 teaspoons salt	**thick**

1. Cook macaroni following label directions; drain.
2. While macaroni cooks, sauté onion, carrot and celery in butter in a large saucepan until soft. Stir in flour, salt and pepper; cook until bubbly.
3. Stir in milk; continue cooking and stirring until sauce thickens and bubbles; add cheese to sauce, stirring until cheese is melted.
4. Combine macaroni, frankfurters and cheese sauce in a large bowl; mix thoroughly. Turn into a 10-cup buttered soufflé or baking dish.
5. Bake in a moderate oven (350°) for 35 minutes or until sauce is bubbly-hot.

Bavarian-Style Knockwurst

Makes 4 servings.

4 bacon slices	¹/₂ teaspoon salt
1 medium-size onion, chopped (¹/₂ cup)	¹/₈ teaspoon pepper
4 cups shredded red cabbage	¹/₄ teaspoon caraway seeds
1 tart apple, pared, quartered, cored and chopped (1 cup)	3 tablespoons cider vinegar
	4 knockwursts (1 pound)
1 tablespoon sugar	Chopped fresh parsley

1. Cook bacon in a large skillet until crisp; remove and drain on paper toweling; crumble. Reserve. Pour drippings into a 1-cup measure then measure 2 tablespoons and return to skillet.
2. Add onion; sauté until tender, about 5 minutes. Add cabbage, apple, sugar, salt, pepper and caraway seeds; stir to coat with pan drippings. Cover; cook over low heat, 10 minutes. Add vinegar.
3. Place knockwursts on top of cabbage. Cover; cook 15 minutes or until knockwursts are hot and cabbage is crisp-tender.
4. To serve: Place cabbage on heated serving platter; arrange knockwursts on top, sprinkle with crumbled bacon and parsley. Serve with boiled potatoes, if you wish.

South-of-the-Border Casserole

Bake at 425° for 25 minutes.

Makes 6 servings.

2 medium-size tomatoes, cored, quartered, seeded and chopped	drained
	1 cup diced Monterey Jack cheese
¹/₃ cup chopped onion	1 cup *sifted* all-purpose flour
1 clove garlic, minced	4 teaspoons baking powder
2 tablespoons chopped fresh parsley	1 tablespoon sugar
	1¹/₂ teaspoons salt
¹/₂ teaspoon salt	1 cup yellow cornmeal
1 package (1 pound) frankfurters	1 cup milk
	2 eggs
1 can (4 ounces) diced green chilies,	¹/₄ cup vegetable oil

1. Combine chopped tomatoes, onion, garlic, parsley and salt in a small bowl; cover. Chill. Preheat oven to 425°.
2. Split frankfurters lengthwise, but do not cut through. Divide the green chilies and cheese between each split frankfurter.
3. Sift flour, baking powder, sugar and salt into a bowl. Stir in cornmeal. Combine milk, eggs and oil in a small bowl. Add to dry ingredients; stir just until smooth.
4. Pour into a buttered 13 × 9 × 2-inch baking pan;

spread evenly. Arrange frankfurters in a double row over cornmeal batter.
5. Bake in a preheated hot oven (425°) for 25 minutes or until cornbread tests done when a wooden pick is inserted in center. Let cool 10 minutes. Serve with chopped tomato mixture.

Bavarian Skillet Supper

Chicken hot dogs are found in the meat department, next to the regular frankfurters.

Makes 6 servings.

1 package (1 pound) chicken frankfurters	seeds
	2 tablespoons light brown sugar
2 tablespoons margarine	1 package (10 ounces) frozen lima beans
1 large onion, sliced	¹/₂ cup beer or beef broth
1 clove garlic, minced	
1 can (29 ounces) sauerkraut, drained	Parsley Potatoes *(recipe follows)*
1 teaspoon caraway	

1. Score each frank, then cut into thirds and brown quickly in margarine in a large skillet; remove with slotted spoon and reserve. Sauté onion and garlic until soft; stir in drained sauerkraut, caraway seeds, brown sugar and lima beans and toss to coat well; place franks on top; pour beer or broth over; cover.
2. Cook over low heat 30 minutes or until flavors are blended. Arrange Parsley Potatoes in a ring around edge of skillet.

Parsley Potatoes: Pare and boil 6 to 8 medium-size potatoes in boiling salted water in a large saucepan 25 minutes or until tender when pierced with a fork; drain water from pan. Return potatoes to heat and toss over low heat 3 minutes. Roll in 1/4 cup chopped fresh parsley and arrange around skillet.

Bockwurst
Plump sausage links, pale gray in color, made from veal and pork, seasoned with a variety of herbs and spices. Bockwurst is a German specialty most often served and enjoyed with beer. To prepare, cook slowly in a frying pan until thoroughly done.

Pictured opposite (from left front): All-American Dogs, page 532; Mediterranean Dogs, page 533; Reuben Dogs, page 532; Pepper and Onion Dogs, page 533; (in cast-iron skillet) Frankfurter and Potato Omelet, page 533; (in soufflé dish) Frankfurter and Macaroni Bake, page 533; Bavarian-Style Knockwurst, page 534; South-of-the-Border Casserole, page 534.

Bratwurst

A mildly seasoned pork or veal link sausage of German origin which means "frying sausage." Bratwurst is popular in many parts of Europe and also made in the United States, particularly where people of German or Scandinavian heritage live.

The meat and seasonings used to make bratwurst vary from country to country. Since it is a fresh sausage, it must be cooked thoroughly before eating. Bratwurst can be pan-fried, braised, broiled or grilled.

Bratwurst and Onions in Beer

Grill sausages 10 minutes.

Makes 4 servings (2 sausages each).

8 bratwursts (2 12-ounce packages)	seeds, crushed
3 medium-size onions, sliced	¹/₂ teaspoon salt
2 tablespoons vegetable oil	1 can (12 ounces) beer
1 teaspoon caraway	8 frankfurter rolls or bratwurst buns, split and toasted

1. Brown bratwursts on grill close to grayed coals, about 10 minutes.
2. While sausages brown, sauté onions in oil in large saucepan on grill 2 to 3 minutes; stir in caraway seeds, salt and beer; heat to boiling. Add sausages; cover and keep saucepan on side of grill to heat at least 10 minutes. Serve on toasted frankfurter rolls or bratwurst buns.

Note: Bratwursts can be broiled or pan-fried to brown.

Beer-Braised Sausages

Makes 6 servings.

2 pounds pork sausages	or ale
4 medium-size onions, thinly sliced	¹/₂ teaspoon leaf thyme, crumbled
1 can or bottle (12 ounces) beer	¹/₂ teaspoon salt
	¹/₄ teaspoon pepper

1. Prick sausages all over with fork. Cook in a large skillet, turning occasionally, until brown. Remove sausages to paper toweling to drain.
2. Pour off all but 3 tablespoons fat. Add onions to skillet; sauté until soft, about 10 minutes.
3. Add beer, thyme, salt and pepper. Heat to boiling; lower heat; simmer, covered, 10 minutes.
4. Return sausages to skillet. Cover and simmer 25 minutes. Serve with mashed potatoes, if you wish.

Bologna

American bologna bears little resemblance to the original mild sausage from Bologna, Italy. Our bologna is made from beef only or a combination of pork and beef. The meat is finely ground, seasoned, cooked and smoked. The two most familiar kinds of bologna are large sausage and ring. The large sausage is widely available presliced and sealed in transparent packages or sold in bulk and sliced to order in the delicatessen of some supermarkets.

Barbecued Bologna Kabobs

Makes 4 servings.

1 pound unsliced bologna	2 tablespoons chili sauce
16 2-inch pieces green celery	2 tablespoons molasses
2 tablespoons prepared mustard	4 cherry tomatoes

1. Cut bologna into 1¹/₄-inch chunks; thread with celery on 4 skewers. Place on rack over a broiler pan.
2. Combine mustard, chili sauce and molasses; brush over kabobs. Broil 5 inches from heat for 10 minutes or until glazed, turning often. To serve: Place a cherry tomato on the end of each skewer.

Alsace Kabob Dinner

Makes 4 servings.

1 pound kielbasa	mustard
1 can (16 ounces) small white onions, drained	1 large cooking apple, pared, quartered, cored and finely chopped
¹/₂ cup currant jelly	
¹/₄ cup apple juice	1 can (16 ounces) sauerkraut, drained and rinsed
¹/₈ teaspoon ground cinnamon	
¹/₄ teaspoon prepared	¹/₃ cup dry white wine

1. Cut sausage crosswise into 1-inch diagonal slices. Arrange slices of sausage alternately with onions on four 10- or 12-inch skewers.
2. Combine jelly with apple juice, cinnamon and mustard in a small saucepan. Heat, stirring constantly, over low heat until jelly melts. Brush sauce over kabobs.
3. Broil until edges of meat begin to brown. Turn; brush other side and broil until it begins to brown.
4. Combine apple, sauerkraut and wine in a medium-size saucepan. Cover; simmer until apples are tender, about 10 minutes.
5. To serve, spoon sauerkraut mixture on warm platter. Arrange broiled sausage skewers on top.

Creamy Corn and Sausage Casserole

Bake at 400° for 20 minutes.

Makes 6 servings.

**1 pound bulk pork
   sausage**
**1 large onion,
   chopped (1 cup)**
**2 cans (16 ounces
   each) cream-style
   corn**
4 eggs, lightly beaten
**1/4 to 1/2 teaspoon
   salt**

1/8 teaspoon pepper
**1/8 teaspoon leaf
   thyme, crumbled**
**1/8 teaspoon ground
   mace or nutmeg**
**2 cups fresh bread
   crumbs (4 slices
   stale firm-textured
   bread)**

1. Fry sausage in a large heavy skillet over moderately high heat, breaking up clumps, until uniformly browned, crumbly and cooked through, 10 to 15 minutes. Transfer to a medium-size bowl with a slotted spoon; reserve. Drain sausage drippings into a 1-cup measure; return 2 tablespoons to skillet; reserve remainder.
2. Stir-fry onion in drippings 10 minutes over moderate heat until limp and lightly browned. Transfer to a large bowl; mix in corn, eggs, salt, pepper, thyme and nutmeg. Spoon half of corn mixture into a buttered 9 × 9 × 2-inch baking dish; arrange sausage evenly on top; spoon in remaining corn mixture. Mix bread crumbs with 2 tablespoons reserved sausage drippings; scatter mixture evenly over all.
3. Bake, uncovered, in a hot oven (400°) for 20 minutes or until bubbling and browned.

Quick Choucroute Garni

Makes 6 servings.

**1 package (8 ounces)
   brown-and-serve
   sausage**
**1 package (1 pound)
   knockwursts**
**2 packages (1 pound
   each) sauerkraut**
**1 teaspoon caraway
   seeds**
1/8 teaspoon ground

cloves
1 cup dry white wine
**1 medium apple,
   pared, quartered,
   cored and sliced**
**1/4 cup packed light
   brown sugar**
**2 cans (16 ounces
   each) small white
   potatoes, drained**

1. Cook sausages in a large skillet following label directions.
2. Score each knockwurst diagonally. Add to skillet; cook, turning frequently, until slightly browned. Add sauerkraut, caraway, cloves, wine, apple and brown sugar. Bring to boiling; lower heat; cover; simmer 20 minutes. Add potatoes; heat.

Smoked Meat
Foods such as ham, pork, bacon and sausages that are flavored and preserved by smoking. The meat is first cured or salted, then it is hung or placed in a chamber where a wood-chip fire is smoldering into a dense smoke. The smoke flavors the food and the heat dries the food to aid in preserving it. The flavor of the smoke will depend on the type of wood burned. Oak and hickory are the most popular but juniper and beech are also used. Smoking was one of the most convenient and reliable methods of preserving meat for long storage before the invention of refrigerators and freezers.

Champagne Choucroute with Smoked Meats

Makes 12 servings.

4 pounds sauerkraut
**1 medium-size onion,
   thinly sliced**
**4 tablespoons butter
   or margarine**
**1/2 pound slab bacon,
   halved**
**1 large carrot, cut in
   1-inch chunks**
3 whole cloves
1 bay leaf
1/3 cup gin
**1 can (13 3/4 ounces)
   chicken broth**
**1 cup champagne or
   white wine**

**1 pound Canadian
   bacon, in one piece**
**Boiled New Potatoes
   and Onions (recipe
   follows)**
**4 fully cooked
   knockwurst (about
   1 pound)***
**5 to 6 fully cooked
   weisswurst or
   bockwurst (white
   veal sausage)*
   (about 1 pound)**
**1/2 pound fully cooked
   cocktail sausage**

1. Rinse the sauerkraut well; drain. Squeeze dry.
2. Sauté the sliced onion in 3 tablespoons of the butter in a large, heavy kettle or Dutch oven until golden brown. Add the sauerkraut. Cook, stirring often, for 5 minutes longer.
3. Add the bacon, carrot with a clove stuck into 3 of the chunks, bay leaf, gin and chicken broth. Bring to boiling. Lower heat; simmer, covered, for 1 1/2 to 2 hours, or until the bacon is tender.
4. Add the champagne and Canadian bacon. Cook, covered, for 30 minutes longer or until heated through.
5. Prepare the Boiled New Potatoes and Onions.
6. Meanwhile, brown the knockwurst, weisswurst and cocktail sausages on all sides in the remaining tablespoon of butter in a large skillet over medium heat. Add to the kettle with the sauerkraut mixture. Cook, covered, for 5 to 10 minutes longer, or until the sausage is heated through.
7. To serve, remove the meats and sausage to a cutting board. Slice or dice the Canadian bacon and cut up the sausages, if you wish. Arrange the sauerkraut and meats on a heated deep platter. Serve the potatoes and onions separately.

Any variety of fully cooked or smoked sausage may

(continued)

be substituted, pound for pound, for knockwurst, weisswurst or bockwurst, or cocktail sausages. You may be able to find lower-sodium meats and sausages in your area.

Boiled New Potatoes and Onions: Cook 16 red new potatoes, with their skins on, in boiling salted water for 20 minutes, or until tender. Drain. Keep warm. Cook 8 medium-size yellow onions in boiling salted water for 30 minutes, or just until tender. Drain and cut in half. Keep warm. (If red new potatoes are not available, use red potatoes, halved or quartered.)

Italian Sausages with Vegetables

Makes 4 servings.

1 pound sweet or hot Italian sausages, or a combination of both	**frozen baby lima beans**
1/2 cup chopped celery	**2 cans (12 ounces each) whole-kernel corn with sweet peppers**
1 package (10 ounces)	

1. Cut sausages into 1/2-inch slices. Cook in large skillet until well browned, 15 minutes. Push sausages to one side; sauté celery until soft.
2. Stir in frozen limas and corn. Simmer 10 minutes or until heated through.

Kielbasa   A highly seasoned beef and pork sausage of Polish origin. It comes shaped in hot-dog-like links or a horseshoe-link shape, about 1 1/2 inches in diameter. Most kielbasa are fully cooked and smoked but are also sold as fresh or smoked, uncooked sausages. Kielbasa can be boiled in water for 30 minutes or broiled or panfried until well browned.

Kielbasa and Kraut

Makes 4 servings.

1 can (27 ounces) sauerkraut, drained	**seeds**
1 teaspoon leaf basil, crumbled	**1 pound kielbasa**
1/2 teaspoon celery	**3 tablespoons brown sugar**
	1/2 cup hot water

1. Mix sauerkraut with basil and celery seeds in a 6-cup baking dish.
2. Remove skin from the sausage and make several deep cuts, 1 inch apart, in the meat; push sausage halfway down into sauerkraut.

Pictured opposite:
Hot Potato-Kielbasa Salad, page 695; Kielbasa and Kraut, page 539.

3. Dissolve brown sugar in hot water in a 1-cup measure; drizzle over the sausage and sauerkraut; cover.
4. Bake in a moderate oven (350°) for 1 hour or until sausage is tender and sauerkraut is heated through.

Hot Sausage and Mozzarella Roll

Bake at 375° for 30 minutes.

Makes 8 servings.

2 loaves (1 pound each) frozen plain bread dough	**shredded**
	1/4 cup freshly grated Parmesan cheese
1 1/2 pounds hot Italian sausages, casings removed	**1/4 cup chopped fresh parsley**
1 large onion, chopped (1 cup)	**1 egg yolk beaten with 2 tablespoons water**
1 package (8 ounces) mozzarella cheese,	**2 tablespoons sesame seeds** *(optional)*

1. Thaw dough in refrigerator overnight or at room temperature for about 1 hour, just until soft enough to yield to pressure of a finger.
2. Meanwhile, prepare filling: Place sausages and onion in a large skillet; cook 10 minutes, stirring often, breaking up meat with the side of a spoon. Transfer sausage and onion to a plate with a slotted spoon; refrigerate.
3. Pat out 1 piece of dough to flatten on a lightly floured surface. Roll dough into a 14 × 9-inch rectangle; sprinkle with half the cooled sausage, cheeses and parsley. Roll up dough starting with 1 long side, enclosing filling like a jelly roll. Preheat oven to 375°.
4. Transfer roll, seam-side down, to a lightly greased cookie sheet and tuck ends under. Brush with egg mixture. Repeat with remaining dough and filling; place second roll several inches from first on same cookie sheet. Brush with egg mixture; sprinkle with sesame seeds, if you wish.
5. Bake in a preheated moderate oven (375°) for 30 minutes or until crust is golden brown.
6. Remove loaves to a serving platter and cut into 1 1/2-inch slices to serve.

Sausage and Apple Skillet

Here's a simple and popular combination for a quick main dish.

Makes 4 servings.

1 package (1 pound) pork sausage links	**1 can (20 ounces) unsweetened apple slices, undrained**
2 large onions, sliced	

1. Place sausages in a large skillet; cook over low heat until lightly browned, about 10 minutes or until no

(continued)

pink shows in center. Remove sausages to a plate. Pour off all but 2 tablespoons fat from skillet.
2. Add onion slices; sauté until tender and light brown; stir in apples and sausages. Cook, stirring often, over low heat for 5 minutes. Serve with brown bread, if you wish.

Sausages in Onion and Apple Sauce

Makes 6 servings.

6 tablespoons butter	1/2 cup dry white wine
4 large onions, thinly sliced	3 Golden Delicious apples, pared, quartered and cored
1 teaspoon salt	Sugar
1/4 teaspoon pepper	Salt
Large pinch sugar	Ground nutmeg
12 fresh pork sausages	

1. Heat 2 tablespoons of the butter in a large skillet. Add onions, salt, pepper and sugar, Cook over low heat for 40 minutes, stirring occasionally, until onions are soft and nicely browned. Remove onions with a slotted spoon.
2. Add 2 more tablespoons of butter to skillet. Cook sausages over medium heat, turning occasionally, 10 minutes or until nicely browned and cooked through. Remove from skillet.
3. Pour off all fat from skillet. Add wine, stirring and scraping any brown bits in the skillet. Cook until wine is reduced to 2 tablespoons. Return onions and sausages to skillet; cover; simmer 10 minutes.
4. While sausages are simmering, heat remaining butter in a small skillet. Add the apples, sprinkle with sugar, a pinch of salt and nutmeg. Cook 5 to 6 minutes, shaking the pan occasionally, until apples are soft and lightly browned. Add apples to sausage mixture in skillet.

Italian Sausage Strata

Bake at 325° for 1 hour.

Makes 4 servings.

1/2 pound Italian sausages (sweet, hot or combination)	tomatoes, drained
	1/2 loaf Italian bread
1/2 cup chopped green pepper	3 eggs
	2 1/2 cups milk
1 medium-size onion, chopped (1/2 cup)	1 teaspoon salt
	1 tablespoon grated Parmesan cheese
1 can (16 ounces)	

1. Remove casing from sausages. Brown sausage in a large skillet about 10 minutes, breaking up with a wooden spoon as it browns. Stir in green pepper and onion. Cook another 5 minutes; add tomatoes, breaking up pieces. Cook 15 minutes to remove most of the liquid.
2. Slice bread; place half the slices in bottom of buttered 8 × 8 × 2-inch baking pan; spread with meat mixture. Top with remaining bread.
3. Beat eggs in medium-size bowl. Stir in milk and salt. Pour over bread. Sprinkle with cheese. Cover and refrigerate at least 1 hour or overnight.
4. Bake in a moderate oven (325°) for 1 hour or until puffed and golden. Remove to wire rack. Let stand 10 minutes before serving.

Sausage-Spaghetti Bake

Chunks of sweet Italian sausage are the "meatballs" in this easy-serve specialty.

Bake at 375° for 30 minutes.

Makes 6 servings.

1 pound sweet Italian sausages, sliced in 1-inch pieces	1 teaspoon sugar
	1/2 teaspoon Italian herb seasoning mix, crumbled
1 clove garlic, minced	
1 can (35 ounces) plum tomatoes	1 package (1 pound) thin spaghetti
1 can (8 ounces) tomato sauce	1/2 cup grated Parmesan cheese
1/2 cup water	

1. Brown sausages slowly in large skillet; push to one side. Add the garlic and sauté 2 minutes; pour off all fat.
2. Stir in tomatoes, tomato sauce, water, sugar and herb seasoning. Bring to boiling; simmer, covered, for 30 minutes to blend flavors.
3. While sauce simmers, cook spaghetti following label directions; drain well.
4. Spoon about half of spaghetti into a 13 × 9 × 2-inch baking dish; top with half of the meat sauce. Repeat with remaining spaghetti and sauce to make 2 layers of each; sprinkle with cheese.
5. Bake in a moderate oven (375°) for 30 minutes or until bubbly-hot. Let stand for 5 minutes, then cut into 6 equal-size servings. Lift out with wide spatula.

Sausage-Stuffed Zucchini

Bake at 350° for 30 minutes.

Makes 4 servings.

8 medium-size zucchini (about 3 1/2 pounds)	1 teaspoon leaf basil, crumbled
	1/2 teaspoon salt
1 pound sweet Italian sausages	1/4 teaspoon pepper
1 large onion, finely chopped (1 cup)	1/2 cup grated Parmesan cheese
	1/2 cup packaged bread crumbs
1/4 cup chopped fresh parsley	2 eggs, slightly beaten

1. Halve zucchini lengthwise. Cook in boiling water in a kettle or Dutch oven just until barely tender, about 10 minutes. Drain; scoop out seeds with tip of

teaspoon, leaving shell about $1/4$- to $1/2$-inch thick. Chop the scooped-out portion very finely.

2. Remove casings from sausages; cook sausages slowly in a large skillet, breaking up with a spoon as it cooks, until no trace of pink remains. Stir in onion, parsley, basil, salt and pepper. Cook, stirring occasionally, until onion is tender, about 5 minutes.

3. Remove from heat; stir in chopped zucchini, Parmesan, bread crumbs and eggs, mixing well. Fill shells with mixture, dividing equally and mounding slightly. Arrange shells close together in a 13 × 9 × 2-inch baking pan.

4. Bake in a moderate oven (350°) for 30 minutes or just until filling is hot.

Knockwurst
Also called knackwurst, this German sausage looks like a fat frankfurter. It's made of finely chopped pork and beef and is seasoned like frankfurters but with a touch of garlic. It is fully cooked and smoked so it needs only to be reheated in water or panfried, broiled or grilled until browned.

Kidney Beans with Knockwurst

Bake at 350° for 45 minutes.

Makes about 10 servings.

1 package (1 pound) dried red kidney beans, rinsed	halved, seeded and diced
10 cups water	1 tablespoon sweet paprika
4 knockwursts or 8 frankfurters	1 teaspoon leaf marjoram, crumbled
1 tablespoon vegetable oil	1 can (28 ounces) whole tomatoes
1 large onion, chopped (1 cup)	1 teaspoon salt
1 large green pepper,	$1/2$ teaspoon pepper

1. Combine beans and water in a large kettle. Cover; let soak overnight. Or, to quick-soak, bring to boiling; cover; boil 2 minutes; remove from heat; let stand 1 hour.

2. Bring beans to boiling; lower heat and cover partially. Simmer 30 minutes or until beans are almost tender; drain; remove from kettle.

3. Cut knockwursts or frankfurters into $3/4$-inch slices. Heat oil in kettle; add slices; sauté until lightly browned, stirring frequently. Add onion and green pepper; cook until soft. Stir in paprika and marjoram; cook 2 minutes. Add beans, tomatoes with their liquid, salt and pepper. Simmer 2 minutes, breaking up tomatoes with a spoon. Spoon into 3-quart baking dish; cover.

4. Bake in a moderate oven (350°) for 45 minutes or until beans are tender and most of the liquid is absorbed.

Grilled Knockwurst or Franks

Makes 8 servings.

8 knockwursts or 16 frankfurters	**Barbecue Sauce (recipe follows)**
$1/2$ recipe Piquant	

1. Split knockwursts lengthwise but don't cut all the way through. For frankfurters, slash crosswise, 1 inch apart and halfway through (they'll curl as they cook).

2. Grill knockwurst or franks, basting often with Piquant Barbecue Sauce until browned and sizzling hot.

Piquant Barbecue Sauce

Makes about $3^{1}/4$ cups.

1 large onion, finely chopped (1 cup)	**tomato puree**
1 clove garlic, finely chopped	**$1/2$ cup firmly packed brown sugar**
3 tablespoons butter or margarine	**$1/2$ cup lemon juice**
1 can (16 ounces)	**$1/2$ cup bottled steak sauce**
	1 tablespoon salt

Sauté onion and garlic in butter in a large saucepan until golden, about 5 minutes. Stir in puree, sugar, lemon juice, steak sauce and salt. Bring to boiling; lower heat. Simmer, partially covered, stirring occasionally, for 20 minutes.

Italian Fiesta Sausages

Grill 20 to 30 minutes.

Makes 4 servings.

$1^{1}/2$ pounds Italian-style sausages, sweet or hot (8 to 10 sausages)	**2 small red peppers, quartered and seeded**
2 medium-size zucchini, split lengthwise, then cut in half	**1 small onion, peeled and halved**
	$1/2$ cup Italian or oil and vinegar salad dressing

1. Alternate sausages, zucchini and peppers on skewers; thread $1/2$ onion on the end of each skewer; brush generously with salad dressing.

2. Grill about 5 inches from heat over grayed coals, turning skewers often and brushing with dressing, 20 minutes or until sausages are cooked through.

Grilled Knockwurst with Fruit Glaze

Grill 10 to 15 minutes.

Makes about 5 cups.

6 tablespoons grape jelly	**¹/₄ teaspoon ground cloves**
3 tablespoons chili sauce	**1 pound knockwurst, Polish sausage or frankfurters, scored**
1 tablespoon prepared mustard	

1. Heat jelly, chili sauce, mustard and cloves in small saucepan, stirring occasionally, just until smooth.
2. Grill sausages about 5 inches from grayed coals, brushing often with glaze, just until heated through, 10 to 15 minutes.

Sausage and Chicken Livers en Brochette

Grill about 5 minutes.

Makes 4 servings.

¹/₂ pound chicken livers, washed and halved	**cut into 2-inch pieces**
1 package (8 ounces) brown-and-serve sausage, cut in half	**2 tablespoons soy sauce**
3 bacon slices, cut in 1¹/₂-inch pieces	**2 tablespoons Worcestershire sauce**
1 red cooking apple, quartered, cored and cut into chunks	**1 tablespoon lemon juice**
1 bunch green onions,	**¹/₄ teaspoon leaf thyme, crumbled**

1. Alternate pieces of liver, sausage, bacon, apple and onion on skewers.
2. Combine soy and Worcestershire sauces, lemon juice and thyme in a small cup.
3. Place skewers on grill 5 to 6 inches over grayed coals for 6 to 8 minutes or until cooked through. Turn and brush often with soy sauce mixture. Serve with hot cooked rice, if you wish.

Sausage and Chicken Livers en Brochette, page 543; Italian Fiesta Sausage, page 541; Grilled Knockwurst with Fruit Glaze, page 542.

MICROWAVE COOKING

Principles of Microwave Cooking

Starting temperature: Whether you're cooking, heating or defrosting, the warmer the food, the shorter the cooking time. Starting with room temperature food is advisable.

Positioning: Before microwaving, place unevenly shaped food with larger, thicker portion toward outside of dish, and smaller, thinner portion toward the center.

Volume: Small amounts take less time to cook than large ones. For example, one potato cooks in about 4 minutes, four potatoes in 12 minutes.

Piece size: Not only will small pieces of food cook faster than large ones, but those that are similar in size will cook more evenly.

Density: Potatoes and other dense foods, as well as massive roasts, cook at a slower rate than light, porous foods such as bread.

Height in oven: The portion of food that is higher than 3 inches cooks faster than parts farther from source of heat. Shield protruding portion with thin strips of aluminum foil for more even cooking.

Boiling: Liquids may boil over before cooking time indicated in recipe, so set probe that will shut off oven when liquid reaches desired temperature.

Stirring: Because microwaves cook foods from outside in, it is necessary to redistribute the heat by stirring cooked portion to the center.

Standing time: Since cooking continues after you remove dish from microwave, let internal heat finish the job, about 1/4 to 1/3 of cooking time, before serving.

Guide to Countertop Microwave Ovens

These ovens come in four sizes; interior capacity is given in cubic feet. **Full-size** (1.1 to 1.6 cu. ft.) hold the largest cookware and amounts of food; they also have the most deluxe features. **Mid-size** (.8 to 1.0 cu. ft.) take up less than space full-size models, but are roomy inside. Come with many special features. **Compact** (.6 to .7 cu. ft.) and **Subcompact** (.3 to .5 cu. ft.) Both are ideal if you're cooking for one or two. Also perfect in a small space or a family room, a dorm, vacation home or office. Subcompacts generally have a limited number of features.

Note: Ovens of the same total cubic foot capacity from different manufacturers can have different interior dimensions, since some are more space-efficient inside than others.

Pictured opposite:
Crown Roast of Pork, page 567.

HOW TO INTERPRET WATTAGE NUMBERS ON MICROWAVES

Each microwave oven has an output wattage, which tells you the amount of microwave energy the oven has for cooking. Wattage is related to an oven's interior size, so, in general, the more cubic feet, the higher the wattage. Ovens range from 400 to 700 watts. Lower wattage ovens (400 to 500) take from a few seconds to a few minutes longer to cook food than higher wattage ovens (600 to 700 watts). Most recipes in magazines, newspapers and cookbooks are written for the high-wattage ovens.

Equivalents in Microwave Cooking Times

600- to 700-watt oven	500- to 600-watt oven	400- to 500-watt oven
15 seconds	18 seconds	20 seconds
30 seconds	35 seconds	45 seconds
1 minute	1 minute, 15 seconds	1 minute, 30 seconds
2 minutes	2 minutes, 30 seconds	2 minutes, 50 seconds
3 minutes	3 minutes, 30 seconds	4 minutes, 15 seconds
4 minutes	4 minutes, 50 seconds	5 minutes, 45 seconds
5 minutes	6 minutes	7 minutes
6 minutes	7 minutes, 15 seconds	8 minutes, 30 seconds
8 minutes	9 minutes, 30 seconds	11 minutes, 15 seconds
10 minutes	12 minutes	14 minutes

Many of Your Stovetop Recipes Can Be Adapted for Use in Your Microwave

• Follow the order of cooking just as it's described in the conventional recipe. Heat, scald, sauté or whatever the instructions say, only do it in the microwave. However, the oil may be eliminated.

• Brown meat, if indicated, but do it in your microwave. The microwave cooks ground meat to perfection every time. After microcooking a roast or other large cut of meat, however, you can achieve a crisper outer surface by placing it in a conventional oven or under a broiler for a short period of time.

• When a recipe calls for a large amount of liquid, reduce the specified amount by half. That's because there is less evaporation of liquid in a microwave oven than on the stovetop.

• For more even cooking, salt vegetables after microwaving.

• When preparing soup, cook the solid ingredients first in the microwave. Then add stock that has been cooked on top of the range and heat until flavors are absorbed.

• Estimate the time needed for cooking. For roasts, poultry, casseroles and stews, figure *about one-quarter to one-half* the time indicated in a conventional recipe. Keep in mind that an extra minute in the microwave can mean a burnt offering. If in doubt, cook for just less than quarter or half of time indicated in the conventional recipe. You can always return the dish to the microwave oven if it's underdone.

If you are comparing a conventional recipe to a similar sounding one developed for the microwave, use the microwave cooking time indicated, less about 20%. Then, check the dish for doneness.

• Test and taste the dish during cooking to determine the flavor, texture and tenderness. You, as a microcook, must stir, poke, taste, test, adjust, improvise and do all the other things you do when cooking over a hot stove.

• If a recipe calls for lots of water in order to cook the dish, don't try to make it in your microwave oven. Pasta, for example, is one food that turns out better when cooked on the stovetop. Soups and stews, however, in which liquid is a small part of the recipe, can be made in the microwave with success.

Baking in the Microwave — It Can Be Done — and Delicious!

Turning out baked products from your microwave oven is probably more a matter of expectations than expertise. If you know what to expect from your microwave oven you can get the best results possible with no disappointments. Here are some tips on what to look for and some delicious examples to illustrate the point.

• Choose glass bakeware so you can see the food as it cooks. You'll be able to check for doneness by looking at the bottom.

• The tests for doneness are different than in conventional baking. In most cases, baked goods will still be underdone at center and will finish cooking and firm up during standing time.

• Cool baked goods directly on heat-proof countertop, rather than on a baking rack. The held-in heat helps finish cooking foods.

• Cakes, whether from mix or from scratch, tend to rise higher in the microwave than in the conventional oven. Underfill cake pans slightly, using extra batter to make cupcakes.

• Avoid the urge to cut or slice until baked goods are cooled.

• For a "browner" look to baked goods, you can substitute brown sugar for some of the granulated sugar in most recipes, and whole wheat flour for not more than 1/4 of the all-purpose flour.

Update on Microwave Ovens

Whether you're buying your first microwave or want to move up to a new model, check out this information. It goes from the basics, such as oven sizes, to state-of-the-art special features.

WHICH MODEL SIZE SHOULD YOU CHOOSE?

• Microwaves run the gamut from no-frills models (great for mainly defrosting and reheating foods) to full-featured (for a lot of cooking). Decide how much and for what purpose you'll be using your microwave before buying it.

• Always compare interior sizes — the oven capacity. (*See "Guide to Countertop Microwave Ovens," on preceding page, for more details.*) Check the maufacturer's booklet to find out if the oven can handle (cook) the amount of food you need and if it's large enough for your favorite microwave-safe cookware. A rule of thumb: the larger your family, the larger capacity you need. Some compact models are designed to hold only frozen food entrées and may not have enough room for one of your dinner plates.

• Where you'll place your microwave also affects your choice. Countertop ovens range from full-size to subcompact. Under-the-cabinet models come in all sizes except full-size. Some ovens can be mounted on, or built into, the wall. There's even an over-the-range microwave oven (1.0 to 1.3 cu. ft. interior) that goes above the cooktop in place of a range hood—but functions as a hood as well!

MICROWAVE PLUS! MULTIFUNCTION OVENS

These three types of microwave ovens perform additional cooking functions. All are able to brown and crisp food.

• *Microwave Convection Oven* Bakes, roasts, broils and toasts or cooks with microwaves alone or with convection cooking. (For the latter method, a fan forces hot air throughout the oven cavity.) Available in full- and mid-size with deluxe features and in over-the-range units.

• *Microwave Thermal Oven* Has upper and lower heating elements like a conventional range. Bakes, roasts, broils and toasts or cooks with microwaves alone or in combination with thermal energy. Compact in size, some can be mounted under the cabinet to free up counter space.

• *Microwave Oven with Browner* An upper heating unit can be turned on after the microwave cooking is completed for final top browning. This feature is available in full-size models only.

EASY-ON-THE-COOK SPECIAL FEATURES

It pays to comparison-shop and see what different model microwave ovens have to offer. Special features are becoming more sophisticated, making less work for the cook! Following are some of the features available.

• *Automatic systems* These give you the ultimate in "computer" cooking! You simply enter the category of food, weight or amount and desired doneness. The oven automatically calculates the correct cooking time and sets power levels to either cook or defrost. Some ovens even have preprogrammed times and power levels for certain foods and recipes.

• **Temperature probes** The probe measures the temperature of a food as it cooks, and then turns the oven off or to a holding temperature when the preset temperature is reached.

• **Special defrost cycles** Provide faster, more even thawing.

• **Electronic controls** Make it easier to set precise times.

• **Rotating antennas, turntables and stirrer fans** These distribute microwaves throughout the oven cavity to insure more even cooking of the food.

Ham and Pineapple Kabobs

A delightful appetizer course, or finger food.
Microwave on Full Power for 8 to 9 minutes.

Makes 2 servings.

1 can (8 ounces) pineapple chunks in pineapple juice	**cloves**
1/2 cup dark corn syrup	**1/2 pound ham steak, cut in 1-inch cubes**
2 tablespoons corn oil	**1 can (8 ounces) sweet potatoes, drained**
1 tablespoon cider vinegar	**1 orange, cut into 12 pieces**
1/8 teaspoon ground	**1 1/2 teaspoons cornstarch**

1. Drain the chunks; reserve 1/2 cup juice.
2. Combine the reserved juice, syrup, oil, vinegar and cloves in a shallow dish.
3. Pierce the ham cubes with a fork. Add the ham, sweet potatoes, pineapple chunks and orange pieces to marinade. Cover; refrigerate overnight; turn frequently.
4. Thread the ham, pineapple chunks and orange pieces on six 8-inch wooden skewers. Arrange spoke-fashion on a microwave-safe plate; place the sweet potatoes between the kabobs.
5. Combine the cornstarch and marinade in a microwave-safe glass bowl until smooth.
6. Microwave on Full Power for 3 minutes, or until thickened, stirring after 1 minute.
7. Baste the kabobs and sweet potatoes with part of the marinade and microwave on Full Power for 3 minutes. Turn the kabobs and baste. Microwave on Full Power for 2 to 3 minutes longer, or until heated through. Serve with the remaining marinade.

Salmon Appetizer Spread

Vary the shape and/or the go-withs; your guests will always come back for more.
Microwave on Full Power for 30 to 45 seconds; then on Half Power for 1 to 1 1/2 minutes.

Makes 2 1/2 cups.

1 small onion, chopped (1/4 cup)	**ounces) salmon, drained and flaked**
1 tablespoon butter or margarine	**1/4 cup chopped parsley**
1 package (8 ounces) cream cheese	**Dash liquid red pepper seasoning**
2 cups shredded Cheddar cheese (8 ounces)	**Chopped parsley** **Thinly sliced pumpernickel**
1 can (7 1/2 or 7 3/4	

1. Microwave the onion and the butter or margarine in a microwave-safe bowl, covered, on Full Power 30 to 45 seconds, or until the onion is tender.
2. Microwave the cream cheese in a large microwave-safe bowl on Half Medium Power 1 to 1 1/2 minutes, or until softened. Stir in the onion-butter mixture, blending well.
3. Add the shredded Cheddar, salmon, 1/4 cup chopped parsley and the pepper seasoning, blending well. Shape the mixture into a ball. Wrap in plastic wrap and chill at least 2 hours.
4. Roll the bottom of the ball in additional chopped parsley, if you wish. Serve with triangles of thinly sliced pumpernickel.

Seafood Mousse

Individual servings of a creamy shellfish appetizer are great for your next dinner party.
Microwave on Full Power for 9 to 11 minutes.

Makes 6 servings.

3 cans (6 ounces each) seafood (lobster, crabmeat, shrimp or a combination), well drained	**1 cup heavy cream** **3 eggs, lightly beaten** **Salt** **Black pepper** **Cayenne pepper**

1. Shred large pieces of seafood into a bowl; set aside.
2. Microwave heavy cream in a 4-cup glass measure on Full Power for 2 to 3 minutes, or until hot.
3. Beat the cream into the eggs in a bowl; add the salt, black and cayenne peppers. Add the seafood, mixing well. Pour into six 6-ounce custard cups, dividing evenly.
4. Microwave on Full Power for 7 to 8 minutes, or until set, rotating and rearranging cups every 2 minutes.
5. Loosen around the edge with a thin-bladed knife; turn out onto serving plates. Serve with canned Newburg sauce, if you wish.

Chile con Queso Dip

Serve with corn chips or taco chips.
Microwave on Full Power for 4 to 7 minutes.

Makes 2 cups.

1 tablespoon butter or margarine
1 small onion, finely chopped (1/4 cup)
1 can (8 ounces) whole tomatoes, drained and chopped
1 can (4 ounces) chopped green

chilies, drained
1/4 teaspoon salt
2 cups shredded Monterey Jack or process American cheese (8 ounces)
1/2 cup mayonnaise
Bottled liquid red pepper seasoning

1. Place the butter or margarine and onion in a 1-quart microwave-safe bowl.
2. Microwave on Full Power for 2 to 3 minutes, or until the onion is tender.
3. Add the chopped tomatoes, chilies, 1/2 teaspoon sugar (if used) and salt.
4. Microwave on Full Power 1 to 2 minutes, or until bubbly. Stir in the cheese and mayonnaise. Microwave on Full Power for 1 to 2 minutes more, or until the cheese melts. Stir in the red pepper seasoning to taste. Transfer to chafing dish; keep warm.

Chunky Vegetable Chowder

This recipe yields enough soup to reheat for lunch later in the week.
Microwave on Full Power for 29 to 31 minutes.

Makes 8 servings.

12 slices bacon
2 cans (10³/4 ounces each) chicken broth
4 cups finely chopped potatoes
2 cups shredded carrot
1 large onion, chopped (1 cup)
1 teaspoon salt

1 teaspoon curry powder
1/4 teaspoon black pepper
2 cans (12 ounces each) evaporated milk
1/4 cup chopped fresh parsley

1. Microwave the bacon in a 3-quart glass microwave-safe dish on Full Power for 5 minutes, or until crisp. Remove with a slotted spoon; reserve the bacon and drippings.
2. Place 2 tablespoons of the drippings and the chicken broth in a 4-quart glass bowl. Stir in the chopped potatoes, carrot, onion, salt, curry powder and black pepper. Cover with vented heavy-duty plastic wrap.
3. Microwave on Full Power for 20 to 22 minutes, or until vegetables are tender, stirring after 10 minutes. Stir in the evaporated milk; cover.

Chunky Vegetable Chowder.

Whole Wheat Pizza.

4. Microwave on Full Power for 4 minutes, or until heated through. Stir in the parsley. Let stand, completely covered, for 5 minutes. Serve half of the chowder topped with 6 slices crumbled bacon.

5. Place the remaining half of the chowder in a large glass bowl. Cover with heavy-duty plastic wrap and refrigerate up to 2 days. Wrap 6 slices bacon in plastic wrap and refrigerate.

To reheat: Vent the plastic wrap. Microwave on Full Power for 6 to 8 minutes, or until heated through, stirring after 3 minutes. Top with crumbled bacon.

Creamy Mushroom Soup

Serve this soup hot or chilled, with a swirl of lightly whipped cream and/or snipped chives, if you wish.

Microwave on Full Power for 9 to 12 minutes.

Makes 4 servings.

2 tablespoons finely chopped onion	**2 teaspoons instant beef bouillon**
2 tablespoons butter or margarine	**¼ teaspoon leaf basil, crumbled**
1 jar (4½ ounces) sliced mushrooms, drained (reserve liquid)	**1 bay leaf**
	Pinch ground black pepper
¼ cup all-purpose flour	**1 cup half-and-half or light cream**

1. Place the onion, butter or margarine and drained mushrooms in a deep 2-quart microwave-safe casserole.

2. Microwave on Full Power for 3 to 4 minutes, or until the onion is soft and translucent.

3. Stir in the flour and bouillon until well blended. Add the water to the reserved mushroom liquid to make 2¼ cups; add to the mushroom mixture and stir well, then stir in the basil, bay leaf and pepper.

4. Microwave on Full Power for 4 to 5 minutes, until

thickened, stirring every minute. Remove the bay leaf. Stir in the half-and-half or cream.

5. Microwave on Full Power for 2 to 3 minutes, or until thoroughly heated.

Whole Wheat Pizzas

At last, a pizza that is totally achievable in the microwave. The whole wheat flour gives the pizza a "browned" look, although for a slightly crisper crust see note at end of recipe.

Microwave on Full Power for about 5 to 5½ minutes.

Makes 4 servings.

1 envelope plus 1 teaspoon active dry yeast	**box**
	Aluminum foil
1 teaspoon sugar	**1½ cups Microwave Tomato Sauce (recipe follows)**
1 cup very warm water	
1½ cups unsifted all-purpose flour	**2½ cups shredded mozzarella cheese (10 ounces)**
1½ cups whole wheat flour	
1½ teaspoons coarse salt	**½ to ¾ cup freshly grated Parmesan cheese (2 to 3 ounces)**
3 tablespoons light olive oil	
Empty 7-ounce cereal	**1 teaspoon leaf oregano, crumbled**

1. Sprinkle the yeast and sugar into ¼ cup of the very warm water in a small custard cup. ("Very warm" water should feel comfortably warm when dropped on wrist.) Place in a loosely closed plastic bag. Let stand for 5 minutes, or until the mixture foams.

2. Place the all-purpose and whole wheat flours, coarse salt, ¾ cup very warm water and olive oil in a large warm bowl of an electric mixer fitted with a dough hook. Beat for 1 to 2 minutes, or mix by hand

(continued)

with a wooden spoon, until the dough leaves the side of the bowl. Blend in the proofed yeast.

3. Turn the dough out onto a lightly floured surface. Knead for 5 minutes, or until smooth and elastic. Place the dough in a greased bowl; turn to bring the greased side up. Cover with a warm, damp cloth.

4. Place the dough in a hot oven (400°) 1 minute. *Turn oven off;* let dough rest for 30 minutes, or until doubled in bulk.

5. Punch the dough down; cover with an inverted bowl; let dough rest for 10 minutes.

6. Make a microwave trivet: Lay the empty cereal box on its back; using scissors, cut in half horizontally to form two 7 × 9 × 1-inch trivets. Cover the top of each with aluminum foil

7. Divide the dough into quarters. Roll or pat each quarter into a 7-inch circle on a floured surface. Prick all over with a fork. Place the dough on the prepared trivet.

8. Microwave, one at a time, on Full Power for 1 minute, 25 seconds. Remove from the oven. Spread with 6 tablespoons of the **Microwave Tomato Sauce.** Top with generous 1/2 cup mozzarella cheese, then 2 tablespoons Parmesan to within 1 inch of the edge of the crust. Sprinkle with 1/4 teaspoon oregano.

9. Microwave on Full Power for 3 1/2 to 4 minutes, rotating once or twice, or until the cheese in the center is melted. Repeat with the remaining dough and topping ingredients.

Note: For a crisper crust: Preheat a conventional oven to hot (450°). Place a cookie sheet in the oven. Prepare a 7-inch circle of dough as directed. Prick. Lightly oil the top of the dough. Invert the dough onto a 7 × 9-inch piece of aluminum foil. Place on the cookie sheet. Bake for 5 minutes. Remove from the oven; continue with step 8.

Microwave Tomato Sauce

This versatile, spicy sauce was developed as topping for Whole Wheat Pizzas, but it can also be spooned over hot pasta.

Microwave on Full Power for 4 to 5 minutes, then on Half Power for 10 to 15 minutes.

Makes 4 cups.

1 tablespoon unsalted butter or olive oil	12 ounces) Italian plum tomatoes
1 medium carrot, finely diced	1 can (6 ounces) tomato paste
1 medium onion, diced	3/4 teaspoon leaf basil, crumbled
1 stalk celery, scraped and finely chopped	1 bay leaf
1 to 2 cloves garlic, finely chopped	1 teaspoon coarse salt
1 can (1 pound,	Black pepper *(optional)*

1. Place the butter or olive oil with the carrot, onion, celery and garlic in a 3-quart glass microwave-safe bowl; cover with wax paper.

2. Microwave on Full Power for 4 to 5 minutes, or until the onion is transparent and the other vegetables are soft. Using potholders, remove the bowl from oven. Add the tomatoes and liquid, tomato paste, basil, bay leaf, salt and pepper, if you wish. Cover with a fresh sheet of wax paper.

3. Microwave on Half Power for 10 to 15 minutes. Taste; adjust seasonings; remove bay leaf. (Tomatoes will still be whole.) Remove bowl from oven.

4. Whirl sauce, part at a time, in the container of an electric food processor or blender until smooth. (Don't overprocess--sauce is nice with texture.)

Apple Upside-Down Cake

Family and guests alike will enjoy nibbling on this sweet snack.

Microwave on Full Power for 14 minutes.

Makes 16 squares.

Glaze:
1/4 cup (1/2 stick) unsalted butter, cut up
1/2 cup granulated sugar
3 tablespoons all-purpose flour
Pinch salt
1 teaspoon ground cinnamon

Topping:
2 pounds (about 5 large) firm apples (Miltons, Gravensteins, early McIntosh or Golden Delicious)
Juice of 1/2 medium-size lemon

Batter:
1 cup plus 2 tablespoons unsifted unbleached all-purpose flour
2 tablespoons granulated sugar
1 teaspoon baking powder
1/2 teaspoon salt
1/4 cup (1/2 stick) unsalted butter, softened
2 extra-large eggs
1 teaspoon vanilla
1/4 cup milk or orange juice
Grated rind of 1/2 lemon

1. Prepare the Glaze: Using your fingertips, blend the 1/4 cup butter or margarine, the brown and granulated sugars, 3 tablespoons flour, salt and cinnamon in a medium-bowl until crumbly. Pat mixture evenly into a greased 8 x 8 x 2-inch-square microwave-safe glass dish.

2. Prepare the Topping: Wash, peel, quarter and slice the apples into large bowl. (You should have 6 cups.) Sprinkle the apples with the lemon juice. Arrange the apple slices over the sugar mixture in 5 overlapping rows. Repeat with remaining apples.

3. Prepare the Batter: Sift together the 1 cup plus 2 tablespoons flour with the 2 tablespoons granulated sugar, the baking powder and salt onto a piece of wax paper. Sift together 2 more times. *(continued)*

Pictured opposite (from top to bottom): Jalapeño Corn Bread, page 552; Apricot-Oatmeal Squares, page 552; Fresh Carrot Loaves, page 552; Apple Upside-Down Cake, page 550.

4. Beat ¼ cup butter in a medium-size bowl with an electric mixer at high speed until light and fluffy. Beat in the eggs, one at a time, and vanilla until well blended. (The mixture may appear curdled.)

5. Using a wooden spoon, alternately stir in the flour in 3 portions and the milk or juice in 2 portions. Stir in the grated lemon rind. (The batter will be thick.) Spread the butter evenly over apples.

6. Microwave the cake on Full Power for 14 minutes or until the cake springs back when lightly touched with fingertip. Invert immediately onto a platter, spooning hot glaze over top. (The glaze will thicken as it cools.) Serve the cake hot or cold.

Note: As the cake stands, the juice exuded by the apples will dissolve the sugar crystals

Fresh Carrot Loaves

Spices add fragrance as well as flavor to this carrot cake.

Microwave on Full Power for 14 minutes, and on Medium-High Power for 2 to 3 minutes.

Makes 2 loaf cakes (12 slices each).

4 cups grated carrot	**2 teaspoons baking**
1½ cups sugar	**soda**
1 cup (2 sticks)	**2 teaspoons ground**
unsalted butter	**cloves**
and/or margarine,	**¾ teaspoon ground**
cut into tablespoon-	**allspice**
size chunks	**¾ teaspoon ground**
½ cup water	**nutmeg**
OR: orange juice	**½ teaspoon salt**
2½ cups unsifted all-	**2 eggs, at room**
purpose flour	**temperature**
1 tablespoon ground	**10X (confectioner's**
cinnamon	**sugar** *(optional)*

1. Lightly butter the bottom and sides of two 8¼ × 4½ × 2⅝-inch microwave-safe glass loaf dishes. Line the bottom and sides of each with strips of wax paper cut to fit.

2. Place the grated carrots, sugar, butter and/or margarine and water or orange juice in a microwave-safe 1½-quart glass bowl. Cover loosely with wax paper.

3. Microwave the carrot mixture on Full Power for 5 minutes or until the mixture begins to boil.

4. Microwave on Medium-High for 2 to 3 minutes longer. Stir the mixture; remove from the microwave and cool.

5. Sift the flour with the cinnamon, baking soda, cloves, allspice, nutmeg and salt onto a sheet of wax paper. Sift again.

6. Beat the eggs in a large bowl of an electric mixer at medium speed until very thick and lemon colored. Add the cooled carrot mixture, then the flour mixture, stirring until the batter is just combined. Divide the batter evenly between the 2 prepared dishes; shield the corners with triangles of aluminum foil.

7. Microwave on Full Power for 9 minutes or until a

wooden pick inserted into the center of the cake comes out clean. Cool the cakes on wire racks. Dust with 10X sugar, if you wish.

Jalapeño Corn Bread

Made with or without the jalapeño peppers — this snack is wholesome either way.

Microwave on Full Power for 8 minutes.

Makes 9 generous pieces.

1 can (16 ounces)	**2 tablespoons sugar**
white corn	**2 teaspoons baking**
1 can (4 ounces)	**powder**
whole green chilies	**1 teaspoon salt**
(optional), drained	**3 eggs, separated**
2 cups plus 2	**3 tablespoons**
tablespoons stone-	**unsalted margarine,**
ground yellow	**melted**
cornmeal	

1. Drain the liquid from corn into a 4-cup measure; reserve the corn. Add enough water to corn liquid to measure 2 cups.

2. Finely chop half of the drained chilies, if using. Cut the remaining chilies into strips. Reserve.

3. Measure the cornmeal, sugar, baking powder and salt into a bowl. Add the slightly beaten egg yolks to the bowl. Stir in the melted margarine and the corn liquid. Beat with a wooden spoon until the mixture is blended. Stir in the reserved corn and the finely chopped green chilies, if using.

4. Beat the egg whites with a pinch of salt in a large bowl until stiff but not dry peaks form. Fold the whites into the batter until no streaks of white remain. Pour the batter into a greased 9½-inch round or square microwave-safe glass pie plate. Arrange the strips of chilies on top in lattice fashion, if using.

5. Microwave the corn bread on Full Power for 8 minutes. Cool the dish directly on a heatproof surface. Cut the cooled cornbread into 3-inch squares.

Apricot-Oatmeal Squares

So easy, even kids can bake these snack squares. So good, they will become a family favorite.

Microwave on Full Power for 7 minutes.

Makes 16 squares.

1½ cups unsifted	**light brown sugar**
unbleached all-	**¾ cup (1½ sticks)**
purpose flour	**unsalted butter or**
1 teaspoon baking	**margarine, cut into**
powder	**tablespoon-size**
½ teaspoon salt	**chunks**
1½ cups	**1 jar (12 ounces)**
old-fashioned	**apricot preserves**
rolled oats	**1 to 2 teaspoons**
½ cup firmly packed	**lemon juice**

1. Sift together flour, baking powder and salt into a

large mixing bowl. Stir in the uncooked oats, then the brown sugar.

2. Using your hands or a pastry blender, cut in the softened butter or margarine until the mixture is crumbly. Place 3 cups of the mixture in a greased square microwave-safe glass baking dish, pressing down to form an even layer.

3. Blend the preserves with lemon juice in a small bowl. Using a spatula, spread the preserves over the crust. Sprinkle the remaining oatmeal mixture over the filling, pressing down gently. (This prevents the crust from crumbling when you cut the squares.)

4. Microwave on Full Power for 7 minutes, rotating once. (The preserves will bubble up during the cooking. The crust may appear somewhat mushy but it will solidify within 15 minutes.) Cool: Cut into squares or bars with a sharp or serrated knife.

Note: The crust mixture may be prepared ahead and refrigerated in a plastic bag.

Tips for Microwaving Chicken

To Microwave: Chicken cooks quickly on the High or Full Power setting and retains its natural juices. In general, a 3-pound whole chicken takes 1 to 1 1/2 hours to roast in a regular oven, but it will cook in less than 30 minutes in a microwave. Here are some tips for cooking chicken in a microwave oven:

● To brown chicken, coat it with butter (not margarine), or use soy sauce, paprika, herbs or a commercial browning sauce.

● Do not salt chicken before cooking. Add salt during the standing time.

● Chicken parts cook best on High or Full Power, but use Half Power for whole birds.

● Choose chicken pieces (breasts, thighs or drumsticks) of equal size so that they will cook evenly.

● When cooking parts, place the larger, thicker parts near the outside and the thinner parts toward the center of the baking dish. Place giblets under the breast.

● Place whole chicken, breast-side down, on a microwave-safe roasting rack in a shallow pan.

● Cover the chicken lightly with wax paper to prevent spattering.

● Microwave on Half Power (50%), 9 minutes per pound, turning the chicken breast-side up after half the cooking time, or until a drumstick moves easily.

● When in doubt about whether the chicken is done, undercook rather than overcook. It's easy to return the chicken to the microwave oven for more cooking. Remember, chicken will continue to cook during the standing time.

● Allow to rest 10 minutes, then carve.

● Because chicken cooks so quickly, added flavors are absorbed more fully if chicken is marinated before cooking.

Chicken Rosemary

Total cooking time: 16 minutes.

Makes 4 servings.

3 cloves garlic, crushed	3 tablespoons fresh lemon juice
1 teaspoon leaf rosemary, crumbled	1 teaspoon salt
1/8 teaspoon chili powder	1/2 teaspoon pepper
1/2 cup dry white wine	1/8 teaspoon cumin powder
1/4 cup olive oil	1 broiler-fryer (3 1/2 to 4 pounds), cut up

1. Combine garlic, rosemary, chili powder, wine, olive oil, lemon juice, salt, pepper and cumin in a 3-quart shallow glass baking dish. Add the chicken pieces, turning several times to coat well. Remove the chicken.

2. Place the baking dish in center of oven; heat the seasoning mixture 3 to 4 minutes on high power until simmering. Add chicken, skin-side down, placing the thicker portions near the edge of the dish. Spoon the mixture over the chicken.

3. Cook, covered with plastic wrap, 4 minutes. Turn the chicken over, spooning mixture over it. Cook 4 minutes. Rotate the dish 1/2 turn. Cook 4 minutes.

4. Remove from oven; cover tightly with aluminum foil; let stand 15 minutes before serving.

Saucy Barbecued Chicken

Lemon juice adds a dimension to basting sauce that gives chicken from the microwave a barbecued quality.

Microwave on Full Power for 30 1/2 to 31 1/2 minutes.

Makes 4 servings.

2 tablespoons margarine or butter	3 tablespoons light brown sugar
1 small onion, chopped (1/4 cup)	1 tablespoon Worcestershire sauce
1 clove garlic, finely chopped	1 teaspoon chicken-flavor instant bouillon
1/2 cup catsup	1 broiler-fryer (2 1/2 to 3 pounds), cut up
1/4 cup bottled lemon juice	
1/4 cup water	

1. Microwave the margarine or butter in a 1-quart glass measure on Full Power for 30 seconds, or until melted. Add the chopped onion and garlic.

2. Microwave on Full Power for 2 minutes, or until the onion is tender. Sir in the catsup, lemon juice, water, brown sugar, Worcestershire sauce and bouillon. Cover loosely with wax paper.

3. Microwave on Full Power for 3 to 4 minutes, or until hot and bubbly.

4. Place the chicken in a 12 x 7-inch shallow

(continued)

Chicken Italia.

microwave-safe dish; pour the sauce over the chicken. Re-cover, using a fresh sheet of wax paper, if you wish.

5. Microwave on Full Power for 25 minutes, or until tender, rearranging the chicken after 10 minutes. Let stand 5 minutes.

Chicken Italia

Cooks 4 servings and freezes 2 to reheat later. The chicken and Italian-flavored sauce are delicious the first and second time around.

Microwave on Full Power for 16 to 18 minutes.

Makes 4 servings.

2 tablespoons all-purpose flour	**taste**
1 jar (15½ ounces) spaghetti sauce with mushrooms	**Garlic powder**
	1 small onion, thinly sliced
1 medium-size tomato, chopped	**½ small sweet green pepper, halved, seeded and cut into strips**
¼ cup rosé wine	
OR: water	**2 cups hot cooked spaghetti**
4 chicken breast halves, skin removed	**Grated Parmesan cheese**
Salt and pepper to	

1. Shake the flour in a 10 x 16-inch oven cooking bag. Place the bag in a 12 x 8 x 2-inch microwave-safe dish. Roll down the top of the bag. Add the spaghetti sauce, chopped tomato and wine or water. Squeeze the bag gently to blend the ingredients.
2. Sprinkle the chicken lightly with salt, pepper and garlic powder. Place chicken in bag; turn the bag gently to coat the chicken. Top the chicken with the onion and green pepper. Close the bag with the nylon tie. Make six ½-inch slits in the top.
3. Microwave the chicken on Full Power for 16 to 18 minutes, or until the chicken is done, rotating the dish after half the cooking time. Let stand for 3 minutes.

4. To serve, spoon the chicken and sauce over the hot cooked spaghetti. Sprinkle with the grated Parmesan cheese.

To Freeze: Place 2 servings of the **Chicken Italia** on a square of heavy-duty aluminum foil. Bundle wrap by bringing 4 corners up together into a pyramid shape, then folding edges together in a series of locked folds. Label, date and freeze.

To Reheat: Remove frozen food from the foil. Place in a 1½ quart microwave-safe casserole. Cover the casserole with vented heavy-duty microwave-safe plastic wrap. Microwave on Half Power for 10 to 12 minutes, or until the chicken is heated through. Serve over hot cooked spaghetti. Sprinkle with the Parmesan cheese.

Chicken with Ratatouille

Chicken with the famous French vegetable stew for a dinner with distinctive flavor.

Microwave on Full Power for 24 minutes, then on Medium-High Power for 18 to 22 minutes.

Makes 4 servings.

1 medium eggplant, peeled and cubed (5 cups)	**1 tablespoon chicken bouillon granules**
4 medium tomatoes, chopped (3 cups)	**2 teaspoons finely chopped fresh garlic**
2 small zucchini, sliced (1½ cups)	**OR: ½ teaspoon garlic powder**
1 large onion, chopped (1 cup)	**1 teaspoon leaf basil, crumbled**
1 medium green pepper, chopped (⅔ cup)	**1 teaspoon sugar**
	¼ teaspoon pepper
1 can (6 ounces) tomato paste	**1 broiler-fryer (2½ to 3 pounds), quartered and skin removed**

1. Place the cut-up eggplant, tomatoes, zucchini, onion and green pepper in a 13 x 9 x 2-inch glass baking dish. Cover with heavy-duty plastic wrap.

2. Microwave on Full Power for 10 minutes, or until the vegetables become slightly limp, rotating dish 1/2 turn after 5 minutes. Add the tomato paste, bouillon granules, garlic, basil, sugar and pepper, stirring until well mixed.

3. Place the chicken in the vegetable mixture, with the thickest meaty pieces to the edge of the dish. Spoon some of the vegetable mixture over the chicken. Recover with a fresh sheet of plastic wrap, if you wish.

4. Microwave on Full Power for 14 minutes. Rearrange the vegetables over the chicken.

5. Microwave on Medium-High Power for 18 to 22 minutes, or until the juices run clear when the chicken is pierced with a fork. Garnish with Italian parsley and serve with a baguette, if you wish.

Chicken with Lemon and Olives

Be sure to marinate the chicken overnight for maximum flavor. The finished dish is even better reheated the second day.

Microwave on Full Power for 3 minutes; then for 15 to 17 minutes. Microwave gravy on High Power for 1 minute.

Makes 4 servings.

1 lemon	1/4 cup dry white wine
2 cloves garlic, finely chopped	OR: water
1/4 teaspoon ground ginger	1 medium-size onion, finely chopped (1/2 cup)
1/4 teaspoon ground cumin	1 medium-size sweet red pepper, halved, cored and cut into 1/4-inch-wide strips
1/4 teaspoon ground cinnamon	
1/4 teaspoon black pepper	1 tablespoon water
1/8 teaspoon cayenne pepper	1 tablespoon flour
2 tablespoons olive oil	20 oil-cured black olives, pitted
1 broiler-fryer chicken (about 3 1/2 pounds), cut into 8 serving pieces	Salt to taste
	1 tablespoon chopped flat-leaf Italian parsley

1. Remove just the outer yellow rind with a swivel-bladed vegetable peeler from half of the lemon. Coarsely chop the rind; reserve. Squeeze and measure out 2 tablespoons of juice from the lemon.

2. Place the rind and the juice in a 12 x 8-inch microwave-safe baking dish. Stir in the garlic, ginger, cumin, cinnamon, pepper, cayenne and olive oil. Add the chicken, turning to coat well. Cover the dish and refrigerate overnight, turning the chicken once or twice.

3. Remove the chicken and set aside. Add the onion to the marinade and stir to mix. Cover the dish with wax paper. Microwave at Full Power for 3 minutes. Stir, arranging the meatier portions toward the outside of the dish. Pour the wine over all.

4. Cover the dish with wax paper. Microwave at Full Power for 15 to 17 minutes; rotate the dish after 10 minutes. Remove the chicken along with the red pepper to a serving dish. Reserve the cooking liquids.

5. Stir together the water and the flour in a microwave-safe 2-cup glass measure until smooth; stir in the wine-cooking mixture. Microwave, uncovered, at Full Power for 1 minute to boiling. Sprinkle the olives and parsley over the chicken. Pour the gravy over all.

Sweet and Sour Chicken and Cabbage

Microwave on Full Power for 19 minutes.

Makes 4 servings.

3 chicken breasts, boned and skinned	5 tablespoons sweet-and-sour reduced-calorie dressing
1 teaspoon sesame seeds	1/4 to 1/2 teaspoon liquid red pepper seasoning
4 cups coarsely shredded red cabbage	1/4 to 1/2 teaspoon curry powder
1 medium-size red onion, thinly sliced (about 1 1/2 cups)	1/8 teaspoon ground cinnamon
1 cup halved seedless green grapes (about 45)	Red and green cabbage leaves

1. Flatten the chicken slightly with a mallet between sheets of wax paper. Arrange the cutlets around the outside of a microwave-safe plate. Cover the chicken with a double thickness of damp microwave-safe paper toweling.

2. Microwave on Full Power for 7 minutes, rotating the plate after 4 minutes if the chicken is cooking unevenly. Cover the chicken completely with heavy-duty microwave safe plastic wrap and let stand for 2 minutes.

3. Place the sesame seeds in a single layer on a small microwave-safe plate.

4. Microwave the seeds on Full Power for 12 minutes, or until the seeds turn golden, rotating the plate after 6 minutes. Set aside.

5. Cut the chicken into 1/4-inch-wide strips. Toss with the shredded red cabbage, the sliced onion, halved grapes, salad dressing, red-pepper seasoning, curry powder and cinnamon in a medium-size bowl until well blended.

6. Spoon into a salad bowl lined with red and green cabbage leaves. Sprinkle with the reserved toasted sesame seeds. Serve immediately.

Antipasto Salad

Microwave on Full Power for 5¹/₂ minutes, then on Half Power for 3 minutes.

Makes 4 servings.

1 piece London broil (10 ounces), cut about 1¹/₂ inches thick, trimmed
1 package (9 ounces) frozen Italian-style green beans
1 medium-size sweet red pepper, cut in ¹/₄-inch-thick rings

1 small onion, thinly sliced (¹/₂ cup)
¹/₄ cup grated Parmesan cheese
5 tablespoons Italian salad dressing
¹/₂ teaspoon salt
¹/₄ teaspoon leaf oregano, crumbled
Pepper to taste

1. Microwave the beef on a microwave-safe plate, uncovered, on Full Power for 1¹/₂ minutes. Turn the meat over.
2. Microwave on Half Power for 3 minutes, or until an instant-reading meat thermometer reads 120° when inserted in the center of beef. Cover the beef with plastic wrap and let stand for 5 minutes.
3. Separate the green beans under cold running water. Arrange the beans in a single layer on a microwave-safe plate. Cover with a double thickness of damp microwave-safe paper toweling.
4. Microwave the beans on Full Power for 4 minutes. Rinse the beans under cold water and drain.
5. Slice the beef thin, cutting across the grain into ¹/₄-inch-thick strips. Place the beef in a bowl with the beans, red pepper, onion, Parmesan, dressing, salt, oregano and pepper; toss to mix. Serve immediately.

Mediterranean Salad

Sole and the luscious produce of the South of France are combined for a light, yet satisfying, main dish.
Microwave on Half Power for 6 minutes, then on Full Power for 12 minutes.

Makes 4 servings.

1 package (12 ounces) frozen sole fillets
¹/₂ pound small new red potatoes, sliced ¹/₄-inch thick
3 plum tomatoes (¹/₂ pound), cut into wedges
20 Niçolse olives, halved and pitted
OR: 1 can (8 ounces) pitted ripe olives (halved, if large)
2 tablespoons

chopped green onion
1 clove garlic, finely chopped
1 tablespoon chopped fresh basil
OR: 1 teaspoon leaf basil, crumbled
¹/₄ teaspoon leaf thyme, crumbled
¹/₂ teaspoon salt
5 tablespoons vinalgrette salad dressing

1. Remove the fish from the package. Arrange in the center of a microwave-safe plate.

2. Microwave the fish uncovered, on Half Power for 6 minutes, turning the fish over after 3 minutes. Cover the defrosted fish with a double thickness of damp microwave-safe paper toweling.
3. Microwave on Full Power for 5 minutes, rotating the dish after 3 minutes if the fish is cooking unevenly. Cover the fish completely with heavy-duty microwave-safe plastic wrap and let stand for 5 minutes.
4. Arrange the sliced potatoes on a microwave-safe plate in a single layer. Cover with a double thickness of wet microwave-safe paper toweling.
5. Microwave on Full Power for 7 minutes; rearrange the potatoes after 5 minutes if cooking unevenly. Rinse the potatoes under cold water; drain and pat dry.
6. Flake the fish into a medium-size salad bowl. Add the potatoes, tomato wedges, halved pitted olives, chopped green onion, garlic, basil, thyme, salt and vinaigrette salad dressing; toss until well blended. Chill for 1 hour before serving. Garnish with carrot curls, if you wish.

Chicken Cordon Bleu

Microwave on Full Power for 13 to 15 minutes.

Makes 4 servings.

2 whole chicken breasts, boned and halved
4 thin slices prosciutto ham
4 slices Monterey Jack cheese
1 egg, beaten

Sauce:
1 to 2 tablespoons

all-purpose flour
2 tablespoons grated onion
¹/₄ cup dry white wine
8 medium mushrooms, sliced
1 cup shredded Monterey Jack cheese
3 tablespoons finely chopped parsley

1. Place each chicken breast in a plastic bag and pound, skin side down, until thin and even. Place a slice each of the ham and cheese on each breast half and fold over. (You may fasten the sides together with wooden picks.)
2. Dip the chicken into the beaten egg, coating evenly. Place, skin side down, in a ring fashion in a shallow round or oval glass dish, leaving the center empty. (Ends may touch each other.) Cover the chicken with wax paper.
3. Microwave on Full Power for 5 minutes. Baste with the drippings. Turn the chicken over and microwave for 4 minutes more, or until the chicken is just tender. Remove the chicken from the dish and set aside. Cover and keep warm.
4. Make the sauce: Stir the flour into the drippings, adding enough to give body. Slowly stir in the grated onion.
5. Microwave on Full Power for 1 minute. Slowly stir in the wine and mushrooms and microwave on Full Power for 2 to 3 minutes, or until the mushrooms are just cooked and the sauce has thickened slightly. Stir

Clockwise from left: Mediterranean Salad, page 556; Antipasto Salad, page 556; Sweet and Sour Chicken and Cabbage, page 555.

in the cheese and microwave for 1 to 2 minutes, or until the cheese is melted.

6. To serve: Place the chicken rolls on a bed of pilaf, if you wish. Spoon sauce over; sprinkle with parsley. (If necessary, reheat on Medium-High Power for 1 to 2 minutes, or until the sauce begins to bubble.) Serve with fluted mushrooms and steamed leeks, if you wish.

Oriental-Style Chicken

A sweet and sour sauce turns chicken into a Chinese dinner.

Microwave on Full Power for 7½ minutes, and on Medium-High Power for 15 to 17 minutes.

Makes 4 servings.

1 can (15½ ounces) pineapple chunks in pineapple juice	3 teaspoons raisins Salt and pepper to taste
2 tablespoons orange juice	1 broiler-fryer (2 to 2½ pounds), cut up
2 tablespoons honey	¼ cup (½ stick) butter or margarine
2 tablespoons dry sherry	1 tablespoon cornstarch
2 teaspoons soy sauce	¼ cup sliced almonds

1. Drain the pineapple juice into a medium-size bowl.

Stir in the orange juice, honey, sherry, soy sauce, raisins, salt and pepper. Reserve the pineapple chunks.

2. Place the chicken in a shallow microwave-safe dish. Pour the sauce over. Cover with plastic wrap. Let stand for 30 minutes.

3. Microwave 2 tablespoons of the butter or margarine in a large shallow glass microwave-safe dish on Full Power for 1 minute, or until melted.

4. Remove the chicken with a slotted spoon to the hot butter in the dish; turn to coat the chicken. Cover with vented heavy-duty plastic wrap. Reserve the sauce.

5. Microwave on Medium-High Power for 15 to 17 minutes, turning the chicken once halfway through cooking. Remove from the oven; cover with aluminum foil; let stand for 5 minutes.

6. Meanwhile, stir a little of the reserved sauce into the cornstarch in a cup, blending well until the mixture is smooth.

7. Microwave the remaining sauce in a 2-cup glass measure on Full Power for 2 minutes, or until bubbly. Stir in the cornstarch mixture and microwave on Full Power for 2 minutes, whisking once. Add the reserved pineapple; pour the sauce over the chicken.

8. Microwave the nuts and remaining 2 tablespoons butter or margarine in a small glass microwave-safe bowl on Full Power for 2½ minutes, stirring after 1 minute. Drain on paper toweling. Garnish the chicken with toasted nuts. Serve over hot cooked rice.

Mexicali Chicken

There's a taste of olé in every bite, thanks to extra spicy seasoning blend.

Microwave on Full Power for 12 to 14 minutes.

Makes 4 servings.

1 broiler-fryer (2¹/₂ pounds), cut up and skin removed
2¹/₂ to 3 tablespoons extra spicy salt-free 14 herb and spice seasoning blend
1 tablespoon vegetable oil
1 fresh lime, cut into wedges
Jalapeño peppers *(optional)*
Sassy Salsa *(recipe follows)*
Tostada chips *(optional)*

1. Arrange the chicken, bone-side up, in a shallow microwave-safe baking dish. Sprinkle with 1 teaspoon of the extra spicy seasoning blend. Loosely cover the chicken with wax paper.
2. Microwave on Full Power for 8 minutes. Turn each piece of the chicken over; drizzle with the oil and sprinkle with the remaining extra spicy seasoning blend. Rotate the dish one-quarter turn. Re-cover.
3. Microwave on Full Power for 4 to 6 minutes, or until chicken is tender. Let stand, covered, 5 minutes. Garnish with lime and fresh jalapeño peppers if you wish. Serve with **Sassy Salsa** and tostada chips if you wish.

Sassy Salsa

A great accompaniment to chicken and grilled fish, or as a dip—any way you serve Sassy Salsa, its punch comes from extra spicy salt-free seasoning blend.

Makes about 2 cups.

2 medium-size ripe tomatoes, chopped (1¹/₂ cups)
1 medium-size onion, chopped (¹/₂ cup)
1 clove garlic, finely chopped
1 tablespoon chopped, seeded jalapeño pepper
1 tablespoon extra spicy salt-free 14 herb and spice seasoning blend

1. Combine the chopped tomatoes, onion, garlic, jalapeño pepper and extra spicy seasoning blend in a small bowl, blending well. Let stand at least 15 minutes to allow the flavors to develop.
2. Serve with **Mexicali Chicken** grilled fish or as a dip with tostadas.

Mexicali Chicken.

Arroz con Pollo.

Arroz con Pollo

This microwave version of the Cuban classic cooks without spattering, so cleanup is fast and easy.
Microwave on Full Power for 43 to 50 minutes.

Makes 8 servings.

4 pounds chicken, skin removed and cut into serving pieces
1¼ teaspoons coarse (kosher) salt
½ teaspoon black pepper
¼ teaspoon sweet paprika
1 package (10 ounces) frozen peas
   OR: artichoke hearts
1 medium-size onion, finely diced, (½ cup)
2 cloves garlic, finely chopped

2 tablespoon olive or peanut oil
1 can (28 ounces) Italian plum tomatoes
2 cups chicken broth
1 bay leaf
2 tablespoons flat-leaf parsley, chopped
Pinch leaf thyme, crumbled
2 cups uncooked rice
½ teaspoon saffron, steeped in 2 tablespoons hot water
1 jar (2 ounces) sliced pimiento, drained

1. Season the chicken with the salt, pepper and paprika. Cook the peas or artichokes following the manufacturer's directions for microwaving.
2. Microwave the onion and garlic in the oil in a 3- to 4-quart microwave-safe casserole, covered with a lid or heavy-duty microwave-safe plastic wrap, on Full Power for 5 minutes, or until onion is transparent. Add the chicken.
3. Microwave, covered, on Full Power for 6 to 7 minutes, turning over the chicken pieces halfway through the cooking time.
4. Add the 2½ cups tomatoes with the liquid, chicken broth, bay leaf, parsley, thyme, rice and steeped saffron and its liquid. Cover tightly.
5. Microwave on Full Power for 10 minutes. Stir; cook 10 minutes more. Stir again. (If the rice seems hard, add the remaining tomatoes and their liquid.) Microwave 10 to 15 minutes more, or until the rice is tender. Stir in the peas or artichokes.
6. Microwave for 2 to 3 minutes or until vegetables are heated through. Garnish with pimiento.

Roast Duckling

Total cooking time: 1 hour.
Makes 4 servings.

1 duckling* (4 to 5 pounds)
Salt

Stuffing *(optional)*
¼ cup orange marmalade

1. Wash bird; dry well. Sprinkle cavity with salt. Stuff neck and main cavity with your favorite stuffing or leave unstuffed. Close openings with skewers or wooden picks. Tie legs together; tie wings to body.

(continued)

Wrap tips of legs and wings with pieces of foil to prevent overcooking. Place bird, breast-side down, in glass baking dish; cover with wax paper (leave paper on while cooking).

2. Cook in microwave 6 minutes per pound (30 minutes for a 5-pound duckling). After 15 minutes, turn bird breast-side up and drain off accumulated fat; continue cooking.

3. Remove from microwave oven; remove foil pieces; remove wax paper; brush skin with orange marmalade. Roast, uncovered, in conventional oven set at hot (400°) for 30 minutes or until skin is crispy-brown and legs move easily.

4. Let duckling stand 10 minutes before carving.

For frozen duckling: Defrost in microwave oven, following manufacturer's specific directions, before starting Step 1.

Herbed Cornish Game Hens

Split Cornish hens are cooked in a fresh mushroom sauce with herbs.

Microwave on Full Power for 8 to 10 minutes, then on Medium-High Power for about 10 minutes.

Makes 2 servings.

2 fresh Cornish game hens	**crushed tomatoes**
2 tablespoons butter or margarine	**2 tablespoons chopped fresh parsley**
1 cup thinly sliced fresh mushrooms	**1 teaspoon leaf tarragon, crumbled**
4 shallots, finely chopped	**1/2 teaspoon salt**
OR: **1 small onion, finely chopped (1/4 cup)**	**1/8 teaspoon pepper**
	1/2 cup dry white wine
1 can (16 ounces)	**2 tablespoons all-purpose flour**

1. Rinse the hens inside and out; pat dry. Split the hens lengthwise with poultry shears or a sharp knife, removing the backbone, if desired.

2. Combine the butter or margarine, mushrooms and shallots or onion in a 12 × 8 inch microwave-safe dish; cover with heavy-duty plastic wrap.

3. Microwave on Full Power for 4 to 6 minutes, or until the mushrooms are tender. Stir in the tomatoes, parsley, tarragon, salt and pepper. Blend the wine and flour in a cup; stir into the tomato mixture; cover with plastic wrap.

4. Microwave on Full Power for 4 minutes.

5. Place the hen halves, bone-side up and with meatier portions toward the edge of the dish, on top of the sauce. Spoon the sauce over the hens; cover with wax paper.

6. Microwave on Medium-High Power for 8 minutes per pound, turning the hens over halfway through the cooking time and recovering with the wax paper.

7. Let stand, covered, for 10 minutes. Test for

doneness after standing time by pricking with a two-tined fork. Juices should run clear when meat is cut near bone.

Microwave Cooking Directions for Turkey

If frozen, thaw turkey first. Thawing in the microwave is not recommended.

First Steps

1. Free the legs from the tucked position. Do not cut the band of skin.

2. Remove the neck and giblets from the neck and body cavities. To microwave, place 3 cups of water, 1/2 teaspoon of salt, the neck, gizzard and heart in a 2-quart microwave-safe casserole and cover. Microwave at Half Power (50%) for 35 minutes. Add the liver, cover and microwave for 10 minutes more. The cooked neck, giblets and stock may be used in making gravy or stuffing.

3. Rinse the turkey and drain well.

4. If desired, stuff the neck and body cavities lightly. Cover the exposed stuffing with plastic wrap.

5. Turn the wings back to hold the neck skin in place. Return the legs to the tucked position. No trussing is necessary.

6. Make Browning Sauce: Microwave 1/2 stick of butter in a microwave-safe bowl at Full Power (100%) for 30 to 40 seconds until melted. Blend in 1/4 teaspoon paprika and 1/8 teaspoon browning and seasoning sauce. Stir well before each use.

To Cook

1. Place the turkey, breast down, in a microwave-safe dish. If the turkey tips, level with a microwave-safe item to cook evenly.

2. Brush the back of the turkey with 1 tablespoon of the Browning Sauce.

3. See the Microwave Cook Schedule for cooking time. Use the Cook Schedule closest to the weight of the turkey. Follow Part I and Part II Cook Times without any delay interruptions.

4. Microwave at Full Power (100%) for Time 1. Rotate the turkey half turn. Microwave for Time 2. Remove and discard the drippings.

5. Turn the turkey, breast up. If stuffed, remove the plastic wrap. Brush with the Browning Sauce. Level if the turkey tips.

6. Microwave at Half Power (50%) for Times 3, 4 and 5. At the end of each time, rotate the turkey quarter turn; discard the drippings; brush the turkey with the Browning Sauce. If over-browning occurs, shield with small pieces of foil. After Time 5, check for doneness. A meat thermometer inserted in the thickest part of the thigh (not touching bone) should register 180° to 185°F.; in the thickest part of the breast, 170°F.; in the center of the stuffing, 160° to 165°F. If all these temperatures have not been reached, cook for Time 6. Recheck the temperatures; cook longer if necessary.

7. Cover the turkey with foil. Let stand for 15 minutes before carving.

Microwave Cooking Schedule for Stuffed or Unstuffed Turkey
Approximate cooking time in 625- to 700-watt microwave ovens

Times	4 lb.	5 lb.	6 lb.	7 lb.	8 lb.	9 lb.	10 lb.	11 lb.	12 lb.
					Weight				
	Part I — Breast down at Full Power (100%)								
1	8 min.	10 min.	12 min.	14 min.	16 min.	18 min.	20 min.	22 min.	24 min.
2	8 min.	10 min.	12 min.	14 min.	16 min.	18 min.	20 min.	22 min.	24 min.
	Part II — Breast up at Half Power (50%)								
3	8 min.	10 min.	12 min.	14 min.	16 min.	18 min.	20 min.	22 min.	24 min.
4	8 min.	10 min.	12 min.	14 min.	16 min.	18 min.	20 min.	22 min.	24 min.
5*	8 min.	10 min.	12 min.	14 min.	16 min.	18 min.	20 min.	22 min.	24 min.
6	8 min.	10 min.	12 min.	14 min.	16 min.	18 min.	20 min.	22 min.	24 min.
Total Cook Time	48 min.	1 hr.	1 hr., 12 min.	1 hr., 24 min.	1 hr., 36 min.	1 hr., 48 min.	2 hrs.	2 hrs., 12 min.	2 hrs., 24 min.

*Check for doneness after Time 5.

Regal Roast Turkey

The microwave produces a great-tasting, juicy turkey. By using a rack to lift turkey from juices you prevent white meat from overcooking.

Microwave on Full Power for 20 minutes, then on Medium-High Power for 7 to 10 minutes per pound.

Makes 6 servings, plus leftovers.

1 turkey (about 14 pounds), defrosted and giblets removed
Salt
¹/₂ cup (1 stick) butter or margarine, melted
¹/₄ cup soy sauce
Frosted Grape Garland (recipe follows)
Fruited Rice Stuffing (recipe in this chapter)
Cauliflower au Gratin (recipe in this chapter)
Orange-Glazed Yams (recipe in this chapter)

1. Wash the turkey; pat dry with paper toweling. Season the turkey and its cavity with salt; tie and truss. Place the turkey, breast side up, on a microwave-safe roasting rack. Brush with a mixture of melted butter or margarine and soy sauce.
2. Microwave on Full Power for 20 minutes. Baste with the drippings.
3. Microwave on Medium-High Power for 7 to 10 minutes per pound, basting with the drippings every 20 minutes.
4. Turn the turkey over midway through the estimated cooking time, continuing to baste. (Any parts that are browning too quickly may be shielded with small pieces of aluminum foil.) Turkey is done when the meat thermometer registers 170°. Check the temperature in several places to insure overall doneness. Let the turkey stand for 15 to 25 minutes before carving. Garnish with the **Frosted Grape Garland**. Serve with **Fruited Rice Stuffing**, **Cauliflower au Gratin**, and **Orange-Glazed Yams**, if you wish.

Frosted Grape Garland: Beat 2 egg whites with a fork in a small bowl until frothy. Break ³/₄ pound seedless red grapes into small clusters; dip into beaten egg whites, coating evenly; shake off the excess. Roll the grapes in 1¹/₂ cups sugar on a sheet of wax paper, coating evenly. Let dry for 1 hour before serving.

Fruited Rice Stuffing

Microwave on Full Power for 6 to 10 minutes.

Makes 6 servings, plus leftovers.

¹/₄ cup (¹/₂ stick) butter or margarine
1 cup sliced almonds
1 cup finely chopped celery
1 medium onion, chopped (¹/₂ cup)
3 cups cooked rice
¹/₂ cup raisins
¹/₄ cup chopped parsley
1 teaspoon salt
¹/₄ teaspoon leaf rosemary, crumbled
¹/₄ teaspoon leaf sage, crumbled
¹/₄ teaspoon leaf thyme, crumbled
¹/₄ teaspoon pepper

1. Place the butter or margarine, nuts, chopped celery and chopped onion in a 2-quart microwave-safe dish. Cover with heavy-duty plastic wrap.
2. Microwave on Full Power for 4 to 6 minutes, or until the celery is tender. Reserve.
3. Combine the cooked rice with the raisins, parsley, salt, rosemary, sage, thyme and pepper in a medium-size microwave-safe glass bowl. Stir in the nut mixture, blending well.
4. Microwave, covered, on Full Power for 2 to 4 minutes, or until heated through.

Regal Roast Turkey, page 561; Fruited Rice Stuffing, page 561; Orange-Glazed Yams, page 562; Cauliflower au Gratin, page 562.

Orange-Glazed Yams

This dish tastes as though oven-baked for hours.
Microwave on Full Power for 7 to 9 minutes.

Makes 6 servings.

**1 can (40 ounces)
    yams, drained**
	**1 tablespoon
	    cornstarch**

1 large orange, peeled and cut into chunks	**¹/₈ teaspoon salt**

**¹/₄ cup firmly packed
    light brown sugar**
	1 cup orange juice
	**1 teaspoon grated
	    orange rind**

**¹/₄ cup granulated
    sugar**
	**2 tablespoons butter
	    or margarine**

1. Arrange the yams and orange chunks in a
1¹/₂-quart microwave-safe round or oval dish. Set
aside.
2. Combine the sugars with the cornstarch and salt in
a 4-cup glass measure. Add the orange juice and rind,
stirring until the cornstarch is dissolved.
3. Microwave on Full Power for 2 minutes, whisking
several times; continue cooking on Full Power for 2
minutes more. Stir in the butter or margarine, until
melted and smooth. Pour the sauce over the yams.
4. Microwave on Full Power for 3 to 5 minutes, or until
heated through.

Cauliflower au Gratin

*A sauced vegetable has never been easier when you
use the microwave and ready-made cheese sauce.*
Microwave on Full Power for 8 to 8¹/₂ minutes.

Makes 6 servings.

**1 head cauliflower
    (about 1 pound)**
1 jar (16 ounces)
	**pasteurized process
	    cheese spread, at
	    room temperature**

1. Wash and trim the cauliflower; shake off the excess
water. Wrap in heavy-duty plastic wrap. Place, core-
side down, on a paper plate.
2. Microwave on Full Power for 3 minutes. Rotate the
plate ¹/₄ turn. Cook for 3 minutes longer or until the
stems on underside are fork-tender. Let stand,
covered, for 3 minutes.
3. Remove the lid from cheese spread. Microwave on
Full Power for 2 to 2¹/₂ minutes, or until hot. Stir.
4. Remove the plastic wrap from the cauliflower. Place
on a serving platter; pour the hot cheese sauce over.
Spoon the unused sauce into a jar; seal and
refrigerate.

After-Thanksgiving Squares

This innovative way with turkey leftovers tastes as good as the big dinner.

Microwave on Full Power for 11 to 14 minutes.

Makes 6 servings.

- 1 package (10 ounces) frozen peas
- 1 package (6 ounces) chicken-flavored stuffing mix
- 1 cup water
- 2 eggs, slightly beaten
- 2 cups diced cooked turkey
- 1/4 teaspoon leaf rosemary, crumbled
- 1 can (10 3/4 ounces) condensed cream of mushroom soup
- 1/4 cup milk
- 2 tablespoons chopped parsley

1. Microwave the peas in a glass bowl on Full Power for 4 to 5 minutes, or until cooked.
2. Combine the stuffing crumbs, seasoning packet, water and eggs in a glass 11 × 7-inch dish. Top with the drained peas and turkey; sprinkle with the rosemary.
3. Combine the soup, milk and parsley in a bowl, blending well; pour over the turkey. Cover with wax paper.
4. Microwave on Full Power for 7 to 9 minutes, or until hot, rotating the dish twice. Let stand, covered, for 5 minutes before cutting into squares.

Curried Turkey Wings

A lively blend of spices lends exotic flair to turkey in just minutes.

Microwave on Full Power for 15 minutes, and on Half Power for 36 minutes.

Makes 4 servings.

- 1 1/2 cups chopped onion
- 2 cloves garlic, finely chopped
- 2 tablespoons vegetable oil
- 1 tablespoon ground coriander
- 1 1/2 teaspoons ground turmeric
- 1 1/2 teaspoons ground cumin
- 1 1/2 teaspoons ground ginger
- 3/4 teaspoon ground red pepper
- 1/4 teaspoon ground cinnamon
- 1/8 teaspoon ground cloves
- 2 turkey wings (about 2 to 2 1/2 pounds)
- 1 1/2 cups turkey broth or chicken bouillon
- 3 tablespoons cornstarch
- 3 tablespoons cold water

1. Combine the chopped onion, garlic and oil in a 2 1/2-quart microwave-safe dish. Stir in the coriander, turmeric, cumin, ginger, red pepper, cinnamon and cloves, mixing well. Cover with vented heavy-duty plastic wrap.
2. Microwave on Full Power for 5 minutes.
3. Meanwhile, cut away and discard the wing tips from the turkey. Separate the first and second sections of the wings at the joints.
4. Add the broth or bouillon to the cooked spice mixture, blending well. Add the turkey pieces, placing the meatiest portions to the outside of dish. Cover with vented heavy-duty plastic wrap.
5. Microwave on Full Power for 5 minutes. Turn the turkey pieces; re-cover.
6. Microwave on Half Power for 18 minutes. Turn the pieces again; re-cover and continue to microwave 18 minutes, or until the meat is easily pierced with a fork. Cool slightly, then separate the meat from the skin and bones. Shred the meat, return to the sauce in dish.
7. Combine the cornstarch and cold water in a cup, mixing well. Stir into the sauce mixture.
8. Microwave, uncovered, on Full Power for 5 minutes, stirring halfway through the cooking time. Serve with hot cooked rice and any or all of the following: chutney, chopped apples, chopped peanuts, chopped tomatoes.

Microwaving Beef Roast

Cover the roast with wax paper to hold in the heat and moisture and to prevent spatter during cooking. (Plastic wrap—including the heavy-duty variety—is not recommended to cover meats, since they would have a steamed quality.) Wax paper is an excellent cover for fruits, too, as well as ground meats, which do not need to be tenderized.

Rotate dish one-quarter turn to promote even cooking. Massive foods such as beef roast which cannot be stirred or rearranged should be rotated a quarter or half turn periodically. (Re-cover with a fresh sheet of wax paper, if you wish.)

Shield areas that receive more energy as soon as they appear cooked. By covering with small pieces of aluminum foil you can prevent overcooking of thinner parts of food, which tend to microwave faster than the meatier parts. Invert roast. It's advisable to turn large items over halfway through estimated cooking time.

Check for doneness this way: Insert an instant-read meat thermometer into thickest portion of boneless roast. Temperature in center should register at least 135°F. on thermometer when done, or 5°F. under desired temperature. (In this case, 140°F. for rare; 160°F. for medium). Not to worry--meat will continue to cook during standing time!

When temperature registers desired pre-doneness, prepare roast for standing time by tenting with aluminum foil to retain heat.

Allow microwaved roast to stand, covered completely in aluminum foil, for at least 20 minutes before carving.

The reason: Food continues to cook after it is removed from the microwave oven. During standing time, food finishes cooking by internal heat transfer. Also, food is easier to carve after appropriate standing time. As a general rule, standing time of one-quarter

(continued)

Microwave Beef Roast (right front), page 564; Fennel Parmesan (right rear), page 564; Broccoli and Cauliflower Ring in Fast Hollandaise (center front), page 565; Chocolate-Dipped Strawberries (left front), page 564; Zabaglione (left rear), page 589.

to one-third of total microwave cooking time is recommended for all dishes.

After prescribed standing time has elapsed, re-check internal temperature, this time for a reading of 140°F. for rare, 160°F. for medium. (Meat is now done.)

Microwave Beef Roast

Boneless beef chuck microwaves to perfection when you follow the how-to's in this chapter.
Microwave on Medium-Low Power for about 1 to 1½ hours.

Makes 6 servings.

3- to 4-pound boneless beef chuck cross rib roast
Fennel Parmesan *(recipe follows)*

Potato Rosettes *(recipe follows)*
Broccoli and Cauliflower Ring *(recipe follows)*

1. Place the meat, fat side down, on a roasting rack in a microwave-safe dish. Cover with wax paper.
2. Microwave on Medium-Low Power for 18 to 22 minutes *per pound,* rotating the dish ¼ turn every 20 minutes.
3. Invert the roast at midpoint of estimated cooking period. (Edges that appear to be overcooking may be shielded with small pieces of aluminum foil during cooking.)
4. Remove the roast when a meat thermometer, inserted into the thickest part, registers 5° F. less than doneness desired (rare to medium, 140° F. to 160° F.).
5. Tent the roast with foil and allow to stand for 5 to 20 minutes before carving. Serve with Fennel Parmesan, Potato Rosettes and Broccoli and Cauliflower Ring with Fast Hollandaise, if you wish.

Fennel Parmesan

A cheesed anise-flavored vegetable complements Microwave Beef Roast.
Microwave on Full Power for 9 minutes.

Makes 6 servings.

3 large bulbs fennel (2 to 2½ pounds)
½ cup water

1 clove garlic, halved
¼ cup shredded fresh Parmesan cheese

1. Remove the stalks and tough outer leaves from fennel. Cut the bulbs lengthwise into ¼-inch-thick slices, keeping the core to retain the fan shape.
2. Place the fennel, water and garlic in a microwave-safe casserole. Cover with vented heavy-duty plastic wrap.
3. Microwave on Full Power for 8 minutes, rotating the dish ¼ turn after 4 minutes. Remove the garlic and pour off the water.
4. Sprinkle the shredded Parmesan over fennel and continue cooking on Full Power for 1 minute. Serve with Microwave Beef Roast, if you wish.

Chocolate-Dipped Strawberries

The microwave makes short shrift of melting chocolate for this simple, yet smashing, grand finale.
Microwave on Full Power for 2 minutes.

Makes about 16.

1 package (6 ounces) semisweet chocolate morsels

1 pint strawberries, rinsed and dried

1. Microwave the chocolate morsels in a 2-cup glass measure on Full Power for 2 minutes, or until melted.
2. Dip the rinsed and dried berries, one at a time, into the melted chocolate, leaving an uncoated rim around the stem. Arrange the berries on a wax paper–lined cookie sheet: Chill for 10 minutes.

Potato Rosettes

An easy styling technique elevates plain mashed potatoes to elaborate dinner party fare.

Microwave on Full Power for 10 to 12 minutes.

Makes 24.

4 large baking potatoes, peeled and quartered	**1 tablespoon grated Parmesan cheese**
¼ cup hot water	**½ teaspoon salt**
¼ teaspoon salt	**1 cup milk**
¼ cup (½ stick) butter or margarine, softened	**1½ teaspoons chopped fresh chives**
¼ cup dairy sour cream	OR: **½ teaspoon dried chives**
	Paprika

1. Place the potatoes in a 1½-quart glass microwave-safe casserole with hot water and ¼ teaspoon salt; covered with vented heavy-duty plastic wrap.
2. Microwave on Full Power for 10 to 12 minutes, or until the potatoes are tender, stirring twice. Drain and mash.
3. Combine the mashed potatoes with the butter or margarine, sour cream, grated Parmesan cheese and the ½ teaspoon salt in a medium-size bowl, blending well.
4. Add the milk gradually, beating with an electric mixer at high speed until smooth; stir in the chives.
5. Fit the pastry bag with a large star tip; fill with the mashed potato mixture; squeeze out rosettes onto a serving dish. Sprinkle with the paprika. Keep warm. Serve with **Microwave Beef Roast**, above, if you wish.

Broccoli and Cauliflower Ring

Microwave on Full Power for 10 to 12 minutes.

Makes 6 servings.

1 large head cauliflower	**Fast Hollandaise (recipe follows)**
2 bunches broccoli	

1. Separate the cauliflower and broccoli into flowerets. Trim off thick stalks (save for another use). Rinse the vegetables, but do not dry.
2. Line the bottom of 2-quart microwave-safe ring pan with the cauliflower. Layer with a ring of the broccoli, placing the stems to the inside of the dish. Repeat the

(continued)

layering until all of the vegetables are used. Cover with vented heavy-duty plastic wrap.

3. Microwave on Full Power for 10 to 12 minutes, or until the vegetables are crisp-tender. Press down on the vegetables to compact them. Let stand for 5 minutes.

4. Drain the water off of the vegetables. Invert into a serving platter. Pour the Fast Hollandaise over. Serve immediately.

Fast Hollandaise: Makes about 2/3 cup. Place 1/2 cup (1 stick) softened butter into a 4-cup glass measure. Beat in 3 egg yolks and 1 to 2 tablespoons fresh lemon juice. Microwave on Full Power for 1 minute, or until warm and slightly thickened, stirring every 15 seconds. (Do not overcook or the sauce will curdle.) Add salt, black pepper and cayenne pepper to taste.

Two-Way Beef Stew

The starting point of more elaborate recipes.

Microwave on Full Power for 11 minutes, then on Half Power for 55 minutes.

Makes enough for two main dish recipes.

2 to 2¹/₂ pounds boneless beef chuck	**¹/₈ teaspoon pepper**
¹/₄ cup *unsifted* **all-purpose flour**	**2 cloves garlic, finely chopped**
1¹/₂ teaspooons salt	**2 tablespoons vegetable oil**
	1¹/₄ cups water

1. Cut the beef into 1¹/₂ x 1¹/₂ x ¹/₂-inch pieces. Dredge the beef with flour, salt and pepper; set aside.

2. Place the garlic and oil in a 4-quart round

Oriental Beef.

microwave-safe dish. Cover with heavy-duty plastic wrap, venting one corner.

3. Microwave on Full Power for 1 minute. Add the beef; cover with vented plastic wrap.

4. Microwave on Full Power for 10 minutes, stirring after 5 minutes. Add the water; cover with vented plastic wrap.

5. Microwave on Half Power for 55 minutes, stirring every 15 minutes.

6. For now, use entire batch to make **Hearty Winter Beef Stew** *(recipe in this chapter).* Or, prepare **Savory Mediterranean Stew** *(see recipe in this chapter)* with half of the beef and cooking liquid. Place the remaining beef and liquid in a freezer container; cover with seal or heavy-duty aluminum foil; freeze; use for **Oriental Beef** *(see recipe in this chapter).*

Oriental Beef

Keep a batch of Two-Way Beef Stew on ice for the basis of this Chinese dinner at a moment's notice.

Microwave on Half Power for 3 to 5 minutes, then on Full Power for 6¹/₂ to 8¹/₂ minutes.

Makes 6 servings.

¹/₂ recipe frozen Two-Way Beef Stew *(recipe in this chapter)*	**pineapple juice, drained and juice reserved**
1 package (14 ounces) frozen Oriental-style vegetables	**2 tablespoons vegetable or peanut oil**
1 medium red pepper, cut into thin strips	**2 teaspoons soy sauce**
4 green onions, thinly sliced	**¹/₈ teaspoon ground ginger**
1 can (8 ounces) pineapple chunks in	**2 cups cooked cellophane noodles**

1. Place frozen **Two-Way Beef Stew** in a microwave-safe container.

2. Microwave on Half Power for 3 to 5 minutes or until defrosted. Spoon into a 2-quart round microwave-safe dish.

3. Add the frozen vegetables, red pepper, green onion, 2 tablespoons of the reserved pineapple juice, vegetable or peanut oil, soy sauce and ginger. Cover with vented heavy-duty plastic wrap.

4. Microwave on Full Power for 6 to 8 minutes, stirring after 3 to 4 minutes. Stir in the pineapple. Cover; continue cooking for 30 seconds. Serve over cooked cellophane noodles, with lychees and mango for dessert, if you wish.

Japanese Beef with Broccoli.

Japanese Beef with Broccoli

Microwave on Full Power for 11 to 12 minutes.

Makes 4 servings.

1 pound beef flank steak	**stems for another use)**
1/3 cup soy sauce	**1 sweet red pepper, halved, seeded and sliced**
1/3 cup sake or white wine	
1/4 teaspoon instant minced garlic	**2 green onions with tops, sliced**
1/4 teaspoon ground ginger	**1 can (81/4 ounces) sliced water chestnuts**
2 tablespoons cornstarch	
1/2 bunch fresh broccoli, cut into flowerets (save	**Parsley Flecked Rice (recipe in this chapter)**

1. Freeze steak for 30 minutes for easier slicing. Thinly slice the partially frozen steak across the grain.
2. Combine the soy sauce, sake or wine, garlic and ginger in a 2-quart glass bowl. Add the sliced steak; cover with plastic wrap; marinate in the refrigerator for at least 6 hours, or overnight.
3. Just before cooking, stir the cornstarch into the marinade. Transfer the steak and marinade to a 2-quart rectangular glass dish. Add the broccoli flowerets, sliced red pepper, green onion and water chestnuts with liquid, mixing well. Cover with wax paper.
4. Microwave on Full Power for 11 to 12 minutes, stirring once. Serve over Parsley Flecked Rice, if you wish.

Crown Roast of Pork

A New Year's dinner from the microwave might include this succulent roast with savory dressing.

Microwave on Full Power for 5 minutes, then on Half Power for 15 to 17 minutes per pound.

Makes 8 servings.

Rice and Sausage Stuffing (recipe in this chapter)	**Garlic clove, halved, or onion powder**
6- to 7-pound crown roast of pork, backbone removed	**Pepper**
	Spiced crabapples
	Parsley sprigs

1. Prepare **Rice and Sausage Stuffing** *(recipe in this chapter)*; refrigerate

(continued)

2. If using, insert microwave meat thermometer between two ribs, so tip is in meaty area on inside of crown and does not touch fat or bone. Place roast on a meat rack with crown ends down. Rub with halved garlic clove or onion powder and pepper. (If you don't have a meat rack, elevate with a saucer or small microwavable bowl turned upside down.)

3. Estimate the total cooking time and divide in half.

4. Microwave for the first 5 minutes on Full Power; reduce power to Half and microwave for the remainder of the first half of cooking time. Turn the roast over, crown side up.

5. Microwave on Half Power the second half of cooking time until 45 minutes of cooking time remains.

6. Fill the cavity with **Rice and Sausage Stuffing.** Cover the stuffing with wax paper. (Leftover stuffing can be placed around the pork or put in a casserole and warmed while the pork is standing.)

7. Microwave for 45 minutes, or until the internal temperature reaches at least 165° F. At the end of cooking time, tent loosely with aluminum foil, shiny side toward meat, for 10 minutes or until the internal temperature reaches 170° F.

8. Transfer the cooked roast to a serving platter and place paper frills over the crown tips. Garnish with spiced crabapples and parsley sprigs.

9. Carve down between the bones. Serve with stuffing.

Country-Style Pork Ribs with Sauerkraut

Old country flavors are brought up to date with this pork favorite.

Microwave on Full Power for 20 minutes, then on Half Power for 15 minutes.

Makes 6 servings.

3 pounds pork loin country-style ribs, trimmed of fat	**1 jar (16 ounces) sweet and sour red cabbage, undrained**
7 cups water	**1 medium onion, chopped (1/2 cup)**
1 jar (24 ounces) sauerkraut, rinsed and drained	**Salt and pepper**

1. Arrange the ribs in a 4-quart microwave-safe dish. Add the water. Cover with vented heavy-duty plastic wrap.

2. Microwave on Full Power for 20 minutes, or until no pink remains. Drain the ribs well.

3. Combine the drained sauerkraut and red cabbage with the liquid in a shallow 2½-quart microwave-safe dish. Arrange the ribs over the top, with the thickest portions facing the outside of the dish and any smaller ribs in the center. Sprinkle with the chopped onion and season with the salt and pepper. Cover with vented plastic wrap.

4. Microwave on Half Power for 15 minutes, shifting slower cooking ribs to outside of dish if the ribs are cooking unevenly.

5. Turn the ribs over. Test with a fork for tenderness. If almost fork tender, remove from the microwave and cover with foil. Let stand at room temperature for 10 minutes, or until the ribs test done.

Southern-Style Ribs

The microwave reduces cooking time for country-style ribs, which are given a final glazing under the broiler.

Microwave on Full Power for 6 to 8 minutes, then on Half Power for 40 minutes. Broil for 15 to 20 minutes.

Makes 4 servings.

1 tablespoon butter or margarine	**lemon juice**
1 medium onion, finely chopped (¹/₂ cup)	**¹/₂ teaspoon dry mustard**
1 clove garlic, finely chopped	**¹/₂ teaspoon salt**
¹/₂ cup catsup	**¹/₈ teaspoon pepper**
¹/₄ cup firmly packed dark brown sugar	**¹/₈ teaspoon liquid red pepper seasoning**
2 tablespoons water	**3 to 3¹/₂ pounds country-style pork loin ribs, cut into pieces**
2 tablespoons freshly squeezed	**1 cup water**

1. Place the butter or margarine, chopped onion and garlic in a small microwave-safe dish.

2. Microwave on Full Power for 1 minute or until the onion is tender. Stir in the catsup, brown sugar, the 2 tablespoons water, lemon juice, dry mustard, salt, pepper and red pepper seasoning, blending well.

3. Microwave on Full Power for 6 to 8 minutes, or until slightly thickened, stirring every 2 minutes. Reserve.

4. Place the ribs in a 14 x 20-inch oven cooking bag; add the 1 cup water. Close the bag loosely with string or ¹/₂-inch strip cut from the open end of the bag. Place bag in a microwave-safe baking dish.

5. Microwave on Half Power for 40 minutes, inverting and rearranging the ribs after 20 minutes. (Use hot pads when handling the bag and dish.)

6. Carefully remove the ribs from the cooking bag; place on the broiler pan; brush with the reserved sauce.

7. Broil, 5 to 7 inches from heat, for 15 to 20 minutes or until cooked and richly glazed, turning and brushing occasionally with sauce.

Pork Tenderloin Oriental

This technique with pork is fast, exotic and flavorful.

Microwave on Medium-Low for 5 to 6 minutes, then on Full Power for 4 to 6 minutes.

Makes 4 servings.

1 pound pork tenderloin	**ginger**
2 tabespoons low-sodium soy sauce	**1 package (1 pound) Oriental-style frozen vegetable combination**
1¹/₂ teaspoons ground	

1. Cut the pork into ¹/₄-inch- thick slices. Combine the

Pork Tenderloin Oriental, page 568.

soy sauce and ginger in a 9-inch microwave-safe pie plate. Dip both sides of the pork into the mixture; arrange in the glass baking dish, with the larger pieces to the outside of the dish. Cover with vented heavy-duty plastic wrap.

2. Microwave on Medium-Low Power for 3 minutes. Turn the meat, rearranging the least cooked parts to the outside of the dish.

3. Microwave on Medium-Low Power for 2 to 3 minutes longer, or until the meat looks cooked. Let stand, covered, while preparing vegetables.

4. Microwave the frozen vegetables in a microwave-safe glass bowl on Full Power for 4 to 6 minutes.

5. Check the pork for final doneness by slicing in the center of the largest piece. If not done, microwave on Medium-Low for 30 to 60 seconds longer. Season to taste. Stir the undrained vegetables into the pork, coating the vegetables with the drippings.

6. To serve, spoon the vegetables onto a serving platter; arrange the pork on top.

Variation: Substitute 1 pound boneless loin pork chops, cut 1/4-inch thick. If using thicker chops, increase the time to 5 minutes before turning them; then cook 4 to 5 minutes more.

Note: In the photo, we show pork with steamed snow peas and julienned carrot. Here's how: Lay 1 cup each snow peas and julienned carrot in the the center of separate sheets of microwave-safe paper toweling; fold all the sides toward the center to enclosed food. Hold the packet under running water until soaked. Place on a glass plate. Microwave on Full Power for 3 to 5 minutes, or until tender. Let stand for 3 minutes.

Rice and Sausage Stuffing

Microwave on Full Power for 10 to 12 minutes.

Makes about 4 cups.

3/4 **pound fresh sausage meat**	**chopped**
3 tablespoons butter or margarine	**2 cloves garlic finely chopped**
2 ribs celery, finely chopped	**2 cups cooked rice**
1/2 **pound fresh mushrooms, sliced**	**Salt and pepper to taste**
1 large onion, finely	**1 tablespoon dried parsley flakes**

1. Crumble the sausage into a hard-plastic colander placed inside a 2- or 3-quart microwave-safe casserole.

2. Microwave on Full Power for 5 to 6 minutes, or until the sausage loses its pink color. Break up with a fork and set aside, draining sausage drippings.

3. Microwave the butter or margarine, celery, mushrooms, onion and garlic in a 2-quart glass microwave-safe dish on Full Power for 5 to 6 minutes. Stir in reserved sausage, cooked rice, salt, pepper and parsley flakes. Cover and refrigerate if not using immediately to fill the cavity of the **Crown Roast of Pork.**

Sweet and Sour Meatballs

You can cook both Sweet and Sour Meatballs and Hot Cooked Rice in the oven, and have both come out piping hot.

Total cooking time: 20 minutes.

Makes 6 servings.

1½ pounds ground chuck	1 green pepper, seeded and sliced
1 medium onion, chopped (½ cup)	½ cup sugar
1 egg	2 tablespoons cornstarch
⅓ cup packaged bread crumbs	1 can (20 ounces pineapple chunks in pineapple juice, undrained
⅓ cup milk	
½ teaspoon salt	
⅛ teaspoon pepper	¼ cup vinegar
3 tablespoons soy sauce	Hot Cooked Rice (*recipe follows*)

1. Combine chuck, onion, egg, bread crumbs, milk, salt, pepper and 1 tablespoon of the soy sauce in a large bowl. Mix well. Shape into 24 meatballs about 1½ inches in diameter. Arrange in an 11¾ × 7½ × 1¾-inch glass baking dish. Cover with wax paper.
2. Cook, covered, in microwave oven 10 to 11 minutes, rotating dish once. Remove from oven. Spoon off drippings or use bulb baster. Sprinkle with green pepper.
3. Combine sugar, cornstarch, remaining soy sauce, pineapple and juice and vinegar in a 4-cup glass measure; stir well. Place, uncovered, in microwave for 6 to 7 minutes or until mixture is bubbly and thickened, stirring several times. Pour sauce over meatballs, mixing lightly to coat.
4. Complete cooking rice (*see recipe that follows*).
5. Return meatballs and sauce in baking dish to oven for 4 to 5 minutes or until heated through.

Note: To make ahead, prepare through step 2. Complete steps 3, 4 and 5 just before serving.

Individual Meatloaves

Cook loaves together, then reheat each one as needed. Or, prepare loaves, freeze and cook one at a time.

Microwave on Full Power for 6 to 7 minutes.

Makes 4 loaves.

1 pound lean ground beef	horseradish
¼ cup packaged bread crumbs	2 teaspoons chopped fresh dill
1 small onion, finely chopped (¼ cup)	OR: ½ teaspoon dried dill, crumbled
¼ cup milk	½ teaspoon salt
1 egg, slightly beaten	Paprika
1 tablespoon prepared	Yogurt-Dill Sauce (*recipe follows*)

1. Combine the beef, crumbs, onion, milk, egg, grated horseradish, dill and salt in a bowl just until blended. Do not overmix. Divide the mixture into 4 equal portions; shape into small loaves.
2. Arrange the loaves in a circle on a microwave-safe plate. Sprinkle each loaf with paprika. Cover with wax paper.
3. Microwave on Full Power for 6 to 7 minutes, rotating the dish ½ turn after 3 minutes. Let stand for 5 minutes. Serve with the **Yogurt-Dill Sauce.**

To reheat: Place the individual loaf on a microwave-safe serving plate; cover with vented heavy-duty plastic wrap. Microwave on Full Power for 2 minutes.

To freeze: Place the uncooked loaves on a cookie sheet; freeze, then wrap separately. Label, date and freeze.

To thaw and cook: Unwrap the individual loaf; place on a microwave-safe plate; cover with wax paper. Defrost in the refrigerator. Microwave on Full Power for 8 to 9 minutes, rotating ½ turn after 3 minutes. Let stand for 5 minutes.

Yogurt-Dill Sauce: Makes 3/4 cup. Combine ½ cup seeded and chopped cucumber with ½ cup plain yogurt, 1 tablespoon chopped fresh dill or 1 teaspoon crumbled dried dillweed, 1 teaspoon minced onion and dash salt (if using) in small bowl, blending well.

Savory Mediterranean Stew

Here's an entrée that will please guests and hostess alike; the flavorful, aromatic stew is a partial make-ahead.

Microwave on Full Power for 9 minutes.

Makes 6 servings.

1 pint pearl onions, peeled	¼ teaspoon leaf rosemary, crumbled
¼ cup water	¼ teaspoon leaf thyme, crumbled
1 can (15 ounces) garbanzo beans, drained	½ recipe Two-Way Beef Stew (*recipe in this chapter*)
1 can (8 ounces) tomato sauce	2 tablespoons snipped Italian parsley
2 tablespoons dry red wine	Fresh rosemary (*optional*)
2 large tomatoes, peeled, seeded and chopped	Puff Pastry Sticks (*recipe in this chapter*)
2 cups sliced mushrooms	

1. Microwave the onions and 1 tablespoon water in a small glass bowl, covered with vented heavy-duty plastic wrap, on Full Power for 1 minute.
2. Combine the onions and liquid with the drained garbanzo beans, tomato sauce, wine, 3 tablespoons water, chopped tomato, mushrooms, rosemary and thyme in a 2-quart microwave-safe dish; cover with vented plastic wrap.
3. Microwave on Full Power for 6 minutes, stirring

All-In-One
Tex-Mex Filling.

after 3 minutes. Add **Two-Way Beef Stew** and liquid; cover.

4. Microwave on Full Power for 2 minutes. Stir in parsley. Garnish with the fresh rosemary, if you wish. Serve with a green salad and **Puff Pastry** Sticks.

Hearty Winter Beef Stew

An inviting stew with a delectable go-with elevates meat and potatoes to gourmet fare.

Microwave on Full Power for 5 to 7 minutes.

Makes 6 servings.

Two-Way Beef Stew (see recipe in this chapter)
1 bunch broccoli
1 sweet red pepper
1 sweet yellow pepper
2 cups sliced mushrooms
1 envelope brown gravy mix

1. Place **Two-Way Beef Stew** in a 2-quart round microwave-safe dish.
2. Trim the broccoli; remove the stalks and save for another use. Cut the broccoli into flowerets. Add to the stew.
3. Halve and seed the peppers. Cut into strips and then in half crosswise. Add to the stew with sliced mushrooms; stir.
4. Prepare the gravy mix following envelope directions. Add to the stew. Cover with vented heavy-duty plastic wrap.
5. Microwave on Full Power for 5 to 7 minutes, stirring after 2$\frac{1}{2}$ to 3$\frac{1}{2}$ minutes. Serve with baked potatoes topped with sour cream, red caviar and chopped chives, if you wish.

All-In-One Tex-Mex Filling

Microwave extra filling to keep on hand for last-minute meals or snacks. Wrapped in heavy-duty aluminum foil, this filling keeps well in the freezer. Perfect for burritos, enchiladas or tacos.

Microwave on Full Power for 26 to 31 minutes.

Makes 6 cups.

2 pounds ground pork sausage
1 large onion, chopped (1 cup)
2 envelopes (1$\frac{1}{4}$ ounces each) taco seasoning mix
1 can (28 ounces) whole tomatoes, cut up
2 cans (16 ounces each) red kidney beans, drained
2 cans (4 ounces each) chopped green chilies, drained
8 taco shells
Shredded lettuce
Chopped tomatoes
Shredded cheddar cheese

1. Place the sausage and onion in a 2-quart microwave-safe bowl. Cover with vented heavy-duty microwave-safe plastic wrap.
2. Microwave on Full Power for 8 to 9 minutes, stirring twice to break the sausage into small chunks. Pour off the excess fat through the vented area.
3. Combine the taco seasoning mix, tomatoes, kidney beans, chilies and cooked sausage mixture in a 3- to 4-quart microwave-safe bowl, mixing well. Cover the bowl with vented microwave-safe plastic wrap.
4. Microwave on Full Power for 18 to 22 minutes, stirring every 5 minutes. Let the mixture stand, covered, for 5 minutes. *(continued)*

Sweet and Sour Devil Dogs.

Best-Ever Veal Parmesan.

Sweet and Sour Devil Dogs

This dish is ideal for snacking, surrounded with Jalapeño Corn Bread. It can be made in advance and reheated.

Microwave on Full Power for 8 to 10 minutes.

Makes 6 servings.

1 pound hot dogs (about 10)	sliced
1 can (20 ounces) pineapple chunks in pineapple juice	3 tablespoons light brown sugar
2 tablespoons cornstarch	2 tablespoons honey
1 cup catsup	4 cloves garlic, finely chopped
1 large onion, thinly	1/4 teaspoon salt
	1/4 cup fresh lemon juice

1. Slice the hot dogs crosswise into thirds. Drain the pineapple, reserving 1/2 cup of the juice. Blend the juice with the cornstarch.
2. Combine the catsup, the onion rings, brown sugar, honey, garlic, salt and lemon juice in a 2-quart microwave-safe casserole. Stir in the pineapple juice and cornstarch mixture. Add the hot dogs, stirring to coat. Cover with the casserole lid or vented heavy-duty microwave-safe plastic wrap.
3. Microwave on Full Power for 5 to 6 minutes or until the sauce is bubbly and hot. Add the pineapple chunks. Cover the casserole.
4. Microwave on Full Power for 3 to 4 minutes or until heated throughout. Garnish the top of the casserole with a lattice of mustard, if you wish.

Best-Ever Veal Parmesan

This veal dish shows the convenience and efficiency of the microwave oven.

Microwave on Full Power for 45 seconds, then on Medium High Power for 8 minutes.

Makes 8 servings.

1/2 cup (1 stick) butter or margarine	3/4 teaspoon paprika
3/4 cup packaged bread crumbs	1/2 teaspoon salt
1/3 cup plus 3 tablespoons grated Parmesan cheese	1/4 teaspoon pepper
3/4 teaspoon leaf basil, crumbled	11/4 pounds veal cutlet, pounded 1/4 inch thick
3/4 teaspoon leaf oregano, crumbled	1 cup bottled spaghetti sauce
	1 cup shredded mozzarella cheese

1. Microwave the butter or margarine in a large shallow microwave-safe dish on Full Power for 45 seconds, or until melted.
2. Combine the crumbs with 1/3 cup Parmesan, the basil, oregano, paprika, salt and pepper on a sheet of wax paper.
3. Cut the veal into serving-size pieces; dip in the

5. Divide the filling in half (about 3 cups each). Spoon half of the filling into a serving bowl. Serve as a filling for tacos with shredded lettuce, chopped tomatoes and shredded Cheddar cheese. Garnish with lime wedges and green chili peppers, if you wish. Freeze remainder of filling.

melted butter to coat, then in the crumb mixture until well covered. Place in microwave-safe dish and cover with wax paper.

4. Microwave the veal on Medium-High Power for 5 minutes, or until the juices are no longer pink. Drain. Top with spaghetti sauce. Sprinkle with the mozzarella and remaining 3 tablespoons Parmesan cheese. Cover the dish.

5. Microwave on Medium-High power for 3 minutes, or until heated through. Serve the veal with vermicelli and roasted red and green peppers, if you wish.

Mexican Sausage Casserole

A spicy meat main dish gets its taste of olé from liquid red pepper seasoning.

Microwave on Full Power for 18 to 20 minutes.

Makes 4 servings.

1 pound sweet Italian sausage, casings removed	chopped
	1/2 teaspoon ground cumin
2 cups sliced zucchini	1/4 teaspoon liquid red pepper seasoning
1 cup sliced onion	
2 cups cooked rice	1/2 cup grated Parmesan cheese
1 can (1 pound) whole tomatoes, coarsely	

1. Microwave the sausage in a deep 2-quart microwave-safe casserole on Full Power for 2 minutes. Break up with a spoon; microwave for 2 minutes longer. Remove with a slotted spoon; reserve.

2. Microwave the zucchini and onion in the same casserole on Full Power for 4 minutes, stirring once; remove and add to the sausage.

3. Place half the cooked sausage in the same casserole; add 1 cup of the cooked rice and half the zucchini and onion. Repeat the layering.

4. Combine the tomatoes and liquid, cumin and liquid red pepper seasoning; pour over the casserole. Sprinkle with the grated Parmesan cheese.

5. Microwave, uncovered, on Full Power for 10 to 12 minutes, or until the cheese begins to form a crust. Let stand for 3 minutes.

Microwave Oven Method For Fish

Fish cooks quickly in a microwave oven and retains its natural flavor because of its high moisture content. Fish tests done the moment it becomes opaque and easily flakes when pierced with a fork. The fish will continue to cook during standing time, so test for doneness at the earliest moment.

Directions for fresh fish:

1. Place thicker portion of fish and large pieces toward outside of microwave-safe dish.

2. Season with 1/2 teaspoon salt, pepper to taste, 1 tablespoon fresh lemon juice and 1 tablespoon butter per 1 pound of fish. Cover dish with glass lid or cover tightly with microwave-safe plastic wrap.

3. Microwave at Full Power for 6 to 7 minutes for 1 pound of fillets, or 8 to 9 minutes for 2 pounds of fillets. Do not overcook.

4. Let fish stand, covered, 5 minutes.

Directions for frozen fish:

Thaw fish fillets in original package in glass baking dish. Microwave at defrost setting for 10 to 12 minutes for 1 pound. Let stand 5 minutes. Proceed with cooking directions for fresh fish in Steps 1 through 3 above.

Salmon Supreme

A dish for special occasions -- fresh salmon fillets served on microwaved asparagus, topped with a hollandaise sauce.

Microwave on Medium-High Power for 8 minutes.

Makes 6 servings.

6 salmon fillets (about 6 ounces each)	lemon juice
	Microwave Asparagus (recipe follows)
Salt and white pepper to taste	
3 tablespoons fresh	Hollandaise Sauce (recipe follows)

1. Arrange the salmon fillets in a single layer in a microwave-safe dish. Season with the salt and pepper. Sprinkle with the lemon juice. Cover the dish with vented microwave-safe plastic wrap.

2. Microwave on Medium-High Power for 8 minutes, or until the fish flakes easily, turning the fillets and basting after 4 minutes. Serve with Microwave Asparagus and Hollandaise Sauce.

Salmon Supreme, page 573; Microwave Asparagus, page 574; Hollandaise Sauce, page 574.

Microwave Asparagus

Asparagus microwaves to perfection.

Microwave on Full Power for 10 to 15 minutes.

Makes 6 servings.

2 pounds fresh asparagus	**¹/₂ cup water** **¹/₂ teaspoon salt**

1. Wash the asparagus. Snap off the tough ends. Arrange the asparagus, buds toward the center, in a large shallow microwave-safe dish with the water and salt. Cover the dish with vented heavy-duty microwave-safe plastic wrap.
2. Microwave on Full Power for 10 to 15 minutes until tender, rearranging once so spears on the outside are brought to the middle. Serve with Hollandaise Sauce spooned over.

Hollandaise Sauce

Microwave on Medium-High Power for 2 minutes.

Makes about ¹/₂ cup.

¹/₄ cup (¹/₂ stick) butter **Juice of ¹/₂ lemon**	**3 egg yolks** **¹/₄ teaspoon salt**

1. Microwave the butter in a microwave-safe 1-cup measure on Medium-High Power for 1 minute or until melted. Beat in the lemon juice, egg yolks and salt, in that order, until the mixture is smooth.
2. Microwave on Medium-High Power for 1 minute, stirring every 15 seconds. For a thicker sauce, cook for 15 seconds longer.

Alaska Salmon with Vegetables

Salmon, carrot, zucchini and onion cook with a herbed lemon-lime baste.

Microwave on Medium-High Power for 7 to 12 minutes.

Makes 4 servings.

4 salmon steaks (about 6 ounces each), thawed if necessary	**3 tablespoons fresh lemon juice**
2 carrots, trimmed and cut into julienne pieces	**3 tablespoons fresh lime juice**
1 large zucchini, trimmed and cut into julienne pieces	**2 tablespoons chopped fresh parsley**
1 small onion, cut into vertical slices	**¹/₂ teaspoon leaf thyme, crumbled** **¹/₂ teaspoon salt**
¹/₃ cup olive or vegetable oil	**¹/₄ teaspoon pepper** **Lemon and lime slices for garnish**

1. Arrange the salmon in a 9 × 13-inch microwave-safe dish, with the thickest portion toward the outer edge of the dish. Combine the carrot, zucchini and onion pieces; tuck into the body cavity area of salmon.
2. Combine the oil, lemon and lime juices, parsley, thyme, salt and pepper in a small bowl. Brush over the salmon and vegetables. Cover with wax paper.
3. Microwave on Medium-High Power for 7 to 12 minutes, turning the dish ¹/₄ turn halfway through cooking time, or until the fish flakes when tested with a fork. Brush with the remaining lemon-lime baste and garnish with lemon and lime slices, if you wish.

Dilled Shrimp and Cucumber

Microwave on Full Power for 5 minutes.

Makes 4 servings.

1 cucumber, peeled, halved lengthwise, seeded and sliced ¹/₂-inch thick	**5 tablespoons herb reduced-calorie salad dressing**
¹/₂ teaspoon salt	**2 tablespoons chopped fresh dill**
4 ounces macaroni twists	**1 tablespoon plus 2 teaspoons lemon juice**
6 ounces peeled and deveined frozen shrimp	**¹/₄ teaspoon caraway seeds**
6 frozen asparagus spears, separated	**Freshly ground black pepper**

1. Toss the peeled and sliced cucumber in a colander with ¹/₂ teaspoon salt. Let stand for 10 minutes to drain.
2. Cook the macaroni or other pasta in boiling salted water following package directions. Rinse under cold water and drain. Set aside.
3. Arrange the frozen shrimp in a single layer on a microwave-safe plate. Cover with a double thickness of wet microwave-safe paper toweling.
4. Microwave on Full Power for 3 minutes. Rinse under cold running water and drain thoroughly.
5. Arrange the frozen asparagus in a single layer on a microwave-safe plate. Cover with a double thickness of microwave-safe wet paper toweling.
6. Microwave on Full Power for 2 minutes. Thoroughly rinse the asparagus and cucumbers; drain thoroughly.
7. Place the cooked macaroni, shrimp, asparagus and cucumber in a medium-size bowl. Toss with salad dressing, dill, lemon juice, caraway and ground pepper until well blended. Serve on individual salad plates. Garnish each with thin-sliced cucumber and a sprig of dill, if you wish.

Pictured opposite:
Oriental Shrimp and Vegetables, page 573.

Oriental Shrimp and Vegetables

Total cooking time: 13 minutes.

Makes 6 servings.

2 tablespoons butter
or margarine
4 green onions, sliced
($^1/_2$ cup)
1 tablespoon
cornstarch
$^1/_4$ cup soy sauce
1 can (8 ounces) water
chestnuts, drained
and sliced
1 can (8 ounces)
sliced bamboo
shoots, drained

1 can (4 ounces)
mushroom pieces,
drained
1 envelope instant
chicken broth
$^1/_4$ teaspoon ground
ginger
1 pound frozen shelled
and deveined
shrimp
1 package (6 ounces)
frozen snow peas

1. Combine butter and onions in a 2-quart glass casserole. Cook, uncovered, in microwave 2 to 3 minutes or until bubbly.
2. Combine cornstarch and soy sauce; stir into casserole along with water chestnuts, bamboo shoots, mushrooms, chicken broth, ginger and shrimp.
3. Cook, covered, in microwave 8 minutes. Stir in snow peas and cook, covered, 3 to 4 minutes longer or until mixture boils and shrimp are firm. Serve over hot cooked rice, if you wish.

Saucy Kabobs

A tasty bite of shrimp and chicken, basted with a sweet and sour marinade.

Microwave on Full Power for 8 to 10 minutes.

Makes 8 servings.

1 can (8 ounces)
pineapple chunks in
natural juice
$^1/_2$ cup salt-free steak
sauce
$^1/_4$ cup honey
1 teaspoon salt-free
lemon and herb and
spice seasoning
blend
$^1/_2$ pound medium

shrimp, shelled and
deveined
1 chicken breast,
boned, skinned and
cut into 16 pieces
1 large sweet red
pepper, seeded and
cubed
2 teaspoons
cornstarch

1. Drain the pineapple juice into a shallow baking dish. Add the salt-free steak sauce, honey and seasoning blend. Add the shrimp, chicken and red pepper, turning to coat. Cover and marinate the chicken mixture in the refrigerator at least 1 hour.
2. Alternately skewer the pineapple, chicken, shrimp and red pepper on 8 eight-inch bamboo skewers; reserve the marinade. Arrange the skewers hanging on the rim of 11 × 7-inch microwave-safe baking dish. Cover the skewers with wax paper.
3. Microwave on Full Power for 5 to 7 minutes or until the chicken and the shrimp are just tender, rotating the dish once. Let stand, covered, for 3 minutes.
4. Combine the reserved marinade with the cornstarch in a 2-cup microwave-safe measure, blending well.
5. Microwave on Full Power for 3 minutes or until thickened. Serve the sauce over the kabobs.

Chunky Vegetable Gumbo with Shrimp

The microwave oven helps to retain the vitamins of fresh vegetables.

Microwave on Full Power for 32 to 38 minutes.

Makes 6 servings.

6 slices bacon, diced
3 cups chopped fresh
okra
OR: 1 package
(10 ounces) frozen
okra, chopped
$^1/_3$ cup vegetable oil
$^1/_3$ cup all-purpose
flour
$1^1/_4$ cups diced celery
$^3/_4$ cup chopped green
onion
1 medium-size onion,
chopped ($^1/_2$ cup)
3 cloves garlic, finely
chopped
1 small yellow squash,
thinly sliced
1 small zucchini, thinly
sliced
1 cup diced sweet

green pepper
2 bay leaves
$3^1/_2$ cups chicken
broth
$^1/_4$ cup finely chopped
parsley
$^1/_2$ teaspoon salt
$^1/_2$ teaspoon pepper
$^1/_2$ teaspoon leaf
thyme, crumbled
$^1/_4$ teaspoon cayenne,
or to taste
1 teaspoon
Worcestershire
sauce
1 pound medium-size
shrimp, shelled and
deveined
$^3/_4$ teaspoon filé
powder *(optional)*

1. Microwave the diced bacon, uncovered, in 2-quart microwave-safe dish on Full Power for 3 minutes or until crisp. Remove the bacon with a slotted spoon and reserve.
2. Microwave the okra in the bacon drippings on Full Power for 7 minutes or until tender, stirring occasionally.
3. Microwave the oil in a 3-quart microwave-safe plastic casserole, uncovered, on Full Power for 2 to 3 minutes or until hot. Stir in the flour until blended.
4. Microwave the flour mixture on Full Power for 7 to 8 minutes or until cinnamon-colored, stirring often. Stir in the celery, onions and garlic.
5. Microwave, uncovered, on Full Power for 4 minutes or until crisp-tender, stirring once. Stir in the okra mixture, squash, zucchini, green pepper and bay leaves. Add the chicken broth, parsley, salt, pepper, thyme, cayenne and Worcestershire sauce, blending well. Cover the dish with vented heavy-duty microwave-safe plastic wrap.
6. Microwave on Full Power for 7 to 9 minutes or until the vegetables are tender, stirring occasionally. Stir in the reserved bacon and the shrimp. Cover.
7. Microwave on Full Power for 2 to 4 minutes or until

Chunky Vegetable Gumbo with Shrimp, page 576.

the shrimp just begins to curl. Stir in the filé powder (if using). Remove the bay leaves. Taste and adjust the seasonings. Serve over hot cooked rice, if you wish.

Microwave Manicotti

Appropriately named, this pasta dish can be made entirely in the microwave. But, if you wish, cook the manicotti noodles on the stovetop.

Microwave on Full Power for 34 minutes.

Makes 5 servings.

6 cups very hot water	**squeezed dry**
1 tablespoon vegetable oil	**2 cups shredded mozzarella cheese (¹/₂ pound)**
1 teaspoon salt	
1 package (8 ounces) manicotti noodles	**1 container (15 ounces) ricotta cheese**
1 jar (16 ounces) spaghetti sauce with meat	**¹/₄ cup grated Parmesan cheese**
1 cup water or dry red wine	**2 eggs, beaten**
	¹/₂ teaspoon salt
2 packages (10 ounces each) frozen chopped spinach, thawed and	**¹/₄ teaspoon pepper**
	¹/₄ teaspoon ground nutmeg

1. Place the water in a 4-quart microwave-safe casserole. Cover with heavy-duty plastic wrap. (Do not vent.)
2. Microwave on Full Power for 8 minutes, or until the water comes to boiling. Very carefully remove plastic wrap towards you; add oil, 1 teaspoon salt and manicotti noodles; stir. Re-cover.
3. Microwave on Full Power for 6 minutes, or until the noodles are al dente, stirring once. Drain in a colander.
4. Microwave the spaghetti sauce with water or dry red wine in a 2-quart microwave-safe bowl, on Full Power for 5 minutes, or until hot.
5. Combine the drained spinach, 1 cup of the mozzarella, the ricotta and Parmesan cheeses, beaten eggs, salt, pepper and nutmeg in large bowl, blending well. Stuff the cheese mixture into the manicotti noodles; place in a large shallow microwave-safe dish. Top with spaghetti sauce. Cover with wax paper.
6. Microwave on Full Power for 15 minutes, rotating twice. Sprinkle with the remaining mozzarella cheese. Let stand, covered, for 5 minutes.

Lighthearted Lasagne

Microwave on Full Power for 17 to 19 minutes, then on Medium-High Power for 20 minutes.

Makes 6 servings.

1 pound ground raw turkey	**¹/₂ teaspoon leaf basil, crumbled**
1 jar (32 ounces) spaghetti sauce	**1 tablespoon leaf parsley flakes, crumbled**
¹/₂ cup red wine	
1 teaspoon fennel seeds	**8 packaged lasagne noodles, uncooked**
¹/₄ teaspoon garlic powder	**8 ounces low-fat mozzarella cheese, sliced**
16 ounces cottage cheese	**¹/₄ cup sliced ripe olives**
¹/₂ cup grated Parmesan cheese	

1. Crumble the turkey into a 2-quart glass microwave-safe bowl. Stir in ¹/₂ cup spaghetti sauce. Stirring

(continued)

Microwave Manicotti.

midway through the cooking, microwave on Full Power for 4 to 5 minutes.

2. Stir the sauce again and pour the remaining spaghetti sauce into a bowl. Pour the wine into the sauce jar, replace the lid, and shake vigorously to loosen the remaining sauce in the jar. Pour the contents of the jar into the bowl along with the fennel seeds and the garlic powder. Cover the bowl with heavy-duty plastic wrap; microwave on Full Power for 7 to 8 minutes, or until bubbly.

3. In a small bowl, combine the cottage cheese, Parmesan cheese, basil and parsley; set aside.

4. To assemble the lasagne, pour 1/3 of the hot spaghetti sauce mixture into a 2-quart rectangular dish; level. Place 3 lasagne noodles in the dish, pressing to make contact with the sauce. Break off part of another lasagne noodle to fit across the end of the dish. Spread 1/2 of the cottage cheese mixture on the noodles. Arrange half of the sliced mozzarella on the top. Pour half of the remaining hot spaghetti sauce into the dish; level. Repeat the layers, with the remaining sauce as the final layer. Distribute olives over the top.

5. Cover the dish with heavy-duty plastic wrap or 2 layers of regular plastic wrap. Microwave on Full

Quiche Lorraine, page 579.

Quick Old-fashioned Shepherd's Pie.

Power for 6 minutes, then on Medium-High Power (70°) for 20 minutes. Do not remove the cover. Let stand for 20 to 30 minutes before serving so that the noodles can finish cooking.

Quick Old-fashioned Shepherd's Pie

One of Grandmother's cherished recipes is easily adapted for use in the microwave.

Microwave on Full Power for 10 to 15 minutes.

Makes 6 servings.

2 cups cubed cooked turkey, chicken or beef	**1/2 cup milk**
	1/4 cup dry sherry OR: water
1 package (20 ounces) frozen broccoli, cauliflower and carrot mix	**1/2 teaspoon leaf tarragon, crumbled**
	Pepper to taste
1/4 cup frozen chopped onion	**Frozen hash brown potatoes, cooked, following package directions**
1 can (10³/4 ounces) condensed cream of chicken soup	**OR: 2 cups mashed potatoes**

1. Layer the turkey, chicken or beef with the frozen vegetable mix and onion in a 2-quart microwave-safe dish.

2. Combine the soup, milk, sherry or water, tarragon and pepper in a bowl, blending well. Pour the liquid over the vegetable layer. Arrange the hash browns or mashed potatoes evenly over the top.

3. Microwave on Full Power for 10 to 15 minutes or until heated through.

Quiche Lorraine

This main-dish pie calls for cooking the filling and crust separately.

Microwave on Full Power for 7¹/₂ minutes.

Makes 6 servings (9-inch pie).

1 cup shredded Swiss cheese	**shell, baked following package directions**
1 cup diced fully-cooked canned ham	
1 tablespoon finely chopped green onion	**1 cup half-and-half or light cream**
	4 eggs, beaten
1 frozen 9-inch pie	**¹/₂ teaspoon pepper**
	Pinch ground nutmeg

1. Sprinkle ²/₃ cup of the Swiss cheese, the diced ham and the green onion evenly over the baked pie shell.
2. Combine the half-and-half or light cream with eggs, pepper and nutmeg in a 1-quart microwave-safe bowl.
3. Microwave, uncovered, on Full Power for 4¹/₂ minutes, stirring after 3 minutes. Stir again and pour into the prepared crust. Cover with wax paper.
4. Microwave the quiche on Full Power for 3 minutes, rotating the quiche halfway through. The quiche is done when a knife inserted in the center comes out clean; otherwise heat 1 minute more. Sprinkle the pie with the remaining Swiss cheese. Cover the top with wax paper and let stand for 5 minutes. Garnish with strips of cooked ham, if you wish.

Jiffy Enchiladas

Nacho cheese soup/dip is a convenient flavor enhancer for cooked turkey or chicken enchiladas.

Microwave on Full Power for 10 to 12 minutes.

Makes 6 servings.

1 medium onion, chopped (¹/₂ cup)	**chopped (¹/₂ cup)**
	1 can (11 ounces) condensed nacho cheese soup/dip
1 tablespoon butter or margarine	
1 small clove garlic, finely chopped	**³/₄ cup milk**
	6 corn tortillas
¹/₄ teaspoon cumin	**Vegetable oil**
2 cups shredded cooked turkey or chicken	**Shredded Cheddar cheese**
	Chopped tomato
1 small tomato,	

1. Microwave the onion, butter or margarine, garlic and cumin in a 2-quart microwave-safe bowl, covered, on Full Power for 2 minutes, or until the onion is tender.
2. Stir in the turkey or chicken, ¹/₂ cup chopped tomato and ¹/₄ cup undiluted soup; set aside.

3. Stir the remaining soup in a small bowl; gradually stir in the milk until blended.
4. Brush the tortillas with oil; stack in a 10 × 6-inch microwave-safe dish. Cover with heavy-duty plastic wrap.
5. Microwave on Full Power for 2 minutes, or until the tortillas are softened. Remove from the baking dish; set aside.
6. Pour ¹/₄ cup soup/milk mixture into the same dish. Spread ¹/₄ cup turkey mixture over each tortilla. Roll up; place seam-side down in dish. Pour the remaining soup mixture over the enchiladas. Cover with vented plastic wrap.
7. Microwave on Full Power for 6 to 8 minutes, or until hot, turning the dish occasionally. Let stand, covered, for 2 minutes. Garnish with the cheese and tomato.

Fettuccine in California Pistachio Sauce

The pistachios add a delicate green color, which contrasts beautifully with the pasta.

Microwave on Full Power for 5 to 6 minutes, then on Low Power for 1 to 2 minutes.

Makes 6 servings.

1 medium onion, chopped (¹/₂ cup)	**6 ounces fettuccine noodles, cooked and drained**
3 tablespoons butter or margarine	
1 clove garlic, finely chopped	**¹/₂ cup coarsely chopped shelled natural pistachios**
1 cup half-and-half or light cream	**2 tablespoons chopped parsley**
Salt and pepper	**Grated Parmesan cheese**
2 eggs, beaten	

1. Combine the onion, butter or margarine and garlic in a 4-cup glass measure.
2. Microwave on Full Power for 3 to 4 minutes. Stir in the half-and-half, salt and pepper.
3. Microwave on Full Power for 2 minutes, or until the mixture comes to boiling. Stir a small amount of the hot mixture into the eggs; blend the eggs back into the mixture.
4. Microwave on Low Power for 1 to 2 minutes, or until the mixture just begins to thicken. Toss with the hot pasta, pistachios and parsley. Serve with the Parmesan cheese.

Microwavable Vegetables

Microwave ovens have made vegetable cooking simpler than boiling water. Tender-crisp, brightly colored, perfectly cooked vegetables are ready in just seconds. Less water and cooking time are required to microwave vegetables so that textures, flavors, vitamins and minerals remain intact. Vitamin C, especially, is sensitive to overcooking.

Microwaving fresh vegetables requires no special equipment, but a few easy rules apply. Always use microwave-safe containers that allow microwave energy to pass through.

Glass, pottery, china, paper and thermoplastic are the most common materials used in the microwave. Plastic cooking bags, but not those from the produce department, may be used. Tie bags shut with string, not twist ties.

Paper toweling, napkins, plates and bags make convenient disposable cooking containers. Be careful to use plastic or wax-coated plates at low temperatures; high temperatures may melt the wax or cause colors to run into the food. Also, be sure the paper towels are all paper and do not contain synthetics that may not withstand high heat.

Glass, ceramic lids and heavy-duty microwave-safe plastic wrap make good covers for containers for most vegetables because they hold in steam. Do not use lightweight plastic wraps, which have a tendency to split during cooking and melt into the food. Use caution when uncovering a cooked dish.

Wax paper works best for covering mushrooms, onions, tomatoes and moist vegetables. It allows some steam to escape so the vegetables do not become soggy.

Microwave potatoes, squash and yams whole. Remember to pierce to allow steam to escape.

There are a few basic techniques used in microwave cooking. Use this as a reference guide.
- All vegetables should be cooked on Full Power (100%). Remember that microwave ovens do vary in wattage output.
- Cooking time depends on the quantity, size, freshness and moisture content of the vegetables. Standing time is as important as actual cooking time, especially when microwaving vegetables. They will continue to cook even after the heat generated by microwaves has ceased. Overcooked vegetables turn dry and tough.
- Vegetables should be cooked only until bright and tender-crisp when pierced. Potatoes, yams and squash should give slightly when pressed. Test for doneness after the recommended standing time.
- In general, estimate cooking time of about 6 to 7 minutes per pound of vegetables. Stir or rotate after 3 minutes; bring the center portion toward the outside of the dish, for more even cooking.

After the minimum cooking time, let stand, then check for doneness. If necessary, cook in 1-minute intervals.

Note: Dried peas and beans are better cooked in a conventional oven or on a range.

- To cook several large individual vegetables (potatoes or squash) place them in a circle for more even cooking, leaving about one inch between. Arrange them in a single layer rather than on top of each other.

Cut vegetables into uniform sizes and shapes. Potatoes should be placed with the thickest portions to the outside. Those with thick, tough stalks, such as broccoli, should be arranged with the tips toward the center.
- Stir and rotate vegetables (especially large quantities) midway through cooking time to prevent uneven cooking.
- Salt vegetables only after they are cooked because salt draws liquid out of food and interferes with the microwave cooking pattern. Other seasonings may be used.

Here is a medley of tips and hints to help you:
- To blanch vegetables for crudité platters or to add to casseroles: Slightly undercook vegetables and let stand, covered, 1 minute. Place vegetables in ice water to stop cooking. Spread vegetables on paper toweling to absorb any excess moisture.
- To soften the tough skins of winter squash, place squash on the oven floor. Microwave, uncovered, on Full Power for 1 minute. Let stand 1 minute before cutting.
- Easy mashed potatoes: Cube potatoes. Add a small amount of water. Cook, tightly covered, until soft. Season and mash with milk or cream.
- For softer vegetables, increase the amount of water and cooking time.
- Recipes made with sour cream, eggs or cream should be cooked at a slightly lower setting to avoid curdling.
- Add butter or margarine with water before cooking vegetables. For soft moist vegetables, such as mushrooms and spinach, substitute equal amounts butter or margarine for water.
- Sprinkle vegetables with grated or shredded cheese during the standing time and toss before serving.
- Don't hesitate to experiment with fresh herbs. Add to vegetables during standing time.
- Substitute beef, chicken or vegetable broth for water. The result is richer tasting vegetables.

VEGETABLE	QUANTITY	WATER	PREPARATION TIPS	COOKING TIME	STANDING TIME
Artichoke	1 medium-size	1/4 cup	Turn upside down in small dish or custard cup. Cover with plastic wrap.	5-7 min. (stem should be fork tender)	5 min. covered.
Asparagus Spears	1 pound	3 Tbs.	Snap off tough ends. Arrange buds toward center of dish, cover with plastic wrap.	5 min.	5 min. covered.
Beans (green, wax)	1 pound	1/2 cup	Snap ends and pull off strings. Cover with plastic wrap or lid.	12-15 min. Stir every 5 min.	5 min. covered.
Beets	6	1 1/2 cups	Wash. *(Do Not Peel.)* Cover with lid or plastic wrap.	14-16 min. Turn after 7 min.	5 min. covered. Let cool, peel.
Broccoli Spears	1 1/2 pounds	—	Place buds toward center of plate. Cover with lid or plastic wrap.	8-10 min. Rotate dish or plate after 5 min.	4 min. covered.
Brussels Sprouts	1 pound	2 Tbs.	Cover with lid or plastic wrap.	6-7 min. Stir after 3 min.	3-5 min. covered. Stem ends should be fork tender.
Cabbage	1 pound	2 Tbs.	Discard wilted outer leaves. Cover with lid or plastic wrap.	4-6 min. (shredded) 6-8 min. (wedges) Stir or turn 1/2 way through cooking.	3 min. covered.
Carrots	1 pound	1/4 cup	Slice in uniform size or leave whole. Cover with lid or plastic wrap. through cooking.	6-7 min. (slices) 8-9 min. (whole) Stir or rotate 1/2 way	5 min. covered.
Cauliflower	1 1/2 pounds	2 Tbs.	Remove outer leaves. Trim stem end. Separate flowerets or leave head whole. Cover with lid or plastic wrap.	6-8 min. (flowerets) 10-11 min. (whole) Stir or rotate head 1/2 way through cooking.	4-5 min. covered.
Corn on the Cob	1 ear	—	Secure husk closed with string. (Or shuck and wrap in plastic.) Place on paper toweling on microwave floor.	3-4 min. per ear. Turn each 1/2 way through cooking.	2-3 min. per ear.
Greens (kale & mustard)	1 1/4 pounds	—	Rinse and coarsely chop. Cover with lid or plastic wrap.	7-8 min. Stir after 3 min.	2 min. covered.
Mushrooms	1 pound	2 Tbs. *or* 2 Tbs. butter	Cut to even shapes. Cover with wax paper.	4-6 min. Stir after 2 min.	2 min. covered.
Onions	1 pound	—	Quarter, slice or leave whole. Cover with wax paper.	4-6 min. Stir after 2 min.	5 min. covered.
Peas	2 1/2 pounds (3 cups)	1/4 cup	Shell and rinse. Cover with lid or plastic wrap.	9-13 min. Stir after 5 min.	5 min. covered.
Potatoes (baking, sweet potatoes, yams)	1	—	Pierce skin on 4 sides with fork. Place on paper toweling on microwave floor. Arrange 1 on floor, 2 side by side, 4 or more in spoke fashion.	4-5 min. Add 2-3 min. per potato. Turn each 1/2 way through cooking.	5-10 min. covered. Should give to slight pressure.
Spinach	1 pound	—	Rinse; shake excess water. Cover with lid or plastic wrap.	5-7 min. Stir after 3 min.	2 min. covered.
Squash (winter)	1 medium-size	—	Cut and remove seeds. Place on plate with hollow side up. Cover with plastic wrap.	10-12 min. Rotate after 5 min.	5 min. covered.
Squash (summer)	1 pound	2 Tbs.	Cover with lid or plastic wrap.	6-7 min. Stir after 3 min.	3 min covered.
Turnips	1 pound	3 Tbs.	Cut into cubes. Cover with lid or plastic wrap.	7-9 min. Stir after 3 min.	3 min. covered.

East Indian Vegetable Casserole

This meatless casserole will delight even the heartiest of eaters. Fresh vegetables team with rice, nuts and a hint of spices, all topped off with mozzarella.

Microwave on Full Power for 25 to 26 minutes.

Makes 6 servings.

1 cup coarsely chopped green pepper	**cardamom**
¾ cup chopped onion	**¼ teaspoon ground nutmeg**
2 tablespoons butter or margarine, melted	**¼ teaspoon liquid red pepper seasoning**
1 cup uncooked long-grain rice	**2 cups beef broth**
¾ cup diagonally sliced celery	**¾ cup raisins**
¾ cup sliced carrot	**½ cup chopped dry roasted peanuts or cashews**
¼ teaspoon ground	**1 package (8 ounces) mozzarella cheese, thinly sliced**

1. Microwave the green pepper, onion and melted butter or margarine in a deep 2-quart microwave-safe casserole on Full Power for 4 minutes, stirring once. Stir in the rice, celery, carrot, cardamom, nutmeg and liquid red pepper seasoning.
2. Microwave beef broth, uncovered, in a 2-cup glass measure on Full Power for 3 to 4 minutes, or until boiling. Add the raisins; let stand for 1 minute.
3. Stir the cooked broth into the rice. Cover with vented heavy-duty plastic wrap.
4. Microwave on Full Power for 15 minutes, or until all the liquid is absorbed, stirring once. Sprinkle the nuts on the casserole; arrange the cheese slices on top.
5. Microwave, uncovered, on Full Power for 3 minutes, or until cheese melts. Let stand for 3 minutes.

Savory Oriental Vegetables

This accompaniment dish is a favorite because it's easy, fast and flavorful.

Microwave on Full Power for 5 minutes.

Makes 2 servings.

¼ cup frozen snow peas, thawed and stringed	**julienne strips**
¼ cup julienne carrots	**2 tablespoons soy sauce**
¼ cup julienne zucchini	**2 tablespoons sesame oil**
¼ cup broccoli flowerets	**½ cup chopped green onion**
1 small onion, cut into	**2 or 3 tablespoons sesame seeds**

1. Place the snow peas, carrots, zucchini, broccoli and onion in a small microwave-safe dish.
2. Combine the soy sauce and sesame oil and stir into the vegetables. Cover with vented heavy-duty plastic wrap.

3. Microwave on Full Power for 5 minutes. Garnish with chopped green onion and sesame seeds.

Microwave Artichokes

Microwave on Full Power for 10 to 15 minutes.

Makes 2 servings.

2 medium artichokes	**Vinaigrette Dressing**
¼ cup water	***(recipe follows)***

1. Trim the artichokes; place in a square glass dish; add ¼ cup water. Cover with vented heavy-duty plastic wrap.
2. Microwave on Full Power for 10 to 15 minutes, or until base is tender when pierced with a knife, rearranging twice during cooking. Let stand for 5 minutes.
3. Serve hot or cold with Vinaigrette Dressing.

Vinaigrette Dressing: Makes ½ cup. Place 2 tablespoons red wine vinegar, ⅛ teaspoon salt and dash pepper in a small jar with a tight-fitting lid; cover; shake well. Gradually add 3 tablespoons olive oil, covering jar tightly and shaking well between additions.

Rainbow Stuffed Peppers

Colorful peppers encase a savory crabmeat filling.

Microwave on Full Power for 15 minutes.

Makes 6 servings.

6 large sweet green, red or yellow peppers	**¼ cup lemon juice**
½ cup (1 stick) butter or margarine	**1 package (8 ounces) herb-seasoned stuffing mix**
¼ cup diced celery	**1 can (6 ounces) crab-meat**
1 small onion, finely chopped (¼ cup)	**1 jar (2 ounces) pimiento, drained and chopped**
½ cup water	

1. Cut a thin slice from the pepper tops; scoop out the membrane and seeds. Arrange the peppers, cut side down, in a large shallow microwave-safe dish. Cover the peppers with heavy-duty microwave-safe plastic wrap.
2. Microwave on Full Power for 7 minutes or until the peppers have softened. Remove the peppers with a slotted spoon to paper toweling.
3. Drain the liquid from the baking dish. Add the butter or margarine, celery and onion to the dish.

(continued)

Pictured opposite:
Rainbow Stuffed Peppers.

4. Microwave on Full Power for 3 minutes, stirring twice. Add the water, lemon juice, stuffing, crab with its liquid and the pimiento. Spoon the stuffing into the peppers.
5. Microwave on Full Power for 5 minutes or until the celery is heated through.

Comfort Carrot Ring

Southern Comfort liquor adds flavorful distinction to this carrot ring.

Microwave on Full Power for 20 minutes, then on Half Power for 10 minutes.

Makes 6 servings.

2 pounds carrots, trimmed and peeled	**2 tablespoons Southern Comfort**
1/2 cup water	**1 tablespoon dark brown sugar**
1/2 teaspoon salt	**1/2 to 1 teaspoon salt**
1/4 cup (1/2 stick) butter or margarine	**1/2 teaspoon ground pepper**
2 egg yolks, lightly beaten	

1. Combine the carrots, water and salt in a 3-quart microwave-safe casserole.
2. Microwave on Full Power for 20 minutes, turning dish 1/4 turn after 9 minutes. Drain thoroughly.
3. Press the carrots through a coarse sieve with the back of a spoon. Stir in the butter or margarine, egg yolks, liquor, sugar, salt and pepper.
4. Butter a 1-quart microwave-safe casserole. Place a small glass in the center of the dish; grease the glass. Pack the carrot mixture in an even layer. Cover with vented heavy-duty plastic wrap.
5. Microwave on Half Power for 10 minutes, or until hot. Cool for 10 minutes. Twist the glass to remove; invert the dish onto a serving platter.

Cheese and Onion Soufflé

Evaporated milk makes this savory soufflé extra creamy.

Microwave on Full Power for 5 minutes, then on Low Power for 10 minutes, then on Half Power for 12 minutes.

Makes 6 servings.

1/4 cup all-purpose flour	**2 cups shredded Muenster cheese (8 ounces)**
1/2 teaspoon salt	**1/2 cup chopped green onion**
1/4 teaspoon dry mustard	**6 eggs, separated**
1 can (13 ounces) evaporated milk	**1 teaspoon cream of tartar**
Few drops liquid red pepper seasoning	**Sliced green onion**

1. Blend the flour, salt and mustard in a 6-cup microwave-safe casserole. Slowly stir in the evaporated milk and red pepper seasoning with a wire whip.
2. Microwave on Full Power for 4 minutes, stirring mixture every 2 minutes, or until thickened. Stir the shredded cheese and chopped green onion into the hot sauce.
3. Microwave on Full Power for 1 minute, or until cheese melts.
4. Beat the egg whites with the cream of tartar in the large bowl of an electric mixer at high speed until stiff but not dry. Without washing beaters, beat the yolks in a medium-size bowl of an electric mixer at high speed until thick and lemon colored.
5. Reduce the mixer speed to low; gradually pour the cheese sauce over the yolks, beating until well blended. Gently pour the mixture over the egg whites; fold together just until combined. Pour the mixture into ungreased 10-cup soufflé dish.
6. Microwave on Low Power for 10 minutes, rotating the dish one-quarter turn every 5 minutes.
7. Microwave on Half Power for 12 minutes longer, rotating the dish one-quarter turn every 4 minutes, or until the soufflé has risen, with a puffed edge; top with sliced green onion. Serve at once.

Black-eyed Pea Stew

Leftover cooked peas and sausage are the basis of a great Sunday night supper.

Microwave on Full Power for 17 to 18 minutes.

Makes 4 servings.

1 medium onion, chopped (1/2 cup)	**1 can (about 15 ounces) tomatoes**
1 clove garlic, finely chopped	**1 cup water**
1 tablespoon vegetable oil	**1 potato, diced**
1 2/3 cups cooked California black-eyed peas	**1/4 pound sliced, fully cooked Polish sausage**
OR: 1 can (16 ounces) black-eyed peas	**1/2 teaspoon salt**
	1/4 teaspoon leaf oregano, crumbled
	1/8 teaspoon pepper

1. Place the chopped onion, garlic and oil in a 2-quart microwave-safe dish; cover with wax paper.
2. Microwave on Full Power for 2 to 3 minutes, or until the onion is tender. Add the drained black-eyed peas, tomatoes, water, potato and sausage. Stir in the salt, oregano and pepper. Cover with wax paper.
3. Microwave on Full Power for 15 minutes, or until the potato is tender and the stew is thickened, stirring every 3 minutes.

Savory Parmesan Potatoes

A delightfully easy potato side dish that is the perfect accompaniment to roast beef.

Microwave on Full Power for 10 minutes.

Makes 4 servings.

**2 large baking
 potatoes
2 tablespoons butter
 or margarine,
 melted
3 tablespoons grated
 Parmesan cheese
1 tablespoon**

**packaged
 unseasoned bread
 crumbs
¹/₄ teaspoon salt
¹/₈ teaspoon garlic
 powder
Dash paprika**

1. Wash the potatoes and cut crosswise into ³/₈-inch slices. Arrange in a single layer on a microwave-safe plate or in a shallow baking dish. Brush with the melted butter or margarine.
2. Combine the grated Parmesan cheese with unseasoned bread crumbs, salt, garlic powder and paprika in a cup. Sprinkle evenly over the potatoes.
3. Microwave on Full Power for 10 minutes, or until the potatoes are tender, turning ¹/₄ turn every 2 or 3 minutes.
4. Remove from the oven. Cover with heavy-duty plastic wrap and let stand for 3 minutes before serving.

How to Bake Potatoes in a Microwave Oven

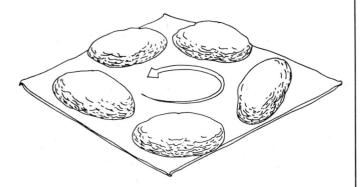

Scrub, dry and prick potatoes. Place 1 inch apart on microwave-safe paper toweling in oven. Microwave on high power, following these guidelines: 1 potato cooks for 5 to 6 minutes; 2 for 6 to 8; 3 for 8 to 10; 4 for 10 to 12 and 5 for 12 to 14. Remember to turn potatoes over after the total cooking.time. (**Note:** Microwave oven cooking times and instructions vary. Check the manufacturer's manual.)

How to Blossom a Baked Potato

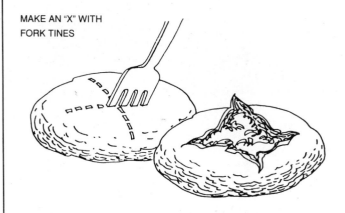

MAKE AN "X" WITH FORK TINES

PUSH SKIN FROM BOTH ENDS FORCING THE "MEAT" TO BLOSSOM

Cottage Cheese Topping

A medium-size baked potato has approximately 90 to 100 calories. The cottage cheese topping has about 90 calories a serving. This combination makes a satisfying lunch or light supper for under 200 calories per serving.

Microwave on Low Power for 3 to 4 minutes.

Makes enough topping for about 4 potatoes.

**2 cups (1 pint) small-
 curd, low-fat
 cottage cheese
¹/₂ cup finely grated
 carrot
¹/₄ cup finely grated
 radish
¹/₄ cup finely chopped**

**sweet green pepper
¹/₄ cup thinly sliced
 green onions,
 including some
 green tops
¹/₄ teaspoon salt
¹/₄ teaspoon black
 pepper**

1. Microwave the cottage cheese in a 1-quart microwave-safe bowl on Low Power for 3 to 4 minutes, stirring every minute, until the cottage cheese is just warmed to room temperature. (Heating the cottage cheese avoids cooling off hot potatoes. Watch carefully, however, because overheating can cause the cheese to separate.)
2. Stir in the grated carrot, radish, chopped green pepper, green onion, salt and pepper, mixing well. Divide the topping evenly over the opened potatoes.

Cottage Cheese Topping for Baked Potato, page 585.

Taco Topping for Baked Potato.

Dilly Oil and Vinegar Topping.

Taco Topping

Placing the sour cream and cheese in the center of the potatoes and covering with hot meat sauce allows these ingredients to melt without additional microwaving.

Microwave on Full Power for 7 to 9 minutes.

Makes enough filling for about 4 medium-size potatoes.

1 pound lean ground beef	**chopped canned mild green chilies**
1 medium-size onion, chopped (1/2 cup)	**1 teaspoon salt**
1/4 cup chopped sweet green pepper	**1/2 cup shredded sharp Cheddar cheese (2 ounces)**
1 can (8 ounces) tomato sauce	**1/2 cup dairy sour cream**
2 tablespoons, or more to taste,	**Diced tomatoes and shredded lettuce**

1. Microwave the beef, onion and green pepper in a 2-quart microwave-safe casserole on Full Power for 7 to 9 minutes, breaking up and stirring every 2 minutes, until the meat is no longer pink and the vegetables are tender. Drain off the fat.

2. Stir in the tomato sauce, chilies and salt, blending well.

3. Just before serving, slash the tops of the potatoes and divide the cheese and the sour cream evenly into the centers. Cover with the hot meat sauce. Garnish with the diced tomatoes and shredded lettuce.

Dilly Oil and Vinegar Topping

This topping gives a nostalgic "potato salad" flavor to microwaved potatoes.

Microwave on Full Power for 1 to 3 minutes.

Makes 1 1/2 cups (enough topping for 4 to 6 potatoes).

3/4 cup olive oil	**vinegar**
1/2 cup chopped green onion, including some of the green top	**1/2 cup chopped dill pickle**
	1/2 teaspoon dillweed
	1/2 teaspoon salt
1/3 cup red wine	**1/8 teaspoon pepper**

1. Microwave 1 tablespoon of the olive oil and the green onions in a 1-quart microwave-safe casserole on Full Power for 1 to 3 minutes or until the green areas have brightened and the white areas are slightly softened.

2. Add the remaining olive oil, the vinegar, chopped pickle, dillweed, salt and pepper, blending well. Spoon into the microwave-baked potatoes which have been slashed open.

Carrots a L'Orange

Total cooking time: 10 minutes.

Makes 4 servings.

3 cups thinly sliced
carrots
(5^1/$_2$ medium-size)
^{1}/$_4$ teaspoon ground
ginger
^{1}/$_2$ teaspoon seasoned

salt
^{1}/$_4$ cup orange juice
2 tablespoons butter
1 tablespoon chopped
fresh parsley

1. In a 1^1/$_2$-quart glass baking dish, stir the carrots, ginger, salt and juice; blend well. Dot with butter.
2. Cover with plastic wrap; cook 5 minutes; stir. Cook 5 minutes more or until carrots are just tender. Sprinkle with parsley.

Sausage-Stuffed Onions

Sweet onions make the perfect containers for a savory sausage and cornbread mixture.
Microwave on Full Power for 28 minutes.

Makes 8 servings.

8 medium-size sweet
onions
^{1}/$_2$ cup water
1 teaspoon salt
1 package (1 pound)
bulk sausage
1^1/$_2$ cups water
^{1}/$_2$ cup (1 stick) butter
or margarine

1 small sweet green
pepper, halved,
seeded and diced
1 package (8 ounces)
cornbread stuffing
mix
Fresh basil leaves and
sweet red pepper
for garnish

1. Peel the onions and arrange in a large shallow microwave-safe casserole. Add the ^{1}/$_2$ cup water to the casserole and sprinkle with salt. Cover the casserole with heavy-duty microwave-safe plastic wrap.
2. Microwave on Full Power for 12 minutes, rotating the dish one-half turn after 6 minutes. Remove the onions from the microwave and allow to stand while making stuffing.
3. Shape sausage into 8 equal patties and arrange in a 2-quart shallow microwave-safe casserole.
4. Microwave the patties on Full Power for 8 minutes, rotating the dish one-half turn after 4 minutes. Remove from the microwave and let stand while preparing the stuffing.
5. Place the 1^1/$_2$ cups water, butter or margarine and diced green pepper in a 6-cup casserole; cover.
6. Microwave the green pepper on Full Power for 6 minutes. Stir in the cornbread stuffing mix until well blended. Let stand while preparing the onions.
7. Loosen and remove the inner rings from the onions and reserve for another recipe. Drain the water from the casserole and return the onions to the dish.
8. Drain the sausage on paper toweling. Crumble and toss with stuffing. Spoon into the onions, dividing evenly.

9. Microwave the onions, uncovered, on Full Power for 2 minutes or until heated through. Garnish with fresh basil leaves and red pepper, if you wish.

Meat and Vegetable Pie

A vegetable pie with a bottom layer of zesty ground meat. Serve with cinnamon-flavored applesauce and whole-wheat Italian bread.

Makes 6 servings.

Vegetable Mixture:
1 package (16 ounces)
frozen mixed
vegetables in small
pieces
^{1}/$_4$ cup water
1 tablespoon butter or
margarine
1 tablespoon all-
purpose flour
^{1}/$_2$ cup beef broth
^{1}/$_2$ teaspoon leaf
thyme, crumbled
Pinch pepper

Meat Mixture:
^{1}/$_2$ cup fresh bread
crumbs
1 tablespoon grated
onion
1 egg, slight beaten

2 tablespoons catsup
2 tablespoons milk
1^1/$_2$ teaspoons Dijon-
style mustard
^{3}/$_4$ teaspoon salt
^{1}/$_2$ teaspoon leaf
thyme, crumbled
^{1}/$_4$ teaspoon pepper
1^1/$_2$ pounds ground
beef

Potato Topping:
1 cup water
^{1}/$_2$ cup milk
1 tablespoon butter
6 tablespoons instant
mashed potato
granules
2 tablespoons grated
Parmesan cheese

1. Prepare the Vegetable Mixture: Place the frozen vegetables in a microwave-safe 8 x 8 x 2-inch square baking dish. Pour in the ^{1}/$_4$ cup water. Cover the dish with pleated plastic wrap. Microwave at Full Power for 7 minutes, stirring once. Drain the vegetables in a colander.
2. Place the butter in a 4-cup microwave-safe glass measure. Microwave, uncovered, at Full Power for 45 seconds to melt. Stir in the flour until smooth. Mix in the beef broth, thyme and pepper. Microwave, uncovered, at Full Power for 2 to 2^1/$_2$ minutes or until boiling. Whisk until smooth. Mix the broth mixture with the vegetables in a small bowl. Set aside.
3. Prepare the Meat Mixture: Combine the bread crumbs, grated onion, egg, catsup, milk, mustard, salt, thyme, pepper and meat in the same 8-inch-square dish; mix well. Pat the meat mixture into an even layer over the bottom of the dish. Cover the meat with wax paper.
4. Microwave the meat at Full Power for 8 minutes. Carefully drain off the liquid. Set aside.
5. Prepare the Potato Mixture: Combine the 1 cup water, ^{1}/$_2$ cup milk and 1 tablespoon butter in the same 4-cup measure used above. Microwave, uncovered, at Full Power for 4 to 4^1/$_2$ minutes just to boiling. Mix in the instant potato granules and the Parmesan cheese.

(continued)

6. To assemble the pie: Spread the potatoes in an even layer over the meat. Top with the vegetable mixture, spreading evenly. Cover the top with wax paper. Microwave the pie at Full Power for 2 minutes to heat through. Let the pie stand for 5 minutes before serving.

Bulgur, Gazpacho-Style

This also makes a good cold salad.
Microwave at Full Power for 9 minutes and at Half Power for 7 minutes.

Makes 6 servings.

3 tablespoons olive oil
1/4 cup sliced green onions, both white and green parts
1/4 cup diced sweet green pepper
1 cup bulgur
1 can (6 ounces) spicy-hot tomato-vegetable juice
1 can (10 1/2 ounces) condensed beef broth

Juice of 1 lime
1 teaspoon leaf thyme, crumbled
1/4 teaspoon garlic powder
1 large tomato, chopped
1 medium-size cucumber, pared and chopped
1/4 cup chopped fresh parsley

1. Place the oil in a shallow, round microwave-safe casserole, about 9 inches in diameter. Stir in the green onion, green pepper and bulgur. Cover with microwave-safe plastic wrap. Microwave at Full Power for 3 minutes.
2. Add the vegetable juice, beef broth, lime juice, thyme and garlic powder. Cover with microwave-safe plastic wrap, pleated slighty at one side to vent. Microwave at Full Power for 6 minutes. Then microwave at Half Power for 7 to 8 minutes until the bulgur is tender. Mix in the tomato, cucumber and parsley. Let stand, covered, on solid surface for 5 minutes. Garnish with cucumber slices, lime slices and parsley, if you wish.

Hot Cooked Rice

Makes 4 cups.

2 cups water
1 cup uncooked long-grain rice

1 teaspoon salt
1 teaspoon vegetable oil

1. Combine water, rice, salt and oil in a 1 1/2-quart casserole.
2. Heat, covered, in microwave 5 to 6 minutes or until mixture comes to boiling. Remove from oven; let stand 10 minutes.
3. *Return, covered, to microwave 3 to 4 minutes. Let stand 5 minutes. Fluff with fork.
Complete the microwave cooking of the rice in this step; then when oven is free, complete step 5 of Sweet and Sour Meatballs.

Curried Vegetable Salad

Microwave on Full Power for 12 minutes and on Half Power for 1 1/2 minutes.

Makes 6 servings.

1 1/2 pounds red potatoes, unpeeled and diced
2 tablespoons butter or margarine, softened
2 cups cauliflower flowerets (about 8 ounces)
1 cup cross-cut green beans (about 4 ounces)
6 asparagus spears, cut in 1/2-inch-thick slices (about

1/2 pound)
1/4 cup diced sweet green pepper
1/4 cup diced sweet red pepper

Curry Dressing:
1/2 cup plain yogurt
1 to 2 tablespoons grated lime rind
1 to 1 1/2 tablespoons lime juice
1 1/2 teaspoons curry powder

1. Combine the potatoes and butter in a 3-quart microwave-safe casserole. Cover with microwave-safe plastic wrap. Microwave at Full Power for 7 to 9 minutes until the potatoes are tender, gently shaking the dish twice. Remove to a large bowl with a slotted spoon.
2. Add the cauliflower to the casserole. Cover with plastic wrap. Microwave at Full Power for 2 minutes until tender-crisp. Add to the potatoes.
3. Add the beans to the casserole. Cover with plastic wrap. Microwave at Full Power for 1 to 2 minutes until tender-crisp. Add to the potato mixture.
4. Add the asparagus and peppers to the casserole. Cover with plastic wrap. Microwave at Full Power for 2 to 3 minutes until tender-crisp. Add to the potatoes.
5. Prepare the Curry Dressing: Combine the yogurt, lime rind, lime juice and curry in a 1-cup microwave-safe measure. Cover with plastic wrap. Microwave at Half Power for 1 1/2 to 2 minutes until warm. Whisk until smooth. Stir half of the dressing into the vegetable mixture.
6. Arrange the vegetable mixture on lettuce, if you wish. Pass the remaining Dressing.

Parsley-Flecked Rice

A small quantity of chopped parsley adds so much to plain rice. Leftovers, if any, are easy to reheat in the microwave.

Microwave on Full Power for 5 minutes, then on Medium Power for 15 to 17 minutes.

Makes 4 servings.

1 1/2 cups uncooked long-grain rice
2 2/3 cups water
1 teaspoon salt

4 teaspoons butter or margarine
3 tablespoons chopped parsley

1. Place the rice, water, salt and butter or margarine in

a deep 2-quart microwave-safe casserole or bowl. Cover with vented heavy-duty plastic wrap.
2. Microwave on Full Power for 5 minutes. Carefully remove the plastic wrap; stir with a fork; re-cover, with a fresh sheet of plastic wrap, if you wish.
3. Microwave on Medium Power for 15 to 17 minutes, or until the water is almost entirely absorbed. Let stand, covered, for 2 to 3 minutes on a flat surface.
4. Remove the covering and gently toss the parsley into the rice with a fork.

Note: To reheat cooked rice, cover and microwave on Full Power for 1 minute per cup of rice.

Pear Sundae With Almond Fudge Sauce

Canned pear halves and a few other stock ingredients make a spectacular dessert with remarkable speed in the microwave.

Microwave on Full Power for 2 minutes.

Makes 4 servings.

1 package (6 ounces) semisweet chocolate pieces
1/4 cup milk or half-and-half
2 tablespoons butter or margarine
1/2 teaspoon almond
extract
1 can (16 ounces) Bartlett pear halves, drained
Vanilla ice cream
Blanched almond slices *(optional)*

1. Place the chocolate, milk, butter or margarine and almond extract in 4-cup microwave-safe measure.
2. Microwave on Full Power for 2 minutes, or until the mixture comes to boiling, stirring every minute. Cool.
3. For each serving, place 2 pear halves in a dessert dish. Top with a scoop of ice cream and warm sauce. Garnish with almonds, if you wish.

Raisin Bread Pudding with Whiskey Sauce

This is a new-fashioned version of the timeless classic.

Microwave on Full Power for 13 minutes.

Makes 6 servings.

7 slices raisin bread, cubed (about 4 cups)
1/3 cup firmly packed light brown sugar
1/4 teaspoon salt
2 cups milk
1/4 cup (1/2 stick) butter, cut up
2 eggs, beaten
Whiskey Sauce *(recipe follows)*

1. Spread the bread in a 10 x 6-inch glass dish. Sprinkle with the sugar and salt.
2. Microwave the milk and butter in 4-cup glass measure on Full Power for 4 minutes, or until hot.

Whisk in the beaten eggs; pour over the bread cubes in the dish.
3. Microwave on Full Power for 9 minutes, or until a knife inserted in the center comes out clean, rotating once. Pour the **Whiskey Sauce** over individual servings.

WHISKEY SAUCE: Makes about 1/2 cup. Mix 1/3 cup sugar and 2 tablespoons bourbon in a 2-cup glass measure; stir in 1/4 cup (1/2 stick) butter, cut up. Microwave on Full Power for 2 minutes, or until the mixture is bubbly. Stir some of the sauce into 1 beaten egg; pour back into the bourbon mixture, and whisk until smooth.

Zabaglione

This light, wine-based dessert should be whipped up while guests are completing the main course.

Microwave on Full Power 2 to 4 1/2 minutes.

Makes 6 servings.

1/2 cup Marsala wine or liqueur
5 egg yolks
1 whole egg
2 tablespoons sugar

1. Microwave the wine or liqueur in a large microwave-safe glass bowl on Full Power for 1 to 3 minutes, or until the alcohol has evaporated. Add the yolks, whole egg and sugar, beating until well blended.
2. Microwave for 1 to 1 1/2 minutes, or just until mixture thickens, beating with a whisk every 15 seconds. Serve immediately in wine goblets.

Toasted Coconut Flan

As cool and creamy a treat as any you'll find, in one-quarter the time it takes in the conventional oven.

Microwave on Full Power for 8 to 9 minutes, then on Medium-High Power for 6 to 7 minutes.

Makes 8 servings.

1/2 cup sugar
2 tablespoons water
2 cups half-and-half or light cream
3/4 cup sweetened condensed milk (not evaporated milk)
1 tablespoon cornstarch
3 eggs, well beaten
1/4 teaspoon ground nutmeg
1/2 cup toasted coconut

1. Combine the sugar and water in a 9-inch round glass microwave-safe cake dish.
2. Microwave on Full Power for 4 to 5 minutes, or until just golden. Remove from the oven; cover with wax paper. (Mixture will continue to brown while standing.)
3. Whisk together the half-and-half or light cream,

(continued)

sweetened condensed milk and cornstarch in a medium-size microwave-safe bowl.

4. Microwave on Full Power for 3 minutes, stirring occasionally. Stir a small anount of the milk mixture into the eggs, then stir the egg mixture back into the milk; stir in the nutmeg.

5. Microwave on Full Power for 1 minute, stirring once. Remove wax paper from cake dish. Pour the cream mixture into the prepared dish.

6. Fill a 9-inch microwave-safe glass pie plate with 1¼ cups hot water. Place the cake dish in the glass pie plate. Carefully place in the oven.

7. Microwave on Medium-High Power for 6 to 7 minutes. (Center will still be soft but will set upon standing.) Remove the cake dish from the pie plate. Let cool directly on a heat-resistant countertop 10 minutes. Chill before turning out onto serving plate. Sprinkle with toasted coconut. Cut into wedges to serve.

Perfect Poached Pears

These pears are poached in a syrup flavored with a vanilla bean. If vanilla bean is unavailable, substitute vanilla extract, adding the extract to the recipe after the syrup has been cooked; otherwise, the flavor of the vanilla extract will evaporate during cooking.

Microwave on Full Power for 10 minutes, 25 seconds.

Makes 2 servings.

2 cups water	**vanilla extract**
¾ cup sugar	**2 medium-size Bosc**
1 vanilla bean (1 inch	**pears (7 ounces**
long	**each)**
OR: **¾ teaspoon**	**1 wedge of lemon**

1. Combine the water, sugar and vanilla bean in a microwave-safe 1-quart glass measure. Microwave on

Perfect Poached Pears.

Full Power for 2 minutes, 25 seconds, or until the mixture boils. Stir to blend.

2. Microwave, uncovered, on Full Power for 5 minutes more. Using potholders, transfer the hot syrup to a shielded countertop. Remove the vanilla bean. (If using the vanilla extract, stir in at this point.)

3. Using a swivel-bladed vegetable peeler, peel the skin from pears, leaving the stems intact. Place each pear in a glass dessert dish. Squeeze lemon juice over each whole pear. Pour half the syrup over each pear. Loosely cover each with wax paper.

4. Microwave the pears on Full Power for 3 minutes. Using potholders, transfer the dish containing the pears to a shielded countertop.

Note: If you wish, place the dried used vanilla bean in a canister of sugar to flavor it for baking or desserts.

Plum Pudding

Once a time-consuming dish to steam (2 hours or more), plum pudding cooked in the microwave is ready in just 15 minutes.

Microwave on Half Power for 15 minutes.

Makes 8 servings.

2 cups unseasoned	**concentrate**
bread crumbs	**½ cup (1 stick)**
1 cup all-purpose flour	**unsalted butter or**
¼ cup firmly packed	**margarine, softened**
light brown sugar	**½ cup brandy**
¼ cup dark molasses	**or sherry**
1 teaspoon baking	**2 eggs**
soda	**1½ cups raisins**
1 teaspoon ground	**Candied pineapple**
cinnamon	**and red and green**
½ teaspoon ground	**cherries**
nutmeg	**Hard Sauce Balls**
½ cup orange juice	*(recipe follows)*

1. Combine the bread crumbs with the flour, brown sugar, molasses, baking soda, cinnamon, nutmeg, orange juice concentrate, butter or margarine, brandy or sherry, eggs and raisins in a large bowl, blending well.

2. Place the mixture in 1½-quart microwave-safe bowl, pushing down slightly. Cover the top of the mixture with aluminum foil to prevent drying. Cover the bowl completely with heavy-duty microwave-safe plastic wrap. (Do not vent).

3. Microwave on Half Power for 15 minutes or until pudding starts to pull away from side of bowl and a skewer inserted into the center of the pudding comes out clean. Let the pudding stand for 10 minutes.

4. Place a serving platter on top of the bowl; invert. Garnish the pudding with candied pineapple and red and green cherries, if you wish. Serve with chilled **Hard Sauce Balls**.

Hard Sauce Balls: Makes 10. Soften 1 cup (2 sticks) butter or margarine in medium-size bowl. Knead in 1½ cups 10X (confectioners') sugar and 1 tablespoon

Plum Pudding,
page 590.

brandy or rum. Shape the mixture into balls, using about 2 tablespoons mixture for each. Spread 1 cup toasted flaked coconut on a sheet of wax paper. Roll balls in coconut. Chill before serving.

Fudge Brownies

This fudgy brownie recipe proves that the microwave can be used to prepare every part of a meal.

Microwave on Half Power for 8 to 9 minutes, then on Full Power for 2 to 3 minutes.

Makes 25 brownies.

1/3 **cup butter or margarine**	3/4 **cup all-purpose flour**
2 **squares (1ounce each) unsweetened chocolate**	1/4 **to** 1/2 **cup coarsely chopped nuts (optional)**
1 **cup sugar**	**Brownie Frosting (recipe follows)**
2 **eggs, lightly beaten**	
1 **teaspoon vanilla**	

1. Place the butter or margarine and unwrapped chocolate in a 2-quart microwave-safe bowl.

2. Microwave on Half Power for 1 to 2 minutes, or until the butter is completely melted. Let stand for 3 minutes, then stir until the chocolate is melted. If the chocolate hasn't finished melting after stirring, microwave on Full Power for 30 seconds, then stir again.
3. Beat in the sugar, eggs and vanilla until the mixture is smooth and light. Then stir in the flour, mixing well.
4. Pour the batter into a greased 8-inch square microwave-safe pan. Smooth the surface of the batter; sprinkle with the chopped nuts if you don't intend to frost the brownies. Shield the corners of the pan by laying a 2-inch wide strip of aluminum foil diagonally across each corner, smoothing foil down onto the sides of the pan.
5. Microwave on Half Power for 7 minutes, then on Full Power for 2 to 3 mintues, rotating the pan 1/4 turn once.
6. Cover the baked brownies loosely with wax paper; place directly on a flat heat-resistant surface; let stand for 10 minutes. Remove the wax paper; place the pan on a rack to finish cooling.
7. While brownies are cooling, prepare **Brownie Frosting**, if desired. Frost while still slightly warm. Cut into squares.

(continued)

Suggested Variation: Use rum flavoring or orange extract instead of vanilla, using the same flavoring in the frosting.

Brownie Frosting

Microwave on Half Power for 1 minute.

Makes enough frosting to cover an 8-inch square pan.

3 tablespoons butter or margarine	Approximately 1½ cups sifted 10X (confectioners') sugar
1 square (1 ounce) unsweetened chocolate	⅓ cup coarsely chopped nuts
2 tablespoons water	

1. Place the butter or margarine and unwrapped chocolate in a 1-quart microwave-safe bowl.
2. Microwave on Half Power for 1 minute, or until the butter is melted. Let stand for 2 minutes, then stir until all the chocolate is melted. Remove the paper.
3. Add the water until well blended, then stir in enough sifted 10X sugar to make a thick but spreadable frosting.
4. Frost the brownies while they are still warm. Sprinkle with the chopped nuts.

Peanutty Caramel Corn

Prepare popping corn conventionally or in the microwave. You'll need about two 3.5-ounce pouches, regular or salt-free.

Microwave on Full Power for 10 minutes; then on Low Power for 15 minutes.

Makes about 4 quarts.

3 to 4 quarts freshly popped corn	2 cups firmly packed light brown sugar
1 cup (4 ounces) unsalted raw Spanish peanuts	½ cup light corn syrup
½ cup (1 stick) unsalted butter	1 teaspoon vanilla
½ cup (1 stick) unsalted margarine	½ teaspoon baking soda
	¾ teaspoon salt

1. Place the popped corn and the nuts in a 13 x 9 x 2-inch glass baking dish. Keep warm in preheated slow oven (250°).
2. Cut the butter and the margarine into chunks and place in a 3- or 4-quart microwave-safe bowl. Using a wooden spoon, stir in the brown sugar and the corn syrup.
3. Microwave, uncovered, on Full Power for 5 minutes or until the mixture boils; stir to blend.
4. Microwave on Full Power for 5 minutes more. (The syrup should read 250° on a microwave candy thermometer.)
5. Using potholders, remove bowl containing the hot syrup to a shielded countertop. Stir in the vanilla. (The mixture will sputter.) Stir in the baking soda. (The mixture will become opaque.) Stir in the salt.
6. Remove the warmed popped corn from the conventional oven. Stir in the caramel, coating the popped corn evenly.
7. Microwave, uncovered, on Low Power for 15 minutes, stirring once. Remove the dish to a shielded countertop for the popcorn to cool and crisp.

Coconut Crunch Brunch Cake

A quickly prepared coffeecake has a crumb topping and confectioners' sugar glaze.

Microwave on Half Power for 7 mintues, then on Full Power for 7 to 8½ minutes.

Makes 12 servings

Cake:	⅓ cup chopped walnuts or pecans
1 package (18½ ounces) pudding-Included yellow cake mix (reserve ⅓ cup for topping)	⅓ cup reserved cake mix
	¼ cup firmly packed light brown sugar
¾ cup water	½ teaspoon ground cinnamon
⅓ cup vegetable oil	
2 eggs	
	Glaze:
Topping:	½ cup 10X (confectioners') sugar
2 tablespoons butter or margarine, at room temperature	1 to 2 teaspoons milk
½ cup shredded coconut	¼ teaspoon vanilla

1. Combine the cake mix, water, oil and eggs in the large bowl of an electric mixer on low speed until moistened; increase the speed to high; beat for 2 minutes. Pour batter into an ungreased 9 x 13-inch microwave-safe dish.
2. Combine the softened butter or margarine with the coconut, chopped nuts, reserved cake mix, brown sugar and cinnamon in a small bowl until well blended. Sprinkle 1 cup of the topping over the batter; swirl through the batter with a spatula. Reserve the remaining topping.
3. Microwave on Half Power for 7 minutes. Increase the power to Full Power; microwave for 3 minutes. Sprinkle remaining topping evenly over the cake.
4. Microwave on Full Power for 4 to 5½ minutes longer, rotating the pan halfway after 3 minutes, or until a wooden pick inserted in the center comes out clean.
5. Let stand on flat, heat-resistant surface for 10 minutes.

(continued)

Pictured opposite:
Delicious Apple Pie, page 594.

6. Combine the 10X sugar, milk and vanilla in a small bowl, blending well; drizzle over the warm cake.

Editor's Note: If your microwave oven has a multipower setting, "Half Power" in our directions refers to power ratings of 30 to 50%. Baked products will be somewhat different than those baked in conventional ovens: the texture will have a finer grain and crusts will not brown. Use ingredients that have darker colored crusts or add frostings or toppings to light-colored baked goods.

Delicious Apple Pie

Microwave on Full Power for 12 minutes; then bake at 425° for 20 minutes.

Makes 6 servings (9-inch pie).

6 red Delicious apples, peeled, cored and sliced (about 6 cups)	cornstarch
	1/4 teaspoon ground cinnamon
1/2 to 1 cup firmly packed light brown sugar, depending on sweetness of apples	1/4 teaspoon ground nutmeg
	2 frozen 9-inch deep-dish pie crusts, slightly softened
1 1/2 tablespoons	1 egg yolk
	Pinch of salt

1. Preheat the oven to hot (425°).
2. Microwave the sliced apples, brown sugar, cornstarch, cinnamon and nutmeg in a 1 1/2-quart microwave-safe bowl on Full Power for 12 minutes or until the apples are soft and the mixture is thick.
3. Bake one crust in the preheated hot oven (425°) for 10 minutes, following the package directions for an empty pie shell.
4. Using a leaf shape or other decorative cutter, make cutouts on the second crust; brush with a mixture of the beaten egg yolk and a pinch of salt. Place the shapes on a cookie sheet in the conventional oven with the partially baked pie crust.
5. Bake the cutouts and the crust in the hot oven (425°) for 10 minutes longer or until the crust and the cutouts are golden brown.
6. Spoon the apple mixture into the pie shell. Arrange the cutouts over the top.

Puff Pastry Sticks

Microwave on Medium-High Power for 5 to 7 minutes.

Makes 36.

1 package (17 1/4 ounces) puff pastry, partially thawed	seeds
	2 tablespoons poppy seeds
1 egg yolk	2 tablespoons caraway seeds
1 teaspoon water	3/4 teaspoon salt
2 tablespoons sesame	

1. Unfold the sheets of partially thawed pastry; cut lengthwise into 1/2-inch-wide strips, using a very sharp knife. Brush one side of the pastry with the egg yolk mixed with 1 teaspoon of water.
2. Place the sesame, poppy and caraway seeds in separate piles on a sheet of wax paper. Sprinkle each pile with 1/4 teaspoon of the salt.
3. Dip the 12 pastry strips, yolk-side down, into sesame seeds, coating the pastry strips well. Twist each strip several times; place on a wax paper-lined microwave-safe dish. Repeat with the remaining pastry strips and poppy and caraway seeds.
4. Microwave on Medium-High Power for 5 to 7 minutes or until the puff pastry sticks turn light gold in color. (Watch for burning.)

Almond Cheesecake

Cheesecakes are a natural for the microwave. This one's smooth and creamy, with a gingersnap crust.

Microwave on Full Power for 1 to 1 1/2 minutes; then on Medium-High Power for 13 to 15 minutes.

Makes 12 servings.

1 cup gingersnap cookie crumbs	2 packages (8 ounces each) cream cheese, softened
1/2 cup ground almonds	1 teaspoon almond extract
1 1/4 cups sugar	3 eggs
1/4 cup (1/2 stick) butter or margarine, melted	1/4 cup all-purpose flour
1 cup ricotta cheese	

1. Combine the gingersnap cookie crumbs, ground almonds and 1/4 cup of the sugar in a medium-size bowl, mixing well. Stir in the melted butter or margarine, blending until crumbly.
2. Cut a piece of cardboard to fit the bottom of a 9-inch round glass dish and place the cardboard in the dish. Spread the cookie crumb mixture onto the bottom and up the side of the prepared dish.
3. Microwave on Full Power for 1 to 1 1/2 minutes, or until just set; cool the dish directly on a heat-resistant countertop.
4. Beat the ricotta cheese in the large bowl of an electric mixer until smooth. Add the cream cheese, the remaining 1 cup sugar and the almond extract, beating until well blended. Add the eggs, one at a time, beating well after each addition. Stir in the flour. Pour the mixture into cooled crust.
5. Microwave on Medium-High Power for 13 to 15 minutes or until cake pulls away from the side of the

(continued)

Pictured opposite: Almond Cheesecake, page 594; Rocky Road Bars, page 596; Pumpkin Date-Nut Loaf, page 596.

pan. (The center will be soft but will firm upon chilling.) Cool the cheesecake in the dish for 1 hour. Remove the cake from the pan by carefully lifting under the cardboard with 2 spatulas. Chill the cake thoroughly before cutting into wedges.

Banana Cream Pie

Cream fillings are always done better by microwave cooking. Also, you'll find that by making the filling and crust separately, the finished pie will have a less soggy bottom crust.

Microwave on Full Power for 5 minutes.

Makes 6 servings (9-inch pie).

2 cups milk	1 frozen 9-inch deep-
2/3 cup sugar	dish pie crust,
1/2 cup cornstarch	baked following
3 egg yolks, beaten	package directions
2 tablespoons butter	2 ripe bananas, sliced
or margarine,	1/2 cup heavy cream,
melted	whipped
2 teaspoons vanilla	

1. Place the milk, sugar and cornstarch in a 1 1/2-quart microwave-safe bowl; stir to blend.
2. Microwave on Full power for 5 minutes or until the mixture thickens.
3. Add 1 cup of the custard to the beaten yolks in a large bowl, stirring constantly until blended. Add the remaining custard, then the butter or margarine and the vanilla, beating until butter is melted and mixture is smooth.
4. Line the baked pie crust with the bananas; pour the custard over the bananas. Cool. Garnish the pie with dollops of whipped cream.

Rocky Road Bars

An irresistible confection for anyone who loves chocolate!

Microwave on Full Power for 13 to 16 minutes.
Makes 48.

1 1/2 cups all-purpose	2 eggs
flour	1 cup chopped
6 tablespoons	walnuts
unsweetened cocoa	or pecans
powder	3/4 cup multicolored
3/4 teaspoon baking	milk chocolate
soda	candies
1/4 teaspoon salt	2/3 cup miniature
3/4 cup (1 1/2 sticks)	marshmallows
butter or margarine	
3/4 cup sugar	

1. Combine the flour, cocoa, baking soda and salt in a small bowl, mixing well.
2. Beat the butter or margarine and the sugar in the large bowl of electric mixer until light and fluffy. Add

the eggs, one at a time, beating well after each addition. Stir in the dry ingredients just until blended; stir in 1/2 cup of the nuts. Spread the batter into a greased 12 x 8-inch microwave-safe baking dish. Shield the corners with small pieces of aluminum foil.
3. Microwave on Full Power for 10 to 12 minutes or until the cake is not quite set in the center. Remove the foil. Sprinkle the multicolored candies, miniature marshmallows and remaining 1/2 cup nuts over the cake, pressing lightly.
4. Microwave on Full Power for 3 to 4 minutes, or until the marshmallows are soft. Cover the top with aluminum foil. Cool the dish directly on a heat-resistant countertop for 15 minutes. Then cool completely on a wire rack before cutting into 2 x1-inch bars.

Pumpkin Date-Nut Loaf

Use glassware to microwave baked goods, especially loaf breads. When checking for doneness, look through bottom for wet spots.

Microwave on Half Power for 9 to 12 minutes, then on Full Power for 2 to 5 minutes.

Makes one loaf.

Nonstick cooking	1/2 teaspoon ground
spray	ginger
2 tablespoons graham	1 cup canned pumpkin
cracker crumbs	2 eggs
1 1/4 cups *unsifted* all-	1/2 cup firmly packed
purpose flour	brown sugar
1 teaspoon baking	1/4 cup granulated
powder	sugar
1 teaspoon baking	1/2 cup vegetable oil
soda	1/2 cup chopped dates
1/2 teaspoon salt	1/2 cup chopped
1 teaspoon ground	walnuts
cinnamon	10X (confectioners')
1 teaspoon ground	sugar
cloves	

1. Spray an 8 x 4 x 3-inch glass microwave-safe loaf dish with nonstick cooking spray. Coat the dish with graham cracker crumbs.
2. Combine the flour, baking powder, baking soda, salt, cinnamon, cloves and ginger in a small bowl, mixing well.
3. Blend the pumpkin, eggs, brown and granulated sugars and oil in a large bowl. Add the dry ingredients. Stir in the dates and nuts. Pour into the prepared dish; shield the ends with aluminum foil.
4. Microwave on Half Power for 9 to 12 minutes, or until the top looks dry, but the center is still wet. Remove the foil.
5. Microwave on Full Power for 2 to 5 minutes, or until the center is almost dry. Cool on a heat-resistant countertop for 10 minutes. Turn out onto a wire rack to cool.
6. If you wish, dust the top with 10X (confectioners') sugar.

Jamocha Pecan Pie

Microwave on Full Power for 1 minute, 50 seconds, then on Medium-High Power for 10 to 12 minutes.

Makes 6 servings.

2 tablespoons water	**sugar**
2 tablespoons Instant coffee powder	**1 cup light corn syrup**
1 square (1 ounce) unsweetened chocolate	**1¹/₄ cups chopped pecans**
2 tablespoons margarine or butter	**Pattable Pie Crust (recipe follows)**
3 large eggs	**Whipped topping or sweetened whipped cream**
¹/₂ cup granulated	

1. Put the water in a 1-quart glass bowl. Microwave on Full Power 45 to 50 seconds. Add the instant coffee to the water and stir to dissolve.
2. Add the chocolate and margarine to the coffee mixture. Microwave on Full Power for 1 minute, or until the chocolate is melted. Add the eggs, sugar and corn syrup; beat well. Stir in the pecans and pour into the **Pattable Pie Crust**.
3. Rotating the pie a half turn after 5 minutes of cooking, microwave on Half Power (50%) 10 to 12 minutes The pie is done when a knife inserted halfway between the outside and center comes out clean. Cool to lukewarm before cutting. Top each serving with the whipped topping.

Note: We think that this pie tastes best when served warm. To warm a slice of pie, microwave on Medium-High Power for 15 to 20 seconds.

Pattable Pie Crust

1¹/₄ cups unsifted all-purpose flour	**¹/₃ cup oil**
¹/₂ teaspoon salt	**2 tablespoons cold water**

1. Put the flour and salt in a medium mixing bowl. Using a fork, stir the oil into the dry ingredients until well combined. Sprinkle the water over the mixture and stir to make a dough.
2. Use Pam® or an unflavored vegetable spray to coat a 9-inch glass pie plate. Pick up the dough and shape it into a ball. Flatten the ball between your palms until it is about 1 inch thick. Place it in the center of the prepared pie plate. Using your fingers, pat the dough in a uniform thickness onto the bottom and up the side of the pie plate.
3. Around the top rim of the plate, pinch the pastry between your thumb and index fingers to make a fluted edge.
4. Using the same fork, prick the bottom and sides of the crust at 1-inch intervals to prevent puffing during baking.
5. Rotating the pie plate a quarter turn after 2 minutes of cooking, microwave on Full Power for 5 to 6 minutes, or until the pie crust looks opaque and blistered.

Note: This recipe can also be baked in a conventional oven. Preheat the oven to hot (450°). Set the pie plate on the top shelf in the oven. Bake for 8 to 12 minutes, or until the crust is golden brown.

Chocolate Amaretto Cheesecake

This dessert is sinfully rich, yet heavenly easy.

Microwave on Full Power for 2¹/₂ minutes, then on Half Power for 8 minutes, then on Medium-High Power for 12 to 14 minutes.

Makes 12 servings.

¹/₄ cup (¹/₂ stick) margarine	**each) cream cheese**
1¹/₄ cups vanilla wafer cookie crumbs	**1¹/₃ cups sugar**
2 tablespoons amaretto liqueur	**3 eggs**
8 squares (1 ounce each) semisweet chocolate	**1 cup dairy sour cream**
3 tablespoons milk	**¹/₂ teaspoon ground cinnamon**
2 packages (8 ounces	**¹/₂ teaspoon almond extract**
	Sliced toasted almonds

1. Place the margarine in a 9-inch round high-sided glass dish.
2. Microwave on Full Power for 30 seconds, or until melted. Stir in the cookie crumbs and pat mixture on the bottom only.
3. Microwave on Full Power for 2 minutes. Sprinkle amaretto liqueur over the crust.
4. Microwave the chocolate and milk in a large glass mixing bowl on Half Power for 4 minutes; stir. Add cream cheese and microwave on Half Power 4 minutes longer, or until cheese is softened.
5. Beat with an electric mixer at medium-high speed until fluffy. Beat in the sugar. Add the eggs, sour cream, cinnamon and almond extract, blending well. Pour into the prepared crust.
6. Microwave on Medium High Power for 12 to 14 minutes, rotating once midway through cooking. (Center will jiggle slightly when set.) Chill at least 2 hours before serving. (Cheesecake will firm considerably after refrigerating.)
7. Serve topped with whipped cream flavored with 1 to 2 tablespoons amaretto liqueur, if you wish. Garnish with sliced toasted almonds.

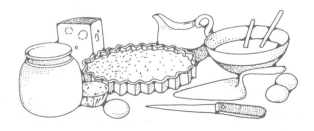

PASTA, GRAINS and DUMPLINGS

Pasta   An Italian term used for the products of a paste made from semolina—milled from durum wheat—and water. Italians have taken the paste or dough and shaped it over 150 ways. Pasta is usually divided into the following types:

Macaroni — A tubular pasta. It can be long rods, short thick tubes, bent into elbow macaroni, and shaped into shells or curls.

Spaghetti — Solid strands of round, flat or curly pasta. Very thin strands are called capelletti d'angelo (angel's hair).

Noodles — These are ribbons of dough which may be cut into different widths or shapes. Most noodles are made with eggs added to the dough. Noodles can be flavored or colored with vegetables such as spinach, carrots or tomatoes.

How much pasta should you cook and serve? It's a matter of personal preference. One pound of spaghetti is sufficient for 6 to 8 first-course or accompaniment servings but makes only 3 to 4 main-dish servings.

Different shapes of pasta are interchangeable in most recipes, but if the size or thickness is different, the amount of pasta needed may have to be adjusted. Dry or uncooked pasta should be substituted by weight, not measurement, because pastas of different shapes will not have the same volume. A cupful of one pasta may differ in weight from a cupful of a differently shaped pasta. Cooked pasta can be substituted cup for cup.

Although dried pasta is widely available in packages, many stores in large cities are carrying freshly made pasta. Some types of pasta can easily be made at home with the aid of a pasta machine. Depending on the model, a pasta machine can either make noodles only or also make shaped pasta. A noodle machine rolls dough between rollers and then cuts it into strips. A pasta maker is equipped with different discs for shaping dough. Electric pasta machines can make numerous pasta products.

How to Cook Pasta

1. Use a large kettle because the pasta needs plenty of room to bubble if it's to cook without sticking.
2. Do not cook more than 1 pound of pasta at a time in the same kettle. It will clump or stick together.
3. Fill a large kettle with water, leaving about 4 inches at the top (for 1 pound of pasta, you should use at least 12 cups of water). Add a drop of olive or vegetable oil (this helps keep pasta from sticking), set

Pictured opposite: (clockwise from upper right): Pepperoni Pasta, page 599; Fusilli with Spinach Pesto, page 600; Spaghetti with Broccoli, Tomatoes and Walnuts, page 600; Tomato Salad Pasta, page 600.

kettle over high heat and bring to a boil. Salt the cooking water or not.

4. When cooking long macaroni or spaghetti, slowly lower a handful at a time into the rapidly boiling water until it softens enough to fit into the kettle. Stir once or twice to separate strands, if necessary.
5. Boil rapidly, uncovered, until a strand of pasta cut in half shows no raw starch in the center—it shows up as a white dot—or until the pasta has no raw starch taste, but *does* feel a bit firm between the teeth (*al dente* is the Italian term for this firm-tenderness).
6. Drain pasta in a large colander the instant it's *al dente*. But do not rinse in cool water unless the pasta is for a salad.
7. If pasta must wait a few minutes before being served, toss with a little oil, set the colander over a kettle containing about 1 inch of simmering water and cover.

Pepperoni Pasta

Makes 4 servings.

1 package (12 ounces) fettuccine noodles	green peppers, halved, seeded and sliced
1/4 cup olive or vegetable oil	1 can (16 ounces) tomatoes
1 large onion, sliced	1 teaspoon leaf oregano, crumbled
2 large cloves garlic, minced	1/2 teaspoon salt
1/2 pound pepperoni sausage, sliced	Freshly grated Parmesan cheese
2 medium-size	

1. Cook pasta following label directions.
2. Meanwhile, heat oil in a large skillet over moderate heat. Add onion, garlic, pepperoni and peppers and cook 5 minutes, stirring often. Add tomatoes, oregano and salt; cover and cook 5 minutes longer, stirring 2 or 3 times to break up tomatoes. Uncover during last minute to thicken sauce slightly.
3. Drain pasta and serve with sauce; sprinkle with grated cheese.

Spaghetti with Broccoli, Tomatoes and Walnuts

Makes 4 servings.

1 package (16 ounces) thin spaghetti or linguine
1/4 cup (1/2 stick) butter or margarine
2 tablespoons olive or vegetable oil
1/2 cup coarsely chopped walnuts
1 pint cherry tomatoes, stems removed
1 large clove garlic, minced
1/2 teaspoon salt
Pinch crushed red pepper
1 teaspoon leaf basil, crumbled
1 medium-size bunch broccoli, cut into 1-inch pieces (about 6 cups)
1/2 to 1 cup chicken broth
1/2 cup grated Parmesan cheese
1/4 cup chopped fresh parsley

1. Cook pasta following label directions.
2. Melt 2 tablespoons of the butter and the oil over moderate heat in a medium-size skillet. Add walnuts and brown lightly. Add the tomatoes and cook, stirring often, 5 minutes or until tomatoes are tender but still hold their shape. Stir in the garlic, salt, pepper, and basil and cook 2 minutes longer. Remove from heat; cover.
3. Add broccoli to pasta during last 5 minutes cooking time. Drain.
4. Melt remaining 2 tablespoons butter in pasta kettle and return pasta and broccoli to kettle. Toss to coat with butter. Add tomato mixture, 1/2 cup of the broth, the cheese and parsley, and toss to blend, adding more broth if mixture seems dry.

Tomato Salad Pasta

Makes 4 servings.

1 package (16 ounces) rigatoni
1 small clove garlic, minced
1/2 teaspoon salt
2 tablespoons red wine vinegar
6 tablespoons olive oil
1/4 teaspoon pepper
1 tablespoon leaf basil, crumbled
4 cups diced ripe tomatoes
1/3 cup diced red onion
1/2 cup small pitted ripe olives
1 package (8 ounces) whole milk mozzarella cheese, finely diced
1/2 cup grated Parmesan cheese

1. Cook pasta following label directions.
2. Mash garlic with salt in a medium-size bowl. Stir in vinegar, oil, pepper and basil. Add the tomatoes, onion and olives and toss to mix.
3. Drain pasta and return to kettle. Add cheeses and toss until heat of pasta begins to melt cheese. Add tomato mixture and toss again.

Fusilli with Spinach Pesto

A year-round version of classic pesto.

Makes 4 servings.

5 cups fresh spinach leaves (about 1/2 pound untrimmed), washed and thoroughly drained
1 package (16 ounces) fusilli, spaghetti or linguine
2 tablespoons olive or vegetable oil
1 large clove garlic
1/2 teaspoon salt
1/4 teaspoon pepper
1 teaspoon leaf basil
1/4 cup walnuts
1 cup ricotta cheese
2 tablespoons freshly grated Parmesan cheese

1. Remove and discard all tough woody stems from spinach.
2. Cook pasta following label directions.
3. Place the oil, garlic, salt and pepper in container of electric blender or food processor. Cover and whirl until garlic is pureed. Add basil and walnuts and whirl again until nuts are finely ground. Add cheeses; whirl until smooth. Start adding spinach leaves, 1 cup at a time, and whirl until smooth. Between additions, scrape mixture down side of container with a rubber spatula.
4. To serve: Stir about 3 tablespoonfuls of the hot pasta cooking water into sauce. Drain pasta and return to kettle. Add sauce and toss.

Pasta with Broccoli

A quick, meatless entrée.

Makes 4 servings.

1 1/2 pounds broccoli
2 large cloves garlic, finely chopped
2 tablespoons olive oil
1 tablespoon butter
1 tomato, cut into 1/2-inch cubes,
OR: 1 cup drained, canned tomatoes, chopped
2 tablespoons anchovy paste
OR: 6 anchovies canned in oil,
mashed
1/2 teaspoon crushed red pepper flakes *(optional)*
1/2 teaspoon salt
1/4 teaspoon black pepper
8 ounces penne, rigatoni or ziti pasta
3 cups boiling water
1/2 cup heavy cream
Grated Romano or Parmesan cheese

1. Trim flowerets from broccoli; cut into bite-size pieces. Reserve stems for soup or other use.
2. Sauté garlic in oil and butter in 10-inch skillet with at least 2-quart capacity, for 30 seconds. Stir in tomato, anchovy paste, red pepper flakes, if using, salt and black pepper. Sauté, stirring, for 1 minute.
3. Add pasta and boiling water, stirring to distribute ingredients evenly. Cover and cook for the least amount of time suggested in the package directions.

Pasta with Broccoli,
page 600.

After 3 minutes, arrange broccoli evenly over top of pasta. Cover and simmer for remaining time or until broccoli is tender and pasta is al dente, or firm but tender.
4. Stir in cream and heat 30 seconds. Toss and serve immediately with cheese.

Fettuccine Alfredo

From Alfredo's in Rome, homemade pasta richly sauced with butter and cheese.

Makes 4 servings.

3 cups *sifted* all-purpose flour	**Cornstarch**
2 teaspoons salt	**1/2 cup (1 stick) butter or margarine, cut in small pieces**
3 eggs	
3 tablespoons olive or vegetable oil	**2 cups freshly grated Parmesan cheese**
1/4 cup cold water	**Freshly ground pepper**

1. Sift flour and salt into a large bowl; make a well in center; add eggs, oil and water. Work liquids into the flour with fingers to make a stiff dough.
2. Turn dough out onto a large pastry board. (Do not add additional flour.) Knead 10 minutes or until dough is as smooth and soft as perfectly kneaded bread dough. Wrap dough in plastic wrap; let rest at room temperature 1 hour.
3. Sprinkle the pastry board with cornstarch. Roll out the dough, a quarter at a time, to a rectangle so thin you can see through it.
4. Fold dough into quarters lengthwise. Slice dough across into 1/4-inch wide strips. Repeat with the remaining quarters of the dough. Unwind strips and allow them to dry on clean towels for 1 hour.
5. Bring water (about 4 quarts) to boiling in large kettle; add 2 tablespoons salt and 1 tablespoon olive or vegetable oil, if you wish. Cook fettuccine 5 minutes or until cooked to tenderness you like. Drain well; turn out onto a heated serving platter.
6. Add pieces of butter and toss with fork and spoon until the butter melts. Add Parmesan and continue to toss until fettuccine is coated and glistening. Grind pepper over the top.

Cannelloni

Bake at 375° for 35 minutes.

Makes enough for two meals (4 servings each).

16 manicotti shells	**1 egg**
1 container (2 pounds) ricotta cheese	**1 teaspoon fennel seeds**
4 ounces feta cheese, crumbled	**1 teaspoon salt**
	1/4 teaspoon pepper
1 package (10 ounces) frozen chopped spinach, thawed, drained and squeezed dry	**Sausage Sauce (*recipe follows*)**
	Creamy Cheese Sauce (*recipe follows*)

1. Cook manicotti following label directions just to *al dente* stage, about 5 minutes. Drain.
2. Combine ricotta, feta, spinach, egg, fennel, salt and pepper in a large bowl. Fill manicotti with mixture

(continued)

using a teaspoon or fit a pastry bag with round tip and press mixture into tubes.

3. Dinner Portion: Arrange 8 manicotti in a single layer in an 11³/₄ × 7¹/₂ × 1³/₄-inch baking dish. Spoon half the Sausage Sauce over manicotti; top with half the Creamy Cheese Sauce.

4. Bake in a moderate oven (375°) for 35 minutes or until bubbly-hot.

5. To freeze: Place 4 manicotti into two 7⁷/₈ × 5³/₈ × 1³/₄-inch aluminum foil containers. Spoon remaining Sausage Sauce and Creamy Cheese Sauce, dividing evenly, over manicotti. Cover securely with foil cover or aluminum foil; label, date and freeze.
Recommended freezer storage: 2 months. To reheat: Bake, uncovered, in a very hot oven (450°) for 45 minutes or until bubbly.

Sausage Sauce

Makes 4 cups.

¹/₂ pound hot or sweet Italian sausages	**tomato paste**
1 large onion, chopped (1 cup)	**1 cup water**
1 clove garlic, minced	**³/₄ teaspoon leaf basil, crumbled**
1 can (16 ounces) tomatoes	**³/₄ teaspoon leaf oregano, crumbled**
1 can (6 ounces)	**1 teaspoon salt**
	¹/₄ teaspoon pepper

1. Remove casings from sausages; cook meat slowly in a medium-size saucepan, breaking up with a spoon as it cooks, until no pink remains. Remove with slotted spoon to paper toweling to drain. Remove all but 1 tablespoon drippings from pan.

2. Sauté onion and garlic in drippings until tender, about 5 minutes. Return sausage to saucepan; add tomatoes, tomato paste, water, basil, oregano, salt and pepper. Bring to boiling; lower heat; simmer sauce, stirring occasionally, 30 minutes or until thickened.

Creamy Cheese Sauce

Makes 3¹/₂ cups.

¹/₃ cup butter or margarine	**3 cups milk**
¹/₄ cup all-purpose flour	**¹/₂ cup grated Parmesan cheese**

Melt butter in a medium-size saucepan; stir in flour and cook until bubbly, about 1 minute. Stir in milk and continue to cook, stirring constantly, until bubbly. Stir in cheese.

Cheese Lasagne Rolls with Spinach

If there is no Cheddar cheese in the refrigerator, any combination, such as Swiss and American, will serve equally well.

Bake at 325° for 20 minutes.

Makes 8 servings.

¹/₄ cup (¹/₂ stick) butter or margarine	**thawed**
¹/₃ cup all-purpose flour	**1 cup grated Parmesan cheese**
¹/₂ teaspoon salt	**¹/₂ pound sharp Cheddar cheese, shredded (2 cups)**
¹/₄ teaspoon pepper	
¹/₄ teaspoon ground nutmeg	**2 teaspoons paprika**
1 quart milk	**2 teaspoons dry mustard**
3 packages (10 ounces each) frozen chopped spinach,	**1 package (1 pound) lasagne noodles**

1. Melt the butter in a large saucepan. Stir in the flour, salt, pepper and nutmeg. Cook, stirring, for 1 minute. Remove from the heat. Gradually stir in the milk. Return to the heat and cook, stirring constantly, until the cream sauce is thickened and bubbly. Set aside.

2. Drain the thawed spinach in a colander, pressing against the sides to remove as much liquid as possible. Transfer to a bowl. Stir in 1 cup of the cream sauce and ¹/₂ cup of the Parmesan until well blended. Set aside.

3. Stir the shredded Cheddar, ¹/₄ cup of the remaining Parmesan, the paprika and dry mustard into the remaining cream sauce until well blended. Set aside.

4. Preheat the oven to slow (325°).

5. Cook the lasagne noodles, following the label directions, just until tender. Drain.

6. Spread the spinach mixture over each lasagne

Chicken Enchiladas in Cheese Cream, page 659; Cheese Lasagne Rolls with Spinach, page 602; "Eggspanable" Eggs with Apricot—Glazed Sausages, page 352.

Rotelle with Shrimp
and Lemon, page 604.

noodle. Roll up the noodles jelly-roll fashion. Place, seam-side down, in a buttered 13 × 9 × 2-inch baking pan.

7. Spoon the remaining cheese sauce over the rolls. Sprinkle with the remaining Parmesan.

8. Bake in the preheated slow oven (325°) for 20 minutes or until thoroughly heated.

To Make Ahead: Prepare the recipe through Step 6. Cover the baking pan and the saucepan of sauce and refrigerate until ready to serve. About 1¹/₂ hours before serving, remove the baking pan and the sauce from the refrigerator and allow them to come to room temperature. Proceed as the recipe directs.

Homemade Egg Noodles

Makes about 1 pound uncooked noodles.

4 eggs	**2³/₄ cups *sifted* all-**
1 teaspoon salt	**purpose flour**

1. Beat eggs well with salt in a medium-size bowl. Stir in 1 cup of the flour, then mix in enough of the remaining flour to form a stiff dough.

2. Turn out onto a lightly floured pastry cloth or board. Knead, adding a little extra flour to keep dough from sticking, 5 minutes or until smooth. Shape into a ball; cover with a bowl turned upside down. Let stand on board about 30 minutes. Divide in half.

3. Roll out, half at a time, into a large thin sheet; hang dough on a towel spread over the back of a straight-back chair. (Another idea is to make a rack by placing a long dowel or broom handle over the back of two chairs.) Let dough hang about 30 minutes or until dry but still workable.

4. Roll up each sheet, jelly-roll fashion; cut into ¹/₄-inch-wide slices. Separate slices, then unroll strips; spread out on board. Let stand to dry, turning several times, about 30 minutes. Cut strips in half, if you wish. Cook, following your favorite recipe.

Lasagna Noodle Beef Loaf

Bake at 350° for 1 hour

Makes 8 servings.

12 flat lasagna noodles	**2 cups milk**
2 pounds ground chuck or round	**1 medium-size onion, minced**
²/₃ cup all-purpose flour	**¹/₄ cup (¹/₂ stick) butter or margarine**
2 teaspoons alt	**3 tablespoons flour**
1 teaspoon leaf thyme, crumbled	**2 cups milk**
2 eggs	**1 envelope or teaspoon instant beef broth**

1. Cook lasagna noodles following label directions; drain; return to pan; cover with cold water.

2. Combine ground chuck, ²/₃ cup flour, salt, thyme and eggs in large bowl; beat at medium speed with electric mixer until blended. Gradually beat in milk and onion.

(continued)

3. Drain noodles; dry on paper toweling. Lightly oil a 6-cup ring mold. Line mold with noodles by placing them crosswise, so that each noodle extends over outer edge, on bottom of mold, then up and over inner edge.

4. Fill center with meat mixture. Bring noodles over filling from inner edge of mold, then outer edge, to enclose mixture. Use a small spatula to tuck noodles into inner edge of mold. Cover mold with foil.

5. Bake in a moderate oven (350°) for 1 hour.

6. About 15 minutes before loaf is done, melt butter in a medium-size saucepan; stir in 3 tablespoons flour. Cook until bubbly, stirring constantly. Remove from heat; gradually stir in milk and instant broth. Cook until thick and bubbly.

7. Remove foil from mold. Pour off all drippings from beef loaf. Invert plate on top of mold. Holding plate and mold together, turn right-side up. Gently remove mold. Spoon some of the hot sauce on top.

Rotelle with Shrimp and Lemon

Makes 4 servings.

12 ounces rotelle, or other spiral or corkscrew-shaped pasta	OR: **1 pound frozen, thawed and drained**
1 cup heavy cream	**1 cup finely chopped fresh herbs, such as parsley, basil, chives**
4 tablespoons (1/2 stick) butter or margarine	
1/8 teaspoon cayenne pepper	**Grated rind of 1 large lemon (1 tablespoon)**
1/4 cup grated Parmesan or Romano cheese	**Juice of 1 large lemon (about 3 tablespoons)**
1 clove garlic, halved	**1 tablespoon capers, coarsely chopped if large**
1 pound medium-size fresh shrimp, shelled and deveined,	**Lemon wedges (optional)**
	Basil leaves (optional)

1. Cook the rotelle in boiling salted water in a large saucepan, following the package direcitons. Drain.

2. Meanwhile, combine the cream, 2 tablespoons of the butter, the cayenne pepper and cheese in a small saucepan. Place over low heat to heat through.

3. Sauté the garlic in the remaining 2 tablespoons of butter in a medium-size skillet; remove the garlic when it begins to brown.

4. Increase the heat to medium-high. Add the shrimp and stir-fry until firm, pink and curled, for about 3 to 5 minutes. Quickly stir in the herbs, lemon rind and juice, and the capers. Remove from the heat.

5. Transfer to a warm serving bowl. Pour the hot cream sauce over the pasta; toss together until well blended. Spoon the shrimp mixture over the pasta; toss. Garnish with the lemon wedges and basil leaves, if you wish.

All-American Macaroni and Cheese

Bake at 350° for 30 minutes.

Makes 4 servings.

1 1/2 cups elbow macaroni, rigati or ziti	**3 tablespoons flour**
	2 1/2 cups milk
1/4 cup (1/2 stick) butter or margarine	**2 tablespoons prepared mustard**
1 cup fresh bread crumbs (2 slices)	**1 teaspoon Worcestershire sauce**
1 large zucchini, sliced	**6 ounces process American cheese**
1 small onion, chopped (1/4 cup)	**1 large tomato**

1. Cook pasta in boiling salted water, following label directions.

2. While pasta cooks, melt margarine in a medium-size saucepan; toss 1 tablespoon with bread crumbs in a small bowl and reserve.

3. Sauté zucchini slices in margarine in saucepan 2 minutes; remove with slotted spoon and reserve. Sauté onion until soft in margarine; stir in flour and cook 1 minute; remove from heat. Gradually stir in milk until smooth. Cook, stirring constantly, 3 minutes; stir in prepared mustard and Worcestershire sauce.

4. Shred 1 cup of the cheese (about 4 ounces) and stir into saucepan until melted; drain pasta and return to kettle; pour sauce over and blend well; pour into an 8-cup shallow casserole.

5. Cut tomato into wedges; make a pretty pattern on macaroni using the zucchini slices, tomato wedges and buttered crumbs; cut remaining cheese into thin slices; place on casserole.

6. Bake in moderate oven (350°) for 30 minutes or until crumbs are golden and casserole is bubbling hot.

Ravioli with Red Pepper and Tomato Sauce

Makes 4 servings.

1 small onion, chopped	**whole tomatoes**
	1/2 teaspoon salt
1 clove garlic, chopped	**1/4 teaspoon leaf basil, crumbled**
1 tablespoon olive oil	**1/4 teaspoon crushed red pepper flakes**
2 medium-size sweet red peppers (6 ounces), halved, seeded and cut into 1/2-inch pieces	**12 ounces mini-round frozen cheese ravioli**
	16 very small asparagus spears
1 cup drained canned	

1. Sauté onion and garlic in oil in medium-size nonstick saucepan until onion is softened, about 3 minutes. Add sweet red pepper; sauté over low heat, stirring constantly, until pepper begins to blister, about 3 minutes.

2. Add tomatoes, salt, basil and red pepper flakes.

Clockwise from left:
Ravioli with Red Pepper
and Tomato Sauce,
page 604; Vealballs with
Dilled Fettucini, page 606;
Confetti Primavera with
Mozzarella, page 605.

Simmer, covered, 10 to 15 minutes or until red pepper
is very soft.
3. Turn tomato mixture into container of food
processor or blender, working in batches, if
necessary. Cover, whirl with on-and-off pulses until
sauce is as coarsely textured or as fine as you wish.
4. Meanwhile, cook ravioli in large pot of lightly salted
water according to package directions.
5. Steam asparagus spears until crisp-tender, 1 to 2
minutes.
6. Drain ravioli, Transfer to 4 serving bowls or plates,
dividing evenly. Spoon red pepper sauce over each.
Garnish each with 4 asparagus spears.

Confetti Primavera with Mozzarella

Makes 4 servings.

4 ounces zucchini	**2 tablespoons olive oil**
4 ounces yellow squash	**1 to 2 tablespoons chopped fresh basil**
4 ounces pared carrots	**1/4 teaspoon salt**
6 ounces vermicelli or thin spaghetti	**1/8 teaspoon pepper**
2 cloves garlic, finely chopped	**3 ounces part-skim-milk lite mozzarella cheese, cut into 1/2-inch cubes**

1. Cut zucchini, yellow squash and carrots into
2¹/₂ × ¹/₄-inch sticks; you should have about 4 cups
total. Set aside.
2. Cook pasta in large pot of boiling salted water

(continued)

according to package directions. During the last 2 minutes of cooking time, add the vegetable sticks. Raise heat to maintain boiling, if necessary. Drain in colander; rinse. Transfer to serving bowl; keep warm.

3. While pasta is cooking, sauté garlic in oil in small skillet until lightly browned; do not let burn. Remove from heat.

4. Add basil, salt and pepper to pasta; toss gently to mix.

5. Divide pasta equally among 4 individual plates or bowls. Place mozzarella over top of each. Spoon garlic and oil over each and serve.

Stuffed Shells Marinara

Great Italian cooks have always known the art of stretching a little meat or fish into a marvelous main dish.

Bake at 350° for 45 minutes.

Makes 8 servings.

1 package (12 ounces) large shell macaroni	crumbled
1 can (7 ounces) chunk light tuna in oil	¼ teaspoon pepper
	1 package (10 ounces) frozen chopped spinach
1 large onion, chopped (1 cup)	2 eggs
1 clove garlic, minced	1 cup fresh bread crumbs (2 slices)
1 can (29 ounces) tomato sauce	1 cup cream-style cottage cheese
2 teaspoons salt	1 teaspoon salt
2 teaspoons leaf basil,	¼ teaspoon pepper

1. Cook macaroni, following label directions, 9 minutes; drain, reserving 1 cup of the cooking water. Place macaroni in a large bowl of cold water.

2. While macaroni cooks, drain oil from tuna into a large skillet; heat; sauté onion and garlic in oil until soft. Stir in tomato sauce, tuna, the 2 teaspoons salt, basil and ¼ teaspoon pepper; simmer 15 minutes to blend flavors. Add reserved 1 cup cooking water to sauce, if it becomes too thick.

3. Cook spinach, following label directions; drain thoroughly. Beat eggs in a medium-size bowl with a wire whisk; add cooked spinach, bread crumbs, cottage cheese, the 1 teaspoon salt and ¼ teaspoon pepper and stir until well blended.

4. Drain macaroni, 1 portion at a time, on paper toweling; fill each shell with 1 teaspoon of spinach-cheese mixture. Spoon half of the sauce into a shallow 12-cup casserole. Arrange stuffed pasta shells over sauce; drizzle on remaining sauce. Cover casserole with aluminum foil.

5. Bake in a moderate oven (350°) for 45 minutes or until shells are tender and casserole is bubbly-hot.

Note: Elbow macaroni or ziti can be substituted for shells. Spoon half the cooked pasta over sauce; top with a layer of spinach-cheese filling, remaining pasta and, finally, sauce. This recipe can be divided easily,

with half spooned into a 9 × 9 × 2-inch baking dish lined with heavy-duty aluminum foil. Seal, label, date and freeze. When solid, remove foil package from baking dish. When ready to serve, peel foil from frozen pasta; place in original baking dish. Bake in a moderate oven (350°) for 1 hour.

Vealballs with Dilled Fettuccine

Bake at 400° for 15 minutes.

Makes 4 servings

Vealballs:	Dill Sauce:
6½ ounces finely grounded veal (14% fat)	¼ cup plain yogurt
	2 tablespoons dairy sour cream
1 tablespoon dry bread crumbs	1 teaspoon lemon juice
1 tablespoon finely chopped onion	1 tablespoon firmly packed snipped fresh dill
1 tablespoon water	
¼ teaspoon grated lemon rind	½ teaspoon salt
	⅛ teaspoon white pepper
¼ teaspoon salt	
¼ teaspoon pepper	6 ounces egg fettuccine

1. Preheat the oven to hot (400°).

2. Prepare the Vealballs: Combine the veal, bread crumbs, onion, water, lemon rind, salt and pepper in a medium-size bowl. Shape into about 20 meatballs, using a rounded measuring teaspoonful for each. Arrange the meatballs on a rack in a small pan.

3. Bake in the preheated hot oven (400°) for 15 minutes, or until no longer pink in the center.

4. Meanwhile, prepare the Dill Sauce: Combine the yogurt, sour cream, lemon juice, dill, salt and white pepper in a medium-size bowl.

5. Cook the fettuccine in a large pot of salted boiling water, following the package directions. Drain. Turn into a serving bowl. Add the Dill Sauce; toss to coat well. Add the Vealballs. Serve immediately. Garnish with fresh dill sprigs, if you wish.

Ziti Casserole

Bake at 350° for 40 minutes.

Makes 8 servings.

1 package (1 pound) ziti	½ cup grated Parmesan cheese
1 container (15 ounces) ricotta cheese	1 egg
	¾ teaspoon salt
	¼ teaspoon pepper
4 ounces mozzarella cheese, diced	1 jar (32 ounces) spaghetti sauce

1. Cook ziti following label directions; drain.

2. While pasta cooks, make the filling. Combine ricotta, mozzarella, Parmesan, egg, salt and pepper in a large bowl.

Lasagna.

3. Layer ziti, filling and spaghetti sauce in a 13 × 9 × 2-inch baking dish, starting and ending with sauce.
4. Bake in a moderate oven (350°) for 40 minutes or until bubbly-hot.

Lasagna

Bake at 350° for 45 minutes.

Makes 8 servings.

1 pound sweet Italian sausages OR: **1 pound ground beef**	**(from a 1-pound package** **1 carton (15 ounces) ricotta cheese**
1 large onion, chopped (1 cup)	**1 egg**
1 teaspoon leaf oregano, crumbled	**1 package (8 ounces) mozzarella cheese, thinly sliced**
1 jar (32 ounces) spaghetti sauce	**¹/₄ cup grated Parmesan cheese**
12 lasagna noodles	

1. Remove casing from sausages, if used. Cook sausage or beef in a large saucepan, breaking it up as it browns. Add onion and oregano; sauté until onion is soft. Drain all fat. Add spaghetti sauce. Cover; simmer over low heat 15 minutes.
2. Cook noodles following label directions; drain and place in a bowl of cold water to keep from sticking.
3. Mix ricotta and egg in a bowl.
4. To assemble: Drain noodles well. Spoon ¹/₄ of the sauce on the bottom of a 13 x 9 x 2-inch baking dish. Arrange 4 strips of noodles over the sauce; spoon on ¹/₂ of the ricotta cheese mixture, ¹/₃ of the mozzarella, ¹/₃ of the Parmesan cheese and ¹/₄ of the sauce. Repeat with 4 more lasagna noodles, remaining ricotta, ¹/₃ mozzarella and ¹/₃ of the Parmesan. Top with remaining noodles, sauce, mozzarella and Parmesan.
5. Bake in a moderate oven (350°) for 45 minutes or until bubbly hot. Cool 10 minutes before serving.

Pasta In Carbonara Sauce

Makes 6 servings.

1 pound tubular pasta (macaroncelli or ziti)	**crushed red pepper** **1 cup light cream or half-and-half**
¹/₂ pound sliced bacon	**Grated Parmesan**
¹/₄ to ¹/₂ teaspoon	**cheese (optional)**

1. Cook pasta following label directions; drain.
2. Cut bacon crosswise into 1-inch pieces. Cook in large skillet until brown and crisp. Pour off drippings; return 4 tablespoonfuls to skillet.
3. Stir pepper into drippings in skillet and heat a few seconds for flavors to blend. Add cream; heat to boiling. Toss with hot pasta until well coated. Serve with Parmesan cheese.

Mushroom-Cheese Lasagna Rolls

Bake at 375° for 30 minutes.

Makes 6 servings.

12 ruffled-edge lasagna noodles (from a 1-pound package)	1/4 cup (1/2 stick) butter or margarine
1 tablespoon vegetable oil	3/4 pound fresh mushrooms, quartered
1 carton (15 ounces) ricotta cheese	1 jar (21 ounces) Italian cooking sauce
1 package (8 ounces) mozzarella cheese, coarsely shredded	OR: 1 jar (16 ounces) meatless spaghetti sauce
2 eggs	1 teaspoon Italian herb seasoning mix
1/4 cup chopped fresh parsley	1 teaspoon sugar
1 1/2 teaspoons salt	1/4 teaspoon crushed red pepper
1/4 teaspoon ground nutmeg	

1. Slide lasagna noodles, one at a time, into a kettle of boiling salted water, to which you've added the tablespoon of vegetable oil. Cook until just tender but firm. Drain; return to kettle. Cover with cold water.
2. Combine ricotta, half of the mozzarella cheese (1 cup), eggs, parsley, 1/2 teaspoon salt and nutmeg in a bowl.
3. Melt butter in a large skillet. Add mushrooms; sauté over high heat just until wilted. remove from heat.
4. Combine cooking or spaghetti sauce, seasoning mix, sugar, remaining 1 teaspoon salt and red pepper. Spoon half of sauce into 13 x 9 x 2-inch baking dish.
5. Lift noodles, one at a time, from water; drain on paper toweling; Spread with 1/4 cup of the cheese mixture; place 3 or 4 mushroom quarters along narrow end and roll up, jelly-roll fashion. Place, seam-side down, in baking dish. Spoon sauce over rolls; cover dish with foil.
6. Bake in a moderate oven (375°) for 25 minutes. Remove foil; sprinkle with remaining mozzarella cheese and top with any leftover mushrooms. Bake 5 minutes longer.

Spaghetti and Meatballs

Bake at 400° for 20 minutes.

Makes 8 servings.

2 pounds ground round	vegetable oil
1 cup fresh bread crumbs (2 slices)	1 can (28 ounces) tomatoes
2 eggs	1 can (6 ounces) tomato paste
1/4 cup milk	1 teaspoon salt
1 1/2 teaspoons salt	1/4 teaspoon pepper
1/4 teaspoon pepper	1 teaspoon leaf basil, crumbled
1 teaspoon Worcestershire sauce	1 teaspoon leaf oregano, crumbled
1 medium-size onion, chopped (1/2 cup)	1 package (1 pound) thin spaghetti
1 clove garlic, chopped	Grated Parmesan cheese
2 tablespoons	

1. Combine beef, bread crumbs, eggs, milk, salt, pepper and Worcestershire in a large bowl; mix well. Shape into meatballs, using about a tablespoon of

Mushroom-Cheese Lasagna Rolls.

mixture for each. Place meatballs on jelly-roll pan or other shallow, rimmed pan.

2. Bake meatballs in a hot oven (400°) for 20 minutes or until browned.

3. While meatballs are browning, make sauce. Sauté onion and garlic in oil in a large saucepan until tender, about 3 minutes.

4. Add tomatoes, breaking up with a spoon, tomato paste, salt, pepper, basil and oregano. Bring to boiling; lower heat; simmer 10 minutes, stirring occasionally.

5. Add browned meatballs to sauce; cover; let simmer, uncovered, for 45 minutes, stirring occasionally.

6. Cook spaghetti following label directions; drain. Serve sauce and meatballs over spaghetti; sprinkle with Parmesan cheese.

Lasagna with Cottage Cheese

Bake at 350° for 35 minutes.

Makes 8 servings.

1 large onion, chopped (1 cup)	**sliced oil-cured black olives (about 12)**
2 cloves garlic, minced	**12 strips lasagna noodles (about 1/2 pound)**
1 tablespoon olive oil	
1/2 pound ground round	**1 container (16 ounces) creamed cottage cheese**
1 jar (15 1/2 ounces) marinara or spaghetti sauce	
1 teaspoon leaf oregano, crumbled	**1 package (8 ounces) mozzarella cheese, cut into 8 slices**
1/2 teaspoon crushed red pepper flakes	**1/3 cup grated Parmesan or Romano cheese**
1/2 teaspoon salt	
1/2 teaspoon sugar	
1/2 cup pitted and	

1. Sauté onion and garlic in oil in a large skillet until soft; add beef and cook until browned. Drain fat.

2. Stir in marinara sauce, oregano, red pepper flakes, salt and sugar. Simmer, covered, 15 minutes. Stir in olives.

3. Cook lasagna noodles, following label directions; lift out carefully with a slotted spoon; place in a large bowl of cold water until ready to use.

4. Lift lasagna noodles from water, 1 at a time; drain well.

5. Spread 3 or 4 tablepoons sauce in bottom of an 11 3/4 × 7 3/4 × 1 3/4-inch baking dish. Place 4 noodles, slightly overlapping, in dish; spread half of the cottage cheese, then half the mozzarella on top; spoon on 1/3 of the sauce. Repeat with 4 more noodles, remaining cottage cheese, remaining mozzarella and 1/3 more of

the sauce. Top with remaining 4 noodles and spread with rest of sauce. Sprinkle with grated Parmesan cheese. Cover with foil.

6. Bake in a moderate oven (350°) for 15 minutes. Remove foil and bake 20 minutes longer or until slightly browned on top. Let stand 15 minutes before cutting into squares.

Homemade Ravioli

Makes 6 to 8 servings.

3 cups *sifted* all-purpose flour	*follows)*
	OR: **Spinach Filling (*recipe follows*)**
2 teaspoons salt	
3 eggs	**Homemade Tomato Sauce (*recipe follows*)**
2 tablespoons olive or vegetable oil	
1/4 cup water	**1/2 cup freshly grated Parmesan cheese**
Ricotta Filling (*recipe*	

1. Sift flour and salt onto a large wooden board; make a well in the center; add the eggs, oil and water. Work liquids into the flour with fingers to make a stiff dough. (Or make dough in a large bowl, but it's not as much fun.)

2. Knead dough on board (do not add additional flour) for 10 minutes or until smooth and soft as perfectly kneaded bread dough.

3. Wrap dough in plastic wrap. Let stand 15 minutes. Cut into quarters; keep dough you are not working with wrapped in plastic to prevent it from drying out.

4. Roll out dough, one quarter at a time, on the wooden board (do not use additional flour) to a 12 x 4 1/2-inch rectangle. (This takes a lot of pressure with rolling pin.) Repeat with remaining quarters of dough.

5. To shape the ravioli, place 24 teaspoonfuls of filling, in 3 evenly spaced rows of 8 teaspoonfuls each, on one of the rolled-out strips. Cover with the second rolled-out strip and cut between mounds of filling with a fluted pastry wheel. Repeat with the remaining 2 rolled-out strips of ravioli dough. (The ravioli can be cooked at once or placed in a single layer on cookie sheets until you are ready to cook them.)

6. Bring water (about 4 quarts) to boiling in a large kettle. Cook ravioli, 24 at a time, 10 minutes; remove with slotted spoon to heated serving dish; top with half the Homemade Tomato Sauce and half the grated Parmesan cheese. Repeat with remaining ravioli, sauce and cheese.

Ricotta Filling: Combine 1 cup of ricotta or cream-style cottage cheese and 1/2 cup freshly grated Parmesan cheese in a small bowl; stir in 1 beaten egg and 2 tablespoons chopped fresh parsley. Chill until you are ready to use. Makes enough filling for 48 ravioli.

Spinach Filling: Sauté 1 small onion, minced, in 1/4 cup butter or margarine in a large saucepan until tender. Stir in 1 package (10 ounces) frozen chopped

(continued)

spinach that has been thawed, drained and squeezed dry. Cook spinach until most of the moisture has evaporated, stirring often. Remove from heat. Cool. Stir in 1 egg, $1/2$ cup grated Parmesan cheese and $1/8$ teaspoon ground nutmeg. Chill until you are ready to use. Makes enough filling for 48 ravioli.

Homemade Tomato Sauce

Makes about 5 cups.

1 large onion, chopped (1 cup)	tomato paste
1 clove garlic, minced	2 teaspoons leaf basil, crumbled
$1/4$ cup olive oil	1 teaspoon salt
1 can (35 ounces) plum tomatoes	Sugar
1 can (6 ounces)	1 cup water

Sauté onion and garlic in oil until soft in a large saucepan; stir in tomatoes, tomato paste, basil, salt, sugar to taste and water. Heat to bubbling; lower heat; simmer, uncovered, stirring frequently, 45 minutes or until sauce has thickened.

Garden-Style Spaghetti

Makes 6 servings.

1 small bunch broccoli (about $1 1/4$ pounds)	$1 1/2$ teaspoons salt
2 small zucchini	$1/4$ teaspoon black pepper
1 pound green beans, cut into 1-inch lengths ($1 1/2$ cups)	$1/2$ pound mushrooms, thinly sliced
1 package (1 pound) spaghetti	$1/2$ pound peas, shelled OR: $1/2$ cup frozen green peas
6 tablespoons olive or vegetable oil	$1/4$ cup chopped fresh parsley
1 large clove garlic, chopped	$1/4$ teaspoon crushed red pepper
3 to 4 ripe tomatoes, cut into 1-inch cubes (3 cups)	$1/4$ cup ($1/2$ stick) butter or margarine
$1/4$ cup chopped fresh basil OR: 1 teaspoon leaf basil, crushed	$3/4$ cup heavy cream
	$2/3$ cup grated Parmesan cheese

1. Wash and trim broccoli; cut into bite-size pieces (4 cups). Trim zucchini; cut into quarters lengthwise, then cut into 1-inch lengths ($1 1/2$ cups).
2. Cook broccoli, zucchini and beans in boiling salted water until crisply tender, about 5 minutes; drain. Place in large bowl.

Garden-Style Spaghetti.

3. Cook spaghetti following label directions; drain.

4. Heat 3 tablespoons oil in large saucepan; stir in garlic; add tomatoes. Cook, stirring gently, over medium heat, 5 minutes. Stir in basil, 1/2 teaspoon of the salt and black pepper. Cover; reserve.

5. Heat remaining oil in large skillet or Dutch oven (large enough to hold spaghetti and vegetables). Stir in mushrooms; cook and stir 3 minutes; stir in peas, parsley, remaining 1 teaspoon salt and the crushed red pepper; cook 1 minute; add to vegetables in bowl; toss to mix.

6. Melt butter in same skillet; stir in cream and cheese. Cook over medium-high heat, stirring constantly until smooth. Add spaghetti; toss to coat well. Drain any juice from tomatoes into skillet, reserving tomatoes. Add vegetables to skillet; toss and stir over low heat until heated through. Serve with tomatoes spooned over each serving.

Spaghetti with Meat Sauce

Makes 4 servings.

2 tablespoons olive or vegetable oil	**2 tablespoons chopped fresh parsley**
1 medium-size onion, chopped (1/2 cup)	**1 bay leaf**
1 clove garlic, minced	**1 teaspoon leaf basil, crumbled**
1 pound ground beef or chuck	**1 teaspoon salt**
1 can (35 ounces) plum tomatoes	**1 teaspoon sugar**
1 can (6 ounces) tomato paste	**1/8 teaspoon pepper**
1/2 cup water	**1 package (16 ounces) spaghetti**
1/4 cup chopped celery	**Grated Parmesan cheese**

1. Heat oil in a large saucepan. Add onion and garlic; sauté just until onion is soft; push to one side.

2. Add ground beef; cook until well browned, breaking up into chunks. Stir in tomatoes, tomato paste, water, celery, parsley, bay leaf, basil, salt, sugar and pepper.

3. Bring to boiling; partially cover and simmer, stirring several times, 1 hour or until sauce is thick. Skim off any fat; remove bay leaf.

4. Cook spaghetti following label directions; drain.

5. Spoon cooked spaghetti and meat sauce onto individual plates. Toss and serve with grated Parmesan cheese.

A Roster of Rice

White Rice Dubbed "regular" because it is the most familiar and popular. Hull, bran and polishings have been removed, leaving a snow-white grain. The size regulates price: *short-grain* and *medium-grain* rice are the thriftiest. These cook moist and tender, and are an ideal choice for casseroles, puddings and croquettes. *Long-grain* rice, at a few pennies more a pound, cooks fluffier and flakier and is preferred for serving as a vegetable or a base for curry. Most white rice is enriched, but let the label be your guide.

Processed White Rice The term *parboiled* or *converted* on a package of rice simply means that the grains have been partly cooked before milling, with special care taken to protect the vitamins and minerals in the outer layer. This rice is long-grain with a light golden color; it cooks the same as regular rice.

Precooked White Rice It's called *instant* because it needs only the briefest cooking. It is milled from special long-grain rice, is enriched and comes plain and seasoned.

Brown Rice This is whole-grain rice with only the outer hull removed. The cooking time for brown rice is longer than for regular white rice, and its savory, nutlike flavor makes it a perfect partner for meat or game.

Wild Rice This is not a true rice, but the seed of a water grass native to some of our northern states. Supply is limited and the gathering, which is done by hand from small boats, is laborious -- the reasons for its sky-high price. When cooked, these long, slender, gray-brown grains have a sweet, nutlike flavor. Wild rice is available as is or mixed with long-grain white rice.

Seasoned Rice These are quick-to-fix, convenience foods. The seasonings are mixed with the rice before packaging. Take your pick of beef, chicken, chili, cheese, curry, herb, pilaf or saffron (yellow) rice flavors. Frozen seasoned rice is the easiest to fix; just heat and serve.

Specialties Just name your choice and it's probably available. In the grocery department, you will find Chinese fried rice in little cardboard buckets; Spanish rice packages that need only the addition of tomatoes; packaged rice mixed with thin pasta sticks and seasoned with chicken, cheese or tomato; rice pudding in boxes for a quick dessert.

How Much Rice Should You Cook?

Rice swells 3 to 4 times as it cooks. Use this chart for reference:

RICE	UNCOOKED	COOKED	SERVINGS
Long-Grain White Rice	1 cup	3 cups	3 to 4
Processed Converted White Rice	1 cup	4 cups	4 to 6
Precooked Instant White Rice	1 cup	2 cups	2 to 3
Brown Rice	1 cup	4 cups	4 to 6
Wild Rice	1 cup	4 cups	4 to 6

How to Cook Rice Perfectly

To Boil: Measure 2 to 2½ cups water (as label directs), 1 tablespoon butter or margarine and 1 teaspoon salt into heavy, medium-size saucepan. Bring to boiling. Stir in 1 cup uncooked, long-grain or processed (converted) white rice; let return to a boil, then adjust heat so water bubbles gently. Cover pan snugly and cook 14 to 25 minutes (following label directions) until rice is fluffy and water absorbed. Fluff with a fork.

To Steam: Measure 2½ cups of water, 1 tablespoon butter or margarine and 1 teaspoon salt into the top of a double boiler; bring to boiling over direct heat, then stir in 1 cup uncooked, long-grain or processed (converted) white rice; cover. Place top of double boiler over bottom (half-filled with boiling water); turn heat to medium, and cook 45 minutes or until water is absorbed and rice fluffy. Fluff with a fork.

To Bake: Combine 1 cup uncooked, long-grain or processed (converted) white rice with 1 teaspoon salt and 1 tablespoon butter or margarine in a 4- or 6-cup baking dish. Pour in 2½ cups *boiling* water; stir; cover. Bake in moderate oven (350°) 1 hour or until water is absorbed and rice tender. Fluff with a fork. Serves 4 to 6.

Paella Valenciana

Bake at 375° for 45 minutes.

Makes 6 servings.

1 broiler-fryer, cut up (about 3 pounds)
1 clove garlic, finely chopped
¼ cup olive or vegetable oil
1 large onion, chopped (1 cup)
1 chorizo (Spanish sausage), sliced ½ inch thick,
OR: **½ cup diced cooked ham**
1½ cups uncooked long-grain rice
6 strands saffron, crushed
2 cans (10 ounces
each) condensed chicken broth
1 cup water
1 teaspoon salt
1 bag (1 pound) frozen, shelled and deveined shrimp, thawed
1 can (4 ounces) pimiento, drained and cut into chunks
1 bag (1 pound) frozen peas
1 dozen small clams, scrubbed
1 dozen mussels, scrubbed (optional)

1. Brown the chicken and garlic in the oil in a large skillet; remove and reserve.
2. Preheat the oven to moderate (375°).
3. Sauté the onion in the pan drippings until soft, then add the chorizo or ham and sauté for 3 minutes; push to one side; sprinkle the rice in the pan and cook, stirring constantly, until the grains are golden; add the saffron, chicken broth, water and salt; bring to boiling; pour into a 12-cup paella dish or shallow casserole; add the browned chicken and cover the casserole.
4. Bake in the preheated moderate oven (375°) for 45 minutes; add the shrimp, pimiento and peas; top with the clams and mussels, if using; cover. Bake for 15 minutes longer or until the shrimp and rice are cooked and the cooking liquid is absorbed.

Rice Imperatrice with Cherry Sauce

Makes 10 servings.

½ cup uncooked long-grain rice
2 cups water
2¼ cups milk
1 envelope unflavored gelatin
¼ cup cold water
2 eggs
½ cup sugar
1 teaspoon vanilla
1 cup heavy cream, whipped
Cherry Sauce (recipe follows)

1. Cook rice in the 2 cups water in a medium-size saucepan, stirring occasionally, 30 minutes, or until all the water is absorbed. Add 1¼ cups of the milk to rice; simmer 30 minutes longer or until milk is absorbed. Cool.
2. Soften gelatin in cold water.
3. Beat eggs lightly in top of a double boiler; add sugar and remaining milk. Cook over simmering water, stirring constantly, until mixture coats a spoon. Add vanilla and softened gelatin; stir until the gelatin is completely dissolved. Turn into a large bowl; stir in the rice.
4. Chill custard mixture over ice and water, or in refrigerator, stirring often, until mixture starts to thicken. Fold in whipped cream. Turn into a 6- or 8-cup mold. Refrigerate 3 hours or until firm. Unmold on serving plate. Garnish with additional whipped cream and cherries from Cherry Sauce, if you wish. Serve with Cherry Sauce.

Cherry Sauce: Reserve a few cherries from a 21-ounce can cherry pie filling for garnish. Turn remaining pie filling into container of electric blender. Whirl until smooth. Stir in 2 tablespoons brandy and a few drops red food coloring, if you wish. Chill before serving.

Wild Rice

Makes about 10 servings.

2 cups wild rice
Boiling water
3 cans (13¾ ounces each)
chicken broth
¾ cup water
2 tablespoons butter

Wash rice in colander under cold running water. Transfer to a large saucepan or Dutch oven. Cover with boiling water; let cool to lukewarm. Drain and return to saucepan. Repeat soaking with boiling water and draining twice more. Return drained rice to saucepan. Add chicken broth and water. Cover; bring to boiling. Uncover; lower heat, simmer about 30 minutes or until just tender and liquid is almost evaporated. Drain; stir in butter until melted.

Chinese Fried Rice
with Chicken.

Chinese Fried Rice with Chicken

Makes 6 servings.

1½ cups long-grain
   white rice
1¼ pounds boneless
   chicken breasts
   OR: chicken thighs,
   skinned and cut
   into ½-inch chunks
¼ cup soy sauce
¼ teaspoon pepper
3 tablespoons
   vegetable oil
2 eggs, slightly beaten
2 cups fresh bean

   sprouts
2 cups small broccoli
   flowerets
1 large sweet red or
   green pepper,
   halved, seeded and
   cut into ¼-inch dice
   (1 cup)
2 green onions, thinly
   sliced
2 tablespoons dry
   sherry or water

1. Cook rice following package directions.
2. Meanwhile, place chicken in a medium-size bowl.
Mix soy sauce and pepper in a cup. Add 1 tablespoon
to chicken; toss to mix.
3. Heat 1 tablespoon of the oil in a wok or large skillet
over high heat. Add eggs; cook, stirring, until lightly
set, about 15 seconds. Remove with slotted spoon to
a small plate; keep warm.
4. Add remaining oil to wok. Add chicken pieces; stir-
fry until cooked through, about 4 minutes. Remove
with slotted spoon to a bowl; keep warm.
5. Add bean sprouts, broccoli, red pepper and green
onion to wok. Stir-fry for 1 minute. Add sherry; cover;
cook for 2 minutes.
6. Add cooked hot rice, chicken and remaining soy
mixture. Toss until rice is evenly coated. Gently stir in
eggs, breaking them up. Serve at once.

Chinese Fried Rice with Pork

Makes 4 servings.

3 tablespoons soy
   sauce
2 tablespoons sherry
1 teaspoon sugar
½ pound boneless
   pork loin, cut in
   ½-inch cubes
4 tablespoons
   vegetable oil
1 large onion,
   chopped (1 cup)
2 cloves garlic,

   minced
3 cups cold cooked
   rice
1 can (8½ ounces)
   green peas, drained
1 can (4 ounces)
   whole mushrooms,
   drained
3 eggs
½ teaspoon salt
1 tablespoon chopped
   fresh parsley

1. Combine soy sauce, sherry and sugar in a medium-
size bowl. Add pork cubes and allow to marinate in
refrigerator for at least 1 hour. Drain; reserve
marinade.
2. Heat 2 tablespoons of the oil in a large skillet; stir-
fry pork 3 minutes. Add onion and garlic; stir-fry 2
minutes longer. Push the mixture to side of skillet.
3. Heat remaining oil in center of skillet. Add rice; stir-
fry 1 minute. Add peas, mushrooms and reserved
marinade. Mix well.
4. Clear center of pan. Beat eggs lightly with salt in a
small bowl; pour into center of skillet. When eggs
begin to set, scramble and mix with rice mixture.
Serve hot, sprinkled with parsley.

Curried Orange Rice

Makes 6 servings.

¹/₄ cup (¹/₂ stick) butter or margarine	grain rice
1 medium-size onion, thinly sliced	1 cup orange juice
	1 cup chicken broth
2 teaspoons curry powder	1 teaspoon salt
	¹/₂ cup raisins
1 cup uncooked long-	1 bay leaf

1. Melt butter in a heavy saucepan or flameproof casserole; sauté onion until soft and golden, but not brown. Stir in curry and rice; cook 2 minutes longer, stirring constantly.
2. Add orange juice, chicken broth, salt, raisins and bay leaf; stir with fork. Bring to boiling; lower heat; cover; simmer 15 to 20 minutes or until rice is tender and liquid has been absorbed. Remove bay leaf before serving.

Pilaf   Rice or bulgur (cracked wheat) cooked in a savory broth, often with small bits of meat or vegetables, herbs and spices.

Zucchini Boats with Bulgur Pilaf

Bake at 350° for 20 minutes.
Makes 8 to 10 servings.

¹/₄ cup chopped shallots OR: green onion	¹/₂ cup tomato juice
	³/₄ teaspoon salt
2 tablespoons butter or margarine	¹/₄ teaspoon ground pepper
1 sweet red pepper, cored, seeded and finely chopped	¹/₈ teaspoon ground allspice
	8 to 10 medium-size zucchini (5 or 6 inches long), halved lengthwise
1 cup bulgur	
2 cups water OR: chicken broth	

1. Sauté the shallots in the butter in a medium-size heavy saucepan for 5 minutes. Add the red pepper; sauté, stirring, for 4 to 5 minutes. Stir in the bulgur, water, tomato juice, salt, pepper and allspice. Bring to boiling. Lower the heat; simmer, covered, for 15 minutes. Remove from the heat. Let stand, tightly covered, for 15 to 20 minutes.
2. Cook the zucchini in boiling salted water to cover in a large skillet, for 8 minutes, or until tender. Drain. Run under cold water. Scoop out the insides, leaving a ¹/₄- to ¹/₂-inch shell. Spoon the bulgur pilaf into the zucchini shells. Serve hot or at room temperature. To serve hot, bake the zucchini in a shallow baking dish, loosely covered with foil, in a preheated moderate oven (350°) until heated through, 20 minutes.

Mushroom Pilaf

Toasting the rice first gives it a marvelous, nutty flavor.
Makes 8 servings.

¹/₂ pound mushrooms	2 tablespoons chopped fresh parsley
6 tablespoons olive or vegetable oil	3 envelopes or teaspoons instant chicken broth
2 cups uncooked long-grain rice	
¹/₂ cup toasted slivered almonds	5 cups water

1. Wash mushrooms; pat dry; trim; chop. Sauté lightly in 2 tablespoons of the oil in a large skillet; remove with a slotted spoon and set aside.
2. Stir rice and remaining 4 tablespoons oil into the same pan; heat slowly, stirring constantly, until rice is toasty-golden.
3. Stir in the mushrooms, almonds, parsley, chicken broth and water. Bring to boiling; cover.
4. Simmer 25 minutes or until rice is tender and liquid is absorbed. Fluff up rice with a fork just before serving.

Polenta Parmesan

A buttery, fragrant northern Italian specialty.
Bake at 400° for 30 minutes.

Makes 12 servings.

6 cups water	6 tablespoons (³/₄ stick) butter, melted
2 teaspoons salt	
2 cups cold water	
2 cups yellow cornmeal	1 cup freshly grated Parmesan cheese

1. Combine the 6 cups water and salt in large kettle or Dutch oven; bring to boiling. Stir cold water and cornmeal together in bowl; pour into boiling water and bring to boiling again, stirring constantly. Lower heat; simmer 5 minutes, stirring until very thick. *Caution*: Hot mixture bubbles and spatters unless heat is very low.
2. Turn cooked cornmeal into an oiled 15 ¹/₂ × 10 ¹/₂ × 1-inch jelly-roll pan. Spread evenly with a spatula; cool, then chill 2 hours or overnight.
3. Turn out onto wooden surface. Cut into ovals or rounds with cookie cutters.
4. Arrange polenta, overlapping, in buttered 11 × 7 × 1¹/₂-inch baking dish. Drizzle butter over and sprinkle with ¹/₂ cup of the Parmesan cheese.
5. Bake in a hot oven (400°) for 30 minutes. Sprinkle remaining Parmesan cheese over top and broil 6 inches from heat for 10 minutes or until bubbly and browned.

Pictured opposite: Homemade Ravioli, page 608.

Jambalaya
A traditional Creole dish of rice, ham, tomato, seafood, green pepper and seasonings.

Jambalaya

Makes 8 servings.

1 broiler-fryer (about 2^1/$_2$ pounds)	1 pound cooked ham, cubed
2 cups water	1 can (16 ounces) tomatoes
3 teaspoons salt	
^{1}/$_4$ teaspoon pepper	1 large green pepper, halved, seeded and chopped
1 bay leaf	
2 large onions, chopped (2 cups)	^{1}/$_2$ teaspoon leaf thyme, crumbled
1 large clove garlic, crushed	^{1}/$_4$ teaspoon cayenne
^{1}/$_4$ cup (^{1}/$_2$ stick) butter or margarine	1 cup uncooked long-grain rice

1. Place chicken in a large kettle or Dutch oven; add water, salt, pepper, and bay leaf; bring to boiling; reduce heat; cover.
2. Simmer 45 minutes or until chicken is tender; remove chicken from broth; reserve. When cool enough to handle, remove meat from bones; cut into cubes; reserve.
3. Pour broth into a 2-cup measure; remove bay leaf; add water, if necessary, to make 2 cups; reserve.
4. In same kettle, sauté onions and garlic in butter or margarine until soft; add ham, tomatoes, green pepper, thyme, cayenne and reserved chicken and broth. Heat to boiling; stir in rice; reduce heat; cover. Simmer, following rice label directions for cooking.
5. Serve in large bowls.

Kasha
Buckwheat kernels or groats that are cooked in liquid and served in place of rice, potatoes or other starches.

Fruited Kasha

Makes 8 servings.

1^1/$_4$ cups kasha (cracked buckwheat)	^{3}/$_4$ cup sliced green onions
1 egg	3 tablespoons butter or margarine
2^1/$_2$ cups boiling water	1 cup diced dried apricots
2 envelopes instant vegetable broth	

1. Heat a large skillet over medium heat. Mix kasha and egg in small bowl; add to skillet. Cook, stirring constantly, until dry and slightly toasted. Stir in boiling water and vegetable broth. Cover; simmer 15 minutes. (This can be done ahead of time.)
2. Before serving, sauté onions in butter in a large saucepan until tender, about 3 minutes; add apricots and kasha and heat through.

Risotto with Chicken Livers

An easy, simple-to-prepare main dish of rice, vegetables and chicken livers.

Makes 4 servings.

1 pound chicken livers, halved	1 cup uncooked long-grain rice
^{1}/$_4$ cup all-purpose flour	1 can (4 ounces) mushroom stems and pieces
1 teaspoon salt	
^{1}/$_4$ teaspoon pepper	2 envelopes or teaspoons instant chicken broth
^{1}/$_4$ cup (^{1}/$_2$ stick) margarine	
1 medium-size onion, chopped (^{1}/$_2$ cup)	^{1}/$_2$ teaspoon salt
^{1}/$_2$ cup diced carrot	^{1}/$_4$ teaspoon pepper
^{1}/$_2$ cup sliced celery	2^1/$_2$ cups boiling water
	Chopped fresh parsley

1. Shake chicken livers with flour, salt and pepper in a plastic bag until coated.
2. Melt margarine in a large skillet. Brown livers over low heat on both sides. Remove with slotted spoon; keep warm.
3. Sauté onion, carrot and celery in same skillet until crisp-tender, about 5 minutes. Add rice, mushrooms with liquid, instant chicken broth, salt, pepper and boiling water.
4. Heat to boiling; lower heat; stir rice mixture well; cover. Simmer 15 minutes. Spoon browned chicken livers over rice; cover. Simmer 15 minutes longer or until liquid is absorbed and rice is tender. Fluff up rice. Garnish with chopped parsley.

Dumpling
Almost every cuisine in the world has its version of the dumpling. The ancestor of dumplings is probably from the Chinese. Marco Polo, on his travels in China, returned to Italy not only with noodles which developed into pasta, but also with meat-filled dumplings which became ravioli. Only the stuffing ingredient separates the two dumplings. Dumplings can be low-cost meal-stretchers—cooked in soup or stews—or can be made into delicious desserts.

Americans think of dumplings as small spoonfuls of dough dropped into boiling soup or stews, or baked apple dumplings. Some dumplings, such as the elegant French quenelles (light-as-a-feather fish dumplings in a rich sauce), can be served as a main course or appetizer. The Italian gnocchi is made from potatoes, semolina or a spinach-and-ricotta mixture and is usually served as a separate course, in place of pasta. Chinese dumplings are savory or sweet. Savory dumplings are filled with pork, shrimp or egg and vegetables. Sweet Chinese dumplings are filled with dried fruits, nuts, or bean pastes. Czechoslovakian dumplings include liver and fruit-stuffed dumplings and some flavored with poppy seeds.

The word "dumpling" may have originated from *dumpf*, a German word meaning damp and moist, or a thick, misshapen lump.

Ukrainian Potato Dumplings

Makes 8 servings.

2¼ cups *sifted* all-
    purpose flour
1 cup minus
    2 tablespoons
    boiling water
1 teaspoon vegetable

oil
½ cup (1 stick) butter
    or margarine,
    melted
Potato Filling *(recipe
    follows)*

1. Place flour in a large bowl; add water and oil slowly, stirring constantly with a fork, until mixture is crumbly; let stand until cool.
2. Knead dough on a lightly floured surface until soft and smooth. Cover dough with a bowl; let stand 15 minutes.
3. Divide dough in half, keeping other half covered. Shape into a roll about 12 inches long; cut into 12 pieces. Roll each piece on lightly floured surface to a 5- to 6-inch round; repeat with remaining dough.
4. Place a generous tablespoonful of cooled Potato Filling in center of each dumpling wrapper. Gather edges of dough together; pinch together securely at the top. Place filled dumplings on wax paper; cover with damp towel.
5. Drop dumplings, 2 or 3 at a time, in a large saucepan of rapidly boiling salted water. Stir gently so dumplings do not stick to pan. Cook 2 to 3 minutes. Remove with slotted spoon; drain; place in serving dish. Pour melted butter over dumplings and serve with sausage and sour cream, if you wish.

Potato Filling: Pare 3 pounds potatoes and cook in boiling salted water until tender; drain. Mash, then beat in ½ teaspoon salt and ¼ teaspoon pepper. Cool to room temperature.

Gnocchi
The Italian word for dumpling. Gnocchi, pronounced NOH-kee, can be made from potatoes, farina, cornmeal or other grain.

Two-Cheese Gnocchi

Bake at 400° for 30 minutes.

Makes 4 servings.

5 cups water
1 teaspoon salt
1 cup enriched farina
2 eggs, beaten
4 ounces Swiss
    cheese, shredded

(1 cup)
¼ teaspoon pepper
¼ cup (½ stick) butter
    or margarine
1 cup grated
    Parmesan cheese

1. Heat water with salt to boiling in a large saucepan; sprinkle in farina and stir until well blended; lower heat; simmer 15 minutes.
2. Remove saucepan from heat; beat in eggs, Swiss cheese and pepper. Return saucepan to heat; cook, stirring constantly, until mixture thickens, about 3 minutes.

3. Pour mixture into a buttered 13 × 9 × 2-inch baking dish; chill 30 minutes or until set.
4. Cut mixture into 1½-inch diamonds and arrange in overlapping pieces in a 2-quart shallow baking dish.
5. Melt butter in a small saucepan; drizzle over gnocchi; top with Parmesan.
6. Bake in a hot oven (400°) for 30 minutes or until tops of gnocchi are golden.

Italian Spinach Dumplings with Cheese Sauce

Makes 4 servings.

2 packages (10 ounces
    each) frozen
    chopped spinach
4 teaspoons salt
½ teaspoon ground
    nutmeg
¼ teaspoon pepper
1 egg, lightly beaten
½ cup ricotta

cheese
6 tablespoons flour
8 cups water
1 tablespoon
    margarine
Cheese Sauce *(recipe
    follows)*
¼ cup grated
    Parmesan cheese

1. Defrost spinach; drain thoroughly, pressing with a spoon to squeeze out all liquid. Chop finely or puree in a blender or food processor.
2. Combine spinach, 1 teaspoon of the salt, nutmeg, pepper, egg and ricotta in a large bowl. Gradually add flour, using enough to make a firm mixture. With floured hands, form mixture into 1-inch balls. Place on a plate. Chill 30 minutes or longer.
3. Combine water, margarine and remaining 3 teaspoons salt in a large saucepan. Bring to boiling. Drop balls gently, several at a time, into water. Cook, uncovered, 8 minutes, or until balls rise to top and are tender. If they stick to bottom of pan, loosen with a spoon.
4. When they are done, lift out with a slotted spoon and keep warm. Pour Cheese Sauce over dumplings. Serve immediately. Sprinkle each serving with grated Parmesan cheese.

Cheese Sauce

Makes about 1½ cups.

3 tablespoons
    margarine
3 tablespoons flour
1½ cups milk
¼ cup grated

Parmesan cheese
¼ teaspoon salt
Pinch pepper
Pinch ground nutmeg

1. Melt margarine in a small saucepan. Blend in flour to form a smooth paste; cook, stirring, over low heat, 2 minutes or until bubbly.
2. Gradually add milk, stirring constantly. Cook over low heat, 5 minutes or until thickened. Add cheese, salt, pepper and nutmeg; reheat.

Gnocchi Parisienne

Make this ahead and refrigerate until ready to bake.
Bake at 350° for 20 minutes.

Makes 4 servings.

1 cup water	**cheese**
¼ cup (½ stick) butter or margarine	**½ teaspoon dry mustard**
¼ teaspoon salt	**4 eggs**
⅛ teaspoon cayenne	**1 tablespoon salt**
1 cup plus 2 tablespoons *sifted* **all-purpose flour**	**Mornay Sauce** *(recipe follows)*
¼ cup freshly grated Parmesan	**2 tablespoons butter or margarine**

1. Combine water, butter, the ¼ teaspoon salt and cayenne in a medium-size saucepan. Bring to boiling.
2. Combine flour, Parmesan cheese and mustard in a small bowl. When liquid is boiling rapidly and butter is melted, dump in flour mixture all at once and, stirring rapidly, continue to stir for 30 seconds or until paste comes away from sides of pan and forms a ball.
3. Add the eggs, 1 at a time, beating until paste is smooth and shiny.
4. Fill a large deep skillet half full with water, add the 1 tablespoon of salt and bring to boiling.
5. With two tablespoons dipped into the hot water, mold dough into egg shapes and drop them into the water. Lower heat so that water just simmers and poach a few at a time for about 15 minutes or until firm, turning each over occasionally with a slotted spoon. Drain on cookie sheet; cover and refrigerate while making sauce.
6. Spread half of the Mornay Sauce in a 2-quart shallow baking dish. Arrange gnocchi in dish; top with remaining sauce.
7. Bake in a moderate oven (350°) for 20 minutes or until sauce is bubbly-hot.
8. Dot with remaining 2 tablespoons butter; place under broiler just until top is glazed and brown.

Mornay Sauce

Makes 3 cups.

2 cups milk	**¼ teaspoon salt**
1 bay leaf	**Dash cayenne**
Slice of onion	**½ cup heavy cream**
A few peppercorns	**½ cup freshly grated Parmesan cheese**
6 tablespoons butter or margarine	
6 tablespoons flour	**½ teaspoon dry mustard**

1. In a small saucepan, heat milk, bay leaf, onion and peppercorns until hot.
2. In a large saucepan, melt butter. Stir in flour, salt and cayenne. Remove from heat; strain the hot milk into it, stirring until mixture is smooth.
3. Stir in cream, Parmesan and mustard; return to

heat and cook over low heat for 3 minutes, stirring frequently.

Quenelle A delicate fish, poultry or meat dumpling bound with eggs, poached in hot liquid, then served with a sauce.

Quenelles of Turkey au Gratin

Makes 4 servings.

1 cup water	**¼ cup (½ stick) butter (for sauce)**
1 teaspoon salt	
¼ cup (½ stick) butter	**6 tablespoons all-purpose flour (for sauce)**
1 cup *sifted* **all-purpose flour**	
3 eggs	**1¼ cups milk**
1 pound ground raw turkey	**½ cup dry vermouth or other dry white wine, heated**
½ teaspoon ground nutmeg	
½ teaspoon salt	**Pinch salt**
½ teaspoon white pepper	**Pinch ground mace**
	Pinch cayenne
2 to 3 tablespoons heavy cream	**½ cup heavy cream**
	Lemon juice
6 cups chicken broth	**¼ cup grated Parmesan cheese**
1 small bay leaf	**Paprika**

1. Bring water to boiling with salt in a saucepan; add ¼ cup butter and when it has melted, remove from heat and stir in flour all at once. Return to low heat and beat until mixture forms a ball and leaves side of pan. Remove from heat.
2. Beat in the eggs, 1 at a time, beating well after each addition. Cool slightly, then stir in ground turkey, nutmeg, salt and white pepper. Beat very well with a wooden spoon or a portable electric mixer. The mixture should be worked to a very smooth, sticky paste. Chill mixture in refrigerator for at least an hour or until you are ready to cook.
3. Before cooking, beat in 3 tablespoons heavy cream, 1 spoonful at a time, until mixture is slightly softer but still stiff enough to be shaped. Using two tablespoons dipped in cold water, or your hands, also dipped in cold water, shape 16 quenelles in ovals or as sausages, approximately 3 inches long and 1 inch in diameter, at the widest point.
4. Pour enough chicken broth into a large skillet to make a 2-inch depth; add bay leaf and bring to boiling. (Use two skillets if you have them.) Add quenelles in a single layer and lower heat to a simmer. Cover. Poach gently for 15 to 20 minutes. Test one quenelle to see if it is firm, opaque and that its juices run clear. When all are done, drain on paper toweling and keep warm. Reserve 1¼ cups liquid for sauce.
5. To make a sauce, melt ¼ cup butter in a saucepan and when bubbling, stir in 6 tablespoons flour. Cook for 2 or 3 minutes, then gradually stir in reserved liquid until smooth with a wire whisk. Stir in milk and wine.

Spaghetti with Meat Sauce, page 611.

Cook until smooth and very thick. Season with salt, mace and cayenne. Stir in 1/2 cup heavy cream until sauce is a little thinner but still thick enough to coat a spoon. Adjust seasonings, adding a little lemon juice, or more wine, to taste.

6. Place quenelles in a single layer in a buttered, shallow baking pan. Cover with sauce. Sprinkle with Parmesan cheese and paprika. Place baking pan 4 inches from broiler. Broil about 10 minutes or until top is brown and sauce is bubbling.

PIES

Pie   A dish of meat, fish, poultry or fruit covered with a crust and baked. The crust is usually a pastry, but a pie can be covered with biscuits, mashed potatoes, crumbs or meringue. Here are recipes for main-dish and dessert pies.

MAIN-DISH PIES

English Pub Pie

Bake at 350° for 1 hour, 40 minutes.

Makes 12 servings.

2 whole chicken breasts (about 12 ounces each)	**Flaky Pastry (*recipe follows*)**
1/2 pound cooked ham, diced	**4 hard-cooked eggs, peeled**
1 can (6 ounces) chopped mushrooms	**1 egg**
	1 tablespoon plus 1 1/2 cups water
1/2 cup chopped fresh parsley	**1/2 teaspoon leaf tarragon, crumbled**
2 teaspoons salt	**1 envelope unflavored gelatin**

1. Bone and skin chicken; dice; reserve skin and bones for step 7.
2. Mix ham and chicken in a large bowl. Fold in mushrooms and liquid, parsley and 1 teaspoon of the salt until well blended.
3. Roll out 3/4 of Flaky Pastry to a 16 × 12-inch rectangle on a lightly floured pastry board. Fit into a 9 × 5 × 3-inch loaf pan, pressing pastry into bottom and sides of pan.
4. Spoon 1/3 of meat mixture into pan; place hard-cooked eggs down center of filling; spoon remaining filling around and on top of eggs.
5. Preheat oven to 350°. Roll out remaining pastry to a 10 × 6-inch rectangle on a lightly floured pastry board. Cut out two 1/2-inch vents near the center of pastry. Arrange pastry over filling; trim to 1/2 inch; turn under and flute edges to make a stand-up rim. Cut pastry trims into leaf and stem shapes. Beat egg with 1 tablespoon water in a cup; brush pastry with egg; arrange pastry trims in design. Brush again with egg wash.
6. Bake in preheated moderate oven (350°) for 1 hour and 40 minutes, brushing with egg after 1 hour, or until pastry is golden and filling bubbles through vents in pastry. Cool in pan.
7. While pie bakes, combine chicken bones and skin, 1 1/2 cups water, remaining salt and tarragon in medium-size saucepan. Heat to boiling; cover saucepan; lower heat; simmer 45 minutes. Strain broth into a 2-cup measure; skim off fat as it rises to the surface. You should have a cup of broth. If not, add water. Chill.
8. After pie is baked, sprinkle gelatin over chilled broth to soften. Pour mixture into a small saucepan; heat until gelatin dissolves. Gradually pour broth through the two vents in pastry. Cool pie on wire rack 1 hour; chill overnight.

Flaky Pastry: Sift 3 cups *sifted* all-purpose flour and 1 teaspoon salt into a large bowl. Cut in 1 cup shortening with a pastry blender until mixture is crumbly. Sprinkle 6 to 8 tablespoons ice cold water over mixture, 1 tablespoon at a time; mix lightly with a fork, just until pastry holds together and leaves the side of the bowl clean. Gather into a ball. Makes enough pastry for one 9 × 5 × 3-inch pan or two-crust 10-inch pie.

Beef and Vegetable Pie

Bake at 400° for 30 minutes.

Makes 6 servings.

1 package piecrust mix	**1 envelope (3/4 ounce) instant brown gravy mix**
1 large onion, chopped (1 cup)	
2 carrots, sliced (1 cup)	**2 tablespoons chopped fresh parsley**
2 cups chopped green cabbage	**1 teaspoon salt**
2 tablespoons butter or margarine	**1/2 teaspoon leaf savory, crumbled**
1 pound ground chuck	**1/4 teaspoon pepper**
1 cup hot water	**1 egg, slightly beaten**

1. Prepare piecrust mix following label directions; chill 30 minutes.
2. Meanwhile, sauté onion, carrots and cabbage in hot butter or margarine in large skillet, stirring often, until tender and slightly browned, about 15 minutes. Remove to a large bowl.
3. In same skillet, sauté meat over high heat, stirring constantly, until it loses its pink color. Lower heat, stir in water; cook and stir to loosen browned bits in pan. Stir in gravy mix, parsley, salt, savory and pepper; cover, simmer 5 minutes; add to vegetables.
4. Preheat oven to 400°. Roll pastry to a 16-inch round on a lightly floured surface. Carefully slide a

(continued)

Pictured opposite (from top): English Pub Pie, page 621; Beef and Vegetable Pie, page 621; Italian Cheese and Vegetable Pie, page 622.

cookie sheet under pastry to within 1 inch from edge of cookie sheet. Spoon meat and vegetable mixture onto pastry half on cookie sheet 2 inches in from edge; fold other half over to make a half circle. Press edges together to seal firmly; turn up and crimp edges. Mix egg with 1 tablespoon water; brush over top of pie. Make a few slits in top for steam to escape.

5. Bake in a preheated hot oven (400°) for 30 minutes or until golden brown. Slide onto a cutting board; cut into slices for serving. Garnish with parsley and tomatoes, if you wish.

Top-Notch Tuna Pie

Bake at 325° for 45 minutes.

Makes 8 servings.

1 1/2 cups uncooked long-grain rice	1 can (16 ounces) whole-kernel corn, drained
4 eggs	3/4 cup milk
1 can (7 ounces) tuna, drained and flaked	1/4 teaspoon salt
6 ounces Swiss cheese, shredded (1 1/2 cups)	1/4 teaspoon pepper
	1/2 teaspoon dried parsley flakes

1. Cook rice following label directions; cool slightly.
2. Beat 2 of the eggs in a large bowl until frothy. Stir in rice. Press rice mixture into buttered 10-inch pie plate to form a crust.
3. Layer in order: tuna, cheese and corn.
4. Beat remaining eggs until frothy in a small bowl. Stir in milk, salt, pepper and parsley. Pour mixture over the layers in pie plate.
5. Bake in a slow oven (325°) for 45 minutes.

Italian Cheese and Vegetable Pie

Bake at 375° for 45 minutes.

Makes 6 servings.

3 tablespoons vegetable or olive oil	tomato sauce
2 medium-size zucchini, sliced thin	1/2 teaspoon leaf oregano, crumbled
2 medium-size onions, sliced thin	Dash pepper
2 1/2 teaspoons salt	1 container (15 ounces) ricotta cheese
1 clove garlic, crushed	4 eggs
3 tablespoons chopped fresh parsley	1 1/2 cups milk
1 can (16 ounces) tomatoes	1 package (8 ounces) refrigerated crescent rolls
1 can (8 ounces)	4 ounces (1/2 package) mozzarella cheese, sliced

1. Heat 2 tablespoons of the oil in large skillet; add zucchini and onions. Sauté, stirring often, until tender, about 10 minutes. Stir in 1 teaspoon of the salt; remove mixture to bowl.

2. In same skillet in remaining oil, sauté garlic and parsley, stirring constantly, 1 minute; add tomatoes, tomato sauce, oregano, 1/2 teaspoon of the salt and the pepper. Cook, stirring occasionally and mashing the tomatoes with a spoon, 15 minutes or until reduced to 2 cups.
3. Beat ricotta cheese, eggs and remaining 1 teaspoon salt in large bowl; gradually beat in milk. Preheat oven to 375°.
4. Line a fluted 10-inch quiche dish or 10-inch pie plate with unrolled and separated crescent rolls, overlapping slightly and pressing edges of dough triangle rolls together. Spread vegetables in bottom of shell; spoon about 1/4 cup tomato sauce over. Set dish on oven shelf, then pour in cheese mixture.
5. Bake in a preheated moderate oven (375°) for 40 minutes or just until set in center. Arrange cheese slices on top of pie; spoon some of the tomato sauce in between slices. Bake 5 minutes longer or until cheese is melted. Garnish with parsley, olives and rolled anchovies, if you wish. Serve in wedges with remaining tomato sauce.

Broccoli, Mushroom and Sweet Pepper Custard Pie

In this pie we've eliminate practically all the cheese and oil, reduced the amount of eggs and substituted skim milk for whole.

Bake at 350° for 25 to 30 minutes.

Makes 6 servings.

1 package (10 ounces) frozen broccoli stalks, thawed	vegetable oil
1/2 cup coarsely chopped sweet green pepper	1/2 cup sliced mushrooms
1/2 cup coarsely chopped sweet red pepper	3/4 cup skim milk
1/2 cup coarsely chopped onion	3 eggs
1 clove garlic, finely chopped	1 teaspoon salt
1 teaspoon olive or	1/4 teaspoon leaf basil, crumbled
	1/8 teaspoon cayenne pepper
	2 tablespoons shredded part-skim milk cheese, such as Swiss

1. Slice broccoli into 1-inch pieces; drain on paper toweling. Arrange in well-greased 9-inch pie plate.
2. Preheat oven to moderate (350°).
3. Sauté green and red peppers, onion and garlic in oil in nonstick skillet over medium to low heat for 3 minutes. Add mushrooms; cook until tender and most of the liquid has evaporated, 2 minutes. Spoon vegetables over broccoli in pie plate.
4. Beat together milk, eggs, salt, basil and cayenne pepper in 2-cup glass measure; pour over vegetables.
5. Bake in preheated moderate oven (350°) for 25 to 30 minutes or until knife inserted near center comes out clean. Sprinkle with cheese. Broil until golden brown. Cool on wire rack 10 minutes before slicing.

From top: Broccoli, Mushroom and Sweet Pepper Custard Pie, page 622; Browned Cabbage and Mushroom Pirog, page 624; Vegetable Pasties, page 624.

Browned Cabbage and Mushroom Pirog

The roasted kasha adds a nutty flavor to these individual pies. Substitute cooked brown rice if you can't find the kasha in the grain or ethnic section of your supermarket or in a specialty food shop.

Bake at 375° for 35 minutes.

Makes 10 servings.

¹/₂ **cup roasted kasha**	**4 hard-cooked eggs,**
1 egg, well beaten	**coarsely chopped**
1 cup chicken broth	**3 tablespoons**
1 large onion, coarsely	**chopped fresh dill**
chopped (1 cup)	OR: **3 teaspoons**
6 tablespoons butter	**dried dillweed**
or margarine	**1 teaspoon salt**
2¹/₂ **cups coarsely**	¹/₄ **teaspoon pepper**
chopped	**2 packages (11 ounces**
mushrooms (about	**each) piecrust mix**
8 ounces)	³/₄ **cup dairy sour**
8 cups finely chopped	**cream**
green cabbage	**1 green onion, finely**
(about 1¹/₂ pounds)	**chopped**

1. Toss kasha with half the beaten egg in small saucepan until grains are well coated. Cook over medium-high heat, stirring constantly, until grains are dry and separate. Gradually stir in the chicken broth. Reduce heat to low; cover and cook 10 minutes or until all liquid is absorbed. Set aside.

2. Sauté the onion in butter in large skillet for 2 minutes. Add mushrooms and sauté 3 minutes more. Add cabbage and sauté 3 minutes more. Add cabbage and sauté 8 to 10 minutes, stirring occasionally (skillet will be quite full), until cabbage is wilted and mixture is lightly browned. Remove from heat. Stir in chopped egg, 2 tablespoons of the chopped dill or 2 teaspoons of the dillweed, the salt, pepper and kasha.

3. Spoon cabbage mixture equally into ten 1-cup aluminum-foil baking tins or casseroles.

4. Prepare 2 packages piecrust mix following label directions. Divide each recipe of pastry into 5 equal portions. Keep all portions wrapped in plastic wrap and refrigerated except one that is being rolled. Roll out one piece of dough on lightly floured surface into circle 1-inch larger than top of baking dish. Cut decorative designs or vents in top for steam to escape.

5. Preheat oven to moderate (375°).

6. Fit pastry over filling. Trim overhang to 1 inch, if necessary; fold under to make a stand-up edge, allowing just enough overlap to grip edge of casserole; flute. Brush top with a little of remaining egg. Repeat with remaining dough and tins.

7. Bake in preheated moderate oven (375°) for 35 minutes or until crust is golden brown. Cool 10 minutes before serving.

8. Meanwhile, combine sour cream, remaining dill or dillweed and green onion in small bowl until well blended and smooth. Serve with pirogs.

Vegetable Pasty

These individual Cornish pies are excellent without the usual beef or pork. Serve with dill pickles and a splash of catsup. Simple, but delicious.

Bake at 400° for 45 minutes.

Makes 6 servings.

1 package (11 ounces) piecrust mix	**and cut into $1/4$-inch cubes (about $3/4$ cup)**
3 medium-size all-purpose potatoes (about 1 pound), pared and cut into $1/4$-inch cubes (about $1^1/4$ cups)	**$3/4$ cup chopped onion**
	$1/4$ cup finely chopped carrot
	$1/2$ teaspoon salt
1 small to medium-size rutabaga ($1/3$ pound), pared	**$1/2$ teaspoon poultry seasoning**
	$1/4$ teaspoon pepper
	2 tablespoons butter

1. Prepare piecrust mix following label directions.
2. Combine potatoes, rutabaga, onion, carrot, salt, poultry seasoning and pepper in medium-size bowl; mix well.
3. Preheat oven to hot (400°).
4. Divide dough into 6 equal portions. Keep all portions wrapped in plastic wrap and refrigerated except one that is being rolled. Roll out each piece of dough on lightly floured board into 8 × 5-inch rectangle.
5. Place about $1/2$ cup of the filling along one-half of one rectangle. Top with 1 teaspoon of the butter. Moisten edges with water. Fold dough in half over filling; press edges firmly together. (Be careful not to tear dough on pointed corners of vegetables; pasties will be very plump with filling.) Trim with scissors to make neat edge. Crimp to make decorative edge. Repeat with remaining dough and filling. Place pasties on large cookie sheet.
6. Bake in preheated hot oven (400°) for 45 minutes or until vegetables are tender and crust is golden brown. (If pasties brown too quickly, cover loosely with foil.)

Onion Pie

Bake at 375° for 35 minutes.

Makes one 10-inch pie.

6 large onions, sliced	**$1^1/2$ cups milk**
$1/4$ cup ($1/2$ stick) butter or margarine	**1 package piecrust mix**
2 tablespoons flour	**2 hard-cooked eggs, sliced**
1 teaspoon salt	
$1/4$ teaspoon pepper	

1. Cook onion slices in boiling salted water to cover in

a large saucepan 10 minutes or just until tender-firm; drain well.
2. While onions cook, melt butter in a medium-size saucepan. Blend in flour, salt and pepper; slowly stir in milk. Cook, stirring constantly, until sauce thickens slightly and bubbles 3 minutes. Remove from heat.
3. Preheat oven to 375°. Prepare piecrust mix following label directions. Roll out $2/3$ to a 14-inch round on lightly floured surface; fit into 10-inch pie plate. Trim overhang to $1/2$ inch.
4. Arrange onions on bottom crust; top with eggs; pour sauce over. Roll out remaining pastry to a 12-inch round; cut several slits near center. Place over filling; pinch edges to seal. Turn edge up and in to seal in juices.
5. Bake in a preheated moderate oven (375°) for 35 minutes or until pastry is golden and juices bubble up near center. Cool on wire rack. Serve warm.

Spanakopita

Spanakopita   A Greek spinach pie with a filling of cooked spinach, feta cheese, eggs and seasonings, baked in a phyllo crust. It is served warm or at room temperature and can also be made into small, triangular appetizers.

Spanakopita

Bake at 375°, then at 350° for 1 hour.

Makes 12 servings.

1 cup (2 sticks) butter or margarine	**2 tablespoons farina (cream of wheat)**
1 bunch green onions, chopped	**$1/2$ cup chopped fresh parsley**
2 packages (10 ounces each) frozen chopped spinach	**$1/2$ cup chopped fresh dill**
	$1/2$ teaspoon salt
6 eggs, lightly beaten	**$1/4$ teaspoon pepper**
8 ounces feta cheese, crumbled	**1 package (16 ounces) frozen phyllo or strudel pastry leaves**
1 container (8 ounces) cottage cheese	

1. Melt butter in small saucepan. Butter a 13 × 9-inch baking dish.
2. Sauté green onions in 2 tablespoons of the butter in a large skillet until tender.
3. Cook spinach in a large saucepan following label directions. Drain, pressing out as much liquid as possible.
4. Combine onions, spinach, eggs, feta cheese, cottage cheese, farina, parsley, dill, salt and pepper in a large bowl.
5. Preheat oven to 375°. Unfold phyllo or strudel leaves and place between damp towels to keep from drying. Remove leaves, one at a time, and place in baking dish; brush each with melted butter. (Cut leaves to fit baking dish, if necessary.) Repeat until there are 6 layers of buttered leaves in dish.

(continued)

Ricotta Pie.

6. Spread spinach mixture evenly over the layers.
7. Butter and stack 8 more phyllo leaves on top of spinach mixture. Mark top leaf lightly in squares with a sharp knife. Cut partially through in square pattern.
8. Place spanakopita in a preheated moderate oven (375°). Immediately lower oven temperature to 350°. Bake about 1 hour or until golden brown and puffed. Cool slightly; cut into squares all the way through.

Ricotta Pie

Bake at 350° for 1 hour, 15 minutes.

Makes 8 servings.

1³/₄ cups *sifted* all-purpose flour	ricotta cheese
¹/₄ teaspoon salt	1 package (8 ounces) smoked mozzarella, cut into ¹/₄-inch cubes
³/₄ cup (1¹/₂ sticks) unsalted butter or margarine	
3 egg yolks, slightly beaten	¹/₄ pound Genoa salami in one piece, cut into ¹/₄-inch cubes
2 to 3 tablespoons ice water	
4 eggs	1 tablespoon grated Parmesan cheese
1 container (15 ounces) whole-milk	¹/₂ teaspoon pepper

1. Sift the flour and salt into a large bowl. Cut in the butter until crumbly. Add the yolks and 2 tablespoons of the water, tossing with a fork. Work the dough until soft enough to gather into a ball; add the additional tablespoon of water, if necessary. Wrap; chill for 1 hour.

2. Beat the eggs and ricotta until smooth. Stir in the mozzarella, salami, Parmesan and pepper.
3. Reserve a third of the dough; cover. Roll the remaining dough on a lightly floured surface into a 12-inch round. Ease into a 9-inch springform pan. Press the dough over the bottom and sides. Prick with a fork. Spoon the filling into the pan.
4. Preheat the oven to moderate (350°).
5. Roll the reserved dough into a 10-inch round. Center on top of the filling. Moisten the edges of the top and bottom crusts with water; pinch together to seal. Set the pan on a cookie sheet.
6. Bake in the preheated moderate oven (350°) for 1 hour and 15 minutes. Cool in the pan on a rack for 35 minutes. Carefully remove the sides. Serve warm.

Greek Chicken Pie

Bake at 400° for 30 minutes.

Makes 8 servings.

1 broiler-fryer (about 3 pounds), cut up	¹/₂ cup (1 stick) butter
1 teaspoon salt	6 tablespoons flour
¹/₄ teaspoon pepper	1 teaspoon salt
3 cups thinly sliced carrots	¹/₄ teaspoon pepper
1¹/₂ cups sliced celery	¹/₂ cup light cream
1 large onion, chopped (1 cup)	2 tablespoons lemon juice
1 package (9 ounces) frozen artichoke hearts	¹/₂ package piecrust mix
	1 egg beaten with 1 tablespoon water

1. Put chicken in large kettle or Dutch oven. Add just enough water to cover. Bring to boiling; skim off foam. Add the 1 teaspoon salt and ¹/₄ teaspoon pepper; lower heat; cover. Simmer 30 minutes or until chicken is tender. Remove chicken from broth to a large bowl; let cool.
2. Add carrots, celery, onion and artichoke hearts to broth. Simmer until tender, 15 minutes. Drain; reserve broth and vegetables. Measure broth; add water to make 3 cups.
3. Skin and bone chicken; cut into bite-size pieces. Add vegetables to chicken.
4. Heat butter in a large saucepan; add flour and remaining salt and pepper. Cook and stir 1 minute. Stir in chicken broth and cream. Cook, stirring constantly, until thickened and bubbly. Stir in lemon juice, chicken and vegetables. Spoon into shallow 2-quart or 11 × 7 × 2-inch baking dish.
5. Preheat oven to 400°. Prepare pie-crust mix following label directions. Roll out on floured surface; cut into ³/₄-inch strips with a pastry wheel. Fit over filling in lattice pattern. Join strips around edge of dish with an edging strip. Pinch to seal; flute. Brush pastry with egg and water.
6. Bake in a preheated hot oven (400°) for 30 minutes or until pastry is golden and filling is bubbly-hot.

Tamale Pie

Spicy corned beef with a cornmeal crust gives this "Tex-Mex" pie a zingy combination of flavors.

Bake at 400° for 1 hour.

Makes 6 servings.

1½ cups yellow
    cornmeal
¾ teaspoon salt
1 cup cold water
3 cups boiling water
2 tablespoons
    vegetable oil
1 medium-size onion,
    chopped (½ cup)
½ cup chopped green
    pepper
1 clove garlic, minced
1 can (12 ounces)
    corned beef*,
    chopped
2 cans (8 ounces

each) tomato sauce
2 to 3 tablespoons
    chili powder
½ to ¾ teaspoon salt
½ teaspoon ground
    cumin
4 ounces Cheddar
    cheese, shredded
    (1 cup)
OR: 6 slices
    American cheese,
    cut into ¼-inch
    pieces
¾ cup pitted ripe
    olives, halved

1. Mix cornmeal, salt and cold water in a medium-size saucepan. Stir in boiling water; bring to boiling; cook over moderate heat, stirring frequently, until mixture is thick, about 3 to 5 minutes. Remove from heat. Cool.
2. Meanwhile, heat oil in large skillet; sauté onion, green pepper and garlic until golden and tender, but not brown.
3. Break up corned beef in skillet; add tomato sauce, chili powder, salt and cumin. Stir over moderate heat until mixture comes to boiling. Remove from heat; add cheese and olives; stir until cheese is melted.
4. Line the sides, but not the bottom, of a buttered, 2-quart, deep ovenproof casserole with ¾ of the cornmeal mixture using a metal spatula. (Dip spatula in cold water to make spreading easier.)
5. Spoon corned beef mixture into center of casserole; spoon remaining cornmeal around edges on top of casserole, leaving a 2- to 3-inch center. Using a wet metal spatula, spread cornmeal smoothly over top and towards edges of casserole, sealing completely.
6. Bake in a hot oven (400°) for 1 hour or until lightly browned on top and bubbling in the middle. Let stand 15 minutes before serving. Garnish with green pepper rings, if you wish.

For the corned beef, substitute 1 can (16 ounces) chili with beans and 1 can (16 ounces) red kidney beans, drained, and use only 1 can tomato sauce.

Greek Chick-Pea Salad, page 696; Greek Chicken Pie, page 626.

Hamburger-Vegetable Pie

Bake at 450° for 15 minutes.

Makes 6 servings.

1 medium-size onion, chopped (1/2 cup)	1 teaspoon dried parsley flakes
1 to 2 cloves garlic, minced	1/2 teaspoon leaf rosemary, crumbled
1 tablespoon vegetable oil	1 can (16 ounces) whole-kernel corn, drained
1 1/2 pounds lean ground beef	1 package (10 ounces) frozen green peas
1 can (16 ounces) tomatoes	2 packages (4.5 ounces each) refrigerated buttermilk biscuits
1 can (6 ounces) tomato paste	
2 teaspoons salt	
1/4 teaspoon pepper	

1. Sauté onion and garlic in oil in a large skillet until tender, about 5 minutes. Add beef and cook, stirring occasionally with fork, until brown. Drain off excess fat. Add tomatoes, tomato paste, salt, pepper, parsley flakes and rosemary. Bring to boiling; lower heat; simmer 15 minutes.
2. Preheat oven to 450°. Remove skillet from heat. Stir in corn and peas; heat thoroughly. Spoon into a 3-quart shallow baking dish. Arrange refrigerated biscuits over top.
3. Bake in a preheated very hot oven (450°) for 15 minutes or until biscuits are golden brown. Let stand 10 minutes before serving.

Empanada Pies

Bake at 450° then at 400° for 30 minutes.

Makes 8 pies.

3/4 pound ground chuck	1/4 cup raisins
2 to 3 tablespoons chili powder	1/4 cup blanched almonds, chopped
2 tablespoons butter or margarine	1 egg yolk, lightly beaten
1 small onion, minced (1/4 cup)	1 package (17 1/4 ounces) pre-rolled frozen puff pastry
1/4 teaspoon salt	
1/8 teaspoon pepper	1 egg white, lightly beaten
2 tablespoons catsup	

1. Cook and stir chuck in a heavy skillet until no pink remains. Stir in chili powder; cook 1 minute. Transfer meat mixture to a colander to drain off all fat and cool to room temperature. Wipe skillet clean with paper toweling.
2. Melt butter in same skillet; sauté onion until tender, about 3 minutes; cool. Combine drained beef and onion in a medium-size bowl. Stir in salt, pepper, catsup, raisins, almonds and egg yolk. Refrigerate until cold.

3. Thaw frozen pastry sheets 20 minutes at room temperature or until pliable, but still very cold. Roll out each sheet on a lightly floured surface to a 13-inch square; divide into 4 equal quarters; repeat with second sheet.
4. Divide filling equally among the 8 pastry squares, leaving a 1-inch border of uncovered pastry on all sides. Brush borders generously with some of the beaten egg white. Fold squares diagonally in half to form triangles. Press edges firmly together, then press with tines of fork to seal securely. Brush tops with egg white. Pierce each top in center with small paring knife to allow steam to escape. Arrange pies 1 inch apart on cookie sheets. Place in freezer while oven heats.
5. Preheat oven to very hot (450°). Place pies in oven. Immediately lower temperature to hot (400°). Bake pies for 30 minutes.

Spicy Green Tomato Pie

Bake at 425° for 15 minutes, then at 350° for 45 minutes.

Makes one 9-inch pie.

8 medium-size green tomatoes	1/2 cup light corn syrup
3/4 cup firmly packed light brown sugar	1 tablespoon lemon juice
1/3 cup cornstarch	1 package piecrust mix
1 1/2 teaspoons ground cinnamon	1 tablespoon butter
1 teaspoon ground nutmeg	Milk
1/4 teaspoon salt	Sugar

1. Drop tomatoes, 3 or 4 at a time, into boiling water; leave 3 minutes or until skin is loosened. Lift out with slotted spoon; dip in cold water. Pat dry with paper toweling; peel, core and thinly slice (6 cups).
2. Combine sugar, cornstarch, cinnamon, nutmeg and salt in large bowl; mix well. Stir in corn syrup and lemon juice. Add tomatoes and gently stir to coat thoroughly. Let stand while preparing piecrust.
3. Preheat oven to 425°. Prepare piecrust following label directions. Roll out half the pastry to a 12-inch round on a lightly floured surface; fit into a 9-inch pie plate. Trim overhang to 1/2 inch. Roll out remaining pastry to an 11-inch round; cut small slits near center for steam to escape.
4. Spoon filling into pastry-lined pie plate, using as much of the liquid as will fit into the pie shell; dot with butter. Fit top pastry over pie; trim overhang to 1/2 inch; turn edge under, flush with rim, and flute edge. Brush top with milk; sprinkle with sugar.
5. Bake in preheated hot oven (425°) for 15 minutes. Lower oven temperature to moderate (350°); cover top of pie with foil and place foil on rack below pie to catch any juices. Continue baking 45 minutes or until pastry is golden and juices bubble in air vents. Remove foil for last 15 minutes if crust is not browning enough. Cool pie on wire rack before serving.

DESSERT PIES

Strawberry-Rhubarb Cream Pie

Bake crust at 375° for 8 to 10 minutes.

Makes 8 servings.

Gingersnap Crust:
1½ cups ground gingersnap cookie crumbs (about 26 gingersnaps)
2 tablespoons sugar
¼ cup melted butter or margarine

Filling:
1 package (16 ounces) frozen rhubarb (about 3 cups)
OR: 1 pound fresh rhubarb, trimmed and cut into 1-inch pieces

1 cup strawberries, washed, hulled
¾ cup plus 2 tablespoons sugar
3 slices (⅛-inch thick) gingerroot
2 envelopes unflavored gelatin
⅓ cup cold water
3 egg whites
½ cup heavy cream
½ teaspoon vanilla
Garnish (optional):
½ cup heavy cream, whipped
Fresh strawberries
Fresh mint leaves

1. Preheat the oven to moderate (375°).

2. Gingersnap Crust: Combine gingersnap crumbs and sugar in small bowl. Stir in melted butter until well blended. Press crumbs evenly over bottom and sides of 9-inch pie plate.

3. Bake in preheated moderate oven (375°) for 8 to 10 minutes. Cool on wire rack. Refrigerate until ready to fill.

4. Filling: Combine rhubarb, strawberries, 1/2 cup of the sugar and gingerroot in medium-size saucepan. Cook over medium heat, stirring occasionally, until fruit is well cooked, about 15 minutes. Remove from heat. Remove gingerroot.

5. Meanwhile, sprinkle gelatin over cold water in measuring cup; let stand to soften, about 5 minutes.

6. Add softened gelatin to hot rhubarb mixture, stirring until gelatin is completely dissolved, about 1 minute. Blend mixture in blender or food processor just until smooth. Pour into bowl. Place bowl in larger bowl of ice water. Chill, stirring occasionally, until mixture is partially set; mixture will mound when dropped from spoon. Remove from ice water and set aside.

7. Beat egg whites in small bowl until soft peaks form. Gradually add 1/4 cup of the sugar, beating until stiff, shiny peaks form.

8. Beat cream, the 2 tablespoons sugar and vanilla in small bowl until stiff.

(continued)

Strawberry-Rhubarb Cream Pie.

9. Gently fold egg whites and whipped cream into fruit mixture. Mound into pie crust. Refrigerate for 1 to 2 hours or until set. Garnish with whipped cream, strawberries and mint leaves, if you wish.

Frozen Orange 'n' Cream Pie

Ice cream and a store-bought chocolate piecrust are the beginnings for this frosty pie.

Makes 8 servings.

1 quart vanilla ice cream	**4 orange sections**
1 package (6 ounces) chocolate-flavored ready-to-use piecrust	**1 square (1 ounce, semisweet chocolate, melted Pressurized whipped cream**

1. Soften the ice cream in a chilled large bowl. Carefully spoon into the pie shell, spreading evenly with a metal spatula. Cover the ice cream with plastic wrap; freeze the pie until solid.
2. Dip one end of each orange section into the melted chocolate. Arrange on the cookie sheet. Refrigerate for 30 minutes or until the chocolate is set.
3. To serve, carefully run a sharp knife under the dipped orange section to loosen from the cookie sheet. Garnish the pie with the whipped cream and orange sections.

Note: To remove the piecrust to serving dish, remove the plastic cover from the pie and set aside. Freeze the crust in its aluminum foil pan for several hours. Carefully turn back the sides of the foil pan; lift the crust from the pan and set in the plastic cover. Refreeze for several hours or until very firm. Fill as directed in the above recipe.

Luscious Lime Chiffon Pie

Makes one 9-inch pie.

14 to 15 shortbread cookies	**4 eggs, separated**
2 tablespoons butter or margarine	**1 cup sugar**
1/2 cup chopped pecans or walnuts	**1 tablespoon grated lime rind**
1 envelope unflavored gelatin	**1/2 cup lime juice**
1/4 cup cold water	**Green food coloring (*optional*)**
	1/2 cup heavy cream, whipped

1. Crush cookies in a plastic bag with rolling pin.* (Makes about 1 cup.) Melt butter in a medium-size heavy skillet; stir in pecans and cookie crumbs; stir over low heat 1 minute. Press firmly over bottom and side of a 9-inch pie plate. Chill piecrust while preparing filling.
2. Sprinkle gelatin over water in a cup; let soften 5 minutes. Set cup in pan of simmering water, stirring

often, until gelatin is completely dissolved. Remove from heat.
3. Beat egg yolks with 1/2 cup of the sugar until very light and fluffy in a large bowl; stir in lime rind, lime juice and gelatin. Place bowl in pan of ice water to chill; stir often until mixture begins to thicken. Tint mixture a pale green with a few drops of green food coloring, if you wish.
4. While gelatin mixture chills, beat egg whites until foamy-white; gradually beat in remaining sugar until meringue stands in soft peaks.
5. Fold whipped cream, then meringue into gelatin mixture until no streaks of white remain. Spoon into chilled piecrust. Chill 4 hours or until filling is firm.
6. Garnish with lime slices and sprigs of mint, if you wish.
* *Cookies may be whirled in blender. The crumbs will be much finer and the crust different in texture.*

Strawberry Chiffon Pie

Bake at 350° for 8 minutes.

Makes 8 servings.

1 1/3 cups crushed vanilla wafers	**1 pint strawberries, washed, hulled and pureed**
1/4 cup (1/2 stick) butter or margarine, melted	**2 egg whites**
2 tablespoons sugar	**1/4 cup sugar**
1 envelope unflavored gelatin	**1/2 cup heavy cream, whipped**
1/4 cup water	**14 whole vanilla wafers**

1. Preheat oven to 350°.
2. Mix vanilla wafer crumbs with butter and sugar until thoroughly blended. Press firmly over bottom and up side of 9-inch pie plate to form a crust.
3. Bake crust in a preheated moderate oven (350°) for 8 minutes. Remove from oven; let cool completely on a wire rack.
4. Sprinkle gelatin over water in a small saucepan; let stand 5 minutes to soften. Heat over low heat, stirring

Frozen Orange 'n' Cream Pie.

Chocolate Chiffon Pie.

constantly, until gelatin dissolves. Stir into pureed berries; chill until mixture is almost set.

5. Beat egg whites in a small bowl with electric mixer at high speed until soft peaks form. Gradually add sugar, beating constantly until whites are stiff and glossy. Fold whites and whipped cream into pureed strawberry mixture.

6. Pour filling into cooled crust. Insert whole vanilla wafers around edge of filling to garnish. Chill 4 hours or until set.

Chocolate Chiffon Pie

Makes 8 servings.

¹/₄ cup (¹/₂ stick) butter or margarine	**unsweetened chocolate**
2 cans (3¹/₂ ounces each) flaked coconut, toasted	**6 eggs, separated**
	2 teaspoons vanilla
	¹/₂ teaspoon cream of tartar
3 envelopes unflavored gelatin	
2 cups sugar	**1 cup heavy cream, whipped**
1 teaspoon salt	**Maraschino cherries and candies (optional)**
2²/₃ cups water	
4 squares	

1. Melt butter in a medium-size saucepan. Stir in coconut; remove from heat. Press mixture against side and bottom of 9-inch pie plate. Refrigerate.

2. Combine gelatin, 1 cup of the sugar, the salt, water and chocolate in a saucepan. Place over low heat until chocolate melts and sugar dissolves. Remove from the heat.

3. Beat yolks slightly in a medium-size bowl. Stir a little hot chocolate mixture into yolks; return to the saucepan. Heat, stirring occasionally, just until boiling. Transfer to bowl; cool over ice water, stirring occasionally, until mixture mounds. Add vanilla.

4. Beat egg whites and cream of tartar in a large bowl until foamy. Gradually beat in remaining 1 cup sugar until meringue forms stiff glossy peaks; do not underbeat. Fold meringue into chocolate mixture; chill briefly. Mound into coconut shell. Refrigerate until firm, about 4 hours.

5. Garnish with whipped cream, and maraschino cherries and candies, if you wish.

Shoofly Pie

Bake at 350° for 30 minutes.

Makes one 9-inch pie.

1¹/₂ cups *sifted* all-purpose flour	**¹/₄ teaspoon salt**
1 cup firmly packed light or dark brown sugar	**¹/₂ teaspoon baking soda**
	²/₃ cup hot water
	²/₃ cup dark molasses
¹/₂ cup (1 stick) butter or margarine	**1 unbaked 9-inch pastry shell**

1. Combine the flour, brown sugar, butter or margarine and salt and rub the mixture between the hands to form crumbs. Preheat oven to 350°.

2. Dissolve the baking soda in the water and combine with molasses. Pour into pastry shell. Sprinkle evenly with crumbs.

3. Bake in a preheated moderate oven (350°) for 30 to 40 minutes or until filling is set. Cool on wire rack.

Black Walnut Chess Pie

Bake at 375° for 45 minutes.

Makes one 7½-inch pie.

1 unbaked 7½-inch pastry shell
½ cup (1 stick) butter, softened
1 cup sugar
3 tablespoons flour
⅛ teaspoon salt

3 egg yolks
1 small can evaporated milk (⅔ cup)
1 teaspoon vanilla
½ cup chopped black walnuts

1. Prepare pastry shell; chill. Preheat oven to 375°. Beat butter and sugar in a medium-size bowl until well mixed. Add flour, salt, egg yolks and evaporated milk. Beat with rotary beater until well mixed. Stir in vanilla and walnuts. Pour into unbaked shell.
2. Bake on lower shelf of a preheated moderate oven (375°) for 45 minutes or until center is almost set but still soft. Cool thoroughly on wire rack.

Deep-Dish Apple Pie

A deep layer of juicy, lightly spiced apples topped with a golden-crisp pastry crust.

Bake at 425° for 45 minutes.

Makes one 10-inch pie.

10 medium-size apples (McIntosh, Granny Smith), pared, quartered, cored and sliced (10 cups)
⅓ cup firmly packed light brown sugar
⅓ cup granulated sugar
3 tablespoons flour
1 teaspoon ground cinnamon

¼ teaspoon ground cloves
¼ teaspoon ground allspice
1 package piecrust mix
2 tablespoons butter or margarine
Water
1 tablespoon granulated sugar

1. Combine apples, brown sugar, the ⅓ cup granulated sugar, flour, cinnamon, cloves and allspice in a large bowl; toss lightly to mix. Let stand while making pastry.
2. Prepare piecrust mix following label directions. Roll out on a lightly floured surface to a 12-inch round. Cut several slits near center to let steam escape.
3. Preheat oven to 425°. Spoon apple mixture into a 10-deep pie plate; dot with butter. Cover with pastry; fold edges under, flush with sides of dish. (Pastry should be inside dish.) Pinch to make a stand-up edge; flute. Brush lightly with water; sprinkle with remaining 1 tablespoon of sugar.
4. Bake in a preheated hot oven (425°) for 45 minutes or until pastry is golden and juices bubble up. (Place a piece of aluminum foil on rack under pie to catch any juices that may run over.) Cool at least 1 hour. Serve in individual bowls; pass sour cream, or serve with softened vanilla ice cream.

Amaretto-Cherry Cheese Pie

Bake at 350° for 40 minutes.

Makes 8 servings.

2 packages (8 ounces each) cream cheese
1 can (12 ounces) almond cake filling
3 eggs
¼ teaspoon salt
2 tablespoons amaretto liqueur

¼ teaspoon almond extract
¼ cup sugar
4 tablespoons slivered or sliced blanched almonds
1 can (21 ounces) cherry pie filling

1. Preheat oven to 350°.
2. Beat cream cheese in a medium-size bowl with electric mixer until smooth and fluffy. Beat in almond filling, eggs, salt, liqueur and almond extract until mixture is well blended. Pour mixture into a 9-inch pie plate.
3. Bake in center of a preheated moderate oven (350°) for 10 minutes.
4. Blend sugar and 2 tablespoons of the almonds in a cup; sprinkle over top of pie. Continue baking 30 minutes longer or until pie is puffed and golden. (Filling will sink as it cools.) Remove pie to wire rack; cool. Spoon cherry pie filling over baked pie; top with remaining almonds.

Virginia Pecan Pie

Bake at 350° for 45 minutes.

Makes one 9-inch pie.

½ package piecrust mix
4 eggs
1 cup sugar
¼ cup all-purpose flour

½ teaspoon salt
1½ cups dark corn syrup
1 teaspoon vanilla
1 cup pecan halves

1. Prepare piecrust mix for a single crust, following label directions. Roll out to a 13-inch round on a lightly floured board; fit into a 9-inch pie plate. Trim overhang to 1 inch; turn under, flush with rim; flute to make a stand-up edge. Preheat oven to 350°.
2. Beat eggs slightly in a medium-size bowl. Stir in sugar, flour, salt, corn syrup and vanilla. Pour into prepared shell; arrange pecan halves in pattern on top. Or, chop pecans coarsely; sprinkle into shell before adding filling.
3. Bake in a preheated moderate oven (350°) for 45 minutes or until center is almost set but still soft. (Do not overbake, for filling will set as it cools.) Cool on wire rack. Serve with whipped cream, if you wish.

Pictured opposite:
Virginia Pecan Pie.

Caramel Custard Pear Pie

Bake at 400° for 45 minutes.

Makes one 9-inch pie.

1/2 **package piecrust mix**
4 **pears (about 2 pounds)**
1 **tablespoon lemon juice**
1 **tablespoon coarsely shredded lemon rind**
2 **teaspoons finely**

chopped preserved ginger (in syrup)
1/2 **cup firmly packed light brown sugar**
2 **eggs**
1 **cup light cream or half-and-half**
1/4 **cup granulated sugar**

1. Prepare piecrust mix following label directions. Roll out on lightly floured surface to a 12-inch round; fit into a 9-inch pie plate. Turn edge under; pinch to make stand-up edge; flute or make rope edge.
2. Preheat oven to 400°. Peel pears, quarter, core and cut into eighths. Toss pear pieces with lemon juice in large bowl. Arrange, petal fashion, starting at outside edge, in 2 circles in bottom of pie shell. Sprinkle lemon rind, ginger and brown sugar evenly over pears; cover loosely with foil.
3. Bake in a preheated hot oven (400°) for 30 minutes.
4. Beat eggs slightly in small bowl; beat in cream; pour over pears.
5. Continue baking 15 minutes or until custard is almost set in center. Cool on wire rack 2 hours before serving.
6. Shortly before serving, melt granulated sugar in small heavy skillet; continue heating until mixture is light brown; cool slightly. Drizzle from the tip of a spoon in a back-and-forth motion over pie. If you wish to make the "spun-sugar" top, let the last tablespoon of syrup cool until syrupy thick; wave the spoon in a circular motion over center of pie to "spin" sugar in threads. If syrup hardens, place over low heat.

Caramel Custard Pear Pie.

Maple Pecan Pie

Thrifty New Englanders used butternuts as a substitute for pecans.

Bake at 375° for 15 minutes, then at 350° for 25 minutes.

Makes one 9-inch pie.

4 **eggs**
2/3 **cup sugar**
1/2 **teaspoon salt**
6 **tablespoons butter or margarine, melted**

1 **cup maple or maple-blended syrup**
1 **to 1 1/2 cups pecan halves**
1 **unbaked 9-inch pastry shell, chilled**

1. Beat eggs slightly in medium-size bowl; blend in sugar, salt, butter and syrup. Preheat oven to 375°.
2. Place pecans in pastry shell (reserve a few to arrange on top, if you wish). Pour in syrup mixture.
3. Bake in a preheated moderate oven (375°) for 15 minutes; lower oven temperature to 350°. Bake 25 minutes longer or until center is almost set but still soft. (Do not overbake, as filling will set as it cools.) Cool on wire rack. Serve with whipped cream, if you wish.

Lemon Sponge Pie

This Amish specialty from Pennsylvania has a layer of lemon custard topped with lemon sponge cake.

Bake at 350° for 35 minutes.

Makes 6 servings.

1/2 **package (11 ounces) pie crust mix**
4 **eggs, separated**
2/3 **cup sugar**
2 **tablespoons all-purpose flour**
1 **tablespoon grated lemon rind**

1/3 **cup lemon juice**
2/3 **cup milk**
2 **tablespoons butter or margarine, melted**
Whipped cream and lemon slices *(optional)*

1. Prepare the pie crust mix, following label directions for a 9-inch pastry shell with a high fluted edge; chill.
2. Preheat the oven to moderate (350°).
3. Beat egg whites in a large bowl until foamy. Add 2 tablespoons of the sugar slowly, beating until meringue forms soft peaks.
4. Beat egg yolks and the remaining sugar in a medium-size bowl until thick and light. Beat in flour, lemon rind and juice, milk and butter until smooth. Fold into meringue until no streaks of white remain. Pour into the pastry shell.
5. Bake in the preheated moderate oven (350°) for 35 minutes, or until top is golden brown. Do not overbake. Cool on a wire rack. Serve warm or chilled. Garnish with whipped cream and lemon slices, if you wish. Refrigerate leftovers.

Spiced Raisin Pie (lattice-topped), page 636; Lemon Sponge Pie, page 634; Green Applie Pie, page 635.

Green Apple Pie

The original English ancestor of this pie was the Marlborough Pie, traditionally made with applesauce, as apples were dried for long keeping over the winter. This version departs from the traditional by layering tender apple slices with creamy lemon custard.

Bake at 400° for 15 minutes; then at 350° for 30 minutes.

Makes 6 servings.

3 medium-size Granny Smith or Greening apples
¹/₄ cup apple juice or cider
3 tablespoons sugar
1 package (11 ounces) pie crust mix
3 eggs
²/₃ cup sugar
¹/₂ teaspoon ground cinnamon

1 tablespoon lemon juice
1 cup light cream or half-and-half
2 tablespoons butter or margarine, melted
1 tablespoon milk
2 tablespoons sugar
Whipped cream and apple slices (optional)

1. Pare, quarter and core apples; cut into very thin slices. Combine with apple juice and the 3 tablespoons sugar in a large saucepan. Cook, gently stirring occasionally, until apple slices are translucent and just tender, about 5 minutes.
2. Preheat the oven to hot (400°).
3. Prepare the pie crust mix following label directions for a 9-inch pastry shell with a high fluted edge. Roll out the remaining half of pastry; cut out 6 large "leaves." Mark each "leaf" with the back of a knife to simulate veins; reserve.
4. Beat eggs in a large bowl until foamy. Stir in apple slices and any remaining syrup, the ²/₃ cup sugar, the cinnamon, lemon juice, cream and butter. Pour the filling into the pastry shell. Brush the pastry leaves with milk; sprinkle with the 2 tablespoons sugar. Arrange on filling, like spokes in a wheel. (Or, you may roll out the pastry, cut vents, and cover pie completely.)
5. Bake in the preheated hot oven (400°) for 15 minutes. Lower the oven temperature to moderate (350°) and continue baking 30 minutes longer. Filling may be a little soft in the center but will set as it cools. Cool on a wire rack. Garnish with whipped cream and apple slices, if you wish. Serve at room temperature. Keep any leftovers refrigerated.

Spiced Raisin Pie

Akin to the Pennsylvania Dutch "Rosina Boi," or, with the addition of chopped nuts, sometimes known as "Funeral Pie." The latter was customarily brought as a gift of food to a bereaved family.

Bake at 425° for 40 minutes.

Makes 6 servings.

1 package (12 ounces) seedless raisins	cinnamon
1 cup firmly packed light brown sugar	2 tablespoons cornstarch
1/2 teaspoon salt	1/4 cup lemon juice
2 cups water	2 tablespoons water
2 tablespoons butter or margarine	1 package (11 ounces) pie crust mix
1 tablespoon grated lemon rind	1 egg, beaten
1/2 teaspoon ground	Vanilla ice cream *(optional)*

1. Combine raisins, sugar, salt, the 2 cups water and butter in a large saucepan. Bring to boiling; lower heat slightly. Cook, stirring occasionally, for 5 minutes. Stir in lemon rind and cinnamon. Remove from the heat.
2. Blend cornstarch with lemon juice and 2 tablespoons water in small bowl until smooth; stir into the raisin mixture. Cook, stirring constantly, until the mixture thickens and bubbles, 1 minute.
3. Preheat the oven to hot (425°).
4. Prepare the pie crust mix, following directions for a 9-inch double-crust pie. Line a 9-inch pie plate with pastry; spoon in the raisin filling.
5. Cut top crust into 1/2-inch strips. Weave over filling in a lattice design. Trim overhang to 1 inch; fold under, flush with rim. Pinch to make a stand-up edge; flute.
6. Brush beaten egg wash over the pastry for a shiny crust.
7. Bake in the preheated hot oven (425°) for 40 minutes, or until juices bubble up and pastry is golden brown. Cool on a wire rack. Serve warm with scoops of vanilla ice cream, if you wish.

Banana Cream Pie

Creamy-smooth, and oh, so delicious!

Makes one 9-inch pie.

1/2 package piecrust mix	1/4 teaspoon salt
2/3 cup sugar	3 cups milk
3 tablespoons flour	2 teaspoons vanilla
2 tablespoons cornstarch	3 medium-size ripe bananas
	1 cup heavy cream

1. Prepare piecrust mix following label directions for a baked pastry shell.
2. Combine sugar, flour, cornstarch and salt in a large saucepan. Stir in milk slowly.
3. Cook, stirring constantly, over moderate heat, until mixture thickens and bubbles. Continue cooking and stirring until mixture is very thick, about 6 minutes longer.
4. Beat eggs in a medium-size bowl until frothy. Stir in half of the cooked mixture until blended. Return to saucepan, blending in mixture. Cook 2 minutes more over low heat, stirring constantly.
5. Remove from heat; stir in vanilla. Place a piece of plastic wrap directly on surface; cool.
6. Peel and slice bananas into pie shell. Pour cooled cream filling over bananas; chill several hours. Whip cream in a medium-size bowl until stiff. Spoon over top of pie.

Chocolate Mousse Pie

A unique pie that uses part of the mixture to form its shell.

Bake at 350° for 25 minutes.

Makes one 9-inch pie.

Packaged bread crumbs	**2/3 cup sugar**
8 squares semisweet chocolate	**1 teaspoon vanilla**
1/4 cup boiling water	**1/8 teaspoon salt**
8 eggs, separated (whites should be at room temperature)	**1/2 cup cherry preserves**
	1 cup heavy cream, whipped

1. Grease a 9-inch pie plate; dust with bread crumbs.
2. Place chocolate in top of double boiler over hot, not boiling, water. Add boiling water. Cook over low heat, stirring occasionally, until chocolate is almost melted. Remove from heat and continue to stir until smooth. Cool slightly.
3. Beat egg yolks in small bowl with electric mixer at high speed until thick and pale lemon-colored, about 5 minutes. Gradually add sugar; continue beating 5 minutes longer until very thick. Blend in vanilla and chocolate.
4. Preheat oven to 350°. Beat egg whites and salt in large bowl with clean beaters until stiff but not dry. Gradually fold half the whites into chocolate mixture, then fold chocolate into remaining whites, folding only until no streaks of white remain. Spoon part of mousse mixture into prepared pie plate so it just comes level with edge of plate.
5. Bake in a preheated moderate oven (350°) for 25 minutes. Turn off oven heat and leave pie in oven 5 minutes longer. Remove and cool on wire rack 2 hours. As pie cools, mixture will form a shell.
6. Cover and refrigerate remaining uncooked mousse. When the shell has cooled completely, spread cherry preserves over bottom; fill with chilled mousse; chill 2 to 3 hours. Pipe cream through pastry bag around edge. Garnish with chocolate curls and maraschino cherries, if you wish.

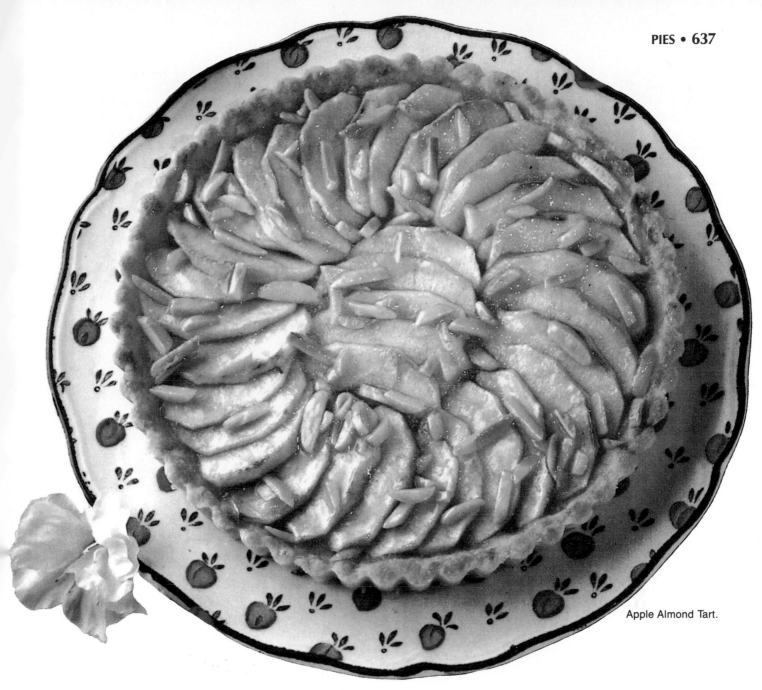

Apple Almond Tart.

Apple-Almond Tart

Bake at 350° for 10 minutes, and then for 35 minutes.
Makes 6 servings.

1¼ cups *sifted* all-
 purpose flour
¼ cup slivered
 blanched almonds,
 toasted and ground
⅛ teaspoon salt
¼ cup sugar
½ cup (1 stick) cold
 unsalted butter
2 egg yolks, lightly
 beaten
1 teaspoon vanilla

4 Granny Smith or
 other tart apples
 (about 1½ pounds)
½ cup sugar
1 tablespoon lemon
 juice
2 tablespoons water
¼ cup slivered
 blanched almonds
2 tablespoons apple
 jelly

1. Combine flour, ground almonds, salt and the ¼ cup sugar in a medium-size bowl. Cut in butter with a pastry blender until mixture is crumbly. Stir in egg yolks and vanilla until blended. Gather dough into a ball. Flatten dough and press into a 9-inch tart pan with removable bottom. Chill 30 minutes. Prick bottom of shell with fork. Preheat oven to 350°.
2. Bake in a preheated moderate oven (350°) for 10 minutes. Remove from oven to wire rack.
3. Pare, core and cut apples into slices. Cook 2 cups of the slices, ¼ cup of the sugar, lemon juice and water in a medium-size saucepan, stirring occasionally, until apples are soft, about 20 minutes. Beat with a spoon; cool. Spread apple sauce over bottom of pastry shell.
4. Toss remaining apple slices with remaining ¼ cup sugar. Arrange slices on top of the apple sauce. Sprinkle with slivered almonds.
5. Bake in a moderate oven (350°) for 35 minutes, or until apples are tender.

(continued)

Apricot-Prune Lattice Pie, page 639.

6. Place tart under broiler with top 3 to 4 inches from heat until apples are lightly browned. Remove to wire rack. Melt apple jelly in a small saucepan over low heat; brush over top of slices to glaze. Cool completely.

Nesselrode The foods created by the French chef of Count Karl Robert Nesselrode, a Russian count who lived from 1780 to 1862 and loved good eating. The most famous dish created and named in his honor was a dessert using chestnut pieces, candied peel, cherries, raisins and currants flavored with maraschino liqueur and mixed with cream, then frozen in a mold. Today, Nesselrode sauces are commercially bottled containing candied fruits and peel in a heavy syrup. Use them for desserts.

Nesselrode Pie

Bake at 375° for 8 minutes.
Makes one 9-inch pie.

**1¼ cups vanilla wafer
or shortbread
cookie crumbs**
**2 tablespoons sugar
(for crust)**
**3 tablespoons butter
or margarine,
melted**
¼ cup rum or brandy
**½ cup mixed candied
fruits**
¼ cup raisins

**1 jar (10 ounces)
marrons (chestnuts)
in syrup**
**1 envelope unflavored
gelatin**
¼ cup cold water
4 eggs, separated
**⅔ cup sugar (for
filling)**
¼ teaspoon salt
**½ cup heavy cream,
whipped**

1. Preheat oven to 375°. Combine crumbs, the 2 tablespoons sugar and butter in a small bowl; press firmly over bottom and side of a buttered 9-inch pie plate.
2. Bake in a preheated moderate oven (375°) for 8 minutes or until set. Cool completely on wire rack.
3. Pour rum over candied fruits and raisins in a small bowl; let stand 30 minutes. Drain marrons; reserve 3 or 4 for garnish; chop remaining coarsely.
4. Sprinkle gelatin over water in a 1-cup measure. Let stand 5 minutes to soften; place cup in pan of simmering water until gelatin dissolves; remove from heat.
5. Combine egg yolks, ⅓ cup of the remaining sugar and the salt in a small bowl. Beat with electric mixer on high speed until very light, about 5 minutes.
6. Combine fruit mixture with gelatin; fold into yolk mixture along with chopped marrons. Chill until mixture is thick enough to mound.
7. Meanwhile, with clean beaters, beat egg whites until foamy-white in large bowl. Gradually beat in remaining sugar; continue beating until meringue forms soft peaks. Fold in yolk mixture and whipped cream. Spoon into prepared shell, piling high. (If mixture is too soft, chill briefly.)
8. Chill at least 4 hours. Decorate with additional whipped cream and reserved marrons.

Lemon Meringue Pie

Bake at 350° for 15 minutes.
Makes one 9-inch pie.

**½ package piecrust
mix**
**1½ cups sugar (for
filling)**
½ cup cornstarch
¼ teaspoon salt
2½ cups water
4 eggs, separated

3 tablespoons butter
**1 tablespoon grated
lemon rind**
½ cup lemon juice
**¼ teaspoon cream of
tartar**
**½ cup sugar (for
meringue)**

1. Prepare piecrust mix; fit into a 9-inch pie plate

making a high stand-up edge. Prick shell all over with a fork. Bake following label directions. Cool.
2. Combine the 1½ cups sugar, cornstarch and salt in a large saucepan; gradually stir in water.
3. Cook over medium heat, stirring constantly, until mixture thickens and boils. Cook 1 minute; remove from heat.
4. Beat egg yolks slightly in a small bowl; slowly blend in about ½ cup of the hot cornstarch mixture; stir back into remaining mixture in saucepan. Cook over low heat, stirring constantly, 2 minutes. (Do not overcook.)
5. Stir in butter, lemon rind and juice; pour into cooled pastry shell. Press a piece of plastic wrap directly on filling to prevent formation of a skin. (Remove before topping pie.) Refrigerate for at least 4 hours.
6. Preheat oven to 350°. Beat egg whites with cream of tartar in a small bowl until foamy. Slowly add remaining ½ cup sugar, 1 tablespoon at a time, beating at high speed until stiff peaks form.
7. Grease and flour a small cookie sheet. Shape or pipe meringue into 6 to 8 small mounds on cookie sheet.
8. Bake in preheated moderate oven (350°) for 15 minutes or until meringues are golden. Cool on cookie sheet. Place on chilled pie.

Apricot-Prune Lattice Pie

Chopped whole lemon and port wine provide exciting flavor accents in this luscious dried fruit mixture that goes into a flaky sour cream pastry.

Bake at 425° for 35 minutes.

Makes one 9-inch pie.

**½ cup (1 stick) butter
or margarine**
**2 cups *sifted* all-
purpose flour**
**2 tablespoons sugar
(for pastry)**
**½ cup dairy sour
cream**
**1 package (8 ounces)
dried apricots,
diced (about
1½ cups)**
**1 cup diced pitted
prunes**
1½ cups water

**½ cup sugar (for
filling)**
**2 teaspoons
cornstarch**
**½ whole lemon,
coarsely chopped
(about ¼ cup)**
**2 tablespoons tawny
port wine or sweet
sherry**
**1 tablespoon sugar
(for topping)**
**1 tablespoon chopped
walnuts or pecans**

1. Cut butter into flour with pastry blender until mixture is crumbly. Add sugar and sour cream; mix lightly with

(continued)

Lemon Meringue Pie, page 639.

a fork until dough holds together and starts to leave side of bowl clean. Gather dough together with hands and knead a few times. Wrap in wax paper; chill at least 1 hour.

2. Combine apricots, prunes and water in a medium-size saucepan; bring to boiling. Simmer, covered, 5 minutes. Mix sugar and cornstarch; stir into boiling mixture; cook, stirring often, 5 minutes. Remove from heat; stir in lemon and port wine.

3. Roll out 2/3 of pastry on lightly floured surface to a

12-inch round; fit into a 9-inch pie plate; trim overhang to 1/2 inch. Pour in the apricot-prune filling.

4. Preheat oven to 425°. Roll out remaining pastry to a 10-inch round. Cut into 10 strips; weave strips over filling. Turn edge under flush with rim; flute edge. Brush top with water; mix sugar and nuts; sprinkle over pie.

5. Bake in preheated hot oven (425°) for 35 minutes or until pastry is golden and filling is bubbling hot. Cool on wire rack. Serve slightly warm.

Pumpkin-Mince Pie

Bake at 425° for 15 minutes, then at 350° for 35 minutes.

Makes 8 servings.

1¹/₃ cups ready-to-use mincemeat	cinnamon
2 teaspoons grated orange rind	¹/₂ teaspoon ground nutmeg
1 nine-inch unbaked pastry shell with a high fluted edge	¹/₂ teaspoon ground ginger
2 eggs	¹/₄ teaspoon salt
1 can (14 ounces) sweetened condensed milk	1 can (16 ounces) pumpkin
1 teaspoon ground	¹/₂ cup heavy cream, whipped
	Slivers of orange rind

1. Preheat oven to 425°. Combine mincemeat and grated orange rind in a 2-cup measure; spoon into pastry shell, spreading evenly.
2. Beat eggs in a large bowl until frothy. Stir in milk, cinnamon, nutmeg, ginger, salt and pumpkin. Mix well until smooth. Pour over mincemeat layer in pastry shell.
3. Bake pie in a preheated hot oven (425°) for 15 minutes; lower heat to moderate (350°) and continue baking for 35 minutes or until the tip of a knife, when inserted into filling 1 inch from edge, comes out clean. Cool pie on wire rack. Garnish with whipped cream and orange slivers.

Fresh Blueberry Pie

Bake at 425° for 15 minutes, then at 350° for 35 minutes.

Makes one 9-inch pie.

4 cups (2 pints) fresh blueberries (or equivalent frozen, or canned, drained blueberries)	¹/₄ teaspoon ground cloves
	¹/₄ teaspoon ground cinnamon
1 cup sugar	1 package piecrust mix
¹/₄ cup all-purpose flour	3 tablespoons butter or margarine
¹/₄ teaspoon salt	Milk or cream
2 teaspoons grated lemon rind	Sugar

1. Gently wash berries; drain well; place in a large bowl. Sprinkle with sugar, flour, salt, lemon rind, cloves, cinnamon; toss to mix. Preheat oven to 425°.
2. Prepare pastry; roll out half the pastry to a 13-inch round; fit into a 9-inch pie plate. Spoon blueberry mixture into bottom crust; dot with butter. Roll remaining pastry to a 12-inch round; cut slits in top for steam to escape. Cover pie; trim overhang to 1 inch. Pinch edges together; flute to make a stand-up edge. Brush crust with milk or cream; sprinkle with sugar.

Press a collar of foil around edge of pie to prevent overbrowning.
3. Bake in a preheated hot oven (425°) for 15 minutes; lower heat to moderate (350°) and bake 10 minutes; remove foil collar. Continue baking 25 minutes or until pastry is golden and juices bubble. Cool at least 1 hour on wire rack.

Fresh Cherry Pie

Bake at 425° for 45 minutes.

Makes one 9-inch pie with lattice crust.

1 package (11 ounces) piecrust mix	(16 ounces each) pitted sour red cherries, drained
¹/₂ cup ground blanched almonds	1¹/₄ cups sugar
4 cups pitted fresh sour cherries OR: 2 cans	2 tablespoons quick-cooking tapioca
	¹/₄ teaspoon salt

1. Combine piecrust mix with almonds in a medium-size bowl; prepare piecrust mix following label directions.
2. Mix cherries, sugar, tapioca and salt in a medium-size bowl. Toss lightly to coat fruit; let stand 20 minutes.
3. Roll out half of pastry to a 12-inch round on a lightly floured surface; fit into a 9-inch pie plate; trim overhang to ¹/₂ inch. Spoon cherry mixture into prepared pastry shell. Preheat oven to 425°.
4. Roll out remaining pastry to an 11-inch round. Cut in ¹/₂-inch strips with a pastry wheel or knife. Weave strips into lattice over filling. Turn ends under; flute. Tear off 2-inch piece of aluminum foil; crumple lightly over fluted edge to keep edge from over-browning.
5. Bake in a preheated hot oven (425°) for 30 minutes; remove foil; continue baking 15 minutes or until pastry is brown and filling bubbly. Serve warm with vanilla ice cream, if you wish.

Fresh Peach Pie

Bake at 425° for 15 minutes, then at 350° for 35 minutes.

Makes one 9-inch pie.

¹/₂ cup sugar	juice
3 tablespoons flour	¹/₄ teaspoon almond extract
¹/₂ teaspoon ground cinnamon	1 package piecrust mix
¹/₄ teaspoon salt	Milk or water
6 large ripe peaches (about 2¹/₂ pounds)	Sugar
1 tablespoon lemon	

1. Combine sugar, flour, cinnamon and salt in a small bowl.
2. Drop peaches into boiling water for 30 seconds;

(continued)

drain. Rinse with cold water. Peel, halve, pit and slice into a large bowl. Sprinkle with lemon juice and almond extract; toss to coat. Add sugar mixture; mix gently.

3. Preheat oven to 425°. Prepare piecrust mix following label directions. Roll out ²/₃ to a 12-inch round on a lightly floured surface; fit into a 9-inch pie plate. Trim edge to a 1-inch overhang. Spoon in filling.

4. Roll out remaining pastry to an 11-inch round; cut into 10 strips. Weave strips over top of pie, pressing strips firmly to bottom crust. Turn edges under, flush with rim; press to make a stand-up edge; flute. Brush with milk or water; sprinkle on sugar.

5. Bake in a preheated hot oven (425°) for 15 minutes. Lower heat to moderate (350°); bake 35 minutes longer or until pastry is golden brown and juices are bubbly. Cool.

PIZZAS

Pizza   The Italian word for pie. Pizza has become a popular American snack food. It can be made from any number of ingredients.

Pizza Rustica

Bake at 350° for 50 minutes.

Makes one 12-inch double-crust pizza.

1 package hot roll mix OR: Easy Pizza Dough (*recipe follows*)	shredded
	¹/₄ pound salami, finely diced
³/₄ cup plus 2 tablespoons very warm water	¹/₃ cup sliced green onions
1 container (15 ounces) ricotta cheese	3 tablespoons chopped fresh parsley
1 package (8 ounces) mozzarella cheese,	1 teaspoon leaf oregano, crumbled
	1 teaspoon salt
	3 eggs, slightly beaten

1. Sprinkle yeast from hot roll mix into very warm water in medium-size bowl; stir until dissolved. ("Very warm water" should feel comfortably warm when dropped on wrist.) Gradually work in flour of hot roll mix to form a fairly stiff dough. Place dough in an oiled bowl; cover. Let rise in warm place until double in volume, about 30 minutes.

2. Meanwhile, prepare filling: Combine ricotta, mozzarella, salami, green onions, parsley, oregano, salt and eggs, reserving about 2 tablespoons of the beaten egg for brushing.

3. Preheat oven to 350°. Punch dough down and divide in half. Lightly oil a 12-inch pizza pan. Stretch one half of dough to fit pan, pressing dough against side of pan to make an edge. Brush edge with reserved beaten egg. Spoon filling over dough. Roll remaining half of dough to a 12-inch round; fit over filling, pressing edges together. Prick entire surface with a two-tined fork. Cut decorations from trimmings. Brush top with egg. Decorate top. Brush decorations.

4. Bake in a preheated moderate oven (350°) for 50 minutes or until golden brown. Cover top with foil if pizza is browning too fast. Let stand 15 minutes before cutting into wedges to serve.

Sausage and Pepper Pizza

Bake at 450° for 25 minutes.

Makes one 14-inch pizza.

Cornmeal Easy Pizza Dough (*recipe in this chapter*)	1 green pepper, halved, seeded and cut into strips
¹/₂ pound sweet Italian sausages	1 red pepper, halved, seeded and cut into strips
1 can (15 ounces) tomato sauce with tomato bits	2 small onions, sliced
¹/₄ cup grated Parmesan cheese	1 package (8 ounces) mozzarella cheese, shredded

1. Lightly oil a 14-inch round pizza pan; sprinkle lightly with cornmeal. Roll and stretch pizza dough to fit pan. Let rise 20 minutes.

2. Preheat oven to 450°. Remove sausage from casings; sauté meat in large skillet until no longer pink. Add tomato sauce; cook, stirring often, until juices have evaporated and mixture is almost dry, about 5 minutes. Remove from heat; cool slightly. Spread meat mixture over dough; sprinkle with Parmesan cheese.

3. Bake in a preheated very hot oven (450°) for 10 minutes; remove from oven. Arrange peppers and onions over top; sprinkle with cheese. Return to oven. Bake 15 to 20 minutes longer or until crust is golden brown and cheese is melted and bubbly. Cut into wedges to serve.

Easy Pizza Dough

Makes one thick 14-inch round crust or two thin 12-inch round crusts.

1 package active dry yeast	3¹/₄ cups *sifted* all-purpose flour
¹/₂ teaspoon sugar	1¹/₂ teaspoons salt
1 cup very warm water	

1. Sprinkle yeast and sugar into very warm water in a 1-cup measure. ("Very warm water" should feel comfortably warm when dropped on wrist.) Stir to dissolve and allow to stand 10 minutes or until mixture begins to bubble.

2. Combine flour and salt in a large bowl; make a well in the center; pour in yeast mixture; gradually work in flour to form a stiff dough.

3. Turn out onto lightly floured surface. Knead until smooth and elastic, about 5 minutes, using only as much flour as necessary to keep dough from sticking.

4. Place in lightly oiled medium-size bowl; turn dough to coat all over with oil. Cover with clean towel. Let rise in a warm place away from drafts 45 minutes or until double in volume. Punch down and use as directed.

Pizza, Mariner's Style

Bake at 450° for 15 to 20 minutes.

Makes two 12-inch pizzas.

1 loaf (1 pound) frozen plain bread dough, thawed overnight in refrigerator	**mushrooms, drained**
1 jar (15½ ounces) thick Italian-style cooking sauce	**2 jars (6 ounces each) marinated artichoke hearts, drained**
1 can (7 ounces) tuna, drained	**1 package (8 ounces) mozzarella cheese, finely diced**
1 can (5¾ ounces) pitted ripe olives	**2 cans (2 ounces each) rolled anchovy fillets, drained**
2 jars (2½ ounces each) whole	**Parsley sprigs**

1. Divide dough in half; stretch to fit two lightly oiled 12-inch pizza pans, pressing against bottoms and sides of pans, keeping dough slightly thicker on edges. Allow crusts to rest 10 to 15 minutes.

2. Preheat oven to 450°. Spread half of sauce on each pizza. Break up tuna; divide between pizzas. Alternate olives and mushrooms around edge; arrange artichokes on pizza; top with cheese.

3. Bake in a preheated very hot oven (450°) for 15 to 20 minutes or until crusts are golden. Garnish with anchovy and parsley.

South-of-the-Border Pizza

Bake at 450° for 15 minutes.

Makes one 12-inch pizza.

¾ pound ground chuck	**whole mild green chilies, drained and cut into strips**
1 can (7½ ounces) taco sauce	**1 package (8 ounces) natural Monterey Jack cheese slices**
1¼ cups buttermilk baking mix	**Sliced green onion**
½ cup yellow cornmeal	**Shredded lettuce**
½ cup milk	**Pickled red cherry peppers**
1 can (4 ounces)	

1. Brown meat lightly in large skillet; stir in taco sauce;

cook, uncovered, 5 minutes or until almost dry. Remove from heat. Cool.

2. Preheat oven to 450°. Combine baking mix and cornmeal in a large bowl; add milk; mix with a fork until moistened; press, with floured hands, on lightly greased cookie sheet to a 12-inch round. Spread meat mixture over dough to edge. Arrange chilies and cheese over meat.

3. Bake in a preheated very hot oven (450°) for 15 minutes or until edges are brown and cheese is melted. Sprinkle with green onions and shredded lettuce; garnish with pickled red cherry peppers.

Overstuffed Italian Bread Pizza

Makes 4 pizzas.

1 large loaf Italian bread (about ½ pound), cut in half horizontally and vertically	**package)**
	¼ cup drained roasted red peppers (part of 7-ounce jar), cut into strips
½ cup prepared marinara spaghetti sauce	**8 oil-cured black olives, halved and pitted**
1 package (8 ounces) shredded mozzarella cheese	**2 tablespoons grated Parmesan cheese**
16 slices pepperoni (part of 3½-ounce	**1 teaspoon olive oil**
	½ teaspoon leaf oregano, crumbled

1. Place bread on broiler rack. Broil 4 inches from heat, 2 minutes on each side or until crisp.

2. Spread cut sides of bread with marinara sauce. Sprinkle with mozzarella cheese and top with pepperoni, peppers, olives, Parmesan, oil and oregano, dividing ingredients equally.

3. Broil pizzas 2 minutes until cheese is melted and bubbly.

Overleaf: Sausage and Pepper Pizza, page 642; (insets from top) South-of-the-Border Pizza, page 643; Pizza Rustica, page 642; Pizza Mariner's Style, page 643.

POULTRY

Poultry A domesticated bird raised for food, poultry includes chicken, turkey, Rock Cornish game hen, duckling and goose. Chicken is the all-American favorite, although turkey is a close second. Rock Cornish game hens are gaining in popularity, especially among white-meat fanciers. These tender, plump-breasted little birds are nearly all white meat. Ducklings and geese are neither as plentiful nor as popular as chicken, turkey or game hen, but they are very good and not exorbitantly priced. For additional information, see specific bird.

How to Stuff and Truss Poultry

Rinse the bird completely clean with cold running water, inside and out. Pat dry with paper toweling. Rub the cavity lightly with salt.

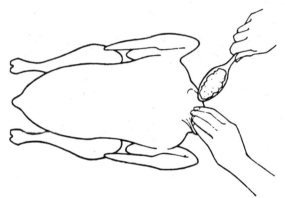

1. Spoon stuffing lightly into neck (do not pack, for stuffing expands during cooking). Pull neck skin over opening and fasten to back with a skewer or wooden pick.

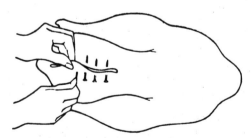

2. Stuff body cavity lightly. Close opening by running skewers or wooden picks through skin from one side of opening to the other; lace securely with string, crisscross fashion. Or, sew it closed with large needle and thread.

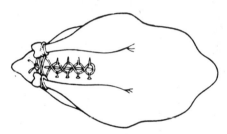

3. Loop the same string around the drumstick ends and tie them together, then fasten them to the tailpiece of the bird.

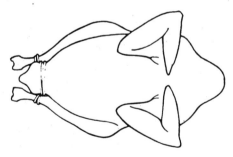

4. Fold wings up and under the back; this will help brace the bird in the roasting pan. Brush lightly with melted butter or margarine and place the bird, breast-side up, in a roasting pan.

Or, if barbecuing on a spit, press wings close to the breast. Run a string around and under the bird to completely encircle it, securing wings snugly against the breast. The bird should be tied so that it makes a compact bundle.

Pictured opposite:
Chicken Ragout with Peas and Mushrooms, page 650.

How to Cut and Bone a Chicken

1. Place chicken breast side up. Using a sharp knife, make lengthwise slit through skin and flesh from neck to cavity. Turn bird over and repeat cut.

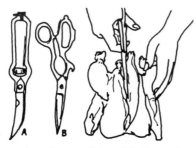

2. Using poultry shears (a) or kitchen shears (b), cut right through bones (ribs). Cutting to one side of breastbone is easier than cutting through it.

3. Turn chicken over. Cut through bones, cutting to one side of the backbone. You may remove backbone. A small bird is cut this way for serving.

4. For quartering chicken, continue using shears. Cut across half the bird, following the natural division just below the rib cage and the breastbone.

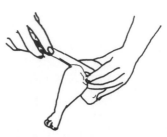

5. Thigh may be left attached to leg for broiling; but for frying, bend leg joint. Cut through joint with a sharp knife, separating leg from the thigh.

6. To separate wing from the breast, bend joint. Cut through joint with a sharp knife. The chicken will now be in eight pieces and ready for frying.

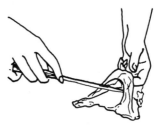

7. If your recipe calls for skinned chicken breasts, use a sharp, small paring knife to start, then slip fingers between skin and flesh and peel skin.

8. To bone chicken breast, use a small paring knife. Cut meat away from rib bones with quick little strokes, feeling your way along with your fingers.

Chicken

No other food is as widely used in the world as chicken. A chicken in your shopping cart promises a good meal at a reasonable price. Dollar for dollar, chicken is hard to beat.

Chickens are descendants of a wild jungle bird from southeastern Asia, hunted by man for food as early as 1400 B.C. Some 800 years later, the Greeks and Romans were breeding the now domesticated bird not only for meat, but eggs as well. Jamestown settlers brought chickens for food and used their feathers to make beds.

Chickens have come a long way from the jungle to the barnyard to today's scientifically operated farms. Our modern birds are scientifically bred and fed a special diet to make them plump, tender and juicy. Whereas it once took months to raise a bird for market, it now takes just weeks, and the savings are reflected in the price at your supermarket. Efficient processing, Federal inspection and grading, and speedy, refrigerated transportation all guarantee carefully controlled quality of the chickens marketed today.

The chicken you buy is produced for its meat. Broiler-fryer chickens differ from egg-producing chickens the same way beef cattle differ from dairy cows.

Chicken is an excellent source of high-quality protein, rich in the essential amino acids needed for building, maintaining and replacing the body's muscles and tissues. It is low in saturated fat and lower than most meats in total fat content. A $3^{1}/_{2}$ ounce serving of skinless, broiled chicken breast has only 115 calories, 185 with the skin on. It's an excellent source of niacin and iron.

Buying and Storing: Chicken is available in a variety of types and products, fresh, frozen or canned.

Broiler-fryer This meaty, all-purpose chicken accounts for 90% of the chickens sold in this country. Marketed at 7 to 9 weeks old, it weighs 2 to $3^{1}/_{2}$ pounds.

Roaster Slightly larger and older than a broiler-fryer, this chicken is marketed at 16 weeks and weighs $3^{1}/_{2}$ to 6 pounds.

Stewing chicken, hen or fowl This chicken is mature and less tender than a broiler-fryer or roaster and is best stewed or made into soup. It may be a year or a little older. A fowl will weigh about $2^{1}/_{2}$ to $3^{1}/_{2}$ pounds; a stewing chicken or hen can weigh $4^{1}/_{2}$ to 6 pounds.

Capon A male chicken that has been castrated so that it grows plump and tender. A capon weighs 4 to 7 pounds.

Rock Cornish game hen This is a special breed of small-size chicken that weighs $1^{1}/_{2}$ pounds or less. Usually sold frozen but available fresh in some large cities, it can be roasted, broiled, fried or baked.

Broiler-fryer chicken parts In many markets today, it is possible to buy only those parts of the chicken you want—all breasts, for example, or thighs, drumsticks, wings or backs.

Boneless, skinless breasts, called chicken cutlets, are very popular.

Chicken giblets, which include the gizzard, liver and heart, may be used for tasty, inexpensive, nutritious dishes.

In addition to the more familiar chicken types, new chicken products are finding their way into supermarkets—chicken frankfurters, chicken bologna, chicken luncheon meat. You will also find numerous canned, boned chicken products and frozen chicken dinners or fried parts.

How Much to Buy: A whole broiler-fryer is 53 percent edible. A 3-pound chicken yields approximately 3 cups cooked edible meat. In an average 3-pound bird, each breast half weighs about $7^{1}/_{2}$ ounces and contains about 5 ounces of edible meat. Each wing weighs about $3^{1}/_{2}$ ounces, yields 1 ounce of meat. Each drumstick weighs about $3^{1}/_{2}$ ounces, yields 2 ounces of meat. Each thigh weighs about $4^{1}/_{2}$ ounces, yields about $2^{1}/_{2}$ ounces meat. The back-neck weighs about 8 ounces, gives only 2 ounces meat. The giblets weigh about 2 ounces each.

Here are some rules to follow in deciding how much chicken to buy. You may want to increase these portions for big eaters in the family.

Chicken for frying: Allow $3/_{4}$ to 1 pound per serving.

Chicken for roasting: Allow $3/_{4}$ to 1 pound per serving.

Chicken for broiling or barbecuing: Allow $1/_{2}$ chicken or 1 pound per serving.

Chicken for stewing Allow $1/_{2}$ to 1 pound per serving.

Storing: Chicken, whether cut-up or whole and packed on trays, can be stored in the original wrapper. Store in the coldest part of the refrigerator and cook within 2 days. Chicken bought in bags should be removed from the bags and rinsed under cool, running water. Pat dry with paper toweling, then cut into portions desired and rewrap in foil or plastic wrap. Refrigerate and use within 2 days. If you plan to keep it for a longer period, you should freeze it.

Uncooked chicken can be frozen whole or in parts in suitable freezer wrap. Plastic freezer bags can also be used. Press all the air out of each package; seal, label and freeze for up to 6 months at 0° F.

Cooked whole chicken or parts can be wrapped as above for freezing. If the chicken was stuffed, remove stuffing and wrap separately. Chicken cooked in a sauce or gravy should be packed in a rigid container with a tight-fitting lid. Allow $1/_{2}$ inch at the top for expansion. Cooked chicken may be kept for up to 2 months at 0°F.

Thaw chicken in the refrigerator, or use a microwave oven. Do not refreeze thawed cooked or uncooked chicken.

To Cook: Chickens can be roasted, baked, broiled, sautéed, stir-fried, fried, braised, steamed, stewed or grilled.

Cooked Chicken Safety Tips

Since chicken is a popular picnic food, take special precautions against spoilage.

● Chicken that has been fried, baked or broiled with no sauce should be chilled quickly in the refrigerator before packing. It is then safe at room temperature (70°F) for up to 4 hours.
● On warm days, pack the chicken in an insulated container or ice chest.
● Chicken salad or creamed chicken should always be kept refrigerated until eating time.

Storing Cooked Chicken

Cooked chicken can be safely refrigerated for no more than 2 to 3 days in the coldest part of your refrigerator. It can also be frozen, packaged the same way as fresh chicken, but the recommended freezing period is only 2 months.

Cooking Time for Chicken Parts

Part	Temperature	Time
4 Chicken Wings	350°	25 to 27 minutes
1 Half Breast	350°	25 to 27 minutes
2 Chicken Thighs	375°	22 minutes
1 Leg-Thigh Combination	375°	35 minutes

Chicken Ragout with Peas and Mushrooms

The delicate flavor of tarragon makes this French stew extra special.

Makes 4 to 6 servings.

1/4 cup all-purpose flour	tarragon, crumbled
1 broiler-fryer (about 3 pounds), cut up	1 teaspoon salt
1/3 cup olive or vegetable oil	1/4 teaspoon freshly ground pepper
2 medium-size onions, sliced	2 bay leaves
2 cloves garlic, chopped	1 can (13 3/4 ounces) chicken broth
1 pound mushrooms, sliced	1 cup dry white wine
1 teaspoon leaf	3 tablespoons flour
	1/4 cup water
	1 package (10 ounces) frozen peas

1. Place 1/4 cup flour and the chicken in plastic bag; shake to coat chicken thoroughly.
2. Heat oil in large skillet; brown chicken on both sides; remove to heavy kettle or Dutch oven. Drain oil and return 3 tablespoons to skillet.
3. Add onions, garlic and mushrooms to skillet; sauté, stirring occasionally, until onions are tender. Add tarragon, salt, pepper, bay leaves, chicken broth and wine; heat; pour over chicken. Simmer, covered, 1 hour or until chicken is tender.

4. Blend remaining 3 tablespoons flour with water in cup; stir into stew. Add peas; bring to boiling. Cook and stir until sauce thickens and peas are tender.

Roast Chicken with Cherry Sauce

Makes 2 servings.

2 tablespoons sugar	cornstarch
2 tablespoons white vinegar	1/2 cup chicken broth
1 large navel orange	1 tablespoon orange-flavored liqueur (optional)
1 lemon	
1 can (16 ounces) pitted sour cherries	1 deli-roasted whole chicken (about 2 1/2 pounds)
1 tablespoon	

1. Combine sugar and vinegar in a medium-size saucepan. Heat until sugar caramelizes and becomes amber in color. (Do not overcook.)
2. Pare rinds thinly from orange and lemon with a sharp knife, cutting colored part only (no white). Cut rinds into thinnest possible strips. Reserve fruits for another use. Combine orange and lemon strips in a saucepan with water to cover; bring to boiling; remove from heat; let stand 3 minutes; drain.
3. Drain cherries; add juice to saucepan. Stir cornstarch into chicken broth; stir into juice in saucepan. Cook, stirring constantly, until sauce thickens and clears. Add drained cherries, reserved rinds and orange liqueur, if using. Heat just until mixture starts to bubble. Serve with deli-roasted chicken.

Stuffed Roast Chickens

Roast at 350° for 1 3/4 to 2 hours.

Makes 8 servings.

2 tablespoons leaf rosemary, crumbled	each)
2 tablespoons leaf tarragon, crumbled	1 teaspoon salt
1/3 cup dry white wine or chicken broth	1/2 teaspoon freshly ground pepper
1/2 cup (1 stick) butter or margarine	1 fresh pear, cored and chopped
2 whole broiler-fryers (3 1/2 pounds	1 package (6 ounces) wild rice mix, cooked following label directions

1. Combine rosemary and tarragon with wine in a small bowl; let stand 1 hour. Strain, reserve liquid. Blend butter into herbs.
2. Sprinkle cavity of each chicken with part of the salt and pepper; add 1 tablespoon herb butter. Loosen skin over breast; press in about 2 tablespoons of the herb butter.
3. Sauté chopped pear in half of remaining herb butter. Blend with cooked wild rice. Stuff chickens with wild rice; truss.
4. Melt remaining herb butter; brush over birds.

Stuffed Roast Chicken, page 650.

Sprinkle with remaining salt and pepper. Combine the remaining herb butter with an equal amount of reserved wine or broth.

5. Roast in a moderate oven (350°) for 1³/₄ to 2 hours or until leg moves easily and juices are no longer pink, basting often with herb-wine mixture.

6. Serve with sautéed zucchini, broccoli, yellow squash and carrots, if you wish.

Herbed Spit-Roasted Chicken

Makes 4 to 6 servings.

3 tablespoons minced fresh rosemary OR: **2 tablespoons leaf rosemary, crumbled**	**Dry white wine** OR: **chicken broth** **¹/₂ cup (1 stick) butter or margarine**
3 tablespoons minced fresh tarragon OR: **2 tablespoons leaf tarragon, crumbled**	**1 teaspoon salt** **¹/₄ teaspoon freshly ground pepper** **1 roasting chicken (about 3¹/₂ to 4 pounds)**

1. Combine fresh rosemary and tarragon in a small bowl. If you are using dried herbs, combine with ¹/₃ cup dry white wine or broth in a small bowl. Let stand 1 hour. Strain; reserve liquid. Add butter to the herbs; blend thoroughly.

2. Sprinkle the cavity of the chicken with part of the salt and pepper and put in about 1 tablespoon of the herb butter. Carefully loosen the skin over the breast with your fingers and press in about 1 to 2 tablespoons of the herb butter. Truss the bird, balance it on the spit and fasten it securely.

3. Melt the remaining herb butter and brush over bird. Sprinkle it with remaining salt and pepper. Combine the remaining melted herb butter with an equal quantity of wine or broth, or, if using dried herbs, with reserved wine or broth.

4. Roast the chicken for about 2¹/₂ hours, basting it frequently with the butter-wine mixture. If possible, put a pan under the bird while roasting to catch the juice. Skim off the fat and pour a little juice over each piece of carved chicken just before serving.

Lemon-Broiled Chicken

Makes 4 servings.

2 broiler-fryers, halved or quartered (about 2 pounds each) **Salt and pepper**	**¹/₄ cup (¹/₂ stick) butter or margarine** **Juice of ¹/₂ lemon**

1. Sprinkle chicken with salt and pepper. Melt butter in a small saucepan; stir in lemon juice; brush lemon-butter on chickens.

(continued)

2. Place chickens, skin-side down, on rack of broiler pan and broil 6 inches from heat 20 to 25 minutes, brushing occasionally with lemon-butter.

3. Turn chickens; brush with remaining lemon-butter and broil 15 to 20 minutes longer or until nicely browned.

Note: If chickens brown too quickly, reduce heat or move farther away from broiler unit.

Beer-Batter Fried Chicken

Crispy chicken prepared with a light coating of beer batter.

Makes 8 servings.

1³/₄ cups *sifted* all-purpose flour	beer
1¹/₂ teaspoons salt	Vegetable oil
¹/₂ teaspoon pepper	2 broiler-fryers
1 can (12 ounces)	(2¹/₂ pounds each), cut up

1. Combine flour, salt and pepper in a medium-size bowl. Beat in beer with a wire whisk or rotary beater until smooth. Let stand 30 minutes.

2. Pour enough vegetable oil in a large skillet or saucepan to make a 1-inch depth. Heat to 375° on a deep-fat frying thermometer or until a cube of bread turns golden within about 60 seconds.

3. Dip chicken pieces into beer batter, a few at a time, allowing excess to drain back into bowl.

Beer-Batter Fried Chicken.

4. Fry chicken pieces, turning once, for 30 minutes or until chicken tests done. Place on paper toweling to drain. Keep warm in a very slow oven (250°) until all chicken is fried. Garnish chicken with parsley and serve with onion rings, if you wish.

Velvet Sliced Chicken

Makes 4 servings.

1 chicken breast (about 14 ounces), halved	snow peas, halved or ¹/₂ of a 7-ounce package frozen snow peas
8 egg whites (1 cup)	1 tablespoon dry sherry
3 tablespoons cornstarch	¹/₂ teaspoon sugar
1 teaspoon salt	2 tablespoons minced cooked bacon or ham
³/₄ cup chicken broth	
2 cups peanut or corn oil	
¹/₄ pound fresh	Green onion

1. Skin and bone chicken. Flatten pieces between sheets of wax paper to ¹/₈-inch thickness using a meat mallet or rolling pin. Cut breast pieces in half lengthwise, then cut into 1-inch pieces to make 1 × 1 × ¹/₈-inch slices (about ³/₄ cup).

2. Beat egg whites in large bowl with rotary beater until foamy. Stir in chicken.

3. Combine cornstarch and salt in a small bowl; stir in chicken broth slowly until blended. Pour into chicken mixture.

4. Heat oil in wok or skillet to 300° on deep-fat frying thermometer. Stir chicken mixture; pour into hot oil.

5. Turn mixture gently with slotted spoon as egg white sets and chicken turns white (about 2 minutes).

6. Pour oil and chicken into strainer placed over a bowl to drain.

7. Wipe wok clean. Return 1 tablespoon of the oil to wok; reheat. Place chicken mixture and snow peas in wok; stir-fry 1 minute. Sprinkle with sherry and sugar. Stir 1 more minute. Sprinkle with bacon; garnish with green onion.

Chicken Risotto

Makes 4 servings.

1 broiler-fryer (2¹/₂ pounds), cut up	chicken broth
	Water
1 package (7¹/₂ ounces) risotto rice mix	1 jar (3 ounces) pimiento-stuffed olives, drained
1 can condensed	

1. Place chicken pieces, skin-side down, in a large skillet over very low heat. (Do not add fat.) Cook chicken slowly in its own fat until skin side is a rich brown, about 10 minutes; turn; brown other side. Remove chicken from skillet with tongs.

2. Add rice and seasoning packet from mix to pan drippings; stir to coat rice with drippings.

3. Pour chicken broth into a 4-cup measure; add water to measure 2½ cups. Stir into rice mixture; bring to boiling. Arrange chicken pieces over mixture. Lower heat; cover. Simmer 20 minutes or until chicken is tender and liquid is absorbed. Stir in olives; fluff up rice.

Ginger Chicken

Grill for 35 minutes.

Makes 4 servings.

2 chicken breasts, halved	ginger
	¼ teaspoon salt
2 tablespoons sesame seeds	Dash pepper
	½ cup vegetable oil
1 teaspoon ground	

1. Wash chicken; pat dry. Put in a large, shallow dish.
2. Crush 1 tablespoon of the sesame seeds; mix with ginger, salt, pepper and oil. Pour over chicken; turn chicken over to coat with mixture. Cover; refrigerate 1 hour.
3. Remove from marinade; add remaining sesame seeds to marinade.
4. Grill chicken 6 inches from hot coals, skin-side up, for 15 minutes; turn and brush with marinade. Grill 20 minutes longer; turn often and brush with marinade.

Chicken Provençale

Set the mood for an evening in the south of France with a variety of appetizers: fresh mushrooms marinated in herbed salad dressing; drained, canned artichoke hearts, tossed with garlic mayonnaise; slices of store-bought pâté or quiche; and crunchy breadsticks. And for dessert, what could be simpler than cheese and fruit.

Makes 8 servings.

2 broiler-fryers (3½ pounds each), cut up	1 can (28 ounces) Italian-style plum tomatoes, coarsely chopped
⅓ cup all-purpose flour for coating, or as needed	1 cup dry white wine
¼ cup olive oil, or as needed	2 teaspoons leaf thyme, crumbled
1 teaspoon salt	1 teaspoon fennel seeds, slightly crushed
¼ teaspoon pepper	
2 medium-size onions, chopped	2 bay leaves
	Pinch saffron *(optional)*
3 cups thickly sliced celery	1 large navel orange
2 cloves garlic, finely chopped	3 cups hot cooked rice

1. Wash chicken. Pat dry with paper toweling. Coat lightly with flour, shaking off excess.

Chicken Provençale.

2. Heat 2 tablespoons of the oil in large flameproof casserole. Brown chicken in batches, adding more oil as necessary. As chicken browns, transfer to plate. Season with salt and pepper.
3. Pour off all but 2 tablespoons fat from casserole. Sauté onions and celery in casserole for 3 minutes. Add garlic; sauté 30 seconds.
4. Add tomatoes, wine, thyme, fennel, bay leaves and saffron, if using; scrape up any browned bits from bottom of casserole with wooden spoon. Return chicken to casserole.
5. Remove outer rind (without white pith) of orange with a vegetable peeler. Add rind to casserole; reserve peeled orange. Bring to boiling. Lower heat; cover; simmer 20 minutes or until chicken is tender.
6. To serve, section reserved peeled orange and arrange on top. Serve with rice.

Chicken in a Basket

Makes 8 servings.

1½ cups all-purpose flour	2 eggs
	¼ cup water
2 teaspoons salt	2 broiler-fryers (2½ to 3 pounds each), quartered
1 teaspoon sugar	
1 teaspoon paprika	
½ teaspoon pepper	Vegetable oil for frying

1. Combine flour, salt, sugar, paprika and pepper in shallow baking dish. Beat eggs and water in another dish.
2. Dip chicken pieces, 1 at a time, into flour mixture to

(continued)

coat lightly. Then dip each piece in egg mixture. Roll again in flour, turning to coat completely.

3. Pour enough vegetable oil into large saucepan or Dutch oven to make a 2-inch depth. Heat to 350° on deep-fat thermometer.

4. Fry the leg and thigh quarters about 18 minutes and the breast and wing quarters 12 minutes. Cool; refrigerate.

Easy Oven Chicken and Vegetables

Golden brown chicken with leeks and mushrooms is an easy main dish.

Bake at 375° for 1½ hours.

Makes 6 servings.

2 cups sliced leeks (white part only)	**(1½ pounds)**
1 pound mushrooms	**¼ cup vermouth or dry white wine**
2 tablespoons butter or margarine	**1 can condensed cream of mushroom soup**
6 chicken legs (1½ pounds)	**¼ teaspoon pepper**
6 chicken thighs	

1. Preheat oven to 375°. Sauté leeks and mushrooms in butter in a large skillet, stirring frequently until tender, about 5 minutes. Transfer to a 13 × 9 × 2-inch baking dish.

2. Arrange chicken pieces, skin-side up, on vegetable mixture.

3. Mix wine, soup and pepper in a 2-cup measure. Pour over chicken, covering completely.

4. Bake in a preheated moderate oven (375°) for 1½ hours, basting occasionally, or until chicken is tender.

Curried Limas and Chicken Wings

A hearty, mildly seasoned casserole with peas and carrots.

Bake at 350° for 30 minutes.

Makes about 8 servings.

1 pound dried lima beans	**(1½ cups)**
8 cups water	**2 teaspoons curry powder**
8 chicken wings (about 1¼ pounds)	**¼ teaspoon ground cinnamon**
¼ cup (½ stick) butter or margarine	**2 tablespoons flour**
1 large onion, chopped	**2 teaspoons salt**
3 carrots, sliced	**1 cup milk**
	1 package (10 ounces) frozen peas

1. Pick over beans and rinse under running water. Combine beans and water in a large kettle; cover, let soak overnight. Or, to quick-soak, bring to boiling, boil 2 minutes, remove from heat; let stand 1 hour.

2. Bring soaked beans to boiling; lower heat; partially cover and simmer 35 minutes or until beans are almost tender.

3. Cut each chicken wing at joint to separate the 2 large sections. Melt butter in a large skillet; add wings and cook slowly until brown on all sides. Remove to paper toweling as they brown.

4. Add onion, carrots, curry powder and cinnamon to fat remaining in skillet. Sauté until onion is tender. Stir in flour and salt. Drain beans, reserving liquid. There should be 2 cups liquid; if not, add water to make that amount.

5. Add reserved liquid to flour mixture; cook, stirring constantly, until thickened and boiling. Add milk and peas; bring to boiling. Combine beans, chicken wings and curry sauce in a 3- to 4-quart baking dish; cover.

6. Bake in a moderate oven (350°) for 30 minutes or until beans are tender, stirring once halfway through baking.

Chicken Fricassee

Bake at 350° for 2 hours.

Makes 4 servings.

1 broiler-fryer (about 3½ pounds), cut up	**¼ cup (½ stick) butter or margarine, softened**
1 can condensed chicken broth	**¼ cup all-purpose flour**
12 small white onions, peeled	**¾ cup heavy cream**
1 small onion, stuck with 4 cloves	**½ pound mushrooms, sliced**
1 small carrot, diced	**OR: 2 cans (4 ounces each) sliced mushrooms, drained**
3 tablespoons chopped fresh parsley	**¼ teaspoon leaf thyme, crumbled**
2 teaspoons salt	**½ teaspoon paprika**
3 peppercorns	
1 bay leaf	

1. Tear off a 22-inch length of 18-inch-wide heavy-duty foil. Place in center of reusable giant round aluminum foil casserole, 9¼ × 2⅞ inches (about 10 cups). Press foil up and around inside of casserole, leaving enough foil to seal tightly.

2. Arrange chicken pieces in foil-lined casserole. Add soup, white onions, onion stuck with cloves, carrot, parsley, salt, peppercorns and bay leaf. Close and seal foil.

3. Bake in a moderate oven (350°) for 1 hour, 45 minutes. Carefully open foil. With tongs or slotted spoon, remove onion stuck with cloves and bay leaf. Mix butter with flour and drop, bit by bit, into liquid, stirring well as you do. Then add heavy cream, mushrooms and thyme, stirring well again. Re-seal foil.

4. Continue baking 15 minutes longer or until sauce is thickened. Sprinkle with paprika before serving.

Pictured opposite: Curried Limas and Chicken Wings.

Stir-Fry Chicken Wings

You can use whichever chicken parts are on special at your market.

Makes 6 servings.

1 pound chicken wings	**vegetable oil**
¹/₂ teaspoon salt	**1 cup thinly sliced celery**
1 bunch green onions	**1 cup frozen peas**
2 large carrots	**3 tablespoons water**
2 red or green sweet peppers	**Sweet-Sour Sauce** *(recipe follows)*
2 tablespoons	**3 cups hot cooked rice**

1. Cut chicken wings at each joint to separate. Sprinkle salt in a large, heavy skillet; heat; add chicken wings and brown about 5 minutes on each side; remove with slotted spoon; reserve.
2. Trim green onions; cut tops and white part into 2-inch pieces; pare carrots and cut into long, diagonal pieces; seed peppers and cut into long strips.
3. Add oil to skillet; stir-fry onions, carrots and peppers in oil; add chicken wings, celery, frozen peas and water; cover skillet and steam 15 minutes; add Sweet-Sour Sauce; cook 3 minutes. Serve with hot cooked rice.

Sweet-Sour Sauce: Combine ¹/₃ cup firmly packed brown sugar and 4 teaspoons cornstarch in a small saucepan; stir in 1 cup water, 1 teaspoon or envelope instant chicken broth, 3 tablespoons cider vinegar and 3 tablespoons soy sauce. Bring to boiling, stirring constantly; let bubble 2 minutes. Makes 1¹/₂ cups.

Stir-Fry Chicken Wings.

Brunswick Stew

Brunswick Stew   This southern stew with many variations was usually made from squirrel. It is now made with chicken, corn, tomatoes and lima beans, slowly simmered to develop its delicious flavor. How it originated is not certain. Several counties in the South named Brunswick have laid claim to originating this dish sometime around the 1820's.

Brunswick Stew

Makes 6 servings.

2 bacon slices, diced	**2 cups fresh lima beans**
1 frying or roasting chicken (3¹/₂ to 4 pounds), cut up	**OR: 1 package (10 ounces) frozen lima beans**
OR: A rabbit of the same size	**2 cups freshly cut corn kernels**
3 tablespoons flour	**OR: 1 package (10 ounces) frozen whole-kernel corn**
1¹/₂ teaspoons salt	
¹/₂ teaspoon pepper	
¹/₈ teaspoon cayenne	
3 medium-size onions, sliced	**¹/₂ pound okra, sliced**
1¹/₂ cups water	**OR: 1 package (10 ounces) frozen cut okra**
4 ripe tomatoes, peeled and chopped	
OR: 1 can (16 ounces) tomatoes	**2 tablespoons chopped fresh parsley**
1 red pepper, seeded and diced	**1 tablespoon Worcestershire sauce**
¹/₂ teaspoon leaf thyme, crumbled	

Top Stove Method:
1. Cook bacon until crisp in a large kettle or Dutch oven; remove bacon with slotted spoon; reserve.
2. Shake chicken pieces with flour, salt, pepper and cayenne in plastic bag to coat well. Brown pieces, a few at a time, in bacon drippings. Stir in onions; sauté 5 minutes. Add water, tomatoes, pepper and thyme. Bring to boiling; return all chicken pieces to kettle; lower heat; cover. Simmer 45 minutes or until chicken is almost done.
3. Add lima beans, corn, okra, parsley and Worcestershire sauce; return to boiling; lower heat; cover. Continue cooking 15 minutes longer or until vegetables are tender. Serve sprinkled with reserved bacon and additional parsley.

Slow-Cooker Method:
Cook bacon and brown chicken and onions following

Top Stove Method: place in electric slow cooker. Add 1 cup water, tomatoes, pepper and thyme; cover. Cook on low 6 to 8 hours or until chicken is almost done. Add remaining ingredients. Cover and cook on high 25 minutes or until vegetables and chicken are tender. Sprinkle with bacon and additional parsley.

Walnut Chicken.

Walnut Chicken

This fast-cooking Cantonese recipe is nutty and flavorful.

Makes 4 servings.

1 tablespoon
  cornstarch
3 tablespoons soy
  sauce
1 tablespoon dry
  sherry
1/2 teaspoon ground
  ginger
1 pound boneless
  chicken breasts, cut
  into 1-inch pieces
4 tablespoons

vegetable oil
1/3 cup sliced green
  onions (1-inch long)
1 clove garlic, minced
1/2 pound fresh snow
  peas, tips and
  strings removed
OR: 1 package (7
  ounces) frozen
  snow peas, partially
  thawed
1 cup walnut pieces

1. Combine cornstarch, soy sauce, sherry and ginger in a medium-size bowl; add chicken pieces; let stand 15 minutes.
2. Meanwhile, heat wok or large skillet; add 3 tablespoons of the oil; heat until smoking; add green onions, garlic and snow peas. Cook 3 minutes, stirring mixture with slotted spoon. Remove mixture to a bowl.
3. Add remaining oil to wok; heat; add chicken pieces until done and soy mixture begins to coat chicken, about 5 minutes. Add walnuts and vegetable mixture. Toss until mixed. Serve with hot cooked rice, if you wish.

Herb-Roasted Chicken

Bake at 375° for 2 1/2 hours.

Makes 6 servings.

1 roasting chicken
  (about 5 pounds)
1 teaspoon salt
1/4 teaspoon pepper
Buttery Bread Stuffing
  (recipe follows)
1/2 cup (1 stick) butter
  or margarine,
  melted
1 tablespoon chopped
  chives

1 tablespoon chopped
  fresh parsley
1/2 teaspoon leaf
  rosemary, crumbled
1/2 teaspoon leaf
  thyme, crumbled
1 clove garlic, minced
2 tablespoons flour
1 can (13 3/4 ounces)
  chicken broth
1/2 cup dry white wine

1. Sprinkle chicken neck and body cavities with salt and pepper.
2. Stuff neck and body cavities lightly with Buttery Bread Stuffing. Skewer neck skin to back; close body cavity and tie legs to tail. Place chicken on rack in

(continued)

roasting pan. Combine melted butter with chives, parsley, rosemary, thyme and garlic. Brush part of mixture over chicken.

3. Roast in a moderate oven (375°), basting every 30 minutes, 2½ hours or until tender. Remove strings or skewers. Transfer to serving platter.

4. Pour off excess fat from roasting pan. Stir flour into pan drippings and cook, stirring constantly, 1 minute. Blend in chicken broth and wine; cook, stirring constantly, until mixture thickens. Serve separately.

Buttery Bread Stuffing

Makes 5 cups.

4 cups firm white bread cubes (8 slices)	**1 cup finely chopped celery with leaves**
½ cup (1 stick) butter or margarine	**¼ cup chopped fresh parsley**
3 medium-size onions, finely chopped (1½ cups)	**1 teaspoon poultry seasoning**
	1 teaspoon salt
	¼ teaspoon pepper

1. Place bread cubes in single layer on jelly-roll pan. Roast in a moderate oven (375°) for 10 minutes.

2. Melt butter in a large skillet; sauté onions and celery until tender, 5 minutes. Add bread cubes, parsley, poultry seasoning, salt and pepper; toss until thoroughly moistened.

Scaloppine with Orange Sauce.

Scaloppine with Orange Sauce

Makes 4 servings.

2 whole chicken breasts (about 14 ounces each), boned, skinned and halved OR: **4 rib pork chops (each ½-inch thick), boned**	**2 large navel oranges**
	1 tablespoon olive oil
	1 tablespoon butter or margarine
	1 small onion, minced (¼ cup)
1 teaspoon salt	**2 teaspoons tomato paste**
¼ teaspoon pepper	**1 cup chicken broth**
Flour	**2 tablespoons minced fresh parsley**

1. Place chicken breast halves or pork between sheets of wax paper and pound firmly with a meat mallet or rolling pin until they are ¼-inch thick or thinner. Sprinkle with salt and pepper; dip in flour and pat briskly to remove excess.

2. Grate the rind of 1 orange; reserve. Cut off all remaining rind and white from both oranges. Cut each in half lengthwise, then cut crosswise into ½-inch slices.

3. Heat oil and butter in large skillet. Add scaloppine and sauté until golden on both sides, about 5 minutes for chicken and 8 minutes for pork. Remove to platter; keep warm.

4. Add onion to skillet; sauté until soft but not brown, about 3 minutes. Stir in tomato paste, chicken broth and rind. Return scaloppine to pan; cover; simmer until tender, about 5 minutes for chicken and 8 minutes for pork.

5. When scaloppine is tender, remove to warm platter. Add orange slices to sauce in skillet and heat through. Spoon over scaloppine. Sprinkle with parsley. Garnish with parsley sprigs, if you wish.

Chicken Cacciatore

No one will guess you haven't worked on this all day.

Makes 4 servings.

1 broiler-fryer (2½ pounds), cut up	**mushrooms**
1 medium-size onion, chopped (½ cup)	**1½ teaspoons chopped fresh basil**
1 jar (14 ounces) spaghetti sauce with peppers and	OR: **½ teaspoon dried basil, crumbled**

1. Dry chicken well; place pieces, skin-side down, in large skillet over very low heat. (Do not add fat.) Cook chicken slowly in its own fat until skin side is a rich brown, about 10 minutes; turn; brown other side.

2. Push chicken to one side; sauté onion in drippings until soft. Stir in spaghetti sauce and basil; cover and simmer 20 minutes. Taste; add salt, if you wish. Serve with spaghetti and crusty bread, if you wish.

Tunisian Baked Chicken.

Tunisian Baked Chicken

Bake at 375° for 45 minutes.

Makes 8 servings.

4 whole chicken breasts (about 12 ounces each), split	minced
	3/4 teaspoon ground cumin
3 tablespoons all-purpose flour	1/2 teaspoon paprika
1 teaspoon salt	Pinch cayenne pepper
1/4 teaspoon pepper	1/2 cup chicken broth
3 tablespoons vegetable oil	Juice of 1 small lemon
	1 small lemon, thinly sliced
1 1/2 cups coarsely chopped onion (about 2 medium-size onions)	1/3 cup halved pimiento-stuffed green olives
2 cloves garlic,	1 tablespoon chopped parsley

1. Pat chicken dry with paper toweling. Combine flour, salt and pepper on wax paper. Turn chicken in flour mixture to evenly coat; shake off excess.
2. Sauté chicken pieces a few at a time in oil in a large skillet; remove pieces to a 13 × 9 × 2-inch baking dish as they brown, arranging in a single layer.
3. Preheat the oven to moderate (375°).
4. Add onion, garlic, cumin, paprika and cayenne to the skillet; sauté until onion is slightly softened. Stir in chicken broth and the juice of 1 small lemon, scraping up any browned bits from bottom of the skillet. Bring to boiling; pour over chicken. Arrange lemon slices over chicken.
5. Bake, covered, in the preheated moderate oven (375°) for 40 minutes. Uncover; sprinkle with olives.

Bake, uncovered, for 5 minutes or until chicken is tender. Sprinkle with parsley. Serve.

Chicken Enchiladas in Cheese Cream

Extra chicken breasts stored in your freezer? Put them to good use in this rich Tex-Mex main dish.

Bake at 400° for 20 minutes.

Makes 12 servings.

2 whole boneless, skinned chicken breasts (about 1 pound), halved	1/2 teaspoon ground cumin
	1/2 teaspoon salt
1/2 cup water	1/4 teaspoon leaf oregano, crumbled
2 cloves garlic, thinly sliced	1/4 teaspoon pepper
1 large onion, finely chopped (1 cup)	1/4 cup all-purpose flour
3 tablespoons butter or margarine	1 cup chicken broth
	1 cup heavy cream
1 clove garlic, finely chopped	1/2 pound Monterey Jack cheese, shredded (2 cups)
2 cans (3 1/2 ounces each) whole green chilies, seeded, rinsed and chopped	1/4 to 1/3 cup vegetable oil
	12 corn tortillas (6-inch)
1 tablespoon chili powder	6 green onions, trimmed and sliced

1. Place the chicken breasts in a medium-size saucepan. Add the water and sliced garlic. Cover. Bring to a simmer. Cook just until tender, about 15

(continued)

minutes. Cool. Remove the chicken and reserve the broth. Cut the chicken into thin julienne strips. Set aside in a bowl.

2. Sauté the onion in the butter in a medium-size skillet just until soft, about 5 minutes. Add the chopped garlic; sauté for 1 minute. Add the chilies, chili powder, cumin, salt, oregano and pepper; cook for 1 minute. Stir in the flour until well combined; cook for 1 minute, stirring.

3. Stir in the reserved cooking broth, the 1 cup of chicken broth and heavy cream. Cook over medium heat, stirring frequently, until the mixture thickens, about 10 minutes. Remove from the heat. Stir in 1 cup of the shredded cheese until melted.

4. Combine 1 cup of the cheese sauce with the reserved chicken.

5. Preheat the oven to hot (400°).

6. Heat the vegetable oil in a small skillet until hot. Dip the tortillas one at a time in the hot oil, just until limp, about 5 to 10 seconds on each side; do not let them become crisp. Place on a work surface.

7. Divide the chicken filling equally along the center of each tortilla. Top each with sliced green onions. Roll up the tortillas and place, seam-side down, in 2 rows in a 13 × 9 × 2-inch baking dish. Pour the remaining cheese sauce evenly over the tortillas. Sprinkle with the remaining 1 cup of cheese.

8. Bake in the preheated hot oven (400°) for 20 minutes or until bubbly. Garnish with extra sliced green onions, if you wish.

Caribbean Chicken and Squash Stew

Makes 8 servings.

1 broiler-fryer (3 pounds), cut up	butt, cut into 1/2-inch cubes
2 tablespoons vegetable oil	1/4 cup shredded coconut
2 medium-size onions, sliced	2 large sweet potatoes (1 pound), pared and cut into cubes
1/2 to 1 teaspoon crushed red pepper	
1/2 teaspoon leaf thyme, crumbled	1 medium-size butternut squash (1 1/2 pounds), pared, seeded and cut into wedges
1 can condensed chicken broth	
1 can (16 ounces) stewed tomatoes	
1 teaspoon salt	1 package (10 ounces) frozen peas
1 pound smoked pork	Hot cooked rice

1. Brown chicken, a few pieces at a time, in oil in large Dutch oven or heavy kettle; remove pieces as they brown. Add onions to drippings in pan and sauté until golden; stir in crushed red pepper and thyme. Return chicken pieces to pan.

2. Add chicken broth, tomatoes, salt, pork, and coconut. Bring to boiling; lower heat; cover. Simmer 15 minutes. Add sweet potatoes and squash. Simmer 35 to 40 minutes longer or until chicken and

vegetables are tender. Stir in peas; cook 5 minutes. Serve with rice.

Sweet-and-Sour Apricot-Glazed Chicken Thighs

Bake at 375° for 45 minutes.

Makes 4 servings.

8 chicken thighs (2 1/2 pounds)	style mustard
1 teaspoon salt	Cooked rice (optional)
1/4 teaspoon pepper	Raisins (optional)
1/2 cup apricot jam	Almond slivers (optional)
2 tablespoons bottled chili sauce	Chopped parsley (optional)
1 tablespoon Dijon-	

1. Preheat the oven to moderate (375°).

2. Pat chicken dry. Sprinkle with salt and pepper. Place chicken, skin-side up, in a 13 × 9 × 2-inch baking dish.

3. Combine apricot jam, chili sauce and mustard in small bowl. Force mixture through a small strainer with the back of a spoon.

4. Bake in the preheated moderate oven (375°) for 25 minutes. Brush skin side of chicken with half the apricot glaze. Bake 20 minutes more or until tender, brushing with the remaining glaze. Serve on a bed of hot cooked rice with raisins, almond slivers and chopped parsley, if you wish.

Arroz Con Pollo

Spain's classic chicken bakes neatly in a casserole together with golden saffron, rice, tomatoes, and peas. With canned and frozen foods trimming preparation time, it's oven-ready in minutes.

Broil for 8 to 10 minutes; bake at 375° for 45 minutes, and then for 15 minutes.

Makes 6 servings.

1 broiler-fryer (about 3 pounds), cut up	1 can (16 ounces) tomatoes, undrained
3 tablespoons olive oil	2 envelopes or teaspoons instant chicken broth
1 teaspoon salt	
1/4 teaspoon pepper	
1/2 teaspoon paprika	1 bay leaf
1 cup frozen chopped onion	1 1/4 cups uncooked long-grain rice
1 clove garlic, crushed	
1/4 teaspoon crushed saffron	1 package (10 ounces) frozen peas, thawed
1/2 teaspoon leaf oregano, crumbled	1 canned pimiento, slivered
1 cup water	

1. Rub chicken pieces with 1 tablespoon of the olive oil, then sprinkle with 1/4 teaspoon of the salt, 1/8 teaspoon of the pepper and all of the paprika. Place

Sweet-and-Sour
Apricot-Glazed Chicken
Thighs, page 660.

Caribbean Chicken and
Squash Stew, page 660.

skin side up on a foil-lined shallow baking pan and broil, 5 inches from the heat, 8 to 10 minutes or until nicely browned.

2. Meanwhile, sauté onion and garlic in a large heavy skillet over fairly high heat in remaining 2 tablespoons olive oil 3 to 4 minutes until limp. Mix in saffron and oregano and heat, stirring, 1 to 2 minutes. Stir in water, tomatoes, instant chicken broth, bay leaf, remaining ³/₄ teaspoon salt and ¹/₈ teaspoon pepper. Simmer 1 to 2 minutes, breaking up tomatoes; add rice and bring to boiling, continuing to stir.

3. Pour all into a 3-quart casserole; arrange browned chicken pieces on top, pushing them down into liquid slightly. Cover.

4. Bake in a moderate oven (375°) for 45 minutes or until rice is almost tender and almost all liquid is absorbed. Fork up rice mixture a bit; add peas and pimiento, distributing them attractively in and around chicken pieces and pushing most of them down into rice mixture. Re-cover and bake 15 minutes longer until peas are cooked through. Remove bay leaf.

Hong Kong Chicken

Bake at 350° for 1¹/₂ hours.

Makes 4 servings.

1 broiler-fryer (about 3 pounds)	**¹/₄ cup soy sauce**
¹/₄ **cup water**	**¹/₄ cup honey**
¹/₄ **cup dry sherry**	**2 teaspoons seasoned salt**

1. Cut chicken into quarters; arrange in a single layer in a 13 × 9 × 2-inch baking dish.

2. Mix water, sherry, soy sauce, honey and seasoned salt in a small bowl; pour over chicken, turning to coat on all sides; cover. Marinate chicken in refrigerator about 4 hours or overnight.

3. About 2 hours before serving time, remove chicken from refrigerator; let stand at room temperature 30 minutes, then drain; reserve marinade. Arrange chicken, skin-side up, on rack over broiler pan or in a shallow baking pan with a rack. Brush generously with part of the marinade.

4. Bake in a moderate oven (350°), basting with remaining marinade every 20 minutes, 1¹/₂ hours or until chicken is tender and deep golden brown.

Silo Chicken

Grill for 40 minutes.
Makes 6 servings.

3 small chickens or
large Cornish game
hens (1½ to
2 pounds each)
½ lemon
1½ teaspoons coarse
salt
1 teaspoon finely
chopped fresh sage
OR: ⅓ teaspoon leaf
sage, crumbled
½ teaspoon snipped
fresh chives
¼ teaspoon mild
paprika
OR: ¼ teaspoon
mild ground chilies
⅛ teaspoon cayenne

pepper
1 jar (12 ounces)
apricot preserves
½ cup chicken broth
1 tablespoon soy
sauce
1 tablespoon Dijon-
style mustard
½ teaspoon chopped
fresh thyme
OR: ⅛ teaspoon leaf
thyme
1 teaspoon grated
lemon rind
½ teaspoon black
pepper
Vegetable oil

1. Remove the backbones from the chickens or hens.
Cut each chicken in half through the breast. Wipe the
chicken with damp paper toweling. Pound gently with
the flat side of a cleaver or the bottom of a heavy
saucepan to flatten the chicken as much as possible.
2. Squeeze the lemon over the chicken. Sprinkle with
the salt, sage, chives, paprika and cayenne. Wrap the
chicken in wax paper and place in a 13 × 9 × 2-inch
baking pan. Refrigerate overnight.
3. Let the chicken stand at room temperature for 1
hour before grilling.
4. Combine the apricot preserves, chicken broth, soy
sauce, mustard, thyme, lemon rind and pepper in a
saucepan. Bring to boiling. Lower the heat and
simmer for 5 minutes. Let cool.

Sautéed Chicken Breasts with Oranges, page 666.

5. Prepare the charcoal for grilling, or preheat the gas
unit.
6. Place the chicken halves, skin-side down, on the
grid. Sear over high heat until browned, 2 to 3
minutes. Turn the chicken over and brown the other
side. Remove the chicken from the grid.
7. Cover the grid with heavy-duty aluminum foil; punch
ventilation holes every 2 inches. Brush the foil lightly
with the oil.
8. Return the chicken to the foil, skin-side up. Baste
well with the apricot mixture. Cover the grill with the
dome. Cook, basting about every 5 minutes with the
apricot mixture, until the juices run clear when the
chicken is pierced with a fork and the meat is no
longer pink near the bone, about 40 minutes.

Note: To make a barbecue cover or dome, see
instructions in chapter Meat, following recipe Tulsa
Rib.

Hot Chicken Salad

A tasty old-fashioned casserole.
Bake at 350° for 45 minutes.

Makes 10 servings.

3 cups cooked bite-
size chicken pieces
(about ¾ pound)*
3 cups thinly sliced
celery
3 cups cooked rice
1 medium-size onion,
chopped (½ cup)
1 box (10 ounces)
frozen peas, thawed
1½ cups mayonnaise

or salad dressing
3 tablespoons lemon
juice
1 teaspoon salt
¼ teaspoon pepper
¼ cup (½ stick) butter
or margarine
⅓ cup all-purpose
flour
3 cups chicken broth
½ cup sliced almonds

1. Preheat the oven to moderate (350°). Grease a
13 x 9 x 2-inch baking pan.
2. Combine the chicken pieces, celery, rice, onion
and peas in a large bowl. Stir in the mayonnaise,
lemon juice, salt and pepper; mix well.
3. Melt the butter in a medium-size saucepan over
medium heat. Stir in the flour. Cook, stirring
constantly, for 1 minute or until the mixture is
thickened and bubbly. Gradually pour in the chicken
broth. Cook, stirring constantly, until the sauce is
thick and smooth, about 2 minutes.
4. Pour the sauce over the chicken mixture; stir to
combine thoroughly. Spoon into the prepared pan.
Sprinkle with the almonds.
5. Bake in the preheated moderate oven (350°) for
45 minutes or until bubbly hot.

To Make Ahead: Complete Step 2 of the recipe,
cover the bowl and refrigerate until ready to bake.
About 30 minutes before ready to bake, remove from
the refrigerator and allow to come to room
temperature. Proceed with the recipe.

*About 2 pounds of whole chicken breasts or a 3-
pound broiler-fryer will yield 3 cups of cooked
chicken pieces.*

Silo Chicken, page 662; Oh My! Potato Salad, page 695; Herbed Tomatoes and Onions, page 785.

Food for Thought...

Chicken is well suited to most all dietary needs, providing complete protein at a moderate cost. It is a short-fibered meat, easy to digest, and calorie-conscious consumers concerned with nutrition naturally think of chicken when dieting.

● Chicken contains fewer calories than most meats. A 3¹/₂-ounce serving of broiled chicken (without the skin) has only about 136 calories, but provides 31.2 grams of protein or 52% of the average adult daily requirements, plus vitamin A, thiamine, riboflavin, niacin, iron and phosphorus.

● Chicken is lower in fats than most red meats. Three ounces of broiled chicken, even with the skin, yields about 9 grams of fat. That amount is doubled or tripled in an equal portion of other meats. Chicken skin contains about 17% fat, a small amount compared to the flavor it offers, and two-thirds of the fat is unsaturated.

● Team chicken with low-calorie vegetables — broccoli, tomatoes, zucchini — instead of starchy fillers.

● Cook chicken in low-cal ways — poached in defatted broth, sautéed in a nonstick skillet without oil.

● If you are really counting the calories, don't eat the skin. Perk up the flavor with herbs and spices such as rosemary, tarragon, or dill.

Orange-Glazed Baked Chicken

To reduce cholesterol intake, remove all visible fat from the chicken.

Bake at 350° for 1 hour.

Makes 8 servings.

2 broiler-fryers (2¹/₂ pounds each), cut into quarters	orange rind
1 clove garlic, crushed	¹/₂ teaspoon dry mustard
1 cup orange juice	¹/₄ teaspoon ground nutmeg
1 tablespoon grated	1 orange, thinly sliced

1. Preheat the oven to moderate (350°).
2. Wash the chicken; pat dry. Place in a large roasting pan. Rub the chicken skin with the garlic.
3. Combine the orange juice, orange rind, mustard and nutmeg; pour over the chicken.
4. Bake, uncovered, in the preheated moderate oven (350°), basting frequently, until tender and well browned, about 1 hour. Garnish with the orange slices.

Quick Crispy Skillet Chicken

A fast and easy pan-sauteéd chicken, complete with vegetables and gravy.

Makes 6 servings.

3 whole boneless chicken breasts, skinned, and halved (about 1³/₄ pounds)	crumbs
	¹/₃ cup finely chopped walnuts
3 tablespoons all-purpose flour	Crisp-Cooked Vegetables
1 teaspoon salt	2 tablespoons vegetable oil
¹/₄ teaspoon ground pepper	2 tablespoons butter or margarine
2 eggs	Sherry Pan Gravy (*recipe follows*)
1 tablespoon milk	Watercress (*optional*)
²/₃ cup fine dry bread	

1. Trim chicken of all excess fat. Place chicken in single layer on wax paper.
2. Mix flour, salt and pepper in small bowl; sprinkle over chicken; turn to coat sides.
3. Beat together eggs and milk in shallow bowl. Mix bread crumbs and walnuts on wax paper. Dip each chicken breast in egg mixture to coat, letting excess drip back into bowl. Turn in crumb mixture to coat evenly; pat lightly with hand to help crumbs stick. Place breaded breasts in single layer on small cookie sheet. Freeze briefly to set coating, about 5 minutes.
4. Prepare Crisp-Cooked Vegetables.
5. Heat oil and butter in large heavy skillet over medium-high heat until bubbly. Add chicken breasts in single layer; brown 2 minutes on each side. Lower heat; continue cooking 4 to 5 minutes longer on each side or until chicken is firm to the touch. Remove from skillet. Keep warm.
6. Prepare Sherry Pan Gravy.
7. Arrange chicken on warm platter with vegetables. Garnish with watercress, if you wish. Serve with gravy and rice.

Sherry Pan Gravy: After the chicken has been removed from the skillet, add 3 to 4 tablespoons dry sherry and 1 can (13³/₄ ounces) chicken broth to skillet. Bring to boiling, scraping up browned bits from bottom and side of skillet. Stir together 3 tablespoons all-purpose flour and ¹/₃ cup water in a cup to make a smooth paste. Stir into skillet; continue cooking and stirring until sauce thickens. Lower heat; simmer 2 minutes. Season to taste with salt and pepper. Pour into gravy boat. Makes 1³/₄ cups.

Chicken Paprika with Spatzle

Paprika-flavored chicken in sour cream sauce, served with tender homemade dumplings.

Makes 6 servings.

1 broiler-fryer (3 to 3¹/₂ pounds), cut up	chopped (1 cup)
	2 tablespoons paprika
¹/₂ cup all-purpose flour	1 cup chicken broth
1¹/₂ teaspoons salt	1 cup light cream or half-and-half
¹/₄ teaspoon pepper	¹/₂ cup dairy sour cream
¹/₂ cup (1 stick) butter or margarine	Spatzle (*recipe follows*)
1 large onion,	

1. Shake chicken in plastic bag with flour, 1 teaspoon of the salt and pepper until coated. Reserve 2 tablespoons of the flour mixture.
2. Brown chicken in butter in a large skillet, removing pieces as they brown to plate. Pour pan fat into a measuring cup. Return 3 tablespoons to skillet.
3. Sauté onion in fat until light golden brown, about 10 minutes. Add paprika, remaining ¹/₂ teaspoon salt and chicken broth. Bring to boiling; lower heat; return chicken, turning to coat. Cook, covered, 30 minutes or until chicken is tender. Remove chicken; keep warm.
4. Stir in light cream. Make a paste of the reserved 2 tablespoons flour mixture and sour cream; slowly stir into skillet. Cook, stirring constantly, over low heat until thickened. *Do not boil.* Return chicken. Serve over Spatzle. Sprinkle with chopped parsley, if you wish.

Pictured opposite (from top left): Mama's Chicken Soup with Fluffy Matzo Balls, page 727; Orange-Glazed Baked Chicken, page 664; Carrot-Yam Tzimmes, page 764; Dilled Green Beans, page 760; Matzo Honey Cake, page 167.

Quick Crispy
Skillet Chicken,
page 664.

Spatzle

Makes 6 servings.

3 cups *sifted*
   all-purpose flour
1 teaspoon salt
1/8 teaspoon white
   pepper

3 eggs, slightly beaten
1 cup water
1/4 cup (1/2 stick) butter
   or margarine,
   melted

1. Combine flour, salt and pepper in a medium-size bowl; make well in center. Add eggs and water to well and mix thoroughly.
2. Scoop up dough on a spatula and cut off small pieces with knife into boiling salted water. As spatzle rises to the top, remove with slotted spoon and put in covered bowl until all are made. Toss with butter; keep warm.

Sauteéd Chicken Breasts with Oranges

Serve with steamed broccoli flowerets.
Makes 4 servings.

2 whole boneless,
   skinned chicken
   breasts (about
   1 pound), halved
1/4 teaspoon leaf
   thyme, crumbled
1/4 teaspoon salt
1/8 teaspoon pepper
1/4 cup finely chopped

shallots
OR: chopped green
   onion, white part
   only
2 tablespoons butter
2 large navel oranges,
   peeled and
   sectioned

1. Place the chicken breasts between 2 sheets of dampened wax paper. Pound to 1/4-inch thickness with a rolling pin or the flat side of meat mallet.

Sprinkle with the thyme, salt and pepper.
2. Sauté the chicken and shallots in the butter in a large nonstick skillet until the chicken is browned, 2 to 3 minutes on each side. Add the orange sections. Cook, turning the chicken breasts for 1 to 2 minutes more or until the juices are slightly thickened.

Chicken Tarragon

Makes 4 servings.

2 whole chicken breasts (14 ounces each), split	**(white part)**
	¼ pound mushrooms, chopped
2 tablespoons flour	**1½ teaspoons chopped fresh tarragon**
½ teaspoon salt	
⅛ teaspoon pepper	
1 tablespoon butter or margarine	**OR: ½ teaspoon leaf tarragon, crumbled**
1 tablespoon vegetable oil	**½ cup dry white wine or chicken broth**
½ cup chopped leeks	

1. Skin and bone chicken. Flatten slightly between sheets of wax paper with rolling pin. Combine flour, salt and pepper on wax paper. Coat chicken in flour.
2. Heat butter and oil in large skillet. Sauté leeks, mushrooms and tarragon until softened. Add chicken to pan. Sauté 3 minutes; turn.
3. Stir in wine; cook 3 more minutes.

Scaloppine with Lemon Zest

Makes 4 servings.

2 whole chicken breasts (about 14 ounces each), boned, skinned and halved	**1 tablespoon vegetable oil**
	1 tablespoon butter or margarine
OR: 4 rib pork chops (each ½-inch thick), boned	**½ teaspoon leaf rosemary, crumbled**
	1 large clove garlic, minced
½ teaspoon salt	**¼ cup dry white wine**
¼ teaspoon pepper	**½ cup chicken broth**
Flour	**½ cup dairy sour cream**
1 lemon	

1. Place chicken breast halves or pork between sheets of wax paper and pound firmly with a meat mallet or rolling pin until they are ¼-inch thick or thinner. Sprinkle with salt and pepper; dip in flour and pat briskly to remove the excess.
2. Remove rind from lemon (yellow part only) with vegetable parer. Stack strips on a chopping board and cut crosswise into fine julienne strips.
3. Heat oil and butter in large skillet. Sauté scaloppine until golden brown on both sides, about 5 minutes for chicken and 8 minutes for pork.
4. Sprinkle rosemary and garlic over scaloppine and shake the pan to distribute evenly for about 30 seconds. Add wine and chicken broth. Cook, uncovered, until the pan liquid has reduced a little.
5. Remove scaloppine to warm platter. Stir sour cream and half of the lemon rind into liquid in skillet. Heat over low heat, but do not boil. Pour sauce over scaloppine and sprinkle with remaining lemon rind.

Low-Calorie Coq au Vin

Here's a streamlined version of France's classic chicken in wine dish. We've replaced the stewing chicken with a trim, young fryer (extra tender, too) and lean Canadian bacon takes the place of fatty salt pork.

Makes 4 servings at 299 calories each.

1 broiler-fryer, cut up (about 2¼ pounds)	**1 tablespoon dried parsley flakes**
2 slices Canadian bacon, cut in strips	**2 cups dry red wine**
	1 can (3 or 4 ounces) sliced mushrooms
½ teaspoon garlic powder	**1 can (8 ounces) small white onions**
1 bay leaf	**2 tablespoons flour**
½ teaspoon leaf thyme, crumbled	**¼ cup cold water**

1. Arrange the chicken, skin-side down, in a cold, nonstick skillet. Cook over medium heat, allowing chicken to brown in its own melting fat. Add the Canadian bacon; brown lightly. Drain off any accumulated fat.
2. Add garlic powder, bay leaf, thyme, parsley flakes and wine to chicken. Drain the mushrooms and onions and add liquids to skillet. Reserve drained vegetables. Bring to boiling; cover. Lower heat; simmer 45 minutes or until chicken is tender.
3. Add drained mushrooms and onions. Simmer, uncovered, 5 minutes or until the liquid is reduced to about 1 cup. Remove bay leaf. Combine the flour and cold water; stir into simmering liquid. Cook, stirring constantly, until the sauce thickens and bubbles 3 minutes. Taste and add salt and pepper, if you wish.

Yakitori

Grilled on a hibachi or broiled in an oven, these bite-size bits of skewered chicken get their special flavor from a teriyaki sauce. Yaki *means grilled and* teri *means bird.*

Makes 4 servings.

2 whole chicken breasts (about 12 ounces each)	**sauce**
	1 tablespoon sugar
1 small onion	**1 tablespoon minced fresh ginger**
¾ cup sake* or dry sherry	**OR: 1 teaspoon ground ginger**
¾ cup Japanese soy	

1. Skim and bone chicken. Cut into 1-inch pieces. Cut onion into 8 wedges. *(continued)*

2. Thread pieces of chicken and onion alternately on each of 12 short bamboo skewers.
3. Combine sake, soy sauce, sugar and ginger in a medium-size skillet. Bring to boiling; lower heat and simmer 15 minutes or until sauce has been reduced to 1¼ cups. Dip skewers into sauce.
4. Grill about 4 inches above medium coals for 2 to 3 minutes; turn and brush with sauce. Grill until chicken is tender, about 3 minutes longer, brushing with sauce. Place skewers on serving platter; garnish with watercress, if you wish.
* A fermented rice beverage.

Rock Cornish Game Hen
This is a specially bred, very small chicken that weighs 1½ pounds or less. It was developed from an English breed called Cornish hen. It is available frozen or fresh in supermarkets across the country. Allow half a 1½-pound or a whole 1-pound game hen per person.

Cornish Game Hens, French-Style

Bacon strips placed over the birds keeps them moist and oranges add a tart flavor.

Bake at 400° for 10 minutes, then at 350° for 1 hour.

Makes 4 servings.

4 Rock Cornish game hens (about ¾ to 1 pound each), thawed if frozen	or margarine
	¼ cup finely chopped shallots or green onion tops
1 teaspoon salt	¼ cup red currant jelly
½ teaspoon pepper	1 teaspoon dry mustard
1 small orange, cut into quarters and seeded	¾ teaspoon salt
4 bacon slices	½ teaspoon leaf tarragon, crumbled
5 to 6 navel or Valencia oranges	⅛ teaspoon cayenne
2 tablespoons butter	

1. Sprinkle inside of birds with salt and pepper; put 1 orange quarter into the cavity of each bird. Truss each bird by tying the legs and wings close to the body.
2. Cut bacon slices in half; cover the breast of each bird with two halves. Place the birds in a shallow roasting pan.
3. Bake in a hot oven (400°) for 10 minutes; lower oven temperature to moderate (350°); roast for an additional 45 minutes.
4. Grate rind from one orange (1 tablespoon). Cut orange rind from 2 more oranges with a vegetable parer or sharp knife (do not include white); cut rind into thin julienne strips. With a sharp knife, remove remaining white membrane from the 3 oranges over a large bowl to catch juice; then section.
5. Drain juice into a measuring cup. Squeeze juice from remaining oranges to make 1 cup orange juice; reserve.

6. Melt butter in a medium-size skillet; add shallots; cook until shallots are soft but not browned. Stir in jelly and the orange rind, mustard, salt, tarragon and cayenne; cook until jelly is melted. Stir in orange juice; bring sauce to boiling.
7. Remove birds from oven; remove string and bacon. Carefully pour off all fat from roasting pan. Pour orange sauce over birds. Return to oven and bake an additional 15 minutes, basting frequently.
8. Remove from oven; place on heated serving platter. Place roasting pan on top of stove; bring sauce to boiling; add reserved orange sections and julienne orange strips; heat to boiling. Spoon a little sauce over each bird. Serve with remaining sauce. Garnish with parsley, if you wish.

Green Chile-Stuffed Cornish Game Hens

Bake at 350° for 1 hour 15 minutes.

Makes 8 servings.

4 Rock Cornish game hens (about 1¼ to 1½ pounds each)	creamed corn
	2 green chilies, seeded and chopped (from a 4-ounce can)
1 teaspoon leaf oregano, crumbled	
1½ teaspoons salt	2 tablespoons butter or margarine
¼ teaspoon pepper	2 tablespoons vegetable oil
1½ cups cornbread stuffing mix (from an 8-ounce package)	1 pound yellow squash, cut into ¼-inch slices
1 can (8 ounces)	

1. Thaw hens, if frozen; rub inside and out with oregano, salt and pepper.
2. Combine cornbread stuffing, corn and green chilies in a medium-size bowl; mix with fork until thoroughly moistened. Stuff body cavities lightly. Close body cavity with poultry pins and string; tie legs to tail.
3. Brown hens, two at a time, slowly on all sides in butter and oil in a large skillet. Remove to wax paper.
4. Tear off 4 large pieces of 18-inch-wide heavy-duty foil (large enough to wrap around hens).
5. Divide squash evenly among foil pieces; place a hen in center of squash; bring foil up over hens and wrap securely. Place on cookie sheet or directly on middle shelf of oven.
6. Bake in a moderate oven (350°) for 1 hour; unwrap hens, folding foil back; bake an additional 15 minutes to brown skin. Serve ½ hen per person.

Pictured opposite:
Green Chile-Stuffed Cornish Game Hens.

Stuffed Cornish Hens in Herb Butter

Roast at 400° for 50 minutes.

Makes 4 servings.

4 Rock Cornish game hens (about 1 pound each)	1/2 teaspoon leaf tarragon, crumbled
1/4 cup (1/2 stick) butter, softened	1/2 teaspoon salt
1/4 cup chopped fresh parsley	Brown Rice Stuffing (recipe follows)
	1 tablespoon flour
	1/2 dry white wine

1. Remove giblets from hens. Simmer giblets in 1 cup salted water in a small saucepan until tender, about 45 minutes. Strain; reserve livers; measure broth. You should have 3/4 cup.
2. Blend butter, parsley, tarragon and salt in a small bowl. Loosen the breast skin from the meat on each of the hens with your fingers. Slide about 1 teaspoon of the butter mixture under the breast skin of each hen.
3. Prepare Brown Rice Stuffing and spoon loosely into cavity of each hen. Tie legs together; bend wing tips under hens. Arrange hens in shallow roasting pan. Spread remaining butter mixture into hens.
4. Roast in a hot oven (400°), basting often, about 50 minutes or until hens are golden and juices run clear. Arrange hens on heated platter.
5. Add reserved giblet cooking broth to drippings in roasting pan, stirring to loosen brown bits; pour liquid into small saucepan. Blend flour with wine in a cup; pour into saucepan. Cook, stirring constantly, until sauce thickens and bubbles, 3 minutes. Spoon over hens. Sprinkle with additional parsley, if you wish.

Brown Rice Stuffing: Bring 1 1/2 cups water and 1/2 teaspoon salt to boiling in a small saucepan; stir in 1/2 cup brown rice. Lower heat; cover; simmer until tender, about 40 minutes. Heat 2 tablespoons butter in a small skillet; stir in 2 tablespoons finely chopped onion, 2 tablespoons finely chooped celery and 2 tablespoons finely chopped carrot. Sauté 5 minutes. Cut up reserved cooked livers from hen and add to vegetables with 2 tablespoons dry white wine. Cover; simmer 3 to 4 minutes; stir into rice; toss to mix.

Grilled Cornish Game Hens

Makes 6 servings.

6 Cornish game hens (3/4 to 1 pound each)	1 teaspoon leaf rosemary, crumbled
1 teaspoon salt	OR: 1 tablespoon fresh rosemary, chopped
1/2 teaspoon pepper	
1/2 cup (1 stick) butter, melted	Fresh rosemary (optional)
3 tablespoons lemon juice	

1. Truss birds. Rub skin with salt and pepper. Arrange on a barbecue spit, head to tail.

2. Combine melted butter, lemon juice and rosemary in a bowl.
3. Attach the spit to electric rotisserie. Grill hens over hot coals, basting with seasoned buter, 1 to 1 1/4 hours or until meat is no longer pink near bone. Garnish with fresh rosemary, if you wish.

Lemon-Roasted Cornish Hens

Roast at 375° for 50 minutes.

Makes 4 servings.

2 lemons	each)
3 tablespoons butter or margarine, softened	2 tablespoons vegetable oil
1 teaspoon salt	1 small onion, sliced
1/4 teaspoon pepper	1 clove garlic, crushed
2 teaspoons chopped fresh mint	1 cup chicken broth
OR: 1/2 teaspoon dried mint, crumbled	2 teaspoons cornstarch
	1 tablespoon water
	Chopped fresh mint or parsley
4 Rock Cornish game hens (3/4 to 1 pound	Watercress (optional)

1. Grate enough lemon rind to make 1 teaspoon. Peel thin yellow rind from remaining lemon; cut in julienne strips to make about 2 tablespoons; reserve. Squeeze enough lemon juice to make 1/4 cup.
2. Mix butter, grated lemon rind, salt, pepper and mint. Rub mixture over hens. Place in shallow small roasting pan.
3. Roast in a moderate oven (375°), basting often, for about 50 minutes or until hens are golden and juices run clear when skin is pierced. Arrange on heated platter.
4. While hens cook, prepare lemon sauce. Heat oil in medium-size saucepan; sauté onion 5 minutes. Stir in reserved julienne lemon peel and garlic; cook and stir 1 minute. Add chicken broth; bring to boiling. Mix cornstarch with water; stir into boiling sauce; boil 1 minute. Stir in reserved lemon juice; remove from heat.
5. Spoon a little sauce over each hen on platter; sprinkle with additional chopped mint or parsley. Garnish with watercress and serve with steamed fresh asparagus, if you wish.

Capon   A male chicken, castrated while young so that it will grow plump and tender in a matter of months. A capon is marketed at 16 weeks of age and weighs from 4 to 7 pounds. It has a high proportion of white meat and a delicious flavor. It is excellent roasted, stewed or braised.

Roast Young Capon with Wild Rice Stuffing

Bake at 350° for 1³/₄ hours.

Makes 6 servings.

1 capon (5 to 6 pounds)
8 tablespoons (1 stick) butter or margarine
Salt and freshly ground black pepper to taste
1 small clove garlic, minced
1 large onion, finely chopped (1 cup)
¹/₂ cup finely diced green pepper
¹/₂ cup finely diced celery with leaves
¹/₂ cup sliced mushrooms
2 cups cooked wild rice
¹/₂ cup chopped toasted almonds
¹/₄ teaspoon ground sage
¹/₄ teaspoon leaf thyme, crumbled

1. Rub the capon inside and outside with 2 tablespoons of the butter. Sprinkle inside with salt and pepper.
2. Heat 4 tablespoons of the butter in a skillet and cook the garlic, onion, green pepper and celery, stirring until onion is translucent.
3. In a separate skillet, cook the mushrooms in remaining butter until mushrooms are wilted.
4. Combine the wild rice, onion mixture, mushrooms, almonds, sage and thyme. Add salt and pepper to taste. Stuff the capon with the mixture. Truss capon.
5. Place the capon, breast-side up, on a rack in a roasting pan.
6. Bake in a moderate oven (350°), basting frequently with pan juices, for 20 to 25 minutes to the pound, about 1³/₄ hours.

Duckling

Duckling   Duck breeders prefer to use the term "duckling" for their commodity, since it more aptly denotes the very young, American-raised ducks that are sold.

Duck is seldom served at everyday meals. It has been largely reserved for special holiday meals or restaurant fare. In America, chicken and turkey will probably continue to outrank duck in popularity, but to immigrants from China, France, Czechoslovakia, Poland, Hungary and Germany, duck will remain number one. In those countries, ducks are highly regarded and great quantities are consumed.

The Chinese cuisine boasts hundreds of ways of preparing all parts of the duck. Ducks are roasted, salted and dried, boiled in soups or braised in soy sauce. Duck skin is served as a tasty morsel wrapped inside Mandarin pancakes; the meat is stir-fried with vegetables and the bones are used to flavor soup.

Duck feet, gizzards and livers are also considered to be great delicacies.

Long Island ducks, well known in the culinary world, are descendants of the White Peking ducks of China, which were first imported into New york in 1873 by a Yankee trader. Offspring of those ducks were raised in Connecticut, then transferred to eastern Long Island. Soon duck farms flourished on the Island, and the Long Island duckling has come to be known as a breed or type of duck.

Today, because of the skyrocketing cost of farmland, there are very few duck farms left on the Island, although Long Island will always be associated with duckling. The bulk of today's duck farms are located primarily in Wisconsin, Indiana, and Virginia.

Ducklings are frozen for shipment throughout the country. In some areas fresh, ice-chilled ducklings are available. An average duckling weighs from 4 to 6 pounds. Allow one-quarter to one-half duckling per person. Poultry shears can be used to cut the bird neatly into quarters.

Roast Ducklings with Kasha Stuffing

Roast at 350° for 2 to 2¹/₂ hours.

Makes 8 servings.

2 ducklings (4 to 5 pounds each), thawed, if frozen
¹/₂ teaspoon salt
¹/₄ teaspoon pepper
1 cup buckwheat groats (kasha)
1 egg
2 cups boiling water
1 large onion, chopped (1 cup)
¹/₂ cup chopped
carrots
¹/₂ cup chopped celery
¹/₂ cup chopped fresh parsley
¹/₄ pound mushrooms, chopped
1¹/₂ teaspoons salt
¹/₂ teaspoon pepper
1 cup sweetened Concorn grape wine
1 teaspoon grated orange rind

1. Remove livers and giblets from ducklings; dice livers; reserve. Remove as much of the yellow fat from ducklings as possible; dice. Sprinkle the ducklings inside and out with the ¹/₂ teaspoon salt and ¹/₄ teaspoon pepper.
2. Mix kasha and egg in a small bowl. Heat the diced fat in a large skillet until brown and crisp. Add the kasha mixture and stir until lightly browned. Stir in the boiling water; simmer for 15 to 20 minutes or until all liquid is absorbed. Stir in livers, onion, carrots, celery, parsley, mushrooms and the remaining salt and pepper; allow mixture to cool.
3. Stuff ducklings with kasha mixture. Skewer openings closed and place ducklings on a rack in a large open roasting pan. Prick skin with a two-tined fork, especially around thighs and back, to allow fat to escape as ducklings roast.
4. Roast in a moderate oven (350°) for 1 hour. Baste with a mixture of the wine and orange rind every 20 minutes for the next 1 to 1¹/₂ hours or until leg of bird can be moved up and down easily.

Chinese Roast Duck

Roast at 350° for 2 hours, then at 400° for 5 minutes.

Makes 4 servings.

1 duckling (about 5 pounds)	2 cups boiling water
2 teaspoons salt	2 tablespoons honey
4 green onions	Spicy Duck Sauce (recipe follows)

1. Rub duckling inside and out with salt; stuff onions inside cavity; tie legs of duckling together. Place on rack in roasting pan. Mix boiling water and honey; pour over duckling, letting water run into roasting pan. Duckling should not touch water.
2. Roast in a moderate oven (350°) for 1 hour. Prick skin to drain excess fat. Continue roasting until deep brown and juices run clear, 1 to 1¼ hours longer.
3. Increase oven temperature to 400°. Brush duckling with Spicy Duck Sauce; return to oven and roast 5 minutes. Serve remaining sauce as a dip for duckling.

Spicy Duck Sauce: Combine ½ teaspoon crushed anise seeds, ½ teaspoon ground cinnamon, ½ teaspoon ground ginger, ⅛ teaspoon ground allspice, 2 tablespoons dry sherry, 2 tablespoons honey, 1 tablespoon chili sauce, 1 tablespoon soy sauce and 1 clove garlic, minced. Let stand at least 2 hours for flavors to blend. Makes about ⅓ cup.

Easy Roast Ducklings

Ducklings used to be raised only on Long Island from birds first brought from China. Today most ducklings are raised in the Midwest, so they shouldn't be called "Long Island Ducklings."

Roast at 350° for 1 hour, 45 minutes.

Makes 4 servings.

2 frozen ducklings (about 4 pounds each), thawed	¾ cup orange marmalade
Salt and pepper	¼ cup Grand Marnier
1 cup chopped celery	2 oranges, cut into wedges
1 cup chopped carrot	Strawberries

1. Season the ducklings with the salt and pepper; secure the neck skin; tie the wings and legs with string.
2. Sprinkle the celery and carrots on the bottom of a shallow roasting pan and add ducklings.
3. Roast in a moderate oven (350°), pricking the ducklings with a two-tined fork several times, to drain fat, for 1 hour, 15 minutes, or until richly golden.

4. Pour off all the fat from the pan. Combine the orange marmalade and Grand Marnier in a small saucepan. Heat until bubbly. Brush generously over the ducklings in the roasting pan.
5. Roast for 30 minutes longer, brushing several times, or until richly glazed. Serve on a heated serving platter and garnish with the orange segments and strawberries, if you wish.

Duck with Orange

Roast at 425° for 20 minutes, then at 350° for 1½ hours.

Makes 3 to 4 servings.

1 frozen duckling (4 to 5 pounds), thawed	¼ teaspoon pepper
1 carrot, sliced	3 oranges
1 medium-size onion, sliced	1 lemon
4 tablespoons butter	2 tablespoons sugar
1 can (13¾ ounces) chicken broth	3 tablespoons red wine vinegar
1 teaspoon salt	2 tablespoons Cognac
	1 tablespoon cornstarch

1. Remove wing tips and giblets from duckling; cut up giblets; sauté with carrot and onion in 2 tablespoons of the butter in large saucepan 10 minutes. Stir in broth. Simmer, partially covered, 1 hour. Strain and reserve.
2. Remove fat from cavity of duckling; sprinkle cavity with salt and pepper. Prick duck with a 2-tined fork. Truss; place on rack in roasting pan, breast-side up.
3. Roast in hot oven (425°) for 20 minutes. Lower heat to moderate (350°); roast 1½ hours or until tender.
4. Meanwhile, remove peel from 2 of the oranges and the lemon with vegetable parer. Cut peel into julienne strips. Poach in water to cover in small saucepan 5 minutes; drain; rinse with cold water and reserve.
5. Trim all white from the 2 oranges; section, removing membranes. Reserve. Squeeze juice from remaining orange.
6. Combine sugar and vinegar in a medium-size saucepan. Cook over medium heat until mixture comes to boiling and turns a golden amber color. (Watch carefully so it does not burn.) Remove from heat; stir in orange juice. Stir Cognac and cornstarch together in small cup; stir into pan. Heat to boiling, stirring until thickened and clear. Add remaining butter and the peel; keep warm.
7. When duck is done, untruss; cut into quarters. Arrange on warm platter. Top with sauce and orange sections.

Pictured opposite:
Easy Roast Ducklings.

How to Carve Duckling

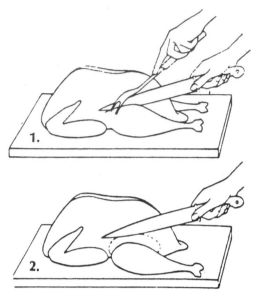

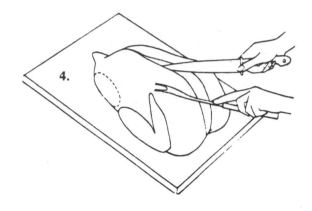

1. and **2.** Holding duckling leg firmly with fork, sever skin at inside hip joint, then pull leg away from body and cut through joint to remove leg. Repeat on other side.

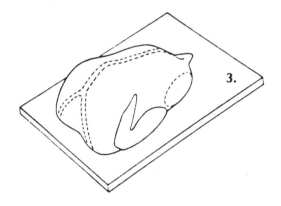

3. Remove wishbone by cutting around area indicated by dotted lines; pull bone out with a fork.

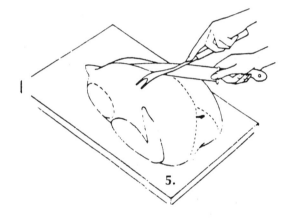

4. and **5.** Anchoring the duckling firmly with the fork, make a cut the length of the ridge of the breastbone, then slide knife down along ribs, first on one side, then the other, to loosen breast meat. Finally, remove the wings by cutting through the shoulder joints.

Spit-Roasted Duckling

Makes 2 servings.

1 frozen duckling (4 to 5 pounds), thawed
¼ cup honey
2 tablespoons lemon juice
1 tablespoon soy sauce
1 teaspoon paprika

1. Remove as much of the fat as possible from the cavity of the duckling.
2. Combine honey, lemon juice, soy sauce and paprika in a cup.

3. Balance duckling in center of spit, securing it with prongs at ends.
4. Place spit about 6 inches from hot coals. Roast 30 minutes; brush with honey mixture. Continue roasting, brushing every 15 minutes, for 2 to 2½ hours, or until skin is crisp and dark and juices run clear when thigh is pierced with a fork.

Note: Prepare the charcoal fire an hour before cooking the duck. You will need 80 briquets. Before starting fire, place a rectangular aluminum foil pan, about the same length and width as the duckling, in the center of the grill and arrange half the briquets all around it. Start your fire.

Goose

These birds are less frequently seen in markets than chickens, turkeys or ducklings, but quick-frozen geese are beginning to appear in the big-city areas with some regularity.

Geese are tender and rich. They can weigh anywhere from 5 to 15 pounds but more commonly weigh from 10 to 12 pounds. Allow 3/4 to 1 pound of ready-to-cook goose per serving.

Geese have been domesticated since antiquity. They are the subject of many tales in different countries. Geese are the traditional holiday birds of many European countries. The fattened liver of geese, called *foie gras,* is highly prized in France and throughout the world. Geese by-products such as feathers and down are used extensively for pillows, quilts and jackets or coats.

Roast Goose with Fruit Stuffing

Roast at 325° for 3 1/2 hours.

Makes about 10 servings.

1 frozen young goose (about 10 pounds)	1/2 teaspoon ground cinnamon
1 package (8 ounces) mixed dried fruits	1/2 teaspoon ground nutmeg
1 cup orange juice	1/4 teaspoon ground cloves
10 slices white bread, toasted and diced	Apricot brandy
1/2 teaspoon ground gingerr	Giblet Gravy *(recipe follows)*

1. Thaw goose 2 or 3 days in refrigerator. Remove giblets; also remove any large pieces of fat from inside goose.
2. Dice the fruits; combine with orange juice in small bowl; let stand about 30 minutes.
3. Combine bread, ginger, cinnamon, nutmeg and cloves in large bowl; pour the fruit mixture over; toss until evenly moistened (mixture will seem somewhat dry).
4. Stuff about 1 cup fruit dressing in neck cavity; fold skin over and hold in place with wing tips or skewers.
5. Stuff remaining dressing into body cavity. Close vent with skewers or sew with needle and thread.
6. Place goose on rack in shallow pan; pierce with 2-tined fork in fatty areas around legs and wings. Do not cover; do not add water.
7. Roast in a slow oven (325°) for 1 hour; remove the accumulated fat from pan. Drain fat twice more, roasting goose 3 hours in all. Then brush goose with apricot brandy; roast 30 minutes longer, brushing with apricot brandy every 10 minutes. Remove to heated platter. To serve: Carve breast into thin slices and separate the drumsticks and thighs at joints. Garnish the platter with chicory and red grapes, if you wish.

Giblet Gravy: Cook neck, gizzard and heart in salted water in small saucepan (with celery tops, if you wish) 2 hours, or until tender; add liver; cook for 15 minutes longer. Drain broth into a 2-cup measure, adding water, if needed, to make 2 cups. Dice meat, discarding bone and gristle. Measure 1/4 cup of drippings from roasting pan into medium-size saucepan; stir in 1/4 cup of all-purpose flour until well blended. Stir in the 2 cups broth; cook and stir until the mixture thickens and bubbles for 3 minutes. Stir in the diced giblets and 1 tablespoon chopped parsley. Taste and add salt and pepper. Makes about 2 1/2 cups.

Crisply Roasted Goose

In days of old, a roast goose was the festive bird of Christmas. Today it's eaten year-round.

Roast at 325° for 2 hours, 30 minutes.

Makes 8 servings, plus leftovers.

1 frozen goose (8 to 10 pounds), thawed	and diced
Salt and pepper	2 stalks celery, diced
1 small onion, chopped (1/4 cup)	Pan Gravy *(recipe follows)*
2 large carrots, pared	Sugared Grapes *(recipe follows)*

1. Remove the neck and giblets from the goose and cook immediately for goose broth. Remove the excess fat from the body cavity and neck skin. Season with the salt and pepper; stuff with the chopped onion, carrots and celery; truss the goose with string.
2. Place the goose, breast-side up, on a rack in a large roasting pan. Insert a meat thermometer into the inside thigh muscle, if you wish.
3. Roast in a slow oven (325°) for 2 hours, 30 minutes, removing the fat and pricking with a two-tined fork while roasting, or until the temperature on the meat thermometer reaches 165° and the drumstick moves easily. Serve with the Pan Gravy; garnish the platter with the Sugared Grapes, if you wish.

Sugared Grapes: Wash and dry 1 bunch of green and 1 bunch of red seedless grapes and 1 bunch of dark grapes; break into small bunches. Arrange on a cookie sheet or jelly-roll pan. Beat 2 egg whites and 2 tablespoons sugar in a small cup. Brush the grapes generously with the egg mixture. Sprinkle generously with 2 tablespoons granulated sugar, let dry for 30 minutes. Sprinkle with additional granulated sugar. Allow to dry at most 2 hours.

Pan Gravy: Pour off all the fat from the roasting pan. Place the pan over low heat. Add 1/4 cup of dry white wine or water, scraping up any browned bits from the bottom of the pan. Remove from the heat; set aside. Melt 1 tablespoon butter in a medium-size saucepan. Stir in 1 tablespoon all-purpose flour until smooth. Cook over low heat, stirring, about 3 minutes. Add 1 can (13 3/4 ounces) of chicken broth and liquid from the roasting pan. Bring to boiling, stirring constantly. Lower the heat and simmer 5 minutes. Add a pinch of pepper. Pour into a warmed gravy boat and serve.

Turkey

Traditionally a Thanksgiving food, turkey is marketed year-round and can do much more than make its once-a-year appearance as the "big bird" at the holiday table.

The majority of turkeys are marketed frozen but are becoming increasingly more available as parts, roasts, steaks or cutlets and made into such products as frankfurters, luncheon meat and turkey "ham."

Turkey Talk

Buying and Storing: The types of turkey sold include the following:

Fresh or Frozen Whole--Labeled hen or tom turkey, there is no difference in quality. The difference is only in the size of the birds. Hens weigh up to about 15 pounds. Tom turkeys are larger. Both are equally tender. Tenderness of turkeys is dependent on the age of the live bird, not its gender.

Frozen Prestuffed Turkey--Available in a broad range of sizes from small to nearly 20 pounds. Do not attempt to stuff and freeze your own bird. Since home-frozen birds cannot be frozen as quickly as commercially frozen, they can be a source of bacterial contamination.

Frozen Self-Basting Turkey--Injected with a mixture of vegetable oil, water, salt, emulsifiers, coloring and artificial flavor, this type of turkey is juicy after roasting.

Turkey Parts—Turkey breasts, thighs, wings and drumsticks are sold separately just as chicken parts are.

Turkey Cutlets--Cut from the breast meat, these thin steaks can replace veal scaloppine in recipes at a fraction of the cost. As with veal, the cutlets are thinly sliced, then pounded in order to break the connective tissue that tightens when cooked.

Ground Turkey--This economical cut is made by grinding the dark thigh meat and skin. It may be sold in a 3-pound sausage-shape roll or packaged like other ground meats. Use it in recipes calling for ground raw meat.

Frozen Boneless Turkey Roast--Pieces of white and dark meat in natural proportions, or white or dark meat only, in a foil pan.

Smoked Turkey–A gourmet item, it's ready to slice and eat. It has been cured, smoked and thoroughly cooked.

When buying turkeys under 12 pounds, allow 3/4 to 1 pound per serving. When buying birds weighing more than 12 pounds, allow 1/2 to 3/4 pound per serving. Remember, a bigger bird is a better buy and it will provide you with leftovers.

THAWING
Conventional (Long) Method
Thawing time: 3 to 4 days, about 24 hours for each 5 pounds of whole frozen turkey.

STORING
Fresh turkeys Refrigerate at all times. Cook within 1 to 2 days of purchase

Frozen whole turkeys Store in original wrapper for up to 12 months at 0°F. or lower.
- Leave the turkey in its original wrapper.
- Place the frozen turkey on a tray in the refrigerator.

Cold Water (Short) Method
Thawing time: about 30 minutes per pound of whole frozen turkey.
- Leave the turkey in its original wrapper.
- Place the turkey in the sink or a large pan.
- Completely cover with cold water.
- Change the water every 30 minutes
- Keep immersed in cold water at all times.

Note:*Never* thaw at room temperature. Once thawed, cook or refrigerate immediately

STUFFING
When? Just before you roast your turkey is the time to stuff it. You run the risk of food poisoning if you do this earlier.

How much? Allow 3/4 cup stuffing per pound of bird for turkeys weighing more than 10 pounds; 1/2 cup stuffing per pound for smaller birds.

Note: *Never* freeze stuffing that is in a cooked or raw bird. Remove all the stuffing from the cooked bird, wrap separately and refrigerate.

COOKING A TURKEY
Cooking that big bird may be intimidating, but don't get "turkey trauma." Today's turkeys are marketed at a young age so they are meaty and tender; it's no longer necessary to cook them to tenderize.

The best way to cook a turkey is in an open pan. Spread butter, margarine, solid shortening or vegetable oil lightly over the skin before roasting to prevent cracking and promote a mouthwatering golden brown color. Once the turkey is brown, cover the breast loosely with a tent of aluminum foil to prevent further browning. Try to use a pan no more than 2" deep so it doesn't shield the heat from the drumstick area and increase the roasting time.

TESTING FOR DONENESS
- Meat thermometer inserted in meatiest part of thigh next to the body but not touching the bone reads 180°F to 185°F. If the turkey is stuffed, insert the thermometer in the center of stuffing. It should read 150° to 155°F.
- Turkey juices run clear.
- Drumsticks move up and down easily

RESTING PERIOD
Let turkey stand at room temperature for 20 minutes. This allows the juices to settle and the meat to firm up for easier carving.

TURKEY VALUE
Buy a turkey weighing between 14 and 16 pounds for the best value. It will have a more meaty breast than birds of lower weights.

TO ROAST AN UNSTUFFED TURKEY
Place a 14- to 15-pound turkey, breast-side up, on a rack in a shallow roasting pan. Brush with melted

butter. Roast in a slow oven (325°) for 4½ to 5½ hours. Baste occasionally. A stuffed turkey will take about 1 hour longer to be done. This turkey will serve 14 to 16 people with ample left over for seconds.

How To Carve A Roast Turkey

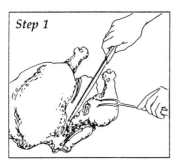
Step 1

Step 1. Removing the legs: Press the leg away from the body. The joint connecting the leg may snap free; if not, sever it with a knife. Carefully cut the dark meat completely from the body contour with a knife.

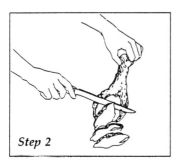
Step 2

Step 2. Slicing the dark meat: Separate the drumstick from the thigh by cutting through the connecting joint. Tilt the drumstick and cut off even slices.

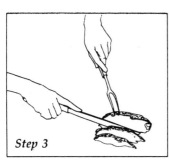
Step 3

Step 3. Slicing the thigh: Hold the thigh firmly with a fork. Cut off even slices parallel to the bone.

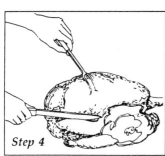
Step 4

Step 4. Preparing the breast: In preparing the breast for easy slicing, place the knife parallel and as close to the wing as possible. Make a deep cut into the breast, cutting right to the bone to create your base cut. All the breast slices will stop at this vertical cut.

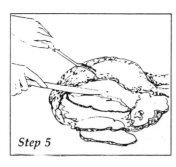
Step 5

Step 5. Carving the breasts: After the base cut, begin to slice the breast. Carve downward, ending at the base cut. Start each new slice slightly up on breast. Keep the slices thin and even.

Timetable for Roasting Turkey (325°)

Bird Weight (pounds)	Stuffed (hours)	Unstuffed (hours)
6 to 8	3 to 3½	2½ to 3½
8 to 12	3½ to 4½	3 to 4
12 to 16	4 to 5	3½ to 4½
16 to 20	4½ to 5½	4 to 5
20 to 24	5 to 6½	4½ to 5½

Roast Turkey

Roast at 325° for about 4 hours.

Makes 8 servings.

1 turkey (about 12 pounds)
Traditional Sage Stuffing (recipe follows)
1 cup (2 sticks) butter, melted
Salt and pepper
Giblet Gravy (recipe follows)

1. Thaw turkey if frozen; remove giblets and neck.
2. Stuff body cavity loosely with Traditional Sage Stuffing; close with skewers and string. Stuff neck cavity with Sausage Stuffing variation (or use Traditional Stuffing in neck cavity also, if you wish). Close cavity. Tie legs together; fold wings under bird. Place bird, breast-side up, on rack in roasting pan. Brush with melted butter; sprinkle with salt and pepper. Insert meat thermometer into thickest part of thigh without touching bone. A "tent" of foil may be placed loosely over turkey to delay browning. Remove foil for last half hour of roasting.
3. Roast in a slow oven (325°) for about 4 hours or until meat thermometer registers 185° or the drumstick and thigh move easily. Brush turkey occasionally with butter during baking. When turkey is done, remove from oven to carving board and let stand 20 minutes to make carving easier. Serve with Giblet Gravy.
4. After turkey is served and dinner is over, remove all stuffing from turkey cavity before refrigerating both leftover turkey and stuffing.

Giblet Gravy

Makes about 5 cups.

Turkey neck and giblets
1 medium-size onion, chopped (½ cup)
Few celery tops
1 teaspoon salt
Dash pepper
1 bay leaf
4 cups water
½ cup all-purpose flour
1 cup water

1. Combine turkey neck, giblets (except liver), onion,

(continued)

celery tops, salt, pepper, bay leaf and the 4 cups water in a medium-size saucepan.
2. Heat to boiling; lower heat; cover. Simmer 1 hour and 40 minutes; add liver. Simmer 20 minutes longer or until tender.
3. Strain broth; measure; add more water if necessary to make 4 cups. Chop giblets; reserve.
4. After turkey is removed from roasting pan, remove rack. Tilt pan and pour off all but 1/2 cup of fat. Add flour; stir over low heat until bubbly.
5. Add the 4 cups giblet broth and the remaining 1 cup water to pan; stir and scrape over low heat until all brown bits are dissolved. Cook, stirring constantly, until gravy thickens and bubbles. Lower heat; simmer 5 minutes. Stir in chopped giblets. Taste; add additional salt and pepper, if needed.

Traditional Sage Stuffing

Makes about 10 cups.

36 slices bread, cubed	**ground pepper**
1 cup (2 sticks) butter	**3 tablespoons leaf**
or margarine	**sage, crumbled**
3 medium-size onions,	**2 eggs**
chopped (1 1/2 cups)	**1 1/2 cups chicken**
3 cups chopped	**broth**
celery, with tops	**1/2 cup chopped**
1 teaspoon salt	**parsley**
1/2 teaspoon freshly	

1. Dry bread in a very slow oven (250°); place in a large bowl. (You should have 12 cups.)

Roast Turkey, page 677.

2. Melt butter in large skillet. Sauté onion and celery until tender, about 15 minutes. Add to bread with salt, pepper and sage.
3. Beat eggs lightly in a small bowl; stir into stuffing. Add enough of the chicken broth to make a moist mixture. Stir in parsley.
4. Stuff turkey cavity lightly. Spoon any extra stuffing into a buttered casserole. Spoon a little extra chicken broth over top and bake, covered or uncovered, with turkey during last half hour of roasting.

Sausage Stuffing: Brown 1/4 pound pork sausage in skillet, breaking into small pieces with a fork. Drain on paper toweling. Add to 1/4 of the Traditional Sage Stuffing mixture; mix well. Use to stuff neck cavity. Makes about 3 cups.

Turkey in Puff Pastry

Bake at 400° for 1 1/2 hours, then at 400° for 30 minutes.

Makes 6 servings.

1 frozen turkey roast	**frozen puff pastry**
in pan with giblet	**1 can (4 3/4 ounces)**
gravy packet	**liver pâté**
(32 ounces)	**1 egg, beaten**
1 package (10 ounces)	

1. Roast turkey in a hot oven (400°) for 1 1/2 hours, following label directions. Remove from oven to a wire rack. Remove paper lid; let cool 30 minutes.
2. Meanwhile, remove puff pastry from package; let soften at room temperature for 20 minutes.
3. Increase oven temperature to 450°.
4. Overlap pastry sheets along long edges on a well-floured surface. Flour rolling pin. Roll out from center to a 14 x 16-inch rectangle, being careful not to tear pastry. Trim edges even, if desired.
5. Lift turkey roast from pan (reserve pan drippings for gravy); remove skin. Cover top and side of roll with liver pâté, spreading evenly with a wet spatula.
6. Insert forks on end of turkey roll; lift up and place, pâté-side down, onto center of pastry rectangle. Bring ends of pastry over top of turkey; fold over to seal. Turn over; place sealed edge down onto a shallow baking pan. Use trimmings to cut decorative crescents for top, brushing with beaten egg for a shiny crust.
7. Lower oven temperature to 400°. Immediately place pastry-covered turkey roll into oven. Bake 30 minutes or until pastry is golden brown. Remove from oven. Place on serving platter. Let stand 15 minutes for easier cutting.
8. Meanwhile, place reserved pan drippings and

Pictured opposite (from the top):
Deviled Lamb Shanks, page 492;
Braised Beef Rolls, page 447;
Turkey in Puff Pastry, page 678.

frozen turkey giblet gravy packet in a small saucepan with 3/4 cup water; bring to boiling and cook 1 minute. Serve with turkey. Garnish platter with cling peaches filled with cranberry orange relish and watercress, if you wish.

Stuffed Turkey Breast

The turkey breast is wrapped around a prosciutto and Fontina cheese stuffing.

Roast at 325° for 2 hours, 15 minutes.

Makes 10 servings.

1 fresh or frozen bone-in turkey breast (6 to 6½ pounds), thawed if frozen	or margarine
	6 ounces thinly sliced prosciutto
2 cups fresh bread crumbs	1 cup shredded Fontina cheese
1½ cups chopped parsley	1 can (13¾ ounces) chicken broth
1 egg, slightly beaten	OR: 2 cups water
1 leek, washed and sliced (¾ cup)	4 teaspoons cornstarch
2 teaspoons finely chopped garlic	2 tablespoons cold water
½ cup (1 stick) butter	Salt and pepper to taste

1. To bone the turkey breast, place, skin-side down, on a cutting board. Using a thin-bladed knife, cut between the bone and flesh, keeping the point of knife close to bone so as not to pierce the meat; pull the bone away as you loosen it. When you get to the base of the breastbone, be careful not to cut through the skin. (Save the bone for soup.)
2. Place the boned turnkey breast, skin-side down, on a work surface. Trim off the excess fat. Cut away the pointed oval fillet from each side of the breast; set aside. Make horizontal slits in the thickest part of the breasts, without cutting all the way through. Open the slits toward the top of the breast; pound slightly with the base of your hand or a mallet to make the meat an even thickness. Set aside.
3. Combine the bread crumbs, parsley and egg in a large bowl.
4. Sauté the leek and garlic in 2 tablespoons of the butter in a small skillet until soft, 5 minutes. Add to bread crumb mixture.
5. Overlap half of the prosciutto slices over the turkey. Sprinkle with the Fontina. Distribute the bread crumb stuffing over the cheese. Top with the remaining prosciutto; press down gently to compact. Lay the reserved breast fillets, end to end, lengthwise, down the center. Roll the breast up from one long side; fasten with skewers to hold its shape. Bring the skin up and over the turkey from both ends; fasten with skewers. Wrap the turkey in a double thickness of cheesecloth. Tie in 4 or 5 places with string. Place, seam-side down, in a small roasting pan. Melt the remaining 6 tablespoons of butter in a saucepan. Pour over the turkey to soak the cheesecloth. The turkey

can be prepared to this point, 3 hours in advance, and refrigerated.
6. Roast in a preheated moderate oven (325°), basting often with the pan drippings, for 2 hours and 15 minutes, or until a meat thermometer inserted into the thickest part registers 185°. Remove the turkey to a cutting board. Let stand for 20 minutes before unwrapping and slicing. Reserve the pan drippings for the gravy. Serve the turkey hot or warm with the pan gravy.
7. Meanwhile, prepare the gravy: Tilt the roasting pan carefully and pour off the fat. Add the chicken broth to the pan. Stir over low heat, scraping up the browned bits from the bottom of the pan. Strain into a small saucepan. Skim off and discard any fat. Bring to boiling. Mix the cornstarch with the cold water in a small cup until smooth. Stir into saucepan. Return to boiling. Cook, stirring, for 1 minute until thickened and smooth. Add the salt and pepper to taste.

Turkey and Pistachio Terrine

Bake at 300° for 2½ hours.

Makes about 24 servings.

⅓ cup chopped shallots or green onions	¾ pound ground fatback
2 tablespoons butter or margarine	1 egg
	½ teaspoon leaf thyme, crumbled
½ pound chicken livers, connective tissue removed	½ teaspoon leaf marjoram, crumbled
2 teaspoons salt	½ teaspoon ground allspice
½ teaspoon pepper	⅓ cup shelled whole pistachio nuts
½ cup dry vermouth	¾ pound sliced bacon
1¼ pounds ground turkey	2 bay leaves
¾ pound ground pork	

1. Sauté the shallots in the butter in a medium-size skillet for 3 minutes. Add the chicken livers, ½ teaspoon of the salt and ¼ teaspoon of the pepper. Sauté just until the livers are tender but still pink inside, about 5 minutes. Stir in the vermouth. Bring to boiling, scraping up any browned bits from the bottom of the pan with a wooden spoon. Remove from the heat. Cool.
2. Combine the turkey, pork, fatback, egg, the remaining salt and pepper, thyme, marjoram, allspice and pistachio nuts in a bowl; mix well. Drain the wine with the shallots from the livers into the bowl with the meat; mix well.
3. Preheat the oven to slow (300°).
4. Line a 6- to 8-cup loaf pan or terrine with the bacon, allowing the ends to overhang the sides by 2 inches. Reserve 2 or 3 pieces to cover the top. Press a third of the meat mixture into the bottom of the pan. Arrange half of the chicken livers over the meat; gently press into the meat mixture. Top with another layer of the meat, then the remaining livers, and a final

Turkey and Pistachio Terrine, page 680; Cassis Punch Royale, page 76.

layer of meat. Smooth the top. Gently rap the pan on a counter to pack. Bring the ends of the bacon up and over the top. Cover the top with the remaining bacon; add the bay leaves. Cover tightly with foil. Place the loaf pan in a deep roasting pan. Place on the oven rack. Pour boiling water into the roasting pan so it comes halfway up the sides of the loaf pan.

5. Bake in the preheated slow oven (300°) for 2 hours. Remove the foil; bake until a meat thermometer registers 160°, another 30 minutes. Remove the pan from the water bath. Cool on a rack for 1 hour. Replace the foil over the top. Weight the terrine with another pan filled with cans. Refrigerate overnight.

6. Unmold the terrine. Carefully scrape off the fat and any jellied liquid. Wrap the terrine in plastic wrap. Refrigerate until serving time. Garnish with thyme sprigs, if you wish, and serve with toasted French bread and cornichons.

To Make Ahead: Refrigerate the terrine, wrapped, for 3 to 4 days.

Couscous

The name of a stew which is the national dish of several North African countries and takes its name from the couscous grain that is an integral part of it. (Couscous is a fine semolina ground from the endosperm of durum wheat.) The stew is made in a *couscousier*, a pan consisting of two parts: a large bottom section in which the stew is cooked, and a perforated top, similar to a colander, which holds the semolina as it steams over the stew. Couscous is served on a large, rimmed platter with butter stirred in; the stew is arranged on top. Traditionally, a peppery relish is served as an accompaniment.

Moroccan Couscous

Makes 16 servings.

2 pounds couscous (coarse semolina)
6 cups boiling water, well salted
8- to 10-pound frozen turkey, thawed
6 large onions, coarsely chopped (6 cups)
1/2 cup (1 stick) butter or margarine
1/2 cup olive or vegetable oil
1 tablespoon salt
1 teaspoon black pepper
1/2 teaspoon ground turmeric
1/4 teaspoon cayenne (optional)
1 teaspoon saffron threads, crushed
1 3-inch piece stick cinnamon
Water

5 tomatoes, fresh or canned, peeled, seeded and chopped (5 cups)
6 carrots, scraped and cut in 1 1/2-inch chunks
1 pound zucchini, cut in 1 1/2-inch lengths
3 or 4 turnips, cut in quarters (optional)
1 large or 2 small acorn squash, peeled, seeded and cut in 1 1/2- to 2-inch chunks
3 cups cooked chick-peas (garbanzos), rinsed and drained, if canned
Harissa Sauce (recipe follows)
1 cup raisins, soaked in liquid from stew

1. If you have a couscousier, prepare semolina by placing it in a large bowl and pouring over it 2 cups of the boiling salted wter. Let stand 20 minutes, fluffing grain occasionally with a fork. Repeat, adding water and fluffing twice at 20-minute intervals. Line the top

(continued)

of the couscousier with a double thickness of clean cheesecloth; add couscous and set aside. If you do not have a couscousier, steam couscous grain in water or broth from stew, following instructions on package. Set aside and keep warm.

2. Cut turkey in stew-size chunks, including bones in wings, legs and thighs. Cut thick breast meat in boneless chunks. Place turkey, chopped onions, butter and oil in the bottom of the couscousier or in an 8-quart soup pot. Add salt, pepper, turmeric, cayenne, saffron and cinnamon.

3. Cook gently, covered, for 20 minutes, swirling pan and stirring occasionally until meat and onion take on a golden color and look slightly braised. Add enough water to come just to the level of the meat. Cover and simmer for 1½ to 2 hours or until meat is tender. Skim off excess fat. Stew can be prepared in advance to this point.

4. Half an hour before serving, add tomatoes, carrots, zucchini and turnips; simmer until tender. At the same time, place the prepared top of couscousier with the grain over the bottom and seal around rim by wrapping it in aluminum foil. Cover top and let couscous grain steam as vegetables cook, fluffing by tossing it with a fork 2 or 3 times during the process. Add acorn squash and chickpeas to stew and cook until tender.

5. Prepare Harissa Sauce.

6. To serve couscous, portion couscous into large, individual bowls (old-fashioned soup plates would be perfect), make a well in the center and in it put meat, vegetables and broth. Top with raisins. Serve with Harissa Sauce.

Harissa Sauce
(Red Pepper Sauce)

Makes about 1²⁄₃ cups.

¹⁄₃ cup crushed, red peppers	1½ cups liquid from stew
2 cloves garlic, peeled	Juice of ½ lemon
2 teaspoons caraway seeds	1 tablespoon minced fresh parsley
1 teaspoon fennel seeds	1 tablespoon minced fresh green coriander, if available
½ teaspoon salt	
3 tablespoons olive oil or as needed	

Grind red peppers, garlic, caraway, fennel seeds and salt in a mortar and pestle or in a spice mill. Stir in 1 teaspoon olive oil. This can be done in advance and kept in the refrigerator. Just before serving, stir 2 teaspoons of this mixture into 1½ cups of broth from

stew, adding 2 tablespoons olive oil and lemon juice. Adjust seasonings, adding salt, if needed. Stir in chopped parsley and coriander. Serve in small sauce bowl, to be spooned over couscous.

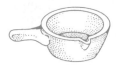

Turkey Crêpes with Cheese Sauce

Bake at 375° for 15 minutes.

Makes 6 servings.

½ cup uncooked long-grain rice	1 small onion, chopped (¼ cup)
3 tablespoons butter or margarine	¾ pound ground turkey
2 tablespoons all-purpose flour	½ cup thawed frozen peas
½ teaspoon salt	¼ teaspoon leaf rosemary, crumbled
¼ teaspoon pepper	¼ teaspoon leaf thyme, crumbled
1 cup water	¼ teaspoon dry mustard
5 tablespoons instant nonfat dry milk powder	Crêpes (recipe follows)
4 ounces Swiss cheese, shredded (1 cup)	

1. Cook rice, following label directions; reserve.

2. Melt 2 tablespoons of the butter in a small saucepan. Blend in flour, ¼ teaspoon of the salt and ⅛ teaspoon of the pepper; cook 1 minute. Stir water into dry milk in a small bowl until blended; stir into saucepan. Cook, stirring constantly, until mixture thickens and bubbles. Remove from heat; add cheese, stirring until melted; reserve.

3. Sauté onion in remaining 1 tablespoon butter in a large skillet until tender. Add turkey, stirring constantly, until turkey loses its pink color. Stir in cooked rice, peas, rosemary, thyme, mustard, and the remaining salt and pepper. Add ⅔ of the reserved cheese sauce, stirring until blended.

4. Spoon a heaping tablespoonful of the turkey mixture on each Crêpe; roll up. Repeat until all Crêpes are filled. Arrange Crêpes in a shallow baking dish. Spoon remaining cheese sauce over Crêpes.

5. Bake in a moderate oven (375°) for 15 minutes or until sauce is bubbly and lightly browned.

Crêpes: Combine 2 eggs, 5 tablespoons instant nonfat dry milk, 1 cup water, 1 cup all-purpose flour, ¼ teaspoon salt and 2 tablespoons melted margarine in the container of electric blender; whirl until smooth. Or, combine all ingredients in a medium-size bowl; beat with a whisk or beater until smooth. Refrigerate batter at least 1 hour. Heat a 7-inch skillet until hot; rub about ¼ teaspoon margarine on bottom of skillet, just to film. Pour in about 3 tablespoons crêpe batter. Tilt and turn skillet to spread batter evenly over

(continued)

bottom. Cook crêpe until lightly browned on bottom; turn over and brown on other side. Stack cooked crêpes with wax paper between until ready to use. Makes 12 crêpes.

Note: Crêpes can be prepared ahead and refrigerated or frozen wrapped in a plastic bag.

Turkey and Carrot Loaf

Bake at 375° for 1 hour.

Makes 6 servings.

1¹/₂ pounds ground turkey	1 teaspoon salt
2¹/₄ cups grated carrots (about 4 medium-size)	¹/₄ teaspoon pepper
	1¹/₄ cups dairy sour cream
1 cup chopped fresh parsley	1 chicken bouillon cube
1 small onion, chopped (¹/₄ cup)	³/₄ cup boiling water
	1 tablespoon flour
¹/₂ cup packaged bread crumbs	2 tablespoon dry sherry

1. Combine turkey, 1¹/₂ cups of the carrots, ¹/₂ cup of the parsley, the onion, bread crumbs, salt, pepper and 1 cup of the sour cream in a large bowl; mix well.
2. Press ¹/₃ of the mixture firmly into an 8¹/₂ × 4¹/₂ × 2¹/₂-inch loaf pan. Sprinkle remaining carrots over top. Press half remaining turkey mixture over carrots; sprinkle with remaining parsley. Top with remaining turkey mixture; press down firmly. Run a metal spatula around sides of pan to loosen. Invert loaf onto greased small shallow baking pan.
3. Bake in a moderate oven (375°) for 1 hour or until golden brown. Transfer loaf to a warm serving platter.
4. Add bouillon cube to boiling water in a cup; stir to dissolve. Sprinkle flour into pan drippings; cook 1 minute. Stir in bouillon mixture. Cook, stirring constantly, until sauce thickens and bubbles. Stir a little of the hot sauce into the remaining ¹/₄ cup sour cream in a small bowl. Return blended mixture to saucepan; stir in sherry. Cook, stirring constantly, just until sauce is hot. Add salt and pepper to taste. Slice; spoon sauce over top.

Roast Turkey Breast

Discard the skin and turkey breast is relatively low in calories.

Roast at 325° for 3 hours.

Makes 16 three-ounce servings at 145 calories each.

1 turkey breast, fresh or thawed, frozen	(about 5 pounds) Salt and pepper

1. Place turkey breast on rack in roasting pan; sprinkle with salt and pepper. Place meat thermometer in thickest part of breast, not touching bone.

2. Roast in slow oven (325°) for 3 hours or until thermometer registers 185°.
3. Remove from oven; let stand 20 to 30 minutes for easier carving. Remove all skin and slice thinly.

Low-Calorie Turkey Scaloppine

Economical and low-calorie turkey breast takes the place of veal in this classic recipe.

Makes 4 servings at 210 calories each.

2 tablespoons flour	¹/₄ cup dry white wine
3 tablespoons grated Romano cheese	1 tablespoon butter or margarine
1 teaspoon garlic salt	1 small onion, chopped (¹/₄ cup)
1 teaspoon dried parsley flakes	1 can (2 ounces) sliced mushrooms
1 pound turkey-breast steaks	Lemon wedges

1. Combine flour, cheese, garlic salt and parsley flakes on wax paper. Press turkey steaks into mixture to lightly coat both sides.
2. Combine wine and butter or margarine in large nonstick skillet; heat to steaming. Add turkey steaks and onion. Cover; simmer 6 minutes.
3. Uncover skillet; continue cooking until liquid evaporates and turkey steaks brown in remaining butter. Turn once to brown evenly. Remove to hot platter; keep warm.
4. Pour mushrooms with liquid into same skillet. Boil over high heat 1 or 2 minutes, stirring in brown bits. Pour over steaks. Garnish with lemon wedges. (For a colorful touch, dip the ends of the lemon wedges in parsley flakes.) Serve at once.

Barbecued Turkey Legs

Grill 1 hour and 45 minutes.

Makes 6 servings.

2 packages (2¹/₂ pounds each) fresh or frozen turkey legs	1 envelope garlic-flavored salad-dressing mix
1 container (8 ounces) plain yogurt	1 tablespoon lemon juice

1. Thaw turkey legs if frozen; dry with paper toweling. Combine yogurt, salad-dressing mix and lemon juice in shallow dish large enough to hold legs in one layer. Brush legs with yogurt mixture; cover; refrigerate overnight.
2. Wrap legs in individual foil packets, reserving yogurt. Place on grill 5 to 6 inches from grayed coals, 1 hour.
3. Unwrap and place legs on grill to brown. Brush with reserved yogurt, turning often.
4. Continue to grill 45 minutes until juices run clear when pierced with fork. Heat any remaining marinade to serve with turkey.

Low-Calorie Oven-Fried Turkey Cutlets

Bake at 425° for 12 minutes.

Makes 4 servings at 263 calories each.

1 egg	steaks
2 tablespoons vegetable oil	1/2 cup seasoned packaged bread crumbs
1 pound turkey-breast	

1. Preheat oven to 425°. Fork-whip egg and oil together in shallow dish. Dip turkey-breast steaks into egg mixture, then into bread crumbs to lightly coat both sides.
2. Place crumbed steaks on a non-stick cookie sheet.
3. Bake in a preheated hot oven (425°) for 12 minutes or until steaks are golden brown and cooked through. Serve with tomato sauce, if you wish.

Lemon-Dill Meatballs with Artichokes

Delicate nuggets of turkey, flavored with lemon and dill, sauced with lemon, capers and artichoke hearts, make for true company fare.

Makes enough for two meals (4 servings each).

4 slices white bread	1 can condensed chicken broth
1/4 cup milk	3 3/4 cups water
2 pounds raw ground turkey or chicken	1/2 cup (1 stick) butter or margarine
1/4 cup grated onion	1/2 cup all-purpose flour
2 eggs	1/4 cup lemon juice
1 tablespoon chopped fresh dill	2 tablespoons drained capers
OR: 1 teaspoon dillweed	2 cans (16 ounces each) artichoke hearts, drained and each cut in half
1 tablespoon grated lemon rind	
1 teaspoon salt	
1/4 teaspoon pepper	

1. Soak bread in milk in a large bowl; crumble or mash with fork. Add turkey, onion, eggs, dill, lemon rind, salt and pepper; mix thoroughly. Refrigerate 1 hour.
2. Moisten palms of hands. Shape meat mixture into 32 meatballs (2 level tablespoonfuls each).
3. Combine chicken broth and water in a large skillet; bring to boiling. Add meatballs in a single layer. (You may have to do this twice.) Lower heat; cover. Simmer 15 minutes. Remove meatballs with slotted spoon to a shallow dish; cover loosely with wax paper to prevent drying.
4. Strain poaching liquid through a cheesecloth-lined strainer into a 4-cup glass measure. (You should have 4 cups liquid.) Add water, if necessary.
5. Melt butter in same skillet; stir in flour and cook until bubbly, 1 minute. Stir in poaching liquid and continue to cook until thickened and bubbly. Stir in lemon juice and capers. Return meatballs; add artichokes; heat thoroughly.
6. Dinner Portion: Spoon half the meatballs, artichokes and sauce into a shallow serving casserole. Garnish with lemon wedges and parsley, if you wish.
7. To freeze: Spoon 4 meatballs, a few artichoke halves and some sauce (about 1/3 cup each) into individual boilable bags; heat-seal. Label, date and freeze. Recommended freezer storage: 2 months. To reheat: Bring water to boiling in a medium-size saucepan. Place boilable bag into water; bring bag to boiling; boil 15 minutes. Remove bag from water; cut off top of bag with scissors; slide mixture into serving casserole or individual serving dishes.

How to Grill Turkey

● Marinades help tenderize, lubricate and flavor turkey cuts; allow meat to marinate for at least 4 hours or overnight, covered and refrigerated.
● Baste sparingly while grilling. Dripping sauce may cause coals to burst into flames and dry the cuts.
● Never flip turkey cuts with a fork; it pierces the meat, allowing valuable juices to escape.
● Serve immediately after cooking. If held too long in a warming oven, turkey tends to dry and toughen.

Be careful not to overcook turkey cuts. Lower temperatures and frequent basting seal in juices and flavor. Fresh white-meat cuts and ground turkey meat are cooked and safe for consumption when the internal cooking temperature has reached 165°, and dark meat when the internal temperature has reached 175°. Cook fresh turkey tenderloins, ground turkey and drumstick steaks until the meat springs back when touched and the inside is no longer pink.

SALADS and SALAD DRESSINGS

Salad   A salad, perhaps more than any other type of food, can be served as any course of a meal. Tart, marinated vegetables, dished up in small portions, make splendid first courses. Frilly, green delicately dressed salads accompany meats to perfection. A salad made with meats, poultry, eggs, seafood or cheese becomes the main course. A salad laden with fruit and enriched with cream or yogurt can easily double as dessert.

The word "salad" is derived from *sal*, the Latin word for salt. Salt was used in the early days not only to flavor edible plants but to preserve plants for eating during the winter when they were not available.

How to Make a Perfect Jellied Mold

Mixing: Follow directions carefully when dissolving gelatin, as mixture should be sparkling-smooth, with no tiny granules clinging to the bowl.

Fruit-flavored gelatin will dissolve quickly in hot water. Unflavored gelatin can be dissolved either of these ways: (1) Soften in cold water, then dissolve in a hot liquid -- or heat softened gelatin over hot water (as in a double boiler) until dissolved; or (2) mix dry gelatin with sugar, then add liquid; heat, following specific recipe directions.

Chilling: Place dissolved gelatin in the refrigerator to chill until syrupy-thick (consistency should be like an unbeaten egg white). Gelatin sets first at the bottom and sides of the bowl, so stir occasionally for even thickening.

In a hurry? Follow suggestions on package label or hasten setting either of these ways: (1) Pour the gelatin mixture into shallow pan and place in refrigerator. (2) Set bowl of gelatin mixture in a larger bowl of ice and water. Keep on the kitchen counter where you can watch it, as it gels fast.

Gelatin set too quickly? Place the bowl over simmering water and heat, stirring constantly, until melted. Then start chilling again, as if it were freshly mixed.

Layering: Like a fancy design on the top? Place mold in a larger pan of ice and water (the pan should be deep enough so the ice and water will come to within one inch of top of mold). Spoon about a 1/4-inch-thick layer of syrupy gelatin into a mold and chill just until beginning to be sticky-firm. Arrange foods to make the design you wish on top of it; carefully spoon on another thin gelatin layer barely to cover; chill just until sticky-firm. This is important whenever you add one layer on top of another, so layers will hold together. This way a layered mold will turn out beautifully firm without one layer slipping from another.

Make any remaining layers this way: Keep rest of gelatin syrupy-thick. (On a cool day keep it at room temperature, or watch it if it is necessary to keep it refrigerated.) Fold in other recipe ingredients, then spoon mixture carefully on top of the already-set layer while it is still sticky-firm.

Setting: Place mold in a far corner of your refrigerator where it can chill without being disturbed. Most molds can be turned out at their prettiest if chilled overnight. Large ones, or those heavy with fruits or vegetables, need at least 12 hours' chilling. Usually, small molds are firm enough to turn out after 3 or 4 hours chilling.

How to Make Perfect Green Salads

- Begin with chilled, crackly-crisp greens. Use more than one variety: dark with light; mild with tangy.
- Tear, rather than cut, greens into bite-size pieces.
- Choose the salad dressing carefully. A thin French or Italian dressing goes well with plain or mixed greens, as does a simple oil and vinegar dressing.

Green Salads

The perfect addition to a summer meal--or a delicious entreé when made with chilled meats and cheeses.

MOST POPULAR SALAD GREENS:

- **Iceberg,** the best-known lettuce, has a nice crisp texture and stores well. After purchasing, wash, dry well, and store the lettuce in a large plastic bag or a tightly covered plastic container, with a drainage space, in the refrigerator.

- **Romaine lettuce** has long dark green outside leaves with lighter, almost yellow inside leaves. The darker green leaves have the higher vitamin content, so use as much of these leaves as possible, discarding only the bruised parts.

- **Boston** or **butterhead lettuce** has tender, velvety leaves that separate easily and a delicate flavor. Wash just before serving in a bowl of very cold water and blot dry on paper towels.

- **Leaf lettuce,** also known as **red-tipped lettuce** or **oakleaf lettuce,** grows in large leafy bunches. The tender long leaves are delicate and should be washed just before serving.

Pictured opposite: Coleslaw Vinaigrette with Cherry Tomatoes, Olives and Capers, page 688; Wilted Red Cabbage Slaw with Bacon and Peppers, page 688; Cabbage and Apple Slaw with Walnuts, page 688.

NICE SALAD ADDITIONS:

- **Belgian endive,** an imported green, is more expensive than other greens and therefore used sparingly in salads. Sliced lengthwise, the long slender leaves add an elegant touch.
- **Curly endive** or **chicory** has long, narrow, curly dark green outer leaves and pale green inner leaves. A slightly bitter taste makes them a good choice to combine with other, milder greens.
- **Green and red cabbage,** shredded into a salad, add color and texture.
- **Spinach** has a crisp texture, slightly biting taste and lots of vitamins in its dark green leaves.

Wilted Red Cabbage Slaw with Bacon and Peppers

Makes 6 servings.

1 small head red cabbage (1¼ pounds)	1 large clove garlic, minced
2 medium-size sweet red peppers, halved, seeded and thinly sliced	¼ cup red wine vinegar
	1½ tablespoons brown sugar
6 bacon slices	½ teaspoon salt
	½ teaspoon pepper

1. Trim outer leaves from cabbage; quarter, core and shred cabbage. (You will need about 7 cups.) Combine in a large bowl with red peppers.
2. Cook bacon in a large skillet until crisp. Drain on paper toweling; crumble and reserve. Measure bacon drippings; reserve ¼ cup.
3. Return bacon drippings to skillet. Sauté garlic until soft, but not browned. Add vinegar, sugar, salt and pepper; bring just to boiling. Pour hot dressing over cabbage; add crumbled bacon and toss well. Serve immediately.

Cabbage and Apple Slaw with Walnuts

Makes 4 servings.

1 small head Savoy cabbage (1 pound)	⅛ to ¼ teaspoon liquid hot pepper seasoning
½ cup mayonnaise or salad dressing	
3 tablespoons lemon juice	2 green or red apples, quartered, cored and thinly sliced
1 tablespoon honey	
½ teaspoon salt	½ cup coarsely chopped toasted walnuts (see Note below)
¼ teaspoon ground allspice	

1. Trim outer leaves from cabbage; quarter, core and shred cabbage. (You will need about 6 cups.) Turn into a large bowl.
2. Combine mayonnaise, lemon juice, honey, salt,

allspice and hot pepper seasoning in a small bowl; mix thoroughly. Pour dressing over cabbage and toss to coat. Cover; refrigerate about 1 hour.
3. When ready to serve, arrange apple slices around edge of bowl; fill center with walnuts. Toss again before serving.

Note: To toast walnuts, place in small, shallow baking pan. Bake in a moderate oven (350°) for 15 minutes.

Coleslaw Vinaigrette with Cherry Tomatoes, Olives and Capers

Makes 4 servings.

1 small head cabbage (1 pound)	capers, drained and chopped
¼ cup pimiento-stuffed green olives, sliced	½ teaspoon salt
	⅛ teaspoon pepper
	¼ teaspoon crushed red pepper
⅓ cup olive oil	
3 tablespoons red wine vinegar	1 cup cherry tomatoes, halved
1 small red onion, diced (¼ cup)	¼ cup chopped fresh parsley
1 tablespoon	

1. Trim outer leaves from cabbage; quarter, core and chop cabbage (6 cups). Combine cabbage in a large bowl with olives.
2. Combine oil, vinegar, onion, capers, salt, pepper and crushed red pepper in a large screw-top jar. Cover; shake well. Pour dressing over cabbage and toss to coat. Cover; refrigerate several hours.
3. To serve: Top with cherry tomatoes; sprinkle with parsley. Toss again before serving.

Chicken and Rotelle Salad

Makes 8 servings.

1 broiler-fryer (about 3 pounds), cut up	1½ teaspoons leaf basil
1 package (1 pound) rotelle (spiral pasta)	1 teaspoon salt
	½ cup grated Parmesan cheese
1 cup olive oil	
4 cups fresh parsley leaves	Romaine leaves
	1 pint cherry tomatoes, cut into halves
¼ cup pine nuts (pignoli) or walnuts	
2 large cloves garlic, minced	¼ cup pitted ripe olives

1. Simmer chicken in water to cover in a large saucepan until tender, about 40 minutes; cool. Skin, bone and cut into strips. Cover and refrigerate.
2. Cook rotelle following label directions; drain. Rinse with cold water; drain again; turn into large salad bowl.
3. Combine olive oil, parsley, pine nuts, garlic, basil and salt in the container of an electric blender; cover and whirl until parsley is finely chopped. Pour into a

Chicken and Rotelle Salad, page 688.

small bowl; stir in cheese. Edge salad bowl with romaine leaves.

4. Toss rotelle with half the dressing; mound chicken in center of bowl; edge bowl with tomatoes and olives. Serve at room temperature with remaining dressing.

Herbed Walnut, Mushroom and Orange Salad

Makes 8 servings.

1/2 pound shelled walnuts (2 cups)	**Leaf lettuce**
2 cans (13³/4 ounces each) chicken broth	**4 navel oranges, peeled and sliced**
2 bay leaves	**1 pound mushrooms, sliced**
1/4 cup chopped onion	**6 green onions, trimmed and sliced**
1/4 cup chopped carrots	**Red Wine Vinegar Dressing (recipe follows)**
1/4 cup chopped parsley	

1. Cook the walnuts in boiling water to cover in a saucepan, for 5 minutes. Drain. Rub in paper toweling to remove the skins. Remove any remaining skins with the point of a sharp knife.

2. Return the nuts to the saucepan. Add the broth, bay leaves, onion, carrots and parsley. Simmer for 20 minutes. Drain; chill the nuts and vegetables. (Save the broth for a soup or other uses.)

3. To serve, line platter with the lettuce. Arrange the orange slices, mushrooms, green onions and walnuts over the lettuce. Pour the dressing over all.

To Make Ahead: The walnuts and dressing can be prepared a day ahead. The salad can be assembled, without the dressing, several hours before; tightly cover and refrigerate.

Red Wine Vinegar Dressing: Combine 1 cup olive oil, 2 tablespooons lemon juice, 2 tablespoons red wine vinegar, 1 teaspoon dry mustard, 1 teaspoon leaf basil, crumbled, 2 cloves garlic, finely chopped, 1/2 teaspoon salt and 1/4 teaspoon pepper in a jar with a tight-fitting lid. Cover; shake well. Reserve. Shake well again before serving.

The ideal Salad Bar for a party (clockwise from top right): Tossed Green Salad with Toppings, page 690; Fresh Fruit Salad with Tangerine Dressing, page 691; Tomato Aspic Rectangles, page 691; Marinated Tomato-Rice Salad, page 691; 3-Vegetable Relishes in separate bowls, page 692; Tuna-White Bean Salad, page 693; Chicken-Macaroni Salad, page 692; Green Potato Salad, page 692; Platter of Cold Cuts and Vegetables, page 693; Condiments, page 693.

Tossed Green Salad

Prepare any or all of the following ingredients ahead of time and keep them well wrapped in the refrigerator until ready to arrange salad bar. Greens should be washed and dried; endive separated into leaves. Vegetables should be washed and peeled, when appropriate, and cut into serving pieces. Each can be arranged in individual serving dishes or crocks, or you can group them on platters. Serve with assorted dressings and Basic Vinaigrette and Variations.

Romaine lettuce
Iceberg lettuce
Boston lettuce

Little carrot sticks
Sliced summer squash
Cherry tomatoes

Bibb lettuce
Spinach leaves
Belgian endive
Shredded cabbage
Watercress
Chopped parsley
**Blanched broccoli
  flowerets**
**Peeled blanched
  finger carrots**
Sliced green onions
Alfalfa sprouts
Sliced radishes
Sliced mushrooms

Tomato wedges
**Diced sweet red
  pepper**
Diced avocado
**Blanched asparagus
  spears**
Celery sticks
Artichoke hearts
**Finely chopped red
  onion**
Diced cucumber
Croutons
Cheese cubes

Fresh Fruit Salad with Tangerine Dressing

Makes 12 servings.

1 medium-size ripe pineapple, peeled, cored and cut into 1-inch cubes
1 small ripe honeydew or crenshaw melon, halved, seeded and scooped into melon balls
1 small ripe cantaloupe, halved, seeded and scooped into melon balls
5 medium-size bananas, cut diagonally into ½-inch-thick slices
3 large oranges, peeled, sectioned and seeded
3 cups seedless green grapes (about 1 pound)
1 pint strawberries, hulled
2 Red Delicious apples, cored and cut into thin wedges
1 can (6 ounces) frozen tangerine juice concentrate, partially thawed
2 tablespoons fresh lime or lemon juice
¼ cup sugar (optional)

1. Combine pineapple, melon balls, banana, orange, grapes, strawberries and apple in a large bowl.
2. Combine tangerine juice, lime juice and sugar, if using, in a small screw-top jar. Cover; shake well to blend. Pour over the fruit salad. Toss to coat. Cover; refrigerate for several hours.
3. Just before serving, toss again.

Tomato Aspic Rectangles

Make this cool refreshing aspic in a large pan; then just cut into individual servings.

Makes 18 servings.

3 envelopes unflavored gelatin
1 can (18 ounces) tomato juice
1 can (35 ounces) whole tomatoes, undrained
1 cup chicken broth OR: water
1 cup diced celery
1 large onion, chopped (1 cup)
¼ cup chopped fresh dill
OR:1 tablespoon dillweed
3 cloves garlic, sliced
1 tablespoon sugar
1 teaspoon salt
1 tablespoon lemon juice
½ teaspoon Worcestershire sauce
Leafy green lettuce
Lemon slices and sprigs of dill for garnish

1. Sprinkle gelatin over 1 cup of the tomato juice in a small bowl; let stand to soften.
2. Combine the remaining tomato juice, whole tomatoes, chicken broth, celery, onion, dill, garlic, sugar and salt in a large saucepan. Bring to boiling. Lower heat; simmer, uncovered, stirring occasionally,

for 30 minutes. Remove from heat. Stir in softened gelatin mixture until dissolved. Cool slightly.
3. Work tomato mixture through a food mill or sieve with a rubber spatula, into a large bowl. Discard solid pulp. Measure the liquid and add enough water to make 6 cups. Stir in lemon juice and Worcestershire.
4. Pour into a 13 × 9 × 2-inch baking pan. Cover; refrigerate overnight.
5. Cut aspic into 18 rectangles, 3 × 2 inches. Transfer each with a small spatula onto a bed of lettuce on a platter or salad plate. Garnish with lemon slices and dill sprigs.

Marinated Tomato-Rice Salad

Make several hours or a day ahead; then unmold just before serving.

Makes 12 servings.

7 medium-size ripe tomatoes (about 2 pounds), cored
½ cup cider vinegar
1 tablespoon leaf basil, crumbled
1 tablespoon sugar
2 small cucumbers, pared, halved,
seeded and diced (about 1½ cups)
1 cup chopped parsley
½ cup olive oil
9 green onions, thinly sliced
3 cups brown rice
1 teaspoon salt
½ teaspoon pepper

1. Prepare a tomato rose for the garnish: Starting at the bottom of one of the tomatoes, cut the skin of the tomato with a vegetable peeler in one long continuous strip, about ¾ inch wide. Starting with the end you first removed, roll the strip, skin-side out, into a rose shape. Cover with damp paper toweling and refrigerate until needed.
2. Cut 5 of the remaining tomatoes, plus the peeled tomato, into ¾-inch cubes. Place in a medium-size bowl. Add the vinegar, basil and sugar; stir to mix well. Cover; marinate in the refrigerator for 1 hour.
3. Cook the rice following label directions. Drain; cool to room temperature.
4. Combine the rice, cucumber and parsley in a large bowl. Stir in the olive oil. Add the green onion, marinated tomatoes, salt and pepper; stir to mix well.
5. Pack 3 cups of the rice mixture into a 3½-quart bowl. Cut the remaining tomato into ¾-inch cubes. Arrange the cubes, skin-side out, in a ring around the outside of the bowl. Add the remaining rice mixture to the bowl; pack well. Cover; refrigerate for 1 hour.
6. To serve, gently run a thin spatula around the inside of the bowl. Invert the salad onto a large serving plate. Garnish the top with the tomato rose.

Three Vegetable Relishes

These three colorful grated raw vegetables — radish, carrot and beet — are marinated in vinegar and then individually flavored. Serve in small quantities as a relish or condiment.

Makes 6 servings of each relish.

3 cups shredded peeled carrots, (about 6 medium-size carrots)
3 cups shredded peeled raw beets, (about 3 medium-size beets)
3 cups shredded radish (about 24 medium-size radishes)
1 cup white vinegar
3 teaspoons salt
4$^1/_2$ cups water
$^1/_2$ cup orange juice
6 tablespoons olive oil
3 teaspoons sugar
3 teaspoons grated orange rind
$^3/_4$ teaspoon ground nutmeg
$^3/_4$ teaspoon dried mint, crumbled
$^3/_4$ teaspoon ground cumin
$^3/_4$ teaspoon pepper

1. Place carrots, beets, and radishes in 3 separate bowls. Add $^1/_3$ cup vinegar, 1 teaspoon salt and 1$^1/_2$ cups water to each bowl. Stir to mix. Cover; refrigerate at least 1 hour. Drain each bowl separately; rinse under cold water. Return each vegetable to a separate bowl.
2. Pour $^1/_4$ cup orange juice into carrots, and remaining $^1/_4$ cup orange juice into beets. Stir 2 tablespoons olive oil and 1 teaspoon sugar into each bowl; toss well to mix.
3. Add 1$^1/_2$ teaspoons of the orange rind to the carrots and the remaining 1$^1/_2$ teaspoons orange rind to the beets. Add nutmeg to the carrots, mint to the beets, and cumin to the radishes. Add $^1/_4$ teaspoon pepper to each bowl. Toss each vegetable to mix well. Cover; refrigerate.
4. Just before serving, toss each vegetable and drain excess dressing. Mound vegetables into 3 separate serving bowls.

Green Potato Salad

Makes 12 servings.

5 pounds small new potatoes, uniform in size
$^1/_3$ cup dry white wine (optional)
24 medium-size green onions
1 medium-size cucumber
2 medium-size sweet green peppers, halved, seeded and
cut into $^1/_4$ -inch dice
1 cup chopped parsley
$^1/_3$ cup lemon juice
1 tablespoon Dijon-style mustard
2 teaspoons leaf tarragon, crumbled
1$^1/_2$ teaspoons salt
$^1/_2$ teaspoon pepper
$^1/_2$ cup olive oil

1. Cook the potatoes in enough boiling salted water to cover in a kettle or Dutch oven until fork-tender, 15 to 20 minutes. Drain. When cool enough to handle, peel; cut into $^1/_4$ -inch thick slices. Place in a large bowl. Pour the wine, if you wish, over the warm potatoes.
2. Thinly slice the green onions, keeping the white part separate from the green; you should have about 1 cup of the white and about 1$^1/_2$ cups of the green. Add the white to the potatoes.
3. Pare, halve and seed the cucumber. Cut into $^1/_4$-inch dice. Add along with the green pepper to the potatoes.
4. Combine the green portions of the onions, the parsley, lemon juice, mustard, tarragon, salt and pepper in the container of an electric blender or food processor. Cover; whirl until pureed. With the machine running, pour in the olive oil. Process until well blended. Pour the dressing over the salad. Toss to coat. Cover; refrigerate.
5. Serve the salad chilled.

Chicken-Macaroni Salad

You can use light or dark meat or a combination of both for the salad, or leftover turkey, if you like. Roasting the peppers adds an extra special flavor.

Makes 12 servings.

3 large sweet red peppers, halved
1 package (1 pound) small elbow macaroni
1$^1/_2$ cups mayonnaise
1$^1/_2$ cups dairy sour cream
4 hard-cooked eggs, chopped
$^1/_4$ cup lemon juice
3 tablespoons prepared mustard
2 tablespoons drained capers
1 teaspoon salt
$^1/_4$ teaspoon pepper
4 cups cubed cooked chicken (about 2 pounds uncooked boneless chicken breast)
2 cans (5.7 ounces each) pitted black colossal olives, drained
2 medium-size onions, grated
2 cups finely chopped celery

1. Arrange the pepper halves, skin-side up, on a cookie sheet. Broil 6 inches from the heat, turning once, until charred and soft, 5 to 8 minutes. Peel and remove seeds, Slice the peppers into 1 × $^1/_4$-inch strips.
2. Cook the pasta following package directions. Drain and place in a large bowl.
3. Stir together the mayonnaise, sour cream, chopped eggs, lemon juice, mustard, capers, salt and pepper in a medium-size bowl. Spoon the dressing over the pasta. Add the chicken. Toss to blend well.
4. Reserve 8 red pepper strips for garnish. Chop the remaining strips and add to the salad. Reserve 8 olives for garnish. Chop the remaining olives and add to the salad along with the onion and celery. Toss well to mix. Cover; refrigerate until ready to serve, up to 3 hours. (Add more mayonnaise or sour cream just before serving if the salad is too dry.)

5. For garnish, fold each of the reserved pepper strips in half. Insert the ends of each into a pitted olive. Mound the salad into a salad bowl. Garnish with the stuffed olives

Platter of Meats with Accompanying Breads

Serve a platter of cold cuts so your guests can create their own Chef's Salad. Be sure to garnish the platter with colorful vegetables such as radish roses, celery brushes, broccoli flowerets and endive. Include any or all of the following.

Sliced roast beef
Sliced roast chicken
Sliced turkey
Sliced smoked ham
Thinly sliced salami or
   pepperoni

Shredded Cheddar
   cheese
Basketful of bread
   sticks, small dinner
   rolls and assorted
   breads

Tuna–White Bean Salad

This attractive salad, flecked with bits of purple and green, can be made 1 or 2 days ahead.
Makes 12 servings.

1 package (1 pound)
   dried Great
   Northern beans
2 quarts water
2 cans (7 ounces
   each) solid white
   tuna packed in oil,
   drained and flaked
2 large red onions,
   finely chopped
   (3 cups)

1 package (10 ounces)
   frozen peas, thawed
1/2 cup olive oil
1/3 cup fresh lemon
   juice
2 teaspoons leaf
   oregano, crumbled
1 1/2 teaspoons salt
3/4 to 1 teaspoon
   pepper
1 lemon for garnish

1. Pick over the beans; rinse under cold water. Soak the beans overnight in enough water to cover in a large bowl. Drain; rinse.
2. Combine the beans and the 2 quarts of water in a kettle or Dutch oven. Bring to boiling. Lower the heat; simmer for 35 to 45 minutes or just until tender. Drain; cool to room temperature.
3. Combine the beans, tuna and red onion in a large bowl. Reserve 1/3 cup peas for garnish. Add the remaining peas to the salad.
4. Combine the oil, lemon juice, oregano, salt and pepper in a screw-top jar; shake well to blend. Pour over the salad. Toss gently to coat. Cover; refrigerate until ready to serve.
5. Make a lemon basket for garnish: Draw a 1/2-inch-wide strip with a pencil down the center of one half of the lemon; this will form the handle. Cut down into the center of the lemon following the outlines of the handle. Starting at the ends of the lemon, cut horizontally in toward the center strip. Remove the wedges from the top half of the lemon. Cut out the

lemon from the underside of the handle. Scoop out the pulp from the bottom half of the lemon. Fill the basket with the reserved peas.
6. To serve, mound the salad in a large serving bowl. Garnish with the lemon basket.

Condiments

To complete your salad bar, include an attractive selection of any or all of the following condiments. Arrange some in individual serving dishes and crocks and others on a platter.

Mustard
Mayonnaise
Sour cream
Horseradish
Taco sauce
Black olives
Green olives
Dill pickle slices
Sweet gherkins
Raisins

Pickled pearl onions
Pickled herring
Bacon bits
Chopped hardcooked
   eggs
Chopped nuts
Capers
Mango chutney
Spiced peaches
Dates

Beet Salad

Makes 4 servings.

1 jar (16 ounces)
   pickled beets,
   drained
   OR: 1 can (16
   ounces) sliced
   beets, drained
Lemon Vinaigrette
   Dressing (*recipe*

follows)
1 navel orange
1 small onion,
   chopped (1/4 cup)
Lettuce
3 tablespoons
   chopped parsley

1. Arrange beets in a shallow dish; drizzle with half of the Lemon Vinaigrette Dressing.
2. Use a sharp knife to peel orange. Cut into thin slices; cut slices in half.
3. Arrange orange slices over beets; spread onion over orange. Pour remaining dressing over all. Cover; refrigerate 30 minutes.
4. Place small lettuce leaf on each of 4 chilled salad plates. Arrange beet salad over lettuce. Spoon a little dressing over each serving; sprinkle with parsley.

Lemon Vinaigrette Dressing

Makes about 1/4 cup.

3 tablespoons olive or
   vegetable oil
1 tablespoon lemon
   juice
1/4 teaspoon salt

1/8 teaspoon pepper
1/8 teaspoon dry
   mustard
1 teaspoon finely
   chopped parsley

Measure all ingredients into a small bowl. Use a wire whisk to blend thoroughly.

Rice and Vegetable Salad

An easy-to-carry salad that does not wilt.

Makes 8 servings.

1 cup uncooked brown rice
1 cup chopped celery
1 cup chopped green onions
1 cup shredded carrots
1 cup shredded zucchini
1 cucumber, pared, seeded and chopped
1/4 cup chopped fresh parsley
1/2 cup white wine vinegar
1/2 cup olive or vegetable oil
1 1/2 teaspoons salt
1 large tomato
4 lemon slices, halved
8 ripe olives
Parsley sprigs

1. Cook rice following label directions; cool; chill 1 hour or until cold.
2. Add celery, onions, carrots, zucchini, cucumber, parsley, vinegar, oil and salt to chilled rice; toss to mix well. Spoon salad into shallow plastic container with a snap-on cover. Cover; refrigerate.
3. To serve: Spoon into bowl. Cut tomato into 4 slices (chop the ends and add to salad); cut each slice in half; arrange on top of salad with lemon slices and olives. Garnish with parsley sprigs.

Steak Salad with Spinach and Red Onion

Makes 4 servings.

1 pound boneless sirloin or blade steak
1 teaspoon salt
1 teaspoon pepper
1 1/2 pounds salad bar vegetables (about 9 cups), including 5
cups spinach leaves and 4 cups mixture of mushroom slices, red onion slices and cherry tomatoes
1 cup blue cheese dressing*

1. Sauté steak without oil in small nonstick skillet about 3 minutes on each side for medium rare, or longer for desired doneness. Transfer to cutting board. Season both sides with salt and pepper.
2. Line large shallow salad bowl with spinach leaves. Arrange mushrooms, red onion, meat and tomatoes in circular pattern.
3. To serve, pour blue cheese dressing over salad; toss well to coat. Serve immediately.

Purchase blue cheese dressing from salad bar or prepare your own:
Combine 1/2 cup (2 ounces) crumbled blue cheese, 1/2 cup mayonnaise and 1 teaspoon Dijon-style mustard.

Rice and Vegetable Salad, page 694; Herb-Cheese Filled Bread, page 122; Lamb and Mushroom Kabobs, page 491; Jumbo Double Chocolage Chip Cookies, page 222.

Steak Salad with Spinach and Red Onions, page 694.

Hot Potato-Kielbasa Salad

Makes 6 servings.

**3 pounds small red
  potatoes**
1 pound kielbasa
³/₄ cup water
**1 medium-size onion,
  chopped (¹/₂ cup)**
**2 tablespoons
  vegetable oil**
1 tablespoon flour
¹/₂ cup vinegar

2 tablespoons sugar
**1 teaspoon caraway
  seeds**
**¹/₂ teaspoon celery
  seeds**
¹/₈ teaspoon pepper
¹/₂ cup sliced radishes
**¹/₂ cup chopped fresh
  parsley**

1. Scrub potatoes; cut in quarters. Cook in boiling
salted water in a large saucepan until tender; drain.
2. Cut kielbasa into 1¹/₂-inch lengths; cut three slits in
each piece, cutting almost to bottom. Combine with ³/₄
cup water in a small saucepan. Bring to boiling; cover.
Lower heat; simmer 3 minutes. Drain, saving ¹/₂ cup
of the cooking liquid; keep kielbasa warm.
3. Sauté onion in oil in a large skillet until lightly
browned, stirring often. Blend in flour until smooth. Stir
in reserved cooking liquid, vinegar, sugar, caraway
and celery seeds and pepper. Cook, stirring
constantly, until thick and bubbly.
4. Add potatoes, kielbasa, radishes and parsley; toss
to mix.

Oh My! Potato Salad

Apples give this salad a special texture and taste.

Makes 6 to 8 servings.

**2¹/₂ pounds new
  potatoes (about
  5 cups)**
**3 sweet apples, such
  as Red Delicious or
  McIntosh**
**2 tablespoons lemon
  juice (1 lemon)**
**1 cup finely chopped
  onion (1 large)**
1 cup thinly sliced dill

**pickles
  (3 to 4 pickles)**
**2 tablespoons capers,
  drained**
1 teaspoon caper juice
**1 cup mayonnaise or
  salad dressing**
¹/₂ teaspoon salt
¹/₄ teaspoon pepper
Watercress (optional)

1. Cook the potatoes in their skins in boiling water in a

(continued)

large covered saucepan until just tender, about 20 to 25 minutes; the centers should not be soft. Drain. Rinse briefly under cold running water; drain.

2. Meanwhile, peel, core and slice the apples. Place in a large bowl, sprinkling with the lemon juice as you cut them. Add the onion, pickles, capers, caper juice and mayonnaise. Toss lightly to combine.

3. Peel the potatoes while still warm. Cut into thin slices. Fold into the apple mixture. Add the salt and pepper. Serve slightly warm or chilled. Garnish with the watercress, if you wish.

Greek Chick-Pea Salad

Here is a delicious salad which only takes a few minutes to prepare. It can be assembled early in the day and the cheese and garnish added just before serving.

Makes 8 to 10 servings.

2 teaspoons Dijon mustard	1 medium-size red onion, sliced and separated into rings
1 1/2 teaspoons salt	
1 1/4 cups olive or vegetable oil	4 ounces feta cheese, crumbled
1/2 cup lemon juice	
1/4 teaspoon ground pepper	2 tablespoons chopped fresh parsley
2 cans (20 ounces each) chick-peas, drained	Lettuce leaves

1. Combine mustard, salt, oil, lemon juice and pepper in container of electric blender; whirl until smooth. (Or, shake well in a 1-quart screw-top jar.)

2. Combine chick-peas and onion in a large bowl. Pour dressing over and toss. Refrigerate 1 hour. (May be prepared several days in advance.)

3. Just before serving, add cheese and parsley; toss. Spoon into lettuce-lined salad bowl.

Hot Nachos Salad

Makes 4 servings.

1 large head iceberg lettuce, finely shredded	pimiento-stuffed olives or thinly sliced canned jalapeño peppers to taste
2 cans (15 ounces each) chili with beans, heated	
1 medium-size red or white onion, chopped (1/2 cup)	4 ounces Monterey Jack or sharp Cheddar cheese, shredded (1 cup)
1 cup coarsely crushed taco chips	Bottled Italian salad dressing and/or dairy sour cream
1/2 cup sliced	

1. Arrange lettuce in a fairly deep platter or shallow serving bowl.

2. Spoon chili in center of lettuce.

3. Sprinkle chili with onion, chips, olives and cheese; toss lightly. Serve dressing and sour cream separately.

Taco Salad in Lettuce Leaves

Makes 6 servings.

1 pound ground round	tomato (2 medium-size)
1 package (1 1/8 ounces) taco seasoning mix	1/2 cup sliced pitted ripe olives
3/4 cup water	1 jar (8 ounces) taco sauce
1 can (16 ounces) pinto beans, drained and rinsed	Dairy sour cream
12 large lettuce leaves	1 can (6 ounces) frozen avocado dip, thawed
6 ounces Cheddar cheese, shredded (1 1/2 cups)	OR: 1 cup homemade guacamole
1 cup diced fresh	

1. Brown meat in a large skillet. Drain and discard all fat. Return meat to pan; stir in taco seasoning mix, water and beans. Cook 15 minutes, stirring frequently. Remove from heat and let cool to lukewarm.

2. Roll up each lettuce leaf and arrange on one half of a large platter. Spoon meat mixture on the other half and top with cheese, tomato and olives. Put taco sauce, sour cream and avocado dip in separate bowls.

To serve: Let everyone put some meat mixture on a leaf of lettuce; top with taco sauce, sour cream or avocado dip. Wrap meat mixture up in lettuce and eat up!

Winter Salad of Julienne Vegetables

Makes 8 to 10 servings.

4 to 6 carrots, cut into julienne (1 1/2 × 1/4-inch) pieces (about 2 cups)	1/8 teaspoon cayenne pepper
	3 tablespoons lemon juice
1/2 pound snow peas, strings removed, cut lengthwise into 1/4-inch strips	3 tablespoons peanut oil
	2 tablespoons soy sauce
1 large fennel bulb, washed	1 tablespoon honey
1 teaspoon grated fresh gingerroot	1 head radicchio,* separated into leaves
1/2 teaspoon finely chopped garlic	1 head romaine, separated into leaves

1. Place the carrots in a metal strainer. Immerse in a

(continued)

Pictured opposite: Taco Salad in Lettuce Leaves.

large pot of boiling salted water. Cook until crisp-tender, 1 to 2 minutes. Life out the strainer and drain; plunge carrots into ice water in a bowl. In the same boiling water, immerse snow peas in strainer until just bright green, 5 seconds. Drain; add to the carrots in ice water. Drain the vegetables well. Place in large bowl.

2. Trim stalks from the fennel. Cut the bulb in half lengthwise. Remove the core from each half. Cut fennel lengthwise into very thin slices. Add to the other vegetables. Refrigerate.

3. Mix the gingerroot, garlic, cayenne, lemon juice, oil, soy sauce and honey. Let stand for 30 minutes.

4. To serve, toss the vegetables with dressing. Arrange radicchio and romaine around the edge of the serving plate. Spoon salad in the center.

Radicchio is a peppery-tasting, red-leafed Italian lettuce.

Orange Avocado Salad

Makes 6 servings.

1 medium-size head romaine	avocado Lemon Dressing
3 large navel oranges	*(recipe follows)*
1 large firm ripe	

1. Tear the romaine into bite-size pieces into a large salad bowl. Cut rind off oranges; section oranges into a small bowl.

2. Just before serving, peel, pit and slice avocado. Arrange avocado and oranges over romaine. Drizzle 1/3 to 1/2 cup Lemon Dressing over salad; toss gently.

Lemon Dressing

Makes 3/4 cup.

1/4 cup fresh lemon juice	1/4 teaspoon sugar
1/2 teaspoon salt	1/4 teaspoon dry mustard
1/8 teaspoon pepper	1/2 cup vegetable oil

1. Beat lemon juice, salt, pepper, sugar and dry mustard in a medium-size bowl.

2. Beat in the oil in a slow, steady stream; refrigerate. Stir well just before serving.

Grape and Endive Salad

Makes 12 servings.

3 tablespoons lemon juice	3 cups seedless green or red grapes
1/4 cup olive oil	1 cup sliced celery
1 tablespoon honey	2 heads Belgian endive, sliced
1/4 teaspoon ground cardamom	Celery leaves and grapes for garnish
Dash salt	

Mix lemon juice, oil, honey, cardamom and salt in a

Bean Sprouts and Tomato Salad, page 699.

Louisiana Salad, page 700.

large bowl; toss in grapes and celery. Chill about 1 hour; toss in endive. Garnish with crisp celery leaves and a cluster of grapes.

Bean Sprouts and Tomato Salad

Makes 4 servings.

1 can (16 ounces)
  bean sprouts,
  rinsed and drained
1 cup cherry
  tomatoes, cut into
  halves
1/2 cup seeded and
  slivered cucumber
1/3 cup chopped fresh
  parsley
3 tablespoons olive or

vegetable oil
1 tablespoon red wine
  vinegar
1/2 teaspoon salt
1/8 teaspoon pepper
1/4 teaspoon leaf basil,
  crumbled
Pinch paprika
1 large clove garlic,
  crushed

1. Toss bean sprouts, tomatoes, cucumber and parsley together in a bowl. Cover; refrigerate 30 minutes.
2. Measure oil, vinegar, salt, pepper, basil and paprika into a cup or bowl; add crushed garlic. Blend with a wire whisk.
3. Just before serving, pour dressing over salad; mix lightly. Spoon onto 4 chilled salad plates. Garnish with fresh parsley, if you wish.

Winter Fruit Salad with Honey-Lemon Dressing

Makes 6 servings.

3 large red apples
1 tablespoon lemon
  juice
1 pound red grapes
1 large red onion
2 bunches watercress,
  stems removed

2 tablespoons honey
2/3 cup lemon juice
1/4 cup vegetable oil
1/2 teaspoon salt
1/8 teaspoon pepper
1/4 cup finely chopped
  red onion

1. Wash, core and slice the apples. Toss with the 1 tablespoon of lemon juice in a bowl. Divide the grapes into clusters. Peel the onion; thinly slice.
2. Arrange the watercress around the outside edge of a large platter or serving bowl. Arrange the apples, grapes and onion on the platter. Reserve.
3. Combine the honey, the 2/3 cup of lemon juice, the oil, salt, pepper and chopped red onion in a large jar with a tight-fitting lid. Shake until the honey has dissolved. Spoon 3 tablespoons of the dressing over the apples and onion. Cover the salad tightly with plastic wrap. Refrigerate both the salad and dressing until ready to serve. Pass the dressing.

To Make Ahead: The dressing can be made a day ahead; the salad, several hours.

Louisiana Salad

Yellow peppers from Holland add to this colorful salad.

Makes 6 servings.

1 small green pepper	**snow peas, thawed**
1 small red pepper	**1 large head Boston**
1 small yellow pepper	**lettuce**
1/4 pound Chinese	**1 head Bibb lettuce**
snow peas	**Chive-Onion Dressing**
OR: 1 package	***(recipe follows)***
(6 ounces) frozen	

1. Halve and seed the green, red and yellow peppers. Cut into julienne slices, Trim the snow peas.
2. Wash and dry the Boston and Bibb lettuces. Break the leaves into bite-size pieces; place in a medium-size salad bowl. Scatter the pepper slices and snow peas over the lettuce. Cover and refrigerate.
3. When ready to serve, pour Chive-Onion Dressing over salad; toss.

Chive-Onion Dressing

Makes about 3/4 cup.

1/2 cup olive or	**2 teaspoons snipped**
vegetable oil	**chives**
1/4 cup red wine	**1/4 teaspoon salt**
vinegar	**Dash freshly ground**
1 tablespoon finely	**pepper**
chopped red onion	

Combine the oil, vinegar, onion, chives, salt and pepper in a jar with a tight-fitting lid. Shake well to blend. Let stand for several hours. Always shake just before using.

Sunset Salad

A dessert salad that's good with a soup and sandwich for lunch.

Makes 8 servings.

2 envelopes	**juice)**
unflavored gelatin	**1/2 cup water**
1/4 cup sugar	**1 cup orange juice**
1/2 teaspoon salt	**1/4 cup cider vinegar**
1 can (20 ounces)	**1 1/2 cups shredded**
crushed pineapple	**carrots (about 3)**
in pineapple juice,	**Fruit Dressing (*recipe**
drained (reserve	**follows*)**

1. Mix gelatin, sugar and salt in a small saucepan; stir in reserved juice from pineapple and water. Heat slowly, stirring constantly, until gelatin dissolves; stir in orange juice and vinegar; pour into a large bowl.
2. Refrigerate until mixture is as thick as unbeaten egg white, about 1 hour.
3. Stir in crushed pineapple and carrots; pour into

6-cup mold or 8 × 8 × 2-inch pan. Refrigerate until firm. Serve with Fruit Dressing.

Fruit Dressing: Combine 1 cup dairy sour cream, 1 teaspoon grated orange rind and 2 tablespoons honey in a small bowl. Beat until smooth; chill. Makes about 1 cup.

German Potato Salad

Makes 6 servings.

6 medium-size	**1 1/2 tablespoons flour**
potatoes (about	**2 tablespoons sugar**
2 pounds)	**1 teaspoon salt**
6 bacon slices	**1/4 teaspoon pepper**
1 medium-size onion,	**1/4 cup cider vinegar**
chopped (1/2 cup)	**1 cup water**
1 cup chopped celery	

1. Cook potatoes in boiling water to cover in a large saucepan just until tender, about 20 minutes. Drain; peel and slice into a large bowl; cover.
2. Cook bacon in a large skillet until crisp; drain on paper toweling. Pour off drippings; measure 1/4 cup and return to skillet.
3. Sauté onion and celery in drippings until soft. Stir in flour, sugar, salt, pepper, vinegar and water. Cook, stirring constantly, until mixture is thickened. Pour over potatoes; toss lightly to coat. Crumble bacon and sprinkle over top. Serve warm.

Pinto Bean Salad

Makes 6 servings.

1 cup dried pinto	**(1 small)**
beans (1/2 pound)	**1 cup sliced fennel**
4 cups water	**4 ounces Swiss**
2 cups torn fresh	**cheese, cubed**
spinach leaves,	**Tangy Mustard**
loosely packed	**Dressing (*recipe**
1 cup sliced zucchini	**follows*)**

1. Pick over beans and rinse under running water. Combine beans and 4 cups cold water in a large kettle. Bring to boiling; cover; simmer 1 1/2 hours or until beans are firm-tender. Drain; chill several hours.
2. To serve: Arrange spinach, zucchini-fennel, Swiss cheese and beans in a large salad bowl. Pour dressing over all; toss to coat evenly.

Tangy Mustard Dressing: Combine 3/4 cup mayonnaise or salad dressing, 2 tablespoons vinegar, 1 tablespoon lemon juice, 2 tablespoons grated onion, 1 tablespoon Dijon mustard, 1/2 teaspoon salt, 1/4 teaspoon cracked black pepper in a small bowl. Refrigerate, covered, at least 1 hour. Makes 1 cup.

Pictured opposite: Sunset Salad (top); German Potato Salad.

Turkey Salad with Corn and Green Beans.

Turkey Salad with Corn and Green Beans

All-American ingredients make this colorful salad a great choice for lunch or dinner. Serve it with crusty bread or corn chips.

Makes 4 servings.

³/₄ pound cooked turkey breast
1 package (10 ounces) frozen whole kernel corn
¹/₂ pound fresh green beans, trimmed
2 medium-size carrots, pared and trimmed
Salt.
¹/₃ cup mayonnaise

¹/₃ cup dairy sour cream
1 tablespoon lemon juice
¹/₂ teaspoon liquid red-pepper seasoning
2 tablespoons chopped fresh cilantro,
OR: chopped fresh parsley

1. Cut turkey into 1 × ¹/₄ × ¹/₄-inch strips.

2. Place frozen corn and 2 tablespoons water in small saucepan. Bring to boiling over high heat. Cover. Lower heat and simmer for 3 minutes. Drain and cool.
3. Cut beans into 1¹/₂-inch lengths. Halve carrots lengthwise. Cut into ¹/₄-inch-thick slices.
4. Bring 2 quarts water and 1 teaspoon salt to boiling in medium-size saucepan. Add beans and carrots. Cook, uncovered, at rapid boil for 5 minutes. Drain. Cool under cold running water. Drain.
5. To prepare dressing, combine mayonnaise, sour cream, lemon juice, liquid red-pepper seasoning and ³/₄ teaspoon salt in small bowl.
6. Combine turkey and cooled, well-drained vegetables, cilantro and dressing in large serving bowl. Toss to mix well. Cover and refrigerate for at least 1 hour or overnight. Stir lightly before serving.

Note: For an attractive buffet presentation, arrange the turkey, corn, green beans and carrots in separate mounds on a large serving platter. Spoon the dressing in ribbons over the salad. Toss just before serving.

SALADS AND SALAD DRESSINGS • 703

Shrimp and Cantaloupe Salad

Makes 4 servings.

1 large cantaloupe	chestnuts
1 small ripe avocado	1/2 cup vegetable oil
3 tablespoons lemon juice	2 tablespoons vinegar
3/4 pound raw shrimp, shelled, deveined and cooked OR: 1/2 pound frozen shelled and deveined shrimp, cooked	2 tablespoons chopped bottled chutney
	1/4 teaspoon salt
	1/4 teaspoon curry powder
	Pinch pepper
1/2 cup sliced water	Romaine leaves

1. Quarter cantaloupe; scoop out seeds. Loosen fruit from rind with a grapefruit knife; cut loosened fruit into 6 crosswise slices.
2. Halve, pit and peel avocado; cube into a medium-size bowl. Sprinkle cubes with 1 tablespoon of the lemon juice. Add shrimp and water chestnuts; toss lightly; chill.
3. Combine oil, vinegar, chutney, salt, curry powder, pepper and remaining lemon juice in a small bowl; mix well.
4. To serve: Arrange cantaloupe on romaine leaves; spoon shrimp mixture over cantaloupe; spoon dressing over salad.

Caesar Salad

Just the right combination and quality of ingredients give this simple, yet justly famous salad its distinctive taste. It was created by a restaurateur named Caesar Cardini in Tijuana, Mexico, in the early 1920's.

Caesar Salad

Makes 6 servings.

3/4 cup olive oil	1/8 teaspoon pepper
1 clove garlic, crushed	1/2 teaspoon Worcestershire sauce
3 slices white bread	
3 tablespoons lemon juice	1 egg
6 flat anchovy fillets, finely chopped	1 large head romaine lettuce
1/2 teaspoon salt	1/2 cup freshly grated Parmesan cheese
1/2 teaspoon dry mustard	

1. Combine olive oil and garlic in cup; let stand several hours or overnight. Remove and discard garlic.
2. Cut bread into small cubes. Heat 1/4 cup of the garlic oil in a large skillet. Add bread cubes, spread in a single layer. Sauté, stirring frequently, until golden brown. Drain on paper toweling.
3. Combine the remaining 1/2 cup garlic oil, lemon juice, anchovies, salt, mustard, pepper and Worcestershire in a large salad bowl.
4. Place egg in small bowl of hot water; let stand 10 minutes or until just at room temperature.
5. Tear romaine leaves into bowl in bite-size pieces, removing any coarse ribs. (You should have about 12 cups, or 3 quarts, torn leaves.)
6. Top greens with half of the Parmesan cheese. Break egg over salad. Toss salad, spooning from bottom of bowl each time, until greens are evenly coated with dressing. Sprinkle with remaining Parmesan cheese and bread cubes. Toss and serve immediately.

Hearts of Romaine with Roquefort Dressing

Makes 6 servings.

6 heads romaine	1/4 teaspoon salt
1 cup olive oil	1/4 teaspoon seasoned pepper
1 egg	
3 tablespoons lemon juice	3 ounces Roquefort cheese, crumbled (1/2 cup)
2 teaspoons red wine vinegar	
1/2 teaspoon dry mustard	2 tablespoons heavy cream

1. Wash romaine thoroughly; drain. Strip away outer leaves (save for another salad later) until all that remains are the small, lighter green leaves in the center of the head. Split each heart in half.
2. Place 1/4 cup of the olive oil, egg, lemon juice, vinegar, mustard, salt and pepper in container of electric blender. Cover. Whirl at medium speed until mixture starts to thicken. Pour in remaining oil in a thin stream (mixture will become quite thick). Whirl a few seconds on highest speed.
3. Turn dressing into a bowl. Fold in Roquefort cheese and cream. Divide romaine among 6 salad plates. Spoon some dressing over; pass remainder.

Asparagus Vinaigrette

Makes 6 servings.

2 1/2 pounds asparagus	1 tablespoon chopped fresh parsley
2/3 cup olive or vegetable oil	
1/3 cup white wine vinegar	1 tablespoon chopped green onion
1/2 teaspoon Dijon mustard	1 tablespoon sweet pickle relish
1/2 teaspoon salt	1 tablespoon chopped pimiento
1/8 teaspoon pepper	

1. Wash and trim asparagus. Cook until just tender, 10 to 13 minutes; drain. Rinse with cold water to stop

cooking; drain on paper toweling. Arrange on platter; chill.

2. Combine oil, vinegar, mustard, salt, pepper, parsley, onion, relish and pimiento in jar with screw-top. Shake well. Chill 2 hours for flavors to develop.

3. Spoon dressing over asparagus about 1/2 hour before serving.

Rice Salad Niçoise

Makes 8 servings.

11/2 cups uncooked long-grain rice	romaine or iceberg lettuce
1 can (16 ounces) cut green beans, drained	2 tomatoes, cut into wedges
3/4 cup vegetable oil	1 small red onion, sliced
1/4 cup red wine vinegar	2 hard-cooked eggs, sliced
2 cloves garlic, minced	1 can (2 ounces) rolled anchovy fillets with capers, drained
1 teaspoon salt	
1/4 teaspoon pepper	2 cans (61/2 ounces each) tuna, drained
1/4 teaspoon leaf thyme, crumbled	1 can (6 ounces) pitted ripe olives, drained
1 medium-size head	

1. Cook rice following label directions.

2. Combine rice, beans, oil, vinegar, garlic, salt, pepper and thyme in a large bowl; mix gently to coat thoroughly. Cover. Chill several hours, mixing occasionally.

3. To arrange: Line large salad plate with romaine. Press rice and bean mixture into a 9-inch ring mold, pressing down to fit; turn upside down in center of salad plate; lift off mold. Arrange tomatoes, onion, eggs, anchovies, tuna broken in large chunks and olives around rice.

Frozen Fruit Salad

Makes 12 servings.

5 ripe bananas	(about 2/3 cup; reserve juice)
1 can (20 ounces) crushed pineapple, drained	2 containers (16 ounces each) dairy sour cream
11/2 cups sugar	
1/4 cup lemon juice	1 can (6 ounces) pecans, chopped (about 12/3 cups)
1 jar (8 ounces) maraschino cherries, chopped	

1. Mash bananas in a large bowl. Add drained pineapple, sugar, lemon juice, chopped cherries and their juice. Stir until blended.

2. Fold in sour cream and chopped pecans. Blend well. Turn mixture into a 10-cup ring mold. Cover with aluminum foil. Freeze 8 hours or until firm; unmold.

Endive Crown Salad

Makes 8 servings.

1 small head romaine	8 radishes, trimmed and sliced
1 head Boston lettuce	French Dressing (recipe follows)
2 heads Belgian endive, quartered lengthwise	

1. Break romaine and Boston lettuce into bite-size pieces in a large salad bowl.

2. Stand endive quarters in greens to form a circle; place radishes in center.

3. Serve with French Dressing.

French Dressing: Combine 3/4 cup vegetable oil, 1/4 cup wine vinegar or cider vinegar, 1/2 teaspoon dry mustard, 1/2 teaspoon sugar, 1/2 teaspoon salt, 1/4 teaspoon Worcestershire sauce and a dash of garlic powder in a jar with a tight lid. Shake well to mix. Makes 1 cup.

Wilted Lettuce

Makes 4 servings.

8 cups loosely packed lettuce leaves	1 tablespoon sugar
4 bacon slices	1/2 teaspoon salt
1/2 cup sliced green onions	1/8 teaspoon pepper
	1/3 cup tarragon-flavored vinegar

1. Wash leaf lettuce in running water; dry on paper toweling; tear dry leaves into a large salad bowl.

2. Cook bacon until crisp in skillet; crumble; reserve.

3. Add green onions, sugar, salt, pepper and vinegar to bacon drippings in skillet. Cook 2 minutes.

4. Pour hot dressing over lettuce. Sprinkle with bacon. Toss to coat greens evenly.

Creamy Chicken Mousse

Makes 6 servings.

2 envelopes unflavored gelatin	1 can (63/4 ounces) chunk chicken, drained and chopped
11/4 cups cold water	
1 envelope or teaspoon instant chicken broth	1/2 cup chopped celery
Radish slices	1 tablespoon chopped green onion
Halved pitted ripe olives	1 tablespoon lemon juice
1 can (103/4 ounces) condensed cream of chicken soup	Pinch pepper
	1/2 cup heavy cream
	Boston lettuce

1. Sprinkle gelatin over 1 cup of the water in a small

Rice Salad Nicoise, page 704.

saucepan. Let stand 5 minutes to soften. Stir over very low heat until gelatin is dissolved. Stir in chicken broth.

2. Remove ¼ cup of the gelatin mixture to a 1-cup measure; stir in the remaining ¼ cup water. Pour into an 8 × 4 × 3-inch loaf pan; refrigerate until syrupy. Arrange radish slices and olive halves in a decorative pattern in gelatin; refrigerate until firm.

3. Meanwhile, combine remaining gelatin mixture, cream soup, chicken, celery, green onion, lemon juice and pepper in a medium-size bowl; refrigerate until slightly thickened.

4. Whip cream in a small bowl until stiff; fold into chicken mixture. Carefully pour over set layer in loaf pan. Cover; refrigerate about 3 hours or until set. Unmold onto lettuce-lined serving plate.

Creamy Vegetable Slaw

Makes 6 servings.

1 small cabbage
  (1 pound)
2 carrots
1/2 bunch red radishes
1 small green pepper,
  halved, seeded and
  cut into 1-inch
  chunks
1 celery stalk, cut into
  1-inch chunks
2 green onions, cut
  into 1-inch pieces

1/3 cup mayonnaise
1/3 cup dairy sour
  cream
1 tablespoon cider
  vinegar
2 teaspoons sugar
3/4 teaspoon salt
2 teaspoons prepared
  Dijon mustard
Dash liquid hot pepper
  seasoning

1. Trim cabbage of outer leaves; quarter and core; cut into pieces. Feed cabbage pieces into container of electric food processor fitted with metal shredding blade. Empty cabbage in a large bowl. Shred carrots; add to cabbage. Using the slicing blade, slice radishes. Add to cabbage. Using the metal chopping blade, chop green pepper, celery and onions in food processor; toss with cabbage mixture in bowl.
2. Combine mayonnaise, sour cream, vinegar, sugar, salt, Dijon mustard and hot pepper seasoning in container of food processor fitted with metal chopping blade. Cover and process quickly or just until well mixed. Pour dressing over cabbage mixture and toss to coat. Cover; refrigerate at least 1 hour. Toss again before serving.

Cool Cucumber-Pineapple Mold

Makes 8 servings.

2 medium-size
  cucumbers
1 can (20 ounces)
  crushed pineapple
  in pineapple juice
1 package (6 ounces)
  lime-flavored
  gelatin

2 cups boiling water
1/4 cup cider vinegar
1/2 cup mayonnaise
1/2 cup dairy sour
  cream
2 teaspoons salt
1/2 teaspoon dillweed

1. Pare cucumbers; halve; remove seeds. Shred on smallest side of food shredder; drain thoroughly, pressing out as much liquid as possible.
2. Drain juice from pineapple into a 1-cup liquid measure. Add water to make 1 cup liquid. Reserve.
3. Dissolve gelatin in boiling water in a medium-size bowl. Stir in reserved pineapple juice and vinegar. Place bowl in a pan of ice and water to speed setting. Chill, stirring often, until as thick as unbeaten egg white.
4. Stir in cucumbers, pineapple, mayonnaise, sour cream, salt and dillweed.
5. Continue to chill over ice and water until mixture again becomes as thick as unbeaten egg white.
6. Pour into an 8-cup mold. Chill until firm, about 4 hours. To unmold: Run a thin-bladed knife around top edge of mold. Dip mold very quickly in and out of hot water. Invert serving plate over top of mold; turn plate upright with mold; shake gently to loosen; lift off.

Creamy Vegetable Slaw.

Refrigerate until ready to serve. Garnish with lettuce or chicory, if you wish.

The Perfect Chef's Salad

You can vary this recipe by substituting ham or turkey for the chicken, and Swiss or Cheddar for the blue cheese.

Makes 6 servings.

2 whole chicken breasts	juice
3 cups torn Boston lettuce	2 tomatoes, cut into thin wedges
3 cups torn romaine leaves	3 hard-cooked eggs, sliced
1 cup sliced celery	4 ounces blue cheese, crumbled
6 bacon slices	Herb Vinaigrette
1 ripe avocado	Dressing *(recipe
1 tablespoon lemon	follows)*

1. Cook chicken by boiling in water, broiling or microwaving; cool. Skin and bone; chill; then cut into thin slices.
2. Combine lettuce, romaine and celery in a large bowl; cover; refrigerate.
3. Cook and crumble bacon.
4. Halve avocado; peel and pit. Cut into cubes; sprinkle with lemon juice.
5. Place tomatoes, avocado, chicken, bacon, eggs and cheese over greens.
6. Pour 1/3 of the Herb Vinaigrette Dressing over the salad just before serving; toss gently to coat. Pass the rest of the dressing.

Herb Vinaigrette Dressing

Makes 1 1/4 cups.

3/4 cup vegetable oil	1/4 teaspoon seasoned pepper
1/2 cup tarragon-flavored vinegar	1/4 teaspoon leaf basil, crumbled
3/4 teaspoon salt	

Place all ingredients in a jar with a tight-fitting lid. Cover. Refrigerate to mellow flavors. Shake just before pouring over salad.

Bibb Lettuce Mimosa

Makes 8 servings.

4 heads Bibb lettuce OR: 2 heads Boston lettuce	finely chopped Creamy Italian Dressing *(recipe follows)*
2 hard-cooked eggs,	

Wash lettuce; dry on paper toweling. Remove outer leaves of Bibb lettuce; line salad bowl. Cut hearts of lettuce into 4 or 6 wedges through core. Arrange spoke-fashion over bed of lettuce in bowl. Sprinkle with chopped eggs. Ladle some of dressing over salad; pass remainder at table.

Creamy Italian Dressing

Makes about 1 1/2 cups.

1 egg	1/8 teaspoon sugar
1 tablespoon Dijon mustard	2 tablespoons lemon juice
1/2 small onion	1/4 cup red wine vinegar
1/2 teaspoon salt	1 cup olive or vegetable oil
1/4 teaspoon pepper	
1 clove garlic	

1. Combine egg, mustard, onion, salt, pepper, garlic, sugar, lemon juice and vinegar in the container of an electric blender. Cover. Whirl until smooth.
2. Add oil slowly through center of blender cover while blender is running. Dressing will be quite thick. Refrigerate at least 1 hour to blend flavors.

Rosé Wine Mold

Fresh fruits sparkle brightly in a tender pink wine gel.

Makes 6 servings.

3 envelopes unflavored gelatin	washed, hulled and halved
1/3 cup sugar	1 large orange, peeled, sectioned and cut into small pieces
2 cups cold water	
2 tablespoons lemon juice	Orange Sour Cream Dressing *(recipe follows)*
1 bottle (3 1/4 cups or 750 ml.) rosé wine	
1 cup honeydew melon balls	Frosted grapes and orange slices for garnish *(optional)*
1 cup strawberries,	

1. Combine gelatin and sugar in a small saucepan; stir in 1 cup of the water. Heat and stir over very low heat until gelatin is dissolved. Remove from heat; stir in remaining water and the lemon juice. Pour into large bowl; add wine. Chill until partially set, about 1 hour.
2. Fold in melon balls, strawberries and orange sections. Pour into 7-cup mold. Chill until set, about 4 hours.
3. To unmold: Loosen edges with small spatula; quickly dip into warm water. Turn upside down on serving platter; shake gently.
4. Serve with Orange Sour Cream Dressing and garnish with frosted grapes and orange slices, if you wish.

Orange Sour Cream Dressing: Grate 1 teaspoon rind from 1 large orange. Cut orange and squeeze to extract 2 tablespoons juice. Combine orange rind and juice, 1 container (8 ounces) dairy sour cream, 2 tablespoons honey and 1/4 teaspoon ground ginger in a small bowl; blend well. Chill. Makes about 1 1/4 cups.

Spring Potato Salad

Makes 6 servings.

1 cup low-fat cottage cheese	dillweed
1 cotainer (8 ounces) plain yogurt	1/4 cup sliced green onion
1 clove garlic, minced	4 cups cubed cooked potatoes
1 1/2 teaspoons salt	1 cup sliced radishes
1/4 teaspoon pepper	1 cup diced unpared cucumber
1/4 teaspoon	

Sieve cheese into a large bowl. Add yogurt, garlic, salt, pepper, dillweed, green onion and cubed potatoes. Mix well; chill 2 hours. Add radishes and cucumbers 30 minutes before serving; toss gently. Spoon into lettuce-lined salad bowl.

All-American Potato Salad

The old family favorite that prompts friends to ask, "May I have your recipe?"

Makes 6 servings.

6 medium-size all-purpose potatoes	3/4 cup mayonnaise or salad dressing
1/4 cup vegetable oil	1/4 cup light cream
1/4 cup cider vinegar	3 hard-cooked eggs, diced
1 medium-size onion, chopped	1 cup sliced celery
2 1/2 teaspoons salt	Boston lettuce
1/4 teaspoon pepper	

1. Cook potatoes just until tender, about 20 minutes, in boiling salted water in a large kettle or saucepan; drain. Peel potatoes and cut into thin slices; place in a large bowl.
2. Combine oil, vinegar, onion, salt and pepper in a jar with a screw-top; cover jar and shake to mix. Pour dressing over potatoes and toss to blend well. Cover bowl; chill at least 3 hours.
3. Just before serving, stir mayonnaise with light cream in a small bowl until smooth; pour over potatoes and toss to coat. Add diced eggs and celery and toss lightly. Line a salad bowl with Boston lettuce; fill bowl with salad; garnish with slices of celery and red pepper, if you wish.

Cucumber Salad

Makes 6 servings.

3 medium-size cucumbers	vinegar
1 1/2 tablespoons sliced green onion	1 1/2 teaspoons sugar
3 tablespoons white	1/2 teaspoon salt
	1/4 teaspoon pepper

1. Pare and thinly slice cucumbers; place in serving dish.

2. Add green onion, vinegar, sugar, salt and pepper; toss gently to coat. Cover with plastic wrap. Place in freezer section of refrigerator for a few minutes, just until chilled.

Macaroni Shell Salad

Macaroni shells elegantly dressed with sour cream and light cream. You can vary the pasta, if you like, but the flavor is still delightful.

Makes 12 servings.

1 package (1 pound) small shell macaroni	2 teaspoons salt
1 cup mayonnaise or salad dressing	1/2 teaspoon pepper
1 container (8 ounces) dairy sour cream	2 cups sliced celery
3/4 cup light cream or half-and-half	1 medium-size green pepper, seeded and diced (1 cup)
	1 medium-size red onion, chopped (1/2 cup)

1. Cook macaroni following label directions; drain. Rinse with cold water. Drain well.
2. Mix mayonnaise, sour cream, light cream, salt and pepper in a large bowl until smooth.
3. Add macaroni, celery, green pepper and red onion to mixture. Toss gently to coat with dressing. Chill 2 to 3 hours.

Tomato Ring with Eggs and Curried Herring Salad

Makes 12 servings.

2 envelopes unflavored gelatin	sauce
3 1/2 cups tomato juice	1/4 teaspoon salt
3 tablespoons tomato paste	Lettuce
1/3 cup lemon juice	Eggs Romanoff (recipe follows)
2 teaspoons Worcestershire	Curried Herring Salad (recipe follows)

1. Sprinkle gelatin over 1 cup of the tomato juice in a large saucepan; let stand 5 minutes to soften. Heat, stirring often, until gelatin is dissolved; remove from heat.
2. Blend in tomato paste, lemon juice, Worcestershire sauce, salt and remaining tomato juice. Pour into a 4-cup ring mold. Chill several hours or until firm. Loosen gelatin around top of mold with tip of knife. Dip mold in and out of hot water.
3. Center over serving platter. Unmold. Garnish with lettuce and Eggs Romanoff. Spoon Curried Herring Salad into center.

Pictured opposite:
Lasagna with Cottage Cheese, page 609; Spring Potato Salad, page 708; Creamy Cottage Cheese Dessert, page 341.

Eggs Romanoff

Makes 12 servings.

6 hard-cooked eggs	mustard
1/2 cup mayonnaise	Red and black
1 teaspoon Dijon	lumpfish caviar

Halve eggs lengthwise. Press egg yolks through a fine sieve into a small bowl. Add mayonnaise and mustard; blend well. Stuff yolk mixture into whites. Garnish tops with red and black lumpfish caviar.

Curried Herring Salad

Makes 12 servings.

2 jars (8 ounces each) pickled herring in wine sauce, drained	2 teaspoons curry powder
3/4 cup mayonnaise	1/4 teaspoon salt
1/2 cup dairy sour cream	2 red apples, quartered, cored and diced (2 cups)
1 teaspoon prepared mustard	1 medium-size onion, diced (1/2 cup)

1. Dice herring pieces, reserving a few pieces for garnish.
2. Blend mayonnaise, sour cream, mustard, curry powder and salt in large bowl. Fold in herring, apples and onion. Chill several hours.
3. To serve: Spoon salad into the center of the tomato aspic ring. Garnish with strips of reserved herring.

Lemon French Dressing

Makes 1 1/3 cups.

1 cup olive or vegetable oil	(basil, dill, marjoram, oregano, thyme)
1/3 cup lemon juice	
1/2 teaspoon dry mustard	OR: 2 teaspoons dried herbs (1/2 teaspoon basil,
1/2 teaspoon paprika	
1 teaspoon sugar	1/2 teaspoon marjoram, 1/2 tea-
1 teaspoon salt	
1/4 teaspoon pepper	spoon oregano,
2 tablespoons finely snipped fresh herbs	1/2 teaspoon thyme)

Combine oil, lemon juice, mustard, paprika, sugar, salt and pepper in a medium-size jar with a tight-fitting lid; cover; shake. Add herbs; shake again. Refrigerate; shake again before using.

Low-Calorie Thousand Island Dressing

Makes 1 1/2 cups.

2 tablespoons finely chopped green pepper	chopped canned pimiento
1 tablespoon finely chopped celery	3/4 cup chili sauce
1 tablespoon finely	1 cup low-calorie mayonnaise

Combine all ingredients; mix well.

Green Goddess Dressing

Use on seafood salads and romaine lettuce.

Makes 2 1/2 cups.

8 anchovy fillets, mashed	tarragon, crumbled
2 green onions, finely chopped	2 cups mayonnaise or salad dressing
1/4 cup finely chopped parsley	2 tablespoons white wine vinegar
1 teaspoon leaf	3 tablespoons finely chopped chives

Combine the anchovies, green onions, parsley and tarragon in a small bowl; mix well. Fold into the mayonnaise. Stir in the vinegar and chives. Refrigerate until ready to use.

Provençal Tomato Dressing

Makes about 2 cups.

1 cup tomato juice	mustard
1/4 cup olive or vegetable oil	1 teaspoon leaf basil or oregano, crumbled
3 tablespoons wine vinegar	2 tablespoons chopped fresh parsley
2 cloves garlic, crushed	
1 teaspoon anchovy paste	1/2 teaspoon salt
1/2 teaspoon dry	1/4 teaspoon pepper

Combine tomato juice, oil, vinegar, garlic, anchovy paste, mustard, basil, parsley, salt and pepper in a medium-size jar with a tight-fitting lid; cover; shake. Refrigerate; shake again before using.

Basic Vinaigrette and Variations

Makes about 2 cups.

1 1/2 cups olive oil OR: 3/4 cup olive oil and 3/4 cup vegetable oil	1/3 cup wine vinegar OR: fresh lemon juice
	2 teaspoons salt
	1/2 teaspoon pepper

Combine the oil, vinegar, salt and pepper in a screw-

Clockwise from top: Provençal Tomato Dressing, page 710; Lemon French Dressing, page 710; Low-Calorie Thousand Island Dressing, page 710; Green Goddess Dressing, page 710.

top jar. Shake well to blend. Serve at room temperature.

Herb Vinaigrette: Crumble 1 tablespoon of leaf basil or oregano, or a mixture of half of each. Add to the jar with the remaining ingredients.

Garlic Vinaigrette: Mash 1 or 2 large chopped garlic cloves with $1/2$ teaspoon of the salt. Add to the jar with the other ingredients.

Mustard Vinaigrette: Add 1 tablespoon Dijon-style mustard to the jar with the other ingredients.

SAUCES, GLAZES, FROSTINGS and STUFFINGS

Sauce   A sauce is used either to enhance the flavor of other foods or to bind foods together. What would spaghetti be without a hearty meat sauce; what would spareribs be without a barbecue sauce? A soufflé or croquette would never hold together without a basic white sauce. The success of many recipes depends upon the sauce. And, a sauce can make a good dish taste even better.

Basic White Sauce

Makes 2 cups.

Thin Sauce:
2 tablespoons butter
    or margarine
2 tablespoons flour
1/2 teaspoon salt
1/8 teaspoon pepper
2 cups milk
Uses: Cream soups,
    chowders,
    casseroles, sauces.

Medium Sauce:
1/4 cup (1/2 stick) butter
    or margarine
1/4 cup all-purpose
    flour
1/2 teaspoon salt

1/8 teaspoon pepper
2 cups milk
Uses: Creamed
    dishes, sauces,
    gravies.

Thick Sauce:
6 tablespoons (3/4
    stick) butter or
    margarine
6 tablespoons all-
    purpose flour
1/2 teaspoon salt
1/8 teaspoon pepper
2 cups milk
Uses: Soufflés,
    croquettes, patties.

1. Melt butter over *low* heat in medium-size, heavy saucepan. It should just melt--not bubble and turn brown. (Use a wooden spoon or wire whisk for stirring.)
2. Have the flour, salt and pepper measured and ready. Stir quickly into melted butter, then cook, stirring constantly, just until it bubbles.
3. Now stir in the milk *slowly.* (This helps to keep sauce from lumping.) Continue cooking and stirring from bottom of pan until sauce thickens and bubbles 3 minutes.

New Delhi Cream: Blend 1/2 cup mayonnaise or salad dressing, 1/2 teaspoon grated onion and 1/4 teaspoon curry powder into 1 cup of hot Thin White Sauce. Delicious on green peas. Makes 1 1/2 cups.

Old-Fashioned Cheese Sauce: Stir 1 cup (4 ounces) shredded Cheddar cheese and 1/4 teaspoon dry mustard into 1 cup hot Thin White Sauce. Serve the sauce over cauliflower, broccoli or green beans. It's also good over poached fish fillets. Makes 1 1/4 cups.

Anchovy Sauce: Blend 1 teaspoon anchovy paste into 1 cup hot Thin White Sauce. Serve the sauce over freshly boiled potatoes or green peas. Makes 1 cup.

Spring Egg Sauce: Stir in 1 chopped hard-cooked egg, 1 tablespoon cut chives and a dash of seasoned salt into 1 cup hot Medium White Sauce. Serve over cooked, well-drained spinach. Makes 1 1/4 cups.

Pink Sauce: Stir 2 tablespoons catsup and 2 teaspoons prepared horseradish into 1 cup hot Medium White Sauce. Spoon it over a freshly cooked head of cauliflower. Makes about 1 cup.

Béchamel Sauce

Makes about 1 cup.

2 tablespoons butter
2 tablespoons flour
1/4 teaspoon salt

Dash pepper
Dash ground nutmeg
1 cup milk

Heat butter in a small saucepan. Stir in the flour, salt, pepper and nutmeg. Cook until bubbly, about 1 minute. Remove from heat; stir in the milk with a wire whisk. Return to heat and cook, stirring constantly until thickened and bubbly.

Béarnaise Sauce

Makes 1 cup.

1 tablespoon minced
    onion or shallot
1/2 teaspoon leaf
    tarragon, crumbled
1/8 teaspoon pepper
1/2 cup dry white wine
1 tablespoon tarragon
    vinegar

2 egg yolks
1/2 cup (1 stick) butter
    or margarine,
    melted
Dash cayenne
1 teaspoon chopped
    fresh parsley

1. Combine onion, tarragon, pepper, wine and vinegar in a small saucepan. Heat to boiling, then simmer, uncovered, 8 to 10 minutes, or until liquid measures about 1/3 cup. Strain into a cup.
2. Beat egg yolks slightly with wire whisk in the top of

(continued)

Pictured opposite (clockwise from top left):
Creamy Custard Sauce, page 716; Hot Fudge
Sauce, page 716; Raspberry Sauce, page 715.

a double boiler; stir in about ⅓ cup of the melted butter. Place over *simmering* water.

3. Beat in strained liquid, alternately with remaining butter; continue beating until mixture is fluffy-thick. Remove from heat at once. Stir in cayenne and parsley.

Foolproof Hollandaise Sauce

Makes ¾ cup.

3 egg yolks	**¼ teaspoon salt**
2 tablespoons lemon juice	**½ cup (1 stick) butter, melted (keep hot)**

1. Rinse container of electric blender with hot water. Add egg yolks, lemon juice and salt. Cover. Whirl to combine.
2. Remove lid; pour in hot butter gradually with motor still on. Whirl until sauce thickens, about 30 seconds.
3. Pour into small bowl and keep warm over hot water, if not using immediately.

Polonaise Sauce

Serve over hot, cooked asparagus, cauliflower, broccoli or Brussels sprouts.

Makes about ¾ cup.

6 tablespoons (¾ stick) butter or margarine	**1 tablespoon chopped fresh parsley**
½ cup coarse fresh bread crumbs	**1 hard-cooked egg, pressed through a sieve**

1. Melt butter in a small skillet; stir in bread crumbs. Heat slowly, stirring often, just until crumbs are lightly toasted. Remove from heat; stir in parsley.
2. Spoon over the vegetable; garnish with egg.

Real Red Chili Sauce

Makes 5 pints.

18 medium-size tomatoes	**vinegar**
3 large onions, cut up	**1 tablespoon celery seeds**
3 large sweet red peppers, halved, seeded and cubed	**1 tablespoon mustard seeds**
¾ cup sugar	**¼ cup finely chopped preserved ginger**
1 tablespoon salt	**3 tablespoons mixed pickling spices**
2 cups cider or distilled white	

1. Wash five 16-ounce preserving jars with 2-piece lids in hot soapy water; rinse. Place jars on rack in large kettle or water-bath canner. Cover with hot water until ready to fill. Cover lids with very hot water in a separate pan.

2. Wash and core tomatoes; cut in eighths. Put tomatoes, onions and red peppers through coarse blade of food grinder.
3. Combine ground vegetables with sugar and salt in a large kettle. Simmer 30 minutes, stirring frequently.
4. Stir in vinegar, celery seeds, mustard seeds and ginger. Tie pickling spices in a piece of cheesecloth; push down into vegetables Cook, stirring frequently, until thickened, about 40 minutes. Remove spice bag.
5. Drain jars. Ladle sauce into hot jars, filling to within ½ inch of top. Wipe rims; seal jars. Process 15 minutes in boiling water bath; cool; label. Store in cool, dry place.

Orange-Spice Barbecue Sauce

It gives a golden-glaze goodness to grilled ducklings. Delicious with pork chops and chicken, too.

Makes 1½ cups.

¼ cup sugar	**cloves**
2 tablespoons cornstarch	**1 cup orange juice**
½ teaspoon ground allspice	**2 tablespoons cider vinegar**
½ teaspoon ground	**¼ cup (½ stick) butter or margarine**

Combine sugar, cornstarch, allspice and cloves in a small saucepan; stir in orange juice and vinegar. Cook, stirring constantly, until sauce thickens and bubbles for 1 minute. Stir in butter until blended.

Lemon Blender Mayonnaise

A winner with seafood salads.

Makes 1¼ cups.

1 egg OR: 2 egg yolks	**or fresh-frozen lemon juice, thawed**
1 teaspoon Dijon mustard OR: ½ teaspoon dry mustard	**OR: 1 tablespoon vinegar**
½ teaspoon salt	**1 cup vegetable oil**
2 tablespoons fresh	**1 tablespoon chopped parsley**

1. Break egg into container of electric blender or food processor. Add mustard, salt, lemon juice and ¼ cup of the oil; cover. Whirl on low speed.
2. With machine running, pour in remaining oil in a steady stream through removable part of lid. Stir in parsley; refrigerate.

Homemade Meat Sauce

Makes 12 cups.

1 large onion,
    chopped (1 cup)
2 cloves garlic,
    minced
1/4 cup vegetable oil
1 pound ground round
    or chuck
2 Italian sausages,
    chopped
2 cans (35 ounces
    each) plum
    tomatoes

2 cans (6 ounces
    each) tomato paste
2 tablespoons sugar
1 tablespoon leaf
    oregano, crumbled
1 tablespoon leaf
    basil, crumbled
1 tablespoon salt
1/2 teaspoon pepper
1/4 cup grated
    Parmesan cheese

1. Sauté onion and garlic in oil until soft in a large
kettle; brown beef and sausage in same kettle. Pour
off all but 2 tablespoons drippings.
2. Stir in tomatoes, tomato paste, sugar, oregano,
basil, salt and pepper. Simmer, uncovered, stirring
frequently, 45 minutes or until sauce thickens. Stir in
Parmesan cheese.

Quick Red Clam Sauce

Makes about 3 cups.

1 large onion,
    chopped (1 cup)
4 cloves garlic,
    minced
1/4 cup olive or
    vegetable oil
2 cans (6 1/2 to 8
    ounces each)
    minced clams
6 medium-size
    tomatoes, peeled

and coarsely
    chopped
1 teaspoon salt
1/2 teaspoon pepper
1/2 teaspoon leaf basil,
    crumbled
1/2 teaspoon leaf
    oregano, crumbled
2 tablespoons
    chopped fresh
    parsley

Sauté onion and garlic in olive oil in a medium-size
saucepan until soft. Drain liquid from clams into
saucepan, reserving clams. Add tomatoes, salt,
pepper, basil and oregano; bring to boiling; lower
heat. Simmer, uncovered, 15 minutes, stirring
occasionally, until sauce is thickened the way you like
it. Mix in clams and parsley and heat 5 minutes
longer.

Raspberry Sauce

Makes 1 1/2 cups.

1 package (10 ounces)
    frozen red
    raspberries, thawed

1/4 cup sugar
2 tablespoons kirsch
    or light rum

Put raspberries into the container of an electric
blender; add sugar; cover; blend on high speed until

smooth. Strain through a sieve over bowl to remove
seeds. Cover with plastic wrap; chill. Stir in kirsch just
before serving.

Chinese Sweet-Sour Sauce

Makes 1 1/4 cups.

1/4 cup firmly packed
    brown sugar
2 tablespoons
    cornstarch
1/2 teaspoon seasoned
    salt
3/4 cup pineapple juice

1/4 cup water
2 tablespoons cider
    vinegar
2 tablespoons honey
2 teaspoons soy
    sauce

1. Mix brown sugar, cornstarch and seasoned salt in a
small saucepan; blend in pineapple juice, water, cider
vinegar, honey and soy sauce. Cook and stir until the
sauce thickens and bubbles, 1 minute.
2. Pour over crisp-cooked vegetables in a large skillet;
toss to mix well; cover. (See Note.)
3. Simmer 5 to 8 minutes or just until the vegetables
are tender.
Note: To prepare and crisp-cook the vegetables, cut
pared carrots into thin pennies, green pepper into very
thin rings and cabbage into thin shreds. (You should
have about 6 cups.) Heat 2 tablespoons of vegetable
oil in a large skillet. Add vegetables; toss to coat with
oil. Cook and stir 2 to 3 minutes or until shiny-moist.

Savory Cranberry Sauce

*A sophisticated and delicious way with cranberry
sauce.*
Makes about 3 1/2 cups.

1 package (12 ounces)
    fresh or frozen
    cranberries
1 cup sugar

1 cup dry red wine
2 teaspoons
    cornstarch

1. Combine cranberries, sugar and 3/4 cup of the wine
in a medium-size saucepan. Cook over medium heat,
stirring occasionally, until cranberries just start to pop
their skins.
2. Dissolve cornstarch in remaining 1/4 cup wine; stir
into cranberry mixture. Continue to cook, stirring
constantly, just until sauce thickens and bubbles; cool;
chill.

Creamy Custard Sauce

Makes 1 1/2 cups.

3 egg yolks
3 tablespoons sugar
3/4 cup milk, scalded

1 teaspoon vanilla
1/2 cup heavy cream, whipped

1. Beat egg yolks and sugar until light and fluffy in small bowl with electric mixer. Gradually beat in scalded milk. Pour mixture back into saucepan; cook, stirring constantly, over moderate heat until custard thickens slightly. Remove from heat; pour into small bowl; stir in vanilla; cover; chill.
2. Just before serving, fold in whipped cream.

Hot Fudge Sauce

Makes 2 1/4 cups.

4 squares unsweetened chocolate
2 tablespoons butter or margarine

3/4 cup boiling water
1 3/4 cups sugar
1/4 cup light corn syrup
2 teaspoons vanilla

1. Chop chocolate coarsely; combine with butter and boiling water in a large saucepan. Heat over low heat, stirring constantly, until chocolate is melted. Add sugar and corn syrup.
2. Bring mixture slowly to boiling; lower heat; simmer gently, 8 minutes. Watch carefully, but do not stir. Test on ice cream or an ice cube, until it firms up as you like it. Add vanilla. Serve while warm. Refrigerate any leftover sauce in screw-top jar.
3. To reheat: Remove cover from jar. Put jar in saucepan of water. Heat, stirring occasionally, until sauce is softened enough to pour.

Apricot-Orange Winter Barbecue Sauce

Makes 1 1/2 cups.

1 medium-size onion, chopped (1/2 cup)
1 clove garlic, minced
2 tablespoons vegetable oil
1 can (17 ounces) apricot halves
1/4 cup cider vinegar
3 tablespoons undiluted frozen orange juice

concentrate
3 tablespoons light brown sugar
1 teaspoon dry mustard
1/2 teaspoon ground ginger
1/2 teaspoon salt
3 to 4 drops liquid hot pepper seasoning

1. Sauté onion and garlic in oil in a medium-size saucepan until tender, about 5 minutes.
2. Drain apricot halves (reserve syrup for gelatin dessert). Place in container of electric blender; cover. Whirl just until smooth. Add cider vinegar, orange juice concentrate, brown sugar, mustard, ginger, salt and hot pepper seasoning. Cover; whirl just until blended.
3. Stir mixture into onion; bring to boiling, stirring constantly. Lower heat; simmer, uncovered, until mixture thickens, about 15 minutes. Cool before storing in containers. Refrigerate for up to 2 weeks.
4. To use: Serve with broiled or roasted meats or brush over chicken pieces before baking, or brush over ham or spareribs for last 30 minutes of baking.

Mandarin Orange Sauce

Makes 2 cups.

1/3 cup sugar
2 tablespoons cornstarch

1 can (11 ounces) mandarin oranges
1/2 cup orange juice

1. Combine sugar and cornstarch in a medium-size saucepan.
2. Drain syrup from mandarin oranges into saucepan; add orange juice. Heat to boiling, stirring constantly, until thickened; add drained oranges.

Butterscotch Sauce

Makes about 1 3/4 cups.

1 1/2 cups packed brown sugar
1/2 cup dark corn syrup
1/2 cup water

1/2 teaspoon salt
2 tablespoons butter or margarine
1 teaspoon vanilla

1. Combine sugar, corn syrup, water and salt in a medium-size heavy saucepan.
2. Cook over low heat, stirring constantly until sugar dissolves; stir in butter.
3. Heat to boiling; cook, without stirring, until candy thermometer reads 230°. (A fine thread spins from the end of a fork when dipped into hot syrup.) Pour into a bowl and stir in vanilla; cool. Serve warm over pudding or desserts.

Rum Raisin Sauce

Makes 1 1/2 cups.

1 cup raisins or dried currants
1 cup water
1/4 cup sugar

2 teaspoons cornstarch
1 teaspoon rum extract

1. Combine raisins and water in medium-size saucepan; bring to boiling; lower heat; simmer for 5 minutes.
2. Combine sugar and cornstarch; stir into mixture. Stir and cook until clear, about 5 minutes. Stir in extract; refrigerate.

Low-Cal Sugar-Free Strawberry Sauce

Makes 2 cups at 7 calories per tablespoonful.

**1 bag (16 ounces)
frozen whole
unsweetened
strawberries
¹/₄ cup cold water**

**2 teaspoons
cornstarch
Sugar substitute to
taste**

1. Remove frozen strawberries from bag to a saucepan; allow to thaw.
2. Combine cold water and cornstarch in a cup; stir until dissolved. Add to strawberries.
3. Place strawberries over moderate heat; cook, stirring constantly, until sauce bubbles and clears. Remove from heat. Stir in sugar substitute. Cool. Serve over low-fat ice milk or sponge cake. Sauce may be served hot over pancakes, French toast, crêpes or dessert omelets.

Brandied Fruit Sauce

Delicious served over ice cream, plain cakes or puddings.

Makes 3¹/₂ cups.

**¹/₂ cup golden raisins
1 package (6 ounces)
dried apricots
1 cup water
1 can (8¹/₄ ounces)
pineapple chunks in
syrup
1 3-inch piece stick**

**cinnamon
¹/₂ cup brandy
¹/₄ cup grenadine
syrup
2 tablespoons
maraschino
cherries (optional)**

1. Combine raisins and apricots with water in medium-size saucepan. Let stand 10 minutes to soften fruits.
2. Drain pineapple; add syrup to pan with cinnamon stick. Bring to boiling; lower heat; simmer 5 minutes until apricots are soft, but not mushy. Stir in brandy, grenadine, pineapple chunks and cherries. Pour into a container. Cover and store in refrigerator for at least a week. Mixture will thicken slightly on standing.

Glaze   A sweet or savory coating brushed on or applied to foods to give them a glossy, attractive appearance. Hot meat such as ham can be glazed with a sugar or fruit syrup. Cold meat such as chicken can be glazed with aspic or mayonnaise mixed with gelatin. Cakes are glazed with a thin icing; nuts are glazed with candy.

Doughnut Glazes

Each glaze makes about ²/₃ to ³/₄ cup.

Vanilla: Combine 2 cups 10X (confectioners') sugar, 2 tablespoons milk and 1 teaspoon vanilla in a small bowl until smooth. If glaze is too thick to dip or drizzle, stir in more milk.

Lemon: Combine 2 cups 10X (confectioners') sugar, 2 tablespoons milk, 1 teaspoon grated lemon rind and 2 teaspoons lemon juice in a small bowl until smooth.

Orange: Combine 2 cups 10X (confectioners') sugar, 1 teaspoon grated orange rind and 2 to 3 tablespoons orange juice in a small bowl until smooth.

Mint: Follow directions for Vanilla Glaze but omit vanilla and add ¹/₄ teaspoon mint extract and a drop of green food coloring.

Chocolate: Melt 2 squares semisweet chocolate with 2 tablespoons butter or margarine in small saucepan; stir in 1 cup 10X (confectioners') sugar and 3 to 4 tablespoons milk until smooth.

Maple: Combine 2 cups 10X (confectioners') sugar, ¹/₄ cup maple-flavored syrup and 1 to 2 tablespoons water in a small saucepan; heat to boiling; use while warm.

Honey: Combine ¹/₂ cup honey and 1 cup 10X (confectioners') sugar in small saucepan. Heat over low heat just to boiling; use while warm.

Cranberry-Apple Glaze

Makes 2 cups.

**2 cups cranberry-
apple drink
2 tablespoons
cornstarch**

**1 teaspoon
Worcestershire
sauce
8 whole cloves**

1. Blend ¹/₄ cup of the cranberry drink into cornstarch in small cup. Stir into remaining cranberry drink in small saucepan. Add Worcestershire sauce and cloves.
2. Bring to boiling, stirring constantly, 1 minute until thickened. Remove from heat. Cool and pour into containers. Refrigerate, covered, up to a week.
3. To use: Stir gently. Brush over ham or spareribs for last 40 minutes of baking.

Sugar Glaze

Makes ³/₄ cup (enough to drizzle over 28 cupcakes).

**1¹/₂ cups 10X
(confectioners')
sugar**

**4 teaspoons corn
syrup
4 teaspoons water**

Combine ingredients in bowl over simmering water. Heat until smooth.

Deep Chocolate Glaze

Makes 1/3 cup.

3 tablespoons butter	**semisweet**
1/2 cup (3 ounces)	**chocolate pieces**

Combine the butter and chocolate in the top of a double boiler. Place over simmering water; stir constantly until smooth. Use while still warm. The glaze will harden as it sits.

Rich Butter Cream Frosting
(A Basic Recipe)

Makes 2 cups (enough to frost 28 cupcakes).

1/2 cup (1 stick) butter	**10X (confectioners')**
or margarine	**sugar**
1 egg yolk	**3 tablespoons milk**
1 package (1 pound)	**1 teaspoon vanilla**

Beat butter with egg yolk in a medium-size bowl with electric mixer until soft. Beat in 10X sugar alternately with milk and vanilla, until smooth and spreadable.

Lemon or Orange Butter Cream Frosting: Follow Basic Recipe but omit vanilla. Add 2 teaspoons grated lemon or orange rind and substitute 3 tablespoons lemon or orange juice for the 3 tablespoons milk.

Mocha Butter Cream Frosting: Follow Basic Recipe but omit milk and vanilla. Dissolve 2 teaspoons instant coffee in 3 tablespoons boiling water.

Honey-Cream Cheese Frosting

Makes 2 cups (enough to frost 24 to 26 cupcakes).

2 packages (3 ounces	**10X (confectioners')**
each) cream	**sugar**
cheese, softened	**6 tablespoons honey**
1 package (1 pound)	

Beat cream cheese in a medium-size bowl with electric mixer until soft. Beat in 10X sugar alternately with honey until smooth and spreadable.

Stuffing
A sweet or savory filling used to stuff poultry, fish, meat, vegetables or fruit. Also called dressing, stuffing may be made with a wide variety of ingredients.

When stuffing poultry, stuff just before roasting. The bird should be stuffed lightly because the stuffing will expand during roasting. Allow 3/4 cup prepared stuffing for each pound of poultry over 10 pounds in weight. Allow 1/2 cup stuffing per pound for smaller birds.

Stuffing can also be baked separately in a covered, greased casserole; allow 25 to 45 minutes to heat through. To keep it moist, spoon some broth over the stuffing as it bakes.

Quantity Reference Chart for Stuffing

Amount of Stuffing	Size of Bird It Will Stuff	Number of Servings
2 cups	3 to 4 pounds	2 to 3
3 cups	5 to 6 pounds	4 to 5
4 cups	6 to 8 pounds	6
6 cups	8 to 10 pounds	8
8 cups	10 to 12 pounds	10
12 cups	12 to 15 pounds	12 to 14
16 cups	15 to 20 pounds	18 to 20

Flavoring Stuffings
When making stuffings for poultry, try flavoring them with combinations of ingredients and seasonings, such as sautéed onions, celery, mushrooms or sausage; mixed dried fruits, apples, oranges, raisins, cranberries, spinach, parsley, sage, marjoram or thyme.

Combinations that marry well with seafood include other seafoods, such as chopped shrimp, crab, lobster, scallops, oysters or clams. Fill mild-flavored fillet rolls such as sole, snapper, cod or flounder with spinach, chives, dill, tarragon, wine, cheese and nuts. As with poultry, sautéed onions, celery and mushrooms work well.

Meat stuffings might include other forms of the meat being stuffed, such as ground pork or lamb stuffing in a crown roast of pork or lamb. Sautéed onions, celery and mushromms accompany meat stuffings nicely. The particular type of meat will determine exactly what flavor combination you might like. Some that work well with one meat would not work with others, such as pork and sauerkraut versus lamb and sauerkraut. Individual taste and preference will determine combinations when selecting meat stuffings. A general rule of thumb to remember is to serve rich stuffings with milder meat, poultry or fish and lighter stuffings with richer meats.

Tips on Preparing Stuffings
1. When preparing stuffings, chop as many ingredients as possible in advance. Store the ingredients in individual containers in the refrigerator and mix together just before ready to use.
2. Stuff the bird, roast or fish just before cooking. Pre-stuffing is a sure way to increase the risk of bacteria growth that could lead to food poisoning. To reduce the risk of food poisoning even more, never stuff anything that is to be frozen, before or after cooking.

(continued)

Pictured opposite: Yakitori, page 667.

Never allow stuffing to remain in foods after serving. Remove stuffing and store both stuffing and stuffed food separately in covered containers in the refrigerator.

3. If using raw pork sausage in a stuffing, sauté until no longer pink in a skillet before combining with other ingredients.

4. Spoon or drop stuffing loosely in the item to be stuffed. If packed too tightly, the stuffing will become heavy when heated, due to expansion.

5. Allow about $1/2$ to $3/4$ cup of stuffing per pound of food to be stuffed. Any leftover stuffing that does not fit into the food to be stuffed should be placed in a separate lightly greased baking dish and baked along with the stuffed food during the last $3/4$ to 1 hour of baking.

Old-fashioned Bread Stuffing

Makes about 12 cups.

1 large onion, chopped (1 cup)	$1/4$ teaspoon pepper
1 cup (2 sticks) butter or margarine	1 can ($13^3/4$ ounces) chicken broth
1 cup finely chopped celery	14 cups soft white bread cubes (28 slices)
2 teaspoons poultry seasoning	$1/2$ cup chopped fresh parsley
$1/2$ teaspoon salt	

Sauté onion in butter in a large skillet until soft, but not brown. Stir in celery, poultry seasoning, salt, pepper and chicken broth. Bring to boiling, then pour over bread and parsley in a large bowl. Toss lightly until evenly moist.

Chestnut Stuffing

Bake at 475° for 15 minutes, then at 325° for 1 hour.

Makes about 10 cups.

1 pound fresh chestnuts OR: 1 can (10 ounces) water-packed chestnuts	chopped (1 cup)
	1 large apple, grated (1 cup)
$1/2$ cup (1 stick) butter or margarine	2 cups water
1 large onion,	2 packages (8 ounces each) herb-seasoned stuffing mix

1. Wash fresh chestnuts; cut slits in each shell; place in a shallow baking pan.
2. Bake in a preheated very hot oven (475°) for 15 minutes. Remove from pan; when cool enough to handle, shell and skin.
3. Cook shelled chestnuts, covered, in boiling salted water to cover, in a medium-size saucepan, about 5 minutes or until tender; drain; chop fine. Or, drain and chop canned chestnuts.

4. Melt butter in a large saucepan, sauté onion until soft; stir in apple and chestnuts; sauté 2 minutes. Add water; heat to boiling. Stir in stuffing mix until evenly moist.
5. Stuff turkey; or, if baking stuffing separately, spoon into a buttered 12-cup baking dish. Cover with foil.
6. Bake in a slow oven (325°) during the last hour the turkey roasts.

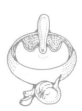

Corn Sausage Stuffing

Makes 10 cups.

1 pound bulk pork sausage	parsley flakes
3 medium-size onions, chopped ($1^1/2$ cups)	$1^1/2$ teaspoons poultry seasoning
8 cups day-old white bread cubes (16 slices)	1 teaspoon salt
	$1/4$ teaspoon pepper
1 tablespoon dried	1 can (about 17 ounces) cream-style corn

1. Cook sausage in a large skillet, stirring to break up, until browned. Remove sausage from skillet. Pour off all but $1/4$ cup sausage fat. Cook onions in fat until soft.
2. Combine bread cubes with parsley, poultry seasoning, salt and pepper in a large bowl. Add onion mixture, sausage and corn and toss until well combined.

Potato Stuffing

Makes $4^1/2$ cups.

$1^1/2$ pounds potatoes	4 cups soft white bread cubes (8 slices)
$1/2$ teaspoon salt	
$1/4$ teaspoon pepper	$1/2$ cup chopped fresh parsley
1 large onion, diced (1 cup)	$1/2$ teaspoon poultry seasoning
$1/2$ cup (1 stick) butter or margarine	

1. Pare and dice potatoes. Cook, covered, in boiling salted water to cover in a large saucepan until fork-tender. Measure and reserve $1/2$ cup of the potato water; drain and discard remaining water. Heat potatoes over low flame a few minutes to dry.
2. Mash potatoes in a large bowl. Add the $1/2$ cup reserved potato water, salt and pepper; beat until fluffy-smooth. Reserve.
3. Sauté onion in butter in a small skillet until lightly browned. Add onion, bread cubes, parsley and poultry seasoning to potato mixture; mix until evenly moist.

Herb Stuffing

Makes 12 cups.

2 cups finely chopped celery	herb-seasoned cubed stuffing mix
1 medium-size onion, chopped (1/2 cup)	1 teaspoon leaf sage, crumbled
1/2 cup (1 stick) butter or margarine	1 can condensed chicken broth
1 package (14 ounces)	3/4 cup water

Cook celery and onion in butter in a large skillet until tender but not browned, about 15 minutes. Combine stuffing mix and sage in a large bowl. Add celery mixture, broth and water; toss until well mixed.

Wild Rice Stuffing

Makes about 3 cups.

1/4 cup (1/2 stick) butter or margarine	1 package (6 ounces) white and wild rice mix
1/4 pound mushrooms, chopped OR: 1 can (3 or 4 ounces) chopped mushrooms	2 1/2 cups boiling water
	1/3 cup chopped fresh parsley
	1/4 cup pine nuts

1. Melt butter in a large heavy saucepan; sauté chopped fresh mushrooms until soft. (Or, drain liquid from canned mushrooms into a 2-cup measure and use as part of the 2 1/2 cups of water. Sauté chopped canned mushrooms in butter for 2 minutes.)
2. Stir white and wild rice into saucepan; sauté for 2 minutes. Blend in boiling water and packet of seasoning; cover saucepan; lower heat to simmer.
3. Cook 25 minutes or until liquid is absorbed; stir in chopped parsley and pine nuts.

Savory Thanksgiving Stuffing

Use to stuff turkey, or bake separately at 350° for 35 minutes.

Makes 14 cups (enough for a 12- to 14-pound turkey).

2 large onions, diced (2 cups)	7-ounce loaves)
2 cups diced celery	1/3 cup chopped parsley
2 cloves garlic, finely chopped	2 teaspoons ground sage
6 tablespoons butter or margarine	1 teaspoon poultry seasoning
15 cups cubed day-old French bread (two	1/2 teaspoon pepper
	3 cups chicken broth

1. Sauté the onions, celery and garlic in 4 tablespoons of the butter in a skillet for 3 minutes or until the onions soften.
2. Combine the sautéed vegetables, bread cubes, parsley, sage, poultry seasoning and pepper in a large bowl. Mix well.
3. Melt remaining 2 tablespoons of butter in a saucepan. Add the butter and chicken broth to the stuffing; toss to mix. Stuff the turkey and roast. Or, spoon into a 13 x 9 x 2-inch baking pan or other shallow baking dish. Bake, uncovered, in a preheated moderate oven (350°) for 35 minutes or until heated through.

Cranberry Cornbread Stuffing

This tasty berry stuffing zips up chicken, turkey or duck.

Use as stuffing, or bake separately at 350° for 45 minutes.

Makes 16 cups (enough for a 14- to 16-pound turkey).

2 cups cranberries, fresh or frozen, thawed if frozen	2 medium-size celery stalks, diced (1/2 cup)
1 cup water	1 medium-size onion, finely chopped (1/2 cup)
1/2 cup sugar	1/4 cup chopped parsley
1 pound sausage meat	
8 cups crumbled cornbread (homemade or store-bought cornbread)	2 teaspoons leaf thyme, crumbled
	2 teaspoons leaf marjoram, crumbled
2 large Red Delicious apples, pared, cored and diced (about 3 cups)	1/2 teaspoon salt
	1/4 teaspoon pepper

1. Combine the cranberries, water and sugar in a medium-size saucepan. Bring to boiling. Lower the heat; simmer for 10 minutes. Drain well. Transfer to a large bowl.
2. Sauté the sausage in a medium-size skillet, breaking up into small pieces with a wooden spoon, until lightly browned and no longer pink, about 5 minutes. Drain the excess fat. Combine with the cranberries in the bowl.
3. Add the cornbread, apples, celery, onion, parsley, thyme, marjoram, salt and pepper to the cranberry-sausage mixture; toss gently to mix.
4. Stuff the turkey and roast according to your favorite recipe. Or, spoon the stuffing into a greased, shallow 4 1/2-quart baking dish. Bake, covered, in a preheated moderate oven (350°) for 45 minutes or until heated through. Uncover for the last 10 minutes of baking time for a crusty top.

Jiffy Stuffing

For stuffing in minutes to serve with any poultry dish, look at the assortment of packaged stuffing mixes on the supermarket shelf. For a distinctive touch, stir in 1 tablespoon orange rind, 1 teaspoon lemon rind, 1/4 cup chopped walnuts, almonds or peanuts or 2 tablespoons chopped celery leaves or parsley.

SOUPS and SNACKS

Soup   The word comes from the Latin *suppa.* It is basically a liquid food that can be served as a main course or an appetizer. A soup can be clear or creamy, hearty or light, sweet or savory, hot or cold.

Making soup from scratch is an old-fashioned way of cutting food costs which still holds true today. A soup kettle can be the repository for odds and ends of vegetables and meat or poultry bones. If time is short, rely on canned broths and soup mixes.

Soup-Calorie Cruncher

Eating soup takes more time and concentration than most solid foods.
If the soup is nice and hot, you'll be foreced to relax and carefully sip each spoonful no matter how ravenous you are. This process allows plenty ot time for satiety signals to reach your brain before you've actually eaten very much. The intestinal hormones that tell your brain you are FULL are released faster, due to the fact that liquids empty more quickly from stomach to intestine.

Soup is high on volume.
Once you've finished a big bowl of soup, your stomach is likely to feel just as full and warm as it would after eating an entire meal of more solid (and more fattening) foods. A cup of soup before a meal will naturally diminish the amount of other foods you eat.

Soups tend to be low on calories and saturated fat.
Especially those that are prepared with a low-fat beef or poultry consommé, seafood or vegetable broth. There are exceptions to this rule—but if you look at the following list of tricks for reducing fat consumption, you'll see how soup can fill the bill every time.
• Serving soup as a main course is an easy way to cut down on your consumption of red meat per sitting and still enjoy the taste. Only one-half pound of meat can flavor enough soup to serve the entire family.
• Soup is a delicious way to enjoy eating leaner cuts of meat and poultry. Trim off all visible fat before cooking or skim all excess fat off the top ot the soup before serving.
• The amount of fatty cheese or heavy cream called for in soup recipes can easily be reduced or replaced by low-fat dairy alternatives, e.g., skim milk, grated Parmesan cheese or yogurt. Yogurt can be used to replace the cream in soups, if you stir it in after taking the soup off the stove.

• Soups are a tasty way to combine low-fat vegetable proteins, e.g., grains and legumes, To limit the number of meals which contain animal proteins, prepare soups which combine rice, corn or wheat pasta with peas or beans.

Eating soup is likely to help you change your dietary habits for the better—nutrition-wise.
Examination of the results from two large U.S. governmental studies has shown that people who consume more soup and dairy products tend to eat the least amount of sugary foods and drinks. They tend to consume an average amount of all foods and show the fewest signs of nutrition problems. By slowing down your dietary pace, soup can help you break the tendency to overeat. It will force you to sit down and concentrate on the fact that you're eating.

Soup is easy to prepare.
This is an advantage, diet-wise, because it cuts down on time in the kitchen where the temptation to nibble can get the best of you. If you use commercially prepared products, making soup is as easy as boiling water. If you make your own, you can prepare large quantities at one time and refrigerate or freeze the rest in small quantities—ideal for quick meals or snacks.

Stock   A flavorful liquid made by cooking ingredients in water for many hours until most of the ingredients disintegrate into the liquid. Any remaining particles are strained and the stock can be boiled to reduce volume and to concentrate the flavor.

A stock is used to prepare soups, gravies and sauces. It differs from a broth in that the ingredients in a broth are cooked just until tender so that the ingredients can also be eaten rather than discarded or dissolved in the cooking liquid.

Broth   A clear meat, fish, poultry or vegetable stock or a combination made from these ingredients. Broth is often used interchangeably with stock and bouillon. A broth can be frozen, but be sure to leave adequate space in the container to allow for expansion. Keep some on hand to make soups and sauces, to moisten stuffings, and to cook rice or vegetables.

Basic beef and chicken broths are wonderfully delicious by themselves, but they are also the start of some equally fabulous variations. Make them on a day you have a little time. Let them bubble leisurely until their rich broth has captured all the goodness from the meat and vegetables. You may want to use some right away; if not, just pack them away in the freezer.

Pictured opposite: Pistou, page 724.

Pistou

This basil-scented soup, famed along the Mediterranean coast of France, is hearty and economical.

Makes 6 servings.

4 large carrots, pared and diced
2 medium-size potatoes, pared and diced
2 leeks, thinly sliced
4 teaspoons salt
1/8 teaspoon pepper
10 cups water
1/2 pound green beans, cut into 1-inch pieces
1 cup very thin noodles
1/2 cup fresh bread crumbs (1 slice)
1 can (16 ounces) red kidney beans, drained
1/4 cup finely chopped fresh basil leaves OR: 4 1/2 teaspoons leaf basil, crumbled
1/4 cup tomato puree
3 cloves garlic, crushed
1/4 cup grated Parmesan cheese
1/2 cup olive or vegetable oil

1. Combine carrots, potatoes, leeks, salt, pepper and water in a large kettle; bring to boiling. Lower heat; cover.
2. Simmer, stirring several times, 1 hour. Add green beans, noodles and bread crumbs; stir to blend in bread crumbs. Cover kettle; simmer 15 minutes. Add kidney beans; simmer 10 minutes.
3. When ready to serve, combine fresh basil, tomato puree and garlic in a heated soup tureen. Add Parmesan cheese and oil, a few drops at a time, stirring until well combined. Add 1 cup of the hot soup, stirring vigorously; then slowly ladle in the remaining soup.

Old-Fashioned Beef and Vegetable Soup

Makes 8 servings.

1 1/2 quarts Basic Beef Broth *(recipe in this chapter)*
2 potatoes, peeled and diced (2 cups)
2 carrots, pared and sliced
1 cup sliced celery
2 small onions, peeled and quartered
1 can (16 ounces) tomatoes
2 teaspoons salt
1/8 teaspoon pepper
1/2 head green cabbage, shredded (2 cups)
1 cup frozen whole-kernel corn
3 cups diced boiled beef (from Basic Beef Broth)
1 tablespoon chopped parsley

1. Heat Beef Broth to boiling in a large saucepan or kettle; add potatoes, carrots, celery, onions, tomatoes,

salt and pepper; heat to boiling again; reduce heat; cover; simmer 20 minutes.
2. Stir in cabbage, corn and meat; simmer 10 minutes longer or just until all vegetables are crisp-tender. Sprinkle with parsley.
3. Ladle into soup bowls.

Split Pea Soup

Makes 6 to 8 servings.

1 ham bone
8 cups water
1 package (1 pound) dried split green peas
4 medium-size carrots,
pared and diced
1 medium-size onion, chopped
1 bay leaf
Salt and pepper

1. Combine ham bone, water, split peas, carrots, onion and bay leaf in a large kettle. Bring to boiling; cover; simmer 1 hour or until peas are soft.
2. Remove ham bone; cut off bits of meat and add to soup. Taste and season with salt and pepper, if needed; remove bay leaf.

Borscht
There are as many recipes for this Russian and Polish soup as there are spellings—thick or thin, meat or meatless, hot or cold. Usually, but not always, borscht is made with beets, and traditionally served topped with sour cream. The most authentic recipes are made with a fermented liquid called kvas, brewed from rye bread, water, sugar, yeast and flour.

Borscht

Adding grated fresh beets to soup just before serving gives a beautiful red color. May be served hot or chilled.

Makes 6 servings.

2 carrots, pared and sliced (1 cup)
1 1/2 cups shredded raw beets
1 turnip, pared and diced (3/4 cup)
1 medium-size onion, sliced
1 cup water
2 tablespoons cider or distilled white vinegar
2 teaspoons salt
1 teaspoon sugar
6 cups Basic Beef Broth (for recipe, see BROTH)
2 cups diced boiled beef (from Basic Beef Broth)
1/2 small head cabbage, shredded (3 cups)
Dairy sour cream
Sliced rye bread

1. In a kettle combine carrots, 1 cup beets, turnip, onion, water, vinegar, salt and sugar.
2. Bring to boiling; reduce heat, cover; simmer 20 minutes. Add Beef Broth, beef and cabbage. Simmer 10 to 15 minutes longer or until all vegetables are tender.

Onion Soup.

3. Stir in remaining ¹/₂ cup beets. Ladle into soup bowls. Top with sour cream. Serve with rye bread.

For chilled soup: Refrigerate at least 4 hours before serving.

Note: Instead of Basic Beef Broth, substitute 4 cans (13³/₄ ounces each) beef broth and 2 cups diced roast beef.

Onion Soup

Bake at 425° for 10 minutes, then broil quickly to brown.

Makes 6 servings.

4 large onions, sliced
¹/₄ cup (¹/₂ stick) butter
  or margarine
6 cups beef broth
Salt and pepper
6 slices French bread,
  toasted
¹/₂ cup grated
  Parmesan cheese
1 ounce Gruyère or
  Swiss cheese,
  shredded (¹/₄ cup)

1. Sauté onions in butter in Dutch oven for 15 minutes or until lightly browned. Stir in beef broth. Bring to boiling; lower heat; cover; simmer 30 minutes. (Soup may be prepared ahead to this point. Reheat and add the bread and cheese just before serving.) Add salt and pepper to taste.

2. Preheat oven to 425°. Ladle soup into 6 ovenproof soup bowls or six 12-ounce custard cups or an 8-cup casserole. Lay bread slices on top; sprinkle with cheeses. Place bowls or cups in a jelly-roll pan or shallow baking pan.

3. Bake in a preheated hot oven (425°) for 10 minutes, then place under preheated broiler and broil until top is bubbly and lightly browned.

Cream of Asparagus Soup

Velvety smooth with the fresh taste of just-cooked asparagus.

Makes 6 servings.

2 pounds asparagus
1 small onion, finely
  chopped
¹/₄ cup (¹/₂ stick) butter
  or margarine
2 tablespoons flour
1 can (13³/₄ ounces)
  chicken broth
1 cup heavy cream
¹/₈ teaspoon ground
  nutmeg

1. Wash and trim asparagus; cut into 1-inch pieces.

(continued)

Cook in boiling salted water to cover just until tender, 10 to 13 minutes. Drain, reserving 1½ cups of the cooking water.

2. Place cooked asparagus and reserved liquid in container of electric blender; whirl until mixture is smooth.

3. Sauté onion in butter in large saucepan until tender but not brown, about 3 minutes. Stir in flour; cook over low heat until bubbly, about 1 minute. Gradually stir in chicken broth. Bring to boiling, stirring constantly. Lower heat; simmer 3 minutes. Add asparagus puree, ½ cup of the cream and the nutmeg. Bring just to boiling.

4. Whip remaining cream in a small bowl until soft peaks form. Serve soup hot or cold with a dollop of cream on each serving.

Mushroom and Leek Soup

Makes 8 servings.

1 pound mushrooms, sliced (4 cups)	**flour**
1 bunch leeks, white part only, sliced (2 cups)	**1 teaspoon salt**
	¼ teaspoon white pepper
½ cup (1 stick) butter or margarine	**3 cans (13¾ ounces each) chicken broth**
¼ cup all-purpose	**1 cup light cream or half-and-half**

1. Sauté mushrooms and leeks in butter in a large saucepan or Dutch oven until tender, about 5 minutes. Stir in flour, salt, pepper and 2 cans of the chicken broth. Cook, stirring constantly, until mixture comes to boiling. Lower heat; cover; simmer 20 minutes.

2. Remove from heat; cool slightly. Pour mixture, a little at a time, into container of electric blender; cover; whirl until pureed. Pour into a large bowl. When all the soup is pureed, return to saucepan.

3. Add remaining can of chicken broth and the light cream; heat until thoroughly hot. Garnish with whipped cream and chopped parsley, if you wish.

Mushroom Barley Soup

Serve with thick slices of Challah for a hearty one-dish meal.

Makes about 8 servings.

1 fresh beef brisket (flanken) (about 4 pounds)	**4 carrots, diced (2 cups)**
4 quarts water	**2 cups sliced celery**
8 envelopes or teaspoons instant vegetable broth	**½ cup chopped fresh parsley**
	1 cup fine barley
1 tablespoon salt	**1 pound mushrooms, sliced**
2 large onions, chopped (2 cups)	**2 teaspoons salt**
	½ teaspoon pepper

1. Place brisket in a large kettle or Dutch oven. Add water and instant broth; stir to mix. Add 1 tablespoon salt, onions, carrots, celery and parsley. Bring to boiling; lower heat; cover; simmer 3 hours or until beef is tender but still holds its shape. Cool, then refrigerate brisket in the broth overnight.

2. The next day, skim the fat from the surface. Remove the brisket from the broth. (Brisket can be served cold with Potato Kugel, q.v.)

3. Add barley to soup. Bring to boiling; lower heat; simmer 40 minutes. Add mushrooms, the remaining salt and pepper and simmer 20 to 30 minutes longer or until barley is tender.

Beef and Barley Soup

Makes 6 servings.

3 pounds meaty cross-cut beef shank or neck	**½ cup chopped fresh parsley**
	1 bay leaf
¼ cup all-purpose flour	**2 teaspoons salt**
	½ teaspoon pepper
¼ cup vegetable oil	**½ teaspoon leaf thyme, crumbled**
¾ cup pearl barley	
2 carrots, cut into quarters lengthwise	**½ teaspoon leaf savory, crumbled**
1 medium-size onion, thinly sliced	**2 cans (13¾ ounces each) beef broth**

1. Dredge meat with flour. Brown in oil on all sides in large kettle.

2. Combine meat with barley, carrots, onion, parsley, bay leaf, salt, pepper, thyme, savory and beef broth in the kettle.

3. Cover and cook on low heat for 2 hours or until beef and barley are tender. Remove meat; discard bones and dice meat. Return to soup.

4. Taste for seasoning; add additional salt or thyme, if you wish.

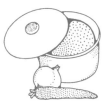

Cream of Broccoli Soup

Makes 6 servings.

1 bunch fresh broccoli (about 1½ pounds)	**2 cans (13¾ ounces each) chicken broth**
1 medium-size onion, chopped (½ cup)	**½ teaspoon salt**
	Dash cayenne
2 tablespoons butter or margarine	**1 cup light cream or half-and-half**
1 potato, pared and diced (1 cup)	**⅛ teaspoon ground nutmeg**

1. Trim outer leaves and tough ends from broccoli.

Separate stalks and cut into 2 or 3 shorter lengths. Parboil in boiling salted water in a large saucepan 5 minutes; drain well.

2. Sauté onion in butter in a large saucepan for 5 minutes, until soft but not brown. Add potato, chicken broth, salt and cayenne. Heat to boiling; lower heat; simmer 15 minutes. Add broccoli, reserving a few flowerets for garnish; simmer 5 minutes longer or until vegetables are tender.

3. Pour mixture, half at a time, into the container of electric blender; cover; whirl until smooth. Return mixture to saucepan; add cream and nutmeg; bring to boiling (if soup is too thick, add more cream or milk). Taste and add more salt, if needed. Garnish with reserved flowerets.

Mama's Chicken Soup with Fluffy Matzo Balls

Prepare this soup a day ahead so you can chill it and then easily remove the fat.

Makes 8 servings (plus chicken for another meal).

1 stewing chicken, about 4 pounds	1 large parsnip, trimmed, scrubbed and quartered
2 quarts water	2 sprigs fresh dill
1 whole onion, peeled	1/2 teaspoon salt
2 whole carrots, scraped	1/4 teaspoon pepper
4 celery stalks, including tops, cut into 3-inch lengths	Fluffy Matzo Balls *(recipe follows)*

1. Wash the chicken. Place in a deep pot; add the water, onion, carrots, celery, parsnip, parsley, dill, salt and pepper. Bring to boiling; lower the heat and simmer, covered, until the chicken is tender, about 2 hours.

2. Remove the chicken and refrigerate for another use. Strain the soup into a large bowl, reserving cooked carrots. Chill the broth. Thinly slice the carrots and reserve.

3. To serve, skim the fat from the soup. Reheat the soup in a saucepan with the reserved carrots. Transfer to a tureen. Add the matzo balls.

Fluffy Matzo Balls

Beaten egg white is used to make a fluffier matzo ball. There is no need to add chicken fat, which is high in cholesterol.

Makes 8 servings (2 per serving).

3 eggs, separated	Salt
1/4 cup seltzer	1/8 teaspoon white pepper
1 tablespoon chopped parsley	3/4 cup matzo meal

1. Beat the egg yolks in a medium-size bowl with a fork until lemon-colored. Stir in the seltzer, parsley, 1/2 teaspoon of salt and the pepper.

2. Beat the egg whites in a small bowl until stiff peaks form; fold into the egg yolk mixture. Gently stir in the matzo meal. Chill for at least 1 hour.

3. Pour water into a Dutch oven or large saucepan to a depth of at least 2 inches; add 1/4 teaspoon salt. Bring to boiling.

4. Form the matzo mixture into sixteen 1-inch balls. Drop into the boiling water. Lower the heat and simmer for 20 minutes or until cooked through.

Mulligatawny Soup

This classic soup has its origins in India and is richly flavored with exotic curry.

Makes 6 servings.

3 medium-size carrots, pared and sliced	chopped
2 celery stalks, sliced	5 teaspoons curry powder
6 cups Basic Chicken Broth *(see above)*	1 teaspoon salt
3 cups diced cooked chicken (from Basic Chicken Broth)	1/4 cup all-purpose flour
1 large onion, chopped (1 cup)	1 tablespoon lemon juice
1/4 cup (1/2 stick) butter or margarine	2 cups hot cooked rice
1 apple, pared, quartered, cored and	1/4 chopped fresh parsley
	6 lemon slices *(optional)*

1. Cook carrots and celery in 1 cup Chicken Broth in a medium-size saucepan 20 minutes or until tender. Add chicken; heat just until hot; cover; keep warm.

2. Sauté onion until soft in butter or margarine in Dutch oven; stir in apple, curry powder and salt; sauté 5 minutes longer or until apple is soft; add flour. Gradually stir in remaining chicken broth; heat to boiling, stirring constantly; reduce heat; cover; simmer 15 minutes.

3. Add vegetables and chicken with the broth they were cooked in; bring just to boiling. Stir in lemon juice.

4. Ladle into soup plates or bowls; pass hot cooked rice and chopped parsley and lemon slices, if you wish, as a garnish.

Overleaf: Gazpacho, page 730.

Gazpacho   Enjoyed in the sunny south of Spain, gazpacho is a chilled, salad-like tomato soup. The word is derived from the Moorish, meaning "soaked bread." It makes a lively meal-opener that's rich in vitamin C.

Gazpacho

Makes 6 servings.

2 cloves garlic, crushed	2 cups tomato juice
2 pounds medium-size tomatoes (about 6), peeled and chopped	1 cup water
	$1/4$ cup olive or vegetable oil
1 medium-size cucumber, pared and cut in chunks	$1/2$ teaspoon salt
	$1/4$ teaspoon freshly ground black pepper
1 large green pepper, seeded and chopped	Cucumber slices (optional)
2 slices white bread, trimmed and crumbled (1 cup)	$1/2$ cup chopped green onions
	$1/2$ cup packaged garlic croutons
$1/4$ cup red wine vinegar	$1/2$ cup chopped green pepper

1. Combine garlic, tomatoes, cucumber, green pepper, bread and vinegar in container of electric blender; cover; whirl until smooth.
2. Press mixture through sieve, discarding the solids. Add tomato juice, water, oil, salt and pepper to the tomato liquid; chill well.
3. Serve in chilled bowls; garnish with cucumber, green onions, croutons and green pepper.

Turkey Soup with Egg Dumplings

Makes 6 servings.

$1/2$ cup *sifted* all-purpose flour	$1/2$ teaspoon leaf thyme, crumbled
$1/4$ teaspoon salt	$1/8$ teaspoon turmeric
2 tablespoons butter or margarine, softened	1 medium-size onion, chopped ($1/2$ cup)
2 eggs, beaten	1 package (10 ounces) frozen whole-kernel corn
6 cups Turkey Broth (*recipe in this chapter*) or canned chicken broth	1 package (10 ounces) frozen baby lima beans
1 teaspoon salt	1 cup chopped cooked turkey
$1/8$ teaspoon pepper	

1. Sift flour with $1/4$ teaspoon salt. Stir into butter in medium-size mixing bowl. Add eggs, beating until well blended.
2. Bring broth to boiling in a large saucepan or kettle with 1 teaspoon salt, pepper, thyme and turmeric. Add onion, corn, beans and turkey. Return soup to boiling.

3. Drop dumpling batter by the spoonful into boiling soup to make 12 dumplings. Lower heat to keep soup simmering; cover and cook 20 minutes or until dumplings are cooked through.
4. Serve in warm soup plates or bowls.

Cream of Turkey Soup

Makes 6 servings.

1 teaspoon salt	1 small parsnip, pared and chopped ($1/2$ cup)
$1/8$ teaspoon pepper	
5 cups Turkey Broth or Basic Chicken Broth (*recipe follows*)	1 tablespoon dry sherry (*optional*)
	$1/2$ cup light cream
1 large carrot, pared and chopped	1 cup chopped cooked turkey
$1/2$ cup chopped celery	2 tablespoons chopped parsley or watercress
2 medium-size leeks, washed well and chopped (1 cup)	

1. Add salt and pepper to broth in a large saucepan; heat to boil. Add carrot, celery, leeks and parsnip. Lower heat; simmer until vegetables are barely soft, about 20 minutes. Remove from heat.
2. Pour soup through strainer into bowl. Puree vegetables in electric blender. Return puree and broth to pan. Add sherry, cream and turkey to soup.
3. Heat just to simmering over medium heat. Do not boil. Add parsley; serve.

Basic Chicken Broth

It is well worthwhile to make homemade chicken broth. This recipe gives you enough broth and meat to make 2 soups and even extra meat for a salad or casserole, if you wish.

Makes 12 cups.

2 broiler-fryers (3 to $3^{1}/2$ pounds each)	2 celery stalks
	2 celery tops
Chicken giblets	3 sprigs parsley
2 medium-size carrots, pared	1 leek, washed well
	Water
1 large parsnip, pared	2 tablespoons salt
1 large onion, chopped (1 cup)	12 peppercorns

1. Combine chicken, chicken giblets, carrots, parsnip, onion and celery in a large kettle; tie celery tops, parsley and leek together with a string; add to kettle. Add enough cold water to cover chicken and vegetables, about 12 cups.
2. Heat slowly to boiling; skim; add salt and peppercorns; reduce heat. Simmer very slowly for 1 to $1^{1}/2$ hours or until chicken is very tender. Remove meat and vegetables from broth, discard the bundle of greens.

3. Strain broth through cheesecloth into a large bowl. (There should be about 12 cups.) Use this delicious broth in the following soup recipe or in any of our recipes calling for chicken broth.

4. When cool enough to handle, remove and discard skin and bones from chicken; cut meat into bite-size pieces; use as called for in following recipe, or use in salads, casseroles, etc. To store in refrigerator up to 3 or 4 days, keep in covered container. To freeze, pack in small portions (1 or 2 cups) in plastic bags or freezer containers, to use as needed.

5. To store in refrigerator up to 4 days, leave fat layer on surface of broth until ready to use, then lift fat off and discard, or use in other cooking. To freeze, transfer broth to freezer containers, allowing space on top for expansion. Freeze until ready to use (3 to 4 months maximum).

Turkey Broth

Makes 8 cups.

Carcass of 12- to 14-pound turkey	**quartered**
2 quarts water	**1 onion, quartered**
2 celery stalks, broken in half	**6 peppercorns**
1 carrot, pared and	**1 large bay leaf**
	1 tablespoon salt

1. Combine all ingredients in large kettle. Bring to boiling; lower heat to simmer. Cook uncovered 2 to 3 hours. Strain through colander.

2. When bones are cool enough to handle, remove meat and use in recipes. Chill broth in refrigerator. Remove fat from surface of broth.

Basic Beef Broth

This flavorful beef broth is the basic stock for a variety of soups to follow.

Makes 14 cups.

2¹/₂ pounds brisket, boneless chuck, or bottom round, in 1 piece	**2 medium-size yellow onions, peeled**
2 pounds shin of beef with bones	**2 celery stalks with leaves**
2 3-inch marrow bones	**1 turnip, pared and quartered**
1 veal knuckle (about 1 pound)	**1 leek, washed well**
Water	**3 large sprigs parsley**
8 teaspoons salt	**12 peppercorns**
2 carrots, pared	**3 whole cloves**
	1 bay leaf

1. Place beef, shin of beef, marrow bones and veal knuckle in a large kettle; add water to cover, about 4 quarts. Heat to boiling; skim off foam that appears on top. Add salt, carrots, onions, celery, turnip and leek; tie parsley, peppercorns, clove and bay leaf in a small cheesecloth bag; add to kettle. Push under the liquid and add more water, if needed.

2. Heat to boiling; cover; reduce heat; simmer very slowly 3¹/₂ to 4 hours or until meat is tender. Remove meat and vegetables from broth.

3. Strain broth through cheesecloth into a large bowl. (There should be about 14 cups.) Use this broth in the following soup recipe or in any of our recipes calling for beef broth.

4. When meat is cool enough to handle, remove and discard bones. Trim large pieces of meat and save for other recipes, if you wish. Cut trimmings and shin beef into bite-size pieces; use as called for in following recipe. To store in refrigerator up to 3 to 4 days, keep in covered container. To freeze, pack in small portions (1 or 2 cups) in plastic bags or freezer containers, to use as needed.

5. To store in refrigerator up to 4 days, leave fat layer on surface of broth until ready to use, then lift off and discard before heating. To freeze, transfer broth to freezer containers, allowing space on top for expansion. Freeze until ready to use (3 to 4 months maximum).

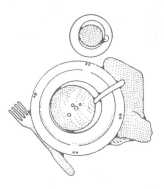

Stracciatella

Makes 8 servings.

1 pound spinach, washed and trimmed	**¹/₄ cup grated Parmesan cheese**
OR: 1 package (10 ounces) frozen leaf spinach	**Pinch ground nutmeg**
	5 cans (13³/₄ ounces each) chicken broth (about 8 cups)
3 eggs	**1 tablespoon lemon juice**
Pinch salt	

1. Cook fresh spinach in a large saucepan, covered, until leaves just wilt; or cook frozen spinach following label directions. Drain; squeeze out as much water as possible, then chop coarsely.

2. Beat eggs in a medium-size bowl with salt, Parmesan and nutmeg. Stir in 1 cup of the chicken broth.

3. Heat remaining broth to boiling in a large saucepan. Pour egg mixture slowly into boiling broth, stirring gently with a wire whisk. Stir in spinach; lower heat. Add lemon juice and simmer about 3 minutes longer, beating constantly.

Egg Drop Soup

Try this famous Chinese soup as the first course for your next dinner party.

Makes 6 servings.

4 cups chicken broth	**1 tablespoon water**
4 green onions, sliced	**Green Onion Fans**
1 bay leaf	***(recipe follows)***
2 eggs	

1. Bring the chicken broth, sliced green onions and bay leaf to boiling in a large saucepan. Lower the heat and simmer for 10 minutes.
2. Beat the eggs and water in a cup until well blended with a fork.
3. Bring the broth mixture to boiling, stir in the beaten egg, just until set. Remove from the heat.
4. Ladle into soup bowls and garnish with Green Onion Fans.

Green Onion Fans
Makes 6 servings. Trim 6 green onions and cut to a 6-inch length from bottom. Cut lengthwise down green leaves to separate into many peices. Let stand in ice water until green leaves curl.

Cucumber and Potato Soup

Makes 4 to 6 servings.

1 large cucumber, pared, seeded and diced (1½ cups)	**cream of potato soup**
	½ teaspoon salt
¼ cup sliced green onions	**⅛ teaspoon cayenne**
2 tablespoons butter or margarine	**⅛ teaspoon ground nutmeg**
2 cups milk	**1 cup light cream or plain yogurt**
1 can condensed	

1. Sauté cucumber and onions in butter in a large

Egg Drop Soup.

saucepan until soft, about 5 minutes. Stir in milk and potato soup. Bring to boiling, stirring constantly. Lower heat; cover.
2. Simmer, stirring often, 5 minutes. Stir in salt, cayenne, nutmeg and cream or yogurt; heat through. (Do not boil if using yogurt.)
3. Puree mixture, ½ at a time, in container of electric blender or food processor. Cool, then chill several hours. When serving, taste and add additional seasoning, if needed. If chilled soup is too thick, add more milk or cream. Pour into a 2-quart insulated container for toting.

Giblet and Barley Soup

Makes 6 servings.

8 ounces chicken livers (about 9), finely chopped or ground	**nutmeg**
	¼ teaspoon ground cumin
4 ounces chicken gizzards (about 6), finely chopped or ground	**3 tablespoons chopped fresh parsley**
	1 small onion, chopped (¼ cup)
3 envelopes or teaspoons instant chicken broth	**3 tablespoons butter or margarine**
3 cups hot water	**½ cup barley (pearl or instant)**
¼ teaspoon pepper	**3 cups water**
¼ teaspoon ground	**Salt**

1. Combine livers, gizzards, instant broth, water, pepper, nutmeg, cumin, parsley and onion in a large saucepan. Bring to boiling, cover and simmer 15 minutes.
2. Heat the butter in a large saucepan. Sauté the barley for 4 to 5 minutes, stirring and shaking the pan often. Add the water, bring to boiling, cover and simmer 30 minutes; stir occasionally.
3. Add the chicken giblet mixture, cover and cook gently about 15 minutes or until the barley is tender. Taste; add additional salt, if you wish. Serve with a hearty oatmeal bread, if you wish.

Tomato and Rice Soup

Makes 8 servings (about 2 quarts).

1½ pounds top round, cut into 1-inch cubes	**¼ teaspoon leaf marjoram, crumbled**
	5 carrots, pared and sliced ½-inch thick
2 quarts water	
1 can (35 ounces) tomatoes	**5 stalks celery, sliced ½-inch thick**
3 beef bouillon cubes	**1 onion, coarsely chopped**
½ teaspoon pepper	
½ teaspoon leaf thyme, crumbled	**½ cup uncooked white rice**

1. Brown the beef in a large saucepan. Add the water.

Tomato and Rice Soup, page 732.

Bring to boiling. Lower the heat; simmer for 20 minutes, or until the meat is almost tender.
2. Stir in the tomatoes with their liquid, breaking up the chunks with a spoon. Add the bouillon, pepper, thyme and marjoram. Simmer for 1 hour. Add the carrots,celery, onion and rice during the last 30 minutes of cooking.

Harvest Pumpkin Soup

Makes 8 servings.

1 large onion, sliced (1 cup)	**cinnamon**
2 tablespoons butter or margarine	**1/4 teaspoon ground nutmeg**
2 cans condensed chicken broth	**1/8 teaspoon pepper**
1 can (16 ounces) pumpkin	**1 cup light cream or half-and-half**
1 teaspoon salt	**Cinnamon-Sugar Toast Triangles** *(recipe follows)*
3/4 teaspoon ground	

1. Sauté onion in butter in a large saucepan until soft, about 5 minutes. Add 1 can of the chicken broth; bring to boiling; cover; lower heat; simmer 10 minutes.

2. Place 1/2 cup of the onion mixture in container of electric blender; cover. Whirl until smooth. Add remaining onion broth mixture and whirl until smooth. Return to saucepan.
3. Add remaining can of chicken broth, pumpkin, salt, cinnamon, nutmeg and pepper. Stir until smooth. Bring to boiling; cover. Lower heat; simmer 10 minutes.
4. Slowly stir in cream; heat just until thoroughly hot. Serve with Cinnamon-Sugar Toast Triangles, if you wish.

Cinnamon-Sugar Toast Triangles: Blend 3 tablespoons softened butter or margarine with 1 tablespoon sugar and 1/2 teaspoon ground cinnamon in a small bowl. Spread generously on 4 slices of cracked wheat or whole wheat bread. Place on a cookie sheet. Bake in a preheated hot oven (400°) for 8 minutes or until bubbly and golden brown. Cut each bread slice into 4 triangles. Makes 16 triangles.

Minestrone   The word minestrone is based on the Italian words *minestra,* meaning soup, and *one,* a suffix meaning big. Minestrone is a big or hearty vegetable soup the Italians serve as a first course. It is made of numerous vegetables cooked in broth with either beans or pasta added.

Salad Bar Minestrone

Makes 4 servings (2 quarts).

1¼ pound mixed salad bar vegetables (about 7 cups), such as sweet green and red peppers, broccoli flowerets, cauliflower flowerets, carrots, shredded cabbage, celery, onion and chick-peas

½ pound sweet Italian sausage, casings removed, and meat crumbled

1 clove garlic, finely chopped

2 tablespoons olive or vegetable oil

1 can (8 ounces) tomato sauce

1 can (10¾ ounces) condensed beef broth

3 soup cans (10¾ ounces each) water

1 can (19 ounces) white kidney beans (cannellini), undrained

½ teaspoon leaf oregano, crumbled

½ teaspoon salt (optional)

¼ teaspoon pepper

⅓ cup orzo or other small pasta

Grated Parmesan cheese

1. Slice any large salad bar vegetables into bite-size pieces; reserve.
2. Sauté sausage and garlic in oil in large saucepan until meat is no longer pink. Add vegetables. Sauté 2 to 5 minutes or until vegetables just begin to brown. Stir in tomato sauce, broth, water, beans, oregano, salt, if using, and pepper.
3. Simmer, uncovered, 15 minutes, Sprinkle pasta over soup; simmer 15 minutes or until pasta is tender. Serve with Parmesan.

Kidney-Bean Minestrone

Makes 12 servings.

1 cup dried red kidney beans

3 cups water

2 tablespoons butter or margarine

2 tablespoons olive or vegetable oil

1 large leek, chopped
   OR: 1 large onion, chopped (1 cup)

1 clove garlic, minced

2 medium-size carrots, pared and diced

1 large potato, pared and diced

1 cup chopped celery

1 can (16 ounces) tomatoes
   OR: 4 ripe

tomatoes, peeled and chopped

12 cups water

4 envelopes or teaspoons instant beef broth

3 teaspoons salt

2 teaspoons leaf oregano, crumbled

¼ teaspoon pepper

½ cup ditalini or elbow macaroni

2 cups shredded cabbage

1 medium-size zucchini, thinly sliced

Grated Parmesan cheese

1. Pick over beans and rinse under running water. Combine beans and water in a large saucepan. Bring to boiling; cover saucepan. Boil 2 minutes; remove from heat; let stand 1 hour. Return saucepan to heat; bring to boiling; lower heat and simmer 1½ hours or until beans become tender; drain beans.
2. Heat butter and oil in a large kettle; sauté leek and garlic until soft; stir in carrots, potato and celery; sauté 5 minutes. Stir in drained beans, tomatoes, water, instant broth, salt, oregano and pepper.
3. Bring to boiling; lower heat; cover kettle; simmer 30 minutes; return liquid to boiling; stir in ditalini or elbow macaroni and cook 10 minutes; stir in cabbage and zucchini; cook 10 minutes longer.
4. Ladle into heated soup bowls and sprinkle with cheese.

Curried Apple and Chicken Soup

Versatile curry combines well with apple for a smooth colorful soup.

Makes 6 servings.

1 medium-size onion, chopped (½ cup)

¼ cup (½ stick) butter or margarine

2 to 3 cooking apples

2 teaspoons curry powder

1 can condensed

cream of chicken soup

2 cups water

½ teaspoon salt

1 cup light cream or half-and-half

1 tablespoon lemon juice

1. Sauté onion in butter in a large saucepan until soft, about 5 minutes. Coarsely shred enough apple to make about 1 cup; add to saucepan; stir in curry powder. Cook and stir 1 to 2 minutes. Add soup; gradually stir in water.
2. Bring to boiling, stirring often; lower heat; cover. Simmer, stirring often, 10 minutes. Puree, ½ at a time, in container of electric blender. Return to saucepan. Add salt and cream and heat through.
3. Shred remaining apple to make about 1 cup; toss with lemon juice; add to soup just before serving.

For Chilled Soup: Add salt and cream to pureed mixture; cool, then chill several hours. Just before serving, shred remaining apple; toss with lemon juice. Garnish with shredded apple.

Old-fashioned Lentil Soup

Makes 6 servings.

1 ham bone

6 cups water

1¼ cups dried lentils (½ of a 1-pound package)

4 medium-size carrots, pared and sliced

1 large onion, chopped (1 cup)

2 teaspoons salt

1 teaspoon sugar

¼ teaspoon pepper

1 bay leaf

1. Combine ham bone, water, lentils, carrots, onion, salt, sugar, pepper and bay leaf in a kettle; cover;

Salad Bar Minestrone, page 734.

bring to boiling; simmer 1 hour or until lentils are tender.

2. Remove ham bone; pull off meat; add to soup. Remove bay leaf.

3. Serve soup in heated bowls.

Beefy Vegetable Soup

Makes 6 servings.

1¹/₂ **pounds beef chuck or round steak**	**2 whole cloves**
¹/₂ **pound cracked beef bones**	**1 small bay leaf**
	¹/₂ **teaspoon leaf thyme, crumbled**
6 cups water	**1 can (8 ounces) tomato sauce**
1 onion, unpeeled, cut in half	**1 cup sliced carrots**
2 teaspoons salt	**1 cup diced celery**
¹/₄ **teaspoon pepper**	¹/₂ **pound green beans, cut into 1-inch pieces**
1 celery stalk with leaves	**2 cups cooked barley (¹/₂ cup uncooked)**
1 carrot, pared, cut in big chunks	**Chopped fresh parsley**
1 clove garlic, crushed	

1. Place meat and bones in an open 6-quart pressure cooker; add water; bring to boiling; skim scum as it accumulates.

2. Sear cut sides of onion in a hot skillet until very brown; add to soup. Also add salt, pepper, celery stalk, carrot chunks, garlic, cloves, bay leaf, thyme and tomato sauce.

3. Close cover securely; place pressure control on vent pipe (15 pounds if your unit has multipressure selections). Pressure-cook on low heat 50 minutes after control jiggles.

4. Turn heat off and let pressure drop for 5 minutes; then place closed cooker under faucet of running cold water until pressure is down.

5. Remove control and cover carefully. Skim fat from top of soup. Remove meat to platter and cut into spoon-size chunks; cover with plastic wrap and set aside. Discard bones.

6. Strain soup through fine sieve, pressing out all the juices and vegetable puree with back of large spoon. Return broth to pressure cooker and reheat in open pot. Add remaining carrots, celery and green beans; cover securely and bring up to pressure again; cook for about 5 to 6 minutes after the control has started to jiggle.

7. Reduce pressure quickly with cold water. Remove control and cover and add meat and the cooked barley. (Or, you may use cooked rice or noodles.)

(continued)

Taste; add additional salt and pepper, if you wish. Serve in big bowls; sprinkle chopped parsley on top, if you wish.

Won Ton Soup

A light and fragrant soup with pork and green onion dumplings.

Makes 6 servings.

1 pound ground pork	**1 package won ton**
¹/₂ cup chopped green	**wrappers**
onions	**4 cans (13³/₄ ounces**
1 egg	**each) chicken broth**
2 tablespoons soy	**1 package (7 ounces)**
sauce	**frozen snow peas**
2 teaspoons	**3 cups sliced Chinese**
cornstarch	**celery cabbage**

1. Combine pork, onions, egg, soy sauce and cornstarch in bowl; mix well.
2. Place about 1 slightly rounded teaspoonful pork filling on each won ton wrapper. Brush edges of wrapper with a little water to moisten. Bring one side of wrapper over filling; roll up as a cylinder, leaving about ¹/₂ inch of wrapper unrolled at the top. Pull the two ends of cylinder together to meet and overlap under filling, pinching firmly.
3. Place won tons in single layer on cookie sheet as you work. Cover with plastic wrap to prevent drying.
4. Heat 3 to 4 quarts salted water to boiling in large kettle; add half the won tons. After water returns to boiling, lower heat to moderate and cook won tons 5 minutes, uncovered. Lift out to colander with slotted spoon. Repeat with remaining won tons.
5. Combine chicken broth and snow peas in large saucepan; bring to boiling. Cook, covered, 5 minutes; add won tons and cabbage; return to boiling. Serve at once.

Chicken Rice Soup

Makes 12 one-cup servings.

1 broiler-fryer (2	**1 green pepper,**
pounds)	**seeded and diced**
4¹/₂ cups water	**(1 cup)**
1 onion, quartered	**2 carrots, diced**
1 bay leaf	**(1 cup)**
6 sprigs parsley	**¹/₂ cup uncooked long-**
Celery tops	**grain rice**
2 cans (16 ounces	**1 tablespoon salt**
each) tomatoes	**¹/₂ teaspoon pepper**
1 potato diced (1 cup)	**2 envelopes instant**
1 large onion, diced	**chicken broth**
(1 cup)	

1. Place chicken and water in Dutch oven. Add onion, bay leaf, parsley and celery tops. Bring to boiling. Lower heat; cover and cook 1 hour or until chicken is tender. Remove solids from broth to bowl; strain broth; return broth to Dutch oven.
2. While chicken is cooling, prepare vegetables. Add tomatoes, potato, onion, green pepper, carrots, rice, salt, pepper and instant chicken broth to broth in Dutch oven. Simmer, covered, 30 minutes.
3. When chicken is cool enough to handle, skin and bone and cut meat into small pieces (about 2¹/₂ cups). Add to soup. Cover and cook 15 minutes or until vegetables and rice are tender.

Watercress Cream

Makes 6 servings.

2 bunches watercress	**2 teaspoons instant**
2 tablespoons flour	**minced onion**
6 cups skim milk	**2 teaspoons salt**

1. Wash watercress and dry on paper toweling. Set aside 6 sprigs for garnish; chop remaining stems and leaves fine. (You should have about 3 cups.)
2. Combine flour and about ¹/₄ cup of the milk until smooth in a large saucepan; slowly stir in remaining milk, onion and salt. Cook, stirring constantly, until mixture thickens slightly and bubbles 3 minutes. Remove from heat. Stir in chopped watercress.
3. Ladle soup into heated soup plates; float a watercress sprig on each serving. Serve hot.

Chowder
A hearty soup made from a variety of ingredients, although it is most often made from seafood and milk. The word "chowder" is taken from the French word *chaudiére*, a large heavy kettle used in making soups and stews.

New England Fish Chowder

Makes 4 servings.

3 bacon slices, diced	**frozen cod or**
1 large onion,	**haddock fillets, cut**
chopped (1 cup)	**up**
1 potato, pared and	**1 package (10 ounces)**
diced (1 cup)	**frozen mixed**
1 cup water	**vegetables**
1¹/₂ teaspoons salt	**1¹/₂ cups milk**
¹/₈ teaspoon cayenne	**¹/₂ cup light or heavy**
1 bay leaf	**cream**
1 package (12 ounces)	

1. Cook bacon until crisp in a large saucepan; remove with slotted spoon and drain on paper toweling; reserve. Add onion to drippings; sauté until tender but

(continued)

Pictured opposite: New England Fish Chowder.

not brown. Add potato, water, salt, cayenne and bay leaf. Simmer, covered, for 10 minutes.
2. Add fish and vegetables to saucepan; cook 10 minutes longer or just until fish and vegetables are tender.
3. Add milk and cream to saucepan; heat through. Ladle into soup bowls. Sprinkle with reserved bacon.

Scallop Chowder

Makes about 6 servings.

1 package (12 ounces) frozen scallops	1 medium-size onion, chopped (1/2 cup)
3 cups boiling water	1 cup milk
1 teaspoon salt	1 cup chicken broth
2 cups cubed potatoes (about 2 medium)	1/8 teaspoon white pepper
1 cup cubed carrots (3 medium)	2 tablespoons butter or margarine
1 cup sliced celery	Lemon slices

1. Cook frozen scallops in boiling, salted water for 3 minutes or until tender; remove from water with slotted spoon; reserve.
2. Add potatoes, carrots, celery and onion to same water; simmer until tender, about 10 minutes. Stir in milk, chicken broth, pepper and butter. Puree in blender with 1/2 cup of the scallops. Return to pan with remaining whole scallops and reheat. Garnish with lemon slices.

Savory Clam Chowder

Thyme adds its pungent good taste to this hearty chowder that is a variation of the popular Manhattan.
Makes 6 servings.

1 can (28 ounces) tomatoes	(8 1/2 ounces each) minced clams and 1 bottle (8 ounces) clam broth
4 large carrots, pared and sliced	
2 cups chopped celery	1 package (10 ounces) frozen lima beans
2 large onions, chopped (2 cups)	1/4 cup bacon drippings
1 teaspoon salt	1/4 cup all-purpose flour
1/4 teaspoon pepper	
4 cups water	1 tablespoon chopped fresh thyme
24 fresh clams (with juice), chopped OR: 2 cans	

1. Combine tomatoes, carrots, celery, onions, salt, pepper and water in a large kettle; bring to boiling. Lower heat and cover kettle; simmer 40 minutes.
2. Stir in clams, broth and lima beans; simmer 10 minutes.

Pictured opposite: Garden Vegetable Soup.

3. Blend bacon drippings and flour in a cup to make a roux. Drop by spoonfuls into hot liquid; add thyme. Cook, stirring constantly, until mixture thickens slightly and bubbles, 3 minutes. Serve with chowder crackers, if you wish.
Note: When substituting dried leaf thyme for fresh: Measure 1/4 cup of the tomato liquid into a cup. Crumble 1 teaspoon thyme into liquid; let stand 15 minutes. Add thyme and tomato liquid to chowder when adding roux.

Garden Vegetable Soup

Makes 8 cups.

2 tablespoons butter or margarine	1 teaspoon leaf basil, crumbled
2 tablespoons vegetable oil	2 teaspoons salt
1 cup sliced carrots	1/4 teaspoon pepper
1 cup sliced celery, with some of the green leafy tops	1 can (13 3/4 ounces) beef broth
	1/4 pound green beans, washed, trimmed and cut into 1-inch pieces (1 cup)
1 large onion, chopped (1 cup)	
1 clove garlic, crushed	
9 medium-size tomatoes OR: 2 cans (16 ounces each) tomatoes, undrained	1/2 pound zucchini, cut in half lengthwise and thinly sliced (2 cups)
	1/4 cup chopped fresh parsley
1 teaspoon leaf oregano, crumbled	Grated Parmesan cheese

1. Heat butter and oil in Dutch oven; sauté carrots, celery, onion and garlic, 5 minutes.
2. Peel tomatoes; cut in half crosswise. Place strainer over large bowl; remove seeds by squeezing gently. Chop pulp and add to juice in large bowl.
3. Add tomatoes and juice to Dutch oven; add oregano, basil, salt and pepper; cook 15 minutes.
4. Add beef broth and green beans; cook 30 minutes longer, adding zucchini and parsley after 20 minutes. Serve with Parmesan cheese.

Cream of Fresh Tomato Soup

Makes 6 servings.

3 medium-size very ripe tomatoes	3 whole cloves
1 small onion, finely chopped (1/4 cup)	1 small bay leaf
	3 tablespoons butter
1/2 cup finely chopped celery	3 tablespoons flour
	1 teaspoon salt
Pinch sugar *(optional)*	3 cups milk

1. Peel and chop tomatoes; combine with onion, celery, sugar (if used), cloves and bay leaf in a

(continued)

medium-size saucepan. Bring to boiling; lower heat; cover and simmer 15 minutes.

2. Melt butter in a large saucepan. Stir in flour and salt; cook 1 minute; stir in milk. Cook, stirring constantly, until mixture thickens and bubbles, 2 minutes; keep warm.

3. Puree tomato mixture through sieve or food mill. Stir puree slowly into sauce. Heat but do not boil. Serve with croutons, if you wish.

Bisque
This term refers to a thick, rich cream soup, usually made with shellfish or fish. Originally, the word was used for a poultry or game puree.

Lobster Bisque

Makes about 8 servings.

1 medium-size onion, chopped (¹/₂ cup)	6 ounces each) lobster or crab-meat, drained and diced
¹/₂ cup (1 stick) butter or margarine	
³/₄ cup all-purpose flour	3 cups light cream or half-and-half
3 cans condensed chicken broth	2 tablespoons tomato paste
³/₄ cup dry sherry	Salt and pepper to taste
2 cans (about	

1. Sauté onion in butter in a large saucepan. Stir in flour; cook until bubbly. Gradually stir in broth; cook until thickened. Stir in sherry and lobster. Cover; simmer 15 minutes. Stir in remaining ingredients; heat.

Shrimp Bisque

Makes 8 servings.

¹/₂ cup (1 stick) butter	shelled and deveined
1 medium-size carrot, thinly sliced	¹/₃ cup all-purpose flour
1 small onion, chopped (¹/₄ cup)	¹/₂ teaspoon salt
1 bay leaf	2 to 3 teaspoons paprika
¹/₄ teaspoon leaf thyme, crumbled	3 cups milk
¹/₂ cup dry white wine	2 cups half-and-half
³/₄ pound raw shrimp,	Fresh dill sprigs

1. Melt 2 tablespoons of the butter in a large saucepan. Sauté carrot and onion until tender, about 3 minutes. Add bay leaf, thyme, wine and shrimp. Cook just until shrimp turn pink, about 3 minutes. Drain shrimp into a bowl, reserving liquid.

2. Melt remaining 6 tablespoons butter in same saucepan; stir in flour. Cook, stirring constantly, until bubbly. Add reserved shrimp liquid to saucepan along with salt, paprika and milk. Cook, stirring constantly, until mixture thickens.

3. Reserve 8 whole shrimp; coarsely chop remainder.

Add chopped shrimp and vegetables with half-and-half to saucepan; heat thoroughly. Garnish with reserved whole shrimp and fresh dill.

Vichyssoise
A cold leek and potato soup of American origin based on a French soup.

Vichyssoise

Makes 6 servings.

3 leeks (white part only) well washed and thinly sliced	each) chicken broth (3 cups)
1 large onion, thinly sliced	2 medium-size potatoes, peeled and diced
¹/₈ pound (2 ounces) spinach	1 cup milk
2 tablespoons unsalted butter	¹/₂ teaspoon salt
	Dash white pepper
2 cans (13³/₄ ounces	¹/₂ cup heavy cream
	Chopped chives

1. Sauté leek, onion and spinach slowly in butter in a large saucepan for 20 minutes, stirring occasionally.

2. Stir in chicken broth and potatoes; cook 20 minutes longer or until potatoes are tender. Add milk; bring mixture to boiling; remove from heat.

3. Add salt and pepper to taste. Puree soup through sieve or food mill or in electric blender container. Chill several hours.

4. Stir cream into soup. Serve with a sprinkling of chopped chives.

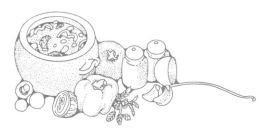

Chilled Spinach Soup

A lovely, pale green, creamy soup with a hint of lemon.

Makes 8 servings.

2 packages (10 ounces each) fresh spinach	1 teaspoon salt
1 medium-size onion, chopped (¹/₂ cup)	¹/₈ teaspoon pepper
	¹/₈ teaspoon ground mace
2 tablespoons butter or margarine	1 teaspoon grated lemon rind
2 cans (13³/₄ ounces each) chicken broth	1 cup light cream or half-and-half

1. Trim spinach; wash leaves well; shake water off.

2. Sauté onion in butter until soft in a large saucepan. Add spinach; cover. (No need to add any water.) Cook

over medium heat 10 minutes or just until leaves are wilted.
3. Add chicken broth, salt, pepper and mace; simmer 5 minutes; cool slightly.
4. Pour soup, part at a time, into container of electric blender; cover. Whirl until smooth.
5. Pour into a large bowl. Stir in lemon rind and cream. Cover; chill several hours or overnight.
6. Pour into chilled serving bowls. Garnish each with a lemon slice, if you wish. Serve icy cold.

Cold Cucumber and Yogurt Soup

A refreshing soup that matches favorably with barbecued foods.

Makes 6 servings.

1 large cucumber	**3 tablespoons finely**
1/4 teaspoon salt	**chopped fresh mint**
2 or 3 cloves garlic,	**OR: 1 tablespoon**
finely chopped	**dried mint,**
1/8 teaspoon pepper	**crumbled**
3 cups plain yogurt	

1. Pare the cucumber. Finely chop or shred the cucumber; place in a colander. Toss with the salt and set aside over a bowl or in the sink to drain for 30 minutes.
2. Mash garlic with mortar and pestle. Or, place in container of electric blender. Cover; whirl briefly until mashed. Add pepper and 3 tablespoons of the yogurt to the mashed garlic in the mortar or blender. Mash or whirl until the mixture is a smooth paste.
3. Combine garlic paste with remaining yogurt in medium-size bowl until well blended. Add cucumber and chopped mint; mix well. Cover; refrigerate until well chilled. If soup seems too thick, thin with a little cold water to desired consistency. Serve in chilled soup bowls.

Chilled Fruit Soup

A traditional Scandinavian dish served as a first course or dessert.

Makes 6 servings.

1 quart cranberry juice	**1 three-inch stick**
cocktail	**cinnamon**
2 cups cold water	**1 pint strawberries,**
3/4 cup sugar	**hulled and halved**
3 tablespoons quick	**2 medium-size**
tapioca	**bananas, peeled**
Rind of 1 medium-size	**and sliced**
lemon	**diagonally**

1. Bring the cranberry juice and water to boiling in a large saucepan; lower the heat to simmer.
2. Stir in the sugar and tapioca. Add the lemon rind and cinnamon stick. Cover; simmer for 15 minutes or until thickened.

3. Remove the lemon rind and cinnamon stick. Cool the soup to lukewarm.
4. Stir in the strawberries and bananas. Refrigerate for 2 hours or until the soup is thoroughly chilled.
Note: Fresh raspberries and green grapes can be used in this recipe.

Cool Avocado Soup

Makes 8 servings (about 5 cups).

2 large ripe avocados	**cream**
1 tablespoon lemon	**1/2 cup buttermilk**
juice	**2 green onions, white**
2 cans (13³/4 ounces	**part only, sliced**
each) chicken	**1/4 teaspoon salt**
broth, chilled	**1 slice lemon for**
1/2 cup dairy sour	**garnish**

1. Peel and pit the avocados. Slice the avocados, reserving several very thin slices for garnish. Brush the reserved slices with 1/2 teaspoon lemon juice to prevent discoloration; cover, refrigerate.
2. Working in batches, combine the chicken broth, sour cream, buttermilk, green onion, avocado, the remaining lemon juice and salt in the container of an electric blender. Cover; whirl until smooth. Pour into a soup tureen. Refrigerate 15 minutes or until thoroughly chilled.
3. To serve, garnish with the reserved avocado slices and a lemon slice.

Buttermilk Shrimp Soup

Makes 6 servings.

1 quart buttermilk	**seeded and**
1 package (8 ounces)	**chopped**
frozen cooked	**6 radishes, sliced**
shrimp	**1 teaspoon salt**
1 cucumber, peeled	**1/4 teaspoon pepper**
and chopped	**1 tablespoon chopped**
(1¹/2 cups)	**fresh dill**
1/2 cup chopped green	**OR: 1 teaspoon**
onions	**dillweed**
1/2 green pepper,	

Combine all ingredients, except dill. Cover and refrigerate at least 12 hours. Add dill just before serving.

Bean and Sausage Soup

Makes 8 servings.

1 pound dried navy beans
8 cups water
1 bay leaf
1 large onion
1 whole clove
1¼ teaspoons salt
3 tablespoons butter or margarine
2 medium-size onions, minced (1 cup)
2 carrots, minced
1 cup minced celery
2 tablespoons tomato paste
4 cans (13¾ ounces each) beef broth
½ teaspoon pepper
½ cup broken thin spaghetti
3 frankfurters, thinly sliced
2 tablespoons minced fresh parsley
1 clove garlic, minced

1. Pick over beans; rinse under running water. Combine with water in a large kettle or Dutch oven. Add bay leaf, onion, clove and ¼ teaspoon of the salt. Bring to boiling; cover. Boil 2 minutes; remove from heat; let stand 1 hour.
2. Return to heat. Bring to boiling; lower heat. Simmer 2 hours or until beans are tender; drain.
3. Heat the butter in a large flameproof casserole or Dutch oven. Cook onions, carrots and celery over low heat until soft but not brown.
4. Add tomato paste, 3 cups of the cooked beans, broth, remaining 1 teaspoon salt and the pepper. Bring to boiling; lower heat. Simmer, covered, 40 minutes. Puree remaining beans; reserve.
5. Add the spaghetti to the soup; cook for 10 minutes or until spaghetti is tender.
6. Add the bean puree and frankfurters; heat through. Taste; add additional seasoning, if you wish.
7. Combine parsley and garlic and sprinkle over soup.

Black Bean Soup

Makes 8 servings.

1 pound dried black beans
Cold water
Ham rind and/or bone
OR: 2 to 3 ham hocks
1 onion, sliced
1 carrot, quartered
2 celery stalks, quartered
1 bay leaf
2 whole cloves
⅛ teaspoon mace
1½ teaspoons salt
Dash cayenne to taste
½ cup dry sherry
OR: 1 tablespoon vinegar
2 hard-cooked eggs, finely chopped
1 lemon, thinly sliced

1. Pick over the beans and wash well. Place in a bowl, add cold water to cover to a depth of 2 inches above the beans and soak overnight.
2. Next day, drain the beans and place in a kettle. Add 8 cups (2 quarts) fresh cold water.
3. Add ham rind, bone or ham hocks, if used, onion, carrot, celery, bay leaf, cloves, mace, salt and cayenne. Bring to boiling; cover and simmer 2½ hours or until the beans are tender.
4. Pass the vegetables and all but 2 cups of the cooked beans with all the liquid through a food mill or sieve. Return pureed mixture to the kettle.
5. Add remaining 2 cups whole beans and sherry or vinegar and bring to boiling. Serve in bowls or soup plates garnished with chopped egg atop lemon slices.

Goulash Soup with Potato Dumplings

A treasured main dish soup in Hungary. Potato Dumplings added at the last minute make a nice variation.

Makes 8 servings.

3 pounds pork shoulder or beef chuck, cut into ¾-inch cubes
1 tablespoon butter or margarine
1 large sweet Spanish onion, sliced (4 cups)
2 tablespoons paprika
1 can condensed beef broth
2 cups water
1 bay leaf
1 teaspoon caraway seeds, crushed
2 teaspoons salt
1 pound carrots, cut into ½-inch chunks
Potato Dumplings (recipe follows)
1 package (9 ounces) frozen cut green beans
Dairy sour cream
Fresh dill sprigs

1. Brown meat, a little at a time, in butter in heavy kettle or Dutch oven; remove pieces to a bowl as they brown. Sauté onion until golden in same pan, about 5 minutes. Add paprika; cook, stirring constantly, over low heat 1 minute. Return all meat to pan.
2. Stir in beef broth, water, bay leaf, caraway seeds and salt. Heat to boiling; lower heat; cover. Simmer 1½ hours; add carrots. Simmer 30 minutes longer or until meat and carrots are just tender.
3. Prepare Potato Dumplings; shape into about 1-inch balls with lightly floured hands.
4. Add beans to Goulash; heat to boiling; simmer 5 minutes. Drop dumplings into stew; cover and simmer 8 to 10 minutes. Serve in soup plates with a dollop of sour cream, a sprig of dill on each serving and warm crusty bread.

Potato Dumplings

Makes 8 servings.

¾ pound potatoes
1 egg
⅓ cup all-purpose flour
2 tablespoons packaged seasoned
bread crumbs
½ teaspoon salt
⅛ teaspoon pepper
1 tablespoon chopped fresh parsley

Pare potatoes; cook in boiling salted water until

(continued)

tender, about 20 minutes. Drain well. Mash or "rice" potatoes; beat in egg, flour, bread crumbs, salt, pepper and parsley until smooth.

Lentil Soup with Sausage

A delicious blend of flavors in a rich, main-dish soup.

Makes 7 cups.

1 cup dried lentils	chopped ($2/3$ cup)
1$1/2$ quarts water (6 cups)	1 pound fresh spinach, washed and trimmed
1 can (8 ounces) tomato sauce	OR: 1 package (10 ounces) frozen chopped spinach, partially thawed
$1/2$ pound sweet Italian sausage	2 teaspoons salt
1 tablespoon olive or vegetable oil	$1/4$ teaspoon pepper
1 large carrot, finely chopped ($1/2$ cup)	$1/4$ cup ditalini or other small pasta
1 large onion, finely chopped (1 cup)	Grated Parmesan cheese
2 celery stalks, finely	

1. Wash lentils and place in large saucepan with water and tomato sauce. Bring to boiling; lower heat; simmer as you continue preparing soup.
2. Remove casings from sausages; heat oil in large skillet; sauté sausage meat, breaking up with a wooden spoon.
3. Stir in chopped carrot, onion and celery; cook until tender-crisp, about 10 minutes.
4. While vegetables cook, coarsely chop spinach. If you are using frozen spinach, cut block into pieces.
5. Add spinach and meat-vegetable mixture to lentils. Stir in salt and pepper; simmer 30 minutes.
6. Add pasta and cook, covered, 10 minutes more or until lentils are tender. Serve hot with grated cheese.

Vegetable Ham Soup

Makes about 8 cups.

3 tablespoons butter or margarine	2 envelopes or teaspoons instant chicken broth
1 medium-size onion, chopped ($1/2$ cup)	2 cups diced potatoes (about 2 medium-size)
1 cup sliced carrots (2 to 3)	1$1/2$ cups julienne-cut cooked ham
1 cup chopped celery (2 stalks)	$1/2$ bunch watercress, cut up (2 cups)
6 cups water	Salt
1 ham bone	Pepper
6 sprigs parsley	
1 bay leaf	

1. Heat butter in kettle or Dutch oven. Sauté onion, carrots and celery until tender. Add water, ham bone, parsley, bay leaf and chicken broth. Bring to boiling; lower heat; cover. Simmer for 30 minutes.
2. Add potatoes and ham; continue to cook until

potatoes are tender, about 15 minutes. Remove bay leaf, parsley and ham bone. Skim fat.
3. Add watercress and cook only until stems are tender. Taste; add salt and pepper, if needed.

Italian Meatball and Escarole Soup

Serve this one-pot supper soup with crusty whole-wheat Italian bread and a salad of crunchy raw vegetables.

Makes 6 servings.

1 pound ground beef	2 tablespoons butter
1 egg	8 cups homemade or canned chicken broth
3 tablespoons water	
3 cloves garlic, minced	$3/4$ pound escarole, rinsed and chopped (about 12 cups)
2 tablespoons chopped fresh parsley	2 tablespoons lemon juice
1 teaspoon salt	Freshly grated Parmesan cheese
$1/4$ teaspoon pepper	
$1/2$ cup uncooked long-grain rice	

1. Combine the beef with the egg, water, 2 cloves garlic, parsley, salt and pepper in a medium-size bowl and blend thoroughly. Shape mixture into 32 small meatballs.
2. Sauté rice and remaining clove garlic in the butter in a large skillet, about 5 minutes or until golden.
3. Bring the broth to boiling in a kettle or Dutch oven.
4. Add meatballs and rice to boiling broth; lower heat; cover; simmer 15 minutes or until meatballs are cooked throughout. (Test one to check.)
5. Add escarole and lemon juice, recover and cook 5 minutes longer. Serve Parmesan cheese separately.

Soup Italiano

Makes 6 servings.

4 slices hard salami, cut into julienne strips	1 can (16 ounces) round bite-size ravioli in meat sauce
2 teaspoons butter or margarine	1 can condensed beef broth
1 cup shredded cabbage	1$1/4$ cups water
1 can (19 ounces) chunky vegetable soup	1 teaspoon Italian herb seasoning mix
1 can (20 ounces) chick-peas, drained	Grated Parmesan cheese

1. Brown salami in butter in a large saucepan. Stir in cabbage; cook 1 minute. Add soup, chick-peas, ravioli, broth, water and Italian seasoning. Heat slowly to boiling; lower heat; simmer 2 minutes.
2. Ladle into large heated soup bowls and sprinkle with Parmesan cheese. Top with croutons, if you wish.

20 Good-for-You Snacks

150 CALORIES OR FEWER

Celery (3 stalks) 10
Broccoli, raw (3 stalks) 96
Carrot, raw 30
Peach, raw 40
Graham cracker (1 whole) 50
Orange juice ($^1/_2$ cup) 55
Cantaloupe (half) 60
Bread, whole wheat (1 slice) 65
Apple 80
Egg (1 boiled) 80
Cottage cheese, 1% fat ($^1/_2$ cup) 80
Peanuts (2 Tbs.) 105
Cheese, Cheddar (1 oz.) 115
Muffin 120
Milk, lowfat (1 cup) 125
Tuna, in water ($^1/_2$ cup) 130
Turkey, white meat (3 oz.) 135
Potato, baked 140
Yogurt, plain (8 oz.) 140
Chicken breast, broiled ($^1/_2$ breast) 150

Popcorn   A wholesome snack food, popcorn is a variety of edible corn. Popcorn kernels are pointed or round with a high proportion of endosperm borne on small cobs or ears. When a kernel of popcorn is exposed to heat, the moisture inside the kernel explodes or expands, producing a mass of starch turned inside out. Yellow and white varieties of popcorn are marketed.

Although oil is often used to pop corn, it is not necessary. Some electric corn poppers use hot air to pop popcorn.

A cup of popped popcorn is only 25 calories. If popped in oil, it is 40 calories. If melted butter or margarine is tossed with the popcorn, the calories can easily double depending on how much is added. In contrast, an ounce of potato chips, which is about a handful or thirteen 2-inch chips, contains 150 calories.

How to Pop Corn

• You'll need a large, heavy skillet or saucepan with a lid. Of, if you own an electric corn popper, follow the manufacturer's directions.
• Use 2 tablespoons of vegetable oil to pop $^1/_3$ cup of corn. That will be enough to cover the bottom of a large skillet and leave plenty of room for the exploding kernels.
• Heat the oil, then drop in a kernel or two to test the popping heat.
• If skillet is hot enough, add corn; cover. Shake skillet over medium heat until popping has almost

ceased. Then take skillet off heat and let stand a few minutes. The yield will be about 4 cups (1 quart) of popped corn.

Homemade Yogurt

Use a homemade, or store-bought, yogurt as a starter.

Makes 4 cups.

1 quart skim milk or reconstituted nonfat dry milk solids	**$^1/_4$ cup instant nonfat dry milk** **3 tablespoons yogurt**

1. Combine the liquid milk with the nonfat dry milk and heat the mixture in a heavy saucepan or in the top of a double boiler until mixture registers 180° on a thermometer.
2. Let milk mixture cool to 113°.
3. Remove scum; mix a little of the warm milk with the yogurt and then stir into the bulk of the milk mixture; mix well. Pour the milk mixture into a very clean, warmed thermos and set aside undisturbed for about 5 hours.
4. It is important that the mixture is not disturbed, otherwise the whey tends to settle out from the curd. An average batch should be thickened in five hours and it should then be refrigerated several hours to thicken further.

Homemade Granola Crunch

Bake at 300° for 1 hour.

Makes 9 cups.

4 cups old-fashioned oats (11 ounces) **1 cup flaked coconut (about 2 ounces)** **1 cup coarsely chopped pecans (4 ounces)** **$^1/_2$ cup unsalted sunflower seeds (2$^1/_2$ ounces)** **$^1/_2$ cup wheat germ (about 2 ounces)** **$^1/_2$ cup firmly packed**	**light brown sugar** **1 teaspoon ground cinnamon** **1 teaspoon salt** **$^1/_2$ cup vegetable oil** **$^1/_2$ cup water** **2 tablespoons honey** **1 teaspoon vanilla** **1 cup raisins** **1 cup coarsely chopped dates (about 5 ounces)**

1. Preheat the oven to slow (300°). Lightly grease a 15$^1/_2$ x 10$^1/_2$ x1-inch jelly-roll pan.
2. Combine the oats, coconut, pecans, sunflower seeds, wheat germ, sugar, cinnamon and salt in a large bowl.
3. Stir together the oil, water, honey and vanilla in a small bowl. Pour over the oat mixture; mix well. Spread the mixture evenly in the prepared jelly-roll pan.
4. Bake in the preheated slow oven (300°) for 1 hour,

(continued)

stirring every 15 minutes, until the mixture is golden brown and slightly crunchy. Cool in the pan on a wire rack. Stir in the raisins and dates. Store in an airtight container.

Croque Monsieur

Makes 4 servings.

8 slices firm white bread, one to two days old
6 tablespoons butter or margarine, softened
12 thin slices cooked ham
4 thin slices Swiss, Gruyère or Muenster cheese
1 tablespoon flour
1/2 teaspoon salt
1/8 teaspoon pepper
Dash paprika or cayenne
1 cup light cream or milk
2 ounces Swiss cheese, shredded (1/2 cup)
3 large eggs
3 tablespoons milk

1. Trim crusts from bread. Spread one side of 4 of the slices with 2 tablespoons of the butter. Top with 2 slices ham, 1 slice cheese and 1 slice ham. Cover with remaining bread slices.
2. Melt 1 tablespoon butter in a medium-size saucepan; blend in flour, salt, pepper and paprika. Slowly stir in cream. Cook, stirring constantly, until thickened and bubbly. Add cheese and cook until melted. Keep warm over low heat.
3. Beat eggs and milk together in a small bowl just until blended. Pour mixture into a pie plate. Dip sandwiches on both sides.
4. Melt the remaining 3 tablespoons butter in a large skillet. Sauté sandwiches, turning once, until golden brown. Add more butter, if needed. Serve with cheese sauce spooned over.

Jumbo Stack Braunschweiger Sandwich

Makes 6 sandwiches.

6 large slices Italian or rye bread, toasted, if desired
Dill Mustard Sauce (recipe follows)
Lettuce leaves
12 slices liver sausage
or Braunschweiger (about 1 pound)
12 thin tomato slices
12 thin cucumber slices
12 thin onion slices

Spread bread or toast with Dill Mustard Sauce. Top one bread slice with lettuce and overlapping slices of liver sausage, tomato, cucumber and onion, using 2 slices of each for each sandwich. Serve open-face.

Dill Mustard Sauce

Makes 1 cup.

1/3 cup dairy sour cream
1/3 cup mayonnaise or salad dressing
3 tablespoons prepared mustard
3 tablespoons chopped dill pickle

Combine ingredients in small bowl.

Sausage-Egg Pita

Makes 4 servings.

1 package (8 ounces) brown-and-serve sausage links, thinly sliced
4 eggs
1/2 cup dairy sour cream
1 tablespoon chopped chives
1/8 teaspoon pepper
2 tablespoons butter or margarine
2 large pita breads, halved crosswise

1. Cook sausage slices in large skillet over medium heat until lightly browned, stirring frequently. Remove from heat; drain sausage slices on paper toweling.
2. Combine eggs, sour cream, chives and pepper in large bowl. Stir in sausages.
3. Melt butter in same skillet. Add sausage-egg mixture and cook just until firm, yet moist, stirring gently with pancake turner.
4. Spoon into pita bread pockets. Serve with sliced cherry tomatoes, if you wish.

Bacon-Spinach Junior Club Sandwiches

The flavor of this sandwich is reminiscent of the popular sweet-sour spinach salad with chopped egg and bacon bits. Called a "junior club," it consists of two bread slices rather than the usual three.

Makes 4 servings.

12 bacon slices
4 eggs
1 medium-size onion, finely chopped (1/2 cup)
1/2 cup mayonnaise
2 tablespoons red wine vinegar
1 tablespoon sugar
1/2 teaspoon salt
Dash pepper
8 slices firm white bread, toasted
Spinach leaves
12 cherry tomatoes

Fry bacon until crisp in large skillet; drain on paper toweling. Remove all but about 1/4 cup drippings from pan. Break eggs, 1 at a time, into hot drippings; fry until firm, breaking yolks with a pancake turner, and turning them over. Transfer to warm platter. Remove and discard all but 1 tablespoon of the drippings from pan.
2. Cook onion in remaining drippings until tender. Remove from heat. Stir in mayonnaise, vinegar, sugar, salt and pepper.

Super Cheese Hero.

3. Spread mayonnaise mixture on each slice of toast. Cover four slices with a layer of spinach leaves, 3 slices bacon, a fried egg and top with more spinach leaves. Cover with remaining slices of toast, mayonnaise-coated-side down. With serrated knife, cut sandwiches into 4 triangles.

4. Alternately spear triangles with cherry tomatoes on 8-inch skewers. Serve on platter garnished with a tomato flower and green onion brushes, if you wish. To make flower garnish, take 2 cherry tomatoes; cut one not quite through into 4 wedges, the other into 6 wedges. Remove pulp. Place the 6-petaled tomato inside the 4-petaled tomato. Cut a 1/2-inch piece of white green onion at the end into crisscross slashes. Spread end out and place in center of tomato flower. For green onion brushes, use 5-inch onions and cut green part into lengthwise shreds about 1 inch long.

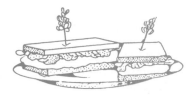

Super Cheese Hero

Makes 1 sandwich.

1/2 **small red pepper, seeded and cut into strips**
1/2 **small green pepper, seeded and cut into strips**
2 teaspoons olive oil
1/8 **teaspoon crushed red pepper**
1/8 **teaspoon leaf basil, crumbled**
1/8 **teaspoon leaf oregano, crumbled**
1 French roll or hero roll
4 thin slices mozzarella cheese
5 flat anchovy fillets

1. Sauté red and green pepper strips in oil in a small skillet until crisp-tender. Sprinkle with red pepper, basil and oregano. Remove from heat.

2. Cut thin slice from the top of roll; scoop out center of roll. Place roll on rack over broiler pan. Broil 4 inches from broiler until lightly browned.

3. Spoon pepper mixture into shell. Top with mozzarella. Broil just to melt cheese. Crisscross anchovy fillets over cheese. Cover filling with top of roll.

Meatball Hero Sandwiches.

Meatball Hero Sandwiches

Bake at 325° for 10 minutes

Makes 9 servings.

9 individual hero rolls	halved, seeded and sliced
1½ pounds ground round	1 red pepper, halved, seeded and sliced
1 egg slightly beaten	1 medium-size onion, sliced
1 tablespoon instant minced onion	1 tablespoon flour
1½ teaspoon salt	¼ cup chili sauce
¼ teaspoon pepper	½ cup water
¼ cup milk	1½ teaspoons light brown sugar
2 tablespoons vegetable oil	½ teaspoon dry mustard
1 green pepper,	

1. Cut a thin slice from the top of each roll; scoop out. Crumble enough insides to make 1¼ cups; reserve. Cover rolls to keep from drying.
2. Combine beef, egg, onion, salt, pepper, milk and the reserved bread crumbs in a medium-size bowl; mix well; shape into 2-inch balls (You should have about 27.)
3. Brown, part at a time, in 1 tablespoon of the oil in a large skillet; remove to a large bowl.

4. Add remaining oil; sauté green and red pepper and onion until tender. Remove to bowl.
5. Stir flour into fat remaining in skillet; heat just until bubbly. Stir in chili sauce and water. Cook, stirring constantly, until sauce thickens and bubbles. Stir in light brown sugar and dry mustard.
6. Add meatball-pepper mixture; cover; simmer 20 minutes.
7. Place rolls on a cookie sheet. Heat in a slow oven (325°) for 10 minutes. Spoon in meatballs and sauce.

Curried Egg Salad Sandwiches

Makes 4 sandwiches.

4 hard-cooked eggs, coarsely chopped	8 slices whole wheat bread
⅓ cup mayonnaise	Softened butter or margarine
1½ teaspoons curry powder	Cucumber slices
¼ teaspoon salt	Boston lettuce

1. Combine eggs, mayonnaise, curry powder and salt in a medium-size bowl; mix thoroughly.
2. Spread all bread slices with butter. Divide the curried egg salad equally among 4 of the slices; top each with thin cucumber slices and crisp lettuce. Place remaining bread on top.

The Reuben

Makes 6 servings.

12 slices pumpernickel or rye bread
1/2 cup bottled Russian or Thousand Island dressing
1/2 pound thinly sliced corned beef
12 thin slices Swiss cheese
1 cup drained sauerkraut
2 tablespoons Dijon mustard
Softened butter or margarine

1. Spread 6 of the bread slices with Russian dressing. Divide corned beef evenly among the slices. Top each with 2 slices of cheese and about 2 tablespoons sauerkraut.
2. Spread remaining bread slices with mustard, and press, mustard-side down, over sandwiches.
3. Spread outside surfaces with butter. Broil or grill sandwiches slowly until cheese melts and bread browns on both sides.

Swiss and Sprout Sandwich

Makes 1 sandwich.

Butter
2 slices pumpernickel bread
2 slices Swiss cheese
Spinach leaves
3 thin slices tomato
Red onion rings
1/2 cup alfalfa sprouts
Mayonnaise

1. Butter bread slices. On one slice, layer cheese, spinach, tomato slices and onion rings.
2. Combine sprouts with enough mayonnaise to moisten. Spoon over sandwich. Top with remaining bread slice.

Tacos

Makes 12 tacos.

1 medium-size onion, chopped (1/2 cup)
1 clove garlic, crushed
2 tablespoons vegetable oil
1 pound ground beef
1 large tomato, peeled and chopped (1 cup)
1 teaspoon leaf oregano, crumbled
1 teaspoon salt
1/8 teaspoon pepper
Vegetable oil for frying
12 corn tortillas
1 small head lettuce, shredded (about 2 cups)
8 ounces Cheddar cheese, shredded (about 2 cups)
3 medium-size tomatoes, peeled and chopped
Red Hot Chile Sauce *(recipe follows)*

1. Sauté onion and garlic in the 2 tablespoons oil until soft in a large skillet, about 5 minutes; add ground beef; cook until brown. Add tomato, oregano, salt and pepper; cook, stirring frequently, 10 minutes or until heated through and thick.
2. To make taco shells: Heat about 1/2 inch of oil in a large skillet to 370° on deep-fat frying thermometer. Drop tortillas into oil, 1 at a time. Using 2 forks, fold tortilla in half. Hold tortilla folded with tines of fork. Fry until tortilla holds its shape and is lightly browned and crisp, about 3 minutes. Drain on paper toweling.
3. To serve: Stuff 3 tablespoons beef filling, some shredded lettuce, shredded cheese and chopped tomatoes into each taco shell. Add a few teaspoonfuls of Red Hot Chile Sauce and garnish with onion rings, if you wish.

Red Hot Chile Sauce

Makes 2 1/2 cups.

2 large tomatoes, peeled and chopped (2 cups)
1 medium-size onion, chopped (1/2 cup)
1 hot green chile (from a 4-ounce can), seeded and chopped
2 tablespoons vegetable oil
1/4 cup lemon juice
1 teaspoon salt
1/4 teaspoon leaf oregano, crumbled
1/8 teaspoon pepper

Combine all ingredients in a medium-size bowl. Store in refrigerator until serving time.

The New York "Deli" Special

Makes 4 servings.

3 tablespoons butter or margarine, softened
1 tablespoon prepared horseradish-mustard
8 small brown-and-serve sourdough rolls
2 packages (3 ounces each) sliced corned beef
2 packages (3 ounces each) sliced pastrami
1 package (6 ounces) sliced Swiss cheese, cut into quarters

1. Combine butter and horseradish-mustard in a small bowl. Cut rolls almost in half, but do not separate. Spread mustard butter on cut rolls; close and press down tops. Place on large cookie sheet.
2. Remove corned beef and pastrami from original packaging. Tear off 2 large pieces of aluminum foil. Place meats in foil; close securely; place on cookie sheet with rolls.
3. Bake rolls following label directions, heating meat at same time and temperature.
4. To assemble: Place 2 strips of Swiss cheese on bottom halves of rolls; divide corned beef on 4 rolls, pastrami on remaining rolls. Press down tops of rolls. Serve 2 sandwiches, 1 corned beef and 1 pastrami per serving, with heated pinto beans and sour pickles, if you wish.

Tomato-Avocado Sandwiches

Makes 6 sandwiches.

4 medium-size tomatoes	1 small ripe avocado
1/4 cup vegetable oil	2 tablespoons lemon juice
2 tablespoons wine vinegar	6 pita breads
1/2 teaspoon salt	1 container (8 ounces) whipped cream cheese
1/4 teaspoon pepper	
1/2 teaspoon leaf tarragon, crumbled	1 red onion, sliced

1. Core tomatoes; cut into thin slices; place in shallow dish. Combine oil, vinegar, salt, pepper and tarragon; pour over tomatoes. Cover. Chill 1 hour.
2. Peel, halve, pit and cut avocado into 12 slices; place in shallow dish. Toss with lemon juice.
3. To assemble: Heat pita bread on a cookie sheet in a very slow oven (250°) for 10 minutes; cut each in half horizontally to make 12 pockets. Spread cream cheese generously inside each pocket. Place tomato slices, avocado and red onion in each half; spoon on additional dressing.

Grilled Open-Face Club Sandwich

Broil for 2 to 3 minutes

Makes 4 servings.

1/4 cup (1/2 stick) unsalted butter, softened	deli roast beef
	1 large ripe tomato, cut into 8 slices
1 tablespoon drained bottled horseradish	8 slices cooked bacon OR: 1/4 cup real bacon bits
2 teaspoons Dijon-style mustard	
8 slices rye bread, lightly toasted	1/2 cup shredded Swiss cheese (2 ounces)
1/2 pound thinly sliced	

1. Adjust the oven rack 6 inches from the broiling element, if using a conventional oven. Preheat the broiler; preheating a toaster oven is not necessary.
2. Combine butter, horseradish and mustard in a small bowl; blend well. Spread evenly on one side of each bread slice.
3. Place the roast beef over the mustard-coated side of each bread slice, dividing equally. Top each with 1 slice of the tomato and 1 slice of the bacon.

Tomato-Avocado Sandwiches.

4. Place 4 of the bread slices on top of the other 4 slices, making 4 open-face double-decker sandwiches.

5. Sprinkle the shredded cheese over the top of each sandwich, dividing equally. Place the sandwiches on the broiler or toaster oven pan.

6. Broil the sandwiches in the oven or toaster oven for 2 to 3 minutes or until the cheese is melted.

Cream Cheese-Date-Nut Sandwich

Makes 1 serving.

1 tablespoon honey	1/4 cup chopped
1 package (3 ounces) cream cheese, softened	walnuts
	2 slices raisin bread
	2 red apple wedges
1/3 cup chopped pitted dates	Mint for garnish *(optional)*

1. Beat honey into cream cheese in a small bowl. Stir in dates and nuts.

2. Spread thickly on 1 bread slice. Top with other bread slice. Cut sandwich into 3 strips. Serve with apple wedges. Garnish with mint, if you wish.

Pepper and Steak Sandwich

Makes 4 sandwiches.

4 round crusty rolls with poppy seeds	strips
	1 small red pepper, halved, seeded and cut into julienne strips
1/4 cup (1/2 stick) butter or margarine, softened	
	1/4 cup vegetable oil
1/2 teaspoon leaf basil, crumbled	2 tablespoons butter or margarine
1/2 teaspoon leaf oregano, crumbled	4 minute or cubed steaks (about 1 1/4 pounds)
1 medium-size onion, thinly sliced	
1 small green pepper, halved, seeded and cut into julienne	1 tablespoon red wine vinegar
	Salt and pepper

1. Cut rolls in half. Combine softened butter with basil and oregano. Spread on each cut half of roll. Place rolls on broiler pan. Broil 4 inches from heat just until lightly browned. Remove; keep warm.

2. Sauté onion, green and red peppers in oil in a large skillet until tender, about 5 minutes. Remove with slotted spoon to platter. Keep warm.

3. Add remaining 2 tablespoons butter to skillet. Sauté steaks on both sides to desired doneness. Remove to platter; keep warm.

4. Add vinegar to pan drippings in skillet. Scrape up brown bits. Cook just until bubbly, but not evaporated. Remove from heat immediately.

5. To assemble: Place a steak on bottom half of roll; top with onion-pepper mixture. Drizzle over some pan juices. Salt and pepper to taste. Cover with top half of roll.

Giant Club Sandwich

Makes 6 servings

1 oval or round 9-inch loaf whole-wheat bread	salad from deli
	1/2 pound thinly sliced Swiss cheese
1/2 cup mayonnaise	2 ripe tomatoes, thinly sliced
1 small head Boston lettuce, separated into leaves	
	1/2 pound thinly sliced baked ham
1/2 pound chicken	

1. Cut loaf horizontally with serrated knife into 4 equal slices. Spread bottom slice with one-third of mayonnaise. Cover with some lettuce; spread with chicken salad.

2. Layer remaining ingredients in following order: second slice of bread spread with one-third of mayonnaise, cheese, lettuce, third slice of bread spread with remaining mayonnaise, tomato, ham, lettuce and top of loaf.

3. Cut into 6 equal slices.

The California Rage

Makes 4 sandwiches.

1/4 cup (1/2 stick) butter or margarine	mayonnaise or salad dressing
1 large onion, thinly sliced	Chicory or iceberg lettuce
4 eggs	1 package (6 ounces) sliced American cheese rounds
8 slices pumpernickel or whole-wheat bread	
1/4 to 1/3 cup	1/2 pound sliced roast beef

1. Melt butter in a large skillet; add onion slices; stir to coat. Cover; lower heat; simmer 20 minutes or just until slices begin to brown. Make 4 indentations in onion mixture. Break eggs, 1 at a time, in a cup and slip into each indentation. Fry eggs to the desired firmness.

2. Meanwhile, spread each of the bread slices with mayonnaise. On 4 slices of the bread add in order: lettuce, 2 cheese rounds, 1/4 of the roast beef, sprinkled lightly with salt and pepper, and 1 fried egg with some of the onions. Top with remaining bread slices, mayonnaise-side down.

VEGETABLES

Vegetable   The word covers a broad range of edible plants, roots and herbs. Vegetables are eaten raw or cooked. Tomatoes, squash, beans, peas and eggplant, though actually fruit botanically, are used as vegetables. In culinary terms, fruits cooked in a savory manner are considered to be vegetables; fruits cooked in a sweet way are desserts. (See also specific vegetables.)

Many vegetables, once grown in other countries, are becoming increasingly available--among them are: chayote, a pear-shaped squash; bitter melon, a warty, 6-inch squash; winter melon, which looks like a watermelon, but its flesh is white and must be cooked. Jicama is a brown, turnip-like root that can be eaten raw or cooked. Spaghetti squash and Jerusalem artichokes are becoming staples in some stores. Serve these unusual vegetables to add variety to everyday meals.

Basic Rules for Cooking Vegetables

• Never overcook vegetables. Vegetables taste and look best and retain their nutrients when they are cooked "tender-crisp"--barely tender, with a slightly crunchy texture.

• Use a small amount of cooking liquid--or simply butter-steam vegetables. Too much water cooks out many of the vitamins and minerals. Invest in a steaming basket; they're inexpensive, easy to use and help retain nutrients.

• Think of vegetables as replacements for other foods. Instead of nutritionally empty, calorie-laden snacks, keep pre-cut raw vegetables in water in the refrigerator. Instead of a second starch in a meal, serve a vegetable; and instead of meat, serve a vegetable main dish occasionally.

Vegetable Preparation

• **Don't overcook!** Vegetables should be cooked only until tender.

• **Boil:** Use a small amount of water, cover with a tight-fitting lid and cook over low heat to minimize loss of vitamins and minerals. Cook until tender.

• **Blanch:** Bring plenty of water to a rolling boil, immerse vegetables and bring water back to a boil for 2 to 4 minutes. Refresh vegetables under icy cold water and use in salads.

• **Steam:** Place a steaming basket, colander or bamboo steamer over 1 1/2 to 2 inches of boiling water, then place prepared vegetables on the rack. Cover the pan, reduce the heat but keep the water boiling and cook until just tender.

• **Stir-Fry:** Place the wok or wide skillet over high heat; when hot, add salad oil and cut-up vegetables.

Pictured opposite:
Stuffed Vegetables, page 755.

Cook uncovered, stirring constantly, just until the vegetables have been lightly coated and slightly cooked (approximately 1 to 2 minutes). Add approximately 1/4 cup of broth to 4 cups of vegetables; then cover and cook, stirring occasionally, until tender. Add more broth if necessary.

• **Microwave:** Cook all vegetables on 100% high power, following the manufacturer's directions. Cover the cooking dish with a casserole lid or heavy-duty plastic wrap. Cooking time depends on the freshness, moisture content and maturity of the vegetable. Remove the vegetables form the microwave after the shortest recommended time, let stand and test for doneness. If the vegetables are still too crisp, microwave further in one-minute segments.

• **Sauté :** Melt butter, margarine or oil in a large skillet. Try a combination of butter and corn oil or olive oil and corn oil. (Butter and olive oil impart flavor, and corn oil allows for cooking over high heat.) Add the prepared vegetables and cook, stirring constantly, until the vegetables are coated lightly, then cover, reduce the heat and cook just until tender.

• **Bake:** Prepare and cut vegetables into thick slices, arrange in a single layer in a baking pan or casserole or place on foil. Dot with butter or oil and bake uncovered until tender.

Try tucking vegetables (*e.g.,* onions, squash and any of the root vegetables) in with the roast and increase the cooking time accordingly.

• **Testing for Doneness:** Cooking time depends on the freshness or maturity of the vegetables. They should be cooked until just tender, that is, until they give slightly, but remain firm when pierced. The color of the vegetable becomes intense when it is cooked until just tender.

• **Serving Suggestions:** Season vegetables after they have been cooked; do not salt the water first.

Snip fresh garden herbs over vegetables before serving or sprinkle with fresh lemon or lime juice.

Vegetable Leftovers   Use up leftovers: Toss steamed, boiled or blanched vegetables into salads. Puree leftover vegetables and add to a chilled cream soup.

VEGETABLE KNOW-HOW

Here's the nutrition lowdown on some of the most popular vegetables, with cooking tips to preserve maximum flavor, color and nutrients.

Asparagus: Iron and vitamins A and C; 11 calories per 1/2 cup. *Steam in a covered skillet over medium heat, 5-10 minutes until asparagus bends slightly.*
Beans (green and yellow): Vitamin A; 15 calories per 1/2 cup. *Steam or stir-fry until crisp-tender.*

(continued)

Beets: Vitamins A and C; 40 calories per ½ cup. *Microwave; grill; steam or serve raw. Wash first; leave nutrient-packed skin intact.*

Bok Choy: Vitamin C and calcium; 15 calories per ½ cup. *Stir-fry; sauté; or serve raw. Separate leaves from stem; cook separately.*

Broccoli: Vitamins A and C, calcium, fiber; 32 calories per stalk. *Blanch to crisp-tender stage; microwave; steam; or stir-fry.*

Carrots: Vitamin A; 50 calories per cup, sliced. *Steam; stir-fry; microwave.*

Cauliflower: Vitamin C and iron; 27 calories per cup. *Microwave; steam; stir-fry.*

Cucumbers: Some vitamins and minerals; 25 calories each. *Scrub skin or peel if waxed.*

Lettuce: Darker leaves contain vitamins A,C, and E; about 15 calories a head. *Best served raw.*

Mushrooms: Trace vitamins and minerals; 20 calories per cup. *Best served raw. May be sautéed.*

Onions: Some vitamin C; 40 calories per dry-skinned onion; 9 calories per green onion. *Cook chopped onion, covered, to mellow flavor.*

Peas: Protein, iron, vitamins A and C; snow peas: 40 calories per ½ cup; garden peas: 60 calories. *Stir-fry snow peas or blanch in boiling water 1 minute; hold blanched peas under cold running water to stop cooking process. Steam fresh peas.*

Peppers (sweet): Vitamins A and C, phosphorus, iron; one contains 15 calories. *Best raw, unpeeled.*

Potatoes: Vitamins, C,B_1, iron, protein; average-size potato contains approx. 90 calories. *Best to cook (and serve) potatoes in skin.*

Spinach: Vitamins A and C, iron, calcium; 14 calories per cup. *Cook briefly in non-aluminum pan to retain color.*

Zucchini: Vitamins A and C; 14 calories per ½ cup. *Serve raw, unpeeled.*

Fresh Fruit and Vegetable Availability

The following fruits and vegetables, thanks to refrigeration and efficient transportation, are usually available all year:

Apples	Cucumbers	Parsnips
Artichokes	Eggplant	Pears
Avocadoes	Escarole	Peas, green
Bananas	Garlic	Peppers, sweet
Beans, green	Grapefruit	Pineapples
Beets	Grapes	Plantains
Broccoli	Greens	Potatoes
Brussels sprouts	Lemons	Radishes
	Lettuce	Spinach
Cabbage	Limes	Squash
Carrots	Mushrooms	Strawberries
Cauliflower	Onions	Sweet Potatoes
Celery	Onions, green	Tomatoes
Chinese cabbage	Oranges	Turnips-rutabagas
	Papayas	
Coconuts	Parsley and herbs	
Corn, sweet		

The following are widely available in the markets during the months indicated:

Apricots—June to August
Asparagus—March to July
Blueberries—June to August
Cantaloupes—April to October
Cherries—May to August
Cranberries—September to December
Honeydews—February to October
Mangoes—March to August
Nectarines—January and February, June to September
Okra—April to November
Peaches—May to September
Persimmons—October to February
Plums and Prunes—June to October
Pomegranates—September to December
Pumpkins—September to December
Tangelos—October to February
Tangerines—November to March
Watermelons—April to September

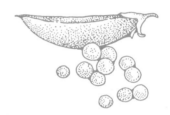

Refrigerating Fresh Fruits and Vegetables

Fruits and vegetables may be stored in the refrigerator for several days. The longer they are refrigerated the greater the vitamin loss, so it is best to eat them as soon after purchase as possible.

Asparagus, broccoli, cabbage, cauliflower, celery, cucumbers, green beans, green onions, green and red peppers, radishes, and greens (kale, spinach, turnip greens, chard and salad greens) should be promptly refrigerated in a covered container, moisture-proof bag or a vegetable crisper.

Apples,apricots, berries, cherries, corn (in husks), grapes, nectarines, peaches, pears, peas (in shell) and plums should be refrigerated loosely covered or in a plastic produce bag with air holes.

The Winter Produce Stall

Besides the year-round favorites (such as bananas, cabbage, carrots, celery, onions, lettuce, sweet red and green peppers and potatoes), winter features an abundance of apples, pears, avocados, grapes, citrus fruits, broccoli, cauliflower, Brussels sprouts, peas, spinach, winter squash and sweet potatoes.

THE ROOTS REVISITED
Don't ignore the earthy goodness of the following root vegetables.

Beets: Cook without trimming the stems or roots too closely, or they'll "bleed." Prepare vitamin A-rich tops as you would spinach. Serve hot sliced beets in an orange glaze, spiced with cloves.

Carrots: Add to soups and stews. Scrub very well; peeling is not necessary. Toss grated carrots with lemon juice, sherry, raisins and chopped nuts. Cut carrots into 2-inch chunks; boil until barely tender. Drain well and roll in orange-mint butter, then in dry bread crumbs; bake.

Parsnips: Parsnips are sweeter after prolonged exposure to cold temperatures; that's why they're best during the winter months. Steam them to bring out their rich nutty flavor. Toss diced cooked parsnips with a thin white sauce; sprinkle with crisp bacon bits and chopped parsley.

Radishes: Serve crisp radishes with butter, coarse salt, pumpernickel bread and icy cold beer.

Rutabagas and turnips: Rutabagas, also called Swedes or Swedish turnips, are golden and larger than white turnips. Rutabaga tops, unlike turnip tops, are not eaten as a separate vegetable. Add a teaspoonful of sugar to the cooking water to improve the mild flavor and sweetness. Mix mashed cooked rutabaga with applesauce. Toss diced cooked turnip with heavy cream and grated Parmesan cheese.

Salsify: Similar in appearance to parsnips, but with grass-like tops, salsify is also called oyster plant. Serve gratinée, with minced chives or shallots. Or mash until creamy; season with butter, salt and pepper.

Celeriac: Also known as celery root. Peel before cooking, adding vinegar to the water. Marinate raw celeriac in a vinaigrette dressing and serve over sliced tomatoes.

Stuffed Vegetables

Bake at 350° for 30 minutes.

Makes 6 servings.

6 medium-size zucchini, halved lengthwise OR: 6 medium-size ripe tomatoes, scooped and drained OR: 1 large eggplant (2¹/₂ to 3 pounds), hollowed out leaving a ¹/₂ -inch shell	¹/₂ **pound hot Italian sausages** 1 small onion, chopped (¹/₄ cup) 1 clove garlic, crushed ¹/₃ cup packaged seasoned bread crumbs ¹/₄ cup grated Parmesan cheese 4 ounces mozzarella cheese, shredded

1. Cook zucchini in boiling salted water in a large skillet for 10 minutes. Drain; scoop out insides, leaving a ¹/₄ -inch shell. Mash insides; drain. Put shells in a shallow baking dish.
2. Remove casings from sausages; break up meat. Cook sausage meat in same skillet 5 minutes. Add onion and garlic; sauté until tender, 3 minutes. Stir in mashed zucchini and bread crumbs. Spoon mixture into shells; sprinkle with cheeses.
3. Bake in a moderate oven (350°) for 30 minutes or until piping-hot.

Lamb-stuffed Acorn Squash

Bake at 375° for 1 hour.

Makes 4 servings.

2 small acorn squash (2 pounds) halved and seeded 1 pound ground lamb 1 medium-size onion, chopped (¹/₂ cup) 2 tablespoons vegetable oil 1 teaspoon mint flakes, crumbled ¹/₄ teaspoon gound cinnamon ³/₄ teaspoon salt	¹/₄ **teaspoon pepper** 2 tablespoons chopped parsley 2 tablespoons dried currants 2 teaspoons vinegar 1 cup frozen mixed vegetables 1 can (8 ounces) tomato sauce 2 tablespoons pine nuts

1. Place squash, cut sides down, in shallow baking pan; add ¹/₂ inch water.
2. Bake in a moderate oven (375°) for 30 minutes; turn cut sides up; bake 10 more minutes.
3. Prepare filling while squash bakes. Sauté lamb and onion in oil in large skillet; stir in remaining ingredients. Cook over low heat 5 minutes to blend flavors.
4. Mound ¹/₂ cup filling in each squash half. (Any extra filling may be wrapped in a foil packet and baked along with squash or frozen.)
5. Bake squash 20 minutes longer or just until heated through.

Artichokes with Mustard Sauce

Makes 6 servings.

6 medium-size artichokes 1 teaspoon salt 1 tablespoon vegetable oil 1 small clove garlic, crushed 3 tablespoons butter or margarine 3 tablespoons	flour 1 tablespoon prepared mustard 1 envelope or teaspoon instant chicken broth 1¹/₂ cups water 1 tablespoon lemon juice

1. Wash artichokes in cold water; cut 1 inch off top,

(continued)

straight across. Cut off stem 1 inch from base. With scissors cut off thorny tip of each leaf.

2. Place artichokes standing upright in a single layer in a large kettle; fill kettle to a depth of 1 inch with boiling water; add 1/2 teaspoon of the salt and oil to water. Cover; simmer 35 to 40 minutes, or until leaves pull out easily and base of artichoke can be easily pierced with a fork. Drain upside down on wire rack.

3. Sauté garlic in butter 1 minute; stir in flour; cook, stirring constantly, just until bubbly; stir in mustard, instant chicken broth, and the remaining 1/2 teaspoon salt until well blended. Stir in water; cook, stirring constantly, until sauce thickens and bubbles 1 minute; stir in lemon juice.

4. To eat artichokes, pull off leaves, one at a time, dip base in sauce, then scrape off its tender flesh with teeth; remove and discard fuzzy choke; cut the artichoke bottom with a knife and dip into sauce.

Marinated Vegetables

To preserve the brightness of the vegetables, prepare no more than a day ahead.

Makes 10 servings.

2 pounds fresh green beans
OR: **2 packages (10 ounces each) frozen whole green beans**
2 cups cooked fresh corn (2 medium-size corn on cob)
OR: **1 package (10 ounces) frozen kernel corn, thawed**
1 package (10 ounces) frozen peas, thawed
1 cup thinly sliced celery (2 large stalks)
1 medium-size onion, chopped (1/2 cup)
1 sweet green pepper, halved seeded and diced
1 jar (4 ounces) pimiento, sliced
3/4 cup distilled white vinegar
3/4 cup vegetable oil
2 tablespoons water
1 teaspoon salt
1/2 teaspoon pepper
1/2 teaspoon paprika

1. Cook the fresh beans in boiling salted water to cover in a large pot for 7 minutes or until crisp-tender. Or, cook the frozen beans following the label directions. Drain. Rinse under cold water. Cut into 2-inch lengths.

2. Combine the beans, corn, peas, celery, onion, green pepper and pimiento in a large, shallow glass baking dish.

3. Combine the vinegar, oil, water, salt, pepper and paprika in a screw-top jar; shake until well blended. Pour over the vegetables; stir to coat well. Cover and marinate overnight in the refrigerator. Drain the marinade before serving, if you wish.

Clockwise from top center: Watermelon Basket, page 337; Sugared and Salted Pecans, page 44; Strawberry-Lemon Punch, page 70; Rolls; Dilled Carrots, page 764; Hot Chicken Salad, page 662; Marinated Vegetables, page 756.

Lemon-Buttered Asparagus

Makes 4 to 6 servings.

2 to 2¹/₂ pounds asparagus
2 tablespoons fresh lemon juice
8 tablespoons (1 stick) butter or margarine
Lemon wedges

1. Wash and trim asparagus. Cook in boiling water just until tender, 10 to 13 minutes.
2. Combine lemon juice and 2 tablespoons of butter in a small saucepan; heat until bubbly. Gradually add remaining butter, stirring until blended.
3. Drain asparagus. Arrange on platter. Spoon lemon butter over asparagus. Garnish with lemon wedges.

Scalloped Asparagus

Here is an elegant way to serve asparagus as a side dish.

Bake at 400° for 15 minutes; then 2 minutes to brown.

Makes 4 servings.

1 pound fresh asparagus
4 tablespoons (¹/₂ stick) butter
1 tablespoon all-purpose flour
1 cup milk
4 hard-cooked eggs,
finely chopped
¹/₂ teaspoon salt
¹/₄ teaspoon cayenne pepper
2 tablespoons fine dry bread crumbs
¹/₂ cup grated Swiss cheese (2 ounces)

1. Preheat the oven to hot (400°). Bring a large saucepan of salted water to boiling. Grease a 1¹/₂-quart shallow baking dish.
2. Snap off tough ends of asparagus; trim off any sandy scales; wash.
3. Add asparagus to boiling water. Cover; lower heat; simmer for 10 minutes or until lower parts of stalks are fork-tender. Drain; transfer to paper toweling to drain further.
4. To prepare cream sauce, melt 1 tablespoon of the butter in a small saucepan. Stir in flour; cook 1 minute. Gradually stir in the milk. Cook, stirring constantly, until the sauce thickens, about 3 minutes. Remove from heat; reserve.
5. Arrange half the asparagus in a layer in a prepared baking dish. Sprinkle with half the chopped egg; dot with 1 tablespoon of the butter; season with salt and cayenne pepper. Arrange another layer with remaining asparagus. Sprinkle the center portion of asparagus with the remaining chopped egg. Pour the reserved cream sauce down the middle of casserole. Sprinkle sauce with bread crumbs and cheese. Dot uncovered portions of asparagus with remaining 2

tablespoons butter to prevent drying out during baking.
6. Bake, covered, in the preheated hot oven (400°) for 15 minutes. Uncover; bake 2 to 3 minutes more or until the top is browned.

Stir-Fried Asparagus

Makes 6 servings.

1 bunch fresh asparagus (about 1¹/₂ pounds)
3 tablespoons peanut oil
2 tablespoons lemon juice
¹/₂ teaspoon salt
¹/₄ teaspoon pepper
1 hard-cooked egg yolk
Chopped fresh parsley
Lemon wedges

1. Break woody ends from asparagus and discard; wash stalks well under running cold water. Cut off tips and set aside; cut stalks diagonally into bias slices about ¹/₄-inch thick and 1-inch long.
2. Heat oil in large skillet or wok. Add sliced stalks; stir-fry 4 to 5 minutes or just until crisply tender; add asparagus tips; stir-fry 2 to 3 minutes longer. Stir in lemon juice, salt and pepper; cook 30 seconds.
3. Spoon asparagus into heated serving dish; sprinkle with chopped or sieved egg yolk and parsley. Serve with lemon wedges.

Lemon-Buttered Asparagus.

Scalloped Asparagus, page 758.

Green Bean Casserole

Makes 8 servings.

1/4 cup olive or
vegetable oil
4 medium-size onions,
sliced
1 1/4 pounds green
beans, cut into 1 1/2-
to 2-inch lengths
1 red or green pepper,
halved, seeded and
cut into strips
1 1/2 teaspoons salt
1 teaspoon leaf

oregano, crumbled
1/2 teaspoon leaf
thyme, crumbled
1/4 teaspoon pepper
1 clove garlic, split
1/2 cup fresh bread
crumbs (1 slice)
1 tablespoon chopped
fresh parsley
3 small tomatoes, cut
into wedges
Rolled anchovies

1. Heat 3 tablespoons of the oil in a large skillet; sauté onions until soft, about 5 minutes. Add green beans, pepper strips, salt, oregano, thyme and pepper. Cook, covered, stirring often, until beans are crisply tender, about 10 minutes. Spoon into 2-quart heatproof casserole.
2. Heat remaining oil in same skillet; add garlic and sauté until brown. Remove garlic and discard. Add bread crumbs and parsley to skillet; toss.
3. Arrange tomatoes over beans; sprinkle with bread crumb mixture. Broil 6 inches from heat until crumbs are brown, about 5 minutes. Top with rolled anchovies, if you wish. Serve hot.

Calico Wax Beans

Makes 4 to 6 servings.

1 pound wax beans,
tipped and cut in
1-inch lengths
OR: 2 cups frozen
wax beans (from a
1 1/2-pound bag)
2 tablespoons
vegetable oil
2 tomatoes, peeled

and chopped
1 teaspoon sugar
1 teaspoon salt
Dash pepper
2 tablespoons water
2 tablespoons
chopped fresh
parsley

1. Sauté beans in oil in a large skillet 5 minutes or just until shiny-moist. Stir in tomatoes, sugar, salt, pepper and water; cover.
2. Simmer, stirring several times and adding a little more water, if needed, 10 minutes or until beans are crisply tender. Sprinkle with parsley and serve.

Dilled Green Beans

Choose crisp, fresh green beans. Remove only the stem end of the beans to reduce vitamin loss during cooking.

Makes 8 servings.

2 pounds green beans, trimmed	fresh dill
2 tablespoons snipped	1½ cups water

Place the green beans flat in a large saucepan or skillet. Add the dill and water. Bring to boiling. Lower the heat and simmer, covered, 10 minutes or until just tender. Drain. Serve with additional fresh dill, if you wish.

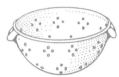

Spicy Brown Beans

Makes 8 servings.

1 package (1 pound) dried red kidney beans	½ cup dark molasses
6 cups water	⅓ to ½ cup brown sugar
2 tablespoons butter or margarine	2 teaspoons salt
1 stick cinnamon	2 to 4 tablespoons white vinegar

1. Pick over the beans; rinse under running water. Place in large kettle; add water; let soak overnight. Or, to quick soak, bring to boiling; boil 2 minutes. Remove from heat; cover and let stand 1 hour. Add butter and cinnamon stick; bring to boiling; lower heat; cover. Simmer, stirring occasionally, 1½ hours or until beans are almost tender. discard cinnamon stick.
2. Add molasses, brown sugar, salt and vinegar; continue cooking, stirring often and adjusting lid to partially cover kettle, 30 minutes longer or until beans are completely tender and sauce is brown and slightly thickened.

Refried Beans

Makes 3 cups.

1 recipe Pinto Beans (recipe in this chapter)	2 ounces longhorn or mild Cheddar cheese, shredded (½ cup)
½ cup bacon drippings or lard	

1. Drain beans and mash in a bowl.
2. Heat drippings in a large skillet over medium heat. Add beans; cook, stirring constantly, until beans are thick and fat has been absorbed. Serve topped with shredded cheese.

Pinto Beans

Makes 4 to 6 servings.

1 pound dried pinto beans	1 teaspoon chili powder
5 cups water	¼ pound salt pork, cut into ¼-inch cubes
1 medium-size onion, chopped (½ cup)	1 teaspoon salt
1 clove garlic, minced	

1. Pick over beans and rinse under running water. Combine beans and enough water to soak in a large kettle; cover; let soak overnight. Or, to quick-soak, bring to boiling; boil 2 minutes; remove from heat. Cover and let stand 1 hour. Drain.
2. Add the 5 cups water, onion, garlic, chili powder and salt pork to beans. Bring to boiling; lower heat; simmer over low heat 2½ hours or until beans are tender. (If beans appear dry, add more water to moisten.) Stir in salt.

Classy Baked Beans

These zesty beans take about 8 hours to prepare, so start them very early in the morning or prepare them a day ahead.

Bake at 275° for 7 hours.

Makes 6 to 8 servings.

1 pound dry, small white (navy) beans	4 tablespoons molasses
2 teaspoons unsalted butter or margarine	5 tablespoons prepared chili sauce
1 clove garlic, crushed	1 tablespoon dry English mustard
1 cup finely chopped onion (1 large)	1 teaspoon curry powder
3 strips bacon, cooked and crumbled	1½ teaspoons salt
2 tablespoons dark brown sugar	½ cup dark rum
2 teaspoons Worcestershire sauce	1½ cups tomato juice, or more as needed
	3 strips uncooked bacon

1. Place the beans in a large pot of boiling water over high heat. Return to boiling. Turn off the heat; let stand for 1 hour.
2. Preheat the oven to very slow (275°). Grease a 1¾-quart bean pot or casserole with the butter. Rub with garlic.
3. Drain the beans. Place in a large mixing bowl. Add the onion, crumbled bacon, brown sugar, Worcestershire, molasses, chili sauce, dry mustard, curry powder, salt and rum. Mix well. Stir in ¼ cup of the tomato juice. Transfer to the prepared bean pot. Place the strips of bacon on top.
4. Bake, covered, in the preheated very slow oven (275°) for 7 hours or until the beans are tender, gently stirring in the additional tomato juice as the liquid is absorbed by the beans.

Dried Beans Expansion One cup of dried beans expands to 2 to 2¹/₂ cups cooked, or enough to serve 3 to 4 people. Prepare a large batch and refrigerate leftovers for up to 1 week or freeze for 4 to 6 months. Reheat gently to retain shape.

Mexican Bean Pot

Bake at 325° for 2 hours.

Makes 6 servings.

1 pound dried pinto beans	**cut into large pieces**
6 cups water	**2 to 4 teaspoons chili powder**
¹/₂ pound hot Italian sausage	**2 teaspoons salt**
1 large onion, chopped (1 cup)	**1 teaspoon leaf basil, crumbled**
2 large green peppers, halved, seeded and	**2 envelopes or teaspoons instant beef broth**

1. Pick over beans and wash; place in a large saucepan and add water; bring to boiling; lower heat; cover saucepan; simmer 1 hour.
2. While beans cook, cut sausage into small pieces; brown in a small skillet; remove with slotted spoon and reserve. Sauté onion until soft; stir in peppers and sauté 2 minutes longer; add chili powder, salt, basil and instant beef broth; cook, stirring constantly, 2 minutes.
3. Transfer cooked beans to a 10-cup casserole with a slotted spoon; reserve cooking liquid; add sausage pieces and sautéed vegetables to cooked beans and mix until well blended. Add enough bean cooking liquid to cover beans.
4. Bake in a slow oven (325°) for 2 hours or until beans are tender and liquid thickens. (If the beans seem too dry, add more cooking liquid.)

New England Baked Beans

Get out your best bean pot and enjoy this stick-to-the-ribs classic.

Bake at 275° for 5 hours.

Makes 6 servings.

1 pound dried navy or pea beans	**syrup**
6 cups water	**3 tablespoons dark molasses**
¹/₂ pound salt pork	**2 tablespoons prepared mustard**
1 large onion, chopped (1 cup)	**1 teaspoon salt**
²/₃ cup maple	

1. Pick over and wash beans. Soak overnight in cold water to cover in a large bowl. Or, to quick soak, bring beans and water to boiling in large kettle; boil 2 minutes, remove from heat; let stand 1 hour.
2. Drain beans; combine with the 6 cups water in a large kettle or Dutch oven. Bring to boiling; lower heat; simmer 45 minutes or until beans are firm-tender.
3. Drain beans, reserving water. Slash salt pork in several places, cutting almost but not quite through. Combine beans and pork with onion in a 2-quart bean pot or deep baking dish.
4. Stir maple syrup, molasses, mustard and salt in a small bowl until blended; stir gently into bean mixture.
5. Pour enough reserved bean water to fill the bean pot and just cover the beans; reserve any remaining water.
6. Bake, covered, in a very slow oven (275°) for 3 hours. Uncover; bake 2 hours longer. Stir beans occasionally during baking and add more reserved water whenever needed.

Sweet-Sour Glazed Beets

Just the right amount of vinegar makes this sauce so good with beets.

Makes 4 servings.

2 bunches beets	**cornstarch**
¹/₄ cup sugar	**¹/₄ teaspoon salt**
1 tablespoon	**¹/₂ cup cider vinegar**

1. Wash beets. Cut off all but 2 inches of tops; leave root end intact.
2. Place beets in saucepan; add water to cover. Bring water to boiling. Cook beets, covered, 35 to 45 minutes (depending on size), or until tender. Drain.
3. Allow beets to cool slightly; trim root and stem ends; slip skins off. Slice beets. (You should get 2 cups.)
4. Combine sugar, cornstarch and salt in a saucepan; add vinegar. Cook over medium heat, stirring constantly until thickened and bubbly.
5. Add beets to sauce; heat 3 minutes, stirring gently.

Broccoli Sauté

Makes 6 servings.

1 bunch fresh broccoli (about 2 pounds)	**3 tablespoons soy sauce**
3 tablespoons peanut or vegetable oil	**¹/₂ teaspoon ground ginger**
2 cups chopped celery	

1. Trim outer leaves and tough ends from broccoli; cut

(continued)

stems and flowerets crosswise into $1/2$-inch-thick slices. (There should be about 6 cups.) Wash; drain.
2. Heat oil in a large skillet; stir in broccoli and celery. Cook, stirring constantly, 4 minutes, or just until wilted. Stir in soy sauce and ginger; cover skillet.
3. Steam 10 to 12 minutes or until vegetables are crisp-tender.

Sesame Broccoli

Makes 8 servings.

1 bunch broccoli (about 2 pounds)	celery
$1/4$ cup ($1/2$ stick) butter	1 can (8 ounces) water chestnuts, drained and sliced
$1/4$ cup water	
1 tablespoon soy sauce	1 tablespoon sesame seeds
1 cup thinly sliced	

1. Trim outer leaves and tough ends from broccoli. Cut stalks and flowerets into 2-inch lengths, then slice lengthwise.
2. Combine butter, water and soy sauce in large skillet; bring to boiling. Stir in the broccoli, celery and water chestnuts; bring to boiling again; cover. Steam 10 minutes or just until broccoli is crisply tender.
3. While broccoli cooks, heat sesame seeds in a small, heavy skillet over low heat, shaking pan constantly, just until lightly toasted; stir into broccoli mixture. Spoon into a heated serving bowl. Serve with more soy sauce to sprinkle over top.

Shannon Vegetable Platter

Makes 12 servings.

12 medium-size boiling potatoes (about 4 pounds)	cabbage
	Boiling water
2 packages (1 pound each) baby carrots	$1/2$ cup (1 stick) butter or margarine
1 large head green	$1/4$ cup chopped parsley

1. Pare the potatoes and carrots. (This can be done the day before. Cover vegetables with cold water in a bowl; refrigerate.)
2. Cook potatoes and carrots, separately, in 2 saucepans of boiling salted water, for 15 minutes or until fork tender. Drain. Return the saucepans to low heat; toss vegetables over the heat to dry. Place on a heated serving platter and keep warm.
3. Cut the cabbage into 12 wedges. Soak in warm salted water in large bowl for 1 minute. Drain. Arrange, overlapping, in a large skillet. Pour boiling water over to cover; cover the skillet; bring to boiling. Lower the heat; simmer for 3 minutes. Remove cabbage and drain on paper toweling. Arrange on the platter with the potatoes and carrots.
4. Heat butter and chopped parsley in a small

saucepan until bubbly. Pour over the vegetables to coat well.

Creamed Brussels Sprouts and Onions

Makes 8 servings.

2 pints Brussels sprouts OR: 2 packages (10 ounces each) frozen Brussels sprouts	onions, peeled
	2 tablespoons butter or margarine
	2 tablespoons flour
	2 cups milk
1 pound small white	Salt and pepper

1. Cook Brussels sprouts and onions in boiling salted water until tender, about 15 minutes; drain; cover to keep warm. If using frozen sprouts, follow label directions.
2. Melt butter in a medium-size saucepan; stir in flour. Cook, stirring constantly, until mixture bubbles; cook 1 more minute. Remove from heat; slowly stir in milk. Return to heat; cook, stirring constantly, until sauce is thickened and bubbly, about 5 minutes. Pour over Brussels sprouts and onions, stirring gently, just to coat well; add salt and pepper to taste.

Carrots Lyonnaise

Cooking carrots this way brings out all their fresh, sweet taste.

Makes 8 servings.

$1/4$ cup ($1/2$ stick) butter or margarine	$1/4$ teaspoon salt
	$3/4$ teaspoon lemon pepper
1 large onion, thinly sliced	2 tablespoons finely chopped fresh parsley
2 pounds carrots, pared and cut into 2-inch sticks	

1. Melt 3 tablespoons of the butter or margarine in a skillet. Sauté onion until tender and golden. Remove from skillet with slotted spoon to a bowl; keep onion warm.
2. Add remaining tablespoon butter or margarine to same skillet. Toss carrots in skillet over medium heat to coat well with butter. Cover; lower heat. Cook 15 minutes or until carrots are tender. Uncover; continue to cook until liquid evaporates. Season carrots with salt, lemon pepper and parsley.
3. Lightly toss onion and carrots together; turn into heated serving dish.

Pictured opposite: Carrots Lyonnaise.

Carrot-Yam Tzimmes

There's nothing more delicious than this traditional mixture of vegetables and fruits, slightly sweetened with honey.

Bake at 350° for 30 minutes.

Makes 8 servings.

2 pounds yams, pared and cut into $3/4$-inch-thick slices	**1 cup orange juice**
	2 tablespoons honey
1 pound carrots, scraped and cut into $3/4$-inch-thick slices	**1 tablespoon grated lemon rind**
	$1/4$ teaspoon ground nutmeg
$1/2$ cup dried prunes	**$1/4$ teaspoon ground ginger**
$1/2$ cup dried apricots	**Orange rind** *(optional)*

1. Cook the yams and carrots in 1 inch of simmering water in a covered saucepan until barely tender, about 15 minutes. Drain.
2. Preheat the oven to moderate (350°).
3. Grease a $2^1/2$-quart casserole. Place the yams and carrots in the casserole; stir in the dried prunes and apricots.
4. Pour the orange juice over the vegetables and fruits. Dot with honey; sprinkle with the lemon rind, nutmeg and ginger.
5. Bake in the preheated moderate oven (350°) for 30 minutes or until fork-tender, stirring gently once or twice. Garnish with thin strips of orange rind, if you wish.

To Make Ahead: Complete Step 1. Place in a large bowl, cover and refrigerate until ready to bake. Remove from the refrigerator and allow to come to room temperature before completing recipe.

Dilled Carrots

Serve chilled as a salad or side dish with roast or barbecued meats or deli sandwiches.

Makes 12 servings.

3 pounds carrots, pared and cut into $1/2$-inch-thick slices	**$1/2$ cup vegetable oil**
	$1/2$ cup red wine vinegar
2 large sweet green peppers, halved, seeded and cut into $1/4$-inch-wide strips	**1 teaspoon Worcestershire sauce**
	1 teaspoon salt
2 large onions, thinly sliced into rings	**$1/2$ teaspoon pepper**
1 can ($10^3/4$ ounces) tomato soup	**$1/4$ cup snipped fresh dill**
	OR: 4 teaspoons dried dillweed
1 cup sugar	

1. Cook the carrots in boiling salted water to cover in a large saucepan until crisp-tender, about 5 minutes. Drain and cool.
2. Combine the carrots, green peppers and onions in a large bowl. Divide the vegetables between two $13^1/2$ x $8^1/2$ x2-inch glass baking dishes.
3. Stir together the soup, sugar, oil, vinegar, Worcestershire, salt and pepper in a 4-cup glass measure. Pour half of the marinade over the vegetables in each dish. Stir gently to combine. Cover and refrigerate for 24 hours. Just before serving, drain the excess marinade, if you wish. Stir in the dill.

Maple-Butter Glazed Carrots

Maple syrup was the popular native-grown sweetener in the years before refined sugar.

Makes 8 servings.

1 cup water	**$1/4$ cup ($1/2$ stick) butter or margarine**
1 teaspoon salt	
2 pounds carrots, pared, cut in half crosswise	**1 teaspoon leaf marjoram, crumbled**
	1 teaspoon salt
$1/4$ cup maple syrup	**$1/4$ teaspoon pepper**

1. Bring water and 1 teaspoon salt to boiling in a medium-size heavy saucepan. Add carrots; return to boiling; cover. Simmer 15 minutes or until carrots are just tender. Drain thoroughly.
2. Cook maple syrup, butter, marjoram, salt and pepper in a large skillet over low heat 2 to 3 minutes or until bubbly and caramel-like in consistency.
3. Add carrots. Toss gently to coat in the maple butter. Cook over high heat, tossing gently, until carrots are glazed and liquid is absorbed.

Creamed Celeriac

Makes 6 servings.

4 large celeriac (about 2 pounds)	**$1/2$ teaspoon salt**
	$1/4$ teaspoon dry mustard
2 tablespoons chopped onion	**Dash pepper**
$1/4$ cup ($1/2$ stick) butter or margarine	**1 small can evaporated milk ($2/3$ cup)**
$1/4$ cup all-purpose flour	

1. Pare celeriac and cut into thin slices. Cook in boiling lightly salted water in a medium-size saucepan 10 minutes or just until tender. (Celeriac darkens when cut, so cook it quickly.) Drain, reserving liquid in a 2-cup measure. Add water, if needed, to make $1^1/3$ cups.
2. While celeriac cooks, sauté onion lightly in butter in a medium-size saucepan. Stir in flour, salt, mustard and pepper; cook, stirring constanty, just until mixture bubbles.
3. Stir in reserved liquid, then evaporated milk. Continue cooking and stirring until sauce thickens and boils 1 minute. Stir in celeriac; heat just to boiling.

Cheese-Stuffed Vegetables; Cold Confetti Meatloaf, page 471.

Cheese-Stuffed Vegetables

This refreshing first course may be made a day ahead.

Makes 4 servings.

1 package (3 ounces)
  cream cheese,
  softened
1 package (2 ounces)
  blue cheese,
  softened
1 teaspoon finely
  chopped onion
1 teaspoon fresh

lemon juice
1 small cucumber,
  pared and trimmed
2 medium-size celery
  stalks, washed and
  trimmed
2 ounces snow peas,
  washed, stem ends
  removed

1. Combine the cheese, onion and lemon juice in a small bowl.
2. Cut the cucumber into $1/3$-inch thick slices. Remove some seeds from the center of each slice with a melon baller to form a small cavity. Spoon 1 teaspoon of the cheese filling into each cavity.
3. Fill the celery stalks with the filling. Cut into $1\frac{1}{2}$-inch-long pieces.

4. Carefully cut open the snow peas on the curved edge. Spoon or pipe 1 teaspoon of the cheese mixture in each.
5. Place the vegetables in a shallow, airtight container lined with damp paper toweling. Cover with another piece of damp paper toweling, then seal with the container cover. Refrigerate for up to 24 hours.

Creamed Celery

Makes 6 servings.

4 cups sliced celery
$1/4$ cup sliced green
  onions
$1/4$ cup ($1/2$ stick) butter
  or margarine
2 tablespoons flour
1 cup canned chicken
  broth

$1/8$ teaspoon pepper
$1/2$ teaspoon
  Worcestershire
  sauce
$1/2$ cup light cream or
  half-and-half
$1/4$ cup toasted
  slivered almonds

1. Sauté celery and onions in butter or margarine in a large skillet 10 minutes until crisp-tender. *(continued)*

2. Sprinkle flour over vegetables, blend in, then add chicken broth. Cook, stirring constantly, until the sauce thickens and bubbles 3 minutes. Stir in the pepper, Worcestershire sauce and cream and heat slowly, stirring, just until hot.

3. Spoon into a serving bowl; sprinkle with toasted slivered almonds.

Red Cabbage

Make 6 to 8 servings.

1 medium-size head red cabbage (about 3 pounds)	1 teaspoon salt
1 medium-size onion, sliced	6 tablespoons sugar
	1 cup cider vinegar
	1¹/₂ cups water
2 large apples, pared and chopped	¹/₄ teaspoon ground allspice
1 tablespoon bacon drippings	1 bay leaf
	2 cloves
	6 peppercorns

1. Remove any bruised and discolored outer leaves from cabbage. Quarter and core cabbage. Slice thinly to make about 12 cups. Combine with onion and apples in a large kettle.

2. Add bacon drippings, salt, sugar, vinegar, water and allspice. Tie bay leaf, cloves and peppercorns in a small piece of cheesecloth. Add to cabbage.

3. Cover and simmer 30 minutes; uncover; simmer 1 hour longer. Remove spice bag. Serve hot. This reheats well.

Drunken Sauerkraut

Makes 6 to 8 servings.

3 strips bacon, chopped	¹/₂ teaspoon caraway seeds
1 cup finely chopped onion	1 can (12 ounces) beer OR: apple cider
1 package (2 pounds) sauerkraut, rinsed and drained	³/₄ cup grated carrot
	Salt and pepper
2 tablespoons brown sugar	1 tablespoon chopped parsley

1. Sauté the bacon in a medium-size heavy pot or Dutch oven until all the fat is rendered, but the bacon is not browned.

2. Add the onion; cook, stirring occasionally, for 4 minutes or until softened.

3. Stir in the sauerkraut, brown sugar, caraway seeds

and beer. Bring to boiling; Lower the heat; simmer, partially covered, 1 hour.

4. Add the carrot. Simmer, partially covered, 30 minutes longer. If the mixture is too wet, raise the heat slightly; cook, uncovered, a little longer. Add the salt and pepper to taste. Sprinkle with the parsley.

Caraway Kraut

Makes 4 servings.

5 bacon slices	1 teaspoon sugar
1 can (16 ounces) sauerkraut, drained	¹/₂ teaspoon caraway seeds
1 can (16 ounces) stewed tomatoes	¹/₄ teaspoon salt
	¹/₈ teaspoon pepper

1. Cut 2 slices of the bacon into 1-inch pieces. Cook until crisp in a medium-size skillet; drain on paper toweling. Cook remaining 3 slices in same pan until almost crisp, then before removing from pan, roll each slice around the tines of a fork to make a curl; drain on paper toweling. Discard all drippings from pan.

2. Combine sauerkraut, tomatoes and liquid, sugar, caraway seeds, salt and pepper in the same skillet; heat to boiling; cover. Simmer 10 minutes.

3. Stir in bacon pieces; spoon into a heated serving bowl. Garnish with bacon curls and parsley, if you wish.

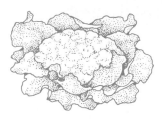

Low-Calorie Cauliflower Supreme

Cauliflower dressed with a low-calorie mock hollandaise sauce. It's a cook-saver, too.

Makes 6 servings at 58 calories each.

1 medium-size cauliflower	juice
¹/₄ cup imitation mayonnaise	1 tablespoon skim milk
1 tablespoon lemon	Paprika

1. Trim green leaves from cauliflower, then separate cauliflower into large flowerets.

2. Cook flowerets in boiling salted water in a large saucepan for 15 minutes or just until crisply tender; drain well.

3. Combine imitation mayonnaise, lemon juice and skim milk in a small saucepan; heat, stirring constantly, just until blended.

4. Spoon cauliflower into a heated serving bowl; pour the sauce over; sprinkle with the paprika.

Cauliflower Italiano

Makes 8 servings.

**1 large cauliflower
(about 3 pounds)
1 can condensed
tomato bisque**

**1 package (8 ounces)
mozzarella cheese,
cut in strips**

1. Trim outer green leaves from cauliflower, but leave head whole. Cook, covered, in boiling salted water in a large saucepan 30 minutes or just until crisp-tender.
2. Lift out carefully; drain well. Place in a broiler-proof dish.
3. Heat tomato bisque to boiling in a small saucepan; spoon over cauliflower; top with cheese strips.
4. Broil 4 inches from heat, 5 minutes or just until cheese melts and starts to bubble. Or, bake in a hot oven (425°) for 10 minutes.

Selecting and Storing Fresh Corn
Yellow or white, corn should have fresh green husks, plump and bright, firm kernels.

Corn should be prepared immediately after purchase or wrapped in plastic and refrigerated for up to two days. Corn becomes less sweet as the natural sugar converts to starch.

Peak season: July-September.

Roasted Corn in Husks

Roast at 400° for 20 minutes.

Remove outer husks; fold back inner ones. Remove silks and spread corn with flavored butter. Pull husks up over corn and tie at open end. (A narrow piece of husk makes an excellent "string.") Place in shallow pan; roast in hot oven (400°) for 20 to 25 minutes. If corn is not picked the same day it is cooked, do not spread with butter before tying. *Do* soak it in cold water for 30 minutes before roasting. Remove husks; serve with butter.

Grilled Corn

Prepare corn as above. Place around edges of grill over hot coals. Turn 2 or 3 times for 15 minutes.

Corn-on-the-Cob with Flavored Butters

Remove husk from corn by peeling back and breaking off end of cob; remove silks. Allow 2 medium-size ears per serving. Fill a large kettle with water; cover; bring to boiling. Add corn, half at a time, if kettle is not large enough for all to cook at once. Boil 5 minutes or just until tender. Remove corn to napkin or towel-lined serving platter, using tongs. Serve hot. Put second

servings in boiling water and repeat as above. Serve with soft seasoned butters.

Dill Butter: Soften 1/2 cup (1 stick) butter in small bowl; stir in 1 1/2 teaspoons freshly snipped dill or 1/2 teaspoon dried dillweed.

Lemon Butter: Soften 1/2 cup (1 stick) butter in small bowl; stir in 2 teaspoons lemon juice.

Chive Butter: Soften 1/2 cup (1 stick) butter in small bowl; stir in 2 teaspoons finely snipped chives.

Garlic Butter: Soften 1/2 cup (1 stick) butter in small bowl; stir in 1/4 teaspoon garlic salt.

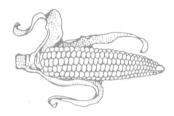

Sweet Corn on the Cob

Grilling corn in its own husk is a great flavor saver.
Roast 15 to 25 minutes.

Makes 4 to 6 servings.

**8 ears fresh corn
Softened butter or
margarine**

**Salt
Pepper**

1. To roast corn in husks, remove only outer husks; fold back inner ones, being careful not to split them; remove silks. Spread corn with butter; sprinkle with salt and pepper. Pull husks back up over ears; tie tips with string to keep corn covered and moist.
2. To roast corn in aluminum foil, husk and remove silks; spread with butter and season with salt and pepper. Wrap well in heavy-duty or double-thick regular aluminum foil.
3. Place corn on grill over gray coals. Roast 15 to 25 minutes, turning several times to grill evenly.

Oven-Fried Eggplant

Bake at 450° for 10 minutes.

Makes 6 servings.

**3 tablespoons low-
calorie ("imitation")
mayonnaise
1 tablespoon water
2 tablespoons lemon
juice (or water)
Pinch garlic powder**

**1/3 cup grated
Parmesan cheese
1/3 cup packaged
bread crumbs
1 medium-size
eggplant
(1 1/4 pounds)**

1. Spray a nonstick cookie sheet or shallow baking pan liberally with vegetable cooking spray (or wipe lightly with vegetable oil).
2. Blend mayonnaise, water, lemon juice and garlic in

(continued)

Rolled Stuffed Eggplant, page 769.

a shallow plate. Combine Parmesan cheese and bread crumbs on wax paper. Preheat oven to 450°.

3. Cut the eggplant lengthwise into ¹/₂-inch-thick slices. Dip each slice into the mayonnaise mixture, turning to coat both sides, then press both sides lightly into the crumb mixture. Arrange each crumb-coated slice in a single layer on the cookie sheet.

4. Bake in a preheated very hot oven (450°) for 5 minutes. Turn slices with a spatula and bake another 5 minutes or more, until coating is crisp and eggplant slices are tender.

Eggplant Parmigiana

Bake at 350° for 30 minutes.

Makes 4 servings.

1 medium-size eggplant (about 1¹/₄ pounds)	**pepper**
1 teaspoon salt	**1 large clove garlic, minced**
¹/₄ cup all-purpose flour	**1 can (8 ounces) tomato sauce**
¹/₂ teaspoon salt	**¹/₂ teaspoon leaf oregano, crumbled**
¹/₄ teaspoon pepper	**1 package (8 ounces) mozzarella cheese, sliced**
¹/₂ cup vegetable oil	
1 medium-size onion, chopped (¹/₂ cup)	**¹/₄ cup freshly grated Parmesan cheese**
¹/₂ cup chopped green	

1. Pare and cut eggplant into 8 slices, ¹/₂- to ³/₄-inch thick. Sprinkle both sides of eggplant slices lightly with the 1 teaspoon salt. Place between paper toweling; weight down with a heavy plate and let stand for 30 minutes. Rinse off slices well and dry on paper toweling.

2. Combine flour, salt and pepper on piece of wax paper. Coat eggplant slices on both sides with the flour mixture.

3. Pour 2 tablespoons of the oil into a large skillet; sauté eggplant slices, a few at a time, adding additional oil as needed. When lightly browned on both sides, drain the slices on paper toweling.

4. Add to the skillet the remaining oil, onion, green pepper and garlic; sauté over low heat, 5 minutes, stirring frequently.

5. Add tomato sauce and oregano; simmer 5 minutes.

6. Spoon half of the tomato sauce mixture into a 1¹/₂-quart shallow baking dish. Arrange eggplant slices on the sauce. Cover with slices of mozzarella and spoon remaining sauce on top. Sprinkle with Parmesan cheese.

7. Bake in a moderate oven (350°) for 30 minutes or until cheese is melted and sauce is boiling.

Braised Endive

Makes 3 to 4 servings.

6 small heads Belgian endive	**1/2 teaspoon seasoned salt**
1 tablespoon lemon juice	**1 tablespoon butter or margarine**

1. Wash endive and halve each lengthwise. Place in a single layer in a medium-size skillet; pour in enough water to cover; add lemon juice and seasoned salt; cover. (Be sure water covers endive completely, for this keeps it from discoloring during cooking.)
2. Bring to boiling; cover and simmer 10 minutes or until crisply tender; drain. Add butter; heat slowly, shaking pan constantly, just until butter melts and bubbles.

Rolled Stuffed Eggplant

Take the work out of entertaining with this make-ahead main dish.

Bake at 450° for 30 minutes.

Makes 15 servings (30 rolls).

4 cloves garlic, finely chopped	**4 eggs**
1 cup vegetable oil	**1/4 cup milk**
2 cans (28 ounces each) crushed tomatoes with puree	**2 eggplant (1 pound each)**
	2 containers (15 ounces each) ricotta cheese
1 can (8 ounces) tomato sauce	**1 package (8 ounces) mozzarella cheese, grated**
1/2 teaspoon salt	
1/2 teaspoon pepper	**1/2 cup grated Parmesan cheese**
4 cups plain bread crumbs	**2 cups chopped parsley**
2 cups *sifted* all-purpose flour	

1. Sauté the garlic in 1 tablespoon of the oil in a large saucepan until golden brown, about 4 minutes. Working in batches, combine the crushed tomatoes, tomato sauce, salt and pepper in a blender. Whirl until smooth. Pour into the saucepan. Bring to boiling. Lower the heat; simmer, partially covered, 30 minutes. Reserve.
2. Combine the crumbs and flour in a large shallow pan. Beat the eggs and milk in a large bowl. Peel the eggplant; cut lengthwise into 1/8-inch-thick slices. Dip into the egg mixture; dredge with the flour mixture, shaking off the excess. Set on wax paper.
3. Working in batches and using about 3 tablespoons of oil per batch, sauté the eggplant in the large skillet until golden, 1 minute per side. Drain on paper toweling.
4. Preheat the oven to hot (450°).
5. Combine the ricotta, mozzarella, Parmesan and parsley in a bowl; mix well. Spread 2 to 3 tablespoons

on one side of each slice of the eggplant. Roll up jelly-roll fashion. Spread 1 cup of the tomato sauce over the bottom of each of two 11 3/4 × 7-inch baking dishes. Arrange the rolls, seam-side down, in a single layer in the dishes. Spoon the sauce over the rolls; save the remainder to pass.
6. Bake, covered, in the preheated hot oven (450°) for 30 minutes or until the sauce is bubbly. Garnish with additional chopped parsley, if you wish.

To Make Ahead: Prepare the dough early in the day; bake just before serving. Or freeze. Defrost in the refrigerator overnight; bake as above.

Braised Leeks

Makes 6 servings.

2 bunches leeks (4 to 5 in a bunch)	**1/2 teaspoon salt**
	1/2 teaspoon celery salt
3 tablespoons butter or margarine	

Trim roots and about 3/4 of the green tops from leeks; split each leek lengthwise; wash well. Arrange pieces, cut-side down, in a large skillet. Add just enough water to cover; heat to boiling; cover. Simmer 5 minutes; drain; return to pan. Add butter; sprinkle with salt and celery salt. Cook slowly, 5 minutes longer, or until leeks are tender.

Lentil Stew

This protein-rich meatless dish features lentils and vegetables. Serve with warm corn bread, cole slaw and milk, if you wish.

Makes 6 servings.

2 medium-size onions, chopped (1 cup)	**tomatoes, undrained but roughly chopped**
1 large green pepper, seeded and chopped	**2 large carrots, thinly sliced**
2 tablespoons vegetable oil	**1/2 to 1 teaspoon leaf oregano, crumbled**
1 1/2 cups dried lentils, washed	**1/4 cup chopped canned pimientos**
4 cups water	**2 teaspoons salt**
1 can (28 ounces)	**1/4 teaspoon pepper**

1. Sauté onions and pepper in heated oil in a large skillet until tender.
2. Add lentils, water, tomatoes, carrots, oregano, pimientos, salt and pepper; mix well. Bring to boiling; lower heat; cover; simmer 45 minutes or until lentils and vegetables are tender.

Carrot-Stuffed Mushrooms

Bake at 350° for 10 minutes.

Makes 8 servings.

8 large fresh
mushrooms
1/4 cup (1/2 stick) butter
or margarine
1 tablespoon lemon
juice
1 pound carrots, pared
and sliced
2 tablespoons orange
marmalade
1/4 teaspoon ground
ginger

1. Remove stems from mushrooms. (Reserve for another use.) Sauté mushrooms in butter and lemon juice until browned, about 3 minutes.
2. Cook carrots in boiling salted water until tender, about 8 minutes. Drain; stir in marmalade and ginger; puree in container of electric blender. Pipe puree through a pastry bag into mushroom caps. Place caps in a shallow baking dish.
3. Bake in a moderate oven (350°) for 10 minutes or until well heated.

Cashew-Mushroom Stroganoff

Makes 4 servings.

1 cup raw cashews or
dry-roasted
cashews
4 tablespoons butter
1 clove garlic, minced
1 medium-size onion,
chopped
1 1/2 pounds
mushrooms, sliced
3 tablespoons
whole wheat flour
1 tablespoon tomato
paste
1 cup water
3 tablespoons tamari
or soy sauce
1 cup dairy sour
cream
2 tablespoons sherry
Salt and pepper

1. Place cashews in a 9-inch pie plate. Toast in a slow oven (250°) for 10 minutes or until lightly browned.
2. Melt 2 tablespoons of the butter in a large skillet. Sauté garlic, onion and mushrooms until soft but not brown, about 4 minutes. Remove to bowl with slotted spoon.
3. Add remaining 2 tablespoons butter to skillet. Stir in flour and tomato paste until smooth. Combine water with tamari; stir into tomato paste mixture, stirring until well blended. Cook, stirring constantly, over medium heat until mixture thickens.
4. Stir in sour cream, sherry, mushrooms and cashews. Heat thoroughly, but do not boil. Taste; add additional salt and pepper, if needed. Garnish with chopped parsley, if you wish.

Creamed Onions

Makes 8 servings.

40 small white onions
6 tablespoons butter
or margarine
6 tablespoons flour
1 1/2 teaspoons salt
1/4 teaspoon white
pepper
1/4 teaspoon ground
nutmeg
3 cups milk
1/2 cup heavy cream

1. Peel onions; cut an "x" in the root end. Cook onions, covered, in boiling salted water in a large saucepan until tender, about 15 minutes. Drain.
2. Melt butter in same saucepan. Stir in flour, salt, pepper and nutmeg; cook 2 minutes. Remove pan from heat; gradually stir in milk and heavy cream until smooth.
3. Bring to boiling; lower heat; simmer about 5 minutes, stirring constantly, until sauce is thick and smooth. Stir in onions.

Batter-Fried Onion Rings

Here's a popular American side dish that's made better with beer batter. You might also like to try the batter on other favorite foods such as shrimp, fish, chicken, or other vegetables.

Makes 6 servings.

1 1/2 cups all-purpose
flour
1 can (12 ounces)
beer, active or flat,
cold or at room
temperature
3 very large yellow
onions or Bermuda
onions
1 quart vegetable oil

1. Combine flour and beer in a large bowl and blend thoroughly, using a rotary beater. Cover; allow batter to stand at room temperature for at least 3 hours. (If batter is too thick, stir in some water.)
2. Twenty minutes before the batter is ready, preheat oven to 200°. Place layers of paper toweling on a jelly-roll pan. Carefully peel the papery skins from the onions so that you do not cut into the outside onion layer. Cut onions into 1/4-inch thick slices. Separate the slices into rings.
3. Pour enough oil in deep fryer or kettle to come 2 inches up the side of the pan. Heat to 375° on a deep-fat frying thermometer.
4. Dip a few onion rings into the batter with metal tongs, then carefully place them in the hot fat. Fry rings, turning them once or twice until they are an even delicate golden color. Transfer to the paper-lined jelly roll pan. To keep warm, place them on the middle shelf of the preheated oven until all the onion rings have been fried.

Glazed Parsnips

These glazed parsnips are excellent with roast meat.
Makes 4 servings.

1 pound parsnips (6 medium-size)	brown sugar
3 tablespoons butter or margarine	1/4 teaspoon salt
1/4 cup firmly packed	1/4 cup cider vinegar
	3 tablespoons orange juice

1. Cook unpared parsnips in boiling salted water to cover in a large saucepan for 10 minutes. Lower heat; simmer 20 minutes longer or until tender but firm. Remove skins while hot; cut parsnips into quarters.
2. Melt butter in a large skillet; stir in sugar, salt, vinegar and orange juice; bring to boiling. Add parsnips and cook over high heat, spooning pan liquid over, about 5 minutes or until well-glazed.

Marinated Black-Eyed Peas

Makes 12 side-dish servings.

2/3 cup vegetable oil	mustard
5 tablespoons red wine vinegar	1/2 teaspoon black pepper
2 medium-size onions, chopped (1 cup)	Dash red pepper flakes
1 cup chopped parsley	1 package (1 pound) black-eyed peas, picked over and rinsed
2 large cloves garlic, crushed	
2 teaspoons leaf basil, crumbled	
1 teaspoon leaf oregano, crumbled	Sweet green pepper rings for garnish (1/2-inch thick)
1/2 teaspoon dry	

1. Combine vegetable oil, red wine vinegar, onion, parsley, garlic, basil, oregano, mustard, black pepper and red pepper flakes in a 4-cup measure. Reserve.
2. Cook peas following label directions. Drain peas in a colander. Place peas in a large bowl. Mix dressing;

Marinated Black-Eyed Peas.

pour over warm peas. Toss gently to mix. Cover with plastic wrap; refrigerate. Marinate overnight, tossing peas once.
3. Line a large platter or serving bowl with green pepper rings. Mound marinated peas in center.

Marinated Black-Eyed Peas Main Dish: To turn this side dish into a main dish, add 1 1/2 cups cubed cooked ham and 1 1/2 cups cubed cheese.

To Clean Black-Eyed Peas: Spread peas on a tray or a large plate. Remove and discard bits of foreign matter or broken or discolored peas. Place the peas in a large bowl of water. Immature beans will have shrunk within their skins and may float to the surface. Remove these along with any loose skins. Rinse the peas in a large colander.

Peas Provençal

Makes 4 to 6 servings.

3 pounds fresh peas in pods, shelled OR: 3 cups frozen peas (from a 1 1/2-pound bag)	2 tablespoons olive or vegetable oil
	2 medium-size tomatoes, peeled and chopped
1 large onion, chopped (1 cup)	1/2 teaspoon salt
1 clove garlic, minced	Dash pepper

1. Cook fresh peas in boiling salted water in a medium-size saucepan for 10 minutes or until tender; drain. If using frozen peas, cook following label directions; drain.
2. While peas cook, sauté onion and garlic in oil until soft in a medium-size skillet; stir in tomatoes, salt and pepper. Cook, stirring often, 20 minutes or until slightly thickened. Stir in peas.

French-Style Green Peas

Makes 6 to 8 servings.

4 pounds fresh peas in pods, shelled OR: 4 cups frozen peas	onions
	1/2 teaspoon salt
	1/8 teaspoon pepper
2 cups shredded lettuce	1/2 cup water
	1/4 cup (1/2 stick) butter or margarine
1/4 cup sliced green	2 tablespoons flour

1. Combine peas, lettuce, green onions, salt, pepper, water and 3 tablespoons of the butter in a large saucepan; heat to boiling; cover. Simmer 10 minutes or until peas are tender.
2. While peas cook, blend remaining 1 tablespoon butter with flour to a paste in a cup.
3. Stir into pea mixture, a small amount at a time; continue cooking and stirring until mixture thickens and boils 1 minute. Spoon into a heated serving bowl.

Stir-Fried Peas Plus

Makes 4 servings.

2 bacon slices	teaspoon instant
18 tiny white onions	chicken broth
(1/2 pound), peeled*	1 teaspoon flour
2 pounds fresh peas,	1/2 cup water
shelled (2 cups)	2 tablespoons
1 small green pepper,	chopped fresh
seeded and cut into	parsley
strips	1 tablespoon butter or
1 envelope or	margarine

1. Cook bacon until crisp in large skillet; remove to paper toweling and reserve. Add onions to drippings in skillet; stir-fry over medium heat for 10 minutes.
2. Add peas to skillet; stir-fry 5 minutes or until peas become bright green. Add green pepper.
3. Blend instant chicken broth, flour and water in small bowl until smooth. Stir into skillet; add 1 tablespoon of the parsley. Cover and cook 3 minutes longer. Stir in remaining parsley and butter until melted. Spoon into heated serving dish; crumble bacon over top.
If tiny white onions are not available, use larger ones, halved or quartered.

Fanned Roast Potatoes

Makes 6 to 8 servings.

12 to 16 small red new	Snipped fresh chives
potatoes	Chopped fresh
8 to 10 tablespoons	tarragon
unsalted butter or	OR: dried leaf
margarine, melted	tarragon, crumbled
Salt and pepper	

1. Cut six to eight 12 × 9-inch rectangles of heavy-duty aluminum foil.
2. Cut 4 or more parallel slices into the potatoes without cutting through. (Place the potatoes in a large spoon before cutting, and you won't cut them all the way through.) Fan-open the potatoes. Place 2 on each piece of foil; pour the butter over. Sprinkle with the salt, pepper, chives and tarragon to taste. Seal the foil to form packets.
3. Place on the grill. Cover. Cook until tender, about 45 minutes.

Parsleyed New Potatoes

Makes 8 servings.

3 pounds small red	1/4 teaspoon salt
new potatoes	1/8 teaspoon pepper
1/4 cup (1/2 stick) butter	2 tablespoons
or margarine,	chopped parsley
melted	

1. Cover the potatoes in a large pot with cold water.

Bring to boiling. Cook 10 to 15 minutes, or until fork-tender. Drain.
2. Cut the potatoes in half and place in a large bowl. Sprinkle with the melted butter, salt, pepper and parsley; toss gently to mix.

Microwave Directions
650 Watt Variable Power Microwave Oven
Ingredient Changes: Cook the potatoes in 1/4 cup water.
Directions: Prick the potatoes with a fork. Place in a 3-quart microwave-safe casserole, placing the larger potatoes at the sides of the casserole. Pour in the 1/4 cup water. Cover. Microwave at full power for 15 to 17 minutes until tender, rearranging the potatoes after 8 minutes to place the less-cooked potatoes at the sides of casserole. When finished cooking, let the potatoes stand covered, 3 minutes. Drain. Place the butter in a 1-cup microwave-safe measure. Microwave, uncovered, at full power for 45 to 60 seconds to melt. Cut the potatoes in half. Lightly toss with the butter, salt, pepper and parsley.

Potato Kugel (Potato Pudding)

Bake at 350° for 1 1/2 hours.
Makes 8 servings.

5 large baking	1 teaspoon baking
potatoes (about	powder
4 pounds)	2 teaspoons salt
3 eggs	3 tablespoons
1 large onion,	vegetable oil or
chopped (1 cup)	melted pareve or
1/3 cup *unsifted* all-	regular margarine
purpose flour	

1. Pare potatoes; shred coarsely directly into a large bowl of cold water. Drain, then rinse in cold running water. Squeeze firmly in toweling to remove as much water as possible.
2. Beat eggs in a large bowl until frothy. Add potatoes, onion, flour, baking powder and salt; stir to blend.
3. Grease a 13 x 9 x 2-inch baking pan. Pour mixture into pan; drizzle top with oil.
4. Bake in a moderate oven (350°) for 1 1/2 hours or until richly browned and crusty. Cut into squares to serve.

French Fries

The term "French fry" means deep-fat fry. Our two-step frying method gets most of the cooking over long before dinner.

Makes 4 servings.

4 medium-size baking	Vegetable oil for deep-
or all-purpose	fat frying
potatoes	

1. Wash and pare potatoes. Cut into long 1/2-inch-wide

Duchess Potato Vegetable Casserole.

slices; cut slices into 1/2-inch strips. Drop strips into a bowl of cold water. Dry on paper toweling before frying.

2. Heat 2 to 3 inches of oil in a large saucepan to 325° on a deep-fat frying thermometer. Place a handful of potatoes in the hot oil. Cook 5 to 6 minutes or until tender, but not brown. Stir the potatoes occasionally to keep them from sticking. Remove potatoes with a slotted spoon as they are cooked and drain on paper toweling. This initial frying may be done several hours ahead of time and potatoes left at room temperature.

3. Reheat oil to 375°. Add the potatoes, a handful at a time, and fry again for 2 to 3 minutes or until golden brown and crisp. Drain on paper toweling; keep warm in a very slow oven (250°). Season with salt.

Duchess Potato Vegetable Casserole

Bake at 425° for 6 minutes.

Makes 12 servings.

12 medium-size potatoes	**1/4 teaspoon pepper**
3 egg yolks	**1/4 cup milk**
3/4 cup (1 1/2 sticks) butter or margarine, melted	**1 package (10 ounces) frozen peas**
1/2 teaspoon salt	**1/2 pound medium-size carrots, pared and sliced**

1. Scrub, pare and cut up potatoes. Cook in boiling

(continued)

water to cover in a large saucepan until tender. Drain and mash (about 6 cups).

2. Beat egg yolks, $1/2$ cup of the butter, salt, pepper and milk in medium-size bowl. Stir into mashed potatoes.

3. Spoon half into shallow 6-cup buttered baking dish. Pipe remaining through a pastry bag in a lattice pattern over top. Drizzle remaining $1/4$ cup melted butter over potatoes.

4. Bake in a very hot oven (425°) for 6 minutes or until golden brown.

5. Cook and drain frozen peas following label directions. Spoon part into spaces in lattice top.

6. Cook carrots in boiling water. Drain. Spoon around edge of baking dish.

Scalloped Potatoes

Creamy smooth with an attractively browned surface, this is a favorite.

Bake at 375° for 1 hour.

Makes 6 to 8 servings.

6 to 8 potatoes (about 3 pounds)	**1$1/2$ teaspoons salt**
3 large onions, sliced thin	**$1/4$ teaspoon pepper**
3 tablespoons flour	**2 cups milk, scalded**
	2 tablespoons butter or margarine

1. Pare and slice potatoes very thinly; parboil in boiling salted water in large saucepan 3 minutes; drain.

2. Layer potatoes and onions in a 10-cup baking dish, sprinkling flour, salt and pepper between layers; pour milk over potatoes; dot with butter; cover.

3. Bake in a moderate oven (375°) for 45 minutes; uncover. Bake 15 minutes longer or until potatoes are tender and top is browned slightly.

Lemony New Potatoes

Makes 6 servings.

2 pounds very small new potatoes	**juice**
$1/3$ cup butter or margarine	**2 tablespoons minced chives**
1 teaspoon grated lemon rind	**$1/2$ teaspoon salt**
1 tablespoon lemon	**$1/8$ teaspoon pepper**
	$1/8$ teaspoon ground cardamom

1. Scrub potatoes well; pare a band from the middle of each one.

2. Place potatoes in a large saucepan; cover with water. Heat to boiling; lower heat; cover; simmer 20 minutes or until tender.

3. Drain potatoes; return to pan. Shake over medium heat to dry.

4. Melt butter; stir in lemon rind and juice. Pour over hot potatoes. Sprinkle with chives, salt, pepper and cardamom. Toss gently to coat potatoes.

Cheese-Stuffed Baked Potatoes

Bake at 425° for 55 minutes, then at 350° for 30 minutes.

Makes 8 servings.

8 large baking potatoes	**1 cup tiny cubes of Swiss cheese**
$1/2$ cup milk	**1$1/2$ teaspoons salt**
$1/4$ cup ($1/2$ stick) butter or margarine	**$1/4$ teaspoon pepper**
$1/2$ cup dairy sour cream	**$1/4$ cup shredded Swiss cheese**

1. Scrub potatoes with a vegetable brush; pat dry on paper toweling. Prick skins with a fork. Place potatoes in a large shallow pan.

2. Bake in a hot oven (425°) for 55 minutes or until potatoes are soft.

3. Cut thin lengthwise slice from top of each potato. Carefully scoop out insides with a teaspoon, leaving a $1/4$-inch shell; place potato flesh in a large bowl. Return shells to pan.

4. Combine milk and butter in a small saucepan; heat until butter melts.

5. Mash potatoes; beat in hot milk mixture until potatoes are fluffy. Stir in sour cream, Swiss cheese cubes, salt and pepper. Spoon back into shells, mounding slightly.

6. Re-bake potatoes in a moderate oven (350°) for 25 minutes; top each with shredded Swiss cheese; bake an additional 5 minutes.

Home-Fried Potatoes

Makes 4 servings.

2 large or 4 medium-size baking potatoes (about 1$1/2$ pounds)	**3 tablespoons vegetable oil**
3 tablespoons butter or margarine	**1 medium-size onion, thinly sliced and separated into rings**
	Salt and pepper

1. Pare potatoes; cut into very thin slices. Heat butter and oil in a heavy 10-inch skillet until a few drops of water will sizzle when flicked into skillet.

2. Spread a thin layer of sliced potatoes in the hot fat; allow to cook until the slices of potato turn a golden brown (about 5 minutes), then layer onion rings and remaining potato slices in skillet. Turn potatoes with a broad, flat turner; allow potatoes to cook until crispy-golden; then turn again.

3. Continue cooking and turning until potatoes are crisp and brown; sprinkle with salt and pepper. Serve at once.

Pictured opposite:
Sweet Potato Kebobs, page 776.

Sweet Potato Kebobs

Makes 6 servings.

2 large sweet potatoes or yams	or margarine
3 green-tipped bananas	2 tablespoons unsweetened pineapple juice
1 large lime	1 tablespoon brown sugar
1/4 cup (1/2 stick) butter	

1. Cook potatoes in boiling salted water just until tender, about 25 minutes. Drain; cool and peel. Peel bananas.
2. Cut potatoes and bananas into 1-to 1 1/2-inch pieces. Cut lime into 6 wedges, then cut each wedge in half crosswise. Thread potatoes, bananas and lime pieces onto long skewers.
3. Melt butter in a small saucepan; stir in pineapple juice and sugar; brush part over vegetables. Place skewers on rack over broiler pan. Broil 5 inches from heat for 10 minutes or until heated through, turning and brushing with butter mixture.

Buttered Sweet Potatoes

Tender golden slices of sweet potato make an excellent accompaniment for either ribs or chicken.
Grill about 35 minutes.

Makes 8 servings.

3 pounds fresh sweet potatoes	2 teaspoons salt
1/3 cup butter or margarine	1/4 teaspoon pepper
	1 tablespoon chopped parsley

1. Pare sweet potatoes; cut into 1/4-inch slices. Place slices on center of a 24-inch length of 18-inch heavy-duty foil or 8 small sheets of foil.
2. Cut butter into small chunks. Place over slices; sprinkle with salt and pepper. Bring ends of foil together evenly; fold over and continue to fold down to top of slices. Fold sides up to make a neat sealed package.
3. Place package directly on hot coals to the side of grill. Grill until potatoes are tender, about 35 minutes, turning package occasionally. Sprinkle slices with parsley before serving.

Candied Sweet Potatoes

Bake at 375° for 30 minutes.

Makes 8 servings.

6 medium-size sweet potatoes	butter
	Salt and pepper
6 tablespoons (3/4 stick) unsalted	1/2 cup firmly packed brown sugar

1. Cook potatoes in boiling salted water in a large saucepan, partly covered, just until tender, about 20 minutes. Drain; peel and cut in half lengthwise.
2. Butter a 13 × 9 × 2-inch baking dish with 2 tablespoons of the butter. Arrange potatoes in dish, sprinkle with salt and pepper. Sprinkle or sieve brown sugar evenly over. Dot with remaining butter.
3. Bake in a moderate oven (375°) for 15 minutes; turn carefully. Continue baking 15 minutes longer or until they are evenly glazed.

Note: Potatoes may be baked several hours ahead and reheated in a moderate oven (350°) for 20 minutes.

Spinach with Mushrooms

Makes 4 servings.

1 pound fresh spinach	chopped
6 medium-size mushrooms	1 tablespoon dry sherry or lemon juice
3 tablespoons vegetable oil	1 teaspoon salt
1 small onion, finely chopped (1/4 cup)	1 teaspoon sugar
1 clove garlic, finely	Dash ground nutmeg

1. Remove stems from spinach; wash leaves well; drain. Wash mushrooms; drain; trim stem ends; cut through stems into thin slices.
2. Heat oil in large skillet or wok; add onion, garlic and mushrooms; stir-fry 3 minutes over medium-high heat. Add spinach; cook, turning and stirring gently 2 to 3 minutes or until spinach is wilted. Stir in sherry, salt, sugar and nutmeg; cook 30 seconds.

Spinach-Cheese Casserole

Bake at 350° for 15 minutes.

Makes 4 servings.

2 bunches (1 1/2 to 2 pounds) spinach, washed, stems removed, slivered to make about 10 cups	6 ounces Cheddar cheese, shredded (1 1/2 cups)
2 tablespoons water	1/2 cup small curd cottage cheese
2 cloves garlic, minced	1/2 teaspoon salt
1/4 cup (1/2 stick) butter or margarine	1/4 teaspoon pepper
	3 cups cooked rice
	6 slices (6 ounces) mozzarella cheese

1. Cook spinach, covered, in a Dutch oven with water

just until limp but still bright green; drain well, pressing out excess moisture. Transfer to bowl.

2. Sauté garlic in 1 tablespoon of the butter until light brown in a small skillet; add remaining 3 tablespoons butter, stirring over low heat until melted.

3. Pour butter-garlic mixture over spinach. Stir in Cheddar and cottage cheese, salt and pepper. Spoon cooked rice into a 1½-quart shallow baking pan; top with spinach mixture.

4. Bake, uncovered, in a moderate oven (350°) until cheeses are melted and blended, about 15 minutes. Cover evenly with mozzarella cheese. Broil until cheese is melted and lightly brown, about 5 minutes.

Wilted Spinach and Lettuce

Country-style wilted lettuce has always been a popular vegetable dish. We've embellished the original with spinach and a touch of mint.

Makes 6 servings.

¾ **pound spinach**	⅓ **cup tarragon-**
1 head Boston lettuce	**flavored vinegar**
4 bacon slices	**1 tablespoon chopped**
1 medium-size onion,	**fresh mint**
sliced	OR: **1 teaspoon dried**
1 tablespoon sugar	**mint, crumbled**
½ **teaspoon salt**	**1 hard-cooked egg,**
⅛ **teaspoon pepper**	**chopped**

1. Wash spinach and lettuce; dry on paper toweling; tear larger leaves into bite-size pieces (about 4 cups each).

2. Cook bacon until crisp in large skillet or Dutch oven; drain on paper toweling. Sauté onion in bacon drippings in skillet until soft but not brown. Add sugar, salt, pepper, vinegar and mint; bring to boiling. Add spinach and lettuce; toss with hot dressing just until wilted. Turn into heated serving dish. Crumble bacon over top; sprinkle with hard-cooked egg.

Succotash

Makes 6 servings.

1 package (10 ounces)	**1 can (about**
frozen baby lima	**16 ounces) stewed**
beans	**tomatoes**
1 package (10 ounces)	**3 tablespoons butter**
frozen whole-kernel	**or margarine**
corn	

1. Cook lima beans following label directions; when almost tender, add corn; bring to boiling; simmer 2 minutes. (If needed, add 1 or 2 tablespoons water to finish cooking, but when done, water should be absorbed.)

2. Stir in tomatoes, heat just until steaming hot; spoon succotash into serving dishes and top each with a pat of butter.

Vegetable-Ham Soufflé Pie

Bake at 425° for 10 minutes, then at 375° for 20 minutes.

Makes 6 servings.

1 cup *sifted* **all-**	**thick and cut into**
purpose flour	**1-inch strips**
¼ **teaspoon salt**	½ **teaspoon salt**
⅓ **cup vegetable**	¼ **teaspoon pepper**
shortening	½ **teaspoon leaf**
2 to 3 tablespoons ice	**marjoram, crumbled**
water	**3 tablespoons butter**
1 cup sliced carrots	**or margarine**
(about 4 small)	**3 tablespoons flour**
3 small onions, each	¾ **cup water**
cut into 6 wedges	**3¾ tablespoons**
¼ **pound mushrooms,**	**instant nonfat dry**
sliced (1 cup)	**milk powder**
1 medium-size	**2 ounces Swiss**
zucchini, cut into	**cheese, shredded**
2 × ¼-inch sticks	**(½ cup)**
¼ **pound cooked ham,**	**3 eggs, separated**
¼ **inch**	

1. Preheat oven to 425°.

2. Sift the 1 cup flour and the ¼ teaspoon salt into a medium-size bowl; cut in shortening with a pastry blender until mixture is crumbly. Sprinkle ice water over mixture; mix lightly with a fork just until pastry holds together and leaves side of bowl clean.

3. Roll out pastry to a 12-inch round on a lightly floured surface. Fit into a 9-inch pie plate. Trim overhang to ½ inch; turn edge under; pinch to make a stand-up edge; flute. Prick shell well all over with a fork.

4. Bake shell in a preheated hot oven (425°) for 10 minutes. (Check shell after 5 minutes. If bubbles have formed, prick again.) Cool on wire rack. Lower oven temperature to 375°.

5. Cook carrots, onions, mushrooms and zucchini in boiling salted water for 5 minutes or until crisp-tender; drain. Turn into large bowl; add ham, the ½ teaspoon salt, pepper and marjoram; mix lightly.

6. Melt butter in a medium-size saucepan; blend in flour; cook 1 minute. Stir the ¾ cup water into dry milk in a small bowl; stir mixture into saucepan. Cook, stirring constantly, until mixture thickens and bubbles. Remove from heat; stir in cheese until melted. Let sauce cool while beating eggs.

7. Beat egg whites in a small bowl with electric mixer until soft peaks form.

(continued)

8. Beat egg yolks until light in a medium-size bowl with same beaters. Beat in cooled cheese sauce. Measure 1/4 cup of the cheese mixture; stir into vegetables. Fold remaining cheese mixture into beaten egg whites until no streaks of white remain.
9. Spoon vegetable mixture into cooled pastry shell. Carefully spoon soufflé mixture over vegetables, spreading to edge of pastry to seal in vegetables.
10. Bake in a preheated moderate oven (375°) for 20 minutes or until soufflé top has puffed and is lightly browned. Serve at once.

Gingered Butternut Squash

Makes 8 servings.

2 butternut squash (about 4 pounds)	**chopped crystallized ginger**
1/4 cup (1/2 stick) butter or margarine	**1 teaspoon salt**
1 tablespoon maple syrup	**1/8 teaspoon pepper**
2 tablespoons finely	**1/4 teaspoon ground nutmeg**

1. Split squash in half, scoop out seeds and membranes. Cook in boiling salted water in skillet 20 minutes or until tender; drain. Cool slightly.
2. Scoop pulp into large bowl. Add butter, syrup, ginger, salt, pepper and nutmeg. Beat with a portable electric mixer until it is well mixed.
3. Spoon into heated serving dish; keep warm.

Spaghetti Squash with Meat Sauce

Makes 4 servings.

1 spaghetti squash (about 3 pounds)	**1 can (28 ounces) tomato puree**
1 pound ground chuck	**1 teaspoon leaf oregano, crumbled**
1 large onion, chopped (1 cup)	**2 teaspoons leaf basil, crumbled**
1 clove garlic, minced	**Salt and pepper**
1 medium-size green pepper, halved, seeded and chopped	**1 cup grated Parmesan cheese**

1. Pour enough hot water into a kettle to make a 1-inch depth. Scrub squash; quarter; place in kettle, rind-side down. Bring to boiling; cover; lower heat. Simmer about 20 minutes or until squash is tender.
2. While squash is cooking, cook ground chuck in a large skillet until brown. Add onion, garlic and green pepper; sauté until onion is tender. Spoon off any excess fat.

3. Add tomato puree, oregano and basil; add salt and pepper to taste. Cover; cook over low heat, stirring occasionally, for 15 minutes.
4. Remove squash from water; scrape out seeds; fluff out strands of squash from shell; discard shell. Serve meat sauce over squash. Sprinkle with cheese.

Quick Squash au Gratin

Toasty croutons and melty Cheddar top squash and onion.

Makes 4 servings.

3 medium-size yellow squash	**cut into small cubes**
1 small onion, sliced	**2 tablespoons butter or margarine**
1/4 cup water	**2 ounces Cheddar cheese, shredded (1/2 cup)**
1 teaspoon salt	
1 slice white bread,	

1. Wash the squash; trim ends, then slice squash 1/4-inch thick. Place the squash slices in a medium-size skillet with the onion, water and salt; cover.
2. Cook, stirring once or twice, 10 to 12 minutes or until tender.
3. While squash cooks, sauté bread cubes in butter just until toasty in a small skillet.
4. Spoon squash and onion into a heated serving bowl; sprinkle with the shredded cheese and toasted bread cubes.

Summer Squash Monterey

Grill 30 minutes.

Makes 6 servings.

6 medium-size yellow squash	**1/3 cup diced red pepper**
1 teaspoon salt	**1/3 cup diced green pepper**
4 ounces Monterey Jack cheese, shredded (1 cup)	**2 tablespoons butter or margarine**

Cut 6 twelve-inch squares of heavy-duty aluminum foil. Cut squash into 1/4-inch diagonal slices; place on foil. Sprinkle over equal amounts of salt, cheese and red and green pepper; dot with butter. Close packet by folding in sides, then rolling up ends. Grill about 5 inches from medium-hot coals about 30 minutes, turning occasionally.

Pictured opposite: Gingered Butternut Squash.

Potato and Leek Pâté

Makes 8 servings.

1½ pounds russet
  baking potatoes
½ teaspoon salt
2 large leeks, washed
  and trimmed
1 envelope unflavored
  gelatin
¼ cup dry white wine
⅓ cup butter or
  margarine, melted
⅓ cup plain yogurt
2 green onions, sliced

2 tablespoons
  chopped chives
¼ teaspoon salt
⅛ teaspoon pepper
Curly lettuce *(optional)*
Chives *(optional)*
Pimiento Vinaigrette
  (recipe follows)
Creamy Celery Seed
  Dressing *(recipe
  follows)*

1. Scrub the potatoes and cook in boiling salted water to cover in a large saucepan just until easily pierced with a fork. Drain. Let cool. Peel. Press through a potato ricer or food mill. Set aside.
2. Trim the green stems from the leeks. Cut the white parts into ½-inch slices. Reserve. Cook the stems in a small amount of boiling water until soft and pliable, 10 minutes. Drain. Cool.
3. Cut the green stems lengthwise on one side; open the stems flat in one piece. Line a greased 7³⁄₈ × 3⁵⁄₈ × 2¼-inch loaf pan with the stems; reserve some to cover the top.
4. Cook the reserved slices of the white part of the leeks in a small amount of boiling water in a saucepan until tender, about 20 minutes. Drain. Chop finely. Stir into the potato.
5. Sprinkle the gelatin over the wine in a small saucepan. Let soften for 5 minutes; stir over low heat to dissolve the gelatin.
6. Add the gelatin, butter, yogurt, green onions, chives, salt and pepper to the potato; mix well. Turn into the prepared pan, smoothing the top. Cover with the reserved leek greens. Cover with plastic wrap. Chill for 5 to 6 hours or until firm.
7. To serve, remove the plastic wrap. Invert onto a cutting board. Cut the pâté into 8 equal slices. Place on individual plates. Garnish with the curly lettuce and chives, if you wish. Spoon the Pimiento Vinaigrette and Creamy Celery Seed Dressing on the plates on either side of the pâté.

To Make Ahead: The pâté can be made up to 2 days ahead, the dressings a day ahead, and refrigerated tightly covered.

Pimiento Vinaigrette: Combine ½ cup olive or vegetable oil, 1 tablespoon lemon juice, 1 tablespoon red wine vinegar, ½ teaspoon dry mustard, 1 clove garlic, finely chopped, ½ teaspoon leaf basil, crumbled, 1 jar (4 ounces) chopped, drained pimiento, ¼ teaspoon salt and ⅛ teaspoon pepper in a jar with a lid. Cover; shake well. Makes 1 cup.

Creamy Celery Seed Dressing: Combine ⅓ cup olive or vegetable oil, ⅓ cup tarragon vinegar, 2 tablespoons sugar, 1 tablespoon whole celery seeds, ½ teaspoon salt, ¼ teaspoon pepper, 1 cup plain yogurt and 1 cup dairy sour cream in a bowl. Mix. Cover; refrigerate until ready to use. Makes 2⅔ cups.

Spicy Chili-Topped Baked Potato

Bake at 400° for 50 minutes.

Makes 4 servings.

4 large baking
  potatoes
1 can (15 ounces) chili
  without beans
Lettuce leaves
2 tablespoons sliced
  green onion

2 ounces Cheddar
  cheese, finely
  shredded (½ cup)
1 medium-size
  avocado, halved,
  pitted, peeled and
  sliced

1. Scrub potatoes well. Prick the skin with a fork to allow steam to escape.
2. Bake on the oven rack in a hot oven (400°) for 50 minutes or until they feel soft when touched. Or, microwave potatoes on high power for 6 minutes. Rearrange and turn potatoes. Microwave 4½ to 6½ more minutes. Cover potatoes with foil or a dish to hold in heat; let stand 5 to 10 minutes.
3. Heat chili in a small saucepan. Just before serving, slit open potatoes by cutting a cross on the top of each. Squeeze each end lightly to open, then using a fork, fluff up inside. Place potatoes on lettuce-lined plates. Top with hot chili, onion and cheese. Serve with avocado slices.

Spicy Chili-Topped Baked Potato.

Potato and Leek Pâté,
page 780.

Surprise Burgers

Makes 8 servings.

$^1/_2$ **pound dried lentils
(1$^1/_4$ cups)**
3 cups water
**1 large onion,
chopped (1 cup)**
1 cup chopped carrots
**3 cups fresh bread
crumbs (6 slices)**
1 egg

1 teaspoon garlic salt
$^1/_2$ **teaspoon leaf
oregano, crumbled**
$^1/_2$ **teaspoon salt**
**3 tablespoons butter
or margarine**
**4 slices American
cheese, each slice
cut into 4 triangles**

1. Wash lentils; add water and bring to boiling in large
saucepan. Lower heat; cover. Cook 15 minutes.
2. Add onion and carrots. Cook 15 minutes more or
until lentils are very tender. Remove from heat. Cool
slightly. Stir in bread crumbs, egg, garlic salt, oregano
and salt.
3. Melt butter in large skillet. Drop lentil mixture by
rounded one-half cupfuls into hot butter. Flatten
mounds into patties with pancake turner or broad
spatula. Cook patties until firm and golden brown on
both sides.
4. Top each patty with 2 cheese triangles; heat until
melted.

Ratatouille   A vegetable stew originating from
Provence in France. It contains eggplant, zucchini,
tomatoes and sweet peppers fried in olive oil, then
gently stewed until soft. Ratatouille is served as a side
dish, or the mixture can be used as a filling for tomato
cups, crêpes or omelets.

Ratatouille

*This is a savory melange of fresh vegetables gently
herbed, seasoned and simmered. Serve warm or at
room temperature as an appetizer or a side dish.*

Makes 16 cups.

**2 medium-size
eggplants
(1$^1/_4$ pounds each)**
**8 medium-size
zucchini (about
2$^1/_2$ pounds)**
**4 large onions (about
1$^1/_4$ pounds)**
**3 medium-size green
peppers (about
1 pound)**
**1 cup olive or
vegetable oil**

**3 to 4 large cloves
garlic, minced**
**1 can (17 ounces)
plum tomatoes,
drained**
$^1/_2$ **cup chopped fresh
parsley**
5 teaspoons salt
$^1/_2$ **teaspoon pepper**
**2 teaspoons leaf
oregano, crumbled**
**2 teaspoons leaf basil,
crumbled**

1. Cut eggplant into $^1/_2$-inch-thick slices, then into 1-
inch cubes. Slice ends off zucchini; cut into $^1/_4$-inch
slices. Slice onions thinly. Halve green peppers;
remove membrane and seeds; cut into $^1/_4$-inch strips.
2. Sauté half the eggplant cubes in $^1/_4$ cup of the oil in

(continued)

a large skillet until lightly browned, about 5 minutes. Remove to large Dutch oven or kettle. Repeat with ¼ cup or more oil and remaining eggplant; remove to Dutch oven.

3. Add ¼ cup more oil to same skillet. Sauté zucchini until tender, about 5 minutes. Remove to Dutch oven.

4. Add the remaining ¼ cup oil to skillet. Sauté onions, green peppers and garlic until soft, about 5 minutes; add to Dutch oven.

5. Add tomatoes, parsley, salt, pepper, oregano and basil to eggplant mixture; stir gently to combine.

6. Simmer mixture over low heat, covered, for 15 minutes. Remove cover; cook 10 minutes longer or until most of juice has evaporated. Serve warm or cool and refrigerate to hold 1 to 2 days. Freeze for longer storage.

Ratatouille-Stuffed Tomatoes: Cut slice off tops of large tomatoes, then hollow out tomatoes carefully. (Use tomato pulp to make soup.) Sprinkle inside of tomatoes very lightly with salt, then turn upside down on paper toweling to drain for an hour. Refrigerate until ready to serve, then fill with ratatouille. Serve as a side dish or as appetizers, using smaller tomatoes.

Hearty Vegetable Stew

Bake at 350° for 45 minutes, then at 375° for 20 minutes.

Makes 8 servings.

3 large onions, sliced	2 teaspoons salt
2 large cloves garlic, minced	¼ teaspoon pepper
2 tablespoons vegetable oil	1 teaspoon leaf basil, crumbled
2 tablespoons butter	1 can (12 ounces) vegetable juice cocktail*
1 pound carrots, pared and cut into 1-inch pieces	1 can (13¾ ounces) beef broth
1 pound new potatoes, washed and quartered	2 cans (20 ounces each) chick-peas, drained
1 head cauliflower (1 pound), separated into flowerets	2 green peppers, halved, seeded and cut into strips
½ pound mushrooms, cleaned and quartered	2 cups fresh bread crumbs (4 slices)
½ small head cabbage, cored and cut into 8 slices	½ cup freshly grated Parmesan cheese
	½ cup chopped fresh parsley

1. Sauté onions and garlic in oil and butter in 4-quart flameproof casserole 5 minutes. Add carrots, potatoes, cauliflower, mushrooms and cabbage. Cook, stirring occasionally, 20 minutes.

2. Sprinkle vegetables with salt, pepper and basil. Add vegetable juice and beef broth. Cover; bring to simmering. Stir in chick-peas and green peppers.

3. Bake, covered, in a moderate oven (350°) for 45

minutes or until potatoes are tender. Remove from oven; raise oven temperature to 375°.

4. Combine bread crumbs, cheese and parsley in medium-size bowl. Spoon over vegetables, covering entire top surface.

5. Bake, uncovered, 20 minutes longer or until crumbs are browned.

Two cans vegetable juice cocktail may be used instead of the beef broth.

Swiss Chard Enchiladas

Makes 6 servings.

2 pounds Swiss chard, washed well	2 hot chilies, fresh or canned, seeds removed
6 tablespoons vegetable oil	1 cup water
1 large clove garlic, finely chopped	Salt
1 teaspoon salt	Vegetable oil
¼ teaspoon pepper	18 corn tortillas
3 medium-size tomatoes (about 18 ounces)	1 cup dairy sour cream
OR: 1 can (16 ounces) tomatoes, drained *(See Note)*	8 ounces mild Cheddar cheese, shredded (1 cup)
1 small onion	1 large onion, thinly sliced, separated into rings
1 clove garlic	

1. Cook the chard in a small amount of water in a kettle, stirring occasionally, for about 5 minutes. Drain and chop coarsely. Heat 2 tablespoons of the oil in a large saucepan and cook the chopped garlic without browning. Add the chard and cook, stirring gently, for about 3 minutes. Add salt and pepper; reserve.

2. Place the tomatoes, onion, garlic, and chilies in the container of an electric blender or food processor; cover and whirl until smooth, but do not overblend. Heat remaining 3 tablespoons oil in a medium-size saucepan; add the blender mixture and cook, stirring and scraping the bottom of the pan, for 5 minutes. Add the water and salt to taste; cook 1 minute longer. Keep warm.

3. Heat ¼-inch of oil in a small skillet. Lower heat and fry tortillas, 1 at a time, briefly on each side until heated through and limp. (They should never become crisp around the edges.) Drain on paper toweling.

4. Spread a rounded tablespoon of tomato sauce across the tortilla; add a little Swiss chard filling and sour cream. Roll loosely; place side by side in a warm 13 × 9 × 2-inch baking dish.

5. Reheat the remaining sauce and pour over the enchiladas. Sprinkle with the cheese and place under

a preheated broiler until cheese melts. Garnish with onion rings.

Note: If using fresh tomatoes, broil until skins blister; peel. If using canned tomatoes, use juice as part of the 1 cup water called for.

Selecting and Storing Tomatoes
Choose red, ripe-looking tomatoes that are plump, free from bruises and not overly soft. Tomatoes may mature somewhat off the vine. If purchased while slightly green, allow to come to good color at room temperature out of direct sunlight.

Never, ever refrigerate tomatoes. Cold ruins their delicate flavor. Store in a dark place at a temperature between 50° and 70°F., if possible, for no more than a week.

Spanish Tomato Cups

Bake at 350° for 20 minutes.

Makes 6 servings.

6 large firm-ripe tomatoes	or margarine
1 package (6 ounces) Spanish rice mix	1 container (4 ounces) processed cheese spread with pimientos
Water	
2 tablespoons butter	

1. Cut a thin slice from top of each tomato; scoop out insides into a 2-cup measure. (There should be 2 cups.) Place tomato cups in a shallow pan.
2. Prepare rice mix with water, butter and the 2 cups tomato pulp, following label directions. Spoon into tomato cups; top each with about 1 tablespoon of the cheese spread.
3. Bake in a moderate oven (350°) for 20 minutes or until heated through. Garnish with sliced ripe olives, if you wish.

Herb-Scented Oven-Dried Tomatoes

Use these in salads, pasta sauce, soups or any dish that would benefit from a sharp tomato flavor. Use sparingly since the flavor is very concentrated.
Bake at 150° for 14 to 17 hours.
Makes 4 half-pints.

6 pounds large, uniform-size plum tomatoes, halved lengthwise	such as rosemary, thyme or oregano
	4 cloves garlic, split
2 tablespoons coarse kosher salt	16 whole black peppercorns
4 sprigs fresh herbs,	Olive and vegetable oils

1. Preheat the oven to very slow (150°).
2. Arrange the tomatoes, cut-side up, on 2 wire racks set over jelly-roll pans; sprinkle with the salt.

3. Bake in the preheated very slow oven (150°) for 14 to 17 hours or until the tomatoes are very wrinkled, deep red and without signs of moisture. Begin checking the tomatoes every hour after 14 hours. (The size of the tomatoes will determine how long they will take to dry out completely.)
4. When ready to can, wash 4 half-pint canning jars and lids and bands in hot soapy water. Rinse. Leave the jars in hot water until needed. Place the lids and bands in a saucepan of simmering water until ready to use.
5. Pack the tomatoes into the clean, hot canning jar. Place 1 herb sprig, 2 pieces of garlic and 4 peppercorns in each jar. Cover with the oils. Seal. Refrigerate for up to 3 months.

Tomatoes Stuffed with Ham Salad

A sour cream–mayonnaise dressing spiked with horseradish and mustard adds zip to this ham salad.

Makes 4 servings.

Horseradish Mayonnaise:	1 cup chopped celery
1/3 cup dairy sour cream	1/4 cup chopped black Greek olives*
2 tablespoons mayonnaise	1/4 cup finely chopped dill pickle
3 teaspoons bottled horseradish	1/4 cup chopped parsley
1 teaspoon Dijon-style mustard	4 medium-size ripe tomatoes
1/8 teaspoon pepper	8 leaves Boston lettuce
3/4 pound deli baked ham, cut into small dice (about 2 cups)	8 whole black Greek olives for garnish

1. Prepare Horseradish Mayonnaise: Combine sour cream, mayonnaise, horseradish, mustard and pepper in large bowl.
2. Add ham, celery, olives, pickle and 3 tablespoons of the parsley; toss gently until all ingredients are evenly coated.
3. Cut each tomato vertically into 6 wedges to within 1/2 inch of bottom. Carefully spoon out center membranes and seeds; save for another use. Stuff tomatoes with ham mixture. Serve on platter lined with Boston lettuce leaves. Garnish with olives and remaining chopped parsley.

For best flavor, use black Greek olives packed in brine. Regular black ripe olives may be substituted.

Tomato-Lima Cups

Makes 6 servings.

1 package (10 ounces) frozen baby lima beans	**vinegar**
3/4 teaspoon salt	**6 medium-size firm-ripe tomatoes**
1/2 teaspoon sugar	**Lettuce leaves**
1/4 teaspoon paprika	**6 pimiento-stuffed green olives**
1/8 teaspoon pepper	**6 small pitted ripe olives**
1/2 cup chopped fresh parsley	**1 canned pimiento, cut in 6 strips**
1/3 cup vegetable oil	
3 tablespoons cider	

1. Cook lima beans, following label directions; drain well; place in a medium-size bowl.
2. Add salt, sugar, paprika, pepper, parsley, vegetable oil and vinegar to beans; toss until well mixed and beans are shiny. Cover with plastic wrap and chill several hours.
3. Heat a pan of water just to boiling. Holding tomatoes one at a time on a slotted spoon, dip into water and hold about 1 minute, then lift out and place in a pie plate to cool. Cut a thin slice from the top of each tomato, then peel off skin. Scoop out the insides with a teaspoon, being careful not to break shells. Turn shells upside down on plate to drain; cover and chill.
4. To serve: Place a large lettuce leaf on each of 6 salad plates; stand a tomato cup on each leaf; spoon lima bean mixture into cups.
5. Slide a green olive onto each of 6 wooden picks, then a pitted ripe olive and a strip of pimiento. Stand one pick in center of each tomato cup. Chill 2 to 3 hours or until serving time.

Crumb-Stuffed Tomatoes

Bake at 350° for 30 minutes.
Makes 6 servings.

3 tablespoons butter or margarine	**parsley**
1 medium-size onion, finely chopped (1/2 cup)	**1/2 teaspoon salt**
	1 teaspoon fresh thyme
1 clove garlic, crushed	**OR: 1/4 teaspoon leaf thyme, crumbled**
1/2 cup packaged bread crumbs	**1/3 cup water**
1/2 cup chopped fresh	**3 large tomatoes**

1. Melt butter in a large skillet; add onion and garlic; sauté until soft. Add bread crumbs, parsley, salt and thyme; add water and mix well.

Pictured opposite:
Tomato-Lima Cups.

2. Cut tomatoes horizontally in half and scoop out pulp. Fill with stuffing. Place in a 13 × 9 × 2-inch baking pan.
3. Bake in a moderate oven (350°) for 30 minutes or until hot.

Herbed Tomatoes and Onions

Makes 6 to 8 servings.

Green leafy lettuce	**crushed**
3 to 4 medium-size ripe tomatoes (1 to 1 1/4 pounds), cut into 1/4-inch-thick slices	**1/4 teaspoon coarse kosher salt**
	1 teaspoon coarse-grained mustard
1 medium-size red onion, thinly sliced	**2 teaspoons lemon juice**
2 tablespoons chopped fresh basil	**1/4 cup olive or vegetable oil**
OR: 2 teaspoons leaf basil, crumbled	**1 to 2 teaspoons wine vinegar**
1 small clove garlic,	**1/4 teaspoon freshly ground pepper**

1. Arrange the lettuce on a serving plate. Overlap the tomato slices with the onion slices over the lettuce. Sprinkle with the basil.
2. Mash the garlic with the salt in a small bowl with the back of a spoon to form a smooth paste. Stir in the mustard, lemon juice, oil and vinegar. Drizzle over the tomatoes. Sprinkle with the pepper.

To Make Ahead: Prepare the dressing the day before or several hours in advance to allow the flavor to develop.

Candied Yams

Bake at 375° for 30 minutes.

Makes 6 servings.

2 large yams or sweet potatoes (about 1 1/4 pounds), scrubbed	**brown sugar**
	2 tablespoons bourbon
	2 tablespoons butter or margarine
1/3 cup light corn syrup	**Chopped pecans (optional)**
2 tablespoons light	

1. Preheat the oven to moderate (375°). Grease a shallow 1-quart baking dish.
2. Cook the yams in boiling salted water to cover in a large saucepan for 30 minutes or just until tender. Drain. When cool enough to handle, peel. Slice crosswise into 1/4-inch-thick slices.
3. Arrange the yams in the prepared baking dish. Stir together the corn syrup, sugar and bourbon in a small bowl. Pour evenly over the yams. Dot with the butter.
4. Bake in the preheated moderate oven (375°), basting several times, for 30 minutes or until glazed

(continued)

and heated through. Sprinkle with chopped pecans, if you wish.

To Make Ahead: Cook the potatoes in the boiling salted water, drain and refrigerate until ready to serve. When ready to serve, proceed as the recipe directs.

Sweet Yam Puffs

Makes 3½ dozen puffs.

1 large sweet potato or yam, cooked and peeled
¼ cup (½ stick) butter or margarine
1 cup milk, scalded
2 cups *sifted* all-purpose flour
1½ cups sugar
1 teaspoon salt
4 teaspoons baking
powder
1 teaspoon ground cinnamon
¼ teaspoon ground nutmeg
¼ teaspoon ground allspice
2 cups whole wheat flour
Vegetable oil for frying

1. Mash yam with butter in a medium-size bowl; stir in milk.
2. Sift together all-purpose flour, sugar, salt, baking powder, cinnamon, nutmeg and allspice. Stir into yam mixture with whole wheat flour. Dough will be a little sticky. Cover bowl; refrigerate 1 hour.
3. Pour oil into a deep skillet to a depth of about 1¼ inches; heat to 360° to 370° on a deep-fat frying thermometer.
4. Pat chilled dough out to ¼-inch thickness on a floured board. Cut into rounds with a 2-inch biscuit cutter. Drop into hot oil, a few at a time; fry until golden brown, about 2½ minutes. Turn with a slotted spoon to brown evenly. Remove to paper towels; cool.

Zucchini à La Grecque

Makes 8 servings.

6 medium-size zucchini, washed and trimmed
1 medium-size onion, minced (½ cup)
3 cloves garlic, minced
2 tablespoons olive oil
1 can (16 ounces)
tomatoes, drained
1 teaspoon coriander seeds
OR: ½ teaspoon ground coriander
1 tablespoon vinegar
¼ teaspoon salt
⅛ teaspoon pepper

1. Score zucchini skin with tines of fork; quarter each lengthwise, then cut into 3-inch-long strips.
2. Cook zucchini in boiling water in a large skillet, covered, 5 minutes, or just until crisp-tender; drain

carefully. Cool slightly and arrange in rows in shallow serving dish.
3. Sauté onion and garlic in oil until soft in a large skillet, about 5 minutes; add tomatoes, breaking up with wooden spoon, and coriander seeds. Cook over medium-high heat, stirring often, until most of the liquid has evaporated. Stir in vinegar, salt and pepper. Spoon tomato mixture over zucchini. Cover with plastic wrap. Chill. Serve at room temperature.

Deviled Cherry Tomatoes

Makes 4 servings.

¼ cup (½ stick) butter
3 tablespoons lemon juice
1 tablespoon prepared mustard
1 tablespoon light
brown sugar
1 pint cherry tomatoes, stemmed and halved
2 tablespoons sliced green onion

Melt butter in a medium-size skillet. Stir in lemon juice, mustard and brown sugar until mixture is smooth and comes to boiling. Add tomatoes; heat thoroughly. Remove from heat; toss with onion.

Vegetable and Tofu Stew

This stew is even better the second day after it is prepared. Serve in large bowls with herbed bread and sweet butter, and a fresh spinach and tomato salad with mustard vinaigrette dressing.

Makes 6 servings.

2 large green peppers, halved, seeded and cut into 2 × ¼-inch pieces (about 2 cups)
½ pound mushrooms, sliced (2 cups)
¾ cup chopped onion
2 cloves garlic, minced
3 tablespoons olive or vegetable oil
2 tablespoons flour
2 cups water
1 can (14½ ounces) sliced baby tomatoes
½ pound zucchini, thinly sliced
1½ teaspoons leaf basil, crumbled
1½ teaspoons dillweed
1 can (15 ounces) blackeyed peas, drained and rinsed
1 pound soybean curd or tofu, preferably firm-style, drained and cut into ½-inch cubes
½ cup grated Parmesan cheese

1. Sauté green peppers, mushrooms, onion and garlic in oil in a large skillet until tender, but not brown.
2. Stir in flour until blended. Remove skillet from heat; stir in water, tomatoes, zucchini, basil and dill. Return to heat; cook, stirring constantly, until zucchini is almost tender.
3. Add peas and tofu; heat thoroughly, stirring very gently, so that tofu does not break up. Sprinkle with Parmesan cheese just before serving.

Cocktail dip served in a green pepper and colorful vegetables make an unusual table decoration.

METRIC CHART

Cup Equivalents (volume)

¼ cup	= 60 ml.
⅓ cup	= 85 ml.
½ cup	= 125 ml.
⅔ cup	= 170 ml.
¾ cup	= 180 ml.
1 cup	= 250 ml.
1¼ cups	= 310 ml.
1½ cups	= 375 ml.
2 cups	= 500 ml.
3 cups	= 750 ml.
5 cups	= 1250 ml.

Spoonful Equivalents (volume)

⅛ teaspoon	= .5 ml.
¼ teaspoon	= 1.5 ml.
½ teaspoon	= 3 ml.
¾ teaspoon	= 4 ml.
1 teaspoon	= 5 ml.
1 tablespoon	= 15 ml.
2 tablespoons	= 30 ml.
3 tablespoons	= 45 ml.

Oven Temperatures

275° F	= 135° C
300° F	= 149° C
325° F	= 165° C
350° F	= 175° C
375° F	= 190° C
400° F	= 205° C
425° F	= 218° C
450° F	= 230° C
500° F	= 260° C

Pan Sizes (linear & volume)

1 inch	= 2.5 cm.
8-inch square	= 20-cm. square (baking pan)
13 x 9 x 1½-inch	= 33 x 23 x 4 cm.
10 x 6 x 2-inch	= 25 x 15 x 5 cm.
13 x 9 x 2-inch	= 33 x 23 x 5 cm.
12 x 7½ x 1½-inch	= 30 x 18 x 4 cm. (baking pans & dishes)
9 x 5 x 3-inch	= 23 x 13 x 8 cm. (loaf pan)
10-inch	= 25 cm. (skillet)
12-inch	= 30 cm. (skillet)
1 quart	= 1 liter (baking dishes)
2 quarts	= 2 liters
5 to 6 cups	= 1.5 liters (ring mold)

Weight (meat, can, and package sizes)

1 ounce	= 28 g.
½ pound	= 225 g.
¾ pound	= 340 g.
1 pound	= 450 g.
1½ pounds	= 675 g.
2 pounds	= 900 g.
3 pounds	= 1.4 kg. (most meats—larger amounts will be weighed in kilograms)
10 ounces	= 280 g. (most frozen vegetables)
10½ ounces	= 294 g. (most condensed soups)
15 ounces	= 425 g.
16 ounces	= 450 g.
1 pound, 24 ounces	= 850 g. (can sizes)

APPROXIMATE EQUIVALENTS FOR BASIC FOODS

Food	Metric	American
Baking powder	4.3 grams	1 teaspoon (approx.)
	30 grams	2½ tablespoons
Breadcrumbs (dry)	90 grams	1 cup
(fresh)	45 grams	1 cup
Butter	15 grams	1 tablespoon
	125 grams	½ cup
	500 grams	2 cups
Cheese	500 grams	1 pound (generous)
(grated)	100 grams	1 cup (scant)
Coffee (medium ground)	85 grams	1 cup
Cornstarch	10 grams	1 tablespoon
Fish	500 grams	1 pound (generous)
Flour (unsifted, all purpose)	35 grams	¼ cup
	70 grams	½ cup
	142 grams	1 cup
	500 grams	3½ cups
(sifted, all purpose)	32 grams	¼ cup
	60 grams	½ cup
	128 grams	1 cup
(sifted, cake and pastry)	30 grams	¼ cup
	60 grams	½ cup
	120 grams	1 cup
Fruit (fresh)	500 grams	1 pound (generous)
(dried)	500 grams	2 cups
Meats	500 grams	1 pound (generous)
(diced)	226 grams	1 cup
Pepper (whole white)	30 grams	3⅚ tablespoons
(whole black)	30 grams	4½ tablespoons
(powdered)	30 grams	4 tablespoons
Rice	240 grams	1 cup
Salt	15 grams	1 tablespoon
Spices (ground)	2½ grams	1 teaspoon
	15 grams	2 tablespoons
Sugar (fine granulated)	5 grams	1 teaspoon
	15 grams	1 tablespoon
	60 grams	¼ cup
	240 grams	1 cup
(confectioners' or icing)	35 grams	¼ cup
	70 grams	½ cup
	140 grams	1 cup
(brown)	10 grams	1 tablespoon
	80 grams	½ cup
	160 grams	1 cup
Vegetables (fresh)	500 grams	1 pound (generous)
(dried)	500 grams	2 cups

METRIC MEASURE CONVERSION

Recipe Calls For	Symbol	Multiply By	To Find	Symbol
teaspoons	tsp.	5	milliliters	ml.
tablespoons	tbsp.	15	milliliters	ml.
fluid ounces	fl. oz.	30	milliliters	ml.
cups	c.	0.24	liters	l.
pints	pt.	0.47	liters	l.
quarts	qt.	0.95	liters	l.
ounces	oz.	28	grams	g.
pounds	lb.	0.45	kilograms	kg.
Fahrenheit	°F.	5/9 (after subtracting 32)	Celsius	C.
inches	in.	2.54	centimeters	cm.
feet	ft.	30.5	centimeters	cm.

Boldface numbers indicate pages with illustrations.

INDEX

Acorn Squash, Lamb-Stuffed 755
After-Thanksgiving Squares 563
Alaska Salmon with Vegetables 574
Alfalfa Wheat Bread 111
All-American
  Burgers 454
  Dogs 532, **535**
  Macaroni and Cheese 604
  Potato Salad 708
  Superburgers 454
  Vanilla Ice Cream 276
All-in-One Tex-Mex Filling 571, **571**
Almond(s)
  Burnt 278
  Butter Cream 152
  Cheesecake 594, **595**
  Crescents 335
  Crunch 276
  Filling 335
  Macaroons 246, **245**
  Praline 182, 254, 326
  -Raspberry Sandwich Cookies 240, **241**
  Tartlets 244, **245**
Alsace Kabob Dinner 536
Amaretti 233
Amaretto-Cherry Cheese Pie 532
Ambrosia 322
  Tarts 329
American Caviar Sampler 48, **48**
Anchovy Eggs 33
Antipasto 25
  Salad 556, **557**
Aperitif 66
Appetizer(s) 25
  Barbecued Chicken Wing 49, **49**
  for a First Course 23
  for a Party 23
  Ham and Walnut 44, **493**
  Puffs, Spinach-Cheese 47
Apple(s)
  -Almond Tart 637 **637**
  and Celery, Stir-Fried 461
  -Bread Pudding 139
  Brûlées, Fresh 309, **306-307**
  Dumplings in Cheese-Walnut Pastry 330, **331**
  -Herb Stuffing 504
  Iced Tea 59
  Mousse with Raspberry-Apple Sauce 288, **331**
  -Nut Strudel 332
  Pancakes 367
  Pastry, Greek 337
  Pie, Deep Dish 632
  Pie Delicious 594, **598**
  Pork Loaf 461
  Relish, Baked 14, **15**
  Sautéed 506, **505**
  Slices, Brandied 20
  -Spice Granola Muffins 126, **126**
  Squares 210, **211**
  Strudel 330, **331**
  -Stuffed Apple 345
  Turnovers, Glazed 334
  Upside-Down Cake 550, **551**
Applesauce Sponge Roll 195
Apricot
  -Apple Quencher 58
  -Banana Ice Cream 283, **282**
  Bars 238
  Bow Ties 335
  Cake Roll 144
  Charlotte Bombe 260, **258**

-Coconut Cookie Bars 207
-Coconut Cookie Squares 228, **227**
  Cream 264
  Glaze 206
  Ice-Cream and Chablis-Ice Bombe 261, **267**
-Oatmeal Squares 552, **551**
-Orange Winter Barbecue Sauce 716, **6**
-Pineapple Jam 9
-Prune Lattice Pie 629, **638**
  Roll 271
-Wheat Germ-Corn Bread 116
-Yogurt Chestnut Bread 112, **92**
  Yogurt Fizz 57
Arroz con Pollo 559, **559**, 660
Artichokes
  Microwave 582
  with Mustard Sauce 755
Asparagus
  Lemon-Buttered 758, **758**
  Microwave 574, **573**
  Scalloped 758, **759**
  Stir-Fried 758
  Vinaigrette 703
  Aspic, Port Wine 24
Avocado
  Dip 32, **33**
  Omelet 364
  Whip 265
Aztec Burgers 458, **459**

Babka, Lemon Cheese 136, **134**
Baby Brownie Cakes 170, **169**
Bacon 531
  Burgers 456, **457**
  Muffins 128
  -Spinach Junior Sandwiches 746
  -Wrapped Scallops in Dijon Sauce 42
Bagna Cauda 28
Baked
  Alaska 280
  Apple Relish 16, **17**
  Beans, Classy 760
  Beans, New England 761
  Creamy Eggs 350
  Double Peach 281
  Fish Balls with Clam Sauce 400
  Ham Steak with Sweet Potatoes 526
  Lentils with Cheese 377
  Meatballs and Spinach Gnocchi 470
  Meat-Stuffed Spanish Onions 472
  Orange Ham with Mustard Fruits 523
  Parsley-Stuffed Lobster 408
  Potato, How to Blossom 585, **585**
  Red Snapper 394
  Salmon and Green Bean Puff 393
  Scrambled Eggs 349
  Stuffed Zucchini 471
Baking in the Microwave 546
Baking Powder Biscuits 123, **124**
Baklava 327
Bambini 55, **52-53**
Banana(s)
  Baked with Pineapple and Honey 341
  Cow 74, **75**
  Cream Pie 596, 636
  Dessert Crêpes 265
  Foster 338

Hawaiian 511
Honey Cream Filling 269
Nut Bread 115
Popsicles 292
-Spice Cake Doughnuts 106, **107**
Split Waffles 132
Bantry Brown Bread 118, **118**
Barbecue(d)
  Beef Short Ribs 441
  Bologna Kabobs 536
  Chicken Wing Appetizer 49, **49**
  Country-Style Spareribs 514
  Grill 422
  Lamb Shank 492
  Sauce, Apricot-Orange 716, **6**
  Sauce, Piquant 541
  Sauce, Texas 420
  Short Ribs 443
  Turkey Legs 684
Basic
  Beef Broth 731
  Cake Batter 203
  Chicken Broth 730
  Cooked Fondant 251
  Cookie Dough 213
  Cream Pudding Filling 199
  Cream Puff Paste 269
  Crêpes 359
  French Mustard 7, **6**
  French Omelet 366
  Vinaigrette Dressing 710
  White Sauce 713
  Yeast Roll 100
Basil
  Breads 96, **97**
  Butter 20, **20**
  Cheese Straws 97, **97**
  Jelly 12, **20**
Batter-Fried Onion Rings 770
Basket of "Fruit"Candies 250
Bavarian
  Cream 262
  Skillet Supper 534
-Style Knockwurst 534, **535**
Bean(s)
  and Sausage Soup 743
  Baked 760
  Baked, New England 761
  Dried, Expansion 761
  Pot, Mexican 761
  Refried 760
  Sprouts and Tomato Salad 699, **698**
Béarnaise Sauce 713
Béchamel Sauce 470, 713
Beef 413
  and Barley Soup 726
  and Beans 423
  and Bulgur 446
  and Lima Bean Stew 424
  and Vegetable Kabobs 423
  and Vegetable Pie 621, **620**
  and Vegetable Stew 424, **425**
  Burgundy 426
  Burgundy, Oven 438, **439**
  Casserole, Cheesaroni 480, **482**
  Cooking 414
  Filet of, Marinated 418
  Glazed 435, **365**
  Gravy 437
  Gulyás 428
  How to Pare Your Bills 415
  Liver, Peppers 'n' 483
  Loaf, Burgundy 462
  Loaf with Mushrooms and Sour Cream 461, **463**
  Loaf with Pastry Crust, Herbed 461
  Oriental 566, **566**

Pan Gravy 421
Paprikash, Magyar 428, **429**
  Pepper Steak 431
  Ragout, New Orleans Style 443
  Roast, Microwave 546, **564-565**
  Rolls, Braised 447, **679**
  Rolls, Italian 435
  Roulade 43, **43**, 444
  Round, Marinated 423
  Sausage over Eggs 353
  Stew, Belgian 419
  Stew, Hearty 419, **412**
  Stew, Hearty Winter 571
  Stew, Texas Chili 426
  Stew, Two-Way 566
  Stroganoff 444
  Sukiyaki 422
  Szechuan 437, **436**
  Tenderizing 415
  Teriyaki 446
  Tostadas 477
  Turnovers, Deviled 467
  with Broccoli, Japanese 567, **567**
  with Sprouts, Stir-Fried 446
  with Vegetables, Stir-Fried 447
Beefsteak Pie 437
Beefy Vegetable Soup 735
Beer-Batter Fried Chicken 652, **652**
Beer-Braised
  Sausages 536
  Short Ribs 438
Beet(s)
  Herring-Stuffed 51
  Pickled 21
  Salad 693
  Sweet-Sour Glazed 761
Beignets, Orange 105, **107**
Belgian
  Beef Stew 419
  Waffles 130
Benne Sticks 51
Best-Ever Veal Parmesan 572, **572**
Bibb Lettuce Minosa 707
Birthday Cakes, Individual 168, **169**
Biscuit(s) 123
  Baking Powder 123, **124**
  Basil 97, **97**
  Buttermilk Ham 125
  Drop 123
  Mini-Herb 125
  Squares, Buttermilk 125
Bismarcks 105, **107**
Bisque
  Lobster 740
  Shrimp 740
Black Bean Soup 743
Blackberry Buckle 265
Black-eyed Peas, Marinated 771, **771**
Black-eyed Pea Stew 584
Black Forest Waffles 132
Black Walnut Chess Pie 632
Blanquette de Veau 448
Blarney Castle Parfait 304, **234**
Blazing Spiced Wine Punch 69
Blini 33
Blintzes, Cheese 268
Blueberry-Bran Muffins 129
Blueberry
  Fool 268
  Jam 9
  Muffins 127
  /Strawberry-Topped Sponge Flan 300
  Topping 343

Blue Cheese Butter 19
Bockwurst 534
Boiled New Potatoes and Onions 539, **10-11**
Bologna 536
  Kabobs, Barbecued 536
  Pickled 34
Bombe 259
  Apricot Charlotte 260, **258**
  Apricot Ice-Cream and Chablis Ice 261, **267**
  Chocolate-Raspberry 260
  Cranberry-Pistachio 260
  Glace 261, **263**
  Strawberry Ice-Cream Brownie 261, **267**
Bonbon(s) 252
  Slices 213, **215**
Borscht 724
Bouillabaisse 406
Bourbon
  Aplesauce Cake 144, **142**
  Balls 249
  Street Pecan Cake 151
Boutons 216, **215**
Braciole 420
Braised
  Beef Rolls 447, **679**
  Endive 769
  Lamb Chops with Vegetables 488
  Lamb Shanks à la Grecque 492
  Leeks 769
  Pork Chops with Cabbage 506
  Stuffed Pork Chops 508
  Twin Shoulders of Lamb 488
  Veal Shoulder Roast 451
Brandied
  Apple Slices 20
  Fruit Sauce 717
Brandy Snaps 205, **204**
Bratwurst 536
  and Onions in Beer 536
Brazilian Chocolate Roll 149, **146-147**
Brazil Nut Chips 44
Bread(s) 83
  Alfalfa Wheat 111
  Apricot-Wheat Germ-Corn 116
  Banana Nut 114, **115**
  Bantry Brown 118, **118**
  Basil, 96, **97**
  Boston Brown, Steamed 113
  Brown, Steamed Ginger 116, **87**
  Carrot-Walnut 116
  Cheese, Georgian 112, **82**
  Chestnut 112, **92**
  Coffee, Golden 90, **48**
  Corn 114
  Cracked Wheat 90
  Cranberry 120, **121**
  Crumbs, Buttered 133
    Dry 138
    Fresh 138
    Seasoned 138
  Cubes 138
    Toasted 138
  Dough, Frozen 111
  Garlic and Onion, Herbed 96
  Herb-Cheese Filled 122, **694**
  Hints for Better 86
  Honey Wheat 89, **87**
  How to Knead and Shape 88, **88**
  Irish Soda 113
  Leftover 138
  Mushroom 91, **92**

Nut and Raisin 96
Onion and Bacon 119
Orange Whole-Wheat 117
Prune 119
Pudding 139
    Apple 139
    Cinnamon Raisin 316
    Orange 313, **313**
    Quick
        How to Mix 85
        Making 85
Raisin, Pumpernickel 111
Rye
    Dark 110
    Old-Fashioned 89
    Seed, Overnight 108, **62-63**
Sticks
    Corn 116
    Garlic 122
Spoon 117
Storing 86
Tea 117
Wheat, Whole 110
Whole-Wheat 92, **92**
Yeast
    Easy 111
    How to Mix, Knead and
        Shape 84
    Making 83
Zucchini 117
Bridie's Irish Scones 123
Bridie's Irish Soda Bread 113
Brioche Dough 386
Brisket of Beef, Oven-Barbe
cued 419
Brittle 247
    Almond 247
    Ginger Sesame 248
    Peanut 248
Broccoli
    and Cauliflower Ring 565,
        564-565
    and Ham Soufflé 359
    Mushroom and Sweet
        Pepper Custard Pie 622,
        623
    Sauté 761
    Sesame 762
Broiled
    Paprika Halibut 395
    Saucy Fish Fillets 389
    Steaks Persillade 432
Broth 723
    Beef, Basic, 731
    Chicken, Basic 730
    Flavorful 404
    Turkey 731
Brown Betty, Peach, 298
Brown Beans, Spicy 760
Browned Cabbage and
    Mushroom Pirog 623, **623**
Brownie(s) 207
    Frosting 592
    Butterscotch, Southern-
        Style 209, **211**
    Carrot 210
    Cream Cheese 209
    Double Chocolate Walnut
        207, **208**
    Fudge 591
    Orange Frosted, Deluxe
        209
    Our Best-Ever 220, **221**
Brown Molasses Cookies
    244, **243, 245**
Brown Rice Stuffing 670
Brown Sugar Syrup 130
Brunswick Stew 656
Brussels Sprouts and
    Onions, Creamed 762
Buckwheat Cakes 119
Bulgur, Gazpacho-Style 588
Buns, Cinnamon, 98
    Hot Cross 135, **134**
    Nutty Maple-Honey 108,
        62-63
Buñuelos 120, **72-73**
Burgers
    All-American 454
    Aztec 458, **459**
    Bacon 456, **457**
    Caesar 458
    California 458, **459**

Cantonese 458, **459**
Chile 456, **457**
Dill 455
Nut 456, **457**
Sour Cream and
    Horseradish 455
    Surprise 781
    Welsh 455
Burgundy
    Beef Loaf 462
    Sauce 462
Burnt Almonds 278
Butter
    Basil 20, **20**
    Blue Cheese 19
    Chili 19
    Chive 767
    Dill, 767
    Garlic 19, 767
    Lemon 767
    Maître d'Hotel 19
    Orange-Honey 368
    Pimiento and Pepper 19
    Plum 19
    Tarragon 17, 19
Butter Cream, Almond 152
    Mocha 187
    Orange 240
Buttered Sweet Potatoes 776,
    511
Butterflied Coconut Shrimp
    40
Buttermilk
    Biscuit Squares 125
    -Lime Sherbet 293
    Pancakes 368
    Shrimp Soup 741, **742**
    Swirl 57, 56
Butter Nut Bars 226, **227**
Butternut Squash, Gingered
    778, **779**
Butterscotch
    Brownie Cake 271
    Crispies 224
    Patties 249
    -Pecan Cream Pudding Fill
        ing 199
    Sauce 716
Buttery Bread Stuffing 658

Cabbage
    and Apple Slaw with
        Walnuts 688, **686**
    Bundles in Paprika Cream
        Sauce 479, **478**
    Stuffed 468
Caesar
    Burgers 458
    Salad 703
Cáfe
    au Lait 61
    Brûlot 61
    Cream Royale 264
    Granité 296, **297**
Cake(s) 143
    à l'Orange 189
    Apple, Swedish 318
    Apple Upside-Down 550,
        551
    Batter, Basic 203
    Bourbon Applesauce 144,
        142
    Bourbon Street Pecan 151
    Brownie 170, **169**
    Buckwheat 119
    Butterscotch Brownie 271
    Carrot 169, **169**
        Family Circle's 156
        Pineapple 172
    Chocolate
        Fudge 148, **146-147**
        Heart 156, **157**
        Nut Upside-Down 161
    Coconut
        Cream 180
        Crunch Brunch 592
        Marmalade 172, **173**
    Colonial Seed 144, **142**
    Cream-Filled Chocolate
        154
    Dad's Golden Car 154, **155**
    Devil's Food 145
        Deep Dark 144, **146-147**

Dobos 176, **177**
Double Banana-Split 272
English Toffee 198, **199**
Family Circle's Big Burger
    152, **153**
Ginger 159
Happy Birthday Teddy Bear
    174, **175**
Honey, Norwegian 180, **181**
How to Frost a 143
Individual Birthday 168,
    169
Layer 182, **137**
Lemon Loaf 281
Matzo Honey 167
Minted Pineapple 158, **310**
Mississippi Mud 144, **142**
Peanut Butter 143, **142**
Pecan Candy 182, **137**
Piña Colada Down-Up 160
Pineapple-Apricot Upside-
    Down 161
Pineapple Chiffon 158
Poppy Seed 201
Prune, Upside-Down 160
Rhubarb Upside-Down 160,
    161
Rice 119
Roll Apricot 144
Sidewalk Sundae 174, **175**
Sour Cream 177
    Walnut 158
Sparkling Cookie 178, **178**
Spice 171, **169**
Sweetheart 153
Storage 143
Walnut, Greek 329
Whiskey 186
Yellow Frosted 153
Caldeirada 404
Calf's Liver, Swiss 483
Calico Wax Beans 759
California
    Burgers 458, **459**
    Pepper Relish 18
    Quiche 375, **374**
Campari, Grapefruit 71, **65**
Canadian Pork Pie 519
Canapés
    How to Decorate and
        Freeze 36
    Party 36
    Shrimp Pâté 26
    Smoked Salmon and
        Cheese 36
    Tartare Steak 36
Candied
    Orange Rind 271
    Sweet Potatoes 776
    Yams 785
Candies, Basket of "Fruit,"
    250
Candies, Jelly 256, **255**
Candy 247
    Temperatures for 248
Canned Tuna Guide 386
Cannelloni 601
Cannoli 285
Cantonese Burgers 248, **459**
Capered Eggs 33
Capers 23
Capon 670
    with Wild Rice Stuffing,
        Young Roast 671
Cappucino 60
Caramel 250
    Coconut Flan 301
    Custard Pear Pie 634, **634**
Caramelized Carrot Swirl
    103, **92**
Caraway Kraut 766
Cardamom Rolls 102, **102**
Caribbean Chicken and
    Squash Stew 660, **661**
Carnitas con Salsa 54, **52-53**
Carrot(s)
    à l'Orange 587
    Brownies 210
    Cakes 169, **169**
    Dilled 764, **756-757**
    Loaves, Fresh 552, **551**
    Lyonnaise 762, **763**

Maple-Butter Glazed 764
-Pineapple Cake 172
-Pineapple Marmalade 8, **6**
-Raisin Cake Doughnuts
    106, **107**
-Relish 15
Ring, Comfort 584
-Stuffed Mushrooms 770
-Walnut Bread 116
-Yam Tzimmes 764, **665**
Zucchini Bar Cookies with
    Cream Cheese Frosting
    234, **235**
Cashew-Mushroom
    Stroganoff 770
Cassata àlla Siziliano 275
Cassis Punch Royale 76, **681**
Cauliflower
    au Gratin 562, **562**
    Italiano 767
    Supreme, Low-Calorie 766
Caviar Sampler, American
    48, **48**
Celeriac, Creamed 764
Celery
    Creamed 765
    Relish 16
Challah 107
Champagne
    Choucroute with Smoked
        Meats 537, **10-11**
    Jelly 14
    Punch 70
Charlotte
    Eggnog, Frozen 271, **270**
    Lemon Curd 342, **343**
    Orange 286
    Strawberry 304
Cheddar
    and Beer Cheesecake 166,
        164-165
    Biscuits 125
    Poppy Strips 31
Cheese(s) 349
    and Bean Enchiladas 380
    and Blueberry Crêpe
        Triangles 360, **48**
    and Grape Compote 323
    and Onion Soufflé 584
    and Wine Fondue 370
    Blintzes 268
    Crisps 30
    Herbed 371
    Lasagne Rolls with
        Spinach 602, **602**
    Lentil Loaf 377
    Muffins 128
    Pancakes with Pear Sauce
        368
    Pie, Amaretto-Cherry 632
    Puffs 32
    Quick Table of Popular 348
    Rolls 32
        Chili 30, **31**
    Sauce 617
    Scones 123
    Soup Soufflé 355
    Squares, Chile 51, **52-53**
    Strata 379
    -Stuffed Baked Potatoes
        774
    -Stuffed Vegetables 765,
        765
    Tart
        Peach-Filled 195, **197**
        Three-, 29
Cheesecake(s) 163
    Almond 594, **595**
    Cheddar and Beer 166,
        164-165
    Chocolate 171, **169**
    Chocolate Amaretto 597
    Chocolate Espresso 166,
        164-165
    Cranberry Nut 167, **137**
    Deluxe, Strawberry 163,
        164-165
    Mini 170, **169**
    Pineapple Coconut 185
    Slim 167
    Valentine 179, **179**
Cheesy Tomato and Garlic
    Loaf 47

Chef's Salad 707
Cherries Jubilee Amandine
    281
Cherry
    -Cheese Waffles 132
    Crisp, Instant 269
    Glaze 180
    -Nut Tarts 324
    Sauce 612
    Tomatoes, Deviled 786
Chestnut
    Butter Filling 191
    Ice Cream Log 284
    Stuffing 720
Chicken(s) 649
    and Cabbage, Sweet and
        Sour 555, **557**
    and Rotelle Salad 688, **689**
    and Squash Stew,
        Caribbean 660, **661**
    and Vegetables, Easy Oven
        654
    Baked
        Orange-Glazed 664, **655**
        Tunisian 659, **659**
    Barbecued, Saucy 553
    Beer-Batter Fried 652, **652**
    Breasts with Oranges,
        Sautéed 666, **662**
    Cacciatore 658
    Cooked, Storing 650
    Cordon Bleu 566
    Enchiladas in Cheese
        Cream 659, **660**
    -Filled Pastry Boats 49
    Fricasée 654
    -Fried Steak with Pan
        Gravy 428
    Ginger 653
    Herb-Roasted 657
    Hong Kong 661
    How to Cut and Bone a 648
    in a Basket 653, **433**
    Italia 554, **554**
    Lemon-Broiled 651
    -Liver Knishes 483
    Livers
        Sherried 48
        with Bacon and Green
            Beans 484
    -Macaroni Salad 692, **690**
    Mexicali 558, **558**
    Oriental-Style 557
    Paprika with Spatzle 664
    Parts, Cooking Time 650
    Pâté with Port Wine Aspic
        24
    Pillows 50, **52-53**
    Provençale 653, **653**
    Ragout with Peas and
        Mushrooms 650, **646**
    Rice Soup 736
    Risotto 652, **528-529**
    Rosemary 553
    Salad, Hot 662
    Scaloppini with Lemon
        Zest 667
    Silo 662, **663**
    Spit-Roasted, Herbed 651
    Stuffed Roast 650, **651**
    Tarragon 667
    Thighs, Sweet-and-Sour
        Apricot-Glazed 660, **661**
    Velvet Sliced 652, **365**
    Walnut 657, **657**
        Strips 50, **52-53**
    Wing Appetizer, Barbecued
        49, **49**
    Wings
        Curried Limas and 654,
            655
        Sesame 50
        Stir-Fry 656, **656**
        with Cherry Sauce, Roast
            650
        with Lemon and Olives 555
        with Ratatouille 554
Chick-Pea Dip 27
Chiffon Cake, Orange 200
    Pineapple 158
Chiffon Pie
    Chocolate 631, **631**
    Luscious Lime 630

Strawberry 630
Chile
Burger 456, **457**
Cheese Squares 51, **52-53**
con Queso Dip 548
Chili
Butter 19
-Cheese Rolls with
Avocado Dip 32, **33**
Meatball Stew 467
Pie Casserole 140, **141**
Ranch-Style 420
Red River 443
Chilled
Fruit Soup 741
Spinach Soup 740
Chimichangas 424
Chinese
Almond Cookies 224
Eggrolls 55
Fried Rice with Chicken
613, **613**
with Pork 613
Mustard Sauce 40
Pork and Ginger Balls 54,
52-53
Roast Duck 673
Roast Pork 509
Steamed Eggs with Pork
352
Sweet-Sour Sauce 715
Chips
Brazil Nut 42
Tortilla 26
Chive
Butter 767
-Onion Dressing 700
Chocolate
-Almond
Meringues 232
Snowdrops 222, **221**
Squares 213, **215**
Amaretto Cheesecake 597
Blancmange 266
Burnt Almond Ice Cream
278, **278**
Cake Doughnuts 105, **107**
Cakes, Cream-Filled 154
Cheesecakes 171, **169**, 218,
215
Chestnut Torte 190
Chiffon Pie 631, **631**
Chip Cookies 207, 222
Double 224
Jumbo Double 222, **694**
Coating 214, 253
Coconut Crisps 237
-Cream Cheese Cupcakes
172, **169**
Cream Cheese Filling 217
Cream Frosting 169
Curls 148, 273
-Dipped Strawberries 564,
564-565
Espresso Cheesecake 166,
164-165
-Filled Mimosa Lemon Roll
286, **287**
Fondue 309
Frosting 176
Fudge Cake 148, **146-147**
Fudge Frosting 149
Glaze 149, 151, 170, 182,
233
-Glazed Bars 236
Go'Rounds 217, **215**
Heart Cake 156, **157**
Hearts 171
Hot, Mexican 66, **72**
Ice Cream Linzer Torte 190,
185
Icing 209, 212
Meringue Torte 148,
146-147
Mousse Pie 636
Nut Upside-Down Cake 161
Orange Torte 187, **188**
-Peanut Butter Frosting 192
-Peanut Butter Torte 192,
192
-Pecan Chess Tart 168, **168**
Pecan Pudding 315

Pistachio Meringues 242,
241
Pretzels 217, **215**
Raisin Cookies 220, 221
-Raspberry Bombe 260
Roll, Brazilian 149, **146-147**
Rosettes 216, **215**
Rum Icebox Cake 284
Rum Raisin Mounds 253
Supreme 272, **273**
Wafers 280
Zabaglione Mousse 289
Choucroute à l'Alsacienne
514
Choucroute Garni, Easy 514
Quick 537
Choucroute with Smoked
Meats, Champagne 537,
10-11
Chow Chow 18
Chowder 736
Chunky Vegetable 548, **548**
Clam 739
Fish, New England 736,
737
Scallop 739
Tuna, Skillet 390
Christmas Stollen 138, **137**
Christmas Tree Cookies 242,
241
Chuck Steak Bordeaux 428
Chunky Vegetable Chowder
548, **548**
Chunky Vegetable Gumbo
with Shrimp 576, **577**
Chutney
Papaya 6
Plum 14
Cinnamon
Buns 98
Filling 101
Nut Coffee Ring 132, **82**
-Raisin Bread Pudding 316
Sugar 210
-Sugar Toast Triangles 733
Yogurt Topping 337
Citrus Cartwheel 67, **67**
Clafouti 266
Clam Cocktail, Curried 64
Clam Sauce, Quick Red 715
Classy Baked Beans 760
Coating, Chocolate 214, 253
Cobbler
Blueberry, Quick 319
Peach 320
Pear, Spicy 320, **321**
Strawberry-Rhubarb 320
Cocido (Spanish Beef Stew)
427
Cockscombs 335
Cocoa 64
Cream Filling 269
Coconut
Cream Cake 180
Cream Filling 181
Crunch Brunch Cake 592
Flake Cookies 246, **245**
Macaroons 181
Marmalade Cake 172, **173**
Milk, Fresh 313
Pudding 312
Raspberry Gems 200
Topping 177, 209
Cod Creole 384
Codfish Cakes 384
Coffee
and Cream, Frozen 64, **65**
Bread, Golden 90, **48**
Butterscotch Swirl Ice
Cream 279
Cake 132
Raisin Spice 133
Cream Filling 149
Dublin Irish 61, **62-63**
Frozen Irish 61, **62-63**
Irish 61
Ring, Cinnamon Nut 132,
82
Vienna, Spiced 60
Cold
Confetti Meatloaf 471, **765**
Cranberry Soufflé 259

Cucumber and Yogurt
Soup 741
Marinated Steak 432, **433**
Stuffed Breast of Veal 452
Coleslaw Vinaigrette with
Cherry Tomatoes, Olives,
and Capers 688, **686**
Collard Greens Quiche 376
Colonial Seed Cake 144, **142**
Colorado Rainbow Trout
Fillets in Mustard Dill Sauce
398
Comfort Carrot Ring 584
Compote(s)
Cheese and Grape 323
Dried Fruit 337
Fresh Pineapple 338
Frosty Cantaloupe 323
Fruit, Wine 337
Peach-Pear 342
Condiments 693, **690**
Confectioners' Glaze 93, 132,
214
Confetti Primavera with
Mozzarella 605, **605**
Cookie(s) 205
Almond, Chinese 224
Almond Raspberry
Sandwich 240, **241**
Bar
Apricot-Coconut 207
Carrot-Zucchini 234, **235**
Mocha 228, **227**
Bow Tie, Crispy 229, **229**
Brown Molasses 244, **243**,
245
Cakes, Frozen Chocolate
243, **243**, **245**
Chocolate Chip 207, 222
Chocolate Raisin 220, **221**
Christmas Tree 242, **241**
Coconut Flake 246, **245**
Date 'n' Oat Bar 205
Dough, Basic 213
Easter 219, **219**
Fruit and Nut 243, **243**, **245**
Gingerbread 224
Goblin' Good 219, **219**
Hanukkah Gelt 225
Lemon Leaf 206, **59**
Lemon Slice 226, **227**
Master Plan for Making 20
from One Kind of Dough
212, **215**
Oatmeal Raisin 237
Oatmeal Sunflower 238
Peanut Butter 235
Pecan 237
Poinsettia 230
Raspberry-Almond 225
Small Sand 247, **245**
Spice, Danish 212, **211**
Squares, Apricot Coconut
228, **227**
Sugar and Spice Jumbo
238
Sugar, Orangy 242, **243**
Sugar, Shamrock 234, **234**
Tiers 239, **241**
Valentine 222, **223**
Cooking Time for Chicken
Parts 650
Cool
Avocado Soup 741
Cucumber-Pineapple Mold
706
Lemon Soufflé 318, **317**
Cooler
Cranberry-Orange 57
Grape 58
Pineapple-Mint 76, **75**
Coq au Vin, Low-Calorie 667
Coquilles St. Jacques 401,
401
Mornay 42
Corn
and Cheese Soufflé 355
Doggies 532
Dollars, Fresh 51
Fresh, Selecting and
Storing 767
Grilled 767
in Husks, Roasted 767

Muffins 128
Omelet 366
on the Cob, Sweet 767
with Flavored Butters 767
Relish, Quick 14
Yankee 13
Sausage Stuffing 720
Cornbread 114, 140
Apricot-Wheat Germ 116
Jalapeño 552, **551**
Sticks 116
-Stuffed Pork Chops 504,
505
Corned Beef 434
Dinner 435
Glazed 434
Kilkenny 434, **118**
-Potato Casserole 434
Cornish Game Hens
French Style 668, **475**
Green Chile-Stuffed 668,
669
Grilled 670
Herbed 560
in Herb Butter, Stuffed 670
Lemon-Roasted 670
Cottage Cheese
Dessert, Creamy 341
Thumb Print 241, **241**
Topping 585, **586**
Cottage Pie 479
Coulibiac 385
Country
Corn Bread 114
Meat Loaf 460
Pâté 25, **24**
Picnic Pâté 519
Pork and Blackeyed Peas
508
-Style Pork Ribs with
Sauerkraut 568
Couscous, Moroccan 681
Crab, Deviled 409
Cracked Wheat Bread 90
Crackers, Poppy Seed-Onion
37
Cranberry-Apple Glaze 717, **6**
Jelly 12
Cranberry
Bread 120, **121**
Cornbread Stuffing 721
Ice 292
Linzer Torte 189, **10-11**
Nut Cheesecake 167, **137**
-Orange Cooler 57
-Orange Liqueur 66
Orange Punch 58
-Pistachio Bombe with
Pineapple Galliano Sauce
260
Relish 15
Crisp 15
Sauce, Savory 715
Topping 167
Cream(s)
Apricot 264
Bavarian 262
Cheese
Brownies 209
Filling 172
Frosting 210, 235
-Date-Nut Sandwich 751
Hard Sauce 169
Loaf 93, **94-95**
Topping 231
Cheesecake, Frozen
Raspberry 286
Egg, Orange, 265
-Filled Chocolate Cakes
154
Meringue 264
of Asparagus Soup 725
of Broccoli Soup 726
of Fresh Tomato Soup 739
of Turkey Soup 730
Papaya, Frozen 296, 310
Pastry 300, 327
Pie
Frozen Orange 'n' 630,
630
Strawberry-Rhubarb 629,
629

Pineapple 264
Puff 268
Paste, Basic 269
Savory 91, **62-63**
Strawberry 269
Rainbow Bavarian 262
Roll
Chocolate, Low-Calorie
318
Raspberry 198, **198**
Royale, Café 264
Rum 285
Creamed
Brussels Sprouts and
Onions 762
Celeriac 764
Celery 765
Onions 770
Creamy
Celery Seed Dressing 780
Cheese Sauce 602
Chicken Mousse 704
Corn and Sausage
Casserole 537
Cottage Cheese Dessert
341
Custard Sauce 716, **712**
Dressing 403
Herb Dip 27
Herbed Tuna 42
Horseradish Sauce 440
Italian Dressing 707
Mushroom Soup 549
Penuche 257
Tapioca with Strawberry-
Wine Sauce 305
Vanilla Filling 151
Vegetable Slaw 706, **706**
Crème au Chocolat, Pots de
267
Brûlée 274
Creole Bouillabaisse 406
Creole-Style Ham and Rice
530
Crêpe(s) 359, 386, 683
Appetizer, Ham and
Cheese 359, **361**
Basic 359
Dessert, Banana 265
Spicy-Nut, Flamed 362,
361
Stick, Zucchini and Onion-
Filed 360, **361**
Triangles, Cheese and
Blueberry 360, **48**
Crescent Lamb Triangles 477
Crescents 218, **215**
Crisp, Cheese 28
Crisp Cranberry Relish 17
Crisply Roasted Goose 675
Crisps, Pita, 25
Crispy Bow Tie Cookies 229,
229
Croissants 97
Flaky, 97
Croque Monsieur 746
Croquette 526
Croutons 138
Garlic 138
Crown Roast of Pork 567, **544**
with Apple-Herb Stuffing
501
with Wild Rice Stuffing 501,
502-503
Cruller(s) 104
French 104, **107**
Crumb Cake, Old-Fashioned
133
Crumb-Stuffed Tomatoes 785
Crumb-Topped Baked Ham,
523
Crunch-Topped Hamburger
Rolls 101, **92**
Crunchy Meat Loaves 464
Cucumber
and Potato Soup 732
-Dill Sauce 392
Dressing 394
Rounds, Dilled Salmon-
Topped 41
Salad 708
Slices, Marinated 23, 41
Smoothie 57, **56**

Cumberland Sauce 523
Cupcake(s) 151
  Chocolate-Cream Cheese
    172, **169**
  Devil's Food 151
  Golden Yellow 200
  Spicy Oatmeal 151, **150**
Curd, Lemon, 8, **6**
Currant-Nut Drops 225
Curried
  Apple and Chicken Soup
    734
  Clam Cocktail 64
  Egg Salad Sandwiches 748
  Egg Strata 139, **141**
  Herring Salad 710
  Limas and Chicken Wings
    654, **655**
  Orange Rice 614, **475**
  Turkey Wings 563
  Vegetable Salad 588
Custard Sauce 315, 332
  Creamy 716, **712**

Dad's Golden Car Cake 154,
  155
Daiquiri 66
  Liqueur 66
Danish
  Apple Dessert 309,
    306-307
  Meatballs with Dill Sauce
    34
  Pastry Dough 334
  Pastry, Tips on Making 335
  Prune 335
  Spice Cookies 212, **211**
  Spritz Cookies 244, **243,
    245**
Darjeeling Punch 70
Dark Rye Bread 110
Date-Apricot Steamed
  Pudding 315
Date 'n' Oat Bar Cookies 205
Date Tea Bread 133
Decorating Frosting 220
Decorator Frosting 176, 226,
  242
Decorator Icing 242
Deep Chocolate Glaze 718
Deep Dark Devil's Food Cake
  145, **146-147**
Deep Dish Apple Pie 632
Delicious Apple Pie 594, **598**
Deluxe Orange-Frosted
  Brownies 209
Dessert 259
Deviled
  Beef Turnover 467
  Cherry Tomatoes 786
  Crab 409
  Egg Patties 354
  Eggs 32
  Hamburgers 455
  Ham Eggs 33
  Lamb Riblets 487
  Lamb Shanks 492, **679**
Devil's Food
  Cake 145
  Cupcakes 151
Dill
  Burgers 455
  Butter 767
  Mustard Sauce 746
  Pickles, Kosher Style 20
Dilled
  Carrots 764, **756-757**
  Creamed Eggs in a Puffy
    Pancake 370, **369**
  Green Beans 760, **665**
  Salmon-Topped Cucumber
    Rounds 41
  Shrimp and Cucumber 574
  Shrimp in Aspic 402
Dilly Oil and Vinegar Topping
  586, **586**
Dip
  Avocado 32, **33**
  Chick-Pea 27
  Chile con Queso 548
  Creamy Herb 27
  Fresh Dill 27
  Garlic Cheese 28

Greek Cucumber 27
Jalapeño Refried Bean 28
Mustard Mayonnaise 48
Olive-Tuna 28
Dobos Cake Ah La Holiday
  176, **177**
Doggies, Corn 532
Dogs
  All-American 532, **535**
  Devil, Sweet and Sour 572,
    572
  Little 532
  Mediterranean 532, **535**
  Peppers and Onion 633,
    535
  Reuben 532, **535**
Double
  Apple Punch 71
  Banana-Split Cake 272
  Chocolate Chip Cookies
    224
  Chocolate Tarts 329
  Chocolate Walnut
    Brownies 207, **208**
  Peach Baked Alaska 281
Doughnut(s) 104
  Banana-Spice Cake 106,
    107
  Cake, 104
  Carrot-Raisin Cake 106,
    107
  Chocolate Cake 105, **107**
  French Market 106, **107**
  Glazes 717
  Jelly 105, **107**
  Whole Wheat Cake 106,
    107
  Yeast Raised 104
  Zucchini-Nut Cake 106, **107**
Dressing
  Basic Vinaigrette and
    Variations 710
  Chive-Onion 700
  Creamy 403
    Celery Seed 780
    Italian 707
  Cucumber 394
  French 704
  Green Goddess 710, **711**
  Herb Vinaigette 707
  Lemon 698
    French 710, **711**
    Vinaigrette 693
  Low-Calorie Thousand
    Island 710, **711**
  Orange Sour Cream 707
  Provençal Tomato 710, **711**
  Red Wine Vinegar 689
  Tangy Mustard 700
  Vinaigrette 582
Dried
  Beans Expansion 761
  Fruit Compote 337
Drinks for a Party, How to
  Dress 67, **67**
Drop Biscuits 123
Drunken Sauerkraut 766, **515**
Dublin Irish Coffee 61
Duchess Potato Vegetable
  Casserole 773, **773**
Duck, Roast, Chinese 673
  with Orange 673
Duckling(s) 671
  How to Carve 674
  Roast 559
    Easy 673, **672**
  Spit-Roasted 674
  with Kasha Stuffing, Roast
    671
Dumpling(s) 616
  Apple 330, **331**
  Potato 442, **441**, 617, 743
  Spinach, Italian 617

East Indian Vegetable
  Casserole 582
Easter Cookies 219, **219**
Easy
  Chocolate Peanut Clusters
    250
  Choucroute Garni, 514
  Fondant Frosting 206

Oven Chicken and
  Vegetables 654
Pizza Dough 642
Roast Ducklings 673, **672**
Yeast Breads 111
Ebi No Kikka Age
  (Chrysanthemum-Shaped
  Shrimp Balls) 40
Eclairs, Chocolate-Glazed,
  Low-Calorie 319
Egg(s) 347
  à la Florentine 350
  Anchovy 33
  Baked
    Creamy 350
    Scrambled 349
  Bake, Onion and 350
  Beef Sausage over 353
  Benedict 352
  Capered 33
  Deviled 32
  Deviled Ham 33
  Divan 354
  Drop Soup 732, **732**
  Egg Foo Yung 363
    Sauce 363
  Glaze 90
  Grading and Storing 347
  Hard-Cooked 347
  Herbed Deviled 32
  in a Puffy Pancake, Dilled
    Creamed 370, **369**
  in Snow 269
  Nippy Deviled 32
  Noodles, Homemade 603
  Optimum Temperature for
    Separating 347
  Patties, Deviled 354
  Patty Muffins 353
  Red Beet 19
  Romanoff 710
  Scotch 352, **433**
  Separating 347
  Strata, Curried 139, **141**
  Stuffed
    Curried 33
    Pickled 32
  Tips on Using 347
  Whites, Beating 347
  with Cheese, Shirred 353
  with Pink Mayonnaise 350
  with Pork, Steamed,
    Chinese 352
  Ziti with Sausage and 354
Eggnog 67, 69
  Brasilia 69
Eggplant
  Meat-Stuffed 471
  Oven-Fried 767
  Parmigiana 768
  Stuffed 769, **768**
Eggrolls, Chinese 55
  Wrappers 55
"Eggspandable" Eggs with
  Apricot-Glazed Sausages
  352
Elegant Pâté 26
Empanada Pies 628
Empanadas, Fruit 336
Enchilada, Casserole, Swiss
  380
Enchiladas
  Cheese and Bean 380
  Cheese, Mexican 380, **381**
  Jiffy 579
  Swiss Chard 782
Endive
  Braised 769
  Crown Salad 704
English Pub
  Pie 621, **620**
  Toffee Cake 198, **199**
Equivalents in Microwave
  Cooking Times 545
Espresso Mousse 289

Fabulous Fudge 256
Family Circle's
  Big Burger Cake 152, **153**
  Carrot Cake 156
Fancy Fingers 214, **215**
Fanned Roast Potatoes 772,
  515

Fast Hollandaise 566
Fast-Rising Yeast Breads 108
Favorite Muffins 128
Fennel Parmesan 564,
  564-565
Fettucine Alfredo 601
  in California Pistachio
    Sauce 579
Figs
  in Port Wine, Ginger 340
  Stuffed with Chocolate 340
    with Lemon Cream 344
Fillet of Flounder with Lobster
  399, **399**
Fillets of Sole in Cucumber
  Sauce 389
Filling
  Almond 335
  All-in-One Tex-Mex 571, **571**
  Banana Honey Cream 269
  Basic Cream Pudding 199
  Butterscotch-Pecan Cream
    Pudding 199
  Chestnut Butter 191
  Chocolate Cream Cheese
    217
  Cinnamon 101
  Cocoa Cream 269
  Coconut Cream 181
  Coffee Cream 149
  Cream Cheese 172
  Creamy Vanilla 151
  Lemon 201
  Orange Cream Pudding
    199
  Pineapple 336
  Potato 617
  Rich Chocolate 287
  Ricotta 609
  Sausage and Pepper 366
  Spinach 609
  Vanilla Custard 319
Fines Herbes 362
Finnish Vanilla Sauce 308
Fish 383
  Bonne Femme 384
  Buying and Storing 383
  Fillets, Broiled Saucy 389
  Okra with 397
  Oven-Fried 392
  Rolls with Clam Sauce,
    Baked 400
  Steaks, Sarasota 389
  Steamed 390
  Stew, Italian 395
  to Cook 383
  Whole, Grilled 395
Fizz, Apricot Yogurt 57
Flaky
  Croissants 97
  Pastry 519, 621
Flamed Spicy-Nut Crêpes
  362, **361**
Flan 360
  Caramel Coconut 301
  Peach and Banana 301
  Spanish Custard 300
  Sponge,
    Blueberry/Strawberry-
    Topped 300
  Toasted Coconut 589
  Triple Fruit 301
Flank Steak, Rolled 431, **430**
  with Dill 432
Flavorful Broth 404
Floating Island, Golden
  Peach 296
Flounder
  and Salmon Roulade 384,
    382
  Fillets North Beach 400
  Florentine 400
  Stuffed 399
  with Lobster, Fillet of 399,
    399
Fluffy
  Matzo Balls 727
  7-Minute Frosting 148
  Tuna Pâté 387, **387**
Fondant 251
  Confections, No-Cook 252
  Cooked, Basic 251
  Logs 252

Fondue 370
  Cheese and Wine 370
  Chocolate 309
  Mexican 371
Foolproof Hollandaise Sauce
  741
Frankfurter 532. See also
  Doggies, Dogs
  and Macaroni Bake 533,
    535
  and Potato Omelet 533,
    535
Freezer Orange French Toast
  139
French
  Chocolate Truffles 250
  Crullers 104, **107**
  Dressing 704
  Fries 772
  Market Doughnuts 106, **107**
  Marrow Bean Casserole
    496
  Omelet 363
  Onion Tart 45
  Sables 216, **215**
  -Style Green Peas 771
  Toast
    Freezer Orange 139
    Orange 379
Fresh
  Apple Brûlées 309,
    306-307
  Apple Nougat Soufflé 357,
    356
  Blueberry Pie 641
  Carrot Loaves 552, **551**
  Cherry Pie 641
  Coconut Layer Cake 182,
    137
  Coconut Milk 313
  Corn Dollars 51
  Dill Dip 27
  Fruit Salad with Tangerine
    Dressing 691, **690**
  Lemonade 59, **59**
  Peach Pie 641
  Pineapple Compote 338
  Strawberry Ice Cream 282,
    283
Frittata 372
  Ratatouille 372, **372**
  with Ham and Mozzarella
    372, **373**
  Zucchini 372
Frosted
  Grape Garland 561
  Yellow Cakes 153
Frosting
  Brownie 592
  Butter Cream 718
  Chocolate 176
  Chocolate Cream 169
  Chocolate Fudge 149
  Chocolate-Peanut Butter
    192
  Cream Cheese 210, 235
  Decorating 220
  Decorator 176, 226, 242
  Easy Fondant 206
  Fluffy 7-Minute 148
  Honey-Butter 210
  Honey-Cream Cheese 718
  Lemon Butter Cream 201
    or Orange Butter Cream
    718
  Light Chocolate Cream
    Cheese 213
  Mimosa-Lemon 287
  Mocha Butter Cream 718
  Orange 209, 212
  Royal 225
  Rum Butter 158
  Silky Chocolate, Mocha
    203
  White Mountain 174
Frosty
  Cantaloupe Compotes 323
  Lemonade 59
Frozen
  Bread Dough 111
  Chocolate Cookie Cakes
    243, **243, 245**
  Coffee 'n' Cream 64, **65**

Eggnog Charlotte 271, **270**
  Fruit Salad 704
  Honey Mousse 288, **277**
  Irish Coffee 61, **62-63**
  Maple Sabayon 266
  Orange 'n' Cream Pie 630, **630**
  Papaya Cream 296, **310**
  Raspberry Cream Cheesecake 286
  Semi-Freddo 302, **303**
  Soufflé Amaretto 259
  Spirits 71
  Strawberry Yogurt 273
  Vanilla Yogurt 274
Fruit
  and Nut Cookies 243, **243, 245**
  Empanadas 336
  -Filled Melon 332, **333**
  Kebabs 67, **67**
  Molded in Sherry Jelly 304
  Salad, Fresh 691, **690**
    Winter 699, **62-63**
  Scones 123
  Smoothie 60, **60**
  Tarts, Mini 218, **215**
  Turnovers 336
Fruitcake 184
  Golden Light 184
  Macadamia-Nut 184
  Plantation 186
Fruited
  Champagne Punch 70
  Kasha 616
  Rice Stuffing 561, **562**
Fudge 256
  Brownies 591
  Cake, Chocolate 148, **146-147**
  Chocolate 257
  Fabulous 256
  Golden 257
  Peanut Butter 256
  Quick and Easy 256, **255**
  Sauce, Hot, 617, **712**
Fudgies 149
Fusilli with Spinach Pesto 600, **598**

Garden
  Mustard Pickles 22
  -Style Spaghetti 610, **610**
  Vegetable Soup 739, **738**
Garlic
  Bread Sticks 122
  Butter 19, 767
  Cheese Dip 28
  Loaf, Cheesy Tomato 45
Gazpacho 730, **728-729**
Georgian Cheese Bread 112, **82**
German Potato Salad 700, **701**
Giant
  Club Sandwich 751
  Cocoa Meringues 232
Giblet
  and Barley Soup 732
  Gravy 675, 677
Ginger
  -Apricot Muffins 12
  Cake 159
  Chicken 653
  Figs in Port Wine 340
  Pound Cake 159
  Sesame Brittle 248
Gingerbread 158, 159
  Cookies 224
  Golden Honey 180, **277**
Gingered Butternut Squash 778, **779**
Glacéed
  Fruit Tarts 326, **327**
  Oranges 323, **475**
  Strawberries 341
Glaze(s) 462, 717
  Apricot 206
  Cherry 180
  Chocolate 149, 151, 170, 182, 233
  Confectioners' 93, 132, 214
  Cranberry-Apple 717, **6**

Deep Chocolate 718
  Doughnut 717
  Egg 90
  Honey 717
  Lemon 116, 717
  Maple 717
  Mint 717
  Orange 200, 717
    Marmalade 200
  Polynesian 510
  Praline 152
  Raspberry 200
  Sour Cream Lemon 170
  Sugar 96, 162, 717
  Valentine Cookie 223
  Vanilla 717
Glazed
  Apple Turnovers 334
  Beef 435, **365**
  Corned Beef 434
  Jelly Doughnuts 105, **107**
  Meat Loaf 462
  Orange Rolls 100, **109**
  Parsnips 771
  Walnuts 251
Glorious Ham 521
Gnocchi 617
  Parisienne 618
  Spinach 470
  Two-Cheese 617
Goblin' Good Cookies 219, **219**
Golden
  Coffee Bread 90, **48**
  Fudge 257
  Honey Gingerbread 180, **277**
  Light Fruitcake 184
  Orange Rolls 112, **82**
  Peach Floating Island 296
  Sponge Layers 301
  Yellow Cupcakes 200
Gold-Filled Pockets 216, **215**
Goodie Drops 216, **215**
Goose 675
  Crisply Roasted 675
  with Fruit Stuffing, Roast 675
Gorgonzola Logs 30
  Toast 30, **10-11**
Goulash 427
  Soup with Potato Dumplings 743
Gourmet Sole Véronique 397
Grand Marnier Christmas Wreaths 239, **241**
Granité, Cafe 296, **297**
  Lemon 296
Granola
  Crunch, Homemade 745
  Fruit Squares 236
  Parfait 290
  with Raisins 239
  -Yogurt Loaves 89
Grape(s)
  and Endive Salad 698
  and Sour Cream "Hats," 302, **302**
  Cooler 58
  Jelly, Low-Calorie 11
  Sugar-Coated 67, **67**
  Sugared 675
Grapefruit
  Campari 71, **65**
  Ice 292
Gravy
  Beef 437
  Giblet 675, 677
  Pan 675
    Beef 421
    Sherry 664
Great-Grandma's Soft Ginger Cake 159
Greek
  Apple Pastry 337
  Chicken Pie 626, **627**
  Chick-Pea Salad 696, **627**
  Cucumber Dip 27
  -Style Lamb Chops 486, **494**
  Walnut Cakes 329
Green
  Apple Pie 635, **635**

Bean Casserole 759
  Beans, Dilled 760, **665**
  Chile Salsa 426
  Chile-Stuffed Cornish Game Hens 668, **669**
  Goddess Dressing 710, **711**
  Grape Ice Block 70
  Onion Fans 732
  Peas, French-Style 771
  Potato Salad 692, **690**
  Salads 687
Griddle Scones 123
Grilled
  Alaska Salmon 392
  Corn 767
  Cornish Game Hens 670
  Knockwurst or Franks 541
    with Fruit Glaze 543, **542-543**
  Open-Face Club Sandwich 750
  Whole Fish 395
Guacamole 28
Guava Fruit Punch 74, **75**
Guide to Countertop Microwave Ovens 545
Gumbo

Halibut
  Broiled Paprika 395
  Poached, Marjoram 397
  Steaks Meunière 395
  Wine-Marinated 394
Ham 520
  and Cheese Appetizer Crêpes 359, **361**
  Mold 531
  Puff 527
  and Pineapple Kabobs 547
  and Potatoes au Gratin 530, **528-529**
  and Rice, Creole-Style 530
  and Swiss in Pastry 527
  and Walnut Appetizers 44, **493**
  Baked, Crumb-Topped 523
    Stuffed 524, **525**
  Croquettes with Mornay Sauce 526
  Glorious 521
  Hoppin' John 'n' 526
  How to Carve a Shank Half 522
  How to Carve a Whole 522
  Lentils with 530
  Loaf with Mustard Sauce 530
  Mousse with Fruit Salad Platter 531
  Roast Fresh 523
  Rolls with Curried Rice 527
  Steak
    Barbecue 524
    Skillet Honey-Glazed 524
    with Sweet Potatoes, Baked 526
    with Mustard Fruits, Baked 523
Hamburger(s) 454. See also Burger(s)
  au Poivre 456
  Deviled 455
  -Vegetable Pie 628
Hanukkah Gelt Cookies 225
Happy Birthday Teddy Bear Cake 174, **175**
Hard Sauce 275
  Balls 590
Harissa Sauce 683
Harvest Pumpkin Soup 733
Hash
  Red Flannel 440
  Hawaiian Sunrise 71
Hazelnut
  Roll 201, **202**
  Torte 186
Hearts of Romaine with Roquefort Dressing 703
Hearty
  Beef Stew 419, **412**
  Vegetable Stew 782
  Winter Beef Stew 571

Herb
  -Cheese Filled Bread 122, **694**
  Onion Rolls 100
  Roasted Chicken 657
  Scented Oven-Dried Tomatoes 783
  -Stuffed Mushrooms 46
  -Stuffed Pork Chops 506
  Stuffing 721
  Vinaigrette Dressing 707
Herbed
  -Baked Scallops 409
  Beef Loaf with Pastry Crust 461
  Cheese 371
  Cornish Game Hens 560
  Deviled Eggs 32
  Garlic and Onion Bread 96
  Spit-Roasted Chicken 651
  Tomatoes and Onions 785, **663**
  Walnut, Mushroom and Orange Salad 689, **502-503**
Herring
  Apple Spread 29
  Salad, Curried 710
  -Stuffed Beets 51
Holiday Punch 69, **10-11**
Hollandaise
  Fast 566
  Sauce 574, **573**
Home-Fried Potatoes 774
Homemade
  Egg Noodles 603
  Granola Crunch 745
  Meat Sauce 715
  Ravioli 609, **615**
  Tomato Juice 64
  Tomato Sauce 610
  Yogurt 745
Honey
  Almond Crunch Ice Cream 275, **277**
  Bubbles 285
  -Butter Frosting 210
  Cake, Norwegian 180, **181**
  -Cream Cheese Frosting 718
  Date-Nut Bars 231
  Raisin Bread 114, 113
  Syrup 285, 328
    Low-Calorie 12
  Wheat Bread 89, **87**
  Whipped Cream 180
Honeydew Ice 293
Honeyed Apple Syrup 338
Hong Kong Chicken 661
  Stir-Fry 516
Hoppin' John 'n' Ham 526
Horseradish 23
Hot
  Apple Spice Sundae 272
  Chicken Salad 662
  Chocolate Soufflé 358
  Cooked Rice 588
  Cross Buns 135, **134**
  Dog Relish 18
  Fudge Sauce 716, **712**
  Herbed Tomato Juice 64, **62-63**
  Mustard 55
  Nachos Salad 696, **391**
  Pepper Jelly 13
  Potato-Kielbasa Salad 695, **538**
  Sausage and Mozzarella Roll 539
  Tuna Bake 387
  Walnut-Stuffed Mushroom Caps 46
How Much Rice Should You Cook? 611
How to Bake Potatoes in a Microwave Oven 585, **585**
How to Blossom a Baked Potato 585, **585**
How to Carve Duckling 674
How to Carve Roast Turkey 677
How to Cook Rice Perfectly 612

How to Cut and Bone Chicken 648
How to Dress Drinks for a Party 67, **67**
How to Grill Turkey 685
How to Knead and Shape Bread 88, **88**
How to Shape Yeast Rolls 99, **99**
How to Stuff and Truss Poultry 647
Huevos Rancheros 353, **72-73**
Hush Puppies 120

Ice 291
  Block, Green Grape 70
  Cranberry 292
  Grapefruit 292
  Honeydew 293
  Orange 292
  Pink Lemonade 292
  Watermelon 293
Icebox Cake 284
  Chocolate Rum 284
  Peppermint 284
Ice Cream
  Apricot-Banana 283, **282**
  Cake
    Piña Colada 344
    Praline 326, **326**
    Tortoni 342
  Chocolate Burnt Almond 278, **278**
  Chocolate Chip, Mint 280
  Coffee Butterscotch Swirl 279
  Fresh Strawberry 282, **283**
  Honey Almond Crunch 275, **277**
  Lemon Cream 283, **282**
  Log, Chestnut 284
  Macaroon 282, **283**
  Peach 281
    Praline 276
  Sandwiches, Plum 279
  Strawberry 278
    One-Step 276
  Vanilla, All-American 276
    Low-Calorie 276
  Walnut Crunch 279
Icing, Chocolate 209, 212
  Decorator 242
  Lemon 206
  Sugar 136
  Sunrise 101
  White 232
Indian
  Pudding 314
  Yogurt Drink 57
Individual Birthday Cakes 168, **169**
  Cheese Soufflés 357
  Meatloaves 570
  Orange Soufflés 358
  Pork Loaves with Orange Sauce 464
Instant
  Cherry Crisp 269
  Mousse au Chocolat 278
  Spumoni 291
Irish
  Coffee 61
    Dublin 61
    Frozen 61, **62-63**
  Stew 487
    Low-Calorie 487
Italian
  Bean and Provolone Bake 377
  Beef Rolls 435
  Cheese and Vegetable Pie 622, **620**
  Fiesta Sausages 541, **542-543**
  Fish Stew 395
  Meatball and Escarole Soup 744
  Sausage Strata 540
  Sausages with Vegetables 539, **528-529**
  Spinach Dumplings with Cheese Sauce 617

Stars 239, **241**

Jalapeño
  Corn Bread 552, **551**
  Refried Bean Dip 28
Jam(s) 8
  Apricot-Pineapple 9
  Blueberry 9
  Freezer, Strawberry-
    Pineapple 12
  Scotch Rhubarb and
    Ginger 9
  Sweet Pepper and Orange
    9
Jambalaya 616
Jamocha Pecan Pie 597
Japanese Beef with Broccoli
  567, **567**
Javanese Curried Noodles
  and Beef 480
Jellies, Neapolitan 254, **255**
Jelly 12
  Basil 12, **20**
  Candies 256, **255**
  Champagne, 14
  Cranberry-Apple 12
  Hot Pepper 12
  Jewels 218, **215**
  Low-Calorie Grape 13
  Muffins 128
  Parsleyed Vermouth 13
  Roll 303
    Old-Fashioned 303
  Vin Chablis 13
  Vin Rosé 13
Jiffy
  Enchiladas 579
  Stuffing 721
Julep 66
Jumbo
  Burger Rolls 455
  Double Chocolate Chip
    Cookies 222, **694**
  Stack Braunschweiger
    Sandwich 746

Kabob Dinner, Alsace 536
Kabobs
  Beef and Vegetable 423
  Lamb and Mushroom 491,
    694
  Napa Valley 389
  Saucy 576
  Scallop 411
    Sweet and Sour 411
Kasha 616
  -Cheese Skillet 371
  Fruited 616
Kebabs, Fruit 67, **67**
Ketchup, Spicy Tomato 23
Key West Pork Stew 516
Kidney-Bean Minestrone 734
Kidney Beans with
  Knockwurst 541
Kidney Pie, Steak and 484
Kielbasa and Kraut 539, **538**
Kilkenny Corned Beef 434,
  118
Kir 76
  Strawberry 76, **78-79**
Knish 483
Knishes, Chicken-Liver 483
Knockwurst
  Bavarian-Style 534, **535**
  Kidney Beans with 541
  or Franks, Grilled 541
  with Fruit Glaze, Grilled
    543, **542-543**
Kuchen 136

Ladyfingers 298
Lamb 484
  à la Grecque, Skillet 480
  and Mushroom Kabobs
    491, **694**
  and Peppers, Pueblo 495
  Beef and Rice Loaf 465
  Braised Twin Shoulders of,
    48
  Burgundy 490, **490-491**
  Chops, Greek-Style 486,
    494
    Provençale 486

  with Vegetables, Braised
    486
  Kabobs with Vegetables
    489, **489**
  Leg of
    How to Carve 485
    Roast Herbed 485
  Ragout, Savory 491
    Springtime 492, **493**
    with Apricots 489
  Riblets, Deviled 487
  Roast, Middle-Eastern
    Style 485
  Shanks
    à la Grecque, Braised
      492
    Barbecued 492
    Deviled 492, **679**
    Rosemary-Braised 491
    Stew, Moroccan 495
  -Stuffed
    Acorn Squash 755
    Zucchini 474
  Supper, South Seas 486
  Triangles, Crescent 477
  with Green Peppers, Spicy
    496
Lasagna 607, **607**
  Noodle Beef Loaf 603
  Rolls, Mushroom-Cheese
    608, **608**
  with Cottage Cheese 609
Lasagne, Lighthearted 577
  Rolls with Spinach,
    Cheese 602, **602**
Leeks, Braised 769
Lemon
  and Lime, Minted 77, **78-79**
  Blender Mayonnaise 714
  -Broiled Chicken 651
  Butter 767
  Butter Cream Frosting 201
  -Buttered Asparagus 758,
    758
  Cheese Balls 136, **134**
    Braid 111, **82**
  Cream Ice Cream 283, **282**
  Curd 8, **6**
    Charlotte with Blueberry
      Topping 342, **343**
  -Dill Meatballs with
    Artichokes 685
  Dressing 698
  Filling 201
  French Dressing 710, **711**
  Glaze 116
  Granité 296
  Icing 206
  Leaf Cookies 206, **59**
  -Lime Marmalade 8, **6**
  Loaf Cake 281
  Meringue Pie 639, **640**
    Tarts 322, **310**
  or Orange Butter Cream
    Frosting 718
  Pound Cake 162
  -Roasted Cornish Hens 670
  Roll, Mimosa, Chocolate-
    Filled 286, **287**
  Sauce 311
  Sherbet 392
  Sirloin 442
  Slice Cookies 226, **227**
  Sponge Pie 635
  Spritzer 59
  Vinaigrette Dressing 693
  Yogurt Cake 345
Lemonade, Fresh 59, **59**
  Frosty 59
  Summertime 59
Lemony New Potatoes 774
  Sponge Cake 194
Lentil(s)
  Soup with Sausage 744
  Stew 769
  with Cheese, Baked 377
  with Ham, Mushrooms and
    Dill, 530
Lettuce
  Bibb, Mimosa 707
  Wilted 704
Light Chocolate Cream
  Cheese Frosting 213

Lighthearted Lasagne 577
Lime Sherbet 294
Linzer
  Squares 217, **215**
  Torte 190
    Chocolate Ice Cream
      190, **185**
Liptauer Cheese Spread 29
Liqueur
  Cranberry-Orange 66
  Daiquiri 66
Little Dogs 532
  Party Cakes 205
Liver. See also Beef Liver;
  Calf's Liver; Chicken Liver
Liver Teriyaki 483
Lobster
  Bisque 740
  Iolani 408
  or Crab Sauce 384
  Parsley-Stuffed, Baked 408
Loin of Pork
  Orange-Glazed 500
  with Baked Apples, Saucy
    498, **515**
Louisiana Salad 700, **699**
Low-Calorie
  Cheesaroni Beef
    Casserole 480, **482**
  Casserole 480, **482**
  Chocolate
    Cream Roll 318
    -Glazed Eclairs 319
  Cauliflower Supreme 766
  Coq au Vin 667
  Grape Jelly 13
  Honey Syrup 14
  Irish Stew 487
  Oven-Fried Turkey Cutlets
    685
  Pancakes 370
  Reuben Brunch Casserole
    378
  Strawberry Nog 66, **68**
  Sugar-Free Strawberry
    Sauce 717
  Thousand Island Dressing
    710, **711**
  Turkey Scaloppine 684
  Vanilla Ice Cream 279
Luscious Lime Chiffon Pie
  630

Macadamia-Nut Fruitcake
  184
  Tarts 328
Macaroni
  and Cheese
    All-American 604
    Shell Salad 708
Macaroon(s) 233
  Almond 246, **245**
  Coconut 233
  Ice Cream 282, 283
  Pine Nut 233
  Tartlets 231, **234**
Magyar Beef Pakrikash 428,
  429
Mai Tai 76, **75**
Maître d'Hotel Butter 19
Mama's Chicken Soup with
  Fluffy Matzo Balls 727, **665**
Mandarin
  Orange Sauce 716
  Pancakes 509
Manicotti, Microwave 577,
  577
Maple
  -Blueberry Topping 132
  -Butter Glazed Carrots 764
  Cream 171
  -Glazed Twists 105, **107**
  Nut Creams 252
  Pecan Pie 634
  Syrup, Ten-Calorie 12
  Walnut Tarts 328
Margaritas 74, 77, **73**
Marinated
  Beef Round 423
  Black-Eyed Peas 771, **771**
  Cucumber Slices 23, 41
  Filet of Beef 418

Tomato-Rice Salad 691,
  690
  Vegetables 756, **756-757**
Marjoram Poached Halibut
  397
Marmalade
  Carrot-Pineapple 8, **6**
  Lemon-Lime 8, **6**
  Strawberry-Orange 8, **6**
Marrow Bean Casserole,
  French 496
Marshmallows 249
Marzipan 251
Matzo
  Balls, Fluffy 727
  Honey Cake 167
Mayonnaise, Blender 714
Meat
  and Vegetable Pie 587
  Piroshki 468, **469**
  Sauce, Homemade 715
  Smoked 537
  -Stuffed Eggplant 471
Meatball(s)
  Baked 470
  Danish 34
  Hero Sandwiches 748, **748**
  in Lemon Sauce with
    Mashed Potatoes 465
  Stew, Chili 467
  Stroganoff 467
  Sweet and Sour 570, **31**
  with Nectarines, Tiny 465
Meat Loaf. See also Beef
  Loaf; Pork Loaf
  and Baked Potato Meal 462
  Cold Confetti 471
  Country 460
  Cumin, Skillet 472, **472**
  Glazed 462
  in Brioche 473, **433**
  Potato-Frosted 468, **469**
  Rolled 460
Meat Loaves
  Crunchy 464
  4 Ways to Shape 460
  Individual 570
Mediterranean
  Dogs 532, **535**
  Salad 556, **557**
Melba Sauce 338
Melon
  Fruit-Filled 332, **333**
  in Sabayon Sauce, 322,
    310
Meringue(s) 232
  Chocolate-Almond 232
    Pistachio 242, **241**
  Cocoa, Giant 232
  Creams 264
  Miniatures 232
  Rice Pudding 316, **317**
  Torte
    Chocolate 148, **146-147**
    Swiss Almond 152
Metric Charts 788
Mexicali Chicken 558, **558**
Mexican
  Bean Pot 761
  Cheese Enchiladas 380,
    381
  Fondue 371
  Hot Chocolate 66, **72**
  Sausage Casserole 573
Microwave
  Adaptation of Stove-top
    Recipes 545
  Artichokes 582
  Asparagua 574, **573**
  Baking, 546
  Beef Roast 564, **564-565**
  Cooking for Turkey 560
  Principles of 545
  Schedule for Stuffed or
    Unstuffed Turkey 561
  Times, Equivalents 545
  Manicotti 577, **577**
  Oven Method for Fish 573
  Ovens, Guide to
    Countertop 545
    Update on 546
  Tomato Sauce 550
Microwavable Vegetables 580

Microwaving
  Beef Roast 563
  Chicken, Tips for 553
Mimosa-Lemon Frosting 287
Mincemeat
  Braid 93, **94-95**
  Roll with Hard Sauce 274
Minestrone 733
  Kidney Bean 734
  Salad Bar 734, **735**
Mini
  Cheesecakes 170, **169**
  Fruit Tarts 218, **215**
  -Herb Biscuits 125
Miniature
  Lemons 252
  Oranges 252
  Sausage-Crêpe Quiches
    54
Mint Chocolate Chip Ice
  Cream 280
  -Pineapple Lemon Sherbet
    294
  Pinwheels 252
Minted
  Lemon and Lime 77, **78-79**
  Pineapple Cake 158, **310**
Mississippi Mud Cake 144,
  142
Mocha
  Bar Cookies 228, **227**
  Butter Cream 187
  Frosting 718
  Lace Roll-Ups 230, **230**
Molasses
  Chips 252
  Coconut Chews, 253
Mold, Tangerine and
  Cranberry 18
Mornay Sauce 526, 618
Moroccan
  Couscous 681
  Lamb Stew 495
Moussaka 476
  Skillet 476
Mousse 288
  au Chocolat, "Instant," 289
  Chocolate Zabaglione 289
  Creamy Chicken 704
  Espresso 289
  Frozen Honey 288, **277**
  Ham 531
  Salmon 41
  Seafood 547
  Strawberry 288
Muffin(s) 126
  Bacon 128
  Blueberry 127
    -Bran 129
  Cheese 128
  Corn 128
    Pecan 127, **127**
  Favorite 128
  Ginger-Apricot 129
  Granola 126, **126**
  Jelly 128
  Pumpkin-Nut 128
  Wheat Germ 128
  Whole Wheat 129
Mulligatawny Soup 727
Mushroom
  and Leek Soup 723
  Barley Soup 723
  Bread Magnifique 91, **92**
  Caps, Hot Walnut-Stuffed
    46
  Carrot-Stuffed 770
  -Cheese
    Lasagna Rolls 608, **608**
    Sauce 392
  Herb-Stuffed 46
  Pickled 22
  Pilaf 614
  Stroganoff 770
Mu Shu Pork 508
Mustard 7
  Basic French 7, **6**
  Fruits 523
  Hot 55
  Mayonnaise Dip 48
  Pickles, Garden 22
  Sauce 43, 530
  Sweet 'n' Hot 7, **6**

Tomato 7
Trio 7

Nachos 45
Napa Valley Kabobs 389
Neapolitan Jellies 254, **255**
Nectarine Cream Torte 187
Nesselrode
  Pie 638-639
  Sauce 312
Never-Fail Cheese Soufflé 357
New Delhi Cream 713
New England
  Baked Beans 761
  Boiled Dinner 440, **440**
  Fish Chowder 736, **767**
  Oyster Scallop 409
New Mexican Pork Chili 516, **517**
New Orleans Pralines 254
Nibbles, Nutritious 46
Nippy Deviled Eggs 32
No-Bake Black Forest Refrigerator Cake 196, **197**
No-Cook Fondant Confections 252
Nog
  Pineapple 57, **56**
  Strawberry, Low-Calorie 66, **68**
Noodles and Beef, Curried, Javanese 480
Normandy Omelet 366
Norwegian Honey Cake 180, **181**
Nougat, Walnut 357
Nut
  and Raisin Bread 96
  Burgers 456, **457**
  Crisps 217, **215**
  Orange Candied 250
Nutritious Nibbles 46
Nutty Maple-Honey Buns 108, **62-63**

Oatmeal
  Bannocks 120
  Raisin Cookies 237
Oh My! Potato Salad 695, 663
Okra with Fish 397
Old-Fashioned
  Beef and Vegetable Soup 724
  Bread Stuffing 720
  Cake Doughnuts 104
  Cheese Sauce 713
  Chocolate Fudge 257
  Crumb Cake 133
  Jelly Roll 303
  Lentil Soup 734
  Rye Bread 89
  Strawberry Shortcake 191
Old German Sauerbraten 442, **441**
Olé Chili Pie 468
Olives, Piquant Pickled 36
Olive-Tuna Dip 28
Omelet(s) 362
  Avocado 364
  Basic French 366
  Corn 366
  Frankfurter and Potato 533, **535**
  French 363
  Normandy 366
  Pork 364, **365**
  Potato Beef 362
  Potato Zucchini 364
  Rolled Shrimp and Sprout 367
  Spanish, Puffy 363, **346**
One-Step Strawberry Ice Cream 276
Onion(s). See also Spanish Onion(s)
  and Bacon Bread 119
  and Egg Bake 350
  Creamed 770
  Fans, Green 732
  -Lemon Relish 13
  Pie 625
  Rings, Batter-Fried 770

Rounds 118
Sausage-Stuffed 587, **29**
Soup 725, **725**
Tart, French 45
Open Fresh Fruit Pie 308, **306-307**
Orange(s)
  Avocado Salad 698, **72-73**
  Beignets 107, **107**
  Bread Pudding 313, **313**
  Butter Cream 240
  Candied Nuts 250
  Charlotte 286
  Cheese Parfaits 304
  Chiffon Cake 200
  Cream Pudding Filling 199
  Cup 67, **67**
  Custard Sauce 315
  Egg Cream 265
  Fondant Dates 252
  French Toast 379
  Frosting 209, 379
  Glacéed 323, **475**
  Glaze 200
  -Glazed Baked Chicken 664, **665**
    Lemon Cups 200
    Loin of Pork 500
    Yams 562, **562**
  -Honey
    Bubble Loaf 133, **134**
    Butter 368
  Ice 292
  in Wine with Honeyed Walnuts 344
  Juice Sparkler 58
  Marmalade Glaze 200
  Peeling an 35
  Rind, Candied 271
  Salmon Patties 383
  Sauce 291
  Sherbet in Orange Cups 295
  Soufflé 318, **475**
  Sour Cream Dressing 707
  -Spice Barbecue Sauce 714
  Stuffed 474, **475**
  Sugared Pecans 249
  Syrup 312
  Whole-Wheat Bread 117
Orangy Sugar Cookies 242, **243**
Oriental
  Beef 566, **566**
  Shrimp and Vegetables 576, **575**
  -Style Chicken 557
Our Best-Ever Brownies 220, **221**
Oven
  -Barbecued Brisket of Beef 419
  Beef Burgundy 438, **439**
  -Fried
    Eggplant 767
    Fish 392
Overnight
  Pickled Vegetables 20, **21**
  Seed Bread 108, **62-63**
Overstuffed Italian Bread Pizza 643
Oyster(s)
  Rockefeller 34, **35**
  Scallop, New England 409
  Stew 409

Pacific Sparkler 58
Paella Valenciana 612, **490-491**
Paillettes 214, **215**
Pancake(s) 367
  Apple 367
  Buttermilk 368
  Cheese 368
  Low-Calorie 370
  Mandarin 509
  Sauce, Pineapple or Orange 12
  Sour Cream Potato 368
  Syrup, Special Low-Calorie 12

with Orange-Honey Butter 368
Pan Gravy 675
Papaya Chutney 14, **6**
Parfait(s)
  Blarney Castle 304, **234**
  Granola 290
  Orange Cheese 304
  Yogurt Lime 290, **290**
Parsley-Flecked
  Potatoes 534
  Rice 588
Parsleyed
  Blue Cheese Spread 30
  New Potatoes 772, **430**
  Vermouth Jelly 13
Parsnips, Glazed 771
Party
  Canapés 34
  Pork Balls 37, **38-39**
  Pretties 214, **215**
Pasta 599
  In Carbonara Sauce 607
  Pepperoni 599, **598**
  with Broccoli 600, **601**
Pastry
  Cream 300, 327
  Flaky 519, 621
  Shell 377
  Sweet 166
Pâté
  Chicken 26
  Country 25, **24**
    Picnic 519
  Elegant 26
  en Groûte, Sausage 26
  Fluffy Tuna 387, **387**
  Potato and Leek 780, **781**
Pattable Pie Crust 597
Peach(es)
  and Banana Flan 301
  and Chocolate Shortcake 132
  and Cream Tart 323
  and Pears, Pickled 22
  and Sour Cream Tarts 324
  Brown Betty 298
  Cobbler 320
  Coupes 287
  -Filled Cheese Tart 195, **197**
  Ice Cream 281
  Melba-Topped Raspberry Soufflé 338, **339**
  -Pear Compote 342
  Praline Ice Cream 276
  Pudding 314
  Spiced 341
Peachy Sherbet 295
Peanut Brittle 248
Peanut Butter
  and Chocolate Layered Fudge 256
  Bars 212, **211**
  Cake 143, **142**
  Cookies 235
  Topping 143
Peanut Clusters, Easy Chocolate 250
Peanutty Caramel Corn 592, **251**
Pear(s)
  -Ginger Pudding with Two Sauces 311, **10-11**
  in White Wine 340
  Perfect Poached 590, **590**
  Poached 308, **306-307**
  Sundae with Almond Fudge Sauce 589
Pea(s)
  Provençal 771
  Stew, Black-Eyed 584
  Stir-Fried 772
Pecan(s)
  Cake, Bourbon Street 151
  Candy Cake 182, 137
  Cookies 237
  Corn Muffins 127, **127**
  Orange Sugared 249
  Sugared and Salted 44, **756-757**
  Tart 328
  Wafers 246, **245**
Penuche, Creamy 257

Pepper(s)
  and Onion Dogs 533, **535**
  and Steak Sandwich 751
  'n' Beef Liver 483
  Relish, California 16
  Stuffed 470, 582, **583**
Peppermint
  Icebox Cake 284
  Patties 252
Pepperoni Pasta 599, **598**
Pepperpot Stew 427
Perfect Poached Pears 590, **590**
Picadillo Tamales 473
Piccalilli 23
Pickle(s)
  Chips, Sweet 21
  Dill, Kosher Style 20
  Mustard 22
Pickled Beets 21
  Bologna 34
  Mushrooms 22
  Peaches and Pears 22
  Shrimp 41
Pie(s) 621
  Apple 632
    Delicious 594, **598**
  Banana Cream 596, 636
  Beef and Vegetable 621, **620**
  Beefsteak 437
  Black Walnut 632
  Caramel Custard Pear 634, **634**
  Cheese 632
  Chicken, Greek 626, **627**
  Chili, Olé 468
  Chocolate Chiffon 631, **631**
  Chocolate Mousse 636
  Cottage 479
  Crust, Pattable 597
  Custard, Broccoli, Mushroom and Sweet Pepper 622, **623**
  Empanada 628
  English Pub 621, **620**
  Fresh
    Blueberry 641
    Cherry 641
    Fruit, Open 308, **306-307**
    Peach 641
  Green Apple 635, **635**
  Italian Cheese and Vegetable 622, **620**
  Lattice, Apricot-Prune 639, **638**
  Lemon Meringue 639, **640**
  Lime Chiffon, Luscious 630
  Meat and Vegetable 587
  Nesselrode 638-639
  Onion 625
  Pecan
    Jamocha 597
    Maple 634
    Virginia 632, **633**
  Pork, Canadian 519
  Pumpkin-Mince 641
  Ricotta, 626, **626**
  Shoofly 631
  Spiced Raisin 636, **635**
  Spicy Green Tomato 628
  Sponge, Lemon 634, **635**
  Strawberry
    Chiffon 630
    -Rhubarb Cream 629, **629**
  Tamale 627
  Tuna, Top-Notch 622
  Vegetable, Hamburger 628
Pilaf 614
  Mushroom 614
Pimiento
  and Pepper Butter 17
  Vinaigrette 780
Piña Colada 76, **75**
  Down-Up Cake 160
  Ice Cream Cake 344
Pineapple
  -Apricot Upside-Down Cake 161
  Chiffon Cake 158
  Coconut Cheesecake 185
  Cream 264

Filling 336
Galliano Sauce 260
Luau Style 336, **511**
-Mint Cooler 76, **75**
Nog 57, **56**
or Orange Pancake Sauce 14
Spears in Rum 322
Yogurt Sherbet 294
Pine Nut Macaroons 233
Pink
  -and-White Frosted Hearts 154, **154**
  Champagne Punch 70
  Grapefruit Snow with Warm Orange Sauce 291, **291**
  Lemonade Ice 292
  Sauce 713
  Tomato Drink 58
Pinto Beans 760
  Salad 700
Pinwheels
  Mint 252
  Raspberry-Nut 226, **227**
Pioneer Sausage Burger Stew 477
Pipérade 351, **351**
Piquant
  Barbecue Sauce 541
  Pickled Olives 36
Pirog, Browned Cabbage and Mushrooms 623, **623**
Piroshki, Meat 468, **82**
Pistou 724, **722**
Pita
  Crisps 27
  Sausage-Egg 746
Pizza 642
  Dough, Easy 642
  Italian Bread, Overstuffed 643
  Mariner's Style 643, **644-645**
  Rustica 642, **644-645**
  Sausage and Pepper 642, **644-645**
  South-of-the-Border 643, **644-645**
  Whole Wheat 549, **549**
Plantation Fruitcake 186
Platter of Meats with Accompanying Breads 693, **690**
Plum
  and Peach Kuchen 136
  Butter 19
  Chutney 14
  -Glazed Spareribs 510, **511**
  Good Pork Chops 508
  Ice Cream Sandwiches 279
  Kuchen 137
  Pudding 590, **591**
  Sherbet 295
Poached
  Pears with Hot Caramel Sauce 308, **306-307**
  Salmon Steaks 393, **396**
Poinsettia Cookies 230
Polenta Parmesan 614
Polonaise Sauce 714
Polynesian
  Glaze 510
  Roast Pork 510
  Spareribs 511
Popcorn 745
  Party Mix 45
  Smoky Bacon Cheese 45
Popovers 122
Poppy Seed
  Cake 201
  -Onion Crackers 37
Popsicles, Banana 292
Pork 496
  and Blackeyed Peas, Country 508
  and Chicken Tablecloth Stainer 518
  and Eggplant Fricassee 519
  and Ginger Balls, Chinese 54, **52-53**
  Balls
    en Brochette 37

in Sour Cream 476
Party 37, **38-39**
Chili, New Mexican 516,
517
Chop and Scalloped Potato
Casserole 506, **507**
Chops
Braised Stuffed 508
Herb-Stuffed 506
Plum Good 508
Savory Stuffed 504
with Cabbage, Braised
506
with Red Cabbage 507,
528-529
Crown Roast of 567, **544**
with Apple-Herb Stuffing
501
with Wild Rice Stuffing
501, **502-503**
Loaf, Apple 461
Loaves with Orange Sauce,
Individual 464
Loin of 598, **515**
Roast, How to Carve 500
Tangy Glazed 500, **512**
Mu Shu 508
Omelets 364, **365**
Pie, Canadian 519
Ribs
Southern Style 568
with Sauerkraut,
Country-Style 568
Roast
Chinese 509
Polynesian 510
Saté 514
Shortcut 513
Shoulder, Spanish 518
Stew
Key West 416
Portuguese 517
San Francisco 516
Sweet and Pungent 513
Tenderloin Oriental 568,
569 with Basil and
Mushroom Stuffing,
Roast 498, **499**
with Noodles, Sweet and
Sour 509
Yam and Apple Skillet 518
Portuguese Pork Stew 517
Port Wine Aspic 24
Potato(es)
and Leek Pâté 780, **781**
and Onions, Boiled New
539, **10-11**
Baked
Cheese-Stuffed 774
Spicy Chili-Topped 780,
780
-Beef Omelet 362
Dumplings 442, **441,** 743
Ukrainian 617
Filling 617
French-Filled 772
-Frosted Meat Loaf 468,
469
Home-Fried 774
How to Bake in a
Microwave Oven 585, **585**
Kugel 772
New
Boiled 539, **10-11**
Lemony 774
Parsleyed 772, **430**
Parsley 534
Roast 772, **515**
Rosettes 565, **564-565**
Salad 695, **663**
All-American 708
German 700, **701**
Green 692, **690**
Oh My! 695, **663**
Spring 708, 709
Savory Parmesan 585
Scalloped 774
Stuffing 720
Vegetable Casserole,
Duchess 773, **773**
Zucchini Omelet 364
Pots de Crème au Chocolat
267

Poultry 647
How to Stuff and Truss 647
Pound Cake 162
Ginger 159
Lemon 162
Sherried 162
Sour Cream 162
Marble 163
Praline 254, 276
Almond 254, 326
Glaze 152
Ice Cream Cake 326, **326**
New Orleans 254
Preheated Ovens for
Baking Bread 113
Preserves 14
Tomato 14
Pretzels, Chocolate 217, **215**
Principles of Microwave
Cooking 545
Profiteroles with Espresso
Sauce 268
Provençal Tomato Dressing
710, **711**
Prune
Danish 335
Oatmeal Bars 237
Pudding 315
Upside-Down Cake 160
Pudding 311
Bread 139, 313, **313**
Chocolate Pecan 315
Cinnamon-Raisin Bread
316
Coconut 312
Custard, Rice 316
Indian 314
Peach 314
Pear-Ginger 311, **10-11**
Plum 590, **591**
Prune 315
Queen of 312
Tropical 314
Rice, Meringue 316, **317**
Steamed
Apple-Date 314
Date-Apricot 315
Surprise, Summer 312, **310**
Pueblo Lamb and Peppers
495
Puff Pastry Sticks 594
Puffy Spanish Omelet 363,
346
Pumpernickel Raisin Bread
111
Pumpkin
Date-Nut Loaf 596, **595**
-Mince Pie 641
'n' Spice Tea Bread 117
-Nut Muffins 128
Punch 69
Champagne 70
Fruited 70
Cranberry Orange 58
Darjeeling 70
Double Apple 71
Fruit, Guava 74, **75**
Holiday 69, **10-11**
Pink Champagne 70
Royal, Cassis 76
Strawberry-Lemon 70
Wine, Blazing Spiced 69
Pushbuttons 218, **215**

Queen of Puddings 312
Quenelles 618
of Turkey au Gratin 618
Quiche(s), 375
California 375, **374**
Collard Greens 376
Lorraine 375, 579, **578**
Miniature Sausage Crêpe
54
Sloppy Joe 376
Tomato-Broccoli 375
Quick
and Easy Fudge 256, **255**
Basic Biscuits 97, **97**
Blueberry Cobbler 319
Choucroute Garni 537
Corn Relish 16
Crispy Skillet Chicken 664,
666

Old-Fashioned Shepherd's
Pie 578, **578**
Red Clam Sauce 715
Squash au Gratin 778

Ragout 443
Rainbow
Bavarian Cream 262
Stuffed Peppers 582, **583**
Venetians 228, **227**
Raisin
Bread, Honey 114, **113**
Pudding with Whiskey
Sauce 589
Spice Coffee Cake 133
Raleigh Buttermilk Ham
Biscuits 125
Ranch-Style Chili 420
Rarebit 371
Welsh 371
Raspberry
-Almond Cookies 225
-Apple Sauce 288
Chocolate Torte 191
Cream Roll 198, **198**
Glaze 200
-Nut Pinwheels 226, **227**
Sauce 260, 715, **712**
Whipped Cream 198
Ratatouille 781
Frittata 372, **372**
-Stuffed Tomatoes 782
Ravioli
Homemade 609, 615
with Red Pepper and
Tomato Sauce 604, **605**
Real Red Chili Sauce 714
Red Beet Eggs 19
Cabbage 766
Slaw, Wilted 688, **686**
Sweet-Sour 506
Flannel Hash 440
Hot Chile Sauce 749
River Chili 443
Snapper, Baked 394
White and Blue Waffle
Shortcake 132
Wine Vinegar Dressing 689
Refried Beans 760
Refrigerator Cake, No-Bake
Black Forest 196, **197**
Regal Peach Crown 298, **299**
Roast Turkey 561, **562**
Relish(es)
Baked Apple 16, **17**
California Pepper 18
Carrot-Raisin 15
Celery 16
Corn, Quick 16
Cranberry 15
Crisp Cranberry 17
Hot Dog 18
Onion-Lemon 15
Ripe Tomato-Pear 16
Sauerkraut 17
Three Vegetable 692, **690**
Yankee Corn 15
Reuben Brunch Casserole
378, **379**
Low-Calorie 378
Reuben Dogs 532, **535**
Rhubarb and Raspberry
Soufflé 390
Upside-Down Cake 160,
161
Rib Roast, How to Carve 418
Ribs
Sweet and Sour 513
Tulsa 422
Rice
and Sausage Stuffing 569
and Vegetable Salad 694,
694
Cakes 119
Cooked, Hot 588
Custard Pudding 316
How Much Should You
Cook? 611
How to Cook Perfectly 612
Imperatrice with Cherry
Sauce 612
Orange, Curried 614, **475**
Parsley-Flecked 588

Roster of 611
Salad Niçoise 704, **705**
Wild 612
with Chicken, Fried,
Chinese 613, **613**
with Pork, Fried, Chinese
613
Rich
Butter Cream Frosting 718
Chocolate Filling 287
Ricotta
Filling 609
Pie 626, **626**
Ripe Tomato-Pear Relish 16
Risotto with Chicken Livers
616
Roast
Beef 421, **421**
Chicken with Curry Sauce
650
Duckling 559
with Kasha Stuffing 671
Fresh Ham 523
Goose with Fruit Stuffing
675
Herbed Leg of Lamb 485
Lamb, Middle-Eastern
Style 485
Pork with Basil and
Mushroom Stuffing, 498,
499
Turkey 677, **678**
Breast 684
Young Capon with Wild
Rice Stuffing 671
Roasted Corn in Husks 767
Rock Cornish Game Hens
668. See also Cornish
Game Hens
Rocky
Road Bars 596, **595**
Roads 250
Roll(s) 98
Basic Yeast 100
Burger, Jumbo 455
Cardamom 102, **102**
Glazed Orange 100, **109**
Hamburger 101, **92**
Herb-Onion 100
Orange, Golden 112, **82**
Sour Cream 101
Yeast, How to Shape 99, **99**
Rolled
Flank Steak 431, **430**
Meat Loaf 460
Roast, How to Carve 418
Shrimp and Sprout Omelet
367
Stuffed Eggplant 769, **768**
Romanoff Roll 196, **197**
Rosé Spritzer 77, **78-79**
Wine Mold
Rosemary-Braised Lamb
Shanks 491
Roster of Rice 611
Rotelle with Shrimp and
Lemon 604, **604**
Roulade, Beef 43, **43**
Roulades, Beef 444
Royal Frosting 225
Rum
Butter Frosting 158
Cream 285
Raisin Sauce 716
Whipped Cream 203
Russian Tea Cakes 238
Rye Bread
Dark 110
Old-Fashioned 89

Sabayon (Zabaglione), Maple
266
Sacher Torte 181, **183**
Saffron Raisin Loaf 103, **92**
Sake 66
Salad(s) 687
Antipasto 556, **557**
Bar Minestrone 734, **735**
Beansprouts and Tomato
699, **698**
Beet 693
Caesar 703

Chef's 707
Chicken and Rotelle 688,
689
Chicken-Macaroni 692,
690
Cucumber 708
Curried Vegetable 588
Dressing(s). See also
Dressing(s)
Endive Crown 704
Frozen Fruit 704
Grape and Endive 698
Greek Chick-Pea 696,
627
Green 698
Potato 692, **690**
Herbed Walnut,
Mushroom and Orange
689, **502-503**
Herring 710
Hot Nachos 696, **391**
Hot Potato-Kielbasa 695,
538
Louisiana 700, **699**
Macaroni Shell 708
Marinated Tomato-Rice
691, **690**
Mediterranean 556, **557**
Niçoise, Rice 704, 705
of Julienne Vegetables
696, **10-11**
Orange Avocado 698,
72-73
Pinto Bean 700
Potato 695, **663**
All-American 708
German 700, **701**
Oh My! 695, **663**
Spring 708, **709**
Rice and Vegetable 694,
694
Shrimp and Cantaloupe
703
Steak 694, **695**
Sunset 700, **701**
Taco 696, **698**
Tossed Green 690, **690**
Tuna-White Bean 693,
690
Turkey 702, **702**
Winter Fruit 699, **62-63**
Salmon
Alaska, Grilled 392
and Green Bean Puff,
Baked 393
Appetizer Spread 547, **30**
Mousse 41
with Cucumber Dressing
394
Patties, Orange 383
Steaks, Poached 393, **396**
Supreme 573, **573**
Timbales 392
with Sour Cream Dill
Sauce, Baked 393
Sandwich(es)
Bacon-Spinach 746
Braunschweiger 746
Cream Cheese-Date-Nut
751
Curried Egg Salad 748
Giant Club 751
Grilled Open-Face Club
750
Meatball Hero 748, **748**
Pepper and Steak 751
Super Cheese Hero 747,
747
Swiss and Sprout 749
The California Rage 751
The New York "Deli"
Special 749
The Reuben 749
Tomato-Avocado 750, **750**
Sangria 71, 74
Spritzer 77, **78-79**
Summer 74
Sarasota Fish Steaks 389
Sassy Salsa 558
Sauce(s) 713
Apricot-Orange Barbecue
716, **6**

Barbecue, Orange-Spice 714
    Piquant 541
Basic White 713
Béarnaise 713
Béchamel 470, 713
Brandied Fruit 717
Burgundy 462
Butterscotch 716
Cardinale 341
Cheese 617, 713
    Creamy 602
Cherry 612
Chile, Red Hot 749
Chinese Mustard 40
Clam 715
Cranberry 715
Cream Cheese Hard 169
Creamy
    Custard 716, **712**
    Horseradish 440
Cucumber-Dill 392
Cumberland 523
Custard 315, 332
Dill Mustard 746
Duck, Spicy 673
Egg 713
Egg Foo Yung 363
Hard 275
Harissa 683
Hollandaise 574, **573**
    Foolproof 714
Hot Fudge 716, **712**
Lemon 311
Lobster or Crab 384
Mandarin Orange 716
Meat 715
Melba 338
Mornay 526, 618
Mousseline 386
Mushroom Cheese 392
Mustard 43, 530
    Sherried 524
Nesselrode 312
Orange 291
    Custard 315
Pineapple Galliano 260
    or Orange Pancake 14
Pink 713
Polonaise 714
Raspberry 260, 715, **712**
    -Apple 288
Red Chili 714
Rum Raisin 716
Sausage 602
Sherry 402
Sour Cream Dill 393
Soy, Dipping 408
Strawberry 304
    Low-Calorie 717
    Wine 305
Sweet and Sour 37, 656, 715
Tartar 385
Tomato
    Homemade 610
    Microwave 550
Vanilla, Finnish 308
Whiskey 589
Yogurt-Dill 570
Saucy
    Barbecued Chicken 553
    Kabobs 576
    Loin of Pork with Baked Apples 498, **515**
Sauerbraten, Old German 442, **441**
Sauerkraut, Drunken 766, **515**
    Relish 17
Sausage(s) 532
    and Apple Skillet 539
    and Chicken Livers en Brochette 543, **542-543**
    and Mozzarella Roll, Hot 539
    and Pepper Filling 366
    and Pepper Pizza 642, **644-645**
    Beer-Braised 536
    Burger Stew, Pioneer 477
    Casserole
        Creamy Corn and 537

Mexican 573
-Egg Pita 746
in Onion and Apple Sauce 540
Italian Fiesta 541, **542-543**
Loaf, Savory 464, **466**
Pâté en Croûte 26
Sauce 602
-Spaghetti Bake 540
Strata, Italian 540
-Stuffed
    Onions 587, **29**
    Zucchini 540
Stuffing 678
    with Vegetables, Italian 539, **528-529**
Sautéed
    Apples 506, **505**
    Chicken Breasts with Oranges 666, **662**
    Steak with Red Wine 429
Savory
    Clam Chowder 739
    Cranberry Sauce 715
    Cream Puffs 91, **62-63**
    Grilled Short Ribs 419
    Lamb Ragout 491
    Mediterranean Stew 570
    Oriental Vegetables 582
    Parmesan Potatoes 585
    Sausage Loaf 464, **466**
    Stuffed Pork Chops 504
    Thanksgiving Stuffing 721
Scallop(s)
    Bacon-Wrapped 42
    Chowder 739
    Herbed-Baked 409
    Kabobs 411
    Kebobs, Sweet and Sour 411
Scalloped Asparagus 758, **759**
    Potatoes 774
Scaloppine with Orange Sauce 658, **658**
Scones 125
    Cheese 123
    Fruit 123
    Griddle 123
    Irish, Bridle's 123
    Whole Wheat 123
Scorpion 74, **75**
Scotch
    Eggs 325, **433**
    Rhubarb and Ginger Jam 9
Seafood Gumbo 397
    Mousse 547
Seltzer 57
Sesame
    Broccoli 762
    Butter Fingers 123
    Chicken Wings 50
    Crunch 253
    Potato Twist Loaf 87, **87**
    Seed Bars 210, **211**
Seviche 42
Shamrock Sugar Cookies 234, **234**
Shannon Vegetable Platter 762, **118**
Shellfish 383
Shells Marinara, Stuffed 606
Shepherd's Pie, Quick Old-fashioned 578, **578**
Sherbet 293
    Buttermilk-Lime 293
    Lemon 293
    Lime 294
    Mint-Pineapple Lemon 294
    Orange in Orange Cups 295
    Peachy 295
    Pineapple Yogurt 294
    Plum 295
    Strawberry 294
Sherried
    Chicken Livers 48
    Mustard Sauce 524
    Pound Cake 162
    Sole 398
Sherry
    Bavarian Cream with Sponge Cake 194

Pan Gravy 664
    Sauce 402
Shirred Eggs with Cheese 353
Shish Kebob 488
Shoofly Pie 631
Shortbread 236
Shortcake(s) 191
    Peach and Chocolate 132
    Strawberry 305
    Waffle 132
Shortcut Pork Saté 513
Short Ribs
    Barbecued 443
    Beef, Barbecued 441
    Beer-Braised 438
    Grilled, Savory 419
Shredded-Wheat Prune Bread 119
Shrimp
    and Cantaloupe Salad 703
    and Cucumber, Dilled 574
    and Sausage Jambalaya 403
    and Scallops in Wine Sauce 411, **410**
    and Vegetables, Oriental 576, **575**
    Balls, Chrysanthemum-shaped 40
    Bisque 740
    Butterflied Coconut 40
    Creole 404, **405**
    Curry 403, **493**
    in Aspic, Dilled 402
    on Chinese Cabbage 406, **407**
    Pâté Canapés 26
    Pickled 41
    Remoulade 404
    Scampi 403
    Stir-Fried 402, **365**
    Toast 40
    with Feta Cheese 403
    with Vegetables, Skewered 402
Sidewalk Sundae Cake 174, **175**
Silky Chocolate Mocha Frosting 203
Silo Chicken 662, **663**
Sirloin
    Lemon 442
    of Beef, with Sauce Bordelaise 437
Skewered Shrimp with Vegetables 402
Skillet
    Cumin Meat Loaf 472, **472**
    Honey-Glazed Ham Steak 524
    Lamb à la Grecque 480
    Moussaka 476
    Steak Meal 431
    Tuna Chowder 390
Slim Cheesecake 167
Sloppy Joe Quiche 376
Sloppy Joes, Spicy 467
Small Sand Cookies 247, **245**
Smoked
    Meat 537
    Salmon
        and Cheese Canapés 36
        Spread in Pumpernickel 29
Smoky Bacon Cheese Popcorn 45
Snacks, 20 Good-for-You 745
Soda Bread, Bridie's Irish 113
Sole
    -Almond Bake 398
    in Cucumber Sauce, Fillets of 389
    Sherried 398
    Véronique, Gourmet 397
Soufflé(s) 354
    Amaretto, Frozen 259
    Apple Nougat, Fresh, 357, **356**
    Broccoli and Ham 359
    Cheese
        and Onion 584
        Individual 357

Never-Fail 357
    Soup 355
Corn and Cheese 355
Cranberry, Cold 259
Hot Chocolate 358
Lemon, Cool 318, **317**
Orange 318, **475**
    Individual 358
Raspberry 338, **339**
Rhubarb and Raspberry 340
Twin Zabaglione 354
Soup(s) 723. See also Bisque; Chowder
    Avocado, Cool 741
    Bean and Sausage 743
    Beef and Barley 726
    Beef and Vegetable 724
    Beefy Vegetable 735
    Black Bean 743
    Buttermilk Shrimp 741, **742**
    Calorie Cruncher 736
    Chicken
        Rice 736
        with Fluffy Matzo Balls 727, **665**
    Cream of Asparagus 725
        of Broccoli 726
        of Fresh Tomato 739
        of Turkey 730
    Creamy Mushroom 549
    Cucumber
        and Potato 732
        and Yogurt, Cold 741
    Curried Apple and Chicken 734
    Egg Drop 732, **732**
    Fruit, Chilled 741
    Garden Vegetable 739, **738**
    Giblet and Parsley 732
    Goulash 743
    Italian Meatball and Escarole 744
    Italiano 744
    Lentil 734
        with Sausage 744
    Mulligatawny 727
    Mushroom
        and Leek 726
        Barley 726
    Onion 725, **725**
    Pumpkin 733
    Spinach, Chilled 740
    Split Pea 724
    Tomato and Rice 732, **733**
    Vegetable Ham 744
    Watercress Cream 736
        with Egg Dumplings, Turkey 730
    Won Ton 736
Sour Cream
    and Horseradish Burgers 455
    Cake with Coconut Topping 177
    Dill Sauce 393
    Lemon Glaze 170
    Marble Pound Cake 163
    Potato Pancakes 368
    Pound Cake 162
    Sunrise Rolls 101
    Waffles with Brown Sugar Syrup, 130, **131**
    Walnut Cake 158
Southern-Style
    Butterscotch Brownies 209, **211**
    Ribs 568
South-of-the-Border
    Casserole 534, **535**
    Pizza 643, **644-645**
South Seas Lamb Supper 486
Soy
    Dipping Sauce 408
    -Flour Waffles 132
Spaghetti
    and Meatballs 608
    Garden-Style 610, **610**
    Squash with Meat Sauce 778

with Broccoli, Tomatoes and Walnuts 600, **598**
    with Meat Sauce 611, **619**
Spanakopita 625, **624**
Spanish
    Custard Flan 300
    Onions, Meat-Stuffed, Baked 472
    Pork Shoulder 518
    Tomato Caps 783
    Veal with Almonds 450
Spareribs 510
    Barbecued Country-Style 514
    Kun Koki 513
    Plum-Glazed 510, **511**
    Polynesian 511
Sparkler
    Orange Juice 58
    Pacific 58
Sparkling Cookie Cake 178, **178**
Spatzle 666
Special Low-Calorie Pancake Syrup 14
Speedy Swiss Steak 444
Spice Cakes with Banana Cream Filling 171, **169**
Spiced
    Coffee Vienna 60
    Peaches 341
    Raisin Pie 636, **635**
    Brown Beans 760
    Chili-Topped Baked Potato 780, **780**
    Duck Sauce 673
    Green Tomato Pie 628
    Lamb with Green Peppers 496
    Oatmeal Cupcakes 151, **150**
    Pear Cobbler 320, **321**
    Sloppy Joes 467
    Szechuan Shredded Beef and Vegetables 438, **445**
    Tomato Ketchup 23
Spinach
    and Lettuce, Wilted 777
    -Cheese
        Appetizer Puffs 47
        Casserole 776
        Strata 140, **141**
    Dumplings with Cheese Sauce, Italian 617
    Filling 609
    Gnocchi 470
    with Mushrooms 776
Spirits, Frozen 71
Spit-Roasted Duckling 674
Split Pea Soup 724
Sponge Cake 192, 194
    Lemony 194
    Sherry Bavarian Cream with 194
    Strawberries 'n' Cream 192, **193**
    Walnut 195
Spoon Bread 117
Spread(s) 29
    Herring Apple 29
    Liptauer Cheese 29
    Parsleyed Blue Cheese 30
    Salmon Appetizer 547, **30**
    Smoked Salmon 29
Spring
    Egg Sauce 713
    Potato Salad 708, **709**
    Vegetable Salad 708, **709**
Springtime Lamb Ragout 492, **493**
Spritz
    Cookie Sandwich 240, **241**
    Cookies, Danish 244, **243, 245**
    Rosettes 214, **215**
Spritzer
    Lemon 59
    Rosé 77, **78-79**
    Sangria 77, **78-79**
Spumoni 291
    Instant 291
Squash au Gratin, Quick 778
Steak(s)

and Kidney Pie 484
au Poivre 427
Marinated, Cold 432, **433**
Meal, Skillet 431
Persillade, Broiled 432
Salad with Spinach and
 Red Onion 694, **695**
Swiss, Speedy 444
with Red Wine, Sautéed
 429
Swiss 430
Steamed
 Apple-Date Pudding with
  Custard Sauce 314
 Boston Brown Bread 113
 Fish 390
 Ginger Brown Bread 116,
  87
Stew
 Beef
  and Lima Bean 424
  and Vegetable 424, **425**
  Belgian 419
  Hearty 419
  Texas Chili 426
 Brunswick 656
 Chili Meatball 467
 Lentil 769
 Pepperpot 427
 Savory Mediterranean 570
 Veal, Milanese 450
Stir-Fried
 Apples and Celery 461
 Asparagus 758
 Beef
  with Sprouts 446
  with Vegetables 447
 Peas Plus 772
 Shrimp 402, **365**
Stir-Fry
 Chicken Wings 656, **656**
 Hong Kong 516
Stock(s) 723
Stollen, Christmas 138, **137**
Storing Cooked Chicken 650
Stracciatella 731
Strawberries
 Chocolate-Dipped 564,
  564-565
 Glacéed 341
 'n' Cream Sponge Cake
  192, **193**
 with Brandied Syllabub 308
Strawberry
 Charlotte with Strawberry
  Sauce 304
 Cheesecake Deluxe 163,
  164-165
 Chiffon Pie 630
 Cream Puffs 269
 Ice Cream 278
  Brownie Bombe 261, **267**
 Kir 76, **78-79**
 Kiwi Tart 324, **325**
 Lemon Punch 70
 Mousse 288
 -Orange Marmalade 8, **6**
 -Pineapple Freezer Jam 12
 -Rhubarb
  Cobbler 320
  Cream Pie 629, **629**
 Sauce 304
 Sherbet 294
 Shortcake, Old-Fashioned
  191
 Shortcakes 305
 Strips 344
 Topping 166, 343
 Wine Sauce 305
 Yogurt Bavarian 262
Strudel 330
 Apple 330, **331**
 Apple-Nut 332
Stuffed
 Baked Ham Maryland-Style
  524, **525**
 Braised Breast of Veal 452,
  453
 Cabbage with Avgolemono
  Sauce 468
 Cornish Hens in Herb
  Butter 670
 Curried Eggs 33

Flounder 399
Fruits 252
Peppers, Italian Style 470
Pickled Eggs 32
Roast Chickens 650, **651**
Shells Marinara 606
Turkey Breast 680, **10-11**
Vegetables 755, **752**
Zucchini 488
Stuffing(s) 718
 Apple-Herb 504
 Bread, Old-Fashioned 720
 Brown Rice 670
 Buttery Bread 658
 Chestnut 720
 Corn Sausage 720
 Cranberry Cornbread 721
 Flavoring 718
 Fruited Rice 561, **562**
 Herb 721
 Jiffy 721
 Potato 720
 Quantity Reference Chart
  718
 Rice and Sausage 569
 Sage, Traditional 678
 Sausage 678
 Thanksgiving 721
 Tips on Preparing 718
 Wild Rice 721
Succotash 777
Sugar(ed)
 and Salted Pecans 44,
  757-757
 and Spice Jumbo Cookies
  238
 Chocolate Wafers 220, **221**
 -Coated Grapes 67, **67**
 Grapes 675
 Icing 136
 Glaze 96, 162, 717
Summer
 Pudding Surprise 312, **310**
 Sangria 74
 Squash Monterey 778
Summertime Lemonade 59
Sun Tea 59
Sundae
 Hot Apple Spice 272
 Pear 589
 Sunshine 272, **272**
Sunflower Oatmeal Cookies
 238
Sunrise Icing 101
Sunset Salad 700, **701**
Super Cheese Hero 747, **747**
Surprise Burgers 781
Swedish
 Apple Cake 318
 Tea Ring 135, **134**
Sweet and Pungent Pork 513
Sweet-and-Sour
 Apricot-Glazed Chicken
  Thighs 660, **661**
 Chicken and Cabbage 555,
  557
 Devil Dogs 572, **572**
 Meatballs 470, **31**
 Pork with Noodles 509
 Ribs 513
 Sauce 37
 Scallop Kebobs 411
Sweet
 Corn on the Cob 767
 'n' Hot Mustard 7, **6**
 Pastry 166
 Pepper and Orange Jam 9
 Pickle Chips 21
 Potatoes
  Candied 776
  Buttered 776, **511**
  Kebobs 776, **775**
 -Sour
  Glazed Beets 761
  Red Cabbage 506
  Sauce 656
 Yam Puffs 786
Sweetheart Cakes 153
Swiss
 Almond Meringue Tarts 152
 and Sprout Sandwich 749
 Calf's Liver 483

Chard Enchilada
 Casserole 380, **391**
 Puff 378
 Steak 430
 Speedy 444
Syllabub 305
Syrup
 Brown Sugar 130
 Honey 285, 328
 Low-Calorie Honey 14
 Honeyed Apple 338
 Orange 312
 Special Low-Calorie
  Pancake 14
 Ten-Calorie Maple 14
Szechuan
 Beef 437, **436**
 Shredded Beef and
  Vegetables, Spicy 438,
  445

Taco(s) 749
 Salad in Lettuce Leaves
  696, **697**
 Tartlets 44
 Topping 586, **586**
Taffy 253
 Vanilla 253
Tamale(s)
 Dough 474
 Picadillo 473
 Pie 627
Tangerine and Cranberry
 Mold 18
Tangy
 Glazed Pork Loin 500, **512**
 Mustard Dressing 700
Tapioca, Creamy 305
Tarragon Butter 19
Tart(s)
 Ambrosia 329
 Apple-Almond 637, **637**
 Cherry-Nut 324
 Chocolate-Pecan Chess
  168, **168**
 Double Chocolate 329
 Fruit, Glazed 326, **327**
 Lemon Meringue 322, **310**
 Macadamia Nut 328
 Maple Walnut 328
 Peaches and Cream 323
 Pecan 328
 Shells, Toasted Coconut
  329
 Strawberry-Kiwi 324, **325**
 Three-Cheese 31
Tartar Sauce 385
Tartare Steak Canapés 36
 Toasted 54, **52-53**
Tartlets
 Almond 244, **245**
 Macaroon 231, **231**
Tea
 Apple Iced 59
 Bread, Date 133
 Cakes, Russian 238
 Ring, Swedish 135, **134**
 Sun, 59
 Tropical 60
Tempura 47, 408
Ten-Calorie Maple Syrup 14
Texas
 Barbecue Sauce 420
 Chili Beef Stew 426
Thailand Stuffed Oranges
 474, **475**
The California Rage 751
 New York "Deli" Special
  749
 Perfect Chef's Salad 707
 Reuben 749
Three-Cheese
 Tart 31
 Vegetable Relishes 692,
  690
Timetable for Roasting
 Turkey 677
Tiny Meatballs with
 Nectarines 465
Tips for Microwaving Chicken
 553
Toast
 Apple-Cheese 378

Gorgonzola 30, **10-11**
Toasted
 Coconut Flan 589
 Coconut Tart Shells 329
 Tartare 54, **52-53**
Toffee, Whipped Cream 199
Tomato(es)
 and Onions, Herbed 785,
  663
 and Rice Soup 732, **733**
 Aspic Rectangles 691, **690**
 -Avocado Sandwiches 750,
  750
 -Broccoli Quiche 375
 Crumb-Stuffed 785
 Cups, Spanish 783
 Drink, Pink 58
 Eye-Opener 71, **48**
 Herb-Scented Oven-Dried
  783
 Juice
  Homemade 64
  Hot Herbed 64, **62-63**
 Ketchup, Spicy 23
 -Lime Cups 785, **784**
 Mustard 7
 -Pear Relish, Ripe 14
 Preserves 14
 Ratatouille-Stuffed 782
 Ring with Eggs and
  Curried Herring Salad
  708
 Salad Pasta 600, **598**
 Sauce, Homemade 610
 Selecting and Storing 783
 Stuffed with Ham Salad
  783, **299**
 Sunrise 58
Top-Notch Tuna Pie 622
Topping(s)
 Blueberry 343
 Cinnamon Yogurt 337
 Coconut 177, 209
 Cottage Cheese 585, **586**
 Cranberry 167
 Cream Cheese 231
 for French Omelet 363
 Maple-Blueberry 338
 Oil and Vinegar, Dilly 586,
  586
 Peanut Butter 143
 Strawberry 166, 343
 Taco 586, **586**
 Whipped Cream 171
Torte(s) 143
 Chocolate
  Chestnut 190
  Meringue 148, **146-147**
  Orange 187, **188**
  -Peanut Butter 192, **192**
 Cranberry Linzer 189, **10-11**
 Hazelnut 186
 Linzer 190
 Nectarine Cream 187
 Raspberry Chocolate 191
 Sacher 181, **183**
 Swiss Almond Meringue
  152
Tortilla Chips 28
Tortoni Ice Cream Cake 342
Tossed Green Salad 690, **690**
Tostadas, Beef 477
Traditional Sage Stuffing 678
Trifle 275
Triple Fruit Flan 301
Tropical
 Queen of Puddings 314
 Refresher 64, **65**
 Tea 60
Trout Meunière 398
Truffles, French Chocolate
 250
Tulsa Ribs 422
Tuna
 Aioli 388, 391
 and Cheese Beanburgers
  388
 Bane, Hot 387
 Chowder, Skillet 390
 Creamy Herbed 42
 Croquettes à l'indienne 388
 Quiche, Canned 386
 Pâté, Fluffy 387, **387**

Peppers 390
Rarebit Pie 388
Turnovers with Mushroom
 Cheese Sauce 390
Tunisian Baked Chicken 659,
 659
Turkey 676
 and Carrot Loaf 684, **682**
 and Pistachio Terrine 680,
  681
 Breast, Roast 684
  Stuffed 680, **10-11**
 Broth 731
 Crepês with Cheese Sauce
  683, **682**
 Cutlets, Oven-Fried, Low-
  Calorie, 685
 How to Carve 677
 How to Grill 685
 in Puff Pastry 678, **679**
 Legs, Barbecued 684
 Meatballs with Artichokes,
  Lemon-Dilled 685
 Roast 677, **678**
  Regal 561, **562**
 Salad with Corn and Green
  Beans 702, **702**
 Scaloppine, Low-Calorie
  684
 Soup with Egg Dumplings
  730
 Talk 676
 Timetable for Roasting 677
 Wings, Curried 563
Twenty Good-for-You Snacks
 745
Twin Zabaglione Soufflés 354
Two-Cheese Gnocchi 617
Two-Way Beef Stew 566

Ukrainian Potato Dumplings
 617
Update on Microwave Ovens
 546
Upside-Down Cake 159
 Chocolate Nut 161
 Pineapple-Apricot 161
 Prune 160
 Rhubarb 160, **161**

Valentine
 Cheesecake 179, **179**
 Cookie Glaze 223
 Cookies 222, **223**
Vanilla
 Custard Filling 319
 Taffy 253
Variety Meats 481
Veal 447
 and Carrot Ragout 449
 and Rice Gremolata 448,
  449
 Balls with Dilled Fettuccine
  606, **605**
 Cutlets and Apples 454
 Parmesan, Best-Ever 572,
  572
 Parmigiana 451
 Piccata 450
 Scallops in Mushroom
  Sauce 451
 Scaloppine Marsala 450
 Schnitzel à la Holstein 451
 Shoulder Roast, Braised
  451
 Stew Milanese 450
 Stuffed Braised Breast of
  452, **453**
 Stuffed Breast of, Cold 452
 with Almonds, Spanish 450
Vegetable(s) 753
 and Tofu Stew 786
 Basic Rule for Cooking 753
 Casserole, East Indian 582
 Cheese-Stuffed 765, **765**
 Gumbo with Shrimp,
  Chunky 576, **577**
 -Ham
  Soufflé Pie 777, **682**
  Soup 744
 Know-How 753
 Leftovers 753
 Marinated 756, **756-757**

Overnight Pickled 20, **21**
  Pastry 625, **623**
  Platter, Shannon 762, **118**
  Preparation 735
  Savory Oriental 582
  Slaw, Creamy 706, **706**
  Stew, Hearty 782
  Stuffed 755, **752**
Velvet Sliced Chicken 652, **365**
Vichissoise 740
Vinaigrette Dressing 582
  Pimiento 780
Vin Chablis Jelly 13
Vin Rosé Jelly 13
Virginia Pecan Pie 632, **633**

Wafers
  Chocolate 280
  Pecan 246, **245**
  Sugared Chocolate 220, **221**
Waffles 130
  Banana Split 132
  Belgian 130

Black Forest 132
Cherry-Cheese 132
Shortcake 132
Sour Cream 130, **131**
Soy-Flour 132
Suzette 302
Walnut(s)
  Chicken 657, **657**
  Crunch Ice Cream 279
  Glazed 251
  Nougat 357
  Sponge Cake 195
Watercress Cream 736
Watermelon
  Basket 337
  Ice 293
Wax Beans, Calico 759
Welsh
  Burgers 455
  Rarebit 371
Wheat Bread, Whole 110
Wheat Germ Muffins 128
Whipped Cream
  Honey 180
  Raspberry 198

Rum, 203
Toffee 199
Topping 171
Whiskey
  Cake 186
  Sauce 589
White
  Icing 232
  Mountain Frosting 174
  -on-White Frosted Hearts 154
Whole Wheat
  Bread 110
  Cake Doughnuts 106, **107**
  Muffins 129
  Pizza 549, **549**
  Scones 123
  "Yamadamia" Bread 92, **92**
Wild Rice 612
  Stuffing 721
Wilted
  Lettuce 704
  Red Cabbage Slaw with Bacon and Peppers 688, **686**

Spinach and Lettuce 777
Wine 77
  Fruit Compote 337
  -Marinated Halibut 394
  Mold, Rosé 707
Winter
  Fruit Salad with Honey-Lemon Dressing 699, **62-63**
  Salad of Julienne Vegetables 696, **10-11**
Won Ton Soup 736

Yakitori 667, **719**
Yams
  Candied 785
  Orange-Glazed 562, **562**
  Puffs, Sweet 786
Yankee Corn Relish 15
Yeast-Raised Doughnuts 104
Yogurt Bavarian, Strawberry 262
  -Dill Sauce 570
  Drink, Indian 57
  Homemade 745

Lime Parfaits 290, **290**
Strawberry, Frozen 273
Vanilla, Frozen 274
Yorkshire Pudding 125

Zabaglione 266, 589, **564**
  Sauce with Fruit 266
Ziti Casserole 606
  with Sausage and Eggs 354
Zucchini à la Grecque 786
  and Onion-Filled Crêpes Stack 360, **361**
  Boats with Bulgur Pilaf 614, **10-11**
  Bread 117
  Frittata 372
  Lamb-Stuffed 474
  -Nut Cake Doughnuts 106, **107**
  Sausage-Stuffed 540
  Stuffed 488
    Baked 471